MASTER THE NEW SAT®

2016

PETERSON'S®

About Peterson's®

Peterson's®, a Nelnet company, has been your trusted educational publisher for over 50 years. It's a milestone we're quite proud of, as we continue to offer the most accurate, dependable, high-quality education content in the field, providing you with everything you need to succeed. No matter where you are on your academic or professional path, you can rely on Peterson's publications and its online information at **www.petersons.com** for the most up-to-date education exploration data, expert test-prep tools, and the highest quality career success resources—everything you need to achieve your educational goals.

For more information, contact Peterson's, 3 Columbia Circle, Albany, NY 12203-5158; 800-338-3282 Ext. 54229; or visit us online at **www.petersons.com**.

ISBN: 978-0-7689-3986-6

Printed in the United States of America

10 9 8 7 6 5 4 3 2 1   18 17 16

Sixteenth Edition

Petersonspublishing.com/publishingupdates

Check out our website at www.petersonspublishing.com/publishingupdates to see if there is any new information regarding the test and any revisions or corrections to the content of this book. We've made sure the information in this book is accurate and up-to-date; however, the test format or content may have changed since the time of publication.

ACCESS 3 SAT® PRACTICE TESTS ONLINE

Go to **www.petersons.com/sat** for instructions on how to access your 3 free online SAT® practice tests.

Sustainability—Its Importance to Peterson's

What does sustainability mean to Peterson's? As a leading publisher, we are aware that our business has a direct impact on vital resources—most importantly the raw material used to make our books. Peterson's is proud that its products are printed at SFI Chain-of-Custody certified facilities and that all of its books are printed on SFI certified paper with 10 percent post-consumer waste using vegetable-based ink.

Supporting the Sustainable Forestry Initiative® (SFI®) means that we only use vendors—from paper suppliers to printers—who have undergone rigorous certification audits by independent parties to demonstrate that they meet the standards.

Peterson's continuously strives to find new ways to incorporate responsible sourcing throughout all aspects of its business.

Contents

PART III: SAT® READING TEST STRATEGIES

PART IV: SAT® WRITING STRATEGIES

PART V: THE NEW SAT® ESSAY

PART VI: SAT® MATH REVIEW

PART VII: FIVE PRACTICE TESTS

PART VIII: APPENDIX

Before You Begin

Whether you have three long months or just four short weeks to prepare for the exam, Peterson's® *Master the NEW SAT*® will help you develop a study plan that caters to your individual needs and personal timetable. These step-by-step plans are easy to follow and remarkably effective. No matter which plan you select, begin by taking a diagnostic practice test.

THE DIAGNOSTIC PRACTICE TEST AND PROCESS

The diagnostic practice test does more than give you testing experience. Easy-to-use diagnostic tables help you track your performance, identify your strengths, and pinpoint areas for improvement. At the end of the diagnostic testing process, you will know which question formats are giving you the most difficulty. You will also know which topics to review in depth and which ones you can spend less time on, whether they are algebra or geometry, literary analysis, or reading charts and graphs. By understanding your testing profile, you can immediately address your weak areas by working through the relevant review chapters, learning the important test-taking tips, and completing the additional practice exercises.

FIVE FULL PRACTICE TESTS IN THIS BOOK

When you have completed your formal review, take the practice tests to sharpen your skills further. Even if you understand the redesigned SAT® perfectly, you still need to practice applying the methods you have learned in Peterson's® *Master the NEW SAT*®. Take the practice tests under simulated test conditions. Find a quiet place where you won't be interrupted, set a timer for the required time for each section, and work through each test as though it were test day. This will help you to get used to the time limits and to learn to pace yourself. If you don't have time to take full-length practice tests, Peterson's® *Master the NEW SAT*® explains how to use timing drills to take shorter sections of the exams to combat your weaknesses, work on your pacing, and increase your level of confidence.

Comprehensive Answer Explanations

At the end of each practice session, read all the answers and explanations, even for the questions that you answered correctly. There are comprehensive explanations for every one of the book's 1,000+ questions! By reading the answer explanations, you can learn from your mistakes.

You'll also find that Peterson's® *Master the NEW SAT*® discusses all of the "big picture issues" other books ignore. For example, it addresses questions such as:

* How is the SAT® really used for college admission?
* When should you take the test?
* How many times should you plan to take the SAT®?
* Do all SAT® scores "count" in the college admissions game?

By addressing these questions, Peterson's® *Master the NEW SAT*® debunks prevailing myths and helps you put the SAT® into its proper perspective. It also serves as your "college guidance counselor," giving you the expert advice you need to apply to college. And when you think about it, that's our number-one goal here. Our objective is to help you dramatically raise your scores so that you can maximize the likelihood of getting into the college of your choice.

HOW THIS BOOK IS ORGANIZED

Peterson's® *Master the NEW SAT*® is divided in to seven parts to facilitate your study:

- Part I explains everything you need to know about the new, redesigned SAT® and provides an overview with examples of the different question types you'll find on the actual test.

- Part II offers a diagnostic test to help you identify your areas of strength and those areas where you need to spend more time in your review sessions.

- Part III explores the Evidence-Based Reading Test section and offers expert strategies for answering each type of question you'll see here.

- Part IV goes into detail about the different questions you'll see on the Writing and Language Test section of the new SAT®. You'll also find a helpful review of Standard English Conventions.

- Part V describes the optional Essay part of the new SAT® and provides strategies for developing a well-supported and coherent response to the essay prompt in this section.

- Part VI offers a thorough review of all math topics you'll see on the Math Test–No Calculator and Math Test–Calculator sections. You'll find helpful information on multiple-choice math strategies, grid-in strategies, numbers and operations, basic algebra, geometry, functions and intermediate algebra, and data analysis, statistics, and probability.

- Part VII has five more tests that provide you with practice for the new SAT® so you can simulate taking the test under timed conditions. Each of the practice tests has detailed answer explanations plus details on how to determine your scores for the Evidence-Based Reading and Writing portion and the two Math sections. You'll also be able to calculate your subscores in the categories of Expression of Ideas, Standard English Conventions, Words in Context, Command of Evidence, Heart of Algebra, Problem Solving and Data Analysis, and Passport to Advanced Math as well as the new cross-test scores for the Analysis in History/Social Studies and Analysis in Science questions.

- Part VIII—Appendix: Parents' Guide to College Admission Testing offers great information for parents in creating a plan to help their teen prepare for college-admissions tests. It discusses the various roles parents play, how to approach teens on this subject matter, and how to work with the guidance counselor. It also provides great tips on how to help teens improve their time management, essential when preparing for standardized tests like the new SAT®.

SPECIAL STUDY FEATURES

Peterson's® *Master the NEW SAT*® was designed to be as user-friendly as it is complete. It includes several features to make your preparation easier. By taking full advantage of all the features presented in Peterson's® *Master the NEW SAT*®, you will become much more comfortable with the SAT® and considerably more confident about getting a good score.

Overview

Each chapter begins with a bulleted overview listing the topics that will be covered in the chapter. You know immediately where to look for a topic that you need to work on.

Summing It Up

Each strategy chapter ends with a point-by-point summary that captures the most important points. The summaries are a convenient way to review the content of these strategy chapters.

Bonus Information

In addition, be sure to look in the page margins of your book for the following test-prep tools:

Note

Notes highlight critical information about the redesigned SAT® format—for example, that in the evidence-based reading questions, the answers will always be directly stated or implied in the passage.

Tip

Tips draw your attention to valuable concepts, advice, and shortcuts for tackling the SAT®. By reading the tips, you will learn how to approach different question types, use process-of-elimination techniques, pace yourself, and, when you need to, guess most effectively.

Alert!

Wherever you need to be careful of a common pitfall or test-taker trap, you'll find an *Alert!* This information reveals and eliminates the misperceptions and wrong turns many people take on the exam.

ACCESS THREE SAT® TESTS ONLINE

Peterson's is providing you with access to three additional SAT® practice tests. The testing content on these three practice tests was created by the test-prep experts at Peterson's. The additional practice will help you boost your test-prep confidence so you can score high on test day. You can access these three practice tests at **www.petersons.com/sat**.

ULTIMATE WORD SUCCESS

Sharpen your skills with hundreds of exercises and practice test questions using our *Ultimate Word Success* eBook. Go to www.petersonspublishing.com and click on the link to access your complimentary copy.

YOU'RE WELL ON YOUR WAY TO SUCCESS

Remember that knowledge is power. By using Peterson's® *Master the NEW SAT*®, you will be studying the most comprehensive SAT®-preparation guide available, and you will become extremely knowledgeable about the SAT®. We look forward to helping you raise your SAT® scores and improve your college prospects. Good luck!

GIVE US YOUR FEEDBACK

Peterson's publishes a full line of books— test prep, career preparation, education exploration, and financial aid. Peterson's publications can be found at high school guidance offices, college libraries and career centers, and your local bookstore and library. Peterson's books are also available as eBooks and online at www.petersonsbooks.com.

We welcome any comments or suggestions you may have about this publication. Your feedback will help us make educational dreams possible for you—and others like you.

TOP 10 STRATEGIES TO RAISE YOUR SCORE

When it comes to taking the SAT®, some test-taking skills will do you more good than others. There are concepts you can learn and techniques you can follow that will help you do your best. Here's our pick for the top 10 strategies to raise your score:

1. **Create a study plan and follow it.** The right SAT® study plan will help you get the most out of this book in whatever time you have.

2. **Don't get stuck on any one question.** Since you have a specific amount of time to answer questions, you can't afford to spend too much time on any one problem.

3. **Learn the directions in advance.** If you already know the directions, you won't have to waste your time reading them. You'll be able to jump right in and start answering questions as soon as the testing clock begins.

4. **If you choose to take the essay portion of the test, it's important to develop your ideas and express them clearly, using examples to back them up.** Your essay doesn't have to be grammatically perfect, but it does have to be focused and organized, and it should explain how the author develops his or her argument.

5. **For the Writing and Language Test multiple-choice questions, think about the simplest, clearest way to express an idea.** If an answer choice sounds awkward or overly complicated, chances are good that it's wrong.

6. **For relevant words in context, be sure to read the sentences around the word carefully.** The SAT® is no longer testing obscure words but instead is focusing on defining words in the context of a passage.

7. **For Evidence-Based Reading Test questions, first skim the passage to see what it's about.** Look for the main ideas, and then tackle the questions that direct you straight to the answer by referring you to a specific line in the passage. Then work on the detailed questions that require a closer reading of the passage.

8. **For the math multiple-choice questions, it can help if you know how to approach the problems.** If you're stuck, try substituting numbers for variables. You can also try plugging in numbers from the answer choices. Start with one of the middle numbers. That way, if it doesn't work, you can strategically choose one that's higher or lower.

9. **For the math grid-ins, you come up with the answer and fill it into a grid.** Be sure to make your best guess, even if you're not sure.

10. **Finally, relax the night before the test.** Don't cram. Studying at the last minute will only stress you out. Go to a movie or hang out with a friend—anything to get your mind off the test!

PART I

SAT® BASICS

All About the SAT®

chapter 1

HOW THE SAT® IS USED FOR COLLEGE ADMISSIONS

The explicitly stated purpose of the SAT® is to predict how students will perform academically as first-year college students. But the more practical purpose of the SAT® is to help college admissions officers make acceptance decisions. When you think about it, admissions officers have a difficult job, particularly when they are asked to compare the academic records of students from different high schools in different parts of the country taking different classes. It's not easy to figure out how one student's grade point average (GPA) in New Mexico correlates with that of another student in Florida. Even though admissions officers can do a good deal of detective work to fairly evaluate candidates, they benefit a great deal from the SAT®. The SAT® provides a single, standardized means of comparison. After all, virtually every student takes the SAT®, and the SAT® is the same for everyone. It doesn't matter whether you hail from Maine, Maryland, or Montana.

So the SAT® is an important test. But it is not the be-all, end-all. Keep it in perspective! It is only one of several important pieces of the college admissions puzzle. Other factors that weigh heavily into the admission process include GPA, difficulty of course load, level of extracurricular involvement, and the strength of the college application itself.

TIP

Are you starting to prepare a little later than you had planned? Don't get upset; it happens. Using the accelerated course, you should be able to cover most of the material within a month. You probably won't have much time to practice, but you'll get the most important facts about the test and be able to take a few sample exams.

WHEN YOU SHOULD TAKE THE SAT® (AND SAT SUBJECT TESTS™)

When you decide which schools you're going to apply to, find out if they require the SAT®. Most do! Your next step is to determine when they need your SAT® scores. Write that date down. That's the one you *really* don't want to miss.

You do have some leeway in choosing your test date. The SAT® is typically offered on one Saturday morning in October, November, December, January, March (or April, alternating), May, and June. Check the exact dates to see which ones meet your deadlines. The first testing dates for the new SAT® are March 5, May 7, and June 4, 2016. Tests are offered on a Sunday, usually the day after each Saturday test date, for students who cannot take the test on Saturday due to religious observance.

What if you don't know which schools you want to apply to? Don't panic! Even if you take the exam in December or January of your senior year, you'll probably have plenty of time to send your scores to most schools.

When you plan to take the SAT®, there is something even more important than the application deadlines of particular schools. You need to select a test date that works best with your schedule. Ideally, you should allow yourself at least two to three months to use this book to prepare. Many students like to take the test in March of their junior year. That way, they take the SAT® several months before final exams, the prom, and end-of-the-year distractions. Taking the test in March also gives students early feedback as to how they are scoring. If they are dissatisfied with their scores, there is ample opportunity to take the test again in the spring or following fall. But your schedule might not easily accommodate a March testing. Maybe you're involved in a winter sport or school play that will take too much time away from SAT® studying. Maybe you have a family reunion planned over spring break in March. Or maybe you simply prefer to prepare during a different time of year. If that's the case, just pick another date.

If the schools you've decided on also require SAT Subject Tests™, here's one good piece of advice: try to take SAT Subject Tests™ immediately after you finish the subject(s) in school. For most of you, this means taking the SAT Subject Tests™ in June. By taking the exam then, you'll save an awful lot of review work. Remember this, too: you have to register for the SAT Subject Tests™ separately, and you can't take the Subject Tests on the same day as the SAT®. So check the dates, think ahead, and plan it out. It's worth it in the end.

HOW YOUR SCORES ARE REPORTED

After you have taken the SAT®, College Board scores your test and creates a score report. We will discuss in detail how the SAT® is scored later in this chapter. You and your high school receive score reports from each SAT® and SAT Subject Test™ that you decide to take.

At the time of registration, you can pick four colleges or universities also to receive your score report. College Board will send your scores to these four schools for free. Within nine days of taking the test, you can change your school selection. If you want to send more than four reports or change your mind more than nine days after your test date, you will have to pay for it.

If you decide to take the SAT®, or any SAT Subject Test™, more than once, you have the option to decide which scores to send to the schools you've picked—scores from one, several, or all test dates.

You may only designate the test date or dates for your score reports; you cannot designate individual test sections. In other words, if you take the SAT® in October, December, and March, you cannot pick the Evidence-Based Reading and Writing score from October, Math score from December, and Essay score from March and ask to have those results sent to the schools of your choice. You can only choose whether to send your complete results from one, two, or all three test dates.

If you choose not to take advantage of this option, all of your scores will be sent to the schools you've selected. However, no score reports will ever be sent without your specific consent. You and your counselor will receive e-mail reminders, asking which scores you want to send, so you have time to make a decision at the time you take the SAT®. You can find more information about this and how colleges and universities use your score reports on the website https://sat.collegeboard.org/register/sat-score-choice.

HOW MANY TIMES YOU SHOULD TAKE THE SAT®

Different colleges evaluate the SAT® in different ways. Some take your highest math, evidence-based reading and writing, and essay scores, even if they were earned on different test days. So if you nailed the math portion in March, the evidence-based reading and writing portion in October, and the essay in December, the colleges will combine those three numbers to maximize your overall score. However, many other colleges won't do that. Some pay most attention to your highest combined score from a single day. Many others will average all of your scores or lend equal weight to all of them.

So what does this mean? It means that you should only take the SAT® when you are truly prepared. There is nothing wrong with taking the SAT® two or three times, as long as you are confident that your scores will improve substantially each time. Let's say that you scored an 1100 on your first SAT®. If you would have been thrilled to have hit 1120, it's probably not worth taking the test again. Most colleges look at SAT® scores in ranges and will not hold 20 points against you. They understand that scoring an 1100 means that you were only one or two questions away from 1120. But if you scored an 1100 and expected to score closer to 1200 or 1300 based on practice testing, then you should probably retake the exam. In other words, it is of little value to take the SAT® multiple times if you expect to earn roughly the same score. But it is worthwhile if you expect to score significantly higher on a second or third try. For more advice about this, see your high school guidance counselor.

HOW TO REGISTER FOR THE SAT®

You should register for the SAT® at least six weeks before your testing date. That way you will avoid late registration fees and increase your chances of taking the exam at your first-choice testing center. You can register through the mail by completing the SAT® registration form found inside *The Student Registration Guide for the SAT and SAT Subject Tests™,* which can be found in your guidance counselor's office." Registering online is probably the quickest and easiest method, and you will receive immediate registration confirmation. You will need to pay by credit card, and you will need to upload a photo with your registration. The photo you provide will become part of your Admission Ticket on test day. For more information, visit https://sat.collegeboard.org/register.

PHOTO IDENTIFICATION

The photo you provided (either uploaded with your online registration or mailed in with the printed registration) becomes part of your Admission Ticket on test day.

Photos must be properly focused with a full-face view. The photo must be clearly identifiable as you, and it must match your appearance on test day. **IMPORTANT:** If you are not easily recognizable in your photo, you will not be admitted to the test center.

Choose a photo that:

- Shows only you—no other people are in the shot
- Shows a head-and-shoulders view, with the entire face, both eyes, and hair clearly visible
- Is properly focused and has no dark spots or shadows
- Only shows a head covering if it is worn for religious purposes

Visit https://sat.collegeboard.org/register/photo-requirements for more information about the required photo ID."

In addition, you are responsible for bringing an acceptable form of identification.

Some acceptable examples include:

- State-issued driver's license
- State-issued nondriver ID
- School identification card
- Passport (required in India, Ghana, Nepal, Nigeria, and Pakistan)
- Government-issued ID
- School ID Form* prepared by your school
- Talent Identification Program ID/Authorization to Test Form (grades seven and eight only); photo not required

*Your school can prepare an ID form for you. This form must include a recognizable photo, and the school seal must overlap the photo. Sign the ID form in the presence of your counselor or principal. You will be asked to sign the ID form again at the test center. This form must be dated and is good only for one year.

GET TO KNOW THE REDESIGNED SAT® FORMAT

The SAT® consists of sections on math, evidence-based reading and writing, and an optional essay. The sections are timed to range from 25 to 65 minutes. The whole test takes 3 hours, plus 50 minutes for the optional essay. Don't worry. There are breaks. The following chart gives you an idea of what to expect. The test sections appear in the following order: Reading Test, Writing and Language Test, Math Test—No Calculator, Math Test—Calculator, and the Essay.

FORMAT OF THE REDESIGNED SAT® TEST

Evidence-Based Reading and Writing

Time—Total: 100 minutes

- Reading Test (65 minutes)
- Writing and Language Test (35 minutes)

Evidence-Based Reading questions based on:

- Passages in U.S. and world literature, history/social studies, and science
- Paired passages
- Lower and higher text complexities
- Words in context, command of evidence, and analysis

Writing and Language questions based on:

- Passages in careers, history/social studies, humanities, and science
- Argument, informative/explanatory, and nonfiction narrative passages
- Words in context, grammar, expression of ideas, and analysis

Question Types

- Multiple-choice with 4 answer choices

Score 200–800

Math

Time—Total: 80 minutes

- One no-calculator section (25 minutes)
- One calculator section (55 minutes)

Content

- Algebra
- Problem solving and data analysis
- Advanced math
- Area and volume calculations
- Lines, triangles, and circles using theorems
- Trigonometric functions

Question Types

- Multiple-choice with 4 answer choices
- Student-produced responses (grid-ins)

Score 200–800

Optional Essay

Time—Total: 50 minutes

Content

- Argument passage written for a general audience
- Analysis of argument in passage using text evidence

Question Type

- One prompt that emphasizes analyzing the argument presented in the passage

Score: 3–12 (Reading: 1–4 scale, Analysis: 1–4 scale, Writing: 1–4 scale)

TIP

On the SAT®, all questions count the same. You won't get more points for answering a really difficult question than you will get for answering a very simple one. Remember that when you're moving through the test. The more time you spend wrestling with the answer to one "stumper," the less time you have to whip through several easier questions.

GET TO KNOW THE SAT® QUESTION TYPES

The question types in the SAT® don't cover a wide variety of topics. They are very limited—no science, no world languages, no social studies. You'll find only questions testing reading comprehension, writing skills, and math skills—skills that you've been working on since kindergarten.

Most of the questions are multiple choice. That's good, because it means the correct answer is right there on the page for you. You just have to find it—easier said than done sometimes, but true. Only the math grid-ins and the essay are student-produced answers. For the grid-ins, you'll need to do the calculations and then fill in bubbles on the answer sheet to show your answers. (More about the answer ovals later in this chapter.) The following pages provide you with a closer look at the question types and question formats that you will find in each section of the SAT®.

SAT® EVIDENCE-BASED READING SECTION

The critical reading section tests your knowledge of words of context, command of evidence in the passages, and your analysis of the passage, including graphics. All the questions are multiple choice. The Evidence-Based Reading section questions are all passage-based. All passages are from previously published sources and cover topics in U.S. and world literature, history/social studies, and science.

Words in Context

Just as the name implies, word-in-context questions assess your ability to determine the meaning of words or phrases in the context of an extended passage. If you do not recognize the meaning of the word, its meaning may be determined by context. Your job is to read the passage and the question, then analyze the answer choices to figure out which one makes the most sense based on the words around it. That means you must look for clues in the passage.

Here is an excerpt from a passage on the opah fish. Following the excerpt are three sample word-in-context questions. Read the passage excerpt and try to answer each question on your own before you read the explanation that accompanies it.

> *Nicholas Wegner of NOAA Fisheries' Southwest Fisheries Science Center in La Jolla, California, is lead author of a new paper on the opah, or moonfish. He and his coauthor, biologist Owyn Snodgrass, discovered that the opah has the unusual ability to keep its body warm, even in the cold depths of the ocean. An excerpt on their findings follows.*

Warm Blood Makes Opah an Agile Predator

New research by NOAA Fisheries has revealed the opah, or moonfish, as the first fully warm-blooded fish that circulates heated blood throughout its body much like mammals and birds, giving it a <u>competitive advantage</u> in the cold ocean depths.

Line The silvery fish, roughly the size of a large automobile tire, is known from oceans around
5 the world and dwells hundreds of feet beneath the surface in chilly, dimly lit waters… .

Fish that typically inhabit such cold depths tend to be slow and sluggish, conserving energy by <u>ambushing</u> prey instead of chasing it. But the opah's constant flapping of its fins heats its body, speeding its metabolism, movement and reaction times, scientists report today in the journal *Science*… .

10 "Before this discovery I was under the impression this was a slow-moving fish, like most other fish in cold environments," Wegner said. "But because it can warm its body, it turns out to be a very active predator that chases down agile prey like squid and can migrate long distances."

Courtesy: NOAA Fisheries

As used in the first paragraph, *competitive advantage* refers to

(A) a way to seek out a mate.

(B) an ability to outperform rivals.

(C) an aptitude for keeping itself moving.

(D) a capacity to conceal itself from predators.

Clues to the meaning of the phrase don't appear until the fourth paragraph: "I was under the impression … like most other fish in cold environments" and "But … it turns out to be a very active predator." Here, you're told that the opah is *unlike* other fish in that it can swim faster and farther and catch more prey. Choices (A), (C), and (D) are specific traits that might help the fish in its environment. But choice (B) is the only one that makes sense in the context of the passage. **The correct answer is (B).**

As it is used in paragraph 3, *ambushing* most nearly means

(A) pursuing for long distances.

(B) moving slowly at first.

(C) hiding and then attacking.

(D) weakening and then killing.

The biggest clue to the meaning of *ambushing* is "instead of chasing it." Because you know that the fish don't chase their prey, you can exclude choice (A). Choices (B) and (D) don't make sense in the context of the sentence because neither is a method for capturing prey, as chasing is. Choice (C), however, makes sense when you consider the context clue. **The correct answer is (C).**

As it is used in paragraph 4, *agile* most nearly means

(A) nimble.

(B) inactive.

(C) strong.

(D) clever.

The clue "very active predator" is your clue that *agile* must mean that the squid provides a challenge for the opah. This eliminates choice (B). Choice (D) can also be eliminated because the context emphasizes physical, not mental abilities. Likewise, you can eliminate choice (C) because the level of activity, not strength, is the focus. Choice (A) fits the context, as it suggests that the squid is able to move quickly and easily. **The correct answer is (A).**

NOTE

In SAT® evidence-based reading questions, the answers will always be directly stated or implied in the passage.

Command of Evidence

The evidence-based reading and writing section of the SAT® requires you to interpret information or ideas in a passage and then use evidence to support your conclusion. This element of the Reading Test, which makes up 20 percent of the questions, works like this: You answer a multiple-choice question in which you analyze a portion of the passage or pair of passages. You then answer a second question requiring you to cite the best evidence in the text for the answer.

The passages include literary texts from U.S. and world literature, as well as nonfiction texts in science and history/social studies. In some cases, related passages are paired and require you to make connections between the texts.

The following is an example of how these "command of evidence" questions work. The passage is a continuation of the NOAA article cited previously, "Warm Blood Makes Opah an Agile Predator."

Gills Show Unusual Design

Wegner realized the opah was unusual when a coauthor of the study, biologist Owyn Snodgrass, collected a sample of its gill tissue. Wegner recognized an unusual design: Blood vessels that carry warm blood into the fish's gills wind around those carrying cold blood back to the body core after absorbing oxygen from water.

5 The design is known in engineering as "counter-current heat exchange." In opah it means that warm blood leaving the body core helps heat up cold blood returning from the respiratory surface of the gills, where it absorbs oxygen. Resembling a car radiator, it's a natural adaptation that conserves heat. The unique location of the heat exchange within the gills allows nearly the fish's entire body to maintain an elevated temperature, known as endothermy,
10 even in the chilly depths.

"There has never been anything like this seen in a fish's gills before," Wegner said. "This is a cool innovation by these animals that gives them a competitive edge. The concept of counter-current heat exchange was invented in fish long before we thought of it."

The researchers collected temperature data from opah caught during surveys off the West
15 Coast, finding that their body temperatures were regularly warmer than the surrounding water. They also attached temperature monitors to opah as they tracked the fish on dives to several hundred feet and found that their body temperatures remained steady even as the water temperature dropped sharply. The 20 fish had an average muscle temperature about 5 degrees C above the surrounding water while swimming about 150 to 1,000 feet below the
20 surface, the researchers found....

A few other fish ... warm certain parts of their bodies ... , boosting their swimming performance. But internal organs, including their hearts, cool off quickly and begin to slow down when they dive into cold depths, forcing them to return to shallower depths to warm up.

Courtesy: NOAA Fisheries

The author discusses the adaptations of some fish in the last paragraph mainly to show that

(A) opah swim faster because they are able to keep themselves warm.

(B) some fish maintain a body temperature warmer than the sea water.

(C) biologists have found evidence that some fish are warm-blooded.

(D) opah have a distinctive design that keeps them warm in cold water.

Which choice provides the best evidence for the answer to the previous question?

(A) Lines 8–10 ("The unique … chilly depths.")

(B) Lines 12–13 ("The concept … of it.")

(C) Lines 14–16 ("The researchers … surrounding water.")

(D) Lines 18–20 ("The 20 fish … researchers found.")

In the first question, the author's intention is to contrast the warming ability of other fish with the warming ability of the opah. Though the passage does note that some fish maintain a body temperature warmer than seawater for a short period, this is not the reason the author includes details about other fish. Thus choice (B) is not correct. Choices (A) and (C) are incorrect because neither idea is noted in the text. **The correct answer is (D).**

The second question asks you to determine which of four segments of the passage provides the best evidence to support your answer to the first question. In this portion of the passage, the author describes the unique body design that gives the opah an edge over other fish in keeping its body warm. Choices (B), (C), and (D) do not provide textual support for the contrast the author makes in the last paragraph. **The correct answer is (A).**

Analysis and Graphics

Two passages in the SAT® reading test include a graphic. Your job is to analyze the passage and interpret the information in the graphic as it relates to the passage. Questions based on the graphic are multiple choice. Here is an example.

John Snow (1813–1858)

John Snow is an iconic figure in epidemiology and public health, best known for his work on cholera, for a famous map, and for organizing the removal of a pump handle in Soho.

Less well-known are his important contributions to anesthesia and to epidemiological *Line* methods, and his engagement in public debates of the time. The breadth and depth of Snow's
5 activities provide a model for population researchers concerned not only with sound method but also with bringing their results to public benefit.

Indeed, though epidemiology is often described as the study of health-related aspects of populations, its methods are applicable to studies of virtually anything in populations, and disciplines which now acknowledge the methods and terminology of epidemiology range
10 from education to crime science and economics.

Snow was born in York on 15 March 1813, one of eight children in a family of modest means. He apprenticed with a surgeon-apothecary in Newcastle from 1827 to 1833, and there witnessed the first epidemic of cholera in the UK. He then moved to London, qualified as physician in 1843 and set up general practice in Soho. Early in his career he became
15 interested in the physiology of respiration in recognition of the major problem of asphyxia of the newborn.

These interests led him to be invited to witness one of the first applications of ether anesthesia in the UK in December 1846. He immediately recognized the importance of ambient temperature and within one month published tables of the vapor pressure of ether. This
20 initiated an important line of research on instruments for administering anesthetics and led to his becoming the most prominent authority on anesthesia in the UK. He administered chloroform to Queen Victoria at the birth of Prince Leopold in 1853.

The second great cholera epidemic arrived in London in 1848, and many attributed its cause to an atmospheric "effluence" or "miasma." Snow's firsthand experience of the disease in 1832, combined with studies of respiration, led him to question miasma theories and to publish the first edition of *On the Mode of Communication of Cholera* in 1849, in which he proposed that cholera was attributable to a self-replicating agent which was excreted in the cholera evacuations and inadvertently ingested, often, but not necessarily, through the medium of water.

When cholera returned in 1853, Snow recognized an ideal opportunity to test his hypothesis by comparing cholera mortality rates in populations of south London supplied by water drawn from sewage-contaminated versus uncontaminated regions of the Thames. He personally carried out a cohort study to make this comparison, recognizing the need to confirm the water source of each case and to assure comparability of the populations concerned.

On 30 August 1854 while involved in these studies, a dramatic cholera epidemic began near his home in Soho, leading to more than 550 deaths within two weeks. Analysis of the addresses of the cholera deaths and interviews of residents of the area led him to suspect that water from a pump on Broad Street was responsible – and he prevailed upon the local council to remove the handle of the pump on 8 September 1854.

Though the epidemic was already in decline by that date, the rapidity of his action, the logic of the analysis, and the pragmatism of the response has made this a classic event in the history of public health, well known to students and practitioners the world over. The combination of these studies provided overwhelming evidence for an infectious agent, known now as *Vibrio cholerae*.

Snow described this work in the second edition of *On the Mode of Communication of Cholera*. He then expanded his public health interests by becoming involved in debates over legislation concerning nuisance industries in London, while maintaining his research and practice in anesthesia until his death in 1858.

The 200th anniversary of Snow's birth provides an occasion to celebrate his achievements, to consider their original context, to discuss their place in contemporary epidemiology, and consider their likely future, not only as the armamentarium of public health, but as a framework of method for science and society.

From "About John Snow," by Professor Paul Fine, London School of Hygiene & Tropical Medicine and The John Snow Society.

> Based on John Snow's map, we can assume that the pump on Broad Street supplied water to the people on all of the following streets except
>
> **(A)** Berwick Street.
>
> **(B)** Blenheim Street.
>
> **(C)** Poland Street.
>
> **(D)** King Street

The passage explains that Snow determined that the pump on Broad Street supplied contaminated water to nearby residents. Deaths from the resulting cholera epidemic are represented in the stacks of lines. You can infer that people living on streets containing stacks of bars used the Broad Street pump. Based on the map, then, people on Blenheim Street may not have used the Broad Street pump. **The correct answer is (B).**

SAT® WRITING AND LANGUAGE SECTION

The SAT® Writing and Language Test consists of multiple-choice questions based on passages. The multiple-choice questions test how well you understand and use standard written English, as well as recognizing words in context and command of evidence in the passages. Analysis of the passages and graphics is also included.

Standard Written English and Words in Context

The Standard Written English questions require you to act as an editor and revise text so that it conforms to the standard rules for punctuation, sentence structure, and usage. In most instances, you will be given a multi-paragraph passage that includes several errors. The most common question format asks you to choose the best alternative to a potential error, identified as an underlined portion of the passage. Here is an example of a question that concerns sentence structure:

> Scientists conducted a series of experiments with chimpanzees in the Democratic Republic of the Congo. The results were astounding. The conclusion, that chimpanzees would eventually learn to cook if provided an oven, could help explain how and when early humans began to cook their food.

> Which choice most effectively combines the sentences at the underlined portion?
>
> **(A)** Democratic Republic of the Congo, and the results were astounding.
>
> **(B)** Democratic Republic of the Congo, the results were astounding.
>
> **(C)** Democratic Republic of the Congo: the results were astounding.
>
> **(D)** Democratic Republic of the Congo, but the results were astounding.

Choice (B) creates a comma splice, which is a form of a run-on sentence, so that's not correct. Likewise, the colon in choice (C) is not correct, as the clause it introduces does not really explain the first part of the sentence. Introducing *but* in choice (D) changes the meaning of the sentences by setting up a contrasting scenario. Only choice (A) maintains the two sentences' meanings and combines them without confusion. **The correct answer is (A).**

The Words in Context section of the test measures your ability to choose appropriate words based on the context of the passage. These questions are multiple choice and include the option to keep the word that is used: NO CHANGE. Here is an example of a Words in Context question.

> There is a debate about whether early humans had the mental capacity to cook. Though it may not seem sophisticated, cooking requires planning, an ability to <u>interrupt</u> gratification, and the complicated use of tools.

(A) NO CHANGE

(B) apprehend

(C) delay

(D) restrain

Here, you must choose the word that makes the most sense in the context. The words *interrupt, apprehend,* and *restrain* don't convey what is meant here—to hold off. Only *delay,* choice (C), conveys that sense. **The correct answer is (C).**

Command of Evidence

To answer the Writing and Language test questions, you must have a firm understanding of the passage in question. Command of Evidence questions measure how well you can analyze the writer's development of his or her theme. The following is an example of this type of question. The excerpt comes from the passage about John Snow.

> The second great cholera epidemic arrived in London in 1848, and many attributed its cause to an atmospheric "effluence" or "miasma." Snow's firsthand experience of the disease in 1832, combined with studies of respiration, led him to question miasma theories and to publish the first edition of *On the Mode of Communication of Cholera* in 1849, in which he proposed that cholera was attributable to a self-replicating agent which was excreted in the cholera evacuations and inadvertently ingested, often, but not necessarily, through the medium of water.

Which choice most effectively establishes the central point of the paragraph?

(A) In 1848, many people thought that cholera was most likely caused by atmospheric "effluence" or "miasma."

(B) John Snow's study, *On the Mode of Communication of Cholera*, combined firsthand experience with studies of respiration.

(C) When the second big cholera outbreak in London occurred in 1848, John Snow questioned existing cholera theories.

(D) Snow questioned the "miasma" theory, proposing instead that a replicating agent could spread through contaminated water.

The question asks you to determine the main idea of the paragraph. Choices (A), (B), and (C) all contain ideas that are important in the paragraph. But choice (D) contains the crux of the paragraph: that Snow questioned the prevailing wisdom and then proposed his own theory about how cholera is transmitted. **The correct answer is (D).**

Analysis and Graphics

One or two of the passages in the Writing and Language portion of the test include graphics. You will be asked to determine how the passage needs to be revised based on the information in the graphic. An excerpt from another passage about John Snow and a sample question illustrate this concept.

> Snow's mapping of the outbreak showed few surprising results. Little Pulteney Street is a case in point. The street is blocks from Broad Street, and closer to two other water pumps. Among residents of the street, there <u>were no cases of cholera</u> reported during the outbreak.

Which choice completes the sentence using accurate data based on the map?

(A) NO CHANGE

(B) was one new case of cholera

(C) were about six new cases of cholera

(D) were more than twenty new cases of cholera

Here, you are being asked to interpret the information in the passage based on the map. If you look closely at the area in question, Little Pulteney Street, you'll see that there are about six bars, and we can infer that each bar represents a case of cholera. **Thus, choice (C) is the correct answer.**

SAT® MATH SECTION

The questions in the math section (Math Test—No Calculator and Math Test—Calculator) address concepts, skills, and practices that are most useful for students after they graduate from high school. There are two question formats for math questions: multiple-choice and grid-ins (student-produced responses).

Multiple-Choice Math

SAT® multiple-choice math questions look like all the other standard multiple-choice math questions you've ever seen. A problem is given in algebra, problem solving, data analysis, advanced math, or additional topics, and four answers are presented from which you must choose the correct answer. The major concepts that you might need in order to solve math problems are given in the test section. You don't need to worry about memorizing these facts, but you do need to know when to use each one. The directions are similar to the following:

Directions: For **Questions 1–15**, solve each problem, choose the best answer from the choices provided, and fill in the corresponding circle on your answer sheet. For **Questions 16–20**, solve the problem and enter your answer in the grid on the answer sheet. Please refer to the directions **before Question 16** on how to enter your answers in the grid. You may use any available space in your test booklet for scratch work.

- The use of a calculator is permitted.

- All variables and expressions used represent real numbers unless otherwise indicated.

- Figures provided in this test are drawn to scale unless otherwise indicated.

- All figures lie in a plane unless otherwise indicated.

- Unless otherwise specified, the domain of a given function f is the set of all real numbers x for which $f(x)$ is a real number.

TIP

A four-function, battery-powered, scientific or graphing calculator is allowed for the math section of the SAT®. You may not use the following: handheld mini-computers, laptop computers, pocket organizers, calculators that print or "talk," or calculators with letters on the keyboard.

Here are some sample multiple-choice math questions. Try them yourself before looking at the solutions that are given.

Michele is at the airport renting a car that costs $39.95 per day plus tax. A tax of 7% is applied to the rental rate, and an additional onetime untaxed fee of $5.00 is charged by the airport where she picks up the car. Which of the following represents Michele's total charge $c(x)$, in dollars, for renting a car for x nights?

(A) $c(x) = (39.95 + 0.07x) + 5$

(B) $c(x) = 1.07(39.95x) + 5$

(C) $c(x) = 1.07(39.95x + 5)$

(D) $c(x) = 1.07(39.95 + 5)x$

The total cost, $c(x)$, can be found by multiplying any daily charges by the number of days, x, and then adding any onetime charges. The daily charges include the $39.95 daily rate and the 7% tax. This can be computed by:

$$\$39.95 + 0.07(\$39.95) = 1(\$39.95) + 0.07(\$39.95) = 1.07(\$39.95)$$

Multiply the daily charge by x and add the one-time charge of $5 to obtain the function rule:

$$c(x) = 1.07(39.95)x + 5$$

The correct answer is (B).

The graph of $y = (3x + 9)(x - 5)$ is a parabola in the xy plane. In which of the following equivalent equations do the x- and y-coordinates of the vertex of the parabola appear as constants or coefficients?

(A) $y = 3x^2 - 6x - 45$

(B) $y = 3x(x - 2) - 45$

(C) $y = 3(x - 1)^2 + (-48)$

(D) $y = (x + 3)(3x - 15)$

The equation $y = (3x + 9)(x - 5)$ can be written in vertex form $y = a(x - h)^2 + k$, where the vertex of the parabola is (h, k). To put the equation in vertex form, first multiply the factors, then complete the square. **The correct answer is (C).**

The same final exam is given to two separate groups of students taking the same class. The students who took the exam on the first floor had a mean score of 84. The students who took the exam on the second floor had a mean score of 78. Which of the following represents the mean score x of both groups of students?

(A) $x = 81$

(B) $x < 81$

(C) $x > 81$

(D) $78 < x < 84$

Many students will select choice (A) as the answer, because 81 is the mean of 78 and 84, but there is no information about the size of the two groups that are being averaged. If the groups were equal in size, choice (A) would be correct. If there were more students on the second floor, then choice (B) would be the correct answer. Similarly if there were more students on the first floor, then choice (C) would be correct. Since we don't know which floor has more students taking the exam or if the number of students is equal we can only say that choice (D) is true. **The correct answer is (D).**

Grid-Ins

Unlike multiple-choice math, the grid-in section of the SAT® does not give you the answers. You have to compute the answer and then fill in your answer in the bubbles on your answer sheet. You may use the Reference Information table earlier in this chapter for these problems also. The directions for the grid-ins are similar to the following:

Directions: Solve each of the following problems and write the arithmetic value of your answer in the open spaces at the top of the correspondingly numbered grid on your answer sheet. Then grid your answer by blackening the ovals that correspond to the decimal point, fraction line, and numbers in your answer.

Notes: If a question has more than one correct answer, grid only one of them.

To grid $4\frac{1}{4}$, use 4.25 or $\frac{17}{4}$. Do not use $4\frac{1}{4}$ as it will be read as $\frac{41}{4}$.

None of these answers requires a minus sign.

Answers may begin in any grid column.

Decimal answers should be entered with the greatest accuracy allowed by the grid.

Here are some examples of these kinds of problems:

The circumference of a circle is 20π. If the area of a sector of the circle with a central angle of $\frac{3\pi}{2}$ is $a\pi$, what is the value of a?

$$C = 2\pi r = 20\pi$$
$$r = 10$$
$$A = \frac{3}{4}\pi r^2 = \frac{3}{4}\pi(10)^2 = 75\pi = a\pi$$
$$a = 75$$

There are 70 students in a school who participate in the music program. If 35% of the students participate in the music program, how many students are in the school?

$$\frac{35}{100} = \frac{70}{x}$$
$$35x = 7000$$
$$x = 200$$

What is one possible solution to the equation $\dfrac{1}{x} + \dfrac{3}{x-1} = -4$?

$$\frac{1}{x} + \frac{3}{x-1} = -4$$
$$x - 1 + 3x = -4x(x-1)$$
$$4x - 1 = -4x^2 + 4x$$
$$0 = -4x^2 + 1$$
$$0 = (-2x + 1)(2x + 1)$$
$$x = \pm 0.5$$

Only 0.5 or $\dfrac{1}{2}$ can be entered in the grid because, as the directions stated, no answer requires a minus sign..

SAT® ESSAY (OPTIONAL)

For the essay, you will be given a previously published passage that examines ideas in the sciences and arts, as well as in civic, cultural, and political life. The passages are written for a broad-based audience, and prior knowledge of the topic is not expected. Your task in writing the essay is to read and comprehend the text sufficiently to write a thoughtful analysis of the passage.

Though the passage contents may vary from test to test, the prompt will not change. You will be asked to explain how the author of the passage builds an argument to persuade an audience. The prompt will likely look something like this:

> As you read the following passage, consider how the author uses the following:
> - Evidence, such as facts, statistics, or examples, to support claims.
> - Reasoning to develop ideas and to connect claims and evidence.
> - Stylistic or persuasive elements, such as word choice or appeals to emotion, to add power
> - to the ideas expressed.

Your response will be evaluated based on your comprehension of the text, as well as on the quality of your analysis and writing. This means that you must show thoughtful understanding of the source text and appropriate use of textual evidence to support your arguments. You will also be expected to organize your ideas in a coherent way and to express them clearly, using the conventions of standard written English. The essay does not elicit your opinion or ask you to use your imagination to write creatively. Instead, your response should depend entirely on the source text to support your analysis. You can learn more about the optional Essay in Chapter 6.

THE SAT® ANSWER SHEET

On the day of the test when you are given your test booklet, you'll also be given a separate answer sheet. For each multiple-choice question, you'll see a corresponding set of answer ovals, also known as bubbles. The ovals are labeled (A) to (D). Remember the following about the answer sheet:

- Answer sheets are read by machines—and machines can't think. That means it's up to you to make sure you're in the right place on the answer sheet every time you record an answer. The machine won't know that you really meant to answer Question 25 when you marked the space for Question 26.

- If you skip a question, list the number on your scratch paper. Don't mark the answer sheet in any way as a reminder. Any stray marks may affect how the machine scores your answer sheet.

- Always check to see that the answer space you have filled in corresponds to the question you are answering.

- Be sure to fill in bubbles completely so that there can be no mistake about which answers you chose.

These seem like simple things, but you'd be surprised how many students fail to do them, especially keeping track of answer lines if they skip a question.

Let's move on to the grid-in responses. These responses are only for questions you will see in the math section. You'll still be filling in ovals, but they will look a little different from the multiple-choice ovals. Here's a sample of the special grid you will use.

TIP

Make sure you're in the right place! Always check to see that the answer space you fill in corresponds to the question you are answering.

← *boxes to write your numerical answer*
← *fraction lines—use at most one per answer*
← *decimal points—use at most one per answer*

At the top of the grid, you'll write in the numerical answer. The slashes that appear in the second row are used for answers with fractions. If you need one of these fraction lines in your answer, darken one of the ovals. The ovals with the dots are for answers with decimal points—use these ovals just as you do the fraction line ovals. In the lower part of the grid, fill in the numbered ovals that correspond to the numbers in your answer.

Here are some examples. Note that for grid-in responses, answers can begin on the left or the right.

HOW THE SAT® IS SCORED

OK, you've filled in all your ovals, and perhaps written an essay. The 3 hours (and 50 minutes if you are taking the optional essay portion) are up (not a minute too soon), and you've turned in your answer sheet and your essay sheet. What next? Off your answers go to the machines at College Board and to the high school and college teachers who have been trained to read and score the essays. The machines can scan the bubble sheets in seconds and calculate a score for most of your test. If you are taking the optional essay portion, two readers will score it based on three criteria: reading, analysis, and writing. Their scores will be combined and reported separately from the main portion of the SAT®.

In scoring the multiple-choice and grid-in sections of the SAT®, the machines give one point for each correct answer. Incorrect answers have no effect on your score. Each reader of your essay uses a rubric against which he or she reads your essay. Each reader then gives your essay a score from 1 to 4. The two scores will be combined to give you an essay subscore.

The result of these calculations for each part of the SAT®—math and evidence-based reading and writing—is your raw score. This is then converted to a scaled score between 400 and 1600. Your essay will be given a score ranging between 6 and 24, and it will be reported separately. These scores will be reported to you and to the colleges you have chosen.

Remember, if you take the SAT® more than once, you can choose whether the school you are applying to receives the scores from each test date or just some of them.

STRATEGIES FOR SAT® SUCCESS

What makes some people better test-takers than others? The secret isn't just knowing the subject; it's knowing specific test-taking strategies that can add up to extra points. This means psyching out the test, knowing how the test-makers think and what they're looking for, and using this knowledge to your advantage. Smart test-takers know how to use pacing and guessing to add points to their score.

NOTE

Because the SAT® can vary in format, scaled scores allow the test-maker to account for differences from one version of the SAT® to another. Using scaled scores ensures that a score of 500 on one SAT® is equivalent to 500 on another.

Pace Yourself

Suppose there are 20 questions in one of the math sections and they need to be answered in 25 minutes. That means that you have 1 minute and 15 seconds to answer each question. But smart test-takers know that's not the best way to use their time. If you use less than a minute to answer the easier questions, you'll have extra time to answer the more difficult ones. That's why learning to pace yourself is so important.

Question Sets in Math Usually Go from Easiest to Most Difficult— You Should, Too

A question set is one set of similar questions within the larger math and evidence-based reading and writing sections. In the math sections, SAT® questions follow the pattern of easiest to hardest. Work your way through the easier questions as quickly as you can. That way you'll have more time for the more difficult ones.

But two words of caution: First, what may be easy to the test-writer may not be to you. Don't panic if Question 3 seems hard. Try to work through it, but don't spend too much time on it if it's a topic such as factoring that has just never been easy for you to understand. Second, work quickly but carefully. Don't work so fast that you make a silly mistake and lose a point that you should have aced.

You Can Set Your Own Speed Limit

All right, how will you know what your speed limit is? Use the practice tests to check your timing and see how it affects your answers. If you've answered most of the questions in the time limit but have a lot of incorrect answers, you'd better slow down. On the other hand, if you are very accurate in your answers but aren't answering every question in a section, you can probably pick up the pace a bit.

It's Smart to Keep Moving

It's hard to let go, but sometimes you have to. Don't spend too much time on any one question before you've tried all the questions in a section. There may be questions later on in the test that you can answer easily, and you don't want to lose points just because you didn't get to them.

The Easy Choice Isn't Always Best

Are you at the end of a math section? Remember, that's where you'll usually find the hardest questions, which means that the answers are more complex. Look carefully at the choices and really think about what the question is asking.

You Don't Have to Read the Directions

What? Yes, you read it correctly the first time—you don't have to read the directions. By the time you actually sit down to take the SAT®, you've read this book, you've taken all the practice tests you could find, and you've read enough SAT® directions to fill a library. So when the exam clock starts ticking, don't waste time rereading directions you already know. Instead, go directly to Question 1.

You're Going to Need a Watch

If you're going to pace yourself, you need to keep track of the time—and what if there is no clock in your room or if the only clock is out of your line of vision? That's why it's a good idea to bring a watch to the test. A word of warning: Don't use a watch alarm or your watch will end up on the proctor's desk.

MAKE AN SAT® STUDY PLAN

As with almost any form of learning, preparing for the SAT® is an investment of time. The more you have, the better your chances of boosting your score significantly. Next, we'll walk you through two different study plans, each tailored to a specific amount of preparation time. Choose the plan that fits your circumstances and adapt it to your needs.

Regardless of how much time you have before the actual exam, your first step should be to take the Diagnostic Test in Part II of this book. After you score it, compute your category percentages to assess your relative strengths and weaknesses. Hang on to the scoring sheet so you know where to get started.

The Complete Course

If you have three or more months to prepare, you should congratulate yourself! This will give you sufficient time to familiarize yourself with the test, learn critical strategies, review grammar and math fundamentals, practice writing, and take full-length tests.

You'll get the most out of your SAT® preparation if you:

- Reread this chapter to ensure that you understand the format, structure, and scoring of the SAT®.
- Take the Diagnostic Test and identify your areas that need improvement.
- Read each and every strategy and review chapter.
- Work through all the examples, exercises, and practice exams.
- Read all the answer explanations.
- Focus on the chapters where your scores show you need to improve.

The Accelerated Course

If you have one month or less to prepare for the SAT® or if you cannot devote a lot of time to studying for any other reason, follow the accelerated course. You'll get the most out of this course if you:

- Reread this chapter to ensure that you understand the format, structure, and scoring of the SAT®.
- Take the Diagnostic Test and identify your areas that need improvement.
- Focus on the chapters that cover material that is most problematic for you and work through all the examples and exercises in these chapters.
- Work through as many practice exams as you can.
- Read all the answer explanations.

NOTE

You may be wondering how you can possibly wade through all this information in time for the test. Don't be discouraged! We wrote this book knowing that some of you would be on very condensed schedules. The information in this section will help you construct a study plan that works for you—one that will help you boost your score no matter how limited your time may be. Remember, though, that practice and targeted study are essential elements of that score boosting, so invest as much time as possible in your SAT® preparation.

TIP

Here's an important point: You don't have to go through the book in order. You might want to start with the topic that you find most difficult, such as functions or grammar, or the question type that you're most unsure about, such as grid-ins. Then move to the next most difficult and so on down the line, saving the easiest topics or question types until the end. If you take the accelerated course, you should definitely take this approach.

MEASURING YOUR PROGRESS

It does seem as if you're on a treadmill sometimes, doesn't it? Question after question after question—are you really getting anywhere? Is all of this studying really working?

The way to find out is to monitor your progress throughout the preparation period, whether it's three months or four weeks. By taking a diagnostic examination at the beginning, you'll establish your skill baseline, and you'll be able to craft the study plan that's right for you. Then, you can either start to read the entire book (if you are taking the complete course) or go directly to the chapters that address your weaknesses (if you are taking the accelerated course). At the end of each chapter, complete the exercises and compare your percentages to your original diagnostic percentages. How have you improved? Where do you still need work? Even if you haven't reached your ultimate performance goal, are you at least applying new test-taking methods?

One Third of the Way Through Your Study

When you are approximately one third of the way through your course of study—this can be after ten days or a month—it's time to take one of the practice tests. When you have finished scoring and reading the answer explanations, compare your scores with your original diagnostic scores. Hopefully, you're doing better. But if you're not, don't panic. At this point in test preparation, it's not unusual to score about the same as you did at the beginning.

What's more important than *what* you scored is *how* you took the practice test. Did you really use the test-taking strategies to which you've been introduced? If you didn't, go back to the strategy chapters and either reread them, if you are doing the complete course, or at least reread the summaries, if you are on the accelerated course. Then continue your review. Read more review chapters and complete the exercises.

Two Thirds of the Way Through Your Study

After you have worked through most of the review chapters (under the complete course plan) or all of the material relating to your areas of weakness (under the accelerated course), it's time to take another practice test. By now, you should be seeing some real improvement in your scores. If you are still having trouble with certain topics, review the problematic material again.

The Home Stretch

For the most part, the last phase of study should involve *less learning* and *more practice*. Take more practice tests! By now, you probably understand how to take the SAT®. What you need is more practice taking the test under simulated test-day conditions to work on your pacing and test-taking strategies.

When you take additional practice exams, be sure to do so in a near-test environment. Keep analyzing your scores to ensure that all of this practice is working. Determine which areas need additional work. Now is the perfect time to take timed drills, whether you are following the complete course or the accelerated course. Because you have already reviewed the chapters, work on your weaknesses by doing timing drills.

The Final Week

One last word of advice: No matter which study plan you select, you should probably take one full, timed practice SAT® the week before you take the actual SAT®. This will get you ready for the big day. But don't take the test the day before the real SAT®. That's a time when you should be relaxing, not cramming.

GETTING READY: THE NIGHT BEFORE AND THE DAY OF THE TEST

If you follow the guidelines in this book, you will be extremely well prepared for the SAT®. You will know the format inside and out; you will know how to approach every type of question; you will have worked hard to strengthen your weak areas; and you will have taken multiple practice tests under simulated testing conditions. The last 24 hours before the SAT® is not the time to cram—it's actually the time to relax. Remember that the SAT® is primarily a test of how you think, not what you know. So last-minute cramming can be more confusing than illuminating.

On the night before the big day, find a diversion to keep yourself from obsessing about the SAT®. Maybe stay home and watch some of your favorite television shows. Or go out to an early movie. Do whatever is best for you. Just make sure you get plenty of sleep.

You should also lay out the following items before you go to bed:

- **Registration ticket:** Unless you are taking the test as a standby tester, you should be able to print your ticket by signing into your College Board account online. Sign in to "My SAT" and click "Print Admission Ticket". The ticket will arrive in the mail if you haven't provided an e-mail address or if you requested that it be sent by mail when you registered.

- **Identification:** Bring photo identification that is accepted by the test center, like a driver's license, a passport, or a school identification card.

- **Pencils:** Make sure you bring at least three No. 2 pencils; those are the only pencils that the machines can read.

- **Calculator:** Consult the College Board's website for a list of permitted calculators, and bring the calculator with which you're most comfortable. Don't pack a calculator that beeps, produces a paper tape, or that is a part of a computer or other device. Also, make sure your calculator has new batteries or bring extras with you just in case.

- **Layered clothing:** You never know what the temperature of the test-taking room will be. By dressing in layers, you can adapt to either a warm or a cold room.

- **Wristwatch:** Your classroom should have an operational clock, but if it doesn't, you want to be prepared. Again, don't wear a watch that beeps, unless you can turn off the alarm function.

- **Snack:** You're not allowed to eat in the room during the test, but you are given two 5-minute breaks. So be armed with a fortifying snack that you can eat quickly in the hallway.

Make sure you allow enough time to arrive at the test site at least 15 minutes before the 8 a.m. arrival time. You don't want to raise your level of anxiety by having to rush to get there.

In the morning, take a shower to wake up and then eat a sensible breakfast. If you are a person who usually eats breakfast, you should probably eat your customary meal. If you don't usually eat breakfast, don't gorge yourself on test day, because it will be a shock to your system. Eat something light (like a granola bar and a piece of fruit) and pack that snack.

SUMMING IT UP

- Learning the SAT® question types is the best way to prepare for the redesigned SAT®. Knowing the test format and question types will relieve test anxiety, because you'll know exactly what to expect on test day.

  1 **Evidence-based Reading:** The answer to every question will be either directly stated or implied in the passage.

  2 **Revising work:** These question sets test your ability to spot and correct grammatical errors, usage problems, and wordiness. You will also be expected to answer questions to improve the development and organization of a particular paragraph or the passage as a whole.

  3 **Multiple-choice math:** A set of reference formulas is given at the beginning of each math section, so you don't have to worry about forgetting an important formula.

  4 **Grid-ins:** You have to calculate the answer and then fill in ovals on the grids provided on the answer sheet. Only the ovals count, so fill in each one correctly.

  5 **Essay (Optional):** You will have 50 minutes to write your essay, which tests reading, analysis, and writing skills. You will be asked to produce a written analysis of a provided source text. You will need to explain how the author has effectively built an argument to persuade his or her audience. The readers are trained to evaluate the essays as first drafts, not polished final products.

- You may use a calculator on the SAT®, but only in one math section. For some questions, you will need to decide if the calculator will help you or slow you down.

- In the math section, questions are generally arranged from easiest to most difficult. Where a question falls in a set provides an instant indication of how difficult it is.

- Every SAT® question is worth 1 point, whether it is an easy question or a difficult one. So nail the easier questions—and quickly accumulate points.

- Fill in the answer bubbles cleanly and completely, or you won't get credit for your answers.

- Random guessing will have little effect on your score, but educated guessing can boost your score.

- Pace yourself and move through the test relatively quickly.

- Relax the evening before the SAT®, but also be sure you're prepared.
  - Assemble the supplies you will need for the test.
  - Pick out what you'll wear and remember to layer your clothes.
  - Be sure your calculator has fresh batteries.

- On the morning of the test, eat breakfast, pack your snack, and leave for the test site in plenty of time to get there at least 15 minutes before the start time.

PART II

DIAGNOSING STRENGTHS AND WEAKNESSES

CHAPTER 2   Diagnostic Test for the SAT®

Diagnostic Test for the SAT®

Before you begin preparing for the SAT®, it's important to know your strengths and the areas where you need improvement. If you find the questions easy for the Reading Test, for example, it would be a mistake to dedicate hours practicing them. Taking the Diagnostic Test in this chapter and then working out your scores will help you determine how you should apportion your study time.

PREPARING TO TAKE THE DIAGNOSTIC TEST

If possible, take the test in one sitting. Give yourself at least 4 hours to complete the Diagnostic Test. The actual test is 3 hours and 45 minutes, and you'll be allowed to take three short breaks—you may even want to have some healthy snacks nearby for a quick break you'll want to take. Simulating the test this way will give you an idea of how long the sections are and how it feels to take the entire test. You will also get a sense of how long you can spend on each question in each section, so you can begin to work out a pacing schedule for yourself.

First, assemble all the things you will need to take the test. These include:

- No. 2 pencils, at least three
- A calculator with fresh batteries
- A timer
- The answer sheet and the lined paper for the essay—provided on the following pages

Set a timer for the time specified for each section, which is noted at the top of the first page of each test section. Stick to that time, so you are simulating the real test. At this point, it's as important to know how many questions you can answer in the time allotted as it is to answer questions correctly.

ANSWER SHEET DIAGNOSTIC TEST

Section 1: Reading Test

1. Ⓐ Ⓑ Ⓒ Ⓓ   12. Ⓐ Ⓑ Ⓒ Ⓓ   23. Ⓐ Ⓑ Ⓒ Ⓓ   33. Ⓐ Ⓑ Ⓒ Ⓓ   43. Ⓐ Ⓑ Ⓒ Ⓓ

2. Ⓐ Ⓑ Ⓒ Ⓓ   13. Ⓐ Ⓑ Ⓒ Ⓓ   24. Ⓐ Ⓑ Ⓒ Ⓓ   34. Ⓐ Ⓑ Ⓒ Ⓓ   44. Ⓐ Ⓑ Ⓒ Ⓓ

3. Ⓐ Ⓑ Ⓒ Ⓓ   14. Ⓐ Ⓑ Ⓒ Ⓓ   25. Ⓐ Ⓑ Ⓒ Ⓓ   35. Ⓐ Ⓑ Ⓒ Ⓓ   45. Ⓐ Ⓑ Ⓒ Ⓓ

4. Ⓐ Ⓑ Ⓒ Ⓓ   15. Ⓐ Ⓑ Ⓒ Ⓓ   26. Ⓐ Ⓑ Ⓒ Ⓓ   36. Ⓐ Ⓑ Ⓒ Ⓓ   46. Ⓐ Ⓑ Ⓒ Ⓓ

5. Ⓐ Ⓑ Ⓒ Ⓓ   16. Ⓐ Ⓑ Ⓒ Ⓓ   27. Ⓐ Ⓑ Ⓒ Ⓓ   37. Ⓐ Ⓑ Ⓒ Ⓓ   47. Ⓐ Ⓑ Ⓒ Ⓓ

6. Ⓐ Ⓑ Ⓒ Ⓓ   17. Ⓐ Ⓑ Ⓒ Ⓓ   28. Ⓐ Ⓑ Ⓒ Ⓓ   38. Ⓐ Ⓑ Ⓒ Ⓓ   48. Ⓐ Ⓑ Ⓒ Ⓓ

7. Ⓐ Ⓑ Ⓒ Ⓓ   18. Ⓐ Ⓑ Ⓒ Ⓓ   29. Ⓐ Ⓑ Ⓒ Ⓓ   39. Ⓐ Ⓑ Ⓒ Ⓓ   49. Ⓐ Ⓑ Ⓒ Ⓓ

8. Ⓐ Ⓑ Ⓒ Ⓓ   19. Ⓐ Ⓑ Ⓒ Ⓓ   30. Ⓐ Ⓑ Ⓒ Ⓓ   40. Ⓐ Ⓑ Ⓒ Ⓓ   50. Ⓐ Ⓑ Ⓒ Ⓓ

9. Ⓐ Ⓑ Ⓒ Ⓓ   20. Ⓐ Ⓑ Ⓒ Ⓓ   31. Ⓐ Ⓑ Ⓒ Ⓓ   41. Ⓐ Ⓑ Ⓒ Ⓓ   51. Ⓐ Ⓑ Ⓒ Ⓓ

10. Ⓐ Ⓑ Ⓒ Ⓓ   21. Ⓐ Ⓑ Ⓒ Ⓓ   32. Ⓐ Ⓑ Ⓒ Ⓓ   42. Ⓐ Ⓑ Ⓒ Ⓓ   52. Ⓐ Ⓑ Ⓒ Ⓓ

11. Ⓐ Ⓑ Ⓒ Ⓓ   22. Ⓐ Ⓑ Ⓒ Ⓓ

Section 2: Writing and Language Test

1. Ⓐ Ⓑ Ⓒ Ⓓ   10. Ⓐ Ⓑ Ⓒ Ⓓ   19. Ⓐ Ⓑ Ⓒ Ⓓ   28. Ⓐ Ⓑ Ⓒ Ⓓ   37. Ⓐ Ⓑ Ⓒ Ⓓ

2. Ⓐ Ⓑ Ⓒ Ⓓ   11. Ⓐ Ⓑ Ⓒ Ⓓ   20. Ⓐ Ⓑ Ⓒ Ⓓ   29. Ⓐ Ⓑ Ⓒ Ⓓ   38. Ⓐ Ⓑ Ⓒ Ⓓ

3. Ⓐ Ⓑ Ⓒ Ⓓ   12. Ⓐ Ⓑ Ⓒ Ⓓ   21. Ⓐ Ⓑ Ⓒ Ⓓ   30. Ⓐ Ⓑ Ⓒ Ⓓ   39. Ⓐ Ⓑ Ⓒ Ⓓ

4. Ⓐ Ⓑ Ⓒ Ⓓ   13. Ⓐ Ⓑ Ⓒ Ⓓ   22. Ⓐ Ⓑ Ⓒ Ⓓ   31. Ⓐ Ⓑ Ⓒ Ⓓ   40. Ⓐ Ⓑ Ⓒ Ⓓ

5. Ⓐ Ⓑ Ⓒ Ⓓ   14. Ⓐ Ⓑ Ⓒ Ⓓ   23. Ⓐ Ⓑ Ⓒ Ⓓ   32. Ⓐ Ⓑ Ⓒ Ⓓ   41. Ⓐ Ⓑ Ⓒ Ⓓ

6. Ⓐ Ⓑ Ⓒ Ⓓ   15. Ⓐ Ⓑ Ⓒ Ⓓ   24. Ⓐ Ⓑ Ⓒ Ⓓ   33. Ⓐ Ⓑ Ⓒ Ⓓ   42. Ⓐ Ⓑ Ⓒ Ⓓ

7. Ⓐ Ⓑ Ⓒ Ⓓ   16. Ⓐ Ⓑ Ⓒ Ⓓ   25. Ⓐ Ⓑ Ⓒ Ⓓ   34. Ⓐ Ⓑ Ⓒ Ⓓ   43. Ⓐ Ⓑ Ⓒ Ⓓ

8. Ⓐ Ⓑ Ⓒ Ⓓ   17. Ⓐ Ⓑ Ⓒ Ⓓ   26. Ⓐ Ⓑ Ⓒ Ⓓ   35. Ⓐ Ⓑ Ⓒ Ⓓ   44. Ⓐ Ⓑ Ⓒ Ⓓ

9. Ⓐ Ⓑ Ⓒ Ⓓ   18. Ⓐ Ⓑ Ⓒ Ⓓ   27. Ⓐ Ⓑ Ⓒ Ⓓ   36. Ⓐ Ⓑ Ⓒ Ⓓ

Section 3: Math Test—No Calculator

1. Ⓐ Ⓑ Ⓒ Ⓓ　4. Ⓐ Ⓑ Ⓒ Ⓓ　7. Ⓐ Ⓑ Ⓒ Ⓓ　10. Ⓐ Ⓑ Ⓒ Ⓓ　13. Ⓐ Ⓑ Ⓒ Ⓓ

2. Ⓐ Ⓑ Ⓒ Ⓓ　5. Ⓐ Ⓑ Ⓒ Ⓓ　8. Ⓐ Ⓑ Ⓒ Ⓓ　11. Ⓐ Ⓑ Ⓒ Ⓓ　14. Ⓐ Ⓑ Ⓒ Ⓓ

3. Ⓐ Ⓑ Ⓒ Ⓓ　6. Ⓐ Ⓑ Ⓒ Ⓓ　9. Ⓐ Ⓑ Ⓒ Ⓓ　12. Ⓐ Ⓑ Ⓒ Ⓓ　15. Ⓐ Ⓑ Ⓒ Ⓓ

16.　17.　18.　19.　20.

(grid-in bubble answer grids for questions 16–20, each with four columns containing fraction bars, decimal points, and digits 0–9)

Section 4: Math Test—Calculator

1. Ⓐ Ⓑ Ⓒ Ⓓ　7. Ⓐ Ⓑ Ⓒ Ⓓ　13. Ⓐ Ⓑ Ⓒ Ⓓ　19. Ⓐ Ⓑ Ⓒ Ⓓ　25. Ⓐ Ⓑ Ⓒ Ⓓ

2. Ⓐ Ⓑ Ⓒ Ⓓ　8. Ⓐ Ⓑ Ⓒ Ⓓ　14. Ⓐ Ⓑ Ⓒ Ⓓ　20. Ⓐ Ⓑ Ⓒ Ⓓ　26. Ⓐ Ⓑ Ⓒ Ⓓ

3. Ⓐ Ⓑ Ⓒ Ⓓ　9. Ⓐ Ⓑ Ⓒ Ⓓ　15. Ⓐ Ⓑ Ⓒ Ⓓ　21. Ⓐ Ⓑ Ⓒ Ⓓ　27. Ⓐ Ⓑ Ⓒ Ⓓ

4. Ⓐ Ⓑ Ⓒ Ⓓ　10. Ⓐ Ⓑ Ⓒ Ⓓ　16. Ⓐ Ⓑ Ⓒ Ⓓ　22. Ⓐ Ⓑ Ⓒ Ⓓ　28. Ⓐ Ⓑ Ⓒ Ⓓ

5. Ⓐ Ⓑ Ⓒ Ⓓ　11. Ⓐ Ⓑ Ⓒ Ⓓ　17. Ⓐ Ⓑ Ⓒ Ⓓ　23. Ⓐ Ⓑ Ⓒ Ⓓ　29. Ⓐ Ⓑ Ⓒ Ⓓ

6. Ⓐ Ⓑ Ⓒ Ⓓ　12. Ⓐ Ⓑ Ⓒ Ⓓ　18. Ⓐ Ⓑ Ⓒ Ⓓ　24. Ⓐ Ⓑ Ⓒ Ⓓ　30. Ⓐ Ⓑ Ⓒ Ⓓ

31.　32.　33.　34.　35.

(grid-in bubble answer grids for questions 31–35, each with four columns containing fraction bars, decimal points, and digits 0–9)

answer sheet

36.

	/	/	
.	.	.	.
	0	0	0
1	1	1	1
2	2	2	2
3	3	3	3
4	4	4	4
5	5	5	5
6	6	6	6
7	7	7	7
8	8	8	8
9	9	9	9

37.

	/	/	
.	.	.	.
	0	0	0
1	1	1	1
2	2	2	2
3	3	3	3
4	4	4	4
5	5	5	5
6	6	6	6
7	7	7	7
8	8	8	8
9	9	9	9

38.

	/	/	
.	.	.	.
	0	0	0
1	1	1	1
2	2	2	2
3	3	3	3
4	4	4	4
5	5	5	5
6	6	6	6
7	7	7	7
8	8	8	8
9	9	9	9

Section 5: Essay

_____

_____

_____

_____

_____

_____

_____

_____

_____

_____

_____

_____

_____

_____

_____

_____

_____

_____

_____

_____

----

answer sheet

SECTION 1: READING TEST

65 Minutes • 52 Questions

TURN TO SECTION 1 OF YOUR ANSWER SHEET TO ANSWER THE QUESTIONS IN THIS SECTION.

Directions: Each passage (or pair of passages) below is followed by a number of multiple-choice questions. After reading each passage, select the best answer to each question based on what is stated or implied in the passage or passages and in any supplementary material, such as a table, graph, chart, or photograph.

QUESTIONS 1–10 ARE BASED ON THE FOLLOWING PASSAGE.

John James Audubon (1785–1851) is known primarily for his bird studies, but as this passage from Ornithological Biography *shows, he wrote about the behavior of other animals as well.*

Black Bear

The Black Bear (*Ursus americanus*), however clumsy in appearance, is active, vigilant, and persevering; possesses
Line great strength, courage, and address; and
5 undergoes with little injury the greatest fatigues and hardships in avoiding the pursuit of the hunter. Like the Deer, it changes its haunts with the seasons, and for the same reason, namely, the desire of
10 obtaining suitable food, or of retiring to the more inaccessible parts, where it can pass the time in security, unobserved by man, the most dangerous of its enemies. During the spring months, it searches for
15 food in the low rich alluvial lands that border the rivers, or by the margins of such inland lakes as, on account of their small size, are called by us ponds. There it procures abundance of succulent roots,
20 and of the tender juicy stems of plants, on which it chiefly feeds at that season. During the summer heat, it enters the gloomy swamps, passes much of its time wallowing in the mud, like a hog, and
25 contents itself with crayfish, roots, and nettles, now and then, when hard pressed by hunger, seizing on a young pig, or perhaps a sow, or even a calf. As soon as the different kinds of berries which grow
30 on the mountain begin to ripen, the Bears

betake themselves to the high grounds, followed by their cubs. In such retired parts of the country where there are no hilly grounds, it pays visits to the maize
35 fields, which it ravages for a while. After this, the various species of nuts, acorns, grapes, and other forest fruits, that form what in the western country is called mast, attract its attention. The Bear is then
40 seen rambling singly through the woods to gather this harvest, not forgetting to rob every Bee tree it meets with, Bears being, as you well know, expert at this operation. You also know that they are
45 good climbers, and may have been told, or at least may now be told, that the Black Bear now and then houses itself in the hollow trunks of the larger trees for weeks together, when it is said to suck
50 its paws. You are probably not aware of a habit in which it indulges, and which, being curious, must be interesting to you. At one season, the Black Bear may be seen examining the lower part of
55 the trunk of a tree for several minutes with much attention, at the same time looking around, and snuffing the air, to assure itself that no enemy is near. It then raises itself on its hind legs, approaches
60 the trunk, embraces it with its forelegs, and scratches the bark with its teeth and claws for several minutes in continuance. Its jaws clash against each other, until a mass of foam runs down both sides of the
65 mouth. After this it continues its rambles. In various portions of our country, many of our woodsmen and hunters who have seen the Bear performing the singular operation just described, imagine that it

GO TO THE NEXT PAGE

www.petersons.com

70 does so for the purpose of leaving behind an indication of its size and power. They measure the height at which the scratches are made, and in this manner, can, in fact, form an estimate of the magnitude of the 75 individual. My own opinion, however, is different. It seems to me that the Bear scratches on the trees, not for the purpose of showing its size or its strength, but merely for that of sharpening its teeth 80 and claws, to enable it better to encounter a rival of its own species during the amatory season. The Wild Boar of Europe clashes its tusks and scrapes the earth with its feet, and the Deer rubs its 85 antlers against the lower part of the stems of young trees or bushes, for the same purpose.

1 As used in line 4, "address" refers to

(A) habitat.

(B) focus.

(C) skill.

(D) direction.

2 What is the most likely reason that Audubon wrote about the black bear?

(A) He wanted to provide more information about another animal to his readers.

(B) He was fascinated by mammals.

(C) He didn't think his readers knew anything about bears.

(D) He wanted to show the commonalities in behavioral patterns of bears and birds.

3 Which of the following quotes from the text provides evidence to support the idea that the bear migrates from one habitat to another?

(A) Lines 7–8 ("Like … seasons")

(B) Line 19 ("it procures … roots")

(C) Lines 53–55 ("the Black Bear … tree")

(D) Line 65 ("After … rambles")

4 Huntsmen and woodsmen claim that the bear scratches tree bark with its teeth and claws to

(A) sharpen its teeth.

(B) mark the tree for winter hibernation.

(C) ward off potential predators by showing its size.

(D) mark the tree so that other animals can't harvest its nuts and acorns.

5 What is the main rhetorical effect of lines 22–28?

(A) To show that the bear is an exceptional predator

(B) To explain why humans might want to hunt bears

(C) To impress the reader with how varied a bear's diet is

(D) To create an image of a bear placidly foraging for food

6 What evidence in the text does Audubon use to support his theory about why bears mark a tree with their teeth and claws?

(A) When foaming at the mouth, the bear scares off predators.

(B) The marks indicate to predators the huge size and power of the bear.

(C) Other animals have similar behaviors designed to strengthen the animal.

(D) The practice makes the bear foam at the mouth, which is a sign of strength to other bears.

7 According to Audubon, how are the claws of the black bear like the tusk of the wild boar?

(A) Both are parts of the body that serve to get food for the animal.

(B) Both animals use these parts of their bodies as a sign of strength.

(C) Both animals use these body parts to defend themselves from human predators.

(D) Both are parts of the body that the animal sharpens to better compete for a mate.

8 The fact that Audubon calls man the bear's "most dangerous" enemy (line 13) indicates that he

(A) is a hunter himself.

(B) has some sympathy for hunted bears.

(C) does not believe that bears are dangerous.

(D) thinks bears are more dangerous than people.

9 What evidence in the text shows that black bears are not vegetarians?

(A) Lines 18–21 ("There it … that season")

(B) Lines 26–28 ("when hard … even a calf.")

(C) Lines 34–35 ("it pays … for a while")

(D) Lines 36–39 ("various species … its attention")

10 How can you tell what assumptions Audubon makes about his reader?

(A) He gives detailed descriptions, suggesting that the reader is interested.

(B) He addresses the reader directly to provide information he thinks the reader doesn't have.

(C) Using comparisons to the deer shows that Audubon assumes readers are more familiar with deer than bears.

(D) Using third-person narration and passive voice indicates that Audubon assumes all of the information is new to the reader.

QUESTIONS 11–21 ARE BASED ON THE FOLLOWING PASSAGE.

Thomas Jefferson wrote in 1787 to his nephew, Peter Carr, a student at the College of William and Mary.

Paris, August 10, 1787

Dear Peter, I have received your two letters of December 30 and April 18 and am very happy to find by them, as well as
Line by letters from Mr. Wythe,* that you have
5 been so fortunate as to attract his notice and good will: I am sure you will find this to have been one of the more fortunate events of your life, as I have ever been sensible it was of mine. I enclose you a
10 sketch of the sciences to which I would wish you to apply in such order as Mr. Wythe shall advise: I mention also the books in them worth your reading, which submit to his correction. Many of these
15 are among your father's books, which you should have brought to you. As I do not recollect those of them not in his library, you must write to me for them, making out a catalogue of such as you think you
20 shall have occasion for in 18 months from the date of your letter, and consulting Mr. Wythe on the subject. To this sketch I will add a few particular observations.

1. Italian. I fear the learning of this
25 language will confound your French and Spanish. Being all of them degenerated dialects of the Latin, they are apt to mix in conversation. I have never seen a person speaking the three languages
30 who did not mix them. It is a delightful language, but late events having rendered the Spanish more useful, lay it aside to prosecute that.

2. Spanish. Bestow great attention on
35 this, and endeavor to acquire an accurate knowledge of it. Our future connections with Spain and Spanish America will render that language a valuable acquisition. The ancient history of a great
40 part of America too is written in that language. I send you a dictionary.

3. Moral philosophy. I think it lost time to attend lectures in this branch. He who made us would have been a pitiful
45 bungler if he had made the rules of our moral conduct a matter of science. For one man of science, there are thousands who are not. What would have become of them? Man was destined for society. His
50 morality therefore was to be formed to this object. He was endowed with a sense of right and wrong merely relative to this. This sense is as much a part of his nature as the sense of hearing, seeing, feeling;
55 it is the true foundation of morality. … The moral sense, or conscience, is as much a part of man as his leg or arm. It

GO TO THE NEXT PAGE

is given to all human beings in a stronger
or weaker degree, as force of members is
60 given them in a greater or less degree. ...
State a moral case to a ploughman and
a professor. The former will decide it
as well, and often better than the latter,
because he has not been led astray by
65 artificial rules.

*George Wythe, a well-respected scholar, the first
American law professor, and one of the signatories
of the Declaration of Independence, became an
important teacher and mentor to Thomas Jefferson.

11 What is the best description of Mr. Wythe
and his relationship to the Jefferson family?

(A) Teacher

(B) Cousin

(C) Family friend

(D) Public servant

12 What is the purpose of Jefferson's letter to
his nephew?

(A) To advise him about his education

(B) To advise him about leading a moral
life

(C) To make sure he will learn a second
language

(D) To keep in touch with his family
while abroad

13 What does Jefferson mean by "lay it aside
to prosecute that" (lines 32–33)?

(A) Support Spain as a world power

(B) Bring legal action against Italy

(C) Pursue studies of Spanish

(D) Engage in the study of Italian

14 Which of the following is the best example
of the paternal tone Jefferson uses with his
nephew?

(A) Lines 6–8 ("I am sure ... your life")

(B) Lines 22–23 ("I will add ...
observations.")

(C) Line 41 ("I send ... a dictionary.")

(D) Line 49 ("Man was ... society.")

15 In lines 56–57, Jefferson compares conscience to a physical limb of the body to
show

(A) that it is natural and present in all
human beings.

(B) how easily we take it for granted.

(C) that without it, humans are powerless.

(D) how mental and physical states are
integrated.

16 What country does Jefferson think will
most closely aligned with the newly independent colonies in the future?

(A) England

B) France

C) Italy

D) Spain

17 By "lost time" (lines 42–43), Jefferson
means

(A) wasted time.

(B) the past.

(C) missing time.

(D) youth.

18 Jefferson tells his nephew not to study
Italian because it's

(A) a degenerated dialect.

(B) not necessary since he already knows
French.

(C) not useful to be multilingual.

(D) too easy to get it mixed up with
Spanish.

19 Which of the following best summarizes
Jefferson's overall view of morality?

(A) Morality is a science that can be
taught by professors and scholars.

(B) Moral philosophy is self-taught.

(C) A sense of morality is part of human
nature.

(D) Humans are moral beings who need
rules to guide their behavior.

Three Generations of the Jefferson Family

Peter Jefferson (b: 1700; d: 1757) – [spouse] Jane Randolph (b: 1721; d: 1776)

[children: 10]

Thomas (b: 1743; d: 1826) – [spouse] Martha Wales (b: 1748; d: 1782)

[children: 6]

(others died before reaching adulthood)

Martha (b: 1772; d: 1836)   Mary (b: 1778; d: 1782)

Martha (b: 1746; d: 1811) – [spouse] Dabney Carr [b: 1743; d: 1773]

[children: 6]

| Peter (b: 1770; d: 1815)

20 How does the family tree best explain Jefferson's concern about Peter's education?

(A) Jefferson was Peter's uncle.

(B) Jefferson didn't have any sons.

(C) Peter's father died when Peter was 3.

(D) Peter was the smartest student in the family.

21 Which of the following best describes the tone of Jefferson's letter to his nephew?

(A) Invested and paternal

(B) Concerned and worried

(C) Objective and matter-of-fact

(D) Distant and preoccupied

QUESTIONS 22–32 ARE BASED ON THE FOLLOWING EXCERPT.

This excerpt is from the article "New Link in the Food Chain? Marine Plastic Pollution and Seafood Safety," by Nate Seltenrich. It has been reproduced from the journal Environmental Health Perspectives.

World plastics production has experienced almost constant growth for more than half a century, rising
Line from approximately 1.9 tons in 1950 to
5   approximately 330 million tons in 2013. The World Bank estimates that 1.4 billion tons of trash are generated globally each year, 10% of it plastic. The International Maritime Organization has banned the
10 dumping of plastic waste (and most other garbage) at sea. However, an unknown portion of the plastic produced each year escapes into the environment— instead of being landfilled, incinerated,
15 or recycled—and at least some of it eventually makes its way to sea.

Plastics that reach the ocean will gradually break down into ever-smaller pieces due to sunlight exposure,
20 oxidation, and the physical action of waves, currents, and grazing by fish and birds. So-called microplastics—variably defined in the scientific literature and popular press as smaller than 1 or 5 mm
25 in diameter—are understood to be the most abundant type of plastic in the ocean. The 5 Gyres' authors* found microplastics almost everywhere they sampled, from near-shore environments to
30 the open ocean, in varying concentrations, and they estimated that particles 4.75 mm or smaller—about the size of a lentil— made up roughly 90% of the total plastic pieces they collected.

35   But the degradation of larger pieces of plastic is not the only way microplastics end up in the ocean. Nurdles—the plastic pellets used as a feedstock for producing plastic goods—can spill from ships or
40 land-based sources, and "microbeads" used as scrubbing agents in personal care products such as skin cleansers, toothpastes, and shampoos, can escape water-treatment facilities and pass into
45 water-sheds with treated water. (In June 2014, Illinois became the first US state to ban the manufacture and sale of products containing microbeads, which have been

documented in the Great Lakes and
50 Chicago's North Shore Channel.)

Marine organisms throughout the food
chain commonly consume plastics of
various sizes. The tiniest microplastics
are small enough to be mistaken for food
55 by zooplankton, allowing them to enter
the food chain at very low trophic levels.
Some larger predators are thought to
confuse nurdles (which typically measure
less than 5 mm in diameter) with fish
60 eggs or other food sources.

Once plastics have been consumed,
laboratory tests show that chemical
additives and adsorbed pollutants and
metals on their surface can desorb (leach
65 out) and transfer into the guts and tissues
of marine organisms ....

Research has shown that harmful
and persistent substances can both
bioaccumulate (or increase in
70 concentration as exposures persist) and
biomagnify (or increase in concentration
at higher trophic levels) within organisms
as they assume some of the chemical
burden of their prey or environment. Yet
75 again, no research has yet demonstrated
the bioaccumulation of sorbed pollutants
in the environment.

Three key questions remain to be
determined. To what extent do plastics
80 transfer pollutants and additives to
organisms upon ingestion? What
contribution are plastics making to the
contaminant burden in organisms above
and beyond their exposures through
85 water, sediments, and food? And, finally,
what proportion of humans' exposure to
plastic ingredients and environmental
pollutants occurs through seafood?
Researchers are moving carefully in the
90 direction of answers to these questions. ...

New laws ... could require handling
plastics more responsibly at the end
of their useful life through recycling,
proper disposal, and extended producer
95 responsibility.

Rolf Halden, director of the Center
for Environmental Security at the
Biodesign Institute at Arizona State
University, advocates for another
100 solution: manufacturing more sustainable

plastics from the start. "We need to design
the next generation of plastics to make
them more biodegradable so that they
don't have a long half-life, they don't
105 accumulate in the oceans, and they don't
have the opportunity to collect chemicals
long-term," he says. "There's just no way
we can shield people from all exposures
that could occur. Let's design safer
110 chemicals and make the whole problem
moot."

*The 5 Gyres Institute addresses plastic pollution in
the ocean.*

---

22 Which of the following is the most common type of plastic found in the ocean?

(A) Nurdles
(B) Microplastics
(C) Microbeads
(D) Plastic pellets

---

23 What evidence from the text helps explain why scientists think it is important to include the study of seafood in their investigations?

(A) Lines 17–22 ("Plastics that ... fish and birds.")
(B) Lines 51–53 ("Marine organisms ... various sizes.")
(C) Lines 62–66 ("chemical additives ... marine organisms")
(D) Lines 86–88 ("what proportion ... through seafood?")

---

24 Which best describes the overall tone of the article?

(A) Neutral and scientific
(B) Emotional and persuasive
(C) Personal and human
(D) Subjective and opinionated

25 What solution does Rolf Halden support to decrease the effects of pollution from plastics on humans?

(A) Passing laws to mandate more rigorous recycling

(B) Developing plastics that are biodegradable

(C) Making plastics that are safe to ingest

(D) Requiring plastic manufacturers to be responsible for the effects of their products

26 This article was written to

(A) share the author's opinion about the environment.

(B) inform the public of the problems of plastic in the ocean.

(C) start a movement to halt all plastic production.

(D) get people to clean up the oceans.

27 What does Halden mean when he says he wants to "make the whole problem moot" (lines 110–111)?

(A) He wants to open it to more debate.

(B) He wants to make it go away.

(C) He wants it to be studied further.

(D) He wants to reduce its significance.

Wastewater and runoff carry microplastics into waterways.

Plastic objects are broken down into smaller pieces by sunlight and surf action.

Marine plastics are often mistaken for food.

Persistent, bioaccumulative, and toxic compounds in seawater preferentially sorb to plastics.

At the same time, constituents of the plastics themselves, such as additives, leach into the tissues of organisms that consume the particles.

More research is needed to learn how these processes ultimately affect body burdens in humans.

Bioaccumulation

Potential plastic-mediated bioaccumulation

Bioaccumulation may be amplified by plastics shuttling pollutants into marine organisms.

GO TO THE NEXT PAGE ▶

diagnostic test

28 Which of the following statements could be learned from the diagram about how plastics disrupt the food chain?

(A) Plastics enter the food chain when small fish eat small pieces of plastic.

(B) Sunlight breaks down larger pieces of plastic that have been tossed in the ocean.

(C) Unfiltered wastewater is often emptied directly into the ocean, even though it is illegal in many places.

(D) People should only eat a limited amount of fish and seafood because they may contain unsafe levels of contaminants.

29 Why did Illinois ban the sale of certain personal care products?

(A) Residues from the products were ending up in the ocean.

(B) The containers couldn't be recycled.

(C) The products were determined to be carcinogenic.

(D) The products contained microbeads that were getting into the water system.

30 Which of the following words would be most helpful in figuring out the meaning of the word "adsorbed" (line 63)?

(A) Absolved

(B) Adhered

(C) Absorbent

(D) Sorbet

31 What evidence does author use to support the idea that plastics in the ocean are a problem for humans?

(A) Ten percent of the world's trash are plastic.

(B) Plastics transfer pollutants and additives to organisms upon ingestion.

(C) Plastics were found in samples from all parts of the ocean.

(D) Experts say we need to design a new kind of plastics that are biodegradable.

32 The main disagreement between the author and Rolf Halden about a solution to the problem of plastic pollution is that the author

(A) advocates new laws and Halden advocates new ways to manufacture plastics.

(B) thinks recycling will resolve the problem, but Halden doesn't think we can ever be safe from exposure.

(C) thinks the plastic manufacturers should be more responsible for their products, but Halden thinks this would be an undue burden on business.

(D) thinks all plastics manufacturing should be stopped and Halden thinks research will find a solution.

QUESTIONS 33–42 ARE BASED ON THE FOLLOWING PASSAGE.

Angel Decora was born Hinookmahiwikilinaka on the Winnebago Reservation in Nebraska in 1871. She worked as a book illustrator, particularly on books by and about Native Americans, and lectured and wrote about Indian art. The story from which this excerpt is taken, "The Sick Child," may be autobiographical.

It was about sunset when I, a little child, was sent with a handful of powdered tobacco leaves and red feathers
Line to make an offering to the spirit who had
5 caused the sickness of my little sister. It had been a long, hard winter, and the snow lay deep on the prairie as far as the eye could reach. The medicine-woman's directions had been that the offering must
10 be laid upon the naked earth, and that to find it I must face toward the setting sun.

I was taught the prayer: "Spirit grandfather, I offer this to thee. I pray thee restore my little sister to health."
15 Full of reverence and a strong faith that I could appease the anger of the spirit, I started out to plead for the life of our little one.

But now where was a spot of earth
20 to be found in all that white monotony? They had talked of death at the house. I hoped that my little sister would live, but I was afraid of nature.

I reached a little spring. I looked down
25 to its pebbly bottom, wondering whether I should leave my offering there, or keep on in search of a spot of earth. If I put my offering in the water, would it reach the bottom and touch the earth, or would it
30 float away, as it had always done when I made my offering to the water spirit?

Once more I started on in my search of the bare ground.

The surface was crusted in some
35 places, and walking was easy; in other places I would wade through a foot or more of snow. Often I paused, thinking to clear the snow away in some place and there lay my offering. But no, my faith
40 must be in nature, and I must trust to it to lay bare the earth.

It was a hard struggle for so small a child.

I went on and on; the reeds were
45 waving their tasselled ends in the wind. I stopped and looked at them. A reed, whirling in the wind, had formed a space round its stem, making a loose socket. I stood looking into the opening. The reed
50 must be rooted in the ground, and the hole must follow the stem to the earth. If I poured my offerings into the hole, surely they must reach the ground; so I said the prayer I had been taught, and dropped my
55 tobacco and red feathers into the opening that nature itself had created.

No sooner was the sacrifice accomplished than a feeling of doubt and fear thrilled me. What if my offering
60 should never reach the earth? Would my little sister die?

Not till I turned homeward did I realize how cold I was. When at last I reached the house they took me in and warmed
65 me, but did not question me, and I said nothing. Everyone was sad, for the little one had grown worse.

The next day the medicine woman said my little sister was beyond hope; she
70 could not live. Then bitter remorse was mine, for I thought I had been unfaithful, and therefore my little sister was to be called to the spirit-land. I was a silent child, and did not utter my feelings; my
75 remorse was intense.

My parents would not listen to what the medicine-woman had said, but clung to hope. As soon as she had gone, they sent for a medicine-man who lived many
80 miles away.

He arrived about dark. He was a large man, with a sad, gentle face. His presence had always filled me with awe, and that night it was especially so, for he
85 was coming as a holy man. He entered the room where the baby lay, and took a seat, hardly noticing any one. There was silence saving only for the tinkling of the little tin ornaments on his medicine-bag.
90 He began to speak: "A soul has departed from this house, gone to the spirit-land. As I came I saw luminous vapor above the house. It ascended, it grew less, it was

GO TO THE NEXT PAGE

gone on its way to the spirit-land. It was
95 the spirit of the little child who is sick;
she still breathes, but her spirit is beyond
our reach…

33 The narrator wants to place her offering
correctly because she

(A) will have to explain her choice to
everyone else.

(B) wants to be trusted with similar tasks
in the future.

(C) thinks doing so will save her little
sister's life.

(D) is afraid of being punished if she
does it incorrectly.

34 How is the sentence "It was a hard struggle
for so small a child" (lines 42–43) different
from the rest of the passage?

(A) It is a change in the voice.

(B) It is a change in tone.

(C) It is a change in tense.

(D) It is a change in the setting.

35 Why didn't the girl's parents send for the
medicine man in the first place?

(A) He was busy helping another family
at the time.

(B) He had to come from a long distance.

(C) They thought the medicine woman
would be able to help their daughter.

(D) They preferred a woman to cure their
female child.

36 What evidence from the text shows the
girl's dilemma in following the medicine
woman's directions?

(A) Lines 9–10 ("the offering … naked
earth")

(B) Lines 19–20 ("But now … white
monotony?")

(C) Lines 34–35 ("The surface … some
places")

(D) Lines 42–43 ("It was … small a
child.")

37 Which title best expresses a theme of the
passage?

(A) Life and Death on the Prairie

(B) A Child's Sacred Memory

(C) Native American Culture

(D) The Offering

38 When the girl says "bitter remorse was
mine" (lines 70–71), she

(A) is sorry that she hurt her sister.

(B) feels badly because she didn't listen
to the medicine woman.

(C) feels angry about being given so
much responsibility.

(D) feels guilty because she feels at fault.

39 Based on the passage, which choice best
describes the narrator's relationship with
her parents?

(A) The parents seem to treat the narrator
as if she were an adult.

(B) The narrator wishes her parents
would give her more responsibility.

(C) The parents love their youngest child,
but not the narrator.

(D) The narrator receives warmth and
validation from her parents.

40 If you were to describe this story to someone who has not read it, which of the following sentences would best summarize
it?

(A) A Native American recalls her
experience of losing her baby sister.

(B) A Native American child is called
upon to make an offering to the
spirits.

(C) A Native American family struggles
with illness in the depths of winter on
the Plains.

(D) A Native American family uses their
religious beliefs to try to save their
daughter.

41 Which of the following best describes the meaning of "thrilled" in line 59?

(A) Excited
(B) Frightened
(C) Pierced
(D) Saddened

42 What lines in the text might convince you that the passage is autobiographical?

(A) Line 21 ("They had … the house.")
(B) Lines 34–35 ("The surface … was easy")
(C) Lines 62–63 ("Not till … cold I was")
(D) Lines 85–86 ("He entered … baby lay")

Directions: The two passages below deal with a related topic. Answer the questions based upon what is stated or implied in the passages and in the additional material provided.

QUESTIONS 43–52 ARE BASED ON THE FOLLOWING PASSAGES.

Passage 1: Fanny Wright was a reformer, author, and orator; unusual occupations for a woman in the early nineteenth century.

Passage 2: Young Robert Emmet was condemned to death for treason after organizing a rebellion against the English in Ireland. He, too, had achieved fame as an orator, with speeches decrying tyranny.

Passage 1—Fanny Wright to a Fourth-of-July Audience at New Harmony, Indiana (1828)

In continental Europe, of late years, the words *patriotism* and *patriot* have been used in a more enlarged sense than
Line it is usual here to attribute to them, or
5 than is attached to them in Great Britain. Since the political struggles of France, Italy, Spain, and Greece, the word *patriotism* has been employed, throughout continental Europe, to express a love
10 of the public good; a preference for the interests of the many to those of the few; a desire for the emancipation of the human race from the thrall of despotism, religious and civil: in short, *patriotism*
15 there is used rather to express the interest felt in the human race in general than that felt for any country, or inhabitants of a country, in particular. And *patriot*, in like manner, is employed to signify a lover of
20 human liberty and human improvement rather than a mere lover of the country in which he lives, or the tribe to which he belongs. Used in this sense, patriotism is a virtue, and a patriot is a virtuous man.

25 With such an interpretation, a patriot is a useful member of society capable of enlarging all minds and bettering all hearts with which he comes in contact; a useful member of the human family,
30 capable of establishing fundamental principles and of merging his own interests, those of his associates, and those of his nation in the interests of the human race. Laurels and statues are
35 vain things, and mischievous as they are childish; but could we imagine them of use, on such a patriot alone could they be with any reason bestowed. …

Passage 2—Robert Emmet to the Court That Condemned Him to Death (1803)

I am charged with being an emissary
40 of France. An emissary of France! and for what end? It is alleged that I wish to sell the independence of my country; and for what end? …

No; I am no emissary. … Sell my
45 country's independence to France! and for what? Was it a change of masters? No, but for ambition. Oh, my country! Was it personal ambition that could influence me? Had it been the soul of my
50 actions, could I not, by my education and fortune, by the rank and consideration of my family, have placed myself amongst the proudest of your oppressors? My country was my idol! To it I sacrificed
55 every selfish, every endearing sentiment; and for it I now offer up myself, O God! No, my lords; I acted as an Irishman, determined on delivering my country from the yoke of a foreign and
60 unrelenting tyranny, and the more galling

GO TO THE NEXT PAGE

yoke of a domestic faction, which is its
joint partner. ... It was the wish of my
heart to extricate my country from this
double riveted despotism—I wished to
65 place her independence beyond the reach
of any power on earth. I wished to exalt
her to that proud station in the world.
Connection with France was, indeed,
intended, but only as far as mutual
70 interest would sanction or require.

Were the French to assume any
authority inconsistent with the purest
independence, it would be the signal for
their destruction ....
75   I wished to prove to France and to
the world that Irishmen deserved to be
assisted ... I wished to procure for my
country the guarantee which Washington
procured for America—to procure an
80 aid which ... would perceive the good,
and polish the rough points of our
character. ...hese were my objects; not to
receive new taskmasters, but to expel old
tyrants. And it was for these ends I sought
85 aid from France ....

Let no man dare, when I am dead,
to charge me with dishonor; let no
man attaint my memory by believing
that I could have engaged in any cause
90 but that of my country's liberty and
independence .... The proclamation of the
provisional government speaks for our
views; no inference can be tortured from
it to countenance barbarity or debasement
95 at home, or subjection, humiliation, or
treachery from abroad. I would not have
submitted to a foreign oppressor, for
the same reason that I would resist the
foreign and domestic oppressor. In the
100 dignity of freedom, I would have fought
upon the threshold of my country, and
its enemy should enter only by passing
over my lifeless corpse. And am I, who
lived but for my country, and who have
105 subjected myself to the dangers of the
jealous and watchful oppressor, and the
bondage of the grave, only to give my
countrymen their rights, and my country
its independence.

---

43 Which of the following statements from
Emmet's speech shows that he thinks he
is a martyr?

(A) Lines 50–53 ("could I not ... your
oppressors")

(B) Lines 64–66 ("I wished to ... on
earth")

(C) Lines 75–77 ("I wished to ... to be
assisted")

(D) Lines 86–87 ("Let no man ... with
dishonor")

---

44 Which of the following of Emmet's statements shows that he thinks he is a patriot?

(A) Line 44 ("No; .... emissary")

(B) Lines 48–49 ("Was it ... influence
me?")

(C) Lines 75–76 ("I wished ... the world")

(D) Lines 91–93 ("The proclamation ...
for our views")

Timeline	
1707	Acts of Union between Scotland and England create the Kingdom of Great Britain
1776–1783	American colonies declare and win independence
1789	French storm the Bastille (prison), fight to end French monarchy
1798	Society of United Irishmen rebel unsuccessfully against British rule
1800	British Parliament passes The Act of Union, abolishing the Irish parliament
1801	United Kingdom of Great Britain and Ireland created
1803	United States purchases Louisiana Territory from France Robert Emmet leads a rebellion in Dublin against the union
1803–1815	Napoleonic Wars in Europe (France vs. European powers)
1808–1833	Spanish wars of independence
1823	France invades Spain to help restore monarchy
1828	Andrew Jackson elected president of United States

45 What events may have led Wright to her conclusion that Europeans have a different view of patriotism? Use the timeline to determine your answer.

(A) The French storming of the Bastille

(B) The establishment of the United Kingdom

(C) The election of Andrew Jackson as president

(D) The Napoleonic Wars changing European government

46 Based on information shown in the timeline, why might France have turned down Emmet's request for help?

(A) France was in the midst of trying to restore the monarchy in Spain.

(B) France was engaged in the drawn-out Napoleonic Wars.

(C) France had fought its own revolution and didn't want to get involved in that of another country.

(D) France was trying to keep the United States from taking Louisiana.

47 Emmet would not fit Wright's definition of a patriot because he

(A) saw no dishonor in his actions.

(B) wanted to free his people.

(C) idolized his own country above all others.

(D) declared the court's sentence to be unjust.

48 Which one of the following statements is true?

(A) Although years apart, both Wright and Emmet were advocating for freedom for their countries.

(B) Emmet was focused on freedom and independence for his own country, while Wright was focused on freedom and independence for all humankind.

(C) Emmet loved his country more than Wright loved her country.

(D) Wright didn't understand tyranny because she lived in a democracy, but Emmet was fighting for the kind of independence the United States won from England.

49 Both passages are excerpts from speeches. How does the tone of Wright's speech compare with that of Emmet's speech?

(A) Both express anger, although in response to different causes.

(B) Wright offers her audience a reasoned defense of her ideas while Emmet expresses anger and passion.

(C) Emmet speaks calmly and rationally, and Wright speaks passionately.

(D) Both provide a reasoned defense of their positions.

50 Which of the following statements is most analogous to Emmet's statement: "In the dignity of freedom, I would have fought upon the threshold of my country, and its enemy should enter only by passing over my lifeless corpse." (lines 99–103)

(A) Never yield to force; never yield to the apparently overwhelming might of the enemy.

(B) With the enemy at their back, with our bayonets at their breasts, in the day of their distress, perhaps the Americans would have submitted…

(C) Give me liberty or give me death.

(D) It is sweet and fitting to die for one's country.

GO TO THE NEXT PAGE

51 Which of the following fits Wright's definition of a patriot?

(A) A person willing to die for their country

(B) A person who fights for improving the lives of others

(C) A person who enlists in the armed forces of his country

(D) A person who loves his country

52 When the British government claims that Emmet is an "emissary" (line 44) of France, they are accusing him of being

(A) an ambassador.

(B) a spy.

(C) a minister.

(D) a mercenary.

STOP

**If you finish before time is called, you may check your work on this section only.
Do not turn to any other section.**

SECTION 2: WRITING AND LANGUAGE TEST

35 Minutes • 44 Questions

TURN TO SECTION 2 OF YOUR ANSWER SHEET TO ANSWER THE QUESTIONS IN THIS SECTION.

Directions: Each passage below is accompanied by a number of multiple-choice questions. For some questions, you will need to consider how the passage might be revised to improve the expression of ideas. Other questions will ask you to consider how the passage might be edited to correct errors in sentence structure, usage, or punctuation. A passage may be accompanied by one or more graphics—such as a chart, table, or graph—that you will need to refer to in order to best answer the question(s).

Some questions will direct you to an underlined portion of a passage—it could be one word, a portion of a sentence, or the full sentence itself. Other questions will direct you to a particular paragraph or to certain sentences within a paragraph, or you'll be asked to think about the passage as a whole. Each question number refers to the corresponding number in the passage.

After reading each passage, select the answer to each question that most effectively improves the quality of writing in the passage or that makes the passage follow the conventions of Standard Written English. Many questions include a "NO CHANGE" option. Select that option if you think the best choice is to leave that specific portion of the passage as it is.

QUESTIONS 1–11 ARE BASED ON THE FOLLOWING PASSAGE.

While most American cities must adapt to constant growth, Detroit is undergoing change as a result of depopulation.

A city of 139 square miles, with a long history of growth and middle-class success, Detroit now faces an unusual, though not entirely novel, situation for U.S. cities: depopulation. **1** Economic transformations caused by recessions, the loss of manufacturing, and other factors have wreaked havoc on the once prosperous city, driving away its middle class and **2** it left behind vast tracts of urban blight. The statistics **3** are staggering— since 1950, some 60 percent of the population has gone elsewhere, leaving the city with

1 Which choice provides the most logical introduction to the sentence?

(A) NO CHANGE
(B) Civic growth caused by the depression
(C) The improvement in living conditions
(D) The decrease in pollution

2

(A) NO CHANGE
(B) having left behind vast tracts of urban blight.
(C) to leave behind vast tracts of urban blight.
(D) leaving behind vast tracts of urban blight.

3

(A) NO CHANGE
(B) are staggering since: 1950 some
(C) are staggering, since 1950 some
(D) are staggering since; 1950 some

4 20,000 new residents. When the people left, thousands of businesses went with them.

City planners have been responding to the challenge of depopulation. Over several years, they have studied their urban spaces and used varying and innovative techniques to **5** require the input of **6** some 30,000 of their residents. Planners have come up with what they call Detroit Future City, a vision that takes the long view and is projected to take some fifty years to implement. Within this plan are different strands of redevelopment, development, and—most dramatically—un-development. **7** Similarly, the strategic plan includes a concept not often seen in U.S. city planning: downsizing, or what some prefer to call "right sizing."

[1] One of the boldest suggestions of the plan is a basic conversion of about one third of all Detroit's urban space. [2] Making the city more compact, the planners **8** reasoned, would save money on services and allow them to devote more resources to a smaller total area. **9** [3] Walking paths, parks, ponds for rainwater collection and retention (the city's sewage system is overburdened), sports fields, meadows, forested areas, campgrounds,

4 Which choice provides information that best supports the claim made by this sentence?

(A) NO CHANGE
(B) 100,000 vacant residences or lots
(C) 50,000 more middle-class residents
(D) 30,000 homeless people

5

(A) NO CHANGE
(B) confirm
(C) solicit
(D) implore

6

(A) NO CHANGE
(B) of some 30,000 of its residents
(C) of some 30,000 of it's residents
(D) of some 30,000 of they're residents

7

(A) NO CHANGE
(B) In fact,
(C) Nevertheless,
(D) Besides,

8

(A) NO CHANGE
(B) insisted
(C) noted
(D) commented

9 For the sake of the cohesion of this paragraph, sentence 3 should be placed

(A) where it is now.
(B) before sentence 1.
(C) before sentence 2.
(D) before sentence 5.

and other green space initiatives would then gradually transform the shutdown area. **[4]** Controversially, the plan suggests shutting down services in certain areas to drive current residents out of them and into neighborhoods being targeted for strengthening. **[5]** The plan also calls for remaining neighborhoods to be **10** transformed but–not by the traditional models of economic growth. **[6]** For example, the city, if organized carefully with viable public transportation options, hopes to create jobs right where people live. In part, the plan is predicated on the idea that within its own various redevelopment areas, or "natural economic zones," people can both live and work in fields that every city **11** has; namely, healthcare, education, government, transportation, and local businesses that meet core needs, such as grocery stores and eating places. The plan is also predicated on the idea that the well-planned urban space generates its own economic success, as well as on the idea that such areas will eventually draw some outside business and industry. Debt-ridden Detroit is definitely going to need the latter. A recent NPR report on Detroit posited that commercial real estate taxes can make up a substantial 70 percent of the revenue for a city.

10

(A) NO CHANGE
(B) transformed—but not by the
(C) transformed but not—by the
(D) transformed, but not by—the

11

(A) NO CHANGE
(B) has; namely, healthcare and education; government and transportation, local businesses
(C) has; namely, healthcare; education; government; transportation; and local businesses
(D) has; namely, healthcare, education, government, transportation; and local businesses

GO TO THE NEXT PAGE

QUESTIONS 12–22 ARE BASED ON THE FOLLOWING PASSAGE.

In a public square on the Indonesian island of Java, dusk falls. Families gather; it is a festival day. Children dart around while, on the edges of the square, vendors **12** hawk snacks and toys. A large screen, lit from behind, stands prominently in the square. A twenty-piece percussion orchestra, or *gamelan*, prepares to play.

13 The scene is modern-day Java, or perhaps Java hundreds of years ago. The performance is *wayang kulit*, or shadow puppetry, one of the world's oldest storytelling **14** traditions its origins stretch back to the ancient spiritual practices of Indonesia's original inhabitants, who believed that the spirits of the ancestors governed the living world. Ceremonial puppet plays addressed the spirits, asking them to help the living.

Over two thousand years ago, islands such as Java, Bali, and Sumatra saw their first **15** Indian migrants, a nation to which Indonesia was linked through trade relations. In the centuries that followed, Indian culture influenced every aspect of Indonesian life.

12

(A) NO CHANGE
(B) stock
(C) advertise
(D) trade

13 At this point, the author is considering deleting the underlined sentence. Should the writer do this?

(A) Yes, because it inserts an irrelevant opinion.
(B) Yes, because it distracts from the main ideas of the paragraph.
(C) No, because it provides a transition from the previous paragraph to this one.
(D) No, because it explains what wayang kulit is.

14

(A) NO CHANGE
(B) traditions and its origins stretch
(C) traditions, its origins stretch
(D) traditions. Its origins stretch

15

(A) NO CHANGE
(B) migrants from India, a nation to which Indonesia
(C) Indian migrants, to which a nation Indonesia
(D) Indian migrants, a nation of people to which Indonesia

The puppet plays reflected these cultural changes. **16** They began to depict narratives from Hindu religious texts, including the *Mahabharata*, the *Ramayana*, and the *Serat Menak*. Traditional Indonesian stories were blended into Hindu epics or lost altogether. Later, when Islam began to spread throughout Indonesia, puppet plays again transformed. The Islamic religion **17** prohibited the display of gods in human form, so Indonesians adapted their art by making flat, leather puppets that cast shadows on a screen. The puppets **18** themselves remain unseen during the performance; only their shadows were visible. *Wayang kulit* was born.

Java is particularly well-known for its continuation of the shadow puppet tradition. **19** Performances arc cpic events, lasting all night long from sunset to sunrise with no break at all. They take place in public spaces and are performed on holidays and at family celebrations. At the center is a large screen, backlit by a gas or electrical light. Behind this screen sits the *dalang*, or shadow master,

16 At this point, the writer is considering adding the following sentence.

> A master of shadow puppetry is called a dalang.

Should the writer do this?

(A) Yes, because it provides relevant and new information about the practice of wayang kulit.

(B) Yes, because it adds an important fact to the paragraph's focus on shadow puppetry.

(C) No, because it repeats information that has already been given.

(D) No, because it distracts from the paragraph's focus on cultural changes.

17

(A) NO CHANGE
(B) discouraged
(C) hindered
(D) restricted

18

(A) NO CHANGE
(B) themselves will remain unseen during the performance
(C) themselves remained unseen during the performance
(D) themselves had been remaining unseen during the performance

19

(A) NO CHANGE
(B) Performances are epic events, lasting from sunset to sunrise with no break.
(C) Performances are epic events, lasting all night long from sunset to sunrise without taking a break.
(D) Performances are epic events, lasting all night.

GO TO THE NEXT PAGE

traditionally a man. He manipulates the puppets—sometimes more than a hundred of them in one show—with rods, voicing and singing all of the roles. **20** Simultaneously, he directs the gamelan, the large percussive orchestra, which consists of percussive instruments, some of which are played by mallets.

Each puppet is carefully crafted, a flat figure that is perforated to project a detailed shadow. Artists begin creating a puppet by tracing the outline of a paper model on leather. The leather figure is painstakingly smoothed and treated before being passed onto another craftsperson, who paints it. Then, the puppet's moving parts—the arms and hands—are added, along with the sticks used **21** to manipulate their parts. These puppets follow an established set of conventions: evil characters have grotesque faces, while noble ones have more refined features. They are highly stylized caricatures, rather **22** then realistic figures.

20 Which choice most effectively maintains the paragraph's focus on relevant information and ideas?

(A) NO CHANGE
(B) Simultaneously, he directs an orchestra.
(C) Simultaneously, he directs an orchestra with instruments, some of which are played by mallets.
(D) Simultaneously, he directs the *gamelan,* the large percussive orchestra.

21

(A) NO CHANGE
(B) to manipulate his parts
(C) to manipulate its parts
(D) to manipulate her parts

22

(A) NO CHANGE
(B) that
(C) than
(D) this

QUESTIONS 23–33 ARE BASED ON THE FOLLOWING PASSAGE

Water issues are hardly unknown to the American Southwest, but they have recently taken on a new urgency.

The arid climate and limited water resources of the American Southwest **[23]** has always influenced the peoples of the region. The Anasazi, ancient people of some of the most inhospitable areas of the Southwest, made a series of accommodations to **[24]** they're hot, arid environment by means of adaptive agricultural practices, cliff-side residences, and elaborate catchment systems.

Today, the American Southwest, **[25]** simplistically defined in this document as encompassing all of Utah, Nevada, New Mexico, Arizona, and California, is the country's fastest-growing **[26]** region. It is home to more than 50 million people who are the source of ever-increasing water demands. Yet, the region is dependent for its water on just two river systems, the Colorado and the Rio Grande, of which the former is unequivocally the primary.

The Colorado supplies water to some 38 million users and irrigates some 300 million acres of farmland, much of it in **[27]** California! However, the mighty Colorado's flow was apportioned almost one hundred years ago to include not just the southwestern United States but also Mexico.

[23]

(A) NO CHANGE
(B) had always influence
(C) have always influenced
(D) is always influenced

[24]

(A) NO CHANGE
(B) their hot, arid environment
(C) there hot, arid environment
(D) its hot, arid environment

[25] Which choice provides the most relevant detail?

(A) NO CHANGE
(B) which has influenced painters as different as Georgia O'Keefe and Agnes Martin,
(C) home to such Native American tribes as the Navajo and Apache,
(D) generally considered a desirable tourist destination,

[26] Which choice most effectively combines the sentences at the underlined portion?

(A) region, but it is home
(B) region; home
(C) region, and it is home
(D) region, home

[27]

(A) NO CHANGE
(B) California. However,
(C) California? However,
(D) California, however,

It was also apportioned according to a volume that simply does not exist in current years; for example, in the years 2001–2006, river water that had been **28** projected to flow versus river water that did flow came up a staggering 34 percent short.

In 2014, the U.S. Department of the Interior warned that the Colorado River basin area "is in the midst of a fourteen-year drought nearly unrivaled in 1,250 years." **29** It further noted that the river's two major reservoirs, Lake Powell and Lake Mead—the once-massive backup systems for years in which drought occurs—were, alarmingly, more than 50 percent depleted. **30** Equally dire, if, more comfortably projected, predictions came out of a recent study, cited in the Proceedings of the National Academy of Science of the United States, that suggested a 50 percent chance of Lakes Powell and Mead reaching a level so low that they become inoperable by the 2020s. **31** For all intensive purposes, the Southwest's water supply is drying up.

28

(A) NO CHANGE
(B) hoped
(C) desired
(D) thought

29 At this point, the writer is considering deleting this sentence. Should the writer do this?

(A) Yes, because it repeats information that has already been presented in the passage.
(B) Yes, because it blurs the paragraph's focus by introducing a new idea.
(C) No, because it illustrates the severity of drought conditions with a specific example.
(D) No, because it introduces the argument that the Southwest's water supply is drying up.

30

(A) NO CHANGE
(B) Equally dire, if more comfortably projected,
(C) Equally dire if more comfortably projected
(D) Equally dire if, more comfortably projected,

31

(A) NO CHANGE
(B) For all intentional purposes,
(C) For all intents and purposes,
(D) For all intended purposes,

32 <u>Compounding</u> the problems of drought, increasing population, and an overly optimistic historical assessment of water resources are problems related to climate change. For example, between 2000 and 2013, temperatures in much of the Southwest rose as much as **33** <u>2 degrees</u>, increasing the negative effects of evapotranspiration, the evaporation of water from the soil. Finally, climate change and drought are leading to the greater prevalence and intensity of fires, including so-called "super fires," a result, in part, of the beetle infestations and dying trees that are weakened by the lack of water.

32

(A) NO CHANGE
(B) Escalating
(C) Inflating
(D) Exaggerating

33 Which choice completes the sentence with accurate data based on the map and its information below

(A) NO CHANGE
(B) 0.8 degrees
(C) 1.2 degrees
(D) 1.4 degrees

Average Temperatures in the Southwestern United States 2000–2014 Versus Long-Term Average

Temperature Increase (°F):

This map shows how the average air temperature from 2000 to 2014 has differed from the long-term average (1895–2014). To provide more detailed information, each state has been divided into climate divisions, which are zones that share similar climate features.

Source: http://www.epa.gov/climatechange/science/indicators/weather-climate/southwest.html

www.petersons.com

GO TO THE
NEXT PAGE

*(vertical text, right margin)* diagnostic test

QUESTIONS 34–44 ARE BASED ON THE FOLLOWING PASSAGE.

Women in Film: Troubling Inequalities

34 In a society in which television and movies have been well documented as **35** <u>influences</u> of social change, current data about women in the movies is far from reassuring. **36** <u>Women simply can't expect to play the leading roles men play or even, in general, to be on-screen for as many minutes as men are in any given film, while there seems to be no end of extraordinary acting talent among women in Hollywood.</u> As for other categories of filmmaking, at least by Oscar standards, women seem barely to exist at all.

34 Which choice most effectively establishes the main topic of the paragraph?

- **(A)** There are many actresses in Hollywood with extraordinary talent, but they cannot seem to get the same roles as men.
- **(B)** Though women land far fewer leading roles than men, in other categories of filmmaking, they do a little better.
- **(C)** Women are not adequately represented in Hollywood, either by the roles they play or by the amount of time they appear on-screen.
- **(D)** The movie industry has the capacity to change, but it has not done so in the area of women in film.

35

- **(A)** NO CHANGE
- **(B)** agents
- **(C)** necessities
- **(D)** factors

36

- **(A)** NO CHANGE
- **(B)** Women simply can't expect to play the leading roles men play or even, in general, while there seems to be no end of extraordinary acting talent among women in Hollywood, to be on-screen for as many minutes as men are in any given film.
- **(C)** Women simply can't expect to play the leading roles men play or to be on-screen for as many minutes as men, and there seems to be no end of extraordinary acting talent among women in Hollywood in general.
- **(D)** While there seems to be no end of extraordinary acting talent among women in Hollywood, women simply can't expect to play the leading roles men play or even, in general, to be on-screen for as many minutes as men are in any given film.

Indeed, **37** women were the protagonists in only 15 percent of the top grossing films of 2013, according to a study conducted at San Diego State University. Other study findings included the fact that when women are on-screen, **38** their marriage status is more identifiable than men. Also, males over age 40 are much more commonly represented on-screen than women in the same age group.

Other inequities have been revealed by Cinemetrics, which strives to gather objective data on movies, and by other organizations. **39** For example, in 2013, lead actresses in full-length films spent 57 minutes on-screen, while lead actors spent 85 minutes on-screen. Compounding the inequity is the tendency of the camera to stay on a female actress longer in a single shot, or stare at **40** them passively, while the camera moves more actively when it shows a male character. In other aspects of films, women **41** are treated even more outrageously. Since the Oscars began in 1928, only 16 percent of all nominees have been women. In fact, there were no women nominees at all in seven categories of achievement for the 2014 Oscars. More significantly, Oscar trends do not seem to be improving over time.

37

(A) NO CHANGE
(B) women were the protagonist
(C) a woman was the protagonists
(D) the protagonists were a woman

38

(A) NO CHANGE
(B) their marriage status is more identifiable than of a men.
(C) their marriage status is more identifiable than that of men.
(D) their marriage status is more identifiable than men's marriage.

39 Which choice most effectively maintains support for claims or points in the text?

(A) NO CHANGE
(B) For example, women direct more documentaries than narrative films.
(C) For example, the highest paid actress in 2013 made $33 million dollars.
(D) For example, women buy about half of movie tickets purchased in the United States.

40

(A) NO CHANGE
(B) him
(C) her
(D) us

41

(A) NO CHANGE
(B) are taken advantage of.
(C) are cheated.
(D) fare even worse.

GO TO THE NEXT PAGE

Some women, however, have managed to shine despite these inequities. Actress Meryl Streep has been nominated for 19 Oscars as of 2015, easily outstripping both male and female competitors for the record of most Academy Award nominations. She is famous for her strong, authoritative roles; she portrayed a powerful—if terrifying—boss in *The Devil Wears Prada* (2006) and a **42** formidable leader in *The Giver* (2014). Streep has received **43** accolades for such parts, as 15 of her 19 Academy Award nominations were in the category of Best Actress in a Leading Role. Even Streep, however, is subject to the inequities of the film industry: in *The Devil Wears Prada* her **44** characters love life was brought to the forefront and depicted as a sacrifice that she, as a woman in power, had to continually make for the good of her career.

42 Which choice gives a second supporting example that is most similar to the example already in the sentence?

(A) NO CHANGE
(B) a mild-mannered bakery owner in It's Complicated (2009)
(C) a talented country singer in A Prairie Home Companion (2006).
(D) a struggling novelist in Manhattan (1979)

43

(A) NO CHANGE
(B) privileges
(C) recognition
(D) attention

44

(A) NO CHANGE
(B) character love life
(C) character's love life
(D) character loves life

STOP

**If you finish before time is called, you may check your work on this section only.
Do not turn to any other section.**

SECTION 3: MATH TEST—NO CALCULATOR

25 Minutes • 20 Questions

TURN TO SECTION 3 OF YOUR ANSWER SHEET TO ANSWER THE QUESTIONS IN THIS SECTION.

Directions: For Questions 1–15, solve each problem, select the best answer from the choices provided, and fill in the corresponding oval on your answer sheet. **For Questions 16–20,** solve the problem and enter your answer in the grid on the answer sheet. The directions **before Question 16** will provide information on how to enter your answers in the grid.

ADDITIONAL INFORMATION:

- The use of a calculator **is not permitted.**

- All variables and expressions used represent real numbers unless otherwise indicated.

- Figures provided in this test are drawn to scale unless otherwise indicated.

- All figures lie in a plane unless otherwise indicated.

- Unless otherwise specified, the domain of a given function f is the set of all real numbers x for which $f(x)$ is a real number.

The number of degrees of arc in a circle is 360.
The number of radians in the arc of a circle is 2π.
The sum of the measures in degrees of the angles of a triangle is 180.

GO TO THE NEXT PAGE

1

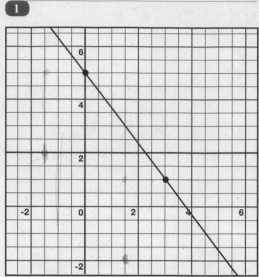

If the line drawn above is translated 3 units to the left and 6 units down, what is the slope of the new line?

(A) $-\dfrac{1}{9}$

(B) $-\dfrac{4}{3}$

(C) $-\dfrac{7}{10}$

(D) -2

2   Catherine is performing a science experiment on the distance traveled by a snail. She sets the snail on her driveway and records the time it takes the snail to crawl to the end of her driveway. She uses the equation $D = 0.4t + 12$, where D is the total distance traveled, in feet, and t represents the time, in minutes. Which of the following statements best interprets the meaning of 12 in Catherine's equation?

(A) It would take the snail 12 minutes to reach the end of the driveway.

(B) The snail began 12 feet from the beginning of the driveway.

(C) The snail traveled a total distance of 12 feet.

(D) The snail traveled at a rate of 12 feet per minute.

3   If $-2x + 5 = 2 - (5 - 2x)$, what is the value of x?

(A) -2

(B) 2

(C) 3

(D) 5

4

The figure shows one square inside another and a rectangle with diagonal T. The best approximation of the value of T, in inches, is given by which of the following inequalities?

(A) $8 < T < 9$

(B) $9 < T < 10$

(C) $10 < T < 11$

(D) $11 < T < 12$

5   The hypotenuse of a right triangle is 13 inches long. If the two legs are in a ratio of 2:3, what is the length, in inches, of the shorter leg?

(A) $\sqrt{13}$

(B) $\sqrt{26}$

(C) $2\sqrt{13}$

(D) $4\sqrt{13}$

6 A grain silo has a maximum capacity of 45,000 cubic feet. It currently contains 32,500 cubic feet of grain. Each week, farmers add 1000 bushels of grain. If one cubic foot is approximately 0.8 bushel, which of the following inequalities can be used to model the number of weeks, w, until the silo reaches its maximum capacity?

(A) $32,500 + 1250w \le 45,000$

(B) $32,500 + 800w \le 45,000$

(C) $32,500 + 1250w \ge 45,000$

(D) $32,500 + 800w \ge 45,000$

7 The graph of $y = (3x - 4)(x + 3)$ is a parabola in the xy-plane. In which of the following equivalent equations do the x- and y-coordinates of the vertex show as constants or coefficients?

(A) $y = 3x^2 + 5x - 12$

(B) $y = 3\left(x - \dfrac{4}{3}\right)\left(x - (-3)\right)$

(C) $y = 3\left(x^2 + \dfrac{5}{3}x - 4\right)$

(D) $y = 3\left(x - \left(-\dfrac{5}{6}\right)\right)^2 - \dfrac{169}{12}$

8 What is the difference when $-x - y$ is subtracted from $-x^2 + 2y$?

(A) $-x^2 - x - 3y$

(B) $x^2 + 3y$

(C) $-x^2 + x + 3y$

(D) $-x^2 + x - 3y$

9 A semitruck has a fuel tank that holds 125 gallons of diesel fuel. When driven at 55 miles per hour, the truck can travel 6 miles on 1 gallon of fuel. If Jorge fills the tank in his truck and drives at 55 miles per hour, which of the following functions d shows the number of gallons of diesel fuel that remains after driving h hours?

(A) $d(h) = 125 - \dfrac{6}{55h}$

(B) $d(h) = 125 - \dfrac{55h}{6}$

(C) $d(h) = \dfrac{125 - 6h}{55}$

(D) $d(h) = \dfrac{125 - 55h}{6}$

10

$$A = \dfrac{M}{M - N}$$

Which of the following expresses M in terms of the other variables?

(A) $M = \dfrac{AN}{A - 1}$

(B) $M = \dfrac{AN}{1 - A}$

(C) $M = \dfrac{N}{A - 1}$

(D) $M = \dfrac{N}{1 - A}$

11 $y = 90x + 75$

Donna bought a sofa with 0% interest for the first 36 months. She makes a small down payment, and then she makes equal monthly payments until she pays off the sofa. The above equation models the number of payments, x, that she makes to pay for a sofa that costs y dollars. How many dollars was Donna's down payment?

(A) 0

(B) 36

(C) 75

(D) 90

12 What is the sum of all values of n that satisfy $2n^2 - 11n + 15 = 0$?

(A) -11

(B) -5.5

(C) 5.5

(D) 15

13 The Matthews family is driving to the beach, which is 480 miles away. The function that represents the distance (in miles) and the time (in hours) it takes them to get to the beach is $f(t) = 480 - 60t$. In this equation, t is the independent variable, and $f(t)$ is the dependent variable. At which point does the graph of the function $f(t) = 480 - 60t$ cross the x-axis?

(A) $(0, 6)$

(B) $(6, 0)$

(C) $(0, 8)$

(D) $(8, 0)$

14 The population of a small town is growing. The town currently has 500 people. Based on the growth of the population in past years, it is estimated that after 1 year the population will be 650. Similarly, it is estimated that after 2 years, the population will be 845, and after 3 years, the population will be 1,099. Which of the following is an expression which represents the town's population growth?

(A) $500 \times 1.3x$

(B) $150x + 500$

(C) $500 \times (1.3)\, x^{-1}$

(D) $650 \times (1.3)\, x^{-1}t$

15 The expression $\dfrac{4x + 1}{x + 2}$ is equivalent to which of the following?

(A) $\dfrac{4 + 1}{2}$

(B) $4 + \dfrac{1}{2}$

(C) $4 + \dfrac{1}{x + 2}$

(D) $4 - \dfrac{7}{x + 2}$

Directions: For **questions 16–20,** solve the problem and enter your answer in the grid, as described below, on the answer sheet.

1. Although not required, it is suggested that you write your answer in the boxes at the top of the columns to help you fill in the circles accurately. You will receive credit only if the circles are filled in correctly.

2. Mark no more than one circle in any column.

3. No question has a negative answer.

4. Some problems may have more than one correct answer. In such cases, grid only one answer.

5. **Mixed numbers** such as $3\frac{1}{2}$ must be gridded as 3.5 or $\frac{7}{2}$.

   If $3\frac{1}{2}$ is entered into the grid as $\boxed{3\ 1/2}$, it will be interpreted as $\frac{31}{2}$, not $3\frac{1}{2}$.)

6. **Decimal answers:** If you obtain a decimal answer with more digits than the grid can accommodate, it may be either rounded or truncated, but it must fill the entire grid.

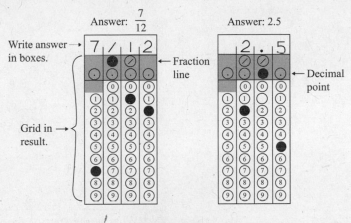

Answer: $\frac{7}{12}$ Answer: 2.5

Write answer in boxes. → Fraction line ← Decimal point ← Grid in result. →

Answer: 201
Either position is correct.

Acceptable ways to grid $\frac{2}{3}$ are:

GO TO THE NEXT PAGE

diagnostic test

16

In the figure above, $AC = BC$. If $m\angle B =$ **50°**, what is the measure of $\angle ECD$? (Do not grid the degree symbol.)

17

$$5x \quad 4y = 13$$
$$x + 2y = 4$$

If (x, y) is a solution of the system of equations above, what is the value of the ratio $\dfrac{x}{y}$?

18 $-9x + 5 = -9(x - b)$

For which value of b will this equation have infinitely many solutions?

19 If $f(x) = 5x + 12$, what is the value of $f(p + 3) - f(p)$?

20 What is the sum of the solutions of the equation $\dfrac{9}{x - 2} + \dfrac{16}{x + 3} = 5$?

STOP

**If you finish before time is called, you may check your work on this section only.
Do not turn to any other section.**

SECTION 4: MATH TEST—CALCULATOR 🖩

55 Minutes • 38 Questions

TURN TO SECTION 4 OF YOUR ANSWER SHEET TO ANSWER THE QUESTIONS IN THIS SECTION.

Directions: For questions 1–30, solve each problem, select the best answer from the choices provided, and fill in the corresponding oval on your answer sheet. **For Questions 31–38,** solve the problem and enter your answer in the grid on the answer sheet. The directions **before Question 31** will provide information on how to enter your answers in the grid.

ADDITIONAL INFORMATION:

- The use of a calculator is **permitted.**

- All variables and expressions used represent real numbers unless otherwise indicated.

- Figures provided in this test are drawn to scale unless otherwise indicated.

- All figures lie in a plane unless otherwise indicated.

- Unless otherwise specified, the domain of a given function f is the set of all real numbers x for which $f(x)$ is a real number.

The number of degrees of arc in a circle is 360.
The number of radians in the arc of a circle is 2π.
The sum of the measures in degrees of the angles of a triangle is 180.

---

1 What is the total savings in purchasing thirty 13-cent lollipops for a class party at a reduced rate of $1.38 per dozen?

- **(A)** $0.35
- **(B)** $0.40
- **(C)** $0.45
- **(D)** $0.50

2 If it costs $1.30 a square foot to lay linoleum, what will be the cost of laying 20 square yards of linoleum? (3 ft. = 1 yd.)

- **(A)** $26.00
- **(B)** $78.00
- **(C)** $156.00
- **(D)** $234.00

GO TO THE
NEXT PAGE

3 Mary wants to determine the average height of the plants in her plant collection. She measures them and finds their heights are 8 inches, 7.5 inches, 11 inches, 6.5 inches, and 14 inches. What is the average height of her plants?

(A) 8 inches

(B) 8.2 inches

(C) 9.4 inches

(D) 10.5 inches

4 A gallon of water is equal to 231 cubic inches. How many gallons of water are needed to fill a fish tank that measures 11″ high, 14″ long, and 9″ wide?

(A) 6

(B) 9

(C) 12

(D) 14

5 The recommended daily protein intake for an adult weighing 50 kg (approximately 110 pounds) is 40 grams. One cup of milk contains 8 grams of protein, and one egg contains 6 grams of protein. Which of the following inequalities represents the possible number of cups of milk, m, and eggs, n, an adult weighing 50 kg could consume in a day to meet or exceed the recommended daily protein intake from these alone?

(A) $8m + 6n \geq 40$

(B) $8m + 6n > 40$

(C) $\dfrac{8}{m} + \dfrac{6}{n} \geq 40$

(D) $\dfrac{8}{m} + \dfrac{6}{n} > 40$

6 Amy is renting a moving van that charges $19.99 per day, plus an additional $0.15 per mile. A tax of 7.5% is applied to both the daily rate and the mileage rate. Which of the following represents the total charge, y, that Amy will pay to rent the van for one day and drive it x miles?

(A) $y = 19.99 + 0.075x + 0.15$

(B) $y = 1.075(19.99) + 0.15x$

(C) $y = 1.075(19.99 + 0.15x)$

(D) $y = 1.075(19.99 + 0.15)x$

7 If nails are bought at 35 cents per dozen and sold at 3 for 10 cents, the total profit on $5\dfrac{1}{2}$ dozen is

(A) 25 cents.

(B) $27\dfrac{1}{2}$ cents.

(C) $31\dfrac{1}{2}$ cents.

(D) 35 cents.

8 A cubic foot of concrete weighs approximately 150 pounds. How many pounds will a similar block of concrete weigh if the edges are twice as long?

(A) 300 pounds

(B) 450 pounds

(C) 800 pounds

(D) 1200 pounds

9 Which of the following expressions is equivalent to $-x(3x - 2) + 2(3 - 2x)$?

(A) $-3x^2 - 6x + 6$

(B) $-3x^2 - 2x + 6$

(C) $3x^2 - 6x + 6$

(D) $3x^2 - 2x + 6$

10 A local organization is giving away t-shirts for its 5-kilometer road race. The cost of the t-shirts is defined by the equation $C(x) = 7x + 60$. The organization gives away the t-shirts for free to people who sign up for the race more than one month in advance and pay the $20 sign-up fee. What is the fewest number of people who must sign up in order for the organization to profit if the only cost is the t-shirts and the only income is the sign-up fee?

(A) 3

(B) 5

(C) 13

(D) 20

11 A small college, which has a population of 2,180 students, recently held a fundraiser in which each male student raised $20, and each female student raised $25 each. Together, they raised a total of $50,000. If x represents the number of male students in the college and y represents the number of female students in the college, which system of equations can be used to represent the scenario?

(A) $\begin{aligned} x + y &= 50,000 \\ 20x + 25y &= 2180 \end{aligned}$

(B) $\begin{aligned} x + y &= 2180 \\ 20x + 25y &= 50,000 \end{aligned}$

(C) $\begin{aligned} x + y &= 2180 \\ 25x + 20y &= 50,000 \end{aligned}$

(D) $\begin{aligned} x + y &= 50,000 \\ 25x + 20y &= 50,000 \end{aligned}$

12 Which of the following is an expression equivalent to $\sqrt[3]{9x^3 y^5 z^6}$?

(A) $3y^2 z^3$

(B) $3xy^2 z^3$

(C) $9^{\frac{1}{3}} xy^2 z^3$

(D) $9^{\frac{1}{3}} xy^{\frac{5}{3}} z^2$

13

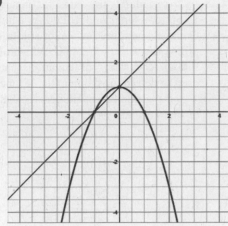

$y = x + 1$

$y = x^2 + 1$

A system of equations and their graphs is shown above. Which of the following are solutions to the system?

I. $(0, 1)$

II. $(1, 0)$

III. $(-1, 0)$

IV. $(0, -1)$

(A) I only

(B) II only

(C) I and III only

(D) II and IV only

14 If $\dfrac{x}{3} - \dfrac{y}{4} = 5$, what is the value of $6y - 8x$?

(A) -120

(B) -60

(C) 60

(D) 120

15 At a restaurant, the rates for meals are $7.50 for a lunch and $12.00 for a dinner. One weekend, the restaurant sold a total of 241 meals for $2523.00. Which of the following systems of equations can be used to determine the number of lunches, x, and the number of dinners, y, that the restaurant sold?

(A)
$$7.5x + 12y = 241$$
$$x + y = 2523$$

(B)
$$12x + 7.5y = 241$$
$$x + y = 2523$$

(C)
$$7.5x + 12y = 2523$$
$$x + y = 241$$

(D)
$$12x + 7.5y = 2523$$
$$x + y = 241$$

16

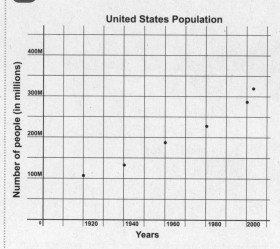

United States Population

The graph shows data representing the population of the United States, where x represents the year, and y represents the number of people, in millions. Which of the following statements is true about the data shown on the graph?

(A) There is a weak correlation between the variables.

(B) There is a strong correlation between the variables.

(C) There is no clear correlation between the variables.

(D) There is an exponential correlation between the variables.

17

The graph shows data representing the gross domestic product (GDP), in trillions of dollars, of China from 1980 through 2013. Which of the following statements best describes the type of function which would represent the data?

(A) A linear function would best represent this data.

(B) A logarithmic function would best represent this data.

(C) A cubic function would best represent this data.

(D) An exponential function would best represent this data.

18 A college graduate goes to work for x dollars per week. After several months, the company gives all the employees a 10% pay cut. A few months later, the company gives all the employees a 10% raise. What is the college graduate's new salary?

(A) $0.90x$

(B) $0.99x$

(C) x

(D) $1.01x$

19. $y < -x + b$

    $y > x - c$

    In the xy-plane, if $(1, 1)$ is a solution to the system of inequalities above, which of the following relationships between b and c must be true?

    (A) $b > c$
    (B) $c > b$
    (C) $|b| > |c|$
    (D) $|c| > |b|$

20. If four triangles are constructed with side lengths indicated below, which triangle will NOT be a right triangle?

    (A) 5-12-13
    (B) 8-15-17
    (C) 9-40-41
    (D) 12-15-18

21. What is the original price of an item if it costs $12.60 at a 10% discount off the selling price?

    (A) $11.34
    (B) $12.48
    (C) $13.86
    (D) $14.00

22. A recipe for a homemade weed killer calls forw $1\frac{1}{3}$ gallons of white vinegar and 2 cups of table salt. Miguel made a large batch of the weed killer and used 7 cups of table salt. If he followed the recipe correctly, how many gallons of white vinegar did he use?

    (A) 4
    (B) $4\frac{2}{3}$
    (C) $5\frac{1}{3}$
    (D) 6

23. A circle has a circumference that is equal to the perimeter of a hexagon. The sides of the hexagon are each 22 inches long. Which of the following is closest to the length of the radius of the circle?

    (A) 7
    (B) 14
    (C) 21
    (D) 28

24 If $(x-4)$ and $(x+2)$ are factors of $f(x)$, which of the following graphs could represent the function $f(x)$?

(A)

(C)

(B)

(D)

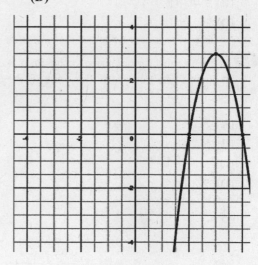

25

	None	1 to 3	4 or more
Group A	8	23	19
Group B	14	21	5
Total	22	44	24

The data in the table above were produced by demographic researchers studying the number of living siblings people have. If a person is chosen at random from Group A, what is the probability that the person has no living siblings?

(A) $\dfrac{4}{25}$

(B) $\dfrac{4}{11}$

(C) $\dfrac{7}{11}$

(D) $\dfrac{22}{25}$

26. During the Apollo 14 mission, astronaut Alan Shepard hit a golf ball on the moon. The height of the ball in meters is modeled by the function $f(t) = -0.81t^2 + 55t + 0.02$, where t is the time in seconds after the ball was hit. What does 0.02 stand for in this equation?

   (A) Acceleration of the ball due to gravity
   (B) Vertical velocity of the ball
   (C) Horizontal velocity of the ball
   (D) Height of the ball before it is hit

27. If k is a positive constant other than 1, which of the following could be the graph of $kx + y = c$?

   (A)

   (C)

   (B)

   (D)

GO TO THE
NEXT PAGE

28 The Cyber Corporation buys a new machine for $80,000. If the machine loses 15% of its value each year, what is its value after 4 years?

(A) $41,760.50

(B) $42,750.50

(C) $48,000.00

(D) $49,130.00

29 The table below shows the total number of medals won by the United States in the last 6 Winter Olympics.

	1994	1998	2002	2006	2010	2014
Number of Medals	12	13	31	25	37	28

How many medals will the United States have to win in the 2018 Winter Olympics in order to increase the average number of medals won by 1?

(A) 29

(B) 31

(C) 32

(D) 36

30 If the expression $\dfrac{6x}{2x+4}$ is written in the form $3 + \dfrac{A}{x+2}$, what is the value of A?

(A) −12

(B) −6

(C) 6

(D) 12

Directions: For **questions 31–38,** solve the problem and enter your answer in the grid, as described below, on the answer sheet.

1. Although not required, it is suggested that you write your answer in the boxes at the top of the columns to help you fill in the circles accurately. You will receive credit only if the circles are filled in correctly.

2. Mark no more than one circle in any column.

3. No question has a negative answer.

4. Some problems may have more than one correct answer. In such cases, grid only one answer.

5. **Mixed numbers** such as $3\frac{1}{2}$ must be gridded as 3.5 or $\frac{7}{2}$. If $3\frac{1}{2}$ is entered into the grid as , it will be interpreted as $\frac{31}{2}$, not $3\frac{1}{2}$.

6. **Decimal answers:** If you obtain a decimal answer with more digits than the grid can accommodate, it may be either rounded or truncated, but it must fill the entire grid.

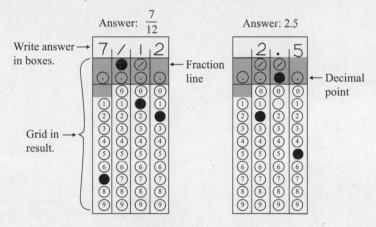

Answer: $\frac{7}{12}$

Write answer in boxes.

Fraction line

Grid in result.

Answer: 2.5

Decimal point

Answer: 201
Either position is correct.

Acceptable ways to grid $\frac{2}{3}$ are:

GO TO THE
NEXT PAGE

diagnostic test

31 What is the value of b in the equation $(3x - 4)(2 - 5x) = ax^2 + bx + c$?

33 In a 3-hour examination of 350 questions, there are 50 mathematical problems. If twice as much time should be allowed for each mathematical problem as for each of the other questions, how many minutes should be spent on the mathematical problems?

32 If $-\frac{1}{4} < -2p + 4 < \frac{3}{4}$, what is one possible value for p?

34 In the 1924–25 season of the National Hockey League (NHL), the Montreal Canadiens won 57% of their games. During the 1947–48 season, they won 33% of their games. If there were twice as many games played in the 1947–48 season as in the 1924–25 season, what percentage of the games did the Montreal Canadiens win in these two seasons of the league? (Do not grid the percentage sign.)

35 A polling company surveys 625 randomly selected registered voters to determine whether a proposed ballot measure might pass. Of those surveyed, 400 voters were in favor of the ballot measure. The polling company reports that the poll results have a conservative margin of error of 4%. If 9000 people actually vote, what is the minimum number of people likely to vote for the ballot measure?

37
$$3x + y = -4$$
$$x + y = 13$$

If (x, y) is a solution for the system of equations above, what is the value of y?

36 The average weight of a medium-sized bottlenose dolphin is 400 pounds. If a particular medium-sized bottlenose dolphin weighs 110% of the average, then how many pounds does the dolphin weigh?

38
$$-3x + 2 = -1$$
$$6x - by = 8$$

What is the value for b that will make the system above have no solution?

STOP

**If you finish before time is called, you may check your work on this section only.
Do not turn to any other section.**

SECTION 5: ESSAY

50 Minutes • 1 Essay

Directions: The essay gives you an opportunity to show how effectively you can read and comprehend a passage and write an essay analyzing the passage. In your essay, you should demonstrate that you have read the passage carefully, present a clear and logical analysis, and use language precisely.

Your essay must be written on the lines provided in your answer booklet. You will have enough space if you write on every line, avoid wide margins, and keep your handwriting to an average size. Try to print or write clearly so that your writing will be legible to the readers scoring your essay.

As you read the passage below, consider how Peter Krapp uses the following:

- Evidence, such as facts, statistics, or examples, to support claims
- Reasoning to develop ideas and to connect claims and evidence
- Stylistic or persuasive elements, such as word choice or appeals to emotion, to add power to the ideas expressed

Adapted from "Penn State Hack Exposes Theft Risk of Student Personal Data" by Peter Krapp, originally published in The Conversation on May 20, 2015. Peter Krapp is a professor of film & media studies at University of California, Irvine. (This passage was edited for length. For the complete article, see http://theconversation.com.*)*

1   Pennsylvania State University's College of Engineering took its computer network offline on May 15 after disclosing two cyberattacks. The perpetrators were able to access information on 18,000 students, who are being contacted this week with the news that their personal identifying information is in hackers' hands.

2   Three days later, the computer network is back online, with new protections for its users. One of the two attacks is ascribed by a forensic cybersecurity corporation retained by Penn State to computers apparently based in China.

3   As a researcher who has published on hacking and hacktivism and serves on the board of the UC Irvine data science initiative, I believe two aspects of this news story deserve particular attention.

Compromising student data

4   Penn State announced last week that the FBI alerted it on November 21, 2014, about an attack with custom malware that started as early as September 2012.

5   Why did it take so long for Penn State to disclose the breach, despite the fact that the experience of large-scale hacks in 2013 and 2014 (against Target, Home Depot, and others) clearly demonstrated an urgent need for quick and full disclosure—both to help the victims and to preserve a modicum of trust?

6   Penn State stated only that any disclosure would have tipped off the perpetrators before their access to the College of Engineering computers could be cut off. Meanwhile, student data may have been compromised for at least six months, maybe longer.

7   Another conspicuous problem with public discussion of events like this is, in fact, the lack of distinction often made in the media between actual appropriation of data (as at Penn State) and mere temporary disabling or defacement of websites (as happened to Rutgers University last month). That is like being unable to make a difference between a grand theft auto and keying a car.

8   The question is, what can universities do to limit the risk to their students?

9   The exposure of student data in higher education is not limited to Social Security numbers or email passwords. Information collected and retained by educational institutions includes full name, address, phone number, credit and debit card information, workplace information, date of birth, personal interests and of course academic performance and grade information.

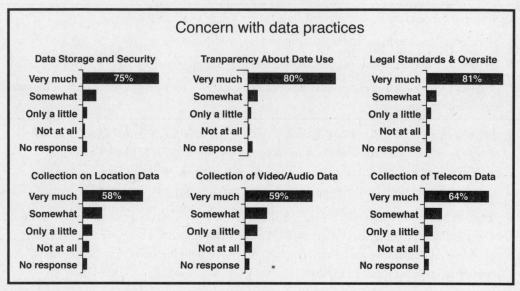

A survey conducted by the Obama administration collected responses from 24,092 individuals on how much they trusted various institutions to keep their data safe. There was a high level of concern around transparency and legal standards.
(https://www.whitehouse.gov/issues/technology/big-data-review)

. . .

10   President Obama only recently called for laws covering data hacking and student privacy. "We're saying that data collected on students in the classroom should only be used for educational purposes," he stated in his speech to the Federal Trade Commission (FTC) earlier this year.

Data privacy concerns

11   If students' right to privacy needs to be protected from the specter of foreign intelligence agencies poking around the Penn State Engineering School, then by the same logic it should be protected also against data-mining by for-profit actors right here in the US.

12   Until May 2014, Google, for instance, routinely mined its apps for education services for advertising and monetizing purposes. When Education Week reported that Google was mining student emails, it quickly led not only to lawsuits but also to landmark legislation. The California Senate Bill 1177 was enacted to prevent educational services from selling student information or mining it for advertising purposes.

13 Yet, almost a year later, students in California remain just as concerned about their data privacy as before—since the new state law was watered down to apply only to K–12 and not to higher education. And when it was disclosed earlier this spring that education publisher Pearson secretly monitored social media to discern references to their content, the legislative response was one that, according to the Electronic Privacy Information Center (EPIC) in Washington, DC, "fails to uphold President Obama's promise that the data collected in an educational context can be used only for educational purposes."

14 Students in higher education nationwide are still in a position where they cannot opt out of the computer services of their learning institutions, and so they have no expectation of privacy.

15 Despite President Obama's promises for safeguarding the privacy of consumers and families, and despite the fact that a number of technology companies concerned with growing consumer distrust recently signed a pledge to safeguard student privacy, neither Google nor Apple signed on.

16 The President's Council of Advisors on Science and Technology (PCAST) was tasked to examine current and likely future capabilities of key technologies, both those associated with the collection, analysis, and use of big data and those that can help to preserve privacy, resulting in a direct recommendation to strengthen US research in privacy-related technologies.

17 And overwhelmingly, respondents to a White House survey recently expressed severe reservations about the collection, storage, and security and use of private information.

18 Maybe it is time for higher education to heed those signals.

Write an essay in which you explain how Peter Krapp builds an argument to persuade his audience that the use of college students' personal information for anything other than educational purposes is a serious violation of privacy and a major breach of computer security. In your essay, analyze how Peter Krapp uses one or more of the features listed above (or features of your own choice) to strengthen the logic and persuasiveness of his argument. Be sure that your analysis focuses on the most relevant features of the passage. Your essay should not explain whether you agree with the writer's claims, but, rather, explain how he builds an argument to persuade his audience.

STOP

If you finish before time is called, you may check your work on this section only.
Do not turn to any other section.

No Test Material On This Page

ANSWER KEY AND EXPLANATIONS

Section 1: Reading

1. C	12. A	23. D	33. C	43. D
2. A	13. C	24. A	34. A	44. B
3. A	14. A	25. B	35. C	45. D
4. C	15. A	26. B	36. B	46. C
5. D	16. D	27. D	37. B	47. B
6. C	17. A	28. A	38. D	48. B
7. D	18. D	29. D	39. A	49. B
8. B	19. C	30. B	40. A	50. C
9. B	20. C	31. C	41. C	51. B
10. B	21. A	32. A	42. C	52. B
11. A	22. B			

READING TEST RAW SCORE [   ]
(Number of correct answers)

1. **The correct answer is (C).** The context here tells us that *address* is not being used to mean direction, choice (D), or habitat, choice (A). *Address* appears in the author's description of the black bear, including qualities that the bear possesses. Since the author later describes the bear as *rambling* and *wandering, address* is not being used to mean *focus*, choice (B). Therefore, the correct answer is choice (C).

2. **The correct answer is (A).** This excerpt is all about the black bear and does not make any direct comparisons to birds, choice (D). It only mentions deer and boars in comparison to bears, so it does not indicate a particular fascination with mammals, choice (B). The shift to second person (lines 43–53) shows that the author assumes that the reader has some knowledge about bears, which makes choice (C) incorrect. Perhaps his readers did not know enough, so he provides further information. Therefore, choice (A) is correct.

3. **The correct answer is (A).** According to this text and the first paragraph, the bear changes location with the seasons, following

food harvests and places where it is safe. All animals seek food, so the bear finding places that have lots of roots does not necessarily show migratory patterns, choice (B). The bear examines the tree trunk to mark territory, choice (C); it is not part of a migration pattern. It continues to wander about, choice (D), with no direction that indicates a new season or a new habitat. Therefore, choice (A) is correct.

4. **The correct answer is (C).** The hunters and woodsmen believe this behavior is designed to scare off predators who would, from the markings on the tree, be able to estimate the size of the bear, choice (C). Choice (A) represents Audubon's claim, not that of the huntsmen and woodsmen. There's no indication that the tree will be used for hibernation, choice (B), nor that such behavior is a way of obtaining food, choice (D).

5. **The correct answer is (D).** The correct answer is (D). Lines 22–28 include the fact that bears may eat livestock, but that is not the main focus, so choices (A) and (B) are incorrect. While the lines do show that the

bear eats a wide range of foods, choice (C), use of phrases such as "wallowing in the mud, like a hog," and "it enters the gloomy swamp," are evidence that the author is creating an image as opposed to making a scientific list of what the bear eats.

6. **The correct answer is (C).** Audubon explains other animal behaviors that are similar and serve the same purpose, leading him to believe that the reason is to keep the bear stronger than his competitors when the mating season starts, choice (C). Foam forming at the mouth is a result of the continuous force used and is a biological response. There is no indication in the text that suggests that the foam has any purpose, so choices (A) and (D) are incorrect. Choice (B) is the position taken by the woodsmen and huntsmen, not Audubon.

7. **The correct answer is (D).** Audubon explains that the bear sharpens its claws and the wild boar sharpens its tusk for the same purpose: to prepare themselves for competition during the mating season, choice (D), not for defense from human predators, choice (C). The bear uses its claws to get food, but Audubon doesn't discuss the use of the wild boar's tusks for getting food, so choice (A) is incorrect. The argument made by the woodsmen and hunters applies to the bear, but it is not the argument supported by Audubon, so choice (B) is incorrect.

8. **The correct answer is (B).** The correct answer is choice (B). This is the only possible conclusion one can reach among those listed. Nothing indicates that Audubon hunts, choice (A), and he never denies that bears are dangerous, choice (D).

9. **The correct answer is (B).** The only choice that references the bear eating meat is choice (B). All of the other options include only plants, nuts, seeds, and other non-meat items.

10. **The correct answer is (B).** Choice (B) is correct because Audubon expresses his assumptions about the reader's knowledge when he draws back from the third person and addresses the reader directly (lines 43–44), remarking that "you well know" and "you also know" about bears' honey

eating and ability to climb). Greater details do not necessarily mean greater interest by a reader, so choice (A) is incorrect. When comparing the bear to the deer, Audubon provides details, so he doesn't assume the reader already knows how they are similar, so choice (C) is incorrect. Audubon switches voice to inject a more personal tone, which is not an assumption about the reader, making choice (D) incorrect.

11. **The correct answer if (A).** The first paragraph of the letter indicates that Wythe and Jefferson have an established relationship and Jefferson believes Wythe had a positive influence on Jefferson's education, thus we can infer that Wythe was a teacher. The letter does not imply any familial relationship or that Wythe and Jefferson are friends—choices (B) and (C)—rather, it shows a more formal connection. There is no indication of how Wythe is employed—choice (D). While he could be a public servant of some kind, that conclusion could not be drawn from the information provided.

12. **The correct answer is (A).** Jefferson's overall concern is that his nephew should receive a solid education, choice (A). This letter has a greater purpose than merely staying in touch, choice (D). His advice about studying languages, choice (C) is part of the overall advise about education, and morality is also a part of his course of study, choice (B).

13. **The correct answer is (C).** The word *prosecute* in this context is used to mean *pursue*, choice (C), as opposed to its more common meaning of using the legal system to sue someone, choice (B). Jefferson is advocating for the study of Spanish, not Italian, choice (D), or support of the government of Spain, choice (A).

14. **The correct answer is (A).** Choice (A) indicates that Jefferson is thinking about his nephew's future and how Peter might evaluate the things that he did as a younger man. The other options show no particular feelings; they are neutral, choices (B) and (C), or express his philosophy, choice (D).

15. **The correct answer is (A).** Jefferson compares conscience to a physical limb of the body to show that it is natural and present in all human beings, choice (A). Choices (B), (C), and (D) may be true, but Jefferson only covers the first point; that morality is as natural as an arm or leg, and is given to all "in a stronger or weaker degree" (lines 58–59).

16. **The correct answer is (D).** In advising Peter about language studies, Jefferson tells him to learn Spanish (lines 34–39). He predicts that it will be valuable in the future because of "connections with Spain and Spanish America", choice (D). He dismisses Italian, choice (C), as unworthy of Peter's attention and doesn't discuss America's future with France, choice (B), or England, choice (A).

17. **The correct answer is (A).** By *lost time*, Jefferson means *wasted time*, choice (A). In his third point, Jefferson tells Peter that he shouldn't bother to study moral philosophy because it is something everyone knows intuitively.

18. **The correct answer is (D).** Jefferson claims that he has never seen anyone who spoke French, Spanish, and Italian who didn't get them confused, choice (D). All three languages are derived from Latin, choice (A), as Jefferson notes, but that is not the reason he gives to avoid the study of Italian. Jefferson does think it is necessary to learn a language other than French, choice (B), because he recommends learning Spanish. Peter is already multilingual, choice (C) because Jefferson claims studying Italian will "confound" his French and Spanish (lines 24–26).

19. **The correct answer is (C).** Jefferson says morality is innate, therefore it doesn't need to be taught. In fact, he argues, teaching it can have a negative effect of being "led astray" (line 64).

20. **The correct answer is (C).** The family tree shows that Peter's father died, choice (C). Jefferson would be likely to help his sister raise her family. The text says that Peter is Jefferson's nephew, so although choice (A) is correct, it is not the best answer. The illustration doesn't show all of Jefferson's children, so choice (B) is incorrect; nor does it show anything about Peter's intelligence, choice (D).

21. **The correct answer is (A).** The correct answer is (A). The letter shows Jefferson to be very involved in ensuring that his nephew gets the best education; he says he's glad Peter will get to study with Jefferson's own mentor, Wythe, who he says greatly influenced his life. There's no indication of preoccupation, choice (D) or worry, choice (B). The letter is personal, not objective (C).

22. **The correct answer is (B).** Microplastics are the most abundant type in the ocean (lines 22–27), choice (B). Nurdles, choice (A), are larger plastics that eventually break down to form microplastics. Microbeads, choice (C), and plastic pellets, choice (D), are types of microplastics.

23. **The correct answer is (D).** It cites one of the three key questions scientists are investigating. Because humans are at the top of the food chain, scientists believe that the accumulation of plastics in the fish/seafood that we eat could affect our health. Marine animals do consume plastics—choice (C)—but that information does not explain the reason for studying seafood in particular. Choice (A) explains how plastics in the ocean can infect fish of all kinds, and choice (B) cites how plastic enters all parts of the food chain. Neither of these supports why scientists want to study seafood in particular.

24. **The correct answer is (A).** The overall tone is neutral, choice (A). The author provides facts and data using scientific terminology and explanations. Nowhere does he attempt to persuade the reader to a particular view, choice (B), inject a personal story, choice (C), or offer his own opinion, choice (D), although he does offer differing viewpoints on possible solutions.

25. **The correct answer is (B).** In lines 101–111, Halden's quote shows that he believes science can find a way to make plastics biodegradable, choice (B), which he says will eliminate the problem. He does not say they will be safe to ingest, but that a new manufacturing process would prevent them

from accumulating and being potentially hazardous. The author states that news laws may help minimize the problem, choices (A) and (D), not Halden.

26. **The correct answer is (B).** The article includes scientific data and explanations of the effects of plastics in the ocean and waterways, offering information to the public, choice (B). He does not call for the public to act in any way, choices (C) and (D), nor offer his own opinion about environmental issues, choice (A).

27. **The correct answer is (D).** In the context of Halden's statement, he says he wants to make the problem so small that it will no longer be a threat, choice (D). He acknowledges that it won't go away completely (lines 107–109) since he believes there will always be some degree of risk of exposure, choice (B). He does advocate further study, choice (C), to find a way to make the plastics biodegradable—but this is unrelated to what he means by the word *moot*.

28. **The correct answer is (A).** Choice (A) is the only choice that refers specifically to the food chain. The other choices may have some bearing on how plastics impact the ocean, but they don't explain disruption to the food chain.

29. **The correct answer is (D).** The author explains that the law was passed to prevent infiltration of these tiny microbeads into the water system (lines 40–50), choice (D). The microbeads were ending up in the Great Lakes and Chicago's waterways. None of the other options are offered as a reason for the law.

30. **The correct answer is (B).** Knowing the meaning of *absorb(ent)*, choice (C), does not assist in understanding the meaning of *adsorb*. The words share the same suffix, but it's the prefix that makes the word less familiar. *Absolve*, choice (A), has the same prefix as *absorb*. *Adhesive* is something that sticks to something else; so *adsorb* must mean when one substance sticks to another, choice (D).

31. **The correct answer is (C).** Choice (C) is the best answer because it includes the concept of harm to humans. Choices (A)

and (B) are facts that by themselves don't show harm. Choice (D) is a part of a direct quote that supports a specific solution; it is not evidence of the problem.

32. **The correct answer is (A).** Choice (A) is correct: the author suggests ways to help reduce the effects of plastics in the environment now through legislation (lines 91–95), and Halden thinks it is possible to design plastics that don't harm humans (lines 101–111). Choice (B) states part of the author's suggestion, but implies that Halden thinks there's no solution. There's no indication that Halden thinks the author's position would be burdensome for business, choice (C), or that the author thinks we should cease producing plastics, choice (D).

33. **The correct answer is (C).** The correct answer is (C). No one at home asks her about the offering once she returns, choices (A) and (D). Although she has been given specific instructions, choice (B), there is no indication that performing this task will lead to other such tasks.

34. **The correct answer is (A).** Choice (A) is correct. In this line, the adult is looking back and comments on the scene; in the rest of the passage, the child narrates as she remembers the events. The tone, choice (B), doesn't change, and the entire passage is told in the past tense, choice (C). The author describes the exterior setting in detail and omits details about the girl's home, but no new setting is introduced.

35. **The correct answer is (C).** Although we are told that the medicine man had to travel quite a distance, choice (B), the family didn't send for him until the medicine woman had given up hope, choice (C). This indicates that they didn't try to reach him earlier and thought the medicine woman would be able to help. This sequence suggests a preference for the medicine woman, though there is no reason stated or implied.

36. **The correct answer is (B).** It shows the girl contemplating how to follow the specific instructions (the spot must be "naked earth") when the ground was covered with snow. Choice (A) describes the instructions given

by the medicine woman; it doesn't explain why they were difficult to follow. Choice (C) describes the variance in the terrain where she was searching for the right spot, but it does not describe any particular conflict. Choice (D) shows the difficulty the girl had because of her age and size, not the dilemma of the directions.

37. **The correct answer is (B).** Choices (A) and (C) are far broader than the content of the excerpt; though both issues are touched upon, they are not themes of the story. Choice (D) narrowly describes one aspect of the story, perhaps a main idea, but not a theme. Choice (B) refers to something that occurred long ago and also suggests the special place where it is kept in the adult's memory.

38. **The correct answer is (D).** Although she meticulously follows the instructions of the medicine woman, choice (B), the girl still feels as if she failed because in the end her sister dies. She feels guilty, choice (D). There is no indication that either choice (A) or choice (C) are true.

39. **The correct answer is (A).** The parents seem oblivious to the natural emotions of a child. Though they give the narrator responsibility and take care of her physical needs (lines 64–65), they don't seem to offer comfort or consolation. The narrator is probably given more responsibility than she wants, which makes choice (B) incorrect. The parents naturally focus on the child likely to die, but there is no indication they prefer the younger child, so choice (C) is incorrect. The narrator seems very alone and her parents display little warmth or affection, making choice (D) incorrect.

40. **The correct answer is (A).** Choice (A) is the best summary of the excerpt because it includes the point of view of a Native American and the idea of loss. Choice (B) only narrowly focuses on the girl following the instructions of the medicine woman. Choice (C) does not capture the concept of the narrative and the point of view, and choice (D) inaccurately implies that the story centers on the reliance of specific religious tenets.

41. **The correct answer is (C).** The modern meaning of *thrilled* is usually choice (A), but in lines 58–59, the author is talking about fear and doubt. Choice (B) would be repetitive. *Sadness*, choice (D), is incorrect because the emotion the narrator feels is describing the feeling more importantly as being sudden and intense.

42. **The correct answer is (C).** Choice (C) uses the first person to describe the author's actions and feelings as a child. The specificity of the detail makes the comment seem like a personal memory. The other options are either less personal descriptions, choice (B), or general observations that could have been made up by any author, choices (A) and (D).

43. **The correct answer is (D).** In choice (D), Emmet acknowledges his death sentence and declares that he is dying for a cause. Choice (C) explains why he asked France for assistance, and choice (B) explains that he was fighting for his country's independence and freedom from tyranny. In choice (A), he defends his actions by saying that he could have stood by and done nothing, given his family's privileged position, but chose instead to defend liberty.

44. **The correct answer is (B).** Choice (B) shows Emmet's pride in his country and his intent to secure independence. Neither choice (A), in which he rhetorically asks if he could be influenced by personal ambition, nor choice (B), in which he denies that he is an emissary, explains his patriotism. Choice (C) is a statement describing Emmet's alignment with an independent government; it is not a display of patriotism.

45. **The correct answer is (D).** The Napoleonic Wars, which lasted for over a decade, continually realigned the monarchies and sovereignties of European nations, choice (D). These kinds of continual changes are likely to make people more responsive to a broader concept of patriotism; one that extends beyond borders and includes freedom from tyranny, wherever it exists. None of the other options applies to all of Europe and its ideology.

46. **The correct answer is (C).** Emmet loved his country and declared his patriotism toward Ireland as his reason for his actions, choice (C). Wright's view was more inclusive, defining it as freeing all people, whatever the country. Emmet's primary focus was on his own people, choice (B), not all of humankind. He defended his actions, choice (A), but this action is unrelated to Wright's concept of a patriot, as is a court that renders an unjust sentence, choice (D).

47. **The correct answer is (B).** Noting the date of Emmet's speech in his defense of his actions prior to his execution, choice (A) is not possible. The Louisiana Purchase by the United States, choice (D), would have given France more resources to help. However, the Napoleonic Wars were draining the French treasury, choice (B), leaving the country overburdened and uninterested in becoming involved elsewhere. The French Revolution had started in 1789, triggering the rise of Napoleon, but this was not directly related to its refusal to aid Emmet.

48. **The correct answer is (B).** Although both Emmet and Wright wanted freedom from tyranny, Emmet's focus was on Ireland and Wright had a broader objective, choice (B). Wright was focused on advancing an expansive concept of patriotism that included other countries, which does not mean that she did not love her country, choice (C), or did not appreciate living in a democratic country, choice (D). She wanted everyone to have the same freedom.

49. **The correct answer is (B).** Choice (D) does not describe the tone of their speeches. A speech can be both logical and emotional. Wright does not show any anger, choice (A). It is Emmet who is passionate and angry and Wright who is calm and reasonable, choice (B), not the other way around, choice (C).

50. **The correct answer is (C).** All the options refer to patriotism, but choice (A) is mostly about perseverance. Choice (B) is speculating on how Americans might react if attacked and suggests submission as one possibility. Choice (D) is a generic, patriotic sentiment. Choice (C) sets up the either-or scenario in which there can only be one of two outcomes: liberty or death. Emmet's statement is analogous because there are only two choices: if the enemy wishes to come into his homeland (symbolized by the word *threshold*), he will defend it to the death.

51. **The correct answer is (B).** Wright says Americans' idea of a patriot is someone who loves his/her country, choice (D), but that idea is too narrow. She explains that Europeans see patriotism as a more expansive concept that extends to freedom for all humans. This idea, she explains, includes working toward the best interests of all human lives, wherever they are, so that they are free from despotism. This statement suggests that she herself holds these ideas, choice (B), and wants others to consider them. Physically fighting for one's country, choices (A) and (C) is an example of vanity

52. **The correct answer is (B).** In this context, an emissary is a spy or an operative who is doing secret work for another country, choice (B), which is why the government is upset. The government wouldn't accuse someone of being an ambassador—an official position as a representative, choice (A). Similarly, a minister is an official head of a government department (C). A mercenary is a paid soldier; there is nothing that suggests the government thinks Emmet is a "hired gun."

Section 2: Writing and Language Test

1. A	10. B	19. B	28. A	37. A
2. D	11. A	20. D	29. C	38. C
3. A	12. A	21. C	30. B	39. A
4. B	13. C	22. C	31. C	40. C
5. C	14. D	23. C	32. A	41. D
6. A	15. B	24. D	33. A	42. A
7. B	16. D	25. A	34. C	43. A
8. A	17. A	26. D	35. B	44. C
9. C	18. C	27. B	36. D	

WRITING AND LANGUAGE TEST RAW SCORE
(Number of correct answers) ☐

1. **The correct answer is (A).** Choice (A) correctly sets up the sentence's focus on the various causes of depopulation and their negative impact. Choices (B), (C), and (D) are incorrect because they present potentially positive developments.

2. **The correct answer is (D).** Choice (D) follows the same parallel construction as the preceding gerund phrase, "driving away its middle class." Choices (A), (B), and (C) are incorrect because they do not demonstrate parallel construction.

3. **The correct answer is (A).** Choice (A) is correct because the dash is being used to indicate the following explanation of what is staggering. Choice (C) is incorrect because it creates a run-on sentence. Choices (B) and (D) are incorrect because they move the punctuation to the wrong part of the sentence.

4. **The correct answer is (B).** Choice (B) correctly maintains the sentence's focus on the effects of depopulation. Choices (A) and (C) are incorrect because they suggest a growth in residency, which contradicts the main argument of the passage. Choice (D) is incorrect because homelessness is unrelated to the main focus of the passage, which is Detroit's depopulation.

5. **The correct answer is (C).** Choice (C) establishes that the planners actively tried to obtain input. Choice (B) is the wrong word choice because it means that the residents have given input, and planners are checking it. Choice (D) is also incorrect, as it connotes asking desperately, which is not suggested by the passage.

6. **The correct answer is (A).** Choice (A) is correct because the plural pronoun "their" refers back to the plural antecedent, "city planners." Choice (B) is incorrect because "it" doesn't agree with "city planners." It *could* refer to the city, but that would be a supposition only. Choices (C) and (D) are incorrect because they are contractions, not possessive pronouns.

7. **The correct answer is (B).** Choice (B) is correct because "in fact" properly suggests an elaboration of the previous sentence. Choice (A) is incorrect because it suggests the second sentence is an equal example, rather than an elaboration of the first. Choice (C) is incorrect because it implies the author is drawing a conclusion despite a contradiction. Choice (D) is also incorrect because it implies that the second sentence is a second example supporting a contrast scenario, which is not the case.

8. **The correct answer is (A).** In choice (A), the sentence explains the planners' logic. Choice (B) implies that there was resistance to their thinking or that their thinking was absolute, which is incorrect. Choices (C) and (D) do not denote the careful calculation that the rest of the sentence implies.

9. **The correct answer is (C).** Sentence 3 should appear before sentence 2, as choice (C) correctly states, because it introduces the idea of shutting down certain areas, which the rest of the sentences build on. Choices (A), (B), and (D) are incorrect because they don't fix the sequence problem created when sentence 3 isn't before sentence 2.

10. **The correct answer is (B).** Choice (B) correctly places the dash so that it separates the two independent clauses. Choices (A), (C), and (D) are incorrect because they place the dash in the wrong place.

11. **The correct answer is (A).** Choice (A) is correct because items in a series should be separated by commas. Choice (B) is incorrect because it is unnecessarily wordy and misuses semicolons. Choice (C) is incorrect because it misuses semicolons. Choice (D) is also incorrect because it incorrectly mixes a semicolon with commas.

12. **The correct answer is (A).** Choice (A) is correct because "hawk" means to call out and sell, which is what vendors at festivals do. Choice (B) is incorrect because, while the vendors may stock merchandise, the author's intent here is to describe *how* they sell that merchandise. Similarly, choices (C) and (D) are incorrect because the vendors are selling—not advertising or trading—goods.

13. **The correct answer is (C).** Choice (C) correctly suggests that this sentence provides a transition between the scene depicted in the first paragraph and the ancient and modern tradition of puppetry, and the writer should not delete it. Choice (A) is incorrect because this sentence is not an opinion. Choice (B) is incorrect because this sentence does not distract from but rather helps in contextualizing the main ideas of the paragraph. Choice (D) is incorrect because it is the following sentence that explains what wayang kulit is.

14. **The correct answer is (D).** Choice (D) correctly uses end punctuation to correct this run-on sentence. Choices (A), (B), and (C) are incorrect because they do not employ the correct punctuation to denote two independent clauses.

15. **The correct answer is (B).** Choice (B) is correct because the phrase, "a nation to which Indonesia had trade relations" should refer to the country of India, not "migrants." Choices (A) and (D) are incorrect because the modifier is misplaced. Choice (C) is incorrect because it is awkward and doesn't make sense.

16. **The correct answer is (D).** Choice (D) is correct because this sentence is tangential to the paragraph's focus on the cultural influences of Hindu culture on the Indonesian way of life. Choice (A) is incorrect because this information is not relevant. Choice (B) is incorrect because this paragraph is not focused on the actual practice of shadow puppetry. Choice (C) is incorrect because this information has not been presented before this sentence.

17. **The correct answer is (A).** Choice (A) reflects the paragraph's emphasis that depicting gods in human form was not allowed under any circumstance. Choices (B), (C), and (D) are incorrect because these words do not suggest complete proscription the way choice (A) does.

18. **The correct answer is (C).** Choice (C) is correct because it places the verb in the past tense. Choice (A) is incorrect because the present tense is an inappropriate shift from the past tense that the rest of the paragraph uses. Choices (B) and (D) are incorrect because the sentence requires the simple past tense.

19. **The correct answer is (B).** Choice (B) conveys both the duration of the events and the lack of interruptions without being redundant or wordy. Choice (A) is incorrect because "all night long" is redundant. Choice (C) is incorrect because it is redundant and wordy; while it is constructed better by omitting "at all," "all night long from sunset to sunrise" is still redundant. Choice (D) is incorrect because it leaves out the lack of interruptions.

20. **The correct answer is (D).** Choice (D) continues the author's use of specific Indonesian terms while editing out unnecessary and redundant information. Choice (A) is incorrect because the mention of "percussive instruments" is redundant. Choices (B) and (C) are incorrect because they leave out relevant information.

21. **The correct answer is (C).** Choice (C) is correct because the pronoun "its" should refer back to the antecedent "the puppet." Choice (A) is incorrect because "their" is plural and "puppet" is not. Choices (B) and (D) are incorrect because "the puppet" is neither male nor female.

22. **The correct answer is (C).** Choice (C) is correct because comparisons require "than," not "then." Choice (A) is incorrect because "then" is an adverb that refers to time. Choices (B) and (D) are incorrect because they don't make sense in the sentence.

23. **The correct answer is (C).** Choice (C) is correct because the sentence subject that includes "arid climate and limited water resources," is a compound subject, which means the verb must also be plural. Choice (A) is incorrect because the subject is plural, and "has" is singular. Choice (B) is incorrect because it is the past perfect instead of the present perfect tense. Choice (D) is incorrect because it is present tense and changes the meaning of the sentence.

24. **The correct answer is (B).** Choice (B) is correct because the sentence requires a possessive pronoun in order to refer back to the Anasazi people. Choice (A) is incorrect because "they're" is a contraction, not a possessive. Choice (C) is incorrect because "there" is an adverb, not a possessive. Choice (D) is incorrect because "its" is singular possessive, while the antecedent here, "people," is plural.

25. **The correct answer is (A).** Choice (A) defines the geographic region in question, which is relevant to the passage's discussion of regional water issues. Choices (B), (C), and (D) are incorrect because they provide information that is outside the scope of the passage's main focus.

26. **The correct answer is (D).** Choice (D) combines the sentences in a way that helps emphasize the connection between the information presented. Choice (A) is incorrect because "but" implies that the two ideas are contradictory. Choice (B) is incorrect because it misuses a semicolon to connect an independent clause and what is now a dependent clause. Choice (C) is incorrect because instead of suggesting an elaboration of the previous sentence, it suggests additional information.

27. **The correct answer is (B).** Choice (B) is correct because the sentence is a statement, and thus it should end in a period. Choice (A) is incorrect because the sentence does not warrant the excitement or surprise that an exclamation point conveys. Choice (C) is incorrect because the sentence is not a question. Choice (D) is incorrect because it creates a run-on sentence.

28. **The correct answer is (A).** Choice (A) is correct because the context of the sentence suggests that a scientific forecast or prediction about water flow has been made about the future. Choices (B) and (C) are incorrect because they reflect subjective impulses and do not maintain with the neutral and scientific tone of the passage. Choice (D) is incorrect because it is vague and fails to suggest a basis in research.

29. **The correct answer is (D).** Choice (D) is correct because the author's main point is that water supplies in both the Colorado River basin area and Lakes Meade and Powell are dwindling. Choice (A) is incorrect because it does not mention the river basin. Choice (B) is incorrect because it does not mention the lakes. Choice (C) is incorrect because it says the water supply of the lakes is improving.

30. **The correct answer is (B).** Choice (B) is correct because the dependent clause "if more comfortably projected" must be set off by commas. Choice (A) is incorrect because it contains one too many commas. Choice (C) is incorrect because it contains no commas. Choice (D) is incorrect because the comma should be before "if."

31. **The correct answer is (C).** Although it may sound otherwise, the conventional expression is "for all intents and purposes," choice (C). Choices (A), (B), and (D) are incorrect.

32. **The correct answer is (A).** Choice (A) is correct because the author's intent is to suggest that there are other factors that make the problems of drought worse and more complicated. Choices (B), (C), and (D) are incorrect because each word emphasizes an increase in severity rather than an increase in the number of factors contributing to problems in the area.

33. **The correct answer is (A).** Choice (A) is correct because the map shows as much as a 2-degree increase of temperatures in the Southwest between the years 2000 and 2013. Choices (B), (C), and (D) are incorrect because they misinterpret the total degree change depicted by the map.

34. **The correct answer is (C).** Choice (C) is correct because this first paragraph establishes that women do not get as many leading roles as men nor do they spend as much time on-screen. Choice (A) is incorrect because it does not stress the number of roles nor the amount of on-screen time. Choice (B) is incorrect because it does not cite the amount of on-screen time, alluding to it only vaguely. Choice (D) is incorrect because it does not note the representation of women in the film industry.

35. **The correct answer is (B).** Choice (B) is correct because only "agents" expresses the idea that television and movies play an active role in causing social change. Choices (A), (C), and (D) are incorrect because they don't suggest a causal relationship to social change.

36. **The correct answer is (D).** Choice (D) is correct because the subordinate clause that begins with "while" is tied to the central premise of the sentence and needs to be at the beginning. Choice (A) is incorrect because at the end of the sentence, the relationship of the clause to the central idea is lost. Choices (B) and (C) are incorrect because they obscure the relationship of the clause to the central idea of the sentence.

37. **The correct answer is (A).** Choice (A) is correct because the noun "women" should agree in number with "protagonists." Choice (B) is incorrect because "protagonists" should be plural. Choice (C) is incorrect because "protagonist" should be singular if it is to agree with the subject. Choice (D) is incorrect because "woman" is not plural.

38. **The correct answer is (C).** Choice (C) clarifies that the comparison is between women's marital status and the marital status of men. Choice (A) is incorrect because it makes an illogical comparison between women's marital status and men in general. Choice (B) is incorrect because it uses the singular "man," meaning that only one man's marriage status is being compared. Choice (D) is incorrect because it compares women's marital status to the grammatically incorrect phrase "men's marriage."

39. **The correct answer is (A).** Choice (A) supports the paragraph's claim that women are underrepresented or underpaid in the film industry. Choices (B) and (D) are incorrect because they don't support the paragraph's main focus that women are underrepresented or underpaid in the film industry. Choice (C) does not support the paragraph's main claim because it doesn't provide data on men's income in comparison.

40. **The correct answer is (C).** Choice (C) is correct because the pronoun should refer to the female actress using "her." Choice (A) is incorrect because it is plural. Choice (B) is incorrect because it is masculine. Choice (D) is incorrect because it is plural and first person.

41. **The correct answer is (D).** Choice (D) maintains the objective and neutral tone of the passage while noting unfavorable comparisons. Choices (A), (B), and (C) are incorrect because the tone of each choice is emotionally charged, which is inconsistent with the objective tone of the passage.

42. **The correct answer is (A).** Streep's role in *The Giver* as described provides another example of Streep in a "strong, authoritative" role. Choices (B), (C), and (D) are incorrect because their roles are not described to be as strong compared to the "formidable leader" presented in choice (A).

43. **The correct answer is (A).** Choice (A) is correct because "accolades" connotes the achievements, honor, and respect that the passage goes on to describe. Choice (B) is incorrect because the awards were not privileges. Choices (C) and (D) are incorrect because they do not connote the honor and respect that "accolades" does.

44. **The correct answer is (C).** The word "characters" should be the possessive "character's," so choice (C) is correct. Choice (A) is incorrect because "characters" is plural instead of possessive. Choice (B) is incorrect because "character" is not possessive. Choice (D) is incorrect because it does not convey the appropriate meaning.

answers DIAGNOSTIC TEST

Section 3: Math Test—No Calculator

1. B	5. C	9. B	13. D	17. 6
2. B	6. A	10. A	14. A	18. 0.55 or
3. B	7. D	11. C	15. D	$\frac{5}{9}$ (5/9)
4. C	8. C	12. C	16. 80	19. 15
				20. 4

MATH TEST—NO CALCULATOR RAW SCORE ☐
(Number of correct answers)

1. **The correct answer is (B).** The slope of a line can be determined by finding the difference in the y-coordinates divided by the difference in the x-coordinates for any two points on the line. Using the points indicated, the slope is $\frac{5-1}{0-3}=-\frac{4}{3}$. Translating the line moves all the points on the line the same distance in the same direction, and the image will be a parallel line. Therefore, the slope of the line is $-\frac{4}{3}$.

2. **The correct answer is (B).** The constant 12 represents the starting distance on the driveway. In other words, before the snail even moved, it was already 12 feet from the beginning of the driveway. Therefore, Catherine must have placed the snail 12 feet from the start of her driveway before she began recording the time it took for the snail to get to the end of her driveway.

3. **The correct answer is (B).** Solve for x:
$$-2x+5=2-(5-2x)$$
$$-2x+5=2-5+2x$$
$$-2x+5=-3+2x \quad \text{Add } 2x \text{ to both sides.}$$
$$5=-3+4x \quad \text{Add } +3 \text{ to both sides.}$$
$$8=4x \quad \text{Divide by 4.}$$
$$2=x$$

4. **The correct answer is (C).** The right triangle, of which T is the hypotenuse, has legs that are 6 inches and 9 inches. Hence,
$$T^2=6^2+9^2$$
$$T^2=36+81=117$$
$$T=\sqrt{117}$$
Therefore, $10<T<11$.

5. **The correct answer is (C).** Let the legs equal $2x$ and $3x$. By the Pythagorean Theorem,
$$(2x)^2+(3x)^2=13^2$$
$$4x^2+9x^2=169$$
$$13x^2=169$$
$$x^2=13$$
$$x=\sqrt{13}$$
The shorter leg measures $2x$, or $2\sqrt{13}$.

6. **The correct answer is (A).** The amount of grain added each week is 1000 bushels. Divide 1000 bushels by 0.8 bushels per cubic foot to obtain 1250 cubic feet per week. So, the total amount of grain in the silo is 32,500 (what is already there) plus $1250w$ (the amount added each week times the number of weeks), which must be less than or equal to the volume of the silo, 45,000 cubic feet.

7. **The correct answer is (D).** The vertex of a parabola is found when the equation is written in the form $y = a(x - h)^2 + k$. You don't need to perform any calculations, because only choice (D) is written in this form.

8. **The correct answer is (C).**
$$-x^2 + 2y - (-x - y) = -x^2 + 2y + x + y$$
$$= -x^2 + x + 3y$$

9. **The correct answer is (B).** Since Jorge's truck is traveling at an average speed of 55 miles per hour and the truck gets 6 miles per gallon, the number of gallons of diesel used each hour can be found by the equation $\frac{55 \text{ miles}}{1 \text{ hour}} \cdot \frac{1 \text{ gallon}}{6 \text{ miles}} = \frac{55}{6}$. The truck uses $\frac{55}{6}$ gallons of diesel per hour, so it uses $\frac{55}{6}h$ gallons of diesel in h hours. The truck's fuel tank has 125 gallons of diesel at the beginning of the trip. Therefore, the function that models the number of gallons of diesel remaining in the tank h hours after the trip begins is $d(h) = 125 - \frac{55h}{6}$.

10. **The correct answer is (A).**
$$A = \frac{M}{M - N}$$
$$A(M - N) = M$$
$$AM - AN = M$$
$$AM - M = AN$$
$$M(A - 1) = AN$$
$$M = \frac{AN}{A - 1}$$

11. **The correct answer is (C).** The down payment is only made once, and the sum of the down payment plus the monthly payments is equal to the cost of the sofa.

12. **The correct answer is (C).** The sum of the values that satisfy the equation is the sum of the solution $2.5 + 3 = 5.5$.
$$2n^2 - 11n + 15 = 0$$
$$(2n - 5)(n - 3) = 0$$
$$2n - 5 = 0, n - 3 = 0$$
$$n = 2.5, n = 3$$

13. **The correct answer is (D).** The graph will cross the x-axis at the point where the function (that is, the y-coordinate) has a value of 0. As result, the following equation needs to be solved:
$$480 - 60t = 0$$
$$-60t = -480$$
$$t = 8$$
Since t represents the independent variable, the point is (8, 0).

14. **The correct answer is (A).** The initial population of the town is 500. The rate of change between consecutive x values (1 year, 2 years, 3 years) is not constant. As a result, the expression cannot be linear, but exponential. Determine the percent of increase of the population from the initial population to that of one year:
$$\frac{650 - 500}{500} = \frac{150}{500} = 0.3$$
Since the population is growing, add the percent of change, in decimal format, to 1 to get 1.3. Therefore, the expression representing the population growth is $500 \times 1.3x$.

15. The correct answer is (D). You can see right away that choice A is not correct, because $(4 + 1)/2 = 2.5$, which is not equivalent to the fraction for all values of x. The three other answer choices all start with a whole number, so to find out which of them is correct, rewrite the given fraction as a mixed number. Since the denominator is $x + 2$ and the numerator includes a $4x$, rewrite it so that it is the sum of two fractions where one has a $4(x + 2)$, or $4x + 8$, in the numerator. Then, simplify the expression until you have a whole number and check the result against the three answer choices to find the correct one.

$$\frac{4x+1}{x+2} = \frac{4x}{x+2} + \frac{1}{x+2}$$

$$= \frac{4x}{x+2} + \frac{8}{x+2} + \frac{1}{x+2} - \frac{8}{x+2}$$

$$= \frac{4x+8}{x+2} + \frac{1-8}{x+2}$$

$$= 4 - \frac{7}{x+2}$$

16. The correct answer is 80. If $AC = BC$, then $m\angle A = m\angle B = 50°$.

In $\triangle ABC$, $m\angle ACB = 180° - (m\angle A + m\angle B)$. So, $m\angle ACB = 80°$. Further, $m\angle ACB = m\angle ECD$ because they are vertical angles. Therefore, $m\angle ECD = 80°$.

17. The correct answer is 6. First, solve for x by multiplying the second equation and adding it to the first one:

$$5x - 4y = 13$$
$$2[x + 2y = 4]$$
$$7x = 21$$
$$x = 3$$

Then, substitute $x = 3$ into the second equation to get the value of y:

$$3 + 2y = 4$$
$$2y = 1$$
$$y = \frac{1}{2}$$

Finally, substitute $x = 3$ and $y = \frac{1}{2}$ into $\frac{x}{y}$ to get the value of the ratio:

$$\frac{x}{y} = \frac{3}{\frac{1}{2}} = 6$$

18. The correct answer is $\frac{5}{9} = 0.55$.
Solve for b:

$$-9x + 5 = -9(x \quad b)$$
$$-9x + 5 = -9x + 9b$$
$$5 = 9b$$
$$\frac{5}{9} = b$$

19. The correct answer is 15. To begin,

$$f(p+3) = 5(p+3) + 12 = 5p + 15 + 12 = 5p + 27.$$

Similarly, $f(p) = 5p + 12$. Thus,

$$f(p+3) - f(p) = 5p + 27 - (5p + 12)$$
$$= 5p + 27 - 5p - 12$$
$$= 15$$

20. The correct answer is 4. Solve for x:

$$\frac{9}{x-2} + \frac{16}{x+3} = 5$$

$$\left(\frac{9}{x-2} + \frac{16}{x+3}\right)(x-2)(x+3) = 5(x-2)(x+3)$$

$$9x + 27 + 16x - 32 = 5x^2 + 5x - 30$$

$$0 = 5x^2 - 20x - 25$$

$$0 = 5(x+1)(x-5)$$

$$x = -1 \text{ or } x = 5$$

To get the sum of the solutions, simply add -1 and 5: $-1 + 5 = 4$.

Section 4: Math Test—Calculator

1. C	**9.** B	**17.** D	**25.** A	**33.** 45
2. D	**10.** B	**18.** B	**26.** D	**34.** 41
3. C	**11.** B	**19.** A	**27.** D	**35.** 5400
4. A	**12.** D	**20.** D	**28.** A	**36.** 440
5. A	**13.** C	**21.** D	**29.** A	**37.** 21.5
6. C	**14.** A	**22.** D	**30.** B	**38.** 4
7. B	**15.** C	**23.** C	**31.** 26	
8. D	**16.** B	**24.** A		

32. $\dfrac{17}{8} > p > \dfrac{13}{8}$ or

$2.125 > p > 1.625$

MATH TEST—CALCULATOR RAW SCORE
(Number of correct answers)

1. **The correct answer is (C).** Buying the lollipops singly would cost: 30 pops × $0.13 per pop = $3.90. The reduced rate is $1.38 per dozen. Thirty pops is $2\frac{1}{2}$ dozen, so the cost for 30 pops is $1.38 × 2.5 = $3.45. The savings with this reduced rate is $3.90 − $3.45 = $0.45.

2. **The correct answer is (D).**

   20 square yards = 180 square feet. At $1.30 per square foot, it will cost 180 × $1.30 = $234.00.

3. **The correct answer is (C).** The sum of the 5 plant heights is 47 inches. The average is found by dividing the sum of the heights by the number of plants: 47 ÷ 5 = 9.4 inches.

4. **The correct answer is (A).** The volume of the fish tank is 11(14)(9) = 1386 cu. in. The amount needed to fill the tank is 1386 ÷ 231 = 6 gallons.

5. **The correct answer is (A).** The amount of protein in m cups of milk is $8m$ grams, and the amount of protein in n eggs is $6n$ grams. The problem asks for the amount to meet *or* exceed the recommended daily intake, which sets up a greater-than-or-equal-to scenario.

6. **The correct answer is (C).** The total charge that Amy will pay is the daily rate, the mileage rate, and the 7.5% tax on both. If Amy drove x miles, then the total charge is $(19.99 + 0.15x) + 0.075(19.99 + 0.15x)$, which can be rewritten as $1.075(19.99 + 0.15x)$.

7. **The correct answer is (B).**

   $5\frac{1}{2}$ dozen nails are bought for $5\frac{1}{2}$ dozen × 35 cents per dozen = 192.5 cents. There are 66 nails in $5\frac{1}{2}$ dozen and 66 ÷ 3 = 22 sets sold at 10 cents per set, so 22 sets × 10 cents per set = 220 cents. The profit is $220 − 192.5 = 27\frac{1}{2}$ cents.

8. **The correct answer is (D).** The weights are proportional to the volumes, and the volumes vary as the cubes of their dimensions. If the edges are doubled, the volume becomes $2^3 = 8$ times as large. Therefore, the weight is $8 \times 150 = 1,200$ pounds.

9. **The correct answer is (B).** Use the distributive property to expand each part of the expression, and then combine like terms.
$$-x(3x - 2) + 2(3 - 2x) = -3x^2 + 2x + 6 - 4x$$
$$= -3x^2 - 2x + 6$$

10. **The correct answer is (B).** One method to find the correct answer is to create an inequality. The income from the sign-up fees for x people is $20x$. For the organization to profit, $20x$ must be greater than the cost of x t-shirts. Therefore, $20x > 7x + 60$ can be used to model the situation. Solving this inequality yields $x > 4.6$. Since there can't be 4.6 people, round the answer up to 5.

11. **The correct answer is (B).** The total number of students, $x + y$, is equal to 2,180, so the answer must be choice (B) or (C). The male students raised $20 each, and the female students raised $25 each. Since x represents the number of male students, then the amount the male students raised is represented by $20x$, and the amount the female students raised is represented by $25y$. The total amount raised is $50,000, so the sum is $20x + 25y = 50,000$. That leaves choice (B) as the only correct answer.

12. **The correct answer is (D).** The cube root of an expression is equal to that expression raised to the $\frac{1}{3}$ power, so
$$\sqrt[3]{9x^3 y^5 z^6} = \left(9x^3 y^5 z^6\right)^{\frac{1}{3}}$$
$$= 9^{\frac{1}{3}} x y^{\frac{5}{3}} z^2$$

13. **The correct answer is (C).** The two intersections of the graphs of the equations are at the points $(0,1)$ and $(-1,0)$. Substituting 0 for x and 1 for y makes both equations true. Also, substituting -1 for x and 0 for y makes both equations true.

14. **The correct answer is (A).** Find the solution to this problem by using the structure of the given equation. Multiplying both sides of the equation $\frac{x}{3} - \frac{y}{4} = 5$ by -24 will clear fractions from the equation and yield $-8x + 6y = -120$.

15. **The correct answer is (C).** If x is the number of lunches sold and y is the number of dinners sold, then $x + y$ represents the number of meals sold during the weekend. The equation $7.5x + 12y$ represents the total amount collected in the weekend. Therefore, the correct system of equations is $x + y = 241$ and $7.5x + 12y = 2523$.

16. **The correct answer is (B).** The scatterplot shows a strong correlation between the variables. As the years increase, the population also increases.

17. **The correct answer is (D).** The points on the graph display a pattern of exponential growth, as a curve could be used to connect them; therefore, an exponential function would best represent the data.

18. **The correct answer is (B).** The graduate starts at x dollars per week. After the pay cut, the graduate receives 90% of the original salary. The 10% raise adds 9% to the salary (10% of 90%), so the new salary is $0.99x$.

19. **The correct answer is (A).** Since $(1, 1)$ is a solution to the system of inequalities, substituting 1 for x and 1 for y in the given system must result in two true inequalities. After this substitution, $y < -x + b$ becomes $1 < -1 + b$ or $2 < b$, and $y > x - c$ becomes $1 > 1 - c$ or $0 > c$. Hence, b is a positive number greater than 2, and c is negative. Therefore, $b > c$.

20. **The correct answer is (D).** If a triangle is a right triangle, then the squares of two sides will add up to the square of the hypotenuse: $12^2 = 144$; $15^2 = 225$; $18^2 = 324$. $144 + 225 \neq 324$.

21. **The correct answer is (D).** If the discount is 10%, then $12.60 is 90% of $14.00.

22. **The correct answer is (D).** To solve for the number of gallons of white vinegar, set up a proportion.

$$\frac{1\frac{1}{3}}{2} = \frac{x}{7}$$

$$2x = \frac{28}{3}$$

$$x = 4\frac{4}{6} = 4\frac{2}{3}$$

23. **The correct answer is (C).** A hexagon with 22-inch sides has a perimeter of 6×22, or 132 inches.

$$C = 2\pi r$$
$$132 = 2\pi r$$
$$132 = 2(3.14)r$$
$$132 = 6.28r$$
$$21.02 = r$$

24. **The correct answer is (A).** Because the function f has $(x - 4)$ and $(x + 2)$ as factors, the function should have zeros when $x - 4 = 0$ and $x + 2 = 0$. The only graph that shows a curve that has x-intercepts at -2 and 4 is choice (A).

25. **The correct answer is (A).** There are a total of $8 + 23 + 19 = 50$ people in Group A. Then, reduce the fraction to find that $\frac{8}{50} = \frac{4}{25}$.

26. **The correct answer is (D).** When $t = 0$, the height of the ball is 0.02 m, so 0.02 represents the height of the ball before it is hit.

27. **The correct answer is (D).** If k is a positive constant other than 1, then the equation

$kx + y = c$ can be rewritten as $y = -kx + c$. If k is positive, then $-k$ is negative, and it must be something other than -1. The only graph with a negative slope other than -1 is answer choice (D).

28. **The correct answer is (A).** If the machine loses 15% of its value each year, then each year its value is 85% of what it was the year before. Therefore, we are looking for the fifth term of a geometric sequence with first term $80,000 at time zero and common ratio 0.85. Using the formula $a_n = a_1 \times r^{n-1}$, we can compute $a_5 = \$80,000 \times (0.85)^4 = \$41,760.50$.

29. **The correct answer is (A).** To find the current average, add all of the medals and divide by 6:

$$\frac{12 + 13 + 31 + 25 + 37 + 28}{6} = \frac{146}{6}$$
$$= 24.3$$
$$\approx 24$$

The new average will have to be 25, but it will be spread over 7 Winter Olympics:

$$\frac{12 + 13 + 31 + 25 + 37 + 28 + x}{7} = \frac{146 + x}{7} = 25$$
$$146 + x = 175$$
$$x = 29$$

30. **The correct answer is (B).** Divide the ratio $\frac{6x}{2x + 4}$ to find the equivalent form, $3 - \frac{12}{2x + 4}$. Simplify the rational expression to obtain $3 - \frac{6}{x + 2}$. Therefore, $A = -6$.

31. The correct answer is 26. Rewrite $(3x-4)(2-5x)$ in the form $ax^2 + bx + c$ to find b:

$$(3x-4)(2-5x) = 3x(2) + 3x(-5x) + (-4)(2) + (-4)(-5x)$$
$$= 6x - 15x^2 - 8 + 20x$$
$$= -15x^2 + 26x - 8$$

Accordingly, $b = 26$.

32. The correct answer is

$$\frac{17}{8} > p > \frac{13}{8} \text{ or } 2.125 > p > 1.625 .$$

Solve the compound inequality for p. Remember to reverse the direction of the inequalities when you divide by -2.

$$-\frac{1}{4} < -2p + 4 < \frac{3}{4}$$
$$-4\frac{1}{4} < -2p < -3\frac{1}{4}$$
$$\frac{17}{8} > p > \frac{13}{8}$$

33. The correct answer is 45. Letting m be the time per regular question, $2m$ is the time per math problem. The total time for all the regular questions is $300m$, and the total time for all the math problems is $50(2m)$. Since the exam is 3 hours, or 180 minutes, $300m + 100m = 180$ minutes, $400m = 180$, and $m = \frac{180}{400} = \frac{9}{20}$. The time to do a math problem is $2\left(\frac{9}{20}\right) = \frac{9}{10}$. All 50 math problems can be done in

$$50\left(\frac{9}{10}\right) = 45 \text{ minutes.}$$

34. The correct answer is 41. The number of games that the Montreal Canadiens played is not provided, but it is given that the ratio of the number of games played in the 1947–48 season to that in the 1924–25 season is 2:1. Problems like this can be solved by plugging in real numbers. Let's say that there were 100 games in the 1924–25 season, so they won 57 of those games. In the 1947–48 season, there were twice as many games, or 200 games, so they won 33% of 200 games, or 66 games. Altogether they won 123 out of 300 games, and this fraction can be simplified to 41 out of 100, or 41%.

35. The correct answer is 5400. Of the number of voters polled, 400 of 625, or 64%, were in favor of the measure. If the margin of error is 4%, the likely population proportion will be between 60% and 68%: 60% of 9000 total voters is $(0.6)(9000) = 5400$.

36. The correct answer is 440. If the dolphin weighs 110% of the average, it weighs 10% more than the average weight of 400 pounds, or $0.10 \times 400 = 40$ pounds. The dolphin weighs $400 + 40 = 440$ pounds.

37. The correct answer is 21.5. First, combine the equations by subtracting $(x + y = 13)$ from $(3x + y = -4)$:

$$3x + y = -4$$
$$\underline{-(x + y = 13)}$$
$$2x = -17$$
$$x = -8.5$$

Then solve for x and substitute into one of the equations to solve for y:

$$-8.5 + y = 13$$
$$y = 21.5$$

38. The correct answer is 4. To find the value that will make the system have no solution, you must show that the two equations are parallel lines. In standard form, parallel lines are equal on the left side of their equations, but not the right. In standard form, the first equation would need to be equal to the second on the left side. Find a factor that you could multiply the first equation with:

$$-3x + 2 = -1$$
$$6x - by = 8$$
$$(-3x + 2y = -1)(-2)$$
$$6x - 4y = 2$$

So $b = 4$.

If $b = 4$, the left side of both equations are equal, but not the right. Therefore, they are parallel.

Section 5: Essay

Analysis of Passage

The following is an analysis of the passage by Peter Krapp, noting how the writer used evidence, reasoning, and stylistic or persuasive elements to support his claims, connect the claims and evidence, and add power to the ideas he expressed. Check to see if you evaluated the passage in a similar way."

Adapted from "Penn State Hack Exposes Theft Risk of Student Personal Data" by Peter Krapp, originally published in The Conversation on May 20, 2015. Peter Krapp is a professor of film & media studies at University of California, Irvine. (This passage was edited for length. For the complete article, see http://theconversation.com.)

1 Pennsylvania State University's College of Engineering took its computer network offline on May 15 after disclosing two cyberattacks. The perpetrators were able to access information on 18,000 students, who are being contacted this week with the news that their personal identifying information is in hackers' hands.

Three days later, the computer network is back online, with new protections for its users.

2 One of the two attacks is ascribed by a forensic cybersecurity corporation retained by Penn State to computers apparently based in China.

3 As a researcher who has published on hacking and hacktivism and serves on the board of the UC Irvine data science initiative, I believe two aspects of this news story deserve particular attention.

Compromising student data

4 Penn State announced last week that the FBI alerted it on November 21, 2014, about an attack with custom malware that started as early as September 2012.

1 *The writer cites a specific example of a computer security breach and uses facts and statistics to show the seriousness of the problem.*

2 *By mentioning that the computer hackers appear to be located in China, the writer underscores the global risks of the security breach.*

3 *The writer establishes his credentials to write about and offer an argument on this topic.*

4 *The writer uses facts and dates to lay the groundwork for the point he is about to make.*

5   Why did it take so long for Penn State to disclose the breach, despite the fact that the experience of large-scale hacks in 2013 and 2014 (against Target, Home Depot, and others) clearly demonstrated an urgent need for quick and full disclosure—both to help the victims and to preserve a modicum of trust?

6   Penn State stated only that any disclosure would have tipped off the perpetrators before their access to the College of Engineering computers could be cut off.

7   Meanwhile, student data may have been compromised for at least six months, maybe longer.

8   Another conspicuous problem with public discussion of events like this is, in fact, the lack of distinction often made in the media between actual appropriation of data (as at Penn State) and mere temporary disabling or defacement of websites (as happened to Rutgers University last month). That is like being unable to make a difference between a grand theft auto and keying a car.

The question is, what can universities do to limit the risk to their students?

9   The exposure of student data in higher education is not limited to Social Security numbers or email passwords. Information collected and retained by educational institutions includes full name, address, phone number, credit and debit card information, workplace information, date of birth, personal interests and of course academic performance and grade information.

5   *The writer poses a rhetorical question to address one aspect of this story that he earlier said deserves "particular attention." His first point is that Penn State took too long to disclose the security breach. He cites two past breaches to support his argument about the need for quick disclosure, and uses evocative words ("help the victims and to preserve a modicum of trust") to emphasize how important early disclosure is.*

6   *The writer states Penn State's justification for delaying disclosure. He uses the word only to imply that Penn State should have been more forthcoming, thus strengthening his own position. At the same time, he presents himself as reasonable because he offers Penn State's argument before going on with his own.*

7   *The writer shows why, in his opinion, Penn State's position is weak.*

8   *The writer now addresses the second point that he feels "deserve[s] particular attention" — The media does not treat breaches like the one at Penn State seriously, often viewing them more like nuisance problems. He supports his view that the media should be able to make a distinction between serious and non-serious security breaches by juxtaposing a significant crime (grand theft auto) with a minor infraction (keying a car).*

9   *The writer shows how dangerous these kinds of security breaches are, using specific examples of the kinds of information that can fall into hackers' hands.*

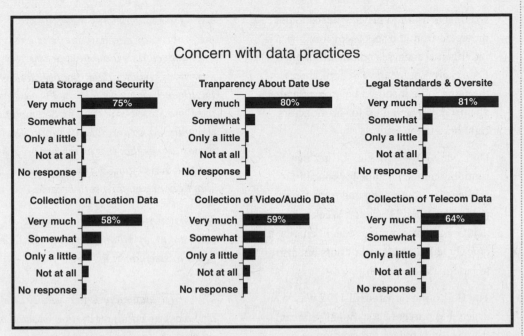

Concern with data practices

10 A survey conducted by the Obama administration collected responses from 24,092 individuals on how much they trusted various institutions to keep their data safe. There was a high level of concern around transparency and legal standards. (https://www.whitehouse.gov/ issues/technology/big-data-review)

. . .

11 President Obama only recently called for laws covering data hacking and student privacy. "We're saying that data collected on students in the classroom should only be used for educational purposes," he stated in his speech to the Federal Trade Commission (FTC) earlier this year this year to the Federal Trade Commission (FTC) earlier this year.

Data privacy concerns

10 *The writer strengthens his viewpoint by providing statistical evidence in the form of a survey that reveals how concerned people are about the safety of their personal data.*

11 *The writer supports his argument by quoting an authority no less than the president of the United States. (He also makes the point that he believes the president's concern is overdue, by saying this statement was made "only recently.")*

12   If students' right to privacy needs to be protected from the specter of foreign intelligence agencies poking around the Penn State Engineering School, then by the same logic it should be protected also against data-mining by for-profit actors right here in the US.

13   Until May 2014, Google, for instance, routinely mined its apps for education services for advertising and monetizing purposes. When Education Week reported that Google was mining student emails, it quickly led not only to lawsuits but also to landmark legislation.

14   The California Senate Bill 1177 was enacted to prevent educational services from selling student information or mining it for advertising purposes.

15   Yet, almost a year later, students in California remain just as concerned about their data privacy as before—since the new state law was watered down to apply only to K–12 and not to higher education.

16   And when it was disclosed earlier this spring that education publisher Pearson secretly monitored social media to discern references to their content, the legislative response was one that, according to the Electronic Privacy Information Center (EPIC) in Washington, DC, "fails to uphold President Obama's promise that the data collected in an educational context can be used only for educational purposes."

17   Students in higher education nationwide are still in a position where they cannot opt out of the computer services of their learning institutions, and so they have no expectation of privacy.

12   *The writer underscores the depth of the problem by pointing out that there are many entities that might access students' computer data: not only foreign intelligence agencies (as was the case with the Penn State breach), but US companies that mine computer data for profit. The writer argues that just as foreign breaches have been recognized as serious, so should domestic for-profit breaches.*

13   *The writer offers a specific example of a US company mining personal data for profit to strengthen his case.*

14   *The writer underscores the validity of his argument by citing legislation enacted to address the problem.*

15   *The writer points out that the final form of the legislation to protect students' data does not extend to college students.*

16   *The writer reinforces his argument that not enough is being done to protect college students' personal data by citing another example of a US company data-mining for profit. He also quotes an authoritative source to support this claim.*

17   *The writer points out a reality that makes and keeps college students vulnerable: "they cannot opt out of the computer services of their learning institutions."*

18 Despite President Obama's promises for safeguarding the privacy of consumers and families, and despite the fact that a number of technology companies concerned with growing consumer distrust recently signed a pledge to safeguard student privacy, <u>neither</u> Google nor Apple signed on.

19 The President's Council of Advisors on Science and Technology (PCAST) was tasked to examine current and likely future capabilities of key technologies, both those associated with the collection, analysis, and use of big data and those that can help to preserve privacy, resulting in a direct recommendation to strengthen US research in privacy-related technologies.

20 And overwhelmingly, respondents to a White House survey recently expressed severe reservations about the collection, storage, and security and use of private information.

21 Maybe it is time for higher education to heed those signals.

18 *The writer underscores college students' vulnerability by pointing out that two major companies (Google and Apple) have refused to sign a pledge to safeguard student privacy.*

19 *The writer points out that an advisory board to the US president has recommended strengthening research on the problem.*

20 *The writer cites a White House survey that reflected "severe reservations about the collection, storage and security and use of private information." The survey shows that despite the measures that have been put in place, the public still feels their data is at risk.*

21 *The writer concludes his argument by saying it's time for colleges (where people are particularly vulnerable) to pay attention to—and act on—the information they have, in order to remedy the situation.*

answers DIAGNOSTIC TEST

Sample Essays

The following are examples of a high-scoring and low-scoring essay, based on the passage by Peter Krapp.

High-Scoring Essay

Peter Krapp builds a well-constructed argument designed to persuade readers that computer hacking is a danger that steals our most valuable possession—personal information—from our most vulnerable people—students. The article focuses on personal information about college students stolen from college computer networks. The writer builds his argument brick by brick. He starts by giving an example of student data stolen from a college by hackers in China, relating his topic to an event that really happened. The writer quickly establishes himself as an expert in the topic so readers can trust his information. Krapp asks and answers questions about the theft of data, goes into more depth about the type of information stolen from college networks, and then briefly touches on the laws, or the lack of laws, to protect students. He points out that data is stolen from students by not only foreign hackers, but also by American companies. The writer finishes with a call for colleges to protect student data, clearly stating his purpose.

The theft of 18,000 students' data from Pennsylvania State University's College of Engineering is a strong example to start the article. Naming the college and identifying the large number of students tells the reader immediately that a single incident affected many people. The location of the hackers shows that protecting the physical location of the data is useless, and it adds a bit of foreign intrigue.

The second paragraph is a single sentence, but accomplishes two important things. It gives the reader his credentials, proving that he is qualified to speak as an authority on the topic. It also provides structure for the next section by telling the reader that the writer will focus on two aspects of the news story.

Krapp reveals the first aspect to be discussed right away—Penn State knew that data was being stolen for six months before doing anything about it. To emphasize just how astonishing Penn State's behavior is, Krapp asks the same question that any reader might ask: Why? He asks the question in words that urge a fast response such as "urgent need" and "help the victims." He demonstrates that Penn State's response is weak by describing the response as "stated only."

The next paragraph starts with "Another conspicuous problem." This phrase presents the second aspect he wants to discuss, which is the media's lack of understanding about the difference between the major problem of stealing data and the minor problem of disabling a website for a short period of time. He helps readers to understand the difference by comparing stealing a car to causing only minor damage to the car.

Krapp follows the reader's natural thought process by asking the next question: If it's a problem, how do we fix it? He presents information in two ways, listing the type of information at risk and displaying bar charts that show the results of a presidential survey on the public's perception of data security.

The section title, "Data privacy concerns," informs readers that Krapp is addressing another concern, the theft of student data by US companies that want to mine data for profit. He gives two examples that are recognized and used by college students: Google and Pearson. He points out that students are particularly vulnerable to theft by the corporations that provide the apps and class materials that students must use for school. The school dictates which apps are to be used, so students "cannot opt out." He touches again on the law, but reveals that it doesn't protect college students. This information reinforces his arguments that college students are vulnerable to data theft. Presenting the facts this way says that college students are not only vulnerable, they are betrayed by the universities, US companies, and laws that should protect them.

The argument Krapp has built leads to a solid conclusion that Krapp states in a single, final sentence that is brief but summarizes the conclusion readers should draw. The brevity of the statement ensures that readers will get the point of the article and remember it in the future. The information that Krapp presents in examples, lists, survey results and bar charts provides a solid foundation for the conclusion that becomes obvious to any reader. Protect student data.

Low-Scoring Essay

Peter Krapp tries to persuade us that students should be allowed to opt out of giving their data to colleges and companies. This would protect them from having their full name, address, phone number, credit and debit card information, workplace information, date of birth, personal interests and of course academic performance and grade information stolen by people like Chinese hackers and companies like Google and Pearson.

Peter Krapp persuades us by giving lots of examples of data being stolen, like Pennsylvania State University's College of Engineering, Target, Home Depot, Google, and Pearson. One of the examples includes a chart that shows how much 24,092 individuals trusted various institutions to keep their data safe. Most of them didn't think their data was safe.

All of this information, charts, and examples that Peter Krapp included in his essay is very convincing. I think we should pass some laws like Peter Krapp suggested. The laws would keep American companies from stealing our data and punish hackers from other countries who steal our data.

All college students should try to opt out of giving away all of their private information because we know the colleges won't protect it. The colleges actually tell students to use apps that they know companies steal data from. This makes college students more vulnerable than anyone else to losing their data.

If companies are going to use the data they take from students, they should pay the students for the data. Then, students might not mind so much if companies take their data because the students would make money from it and college is very expensive.

When I go to college, I will opt out of giving my data to colleges and companies. My information is important to me and I don't want it stolen from me.

COMPUTING YOUR SCORES

To get a sense of your progress in preparing for the SAT®, follow these instructions and the following conversion tables.

To Determine Your Practice Test Scores

1 After you go through each of the test sections (Reading, Writing and Language, Math—No Calculator, and Math—Calculator) and determine which answers you got right, be sure to enter the number of correct answers in the box below the answer key for each of the sections.

2 Your total score on the SAT® diagnostic test is the sum of your Evidence-Based Reading and Writing Section score and your Math Section score. To get your total score, convert the raw score—the number of questions you got right in a particular section—into the "scaled score" for that section, and then you'll calculate the total score. It sounds a little confusing, but we'll take you through the steps.

To Calculate Your Evidence-Based Reading and Writing Section Score

Your Evidence-Based Reading and Writing Section score is on a scale of 200–800. First determine your Reading Test score, and then determine your score on the Writing and Language Test.

1 Count the number of correct answers you got on the **Section 1: Reading Test.** Remember that there is no penalty for wrong answers. **The number of correct answers is your raw score.**

2 Go to Raw Score Conversion Table 1: Section and Test Scores on page 112. Look in the "Raw Score" column for your raw score, and match it to the number in the "Reading Test Score" column.

4 Do the same with **Section 2: Writing and Language Test** to determine that score.

4 Add your Reading Test score to your Writing and Language Test score.

5 Multiply that number by 10. This is your Evidence-Based Reading and Writing Section score.

To Calculate Your Math Section Score

Your Math Section score is also on a scale of 200–800.

1 Count the number of correct answers you got on the **Section 3: Math Test—No Calculator** and the **Section 4: Math Test—No Calculator** practice tests. Again, there is no penalty for wrong answers. **The number of correct answers is your raw score.**

2 Add the number of correct answers on the Section 3: Math Test—No Calculator and the Section 4: Math Test—No Calculator practice tests.

3 Use the **Raw Score Conversion Table 1: Section and Test Scores** on page 112 and convert your raw score into your Math Section score.

To Obtain Your Total Score

Add your score on the Evidence-Based Reading and Writing Section to the Math Section score. This is your total score on this SAT® Practice Test, on a scale of 400–1600.

Subscores Provide Additional Information

Subscores offer you greater details about your strengths in certain areas within literacy and math. The subscores are reported on a scale of 1–15 and include Heart of Algebra, Problem Solving and Data Analysis, Passport to Advanced Math, Expression of Ideas, Standard English Conventions, Words in Context, and Command of Evidence.

Heart of Algebra

The **Heart of Algebra subscore** is based on questions from the Math Test—No Calculator and Math Test—Calculator (Sections 3 and 4) that focus on linear equations and inequalities.

- Add up your total correct answers from these sections:
- Math Test—No Calculator: Questions 1–3, 6, 9, 11, 17, 18
- Math Test—Calculator: Questions 5, 6, 10, 11, 14, 15, 19, 27, 32, 37, 38
- Your Raw Score = the total number of correct answers from all of these questions.
- Use the **Raw Score Conversion Table 2: Subscores** on page 113 to determine your **Heart of Algebra** subscore.

Problem Solving and Data Analysis

The **Problem Solving and Data Analysis subscore** is based on questions from the Math Test that focus on quantitative reasoning, the interpretation and synthesis of data, and solving problems in rich and varied contexts.

- Add up your total correct answers from these sections:
- Math Test—No Calculator: None
- Math Test—Calculator: Questions 1–3, 7, 8, 16–18, 21, 22, 25, 28, 29, 33–36
- Your Raw Score = the total number of correct answers from all of these questions.
- Use the **Raw Score Conversion Table 2: Subscores** on page 113 to determine your **Problem Solving and Data Analysis** subscore.

Passport to Advanced Math

The **Passport to Advanced Math subscore** is based on questions from the Math Test that focus on topics central to your ability to progress to more advanced math, such as understanding the structure of expressions, reasoning with more complex equations, and interpreting and building functions.

- Add up your total correct answers from these sections:
- Math Test—No Calculator: Questions 7, 8, 10, 12–15, 19, 20
- Math Test—Calculator: Questions 9, 12, 13, 24, 26, 30, 31
- Your Raw Score = the total number of correct answers from all of these questions.
- Use the **Raw Score Conversion Table 2: Subscores** on page 113 to determine your **Passport to Advanced Math** subscore.

Expression of Ideas

The **Expression of Ideas subscore** is based on questions from the Writing and Language Test that focus on topic development, organization, and rhetorically effective use of language.

- Add up your total correct answers from Section 2: Writing and Language Test:
- Questions 1, 4, 5, 7–9, 12, 13, 16, 17, 19, 20, 25, 26, 28, 29, 32–35, 39, 41–43
- Your Raw Score = the total number of correct answers from all of these questions.
- Use the **Raw Score Conversion Table 2: Subscores** on page 113 to determine your Expression of Ideas subscore.

Standard English Conventions

The **Standard English Conventions subscore** is based on questions from the Writing and Language Test that focus on sentence structure, usage, and punctuation.

- Add up your total correct answers from Section 2: Writing and Language Test:
- Questions 2, 3, 6, 10, 11, 14, 15, 18, 21–24, 27, 30, 31, 36–38, 40, 44
- Your Raw Score = the total number of correct answers from all of these questions.
- Use the **Raw Score Conversion Table 2: Subscores** on page 113 to determine your **Standard English Conventions** subscore.

Words in Context

The **Words in Context subscore** is based on questions from the Reading Test and the Writing and Language Test that address word/phrase meaning in context and rhetorical word choice.

- Add up your total correct answers from Sections 1 and 2:
- Reading Test: Questions 1, 6, 13, 17, 27, 30, 38, 41, 51, 52
- Writing and Language Test: Questions 5, 8, 12, 17, 28, 32, 35, 43
- Your Raw Score = the total number of correct answers from all of these questions.
- Use the **Raw Score Conversion Table 2: Subscores** on page 113 to determine your **Words in Context** subscore.

Command of Evidence

The **Command of Evidence subscore** is based on questions from the Reading Test and the Writing and Language Test that ask you to interpret and use evidence found in a wide range of passages and informational graphics, such as graphs, tables, and charts.

- Add up your total correct answers from Sections 1 and 2:
- Reading Test: Questions 4, 10, 14, 20, 23, 28, 36, 42, 43, 44
- Writing and Language Test: Questions 1, 4, 13, 16, 25, 29, 34, 42
- Your Raw Score = the total number of correct answers from all of these questions.
- Use the **Raw Score Conversion Table 2: Subscores** on page 113 to determine your **Command of Evidence** subscore.

Cross-Test Scores

The new SAT®also reports two cross-test scores: Analysis in History/Social Studies and Analysis in Science. These scores are based on questions in the Reading Test, Writing and Language Test, and both Math Tests that ask you to think analytically about texts and questions in these subject areas. Cross-test scores are reported on a scale of 10–40.

Analysis in History/Social Studies

- Add up your total correct answers from these sections:
- Reading Test: Questions 11–21, 43–52
- Writing and Language Test: Questions 12, 13, 16, 17, 19, 20
- Math Test—No Calculator: Question 14
- Math Test—Calculator: Questions 11, 16, 17, 25, 29, 34, 35
- Your Raw Score = the total number of correct answers from all of these questions.
- Use the **Raw Score Conversion Table 3: Cross-Test Scores** on page 114 to determine your **Analysis in History/Social Studies** cross-test score.

Analysis in Science

- Add up your total correct answers from these sections:
- Reading Test: Questions 1–10, 22–32
- Writing and Language Test: Questions 25, 26, 28, 29, 32, 33
- Math Test—No Calculator: Questions 2, 13
- Math Test—Calculator: Questions 3, 5, 8, 22, 26, 36
- Your Raw Score = the total number of correct answers from all of these questions.
- Use the **Raw Score Conversion Table 3: Cross-Test Scores** on page 114 to determine your **Analysis in Science** cross-test score.

answers DIAGNOSTIC TEST

Raw Score Conversion Table 1: Section and Test Scores

Raw Score	Math Section Score	Reading Test Score	Writing and Language Test Score	Raw Score	Math Section Score	Reading Test Score	Writing and Language Test Score	Raw Score	Math Section Score	Reading Test Score	Writing and Language Test Score
0	200	10	10	20	450	22	23	40	610	33	36
1	200	10	10	21	460	23	23	41	620	33	37
2	210	10	10	22	470	23	24	42	630	34	38
3	230	11	10	23	480	24	25	43	640	35	39
4	240	12	11	24	480	24	25	44	650	35	40
5	260	13	12	25	490	25	26	45	660	36	
6	280	14	13	26	500	25	26	46	670	37	
7	290	15	13	27	510	26	27	47	670	37	
8	310	15	14	28	520	26	28	48	680	38	
9	320	16	15	29	520	27	28	49	690	38	
10	330	17	16	30	530	28	29	50	700	39	
11	340	17	16	31	540	28	30	51	710	40	
12	360	18	17	32	550	29	30	52	730	40	
13	370	19	18	33	560	29	31	53	740		
14	380	19	19	34	560	30	32	54	750		
15	390	20	19	35	570	30	32	55	760		
16	410	20	20	36	580	31	33	56	780		
17	420	21	21	37	590	31	34	57	790		
18	430	21	21	38	600	32	34	58	800		
19	440	22	22	39	600	32	35				

Conversion Equation 1 Section and Test Scores

Raw Score Conversion Table 2: Subscores

Raw Score (# of correct answers)	Expression of Ideas	Standard English Conventions	Heart of Algebra	Problem Solving Data Analysis	Passport to Advanced Math	Words in Context	Command of Evidence
0	1	1	1	1	1	1	1
1	1	1	1	1	3	1	1
2	1	1	2	2	5	2	2
3	2	2	3	3	6	3	3
4	3	2	4	4	7	4	4
5	4	3	5	5	8	5	5
6	5	4	6	6	9	6	6
7	6	5	6	7	10	6	7
8	6	6	7	8	11	7	8
9	7	6	8	8	11	8	8
10	7	7	8	9	12	8	9
11	8	7	9	10	12	9	10
12	8	8	9	10	13	9	10
13	9	8	9	11	13	10	11
14	9	9	10	12	14	11	12
15	10	10	10	13	14	12	13
16	10	10	11	14	15	13	14
17	11	11	12	15		14	15
18	11	12	13			15	15
19	12	13	15				
20	12	15					
21	13						
22	14						
23	14						
24	15						

Conversion Equation 2 Subscores

Raw Score Conversion Table 3: Cross-Test Scores

Raw Score (# of correct answers)	Analysis in History/Social Studies Cross-Test Score	Analysis in Science Cross-Test Score
0	10	10
1	10	11
2	11	12
3	12	13
4	14	14
5	15	15
6	16	16
7	17	17
8	18	18
9	20	19
10	21	20
11	22	20
12	23	21
13	24	22
14	25	23
15	26	24
16	27	24
17	28	25
18	28	26
19	29	27
20	30	27
21	30	28
22	31	29
23	32	30
24	32	30
25	33	31
26	34	32
27	35	33
28	35	33
29	36	34
30	37	35
31	38	36
32	38	37
33	39	38
34	40	39
35	40	40

Conversion Equation 3: Cross-Test Scores

TEST	ANALYSIS IN HISTORY/SOCIAL STUDIES		ANALYSIS IN SCIENCE	
	QUESTIONS	RAW SCORE	QUESTIONS	RAW SCORE
Reading Test	11–21, 43–52		1–10, 22–32	
Writing and Language Test	12, 13, 16, 17, 19, 20		25, 26, 28, 29, 32, 33	
Math Test—No Calculator	14		2, 13	
Math Test—Calculator	11, 16, 17, 25, 29, 34, 35		3, 5, 8, 22, 26, 36	
TOTAL				

ANALYSIS IN HISTORY/
SOCIAL STUDIES
RAW SCORE (0–35)

CONVERT

ANALYSIS IN HISTORY/
SOCIAL STUDIES
CROSS-TEST SCORE (10–40)

ANALYSIS IN SCIENCE
RAW SCORE (0–35)

CONVERT

ANALYSIS IN SCIENCE
CROSS-TEST SCORE (1–15)

PART III

SAT® READING TEST STRATEGIES

Chapter 3: Evidence-Based Reading Strategies

Evidence-Based Reading Strategies

OVERVIEW

- A closer look at evidence-based reading
- Basic steps for answering evidence-based reading questions
- Tips for taking the Reading Test
- Strategies for answering specific question types
- Exercise: Evidence-Based Reading
- Answer key and explanations
- Summing it up

A CLOSER LOOK AT EVIDENCE-BASED READING

The new SAT® Evidence-Based Reading Test is focused on demonstrating comprehension and reasoning skills through responses to a variety of reading passages. The passages are chosen to reflect the complexity and reading levels appropriate to college and career readiness. The questions will require you to analyze the text and use textual evidence to assess meaning and to support ideas. The emphasis is on using the text to support your answers, and on understanding the overall concepts and how they are developed through the course of the passage.

Passage topics are drawn from U.S. and world literature, historical and social science documents, and scientific writing. There will be four single passages and one paired passage, with a total of 52 questions. The single passages' lengths are between 500–750 words; the paired passage has the same word length between the two passages.

The reading comprehension questions are designed to assess how well you read and understand information. The questions don't test the specifics you have learned in your course work. They are based solely on explicit and implicit information contained in the passage. At least one passage will be accompanied by an informational graphic from which one or more questions will be drawn. These questions require you to analyze the data presented in formats such as tables, graphs, and charts.

NOTE

Note that the evidence-based reading questions are not arranged in order of difficulty. The questions for each passage will generally begin with broader questions about the overall ideas in the text and will then focus on specific portions of the passage.

Question Format

On the new SAT®, each evidence-based reading passage and question set starts with a direction line that looks like this:

Questions 1–10 are based on the following passage.

OR

Questions 1–10 are based on the following passage and supplementary material.

OR

Questions 1–10 are based on the following two passages.

The direction line is followed by a brief introduction to the text. The introduction describes the origin of the passage. Sometimes, the introduction will include additional background information.

The questions for each passage are in standard multiple-choice format with four answer choices each. Most often, these questions ask you to do one of the following:

- Determine central themes and ideas as presented in the passage.
- Determine the author's purpose or point of view of the text.
- Cite textual evidence to support inferences, conclusions, or arguments.
- Cite evidence to illustrate or support interpretations of meaning, mood, or tone of the passage.
- Analyze words and phrases in the context of the passage.
- Analyze information in an accompanying table, graph, chart, etc.

BASIC STEPS FOR ANSWERING EVIDENCE-BASED READING QUESTIONS

To answer the reading questions, follow these five steps:

1 Read the introduction.

2 Read the questions.

3 Read the passage with the questions in mind.

4 Answer the questions.

5 For any question you're not sure of, eliminate obviously wrong answers and take your best guess. Answer all the questions.

Let's look at the five steps in more detail.

1 You don't want to blow past the introductory paragraph because it can be very helpful to you. It might provide some important background information about the passage, or it might set the stage so you know what you're reading about.

2 Read the questions so you know what to look for in the passage. For example, if there's a question about the theme, consider that as you read. If there's a question that references a particular word or phrase, or perhaps a quotation in the text, look for it as you read the passage.

3 Now read the passage as quickly as you can without getting lost. Don't fret over details; focus on the larger ideas and try to follow the sequence, argument, or plot.

④ Answer the questions that are easiest for you. Then tackle the others in order, referring to the text to find and confirm answers as time permits.

⑤ Eliminate answer choices that you know are incorrect and guess at the remaining choices. Remember, there is no penalty for incorrect answers, so be sure not to leave any answer ovals blank.

Now that you're familiar with how to approach evidence-based reading passages and questions, let's try a few.

Sample Reading Passage 1

QUESTIONS 1–4 ARE BASED ON THE FOLLOWING PASSAGE.

José Martí was a Cuban teacher, organizer, writer, and poet. The lyrics to the popular folksong "Guantanamera" were adapted from one of Martí's poems. Although Cuban by birth, he is considered one of the most influential writers in all of Latin America. He died in the battle for Cuba's independence from Spain, a cause to which he had devoted much of his life.

The following excerpt comes from an article by Martí that was published in El Partido Liberal *(Mexico City), March 5, 1892.*

Our America

The prideful villager thinks his hometown contains the whole world, and as long as he can stay on as mayor or humiliate the rival who stole his sweetheart or watch his nest egg accumulating in its strongbox he believes the universe to be in good order, unaware of the
Line giants in seven-league boots who can crush him underfoot or the battling comets in the
5 heavens that go through the air devouring the sleeping worlds. … It is the hour of reckoning and of marching in unison, and we must move in lines as compact as the veins of silver that lie at the roots of the Andes. …

Our youth go out into the world wearing Yankee- or French-colored glasses and aspire to rule by guesswork a country they do not know. … To know is to solve. To know the country
10 and govern it in accordance with that knowledge is the only way of freeing it from tyranny. The European university must yield to the American university. The history of America from the Incas to the present must be taught in its smallest detail, even if the Greek Archons go untaught. Our own Greece is preferable to the Greece that is not ours; we need it more. Statesmen who arise from the nation must replace statesmen who are alien to it. …
15 What a vision we were: the chest of an athlete, the hands of a dandy, and the forehead of a child. We were a whole fancy dress ball, in English trousers, a Parisian waistcoat, a North American overcoat, and a Spanish bullfighter's hat. The Indian circled about us, mute, and went to the mountaintop to christen his children. The black, pursued from afar, alone and unknown, sang his heart's music in the night, between waves and wild beasts.
20 The campesinos, the men of the land, the creators, rose up in blind indignation against the disdainful city, their own creation. We wore epaulets and judge's robes, in countries that came into the world wearing rope sandals and Indian headbands. The wise thing would have been to pair, with charitable hearts and the audacity of our founders, the Indian headband and the judicial robe, to undam the Indian, make a place for the able black, and tailor liberty to
25 the bodies of those who rose up and triumphed in its name. … No Yankee or European book could furnish the key to the Hispanoamerican enigma. So the people tried hatred instead, and our countries amounted to less and less each year. Weary of useless hatred … we are beginning, almost unknowingly, to try love. The nations arise and salute one another. "What are we like?" they ask, and begin telling each other what they are like. … The young men
30 of America are rolling up their sleeves and plunging their hands into the dough, and making

it rise with the leavening of their sweat. They understand that there is too much imitation, and that salvation lies in creating. Create is this generation's password. Make wine from plantains; it may be sour, but it is our wine! …

   Anyone who promotes and disseminates opposition or hatred among races is committing
35 a sin against humanity. … To think is to serve. We must not, out of a villager's antipathy, impute some lethal congenital wickedness to the continent's light-skinned nation simply because it does not speak our language or share our view of what home life should be or resemble us in its political failings, which are different from ours, or because it does not think highly of quick-tempered, swarthy men or look with charity, from its still uncertain
40 eminence, upon those less favored by history who, in heroic stages, are climbing the road that republics travel. But neither should we seek to conceal the obvious facts of the problem, which can, for the peace of the centuries, be resolved by timely study and the urgent, wordless union of the continental soul. For the unanimous hymn is already ringing forth, and the present generation is bearing industrious America along the road sanctioned by our
45 sublime forefathers. From the Rio Bravo to the Straits of Magellan, the Great Cemi,* seated on a condor's back, has scattered the seeds of the new America across the romantic nations of the continent and the suffering islands of the sea!

*Cemi is a deity or ancestral spirit of the Taíno people—one of the indigenous groups of the Caribbean.

1. What is the most likely reason Martí wrote this article?
   (A) To appeal to fellow Latin Americans to be more like the Europeans
   (B) To gain support from fellow Latin Americans to join in a fight against European invaders
   (C) To rally support for himself as a leader of a revolution to free his country from tyranny
   (D) To encourage fellow Latin Americans to educate themselves about their own mixed heritage

Review the introduction and note that Martí was a teacher, writer, and organizer and that he spent a good part of his life fighting for Cuban independence. You can infer from that information that he would try to persuade people to educate themselves. Martí talks about how little his fellow countrymen know of their own heritage and says that they cannot expect to govern themselves unless they understand their own heritage (lines 8–9). Choice (D) pinpoints one rationale Martí gives for education. Overall, the excerpt does not address revolution, nor does Martí present himself as revolutionary. He appeals to pride in one's heritage. These ideas are connected, because Martí believes that his fellow Latin Americans can free themselves through education (lines 9–10: "To know the country and govern it in accordance with that knowledge is the only way of freeing it from tyranny."). **The correct answer is (D).**

2. What does Martí mean by the "vision" referred to in line 15? ("What a vision we were")?
   (A) How others perceive the peoples of Latin America
   (B) A picture of a unified culture
   (C) Martí's ideals about freedom
   (D) The opportunity to create a new beginning

When a question refers to a specific part of the text, quickly reread the line(s) and the surrounding text. In paragraph 3, Martí offers a detailed, mocking description of the disparate parts blended to compose the peoples of Latin America. The picture he paints is of a person comprising various elements of other cultures—none his or her own. This, he says, is how Europeans saw the people of Latin America. The vision is the image others have of them and how it is misunderstood and even hated by others. So, **the correct answer is (A).**

3. Which statement represents Martí's attitude toward education?

   (A) Universal education is of the utmost importance.

   (B) Everyone should learn about Latin American history.

   (C) Education is necessary for new leadership.

   (D) Education should include the study of Greek democracy as a model for freedom.

This question is asking for an overview, so you need to think about the points Martí makes and his overall message. You can eliminate choices (A) and (B) because they are general statements that anyone could make—they are not ideas that are represented in the passage (though they are related). Choice (D) is an incorrect interpretation of the text. Choice (C) is the best answer because Martí says that education is important for new leaders, and these leaders must be well-versed in the history of Latin America. People who are educated about their own country and heritage will rise as leaders and take over for "statesmen who are alien to it" (line 14). **The correct answers is (C).**

4. Which of the following best describes of the overall tone of the article?

   (A) Passionate and resolute

   (B) Angry and bitter

   (C) Scolding and arrogant

   (D) Inflammatory and rebellious

This type of question also requires you to think about the point of view and presentation, which determine the tone. Martí tries to persuade his readers, advising them to wake up to threats from those who don't understand them or hate them (lines 25–27: "No Yankee or European book could furnish the key to the Hispanoamerican enigma. So the people tried hatred instead, and our countries amounted to less and less each year."). His passion comes through in the use of flowery and emotional language: "the hour of reckoning and of marching in unison" (lines 5–6); similes: "move in lines as compact as the veins of silver" (line 6); and metaphors: "sang his heart's music in the night, between waves and wild beasts" (line 19). He expresses a resolve, not anger or bitterness: "Make wine from plantains; it may be sour, but it is our wine!" (lines 32–33). Although Martí admonishes his fellow countrymen for being naïve and for ignoring dangers (lines 3–4: they are "unaware of the giants in seven-league boots who can crush him underfoot"), he does not take the position of preacher. Rather, he speaks as one of the people (lines 5–7: "It is the hour of reckoning and of marching in unison, and we must move in lines as compact as the veins of silver that lie at the roots of the Andes.") Martí does not use inflammatory language; nor does he call for rebellion, choice (D). Rather, he tries to persuade his fellow Latin Americans to unite in spite of their differences and to defend their lands from foreigners who do not understand them. **The correct answer is (A).**

Sample Reading Passage 2

QUESTIONS 1–4 ARE BASED ON THE FOLLOWING TWO PASSAGES.

The following passages discuss theories of how culture and language spread across Europe and Central Asia to form modern European and Asian peoples. Two teams of scientists—one based at the University of Copenhagen and one at the University of Adelaide—presented studies about the DNA of ancient Europeans, based on 170 skeletons found in countries from Spain to Russia.

Passage 1: When Modern Eurasia Was Born

With this new investigation, the researchers confirm that the changes came about as a result of migrations. The researchers think that this is interesting also because later developments in the Bronze Age are a continuation of this new social perception. Things
Line add up because the migrations can also explain the origin of the northern European language
5 families. Both language and genetics have been with us all the way up to the present. Kristian Kristiansen [professor of archaeology at the University of Gothenburg, Sweden] even thinks that it was crucial events that happened during these few centuries, as crucial as the colonization of the Americas.

One of the main findings from the study is how these migrations resulted in huge changes
10 to the European gene-pool, in particular conferring a large degree of admixture on the present populations. Genetically speaking, ancient Europeans from the time post these migrations are much more similar to modern Europeans than those prior the Bronze Age.

Mobile warrior people

The re-writing of the genetic map began in the early Bronze Age, about 5,000 years ago. From the steppes in the Caucasus, the Yamnaya Culture migrated principally westward
15 into North and Central Europe, and to a lesser degree, into western Siberia. Yamnaya was characterized by a new system of family and property. In northern Europe the Yamnaya mixed with the Stone Age people who inhabited this region and along the way established the Corded Ware Culture, which genetically speaking resembles present-day Europeans living north of the Alps today.
20 Later, about 4,000 years ago, the Sintashta Culture evolved in the Caucasus. This culture's sophisticated new weapons and chariots were rapidly expanding across Europe. The area east of the Urals and far into Central Asia was colonized around 3,800 years ago by the Andronovo Culture. The researchers' investigation shows that this culture had a European DNA background.
25 During the last part of the Bronze Age, and at the beginning of the Iron Age, East Asian peoples arrived in Central Asia. Here it is not genetic admixture we see, but rather a replacement of genes. The European genes in the area disappear.

A new scale

These new results derive from DNA analyses of skeletons excavated across large areas of Europe and Central Asia, thus enabling these crucial glimpses into the dynamics of
30 the Bronze Age. In addition to the population movement insights, the data also held other surprises. For example, contrary to the research team's expectations, the data revealed that lactose tolerance rose to high frequency in Europeans, in comparison to prior belief that it evolved earlier in time (5,000–7,000 years ago).

Excerpted from "When modern Eurasia was born," originally published by the University of Copenhagen on June 10, 2015 by the Centre for GeoGenetics and the Natural History Museum of Denmark. (This passage was edited for length. For the complete article, please visit http://news. ku.dk/all_news/2015/06/when-modern-eurasia-was-born/.)

Passage 2: European Invasion: DNA Reveals the Origins of Modern Europeans

What we have found is that, in addition to the original European hunter-gatherers and
35 a heavy dose of Near Eastern farmers, we can now add a third major population: steppe
pastoralists. These nomads appear to have "invaded" central Europe in a previously unknown
wave during the early Bronze Age (about 4,500 years ago).

This event saw the introduction of two very significant new technologies to western
Europe: domestic horses and the wheel. It also reveals the mysterious source for the Indo-
40 European languages.

The genetic results have answered a number of contentious and long-standing questions
in European history. The first big issue was whether the first farmers in Europe were hunter-
gatherers who had learnt farming techniques from neighbours in southeast Europe, or did
they instead come from the Near East, where farming was invented.

45 The genetic results are clear: farming was introduced widely across Europe in one or two
rapid waves around 8,000 years ago by populations from the Near East—effectively the very
first skilled migrants.

At first the original hunter-gatherer populations appear to have retreated to the fringes
of Europe: to Britain, Scandinavia and Finland. But the genetics show that within a few
50 thousand years they had returned, and significant amounts of hunter-gatherer genomic DNA
was mixed in with the farmers 7,000 to 5,000 years ago across many parts of Europe.

Wheeling across Europe

But there was still a major outstanding mystery. Apart from these two groups, the genomic
signals clearly showed that a third—previously unsuspected—large contribution had been
made sometime before the Iron Age, around 2,000 years ago. But by whom?

55 We have finally been able to identify the mystery culprit, using a clever new system
invented by our colleagues at Harvard University.

Instead of sequencing the entire genome from a very small number of well-preserved
skeletons, we analysed 400,000 small genetic markers right across the genome. This made it
possible to rapidly survey large numbers of skeletons from all across Europe and Eurasia.

60 This process revealed the solution to the mystery. Our survey showed that skeletons of the
Yamnaya culture from the Russian/Ukrainian grasslands north of the Black Sea, buried in
large mounds known as kurgans, turned out to be the genetic source we were missing.

*Excerpted from "European invasion: DNA reveals the origins of modern Europeans" by Alan Cooper,
a director at the Australian Centre for Ancient DNA at the University of Adelaide, and Wolfgang
Haak, a senior research fellow at the University of Adelaide. This article was originally published
in The Conversation on March 22, 2015. (This passage was edited for length. For the complete
article, see http://theconversation.com/.)*

1. How do the passages illustrate the contributions of DNA evidence to scientific inquiry?

   (A) Both provide examples of how DNA evidence enabled scientists to fill in gaps in their
   knowledge about human migrations.

   (B) Both describe how DNA analysis is used in scientific investigations.

   (C) The passages imply that DNA evidence can solve evolutionary questions.

   (D) The passages show how scientists solved the mysteries of DNA evidence.

Both passages illustrate how DNA has been used to answer questions about human migration
patterns—questions that had been unresolved before the ability to use DNA as evidence for such
studies, choice (A). Neither passage gives details about the actual scientific methodology as both
are focused on the results. Choices (C) and (D) are not correct interpretations of the passages. **The
correct answer is (A).**

2. Which lines from the text support the idea that migration of human populations can by tracked through DNA testing?

   (A) Lines 1–2: ("With this … migrations.")

   (B) Lines 11–12: ("Genetically … the Bronze Age.")

   (C) Lines 36–37: ("These nomads … 4,500 years ago.")

   (D) Lines 38–40: ("This event … Ind-European languages.")

This type of question requires that you find specific text to support an answer to a question. Although the concept given—that DNA testing was used to track population migrations—can be found in both passages, you only need to review the specific lines given in the answer choices to find the correct answer. Review only the options to find the one that that best supports the concept. Choices (C) and (D) are not directly related to DNA evidence. Choice (A) confirms the idea of migration, but the text does not refer to DNA as the process that tracked the migration. Choice (B) refers to the genetic evidence, another term for DNA, which shows a similarity between ancient and modern Europeans. This evidence illustrates that scientists have been tracking the migration patterns. **The correct answer is (B).**

3. What is the best description of the two passages?

   (A) They show conflicting claims about the migrations.

   (B) They describe different scientific methodologies.

   (C) They provide supplementary information.

   (D) They are written from a different perspective.

When reading paired passages, compare the passages as you read. This question asks you to compare the information. On your first reading, you probably noticed that they do not contradict one another, choice (A); nor do they show different points of view, choice (D). Both passages describe scientific studies and what scientists were able to learn from them, and both describe using DNA as the methodology, so you can eliminate choice (B). But the second passage adds to the information in the first, making them supplements, choice (C), to one another. **The correct answer is (C).**

4. Based on information in the two passages, which of the following statements could be made about scientific inquiry?

   (A) DNA evidence showed why many Europeans are lactose intolerant.

   (B) Research can provide historical information.

   (C) Evidence showed that the steppe pastoralists introduced horses and the wheel to Western Europe.

   (D) Scientific investigation can provide evidence about human history not obtainable through other means.

Like the preceding question, this one asks you to compare the two passages, except this question looks at a topic not directly discussed in the passages but one that is implicit within it—the nature of scientific inquiry. So while choices (A) and (C) are true, neither one answers the question. Choice (B) is also true, but it doesn't address the nature of scientific investigations; it is simply a general statement that could apply to many texts. Choice (D), however, states a fact about scientific inquiry that can be gleaned from the text: Both passages describe how scientists were able to use DNA data to answer questions they were unable to address before the use of DNA testing was available. **The correct answer is (D).**

TIPS FOR TAKING THE READING TEST

You will be allotted 65 minutes to answer the 52 questions in the Reading section. That's a lot of questions in a short period of time. However, you can use some specific strategies and techniques to move through this portion of the SAT® efficiently. Check out these strategies for answering the evidence-based reading questions quickly and accurately.

Answer All of the Questions Before You Start the Next Passage

There won't be time to go back to reread the passages and recheck your answers, so answer every question that you can about the passage. If you don't know an answer, skip the question and return to it when you have answered the other questions in the passage. Check your time, and if you think you can answer one of the skipped questions with a quick reread of part of the passage, go ahead. If not, or if you find it is taking too long, just give it your best guess and then move on. Remember, wrong answers are not held against you, so don't leave anything blank. Make sure you have answered every question for each passage before you move on to the next one.

Remember That the Questions Get More Specific

The question order often holds a key to understanding a passage. The SAT® Reading Test organizes the questions from broader questions about themes, purpose, point of view, and main ideas to more specific questions about explicit and implicit meaning, specific language, and structure of the text. Review the questions and take note of the information they ask for before reading the passage. As you read, underline or make notes to highlight text that may answer a question. Remember, answers will be in the text—either stated or implied.

Paired Passages

For the paired passage, look for the characteristics in each passage that tie them together. Skim the questions so you know what to look for and underline parts of the text that you may want to refer to. Try to form an overview of the two passages. Ask yourself why they are paired: what do they have in common; how are they different. In answering the questions for this type of passage, follow the same strategy: first answer all the questions you are fairly sure about. Then fill in the others based on best guesses, and, if time allows, review the evidence in the text to support your guess and answer the question accordingly. Make sure you have answered all the questions, and then go to the next passage.

Don't Panic When You Read an Unfamiliar Passage

The passages can be unfamiliar. In their attempt to be fair, the test-makers purposely choose a variety of passages. This helps make sure that each test-taker can demonstrate his or her reading and analysis skills. Remember, you're not being tested on your knowledge of the topic but on how well you do the following:

- Understand the author's assumptions, point of view, and theme
- Determine how the author supports the main ideas in the text
- Determine how the author uses specific language to create mood or tone
- Analyze the logical structure of the text
- Analyze overall meaning as well as specific words and phrases in context of the passage

The paired passages have the same types of questions as the single passages. Some of the questions, however, may ask you to synthesize the information presented in the two passages by noting commonalities or comparing them in some way.

Remember That Everything You Need to Know Is Right There in Front of You

The introductory paragraph and the passage have all the information you'll need to answer the questions. Even if the passage is about the price of beans in Bulgaria or the genetic makeup of a wombat, don't worry. It's all right there on the page.

Start with the Passages That Interest You

A point is a point. It doesn't matter if the point comes from answering correctly a question about a piece of fiction or a scientific experiment. If the style and subject matter appeal to you, you will probably go through a passage more quickly and answer the questions more easily. So before you start, quickly check the topics by skimming the titles and introductions. Start with the topics that are most familiar or most interesting. Then work your way down to the ones that you think will be hardest. Make a notation so you know which passages you have completed, and double check that your answers on the answer sheet correspond to the correct question numbers.

Highlight Important Information as You Read the Passages

It pays to be an active reader, and making quick notes is a part of this process. Let the questions guide your notations. Based on the questions, actively use your pencil to look for and bracket the text evidence that addresses questions about the big ideas, themes, and purpose as you read. Use other markings to indicate places in the text that may provide evidence for other questions, for example a specific word or phrase referred to in a question. The questions will be related to the most important information in the passage. If you've highlighted those pieces of information, you'll be able to find them more easily to help answer the questions.

Don't Get Bogged Down in the Details

Remember, you don't have to understand every bit of information. You just have to find the information you need to answer the questions. Don't waste your time trying to analyze technical details or information not related to a question.

Don't Confuse a "True" Answer with a "Correct" Answer

The fact that an answer choice is true doesn't mean it's right. What does that mean? It means that a certain answer choice may be perfectly true—in fact, all of the answer choices may be true. But the *right* answer must be the correct answer to the question that's being asked. Only one of the answer choices will be correct and, therefore, the right choice. Read carefully—and don't be fooled!

STRATEGIES FOR ANSWERING SPECIFIC QUESTION TYPES

As you learned earlier, each reading question asks you to do one of the following:

- Determine central themes and ideas as presented in the passage.
- Determine the author's purpose or point of view of the text.
- Cite textual evidence to support inferences, conclusions, or arguments.
- Cite evidence to illustrate or support interpretation of meaning, mood, or tone of the passage.

- Analyze words and phrases in the context of the passage.
- Analyze quantitative information in an accompanying graphic, such as a table, graph, or chart.

The following tips present strategies for dealing with specific types of SAT® reading questions. You should use these strategies in combination with the basic steps for approaching the reading test. These strategies don't take the place of the basic steps but are extra tools to help you with certain types of questions. These tools work with both single and paired passages on any topic.

1 A broad question about the passage requires you to think about the passage as a whole. Keep this kind of question in mind as you read the passage, noting any references to an overview in the introduction and/or conclusion of the passage.

2 Before you begin, note the subject of the passage and the voice/perspective. These items can often be found in the introduction to the passage. Ask yourself if the author is providing information about a specific topic, making an argument for or against something, or telling a story. Whether fiction or nonfiction, ask yourself who is telling the story and why.

3 Look for evidence of inferences in the text and evaluate how they support the author's ideas.

4 As you read, notice the overall tone and mood of the passage and find textual evidence—specific words or phrases—that contribute to these elements.

5 If there's a question related to a specific word choice, read the surrounding text to verify the context in which the word is used.

6 Examine the graphic illustration specifically in response to the question associated with it. If it asks to apply the illustration to the text, read that portion of the text in conjunction with the graphic illustration.

To help you see how these tips work, read the following introductory paragraph and the passage. Then read each tip and try to use it to help you answer each question before you read the answer explanation.

EXERCISE: EVIDENCE-BASED READING

30 Minutes • 23 Questions

Directions: Each passage or pair of passages below is followed by a number of questions. After reading each passage or pair, choose the best answer to each question based on what is stated or implied in the passage or passages and in any accompanying graphics (such as a table or graph).

QUESTIONS 1–6 ARE BASED ON THE FOLLOWING PASSAGE.

The passage below discusses how Alaska Native cultural practices and heritage are being preserved in the twenty-first century. (For the full article, please visit http://nps.gov.)

Alaska Native cultural practices continue to be a central force in virtually all villages throughout Alaska. In order to maintain cultural knowledge and ensure its survival, Alaska Native people need to learn the best methods of recording and archiving music, dance,

Line and oral history. Along with the expansion of Europeans and Americans into Alaska were
5 accompanying hardships for the indigenous people: epidemic diseases, strong Christian missionary activities, and western educational policies such as English language-only rules. These resulted in decimated populations throughout the entire territory of Alaska, a decline in indigenous languages, and, in many cases, the abolishment of traditional religion and associated music and dance repertoires.

10 Native people are deeply spiritual people; historically, they had a rich ceremonial life that was profoundly expressed through music and dance—core means by which people communicate their identities and beliefs. With the introduction of Christianity, traditional cultures, including aspects such as music and dance, were not viewed favorably by the missionaries. Sadly, most of the missionaries did not tolerate masked dancing and other
15 forms of religious expressions. Dance, language, and ceremonial practices either had to be practiced in secret, or were lost.

In the 1960s, during the Native Solidarity Movement, as Alaska Native people became more politically active their re-identification with their cultures, languages, music, and dance became a banner of their newfound political and social strength. One of the major outcomes
20 of that movement has been a renaissance in traditional music and dance practices, resulting in multiple dance festivals and younger people becoming actively involved in their village dance groups. …

The Fifth Annual Kingikmiut Dance Festival featured a large Russian dance group, as well as the Tikigaq Traditional Dancers of Point Hope and dance groups from Brevig Mission and
25 other villages on the Seward Peninsula. Kingikmiut, or Wales, was once known as the dance capital of the Seward Peninsula. Captain Henry Trollope visited Wales in 1853–54 and wrote "… the place is sort of a capital in these parts and has four dancing houses, which is a very expressive manner of estimating the extent and population for a place." (Ray 1975) Because of its strategic location, Kingikmiut flourished. Before the 1900 and 1917 epidemics, it
30 consisted of two related villages and consolidated into one village once the populations had been decimated by disease. After these terrible epidemics, western educators' English-only policies forced music, dance, and other expressions of traditional Native culture to go underground.

Repression of Native culture by western educators and missionaries was common all over
35 Alaska and is a major reason why many Alaska Native languages are threatened today. In the first part of the twentieth century, traditional dance and music became associated with the old ways and were looked down upon. After the 1960s, a strong revitalization movement arose. Today there is a renaissance in traditional music and dance practices. In Wales and other Seward Peninsula communities, the younger people, who make up a large percentage of the
40 population, have a great thirst for learning to sing and dance their traditional songs.

1. Which of the following best reflects the main idea of the passage?

   (A) There has been a recent surge in interest in Native cultures everywhere.

   (B) Native Alaskans have always tried to preserve their history and culture.

   (C) Western expansion into Alaska resulted in loss of native cultures.

   (D) Native Alaskan traditions were revived in the 1960s.

2. What can you infer about how the U.S. civil rights movement of the 1960s might have influenced the Native Solidarity Movement?

   (A) It was a catalyst for the Native Solidarity Movement, which provided an avenue for political activity and renewed cultural identity.

   (B) It led to new laws that give the Native Alaskan people the right to practice their religion and express their native culture.

   (C) It allowed the Native Alaskan people to rebel against the forced repression of their culture.

   (D) It revived Native Alaskan cultural practices that had been lost.

3. What was the relationship between the missionaries in Alaska and the Native Alaskans?

   (A) The Native Alaskans and missionaries lived in harmony because they had the same religious beliefs.

   (B) The missionaries embraced the Native Alaskans and rescued them from epidemics of disease.

   (C) The Native Alaskans resented the missionaries and tried to make them leave.

   (D) The missionaries repressed native culture and the Native Alaskans rebelled by holding on to their culture.

4. What evidence does the passage provide to suggest that Alaskan culture was influenced by Russia?

   (A) Lines 4–5: ("Along with … indigenous people")

   (B) Line 23: ("The Fifth Annual … dance group")

   (C) Lines 25–26: ("Kingikmiut, or Wales, … Seward Peninsula.")

   (D) Lines 28–29 ("Because of … Kingikmiut flourished.")

5. What conclusion could you infer from the passage?

   (A) Native Alaskan cultures are still thriving.

   (B) Cultural ties are very strong and can't be easily extinguished.

   (C) Many minor native languages are being lost.

   (D) Music and dance is a common way to express one's culture.

6. As used in lines 32–33, "go underground" most nearly means

   (A) hide in a hut

   (B) be practiced in an ice hut

   (C) practice in secret

   (D) be wiped out

QUESTIONS 7–11 ARE BASED ON THE FOLLOWING PASSAGE.

The following is an excerpt from "The Purloined Letter," a short story by Edgar Allan Poe. Poe is best known for writing poems and stories in the horror and mystery genre. However, he is also considered the inventor of detective fiction. The Mystery Writers of America call their awards for excellence in the genre "Edgars," in honor of Poe.

The Purloined Letter

… "Well, then; I have received personal information, from a very high quarter, that a certain document of the last importance, has been purloined from the royal apartments. The individual who purloined it is known; this beyond a doubt; he was seen to take it. It is known,

Line also, that it still remains in his possession."

5   "How is this known?" asked Dupin.

"It is clearly inferred," replied the Prefect, "from the nature of the document, and from the non-appearance of certain results which would at once arise from its passing out of the robber's possession; that is to say, from his employing it as he must design in the end to employ it."

10   "Be a little more explicit," I said.

"Well, I may venture so far as to say that the paper gives its holder a certain power in a certain quarter where such power is immensely valuable." The Prefect was fond of the cant of diplomacy.

"Still I do not quite understand," said Dupin.

15   "No? Well; the disclosure of the document to a third person, who shall be nameless, would bring in question the honor of a personage of most exalted station; and this fact gives the holder of the document an ascendancy over the illustrious personage whose honor and peace are so jeopardized."

"But this ascendancy," I interposed, "would depend upon the robber's knowledge of the

20 loser's knowledge of the robber. Who would dare—"

"The thief," said G., "is the Minister D—, who dares all things, those unbecoming as well as those becoming a man. The method of the theft was not less ingenious than bold. The document in question—a letter, to be frank—had been received by the personage robbed while alone in the royal boudoir. During its perusal she was suddenly interrupted by the

25 entrance of the other exalted personage from whom especially it was her wish to conceal it. After a hurried and vain endeavor to thrust it in a drawer, she was forced to place it, open as it was, upon a table. The address, however, was uppermost, and, the contents thus unexposed, the letter escaped notice. At this juncture enters the Minister D—. His lynx eye immediately perceives the paper, recognises the handwriting of the address, observes the confusion of

30 the personage addressed, and fathoms her secret. After some business transactions, hurried through in his ordinary manner, he produces a letter somewhat similar to the one in question, opens it, pretends to read it, and then places it in close juxtaposition to the other. Again he converses, for some fifteen minutes, upon the public affairs. At length, in taking leave, he takes also from the table the letter to which he had no claim. Its rightful owner saw, but, of

35 course, dared not call attention to the act, in the presence of the third personage who stood at her elbow. The minister decamped; leaving his own letter—one of no importance—upon the table." …

"You looked among D—'s papers, of course, and into the books of the library?"

"Certainly; we opened every package and parcel; we not only opened every book, but we

40 turned over every leaf in each volume, not contenting ourselves with a mere shake, according to the fashion of some of our police officers. We also measured the thickness of every book-cover, with the most accurate ad measurement, and applied to each the most jealous scrutiny of the microscope. Had any of the bindings been recently meddled with, it would have been utterly impossible that the fact should have escaped observation. Some five or six volumes,

45 just from the hands of the binder, we carefully probed, longitudinally, with the needles."

"You explored the floors beneath the carpets?"

"Beyond doubt. We removed every carpet, and examined the boards with the microscope."

"And the paper on the walls?"

"Yes."

50   "You looked into the cellars?"

"We did."

"Then," I said, "you have been making a miscalculation, and the letter is not upon the premises, as you suppose."

"I fear you are right there," said the Prefect. "And now, Dupin, what would you advise me
55 to do?"

"To make a thorough re-search of the premises."

"That is absolutely needless," replied G—. "I am not more sure that I breathe than I am that the letter is not at the Hotel."

7. Which of the following best describes the mystery to be solved in "The Purloined Letter"?

   (A) What information is in the letter?

   (B) What will happen if the letter is exposed?

   (C) Where is the letter?

   (D) Who has the letter?

8. Who is being blackmailed, and by whom?

   (A) The royal lady is being blackmailed by the Minister D.

   (B) The Minister D is being blackmailed by the Prefect G.

   (C) The Prefect G is being blackmailed by Dupin.

   (D) The royal lady is being blackmailed by the Prefect G.

9. What is the most likely reason that Dupin asks the Prefect (G) to describe the search in such detail?

   (A) To make sure the police haven't missed anything

   (B) To look for other clues

   (C) To hear a good story

   (D) To verify his own ideas

10. As used in line 12, "cant" most nearly means

   (A) inclination

   (B) jargon

   (C) music

   (D) inability

11. Which of the following is a line that could be in the letter?

   (A) It would be such an honor to have you in attendance at this surprise gala.

   (B) You know how much I would like to be in your employ again.

   (C) I'm so sorry that this is late notice, but can I meet with you and the prince next week?

   (D) I beg of you to meet me on Monday when the prince is in Monaco.

QUESTIONS 12–17 ARE BASED ON THE FOLLOWING PASSAGE AND SUPPLEMENTARY MATERIAL.

This passage is the introduction to a report from the Office of the Chief Technologist at the U.S. space agency NASA, entitled Emerging Space: The Evolving Landscape of the 21st Century American Spaceflight (http://www.nasa.gov/sites/default/files/files/Emerging_Space_Report.pdf).

America stands today at the opening of a second Space Age. Innovative NASA programs and American entrepreneurs together are transforming the space industry. These initiatives—both at NASA and in the private sector—are expanding the nation's opportunities for

Line exploration and for the economic development of the solar system.

5   Today's space economy extends some 36,000 kilometers (22,369 miles) from the surface of the Earth and includes an array of evidence-based technologies—satellite communications, global positioning satellites, and imaging satellites—on which our economy depends. These technologies are now an integral part of our economy, and they would not exist if not for the over 50 years of research, development, and investment in the enabling technologies by

10   NASA and other government agencies that seeded these efforts and allowed them to bloom. As we expand our activities in the solar system over the next decades, NASA programs and investments will provide the seed and soil that encourage economic development increasingly farther from Earth. The first signs of this are already visible.

The next era of space exploration will see governments pushing technological

15   development and the American private sector using these technologies as they expand their economic activities to new worlds. NASA's next objectives for exploration—visits to asteroids and Mars— are more complex than any previous space mission attempted. They will happen in the context of relatively smaller NASA budgets and an expanding commercial space economy. Teaming with private-sector partners to develop keystone markets like low

20   Earth orbit (LEO) transportation and technological capabilities like asteroid mining will help NASA achieve its mission goals, help the space economy evolve to embrace new ambitions, and provide large economic returns to the taxpayer through the stimulation and growth of new businesses and 21st-century American jobs.

Motivated by an intrinsic desire to explore space, successful American entrepreneurs

25   have pledged and spent hundreds of millions of dollars to develop technologies aimed at fundamentally improving space access. Since 2003, commercial human spaceflight has received $2.5 billion in private investment.[1] At the same time, a new generation of space enthusiasts are engaging directly though small-scale projects. Through cubesats, suborbital and orbital adventures, and citizen science opportunities, the United States is transitioning

30   from a spacefaring nation to a nation of spacefarers.

In addition to executing its scientific and human spaceflight programs, NASA also has a legislated responsibility to "encourage, to the maximum extent possible, the fullest commercial use of space." As part of fulfilling this responsibility, this report examines how NASA has collaborated with American private-sector individuals and companies investing in

35   space exploration, collectively known as "emerging space." Today, more than fifty years after the creation of NASA, our goal is no longer just to reach a destination. Our goal is to develop the capabilities that will allow the American people to explore and expand our economic sphere into the solar system. Although when NASA was founded only a government program could undertake a voyage from the Earth to the Moon, this may not be true in the future. By

40   taking full advantage of the combined talents of government and the American private sector, our next journeys beyond Earth will come sooner and we will catalyze new industries and economic growth in the process.

[1]2013 Commercial Spaceflight Industry Indicators, Commercial Spaceflight Federation.

Project	Citizen Scientist Role	Number of Participants
Be a Martian	Tag rover images and map craters from satellite pictures	1,230,000
IIiTranslate	Help translate NASA's HiRISE project captions into different languages	1,021 new in 2012
International Space Apps Challenge	Develop mobile applications, software, hardware, data visualization, and platforms to address current challenges relevant to space exploration and social need	2,083 from 17 countries in 2012
Lunar Impacts	Independent observers can monitor the rates and sizes of large meteoroids striking the far side of the Moon	26 impact candidates
Rock Around the World	Help Mars scientists better understand the red planet by sending rocks to NASA for analysis	12,461 rocks received
Stardust at Home	Search for the first samples of solid matter from outside the solar system	30,649 from 2006 to 2012
Target Asteroids!	Observe asteroids, to help scientists refine orbits and determine the composition of near-Earth objects (NEOs) in support of the OSIRIS-Rex mission	104 registered users from 23 countries

NASA provides a number of resources for people willing to contribute as citizen scientists. All are available online, meaning all you need is access to the Internet. Software tools are also provided. More than 1.2 million people from 80 countries have participated in NASA's citizen science projects. This table captures just a few of the projects.

12. How did the government investment in space boost the economy?

   (A) It expanded the knowledge about space beyond our solar system.

   (B) It led to the development of popular commercial products.

   (C) It led to human spaceflight programs, which required specialized products.

   (D) It expanded space exploration farther from the Earth.

13. How will the next era of space exploration be different from the past?

   (A) It will include private and public investment.

   (B) It will require citizen participation.

   (C) It will send people to explore and perhaps live on other planets.

   (D) It will be much more expensive.

14. What is meant by: "the United States is transitioning from a spacefaring nation to a nation of spacefarers." (lines 29–30)?

    (A) The United States will no longer be able to use space for warfare.

    (B) People will be more interested in space exploration.

    (C) The United States will be able to dominate space exploration.

    (D) People will be able to travel in space.

15. Which of the following is the best summary of the passage?

    (A) NASA is ushering in a new chapter in the space age that will allow the commercialization of space.

    (B) In the next decades, ordinary people will be able to travel in space.

    (C) NASA is the U.S. agency that is charged with developing space programs.

    (D) The Second Space Age will expand the economy and increase complex technologies in space exploration.

QUESTIONS 16 AND 17 REFER TO THE TABLE.

16. What is the most likely reason that the "Be a Martian" project has so many more participants than the other projects?

    (A) More people are interested in exploring Mars than in other aspects of the program.

    (B) Other projects require more sophisticated/complex technology skills.

    (C) It is the only project that is designed for young people.

    (D) The other projects all require more time as a volunteer.

17. What skills are needed to participate in the NASA projects as a citizen-scientist?

    (A) The ability to identify different kinds of rocks

    (B) The ability to use a telescope

    (C) The ability to use software technology and the Internet

    (D) The ability to locate and recognize the planets and other celestial bodies

QUESTIONS 18–23 ARE BASED ON THE FOLLOWING TWO PASSAGES.

The following passages are excerpted from narratives written by two explorers. Passage 1 is by Sir Earnest Shackleton from of an account he wrote entitled: South! The Story of Shackleton's Last Expedition *(1914–1917).* Passage 2 is part of an account by Hiram Bingham III, from "The Discovery of Machu Picchu," *first published in* Harper's Monthly *magazine in 1913.*

Passage 1

Some intangible feeling of uneasiness made me leave my tent about 11 p.m. that night and glance around the quiet camp. The stars between the snow-flurries showed that the floe had swung round and was end on to the swell, a position exposing it to sudden strains. I started
Line to walk across the floe in order to warn the watchman to look carefully for cracks, and as I
5 was passing the men's tent the floe lifted on the crest of a swell and cracked right under my feet. The men were in one of the dome-shaped tents, and it began to stretch apart as the ice opened. A muffled sound, suggestive of suffocation, came from beneath the stretching tent. I rushed forward, helped some emerging men from under the canvas, and called out, "Are you all right?"

10   "There are two in the water," somebody answered. The crack had widened to about four feet, and as I threw myself down at the edge, I saw a whitish object floating in the water. It was a sleeping-bag with a man inside. I was able to grasp it, and with a heave lifted man and bag on to the floe. A few seconds later the ice-edges came together again with tremendous force. Fortunately, there had been but one man in the water, or the incident might have been
15 a tragedy. The rescued bag contained Holness, who was wet down to the waist but otherwise unscathed. The crack was now opening again. The *James Caird* and my tent were on one side of the opening and the remaining two boats and the rest of the camp on the other side. With two or three men to help me I struck my tent; then all hands manned the painter and rushed the James Caird across the opening crack. We held to the rope while, one by one, the men left
20 on our side of the floe jumped the channel or scrambled over by means of the boat. Finally I was left alone. The night had swallowed all the others and the rapid movement of the ice forced me to let go the painter. For a moment I felt that my piece of rocking floe was the loneliest place in the world. Peering into the darkness; I could just see the dark figures on the other floe.

Passage 2

25   Nor was I in a great hurry to move. The water was cool, the wooden bench, covered with a woolen poncho, seemed most comfortable, and the view was marvelous. On both sides tremendous precipices fell away to the white rapids of the Urubamba River below. In front was the solitary peak of Huay-na Picchu, seemingly inaccessible on all sides. Behind us were rocky heights and impassable cliffs. Down the face of one precipice the Indians had made a
30 perilous path, which was their only means of egress in the wet season, when the bridge over which we had come would be washed away. Of the other precipice we had already had a taste. We were not surprised to hear the Indians say they only went away from home about once a month.

    Leaving the huts, we climbed still farther up the ridge. Around a slight promontory the
35 character of the stone-faced andenes began to improve, and suddenly we found ourselves in the midst of a jungle-covered maze of small and large walls, the ruins of buildings made of blocks of white granite, most carefully cut and beautifully fitted together without cement. Surprise followed surprise until there came the realization that we were in the midst of as wonderful ruins as any ever found in Peru. It seemed almost incredible that this
40 city, only five days' journey from Cuzco, should have remained so long undescribed and comparatively unknown. Yet so far as I have been able to discover, there is no reference in the Spanish chronicles to Machu Picchu. It is possible that not even the conquistadors ever saw this wonderful place. From some rude scrawls on the stones of a temple we learned that it was visited in 1902 by one Lizarraga, a local muleteer. It must have been known long
45 before that, because, -as we said above, Wiener [an Austrian-French explorer], who was in Ollantaytambo in the 70's, speaks of having heard of ruins at a place named "Matcho Picchu," which he did not find.

18. How do the two passages differ in their tone?

    (A) Passage 1 has a tone of surprise, and Passage 2 has a tone of fear.

    (B) Passage 1 has a threatening tone, and Passage 2 has an adventurous tone.

    (C) Passage 1 exhibits a tone of danger, and Passage 2, a tone of awe.

    (D) Passage 1 features a gloomy tone, and Passage 2, a festive tone.

19. What does the passage reveal about Shackleton's character?

(A) He is fearful for himself and others.

(B) He is a risk-taker who likes adventure.

(C) He is a heroic man who likes attention.

(D) He is a leader who puts others first.

20. Which of the following best describes a purpose common to both passages?

(A) They want to tell the world about the dangers of undeveloped places.

(B) They want to tell the world about new and undiscovered places.

(C) They want to persuade others to visit undeveloped places.

(D) They want to persuade people to help develop the locales described.

21. As used in line 16, "unscathed" most nearly means

(A) fearless

(B) not whole

(C) not harmed

(D) harmless

22. What idea in the text leads to the conclusion that Bingham thought he discovered Machu Pichu?

(A) It would take five days to get there from the closest city of Cuzco.

(B) The Native Indians didn't seem to know about it.

(C) He dismisses the others who may have been there.

(D) It was hidden behind thick jungle growth.

23. Based on the two passages, what can be inferred about the nature of expeditions?

(A) They are often dangerous and can't be undertaken alone.

(B) They usually add to the knowledge about a place.

(C) They are good travel destinations for people who enjoy going to little-known places.

(D) They represent undiscovered parts of the world.

ANSWER KEY AND EXPLANATIONS

1. C	6. C	11. D	16. B	20. B
2. A	7. C	12. B	17. C	21. C
3. D	8. A	13. A	18. C	22. C
4. B	9. D	14. D	19. D	23. B
5. B	10. B	15. D		

1. **The correct answer is (C).** The first paragraph in the passage provides a summary. It explicitly states the reasons that the Native Alaskan culture was almost wiped out and what needs to be done to ensure that it is not lost forever. The rest of the passage supports the concepts introduced here.

2. **The correct answer is (A).** Lines 17–19 explain that the Native Solidarity Movement led to increased political activity. Although the passage doesn't mention the civil rights movement by name, the question identifies its era, and the passage states that the Native Solidarity Movement occurred during the same time period. A logical inference, therefore, could be that the civil rights movement had some impact on the Native American Solidarity Movement. There is no information about laws that might have affected Native Alaskans, choice (B). The passage does not indicate that the Native Alaskans rebelled, choice (C). The passage does indicate that the cultural practices have been revived, but the text does not connect the revival, even indirectly, to the civil rights movement.

3. **The correct answer is (D).** The passage does not directly state the relationship of the Native Alaskan people to the missionaries, but it does describe how the missionaries imposed Christianity on them and tried to force the Native Alaskans to abandon their own belief systems. There is no indication of living in harmony, choice (A), nor of the missionaries rescuing them in the face of epidemic disease, choice (B). Although the passage suggests that Native Alaskans may have had reason to resent the missionaries, there is no indication that they tried to make them leave, choice (C).

4. **The correct answer is (B).** The presence of a Russian dance group among other native groups indicates that the Russian culture had been mixed with that of the Native Alaskan groups. Choice (A) does not explain any influences on culture. There is no information that explains the proximity of the Seward Peninsula to Russia, choice (C). Kingikmuit is located on the Seward Peninsula, as described in the passage, but, as in choice (C), the passage does not explain its geographic relationship to Russia, choice (D).

5. **The correct answer is (B).** The main idea of the text shows that although missionaries tried to impose their beliefs on the Native Alaskans, they were not completely successful. The Native Alaskans maintained their belief systems and passed on their traditions in secret when it was not possible to be open about them. Today, these traditions are no longer repressed and are thriving. Overall, this suggests the conclusion in choice (B). Although choice (A) is true, it is neither a conclusion nor an inference; that idea is stated in the text. Both answer choices (C) and (D) are general concepts that could be applied to the Native Alaskan culture, but nothing in the text suggests such a generality.

6. **The correct answer is (C).** The idiom "go underground" means doing something in secret. In this case, the western educators who had come to Alaska forced their own culture onto the Native Alaskans, who then practiced their traditions in secret rather than give them up.

7. **The correct answer is (C).** The conversation in the excerpt reveals, in general terms, the responses listed in the other choices (A), (B), and (D). The mystery to be solved by either the Prefect or Dupin is in locating the letter, choice (C).

8. **The correct answer is (A).** It is the royal lady who has told the Prefect the story, which he retells to Dupin and the narrator (line 1: "I have received personal information, from a very high quarter."). His retelling also describes the identity of the thief (minister D), and the importance of the document (lines 11–12: "that the paper gives its holder a certain power in a certain quarter where such power is immensely valuable.").

9. **The correct answer is (D).** We can infer from his advice (line 56: "To make a thorough re-search of the premises.") that Dupin has an idea about the whereabouts of the letter, which he wants to confirm through the details of the search. Dupin listens carefully, demonstrating that he is interested in the specifics of the investigation. The details confirm his own ideas.

10. **The correct answer is (B).** The word "cant" is used in a statement made by the unnamed narrator. He is commenting about the language of the Prefect's statement. "Jargon" (the language or idiom of a particular group) is the only choice related to language.

11. **The correct answer is (D).** We know that the royal lady is being blackmailed. Therefore, the contents must reveal something she is hiding from the man in the room with her, most likely her husband. Choice (D) is the only one that contains information that is to be kept from the prince.

12. **The correct answer is (B).** The passage describes the space economy and the many products that were developed because of space exploration and then applied to commercial markets. Lines 7–10 explain that these products are now part of our economy. The space program was responsible for introducing new products to the market and new products that people want and buy increase economic activity.

13. **The correct answer is (A).** The passage discusses the inclusion of private investment (lines 14–16). Commercial companies are already gearing up to provide new space services based on the ability to travel in space and explore places beyond Earth. Formerly, space travel was only done by NASA.

14. **The correct answer is (D).** People have always been interested in space but the passage talks about how the next phase of space exploration will include ordinary citizens who will be able to take advantage of the commercialization of space exploration and travel.

15. **The correct answer is (D).** This statement represents the best summary because it states the main idea by providing the two most important aspects of the commercialization of space exploration.

16. **The correct answer is (B).** The table shows that the "Be a Martian" project involves tagging on the Internet, and the table caption explains that participants are provided with any needed software. According to the descriptions of the other projects, they all require some additional skill, for example translating text or doing more complex searches.

17. **The correct answer is (C).** Reading the descriptions, the skill required in all of the projects is how to use the Internet to conduct searches. Even for projects that involve language translation, a participant would have to access the Internet to get the text that needs to be translated.

18. **The correct answer is (C).** The first line of Passage 1 sets the tone of danger (feeling of uneasiness) that continues after the crack in the ice. Although the men aren't killed, the path to the boat was nevertheless full of danger. Passage 2 begins with Bingham's observations that show his appreciation of the beauty of the place. He marvels at the Indians who make their way down the steep precipice on a regular basis (lines 29–31). As Bingham makes his way through the jungle and sees Machu Picchu for the first time, detailed descriptions show awe and surprise at the "wonderful ruins" (line 39).

19. **The correct answer is (D).** Shackleton describes the scene and how he warned to "look carefully for cracks" (line 4), which shows he was checking the ice to make sure he and his men were safe. When he saw the ice cracking, his first instinct was to throw himself down at the edge (line 11) and save one of the men. He made sure the others were safe, leading them back to the boat; he was the last in line to board.

20. **The correct answer is (B).** Both passages record the experiences of men who are drawn to exploring places that most people don't ever see. Both use detailed descriptions of the physical terrain of remote places that are void of other people. There is no call inviting others to join them—just descriptions that inform.

21. **The correct answer is (C).** The surrounding text describes the condition of the man (who was wet down to the waist), and we know from the rest of the text that the water was bitter cold. The word "otherwise" shows that what follows is an exception, so he is—not harmed—except for being wet (and presumably cold).

22. **The correct answer is (C).** In lines 41–47, Bingham describes the others who may have come before him. He remarks on the beauty of the ancient city and how incredible it is that others missed it. Surely the conquistadors would have told others about it; Weiner never found it; and the muleteer didn't understand what he was looking at.

23. **The correct answer is (B).** Both passages describe places about which little was known at the time. Both men undertook the trip and wrote detailed accounts of their experiences so that others could learn about them and perhaps follow their footsteps to gain even more knowledge.

SUMMING IT UP

- You do not need information beyond what is provided by the passage to answer any question.

- Complete familiar and interesting passages first.

- Read the introduction; it often provides background that will help form an overview of the passage.

- Read the questions and their answer choices.

- Read the passage as quickly as possible, marking the text to note information that may be relevant to the questions. Let the questions drive your focus and the notations you make.

- Don't get bogged down in details. Most questions will not be focused on details unless they are used to support a major idea or theme.

- Go back into the passage to find answers as needed.

- Reading Test questions are ordered from those related to the central ideas and overall themes to those involving structural and language-related concepts. Approach each passage by first looking for the big ideas and then the more structural concepts.

- For any question you're not sure of, eliminate obviously wrong answers and take your best guess. Wrong answers are not counted against you, so answer every question.

- Answer every question for a passage before starting the next passage.

- In addition to your Reading Test score, the following subscores and cross-test scores will be provided:
  - Command of Evidence
  - Words in Context
  - Analysis in History/Social Studies
  - Analysis in Science

PART IV
SAT® WRITING STRATEGIES

Writing and Language Test Strategies

chapter 4

OVERVIEW

- A closer look at the Writing and Language Test
- The three most common multiple-choice editing questions
- Expression of ideas questions: Words in context
- Expression of ideas questions: Adding or deleting text
- Expression of ideas questions: Reordering sentences
- Expression of ideas questions: Combining sentences and using words and phrases correctly
- Graphic organizer questions
- Exercise: Writing and Language questions
- Answer key and explanations
- Summing it up

A CLOSER LOOK AT THE WRITING AND LANGUAGE TEST

The Writing and Language Test gives you opportunities to demonstrate your college and career readiness by revising and editing four passages. Each passage is 400–450 words long. There are 11 multiple-choice questions about each one—a total of 44 questions in all. You have 35 minutes to complete this section; that is about 48 seconds per question. If that doesn't sound like enough time to you, be assured that you will be able to answer many of the questions in *fewer* than 48 seconds. You can save up your extra seconds for the harder questions you'll encounter.

One passage of the four will be career-related; for example, this chapter includes a passage on technical writing careers. Another passage will be humanities-related; it might be about visual art, music, theater arts, or literature. For example, this chapter includes a short critical essay on a nineteenth-century novel by British author Jane Austen. The other two passages will be about history/social studies and science. Some of the passages will be accompanied by graphic organizers such as tables, charts, or graphs.

The passages' writing modes will include argument, informative/explanatory text, and nonfiction narrative. For example, this chapter's sample passage on technical writing is an informative/explanatory text. The essay on Jane Austen that appears later in this chapter includes both argument and nonfiction narrative.

Answering the multiple-choice questions on each passage will place you in an editor's role. You will be revising and editing the work of an unspecified writer. You will be asked to improve each passage's development, organization, and use of language. Your tasks will include making sure that each passage conforms to standard rules of English grammar, usage, and punctuation. When a passage is accompanied by one or more graphic organizers, you may need to correct the passage's inaccurate interpretation of data.

These editing and revising goals may sound overwhelming, but don't worry. Every answer is right there on your test page. All you have to do is to select one out of four possible solutions [(A). (B), (C), or (D)] to choose the best use of language.

THE THREE MOST COMMON MULTIPLE-CHOICE EDITING QUESTIONS

The Writing and Language Test contains three primary categories of multiple-choice questions:

❶ Expression of Ideas Questions

More than half of the questions fall into this category. This group includes questions about the following:

- Words in context
- Adding, deleting, or changing text
- Transitional language that smoothly and clearly takes the reader from one idea to another
- Relevant (or irrelevant) details
- Combining sentences to make text more concise and less "choppy-sounding"
- Eliminating awkward language and wordiness
- Reordering sentences so that paragraphs make better sense
- Consistency of style and tone
- Cohesion and precision of language

You will learn how to approach Expression of Ideas questions later in this chapter.

❷ Standard English Conventions Questions

About 45 percent of the questions fall into this category of grammar, usage, and punctuation rules. It includes questions that require you to demonstrate your knowledge of the following:

- Consistent (or inconsistent) verb tenses
- Punctuation
- Sentence structure
- Correct (or incorrect) word usage

The Exercise section of this chapter provides practice with answering some questions from this category. In Chapter 5, you will learn more about grammar, usage, and punctuation questions.

❸ Graphic Organizer Questions

This is the smallest percentage of the three primary categories. There may be only a few questions that deal with graphic organizers on the Writing and Language Test. This type of question asks you to make revising and editing decisions about passages in light of information and ideas conveyed through graphic organizers such as tables, charts, and graphs. However, you will not need to do any mathematical computation in order to answer the questions in this category. Later in this chapter, you will learn how to approach Graphic Organizer Questions.

EXPRESSION OF IDEAS QUESTIONS: WORDS IN CONTEXT

Words in Context questions are perhaps the easiest type of question on the Writing and Language Test. Most of the questions on the test, including Words in Context, do not have a question right before the answer choices. Instead, you should choose the response that corrects the sentence or paragraph and makes the writing stronger. Review the example below.

Jane Austen and Fanny Price

In real life, one **1** <u>was</u> sometimes left out because of actual purposeful wrongdoing on the parts of those doing the leaving out, but sometimes one is simply left out—and **2** <u>realism</u> is beside the point. **3** <u>The second case is much less satisfying to the left-out person, but it is also much more usual.</u> **4** <u>Novels</u> such as Cinderella are satisfying because, in them, it is clearly the nastiness of the villains and villainesses that causes the heroes and heroines to be excluded from pleasurable activities.

4

(A) NO CHANGE
(B) Fairytales
(C) Stories
(D) Articles

First, quickly read the paragraph to get a general sense of its meaning—you don't need to understand every word. Right now you are answering Question 4 only, so don't worry about any errors you might spot in the rest of the paragraph—you will deal with those later in the "Exercise" portion of this chapter.

Question **4** asks you to decide which word best fits the context. Your four choices are:

(A) NO CHANGE (Novels); (B) Fairytales; (C) Stories; and (D) Articles.

Use the context clue such as *Cinderella* to make the best choice. Right away you can eliminate choice (D): Cinderella is *not* an article—most articles are nonfiction. Choice (C) is a possibility: Cinderella *is* a story—set this choice aside for a moment. Is Cinderella a novel? No—novels are long, and the story of Cinderella is fairly short. Eliminate choice (A). Is Cinderella a fairytale? Yes, it is: it has magical elements, and it is a traditional tale that has been passed down for many generations. Is *Fairytales* a better answer than *Stories*? Yes, it is, because this description is more precise. Fairytales are a specific type of story. **The correct answer is choice (B).**

Let's try a Words in Context question that goes with a different passage.

A Technical Writing Career   **11**

Technical **11** communicators, better known as "technical writers," plan, write, and edit instruction manuals, print and online articles, and other documents that transform **12** intense technical information into simpler language that end users can understand.

(A) NO CHANGE
(B) engineers
(C) manuals
(D) workers

Quickly read the one-sentence paragraph to figure out what it is mainly about. Again, focus on the question you're answering (Question 11).

Here are some clue words and phrases that will help you figure out which word belongs after the numeral **11**: *writers; write, and edit*; and *simpler language that . . . users can understand*. To which answer choice do these clues direct you? You can eliminate choice (C), *manuals*: a manual is a thing (a set of instructions), not a person. Might *engineers* (B) and *workers* (D) be writers who write and edit text?

Maybe, but the word *communicators* is the best choice because it is most precise—a writer's main job is to communicate with others by writing understandable sentences, paragraphs, and so on.

Since the word *communicators* already appears in the paragraph after the **11**, **the correct answer choice is (A) NO CHANGE.**

EXPRESSION OF IDEAS QUESTIONS: ADDING OR DELETING TEXT

Here is a question that asks you whether it is a good or bad idea to delete a certain sentence.

When I was in elementary school, I was a shy little girl . . . . The stories I made up always had the same plot: I was carried off by a prince (David) on a flying horse to his castle where I became his wife and got to live in the lap of luxury. **5** From there I would go into elaborate detail about the décor of the castle, how many horses we owned, what colors they were, and so on. It was a silly, childish fantasy, but it comforted me.

5 The writer is considering deleting the underlined sentence. Should the writer do this? Why or why not?

(A) Yes, because it adds unnecessary technical details.
(B) Yes, because it makes the grown-up writer seem silly and childish.
(C) No, because it adds funny details and helps to show that the narrator was a child at the time.
(D) No, because, without this sentence, the last sentence in the paragraph would not make sense.

This question truly casts you in an editor's role. You're asked whether the paragraph would be better or worse if this sentence were deleted. Not only that, you're asked *why* your choice is the correct one.

You can eliminate choice (B). The underlined sentence doesn't make the grown-up writer seem "silly and childish"—it makes her *subject* (her younger self) seem so. The writer explicitly states this in the last sentence of the paragraph—she is having fun making fun of her younger self.

Also eliminate choice (A): this sentence *does* contain details, but they are not technical. How about choice (D)? Would the paragraph's last sentence fail to make sense if the underlined sentence were deleted? Read the first two sentences and the last one *without* the middle (underlined) one. The last sentence still makes sense, so you can eliminate choice (D).

You are left with choice (C). Even if you disagree that the underlined sentence is funny, it definitely "helps to show that the narrator was a child at the time." **The correct answer is choice (C).**

EXPRESSION OF IDEAS QUESTIONS: REORDERING SENTENCES

Next, let's try a question that asks you to reorder sentences in a paragraph.

[1] A few years ago, U.S. government experts predicted that employment of technical writers would grow 1.5 percent from 2012 to 2022, a gain of about 7,400 jobs per year. [2] (This is faster than the average for all occupations on which the U.S. Department of Labor gathers statistics.) [3] This causes a greater need for professionals with the talent and skills to write instructional manuals that users can easily understand and follow. **16** [4] The high-tech and electronics industries continue to change and grow.

16 For the sake of cohesion, sentence 4 should be placed

(A) where it is now.
(B) before sentence 1.
(C) after sentence 1.
(D) after sentence 2.

In this type of question, each sentence in a paragraph is numbered with a numeral in brackets. Your job is to decide whether a specific sentence should stay where it is; move to a different spot in the paragraph; and if it *should* move, where it should go.

The best way to answer this question would be to read the paragraph out loud to yourself. During the SAT®, you won't be able to do that, but try it now if possible. You will probably notice that sentence 4 sounds odd at the end of the paragraph—it seems "tacked on" somehow. So it needs to be moved, but where?

Try each option one at a time. You will discover that this sentence belongs right after sentence 2 (and before sentence 3). Sentence 3 says that "This causes a greater need . . . [for good technical writers]." *What* causes this need? The cause is the fact that "the high-tech and electronics industries continue to change and grow." If sentences 3 and 4 were to swap places, the paragraph would be "most logical"—it would make better sense than it does now, for sure. **The correct answer is choice (D).**

EXPRESSION OF IDEAS QUESTIONS: COMBINING SENTENCES AND USING TRANSITIONAL WORDS AND PHRASES CORRECTLY

Here is a question that asks you to complete two tasks at once: combine two shorter sentences into one longer one and choose the transitional word or phrase that makes the best sense in the new, longer sentence.

Most novel readers do not like it when story events seem artificially "rigged" by the author in order to teach a moralistic lesson. In this novel, Jane Austen rigs **7** events. Whenever Fanny is left out, we can be sure that one or some of the other characters are engaged in something sinful. This is an unrealistic (fairytale) element in what is otherwise a highly developed, realistic novel.

7 Which choice most effectively combines the two sentences at the underlined portion?

(A) events, but whenever Fanny is left out,

(B) events so that whenever Fanny is left out,

(C) events, because, whenever Fanny is left out,

(D) events, and the cause is that whenever Fanny is left out,

Again, the best way to solve this editing problem is to imagine reading the paragraph out loud. If you try one answer choice at a time, you will soon find the one that makes the best sense. In this case, the correct answer is choice (B). The writer is saying that Jane Austen heavy-handedly rigs events in her novel *so that* such and such happens. The transitional words and phrases in the other answer choices (A: *but;* C: *because;* D: *and the cause is that*) do not make good sense in the new, longer sentence or in the paragraph as a whole. **The correct answer is choice (B).**

GRAPHIC ORGANIZER QUESTIONS

Every Writing and Language Test contains one or more passages with graphic organizer(s) such as tables, charts, and graphs. One or more of the questions following such a passage deal with its organizer(s). This type of question asks you to compare information given in the passage to similar information or data that the graphic organizer presents. If the two sets of information are inconsistent, you will need to make editing changes to the passage.

Here is an example:

A TECHNICAL WRITING CAREER

Quick Facts: Technical Writers	
2012 Median Pay	$65,500 per year $31.49 per hour
Entry-Level Education	Bachelor's degree
Work Experience in a Related Occupation	Less than 5 years
On-the-job Training	Short-term on-the-job training
Number of Jobs, 2012	49,500
Job Outlook, 2012–22	15% (Faster than average)
Employment Change, 2012–22	7,400

[Source: http://www.bls.gov/ooh/Media-and-Communication/Technical-writers.htm]

Technical communicators, better known as "technical writers," plan, write, and edit instruction manuals, print and online articles, and other documents. Requirements for this well-paid profession include **17** a bachelor's degree and five to ten years of on-the-job training in a technical field.

17 Which choice most accurately and effectively represents the information in the chart?

(A) NO CHANGE

(B) a bachelor's degree and less than ten years of on-the-job work experience in a related occupation

(C) a master's degree, less than five years of work experience in a related occupation, and a short period of on-the-job training

(D) a bachelor's degree, less than five years of work experience in a related occupation, and a short period of on-the-job training

To find the correct answer choice, you will need to pay close attention to details in the chart. In this case, carefully read the three rows beginning with "Entry-Level Education" and ending with "On-the-job Training." Choice (A) is incorrect because the chart does not specify "five to ten years of on-the-job training in a technical field." Choice (B) is incorrect because the chart does not specify "less than ten years of on-the-job work experience in a related occupation." Choice (C) is incorrect because the chart lists a bachelor's degree, not a master's, as a prerequisite for an entry-level technical writing job. The only answer choice that perfectly matches the chart is choice (D). **The correct answer is choice (D).**

EXERCISE: WRITING AND LANGUAGE QUESTIONS

Directions: Each of the following passages is accompanied by a set of questions. For some questions, you will consider how the passage might be revised to improve the expression of ideas. For other questions, you will consider how the passage might be edited to correct errors in sentence structure, usage, or punctuation. A passage or a question may be accompanied by one or more graphics (such as a table, chart, graph, or photograph) that you will consider as you make revising and editing decisions.

Some questions will direct you to an underlined portion of a passage. Other questions will direct you to a location in a passage or ask you to think about the passage as a whole.

After reading each passage, choose the answer to each question that most effectively improves the quality of writing in the passage or that makes the passage conform to the conventions of standard written English. Many questions include a "NO CHANGE" option. Choose that option if you think the best choice is to leave the relevant portion of the passage as it is.

QUESTIONS 1–11 ARE BASED ON THE FOLLOWING PASSAGE.

Jane Austen and Fanny Price

…In real life, one **1** <u>was</u> sometimes left out because of actual purposeful wrongdoing on the parts of those doing the leaving out, but sometimes one is simply left out—and **2** <u>realism</u> is beside the point. **3** <u>The second case is much less satisfying to the left-out person, but it is also much more usual.</u> Fairytales such as Cinderella are satisfying because, in them, it is clearly the nastiness of the villains and villainesses that causes the heroes and heroines to be excluded from pleasurable activities.

1

(A) NO CHANGE
(B) is
(C) will be
(D) may have been

2

(A) NO CHANGE
(B) purpose
(C) culpability
(D) satisfaction

3 The writer is considering deleting the underlined sentence. Should the writer do this?

(A) Yes, because it does not provide a good transition between the first and third sentences in the paragraph.

(B) Yes, because it fails to support the main argument of the passage: that *Mansfield Park* presents a fairytale conception of being left out.

(C) No, because it identifies important distinctions among three different "cases."

(D) No, because it provides a good transition between the first and third sentences in the paragraph.

[1] When I was in elementary school, I was a shy little girl not unlike Fanny Price of Jane Austen's **4** *Mansfield Park.* [2] Sometimes when I was feeling left out, I would sit on a bench at the very edge of the playground and put spit on my cheeks to simulate tears, in case David Gould, **5** a boy I knew, should pass by and take pity on me. **6** [3] I also had a fairytale conception of being left out (as Fanny and Jane Austen have in this novel). [4] He never did, but it didn't really **7** matter. My imagination would take over from that point. [5] The stories I made up always had the same plot: I was carried off by a prince (David) on a flying horse to his castle where I became his wife and got to live in the lap of luxury. [6] (From there I would go into elaborate detail about the décor of the castle, how many horses we owned, **8** what colors they were and so on.

4 The writer is considering adding the phrase "magnificent work of art" here. Should the writer do this?

(A) Yes, because it identifies the genre of *Mansfield Park.*

(B) Yes, because it sums up the writer's true opinion of the book.

(C) No, because it is an unnecessary and possibly confusing addition.

(D) No, because it contradicts the writer's previous, more critical statement.

5 Which choice provides the most relevant detail?

(A) NO CHANGE

(B) the shortest boy in my classroom

(C) the handsomest boy in the school

(D) my sister's best friend's boyfriend

6 To make this paragraph most logical, sentence 3 should be placed

(A) where it is now.

(B) after sentence 1.

(C) after sentence 4.

(D) after sentence 6.

7 Which choice most effectively combines the two sentences at the underlined portion?

(A) matter, because my imagination

(B) matter; for example, my imagination

(C) matter; in other words, my imagination

(D) matter—consequently, my imagination

8

(A) NO CHANGE

(B) what colors they are and so on.

(C) what colors they will be, and so on.)

(D) what colors they were, and so on.)

In the course of Mansfield Park, Fanny goes through one big suffer-and-be-vindicated cycle (her **9** <u>ultimate</u> marriage to Edmund after many, many years of being left out) and many little suffer-and-be-comforted cycles:

> "Edmund . . . going quietly to another table . . . brought a glass of Madeira to Fanny [who had a headache as a result of being deprived of proper exercise by the thoughtless disregard of others], and obliged her to drink the greater part. She wished to be able to decline it, but the tears which a variety of feelings created, made it easier to swallow than to speak." [*Mansfield Park*, page 513; from *The Complete Novels of Jane Austen*, Modern Library edition]

The little gush of passionate, passive gratefulness that Fanny feels when Edmund "obliges" her to drink the Madeira feels to me similar to the sweet rush of vindicated personal pathos that I felt at the moment in my David Gould fantasy when he would suddenly appear and sweep me up and away from my wrongfully left-out state into one of well-deserved bliss. This way of thinking is childish, self-pitying, and self-deluded; **10** <u>accordingly,</u> Jane Austen (who is usually far more astute) lets Fanny get away with it.

The author rigs things so that whenever Fanny is left out, we can be sure that one or some of the other characters are engaged in something **11** <u>sinful; this</u> is an unrealistic (fairytale) element in what is otherwise a highly developed, realistic novel.

9
(A) NO CHANGE
(B) ill-advised
(C) initial
(D) volatile

10
(A) NO CHANGE
(B) yet,
(C) predictably,
(D) on the other hand,

11
(A) NO CHANGE
(B) sinful, this
(C) sinful: this
(D) sinful (this

QUESTIONS 12–22 ARE BASED ON THE FOLLOWING PASSAGE AND SUPPLEMENTARY MATERIAL.

A Technical Writing Career

Technical communicators, better known as "technical writers," plan, write, and edit instruction manuals, print and online articles, and other documents that transform **12** intense technical information into simpler language that end users can understand.

A typical technical writer

- **13** determines end users' needs and requirements.

- studies product samples and discusses them with designers and developers.

- outlines, writes, and edits documents that support a variety of technical products.

- gathers and/or creates graphics that illustrate instructions and other technical documents.

- writes scripts for online instructional videos.

- decides which medium **14** (how-to manuals, "frequently asked questions" pages, online videos) will most effectively convey the information.

- gathers feedback on products' usability from customers, designers, and manufacturers.

- revises documents to fit product changes.

- works with customer service specialists to improve the end-user experience through product design changes.

Technical writers must be able to fully comprehend complex information. Their work colleagues may include computer hardware engineers, scientists, computer support specialists, and software developers.

12

(A) NO CHANGE
(B) ordinary
(C) complex
(D) varied

13

(A) NO CHANGE
(B) determines end users' needs.
(C) determines and decides end users' needs.
(D) determines the needs of end users and people who will be using the product.

14 Which choice provides the most relevant list of details?

(A) NO CHANGE
(B) (books, magazines, newspapers, television news shows)
(C) (drawing, painting, sculpture, computer-generated graphics)
(D) (keyboards, monitors, hard drives, software, cloud computing)

Quick Facts: Technical Writers	
2012 Median Pay	$65,500 per year $31.49 per hour
Entry-Level Education	Bachelor's degree
Work Experience in a Related Occupation	Less than 5 years
On-the-job Training	Short-term on-the-job training
Number of Jobs, 2012	49,500
Job Outlook, 2012–22	15% (Faster than average)
Employment Change, 2012–22	7,400

[Source: http://www.bls.gov/ooh/Media-and-Communication/Technical-writers.htm]

15 How else can they be expected to communicate with people from such an array of professional backgrounds?

16 [1] Why is the technical writing field growing so quickly? [2] A few years ago, U.S. government experts predicted that employment of technical writers would grow **17** 1.5 percent from 2012 to 2022, a gain of about 7,400 jobs per year. [3] (This is faster than the average for all occupations on which the U.S. Department of Labor gathers statistics.) [4] As the high-tech and electronics industries continue to change and grow, they

15 Which change most effectively ends this paragraph and is also consistent with information provided in the chart?

(A) NO CHANGE

(B) Prior knowledge about such colleagues' fields enables technical writers to understand and translate "tech speak" into clear, useful instructions for users.

(C) It takes years of graduate study to enable a technical writer to understand various work colleagues' fields—a master's degree or Ph.D. in technical writing is advisable.

(D) DELETE the underlined sentence and do not replace it.

16 For the sake of cohesion, sentence 1 should be placed

(A) where it is now.

(B) after sentence 2.

(C) after sentence 3.

(D) after sentence 4.

17 Which choice most accurately and effectively represents the information in the chart?

(A) NO CHANGE

(B) 7.5 percent from 2012 to 2022, a gain of about 7,500 jobs per year.

(C) 15 percent from 2012 to 2022, a gain of about 7,400 jobs per year.

(D) 15 percent from 2012 to 2022, a gain of about 7,400 jobs total.

18 reflect a greater need for professionals with the talent and skills to write instructional manuals that users can easily understand and follow.

Job opportunities **19** abound. This is especially true for applicants with both technical skills and writing skills. Increasingly, consumers rely on technologically sophisticated products in the home as well as in the workplace. **20** In addition—for many people—ordinary daily life requires us to understand complex medical and scientific information. All of these factors are combining to create many new opportunities for technical writers. **21** Remember now, that as older workers retire, their jobs will become vacant. Yet, competition among freelance technical writers will remain **22** lively.

18

(A) NO CHANGE
(B) generate
(C) effect
(D) obligate

19 Which choice most effectively combines the two sentences at the underlined portion?

(A) abound, especially for applicants with
(B) abound, especially is this the case for applicants with
(C) abound; especially positively impacted are applicants with
(D) abound—and especially for those lucky applicants who have acquired

20

(A) NO CHANGE
(B) And another thing: for many people,
(C) I need to make one last point—for many people—
(D) in contrast, for many people,

21

(A) NO CHANGE
(B) As older technical writers retire,
(C) Baby Boomers are retiring these days, so
(D) Smarter job seekers will recall that, as older workers retire,

22

(A) NO CHANGE
(B) competitive
(C) apparent
(D) stagnant

ANSWER KEY AND EXPLANATIONS

Passage 1

1. B	4. C	6. B	8. D	10. B
2. C	5. C	7. A	9. A	11. A
3. D				

1. **The correct answer is (B).** Except for this verb, *was*, the writer uses the present tense throughout the paragraph. Therefore, to be consistent, the correct choice is choice (B).

2. **The correct answer is (C).** The writer is making a distinction between times when a person is left out because other(s) have misbehaved and times when a person is left out, but no one else is at fault, or culpable. Since a noun is needed in the sentence here, *culpability,* choice (C) is the correct answer.

3. **The correct answer is (D).** The writer should not delete the sentence because it provides a good transition between the first and third sentences in the paragraph.

4. **The correct answer is (C).** The writer should not add this phrase here because it is unnecessary and may confuse readers into thinking *Mansfield Park* is a work of visual art, such as a painting.

5. **The correct answer is (C).** It makes sense that a girl would cast the handsomest boy in the school in the role of a prince who saves her from her unhappy state. Choices (A), (B), and (D) are incorrect because, while they are possible choices, they are not as relevant as choice (C).

6. **The correct answer is (B).** Sentence 3 makes the best sense when it follows sentence 1.

7. **The correct answer is (A).** The linking word *because* makes sense in context: the writer is explaining *why* it did not matter that David Gould never noticed or pitied her when she was a shy little girl.

8. **The correct answer is (D).** Choice (D) correctly includes a needed comma following the word were and includes a missing close parenthesis mark.

9. **The correct answer is (A).** The writer is referring to an event that occurs near the end of the novel ("after many, many years of being left out," Fanny finally marries Edmund). The correct choice is (A), NO CHANGE: *ultimate,* meaning "final."

10. **The correct answer is (B).** The transitional word *yet* makes sense in context: the writer is explaining that, even though Jane Austen is usually astute about her characters, in this case the author "lets Fanny get away with" childishness, self-pity, and self-delusion.

11. **The correct answer is (A).** No change is needed because this phrase is correctly punctuated with a semicolon.

Passage 2

12. C	15. B	17. D	19. A	21. B
13. B	16. C	18. B	20. A	22. A
14. A				

12. **The correct answer is (C).** The writer is referring to technical ideas that are the opposite of "simple." The correct choice is (C): *complex*.

13. **The correct answer is (B).** Only choice (B) offers clear and concise wording without redundancy. Therefore, choice (B) is the right answer. Choice (A) is incorrect because end users' "needs" and "requirements" are redundant. Choice (C) eliminates the original redundancy, but then it creates a new one: "determines" and "decides" mean the same thing. Choice (D) is incorrect because it, too, is redundant: "end users" and "people who will be using the product" mean the same thing.

14. **The correct answer is (A).** No change is needed because the writer is using the word *medium* to refer to a genre or method of effectively conveying technical information.

15. **The correct answer is (B).** This sentence clarifies information presented earlier in the paragraph.

16. **The correct answer is (C).** The correct choice is (C) because sentence **[1]** makes the most sense when it follows sentence **[3]**.

17. **The correct answer is (D).** The correct choice is (D) because the last two lines of the chart say that the projected job outlook for technical writers during the ten years from 2012 to 2022 is 15 percent growth, and that during those ten years, the technical writing field will gain 7,400 jobs total. Choices (A), (B), and (C) are incorrect because the statistics they give do not match those shown in the chart.

18. **The correct answer is (B).** The writer is referring to certain changes in the U.S. economy that will produce, result in, or generate more technical writing jobs. The correct choice is (B): *generate*.

19. **The correct answer is (A).** This is the simplest, clearest way to combine the two sentences. Choices (B), (C), and (D) are incorrect because each is either awkward or too wordy or does not match the rest of the passage's style and tone.

20. **The correct answer is (A).** No change is needed because the existing wording is the simplest, clearest way to make this point. It matches the style and tone of the passage while including necessary transitional language.

21. **The correct answer is (B).** This phrase is appropriately specific and best matches the rest of the passage's style and tone.

22. **The correct answer is (A).** The writer's point is that even though many older technical writers will be vacating their jobs as they retire, freelance technical writers will still face competition as they vie for available jobs; thus, the competition will be *lively*.

SUMMING IT UP

- In the Writing and Language test section of the SAT®, there are four passages and 44 multiple-choice questions (eleven questions about each passage). You will have 35 minutes to complete this section.

- The multiple-choice questions in this section put you in an editor's role. Each question consists of an "editing problem" with four possible solutions.

- Some passages are accompanied by informational graphics, such as graphs, charts, tables, and photographs. You'll need to refer to these supplementary graphics to answer a question or two, but no math will be required in this section.

- There are three main categories of multiple-choice questions:

  1 Expression of Ideas questions, including questions on words in context; adding, deleting, or changing text; transitional language; relevant details; combining sentences; eliminating awkward language and wordiness; reordering sentences so that paragraphs make better sense; consistency of style and tone; cohesion and precision of language

  2 Standard English Conventions questions covering grammar, usage, and punctuation

  3 Graphic Organizer questions that ask you to compare information that is in the passage to similar information or data that is presented in a chart, graph, table, or photograph

- In addition to your Writing and Language Test score, the following subscores and cross-test scores will be provided:

  ○ Command of Evidence

  ○ Expression of Ideas

  ○ Words in Context

  ○ Standard English Conventions

  ○ Analysis in History/Social Studies

  ○ Analysis in Science

English Language Conventions Review

OVERVIEW

- **Sentence formation**
- **Conventions of usage**
- **Conventions of punctuation**
- **Summing it up**

This chapter reviews standard English conventions. While we're not attempting to teach you all the rules of punctuation and grammar, we do want you to review those rules that may be tested or that you may need to call on for your own writing.

Each of the three main domains covered in this chapter—sentence structure, conventions of usage, and conventions of punctuation—is broken down into smaller sections. These instructional sections are followed by exercises with answers and explanations. Be sure to read all the answer explanations, even for the questions you answered correctly. Review is an important part of your SAT® preparation.

SENTENCE FORMATION

Sentence Boundaries

Fragments

Basic Rule

Every sentence must have a complete subject and verb, and express a full idea. A group of words that is missing one of these elements is called a sentence fragment or an incomplete sentence.

There are three ways to correct incomplete sentences:

1 Add the fragment to the sentence that precedes it.

Incorrect: Zoologists and wildlife biologists study animals and other wildlife. How they interact with their ecosystems.

Correct: Zoologists and wildlife biologists study animals and other wildlife and how they interact with their ecosystems.

Explanation: The fragment is added to the sentence that precedes it.

2 Add the fragment to the sentence that follows it.

Incorrect: By studying animal behaviors. Wildlife biologists seek to understand how animals interact with their ecosystems.

Correct: By studying animal behaviors, wildlife biologists seek to understand how animals interact with their ecosystems.

Explanation: The fragment is added to the sentence that follows it.

3 Add a subject and verb to the fragment.

Incorrect: Depending on their specialty.

Correct: Depending on their specialty, a wildlife biologist may spend considerable time studying animals in their natural habitats.

Explanation: A subject and verb are added to the fragment.

Run-ons

A run-on sentence occurs when a writer fails to use either end-stop punctuation to divide complete thoughts or suitable conjunctions to join two ideas.

The following rules will help you avoid and fix run-on sentences:

1 Though the result can be short, choppy sentences, the most common way to correct a run-on sentence is to simply divide the sentence using end-stop punctuation.

Incorrect: Zoologists need a bachelor's degree for entry-level positions a master's degree or Ph.D. is often needed for advancement.

Correct: Zoologists need a bachelor's degree for entry-level positions. A master's degree or Ph.D. is often needed for advancement.

2 A more advanced technique is to join independent clauses using a coordinating or subordinating conjunction such as *and, but, though,* or *while*.

Incorrect: Zoologists need a bachelor's degree for entry-level positions a master's degree is often needed for advancement.

Correct: Zoologists need a bachelor's degree for entry-level positions, though a master's degree is often needed for advancement.

Also correct: Zoologists need a bachelor's degree for entry-level position, but a master's degree is often needed for advancement. (Remember that a comma is required when you use a coordinating conjunction to join two independent clauses.)

3 Use a semi-colon when ideas are very closely related in meaning and full end-stop punctuation seems too strong.

Incorrect: Zoologists and wildlife biologists study how animals and other wildlife interact with their ecosystems they work in offices, laboratories, or outdoors.

Correct: Zoologists and wildlife biologists study how animals and other wildlife interact with their ecosystems; they work in offices, laboratories, or outdoors.

Skill Builder: Fragments and Run-ons

Directions: Revise the following sentences to correct fragments and eliminate run-ons.

1. Zoologists and wildlife biologists perform a variety of scientific tests and experiments for example they take blood samples from animals to assess their levels of nutrition, check animals for disease and parasites, and tag animals in order to track them.

2. In order to track potential threats to wildlife. Wildlife biologists often use computer programs.

3. Zoologists and wildlife biologists work to expand our knowledge of wildlife species. Work closely with public officials to develop wildlife management and conservation plans.

4. Herpetologists study reptiles, such as snakes. And amphibians, such as frogs.

5. Some wildlife biologists develop conservation plans and make recommendations on conservation and management issues. To policymakers and the general public.

6. Ecologists study ecosystems. And the relationships between organisms and the surrounding environments.

7. Evolutionary biologists study the origins of species. The changes in their inherited characteristics over generations.

8. Zoologists and wildlife biologists do jobs such as conducting experimental studies they also collecting biological data for analysis.

Answers

In some cases there are many possible correct answers. Here are some examples:

1. Zoologists and wildlife biologists perform a variety of scientific tests and experiments. For example they take blood samples from animals to assess their levels of nutrition, check animals for disease and parasites, and tag animals in order to track them.

2. In order to track potential threats to wildlife, wildlife biologists often use computer programs.

3. Zoologists and wildlife biologists work to expand our knowledge of wildlife species, and work closely with public officials to develop wildlife management and conservation plans.

4. Herpetologists study reptiles and amphibians, such as snakes and frogs.

5. Some wildlife biologists develop conservation plans and make recommendations on conservation and management issues to policymakers and the general public.

6. Ecologists study ecosystems and the relationships between organisms and the surrounding environments.

7. Evolutionary biologists study the origins of species and the changes in their inherited characteristics over generations.

8. Zoologists and wildlife biologists do jobs such as conducting experimental studies and collecting biological data for analysis.

Coordination and Subordination

Basic Rule

Coordinating and subordinating clauses are used to join together clauses and form compound and complex sentences.

Some common coordinating and subordinating conjunctions are:

Coordinating conjunctions	Subordinating conjunctions
and, but, for, nor, or, so, yet	after, although, as, as if, because, before, even if, even though, if, if only, rather than, since, that, though, unless, until, when, where, whereas, wherever, whether, which, while

Basic Rule of Coordinating Conjunctions

Coordinating conjunctions are used to join independent clauses to make compound sentences. In these sentences, each piece of information carries the same weight.

Independent clauses: There was a Treaty of Paris signed in 1763. There was also one signed 1783.

Joined together: There was a Treaty of Paris signed in 1763 and 1783.

When two clauses are joined, if the second remains an independent clause, a comma must be used before the coordinating conjunction.

Independent clauses: There was a Treaty of Paris signed in 1763. There was also one signed 1783.

Joined together: Not only was there a Treaty of Paris signed in 1763, but there was another Treaty of Paris signed in 1783.

Basic Rule of Subordinating Conjunctions

Subordinating conjunctions are used to join independent clauses to make complex sentences. In these sentences, one piece of information is emphasized over another.

Independent clauses: A tax on imported goods from another country is called a tariff. A tax on imported goods from another country to protect a home industry is called a protective tariff.

Joined together: A tax on imported goods from another country is called a tariff while a tax on imported goods from another country to protect a home industry is called a protective tariff.

Here, the subordinate clause is at the end. You can also place a subordinate clause at the beginning of a sentence, as long as you use a comma.

Independent clauses: A tax on imported goods from another country is called a tariff. A tax on imported goods from another country to protect a home industry is called a protective tariff.

Joined together: While a tax on imported goods from another country is called a tariff, a tax on imported goods from another country to protect a home industry is called a protective tariff.

Skill Builder: Subordination and Coordination

Directions: Join the following sentences using subordinating or coordinating conjunctions.

1. A democracy is a form of government that is run for the people. It is also run by the people.

2. A primary source is an original record of an event. A secondary source is something that was written later.

3. The Industrial Revolution ushered in a time of unparalleled human progress. People often forget the damage that this progress did, and continues to do, to the environment.

4. Elizabeth Cady Stanton became famous as an advocate of women's rights. During the Civil War, she was also an ardent abolitionist.

Answers

In some cases there are many possible correct answers. Here are some examples:

1. A democracy is a form of government that is run for the people and by the people.

2. Whereas a primary source is an original record of an event, a secondary source is something that was written later.

3. While the Industrial Revolution ushered in a time of unparalleled human progress, people often forget the damage that this progress did, and continues to do, to the environment.

4. Elizabeth Cady Stanton became famous as an advocate of women's rights, but during the Civil War, she was also an ardent abolitionist.

Parallel Structure

Parallel structure is the repetition of a grammatical form within a sentence. Parallel structure is a hallmark of effective writing and is often used to emphasize ideas and to present compared items in an equal light. Coordinating conjunctions are often used in parallel constructions.

Non-parallel structure: As a child, George Washington Carver enjoyed reading, learned about plants, and he made art.

Parallel structure: As a child, George Washington Carver enjoyed reading, learning about plants, and making art.

Modifier Placement

A modifier is a word, phrase, or clause that adds detail to a sentence. In order to avoid confusion, modifiers should be placed as close as possible to the things they modify.

Examples of a modifiers are underlined in the below sentences.

Employment is <u>highly</u> competitive <u>within the field of marine biology</u>. (The word "highly" modifies our understanding of the competitive nature of finding employment. The phrase "within the field of marine biology" modifies the subject of the sentence, which is "employment.")

The supply of <u>marine</u> scientists <u>far exceeds the demands</u>, and the number of federal and state government jobs is <u>limited</u>. ("Marine" modifies scientists. "Far exceeds the demands" modifies "supply." "Limited" modifies our understanding of "jobs.")

Caution

When the subject of a modifier is unclear, it is considered a dangling modifier.

Incorrect: Not realizing that the job title of marine biologist rarely exists, many people are familiar with the field of marine biology. (What is the first phrase modifying?)

Possible revision: Many people are familiar with the field of marine biology, but most don't realize that the job of "marine biologist" rarely exists.

Caution

Misplaced modifiers occur when a modifier is poorly placed, and it becomes unclear what that modifier is describing.

Incorrect: The term "marine biologist," not just for those that deal with the physical properties of the sea, is actually used for many disciplines and jobs that deal with the study of marine life.

Possible revision: The term "marine biologist" is actually used for many disciplines and jobs that deal with the study of marine life, not just for those that deal with the physical properties of the sea.

Skill Builder: Modifier Placement

Directions: Revise the following sentences to eliminate problems with modifier placement.

1. In fishery science, in the job market, a strong background in advanced mathematics and computer skills is critical for getting a competitive edge.

2. After taking course work a fishery scientist studies in the animal and aquatic sciences fish and marine mammal population dynamics.

3. Another increasingly important field within marine biology, more universities are starting to offer programs in fisheries or wildlife management.

4. As well as their interactions, biological oceanographers study both the biological and physical aspects of the sea.

5. A student may take course work weighted heavily in physics, mathematics, and computer modeling in the field of physical oceanography.

Answers

In some cases there are many possible correct answers. Here are some examples:

1. In fishery science, a strong background in advanced mathematics and computer skills is critical for getting a competitive edge in the job market.

2. After taking course work in the animal and aquatic sciences, a fishery scientist studies fish and marine mammal population dynamics.

3. More universities are starting to offer programs in fisheries or wildlife management, another increasingly important field within marine biology.

4. Biological oceanographers study both the biological and physical aspects of the sea, as well as their interactions.

5. A student in the field of physical oceanography may take course work weighted heavily in physics, mathematics, and computer modeling.

VERB TENSE, MOOD, AND VOICE

Basic Rule

Use the same verb tense whenever possible within a sentence or paragraph. Do not shift from one tense to another unless there is a valid reason.

Incorrect: The Magna Carta *was* signed in 1215 by King John of England and *has been* the first document of its kind to limit the power of the British monarchy.

Correct: The Magna Carta *was* signed in 1215 by King John of England and *was* the first document of its kind to limit the power of the British monarchy.

When to Use the Perfect Tenses

Basic Rule

Use *present perfect* for an action begun in the past and extended to the present.

Example: Scientists at NASA *have seen* an alarming increase in the accumulation of greenhouse gases.

Explanation: In this case, s*cientists at NASA saw* would be incorrect. What they *have seen* (present perfect) began in the past and extends to the present.

Basic Rule

Use *past perfect* for an action begun and completed in the past before some other past action.

Example: Despite their preparations, Lewis and Clark had never encountered the kinds of challenges that awaited them before their expedition.

Explanation: In this case, *never encountered* would be incorrect. The action *had never encountered* (past perfect) is used because it is referring to events prior to their expedition.

Basic Rule

Use *future perfect* for an action begun at any time and completed in the future.

Example: When the American astronauts arrive, the Russian cosmonauts *will have already been* on the International Space Station for six months.

Explanation: In this case, although both actions occur in the future, the Russian cosmonauts *will have been* on the space station before the American astronauts *arrive*. When there are two future actions, the action completed first is expressed in the future perfect tense.

Skill Builder: Verb Tense

Directions: Choose the correct verb tense for each sentence.

1. (was, has been) Founded in Jamestown, Virginia, the House of Burgesses ___ the first representative body founded in the new world.

2. (have been, were) There ___ many great American explorers, but some scholars argue that none are as historically significant as Lewis and Clark.

3. (had never been, never was) Before 1804, Meriwether Lewis ___ on an expedition of any significance, let alone led one.

4. (will have added, has added) By the time this article is published, the United States ___ 250,000 new jobs.

5. (was, has been) Civil Disobedience, or the refusal to obey a government law or laws, ___ one of Martin Luther King, Jr.'s key tactics during the Civil Rights Movement.

Answers

1. **The correct answer is** was. The past tense is used because the action occurred in the past.

2. **The correct answer is** have been. The present perfect tense is used because the sentence refers to an unspecified time in the past.

3. **The correct answer is** had never been. The past perfect tense is used because the sentence contains a past tense action that occurred before another action.

4. **The correct answer is** will have added. The future perfect tense is used because the sentence refers to an action that will be completed before another.

5. **The correct answer is** was. The past tense is used because the action occurred in the past.

Mood

Basic Rule

Mood, as it relates to verb forms, refers to the kind of message the writer intends to communicate.

The *indicative mood* is the most common mood and is used to state facts or opinions.

Example: Zora Neale Hurston's novel *Their Eyes Were Watching God* was forgotten for many years, but is now considered a literary classic.

The *imperative mood* is used when a writer wants to give a directive or make a request. Though not stated, the subject of an imperative sentence is *you*.

Example: Stop pretending that it doesn't matter.

Example: George Washington peered across the Potomac as the frigid wind lashed his face. "Hurry!" he exclaimed. (*Peered* is in the indicative. *Hurry* is in the imperative.)

The *subjunctive mood* expresses a condition contrary to fact, a wish, a supposition, or an indirect command. Although it is going out of use in English, the subjunctive can still be seen in the following forms:

- To express a wish not likely to be fulfilled or impossible to be realized.

  Example: I wish it *were* possible for us to approve his transfer at this time. (It is *not* possible.)

- In a subordinate clause after a verb that expresses a command, a request, or a suggestion.

  Example: It was recommended by the White House *that* the Office of Homeland Security *be* responsible for preparing the statements.

- To express a condition known or supposed to be contrary to fact.

  Example: If George Washington knew what was going on in Congress, he would be rolling in his grave.

- After *as if* or *as though*. In formal writing and speech, *as if* and *as though* are followed by the subjunctive, since they introduce as supposition something not factual. In informal writing and speaking, the indicative is sometimes used.

  Example: Before defecting to France, Benedict Arnold talked as if he were a true American patriot. (He is not.)

Caution

Avoid shifts in mood. Once you have decided on the mood that properly expresses your message, use that mood throughout the sentence or the paragraph. A shift in mood is confusing to the listener or reader; it indicates that the speaker or writer himself has changed his way of looking at the conditions.

Incorrect: It is requested by the White House that a report of Congressional proceedings *be* prepared and copies *should be* distributed to all citizens. (*Be* is subjunctive; *should be,* indicative.)

Correct: It is requested by the White House that a report of the Congressional proceedings *be* prepared and that copies *be* distributed to all citizens.

Voice

Basic Rule

Voice tells us whether the subject of a sentence is the actor or is acted upon. In formal writing, active voice is preferred because it is more immediate and places the reader closer to the action.

Active voice example: According to legend, George Washington chopped down the whole cherry tree.

Passive voice example: According to legend, the cherry tree was chopped down by George Washington.

Skill Builder: Mood and Voice

Directions: In the following sentences, fill-in the correct mood, or identify the correct voice.

1. (was, were) The team of Russian engineers ___ unable to prevent the nuclear reactor in Chernobyl from melting down.

2. (was, were) If climate change ___ not such a threat to life on this planet, the scientific community would not be making such a big deal about carbon emissions.

3. (is, were) If inflation ___ to continue to rise, the effects on the economy would be disastrous.

4. (be, should be) The President asked that the Speaker of the House ___ present when the special announcement was made.

5. (passive or active voice) In a cup made of calcium carbonate sits each stony coral polyp.

6. (passive or active voice) For over 40 years, Henry Clay played a central role on the national political stage.

Answers and Explanations

1. **The correct answer is** "was". This sentence uses the indicative mood and requires the simple past tense.

2. **The correct answer is** "were". The subjunctive is correct because the sentence is making a supposition.

3. **The correct answer is** "were". The subjunctive is correct because the sentence is making a supposition.

4. **The correct answer is** "be". The subjunctive is correct because the subordinate clause after the verb is making a request.

5. **The correct answer is** "passive voice". This sentence is passive because the subject of the sentence is acted upon.

6. **The correct answer is** "active voice". This sentence is active because the subject of the sentence is the actor.

CONVENTIONS OF USAGE

Pronouns

Pronouns substitute for nouns.

Examples: George Washington was born on February 22, 1732, in Pope's Creek, Virginia; *he* was the first American president.

Did you know that Besty Ross and George Washington both went to the same church? *It* was called Christ Church, and *it* was located in Philadelphia.

The following pronoun chart may prove helpful:

NUMBER	PERSON	SUBJECTIVE CASE	OBJECTIVE CASE	POSSESSIVE CASE
Singular	1st person	I	me	mine
	2nd person	you	you	yours
	3rd person	he, she, it, who	him, her, it, whom	his, hers, whose
Plural	1st person	we	us	ours
	2nd person	you	you	yours
	3rd person	they, who	them, whom	theirs, whose

Basic Rule

A pronoun uses the subjective case when it is the subject of the sentence, or when it renames the subject as a subject complement.

Incorrect: That night, George Washington, Robert Morris, and *him* asked Betsy Ross to sew the first flag.

Correct: That night, George Washington, Robert Morris, and *he* asked Betsy Ross to sew the first flag. (*He* is part of the subject of the sentence.)

Incorrect: George Ross is *him.*

Correct: George Ross is *he.* (*He* renames the subject.)

Basic Rule

If a pronoun is the object of a verb or preposition, it is placed in the objective case.

Incorrect: After the plot was discovered, they accused Benedict Arnold and *he* of treason.

Correct: After the plot was discovered, they accused Benedict Arnold and *him* of treason. (*Him* is the object of the verb *accused.*)

Incorrect: Despite the fact that we turned in our marine biology paper late, "A" grades were given to Franklin and *I.*

Correct: Despite the fact that we turned in our marine biology paper late, "A" grades were given to Franklin and *me.* (*Me* is the object of the verb *given.*)

Pronoun Clarity

Avoid ambiguity and confusion by placing a pronoun as close as possible to its antecedent and by making sure that the antecedent is clear.

Incorrect: At the height of his career, Frank Lloyd Wright told an architectural scholar that *he* thought *his* work was improving. (Is Wright talking about his own work or the work of the scholar?)

Correct: At the height of his career, Frank Lloyd Wright told an architectural scholar that he thought *his own* work was improving.

Incorrect: Frank Lloyd Wright and his wife Olgivanna founded a school for aspiring artists in Spring Green, Wisconsin, where they could "learn by doing." (Does *they* refer to the Wrights or the artists?)

Correct: Frank Lloyd Wright and his wife Olgivanna founded a school in Spring Green, Wisconsin, where aspiring artists could "learn by doing."

Possessive Determiners

When a pronoun expresses ownership, it is placed in the possessive case.

Caution

Possessive determiners (its, your, their), contractions (it's, you're, they're), and adverbs (there) are often confused. Remember that personal pronouns that express ownership never require an apostrophe.

Incorrect: Frank Lloyd Wright believed that architectural structures should be in harmony with humanity and *it's* environment.

Correct: Frank Lloyd Wright believed that architectural structures should be in harmony with humanity and *its* environment.

Skill Builder: Pronouns

Directions: In the space provided, identify and explain the pronoun error contained in each statement.

1. The battle for Yorktown was an important turning point in the American Revolution and the British defeat signaled the end of it.

2. The American Bill of Rights was based on the English Bill of Rights; it protected the rights of its citizens.

3. While the Articles of Confederation is less famous than other historical documents like the Declaration of Independence and the Constitution, it's historical significance cannot be overstated.

4. As opposed to Federalists, who favored a strong national government based on the Constitution, Anti-federalists opposed the Constitution. They preferred more power be given to the states.

5. Thomas Paine was an American patriot who's pamphlets *Common Sense* and *The Crisis* help stir the American independence movement.

Answers and Explanations

1. It is unclear whether the "it" at the end of the sentence refers to the American Revolution or the Battle for Yorktown.

2. It is unclear whether the "it" that follows the semi-colon refers to the American or English Bill or Rights or both.

3. "It's" is a contraction; the correct word should be the possessive pronoun "its."

4. It is unclear whether "they" refers to the Federalists or the Anti-federalists.

5. "Who's" is a contraction; the correct word should be the possessive pronoun "whose."

AGREEMENT

Pronoun-Antecedent Agreement

TIP

The third person singular of most verbs ends in "s." First person: *I, we speak;* second person: *you speak;* third person: *he, she, it speaks.* Examples: *He runs. She jogs. It jumps. The man sees. Mary laughs. The child walks.*

A pronoun agrees with the word it refers to (the *antecedent*) in both person and number.

Example: The team of archaeologists examined the fossilized bone with great care to make sure they didn't damage *it.*

Explanation: The pronoun *it* refers to *bone,* the antecedent.

Caution

Remember to use a singular pronoun when you refer to words such as *everyone, everybody, each, every, anyone, anybody, nobody, no one, one, each, either,* and *neither.*

Examples: While all fire departments operate as tight-knit communities, each fireman knows that *his* (not *their*) gear is *his* (not *their*) responsibility.

Despite the fact that many came from wealthy families, each woman who attended the Seneca Falls conference on women's rights risked *her* (not *their*) life and reputation.

None of the programmers could be certain if it was *his* or *her* (not *their*) mistake that caused the computer network to crash.

Caution

Collective nouns present special problems. A *collective* names a group of people or things. Although usually singular in form, it is treated as either singular or plural according to the sense of the sentence:

Singular when members of the group act, or are considered, as a *unit:*

The citizens' *assembly is drafting* a petition that would seek to protect local aquifers from chemical run-off and hazardous waste.

Plural when the members act, or are considered, as multiple individuals:

After one of the longest and most fabled droughts in baseball history, the *Boston Red Sox have* finally overcome the "Curse of the Bambino" to win another World Series.

Common collective nouns include:

assembly, association, audience, board, cabinet, class, commission, committee, company, corporation, council, counsel, couple, crowd, department, family, firm, group, jury, majority, minority, number, pair, press, public, staff, United States

The following short words—though seldom listed as collective nouns—are governed by the same rules. They are singular or plural according to the intended meaning of the sentence.

all, any, more, most, some, who, which

Subject-Verb Agreement

Basic Rule

A verb agrees in number with its subject. A singular subject takes a singular verb. A plural subject takes a plural verb.

Examples: Coral reefs are an important part of the marine ecosystem.

The teacher explained that coral reefs are an important part of the marine ecosystem.

For the following sentence, choose the *correct verb:* (is, am, are)

Booker T. Washington, Frederick Douglass, and W.E.B. DuBois _____ all important historical figures.

Explanation: Remember that the verb must agree with the subject. Since the subject is plural—subjects joined by *and* are plural—a plural verb is needed. The correct response therefore should be:

Booker T. Washington, Frederick Douglass, and W.E.B. DuBois are all important historical figures.

Caution

Sometimes the subject comes after the verb, but the rule still applies.

Choose the *correct verb:* (is, are)

While the lecture has lasted 2 hours already, there _____ still 3 more speakers.

Explanation: Are is correct since the subject *hours* is plural and requires a plural verb:

Caution

There is one major exception to this rule. When the sentence is introduced by the word "there" and the verb is followed by a compound (double) subject, the first part of the subject dictates whether the verb should be singular or plural.

Example: There *is one American astronaut* in the shuttle and four Russian astronauts in the space station.

When compound subjects are joined by *either-or* or *neither-nor,* the verb agrees with the subject closest to the verb.

Examples: Neither the violinist nor *the other musicians have had* much experience performing for an audience

Neither you nor *I am* willing to make the sacrifices required of a professional musician.

Explanation: In the first example, *musicians* (plural) is closest to the verb; in the second example, *I* (singular) is closest to the verb.

Caution

Sometimes a word or a group of words may come between the subject and the verb. The verb still must agree with the simple subject, and the *simple subject is never part of a prepositional phrase.*

Example: Stephen King, the author of hundreds of best-selling novels, novellas, and short stories, *is* also a guitarist and singer in a band.

The simple subject is Stephen King, a singular noun. The verb must be *is.*

Choose the *correct verb:* (was, were)

The causes of the deterioration of coral reefs ____ not known until recently.

Explanation: The simple subject is *causes;* "of the deterioration of coral reefs" is a prepositional phrase. Since the subject is plural, the plural verb *were* is required. So, the correct answer is *were.*

Skill Builder: Agreement

Directions: Follow the principles of agreement and choose the correct word.

1. (is, are) The President and Vice President of the United States of America ____ expected to attend tomorrow's historic ceremony honoring Rosa Parks.

2. (have, has) Either the chair of the department or one of the professors ____ the necessary paperwork.

3. (was, were) In the time of the first settlers, there ____ no antibiotics to prevent outbreaks of disease.

4. (its, their) Because of ____ biodiversity, coral reefs are often called "the rainforests of the sea."

5. (her, their) After a brief introduction, each of the female doctors presented ____ findings at the medical conference.

6. (is, are) Many young people are surprised to find out that the music of Verdi's operas _____ as vibrant and fun as anything on the radio.

7. (his, their) As the conductor took the podium, the musicians finished tuning ___ instruments.

8. (know, knows) Neither Sherlock Holmes nor the detectives of Scotland Yard ___ who the perpetrator is.

9. (is, are) According to preliminary market reports, either Xiaomi or Huawei ___ the biggest smartphone provider in China.

10. (is, are) However, neither the Republicans nor the Democrats ___ satisfied with the language of the new nuclear weapons treaty.

Answers and Explanations

1. **The correct answer is "are".** The plural subject *President and Vice President* requires the plural *are*.

2. **The correct answer is "has."** The verb must agree with the subject closest to it, in this case the singular *one*.

3. **The correct answer is "were".** The plural subject *antibiotics* requires the plural *were*.

4. **The correct answer is "their".** The plural subject *coral reefs* requires the plural *their*.

5. **The correct answer is "her".** The singular subject *each* requires the singular *her*.

6. **The correct answer is "is".** The singular subject *music* requires the singular *is*.

7. **The correct answer is "their".** The plural antecedent *musicians* requires the plural *their*.

8. **The correct answer is "know".** In a *neither-nor* construction, the verb is governed by the closest subject, *detectives*.

9. **The correct answer is "is".** The singular determiner *either* requires the singular verb *is*.

10. **The correct answer is "are".** In a *neither-nor* construction, the verb is governed by the closest subject, *Democrats*.

Skill Builder: Agreement

Directions: Revise the underlined words to eliminate agreement errors. If the underlined word is grammatically correct, write C above it. If a change is necessary, indicate the change and give a grammatical reason for it. Do not make unnecessary changes.

Joseph, one of my best friends, <u>are</u> considering becoming a medical doctor. He and I <u>believe</u>
                                  1   2
that medicine, compared to other professions, <u>are</u> an exciting and fulfilling field. In order to help
                                               3
him decide, he asked each of his friends to give his or her opinion about why medicine would or

would not be a fulfilling career choice. After that, he also asked his parents for their opinions. It

seems that his friends and his mother <u>is</u> in agreement, but his father <u>do</u> not agree.
                                       4   5

Jacob's father feels strongly that the medical profession, unlike other professions, <u>requires</u> an
6

excessive amount of study and is too emotionally taxing. On the other hand, his friends and his

mother <u>agree</u> that while the schooling is rigorous, the practice itself would be very rewarding.
    7

Jacob <u>is</u> still deciding what he wants to be, but he and I <u>has</u> learned that there <u>is</u> always many
    8   9   10

different possible answers to a question.

Answers and Explanations

1. **The correct answer is "is".** The subject, *Joseph*, is singular.

2. **The correct answer is C.** The subject, *He and I*, is plural.

3. **The correct answer is "is".** The subject, *medicine*, is singular.

4. **The correct answer is "are".** The subject, *his friends and his mother*, is plural.

5. **The correct answer is "does".** The subject, *father*, is singular.

6. **The correct answer is C.** The subject, *medical profession,* is singular.

7. **The correct answer is C.** The subject, *friends and mother,* is plural.

8. **The correct answer is C.** The subject, *Jacob*, is singular.

9. **The correct answer is "have".** The subject, *he and I*, is plural.

10. **The correct answer is "are".** The subject, *answers*, is plural.

FREQUENTLY CONFUSED WORDS

The following pages review groups of words that are similar in sound and/or meaning and are generally found to be confusing to students and adults alike. Misunderstanding what they mean or how they are used results in various usage problems. The word groups have been broken down into manageable sections to help you learn them more easily. Do not try to master all the information at once. Study one section at a time.

At the end of each section there is a practice exercise. See how well you do on the exercise by checking your answers against the answers and explanations given. If you do well, go on to the next section. If you find that you have made a number of errors, review the section. It is important that you master each section before moving on to the next one.

Frequently Confused Words: Group 1

a is used before words that start with a consonant sound

an is used before words that start with a vowel sound

> Please give the baby *a* toy.

> He is *an* only child. We put up *a* united front. *(United* begins with a consonant sound—*y*.)

> We spent *an* hour together. *(Hour* begins with a vowel sound, since the *h* is silent.)

and is used to join words or ideas

> We enjoy shopping *and* sightseeing.

> She is a very serious student, *and* her grades are the best in the class.

accept means *to receive* or *to agree* to something

except means *to exclude* or *excluding*

> I'll *accept* the gift from you.

> Everyone *except* my uncle went home.

> My uncle was *excepted* from the group of losers.

advice means *counsel* (noun), opinion

advise means *to offer advice* (verb)

> Let me give you some free *advice*.

> I'd *advise* you to see your doctor.

affect means *to influence* (verb)

effect means *to cause* or *bring about* (verb) or a *result* (noun)

> The pollution *affected* our health.

> Our lawsuit *effected* a change in the law.

> The *effect* of the storm could not be measured.

all ready means *everybody* or *everything ready*

already means *previously*

> They were *all ready* to write when the test began.

> They had *already* written the letter.

all together means *everybody* or *everything together*

altogether means *completely*

> The boys and girls stood *all together* in line.

> His action was *altogether* strange for a person of his type.

desert (DEZZ-ert) means an *arid area*

desert (di-ZERT) means *to abandon,* or *a reward or punishment* (usually plural)

dessert (di-ZERT) means the *final course of a meal*

> I have seen several movies set in the Sahara *desert*.

> The soldier was warned not to *desert* his company.

> We're certain that execution is a just *desert* for his crime.

> He received his just *deserts*.

> We had strawberry shortcake for *dessert*.

in is used to indicate *inclusion, location,* or *motion within limits*

into is used for *motion toward* one place *from* another

> The spoons are *in* the drawer.

> We were walking *in* the room.

> I put the spoons *into* the drawer.

it's is the contraction of *it is* or *it has*

its is a possessive pronoun meaning *belonging to it*

> *It's* a very difficult assignment.

> *It is* a very difficult assignment.

> We tried to analyze *its* meaning.

lay means *to put*

lie means *to recline*

> *To lay:*

> (present)   I lay

> (past)   I laid the gift on the table.

> (present perfect) I have laid

> *To lie:*

> (present)   I lie

> (past)   I lay on my blanket at the beach.

> (present perfect) I have lain

lets is third person singular present of *let*

let's is a contraction for *let us*

> He *lets* me park my car in his garage.

> *Let's* go home early today.

loose means *not fastened or restrained,* or *not tight-fitting*

lose means *to mislay, to be unable to keep, to be defeated*

> The dog got *loose* from the leash.

> Try not to *lose* your umbrella.

passed is the past tense of *to pass*

past means *just preceding* or *an earlier time*

> The week *passed* very quickly.

> The *past* week was a very exciting one.

principal means *chief* or *main* (adjective), or a *leader,* or a *sum of money* (noun)

principle means a *fundamental truth or belief*

> His *principal* support comes from the real estate industry.

> The *principal* of the school called a meeting of the faculty.

> He earned 10 percent interest on the *principal* he invested last year.

> As a matter *of principle,* he refused to register for the draft.

quiet means *silent, still*

quit means *to give up, to discontinue*

quite means *very* or *exactly, to the greatest extent*

> My brother is very shy and *quiet.*

> I *quit* the team last week.

> His analysis is *quite* correct.

raise means *to lift, to erect*

raze means *to tear down*

rise means *to get up, to move from a lower to a higher position, to increase in value*

> The neighbors helped him *raise* a new barn.

> The demolition crew *razed* the old building.

> The price of silver will *rise* again this month.

set means *to place something down* (mainly)

sit means *to seat oneself* (mainly)

To set:

(present)	He sets
(past)	He set the lamp on the table.
(present perfect)	He has set

To sit:

(present)	He sits
(past)	He sat on the chair.
(present perfect)	He has sat

stationary means *standing still*

stationery means *writing material*

> In ancient times, people thought that the earth was *stationary.*

> We bought our school supplies at the *stationery* store.

suppose means *to assume* or *guess*

supposed is the *past tense* and also *past participle* of *suppose*

supposed also means *ought to* or *should* (when followed by *to*)

    I *suppose* you will be home early.

    I *supposed* you would be home early.

    I had *supposed* you would be there.

    I am *supposed to* be in school tomorrow.

than is used to express *comparison*

then is used to express *time* or *a result or consequence*

    Jim ate more *than* we could put on the large plate.

    I knocked on the door, and *then* I entered.

    If you go, *then* I will go, too.

their means *belonging to them*

there means *in that place*

they're is the contraction for *they are*

    We took *their* books home with us.

    Your books are over *there* on the desk.

    They're coming over for dinner.

though means *although* or *as if*

thought is the past tense of *to think*, or *an idea* (noun)

through means *in one side and out another, by way of, finished*

    Though he is my friend, I can't recommend him for this job.

    I *thought* you were serious!

    We enjoyed running *through* the snow.

to means *in the direction of* (preposition); it is also used before a verb to indicate the *infinitive*

too means *very, also*

two is the numeral 2

    We shall go *to* school.

    It is *too* hot today.

    We shall go, *too*.

    I ate *two* sandwiches for lunch.

use means *to employ, put into service*

used is the past tense and the past participle of *use*

> I want to *use* your chair.
>
> I *used* your chair.

used meaning *in the habit of* or *accustomed to,* is followed by *to*

used is an adjective meaning *not new*

> I am *used to* your comments.
>
> I bought a *used* car.

weather refers to *atmospheric conditions*

whether introduces a *choice;* it should not be preceded by *of* or *as to*

> I don't like the *weather* in San Francisco.
>
> He inquired *whether* we were going to the dance.

were is a past tense of *be*

we're is a contraction of *we are*

where refers to *place* or *location*

> They *were* there yesterday.
>
> *We're* in charge of the decorations.
>
> *Where* are we meeting your brother?

who's is the contraction for *who is* (or *who has)*

whose means *of whom,* implying ownership

> *Who's* the next batter?
>
> *Whose* notebook is on the desk?

your is a possessive, showing ownership

you're is a contraction for *you are*

> Please give him *your* notebook.
>
> *You're* very sweet.

Skill Builder: Usage

Directions: Circle the correct word to complete the sentence while adhering to formal, American-English conventions.

1. The patriot Samuel Adams was one of the (principal, principle) organizers of the Boston Tea Party.

2. Merchants in Boston refused to (accept, except) the taxes imposed upon them by the Tea Act of 1773.

3. Though the significance of the Tea Act of 1773 cannot be underestimated, (weather, whether) or not the Tea Act of 1773 led to the American Revolution is hard to say.

4. In late November of 1773, the ship the Dartmouth sailed (in, into) Boston Harbor.

5. Governor Hutchinson was determined to collect the taxes and (adviced, advised) the tea consignees not to back down.

6. More (than, then) 40 tons of tea were thrown into the water during the Boston Tea Party.

7. Tea smuggling was (all ready, already) a significant problem, especially in New York and Philadelphia.

8. The overall (affect, effect) of the Boston Tea Party was to bolster the revolutionary fervor that was sweeping New England.

9. The British Crown reacted swiftly and harshly in order to dispel the idea that they were (loosing, losing) control of the colonies.

10. (All together, Altogether) 342 chests of tea, weighing over 92,000 pounds, were dumped into the water.

Answers

1. principal
2. accept
3. whether
4. into
5. advised
6. than
7. already
8. effect
9. losing
10. altogether

Frequently Confused Words: Group 2

abbreviate means *to shorten by omitting*

abridge means *to shorten by condensing*

>New York is *abbreviated* to NY.

>In order to save time in the reading, the report was *abridged*.

ad is used informally, but in formal usage *advertisement* is correct; similarly: exam (examination), auto (automobile), phone (telephone), gym (gymnasium)

advantage means *a superior position*

benefit means a *favor conferred or earned* (as a profit)

>He had an *advantage* in experience over his opponent.

>The rules were changed for his *benefit*.

aggravate means *to make worse*

annoy means *to bother* or *to irritate*

>Your nasty comments *aggravated* a bad situation.

>Your nasty comments *annoyed* him. (Not: Your nasty comments aggravated him.)

ain't is an unacceptable contraction for *am not, are not,* or *is not,* although *ain't* is sometimes heard in very informal speech

alibi is an *explanation on the basis of being in another place*

excuse is an *explanation on any basis*

>The accused man's *alibi* was that he was in another town when the robbery occurred.

>Whenever he is late, he makes up a new *excuse*.

all ways means *in every possible way*

always means *at all times*

>He was in *all ways* acceptable to the voters.

>He was *always* ready to help.

almost means *nearly, not quite*

most refers to the *greatest amount or number* or to the *largest part, a majority*

>We are *almost* finished writing the book.

>*Most* of the credit should be given to his uncle.

alongside of means *side by side with*

alongside means *parallel to the side*

>He stood *alongside of* her at the corner.

>Park the car *alongside* the curb.

allot means *to give* or *apportion*

> I will *allot* 3 hours for painting the table.

alot is a misspelling of *a lot*

> He earned *a lot* of money. (Better: He earned *a great deal* of money.)

alright is now often employed in common usage to mean *all right* (In formal usage, *all right* is still preferred by most authorities.)

all right means *satisfactory, very well, uninjured,* or *without doubt*

> I'm *alright,* thank you.

> It was his responsibility, *all right.*

alternate, as a noun, means a *substitute* or *second choice*

alternate, as a verb, means to *perform by turns*

alternative means a *choice between two things, only one of which may be accepted*

> She served as an *alternate* delegate to the convention.

> The cook *alternated* green beans and cauliflower on the menu.

> Is there an *alternative* to the proposition? (In less formal usage, *alternative* is not always limited to a choice between *two.)*

alumna means *a female graduate* (plural: alumnae; *ae* rhymes with key)

alumnus means *a male graduate* (plural; alumni; *ni* rhymes with high)

> She is an *alumna* of Mrs. Brown's School for Young Women.

> He is an *alumnus* of City College.

among is used to discuss *more than two* items

between is used to discuss *two* items only

> The work was divided *among* the four brothers.

> She divided the pie *between* Joe and Marie.

amount is used to refer to *a quantity not individually countable*

number is used to refer to *items that can be counted individually*

> A tremendous *amount* of work had piled up on my desk.

> We ate a great *number* of cookies at the party.

annual means *yearly*

biannual means *twice a year* (also semiannual)

biennial means *once in two years* or *every two years*

> Are you going to the *annual* holiday party?

> I received *biannual* car insurance statements in April and in October.

> He gets a new car *biennially.*

anxious means *worried*

eager means *keenly desirous*

> We were *anxious* about our first airplane flight.

> I am *eager* to see you again.

anyways is an incorrect form for *anyway*

anywheres is an incorrect form for *anywhere*

> I didn't want to go *anyway.*

> I couldn't locate her *anywhere.*

aren't I is used informally, but in formal usage *am I not* is correct

> *Am I not* entitled to an explanation?

as is not always as clear as *because, for,* or *since* (also see *like*)

> She wants to cry *because* she is very sad.

as, used as a *conjunction,* is followed by a verb

like, used as a *preposition,* is *not* followed by a verb

> Do as I do, not *as* I say.

> Try not to behave *like* a child.

as…as is used in an *affirmative* statement

so…as is used in a *negative* statement

> She is *as* talented *as* any other actress in the show.

> He is *not so* reliable *as* his older brother.

as good as is used for *comparisons,* not to mean *practically*

> This bicycle is *as good as* the other one.

> They *practically* promised us a place in the hall. (Not: They *as good as* promised us a place in the hall.)

astonish means *to strike with sudden wonder*

surprise means *to catch unaware*

The extreme violence of the hurricane *astonished* everybody.

A heat wave in April would *surprise* us.

at should be avoided when it does not contribute to the meaning of an idea

Where do you live at? may be heard in informal usage, but *Where do you live?* is the correct form.

The group will arrive *about* noon. (not *at about* noon)

awfully is sometimes heard in informal usage. In formal usage, *very* is correct.

This pie is very good. (not *awfully* good)

a while is used after a preposition (noun)

awhile is used in other cases (adverb)

I coached the team for *a while*.

I coached the team *awhile*.

backward and *backwards* both may be used as adverbs

We tried to skate *backward*. (Or: *We tried to skate backwards.*)

bad is used after verbs that refer to the senses, such as *look, feel* (adjective)

badly means *greatly, in a bad manner* (adverb)

He felt *bad* that he could not attend the meeting.

The young man needs a part-time job very *badly*.

been is the past participle of *to be,* used after helping verbs *have, has,* or *had*

being is the *-ing* form of *to be,* usually used after helping verbs *is, am, are, was,* and *were*

I have *been* living here for six years.

He was *being* a troublemaker, so we told him to stay away from us.

being as and *being that* should not be used in standard English. *Because* and *since* are preferable.

Since it was dark, we turned on the lights.

Because he is my friend, I give him a gift.

Skill Builder: Usage

Directions: Circle the correct word to complete the sentence while adhering to formal, American-English conventions.

1. The (abbreviated, abridged) jobs report omitted jobs in the arts in order to make the report more manageable.

2. Detectives often ask criminals if they have an (alibi, excuse) for where they were on the night of a given crime.

3. Animal trainers must (allot, a lot) a significant amount of their work time to building a relationship with their animals.

4. The famous dog trainer Felix Ho is an (alumna, alumnus) of La Trobe University in Melbourne, Australia.

5. Animal care and service workers often divide their time (among, between) training, feeding, grooming, and exercising their animals.

6. Learning how to be an effective animal trainer requires a tremendous (amount, number) of work.

7. Animals form very real bonds with their trainers; likewise, trainers are often (anxious, eager) to see their animals when they have been away.

8. While horse trainers rarely have formal schooling in their field, they can't get their training just (anywhere, anywheres).

9. Becoming a good animal trainer requires experience that can be (awfully, very) difficult to attain.

10. Many animal trainers feel (bad, badly) when they have to leave their animals for long periods of time.

11. (Because, Being that) zookeepers and marine mammal trainers require formal education, they tend to make more money than other animal care professionals.

Answers

1. abbreviated

2. alibi

3. allot

4. alumnus

5. between

6. amount

7. eager

8. anywhere

9. very

10. bad

11. Because

Frequently Confused Words: Group 3

beside means *at the side of*

besides means *in addition to*

> In our tennis game, he played *beside* me at the net.

> We entertained Jim, Sue, and Louise, *besides* the members of the chorus.

better means *recovering*

well means *completely recovered*

better is used with the verb *had* to show desirability

> He is *better* now than he was a week ago.

> In a few more weeks, he will be *well*.

> He *had better* (not *he better)* follow instructions or pay the penalty.

between you and I is the incorrect form, since the object of the preposition *between* should be the objective case *me*, not the subjective case *I*

> *Between you and me,* he has not been very helpful this week.

both means *two considered together*

each means *one of two or more*

> *Both* of the applicants qualified for the position.

> *Each* applicant was given a good reference.

bring means *to carry toward the speaker*

take means *to carry away from the speaker*

> *Bring* the coat to me.

> *Take* money for carfare when you leave.

bunch is used informally to describe a group of people, but in formal usage *group* is preferred

> When he returned to his office, he learned that a *group* of students was waiting for him.

burst is used in present and past tenses to mean *to explode* (or *to break*)

bust and *busted* are incorrect forms of *burst*

> I do hope the balloon will not *burst*.

> He cried when the balloon *burst*. (not *busted*)

but that is sometimes heard in informal usage, but in formal usage *that* is correct

> He never doubted *that* she would visit him.

can means *able*

may implies *permission* or *possibility*

> *I can* eat both desserts.
>
> *May I* eat both desserts?
>
> It *may* snow tonight.

cannot seem is sometimes used informally, but in formal usage *seems unable* is correct

> My elderly uncle *seems unable* to remember his own phone number.

complected should not be used for *complexioned*

> At the beach, the fair-*complexioned* boy stayed under an umbrella.

consistently means *in harmony*

constantly means *regularly, steadily*

> If you give me advice, you should act *consistently* with that advice.
>
> I *constantly* warned him about leaving the door unlocked.

continual means *happening again and again at short intervals*

continuous means *without interruption*

> The teacher gave the class *continual* warnings.
>
> Noah experienced *continuous* rain for forty days.

could of is an incorrect form of *could have,* which can be contracted to *could've* in speech or informal writing

> I wish that I *could've gone.* (Better: I wish that I *could have gone.*)

couple refers to *two; several* or *a few* refers to *more than two*

> Alex and Frieda are the most graceful *couple* on the dance floor.
>
> A *few* of my cousins—Mary, Margie, Alice, and Barbara—will be at the reunion tonight.

data is the Latin plural of *datum,* meaning *information* (*data* is preferred with plural verbs and pronouns, but is now acceptable in the singular)

> *These data* were very significant to the study. (Or: *This data* was very significant to the study.)

did is the past tense of *do*

done is the past participle of *do*

> I *did* whatever was required to complete the job.
>
> I have *done* what you requested.

different than is often used informally, but in formal usage *different from* is correct

> Jack is *different from* his brother.

disinterested means *impartial*

uninterested means *not interested*

> The judge must be a *disinterested* party in a trial.

> I'm an *uninterested* bystander, so I find the proceedings boring.

doesn't is a contraction of *does not* (third person singular)

don't is a contraction of *do not* and is not a substitute for *doesn't*

> She *doesn't* go to school.

> They *don't* go to school.

doubt whether is often heard in informal usage, but *doubt that* is the correct form

> I *doubt that* I will be home this evening.

due to is sometimes used informally at the beginning of a sentence, but in formal usage *because of, on account of,* or some similar expression is preferred

> *Because of* (not *due to*) the rain, the game was postponed. (But: The postponement was *due to* the rain.)

each other refers to *two persons*

one another refers to *more than two persons*

> Jane and Jessica have known *each other* for many years.

> Several of the girls have known *one another* for many years.

either...or is used to refer to choices

neither...nor is the negative form

> *Either* Lou *or* Jim will drive you home.

> *Neither* Alice *nor* Carol will be home tonight.

else than is sometimes heard in informal usage, but in formal usage *other than* is correct

> Shakespeare was rarely regarded by students as anything *other than* the writer of plays.

enthuse or *enthused* should be avoided; use *enthusiastic*

> We were *enthusiastic* when given the chance to travel abroad.

equally as good is an incorrect form; *equally good* or *just as good* is correct

> This bicycle is *just as good* as that one.

> etc. is the abbreviation for the Latin term *et cetera,* meaning *and so forth, and other things.* In general, it is better to be specific and not use *etc.*

> I think that oranges, peaches, cherries, *etc.,* are healthful. (*Etc.* is not preceded by *and*)

everyone, written as one word, is a *pronoun*

every one, written as two words, is used to refer to each *individual*

> *Everyone* present voted for the proposal.

> *Every one* of the voters accepted the proposal.

every bit is incorrect usage for *just as*

> You are *just as* (not *every bit as*) clever as she is.

ever so often means *frequently* or *repeatedly*

every so often means *occasionally* or *now and again*

> He sees his brother *ever so often,* practically every day.

> Since tickets are so expensive, we only attend the theater *every so often.*

expect is sometimes used incorrectly to mean *assume* or *presume*

> I *assume* (not *expect*) that he won the race.

Skill Builder: Usage

Directions: Circle the correct word to complete the sentence while adhering to formal, American-English conventions.

1. (Beside, Besides) needing a bachelor's degree in marine biology, animal science, biology, or a related field, marine mammal trainers often need to have SCUBA certification.

2. Between you and (me, I), training lions does not sound like fun!

3. After a rigorous application process, (both, each) of the trainers were hired.

4. A dog trainer might begin with a simple task such as training a dog to (bring, take) a rubber ball back to him.

5. Young students often ask zookeepers, "(Can, May) I help you feed the animals?"

6. While jobs in kennels, grooming shops, and pet stores is increasing, many advanced animal care professionals such as zookeepers and marine mammal trainers (cannot seem, seem unable) to find work.

7. In jobs surveys, the percentage of nonfarm animal caretakers (consistently, constantly) outnumbers the number of actual animal trainers.

8. Here are a (couple, few) examples of what an animal care specialist might do: give food and water to animals; clean equipment and the living spaces of animals; monitor animals and record details of their diet, physical condition, and behavior; and examine animals for signs of illness or injury.

9. Even though they sound the same, the job of a pet groomer is very (different from, different than) the job of a horse groom.

10. (Because of, Due to) employment growth and high job turnover, job opportunities in the animal care and services field will continue to grow.

11. The starting salary for animal care and service workers is (equally as good, just as good) as the starting salary for nonfarm animal caretakers.

Answers

1. Besides
2. me
3. both
4. bring
5. May
6. seem unable
7. constantly
8. few
9. different from
10. Because of
11. just as good

Frequently Confused Words: Group 4

fewer is used to refer to items that can be *counted*

less is used to refer to something viewed as *a mass,* not as a series of individual items

> I made *fewer* repairs on the new car than on the old one.

> After the scandal, the company enjoyed *less* prestige than it had the previous year.

finalized is used to mean *concluded* or *complete,* usually in informal usage; in formal usage, *completed* is preferred

> Labor and management *completed* arrangements for a settlement.

flaunt means *to make a display of*

flout means *to show contempt, scorn*

> He *flaunted* his new wealth in an ostentatious manner.

> She *flouted* the policeman's authority.

former means *the first of two*

latter means *the second of two*

> The *former* half of the story was in prose.

> The *latter* half of the story was in poetry.

good is an adjective; *good* is often used informally as an adverb, but the correct word is *well*

> She is a *good* singer.

> She sings *well.*

graduated is followed by the preposition *from* when it indicates completion of a course of study

graduated also means *divided into categories or marked intervals*

> He *graduated from* high school last year. (Or: He *was graduated from* high school last year.)

> A *graduated* test tube is one that has markings on it to indicate divisions.

guess is sometimes used informally to mean *think* or *suppose,* but it is incorrect in formal use

> I *think* (not *guess*) I'll go home now.

habit means an *individual tendency to repeat a thing*

custom means *group habit*

> He had a *habit* of breaking glasses before each recital.

> The *custom* of the country was to betroth girls at an early age.

had ought is an incorrect form for *ought* or *should*

hadn't ought is an incorrect form for *should not* or *ought not*

> The men *ought* (not *had ought*) to go to the game now.

> He *ought not* (not *hadn't ought*) to have spoken.

> He *should not* (not *hadn't ought*) have spoken.

hanged is used in reference to a *person*

hung is used in reference to a *thing*

> The prisoner was *hanged* in the town square.

> The drapes were *hung* unevenly.

have got is incorrect usage; *got* should be omitted

> I *have* an umbrella.

healthful is used to express whatever *gives* health

healthy is used to express whatever *has* health

> He follows a *healthful* diet.

> He is a *healthy* person.

hisself is a misspelling of *himself*

> Let him do it *himself.*

humans is used informally to refer to human beings, but in formal usage *human beings* is correct

> He says that love is a basic need of all *human beings*. (But, used as an adjective: He says that love is a basic *human* need.)

if introduces a *condition*

whether introduces a *choice*

> I shall go to Greece *if* I win the prize.

> He asked me *whether* I intended to go to Greece.

if it was implies that *something might have been true in the past*

if it were implies *doubt* or indicates *something that is contrary to fact*

> If your book *was* there last night, it is there now.

> *If it were* summer now, we would all go swimming.

imply means *to suggest* or *hint* at (the speaker *implies*)

infer means *to deduce* or *conclude* (the listener *infers*)

> Are you *implying* that I have disobeyed orders?

> From your carefree tone, what else are we *to infer?*

in back of means *behind*

in the back of (or *at the back of*) means *in the rear of*

> The shovel is *in back of* (behind) the barn.

> John is sitting *in the back of* the theater.

in regards to is an incorrect form for *in regard to*

> He called me *in regard to* your letter.

instance where is sometimes used informally, but the correct term is *instance in which*

> Can you tell me of one *instance in which* such a terrible thing occurred?

irregardless in an incorrect form for *regardless*

> I'll be your friend *regardless* of what people say, even if the people are accurate.

is when and ***is where*** are sometimes used informally, but in formal usage *occurs when* and *is a place where* are correct

> The best scene *occurs when* the audience least expects it.

> My favorite vacation spot *is a place where* there are no telephones.

kind of and ***sort of*** are informal expressions that should be rephrased in formal writing—for instance, *somewhat* or *rather* are preferable

> I am *rather* sorry he retired.

> He was *somewhat* late for the meeting.

kid is used informally to mean *child* (noun) or *to make fun of* (verb), but is incorrect in formal usage

> My cousin is a very sweet *child*.

> They always laugh when you *make fun of me*.

Master the New SAT®

learn means *to acquire knowledge*

teach means *to give knowledge*

> We can *learn* many things just by observing carefully.

> He is one actor who likes to *teach* his craft to others.

least means the *smallest in degree* or *lowest rank*

less means the *smaller* or *lower of two*

> This is the *least* desirable of all the apartments we have seen.

> This apartment is *less* spacious than the one we saw yesterday.

leave means *to go away from* (a verb is NOT used with *leave*)

let means *to permit* (a verb IS used with *let*)

> *Leave* this house at once.

> *Let* me remain in peace in my own house.

lend is a verb meaning *to give to*

loan is a noun denoting *what is given*

borrow means *to take from*

> The bank was willing to *lend* him $500.

> He was granted a *loan* of $500.

> I'd like to *borrow* your electric drill for an hour.

liable means *responsible according to the law*

likely suggests *probable behavior*

> If he falls down the stairs, we may be *liable* for damages.

> A cat, if annoyed, is *likely* to scratch.

libel is a *written and published statement injurious to a person's character*

slander is a *spoken statement of the same sort*

> The unsubstantiated negative comments about me in your book constitute *libel*.

> When you say these vicious things about me, you are committing *slander*.

like is a preposition used to introduce a phrase

as if is used to introduce a clause (a subject and a verb)

as is a conjunction used to introduce a clause

like if is an incorrect form for *like, as,* or *as if*

> It seems *like* a sunny day.

> It seems *as if* it is going to be a sunny day.

> He acted *as* he was expected to act.

many refers to a *number*

much refers to a *quantity* or *amount*

How *many* inches of rain fell last night?

Much rain fell last night.

may of is an incorrect form for *may have*

might of is an incorrect form for *might have*

Note:

Contractions of these terms are unacceptable in formal usage.

He *may have* been there, but I didn't see him.

I *might have* gone to the party if I hadn't been ill.

Skill Builder: Usage

Directions: Circle the correct word to complete the sentence while adhering to formal, American-English conventions.

1. As of 2012, the median annual wage for nonfarm animal caretakers is (less, fewer) than $20,000.

2. During the interrogation, the lawyer (flaunted, flouted) his authority as he questioned the accused thief.

3. In addition to being patient with animals, animal caretakers must also work (good, well) with people!

4. She is one of 2,200 people to (graduate, graduate from) the National Association of Professional Pet Sitters' certification program.

5. While in captivity, many animals develop nervous (customs, habits) such as pacing and over-grooming.

6. While it is usually not required, animal caretakers in shelters (ought, had ought) to attend training programs through the Humane Society of the United States and the American Humane Association.

7. Keepers in zoos plan diets, monitor eating patterns, and clean enclosures in order to maintain (healthful, healthy) animals.

8. Often, the difference between the needs of animals and (human beings, humans) is not as much as you think.

9. (Irregardless, Regardless) of one's education, the number one trait an animal trainer must have is a love for animals.

10. While it does happen, it is (rather, sort of) rare for a groom to be hired who does not have significant prior experience with horses.

11. Animal trainers take good care of their animals because when animals are neglected, they are more (liable, likely) to become aggressive and dangerous.

Answers

1. less
2. flaunted, flouted
3. well
4. graduate from
5. habits
6. ought
7. healthy
8. human beings
9. Regardless
10. rather
11. likely

Frequently Confused Words: Group 5

maybe means *perhaps, possibly* (adverb)

may be shows *possibility* (verb)

> *Maybe* he will meet us later.

> He *may be* here later.

mighty means *powerful* or *great;* it should not be used in formal writing to mean *very*

> He was *very* (not *mighty*) sleepy.

media is the Latin plural of *medium*; it refers to a means of mass communication or artistic expression and is used with a plural verb

> Most *media* that report the news realize their responsibility to the public.

> That artist's favorite *medium* is watercolor.

must of is incorrect form for *must have*

> I *must have* been sleeping when you called. (A contraction of this term is unacceptable in formal usage.)

myself is used as an *intensifier* if the subject of the verb is *I*

myself instead of *I* or *me*, is not correct

> Since I know *myself* better, let me try it my way.

> My daughter and *I* (not *myself*) will play.

> They gave my son and *me* (not *myself*) some food.

nice is used informally to mean *pleasing, good, fine,* but a more exact, less overused word is preferred

    This is *sunny* (or *good* or *fine*) weather (not *nice* weather).

    He is a *good* (or *kind*) person.

nowheres is incorrect usage for *nowhere*

    The dog was *nowhere* to be found.

off of is sometimes used informally, but *off* is correct in formal usage

    Joe was taken *off* the team.

okay (O.K.) is used informally but is to be avoided in formal writing

    Informal: His work is *okay.*

    Formal: His work is *acceptable* (or *good*).

on account of is an incorrect form for *because*

    We could not meet you *because* we did not receive your message in time.

oral means *spoken*

verbal means *expressed in words,* either spoken or written

    Instead of writing a note, she gave him an *oral* message.

    Shorthand must usually be transcribed into *verbal* form.

outdoor is an adjective

outdoors is an adverb

    We spent the summer at an *outdoor* music camp.

    We played string quartets *outdoors.*

owing to is used informally, but in formal usage *because* is preferred

    Because of a change of management, his company canceled the takeover attempt.

people comprise a *united or collective group of individuals*

persons are *individuals that are separate and unrelated*

    The *people* of our city will vote next week.

    Only ten *persons* remained in the theater after the first act.

per is a Latin term used mainly in business: *per diem* (by the day), *per hour* (by the hour). In formal writing, *according to* or *by the* is preferred

    As *per* your instructions... (Better: *According* to your instructions...)

plan on is used informally, but in formal usage *plan to* is correct

    Do you *plan to go* (not *plan on going*) to the lecture?

plenty means *abundance* (noun)

plenty is incorrect as an adverb or adjective

> There is *plenty* of room in that compact car.

> That compact car is *very* large (not *plenty* large).

prefer that than is the incorrect form for *prefer that to*

> I *prefer that to* anything else you might suggest.

put in is incorrect for to *spend, make,* or *devote*

> Every good student should *spend* (not *put in*) several hours a day doing homework.

> Be sure *to make* (not *put in*) an appearance at the meeting.

quit is sometimes used informally to mean *stop,* but in formal usage *stop* is preferred

> Please *stop* your complaining.

quite is used to mean *very* in informal usage, but in formal usage *very* is preferred

> Your comment was *very* (not *quite*) intelligent.

quite a few is used to mean *many* in informal usage, but in formal usage *many* is preferred

> My car has *many* (not *quite a few*) dents.

read where is heard in informal usage, but in formal usage *read that* is correct

> I *read that* the troops were being reviewed today.

real is sometimes used informally instead of *really* or *very,* but in formal usage *really* is correct

> He's a *very* (not *real*) good ballplayer.

> He plays *really* (not *real*) well with the band.

reason is because is used informally in speech, but in formal usage *the reason is that* is correct

> The *reason* she calls *is that* (not *because*) she is lonely. (Or: She calls *because* she is lonely.)

refer back/report back: since *re* means *back* or *again,* the word *back* is redundant and should be omitted

> Please *refer* to your notes.

> Please *report* to the supervisor.

repeat again is redundant; *again* should be omitted

> Please *repeat* the instructions.

respectfully means *with respect and decency*

respectively means *as relating to each, in the order given*

> The students listened *respectfully* to the principal.

> Jane and Lena are the daughters *respectively* of Mrs. Smith and Mrs. Jones.

run is used informally to mean *conduct, manage,* but in formal usage *conduct* or a similar word is preferred

> He wants to *conduct* (not *run*) the operation on a profitable basis.

said is sometimes used in business or law to mean *the* or *this*; in formal usage, *the* or *this* is correct

said is also used incorrectly to mean *told someone*

> When *the* (not *said*) coat was returned, it was badly torn.

> The professor *told us* (not *said*) to study for the examination.

same as is an incorrect form for *in the same way as* or *just as*

> The owner's son was treated *in the same way as* any other worker.

says is present tense of *say*

said is past tense of *say*

> He *says* what he means.

> He *said* what he meant. (*Goes* or *went* should not be used instead of *says* or *said.*)

Skill Builder: Usage

Directions: Circle the correct word to complete the sentence while adhering to formal, American-English conventions.

1. If you are interested in the social and organizational side of businesses, the field of organizational psychology (may be, maybe) the field for you.

2. As the economy continues to grow and more businesses are created, organizational psychology is becoming a (mighty, very) important field.

3. (Because of, On account of) their collaborative work social workers and healthcare professionals, demand for psychologists is expected to increase in tandem with the healthcare industry overall.

4. (Nowhere, Nowheres) is the demand for psychologists growing more than in the field of organization psychology.

5. Because of the importance of talking with patients, clinical psychologists are expected to have good (oral, verbal) communication skills.

6. Psychologists typically work in offices, so if you prefer working (outdoor, outdoors), this might not be the job for you.

7. Over the next decade, the job market for psychologists will continue to grow in large part (because of, owing to) increased demand for psychological services in schools, hospitals, mental health centers, and social services agencies.

8. Most (people, persons) don't realize that there is a difference between a Ph.D. in psychology (a research degree), and a Psy.D. (a clinical degree).

9. While a master's degree is sufficient for some positions, most aspiring psychologists (plan on getting, plan to get) a Ph.D. or a Psy.D.

10. In addition to formal schooling, most clinical psychologists (put in, spend) hundreds of unpaid hours as interns in their fields of specialization.

11. The reason most aspiring psychologists get Ph.D.'s and Psy.D.'s is (because, that) there are more jobs available for psychologists with terminal degrees.

Answers

1. may be
2. very
3. Because of
4. Nowhere
5. oral
6. outdoors
7. because of
8. people
9. plan to get
10. spend
11. that

Frequently Confused Words: Group 6

saw is the past tense of *see*

seen is the past participle of *see*

> We *saw* a play yesterday.

> I have never *seen* a Broadway show.

seem is used in informal speech and writing in the expressions *I couldn't seem to* and *I don't seem to,* but in formal usage:

> We *can't find* the address. (Not: We *can't seem to find* the address.)

seldom ever is used informally, but in formal usage *ever* is redundant and should be omitted, or *if* should be inserted

> I *seldom* swim in January.

> I *seldom if ever* swim in January.

shall is used with *I* and *we* in formal usage; informally, I *will (would)* may be used

will is used with *you, he, she, it, they*

> When an emphatic statement is intended, the rule is reversed

> I *shall* be there today.

> We *shall* pay the rent tomorrow.

> I certainly *will* be there.

> They *shall* not pass.

shape is incorrect when used to mean *state* or *condition*

> The refugees were in *serious condition* (not *shape*) when they arrived here.

should of is an incorrect form for *should have,* which can be contracted to *should've* in speech or informal writing

> You *should've* returned that sweater. (Better: You *should have* returned that sweater.)

sink down is sometimes heard in informal usage, but *down* is redundant and should be omitted

> You can *sink* into the mud if you are not careful.

some time means *a segment of time*

sometime means *at an indefinite time in the future*

sometimes means *occasionally*

> I'll need *some time* to make a decision.

> Let's meet *sometime* next week.

> *Sometimes* I have an urge to watch a late movie on television.

stayed means *remained*

stood means *took or remained in an upright position* or *erect*

> He *stayed* in bed for three days.

> The scouts *stood* at attention while the flag was lowered.

still more yet is redundant; *yet* should be omitted

> There is *still more* to be said.

sure is used informally to mean *surely* or *certainly,* but in formal usage *surely* or *certainly* is preferred

> She *certainly* (not *sure)* is pretty!

> We will *surely* be in trouble unless we get home soon.

testimony means *information given orally*

evidence means *information given orally or in writing; an object* that is presented as proof

> He gave *testimony* to the grand jury.

> He presented written *evidence* to the judge.

than any is used informally in a comparison, but in formal usage *than any other* is preferred

> He is smarter *than any other* boy in the class.

the both is used informally, but in formal usage *the* should be omitted

> I intend to treat *both* of you to lunch.

their, in informal usage, often appears in the construction, "Anyone can lose their card," but since *anyone* takes a singular personal pronoun, *his* or *her* is the correct form

theirselves is an incorrect form for *themselves*

> They are able to care for *themselves* while their parents are at work.

them is the objective case of *they;* it is not used instead of *those* (the plural of *that*) before a noun

> Give me *those* (not *them*) books!

try and is sometimes used informally instead of *try to,* but in formal usage *try to* is correct

> My acting teacher is going to *try to* attend the opening of my play.

unbeknownst to is unacceptable for *without the knowledge of*

> The young couple decided to get married *without the knowledge of* (not *unbeknownst to*) their parents.

upwards of is an incorrect form for *more than*

> There are *more than* (not *upwards of*) 60,000 people at the football game.

valuable means *of great worth*

valued means *held in high regard*

invaluable means *priceless*

> This is a *valuable* manuscript.
>
> You are a *valued* friend.
>
> A good name is an *invaluable* possession.

wait on is sometimes used informally, but in formal usage *wait for* is correct

> We *waited for* (not *on)* him for over an hour.

which is sometimes used incorrectly to refer to people; it refers to things

who is used to refer to people

that is used to refer to people or things

> He decided to wear his orange striped tie, *which* had been a gift from his daughter.
>
> I am looking for the girl *who* made the call.
>
> He finally returned the books *that* he had borrowed.

while is unacceptable for *and, but, whereas,* or *though*

> The library is situated on the south side, *whereas* (not *while*) the laboratory is on the north side.
>
> *Though* (not *while*) I disagree with you, I shall not interfere with your right to express your opinion.

who is, *who am* is used with these constructions:

> It is *I* who *am* the most experienced.

> It is *he* who *is*...

> It is *he or I* who *am*...

> It is *I or he* who *is*...

> It is *he and I* who *are*...

who, whom is used to determine whether to use *who* or *whom* (without grammar rules): *(Who, Whom) do you think should represent our company?*

> Step 1: Change the *who—whom* part of the sentence to its natural order:

> Do you think *(who, whom)* should represent our company?

> Step 2: Substitute *he* for *who*, and *him* for *whom:*

> Do you think *(he, him)* should represent our company?

> Step 3: Since *he* would be used in this case, the correct form is:

> *Who* do you think should represent our company?

whoever, whomever (see *who, whom* above)

> Give the chair to *whoever* wants it (subject of verb *wants*).

> Speak to *whomever* you see (object of preposition *to*).

win is used when you *win* a game

beat is used when you *beat* another player; *beat* is incorrect usage for swindle

> We *won* the contest.

> We *beat* (not *won*) the other team.

> The hustler *swindled* the gambler out of twenty dollars.

without is incorrect usage for *unless*

> You will not receive the tickets *unless* (not *without*) you pay for them in advance.

worst kind and *worst way* are incorrect usages for terms such as *very badly* or *extremely*

> The school is *greatly in need* of more teachers (not *needs teachers in the worst way*).

would of is an incorrect form for *would have,* which can be contracted to *would've* in informal usage

> He *would've* treated you to the movies. (Better: He *would have* treated you to the movies.)

would have is *not* used instead of *had* in an *if* clause

> If I *had* (not *would have*) gone, I would have helped him.

Skill Builder: Usage

Directions: Circle the correct word to complete the sentence while adhering to formal, American-English conventions.

1. In Sir Arthur Conan Doyle's story, "A Scandal in Bohemia," Sherlock Holmes (can't believe, can't seem to believe) that he's been outsmarted by the beautiful and alluring Irene Adler.

2. Forest conservation workers are (seldom, seldom ever) required to have education beyond basic bachelor's degree.

3. According to his fictional biography, Sherlock Holmes's friend, John H. Watson, returns to England in serious (condition, shape) after being wounded in the Second Anglo-Afghan War.

4. (Some time, Sometime) in the near future, the U.S. Forest Service may be forced to undertake its own fire suppression duties, which will result in higher levels of employment.

5. At the end of all Sherlock Holmes stories, Holmes presents (evidence, testimony) that shows how a crime was committed and who it was committed by.

6. According to some scholars, Sherlock Holmes is more recognizable (than any, than any other) fictional detective in the world.

7. The complexity of the Tube, Britain's underground railway system, makes it possible for anyone to lose (his or her, their) way.

8. In the event that they get lost, forest services workers need to be able to take care of (theirselves, themselves) in the wild.

9. If formal schooling is unavailable, aspiring forest and conservation services workers should (try and, try to) gain experience working in forestry related fields.

10. As of 2012, there were (more than, upwards of) 10,000 jobs in the forest and conservation services field.

Answers

1. can't believe
2. seldom
3. condition
4. Some time
5. evidence
6. than any other
7. his or her
8. themselves
9. try to
10. more than

Conventional Expressions

A conventional expression is a phrase or clause that has become a characteristic way of expressing a certain idea. Ironically, despite these expressions being conventional, they are often misused.

Here is a list of commonly misused conventional expressions and their correct usages.

Incorrect Usage	Correct Usage
It's a doggy-dog world	It's a dog-eat-dog world
For all intensive purposes	For all intents and purposes
I'm *suppose to* go running	...supposed to...
statue of limitations	statute of limitations
I could care less	I couldn't care less
Fall by the waste side	Fall by the wayside
Irregardless	Regardless
Escape goat	Scapegoat
I guess we'll *make due*	...make do...
Peak my interest	Pique my interest
The criminal got away *scott free*	...scot free...
I'm waiting with *baited breath*	...bated breath...
Without further adieu	Without further ado
The boy had *free reign*	...free rein...
Hunger pains	Hunger pangs
I *should of* called	...should have...
Don't *step foot* on this carpet	...set foot...
Nipped in the butt	Nipped in the bud
The waiter was at his *beckon call*	...beck and call...
The lawyer made a *mute point*	...moot point...
Case and point	Case in point
The cops were starting to *hone in*	...home in...
One in the same	One and the same

Logical Comparison

Basic Rule

In order for a comparison to make sense, it must be logical and complete.

In an incomplete comparison, what is being compared is unclear.

Incomplete: According to some scholars of U.S. history, the Magna Carta is more important because it was the first document to limit the powers of the King of England.

Complete: According to some scholars of U.S. history, the Magna Carta is more important than the Declaration of Independence because it was the first document to limit the powers of the King of England.

Incomplete: At 864,000 miles across, the Sun is more than 100 times the size.

Complete: At 864,000 miles across, the Sun is more than 100 times the size of Earth.

For a comparison to be logical, you must be comparing the same things.

Illogical: Despite popular opinion, many scholars believe that the political achievements of Thomas Jefferson were much more significant to American history than George Washington. (Thomas Jefferson's achievements are being compared to the person George Washington.)

Logical: Despite popular opinion, many scholars believe that the political achievements of Thomas Jefferson were much more significant to American history than the achievements of George Washington.

Illogical: The distance from the Sun to the planet Neptune is 30 times greater than the Sun and Earth. (This distance from the Sun to Neptune is being compared to the Sun and Earth, not the distance between them.)

Logical: The distance from the Sun to the planet Neptune is 30 times greater than the distance from the Sun to Earth.

Skill Builder: Logical Comparisons

Directions: Revise the following comparisons to make sure they are logical.

1. According to scientists, the brain mass of a dolphin is actually slightly greater than a human.

2. Although they are on the same hemisphere, the average rainfall in South America differs greatly from North America.

3. In the 2015 World Happiness Report, the people of Switzerland ranked happier than America.

4. The tallest mountain in the United States is still 9,000 feet shorter than Nepal.

Answers

1. According to scientists, the brain mass of a dolphin is actually slightly greater than the brain mass of a human.

2. Although they are on the same hemisphere, the average rainfall in South America differs greatly from the average rainfall in North America.

3. In the 2015 World Happiness Report, the people of Switzerland ranked happier than the people of America.

4. The tallest mountain in the United States is still 9,000 feet shorter than the tallest mountain in Nepal.

CONVENTIONS OF PUNCTUATION

End-of-Sentence Punctuation

There are three types of punctuation used to end a sentence: the period, the question mark, and the exclamation mark.

1 A period is used at the end of a sentence that makes a statement.

> *Examples:* Toni Morrison's first novel, *The Bluest Eye,* was published in 1970.
>
> In 1620, the Pilgrims in Plymouth signed the Mayflower Compact.

2 A question mark is used after a direct question. A period is used after an indirect question.

> *Examples: Direct Question*—Were the Federalist Papers written by James Madison, John Jay, or Alexander Hamilton?
>
> *Indirect Question*—Profession Mahin wanted to know if you knew who wrote the Federalist Papers.

3 An exclamation mark is used after an expression that shows strong emotion or issues a command. It may follow a word, a phrase, or a sentence.

> *Examples:* Koko the gorilla knows more than 1,000 sign-language signs and can communicate with humans. Amazing!
>
> One of the most famous quote in American history is Patrick Henry's, "Give me liberty or give me death!"

Within-Sentence Punctuation

The Colon

Basic Rule

The colon is used to precede a list of three or more items or a long quotation.

Examples:

> Christopher Columbus led three ships to the New World: La Nina, La Pinta, and La Santa Maria.
>
> In the United States, there are three branches of government: the Executive, the Legislative, and the Judicial.

Caution

Avoid using the colon after a verb. It can interrupt the natural flow of language.

Incorrect: The Louisiana Purchase included territory that would become: Montana, South Dakota, Nebraska, Kansas, Oklahoma, Arkansas, Louisiana, and Missouri.

Correct: The Louisiana Purchase included territory that would become many of today's states: Montana, South Dakota, Nebraska, Kansas, Oklahoma, Arkansas, Louisiana, and Missouri.

The Semicolon

> **Basic Rule**

A semicolon may be used to separate two complete ideas (independent clauses) in a sentence when the two ideas have a close relationship and they are *not* connected with a coordinating conjunction.

Example: "Inalienable rights" are basic human rights that many believe cannot and should not be given up or taken away; life, liberty, and the pursuit of happiness are some of those rights.

The semicolon is often used between independent clauses connected by conjunctive adverbs such as *consequently, therefore, also, furthermore, for example, however, nevertheless, still, yet, moreover,* and *otherwise.*

Example: In 1783, critics thought William H. Seward foolish for buying the largely unexplored territory of Alaska for the astronomical price of $7 million; however, history has proven that it was an inspired purchase.

> **Caution**

Do not use the semicolon between an independent clause and a phrase or subordinate clause.

Skill Builder: Punctuation

Directions: Decide whether the colons and semicolons are correctly placed in the following sentences or whether another mark of punctuation would be better. Write the correct punctuation on the line provided.

1. He is an excellent student and a fine person; as a result, he has many friends.

2. Because he is such an industrious student; he has many friends.

3. We tried our best to purchase the books; but we were unsuccessful.

4. The students were required to pass the following exit tests: English, science, math, and social studies.

5. The rebuilt vacuum cleaner was in excellent condition; saving us a good deal of expense since we didn't have to purchase a new one.

6. Marie has a very soft voice; however, it is clear and distinct.

7. Don't open the door; the floor is still wet.

8. Don't open the door; because the floor is still wet.

9. To the campers from the city, every noise in the night sounded like a bear: a huge, ferocious, meat-eating bear.

10. We worked for three days painting the house; nevertheless, we still needed more time to complete the job.

11. The telephone rang several times, as a result; his sleep was interrupted.

12. Peter was chosen recently to be vice president of the business; and will take over his duties in a few days.

Answers

1. Correct.
2. Substitute a comma for the semicolon.
3. Substitute a comma for the semicolon.
4. Correct.
5. Substitute a comma for the semicolon.
6. Correct.
7. Correct.
8. Delete the semicolon.
9. Substitute a comma for the colon.
10. Correct.
11. The telephone rang several times; as a result, his sleep was interrupted. (Note the two punctuation changes. The semicolon is placed in front of the conjunctive adverb and the comma after it.)
12. Delete the semicolon; no punctuation is necessary in its place.

The Em-Dash

Basic Rule

Em-dashes are used to set off parenthetical material that you want to emphasize.

Example: Benjamin Franklin's many intellectual pursuits—from printmaking to politics—exemplify his eclectic personality.

Em-dashes can also be used when you are renaming a nearby noun. Typically, you would use a comma to set this clause off, but since it includes commas already, you use an em-dash.

Example: Benjamin Franklin—a printer, writer, inventor, and statesman—was the son of a soap maker.

An em- dash also indicates a list, a restatement, an amplification, or a dramatic shift in tone or thought.

Example: Eager to write for his brother's newspaper, young Benjamin began submitting letters to the editor under the pseudonym, Silence Dogood—they were a hit!

Skill Builder: Punctuation

Directions: Revise the following sentences to eliminate end-of-sentence and within-sentence punctuation errors.

1. Architects design houses, office buildings, and other structures!

2. On any given day, architects might perform the following tasks; prepare structural specifications; meet with clients to determine objectives and structural requirements; direct workers to prepare drawings and documents.

3. Architects are responsible for designing the places where we live: work: play: learn: shop: and eat?

4. Architects design both indoor and outdoor spaces on both public and private projects.

5. Architects often provide various predesign services: from environmental impact studies to cost analyses: depending on a project's needs.

6. For actual blueprints, traditional paper and pencil drafting has been replaced by computer-aided design and drafting (CADD): however, hand-drawing skills are still important during the conceptual stages of a project.

7. Did you know that BIM stands for business information modeling.

8. Architects often collaborate with workers in related fields; civil engineers, urban planners, interior designers, and landscape architects.

9. In addition to years of schooling, being a good architect requires a mix of artistic talent and mathematical ability: it's not easy!

10. The path to becoming an architect requires a college education: a five-year Bachelor of Architecture degree program is typical.

Answers

1. Architects design houses, office buildings, and other structures.

2. On any given day, architects might perform the following tasks: prepare structural specifications; meet with clients to determine objectives and structural requirements; and direct workers to prepare drawings and documents.

3. Architects are responsible for designing the places where we live, work, play, learn, shop, and eat.

4. Architects design both indoor and outdoor spaces on both public and private projects.

5. Architects often provide various predesign services—from environmental impact studies to cost analyses—depending on a project's needs.

6. For actual blueprints, traditional paper and pencil drafting has been replaced by computer-aided design and drafting (CADD); however, hand-drawing skills are still important during the conceptual stages of a project.

7. Did you know that BIM stands for business information modeling?

8. Architects often collaborate with workers in related fields: civil engineers, urban planners, interior designers, and landscape architects.

9. In addition to years of schooling, being a good architect requires a mix of artistic talent and mathematical ability—it's not easy!

10. The path to becoming an architect requires a college education; a five-year Bachelor of Architecture degree program is typical.

Possessive Nouns

The Apostrophe

The apostrophe is usually either misused or omitted because of the writer's failure to proofread his paper or because he is not certain about its use. The apostrophe is used in the following situations:

- To indicate the possessive case *of nouns*. It is not used with possessive pronouns, since such pronouns as *yours, hers, our, theirs*, and *whose* indicate possession already.

- To indicate a *contraction*—the omission of one or more letters.

- To indicate *plurals* of letters, abbreviations, and numbers.

To form the possessive of a noun: If the noun does not end in *s*—whether singular or plural—add an *'s*; if the noun ends in *s* simply add the *'*. Some writers like to add *'s* to all nouns, even those that already end in *s*.

Examples:

The impact of Allen Ginsberg's poem "Howl" on the cultural landscape of the United States cannot be overstated.

A car's headlights are typically wired in parallel so that if one burns out the other will keep functioning.

John Coltrane's skill as a jazz musician is widely recognized.

To form a contraction: Place the apostrophe exactly where the missing letters occur.

Examples: can't = can not

it's = it is

we're = we are

To form plurals of letters, abbreviations, and numbers: Usually the apostrophe is used to form the plurals of lowercase letters (a's, b's, c's, and so on), plurals of abbreviations with periods (Ph.D.'s, R.N.'s), and numbers (3's, 6's). With capital letters, abbreviations without periods, and even with numbers when no confusion results, you have a choice. In either case, the writer should be consistent in his or her style.

Skill Builder: Apostrophe Use

Directions: Revise the following sentences to correct any apostrophe errors.

1. Poet William <u>Wordsworths</u> most famous work is *The Prelude*, which was published in 1850.

2. <u>Its</u> how Wordsworth uses the language of the "common man" that strikes most <u>readers</u>.

3. While most of his <u>poems</u> are considered classics, *The Prelude* stands as one of the crowning <u>achievements</u> of British Romanticism.

4. <u>Wordsworths</u> poem, *The Prelude* was published three <u>months</u> after his death by his wife Mary.

5. <u>Sonnet 18s</u> theme revolves around the idea of expressing <u>ones</u> self through language.

6. From 2008 to 2010, there were approximately 2.9 million <u>R.N.s</u> and 690,000 <u>L.P.N.s</u> working or seeking employment in the nursing workforce.

7. The number of <u>R.N.s</u> in the nursing workforce grew substantially in the <u>2000s</u> by over 24 percent.

Answers

1. Poet William <u>Wordsworth's</u> most famous work is *The Prelude*, which was published in 1850.

2. <u>It's</u> how Wordsworth uses the language of the "common man" that strikes most <u>readers</u>.

3. While most of his <u>poems</u> are considered classics, *The Prelude* stands as one of the crowning <u>achievements</u> of British Romanticism.

4. <u>Wordsworth's</u> poem, *The Prelude* was published three <u>months</u> after his death by his wife Mary.

5. <u>Sonnet 18's</u> theme revolves around the idea of expressing <u>one's</u> self through language.

6. From 2008 to 2010, there were approximately 2.9 million <u>R.N.'s</u> and 690,000 <u>L.P.N.'s</u> working or seeking employment in the nursing workforce.

7. The number of <u>R.N.s</u> in the nursing workforce grew substantially in the <u>2000s</u> by over 24 percent.

Skill Builder: Apostrophe Use

Directions: Circle the word with the correct spelling in the following sentences.

1. According to (statistics, statistic's), 55 percent of the nursing workforce holds a (bachelors, bachelor's) degree or higher.

2. Over the past decade, the average age of (nurses, nurse's) has increased by almost two years for (RNs, RN's) and 1.75 years for (LPNs, LPN's).

3. According to the Board of Registered (Nurse's, Nurses') list of (regulations, regulation's), registered (nurses, nurse's) must have a high school diploma, appropriate pre-licensure schooling, and required certification.

4. Despite teaching similar (skills, skill's), one nursing (program, program's) (requirements, requirement's) can be very different than another (programs, program's) (requirements, requirement's).

5. Many future (RNs, RN's) attend the following types of pre-licensure degree (programs, program's): Associate Degree in Nursing (ADN); Bachelor of Science in Nursing (BSN); Entry Level Masters Program in Nursing (ELM).

6. Based on recent (studies, studies'), an (RNs, RN's) salary is about $50,000 a year.

Answers

1. statistics; bachelor's

2. nurses; RNs; LPNs

3. Nurses'; regulations; nurses

4. skills; program's; requirements; program's; requirements

5. RNs; programs

6. studies; RN's

Items in a Series

Basic Rule

Use a comma between items in a series when three or more items are present. Items can be expressed as words, phrases, or clauses.

Example: The following wildlife biologists study animals based on where they live: limnologists, marine biologists, and terrestrial biologists.

When the items themselves contain commas, use a semi-colon to separate them.

Example: Some kinds of biologists study specific species of animals. For example, cetologists study marine mammals, such as whales and dolphins; entomologists study insects, such as beetles and butterflies; and ichthyologists study wild fish, such as sharks and lungfish.

Skill Builder: Items in a Series

Directions: Revise the following sentences to make sure they are correctly punctuating items in a series.

1. A typical architectural program includes courses on such topics as architectural history, building design, computer-aided design, and math.

2. Architects must possess certain qualities: analytical skills, in order to understand the content of designs, communication skills, in order to communicate with clients, creativity, in order to develop attractive and functional structures, and organizational skills, in order to keep track of big projects.

3. In order to get hired as an architect, you typically need to: complete a professional degree in architecture: gain relevant experience through a paid internship: and pass the Architect Registration Exam.

4. Because of growing concerns about the environment, today's architects need to understand sustainable design, which emphasizes the efficient use of resources, such as energy and water conservation, waste and pollution reduction, and environmentally friendly design, specifications, and materials.

5. In addition to structural plans architects often provide drawings of the air-conditioning heating and ventilating systems electrical systems communications systems plumbing and possibly site and landscape plans.

Answers

1. *No corrections are needed. The sentence read fine as:* A typical architectural program includes courses on such topics as architectural history, building design, computer-aided design, and math.

2. Architects must possess certain qualities: analytical skills, in order to understand the content of designs; communication skills, in order to communicate with clients; creativity, in order to develop attractive and functional structures; and organizational skills, in order to keep track of big projects.

3. In order to get hired as an architect, you typically need to complete a professional degree in architecture, gain relevant experience through a paid internship, and pass the Architect Registration Exam.

4. Because of growing concerns about the environment, today's architects need to understand sustainable design, which emphasizes the efficient use of such resources as energy and water; waste and pollution reduction; and environmentally friendly specifications and materials.

5. In addition to structural plans, architects often provide drawings of the air-conditioning, heating, and ventilating systems; electrical systems; communications systems; plumbing; and possibly site and landscape plans.

Nonrestrictive and Parenthetical Elements

Basic Rule

Nonrestrictive and parenthetical elements provide extra information that is not essential to the meaning or grammatical correctness of a sentence. A nonrestrictive or parenthetical element can be removed from a sentence without making the sentence grammatically incorrect and without interfering with the rest of the sentence's meaning.

Parenthetical elements are identified by *commas*, *parentheses*, or *em-dashes*. While each of these punctuation marks serves a similar purpose, the difference between them is one of emphasis.

Commas indicate a slight interruption.

Example: Toni Morrison, who won the Nobel Prize in Literature in 1993, is a Professor Emeritus at Princeton University.

Parentheses are seen as "quieter" than commas and are reserved for asides that are less important and more tangential than those indicated by commas. They also allow the inclusion of material that doesn't have a specific grammatical connection to the rest of the sentence.

Example: Toni Morrison's novel *Beloved* (1987) explores the themes of love and the supernatural.

Example: While at Princeton, Toni Morrison (the writer) established a special creative workshop for writers and performances called the Princeton Atelier.

If parentheses are used for "quiet" asides, dashes are used when you want to call attention to something. Dashes interrupt the flow of your sentence, thereby calling attention to the information they contain.

Example: Toni Morrison—winner of both the Pulitzer and Nobel Prizes in Literature—is considered one of the greatest writers of her generation.

Skill Builder: Nonrestrictive and Parenthetical Elements

Directions: Select a comma, parentheses, or em-dash, to set off the underlined portion of each sentence.

1. Samuel Clemens <u>1835–1910</u> was born in Florida, Missouri, to John and Jane Clemens.

2. Mark Twain <u>whose given name was Samuel Clemens</u> was the sixth of seven children.

3. In 1861, Sam's dreams of becoming a steamboat pilot ended abruptly <u>the Civil War started</u>.

4. Sam's commitment to the Confederate cause was short-lived <u>he quit the army after just two weeks</u>.

5. Twain's "big break" came with the publication of his short story, "Jim Smiley and His Jumping Frog" <u>1865</u>, which was picked up by papers across the country.

6. After the success of his story, "Jim Smiley and His Jumping Frog," Clemens was hired by the Sacramento Union to visit and report on the Sandwich Islands <u>now Hawaii</u>.

7. Clemens' writings for the Sacramento Union were so popular that <u>upon his return</u> he was asked to undertake a lecture tour across the United States.

8. Like all good writers, Mark Twain <u>Samuel Clemens</u> spent his life observing and writing about life as he saw it, with all of its joys and horrors.

Answers

1. Samuel Clemens (1835–1910) was born in Florida, Missouri, to John and Jane Clemens.

2. Mark Twain, whose given name was Samuel Clemens, was the sixth of seven children. *(Em-dashes might also be acceptable here if the writer wished to emphasize the information.)*

3. In 1861, Sam's dreams of becoming a steamboat pilot ended abruptly—the Civil War started.

4. Sam's commitment to the Confederate cause was short-lived—he quit the army after just two weeks.

5. Twain's "big break" came with the publication of his short story, "Jim Smiley and His Jumping Frog" (1865), which was picked up by papers across the country.

6. After the success of his story, "Jim Smiley and His Jumping Frog," Clemens was hired by the Sacramento Union to visit and report on the Sandwich Islands (now Hawaii).

7. Clemens' writings for the Sacramento Union were so popular that, upon his return, he was asked to undertake a lecture tour across the United States.

8. Like all good writers, Mark Twain (Samuel Clemens) spent his life observing and writing about life as he saw it, with all of its joys and horrors.

The Comma

Basic Rule

In previous sections, we covered the way that commas are used to separate the following:

- Independent clauses that are connected by a coordinating conjunction
- Items in a series
- Nonrestrictive elements

In addition to these uses, commas have several other purposes:

- To set off introductory clauses and phrases.

  Example: The year after winning her Nobel Prize, Toni Morrison published the novel *Jazz*.

- To set off nouns that are being addressed directly.

  Example: Toni Morrison, the Nobel Prize committee commends you on your achievements and thanks you for your contribution to world literature.

- To separate the different parts of dates, addresses, and geographical names.

  Example: Toni Morrison was born on February 18, 1931, in Lorain, Ohio, to Ramah and George Wofford.

- To introduce a titles and quotations.

  Example: Toni Morrison began her lecture, "The Future of Time: Literature and Diminished Expectations," with the line, "Time, it seems, has no future."

- To separate contrasted elements or to indicate a distinct pause or shift.

  Examples: To her handlers, Koko the gorilla seemed thoughtful, almost human.

  You're one of the senator's close friends, aren't you?

- To separate coordinate adjectives that precede the noun they describe. Coordinate adjectives are of equal importance and related meaning.

  Examples: Toni Morrison is rumored to be a fun, entertaining speaker.

Caution

Note how the word *and* can be substituted for the comma. If you cannot substitute *and* without changing the meaning, the adjectives are not coordinate, and no comma is needed.

Example: Toni Morrison is a well-respected American writer.

Unnecessary Punctuation

Unnecessary punctuation can break a sentence into confusing and illogical fragments.

Here are some common mistakes to look out for.

- Don't use a comma to connect independent clauses. This is called a comma splice.

  Incorrect: Toni Morrison grew up in an integrated neighborhood, she did not become fully aware of racial divisions until she was in her teens.

  Possible revision: Toni Morrison grew up in an integrated neighborhood and did not become fully aware of racial divisions until she was in her teens.

TIP

While any punctuation mark can be misused, overused commas tend to be a common problem.

- Don't use a comma between compound elements that are not independent clauses.

   Incorrect: In 1998, Oprah Winfrey, and Danny Glover starred in a film adaptation of Morrison's novel, *Beloved*.

   Possible revision: In 1998, Oprah Winfrey and Danny Glover starred in a film adaptation of Morrison's novel, *Beloved*.

- Do not use an apostrophe when making a noun plural.

   Incorrect: In 2006, the *New York Times Book Review* named *Beloved* the best American novel published in the last 25 year's.

   Possible revision: In 2006, the *New York Times Book Review* named *Beloved* the best American novel published in the last 25 years.

Skill Builder: Commas and Unnecessary Punctuation

Directions: Revise the following sentences to correct errors, with special attention to unnecessary, misused, and missing punctuation marks. In some cases, there are multiple ways to fix these errors. Consider the answers a partial list of possible revisions.

1. The job of an art director is a creative one he or she is responsible for the visual style and images in magazines newspapers product packaging, and movie and television productions.

2. An art director's job includes creating the overall design of a project; and directing others who develop artwork and layouts.

3. People interested in becoming art director's often work as graphic designer's, illustrator's, copy editor's, or photographer's, or in some other art and design related occupation.

4. Some art directors work for advertising and public relations firms and others work in print media and entertainment.

5. In order to become an art director you typically need at least a bachelor's degree in an art or design subject, and previous work experience.

6. Art direction is a management position, that oversees the work of other designers and artists.

7. An art director might choose the overall style or tone, desired for a project, and communicate this vision to the artists he or she manages.

8. In the movie industry an art director might collaborate with a director; in order to determine the look and style of a movie.

9. As of 2012: art directors held about 74,800 jobs.

10. Even though the majority of art directors are self-employed they often work under pressure to meet strict deadlines.

Answers

1. The job of an art director is a creative one; he or she is responsible for the visual style and images in magazines, newspapers, product packaging, and movie and television productions.

2. An art director's job includes creating the overall design of a project and directing others who develop artwork and layouts.

3. People interested in becoming art directors often work as graphic designers, illustrators, copy editors, or photographers, or in some other art and design related occupation.

4. Some art directors work for advertising and public relations firms, and others work in print media and entertainment.

5. In order to become an art director, you typically need at least a bachelor's degree in an art or design subject and previous work experience.

6. Art direction is a management position that oversees the work of other designers and artists.

7. An art director might choose the overall style or tone desired for a project and communicate this vision to the artists he or she manages.

8. In the movie industry, an art director might collaborate with a director in order to determine the look and style of a movie.

9. As of 2012, art directors held about 74,800 jobs.

10. Even though the majority of art directors are self-employed, they often work under pressure to meet strict deadlines.

SUMMING IT UP

- The Standard English conventions reviewed in this lesson are keys to good writing. When you utilize proper sentence structure, grammar, and punctuation, your writing is stronger, clearer, and more focused. That is why using standard English conventions is important for both college writing and any writing you will do in your career.

- The SAT® Writing and Language Test is designed to test your mastery of Standard English conventions. On the test, you will read multiple passages that may cover careers, science, history, or the humanities. The questions will require you to read the passages and select the answers that improve the writing in the passage. The correct answer will be the one that best follows Standard English conventions.

PART V
THE NEW SAT® ESSAY

The Writing Process and the SAT® Essay

chapter 6

OVERVIEW

- **A closer look at the essay question**
- **Prewriting**
- **Writing the introduction**
- **Developing your ideas**
- **Writing the conclusion**
- **The scoring rubric for the SAT® essay**
- **Exercise: Practicing your essay skills**
- **Summing it up**

The Essay section of the SAT® is 50 minutes long. In this time, you need to read the essay prompt and plan and write your essay. It doesn't need to be—and isn't supposed to be—a final, polished version. The high school and college English teachers who will score your essay are trained to view the essays as first drafts. They will be assessing your essay and hundreds of others against a rubric that guides them to look at the essays holistically. They are reading for an overall general impression of your reading, writing, and analyzing skills. Later in this chapter you will analyze a rubric that is similar to the one the scorers will use.

A CLOSER LOOK AT THE ESSAY QUESTION

You will be given one essay prompt and asked to write an analytical essay in response. You won't have a choice of questions to answer. This is good because it saves you time, as you don't have to decide which one to choose. The essay section is made up of a prompt that directs you to read and analyze a high-quality source text. In this text, the author makes an argument or examines a current debate, idea, or trend.

Once you have closely read and analyzed the source text you can begin your planning. You don't need any specific subject-area knowledge to write your essay. The purpose of the essay is to demonstrate for the scorers that you can then analyze it in writing using your own critical reasoning and evidence drawn from the source text.

Pacing Your Writing

You want to use everything you've been taught in English class about the writing process—but sped up to fit within 50 minutes. Pacing yourself is important so that you are able to get your ideas down on paper in a complete, coherent, and unified essay. As you practice writing essays in this chapter and in the practice tests in this book, work out a pacing schedule for yourself. Begin by trying out the following timetable and see how it works for you. If necessary, adjust it as you practice, but be sure to give yourself enough time to finish a complete draft.

225

- Prewriting: 10 to 15 minutes
- Writing the introduction: 4 to 5 minutes
- Writing the body of the essay: 15 to 20 minutes
- Writing the conclusion: 3 to 4 minutes
- Revising: 3 to 5 minutes
- Proofing: 3 to 5 minutes

PREWRITING

Before you begin to write your analysis, read the prompt and the source text. Pay attention to the text author's key claims. Underline the author's key claims. Then circle or highlight evidence the author uses to support those claims. Finally, take notes on important stylistic features or persuasive techniques the author uses in the source text.

You want to spend about 10 to 15 minutes on prewriting, as this will give you time to carefully read the prompt and then read and analyze the source text. Your goals in this planning stage are:

- To identify and underline the author's key claims
- To find and then circle or highlight specific evidence the author uses to support his or her key claims
- To take notes on ways the author has used logic, reasoning, rhetoric (persuasive language techniques), and evidence to convince readers that his or her key claims are valid

Familiarizing Yourself with the Prompt and the Passage

The Essay prompt will not change much at all, no matter when and where you are taking the SAT®. This is great news because it means you can become very familiar and comfortable with the prompt before you take the test. The source text (passage) that accompanies the prompt *will* be new to you; however, it will share important qualities with other passages you will read and analyze as you prepare to write the SAT® Essay.

All passages

- come from high-quality, previously published sources.
- contain arguments written for a broad audience.
- examine ideas, opinions, views, debates, or trends.
- discuss topics in the arts, the sciences, or in civic, cultural, or political life.
- are interesting, relevant, and accessible to college-bound students at your grade level.
- tend NOT to consist of simple pro/con debates on issues.
- strive to convey nuanced views on complex subjects.
- use evidence, logical reasoning, and/or stylistic and persuasive elements.
- are similarly complex: all are challenging—but not *too* difficult—for readers at your grade level.
- do NOT require test-takers to possess prior knowledge on specific topics.

The prompt that introduces the passage will be identical or very similar to this:

> As you read the passage below, consider how [the author] uses the following:
>
> - Evidence, such as facts or examples, to support claims.
> - Reasoning to develop ideas and to connect claims and evidence.
> - Stylistic or persuasive elements, such as word choice or appeals to emotion, to add power to the ideas expressed.

After the passage, the prompt will continue as follows:

> Write an essay in which you explain how [the author] builds an argument to persuade [his/her] audience that [the author's claim is true or valid]. In your essay, analyze how [the author] uses one or more of the features listed above [see bullet points above] (or features of your own choice) to strengthen the logic and persuasiveness of [his/her] argument. Be sure that your analysis focuses on the most relevant aspects of the passage. Your essay should not explain whether you agree with [the author's] claims, but, rather, it should explain how the author builds an argument to persuade [his/her] audience.

It is vital that you read, reread, and thoroughly understand everything the prompt asks you to do. Pay particular attention to the bullet points that tell you exactly what to look for in the passage. Also note that the prompt gives you the option of mentioning other "features of your own choice." Finally, let's take a close look at the last sentence in the prompt (we have capitalized and underlined the word *not*):

> Your essay should <u>NOT</u> explain whether you agree with [the author's] claims, but rather explain how the author builds an argument to persuade [his/her] audience.

In other words, your task is *not* to present your own arguments—the passage author has already done that. Your task is to analyze the author's argument: "explain how the author builds an argument to persuade [his/her] audience."

The people who develop the SAT® believe that if you complete this essay-writing task, your work will exhibit three types of skills:

1. close reading skills
2. analyzing skills
3. writing skills

Organizing Your Essay

Decide how many paragraphs you need to write to develop your analysis of the passage. Remember that length is not a valid substitute for strength. Your answer booklet provides a certain number of pages for your essay. You can't write more than the lines provided, but you can write fewer. It is more important to do a good job of analyzing the passage than it is to fill up all the lines. However, an essay of five sentences won't earn you a high score.

A safe number of paragraphs is five. Use the first paragraph for the introduction and the last one for the conclusion. That gives you three paragraphs to develop your ideas. That doesn't mean that you can't write a fourth or even fifth paragraph in the body of your essay to develop your ideas. It's more important to have a tightly written and well-developed shorter essay than a longer, rambling, repetitious one that you didn't have time to revise or proofread. There is a limit to what you can write in 50 minutes. Use the opportunity that you have for practice in this book to work on your pacing and see how much you can plan and write well in 50 minutes.

WRITING THE INTRODUCTION

Now it's time to write. You've analyzed the prompt and the passage in your prewriting step and identified the author's key claims, use of evidence and reasoning, and stylistic or persuasive language features. Now begin writing your introduction.

In your introduction, it is important to introduce the source text to your reader. State the author's name and the title of the passage. Then give a brief summary of the author's key claim. Two to four sentences should accomplish these tasks.

As you practice writing essays in this book and as you write the real one on test day, keep the following five ideas in mind:

1. In writing your introduction, keep the key words and phrases of the prompt in mind.

2. Avoid being cute, funny, ironic, satiric, overly emotional, or too dramatic. Set the tone or attitude in your first sentence. You want to be sincere, clear, and straightforward.

3. Don't bother repeating the key claims from the source text word for word. A paraphrase in your own words is far better than just copying the words of the source text.

4. In your first paragraph, besides introducing the passage's author, title, topic, and the author's key claim about the topic, make it clear to your readers that you are about to analyze the passage and explain how the author accomplishes his or her persuasive purpose. This can be accomplished in a clear topic sentence.

5. Each sentence should advance your topic and be interesting to your reader.

Skill Builder: Topic Sentence

Directions: Which of the following is the best topic sentence?

1. I agree with the author that the use of motorized boats and watercraft should be limited in freshwater streams and lakes.

2. The author believes that the use of motorized boats and other watercraft should be limited in freshwater ecosystems in order to decrease pollution.

3. In this essay, I will examine the author's argument in favor of limiting the use of motorized boats and watercraft in freshwater streams and lakes.

4. The author introduces her argument with startling statistics on the negative effects of motorized watercraft on freshwater ecosystems; she then builds on those statistics with careful reasoning to reach the logical conclusion that we should limit the use of motorized watercraft in freshwater ecosystems.

Answers and Explanations

Sentence four is the best opening sentence since it states the topic clearly, limits the scope of the essay, and presents the key points of the analysis. Sentence four also implies that the essay writer will expand on these key points in the body of the essay.

Recognizing Effective Introductions

An *effective* introduction often refers to the subject of the essay, explains the value of the topic, or attracts the attention of the reader by giving a pertinent illustration. Ineffective beginnings often contain unrelated material, ramble, and lack clarity.

Skill Builder: Effective Introductions

Directions: Examine the following excerpts from five introductory paragraphs and decide whether each is effective or ineffective. Be able to defend your decision.

1. The pollution of freshwater streams and lakes has become a pretty big problem in the United States. Part of the problem is due to the unrestricted use of motorized boats and other stuff. I mostly agree with the author that something needs to be done about it, but I don't know that you should tell people where they can drive their boats.

2. Freshwater lakes and streams are popular recreational destinations for many Americans. These bodies of water are also the principal ecosystems of many different animals and plants. In her essay, "Bringing Fresh back to Freshwater Lakes and Streams," activist River Pura makes the claim that the unrestricted use of motorized watercraft is to blame for polluting these ecosystems.

3. River Pura makes a very persuasive argument to persuade her audience that motorized boats should be restricted in freshwater streams and lakes. She persuades her audience with some facts and emotional appeals.

4. The author makes an argument to persuade her audience about what she is thought about. It's pollution.

5. Pollution in freshwater ecosystems has been growing over the past decade. Author River Pura, in her essay titled "Bringing Fresh Back to Freshwater Streams and Lakes," claims that motorized watercraft are the primary source of that pollution. While Pura presents her readers with startling statistical information, her argument is anticlimactic and builds to no logical conclusion.

Answers and Explanations

1. *Ineffective.* This paragraph is focused on the topic of the source text, not on the author's writing. Although the prompt specifically says *not* to present opinions on the topic, the writer states that he or she "mostly agrees" with the passage author. Also, the writer uses vague, informal expressions: "pretty big" and "mostly agree."

2. *Effective.* This paragraph effectively introduces the author, the passage title, and the topic. The paragraph also identifies the author's key claim and begins to analyze the author's work.

3. *Ineffective.* While this paragraph identifies the author's key claim, nonspecific phrases like "some facts" and "emotional appeal" weaken the paragraph. Also, the writer uses three different forms of the word *persuade*, which sounds repetitious.

4. *Ineffective.* The paragraph does not introduce the author, the passage title, or the author's key claim. It does not explain that the writer is going to analyze the passage. The writing is poorly constructed and misuses verb tense.

5. *Effective.* This paragraph clearly introduces the source text, highlights the author's key claim, and explains how the passage author fails to build an effective argument.

DEVELOPING YOUR IDEAS

The heart of your essay is the development, or middle paragraphs. In these paragraphs, you must use explanations, details, and examples from the source text to support the main ideas in your essay. All the sentences in the development paragraphs must explain and support your analysis of the source text and must not digress.

In the limited time you have on the Essay section of the SAT®, you can take only 15 to 20 minutes to write the body of your essay. In this time, you need to support your analysis of the author's work with careful reasoning, and back up your analysis with evidence from the source text. Your writing must be coherent, logical, unified, and organized.

Avoid the following three pitfalls in the development of your essay:

1 Using sentences that are irrelevant and contain extraneous material

2 Using sentences that do not follow a logical sequence of thought but seem to jump from one idea to another

3 Using sentences that do not relate to the topic sentence or do not flow from the preceding sentence

Using Transitions

The successful writer uses transitional words and phrases to connect thoughts and provide a logical sequence of ideas. Become familiar with the following list of transitions and use them in your practice essays. They will help make your writing smoother:

therefore	for example	nevertheless
first of all	in any case	but
then	consequently	still
moreover	for instance	yet
secondly	on the other hand	also
indeed	of course	in addition
however	finally	furthermore

Skill Builder: Using Transitions

Directions: In the following three samples, the transition is missing. Supply a transitional word or phrase that will allow the second sentence to follow smoothly or logically from the first.

1. Freshwater ecosystems hold only 0.01% of Earth's water supply. Over half of the people on Earth live near freshwater ecosystems.

2. Human activity comprises the primary threat to freshwater ecosystems. Damming lakes, extracting water, and filling shallow wetlands all lead to the destruction of these ecosystems.

3. Constructing dams and levees can lead to a significant loss of habitat for land animals and plant species. The restricted water flow changes natural water temperatures and impacts marine life.

Answers and Explanations

1. The sentences require a transition that indicates contrast, such as *yet, but, however, still,* or *although.*

   Although freshwater ecosystems hold only 0.01% of Earth's water supply, over half of the people on Earth live near these ecosystems.

2. These sentences require a transition that indicates an example is to follow.

   Human activity comprises the primary threat to freshwater ecosystems; for example, damming lakes, extracting water, and filling shallow wetlands all lead to the destruction of these ecosystems.

3. These sentences require a transition that indicates the idea of addition.

   The construction of dams and levees can lead to a significant loss of habitat for land animals and plant species. Furthermore, the restricted water flow changes natural water temperatures and impacts marine life.

Writing Effectively

There are three important elements that will be considered in scoring an SAT® essay:

1 Reading

2 Analysis

3 Writing

Essays are scored according to how well they meet these three basic criteria. To improve an essay you are writing, ask yourself these questions:

Reading

- Does my essay demonstrate a thorough understanding of the source text?
- Does my essay identify the author's key claims?
- Does my essay explain how the author uses evidence to support his or her key claims?
- Does my essay effectively use evidence from the source text?

Analysis

- Does my essay offer an in-depth evaluation of the author's use of evidence in building and supporting an argument?

- Does my essay offer an in-depth evaluation of the author's use of stylistic or persuasive language features to build and support his or her argument?

- Does my essay use supporting evidence from the passage that is relevant and focused on my task (analyzing the passage)?

Writing

- Does my essay include a precise central claim that is supported with body paragraphs?

- Does my essay include an effective introduction and a strong conclusion?

- Does my essay incorporate a variety of sentence structures? Is each of my sentences clearly written? Does each sentence flow well?

- Is my essay virtually error-free in spelling, grammar, usage, and mechanics?

WRITING THE CONCLUSION

Lewis Carroll, the author *of Alice in Wonderland,* once gave some very good advice for writers. He said, "When you come to the end, stop!"

When you come to the end of your ideas, stop writing the development—and begin writing your conclusion. You can't just end your essay with your last development paragraph. You need to draw your comments together in a strong, clear concluding paragraph.

A good concluding paragraph for your SAT® essay should assure your scorers that you have successfully read, understood, and analyzed the source text. You should be able to do this in three to six sentences written in 3 to 4 minutes. The following are three possible ways to end your essay:

1. Through a *restatement* of your most important or most central idea

2. Through a *summary* of the material covered in the essay

3. Through a *clear statement* about the effectiveness of the passage author's work

Keep in mind that a good conclusion is an integral part of your essay. It may be a review or a restatement, or it may leave your readers with an intriguing question to think about (one that is closely related to your essay, of course). In any case, your conclusion must be strong, clear, and effective.

What *Not* to Say in Your Conclusion

Just as there are good techniques, there are also some very ineffective methods that essay writers may be tempted to use in drawing a composition to a close. Try to avoid falling into the following three traps:

1. Apologizing for your inability to more thoroughly analyze the passage in the allotted time

2. Complaining that the source text did not interest you or that you don't think it was fair to be asked to write an analysis of the source text without giving your own opinions on the topic

3   Introducing material that you will not develop, rambling on about nonpertinent matters, using material that is trite or unrelated, or making a sarcastic joke that indicates your disdain for the topic you just spent 50 minutes writing about

Recognizing Effective Conclusions

Remember that an *effective* concluding paragraph may restate or summarize main idea(s) in your essay, draw a logical conclusion, or offer a strong opinion about the effectiveness of the author's work. An *ineffective* final paragraph introduces new material in a scanty fashion, apologizes for the ineffectiveness of your essay, or is illogical or unclear. Use the following skill-builder exercises to test yourself.

Skill Builder: Effective Conclusions

Directions: Why are the following sentences ineffective in a concluding paragraph?

1. I wish I had more time to write a better, more in-depth analysis, but I find that in the allotted time this is all that I could do.

2. Although I have not mentioned this before, my family enjoys boating on freshwater lakes. We often pick up litter from the water in the hopes of decreasing pollution.

3. This passage was incredibly difficult to understand, and I felt like the author droned on and on about nothing.

Directions: Examine the following five excerpts from concluding paragraphs and decide whether each is effective or ineffective.

4. That's all I have to say about the topic. I know I'm not an expert, but at least this is an actual analysis of the work. I also used a lot of supporting details from the source text. So, I think you should give me at least a 3.

5. While River Pura is a passionate spokesperson for freshwater ecosystems, her argument for limiting the use of motorized watercraft lacks cohesion. Furthermore, a careful examination of the issue shows that motorized watercraft are not the main cause of pollution in freshwater ecosystems. Had Pura taken the time to structure her impassioned pleas around valid statistical evidence, her argument would be stronger.

6. I forgot to mention earlier that the author uses a variety of descriptive words and phrases to appeal to the emotions of readers. She also uses figurative language and makes some illusions to other articles the reader may have read.

7. Protecting the biodiversity of freshwater ecosystems is a topic of importance for all of those who depend upon these ecosystems for survival. River Pura makes a solid case for the restriction of motorized watercraft in freshwater areas. Pura begins her argument with startling facts and statistics designed to capture the reader's attention. She then moves into a well-reasoned discourse that effectively negates any counter-claims opponents might make.

8. In conclusion, the author makes a pretty good case for protecting freshwater ecosystems. However, most people I know aren't going to stop boating because an environmentalist says they should.

Answers and Explanations

1. Don't apologize for doing a poor job. (Maybe your essay is better than you think. And if it *is* bad, why would you want to call attention to its weaknesses?) Also, don't blame the fact that you did a poor job on the time limit.

2. Don't include "asides" like this anywhere in your essay—but especially not in your conclusion. You're supposed to be concluding your analysis, not cramming in extra details that are only loosely related to the topic.

3. Do not complain about the task in the conclusion. Your essay should maintain a formal tone throughout.

4. *Ineffective.* Do not speak directly to or "butter up" the scorers in your concluding paragraph. Maintain a formal tone.

5. *Effective.* This paragraph sums up the key points of the analysis and states the essay writer's opinion of the passage author's persuasive writing.

6. *Ineffective.* Do not introduce new ideas into a concluding paragraph. If you have more information to add that would improve or add depth to your analysis, consider adding another body paragraph. Also, the essay writer has misused the word *illusion*: he or she should have used *allusion*.

7. *Effective.* This paragraph effectively summarizes the key points of the analysis.

8. *Ineffective.* This paragraph gives only a vague summary of the analysis and offers an opinion that is irrelevant to the essay-writing task.

THE SCORING RUBRIC FOR THE SAT® ESSAY

The new SAT® essay will be scored based on a 4-point rubric. Points will be awarded in three areas: reading, analysis, and writing. Each essay will be scored by 2 graders who will give a score of 1 to 4 in each of the three areas. Scores in each area will be reported separately from the other two. For example, a test-taker might earn a score of 3/4/3. This means that the test-taker scored 3 out of 4 points in both reading and writing and 4 out of 4 points in analysis.

All the scorers read the essays against the same rubric developed by the College Board, which administers the SAT®. This rubric guides the scorers in considering overall impression, development, organization, diction, sentence structure, grammar, usage, and mechanics. The rubric also directs scorers in evaluating essay writers' comprehension of the source text, use of relevant evidence from the passage, and their analysis of the passage author's argument. The score guidelines are similar to the following:

Essay Scoring 4 (Advanced)

- *Reading:* shows a comprehensive understanding of the source text, including the author's key claims, use of details and evidence, and the relationship between the two

- *Analysis:* offers an "insightful" and in-depth evaluation of the author's use of evidence and stylistic or persuasive features in building an argument; uses relevant supporting details that address the task

- *Writing:* includes all of the features of a strong essay, including a precise central claim, body paragraphs, and a strong conclusion; incorporates a variety of sentence structures; is virtually free of all convention errors

Essay Scoring 3 (Proficient)

- *Reading:* shows an appropriate understanding of the source text, including the author's key claims and use of details in developing an argument
- *Analysis:* offers an effective evaluation of the author's use of evidence and stylistic or persuasive features in building an argument; uses appropriate supporting details and evidence that are relevant and focused on the task
- *Writing:* includes all of the features of an effective essay, including a precise central claim, body paragraphs, and a strong conclusion; incorporates a variety of sentence structures and is relatively free of common grammatical errors

Essay Scoring 2 (Partial)

- *Reading:* shows some understanding of the source text, including the author's key claims; uses limited textual evidence; incorporates unimportant details
- *Analysis:* offers a limited evaluation of the author's use of evidence and stylistic or persuasive features in building an argument; supporting details are lacking and/or irrelevant to task
- *Writing:* does not provide a precise central claim, nor an effective introduction, body paragraphs and conclusion; incorporates little variety of sentence structures and contains numerous errors in grammar and conventions

Essay Scoring 1 (Inadequate)

- *Reading:* demonstrates little or no understanding of the source text, or the author's use of key claims
- *Analysis:* offers no clear evaluation of the author's use of evidence and stylistic or persuasive features in building an argument; supporting details and evidence are non-existent or irrelevant to task
- *Writing:* lacks any form of cohesion or structure; incorporates little variety in sentence structure and includes significant errors in convention which make it difficult to read

Read the rubric several times. As you practice writing essays for the SAT®, keep this rubric in mind. As you write each essay, try to focus on one or two qualities of good writing that the rubric measures. After you have finished writing your essay, come back to the rubric and see how your essay measures up.

Use the following table to help you. Give yourself anywhere from 1 to 4 points for each quality of good writing.

PRACTICE TEST SCORING TABLE

Reading	_____
Analysis	_____
Writing	_____
Final Score:	_____ / _____ / _____

EXERCISE: PRACTICING YOUR ESSAY SKILLS

Use the following prompt to practice writing an effective essay. Carefully read the prompt and write a response. Make use of the effective writing techniques discussed in this chapter. Use the scoring guide to evaluate your work. Then read and evaluate the three sample responses.

As you read the passage below, consider how the writer uses the following:

- Evidence, such as facts or examples, to support claims

- Reasoning to develop ideas and to connect claims and evidence

- Stylistic or persuasive elements such as word choice, emotional appeal, intellectual appeal, and ethical appeal to add power to the ideas expressed

Henry Clay (1777–1852) served several terms in Congress and was Secretary of State in 1825. In the following speech, given in 1818, he argues that the United States should support South America in gaining independence from Spain.

The Emancipation of South America

1   Spain has undoubtedly given us abundant and just cause for war. But it is not every cause of war that should lead to war…. If we are to have war with Spain, I have, however, no hesitation in saying that no mode of bringing it about could be less fortunate than that of seizing, at this time, upon her adjoining province. There was a time, under certain circumstances, when we might have occupied East Florida with safety; had we then taken it, our posture in the negotiation with Spain would have been totally different from what it is.

2   But we have permitted that time, not with my consent, to pass by unimproved. If we were now to seize upon Florida after a great change in those circumstances, and after declaring our intention to acquiesce in the procrastination desired by Spain, in what light should we be viewed by foreign powers—particularly Great Britain? We have already been accused of inordinate ambition, and of seeking to aggrandize ourselves by an extension, on all sides, of our limits. Should we not, by such an act of violence, give color to the accusation? No, Mr. Chairman; if we are to be involved in a war with Spain, let us have the credit of disinterestedness. Let us put her yet more in the wrong. Let us command the respect which is never withheld from those who act a noble and generous part. I hope to communicate to the committee the conviction which I so strongly feel, that the adoption of the amendment which I intend to propose would not hazard, in the slightest degree, the peace of the country….

3   In contemplating the great struggle in which Spanish America is now engaged, our attention is fixed first by the immensity and character of the country which Spain seeks again to subjugate. Stretching on the Pacific Ocean from about the fortieth degree of north latitude to about the fifty-fifth degree of south latitude, and extending from the mouth of the Rio del Norte (exclusive of East Florida), around the Gulf of Mexico and along the South Atlantic to near Cape Horn, it is nearly five thousand miles in length, and in some places nearly three thousand in breadth….

4   Throughout all the extent of that great portion of the world which I have attempted thus hastily to describe, the spirit of revolt against the dominion of Spain has manifested itself. The Revolution has been attended with various degrees of success in the several parts of Spanish America. In some it has been already crowned, as I shall endeavor to show, with

complete success, and in all I am persuaded that independence has struck such deep root, that the power of Spain can never eradicate it. What are the causes of this great movement?

5   Three hundred years ago, upon the ruins of the thrones of Montezuma and the Incas of Peru, Spain erected the most stupendous system of colonial despotism that the world has ever seen—the most vigorous, the most exclusive. The great principle and object of this system have been to render one of the largest portions of the world exclusively subservient, in all its faculties, to the interests of an inconsiderable spot in Europe….

6   Thus upon the ground of strict right, upon the footing of a mere legal question, governed by forensic rules, the Colonies, being absolved by the acts of the parent country from the duty of subjection to it, had an indisputable right to set up for themselves. But I take a broader and a bolder position. I maintain that an oppressed people are authorized, whenever they can, to rise and break their fetters. This was the great principle of the English Revolution. It was the great principle of our own….

7   In the establishment of the independence of Spanish America, the United States have the deepest interest. I have no hesitation in asserting my firm belief that there is no question in the foreign policy of this country, which has ever arisen, or which I can conceive as ever occurring, in the decision of which we have had or can have so much at stake. This interest concerns our politics, our commerce, our navigation ….

8   I would invoke the spirits of our departed fathers. Was it for yourselves only that you nobly fought? No, no! It was the chains that were forging for your posterity that made you fly to arms, and, scattering the elements of these chains to the winds, you transmitted to us the rich inheritance of liberty.

> Write an essay in which you explain how Henry Clay builds an argument to persuade his audience that the United States should support South America in its efforts to secure freedom from Spain. In your essay, analyze how Clay uses one or more of the features previously listed (or features of your own choice) to strengthen the logic and persuasiveness of his argument. Be sure that your analysis focuses on the most relevant aspects of the passage.
>
> Your essay should not explain whether you agree with Clay's claims, but rather explain how he builds an argument to persuade his audience.

Use the following scoring guide to help you evaluate Sample Essay 1. Then, read our analysis of the essay, as well as suggestions for improvement.

Score Point	Reading	Analysis	Writing
4 (Advanced)	The essay shows a comprehensive understanding of the source text, including the author's key claims, use of details and evidence, and the relationship between the two.	The essay offers an "insightful" and in-depth evaluation of the author's use of evidence and stylistic or persuasive features in building an argument. Supporting details and evidence are relevant and focus on those details that address the task.	The essay includes all of the features of a strong essay, including a precise central claim, body paragraphs, and a strong conclusion. There is a variety of sentence structures used in the essay, and is virtually free of all convention errors.
3 (Proficient)	The essay shows an appropriate understanding of the source text, including the author's key claims and use of details in developing an argument.	The essay offers an "effective" evaluation of the author's use of evidence and stylistic or persuasive features in building an argument. Supporting details and evidence are appropriate and focus on those details that address the task.	The essay includes all of the features of an effective essay, including a precise central claim, body paragraphs, and a strong conclusion. There is a variety of sentence structures used in the essay, and it is free of significant convention errors.
2 (Partial)	The essay shows some understanding of the source text, including the author's key claims, but uses limited use of textual evidence and/or unimportant details.	The essay offers limited evaluation of the author's use of evidence and stylistic or persuasive features in building an argument. Supporting details and evidence are lacking and/or are not relevant to the task.	The essay does not provide a precise central claim, nor does it provide an effective introduction, body paragraphs, and conclusion. There is little variety of sentence structure used in the essay, and significant errors in convention make it difficult to read.
1 (Inadequate)	The essay demonstrates little or no understanding of the source text, or the author's use of key claims. The essay does not utilize textual evidence from the source text.	The essay offers no clear evaluation of the author's use of evidence and stylistic or persuasive features in building an argument. Supporting details and evidence are non-existent or irrelevant to the task.	The essay lacks any form of cohesion or structure. There is little variety of sentence structures and significant errors in convention make it difficult to read.

Sample Essay 1

In his speech to Congress, Henry Clay emphasizes the importance of supporting South America in their revolt against Spain. Clay begins his argument by talking about the significance of the state of Florida, which isn't actually a state yet. Clay urges Congress not to invade Florida (which apparently has been captured by Spain) because it would make the U.S. look bad. Clay's goal is for Spain to be "in the wrong" and for the U.S. to "command the respect which is never withheld from those who act a noble and generous part."

Clay goes on to remind his listeners that the majority of South America is already involved in a Revolution against Spain. This is a key point of persuasion. Finally, Clay makes the comparison between the Revolution in South America and the Revolution against Great Britain. He even goes so far as to "invoke the spirits of our departed fathers" and uses other images like "fly to arms" and "the rich inheritance of liberty." While Clay's argument is okay, it's long-winded and focuses too much on emotional appeal.

Analysis of Sample Essay 1

This response scored a 2/2/2.

- **Reading—2:** The writer demonstrates some comprehension of the source text. In the first paragraph, the writer conveys the basic central claim—*the importance of supporting South America in their revolt against Spain.* The writer also shows a partial understanding of Clay's position on Florida—*Clay's goal is for Spain to be "in the wrong"*—but does not effectively tie it to the central claim. In the following paragraph, the writer correctly identifies Clay's comparison of the South American Revolution to the U.S. Revolution. However, there is little demonstration of the relationship between the central claim and the supporting details. Overall, the writer shows a partial understanding of the source text.

- **Analysis—2:** The response offers a limited analysis of the source text, showing only partial understanding of the task. The writer mentions the *significance of the state of Florida* but then does not elaborate on this significance or explain how Florida's significance contributes to Clay's argument. In the second paragraph, the writer makes note of *a key point of persuasion*; however, there is no further discussion of why South America's revolution against Spain is a key point of persuasion. Furthermore, the writer does not develop the effect of Clay's comparison of the South American Revolution to the U.S. Revolution. While the writer includes the use of *emotional appeal* in the analysis, there is no explanation of it. Overall, this response is only a partially successful analysis.

- **Writing—2:** This response reflects limited cohesion and some skill in the use of language. There is no precise central claim, nor is there an effective introduction and conclusion. Phrases like *isn't actually a state yet* and *which apparently has been captured by Spain* use an informal, almost flippant tone. Calling the source text *long-winded* is subjective and inappropriate for a formal analysis. Overall, this response represents a partially developed essay.

Suggestions for Improvement

1. The response needs a clearly developed introduction that establishes the topic and presents a precise central claim. While the first paragraph makes a start, a precise central claim should briefly summarize the key points that the writer will make in his or her analysis.

2. Each body paragraph should begin with a topic sentence that summarizes the key point of the paragraph. For instance, the writer could begin the second paragraph with the sentence: *Clay begins his argument with reason rather than rhetoric, logically appealing to those who are hesitant to engage in open warfare.*

3. The use of evidence from the source text should directly support key aspects of the essay writer's analysis. Look at this sentence from paragraph 2 of Sample Essay 1: *He even goes so far as to "invoke the spirits of our departed fathers" and uses other images like "fly to arms" and "the rich inheritance of liberty."* The quotations here do not support the writer's analysis of the source text. A better use of quotations might be:

Clay uses emotionally powerful language as a persuasive tool in making the correlation between the U.S. quest for independence from Great Britain and South America's quest for independence from Spain. He wants to inspire the same passionate support for South America's struggle that most of his listeners feel about their own country's revolution, so he uses emotional phrases like "invoke the spirits of our departed fathers," "fly to arms," and "rich inheritance of liberty."

4. The response should include a strong conclusion that restates the thesis, recaps the most important parts of the analysis, or leaves the reader with a final thought. The conclusion should provide a sense of closure on the topic.

5. All SAT® essays should maintain a formal and objective tone. The writer should limit the use of contractions and refrain from using derogatory adjectives like *long-winded* to describe the source text.

Sample Essay 2

In Henry Clay's 1818 address to Congress, he is building an argument to persuade his listeners to support South America in their revolution against Spain. He builds his argument in three different ways. Clay demonstrates an understanding of his audience, underscores the action that they need to take, and closes with an emotional appeal for liberty by referencing the Revolutionary War.

Clay begins building his argument by demonstrating an understanding of his audience. He demonstrates an understanding of his audience when he assures them at the outset of his speech that he is not calling for open warfare against Spain. This is significant because many members of Congress still remembered the bloodshed from the Revolutionary War. Clay reassures his audience and seeks to get them on his side by stating "it is not every cause of war that should lead to war." Once Congresses minds are put at ease, Clay can move onto talking about his central claim.

After Clay reassures his listeners, he then attempts to underscore the amount of involvement they would have to take in the conflict. He is seeking to minimize the nature of the conflict in order to win support for it. Clay says that, "The Revolution has been attended with various degrees of success in the several parts of Spanish America. In some it has been already crowned, as I shall endeavor to show, with complete success...."

Finally, Clay seeks to draw a parallel for his listeners between the revolution they had recently won and the revolution being fought in South America. This is his emotional appeal. Clay is telling his listeners, "Remember your fight for independence? Remember how greatly you desired freedom? This is the same thing." By getting his listeners to remember how passionately they desired freedom from Great Britain, he is hoping to sway their emotions in favor of supporting South America against Spain.

Henry Clay uses logic, minimizing, and emotional appeal to build an argument. He shows that he understands his audience and seeks to give them what they need so that they will agree with him.

Analysis of Sample Essay 2

This essay scored a 3/3/3.

- **Reading—3:** This response demonstrates effective understanding of the source text with appropriate use of evidence through the analysis. In the second paragraph, the author discusses Clay's understanding of his audience and what the audience most fears. Although the source text does not refer explicitly to this fear, the writer picks up on it from a careful reading of the passage. In the next paragraph, the writer cites and discusses a claim Clay makes that supporting South America requires a minimal response. Finally, the last body paragraph paraphrases Clay's emotional call to remember the principles that guided the American Revolution. The writer shows an effective understanding of both the central idea and important details.

- **Analysis—3:** The writer shows an effective understanding of the task by identifying three ways Clay builds his argument (*Clay demonstrates an understanding of his audience, underscores the action that they need to take, and closes with an emotional appeal....*) and then elaborating on each point in the body paragraphs. Each body paragraph carefully evaluates how pieces of evidence from the source text, the author's use of reasoning, or stylistic or persuasive features are used to develop an argument. For example, in the final body paragraph the writer claims that Clay is *getting his listeners to remember how passionately they desired freedom from Great Britain* and explains that this is *to sway their emotions in favor of supporting South America against Spain.* The response could have made stronger use of evidence from the text, offering a direct quote rather than a paraphrase. However, this response shows an effective analysis of the source text using relevant support.

- **Writing—3:** This essay includes most of the features of an effective essay, including a precise central claim and body paragraphs. The introduction and conclusion lack development, although the introduction presents the central claim and the conclusion restates it. There is appropriate variety of sentence structure, and the few errors of convention and grammar do not detract from the overall reading of the response. Overall, this analysis is proficient.

Suggestions for Improvements

1. The author should work to develop a stronger introduction and conclusion. For example, the introduction could explain the significance of the topic, and the conclusion might provide a final thought or statement.

2. Paragraph 3 could further discuss Clay's reasons for minimizing the support needed in South America. While the writer effectively points out Clay's use of minimization, the importance of this technique to Clay's argument is not fully clear.

3. In paragraph 4, the writer paraphrases Clay's emotional appeal. When discussing an author's use of emotional language to persuade listeners to share his point of view or take a certain action, direct quotes from the source text are best.

Sample Essay 3

In 1818, South America was rising in revolt against Spain. Congressman Henry Clay believed that it was in America's best interest to support their neighbors to the south. In his speech to the 1818 Congress, Clay builds an argument tailor-made for his audience, outlining action steps Congress should take while at the same time appealing to their passionate belief in democracy. Through a combination of careful rhetoric, logic, and emotional appeal, Clay hopes to convince Congress to adopt an amendment that would put the U.S. at war with Spain.

Clay begins his argument with careful rhetoric designed specifically for his audience. Clay understands that some may be thinking of the bloodshed of the American Revolution and have no desire to engage in another war. "It is not every cause of war that should lead to war …" Clay maintains. However, Clay goes on to suggest to his audience that, had they acted prior to this moment in time, war might have been avoided. In essence, Clay is telling his audience that he does not condone war; however, Congress has brought about the necessity to engage in war by previous inaction. Clay tells his audience, "There was a time … when … our posture in the negotiation with Spain would have been totally different …" Yet, Clay maintains, that time has passed. Now is the time for more heavy-handed action.

Clay furthers the appeal of his argument by insisting that the action steps he proposes would not lead the country into another violent conflict. Rather, Clay maintains "… the adoption of the amendment which I intend to propose would not hazard, in the slightest degree, the peace of the country…." He uses logic to reason that, because of the size of South America, and because of the success that some South American people have already had in their fight against Spain, the revolution in some areas is already "a complete success." Therefore, Clay is demonstrating to his audience that supporting his amendment poses no risk to them.

Finally, Clay uses an emotional appeal to ultimately convince Congress to pass the amendment. Clay draws a parallel between the ideals of freedom and democracy that underscored the fight for American independence and the ideals of freedom and democracy that are bolstering the fight in South America. His emotional appeal is summed up in the last paragraph of the speech: "I would invoke the spirits of our departed fathers. Was it for yourselves only that you nobly fought? No, no! It was the chains that were forging for your posterity that made you fly to arms …"

Speaking to Congress of the imminent threat of Spain, Henry Clay seeks to persuade his listeners to pass an amendment that would essentially put the fledgling nation at war with another European nation. With careful rhetoric, logic, and emotional appeals, Clay seeks to convince his listeners that freedom is something for which one should always be willing to fight.

Analysis of Sample Essay 3:

This essay scored a 4/4/4.

- **Reading—4:** This response demonstrates thorough understanding of the source text with skillful use of paraphrases and direct quotations. The writer briefly summarizes the main idea of Clay's argument, (*Clay believed that it was in America's best interest to support their neighbors to the south,*) and presents many details from the text, including Clay's reflection that Congress had an opportunity to negotiate with Spain but missed it, to demonstrate why Clay's argument is significant. There are few long direct quotations from the source text. Instead, the author accurately and precisely paraphrases the key points of the speech.

- **Analysis—4:** The writer demonstrates an insightful understanding of the task by identifying three ways Clay builds his argument (*Through a combination of careful rhetoric, logic, and emotional appeal* ...) and then elaborating on each point in the body paragraphs. Each body paragraph carefully evaluates how pieces of evidence from the source text, the author's use of reasoning, or stylistic or persuasive features are used to develop an argument. For example, in the final body paragraph the writer claims that Clay *draws a parallel between the ideals of freedom and democracy that underscored the fight for American independence and the ideals of freedom and democracy that are bolstering the fight in South America.* The response demonstrates a thorough understanding of both the source text and its effect on the audience.

- **Writing—4:** This essay is cohesive and shows an effective command of language, including a precise central claim and body paragraphs. The introduction and conclusion are well developed. There is ample variety of sentence structures and no errors of convention and grammar that detract from the overall reading of the response. Overall, this analysis shows advanced writing proficiency.

Additional Essay Writing Practice

For more practice, carefully read the following prompt and source text. Then write an analysis of the passage. Score your analytical response using the rubric provided.

As you read the passage below, consider how the writer uses the following:

- Evidence, such as facts or examples, to support claims
- Reasoning to develop ideas and to connect claims and evidence
- Stylistic or persuasive elements such as word choice, emotional appeal, intellectual appeal, and ethical appeal to add power to the ideas expressed

---

Padre Island National Seashore separates the Gulf of Mexico from the Laguna Madre, one of a few hypersaline lagoons in the world. The park protects 70 miles of coastline, dunes, prairies, and wind tidal flats teeming with life. It is a safe nesting ground for the Kemp's Ridley sea turtle and a haven for 380 bird species. It also has a rich history, including the Spanish shipwrecks of 1554.

The Importance of the 1554 Shipwrecks

1   In April, 1554, three Spanish *naos* (a type of cargo and passenger ship similar to Columbus's Santa Maria) went aground on Padre Island following a storm that had blown them across the Gulf of Mexico from the coast of Cuba. At the time this was the greatest disaster to ever befall the Spanish fleet in the New World. Tons of treasure bound for Spain was lost in addition to the lives of approximately three hundred passengers and crew who died from hunger, thirst, and attacks by natives as they attempted to walk back to the port of Vera Cruz.

2   But the story of the 1554 shipwreck does not end there, nor does it end with the conclusion of the salvage operations that took place later that year. As with any important historical event, its effects resonate through the centuries and can still be felt today—if one looks for them.

3   First of all, the wrecks were the first documented occurrence of Europeans on the island and one of the first occurrences of Europeans in what was to become Texas. The salvage operation was the first documented instance of Europeans intentionally coming to the island and staying for an extended period.

4   Second, the three ships that wrecked (the Santa Maria de Yciar, the Espiritu Santo, and the San Esteban) are the oldest shipwrecks ever found in North America (excluding the Caribbean and Latin America).

5   Third, when the remains of the ships were discovered in 1967, a private company called Platoro, Ltd. began excavating them. This set off a long legal battle over ownership of the remains, as Texas had no laws governing antiquities at the time. In the long run, the state won its case and the remains were turned over to the National Park Service, who has transferred curation of the artifacts to the Corpus Christi Museum of Science and History, where they may now be viewed.

6   Historian and Marine Archeologist Dr. Donald Keith, President of the Ships of Discovery at the Corpus Christi Museum of Science and History, notes that:

7   "The 1554 shipwrecks are important for a lot of reasons. The 'mining' of them by Platoro caused the State of Texas to realize that shipwrecks and archaeological sites in general are important, and the property of the people and the state. They are cultural resources that have to be cared for. Some of the earliest experiments in the conservation of artifacts from the sea were done on the objects and hull remains that were recovered from the sites that Platoro and the State worked…. The Platoro conflict did lead to the establishment of the Texas Antiquities Committee, which led to the Texas Historical Commission, which led to the discovery and excavation of La Belle [the ship of the French explorer La Salle, found on the Texas coast within the past few years] among other accomplishments."

8   This third and last effect on our present society is undoubtedly the most important, because it resulted in new Texas laws to protect archeological resources. These laws follow the federal Antiquities Act in spirit, which gives federal agencies custody of relics found within their jurisdictions so that they may be properly protected and studied. Thus, instead of ending up in private collections where they become curiosities for a fortunate few, the knowledge derived from the artifacts goes to the public in the form of publications and exhibits in museums and on websites.

9   Bits and pieces of the 1554 wrecks and many other historical events still wash up on the island or can be found emerging from the sands. If you discover something, please remember that the right thing to do is leave it where it is and report it to us, so that we may conduct a proper archeological dig and learn more about the rich history of the island and share our findings (and yours) with the world.

Write an essay in which you explain how the writer builds an argument to persuade his or her audience of the importance of the 1554 shipwrecks. In your essay, analyze how the author uses one or more of the features listed previously (or features of your own choice) to strengthen the logic and persuasiveness of his/her argument. Be sure that your analysis focuses on the most relevant aspects of the passage.

Your essay should not explain whether you agree with the writer's claims, but rather explain how the writer builds an argument to persuade his or her audience.

Score Point	Reading	Analysis	Writing
4 (Advanced)	The essay shows a comprehensive understanding of the source text, including the author's key claims, use of details and evidence, and the relationship between the two.	The essay offers an "insightful" and in-depth evaluation of the author's use of evidence and stylistic or persuasive features in building an argument. Supporting details and evidence are relevant and focus on those details that address the task.	The essay includes all of the features of a strong essay, including a precise central claim, body paragraphs, and a strong conclusion. There is a variety of sentence structures used in the essay, and is virtually free of all convention errors.
3 (Proficient)	The essay shows an appropriate understanding of the source text, including the author's key claims and use of details in developing an argument.	The essay offers an "effective" evaluation of the author's use of evidence and stylistic or persuasive features in building an argument. Supporting details and evidence are appropriate and focus on those details that address the task.	The essay includes all of the features of an effective essay, including a precise central claim, body paragraphs, and a strong conclusion. There is a variety of sentence structures used in the essay, and is free of significant convention errors.
2 (Partial)	The essay shows some understanding of the source text, including the author's key claims, but uses limited use of textual evidence and/or unimportant details.	The essay offers limited evaluation of the author's use of evidence and stylistic or persuasive features in building an argument. Supporting details and evidence are lacking and/or are not relevant to the task.	The essay does not provide a precise central claim, nor does it provide an effective introduction, body paragraphs, and conclusion. There is little variety of sentence structure used in the essay, and significant errors in convention make it difficult to read.
1 (Inadequate)	The essay demonstrates little or no understanding of the source text, or the author's use of key claims. The essay does not utilize textual evidence from the source text.	The essay offers no clear evaluation of the author's use of evidence and stylistic or persuasive features in building an argument. Supporting details and evidence are non-existent or irrelevant to the task.	The essay lacks any form of cohesion or structure. There is little variety of sentence structures and significant errors in convention make it difficult to read.

SUMMING IT UP

- Set a timer for 50 minutes.
- Read the prompt and the source text (passage).
- Jot down notes of the author's central claim, use of evidence, reasoning, or stylistic and persuasive features.
- Plan and write an essay within the 50 minutes.
- Score it against the rubric.

PART VI

SAT® MATH REVIEW

Multiple-Choice Math Strategies

OVERVIEW

- Why multiple-choice math is easier
- Question format
- Solving multiple-choice math questions
- Know when to use your calculator
- Learn the most important multiple-choice math tips
- Summing it up

WHY MULTIPLE-CHOICE MATH IS EASIER

How can one kind of math possibly be easier than another? SAT® multiple-choice math is easier than the math tests you take in class because the answers are right there in front of you. As you know from other standardized tests, multiple-choice tests always give you the answer. You just have to figure out which answer is the correct one. So even if you aren't sure and have to guess, you can use estimating to narrow your choices and improve your odds.

The questions in each multiple-choice math section are arranged from easiest to most difficult. The questions don't stick to one content area. They jump around from algebra to geometry to advanced math to data analysis to statistics and back to algebra in no particular pattern.

QUESTION FORMAT

On the SAT®, each set of multiple-choice math questions starts with directions and a reference section that look like this:

> **Directions: For Questions 1–30,** solve each problem, select the best answer from the choices provided, and fill in the corresponding oval on your answer sheet. **For Questions 31–38,** solve the problem and enter your answer in the grid on the answer sheet. The directions **before question 31** will provide information on how to enter your answers in the grid.

ADDITIONAL INFORMATION:

- The use of a calculator **is permitted.**

- All variables and expressions used represent real numbers unless otherwise indicated.

- Figures provided in this test are drawn to scale unless otherwise indicated.

- All figures lie in a plane unless otherwise indicated.

- Unless otherwise specified, the domain of a given function f is the set of all real numbers x for which is $f(x)$ is a real number.

The information in the reference section should all be familiar to you from your school-work. Know that it's there in case you need it. But remember: the formulas themselves aren't the answers to any problems. You have to know when to use them and how to apply them.

Some multiple-choice questions ask to solve a given equation or system of equations, while others are presented in the form of word problems. Some include graphs, charts, or tables that you will be asked to interpret. All of the questions have four answer choices. These choices are arranged in order when the answers are numbers, usually from smallest to largest, but occasionally from largest to smallest.

SOLVING MULTIPLE-CHOICE MATH QUESTIONS

These five steps will help you solve multiple-choice math questions:

1 Read the question carefully and determine what's being asked.

2 Decide which math principles apply and use them to solve the problem.

3 Look for your answer among the choices. If it's there, mark it and go on.

4 If the answer you found is not there, recheck the question and your calculations.

5 If you still can't solve the problem, eliminate obviously wrong answers and take your best guess.

Now let's try out these steps on a couple of SAT®-type multiple-choice math questions.

Example 1:

$$PQ = PS$$

In the figure above, $x =$

(A) 15°

(B) 30°

(C) 60°

(D) 75°

1 The problem asks you to find the measure of one angle of right triangle PQR.

2 Two math principles apply: (1) the sum of the measures in degrees of the angles of a triangle is 180, and (2) 45-45-90 right triangles have certain special properties. Since $PQ = PS$, $\triangle PQS$ is a 45-45-90 right triangle. Therefore, angle $PQS = 45°$ and angle $PQR = 45 + 15 = 60°$. Therefore, angle $x = 180 - 90 - 60 = 30°$.

3 The correct answer, 30, is choice (B).

Example 2:

If x and y are negative numbers, which of the following is negative?

(A) xy

(B) $(xy)^2$

(C) $(x - y)^2$

(D) $x + y$

1 The problem asks you to pick an answer choice that is a negative number.

2 The principles that apply are those governing operations with signed numbers. Since x and y are negative, choice (A) must be positive. As for choices (B) and (C), as long as x and y are not

www.petersons.com

TIP
Remember the reference information! The reference information at the start of the math section provides valuable information about special right triangles.

equal to each other, both expressions must be positive. (If they're equal, the expression equals zero, and any number other than zero squared gives a positive result.) Choice (D), however, is negative since it represents the sum of two negative numbers.

3 Therefore, the correct answer must be choice (D). If you have trouble working with letters, try substituting easy numbers for x and y in each choice.

KNOW WHEN TO USE YOUR CALCULATOR

Calculators are allowed in the SAT® Math Test—Calculator section, but you won't *need* a calculator to solve any SAT® math questions. Calculators can be helpful in solving most of the problems, whether you use the calculator for simplifying expressions or graphing equations. But remember that your calculator is not some sort of magic brain. If you don't understand the questions in the first place, the calculator won't give you some a solution.

Most calculators that you would use in class are allowed. It is best to use whichever calculator you are already comfortable using instead of trying to learn how to use a new calculator.

The most important thing to remember is to set up your work on paper first, and then plug the information into the calculator. For example, if you have a question that deals with an equation, set up the equation on your scratch paper. Then make your number substitutions on the calculator. This way, you always have something to refer to without having to think, "Oh, nuts, how did I set that up?" as the seconds tick by.

When you use your calculator, check the display each time you enter numbers to make sure you entered them correctly. Make sure to hit the Clear key after each finished operation, otherwise it could get ugly.

ALERT!

Don't automatically reach for your calculator. If it can't help you solve the problem, you'll just waste time fiddling with it. Save the calculator for what it does best, especially simplifying numeric expressions.

LEARN THE MOST IMPORTANT MULTIPLE-CHOICE MATH TIPS

Some of these you've heard before; some will be new to you. Whatever the case, read them, learn them, love them. They will help you.

The Question Number Tells You How Hard the Question Is

Just as in most of the other SAT® sections, the questions go from easy to hard as you work toward the end. The first third of the questions is easy, the middle third is average but harder, and the final third gets more and more difficult. Take a look at these three examples. Don't solve them yet (you'll be doing that in a couple of minutes); just get an idea of how the level of difficulty changes from Question 1 to Question 12 to Question 25.

1. If $x - 2 = 5$, then $x =$

   (A) -10
   (B) $\dfrac{5}{2}$
   (C) 3
   (D) 7

12. For how many integers x is $-7 < 2x < -5$?

    (A) None

    (B) One

    (C) Two

    (D) Three

25. In a set of five books, no two of which have the same number of pages, the longest book has 150 pages and the shortest book has 130 pages. If x pages is the average (arithmetic mean) of the number of pages in the five-book set, which of the following best indicates all possible values of x and only possible values of x?

    (A) $130 < x < 150$

    (B) $131 < x < 149$

    (C) $133 < x < 145$

    (D) $135 < x < 145$

Can you see the difference? You can probably do Question 1 with your eyes closed. For Question 12, you probably have to open your eyes and do some calculations on scratch paper. Question 25 may cause you to wince a little, and then get started on some heavy-duty thinking.

Easy Questions Have Easy Answers—Difficult Questions Don't

The easy questions are straightforward and don't have any hidden tricks. The obvious answer is almost always the correct answer. So for Question 1 the answer is indeed choice (D).

When you hit the difficult stuff, you have to think harder. The information is not straightforward and the answers aren't obvious. You can bet that your first-choice, easy answer will be wrong. If you don't believe it, let's take a look at the solution for difficult Question 25.

25. In a set of five books, no two of which have the same number of pages, the longest book has 150 pages and the shortest book has 130 pages. If x pages is the average (arithmetic mean) of the number of pages in the five-book set, which of the following best indicates all possible values of x and only possible values of x?

    (A) $130 < x < 150$

    (B) $131 < x < 149$

    (C) $133 < x < 145$

    (D) $135 < x < 145$

Yes, it's difficult mostly because the process you have to use to find the solution is difficult. Let's start by eliminating answer choices. Choice (A) is designed to fool you. You see the same information that appears in the word problem, so you figure it's got to be right. Wrong. All it does is say that the shortest book is 130 pages, the longest book is 150 pages, and the average is between 130 and 150. Simple and wrong.

Choice (B) illustrates the reasoning that "no two books have the same number of pages, so the average must be one page more than the shortest book and one page less than the longest." Remember, it's a difficult question, so it's just not that easy an answer.

TIP

Look for shortcuts. SAT® math problems test your math reasoning, not your ability to make endless calculations. If you find yourself calculating too much, you've probably missed a shortcut that would have made your work easier.

Let's skip to the correct answer, which is choice (D), and find out how we got there. First, you want to find the minimum value for x so you assume that the other three books contain 131, 132, and 133 pages. So the average would be:

$$\frac{130+131+132+133+150}{5} = \frac{676}{5} = 135.2$$

So x must be more than 135. Now assume that the other three books contain 149, 148, and 147 pages. Then the average length of all five books would be:

$$\frac{150+149+148+147+130}{5} = \frac{724}{5} = 144.8$$

Then x would be greater than 135 but less than 145.

Be Certain to Answer the Question Being Asked

Suppose that you were asked to solve the following problem:

If $5x + 11 = 31$, what is the value of $x + 4$?

(A) 4

(B) 6

(C) 8

(D) 10

The first step is to solve the equation $5x + 11 = 31$.

$5x+11 = 31$ Subtract 11 from both sides.

$\quad 5x = 20$ Divide both sides by 5.

$\quad\ x = 4$

Remember that the problem does not ask for the value of x, it asks for the value of $x + 4$, so the answer is actually choice (C). Make certain that the answer you select is the answer to the question that is being asked. **The correct answer is** (C).

When Guessing at Hard Questions, You Can Toss Out Easy Answers

Now that you know the difficult questions won't have easy or obvious answers, use a guessing strategy. (Use all the help you can get!) When you have less than a clue about a difficult question, scan the answer choices and eliminate the ones that seem easy or obvious, such as any that just restate the information in the question. Then take your best guess.

Questions of Average Difficulty Won't Have Trick Answers

Let's look again at Question 12:

12. For how many integers x is $-7 < 2x < -5$?

    (A) None

    (B) One

    (C) Two

    (D) Three

This is a bit more difficult than Question 1, but it's still pretty straightforward. There is only one integer between -7 and -5, and that's -6. There's also only one value for integer x so that $2x$ equals -6, and that is -3. Get it? $2(-3) = -6$. So, choice (B) is the correct answer. Trust your judgment and your reasoning; no tricks here.

It's Smart to Work Backward

Every standard multiple-choice math problem includes four answer choices. One of them has to be correct; the other three are wrong. This means that it's always possible to solve a problem by testing each of the answer choices. Just plug each choice into the problem, and sooner or later you'll find the one that works! Testing answer choices can often be a much easier and surer way of solving a problem than attempting a lengthy calculation.

When Working Backward, Always Start from the Middle

When working on multiple-choice math questions, remember that all of the numeric answer choices are presented in order—either smallest to largest, or vice versa. As a result, it's always best to begin with a middle option, choice (B) or choice (C). This way, if you start with choice (C) and it's too large, you'll only have to concentrate on the smaller choices. There, you've just knocked off at least two choices in a heartbeat! Now let's give it a test run!

If $\frac{8}{9}y = \frac{9}{4}$, what is the value of y?

    (A) $\frac{32}{81}$

    (B) $\frac{1}{2}$

    (C) 2

    (D) $\frac{81}{32}$

Start with choice (C), because it will be easier to compute with than choice (B): $\frac{8}{9}(2) = \frac{16}{9} < \frac{9}{4}$

Since choice (C) is too small, the only possible answer is choice (D).

You can check that $\frac{8}{9}\left(\frac{81}{32}\right) = \frac{9}{4}$

The correct answer is (D).

TIP

Leave a paper trail! If you need to set up an equation, jot it down in your test booklet. That way, if you come back to recheck your work, you'll know what you were originally thinking.

Now try this testing business with a more difficult question:

In the xy-plane, the line determined by the points $(8,c)$ and $(c,18)$ passes through the origin. Which of the following could be the value of c?

(A) 10

(B) 11

(C) 12

(D) 13

Start with choice (C), because it may be easier to compute with than choice (B): the line through $(8,12)$ and $(12,18)$ is $y = \frac{18-12}{12-8}x + b$ This equation simplifies to $y = \frac{3}{2}x$, which is a line through the origin. Choice (C) meets the requirements of the problem. **The correct answer is** (C).

It's Easier to Work with Numbers Than with Letters

Because numbers are more meaningful than letters, try plugging them into equations and formulas in place of variables. This technique can make problems much easier to solve. Here are some examples:

If $x - 4$ is 2 greater than y, then $x + 5$ is how much greater than y?

(A) 3

(B) 7

(C) 9

(D) 11

Choose any value for x. Let's say you decide to make $x = 4$. All right, $4 - 4 = 0$, and 0 is 2 greater than y. So $y = -2$. If $x = 4$, then $x + 5 = 4 + 5 = 9$, and so $x + 5$ is 11 more than y. **The correct answer is (D).**

The cost of renting office space in a building is $2.50 per square foot per month. Which of the following represents the total cost c, in dollars to rent p square feet of office space each year in the building?

(A) $c = 2.50(12p)$

(B) $c = 2.50p + 12$

(C) $c = \dfrac{2.50h}{12}$

(D) $c = \dfrac{12h}{2.50}$

Let $h = 100$, then the rent for one month is $250 and the rent for one year is $3,000. The only answer choice that will provide that answer is choice (A). **The correct answer is (A).**

If a question asks for an odd integer or an even integer, go ahead and pick any odd or even integer you like.

In Problems Involving Variables, Pay Careful Attention to Any Restrictions on the Possible Values of the Variables

Consider the following question:

> If $x \geq 2$, which of the following is a solution to the equation $x(x-3)(x+4)(x+2)(3x-5) = 0$?
>
> **(A)** 2
>
> **(B)** 3
>
> **(C)** 4
>
> **(D)** 5

This equation has five solutions, but the problem is only looking for a solution that is at least 2. Set each of the factors equal to 0 and solve for x. The only answer that is greater than or equal to 2 is 3, choice (B). **The correct answer is (B).**

Now, consider this slightly different version of the same problem.

> If $x < -2$, which of the following is a solution to the equation $x(x-3)(x+4)(x+2)(3x-5) = 0$?
>
> **(A)** −3
>
> **(B)** −4
>
> **(C)** −5
>
> **(D)** There is more than one solution.

The solutions to the equation can be found by setting each of the factors equal to zero. So $x = 0$, $x - 3 = 0$, $x + 4 = 0$, $x + 2 = 0$, and $3x - 5 = 0$.

These lead to the solutions $x = 0, 3, -4, -2$, and $\frac{5}{3}$ respectively.

Of these five solutions only −4, choice (B), is less than −2. **The correct answer is (B).**

TIP

The test booklet is yours, so feel free to use it for your scratchwork. Also, go ahead and mark up any diagrams with length or angle information; it helps. But don't waste time trying to redraw diagrams; it's just not worth it.

TIP

For multiple-choice math questions, circle what's being asked so that you don't pick a wrong answer by mistake. That way, for example, you won't pick an answer that gives perimeter when the question asks for an area.

Questions in the Three-Statement Format Can Be Solved by the Process of Elimination

You may find a three-statement format in certain questions in the multiple-choice math section. The best way to answer this kind of question is to tackle one statement at a time, marking it as either true or false. Here is an example:

Note: the figure is not drawn to scale.

In the figure above, lines k and m intersect at a point, and lines k and n intersect at a different point. If $v + s = p + q$, which of the following statements must be true?

  I. $r = w$

 II. $t = s$

III. $q = x$

  (A) I only

  (B) II only

  (C) I and II only

  (D) I, II, and III

Because $v + s = p + q$, we know that $p + q = 180$. Because they both make a straight line, lines m and n must be parallel. Since m and n are parallel, then statements I and II, choice (C), must be true. While statement III might be true, it is only true if line k is perpendicular to lines m and n, and that does not have to be true. **The correct answer is (C).**

When Solving Equations Involving Square Roots or Algebraic Fractions, Make Certain to Check Your Answer

The procedure for solving such equations occasionally results in what are known as *extraneous solutions*. An extraneous solution is a number that is correctly obtained from the equation-solving process, but doesn't actually solve the equation.

Solve for x: $\sqrt{x+4} + 15 = 10$

  (A) -29

  (B) -21

  (C) 21

  (D) There are no solutions.

Let's solve the equation.

$$\sqrt{x+4}+15=10 \qquad \text{Subtract 15 from both sides}$$

$$\sqrt{x+4}=-5 \qquad \text{Square both sides}$$

$$\left(\sqrt{x+4}\right)^2=\left(-5\right)^2$$

$$x+4=25$$

$$x=21$$

It appears that the solution is choice (C). However, if you check the solution $x = 21$ in the original equation, you will see that it doesn't solve it.

$$\sqrt{x+4}+15=10\,?$$

$$\sqrt{21+4}+15=10\,?$$

$$\sqrt{25}+15=10\,?$$

$$5+15 \neq 10.$$

The correct answer is (D).

Using the Measure of an Angle or a Side of Another Shape Can Help You Find a Measure You Need

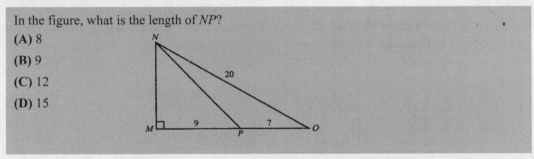

In the figure, what is the length of *NP*?

(A) 8

(B) 9

(C) 12

(D) 15

TIP

Draw a diagram if none is supplied. Drawing a diagram is a great way to organize information. Mark it up with the information you're given, and you'll have a better idea of what you're looking for.

This figure is really two right triangles, *NMO* and *NMP*. Since *NM* is a side of both triangles, once you find the length of that, you can find the length of *NP*. The Pythagorean theorem is what you need:

$NM^2 + MO^2 = NO^2$

$NM^2 + (16)^2 = (20)^2$

Note that 16 and 20 are multiples of 4 and 5, respectively, so you now know that this is a 3-4-5 right triangle, which means that $NM = 12$.

Since you just found out that triangle *NMP* has sides of 9 and 12, it's also a 3-4-5 right triangle, so *NP* must be 15. **The correct answer is (D).**

The Pythagorean Theorem Is Usually Needed to Solve Problems Involving a Right Triangle for Which You Are Given the Lengths of Some of the Sides

The Pythagorean theorem enables you to compute the length of the third side of a right triangle if you know the lengths of the other two sides. It is one of the most useful and common SAT® geometry facts. Consider the problem below.

Line segment $\overline{PQ}$ is tangent to the circle with center O at point T. If T is the midpoint of $\overline{PQ}$, $OQ = 13$, and the radius of the circle is 5, what is the length of $\overline{PQ}$?

(A) 10

(B) 12

(C) 24

(D) 26

This is a tricky question since, at the moment, it doesn't appear to involve any triangles at all. However, you are told that the radius of the circle is 5, and if you draw in radius $\overline{OT}$, you will create triangle OTQ. Use the fact that a tangent line to a circle is perpendicular to the radius at the point of contact to deduce that $\angle OTQ$ is a right angle.

The diagram now depicts right triangle OTQ, and $OT = 5$ and $OQ = 13$. Now, use the Pythagorean theorem to determine that $TQ = 12$, as shown here:

$$OT^2 + TQ^2 = OQ^2$$
$$5^2 + TQ^2 = 13^2$$
$$25 + TQ^2 = 169$$
$$TQ^2 = 144$$
$$TQ = 12$$

Finally, since T is the midpoint of line segment $\overline{PQ}$, the entire length of the line segment is $12 + 12 = 24$. **The correct answer is (C).**

A Reality Check Can Help You Eliminate Answers That Can't Possibly Be Right

Knowing whether your calculations should produce a number that's larger or smaller than the quantity you started with can point you toward the right answer. It's also an effective way of eliminating wrong answers. Here's an example:

> Using his bike, Daryl can complete a paper route in 20 minutes. Francisco, who walks the route, can complete it in 30 minutes. How long will it take the two boys to complete the route if they work together, one starting at each end of the route?
>
> **(A)** 8 minutes
>
> **(B)** 12 minutes
>
> **(C)** 20 minutes
>
> **(D)** 30 minutes

Immediately you can see that choices (C) and (D) are impossible because the two boys working together will have to complete the job in less time than either one of them working alone.

	Daryl	Francisco
$\dfrac{\text{Actual time spent}}{\text{Time needed to do entire job alone}}$	$\dfrac{x}{20}$	$\dfrac{x}{30}$

$$\frac{x}{20} + \frac{x}{30} = 1$$

Multiply by 60 to clear fractions:

$$3x + 2x = 60$$
$$5x = 60$$
$$x = 12$$

The correct answer is (B).

Your Eye Is a Good Estimator

Figures in the standard multiple-choice math section are always drawn to scale unless you see the warning "Note: Figure not drawn to scale." That means you can sometimes solve a problem just by looking at the picture and estimating the answer. Here's how this works:

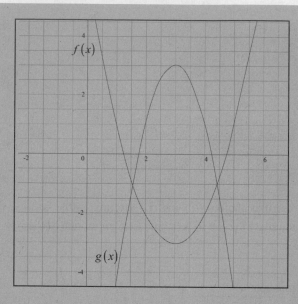

$$f(x) = (x - 3)^2 - 3$$
$$g(x) = -2(x - 3)^2 + 3$$

Graphs of the functions f and g are shown in the xy-plane above. For which of the following values of x does $f(x) + g(x) = 0$?

(A) 1

(B) 2

(C) 3

(D) 4

The sum of the function values is 0 when the function values for f and g are opposites. That appears to be true at $x = 3$. **The correct answer is (C).**

If Some Questions Always Give You Trouble, Save Them for Last

You know which little demons haunt your math skills. If you find questions that you know will give you nightmares, save them for last. They will take up a lot of your time, especially if you're panicking, and you can use that time to do more of the easier questions.

EXERCISES: MULTIPLE-CHOICE MATH

Exercise 1

15 Questions • 18 Minutes

For Questions 1–15, solve each problem, choose the best answer from the choices provided, and put a circle around the correct answer. You may use any available space for scratch work.

ADDITIONAL INFORMATION:

- The use of a calculator is permitted.

- All variables and expressions used represent real numbers unless otherwise indicated.

- Figures provided in this test are drawn to scale unless otherwise indicated.

- All figures lie in a plane unless otherwise indicated.

- Unless otherwise specified, the domain of a given function f is the set of all real numbers x for which $f(x)$ is a real number.

Reference Information

Circle: $C = 2\pi r$ $A = \pi r^2$

Rectangle: $A = lw$

Triangle: $A = \frac{1}{2}bh$ $a^2 + b^2 = c^2$

Rectangular Solid: $V = lwh$

Cylinder: $V = \pi r^2 h$

Sphere: $V = \frac{4}{3}\pi r^3$

Cone: $V = \frac{1}{3}\pi r^2 h$

Rectangular Based Pyramid: $V = \frac{1}{3}lwh$

The number of degrees of arc in a circle is 360.
The number of radians in the arc of a circle is 2π.
The sum of the measures in degrees of the angles of a triangle is 180.

1. In a linear function $f(x)$ with a graph that has a slope of -2.5, if $f(5) = 8$, what is the value of $f(1)$?

    (A) -2
    (B) 3
    (C) 13
    (D) 18

2. Which of the following expressions is equal to 0 for some value of p?

    (A) $|p - 2| - 2$
    (B) $|2 - p| + 2$
    (C) $|p + 2| + 2$
    (D) $|p - 2| + 2$

3. If $f(x) = -3x + 4$, what is $f(-4x)$?

    (A) $-12x - 4$
    (B) $12x + 4$
    (C) $12x - 4$
    (D) $12x^2 - 20x$

4. $$\frac{y}{x} = 4$$
   $$5(x - 1) = y$$

   If (x,y) is the solution to the system of equations above, what is the value x?

    (A) -20
    (B) -5
    (C) 5
    (D) 20

5. Which of the following is equivalent to the expression $5(3x - 2)(2x + 1)$?
   (A) $15x$
   (B) $30x^2 - 10$
   (C) $30x^2 - 5x - 10$
   (D) $25x^2 - 5$.

6. Kathleen is preparing to run her first road race. She begins training by doing intervals of running and walking. The longest interval of running increases by a constant amount each week. The first week she runs for intervals of up to 2 minutes at a time. By the ninth week, she runs for intervals of up to 40 minutes at a time. Which of the following best describes how the time Kathleen spends running changes between her first and ninth weeks?
   (A) Kathleen increases the time of her longest run by 5 minutes each week.
   (B) Kathleen increases the time of her longest run by 4.75 minutes each week.
   (C) Kathleen increases the time of her longest run by 4.5 minutes each week.
   (D) Kathleen increases the time of her longest run by 4.25 minutes each week.

7. If $\dfrac{x + y}{y} = \dfrac{5}{9}$, which of the following must also be true?
   (A) $\dfrac{x}{y} = -\dfrac{4}{9}$
   (B) $\dfrac{x}{y} = \dfrac{14}{9}$
   (C) $\dfrac{x - y}{y} = -\dfrac{4}{9}$
   (D) $\dfrac{x - 2y}{y} = -\dfrac{13}{9}$

8. Which of the following shows the solution set to the equation $\sqrt{x - 1} = x - 7$?
   (A) $\{5, 10\}$
   (B) $\{1\}$
   (C) $\{5\}$
   (D) $\{10\}$

9. A circle whose center is at the origin passes through the point whose coordinates are $(1,1)$. What is the area of this circle?
   (A) π
   (B) 2π
   (C) $\sqrt{2}\pi$
   (D) $2\sqrt{2}\pi$

10. In triangle ABC, $AB = BC$, and $\overline{AC}$ is extended to D. If angle BCD measures $100°$, find the number of degrees in angle B.

   (A) 20
   (B) 40
   (C) 50
   (D) 80

11. Which of the following represents a line that is perpendicular to the line with equation $y = 4 - 2x$?
   (A) $y = 2x + 5$
   (B) $y = -2x + 3$
   (C) $y - 2x = 1$
   (D) $2y - x = 6$

12.
$$x = 3y$$
$$(x - 3)^2 + (y - 1)^2 = 10$$

   How many ordered pairs satisfy the system of equations above?
   (A) 0
   (B) 1
   (C) 2
   (D) infinitely many

13. If $\dfrac{z+6}{z-5} = 5$, what is the value of z?

   (A) $\dfrac{19}{6}$

   (B) $\dfrac{35}{6}$

   (C) $\dfrac{25}{4}$

   (D) $\dfrac{31}{4}$

14. If the expression $(4 + 3i)(2 - 7i)$ is re-written in the form $a + bi$, where a and b are real numbers, what is the value of a? (Note: $i = \sqrt{-1}$)

   (A) 29

   (B) 8

   (C) −13

   (D) −22

15. $x^2 - 6dx = \dfrac{e}{2}$

   In the quadratic equation above, d and e are constants. What are the solutions for x?

   (A) $x = 3d \pm \dfrac{6d - \sqrt{2e}}{2}$

   (B) $x = 3d \pm \dfrac{6d + \sqrt{2e}}{2}$

   (C) $x = 3d \pm \dfrac{\sqrt{36d^2 - 2e}}{2}$

   (D) $x = 3d \pm \dfrac{\sqrt{36d^2 + 2e}}{2}$

Exercise 2

10 Questions • 12 Minutes

For Questions 1–10, solve each problem, choose the best answer from the choices provided, and put a circle around the correct answer. You may use any available space for scratch work.

ADDITIONAL INFORMATION:

- The use of a calculator is permitted.

- All variables and expressions used represent real numbers unless otherwise indicated.

- Figures provided in this test are drawn to scale unless otherwise indicated.

- All figures lie in a plane unless otherwise indicated.

- Unless otherwise specified, the domain of a given function f is the set of all real numbers x for which f(x) is a real number.

1. Mario has made 58 successful 3-point shots in basketball this season. The school record is 92 3-point shots. If he makes 3 more 3-point shots each game, which of the following shows how many 3-point shots he will have made after g additional games?

(A) $3 + 58g$

(B) $92 + 3g$

(C) $58 + 3g$

(D) $58 - 3g$

2. If $a = 5b$, then $\frac{3}{5}a =$

(A) $\frac{5b}{3}$

(B) $3b$

(C) $\frac{3b}{5}$

(D) $\frac{b}{3}$

3. A rectangular door measures 5 feet by 6 feet 8 inches. What is the distance from one corner of the door to the diagonally opposite corner?

(A) 8 feet 2 inches

(B) 8 feet 4 inches

(C) 8 feet 8 inches

(D) 9 feet 6 inches

4. Two ships leave from the same port at 11:30 a.m. If one sails due east at 20 miles per hour and the other due south at 15 miles per hour, how many miles apart are the ships at 2:30 p.m.?
   - (A) 25
   - (B) 50
   - (C) 75
   - (D) 80

5. The line $y = ax - 5$, where a is a constant, is graphed in the xy-plane. If the line contains the point (b,c), which does not lie on either the x- or y-axis, what is the slope of the line in terms of b and c?

   - (A) $\dfrac{c + 5}{b}$
   - (B) $\dfrac{b + 5}{c}$
   - (C) $\dfrac{c - 5}{b}$
   - (D) $\dfrac{b - 5}{c}$

6. Ken received grades of 90, 88, and 75 on three tests. What grade must he receive on the next test so that his average for these four tests is 85?
   - (A) 87
   - (B) 89
   - (C) 90
   - (D) 92

7. There is enough food at a picnic to feed 20 adults or 32 children. If there are 15 adults at the picnic, how many children can still be fed?
   - (A) 6
   - (B) 8
   - (C) 12
   - (D) 16

8. In parallelogram *ABCD*, angle *A* contains 60°. What is the sum of angle *B* and angle *D*?
   - (A) 180°
   - (B) 240°
   - (C) 280°
   - (D) 300°

9. If $4x - 7 \leq 1$, what is the greatest possible value of $4x + 2$?
   - (A) 10
   - (B) 7
   - (C) 3
   - (D) 1

10. If a train covers 14 miles in 10 minutes, what is the rate of the train in miles per hour?
   - (A) 64
   - (B) 76
   - (C) 84
   - (D) 98

exercises

ANSWER KEY AND EXPLANATIONS

Exercise 1

1. D	4. C	7. A	10. A	13. D
2. A	5. C	8. D	11. D	14. A
3. B	6. B	9. B	12. C	15. D

1. **The correct answer is (D).** If the slope is -2.5 and $f(5) = 8$, then use the slope formula to find $f(1)$.

$$\frac{8 - f(1)}{5 - 1} = -2.5$$

$$\frac{8 - f(1)}{4} = -2.5$$

$$8 - f(1) = -10$$

$$8 + 10 = f(1)$$

$$18 = f(1)$$

2. **The correct answer is (A).** The absolute value of an expression is always greater than or equal to 0, so adding a number to the expression will never result in 0. Answer choice (A), which states $|p - 2| - 2 = 0$ when $p = 0$ or 4, is correct.

3. **The correct answer is (B).** If $f(x) = -3x + 4$, then $f(-4x) = -3(-4x) + 4$, and $-3(-4x) + 4 = 12x + 4$.

4. **The correct answer is (C).** If $\frac{y}{x} = 4$ and $5(x - 1) = y$, then $y = 4x$ and $y = 5x - 5$. So, $4x = 5x - 5$ and $x = 5$.

5. **The correct answer is (C).** Multiply the expression to find the equivalent one. Use FOIL.

$$5(3x - 2)(2x + 1) = 5(6x^2 + 3x - 4x - 2) =$$
$$5(6x^2 - x - 2) = 30x^2 - 5x - 10$$

6. **The correct answer is (B).** To find the average increase, divide the change in increase by the number of weeks: $\frac{40 - 2}{9 - 1} = \frac{38}{8} = 4.75$

7. **The correct answer is (A).** If $\frac{x + y}{y} = \frac{5}{9}$, then

$$\frac{x}{y} + \frac{y}{y} = \frac{5}{9}$$

$$\frac{x}{y} + \frac{y}{y} - 1 = \frac{5}{9} - 1$$

$$\frac{x}{y} = -\frac{4}{9}$$

8. **The correct answer is (D).**

$$\sqrt{x - 1} = x - 7 \qquad x = 5, x = 10$$
$$x - 1 = (x - 7)^2 \qquad \sqrt{5 - 1} \, ? \, 5 - 7$$
$$x - 1 = x^2 - 14x + 49 \longrightarrow 2 \neq -2$$
$$0 = x^2 - 15x + 50 \qquad \sqrt{10 - 1} \, ? \, 10 - 7$$
$$0 = (x - 5)(x - 10) \qquad 3 = 3$$

5 is not a solution, but 10 is a solution.

9. **The correct answer is (B).**

$$1^2 + 1^2 = r^2$$
$$2 = r^2$$

$$\text{Area} = \pi r^2 = 2\pi$$

10. **The correct answer is (A).**

    Angle BCA = Angle BAC = 80°.

    There are 20° left for angle B.

11. **The correct answer is (D).** A line that is perpendicular to the line with the equation $y = 4 - 2x$ will have a slope equal to 0.5. If all equations are written in slope–intercept form, only choice (D) will be correct.

12. **The correct answer is (C).** Graph the system of equations. Note that the second equation is a circle that is intersected twice by the line.

13. **The correct answer is (D).**

    $$\frac{z + 6}{z - 5} = 5$$

    $$z + 6 = 5z - 25$$

    $$31 = 4z$$

    $$\frac{31}{4} = z$$

14. **The correct answer is (A).**

    $$\left(4 + 3i\right)\left(2 - 7i\right) = 8 - 28i + 6i - 21i^2$$

    $$\left(4 + 3i\right)\left(2 - 7i\right) = 8 - 22i - 21(-1)$$

    $$\left(4 + 3i\right)\left(2 - 7i\right) = 29 - 22i$$

15. **The correct answer is (D).** Write the equation in standard form, then plug the numbers into the quadratic formula and simplify.

    $$x^2 - 6dx - \frac{e}{2} = 0$$

    $$x = \frac{-b}{2a} \pm \frac{\sqrt{b^2 - 4ac}}{2a}$$

    $$x = \frac{-(-6)}{2} \pm \frac{\sqrt{(-6d)^2 - 4(1)\left(-\frac{1}{2}\right)}}{2(1)}$$

    $$x = 3d \pm \frac{\sqrt{36d^2 + 2e}}{2}$$

Exercise 2

| 1. C | 3. B | 5. A | 7. B | 9. A |
| 2. B | 4. C | 6. A | 8. B | 10. C |

1. **The correct answer is (C).** If Mario already has made 58 shots and will make an additional 3 shots each game, then he will make an additional $3g$ 3-point shots in g games, for a total of $58 + 3g$.

2. **The correct answer is (B).**

3. **The correct answer is (B).**

    5 feet = 60 inches

    6 feet 8 inches = 80 inches

    This is a 6-8-10 triangle, making the diagonal 100 inches, which is 8 feet 4 inches.

4. **The correct answer is (C).** In 3 hours, one ship went 60 miles, the other 45 miles. This is a 3-4-5 triangle as 45 = 3(15), 60 = 4(15). The hypotenuse will be 5(15), or 75.

5. **The correct answer is (A).** Substitute the point (b,c) into the equation $y = ax - 5$ and solve for a to find that $c = ab - 5$ and $a = \frac{c + 5}{b}$.

6. **The correct answer is (A).** He must score as many points above 85 as below. So far he has 8 above and 10 below. He needs another 2 above.

7. **The correct answer is (B).** If 15 adults are fed, $\frac{3}{4}$ of the food is gone. $\frac{1}{4}$ of the food will feed $\frac{1}{4} \times 32$, or 8, children.

8. **The correct answer is (B).** If angle $A = 60°$, then angle $B = 120°$.

    Angle B = Angle D. Their sum is 240°.

9. **The correct answer is (A).**

If $4x - 7 \leq 1$, then $4x + 2$ must be at most 10.

$$4x - 7 + 9 \leq 1 + 9$$
$$4x + 2 \leq 10$$

10. **The correct answer is (C).**

$$10 \text{ minutes} = \frac{1}{6} \text{ hour}$$

In one hour, the train will cover 6(14), or 84, miles.

SUMMING IT UP

- Follow the five-step plan for answering basic multiple-choice math questions:

  1 Read the question carefully and determine what's being asked.

  2 Decide which math principles apply and use them to solve the problem.

  3 Look for your answer among the choices. If it's there, mark it and go on.

  4 If the answer you found is not there, recheck the question and your calculations.

  5 If you still can't solve the problem, eliminate obviously wrong answers and take your best guess.

- In the Math Test—Calculator section, use a calculator where it can help the most: on basic arithmetic calculations, when calculating square roots and percentages, and comparing and converting fractions.

- Always set up your work on paper, then enter the numbers in your calculator; that way, if your calculation becomes confused, you don't have to try to replicate your setup from memory.

- The question number tells you how hard the question will be though some questions may be easier for you.

- Work backward from the answer choices. When you do, start with choice (B) or choice (C).

- Try to work with numbers instead of letters. This will help you avoid unnecessary algebraic calculations.

- Figures in the math section are always drawn to scale unless you see a warning. So use your eye as an estimator if you need to.

Grid-In Strategies

OVERVIEW

- Why grid-ins are easier than you think
- How to record your answers
- Guessing on grid-ins can't hurt you
- Summing it up

WHY GRID-INS ARE EASIER THAN YOU THINK

Let's take a quick break from multiple-choice questions and examine the other kind of question you will see on both the Math Test—No Calculator and Math Test–Calculator sections: grid-ins. These are officially named "student-produced responses," because you have to do the calculations and find the answer on your own; there are no multiple-choice answers from which to choose.

Many students are intimidated by grid-ins. Don't be! Grid-in questions test the exact same mathematical concepts as the multiple-choice questions. The only difference is that there are no answer choices with which to work.

The grid-in questions are in a section of their own and arranged in order of difficulty from easy to hard.

Take a Look at a Grid

The special answer grid has some very different sections. There are blank boxes at the top so you can actually write in your answer. Below the boxes are some ovals that have fraction slashes and decimal points. You fill these in if your answer needs them. The largest section has ovals with numbers in them. You have to fill in the ovals to correspond to the answer you have written in the boxes. Yes, it's a lot to think about, but once you understand how to use them, it's not a big deal.

chapter 8

NOTE

Remember that the student-produced responses will not be negative numbers and won't be greater than 9999.

Here is a sample grid:

ALERT!

A mixed number such as $3\frac{1}{2}$ must be gridded as 7/2 or as 3.5. If gridded as "3 1/2," it will read as "thirty-one halves."

HOW TO RECORD YOUR ANSWERS

On the SAT®, each set of grid-in questions starts with directions that look approximately like this:

Directions: For these questions, solve the problem and enter your answer in the grid, as described below, on the answer sheet.

1. Although not required, it is suggested that you write your answer in the boxes at the top of the columns to help you fill in the circles accurately. You will receive credit only if the circles are filled in correctly.

2. Mark no more than one circle in any column.

3. No question has a negative answer.

4. Some problems may have more than one correct answer. In such cases, grid only one answer.

5. Mixed numbers such as $3\frac{1}{2}$ must be gridded as 3.5 or $\frac{7}{2}$.

   If $3\frac{1}{2}$ is entered into the grid as [3|1|/|2], it will be interpreted as $\frac{31}{2}$, not $3\frac{1}{2}$.

6. **Decimal answers:** If you obtain a decimal answer with more digits than the grid can accommodate, it may be either rounded or truncated, but it must fill the entire grid.

Once you understand the following six rules, you can concentrate just on solving the math problems in this section.

1 Write your answer in the boxes at the top of the grid.

2 Mark the corresponding ovals, one per column.

3 Start in any column.

4 Work with decimals or fractions.

5 Express mixed numbers as decimals or improper fractions.

6 If more than one answer is possible, grid any one.

Now let's look at these rules in more detail:

1. Write your answer in the boxes at the top of the grid. Technically, this isn't required by the SAT®. Realistically, it gives you something to follow as you fill in the ovals. Do it—it will help you.

2. Make sure to mark the ovals that correspond to the answer you entered in the boxes, one per column. The machine that scores the test can only read the ovals, so if you don't fill them in, you won't get credit. Just entering your answer in the boxes is not enough!

3. You can start entering your answer in any column, if space permits. Unused columns should be left blank; don't put in zeroes. Look at this example:

Here are two ways to enter an answer of "150."

4. You can write your answer as a decimal or a fraction. For example, an answer can be expressed as $\frac{3}{4}$ or as .75. You don't have to put a zero in front of a decimal that is less than 1. Just remember that you have only four spaces to work with and that a decimal point or a fraction slash uses up one of the spaces.

For decimal answers, be as accurate as possible but keep it within four spaces. Say you get an answer of .1777; here are your options:

Answers .177 and .178 would both be marked as correct.

Answers .18 or .2 would be marked wrong because they could have been written more accurately in the space provided.

Fractions do not have to be simplified to simplest form unless they don't fit in the answer grid. For example, you can grid $\frac{4}{10}$, but you can't grid $\frac{12}{16}$ because you'd need five spaces. So, you would simplify it and grid $\frac{3}{4}$.

5 A mixed number has to be expressed as a decimal or as an improper fraction. If you tried to grid $1\frac{3}{4}$, it would be scored as $\frac{13}{4}$, which would give you a wrong answer. Instead, you could grid the answer as 1.75 or as $\frac{7}{4}$.

The above answers are acceptable.

The above answer is unacceptable.

⑥ Sometimes the problems in this section will have more than one correct answer. Choose one and grid it.

For example, if a question asks for a prime number between 5 and 13, the answer could be 7 or 11. Grid 7 or grid 11, but don't put in both answers.

Either answer is acceptable, but not both.

GUESSING ON GRID-INS CAN'T HURT YOU

Unfortunately, you cannot receive partial credit for grid-ins. Your answers are either completely correct or completely wrong. But no points are deducted for incorrect responses, so guessing is better than leaving a question blank.

EXERCISES: GRID-INS

Exercise 1

10 Questions • 15 Minutes

Directions: For these questions, solve the problem and enter your answer in the grid following each question, as described below.

1. Although not required, it is suggested that you write your answer in the boxes at the top of the columns to help you fill in the circles accurately. You will receive credit only if the circles are filled in correctly.

2. Mark no more than one circle in any column.

3. No question has a negative answer.

4. Some problems may have more than one correct answer. In such cases, grid only one answer.

5. Mixed numbers such as $3\frac{1}{2}$ must be gridded as 3.5 or $\frac{7}{2}$.

   If $3\frac{1}{2}$ is entered into the grid as [grid showing 3 1 / 2], it will be interpreted as $\frac{31}{2}$, not $3\frac{1}{2}$.

6. **Decimal answers:** If you obtain a decimal answer with more digits than the grid can accommodate, it may be either rounded or truncated, but it must fill the entire grid.

1. If $3x + y = 4$ and $x + 3y = 5$, what is the value of $x + y$?

2. Marion is paid \$24 for 5 hours of work in the school office. Janet works 3 hours and makes \$10.95. How much more per hour does Marion make than Janet? (Ignore the dollar sign in gridding your answer.)

3. If the outer diameter of a cylindrical oil tank is 54.28 inches and the inner diameter is 48.7 inches, what is the thickness of the wall of the tank, in inches?

5. If $r = 25 - s$, what is the value of $4(r + s)$?

4. A car has an average mileage of 30 miles per gallon. If one gallon of gasoline costs \$3.75, how many miles can the car travel on \$20 worth of gasoline?

6. Arc AB is on circle O. If the radius of circle O is 5 centimeters, and angle AOB measures 30°, what is the length of arc AB rounded to the nearest tenth of a centimeter?

7. $\sqrt{4x+5} = 6$

   If x is a solution of the equation above, what is the value of $4x$?

9. In May, Carter's Appliances sold 40 washing machines. In June, because of a special promotion, the store sold 80 washing machines. What is the percent of increase in the number of washing machines sold?

8. A cube with edges 3 centimeters long is made from solid aluminum. If the density of aluminum is approximately 2.7 grams per cubic centimeter, what is the weight of the cube to the nearest tenth of a gram?

10. Find the value of $\left(3\sqrt{2}\right)^2$.

Exercise 2

10 Questions • 15 Minutes

Directions: For these questions, solve the problem and enter your answer in the grid following each question, as described below.

1. Although not required, it is suggested that you write your answer in the boxes at the top of the columns to help you fill in the circles accurately. You will receive credit only if the circles are filled in correctly.

2. Mark no more than one circle in any column.

3. No question has a negative answer.

4. Some problems may have more than one correct answer. In such cases, grid only one answer.

5. Mixed numbers such as $3\frac{1}{2}$ must be gridded as 3.5 or $\frac{7}{2}$.

   If $3\frac{1}{2}$ is entered into the grid as $\boxed{3\ 1\ /\ 2}$, it will be interpreted as $\frac{31}{2}$, not $3\frac{1}{2}$.

6. **Decimal answers:** If you obtain a decimal answer with more digits than the grid can accommodate, it may be either rounded or truncated, but it must fill the entire grid.

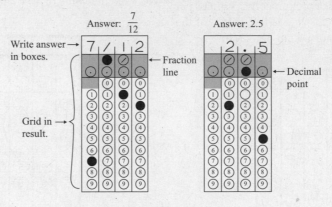

Answer: $\frac{7}{12}$ Answer: 2.5

Answer: 201
Either position is correct.

Acceptable ways to grid $\frac{2}{3}$ are:

1. 53 percent of the 1000 students at Jackson High are girls. How many boys are there in the school?

2. The legs of a right triangle measure $\sqrt{2}$ centimeters and $\sqrt{6}$ centimeters. What is the length of the hypotenuse of the right triangle to the nearest tenth of a centimeter?

3. In a group of 40 students, 25 applied to Columbia and 30 applied to Cornell. If 3 students applied to neither Columbia nor Cornell, how many students applied to both schools?

4. If $x^2 - y^2 = 100$ and $x - y = 20$, what is the value of $x + y$?

5. A gallon of water is added to 6 quarts of a solution that is 50% acid. What percent of the new solution is acid?

7. A plane flies over Denver at 11:20 a.m. It passes over Coolidge, 120 miles from Denver, at 11:32 a.m. Find the rate of the plane in miles per hour.

6. A gasoline tank is $\frac{1}{4}$ full. After adding 10 gallons of gasoline, the gauge indicates that the tank is $\frac{2}{3}$ full. Find the capacity of the tank in gallons.

8. $\frac{x+1}{x-1}=5$

What value of x is a solution of the equation above?

9. What is the median of the set of numbers 2, 3, 4, 5, 6, 7, 8, and 9?

10. $y = x^2 - 8x + 7$

    $y = x - 1$

    If (x, y) is a solution of the system of equations above, what is a possible value of $x + y$?

ANSWERS AND EXPLANATIONS

Exercise 1

1. $3x + y = 4$

    $x + 3y = 5$

    $4x + 4y = 9$

    $4(x + y) = 9$

    $x + y = \dfrac{9}{4}$ **(answer)**

    You would grid 9/4 or 2.25.

2. Marion's hourly wage is $\dfrac{\$24}{5}$, or $4.80.

    Janet's hourly wage is $\dfrac{\$10.95}{3}$, or $3.65.

    $4.80 − $3.65 = $1.15 **(answer)**

    You would grid 1.15. You do not need to worry about the dollar sign.

3. The difference of 5.58 must be divided between both sides. The thickness on each side is 2.79 inches. So you would grid in 2.79 as your answer.

4. $30\left(\dfrac{20}{3.75}\right) = 160$ **(answer)**

5. $r + s = 25$

    $4(r + s) = 4(25) = 100$ **(answer)**

6. The circumference of the circle is $2\pi(5) = 10\pi$.

    $\dfrac{30}{360}(10\pi) \approx 2.61$ or 2.62 **(answer)**

7. $\sqrt{4x + 5} = 6$

    $4x + 5 = 36$

    $4x = 31$ **(answer)**

8. $27(2.7) = 72.9$ **(answer)**

9. When computing the percent of increase (or decrease), use $\dfrac{difference}{original} \times 100$. In this case, the difference is $80 - 40$, which is 40. The original amount sold was 40, so $\dfrac{40}{40} \times 100 = 100\%$ increase. You would grid 100 as your answer.

10. $\left(3\sqrt{2}\right)\left(3\sqrt{2}\right) = 9 \cdot 2 = 18$ **(answer)**

Exercise 2

1. 47 percent of 1000 are boys.

$(0.47)(1000) = 470$ boys **(answer)**

2. $\left(\sqrt{2}\right)^2 + \left(\sqrt{6}\right)^2 = (hypotenuse)^2$

$$2 + 6 = (hypotenuse)^2$$

$$8 = (hyp)^2$$

$$\sqrt{8} = hyp$$

$$2.8 \approx hyp \quad \textbf{(answer)}$$

3.

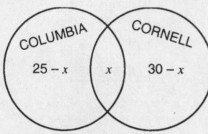

$$25 - x + x + 30 - x = 37$$

$$55 - x = 37$$

$$18 = x$$

18   **(answer)**

4. $x^2 - y^2 = (x - y)(x + y)$

$$100 = 20(x + y)$$

$$5 = (x + y)$$

5   **(answer)**

5.

	No. of quarts	% acid	Amount of acid
Original	6	0.50	3
Added	4	0	0
New	10		3

$\frac{3}{10} = 30\%$ **(answer)**

6. 10 gallons is $\frac{2}{3} - \frac{1}{4}$ of the tank.

$$\frac{2}{3} - \frac{1}{4} = \frac{8 - 3}{12} = \frac{5}{12}$$

$$\frac{5}{12}x = 10$$

$$5x = 120$$

$$x = 24 \quad \textbf{(answer)}$$

7. The plane covers 120 miles in 12 minutes, or $\frac{1}{5}$ hour. In $\frac{5}{5}$, or 1 hour, it covers $5(120)$, or 600 miles. 600 **(answer)**

8. $\frac{x + 1}{x - 1} = 5$

$$x + 1 = 5(x - 1)$$

$$x + 1 = 5x - 5$$

$$6 = 4x$$

$$\frac{6}{4} = x$$

$$x = 1.5 \quad \textbf{(answer)}$$

9. The median is equal to the arithmetic mean of the two numbers in the middle, 5 and 6.

$\frac{5 + 6}{2} = \frac{11}{2} = 5.5$ **(answer)**

10.

$$y = x^2 - 8x + 7$$

$$y = x - 1$$

$$x^2 - 8x + 7 = x - 1$$

$$x^2 - 9x + 8 = 0$$

$$(x - 8)(x - 1) = 0$$

$$x = 8 \text{ or } x = 1$$

If $x = 8$, then $y = 8 - 1 = 7$.

If $x = 1$, then $y = 1 - 1 = 0$.

$x + y = 15$ or $x + y = 1$ **(both answers are acceptable)**

SUMMING IT UP

- When you grid answers to student-produced response questions, follow these six rules:
  1. Write your answer in the boxes at the top of the grid.
  2. Mark the corresponding ovals, one per column.
  3. Start in any column.
  4. Work with decimals or fractions.
  5. Express mixed numbers as decimals or improper fractions.
  6. If more than one answer is possible, grid any one.
- Remember that grid-ins test the same concepts as multiple-choice math.
- The most important advice for grid-ins? Don't be intimidated.

Numbers and Operations Review

OVERVIEW

- Operations with fractions
- Verbal problems involving fractions
- Complex numbers
- Direct and inverse variation
- Finding percents
- Verbal problems involving percent
- Summing it up

OPERATIONS WITH FRACTIONS

The four basic *arithmetic operations* are addition, subtraction, multiplication, and division.

Adding and Subtracting

In adding or subtracting fractions, you must remember that the numbers must have the same (common) denominator.

Add $\frac{1}{3} + \frac{2}{5} + \frac{3}{4}$.

The least number that is divisible by 3, 5, and 4 is 60. Therefore, use 60 as the common denominator. Convert each fraction to fractions with the common denominator, 60, by multiplying each numerator by the same factor as you must multiply the denominator by to result in the common denominator of 60.

$$\frac{20}{60} + \frac{24}{60} + \frac{45}{60} = \frac{89}{60}$$
$$= 1\frac{29}{60}$$

Fractions should be written in the simplest form. Often, in multiple-choice questions, you may find that the answer you have correctly computed is not among the choices but an equivalent fraction is. Be careful!

In simplifying fractions involving large numbers, it is helpful to be able to tell whether a factor is common to both numerator and denominator before a lengthy trial division. Certain tests for divisibility help with this.

chapter 9

TESTS FOR DIVISIBILITY

To test if a number is divisible by:	Check to see:
2	if it is even
3	if the sum of the digits is divisible by 3
4	if the number formed by the last two digits is divisible by 4
5	if its last digit is a 5 or 0
6	if it is even and the sum of the digits is divisible by 3
8	if the number formed by the last three digits is divisible by 8
9	if the sum of the digits is divisible by 9
10	if its last digit is 0

Simplify: $\dfrac{3525}{4341}$

This fraction can be simplified by dividing by 3, since the sum of the digits of the numerator is 15 and those of the denominator add up to 12, both are divisible by 3.

$$\frac{3525}{4341} = \frac{1175}{1447}$$

The resulting fraction meets no further divisibility tests and therefore has no common factor listed above. Larger divisors would be unlikely on the SAT®.

To add or subtract mixed numbers, it is again important to remember common denominators. In subtraction, you must borrow in terms of the common denominator.

Addition:
$$43\frac{2}{5} = 43\frac{6}{15}$$
$$+8\frac{1}{3} = +8\frac{5}{15}$$
$$51\frac{11}{15}$$

Subtraction:
$$43\frac{2}{5} = 43\frac{6}{15} = 42\frac{21}{15}$$
$$-6\frac{2}{3} = -6\frac{10}{15} = -6\frac{10}{15}$$
$$36\frac{11}{15}$$

Multiplying

To multiply fractions, always try to divide common factors where possible before actually multiplying. In multiplying mixed numbers, always rename them as improper fractions first.

Multiply: $\dfrac{2}{3} \cdot \dfrac{10}{11} \cdot \dfrac{99}{110} = \dfrac{18}{55}$

Multiply: $4\frac{1}{2} \cdot 1\frac{2}{3} \cdot 5\frac{1}{5}$

$$\frac{\overset{3}{\cancel{9}}}{\cancel{2}} \cdot \frac{\cancel{5}}{\cancel{3}} \cdot \frac{\overset{13}{\cancel{26}}}{\cancel{5}} = 39$$

Dividing

To divide fractions or mixed numbers, remember to multiply by the reciprocal of the divisor (the number after the division sign).

Divide: $4\frac{1}{2} \div \frac{3}{4} = \frac{\overset{3}{\cancel{9}}}{\cancel{2}} \cdot \frac{\overset{2}{\cancel{4}}}{\cancel{3}} = 6$

Divide: $62\frac{1}{2} \div 5 = \frac{\overset{25}{\cancel{125}}}{2} \cdot \frac{1}{\cancel{5}} = 12\frac{1}{2}$

To simplify complex fractions (fractions within fractions), multiply every term by the least common multiple of all denominators in order to clear all fractions in the given numerator and denominator.

$$\frac{\frac{1}{2}+\frac{1}{3}}{\frac{1}{4}+\frac{1}{6}}$$

The least number that can be used to clear all fractions is 12. Multiplying each term by 12 yields:

$$\frac{\frac{1}{2}+\frac{1}{3}}{\frac{1}{4}+\frac{1}{6}} = \frac{\frac{12}{2}+\frac{12}{3}}{\frac{12}{4}+\frac{12}{6}} = \frac{6+4}{3+2} = \frac{10}{5} = 2$$

$$\frac{\frac{3}{4}+\frac{2}{3}}{1-\frac{1}{2}}$$

Again, multiply by 12.

$$\frac{\frac{3}{4}+\frac{2}{3}}{1-\frac{1}{2}} = \frac{\frac{36}{4}+\frac{24}{3}}{12-\frac{12}{2}} = \frac{9+8}{12-6} = \frac{17}{6} = 2\frac{5}{6}$$

EXERCISES: OPERATIONS WITH FRACTIONS

Directions: Work out each problem in the space provided.

Add:

1. $12\dfrac{5}{6}+2\dfrac{3}{8}+21\dfrac{1}{4}$

2. $\dfrac{1}{2}+\dfrac{1}{3}+\dfrac{1}{4}+\dfrac{1}{5}+\dfrac{1}{6}$

Subtract:

3. $5\dfrac{3}{4}$ from $10\dfrac{1}{2}$

4. $17\dfrac{2}{3}$ from 50

Multiply:

5. $5\dfrac{1}{4}\bullet 1\dfrac{5}{7}$

6. $\dfrac{3}{4}\bullet\dfrac{3}{4}\bullet\dfrac{3}{4}$

Divide:

7. $\dfrac{1}{5}\div 5$

8. $3\dfrac{2}{3}\div 1\dfrac{5}{6}$

Simplify:

9. $\dfrac{\dfrac{5}{6}-\dfrac{1}{3}}{2+\dfrac{1}{5}}$

10. $\dfrac{3+\dfrac{1}{4}}{5-\dfrac{1}{2}}$

Solve:

11. $4\left(\dfrac{1}{6}+\dfrac{1}{12}\right)$

12. $\dfrac{2}{5}\left(\dfrac{1}{3}+\dfrac{1}{4}\right)$

13. $\dfrac{4}{9}+\dfrac{7}{18}-\dfrac{4}{5}$

ANSWERS AND EXPLANATIONS

1.

$$12\frac{5}{6} = 12\frac{20}{24}$$

$$2\frac{3}{8} = 2\frac{9}{24}$$

$$+21\frac{1}{4} = 21\frac{6}{24}$$

$$35\frac{35}{24} = 36\frac{11}{24}$$

2.

$$\frac{1}{2} = \frac{30}{60}$$

$$\frac{1}{3} = \frac{20}{60}$$

$$\frac{1}{4} = \frac{15}{60}$$

$$\frac{1}{5} = \frac{12}{60}$$

$$+\frac{1}{6} = \frac{10}{60}$$

$$\frac{87}{60} = 1\frac{27}{60} = 1\frac{9}{20}$$

3.

$$10\frac{1}{2} = 9\frac{3}{2} = 9\frac{6}{4}$$

$$-5\frac{3}{4}$$

$$4\frac{3}{4}$$

4.

$$\overset{49}{\cancel{50}}\frac{3}{3}$$

$$-17\frac{2}{3}$$

$$32\frac{1}{3}$$

5. $\dfrac{\overset{3}{\cancel{21}}}{\cancel{4}} \cdot \dfrac{\overset{3}{\cancel{12}}}{\cancel{7}} = 9$

6. $\dfrac{3}{4} \cdot \dfrac{3}{4} \cdot \dfrac{3}{4} = \dfrac{27}{64}$

7. $\dfrac{1}{5} \cdot \dfrac{1}{5} = \dfrac{1}{25}$

8. $\dfrac{\cancel{4}}{\cancel{3}} \cdot \dfrac{\overset{2}{\cancel{6}}}{\cancel{4}} = 2$

9. $\dfrac{25-10}{60+6} = \dfrac{15}{66} = \dfrac{5}{22}$

Each term was multiplied by 30.

10. $\dfrac{12+1}{20-2} = \dfrac{13}{18}$

Each term was multiplied by 4.

11.
$$4\left(\frac{1}{6}+\frac{1}{12}\right) = 4\left(\frac{2}{12}+\frac{1}{12}\right)$$

$$= 4\left(\frac{3}{12}\right)$$

$$= \left(\frac{12}{12}\right)$$

$$= 1$$

12.
$$\frac{2}{5}\left(\frac{1}{3}+\frac{1}{4}\right) = \frac{2}{5}\left(\frac{4}{12}+\frac{3}{12}\right)$$

$$= \frac{2^{1}}{5}\left(\frac{7}{12_{6}}\right)$$

$$= \left(\frac{7}{30}\right)$$

13.
$$\frac{4}{9}+\frac{7}{18}-\frac{4}{5} = \frac{8}{18}+\frac{7}{18}-\frac{4}{5}$$

$$= \frac{15}{18}-\frac{4}{5}$$

$$= \frac{5}{6}-\frac{4}{5}$$

$$= \frac{25}{30}-\frac{24}{30}$$

$$= \frac{1}{30}$$

VERBAL PROBLEMS INVOLVING FRACTIONS

Fraction problems deal with parts of a whole.

> If a class consists of 12 boys and 18 girls, what part of the class is boys?

The class consists of 12 boys out 30 total students, or $\frac{12}{30} = \frac{2}{5}$. So, boys represent $\frac{2}{5}$ of the class.

Notice, that to find the solution you must add the boys and girls to find the total number of students. Problems may require more than one calculation as you can see in this example.

> One-quarter of this year's seniors have averages above 90. One-half of the remainder have averages between 80 and 90 inclusive. What part of the senior class have averages below 80?

$\frac{1}{4}$ have averages above 90.

$\frac{1}{2}$ of $\frac{3}{4}$, or $\frac{3}{8}$, have averages between 80 and 90 inclusive.

$\frac{1}{4} + \frac{3}{8} = \frac{2}{8} + \frac{3}{8} = \frac{5}{8}$ have averages 80 and above.

Therefore, $\frac{3}{8}$ of the class have averages below 80.

> 14 is $\frac{2}{3}$ of what number?

$14 = \frac{2}{3}x$

Divide each side of the equation by $\frac{2}{3}$, which is the same as multiplying the reciprocal or $\frac{3}{2}$.

$21 = x$

> If John has p hours of homework and has worked for r hours, what part of his homework is yet to be done?

If John had 5 hours of homework and had worked for 3 hours, you would first find he had $5 - 3$ hours, or 2 hours, yet to do. This represents $\frac{2}{5}$ of his work. Using letters, his remaining work is represented by $\frac{p-r}{p}$.

EXERCISES: VERBAL PROBLEMS INVOLVING FRACTIONS

Directions: Work out each problem. Circle the letter of your choice.

1. A team played 30 games, of which it won 24. What part of the games played did the team lose?

    (A) $\frac{4}{5}$

    (B) $\frac{1}{4}$

    (C) $\frac{1}{5}$

    (D) $\frac{3}{4}$

2. If a man's weekly salary is X and he saves Y, what part of his weekly salary does he spend?

    (A) $\frac{X}{Y}$

    (B) $\frac{X-Y}{X}$

    (C) $\frac{X-Y}{Y}$

    (D) $\frac{Y-X}{X}$

3. What part of an hour elapses between 11:50 a.m. and 12:14 p.m.?

    (A) $\frac{2}{5}$

    (B) $\frac{7}{30}$

    (C) $\frac{17}{30}$

    (D) $\frac{1}{6}$

4. One half of the employees of Acme Co. earn salaries above $18,000 annually. One third of the remainder earn salaries between $15,000 and $18,000. What part of the staff earns below $15,000?

    (A) $\frac{1}{6}$

    (B) $\frac{2}{3}$

    (C) $\frac{1}{2}$

    (D) $\frac{1}{3}$

5. David received his allowance on Sunday. He spends $\frac{1}{4}$ of his allowance on Monday and $\frac{2}{3}$ of the remainder on Tuesday. What part of his allowance is left for the rest of the week?

    (A) $\frac{1}{3}$

    (B) $\frac{1}{12}$

    (C) $\frac{1}{4}$

    (D) $\frac{1}{2}$

6. 12 is $\frac{3}{4}$ of what number?

    (A) 16
    (B) 9
    (C) 36
    (D) 20

7. A piece of fabric is cut into three sections so that the first is three times as long as the second, and the second section is three times as long as the third. What part of the entire piece is the smallest section?

(A) $\frac{1}{13}$

(B) $\frac{1}{9}$

(C) $\frac{1}{7}$

(D) $\frac{1}{3}$

8. If a number is added to both the numerator and denominator of $\frac{4}{7}$, the result is $\frac{8}{9}$. What is the number?

(A) 2

(B) 9

(C) 18

(D) 20

9. A factory employs M men and W women. What part of its employees are women?

(A) $\frac{5}{8}$

(B) $\frac{5}{3}$

(C) $\frac{3}{5}$

(D) $\frac{3}{8}$

10. A motion was passed by a vote of 5:3. What part of the votes cast were in favor of the motion?

(A) $\frac{M}{W}$

(B) $\frac{M+W}{W}$

(C) $\frac{W}{M-W}$

(D) $\frac{W}{M+W}$

11. If the ratio of $x:y$ is 9:7, what is the value of $x + y$?

(A) 2

(B) 16

(C) 63

(D) It cannot be determined from the information given.

12. In a certain class, the ratio of men to women is 3:5. If the class has 24 people in it, how many are women?

(A) 9

(B) 12

(C) 15

(D) 18

13. A rain barrel contains $56\frac{1}{2}$ gallons of water. In the morning, $23\frac{1}{4}$ gallons are used. The level of the rain barrel after it rains increases by $16\frac{3}{4}$ gallons. How many gallons are in the tank after it rains?

(A) $16\frac{1}{2}$

(B) 50

(C) 64

(D) $96\frac{1}{2}$

14. If x is $\frac{2}{3}$ of y and y is $\frac{3}{4}$ of z, what is the ratio of $z:x$?

(A) 1:2

(B) 1:1

(C) 2:1

(D) 3:2

15. Teagan can paint a house in 5 hours and Kevin can paint a house in 8 hours. How many hours will it take them to paint a house if they work together?

(A) 3

(B) $3\frac{1}{13}$

(C) $6\frac{1}{2}$

(D) 13

ANSWER KEY AND EXPLANATIONS

1. C	4. D	7. A	10. A	13. B
2. B	5. C	8. D	11. D	14. C
3. A	6. A	9. D	12. C	15. B

1. **The correct answer is (C).** The team lost 6 games out of 30. $\frac{6}{30} = \frac{1}{5}$

2. **The correct answer is (B).** The man spends $X - Y$ out of X. $\frac{X-Y}{X}$

3. **The correct answer is (A).** 10 minutes elapse by noon, and another 14 after noon, making a total of 24 minutes. There are 60 minutes in an hour. $\frac{24}{60} = \frac{2}{5}$

4. **The correct answer is (D).** One half earn over \$18,000. One third of the other $\frac{1}{2}$, or $\frac{1}{6}$, earn between \$15,000 and \$18,000. This accounts for $\frac{1}{2} + \frac{1}{6}$, or $\frac{3}{6} + \frac{1}{6} + \frac{4}{6} = \frac{2}{3}$ of the staff, leaving $\frac{1}{3}$ to earn below \$15,000.

5. **The correct answer is (C).** David spends $\frac{1}{4}$ on Monday and $\frac{2}{3}$ of the other $\frac{3}{4}$, or $\frac{1}{2}$, on Tuesday, leaving only $\frac{1}{4}$ for the rest of the week.

6. **The correct answer is (A).** $12 = \frac{3}{4}x$. Multiply each side by $\frac{4}{3}$. $16 = x$.

7. **The correct answer is (A).** Let the third or shortest section $= x$. Then the second section $= 3x$, and the first section $= 9x$. The entire piece of fabric is then $13x$, and the shortest piece represents $\frac{x}{13x}$, or $\frac{1}{13}$, of the entire piece.

8. **The correct answer is (D).** Let n be the number that is being added.

$\frac{4+n}{7+n} = \frac{8}{9}$; $9(4+n) = 8(7+n)$;

$36 + 9n = 56 + 8n$; $n = 20$.

9. **The correct answer is (D).** The factory employs $M + W$ people, out of which W are women.

10. **The correct answer is (A).** For every 5 votes in favor, 3 were cast against. 5 out of every 8 votes cast were in favor of the motion.

11. **The correct answer is (D).** Remember, a ratio is a fraction. If x is 18 and y is 14, the ratio $x:y$ is 9:7, but $x + y$ is 32. The point of this problem is that x and y can take on *many* possible values, just as long as the ratio 9:7 is preserved. Given the multiplicity of possible values, it is not possible here to establish *one* definite value for the sum of x and y.

12. **The correct answer is (C).** The ratio of women to the total number of people is 5:8. We can set up a proportion. If $\frac{5}{8} = \frac{x}{24}$, then $x = 15$.

13. **The correct answer is (B).** To find the water remaining in the tank solve:

$56\frac{1}{2} - 23\frac{1}{4} + 16\frac{3}{4}$. The result is

$56\frac{2}{4} - 23\frac{1}{4} + 16\frac{3}{4} = 50$ gallons.

14. **The correct answer is (C).** There are several ways to attack this problem. If x is $\frac{2}{3}$ of y, then $x = \frac{2}{2} \bullet y$. If y is $\frac{3}{4}$ of z, then z is $\frac{4}{3}$ of y, or $z = \frac{4}{3} \bullet y$. Therefore, $z = 2x$.

The ratio of $z{:}x$ is 2:1. You could also plug in a real number and solve. If x is 2, figure out what y and z would be. Therefore, y would be 3 and z would be 4, so the ratio of z to x is 2:1.

15. **The correct answer is (B).** To find how long it will take them to paint the house together solve: $\frac{x}{5} + \frac{x}{8} = 1$. The result is $8x + 5x = 40$, $13x = 40$, $x = 3\frac{1}{13}$.

COMPLEX NUMBERS

A complex number is a number made up of a real number and an imaginary number. It can be written in standard form $a + bi$, where a and b are real numbers and i is an imaginary unit.

$i = \sqrt{-1}, i^2 = -1$

For example, in the complex number $2 + 3i$ the real number is 2 and the imaginary number is $3i$.

Complex numbers can be added, subtracted, multiplied and divided.

Adding Complex Numbers

To add complex numbers, add the real numbers and the imaginary numbers separately.

Sum: $(a + bi) + (c + di) = (a + c) + (b + d)i$

Add: $(2 + 3i) + (8 + 4i)$

Add the real numbers and then the imaginary numbers.

$(2 + 8) + (3i + 4i) = 10 + 7i$

Subtracting Complex Numbers

To subtract complex numbers, subtract the real numbers and the imaginary numbers separately.

Difference: $(a + bi) - (c + di) = (a - c) + (b - d)i$

Subtract: $(2 + 3i) - (8 + 4i)$

Subtract the real numbers and then the imaginary numbers.

$(2 + 3i) - (8 + 4i) = (2 - 8) + (3i - 4i) = -6 - i$

Multiplying Complex Numbers

Multiplying complex numbers is like multiplying polynomials by using the distributive property or the FOIL method.

Product: $(a + bi)(c + di) = (ac) + (adi) + (bci) + (bd)i^2$

Multiply: $3i(-2 + 9i)$

Distribute $3i$ to all of the terms in the parentheses.

$$3i(-2 + 9i) = (3i)(-2) + (3i)(9i)$$
$$= (-3i)(-2) + 27i^2$$
$$= -6i + 27(-1)$$
$$= -27 - 6i \qquad i^2 = (\sqrt{-1})(\sqrt{-1}) = -1$$

Multiply: $(2 + 3i)(8 + 4i)$

Find the sum of the products of the **F**irst terms, the **O**uter terms, the **I**nner terms, and the **L**ast terms of the binomials. The acronym FOIL stands for First Outer Inner Last and will help you to remember how to multiply two binomials.

When simplifying an expression that involves complex numbers simplify i^2 to –1.

$$(2 + 3i)(8 + 4i) = (2 \bullet 8) + (2 \bullet 4i) + (8 \bullet 3i) + (3i \bullet 4i)$$
$$= 16 + 8i + 24i + 12i^2$$
$$= 16 + 32i + 12(-1)$$
$$= 4 + 32i$$

Simplify and write in standard form $a + bi$.

Dividing Complex Numbers

Dividing complex numbers is more complicated because the denominator can not contain a radical. This process is called *rationalizing the denominator*. In order to make the denominator rational you must use its *complex conjugate*. The product of two complex conjugates is always a real number $a^2 + b^2$. The numbers $2 + 8i$ and $2 - 8i$ are examples of complex conjugates, and their product is the real number $2^2 + 8^2 = 4 + 64 = 68$.

Complex conjugates: $(a + bi)$ and $(a - bi)$

Product of Complex conjugates: $(a + bi)(a - bi) = a^2 + b^2$

Simplify: $\dfrac{8}{7i}$

Rationalize the denominator by multiplying the numerator and denominator by i.

$$\frac{8}{7i} = \frac{8}{7i} \bullet \frac{i}{i} = \frac{8i}{7i^2} = \frac{8i}{7(-1)} = \frac{8i}{-7}$$

Simplify: $\dfrac{4 + 2i}{-3 + 5i}$

Rationalize the denominator by multiplying the numerator and denominator by the conjugate for the denominator. Then simplify by combining like terms.

$$\frac{4 + 2i}{-3 + 5i} = \frac{4 + 2i}{-3 + 5i} \bullet \frac{-3 - 5i}{-3 - 5i} = \frac{-12 - 20i - 6i - 10i^2}{9 + 15i - 15i - 25i^2}$$
$$= \frac{-12 - 20i - 6i - 10(-1)}{9 + 15i - 15i - 25(-1)}$$
$$= \frac{-2 - 26i}{9 + 25}$$
$$= \frac{-2 - 26i}{34}$$
$$= \frac{-2}{34} - \frac{26i}{34}$$
$$= \frac{-1}{17} - \frac{13i}{17}$$

Recall that $i^2 = -1$.

Master the New SAT®

EXERCISES: COMPLEX NUMBERS

Directions: Work out each problem. Circle the letter of your choice.

1. **Add:** $(8 + 2i) + (2 - 3i)$
   (A) $15i$
   (B) $5 + 4i$
   (C) $6 + i$
   (D) $10 - i$

2. **Add:** $(-2 - 5i) + (6 + 9i)$
   (A) $4 + 4i$
   (B) $7 + i$
   (C) $8i$
   (D) $8 + 14i$

3. **Subtract:** $(-9 + 4i) - (3 + 7i)$
   (A) $-6 - 3i$
   (B) $-2 + i$
   (C) $-12 - 3i$
   (D) $-i$

4. **Subtract:** $(6 + 3i) - (2 + 9i)$
   (A) $4 - 6i$
   (B) $4 + 12i$
   (C) $8 - 6i$
   (D) $10i$

5. **Multiply:** $(2i)(32i)$
   (A) 64
   (B) -64
   (C) $64i$
   (D) $-64i$

6. **Multiply:** $(-5i)(12 - 3i)$
   (A) $8 + 17i$
   (B) $-15 - 60i$
   (C) $15 + 60i$
   (D) $-8 + 17i$

7. **Multiply:** $(4 - 6i)(1 - 2i)$
   (A) $4 + 12i$
   (B) $4 - 12i$
   (C) $8 + 14i$
   (D) $-8 - 14i$

8. **Multiply:** $(-5 + 3i)(20 - 7i)$
   (A) $-100 - 4i$
   (B) $100 + 21i$
   (C) $-79 + 95i$
   (D) $121 + 95i$

9. **Simplify:** $\dfrac{-5i}{4i + 11}$
   (A) $-4 - 11i$
   (B) $\dfrac{20 - 55i}{137}$
   (C) $\dfrac{-20 - 55i}{137}$
   (D) $4 + 11i$

10. **Simplify:** $\dfrac{17 - i}{3i}$
   (A) $\dfrac{1}{3} - \dfrac{17}{3}i$
   (B) $\dfrac{1}{3} + \dfrac{17}{3}i$
   (C) $-\dfrac{1}{3} + \dfrac{17}{3}i$
   (D) $-\dfrac{1}{3} - \dfrac{17}{3}i$

11. Simplify: $\dfrac{6+14i}{1+2i}$

    (A) $-\dfrac{22}{3}-\dfrac{2}{3}i$

    (B) $-\dfrac{22}{3}+\dfrac{2}{3}i$

    (C) $\dfrac{34}{5}+\dfrac{2}{5}i$

    (D) $-\dfrac{34}{5}-\dfrac{2}{5}i$

12. Simplify: $\dfrac{-3+5i}{-3-4i}$

    (A) $-\dfrac{29}{5}-\dfrac{27}{5}i$

    (B) $-\dfrac{11}{25}-\dfrac{27}{25}i$

    (C) $\dfrac{21}{25}-\dfrac{27}{25}i$

    (D) $\dfrac{11}{7}+\dfrac{27}{7}i$

ANSWER KEY AND EXPLANATIONS

1. D	4. A	7. D	9. C	11. C
2. A	5. B	8. C	10. D	12. B
3. C	6. B			

1. **The correct answer is (D).**

$(8+2i)+(2-3i)=(8+2)+(2i-3i)=10-i$

2. **The correct answer is (A).**

$(-2-5i)+(6+9i)=(-2+6)+(-5i+9i)$
$=4+4i$

3. **The correct answer is (C).**

$(-9+4i)-(3+7i)=(-9-3)+(4i-7i)$
$$=-12-3i$$

4. **The correct answer is (A).**

$(6+3i)-(2+9i)=(6-2)+(3i-9i)$
$$=4-6i$$

5. **The correct answer is (B).**

$(2i)(32i)=64i^2=64(-1)=-64$

6. **The correct answer is (B).**

$(-5i)(12-3i)=(-5i)(12)+(-5i)(-3i)$
$$=-60i+15i^2$$
$$=-60i+15(-1)$$
$$=-15-60i$$

7. **The correct answer is (D).**

$(4-6i)(1-2i)=(4)+(-8i)+(-6i)+(12i^2)$
$$=4+(-14i)+(-12)$$
$$=-8-14i$$

8. **The correct answer is (C).**

$(-5+3i)(20-7i)=-100+(-5)(-7i)+(3i)(20)+(3i)(-7i)$
$$=-100+35i+60i+(-21i^2)$$
$$=-100+95i+21$$
$$=-79+95i$$

9. **The correct answer is (C).**

$$\frac{-5i}{11+4i}=\frac{-5i}{11+4i}\bullet\frac{11-4i}{11-4i}$$
$$=\frac{-5i(11-4i)}{(11+4i)(11-4i)}$$
$$=\frac{-55i+20i^2}{121-44i+44i+16i^2}$$
$$=\frac{-20-55i}{121+16}$$
$$=\frac{-20-55i}{137}$$

10. **The correct answer is (D).**

$$\frac{17-i}{3i}=\frac{17-i}{3i}\bullet\frac{i}{i}$$
$$=\frac{(17-i)(i)}{3i^2}$$
$$=\frac{17i-i^2}{3(-1)}$$
$$=\frac{17i-(-1)}{3(-1)}$$
$$=\frac{1+17i}{-3}$$
$$=-\frac{1}{3}-\frac{17}{3}i$$

11. The correct answer is (C).

$$\frac{6+14i}{1+2i} = \frac{6+14i}{1+2i} \cdot \frac{1-2i}{1-2i}$$

$$= \frac{(6+14i)(1-2i)}{(1+2i)(1-2i)}$$

$$= \frac{6-12i+14i-28i^2}{1-2i+2i-4i^2}$$

$$= \frac{6-12i+14i-28(-1)}{1-2i+2i-4(-1)}$$

$$= \frac{6+2i+28}{1+4}$$

$$= \frac{34+2i}{5}$$

$$= \frac{34}{5} + \frac{2}{5}i$$

12. The correct answer is (B).

$$\frac{-3+5i}{-3-4i} = \frac{-3+5i}{-3-4i} \cdot \frac{-3+4i}{-3+4i}$$

$$= \frac{(-3+5i)(-3+4i)}{(-3-4i)(-3+4i)}$$

$$= \frac{9-12i-15i+20i^2}{9-12i+12i-16i^2}$$

$$= \frac{9-12i-15i+20(-1)}{9-12i+12i-16(-1)}$$

$$= \frac{9-27i+(-20)}{9+(-16)(-1)}$$

$$= \frac{-11-27i}{25}$$

$$= \frac{-11}{25} - \frac{27}{25}i$$

DIRECT AND INVERSE VARIATION

Direct Variation

Two quantities are said to *vary directly* if as one increases, the other increases, and, as one decreases, the other decreases.

For example, the amount of sugar needed in a recipe varies directly with the amount of butter used. The number of inches between two cities on a map varies directly with the number of miles between the cities. The equation $y = ax$ represents direct variation between x and y, and y is said to vary directly with x. The variable a is called the constant of variation. By dividing each side by x, you can see that the ratio for the variable is the constant a.

> Hooke's Law states that the distance d a spring stretches varies directly with the force F that is applied to it. Suppose a spring stretches 15 inches when a force of 9 lbs. is applied. Write an equation that relates d to F, and state the constant of variation.

You are comparing the distance that a spring stretches with the force that is applied, so $\dfrac{d}{15} = \dfrac{F}{9}$.

Solving for d in terms of F, you get $d = \dfrac{5}{3} F$. The constant of variation is $\dfrac{5}{3}$.

> The weight of a person on the moon varies directly with the weight of a person on Earth. A person who weighs 100 lbs. on Earth weighs 16.6 lbs. on the moon. How much would a person who weighs 120 lbs. on Earth weigh on the moon?

Start with the equation $y = ax$ where y is the weight of a person on the moon and x is the weight of a person on Earth.

$$y = ax$$
$$16.6 = a(100)$$
$$0.166 = a$$

The equation $y = 0.166x$ gives the weight y on the moon of a person who weighs x pounds on Earth. To solve the example, substitute $x = 120$ in the equation to determine the weight of the person on the moon.

$$y = 0.166x$$
$$y = 0.166(120)$$
$$y = 19.92$$

A person who weighs 120 lbs. on Earth would weigh 19.92 lbs. on the moon.

Inverse Variation

Two quantities are said to *vary inversely* if as one increases, the other decreases.

For example, the number of workers hired to paint a house varies inversely with the number of days the job will take. A doctor's stock of flu vaccine varies inversely with the number of patients

TIP
Whenever two quantities vary directly, you can find a missing term by setting up a proportion. However, be very careful to compare the same units, in the same order, on each side of the equal sign.

injected. The number of days a given supply of cat food lasts varies inversely with the number of cats being fed.

The equation $xy=a$ where $a \neq 0$ represents inverse variation between x and y, and y is said to vary inversely with x. The variable a is called the constant of variation.

> The number of songs that can be stored on a hard drive varies inversely with the size of the song. A certain hard drive can store 3,000 songs when the average size of the song is 3.75 MB. Write an equation that gives the number of songs y that will fit on the hard drive as a function of the average song size x.

First write an inverse variation equation that relates x and y. Then substitute 3000 in for y and 3.75 in for x.

$$xy = a$$

$$y = \frac{a}{x}$$

$$3000 = a(3.75)$$

$$800 = a$$

The inverse variation equation for this situation is $y = \dfrac{800}{x}$.

EXERCISES: DIRECT AND INVERSE VARIATION

Directions: Work out each problem. Circle the letter of your choice.

1. If 60 feet of uniform wire weigh 80 pounds, what is the weight of 2 yards of the same wire?

   (A) $2\dfrac{2}{3}$ pounds

   (B) 6 pounds

   (C) 8 pounds

   (D) 120 pounds

2. A gear 50 inches in diameter turns a smaller gear 30 inches in diameter. If the larger gear makes 15 revolutions, how many revolutions does the smaller gear make in that time?

   (A) 9

   (B) 12

   (C) 20

   (D) 25

3. The distance a spring stretches varies directly with the force applied to it. If a 4-lb. weight stretches a spring 65.5 in., how many inches will the spring stretch if a 12-lb. weight is applied?

   (A) 262

   (B) $196\dfrac{1}{2}$

   (C) $21\dfrac{1}{3}$

   (D) $16\dfrac{3}{8}$

4. If a furnace uses 40 gallons of oil in a week, how many gallons, to the nearest gallon, does it use in 10 days?

   (A) 4

   (B) 28

   (C) 57

   (D) 58

5. A recipe requires 13 ounces of sugar and 18 ounces of flour. If only 10 ounces of sugar are used, how much flour, to the nearest ounce, should be used?

   (A) 13

   (B) 14

   (C) 15

   (D) 23

6. If a car can drive 25 miles on two gallons of gasoline, how many gallons will be needed for a trip of 150 miles?

   (A) 12

   (B) 10

   (C) 7

   (D) 6

7. A school has enough bread to feed 30 children for 4 days. If 10 more children are added, how many days will the bread last?

   (A) $1\dfrac{1}{3}$

   (B) $2\dfrac{2}{3}$

   (C) 3

   (D) $5\dfrac{1}{3}$

8. The intensity of a sound, I, varies inversely with the square of the distance, d, from the sound. If the distance is reduced by a factor of ¼, by what factor will the intensity of the sound increase?

   (A) 4

   (B) 8

   (C) 12

   (D) 16

9. If 3 miles are equivalent to 4.83 kilometers, then 11.27 kilometers are equivalent to how many miles?

(A) $2\frac{1}{3}$

(B) 5

(C) $6\frac{1}{2}$

(D) 7

10. Suppose the variables x and y vary inversely. If $x = -12$ and $y = 4$, find y when $x = -2$.

(A) 48

(B) 24

(C) −24

(D) −48

ANSWER KEY AND EXPLANATIONS

1. C	3. B	5. B	7. C	9. D
2. D	4. C	6. A	8. D	10. B

1. **The correct answer is (C).** You are comparing feet with pounds. The more feet, the more pounds. This is DIRECT. Remember to rename yards as feet:

$$\frac{60}{80} = \frac{6}{x}$$
$$60x = 480$$
$$x = 8$$

2. **The correct answer is (D).** The larger a gear, the fewer times it revolves in a given period of time. This is INVERSE.

$$50 \bullet 15 = 30 \bullet x$$
$$750 = 30x$$
$$25 = x$$

3. **The correct answer is (B).** The more weight that is applied the farther the spring will stretch.

$$\frac{4}{65.5} = \frac{12}{x}$$
$$4x = 786$$
$$x = 196\frac{1}{2}$$

4. **The correct answer is (C).** The more days, the more oil. This is DIRECT. Remember to rename the week as 7 days.

$$\frac{40}{7} = \frac{x}{10}$$
$$7x = 400$$
$$x = 57\frac{1}{7}$$

5. **The correct answer is (B).** The more sugar, the more flour. This is DIRECT.

$$\frac{13}{18} = \frac{10}{x}$$
$$13x = 180$$
$$x = 13\frac{11}{13}$$

6. **The correct answer is (A).** The more miles, the more gasoline. This is DIRECT.

$$\frac{25}{2} = \frac{150}{x}$$
$$25x = 300$$
$$x = 12$$

7. **The correct answer is (C).** The more children, the fewer days. This is INVERSE.

$$30 \bullet 4 = 40 \bullet x$$
$$120 = 40x$$
$$3 = x$$

8. **The correct answer is (D).**

$$I(d^2) = k$$
$$I(\frac{d}{4})^2 = k$$
$$I(\frac{d^2}{16}) = k$$
$$I = \frac{16k}{d^2}$$
$$I(d^2) = 16k$$

9. **The correct answer is (D).** The more miles, the more kilometers. This is DIRECT.

$$\frac{3}{4.83} = \frac{x}{11.27}$$
$$4.83x = 33.81$$
$$x = 7$$

10. **The correct answer is (B).**

$$xy = k$$
$$(-12)(4) = k$$
$$-48 = k$$
$$-2y = -48$$
$$y = 24$$

FINDING PERCENTS

Percent Equivalents

"Percent" means "out of 100." If you understand this concept, it becomes very easy to rename a percent as an equivalent decimal or fraction.

$$5\% = \frac{5}{100} = 0.05$$

$$2.6\% = \frac{2.6}{100} = 0.026$$

$$c\% = \frac{c}{100} = \frac{1}{100} \cdot c = 0.01c$$

$$\frac{1}{2}\% = \frac{\frac{1}{2}}{100} = \frac{1}{100} \cdot \frac{1}{2} = \frac{1}{100} \cdot 0.5 = 0.005$$

Certain fractional equivalents of common percents occur frequently enough that they should be memorized. Learning the values in the following table will make your work with percent problems much easier.

Percent-Fraction Equivalent Table

$50\% = \frac{1}{2}$	$33\frac{1}{3}\% = \frac{1}{3}$	$12\frac{1}{2}\% = \frac{1}{8}$
$25\% = \frac{1}{4}$	$66\frac{2}{3}\% = \frac{2}{3}$	$37\frac{1}{2}\% = \frac{3}{8}$
$75\% = \frac{3}{4}$	$20\% = \frac{1}{5}$	$62\frac{1}{2}\% = \frac{5}{8}$
$10\% = \frac{1}{10}$	$40\% = \frac{2}{5}$	$87\frac{1}{2}\% = \frac{7}{8}$
$30\% = \frac{3}{10}$	$60\% = \frac{3}{5}$	$16\frac{2}{3}\% = \frac{1}{6}$
$70\% = \frac{7}{10}$	$80\% = \frac{4}{5}$	$83\frac{1}{3}\% = \frac{5}{6}$
$90\% = \frac{9}{10}$		

Most percentage problems can be solved by using the following proportion:

$$\frac{\%}{100} = \frac{part}{whole}$$

Although this method works, it often yields unnecessarily large numbers that are difficult to compute. Following are examples of the four basic types of percent problems and different methods for solving them.

To Find a Percent of a Number

Find 27% of 92.

PROPORTIONAL METHOD

$$\frac{27}{100} = \frac{x}{92}$$

$$100x = 2484$$

$$x = 24.84$$

SHORTER METHOD

Rename the percent as its decimal or fraction equivalent and multiply. Use fractions only when they are among the familiar ones given in the previous chart.

$$\begin{array}{r} 92 \\ \times 0.27 \\ \hline 644 \\ 184 \\ \hline 24.84 \end{array}$$

TIP

To change a fraction to a %, add the % sign and multiply by 100.

Find $12\frac{1}{2}$% of 96.

PROPORTIONAL METHOD

$$\frac{12\frac{1}{2}}{100} = \frac{x}{96}$$

$$100x = 1200$$

$$x = 12$$

DECIMAL METHOD

$$\begin{array}{r} 0.125 \\ \times\ 96 \\ \hline 750 \\ 1125 \\ \hline 12.000 \end{array}$$

FRACTIONAL METHOD

$$\frac{1}{8} \bullet 96 = 12$$

Which method is easiest? It really pays to memorize those fractional equivalents.

To Find a Number When a Percent of It Is Given

7 is 5% of what number?

PROPORTIONAL METHOD

$$\frac{5}{100} = \frac{7}{x}$$
$$5x = 700$$
$$x = 140$$

SHORTER METHOD

Translate the problem into an algebraic equation. In doing this, the percent must be written as a fraction or decimal.

$$7 = 0.05x$$
$$700 = 5x$$
$$140 = x$$

20 is $33\frac{1}{2}\%$ of what number?

PROPORTIONAL METHOD

$$\frac{33\frac{1}{3}}{100} = \frac{20}{x}$$
$$33\frac{1}{3}x = 2000$$
$$\frac{100}{3}x = 2000$$
$$100x = 6000$$
$$x = 60$$

SHORTER METHOD

$$20 = \frac{1}{3}x$$
$$60 = x$$

Just think of the time you will save and the number of extra problems you will solve if you know that $33\frac{1}{3}\% = \frac{1}{3}$.

To Find What Percent One Number Is of Another

90 is what percent of 1500?

PROPORTIONAL METHOD

$$\frac{x}{100} = \frac{90}{1500}$$

$$1500x = 9000$$

$$15x = 90$$

$$x = 6$$

SHORTER METHOD

Put the part over the whole. Simplify the fraction and multiply by 100.

$$\frac{90}{1500} = \frac{9}{150} = \frac{3}{50} \bullet 100 = 6$$

7 is what percent of 35?

PROPORTIONAL METHOD

$$\frac{x}{100} = \frac{7}{35}$$

$$35x = 700$$

$$x = 20$$

SHORTER METHOD

$$\frac{7}{35} = \frac{1}{5} = 20\%$$

18 is what percent of 108?

PROPORTIONAL METHOD

$$\frac{x}{100} = \frac{18}{108}$$

$$108x = 1800$$

Time-consuming long division is necessary to get:

$$x = 16\frac{2}{3}$$

SHORTER METHOD

$$\frac{18}{108} = \frac{9}{54} = \frac{1}{6} = 16\frac{2}{3}\%$$

Once again, if you know the fraction equivalents of common percents, computation can be done in a few seconds.

To Find a Percent Over 100

Find 125% of 64.

PROPORTIONAL METHOD	DECIMAL METHOD	FRACTIONAL METHOD
$\dfrac{125}{100} = \dfrac{x}{64}$	64	$1\dfrac{1}{4} \cdot 64$
$100x = 8000$	$\times 1.25$	
$x = 80$	320	$\dfrac{5}{4} \cdot 64 = 80$
	128	
	$\underline{64\ \ }$	
	80.00	

36 is 150% of what number?

PROPORTIONAL METHOD	DECIMAL METHOD	FRACTIONAL METHOD
$\dfrac{150}{100} = \dfrac{36}{x}$	$36 = 1.50x$	$36 = 1\dfrac{1}{2}x$
$150x = 3600$	$360 = 15x$	$36 = \dfrac{3}{2}x$
$15x = 360$	$24 = x$	$72 = 3x$
$x = 24$		$24 = x$

60 is what percent of 50?

PROPORTIONAL METHOD	FRACTIONAL METHOD
$\dfrac{x}{100} = \dfrac{60}{50}$	$\dfrac{60}{50} = \dfrac{6}{5} = 1\dfrac{1}{5} = 120\%$
$50x = 6000$	
$5x = 600$	
$x = 120$	

EXERCISES: FINDING PERCENTS

Directions: Work out each problem. Circle the letter of your choice.

1. Write 0.2% as a decimal.
   (A) 0.002
   (B) 0.02
   (C) 0.2
   (D) 20

2. Write 3.4% as a fraction.
   (A) $\dfrac{34}{1000}$
   (B) $\dfrac{34}{10}$
   (C) $\dfrac{34}{100}$
   (D) $\dfrac{340}{100}$

3. Write $\dfrac{3}{4}$% as a decimal.
   (A) 0.75
   (B) 0.075
   (C) 0.0075
   (D) 0.00075

4. Find 60% of 70.
   (A) 4200
   (B) 420
   (C) 42
   (D) 4.2

5. What is 175% of 16?
   (A) 28
   (B) 24
   (C) 22
   (D) 12

6. What percent of 40 is 16?
   (A) 20
   (B) $2\dfrac{1}{2}$
   (C) $33\dfrac{1}{3}$
   (D) 40

7. What percent of 16 is 40?
   (A) 20
   (B) $2\dfrac{1}{2}$
   (C) 200
   (D) 250

8. $4 is 20% of what?
   (A) $5
   (B) $20
   (C) $200
   (D) $500

9. 12 is 150% of what number?
   (A) 18
   (B) 15
   (C) 9
   (D) 8

10. How many sixteenths are there in $87\dfrac{1}{2}$?
    (A) 7
    (B) 13
    (C) 14
    (D) 15

ANSWER KEY AND EXPLANATIONS

1. A	3. C	5. A	7. D	9. D
2. A	4. C	6. D	8. B	10. C

1. **The correct answer is (A).**

   $0.2\% = 0.002$
   The decimal point moves to the LEFT two places.

2. **The correct answer is (A).**

   $3.4\% = \dfrac{3.4}{100} = \dfrac{34}{1000}$

3. **The correct answer is (C).**

   $\dfrac{3}{4}\% = 0.75\% = 0.0075$

4. **The correct answer is (C).**

   $60\% = \dfrac{3}{5} \qquad \dfrac{3}{5} \bullet 70 = 42$

5. **The correct answer is (A).**

   $175\% = 1\dfrac{3}{4} \qquad \dfrac{7}{4} \bullet 16 = 28$

6. **The correct answer is (D).**

   $\dfrac{16}{40} = \dfrac{2}{5} = 40\%$

7. **The correct answer is (D).**

   $\dfrac{40}{16} = \dfrac{5}{2} = 2\dfrac{1}{2} = 250\%$

8. **The correct answer is (B).**

   $20\% = \dfrac{1}{5}$, so $\quad 4 = \dfrac{1}{5}x$
   $$20 = x$$

9. **The correct answer is (D).**

   $150\% = 1\dfrac{1}{2}$

   $\dfrac{3}{2}x = 12$

   $3x = 24$

   $x = 8$

10. **The correct answer is (C).**

    $87\dfrac{1}{2}\% = \dfrac{7}{8} = \dfrac{14}{16}$

VERBAL PROBLEMS INVOLVING PERCENT

Certain types of business situations are excellent applications of percent.

Percent of Increase or Decrease

The *percent of increase or decrease* is found by putting the amount of increase or decrease over the original amount and renaming this fraction as a percent.

> Over a five-year period, the enrollment at South High dropped from 1000 students to 800. Find the percent of decrease.

Answer: $\dfrac{1000-800}{1000} = \dfrac{200}{1000} = \dfrac{20}{100} = 20\%$

> A company normally employs 100 people. During a slow spell, the company fired 20% of its employees. By what percent must the company now increase its staff to return to full capacity?

$20\% = \dfrac{1}{5}$ $\dfrac{1}{5} \bullet 100 = 20$

The company now has $100 - 20 = 80$ employees. If it then increases its staff by 20, the percent of increase is $\dfrac{20}{80} = \dfrac{1}{4}$, or 25%.

Discount

A *discount* is usually expressed as a percent of the marked price that will be deducted from the marked price to determine the sale price.

> Bill's Hardware offers a 20% discount on all appliances during a sale week. If they take advantage of the sale, how much must the Russells pay for a washing machine marked at $280?

LONG METHOD

$20\% = \dfrac{1}{5}$

$\dfrac{1}{5} \bullet 280 = \$56$ discount

$\$280 - \$56 = \$224$ sale price

The danger inherent in this method is that $56 is sure to be among the multiple-choice answers.

SHORTCUT METHOD

If there is a 20% discount, the Russells will pay 80% of the marked price.

$80\% = \dfrac{4}{5}$

$\dfrac{4}{5} \bullet 280 = \$244$ sale price

TIP

In word problems, *of* can usually be interpreted to mean *times* (in other words, *multiply*).

A store offers a television set marked at $340 less discounts of 10% and 5%. Another store offers the same television set also marked at $340 with a single discount of 15%. How much does the buyer save by buying at the better price?

In the first store, the initial discount means the buyer pays 90%, or $\frac{9}{10}$, of $340, which is $306. The additional 5% discount means the buyer pays 95% of $306, or $290.70. Note that the second discount must be figured on the first sale price. Taking 5% off $306 is a smaller amount than taking the additional 5% off $340. The second store will therefore have a lower sale price. In the second store, the buyer will pay 85% of $340, or $289, making the price $1.70 less than in the first store.

Commission

Many salespeople earn money on a commission basis. In order to encourage sales, they are paid a percentage of the value of goods sold. This amount is called a *commission*.

A salesperson at Brown's Department Store is paid $80 per week in salary plus a 4% commission on all her sales. How much will that salesperson earn in a week in which she sells $4032 worth of merchandise?

Find 4% of $4032 and add this amount to $80.

4032
×   0.04
$161.28 + $80 = $241.28

Bill Olson delivers newspapers for a dealer and keeps 8% of all money collected. One month he was able to keep $16. How much did he forward to the newspaper?

First, determine how much he collected by finding the number that 16 is 8% of.

$$16 = 0.08x$$
$$1600 = 8x$$
$$200 = x$$

If Bill collected $200 and kept $16, he gave the dealer $200 − $16, or $184.

Taxes

Taxes are a percent of money spent or money earned.

Noname County collects a 7% sales tax on automobiles. If the price of a car is $8532 before taxes, what will this car cost once sales tax is added in?

Find 7% of $8532 to determine tax and then add it to $8532. This can be done in one step by finding 107% of $8532.

$8532
× 1.07
59724
85320
$9129.24

If the tax rate in Anytown is $3.10 per $100, what is the annual real estate tax on a house assessed at $47,200?

Annual tax = Tax rate • Assessed value

= ($3.10/$100)($47,200)

= (0.031) (47,200)

= $1463.20

EXERCISES: VERBAL PROBLEMS INVOLVING PERCENT

Directions: Work out each problem. Circle the letter of your choice.

1. A suit marked at $80 is sold for $68. What is the rate of discount?

   (A) 12%

   (B) 15%

   (C) **20%**

   (D) 85%

2. What was the original price of a radio that sold for $70 during a 20%-off sale?

   (A) $56

   (B) $84

   (C) $87.50

   (D) $90

3. How many dollars does a salesperson earn on a sale of $800 at a commission of 2.5%?

   (A) 20

   (B) 200

   (C) 2,000

   (D) 20,000

4. At a selling price of $273, a refrigerator yields a 30% profit on the cost. What selling price will yield a 10% profit on the cost?

   (A) $210

   (B) $221

   (C) $231

   (D) $235

5. What single discount is equivalent to two successive discounts of 10% and 15%?

   (A) 25%

   (B) 24.5%

   (C) 24%

   (D) 23.5%

6. The net price of a certain article is $306 after successive discounts of 15% and 10% off the marked price. What is the marked price?

   (A) $234.09

   (B) $382.50

   (C) $400

   (D) $408

7. If a merchant makes a profit of 20% based on the selling price of an article, what percent does the merchant make on the cost?

   (A) 20

   (B) 25

   (C) 40

   (D) 80

8. A certain radio costs a merchant $72. At what price must the merchant sell this radio in order to make a profit of 20% of the selling price?

   (A) $86.40

   (B) $90

   (C) $92

   (D) $144

9. A baseball team has won 40 games out of 60 played. It has 32 more games to play. How many of these must the team win to make its record 75% for the season?

   (A) 26

   (B) 28

   (C) 29

   (D) 30

10. If prices are reduced 25% and sales increase 20%, what is the net effect on gross receipts?

   (A) They increase by 5%.

   (B) They decrease by 5%.

   (C) They increase by 10%.

   (D) They decrease by 10%.

11. A salesperson earns 5% on all sales between $200 and $600, and 8% on the part of the sales over $600. What is her commission in a week in which her sales total $800?

    (A) $20
    (B) $36
    (C) $46
    (D) $78

12. If the enrollment at State U. was 3000 in 1998 and 12,000 in 2008, what was the percent of increase in enrollment?

    (A) 400%
    (B) 300%
    (C) 25%
    (D) 3%

13. If 6 students, representing $16\frac{2}{3}\%$ of the class, failed algebra, how many students passed the course?

    (A) 30
    (B) 32
    (C) 36
    (D) 42

14. If 95% of the residents of Coral Estates live in private homes and 40% of these live in air-conditioned homes, what percent of the residents of Coral Estates live in air-conditioned homes?

    (A) 3%
    (B) 3.8%
    (C) 30%
    (D) 38%

15. A salesperson receives a salary of $100 a week and a commission of 5% on all sales. What must be the amount of sales for a week in which the salesperson's total weekly income is $360?

    (A) $6200
    (B) $5200
    (C) $2600
    (D) $720

ANSWER KEY AND EXPLANATIONS

1. B	4. C	7. B	10. D	13. A
2. C	5. D	8. B	11. C	14. D
3. A	6. C	9. C	12. B	15. B

1. **The correct answer is (B).** The amount of discount is $12. Rate of discount is figured on the original price.

$$\frac{12}{80} = \frac{3}{20} \qquad \frac{3}{20} \cdot 100 = 15\%$$

2. **The correct answer is (C).** $70 represents 80% of the original price.

$$70 = 0.80x$$
$$700 = 8x$$
$$\$87.50 = x$$

3. **The correct answer is (A).**

$$2.5\% = \frac{2.5}{100}$$

The commission is $\frac{2.5}{100}(800) = \$20$.

4. **The correct answer is (C).**

$$1.30x = 273$$
$$13x = 2730$$
$$x = \$210 = cost$$

$273 represents 130% of the cost.

The new price will add 10% of cost, or $21, for profit.

New price = $231

5. **The correct answer is (D).** Work with a simple figure, such as 100.

First sale price is 90% of $100, or $90

Final sale price is 85% of $90, or $76.50

Total discount is $100 − $76.50 = $23.50

Percent of discount = $\frac{23.50}{100} = 23.5\%$

6. **The correct answer is (C).**

If marked price = m, first sale price = $0.85m$ and net price = $0.90(0.85m) = 0.765m$

$$0.765m = 306$$
$$m = 400$$

In this case, it would be easy to work from the answer choices.

15% of $400 is $60, making a first sale price of $340.

10% of this price is $34, making the net price $306.

Choices (A), (B), and (D) would not give a final answer in whole dollars.

7. **The correct answer is (B).** Use an easy amount of $100 for the selling price. If the profit is 20% of the selling price, or $20, the cost is $80. Profit based on cost is

$$\frac{20}{80} = \frac{1}{4} = 25\%$$

8. **The correct answer is (B).** If the profit is to be 20% of the selling price, the cost must be 80% of the selling price.

$$72 = 0.80x$$
$$720 = 8x$$
$$90 = x$$

9. **The correct answer is (C).** The team must win 75%, or $\frac{3}{4}$, of the games played during the entire season. With 60 games played and 32 more to play, the team must win $\frac{3}{4}$ of 92 games in all. $\frac{3}{4} \cdot 92 = 69$. Since 40 games have already been won, the team must win 29 additional games.

10. **The correct answer is (D).** Let original price $= p$, and original sales $= s$. Therefore, original gross receipts $= ps$. Let new price $- 0.75p$, and new sales $= 1.20s$. Therefore, new gross receipts $= 0.90ps$. Gross receipts are only 90% of what they were.

11. **The correct answer is (C).** Five percent of sales between $200 and $600 is $0.05(600) =$ $30. 8% of sales over $600 is $0.08(200) =$ $16. Total commission $= \$30 + \$16 = \$46$.

12. **The correct answer is (B).** There was an increase of 9000 students. To determine the percent of this increase in enrollment:

$$\frac{9000}{3000} = 3 = 300\%$$

13. **The correct answer is (A).**

$$16\frac{2}{3}\% = \frac{1}{6}$$

$$6 = \frac{1}{6}x$$

$$36 = x$$

36 students in class: 6 failed, 30 passed

14. **The correct answer is (D).**

$$40\% = \frac{2}{5}$$

$$\frac{2}{5} \text{ of } 95\% = 38\%$$

15. **The correct answer is (B).**

Let s = sales

$$\$100 + 0.05s = 360$$

$$0.05s = 260$$

$$5s = 26,000$$

$$s = \$5200$$

SUMMING IT UP

- If the arithmetic looks complex, try to simplify it first.

- If a problem is given with letters in place of numbers, the same reasoning must be applied as for numbers. If you are not sure how to proceed, replace the letters with numbers to determine the steps that must be taken.

- Fractions should be written in the simplest form. Often, in multiple-choice questions, you may find that the answer you have correctly computed is not among the choices but an equivalent fraction is. Be careful!

- Whenever two quantities vary directly, you can find a missing term by setting up a proportion. However, be very careful to compare the same units, in the same order, on each side of the equal sign.

- To change a decimal to a %, add the % sign and multiply by 100. This has the effect of moving the decimal point two places to the RIGHT. To change a % to a fraction, remove the % sign and divide by 100. This has the effect of putting the % over 100 and simplifying the resulting fraction.

- In problems dealing with percent, you may be presented with certain types of business situations, such as taxes or commissions. For problems asking about the percent of increase or decrease, put the amount of increase or decrease over the original amount and rename that fraction as a percent. A discount is usually expressed as a percent of the marked price that will be deducted from the marked price to determine the sale price.

Basic Algebra Review

chapter 10

OVERVIEW

- Signed numbers
- Linear equations
- Simultaneous equations
- Exponents
- Quadratic equations
- Roots and radicals
- Monomials and polynomials
- Problem solving in algebra
- Inequalities
- Summing it up

SIGNED NUMBERS

To solve algebra problems, you must be able to compute accurately with signed numbers.

Addition: To add signed numbers with the same sign, add the magnitudes of the numbers and keep the same sign. To add signed numbers with different signs, subtract the magnitudes of the numbers and use the sign of the number with the greater magnitude.

Subtraction: When subtracting a positive number from a negative number, add the magnitudes and make the difference (the answer) negative. When subtracting a negative number from a positive number, add the magnitude and make the difference positive. When asked to find the difference or a distance between a negative number and a positive number, the answer will always be positive.

Multiplication: If there is an odd number of negative signs, the product is negative. An even number of negative signs gives a positive product.

Division: If the signs are the same, the quotient is positive. If the signs are different, the quotient is negative.

Practicing these basic operations with signed numbers will help you on the more difficult problems on the SAT® in which these and more complex skills are tested.

EXERCISES: SIGNED NUMBERS

Directions: Work out each problem. Circle the letter next to your choice.

1. When +3 is added to −5, what is the sum?
   (A) −8
   (B) +8
   (C) −2
   (D) +2

2. When −4 and −5 are added, what is the sum?
   (A) −9
   (B) +9
   (C) −1
   (D) +1

3. Subtract −6 from +3.
   (A) −3
   (B) +3
   (C) +18
   (D) +9

4. When −5 is subtracted from +10, what is the result?
   (A) +5
   (B) +15
   (C) −5
   (D) −15

5. (−6)(−3) equals
   (A) −18
   (B) +18
   (C) +2
   (D) −9

6. What is the product of $(-6)\left(+\dfrac{1}{2}\right)(-10)$?
   (A) $-15\dfrac{1}{2}$
   (B) $+15\dfrac{1}{2}$
   (C) −30
   (D) +30

7. When the product of (−4) and (+3) is divided by (−2), the quotient is
   (A) $+\dfrac{1}{2}$
   (B) $+15\dfrac{1}{2}$
   (C) +6
   (D) $-\dfrac{1}{2}$

8. Last winter the meteorology class recorded the daily temperatures. The coldest recorded temperature was −37 degrees Fahrenheit, and the warmest was 38 degrees Fahrenheit. How many degrees warmer was the warmest day than the coldest day?
   (A) −75
   (B) −1
   (C) 1
   (D) 75

9. The highest point in California is Mt. Whitney with an elevation of 14,494 feet. The lowest point is Death Valley with an elevation of −294 feet. How much higher is the base of a tree at the top of Mt. Whitney than a person standing at the lowest point in Death Valley?
   (A) 294 feet
   (B) 14,200 feet
   (C) 14,494 feet
   (D) 14,788 feet

10. A submarine started at an elevation of −1,250 feet, or 1,250 feet below sea level, and it submerged another 25 feet per second. It continued to submerge for 10 seconds. What was its new elevation?
    (A) −1,500 feet
    (B) −1,000 feet
    (C) 250 feet
    (D) 1,500 feet

ANSWER KEY AND EXPLANATIONS

1. C	3. D	5. B	7. C	9. D
2. A	4. B	6. D	8. D	10. A

1. **The correct answer is (C).** In adding numbers with opposite signs, subtract their magnitudes ($5 - 3 = 2$) and use the sign of the number with the greater magnitude (negative).

2. **The correct answer is (A).** In adding numbers with the same sign, add their magnitudes ($4 + 5 = 9$) and keep the same sign.

3. **The correct answer is (D).** Change the sign of the second number and follow the rules for addition.

$$\begin{array}{r} + \quad 3 \\ + \ + \ 6 \\ \hline + \quad 9 \end{array}$$

4. **The correct answer is (B).** Change the sign of the second number and follow the rules for addition.

$$\begin{array}{r} + \quad 10 \\ + \quad \ 5 \\ \hline + \quad 15 \end{array}$$

5. **The correct answer is (B).** The product of two negative numbers is a positive number.

6. **The correct answer is (D).** The product of an even number of negative numbers is positive.

$$\frac{6}{1}\left(\frac{1}{2}\right)(10) = 30$$

7. **The correct answer is (C).**

$$(-4)(+3) = -12$$

Dividing a negative number by a negative number gives a positive quotient.

$$\frac{-12}{-2} = +6$$

8. **The correct answer is (D).** When subtracting a positive number from a negative number, you add the magnitude and make the difference positive. This is like a distance question. It's really asking what the distance is on the number line from -37 to $+38$. Try to picture the number line. Add the magnitudes and make the answer positive:

$$-37 - 38 = -75$$

The difference is 75 degrees.

9. **The correct answer is (D).** This question is really asking about distance between two things, so the answer will be positive. You can figure it is 14,494 feet from the top of Mt. Whitney to sea level, and then another 294 feet to get to the lowest point of Death Valley. Add the two numbers: $14,494 + 294 = 14,788$.

10. **The correct answer is (A).** Find the additional distance submerged. Multiply -25 by 10. When multiplying a negative number by a positive, the product is negative.

$$-25 \times 10 = -250$$

Subtract 250 from $-1,250$. When subtracting a positive number from a negative number, add the magnitude and make the difference (the answer) negative:

$$1,250 + 250 = 1,500$$

The answer is $-1,500$.

TIP

If you have a string of multiplications and divisions to do and the number of negative factors is even, the result will be positive; if the number of negative factors is odd, the result will be negative.

LINEAR EQUATIONS

The next step in solving algebra problems is mastering linear equations. Whether an equation involves numbers or only variables, the basic steps are the same.

Four-Step Strategy

1 If there are fractions or decimals, remove them by multiplication.

2 Collect all terms containing the unknown for which you are solving on the same side of the equation. Remember that whenever a term crosses the equal sign from one side of the equation to the other, it must "pay a toll." That is, it must change its sign.

3 Determine the coefficient of the unknown by combining similar terms or factoring when terms cannot be combined.

4 Divide both sides of the equation by this coefficient.

Solve for x: $5x - 3 = 3x + 5$

$$2x = 8$$
$$x = 4$$

Solve for x: $\dfrac{3}{4}x + 2 = \dfrac{2}{3}x + 3$

Multiply by 12: $9x + 24 = 8x + 36$
$$x = 12$$

Solve for x: $0.7x + 0.04 = 2.49$

Multiply by 100: $70x + 4 = 249$
$$70x = 245$$
$$x = 3.5$$

An equation that is true for every value of the variable is called an **identity**. It has infinitely many solutions. An equation has no solution if no value for the variable will make the equation true.

Solve for x: $0.5(6x + 4) = 3x + 2$

First, simplify each side of the equation. Then solve for x:

$$3x + 2 = 3x + 2$$
$$3x = 3x$$
$$x = x$$

Since $x = x$ is always true, the original equation has infinitely many solutions and is called an *identity*.

Solve for x: $9x + 7 = x + 2(4x + 3)$

First, simplify each side of the equation. Then solve for x:

$$9x + 7 = x + 8x + 6$$
$$9x + 7 = 9x + 6$$
$$7 = 6$$

Since $7 \neq 6$, the original equation has *no solution*.

If you eliminate the variable in the process of solving the equation, then you will have either infinitely many solutions or no solution.

In the equation $ax + 7 = 2x + 3$, for which values of a will the equation have no solutions?

If $a = 2$, the original equation becomes $2x + 7 = 2x + 3$. Since $2x + 7 \neq 2x + 3$ there are *no solutions* that make the equation true.

Real-World Linear Equations

A **literal equation** is an equation that involves two or more variables. You can solve for one variable in terms of the others using the properties of equalities. A **formula** is a literal equation that defines a relationship among quantities. For example, the perimeter of a rectangle can be found using the formula $P = 2l + 2w$, where P = perimeter, l = length, and w = width.

What is the width of a rectangle with perimeter 42 and length 8?

Using the formula $P = 2l + 2w$, where P = perimeter, l = length, and w = width, solve for the variable w.

Substitute the values that you know into the formula.

$$42 = 2(8) + 2w$$
$$42 = 16 + 2w$$
$$42 - 16 = 2w$$
$$26 = 2w$$
$$\frac{26}{2} = w$$
$$13 = w$$

The drama club sold student and adult tickets to its spring play. The adult tickets cost $15 each, and the student tickets cost $10 each. Tickets sales were $4,050. If 120 adult tickets were sold, how many student tickets were sold?

Using the formula $R = 15a + 10s$, where R = revenue from ticket sales, a = adult tickets, and s = student tickets, solve it for the variable s.

Substitute the values that you know into the formula.

$$4050 = 15(120) + 10s$$
$$4050 = 1800 + 10s$$
$$4050 - 1800 = 10s$$
$$2250 = 10s$$
$$\frac{2250}{10} = s$$
$$225 = s$$

The drama club sold 225 student tickets.

EXERCISES: LINEAR EQUATIONS

Directions: Work out each problem. Circle the letter of your choice.

1. If $5x + 6 = 10$, then x equals

   (A) $\dfrac{16}{5}$

   (B) $\dfrac{5}{16}$

   (C) $-\dfrac{5}{4}$

   (D) $\dfrac{4}{5}$

2. Solve for x: $2x - 3 = 4x - 15$

   (A) -6

   (B) -3

   (C) 3

   (D) 6

3. Solve for k: $\dfrac{k}{3} + \dfrac{k}{4} = 1$

   (A) $\dfrac{8}{11}$

   (B) $\dfrac{7}{12}$

   (C) $\dfrac{12}{7}$

   (D) $\dfrac{1}{7}$

4. If $x + y = 12$ and $x - y = 2$, what is the value of xy?

   (A) 10

   (B) 12

   (C) 20

   (D) 35

5. If $7x = 3x + 12$, then $2x + 5 =$

   (A) 10

   (B) 11

   (C) 12

   (D) 13

6. Solve for x: $6x + 7 = 2(3x - 5)$

   (A) 0

   (B) 4

   (C) No solution

   (D) Infinitely many solutions

7. Solve for x: $\dfrac{2x + 9}{7} = \dfrac{3x + 8}{2}$

   (A) No solution

   (B) Infinitely many solutions

   (C) $\dfrac{17}{38}$

   (D) $-\dfrac{38}{17}$

8. Solve for x: $\dfrac{1}{2}(2x + 8) = 4(\dfrac{1}{4}x + 1)$

   (A) Infinitely many solutions

   (B) No solution

   (C) 0

   (D) 8

9. The formula for the area of a triangle is $A = \dfrac{1}{2}bh$. Find the base of the triangle if the area is 28 in.^{2} and its height is 7 in.

   (A) 2 in.

   (B) 8 in.

   (C) 98 in.

   (D) 196 in.

10. For what values of n is $n + 5$ equal to $n - 5$?

    (A) No value

    (B) 0

    (C) All positive values

    (D) All values

11. Membership to Iron gym costs $40 per month plus $30 registration fee. The monthly cost is deducted automatically from your account. If your starting balance is $350, how many months will you be able to go to the gym before you have to add money to your account?

(A) 6

(B) 7

(C) 8

(D) 9

12. Your cell phone plan costs $45 per month plus $0.08 per text message. Your latest bill is $66.04. How many text messages were included in this bill?

(A) 825

(B) 562

(C) 420

(D) 263

ANSWER KEY AND EXPLANATIONS

1. D	4. D	7. A	9. E	11. C
2. D	5. C	8. B	10. C	12. D
3. C	6. D			

1. **The correct answer is (D).**

$$5x = 4$$

$$x = \frac{4}{5}$$

2. **The correct answer is (D).**

$$2x - 3 = 4x - 15$$

$$-2x - 3 = -15$$

$$-2x = -12$$

$$x = 6$$

3. **The correct answer is (C).** Multiply by 12:

$$4k + 3k = 12$$

$$7k = 12$$

$$k = \frac{12}{7}$$

4. **The correct answer is (D).** Add the two equations to cancel the y-variable and solve for x.

$$x + y = 12$$
$$x - y = 2$$
$$2x = 14$$
$$x = 7$$

Substitute the value of x into the addition equation to find the value of y.

$$7 + y = 12$$
$$y = 5$$
$$xy = 35$$

5. **The correct answer is (B).** Solve for x:

$$4x = 12$$
$$x = 3$$
$$2x + 5 = 2(3) + 5 = 11$$

6. **The correct answer is (C).**

$$6x + 7 = 2(3x - 5)$$

$$6x + 7 = 6x - 10$$

$$7 = 10$$

Since $7 \neq 10$, there are no values of x that will satisfy the equation. There is no solution.

7. **The correct answer is (D).**

$$\frac{2x + 9}{7} = \frac{3x + 8}{2}$$

$$2(2x + 9) = 7(3x + 8)$$

$$4x + 18 = 21x + 56$$

$$-17x = 38$$

$$x = -\frac{38}{17}$$

8. **The correct answer is (A).**

$$\frac{1}{2}(2x + 8) = 4(\frac{1}{4}x + 1)$$

$$x + 4 = x + 4$$

All values of x will make this equation true, so there are infinitely many solutions.

9. **The correct answer is (A).** Solve the formula for b. Then substitute in the values of the variables.

$$A = \frac{1}{2}bh$$

$$\frac{2A}{h} = b$$

$$\frac{2(28)}{7} = b$$

$$8 = b$$

10. **The correct answer is (A).** There is no number such that, when 5 is added, you get the same result as when 5 is subtracted. Do not confuse choices (A) and (B). Choice (B) would mean that the number 0 satisfies the equation, which it does not.

11. **The correct answer is (C).**

$$40x + 30 = 350$$
$$40x = 320$$
$$x = 8$$

12. **The correct answer is (D).** Write an equation to model your monthly cell phone bill. Use the variable B for your total bill and t for the number of text messages. Then plug in the given values and solve for t.

$$B = 45 + 0.08t$$
$$\frac{B - 45}{0.08} = t$$
$$\frac{66.04 - 45}{0.08} = t$$
$$263 = t$$

Your latest bill included charges for 263 text messages.

SIMULTANEOUS EQUATIONS

In solving equations with two unknowns, you must work with two equations simultaneously. The object is to eliminate one of the two unknowns and solve for the resulting single unknown.

> Solve for x: $2x - 4y = 2$
>
> $\qquad 3x + 5y = 14$

Multiply the first equation by 5:

$10x - 20y = 10$

Multiply the second equation by 4:

$12x + 20y = 56$

Since the y-terms now have the same numerical coefficients, but with opposite signs, you can eliminate them by adding the two equations. If they had the same signs, you would eliminate them by subtracting the equations.

Add the equations:

$$10x - 20y = 10$$
$$12x + 20y = 56$$
$$\overline{\qquad 22x = 66}$$
$$x = 3$$

Since you were only asked to solve for x, stop here. If you were asked to solve for both x and y, you would now substitute 3 for x in either equation and solve the resulting equation for y.

$$3(3) + 5y = 14$$
$$9 + 5y = 14$$
$$\overline{\qquad 5y = 5}$$
$$y = 1$$

In the previous example, the system of equations has exactly one solution (3, 1). It is also possible for a system of equations to have no solution or infinitely many solutions.

> Solve the system: $-12x + 8y = 2$
>
> $\qquad\qquad 3x - 2y = 7$

Multiply the second equation by 4, so that the x-terms and y-terms have the same numerical coefficients:

$-12x + 8y = 2$

$12x - 8y = 28$

Now add the equations:

$$-12x + 8y = 2$$
$$12x - 8y = 28$$
$$\overline{\qquad\quad 0 = 30}$$

Since $0 \neq 30$, there is no solution to the system.

Solve the system: $3x - 2y = -15$

$$x - \frac{2}{3}y = -5$$

Multiply the second equation by 3, so that the x- and y-terms have the same numerical coefficients:

$3x - 2y = -15$
$3x - 2y = -15$

Now subtract the equations:

$$3x - 2y = -15$$
$$\underline{3x - 2y = -15}$$
$$0 = \quad 0$$

Since $0 = 0$ is an identity, there are infinitely many solutions to the system.

For which value of a will the system $3x - 4y = 12$ have infinitely many solutions?
$$ax - 3y = 9$$

Consider solving each equation for y: $y = \frac{3}{4}x - 3$

$$y = \frac{a}{3}x - 3$$

To have infinitely many solutions, $\frac{3}{4} = \frac{a}{3}$. So $a = \frac{9}{4}$.

Solve the system: $x^2 + y = 9$
$$x - y = -3$$

Add the equations to eliminate the y-variable:

$$x^2 + y = \quad 9$$
$$\underline{x - y = -3}$$
$$x^2 + x = \quad 6$$

Set the equation equal to 0 and solve for x: $x^2 + x - 6 = 0$

Factor to solve for x: $(x - 2)(x + 3) = 0$

$x = 2$ or $x = -3$

Find the corresponding y-values by substituting each value of x into the linear equation.

$2 - y = -3; y = 5$ and $-3 - y = -3; y = 0$

Master the New SAT®

There are 2 possible solutions for the system: (2, 5) and (–3, 0). Check each in both equations.

1st equation: $(x)^2 + y = 9$ and $(x)^2 + y = 9$

$$(2)^2 + 5 = 9 \qquad (-3)^2 + 0 = 9$$
$$9 = 9 \qquad\qquad 9 = 9$$

2nd equation: $(x) - y = -3$ and $(x) - y = -3$

$$(2) - 5 = -3 \qquad (-3) - 0 = -3$$
$$-3 = -3 \qquad\qquad -3 = -3$$

The solutions to the system are (2, 5) and (–3, 0).

Applications of Systems

Systems of equations can be used to solve many real-life problems.

> A company makes and sells computer parts. The material for each part costs $3.00 and sells for $12.75 each. The company spends $1200 on additional expenses each month. How many computer parts must the company sell each month in order to break even?

The break-even point is when the income equals the expenses. The first equation $12.75x = y$ represents the income. The second equation $3x + 1200 = y$ represents expenses.

$$y = 12.75x$$
$$y = 3.00x + 1200$$

Solve the system by subtracting the second equation from the first.

$$y = 12.75x$$
$$\underline{y = 3.00x + 1200}$$
$$0 = 9.75x - 1200$$
$$-9.75x = -1200$$
$$x = \frac{-1200}{-9.75}$$
$$x \approx 123.08$$

To break even, the company would have to sell at least 124 computer parts.

> A couple is planning a vacation. They plan to spend some of the time in Naples, Florida, and the rest of time in Key West. They estimate that it will cost $250 per day in Naples and $325 per day in Key West. If they plan to vacation a total of 8 days and have a budget of $2,375. How many days should the couple spend in each city?

To write the equations, let x = the number of days in Naples and y = the number of days in Key West. The first equation $x + y = 8$ represents the total number of days on vacation. The second equation $250x + 325y = 2375$ represents total cost.

The system of equations is:
$$x + y = 8$$
$$250x + 325y = 2375$$

Solve the system by multiplying the first equation by 325 and then subtract the second equation from the first.

$$325x + 325y = 2600$$
$$\underline{250x + 325y = 2375}$$
$$75x = 225$$
$$x = 3$$

Since $x + y = 8$, if $x = 3$ then $y = 5$. The couple can spend 3 days in Naples and 5 days in Key West.

Solving Systems of Inequalities by Graphing

Systems of inequalities are solved using the same methods as systems of equations. Recall that you must reverse the sign of the inequality if you multiply or divide by a negative value.

You can graph a system of linear inequalities in the coordinate plane. The solution of the system is where the graphs of the inequalities overlap. Recall, that an inequality with a $<$ or $>$ sign, is graphed as a dashed line, while an inequality with a $\leq$ or $\geq$ is graphed with a solid line. A solid line shows that answers along the line are included in the solution set for that inequality.

What system of inequalities is represented by the graph shown?

First write the inequality that represents the region bounded by the solid line, using two points along the line and the slope-intercept formula $y = mx + b$, replacing the equal sign with a comparison symbol.

$y \geq -0.5x + 2$

Then write the inequality that represents the region bounded by the dashed line.

$y < 2x + 1$

The graph shows the intersection of the system $y \geq -0.5x + 2$
$$y < 2x + 1$$

Solve the system of inequalities by graphing:
$$x + 2y \leq 8$$
$$3x - y \geq 3$$

First solve each inequality for y to rewrite in slope-intercept form:

1st inequality: $x + 2y \leq 8$ 2nd inequality: $3x - y \geq 3$

$$2y \leq -x + 8 \qquad\qquad -y \geq -3x + 3$$

$$y \leq -\frac{1}{2}x + 4 \qquad\qquad y \leq 3x - 3$$

Then graph each inequality.

The solution is the region where the graphs overlap.

EXERCISES: SIMULTANEOUS EQUATIONS

Directions: Work out each problem. Circle the letter of your choice.

1. Solve the system for x:

   $-x + 2y = 7$
   $3x - 2y = -3$

   (A) 4.5
   (B) 2
   (C) −2
   (D) −11

2. Solve the system for y:

   $2x - 9y = 4$
   $-x + y = 5$

   (A) 7
   (B) 2
   (C) −2
   (D) −7

3. Solve the system:

   $2y = x + 16$
   $-\dfrac{1}{2}x + y = -2$

   (A) No solution
   (B) Infinitely many solutions
   (C) 0
   (D) All positive values

4. Solve the system for y:

   $x - y^2 = 2$
   $2x + 5y = 7$

   (A) $y = 11, 2.25$
   (B) $y = 0.5, -3$
   (C) $y = 1.75, 17$
   (D) Infinitely many solutions

5. Solve the system:

   $14y = -2x + 23$
   $2(x + 7y) = 23$

   (A) 0
   (B) All negative values
   (C) No solution
   (D) Infinitely many solutions

6. What system of inequalities is shown in the graph?

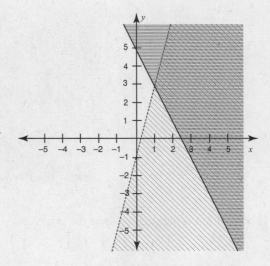

   (A) $y < 4x - 1$
   $\quad\;\; 2x + y \geq 5$

   (B) $y < 4x + 1$
   $\quad\;\; -2x + y \geq 5$

   (C) $y > 4x - 1$
   $\quad\;\; 2x - y \geq 5$

   (D) $y \leq 4x + 1$
   $\quad\;\; 2x + y \geq -5$

7. Budget Rent-A-Car charges $45 a day plus $0.60 per mile driven to rent a car. Zippy Rental charges $40 a day plus $0.70 per mile driven to rent a car. After how many miles would it cost the same amount to rent a car from either Budget Rent-A-Car or Zippy Rental?

   (A) 25 miles
   (B) 50 miles
   (C) 75 miles
   (D) 100 miles

8. A used bookstore sells hardcover books for $5 each and paperback books for $1 each. You buy 13 books for summer reading, and you spend $45. How many more hardcover books than paperback books did you buy?

   (A) 8
   (B) 5
   (C) 4
   (D) 3

ANSWER KEY AND EXPLANATIONS

1. B	3. A	5. D	7. B
2. C	4. B	6. A	8. D

1. **The correct answer is (B).** Add the equations to eliminate y.

$$\begin{aligned} -x + 2y &= 7 \\ 3x - 2y &= -3 \\ \hline 2x &= 4 \\ x &= 2 \end{aligned}$$

2. **The correct answer is (C).** Rewrite the equations and multiply the second equation by 2. Then add the equations to eliminate x.

$$\begin{aligned} 2x - 9y &= 4 \\ -x + y &= 5 \\ 2x - 9y &= 4 \\ -2x + 2y &= 10 \\ \hline -7y &= 14 \\ y &= -2 \end{aligned}$$

3. **The correct answer is (A).** Multiply the second equation by 2 and add to eliminate a variable.

$$\begin{aligned} 2y &= x + 16 \\ -\frac{1}{2}x + y &= -2 \\ \hline -x + 2y &= 16 \\ x - 2y &= 4 \\ \hline 0 &= 20 \end{aligned}$$

Since $0 \neq 20$, there is no solution.

4. **The correct answer is (B).** Eliminate the x-variable and solve for y.

$$\begin{aligned} x - y^2 &= 2 \\ 2x + 5y &= 7 \\ \hline 2x - 2y^2 &= 4 \\ 2x + 5y &= 7 \\ \hline 2y^2 + 5y &= 3 \end{aligned}$$

$$2y^2 + 5y - 3 = 0$$
$$(2y - 1)(y + 3) = 0$$
$$y = \frac{1}{2}, -3$$

5. **The correct answer is (D).**

$$\begin{aligned} 14y &= -2x + 23 \\ 2(x + 7y) &= 23 \\ \hline 2x + 14y &= 23 \\ 2x + 14y &= 23 \\ \hline 0 &= 0 \end{aligned}$$

Since $0 = 0$ is always true, there are infinitely many solutions.

6. **The correct answer is (A).** First write the inequality that represents the region bounded by the dashed line using two points and the slope intercept formula.

$y < 4x - 1$

Then write the inequality that represents the region bounded by the solid line.

$y \geq -2x + 5$

The graph shows the intersection of the system $y < 4x - 1$

$$2x + y \geq 5$$

7. **The correct answer is (B).** The system of equations that represents the cost of renting a car from the places is:

$$y = 45 + 0.6x$$
$$y = 40 + 0.7x$$

Solve this system by subtracting the second equation from the first. The solution is 50 miles.

Rewrite the equations so that you can eliminate the y variable. So:

$$40 = -0.7x + y$$
$$-45 = 0.6x - y$$

Add the second equation to the first to eliminate the y variable: $-5 = -0.1x$. When simplified, $x = 50$. Therefore, 50 is the number of miles it would take for the cost (y) of both rental companies to be equal.

8. **The correct answer is (D).** The system of equations that represents this situation is:

$$x + y = 13$$
$$5x + y = 45$$

Where x represents the number of hardcover books purchased and y represents the number of paperback books purchased. Solve this system by subtracting the first equation from the second.

$$5x + y = 45$$
$$-x - y = -13$$

You are left with $4x = 32$ or $x = 8$. If 8 hardcover books are purchased, then 5 paperback books are purchased. This means that you purchased 3 more hardcover books than paperback books.

EXPONENTS

An exponent is a mathematical notation indicating that a number, called the base, has been multiplied one or more times by itself. For example, in the term 2^3, the 2 is the base and the ^{3} is the exponent. This term means "two times two times two" and is read "two to the third power." The word power tells how many times the base number appears in the multiplication.

$x^3 = x$ times x times x

$x^2 = x$ times x

$x^1 = x$

$x^0 = 1$

TIP
Commit to memory small powers of small numbers that come up in many questions. For example, the powers of 2: 2, 4, 8, 16, 32, . . . the powers of 3: 3, 9, 27, 81, . . . and so on.

The Five Rules of Exponents

1 To multiply powers of the same base, add the exponents.

x^2 times $x^3 = x^{2+3} = x^5$

x^5 times $x^4 = x^{5+4} = x^9$

2 To divide powers of the same base, subtract the exponent of the divisor from the exponent of the dividend.

$$\frac{x^6}{x^2} = x^{6-2} = x^4$$

$$\frac{x^{10}}{x^3} = x^{10-3} = x^7$$

❸ Negative powers represent reciprocals.

$$x^{-1} = \frac{1}{x}$$

$$\left(\frac{x^3}{y^5}\right)^{-2} = \left(\frac{y^5}{x^3}\right)^2 = \frac{y^{10}}{x^6}$$

❹ To find the power of a power, multiply the exponents.

$$(x^2)^3 = x^{(2)(3)} = x^6$$

$$(x^3 y^5)^2 = x^{(3)(2)} y^{(5)(2)} = x^6 y^{10}$$

A variable base with an even exponent has two values, one positive and one negative.

$x^2 = 25$; x could be positive 5 or negative 5.

A variable base can be zero (unless otherwise stated in the problem). In that case, no matter what the exponent, the value of the term is zero.

Is x^4 always greater than x^2? No; if x is zero, then x^4 and x^2 are equal.

When the base is a fraction between 0 and 1, the larger the exponent, the smaller the value of the term.

Which is greater, $\left(\frac{37}{73}\right)$ or $\left(\frac{37}{73}\right)^2$? The correct answer is $\left(\frac{37}{73}\right)$ because $\left(\frac{37}{73}\right)$ is almost $\frac{1}{2}$,

while $\left(\frac{37}{73}\right)^2$ is about $\frac{1}{4}$.

❺ Fractional exponents represent roots.

$$x^{\frac{1}{2}} = \sqrt{x}$$

$$x^{\frac{1}{3}} = \sqrt[3]{x}$$

$$x^{\frac{2}{5}} = \left(\sqrt[5]{x}\right)^2$$

$$= \sqrt[5]{x^2}$$

EXERCISES: EXPONENTS

Directions: Work out each problem. Circle the letter of your choice.

1. $p^8 \times q^4 \times p^4 \times q^8 =$
    (A) $p^{12}q^{12}$
    (B) p^4q^4
    (C) $p^{32}q^{32}$
    (D) $p^{64}q^{64}$

2. $(x^2y^3)^4 =$
    (A) x^6y^7
    (B) x^8y^{12}
    (C) $x^{12}y^8$
    (D) x^2y

3. $\dfrac{x^{16}y^6}{x^4y^2} =$
    (A) $x^{20}y^8$
    (B) x^4y^3
    (C) $x^{12}y^3$
    (D) $x^{12}y^4$

4. If $x^4 = 16$ and $y^2 = 36$, then the *maximum* possible value for $x - y$ is
    (A) -14
    (B) -4
    (C) 8
    (D) 20

5. $a^{-4} \times a^{-3} =$
    (A) $\dfrac{1}{a^{12}}$
    (B) $\dfrac{1}{a^7}$
    (C) a^7
    (D) a^{12}

6. $x^{\frac{2}{3}}x^{\frac{1}{2}} =$
    (A) $\sqrt[3]{x}$
    (B) $\sqrt[5]{x^3}$
    (C) $\left(\sqrt[6]{x}\right)^7$
    (D) $\dfrac{1}{\sqrt[5]{x^2}}$

ANSWER KEY AND EXPLANATIONS

1. A	3. D	4. C	5. B	6. C
2. B				

1. **The correct answer is (A).** The multiplication signs do not change the fact that this is the multiplication of terms with a common base and different exponents. Solve this kind of problem by adding the exponents.

$$p^{8+4} \times q^{4+8} = p^{12}q^{12}$$

2. **The correct answer is (B).** To raise a power to a power, multiply the exponents.

$$x^{(2)(4)}y^{(3)(4)} = x^8 y^{12}$$

3. **The correct answer is (D).** All fractions are implied division. When dividing terms with a common base and different exponents, subtract the exponents. Therefore, $16 - 4 = 12$ and $6 - 2 = 4$.

4. **The correct answer is (C).** x could be positive 2 or negative 2. y could be positive 6 or negative 6. The four possible values for $x - y$ are as follows:

$$2 - 6 = -4$$
$$2 - (-6) = 8$$
$$-2 - 6 = -8$$
$$-2 - (-6) = 4$$

The maximum value would be 8.

5. **The correct answer is (B).** To multiply, add the exponents. The resulting exponent will be negative, which means you need to take the reciprocal.

$$a^{-4} \times a^{-3} = a^{-4+(-3)}$$
$$= a^{-7}$$
$$= \frac{1}{a^7}$$

6. **The correct answer is (C).** To multiply, add the exponents. Then, use the rules for rational exponents to convert to root form.

$$x^{\frac{2}{3}}x^{\frac{1}{2}} = x^{\frac{2}{3}+\frac{1}{2}}$$
$$= x^{\frac{7}{6}}$$
$$= \left(\sqrt[6]{x}\right)^7$$

QUADRATIC EQUATIONS

Roots and Factoring

In solving quadratic equations, remember that there will always be two roots, even though these roots may be equal. A complete quadratic equation is of the form $ax^2 + bx + c = 0$.

Factor: $x^2 + 7x + 12 = 0$

$(x + 3)(x + 4) = 0$

The last term of the equation is positive; therefore, both factors must have the same sign, since the last two terms multiply to a positive product. The middle term is also positive; therefore, both factors must be positive, since they also add to a positive sum.

$(x + 4)(x + 3) = 0$

If the product of two factors is 0, each factor may be set equal to 0, yielding the values for x of -4 or -3.

Factor: $x^2 + 7x - 18 = 0$

$(x + 9)(x - 2) = 0$

Now you are looking for two numbers with a product of -18; therefore, they must have opposite signs. To yield $+7$ as a middle coefficient, the numbers must be $+9$ and -2.

$(x + 9)(x - 2) = 0$

This equation gives the roots -9 and $+ 2$.

Incomplete quadratic equations are those in which b or c is equal to 0.

Solve for x: $x^2 - 16 = 0$

$x^2 = 16$

$x = \pm 4$

Remember, there must be two roots.

Solve for x: $4x^2 - 9 = 0$

$4x^2 = 9$

$x^2 = \dfrac{9}{4}$

$x = \pm\dfrac{3}{2}$

ALERT!

Don't forget: In working with any equation, if you move a term from one side of the equal sign to the other, you must change its sign.

Solve for x: $x^2 + 4x = 0$

Never divide through an equation by the unknown, as this would yield an equation of lower degree having fewer roots than the original equation. Always factor this type of equation.

$x(x + 4) = 0$

The roots are 0 and −4.

Solve for x: $4x^2 - 9x = 0$

$x(4x - 9) = 0$

The roots are 0 and $\dfrac{9}{4}$.

The **quadratic formula** can also be used to find the solutions to quadratic equations $ax^2 + bx + c = 0$ where a, b, and c are real numbers and $a \neq 0$.

$$x = \frac{-b \pm \sqrt{b^2 - 4ac}}{2a}$$

Use the quadratic formula to solve for x: $2x^2 + 7x = 3$

Write the equation in standard form: $2x^2 + 7x - 3 = 0$. Then, identify the values of a, b, and c and substitute them into the quadratic formula.

$a = 2$, $b = 7$, and $c = -3$

$$x = \frac{-b \pm \sqrt{b^2 - 4ac}}{2a}$$

$$x = \frac{-7 \pm \sqrt{(7)^2 - 4(2)(-3)}}{2(2)}$$

$$x = \frac{-7 \pm \sqrt{73}}{4}$$

The solutions are $x = \dfrac{-7 + \sqrt{73}}{4} \approx 0.386$ or $x = \dfrac{-7 - \sqrt{73}}{4} \approx -3.886$

EXERCISES: QUADRATIC EQUATIONS

Directions: Work out each problem. Circle the letter of your choice.

1. Solve for x: $x^2 - 2x - 15 = 0$
   (A) $+5$ or -3
   (B) -5 or $+3$
   (C) -5 or -3
   (D) $+5$ or $+3$

2. Solve for x: $x^2 + 12 = 8x$
   (A) $+6$ or -2
   (B) -6 or $+2$
   (C) -6 or -2
   (D) $+6$ or $+2$

3. Solve for x: $4x^2 = 12$
   (A) $\sqrt{3}$
   (B) 3 or -3
   (C) $\sqrt{3}$ or $-\sqrt{3}$
   (D) $\sqrt{3}$ or $\sqrt{-3}$

4. Solve for x: $3x^2 = 4x$
   (A) $\dfrac{4}{3}$
   (B) $\dfrac{4}{3}$ or 0
   (C) $-\dfrac{4}{3}$ or 0
   (D) $\dfrac{4}{3}$ or $-\dfrac{4}{3}$

5. Solve for x: $2x^2 + 3x = 7$
   (A) $x = \dfrac{3+\sqrt{47}}{4}$, $x = \dfrac{3-\sqrt{47}}{4}$
   (B) $x = \dfrac{3+\sqrt{65}}{4}$, $x = \dfrac{3-\sqrt{65}}{4}$
   (C) $x = \dfrac{-3+\sqrt{47}}{4}$, $x = \dfrac{-3-\sqrt{47}}{4}$
   (D) $x = \dfrac{-3+\sqrt{65}}{4}$, $x = \dfrac{-3-\sqrt{65}}{4}$

ANSWER KEY AND EXPLANATIONS

| 1. A | 2. D | 3. C | 4. B | 5. D |

1. **The correct answer is (A).**

    $(x-5)(x+3) = 0$

    $x = 5 \text{ or } -3$

2. **The correct answer is (D).**

    $x^2 - 8x + 12 = 0$

    $(x-6)(x-2) = 0$

    $x = 6 \text{ or } 2$

3. **The correct answer is (C).**

    $x^2 = 3$

    $x = \sqrt{3} \text{ or } -\sqrt{3}$

4. **The correct answer is (B).**

    $3x^2 - 4x = 0$

    $x(3x - 4) = 0$

    $x = 0 \text{ or } \dfrac{4}{3}$

5. **The correct answer is (D).** Write the equation in standard form:

    $2x^2 + 3x - 7 = 0.$

    $a = 2, b = 3, \text{ and } c = -7.$

    $x = \dfrac{-3 \pm \sqrt{(3)^2 - 4(2)(-7)}}{2(2)}$

    $x = \dfrac{-3 \pm \sqrt{65}}{4}$

    The solutions are $x = \dfrac{-3 + \sqrt{65}}{4}$ or $x = \dfrac{-3 - \sqrt{65}}{4}.$

LITERAL EQUATIONS

There are many equations that can be used to represent common problems, such as distance. The equation to find distance, given rate and time, is written as $d = rt$. This type of equation is called a *literal equation* in which the equation is solved for one variable in particular, such as d in the distance formula. Here are some examples:

Solve for l in the equation $P = 2l + 2w$.

Subtract $2w$ from both sides of the equation. This will eliminate it from the right side of the equation.

$P - 2w = 2l$

Divide both sides of the equation to solve for l.

$$\frac{P - 2w}{2}; \frac{P}{2} - w = l$$

Solve for c in the equation $E = mc^2$.

Divide both sides by m. This will eliminate it from the right side of the equation.

$$\frac{E}{m} = c^2$$

Take the square root of both sides to solve for c.

$$\sqrt{\frac{E}{m}} = c$$

The volume of a cone can be found using the formula $V = \frac{1}{3}\pi r^2 h$. Solve for r.

Divide both sides by h: $\dfrac{v}{h} = \dfrac{1}{3}\pi r^2$

Divide both sides by pi: $\dfrac{v}{\pi h} = \dfrac{1}{3}r^2$

Multiply both sides by 3: $3 \times \dfrac{v}{\pi h} = \dfrac{1}{3}r^2$

Take the square root of both sides: $\sqrt{3 \times \dfrac{v}{\pi h}} = r$

EXERCISES: LITERAL EQUATIONS

Directions: Work out each problem. Circle the letter of your choice.

1. Solve for x in the equation $z = 5x - 25xy$

   (A) $\dfrac{z}{-20y} = x$

   (B) $\dfrac{z}{1 - 5y} = x$

   (C) $\dfrac{z}{5 - 25y} = x$

   (D) $\dfrac{z}{30y} = x$

2. A bakery orders vanilla beans at a cost of $12.45 for a package of 10. There is a shipping cost of $6.00 for all sizes of shipments. Which of the following shows the equation solved for p, the total number of packages purchased, where c is the total cost of the order.

   (A) $p = 6c + 12.45$

   (B) $p = 12.45c + 6$

   (C) $p = \dfrac{c}{12.45} - 6$

   (D) $p = \dfrac{c - 6}{12.45}$

3. The distance between two points is determined by the equation below, where x_1 and x_2 are the x-coordinates of a two points and y_1 and y_2 are the y-coordinates of the two points.

   $$d = \sqrt{(x_2 - x_1)^2 + (y_2 - y_1)^2}$$

   Which shows the equation solved for y_2?

   (A) $y_2 = \sqrt{d^2 - (x_2 - x_1)^2} + y_1$

   (B) $y_2 = \sqrt{d - (x_2 - x_1)} + y_1$

   (C) $y_2 = \sqrt{d - (x_2 - x_1)} + y_1$

   (D) $y_2 = \sqrt{d^2 - (x_2 - x_1)^2} + y_1$

4. The surface area of a cylinder is found using the formula $SA = 2\pi rh + 2\pi r^2$. Which shows the equation solved for h, the height of the cylinder, in simplest form?

   (A) $\dfrac{SA - 2\pi r^2}{2\pi r} = h$

   (B) $\dfrac{SA}{2\pi r} - r = h$

   (C) $\dfrac{SA}{2\pi r} = h$

   (D) $\dfrac{SA}{4\pi r} = h$

5. The formula for converting degrees Fahrenheit to degrees Celsius is shown below.

   $$C = \frac{5}{9}(F - 32)$$

   Which equation shows the formula correctly solved for F?

   (A) $\dfrac{9}{5}(C + 32) = F$

   (B) $\dfrac{\frac{c}{9}}{5} - 32 = F$

   (C) $\dfrac{9}{5}C - 32 = F$

   (D) $\dfrac{9}{5}C + 32 = F$

6. Solve for f: $\dfrac{1}{f} = \dfrac{1}{a} + \dfrac{1}{b}$

   (A) $f = a + b$

   (B) $f = \dfrac{ab}{a + b}$

   (C) $ab = f$

   (D) $f = \dfrac{ba}{b - a}$

ANSWER KEY AND EXPLANATIONS

1. C	3. A	4. B	5. D	6. B
2. D				

1. **The correct answer is (C).** Factor out an x from both terms on the right side of the equation: $z = x(5 - 25y)$

   Divide both sides by $5 - 25y$:

   $$\frac{z}{5 - 25y} = x$$

2. **The correct answer is (D).** The total cost, c, is determined by the equation $12.45p + 6 = c$. To solve for p, subtract 6 from both sides. Then, divide both sides by 12.45 to isolate p.

3. **The correct answer is (A).** To solve for y_2 start by squaring both sides to remove the square root from the right side.

   $$d^2 = (x_2 - x_1)^2 + (y_2 - y_1)^2$$

   Subtract the term $(x_2 - x_1)^2$ from both sides.

   $$d^2 - (x_2 - x_1)^2 = (y_2 - y_1)^2$$

   Take the square root of both sides to eliminate the exponent on the right side.

   $$\sqrt{d^2 - (x_2 - x_1)^2} = y_2 - y_1$$

   Add y_1 to both sides of the equation.

   $$\sqrt{d^2 - (x_2 - x_1)^2} + y_1 = y_2$$

4. **The correct answer is (B).** To solve for the height, h, factor out $2\pi r$ from the terms on the right side of the equation.

   $$SA = 2\pi r(h + r)$$

   Divide both sides of the equation by $2\pi r$.

   $$\frac{SA}{2\pi r} = h + r$$

   Subtract r from both sides of the equation.

   $$\frac{SA}{2\pi r} - r = h$$

5. **The correct answer is (D).** To solve for F, divide both sides by $\frac{5}{9}$ or multiply both sides by $\frac{9}{5}$.

   $$\frac{9}{5}C = F - 32$$

   Add 32 to both sides to isolate F.

   $$\frac{9}{5}C + 32 = F$$

6. **The correct answer is (B).** To solve for f, first multiply both sides of the equation by f to move it into the numerator.

   $$1 = \frac{f}{a} + \frac{f}{b}$$

   Multiply by b and then by a to write the fractions with a common denominator, ab.

   $$1 = \frac{fb}{ab} + \frac{fa}{ab}$$

   Add the fractions.

   $$1 = \frac{fb + fa}{ab}$$

   Multiply both sides of the equation by ab.

   $$ab = fb + fa$$

   Factor f out of the terms on the right side of the equation.

   $$ab = f(b + a)$$

   Divide both sides of the equation by $(b + a)$.

   $$\frac{ab}{a + b} = f$$

ROOTS AND RADICALS

Adding and Subtracting

Rules for adding and subtracting radicals are much the same as for adding and subtracting variables. Radicals must be exactly the same if they are to be added or subtracted, and they merely serve as a label that does not change.

$4\sqrt{2} + 3\sqrt{2} = 7\sqrt{2}$

$\sqrt{2} + 2\sqrt{2} = 3\sqrt{2}$

$\sqrt{2} + \sqrt{3}$ cannot be added

Sometimes, when radicals are not the same, simplification of one or more radicals will make them the same. Remember that radicals are simplified by factoring out any perfect square factors.

$\sqrt{27} + \sqrt{75}$

$\sqrt{9 \cdot 3} + \sqrt{25 \cdot 3}$

$3\sqrt{3} + 5\sqrt{3} = 8\sqrt{3}$

Multiplying and Dividing

In multiplying and dividing, treat radicals in the same way as you treat variables. They are factors and must be handled as such.

$\sqrt{2} \cdot \sqrt{3} = \sqrt{6}$

$2\sqrt{5} \cdot 3\sqrt{7} = 6\sqrt{35}$

$\left(2\sqrt{3}\right)^2 = 2\sqrt{3} \cdot 2\sqrt{3} = 4 \cdot 3 = 12$

$\dfrac{\sqrt{75}}{\sqrt{3}} = \sqrt{25} = 5$

$\dfrac{10\sqrt{3}}{5\sqrt{3}} = 2$

Simplifying

To simplify radicals that contain a sum or difference under the radical sign, add or subtract first, then take the square root.

$$\sqrt{\dfrac{x^2}{9} + \dfrac{x^2}{16}} = \sqrt{\dfrac{16x^2 + 9x^2}{144}} = \sqrt{\dfrac{25x^2}{144}} = \dfrac{5|x|}{12}$$

If you take the square root of each term before combining, you would have $\dfrac{x}{3} + \dfrac{x}{4}$, or $\dfrac{7x}{12}$, which is clearly not the same answer. Remember that $\sqrt{25}$ is 5. However, if you write that $\sqrt{25}$ as $\sqrt{16+9}$, you cannot say it is 4 + 3, or 7. *Always* combine the quantities within a radical sign into a single term before taking the square root.

Radicals

In solving equations containing radicals, always get the radical alone on one side of the equation; then square both sides to remove the radical and solve. Remember that all solutions to radical equations must be checked, as squaring both sides may sometimes result in extraneous roots.

Solve for x: $\sqrt{x+5} = 7$

$x + 5 = 49$

$x = 44$

Checking, we have $\sqrt{49} = 7$, which is true.

Solve for x: $\sqrt{x} = -6$

You may have written the answer: $x = 36$.

Checking, we have $\sqrt{36} = -6$, which is not true, as the radical sign means the positive, or principal, square root only. This equation has no solution because $\sqrt{36} = 6$, not -6.

Solve for x: $\sqrt{x^2 + 6} - 3 = x$

$$\sqrt{x^2 + 6} - 3 = x$$

$$\sqrt{x^2 + 6} = x + 3$$

$$x^2 + 6 = x^2 + 6x + 9$$

$$6 = 6x + 9$$

$$-3 = 6x$$

$$-\frac{1}{2} = x$$

Checking, we have

$$\sqrt{6\frac{1}{4}} - 3 = -\frac{1}{2}$$

$$\sqrt{\frac{25}{4}} - 3 = -\frac{1}{2}$$

$$\frac{5}{2} - 3 = -\frac{1}{2}$$

$$2\frac{1}{2} - 3 = -\frac{1}{2}$$

$$-\frac{1}{2} = -\frac{1}{2}$$

This is a true statement. Therefore, $-\frac{1}{2}$ is a true root.

Roots as Fractional Powers

Roots can also be written as fractional exponents to make them easier for you to work with. The square root of 4, for example, $\sqrt{4}$ can also be written as $4^{\frac{1}{2}}$. The value of a square root includes both the positive and negative root, so $\sqrt{4} = \pm 2$ and $4^{\frac{1}{2}} = \pm 2$.

To write an nth root as a fractional exponents, use the root as the denominator of the fraction under 1 or $\sqrt[n]{x} = x^{\frac{1}{n}}$.

Use the laws of exponents to solve radical expressions and equations.

Simplify: $\sqrt{3x} \times \sqrt{3x}$

(A) $9x^2$

(B) $6x$

(C) $3x^2$

(D) $3x$

Solution: $\sqrt{3x} \times \sqrt{3x} = 3x^{\frac{1}{2}} \times 3x^{\frac{1}{2}}$

$$= (3x)^{\frac{1}{2} + \frac{1}{2}}$$

$$= 3x$$

EXERCISES: ROOTS AND RADICALS

Directions: Work out each problem. Circle the letter of your choice.

1. What is the sum of $\sqrt{12} + \sqrt{27}$?

   (A) $\sqrt{29}$

   (B) $3\sqrt{5}$

   (C) $13\sqrt{3}$

   (D) $5\sqrt{3}$

2. What is the difference between $\sqrt{150}$ and $\sqrt{54}$?

   (A) $2\sqrt{6}$

   (B) $16\sqrt{6}$

   (C) $\sqrt{96}$

   (D) $6\sqrt{2}$

3. What is the product of $\sqrt{18x}$ and $\sqrt{2x}$, where x is greater than 0?

   (A) $6x^2$

   (B) $6x$

   (C) $36x^2$

   (D) $6\sqrt{x}$

4. If $\dfrac{1}{x} = \sqrt{0.25}$, what does x equal?

   (A) 2

   (B) 0.5

   (C) 0.2

   (D) 20

5. Solve for x: $5\sqrt{2x^2} = \sqrt{500}$

   (A) 10

   (B) 100

   (C) $2\sqrt{5}$

   (D) $\sqrt{10}$

6. Solve for x: $8\sqrt{x} + 7 = 3\sqrt{x} + 17$

   (A) -2

   (B) $\sqrt{2}$

   (C) 2

   (D) 4

7. Which expression is equivalent to $\sqrt[5]{4x} + \sqrt[5]{6x}$?

   (A) $\sqrt[5]{10x}$

   (B) $10x^{\frac{1}{5}}$

   (C) $\sqrt[5]{10 + 2x}$

   (D) $4x^{\frac{1}{5}} + 6x^{\frac{1}{5}}$

8. Divide $6\sqrt{45}$ by $3\sqrt{5}$.

   (A) 6

   (B) 9

   (C) 15

   (D) 30

9. $\sqrt{\dfrac{y^2}{25} + \dfrac{y^2}{16}} =$

   (A) $\dfrac{2y}{9}$

   (B) $\dfrac{9y}{20}$

   (C) $\dfrac{y}{9}$

   (D) $\dfrac{|y|\sqrt{41}}{20}$

10. Which expression shows $\dfrac{\sqrt[5]{32} - \sqrt[3]{2}}{\sqrt{8}}$ written in simplest form?

    (A) $\dfrac{3}{\sqrt{2}}$

    (B) $\dfrac{0}{\sqrt{2}}$

    (C) $\dfrac{4 - 1^{\frac{1}{3}}}{\sqrt{2}}$

    (D) $\dfrac{2 - 2^{\frac{1}{3}}}{2\sqrt{2}}$

ANSWER KEY AND EXPLANATIONS

1. D	3. B	5. D	7. D	9. D
2. A	4. A	6. D	8. A	10. D

1. **The correct answer is (D).**

$$\sqrt{12} = \sqrt{4}\sqrt{3} = 2\sqrt{3}$$
$$\sqrt{27} = \sqrt{9}\sqrt{3} = 3\sqrt{3}$$
$$2\sqrt{3} + 3\sqrt{3} = 5\sqrt{3}$$

2. **The correct answer is (A).**

$$\sqrt{150} = \sqrt{25}\sqrt{6} = 5\sqrt{6}$$
$$\sqrt{54} = \sqrt{9}\sqrt{6} = 3\sqrt{6}$$
$$5\sqrt{6} - 3\sqrt{6} = 2\sqrt{6}$$

3. **The correct answer is (B).**

$$\sqrt{18x} \bullet \sqrt{2x} = \sqrt{36x^2} = 6x$$

4. **The correct answer is (A).**

$$\sqrt{0.25} = 0.5$$
$$\frac{1}{x} = 0.5$$
$$1 = 0.5x$$
$$10 = 5x$$
$$2 = x$$

5. **The correct answer is (D).**

Factor $\sqrt{500} = \sqrt{100}\sqrt{5} = 10\sqrt{5}$ so

you get: $5\sqrt{2x^2} = 10\sqrt{5}$.

Factor 5 from each side of the equation:

$$\sqrt{2x^2} = 2\sqrt{5}$$

Square each side:

$$2x^2 = 4 \times 5 = 20 \cdot x^2 = 10 \text{ so } x = \sqrt{10}.$$

6. **The correct answer is (D).** Subtract 7 from each side of the equation: $8\sqrt{x} = 3\sqrt{x} + 10$.

Subtract $3\sqrt{x}$ from each side: $5\sqrt{x} = 10$.

Divide each side by 5: $\sqrt{x} = 2$, $x = 4$.

7. **The correct answer is (D).** The terms under the roots cannot be added because they are not like terms. The terms must remain as $4x$ and $6x$. The fifth root can be rewritten as an exponent of $\frac{1}{5}$.

8. **The correct answer is (A).**

$$\frac{6\sqrt{45}}{3\sqrt{5}} = 2\sqrt{9} = 2 \bullet 3 = 6$$

9. **The correct answer is (D).**

$$\sqrt{\frac{y^2}{25} + \frac{y^2}{16}} = \sqrt{\frac{16y^2 + 25y^2}{400}}$$
$$= \sqrt{\frac{41y^2}{400}} = \frac{|y|\sqrt{41}}{20}$$

10. **The correct answer is (D).** The fifth root of 32 is 2, because $2 \times 2 \times 2 \times 2 \times 2 = 32$.

$$\frac{2 - \sqrt[3]{2}}{\sqrt{8}}$$

The third root of 2 can be rewritten as

$$2^{\frac{1}{3}} : \frac{2 - 2^{\frac{1}{3}}}{\sqrt{8}}.$$

The square root of 8 can be simplified:

$$\sqrt{8} = \sqrt{4 \times 2} = 2\sqrt{2}$$

$$\frac{2 - 2^{\frac{1}{3}}}{2\sqrt{2}}$$

MONOMIALS AND POLYNOMIALS

When we add a collection of expressions together, each expression is called a *term*. *Monomial* means one term. For example, we might say that $2x + 3y^2 + 7$ is the sum of three terms, or three monomials. When we talk about a monomial, we generally mean a term that is just the product of constants and variables, possibly raised to various powers. Examples might be 7, $2x$, $-3y^2$, and $4x^2z^5$. The constant factor is called the *coefficient* of the variable factor. Thus, in $-3y^2$, -3 is the coefficient of y^2.

If we restrict our attention to monomials of the form Ax^n, the sums of such terms are called *polynomials* (in one variable). Expressions like $3x + 5$, $2x^2 - 5x + 8$, and $x^4 - 7x^5 - 11$ are all examples of polynomials. The highest power of the variable that appears is called the *degree* of the polynomial. The three examples just given are of degree 1, 2, and 5, respectively.

In evaluating monomials and polynomials for negative values of the variable, the greatest pitfall is keeping track of the minus signs. Always remember that in an expression like $-x^2$, the power 2 is applied to the x, and the minus sign in front should be thought of as (-1) times the expression. If you want to have the power apply to $-x$, you must write $(-x)^2$.

Combining Monomials

Monomials with identical variable factors can be added together by adding their coefficients. So $3x^2 + 4x^2 = 7x^2$. Of course, subtraction is handled the same way, thus:

$3x^4 - 9x^4 = -6x^4$

Monomials are multiplied by taking the product of their coefficients and taking the product of the variable part by adding exponents of factors with like bases. So, $(3xy^2)(2xy^3) = 6x^2y^5$.

Monomial fractions can be simplified to simplest form by dividing out common factors of the coefficients and then using the usual rules for subtraction of exponents in division. An example might be:

$$\frac{6x^3y^5}{2x^4y^3} = \frac{3y^2}{x}$$

Combine into a single monomial: $\dfrac{8x^3}{4x^2} - 6x$

The fraction simplifies to $2x$, and $2x - 6x = -4x$.

Combining Polynomials and Monomials

Polynomials are added or subtracted by just combining like monomial terms in the appropriate manner. Thus,

$(3x^2 - 3x - 4) + (2x^2 + 5x - 11)$

is summed by removing the parentheses and combining like terms, to yield

$5x^2 + 2x - 15.$

In subtraction, when you remove the parentheses with a minus sign in front, be careful to change the signs of *all* the terms within the parentheses. So:

$$\left(3x^2 - 3x - 4\right) - \left(2x^2 + 5x - 11\right)$$
$$= 3x^2 - 3x - 4 - 2x^2 - 5x + 11$$
$$= x^2 - 8x + 7$$

(Did you notice that $3x^2 - 2x^2 = 1x^2$ but the "1" is not shown?)

To multiply a polynomial by a monomial, use the distributive law to multiply each term in the polynomial by the monomial factor. For example, $2x(2x^2 + 5x - 11) = 4x^3 + 10x^2 - 22x$.

When multiplying a polynomial by a polynomial, you are actually repeatedly applying the distributive law to form all possible products of the terms in the first polynomial with the terms in the second polynomial. The most common use of this is in multiplying two *binomials* (polynomials with two terms), such as $(x + 3)(x - 5)$. In this case, there are four terms in the result, $x \times x = x^2$; $x(-5) = -5x$; $3 \times x = 3x$; and $3 \times (-5) = -15$; but the two middle terms are added together to give $-2x$. Thus, the product is $x^2 - 2x - 15$.

This process is usually remembered as the FOIL method. That is, form the products of First, Outer, Inner, Last, as shown in the figure below.

$(x + 3)(x - 5) = x^2 + (-5x + 3x) - 15$

> If d is an integer, and $(x + 2)(x + d) = x^2 - kx - 10$, what is the value of $k + d$?

The product of the two last terms, $2d$, must be -10. Therefore, $d = -5$. If $d = -5$, then the sum of the outer and inner products becomes $-5x + 2x = -3x$, which equals $-kx$. Hence, $k = 3$, and $k + d = 3 + (-5) = -2$.

Factoring Monomials

Factoring a monomial simply involves reversing the distributive law. For example, if you are looking at $4x^2 + 12xy$, you should see that $4x$ is a factor of both terms. Hence, you could just as well write this as $4x(x + 3y)$. Multiplication using the distributive law will restore the original formulation.

> If $3x - 4y = -2$, what is the value of $9x - 12y$?

Although you seem to have one equation in two unknowns, you can still solve the problem, because you do not need to know the values of the individual variables. Just rewrite:
$9x - 12y = 3(3x - 4y)$. Since $3x - 4y = -2$, $9x - 12y$ is 3 times -2, or -6.

EXERCISES: MONOMIALS AND POLYNOMIALS

Directions: Work out each problem. Circle the letter of your choice.

1. $6x^3(x^2)^3 =$
   (A) $6x^7$
   (B) $6x^8$
   (C) $6x^9$
   (D) $6x^{10}$

2. $(3w^2y^3)^4 =$
   (A) $18w^8y^{12}$
   (B) $18w^6y^7$
   (C) $81w^6y^7$
   (D) $81w^8y^{12}$

3. $5x^3(-3x^8) =$
   (A) $15x^{11}$
   (B) $-15x^{11}$
   (C) $-15x^{24}$
   (D) $15x^{24}$

4. Simplify: $\dfrac{3x^3y - 9x^2}{xy^2}$

   (A) $\dfrac{-6xy}{xy^2}$

   (B) $\dfrac{3x(xy - 3)}{y^2}$

   (C) $\dfrac{3x^2 - 9x}{y}$

   (D) $3x^2 - 9x$

5. $(a^3 + 4a^2 - 11a + 4) - (8a^2 + 2a + 4) =$
   (A) $-3a^2 - 13a$
   (B) $a^3 - 12a^2 - 13a - 8$
   (C) $a^3 - 4a^2 - 9a + 8$
   (D) $a^3 - 4a^2 - 13a$

6. $(4x^3 - 2x + 5) + (8x^2 - 2x - 10) =$
   (A) $4x^3 + 8x^2 - 4x - 5$
   (B) $12x^2 - 4x - 5$
   (C) $12x^3 - 5$
   (D) $4x^3 + 8x^2 + 15$

7. What is the product of $2x^2$ and $3x^3 - x + 4$?
   (A) $6x^6 + 6x^2$
   (B) $6x^5 - 2x^3 + 8x^2$
   (C) $5x^5 - x^2 + 4$
   (D) $6x^5 + 2x^3 + 8x^2$

8. Multiply: $(x^2 - 1)(2x^3 + 5)$
   (A) $2x^5 + 5x^2$
   (B) $-2x^3 - 5$
   (C) $2x^5 - 2x^3 + 5x^2 - 5$
   (D) $2x^6 - 5x^2 - 2x^3 - 5$

ANSWER KEY AND EXPLANATIONS

1. C	3. B	5. D	7. B
2. D	4. B	6. A	8. C

1. **The correct answer is (C).**

$$6x^3(x^2)^3 = (6 \cdot x^3 \cdot (x^2)^3$$
$$= 6 \cdot x^3 \cdot x^{(2 \cdot 3)}$$
$$= 6 \cdot x^3 \cdot x^6$$
$$= 6 \cdot x^9$$
$$= 6x^9$$

2. **The correct answer is (D).**

$$(3w^2 y^3)^4 = (3)^4 \cdot w^{(2 \cdot 4)} \cdot y^{(3 \cdot 4)}$$
$$= 81 \cdot w^8 \cdot y^{12}$$
$$= 81w^8 y^{12}$$

3. **The correct answer is (B).**

$$5x^3(-3x^8)^3 = (5 \cdot x^3 \cdot (-3) \cdot x^8$$
$$= 5 \cdot (-3) \cdot x^3 \cdot x^8$$
$$= -15 \cdot x^{3+8}$$
$$= -15x^{11}$$

4. **The correct answer is (B).** The variable x can be factored out of the all the terms in the numerator and denominator of the fraction:

$$\frac{3x^3 y - 9x^2}{xy^2} = \frac{3x^2 y - 9x^1}{(1)y^2}$$
$$= \frac{3x^2 y - 9x}{y^2}$$

Factor the term $3x$ out of the expression in the numerator: $3x(xy - 3)$

Because y appears in only one of the terms in the numerator, it cannot be factored out of either the numerator or the denominator.

5. **The correct answer is (D).** The term a^3 will remain because there are no other like terms to subtract. Subtract the squared terms: $4a^2 - 8a^2 = -4a^2$; the single variable terms $-11a - 2a = -13a$; and the integer terms $-4 - 4 = 0$. Combining these terms with a^3 gives us $a^3 - 4a^2 - 13a$.

6. **The correct answer is (A).** The only like terms that may be combined are $(-2x) + (-2x) = -4x$ and $+5 + (-10) = 5 - 10 = -5$.

Combine all the terms to get $4x^3 + 8x^2 - 4x - 5$.

7. **The correct answer is (B).** Multiply each term in the polynomial by $2x^2$:

$$2x^2 \times 3x^3 = 6x^5$$
$$2x^2 \times (-x) = -2x^3$$
$$2x^2 \times 4 = 8x^2$$

Combine the products to get $6x^5 - 2x^3 + 8x^2$.

8. **The correct answer is (C).** Use the FOIL method to multiply:

First: $(x^2)(2x^3) = 2x^5$

Outer: $(x^2)(5) = 5x^2$

Inner: $(-1)(2x^3) = -2x^3$

Last: $(-1)(5) = -5$

Combine the terms to get $2x^5 - 2x^3 + 5x^2 - 5$.

PROBLEM SOLVING IN ALGEBRA

When you are working with algebraic word problems, remember that before you begin working you should be absolutely certain that you understand precisely what you need to answer. Once this is done, show what you are looking for algebraically. Write an equation that translates the words of the problem to the symbols of mathematics. Then solve that equation by using the techniques you just learned.

This section reviews the types of algebra problems most frequently encountered on the SAT®. Thoroughly familiarizing yourself with the problems that follow will help you to translate and solve all kinds of verbal problems.

Solving Two Linear Equations in Two Unknowns

Many word problems lead to equations in two unknowns. Usually, one needs two equations to solve for both unknowns, although there are exceptions. There are two generally used methods to solve two equations in two unknowns. They are the method of *substitution* and the method of *elimination by addition and subtraction*.

We'll illustrate both methods via example. Here is one that uses the method of substitution.

> Mr. Green took his four children to the local craft fair. The total cost of their admission tickets was $14. Mr. and Mrs. Molina and their six children had to pay $23. What was the cost of an adult ticket to the craft fair, and what was the cost of a child's ticket?

Expressing all amounts in dollars, let x = cost of an adult ticket and let y = cost of a child's ticket.

For the Greens: $x + 4y = 14$

For the Molinas: $2x + 6y = 23$

The idea of the method of substitution is to solve one equation for one variable in terms of the other and then substitute that solution into the second equation. So we solve the first equation for x, because that is the simplest one to isolate:

$x = 14 - 4y$

and substitute into the second equation:

$2(14 - 4y) + 6y = 23$

This gives us one equation in one unknown that we can solve:

$28 - 8y + 6y = 23$

$-2y = -5; y = 2.5$

Now that we know $y = 2.5$, we substitute this into $x = 14 - 4y$ to get:

$x = 14 - 4(2.5) = 4$

Thus, the adult tickets were $4.00 each, and the children's tickets were $2.50 each.

Here is an example using the method of elimination.

> Paul and Denise both have after-school jobs. Two weeks ago, Paul worked 6 hours, Denise worked 3 hours, and they earned a total of $39. Last week, Paul worked 12 hours, Denise worked 5 hours, and they earned a total of $75. What is each one's hourly wage?

Again, let us express all amounts in dollars. Let x = Paul's hourly wage, and let y = Denise's hourly wage.

For the first week: $6x + 3y = 39$

For the second week: $12x + 5y = 75$

The idea of the method of elimination is that adding equal quantities to equal quantities gives a true result. So we want to add some multiple of one equation to the other one so that if we add the two equations together, one variable will be eliminated. In this case, it is not hard to see that if we multiply the first equation by -2, the coefficient of x will become -12. Now when we add the two equations, x will be eliminated. Hence,

$$\begin{array}{r} -12x - 6y = -78 \\ \underline{12x + 5y = 75} \\ -y = -3 \end{array}$$

Thus, $y = 3$. We now substitute this into either of the two equations. Let's use the first:

$6x + (3)(3) = 39$; $x = 5$.

Thus, Denise makes only $3 per hour, while Paul gets $5.

Word Problems in One or Two Unknowns

Word problems can be broken down into a number of categories. To do *consecutive integer* problems, you need to remember that consecutive integers differ by 1, so a string of such numbers can be represented as $n, n + 1, n + 2, \ldots$

Rate-time-distance problems require you to know the formula $d = rt$. That is, distance equals rate times time.

Here are some examples of several types of word problems.

Movie tickets are $13.50 for adults and $8.00 for senior citizens. On Saturday night, a total of 436 adults and senior citizens attended, and the movie theater collected $4,885.00 from these adults and senior citizens. How many senior citizens were at the movie theater?

To solve the problem, you must write two different equations using the data in the question. Let a be the number of adults and s represent senior citizens.

$a + s = 436$

You also know that $a \times \$13.50$ can be used to find the total amount the movie theater collected for adult tickets and $s \times \$8.00$ to find the total amount collected for senior citizen tickets. Together these dollar amounts total $4885.

$13.5a + 8s = 4885$

Solve using elimination, by multiplying the first equation by -8 to eliminate one of the variables during addition of the equations $(-8)(a + s) = (-8)(436)$

$-8a + -8s = -3488$

Add the equations:

$$-8a + -8s = -3488$$
$$+13.5a + 8s = \ \ 4885$$
$$5.5a = \ \ 1397$$
$$a = \ \ \ 254$$

254 adults attended, so $436 - 254 = 182$ senior citizens were at the movie theater.

> A supermarket places two orders for regular and extra-large packages of paper towels. The first order had 48 regular and 120 extra-large packages and cost $644.40. The second order had 60 regular and 40 extra-large and cost $338.00. What is the difference in cost between a regular and extra-large package of paper towels?

Write two equations using the data given in the question. Use r to represent a regular package of paper towels and e to represent an extra-large package.

$$48r + 120e = 644.40$$
$$60r + 40e = 338$$

Multiply the bottom equation by -3 to eliminate e:

$$(-3)(60r + 40e) = (-3)(338)$$
$$-180r - 120e = -1014$$

Add the 2 equations:

$$48r + 120e = \ \ 644.4$$
$$+ -180r - 120e = -1014$$
$$-132r = -369.6$$
$$r = \ \ \ 2.8$$

The price of a regular package of paper towels is $2.80. To find the price of an extra-large package, substitute 2.8 into one of the equations:

$$(48)(2.8) + 120e = 644.4$$
$$120e = 510$$
$$e = 4.25$$

The difference in cost between an extra-large package and a regular package of paper towels is:

$4.25 - 2.80 = 1.45$

It took Andrew 15 minutes to drive downtown at 28 miles per hour to get a pizza. How fast did he have to drive back in order to be home in 10 minutes?

15 minutes is $\frac{1}{4}$ of an hour. Hence, going 28 miles per hour, the distance to the pizza parlor can be computed using the formula $d = rt$; $d = (28)\left(\frac{1}{4}\right) = 7$ miles. Since 10 minutes is $\frac{1}{6}$ of an hour, we have the equation $7 = r\left(\frac{1}{6}\right)$. Multiplying by 6, $r = 42$ mph.

Fraction Problems

A fraction is a ratio between two numbers. If the value of a fraction is $\frac{2}{3}$, it does not mean the numerator must be 2 and the denominator 3. The numerator and denominator could be 4 and 6, respectively, or 1 and 1.5, or 30 and 45, or any of infinitely many combinations. All you know is that the ratio of numerator to denominator will be 2:3. Therefore, the numerator may be represented by $2x$, the denominator by $3x$, and the fraction by $\frac{2x}{3x}$.

The value of a fraction is $\frac{3}{4}$. If 3 is subtracted from the numerator and added to the denominator, the value of the fraction is $\frac{2}{5}$. Find the original fraction.

Let the original fraction be represented by $\frac{3x}{4x}$. If 3 is subtracted from the numerator and added to the denominator, the new fraction becomes $\frac{3x-3}{4x+3}$.

The value of the new fraction is $\frac{2}{5}$.

$$\frac{3x-3}{4x+3} = \frac{2}{5}$$

Cross-multiply to eliminate fractions.

$$15x - 15 = 8x + 6$$
$$7x = 21$$
$$x = 3$$

Therefore, the original fraction is $\frac{3x}{4x} = \frac{9}{12}$.

EXERCISES: PROBLEM SOLVING IN ALGEBRA

Directions: Work out each problem. Circle the letter of your choice.

1. A train with a heavy load travels from point A to point B at 15 miles per hour. After unloading the load, it travels back from point B to point A at 20 miles per hour. The trip from point A to point B took 1.5 hours longer than the return trip. Which of the following equations can be used to calculate the time, t, it took for the train to go from point A to point B?

   (A) $1.5t = 20t$
   (B) $15t = 20t - 30$
   (C) $t = 20t - 30$
   (D) $15t = 20 + 30$

2. If a fleet of m buses uses g gallons of gasoline every two days, how many gallons of gasoline will be used by 4 buses every five days?

   (A) $\dfrac{10g}{m}$

   (B) $10gm$

   (C) $\dfrac{10m}{g}$

   (D) $\dfrac{20g}{m}$

3. A faucet is dripping at a constant rate. If, at noon on Sunday, 3 ounces of water have dripped from the faucet into a holding tank and, at 5 p.m. on Sunday, a total of 7 ounces have dripped into the tank, how many ounces will have dripped into the tank by 2:00 a.m. on Monday?

   (A) 10

   (B) $\dfrac{51}{5}$

   (C) 12

   (D) $\dfrac{71}{5}$

4. The Olympic world record in 800-meter freestyle swimming is approximately 8 minutes and 15 seconds. Marta is recording her times in seconds, s, for the 800-meter freestyle competition at her school. Which expression below could be used to calculate Marta's time as a percentage of the world record?

   (A) $\dfrac{s}{8.25} \times 100$

   (B) $\left(\dfrac{s}{60} \div 8.15 \right) \times 100$

   (C) $\left(\dfrac{s}{60} \div 495 \right) \times 100$

   (D) $\dfrac{s}{495} \times 100$

ANSWER KEY AND EXPLANATIONS

1. B	2. A	3. D	4. D

1. **The correct answer is (B).** Use the distance formula $d = rt$. The train's rate from point A to point B is 15mph. Its time can be expressed as t. The train's rate from point B to point A is 20mph. Its time can be expressed as $t - 1.5$.

    For the trip from A to B: $d = 15t$

    For the trip from B to A: $d = 20(t - 1.5) = 20t - 30$

    Since the distance from A to B is equal to the distance from B to A, we can set these two expressions equal to each other:

    $15t = 20t - 30$

2. **The correct answer is (A).** Running m buses for two days is the same as running one bus for $2m$ days. If we use g gallons of gasoline, each bus uses $\dfrac{g}{2m}$ gallons each day. So if you multiply the number of gallons per day used by each bus by the number of buses and the number of days, you should get total gasoline usage. That is,

    $\dfrac{g}{2m} \times (4)(5) = \dfrac{10g}{m}$.

3. **The correct answer is (D).** In 5 hours, 4 ounces $(7 - 3)$ have dripped. Therefore, the "drip rate" is $\dfrac{4}{5}$ of an ounce per hour.

    From 5:00 p.m. on Sunday until 2:00 a.m. on Monday is 9 hours, which means the total will be:

    $7 + \dfrac{4}{5} \times 9 = 7\dfrac{36}{5} = \dfrac{71}{5}$

4. **The correct answer is (D).** Convert the world record of 8 minutes and 15 seconds to seconds by multiplying 8 *seconds* × 60 *sec/min* = 480 seconds. Add 15: 480 + 15 = 495 seconds. Divide Marta's time, s, by the world record, 495: $\dfrac{s}{495}$ and multiply by 100 to express it as a percent. So the correct answer is $\dfrac{s}{495} \times 100$.

INEQUALITIES

Algebraic inequality statements are solved just as equations are solved. However, you must remember that whenever you multiply or divide by a negative number, the order of the inequality, that is, the inequality symbol, must be reversed.

> Solve for x: $3 - 5x > 18$

Add -3 to both sides:

$-5x > 15$

Divide by -5, remembering to reverse the inequality:

$x < -3$

> Solve for x: $5x - 4 > 6x - 6$

Collect all x-terms on the left and numerical terms on the right. As with equations, remember that if a term crosses the inequality symbol, the term changes sign.

$-x > -2$

Divide (or multiply) by -1:

$x < 2$

Inequality Symbols

$>$ greater than

$<$ less than

$\geq$ greater than or equal to

$\leq$ less than or equal to

You can solve inequalities in the same way you solve linear equations, except in cases where you multiply or divide by a negative number. In these situations, you must reverse the direction of the inequality symbol.

Properties of Inequalities

In the properties below, assume that a, b, and c are real numbers.

Addition Property of Inequality	Subtraction Property of Inequality
If $a > b$, then $a + c > b + c$	If $a > b$, then $a - c > b - c$
If $a < b$, then $a + c < b + c$	If $a < b$, then $a - c < b - c$
Multiplication Property of Inequality	**Division Property of Inequality**

$c > 0$
 	
     If $a > b$, then $ac > bc$
 	
     If $a < b$, then $ac < bc$
 $c < 0$
 	
     If $a > b$, then $ac < bc$
 	
     If $a < b$, then $ac > bc$
	$c > 0$
	
	     If $a > b$, then $\dfrac{a}{c} > \dfrac{b}{c}$
	
	     If $a < b$, then $\dfrac{a}{c} < \dfrac{b}{c}$
	 $c < 0$
	
	     If $a > b$, then $\dfrac{a}{c} < \dfrac{b}{c}$
	
	     If $a < b$, then $\dfrac{a}{c} > \dfrac{b}{c}$

These properties are also true for inequalities that include the $\leq$ and $\geq$ symbols.

> The meeting room can hold at most 250 people. If 182 people have already been admitted, how many more people can be allowed into the meeting room?

Let x = number of people that can be admitted.

$$182 + x \leq 250$$
$$182 - 182 + x \leq 250 - 182$$
$$x \leq 68$$

There can be at most 68 more people admitted to the meeting room.

> To stay healthy, an adult's goal should be to walk at least 10,000 steps each day. A fitness tracker showed that a person had walked 6,349 steps. What is the possible number of steps this person can take to reach this goal?

Let x = number of steps.

$$6349 + x \geq 10,000$$
$$6349 - 6349 + x \geq 10,000 - 6349$$
$$x \geq 3651$$

The person must walk at least 3,651 more steps.

> Alexander plans on mowing lawns this summer. He charges $20 per lawn. How many lawns will he have to mow in order to earn at least $575?

Let x = number of lawns.

$$20x \geq 575$$

$$\frac{20x}{20} \geq \frac{575}{20}$$

$$x \geq 28.75$$

Alexander must mow at least 29 lawns to earn at least $575.

Use properties of inequality to solve multi-step inequalities.

> The marching band members are making a banner for the pep rally. The banner is in the shape of a rectangle that is 12 ft. long. They have no more than 32 ft. of fringe for the banner. What are the possible widths of the banner?

Let w = width of the banner and l = length of the banner. Use the perimeter formula to find the possible allowable widths.

$$2l + 2w \leq P$$

$$2(12) + 2w \leq 32$$

$$24 + 2w \leq 32$$

$$2w \leq 8$$

$$\frac{2w}{2} \leq \frac{8}{2}$$

$$x \leq 4$$

The width of the banner can be 4 ft. or less.

> A prepaid cell phone has a balance of $40. Calls are $0.04 per minute, and texts are $0.07 per text. If there 342 texts were used, how many minutes can be used for calls?

Let x = number of minutes used on calls and y = number of texts.

$$0.04x + 0.07y \leq 40$$

$$0.04x + 0.07(342) \leq 40$$

$$0.04x + 27.44 \leq 40$$

$$0.04x \leq 12.56$$

$$\frac{0.04x}{0.04} \leq \frac{12.56}{0.04}$$

$$x \leq 314$$

The number of minutes that can be used for calls can be 314 or less.

EXERCISES: INEQUALITIES

Directions: Work out each problem. Circle the letter of your choice.

1. If $3x - 8 \geq 4x$, then
   - (A) $-8 \leq x$
   - (B) $-8 \geq x$
   - (C) $-8 < x$
   - (D) $-8 > x$

2. If $-9x + 7 < 43$, then
   - (A) $x \geq -4$
   - (B) $x \leq -4$
   - (C) $x > -4$
   - (D) $x < -4$

3. The admission to the local carnival is $6. You want to play games that cost $1.50 per game. If you have $30, how many games can you play?
   - (A) At least 24
   - (B) No more than 20
   - (C) Less than or equal to 16
   - (D) Greater than or equal 20

4. You order a bouquet of flowers that contains roses and carnations. You have only $48 to spend. Roses cost $3 each, and carnations cost $1.25 each. How many roses can be in the bouquet if there are 18 carnations in the bouquet? Let r represent the number of roses.
   - (A) $r \geq 8$
   - (B) $r \leq 9$
   - (C) $r \geq 9$
   - (D) $r \leq 8$

5. Bike rentals cost $15 for the first 2 hours and $6 for any additional hours. Ali wants to bike for more than 2 hours, but she only has $35. Which inequality represents the situation, where h is the total number of hours Ali can bike?
   - (A) $6 + 15h \leq 35$
   - (B) $6(h - 2) + 15 \leq 35$
   - (C) $6h + 15 \leq 35$
   - (D) $6(h + 2) + 15 \leq 35$

6. Selena is adding trim to a rectangular tablecloth that measures 108 in. long. If she has 330 in. of trim, what is the greatest possible width of the tablecloth?
   - (A) At most 54 in.
   - (B) At most 57 in.
   - (C) At most 222 in.
   - (D) At most 114 in.

ANSWER KEY AND EXPLANATIONS

   3. C   5. B   6. B

1. **The correct answer is (B).** Subtracting $3x$ from both sides leaves $-8 \geq x$.

2. **The correct answer is (C).**

$$-9x + 7 < 43$$
$$-9x < 36$$
$$x > -4$$

By dividing by -9, you reverse the inequality sign.

3. **The correct answer is (C).**

$$6 + 1.5x \leq 30$$
$$1.5x \leq 24$$
$$\frac{1.5x}{1.5} \leq \frac{24}{1.5}$$
$$x \leq 16$$

4. **The correct answer is (D).**

$$3r + 1.5c \leq 48$$
$$3r + 1.5(18) \leq 48$$
$$3r + 22.5 \leq 48$$
$$3r \leq 25.5$$
$$\frac{3x}{3} \leq \frac{25.5}{3}$$
$$x \leq 8.5$$

There can only be at most 8 roses in the bouquet.

5. **The correct answer is (B).** The cost for the first 2 hours is $15. Subtract the 2 hours from the total number of hours (h), and multiply by $6 an hour to compute the cost for the number of hours over 2. Be sure to add the initial $15 for the first 2 hours:

$$6(h - 2) + 15 \leq 35$$

6. **The correct answer is (B).**

$$2l + 2w \leq 330$$
$$2(108) + 2w \leq 330$$
$$216 + 2w \leq 330$$
$$2w \leq 114$$
$$\frac{2w}{2} \leq \frac{114}{2}$$
$$w \leq 57$$

The tablecloth can be at most 57 in. wide.

SUMMING IT UP

- In complex questions, don't look for easy solutions.

- Always keep in mind what is being asked.

- Keep the negatives and positives straight when you're doing polynomial math.

- Don't be distracted by strange symbols.

- An equation can have one solution, infinitely many solutions, or no solutions.

- Let a, b, and c be real numbers.
    - If $a > b$, then $a + c > b + c$
    - If $a < b$, then $a + c < b + c$
    - If $a > b$, then $a - c > b - c$
    - If $a < b$, then $a - c < b - c$
    - If $c > 0$, then if $a > b$, then $ac > bc$ and if $a < b$, then $ac < bc$
    - If $c < 0$, then if $a > b$, then $ac < bc$ and if $a < b$, then $ac > bc$

- You can graph a system of linear inequalities in the coordinate plane. The solution of the system is where the graphs of the inequalities overlap.

Geometry Review

chapter 11

OVERVIEW

- Geometric notation
- Angle measurement
- Intersecting lines
- Area
- Circles
- Volume
- Triangles
- Parallel lines
- Coordinate geometry
- Summing it up

GEOMETRIC NOTATION

1 A point is represented by a dot, and denoted by a capital letter.

$\bullet\, P$

Point P

2 A *line* can be denoted in two different ways. First, a small letter can be placed next to the line. For example, the diagram below depicts line *l*. The arrowheads on both ends of the line indicate that lines extend infinitely in both directions.

$\longleftrightarrow l$

3 A *line* can also be denoted by placing a small double-headed arrow over two of its points. The diagram below depicts line $\overleftrightarrow{AB}$.

$A \qquad B$

4 A *line segment* is the part of a line between two of its points, which are called the endpoints of the line segment. A line segment is denoted by placing a small line segment over the two endpoints. Thus, the diagram below depicts the line segment $\overline{AB}$.

$A \qquad B$

375

5 The length of a line segment is denoted by placing its two endpoints next to each other. In the diagram below, $CD = 7$.

6 Two line segments that have the same length are said to be *congruent*. The symbol for congruence is $\cong$. Thus, if $AB = 12$ and $EF = 12$, then $\overline{AB}$ is congruent to $\overline{EF}$, or $\overline{AB} \cong \overline{EF}$.

7 A *ray* is the part of a line beginning at one point, called the *endpoint,* and extending infinitely in one direction. A ray is denoted by placing a small one-headed arrow over its endpoint and another point on the ray. The first diagram below depicts the ray $\overrightarrow{AB}$, and the second diagram depicts the ray $\overrightarrow{AC}$.

8 Two lines that cross each other are said to *intersect*. Two lines that do not intersect are said to be *parallel*. The symbol $||$ is used to represent parallel lines. In the diagrams below, line k intersects line l at point P, while lines m and n are parallel, that is, $m || n$.

ANGLE MEASUREMENT

1 When two rays share a common endpoint, they form *angles*. The point at which the rays intersect is called the *vertex* of the angle, and the rays themselves are called the *sides* of the angle.

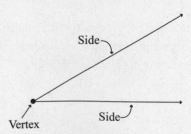

2 The symbol for angle is ∠. Angles can be denoted in several different ways, as shown in the diagram below. The most common way to denote an angle is to name a point on one side, then the vertex, and then a point on the other side as shown in the diagram.

∠ABC or ∠CBA

Angles can also be denoted by writing a letter or a number within the angle, as shown below. If there is no ambiguity, an angle can be named by simply naming the vertex.

3 The size of an angle is measured in *degrees*. The symbol for degree is °. A full circle contains 360°, and all other angles can be measured as a fractional part of a full circle. Typically, the measure of an angle is written in the interior of the angle, near the vertex.

4 A *straight angle* is an angle that measures 180°.

5 A *right angle* is an angle that measures 90°. Note, as shown in the diagram below, the symbol ⌐ is used to represent a right angle.

6 The measure of an angle is denoted by writing the letter m followed by the name of the angle. For example, m∠ *ABC* = 45° tells that angle *ABC* has a measure of 45°.

7 Two angles that have the same number of degrees are said to be *congruent*. Thus, if m∠P = m ∠Q, then ∠P ≅ ∠Q.

8 Two angles whose measures add up to 180° are said to be *supplementary*. Two angles whose measures add up to 90° are said to be *complementary*.

∠*ABC* and ∠*CBD*
are supplementary.

∠*EFG* and ∠*GFH*
are complementary.

9 To convert between degrees and radians:

Degrees to radians:

Multiply the degree measure by $\dfrac{\pi \text{ radians}}{180°}$.

85° to radians:

$$85° = 85\left(\dfrac{\pi \text{ radians}}{180°}\right) = \dfrac{17\pi}{36}$$

Radians to degrees:

Multiply the radian measure by $\dfrac{180°}{\pi \text{ radians}}$.

$\dfrac{\pi \text{ radians}}{6}$ to degrees:

$$\dfrac{\pi}{6} = \left(\dfrac{\pi \text{ radians}}{6}\right)\left(\dfrac{180°}{\pi \text{ radians}}\right) = 30°$$

INTERSECTING LINES

❶ When two lines intersect, four angles are formed. The angles opposite each other are congruent.

$\angle 1 \cong \angle 3$ and

$\angle 2 \cong \angle 4$

❷ When two lines intersect, the angles adjacent to each other are supplementary.

$m\angle 5 + m\angle 6 = 180°$

$m\angle 6 + m\angle 7 = 180°$

$m\angle 7 + m\angle 8 = 180°$

$m\angle 8 + m\angle 5 = 180°$

If you know the measure of any one of the four angles formed when two lines intersect, you can determine the measures of the other three. For example, if $m\angle 1 = 45°$, then $m\angle 3 = 45°$, and $m\angle 2 = m\angle 4 = 180° - 45° = 135°$.

3 Two lines that intersect at right angles are said to be *perpendicular*. In the figure below, $\overline{AB}$ is perpendicular to $\overline{CD}$. This can be denoted as $\overline{AB} \perp \overline{CD}$.

Note that all four of the angles in the diagram above are right angles.

AREA

1 Rectangle = bh

Area = $6 \bullet 3 = 18$

2 Parallelogram = bh

Area = $8 \bullet 4 = 32$

3 Square = s^2

Area = $6^2 = 36$

Area = $\dfrac{1}{2}(10)(10) = 50$

4 Triangle = $\dfrac{1}{2}bh$

Area = $\dfrac{1}{2}(12)(4) = 24$

5 Trapezoid $= \frac{1}{2}h(b_1 + b_2)$

Area $= \frac{1}{2}(5)(16) = 40$

6 Circle $= \pi r^2$

Area $= \pi(6)^2 = 36\pi$

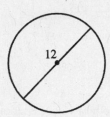

7 Area of a sector of a circle

Area of sector $AOB = \dfrac{m\widehat{AB}}{360} \bullet \pi r^2$

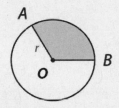

CIRCLES

1 A *circle* is a closed flat figure formed by a set of points all of which are the same distance from a point called the *center*. The boundary of the circle is called the *circumference*, and the distance from the center to any point on the circumference is called the *radius*. A circle is denoted by naming the point at its center, that is, the circle whose center is at point P is called circle P.

❷ A *diameter* of a circle is a line segment that passes through the center of the circle, and whose endpoints lie on the circle. The diameter of a circle is twice as long as its radius. Typically, the letter *r* is used to represent the radius of a circle, and the letter *d* is used to represent the diameter.

$2r = d$

❸ A *chord* of a circle is a line segment both of whose endpoints lie on the circumference of the circle. The chords of a circle have different lengths, and the length of the longest chord is equal to the diameter.

$\overline{AB}$, $\overline{CD}$, and $\overline{EF}$ are chords of circle O. $\overline{EF}$ is also a diameter.

❹ A *tangent* is a line that intersects the circle at exactly one point. A radius drawn to the point of intersection is perpendicular to the tangent line.

$\overline{OQ} \perp \overline{CD}$

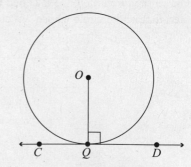

5 A *central angle* is an angle that is formed by two radii of a circle. As the diagram below shows, the vertex of a central angle is the center of the circle.

Central angle ∠ *AOB*

6 A central angle is equal in degrees to the measure of the arc that it intercepts. That is, a 40° central angle intercepts a 40° arc, and a 90° central angle intercepts a 90° arc.

7 An *arc* is a piece of the circumference of a circle. The symbol ⌒ placed on top of the two endpoints is used to denote an arc. For example, $\overset{\frown}{MN}$ is indicated in the figure below.

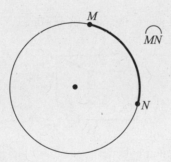

8 Length of an arc of a circle

The measure of an arc is in degrees. The arc's length depends on the size of the circle because it represents a fraction of the circumference.

Length of $\overset{\frown}{AB}$ $= \dfrac{m\overset{\frown}{AB}}{360} \cdot 2\pi r$

If the radius of a circle is 5 cm and the measure of the arc is 45°, then the length of the arc is

$$\frac{45°}{360°} \cdot 2\pi(5) = \frac{5\pi}{4}\,\text{cm}$$

$$= 1.25\pi\,\text{cm}$$

$$\approx 3.93\,\text{cm}$$

9   Area of a sector of a circle

The area of a sector of a circle is the product of the ratio $\dfrac{\text{measure of the arc}}{360°}$ and the area of the circle. If the radius of a circle is 3 cm and the measure of the arc is 60°, then the area of the sector is $\dfrac{60°}{360°} \bullet \pi(3)^2 = \dfrac{9\pi}{6} = \dfrac{3\pi}{2}$ cm².

10   Length of a chord

The length of a chord of a circle is the product of $2r$ and $\sin\left(\dfrac{\text{measure of the central angle}}{2}\right)$. If the radius of a circle is 4 inches and the measure of the central angle is 60°, then the length of the chord is $2(4)\sin\left(\dfrac{60°}{2}\right) = 8\sin(30°) = 4$ inches.

VOLUME

1   The volume of a right rectangular prism is equal to the product of its length, width, and height.

$V = lwh$

$V = (6)(2)(4) = 48$

2   The volume of a cube is equal to the cube of an edge.

$V = e^3$

$V = (5)^3 = 125$

3   The volume of a right circular cylinder is equal to π times the square of the radius of the base times the height.

$V = \pi r^2 h$

$V = \pi(5)^2(3) = 75\pi$

4 The volume of a sphere is equal to $\frac{4}{3}\pi$ times the cube of the radius.

$$V = \frac{4}{3}\pi r^3$$

$$V = \frac{4}{3}\pi(3)^3 = \frac{4}{3}\pi(27) = 36\pi$$

5 The volume of a right square pyramid is equal to $\frac{1}{3}\pi$ times the product of the square of the side and the height.

$$V = \frac{1}{3}s^2h$$

$$V = \frac{1}{3}(2)^2(6)$$

$$V = 8$$

6 The volume of a right circular cone is equal to $\frac{1}{3}\pi$ times the product of the square of the radius and the height.

$$V = \frac{1}{3}\pi r^2h$$

$$V = \frac{1}{3}\pi(6)^2(9)$$

$$V = 108\pi$$

TRIANGLES

1 A *polygon* is a flat closed figure that consists of straight line segments called *sides*. A *triangle* is a polygon with three sides. A *vertex* of a triangle is a point at which two of its sides meet. The symbol for a triangle is $\triangle$, and a triangle can be named by writing its three vertices in any order.

$\triangle ABC$ contains sides $\overline{AB}$, $\overline{BC}$, and $\overline{AC}$, and angles $\angle A$, $\angle B$, and $\angle C$.

2 The sum of the measures of the angles in a triangle is 180°. Therefore, if the measures of any two of the angles in a triangle are known, the measure of the third angle can be determined.

3 In any triangle, the longest side is opposite the largest angle and the shortest side is opposite the smallest angle. In the triangle below, if $a° > b° > c°$, then $\overline{BC} > \overline{AC} > \overline{AB}$.

4 If two sides of a triangle are congruent, the angles opposite these sides are also congruent.

If $\overline{AB} = \overline{AC}$, then $\angle B \cong \angle C$.

5 If two angles of a triangle are congruent, the sides opposite these angles are also congruent.

If $\angle B \cong \angle C$ then $\overline{AB} = \overline{AC}$.

7 In the diagram below, $\angle 1$ is called an *exterior* angle. The measure of an exterior angle of a triangle is equal to the sum of the measures of the two *remote interior* angles, that is, the two interior angles that are the farthest away from the exterior angle.

$m\angle 1 = 115°$

8 If two angles of one triangle are congruent to two angles of a second triangle, the third angles are also congruent.

$\angle D \cong \angle A$

Right Triangles

1 Pythagorean theorem

$(\text{leg})^2 + (\text{leg})^2 = (\text{hypotenuse})^2$

$$4^2 + 5^2 = x^2$$
$$16 + 25 = x^2$$
$$41 = x^2$$
$$\sqrt{41} = x$$

TIP

Remember that in a right triangle, you can use the two legs (the two sides other than the hypotenuse) as base and altitude.

2 Pythagorean triples: These are sets of numbers that satisfy the Pythagorean theorem. When a given set of numbers such as 3-4-5 forms a Pythagorean triple ($3^2 + 4^2 = 5^2$), any multiples of this set, such as 6-8-10 or 15-20-25 also form a Pythagorean triple. The most common Pythagorean triples that should be memorized are:

3-4-5

5-12-13

8-15-17

7-24-25

Squaring the numbers 15 and 39 in order to apply the Pythagorean theorem would take too much time. Instead, recognize the hypotenuse as 3(13). Suspect a 5-12-13 triangle. Since the given leg is 3(5), the missing leg must be 3(12), or 36, with no computation and a great saving of time.

③ The 30°-60°-90° triangle

a) The leg opposite the 30° angle is $\frac{1}{2} \times$ hypotenuse.

b) The leg opposite the 60° angle is $\frac{1}{2} \times$ hypotenuse $\times \sqrt{3}$.

c) An altitude in an equilateral triangle forms a 30°-60°-90° triangle and is therefore equal to $\frac{1}{2}$ hypotenuse $\times \sqrt{3}$.

TIP

Remember the well-known Pythagorean triples, that is, sets of whole numbers such as 3-4-5 for which $a^2 + b^2 = c^2$. On the SAT®, you'll encounter right triangles with sides whose lengths correspond to these values. Other Pythagorean triples are: 5-12-13, 8-15-17, and 7-24-25. Also watch for their multiples, such as 6-8-10 or 15-20-25.

$x = 4$

$y = 5\sqrt{3}$

$z = 12$

$x = 4\sqrt{3}$

④ The 45°-45°-90° triangle (isosceles right triangle)

a) Each leg is $\frac{1}{2} \times$ hypotenuse $\times \sqrt{2}$.

b) The hypotenuse is leg $\times \sqrt{2}$.

c) The diagonal in a square forms a 45°-45°-90° triangle and is therefore equal to the length of one side $\times \sqrt{2}$.

$w = 6$

$x = 8\sqrt{2}$

$y = 5\sqrt{2}$

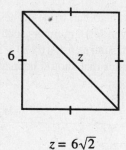

$z = 6\sqrt{2}$

5 One way to solve SAT® questions that involve 30°-60°-90° triangles and 45°-45°-90° triangles is to use right triangle trigonometric relationships. In the triangle below, side $\overline{AB}$ is called the side *adjacent* to $\angle A$, side $\overline{BC}$ is called the side *opposite* $\angle A$, and side $\overline{AC}$ is the *hypotenuse*. Relative to $\angle A$, the trigonometric ratios *sine, cosine,* and *tangent* are defined as shown.

$$\text{sine } a° = \sin a° = \frac{\text{opposite}}{\text{hypotenuse}}$$

$$\text{cosine } a° = \cos a° = \frac{\text{adjacent}}{\text{hypotenuse}}$$

$$\text{tangent } a° = \tan a° = \frac{\text{opposite}}{\text{adjacent}}$$

The table below shows the values of the sine, cosine, and tangent for 30°, 45°, and 60°.

Angle a	$\sin a°$	$\cos a°$	$\tan a°$
30°	$\frac{1}{2}$	$\frac{\sqrt{3}}{2}$	$\frac{\sqrt{3}}{3}$
45°	$\frac{\sqrt{2}}{2}$	$\frac{\sqrt{2}}{2}$	1
60°	$\frac{\sqrt{3}}{2}$	$\frac{1}{2}$	$\sqrt{3}$

By using the values of sine, cosine, and tangent above, problems involving 30°-60°-90° triangles and 45°-45°-90° triangles can also be solved. For example, consider the 30°-60°-90° triangle with hypotenuse of length 8. The computations that follow show how to determine the lengths of the other two sides.

$\text{sine } 60° = \dfrac{\text{opposite}}{\text{hypotenuse}} = \dfrac{y}{8}$. Also, since sine $60° = \dfrac{\sqrt{3}}{2}$, then $\dfrac{y}{8} = \dfrac{\sqrt{3}}{2}$. Cross-multiply to

get $2y = 8\sqrt{3}$, or $y = \dfrac{8\sqrt{3}}{2} = 4\sqrt{3}$. Note that this is the same answer that would be obtained

using the properties of 30°-60°-90° triangles.

$\cos 60° = \dfrac{\text{adjacent}}{\text{hypotenuse}} = \dfrac{x}{8}$. Also, since cos $60° = \dfrac{1}{2}$, then $\dfrac{x}{8} = \dfrac{1}{2}$. Cross-multiply to get

$2x = 8$, or $x = 4$. This, again, is the same answer that would be obtained using the properties of 30°-60°-90° triangles above.

6 Here are two sample problems:

Suppose a building has a handicap ramp that rises 2.5 ft. and forms a 3° angle with the ground. How far from the base of the building is the start of the ramp? Round your answer to the nearest tenth.

$$\tan 3° = \frac{2.5}{x}$$

$$x = \frac{2.5}{\tan 3°}$$

$$x \approx 47.7 \text{ feet}$$

Suppose a 26-ft. wire is attached to the top of a pole and staked in the ground at a 40-degree angle. Estimate the height of the pole.

$$\sin 40° = \frac{x}{26}$$

$$26 \sin 40° = x$$

$$16.7 \text{ ft} \approx x$$

To find how far the stake is from the ground you can use the Pythagorean Theorem:

$$a^2 + b^2 = c^2$$

$$16.7^2 + b^2 = 26^2$$

$$19.9 \text{ ft} \approx x$$

PARALLEL LINES

1 If two parallel lines are cut by a transversal, the alternate interior angles are congruent.

If $\overleftrightarrow{AB} \parallel \overleftrightarrow{CD}$, then
$\angle 1 \cong \angle 3$ and
$\angle 2 \cong \angle 4$.

2 If two parallel lines are cut by a transversal, the corresponding angles are congruent.

If $\overleftrightarrow{AB} \parallel \overleftrightarrow{CD}$, then
$\angle 1 \cong \angle 5$,
$\angle 2 \cong \angle 6$,
$\angle 3 \cong \angle 7$, and
$\angle 4 \cong \angle 8$.

3 If two parallel lines are cut by a transversal, interior angles on the same side of the transversal are supplementary.

If $\overleftrightarrow{AB} \parallel \overleftrightarrow{CD}$, then
$\angle 1$ is supplementary to $\angle 4$ and
$\angle 2$ is supplementary to $\angle 3$.

COORDINATE GEOMETRY

1 Lines and other geometric figures can be positioned on a plane by means of the *rectangular coordinate system*. The rectangular coordinate system consists of two number lines that are perpendicular and cross each other at their *origins* (0 on each of the number lines). The horizontal number line is called the *x*-axis, and the vertical number line is called the *y*-axis.

2 Any point on the plane can be designated by a pair of numbers. The first number is called the *x-coordinate* and indicates how far to move to the left (negative) or to the right (positive) on the *x*-axis, and the second number is called the *y-coordinate* and tells how far to move up (positive) or down (negative) on the *y*-axis. Generically, a point on the plane can be written as (x, y). When two points need to be expressed generically, they are typically written as (x_1, y_1) and (x_2, y_2).

The points (2,3), (−4,1), (−5,−2), (2,−4), and (5,0) are graphed on a coordinate system as shown below.

3 The *slope* of a straight line is a number that measures how steep the line is. Traditionally, the variable *m* is used to stand for the slope of a line. By convention, a line that increases from left to right has a positive slope, and a line that decreases from left to right has a negative slope. A horizontal line has a slope of 0 since it is "flat," and a vertical line has an undefined slope.

Positive Slope   Negative Slope   Zero Slope   Undefined Slope

4 If (x_1,y_1) and (x_2,y_2) are any two points on a line, the slope is given by the formula $m = \dfrac{(y_2 - y_1)}{(x_2 - x_1)}$.

Therefore, for example, if a line contains the points (5,7) and (3,4), the slope would be $m = \dfrac{7-4}{5-3} = \dfrac{3}{2}$. A slope of $\dfrac{3}{2}$ represents the fact that for every 2 units moved horizontally along the *x*-axis, the line rises vertically 3 units.

5 An equation of degree one that contains the variables *x* and/or *y* raised to the first power, but no higher, will always have a straight line as its graph. A very convenient way to write the equation of a line is in the *slope-intercept* form, $y = mx + b$. In this form, *m* represents the slope of the line, and *b* is the *y-intercept,* that is, the point where the graph crosses the *y-axis*.

As an example, consider the line represented by the equation $2x + 5y = 12$. Begin by writing this equation in slope-intercept form.

$2x + 5y = 12$ Subtract $2x$ from both sides

$\quad 5y = -2x + 12$ Divide both sides by 5

$\qquad y = -\dfrac{2}{5}x + \dfrac{12}{5}$

Therefore, the slope of the line is $-\dfrac{2}{5}$, and the *y*-intercept is $\dfrac{12}{5}$. The graph of this line is shown below.

The following are sample problems:

Suppose you were asked to write the equation of the line containing the point (2,1) and having slope 5. Begin by taking the slope-intercept form $y = mx + b$, and substituting $m = 5$, to obtain $y = 5x + b$. To determine the value of the y-intercept b, substitute the coordinates of the point (2,1) into the equation.

$y = 5x + b$ Substitute (2,1)

$1 = 5(2) + b$ Solve for b

$1 = 10 + b$

$b = -9$

Therefore, the equation of the line is $y = 5x - 9$.

6 Suppose you are asked to graph the function $f(x) = 2x + 5$. Begin by recognizing that the slope is 2 and the y-intercept is (0,5). To graph this function, first graph the point (0,5). Then move up 2 units and then to the right 1 unit. This location is (1,7). Starting at (0,5) again, go down 2 units and then to the left 1 unit. This location is (−1,3). Connect these points to form the graph of the function $f(x) = 2x + 5$.

7 You can write an equation of a line from a graph given any two points on the line. First, use the two points to find the slope. Then use the point–slope form of an equation of a line: $y - y_1 = m(x - x_1)$. As an example, consider the graph shown below.

You need to first find the slope using two points on the line.

The slope formula is $m = \dfrac{y_2 - y_1}{x_2 - x_1}$. Use the points (0,3) and (−1,1) to find the slope.

$$m = \frac{y_2 - y_1}{x_2 - x_1} = \frac{1-3}{-1-0} = \frac{-2}{-1} = 2$$

Use the point–slope form and either given point.

$$y - y_1 = m(x - x_1)$$
$$y - 1 = 2(x - (-1))$$
$$y - 1 = 2(x + 1)$$

To write this equation in slope–intercept form, solve for y.

$$y - 1 = 2(x + 1)$$
$$y = 2(x + 1) + 1$$
$$y = 2x + 2 + 1$$
$$y = 2x + 3$$

8 Here is an example of how to write an equation of a line from a verbal model and then graph the equation using the intercepts.

Suppose you purchase holiday gift cards for your family. You have $300 to spend on the cards, and you purchase cards for either $20 or $30. What are three combinations of cards that you can purchase?

To write an equation that represents this situation, first define your variables.

Let x − number of $20 gift cards purchased and y = number of $30 gift cards purchased.

Now write an equation to represent the situation.

$20x + 30y = 300$

Use the intercepts to draw the graph.

$$20x + 30y = 300 \qquad 20x + 30y = 300$$
$$20(0) + 30y = 300 \qquad 20x + 30(0) = 300$$
$$30y = 300 \qquad\qquad 20x = 300$$
$$y = 10 \qquad\qquad x = 15$$

You cannot purchase a fraction of a card, so only the integer combinations can be solutions.

You can purchase fifteen $20 cards and zero $30 cards, six $20 cards and six $30 cards, or zero $20 cards and ten $30 cards.

9 The standard form of the equation of a circle with center at (h,k), and radius r is $(x-h)^2 + (y-k)^2 = r^2$. For example, to graph $y^2 = -x^2 + 64$, first rewrite the equation in standard form: $x^2 + y^2 = 64$. Then identify the radius, $r = 8$, and the center, $(0,0)$. Now plot points that are on the circle: $(0,8)$, $(0,-8)$, $(-8,0)$, and $(8,0)$. Connect the points to draw the circle.

To graph $(x-1)^2 + (y+2)^2 = 4$, first identify the radius, $r = 2$, and the center, $(1,-2)$. Next, plot points that are on the circle. The easiest way to do this is to find points 2 units above, below, left, and right of the center: $(1,0)$, $(1,-4)$, $(-1,-2)$, and $(3,-2)$. Connect the points to draw the circle.

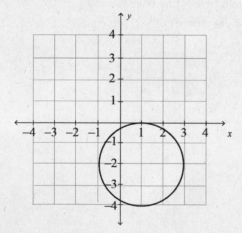

10 Parallel lines have the same slope. Therefore, one way to tell whether two lines are parallel or not is to write them in slope-intercept form and compare the slopes. To write the equation of the line that is parallel to the line $y = 3x + 7$ and contains the point (5,2), begin by noting that the equation of the line we are looking for must have a slope of 3, just like the line $y = 3x + 7$. Thus, it must be of the form $y = 3x + b$.

$$y = 3x + b \qquad \text{Substitute (5,2)}$$
$$2 = 3(5) + b \qquad \text{Solve for } b$$
$$2 = 15 + b$$
$$b = -13$$

Therefore, the equation of the line is $y = 3x - 13$.

11 The slopes of perpendicular lines are *negative reciprocals* of each other. That is, if a line has a slope of $\dfrac{a}{b}$, then the slope of the perpendicular line would be $-\dfrac{b}{a}$. Thus, the line perpendicular to the line with slope $\dfrac{2}{5}$ would have a slope of $-\dfrac{5}{2}$.

To write the equation of the line that is perpendicular to the line $y = \dfrac{1}{2}x - 7$ and contains the point

(4,−3), begin by noting that the equation of the line to be determined has a slope of −2. Thus, the equation must be of the form $y = -2x + b$.

$$y = -2x + b \qquad \text{Substitute } (4,-3)$$
$$-3 = -2(4) + b \qquad \text{Solve for } b$$
$$-3 = -8 + b$$
$$b = 5$$

Therefore, the equation of the line is $y = -2x + 5$.

EXERCISES: GEOMETRY

> **Directions:** Work out each problem. Circle the letter next to your choice.

1. If the angles of a triangle are in the ratio 2:3:7, what is the measure of the smallest angle?
   - (A) 15°
   - (B) 30°
   - (C) 45°
   - (D) 105°

2. What is the volume of a square pyramid with height 34.2 feet and base edges of 25 feet?
   - (A) 285
   - (B) 2,565
   - (C) 7,125
   - (D) 81,225

3. If the radius of a circle is decreased by 10%, by what percent is its area decreased?
   - (A) 10
   - (B) 19
   - (C) 21
   - (D) 81

4. A spotlight is mounted on the ceiling 5 feet from one wall of a room and 10 feet from the adjacent wall. How many feet is it from the intersection of the two walls?
   - (A) 15
   - (B) $5\sqrt{2}$
   - (C) $5\sqrt{5}$
   - (D) $10\sqrt{2}$

5. A sphere has a diameter of 3 cm, and a cone has a height of 10 cm and a radius of 1.5 cm. How much bigger is the volume of the cone than the volume of the sphere?
   - (A) 0.5π
   - (B) π
   - (C) 3π
   - (D) 4.5π

6. In parallelogram $PQRS$, angle P is 4 times angle Q. What is the measure in degrees of angle P?
   - (A) 36
   - (B) 72
   - (C) 125
   - (D) 144

7. If $\overline{PQ} \cong \overline{QS}$, $\overline{QR} \cong \overline{RS}$ and the measure of angle $PRS = 100°$, what is the measure, in degrees, of angle QPS?

   Note: Figure not drawn to scale
   - (A) 10
   - (B) 15
   - (C) 20
   - (D) 25

8. A circle has a radius of 6 cm. What is the area of a sector bounded by a 60° minor arc?
   - (A) π
   - (B) 2π
   - (C) 6π
   - (D) 20π

9. A rectangular box with a square base contains 6 cubic feet. If the height of the box is 18 inches, how many feet are there in each side of the base?
   - (A) 1
   - (B) 2
   - (C) $\sqrt{3}$
   - (D) $\dfrac{\sqrt{3}}{3}$

10. The surface area of a cube is 150 square feet. How many cubic feet are there in the volume of the cube?

    (A) 30

    (B) 50

    (C) 100

    (D) 125

11. Peter lives 12 miles west of his school and Bill lives north of the school. Peter finds that the direct distance from his house to Bill's is 6 miles shorter than the distance by way of his school. How many miles north of the school does Bill live?

    (A) 6

    (B) 9

    (C) 10

    (D) $6\sqrt{2}$

12. A square is inscribed in a circle of area 18π. Find a side of the square.

    (A) 3

    (B) 6

    (C) $3\sqrt{2}$

    (D) $6\sqrt{2}$

13. A carpet is y yards long and f feet wide. How many dollars will it cost if the carpet sells for x cents per square foot?

    (A) $3xyf$

    (B) $\dfrac{xyf}{3}$

    (C) $\dfrac{0.03yf}{x}$

    (D) $0.03xyf$

14. If a triangle of base 6 has the same area as a circle of radius 6, what is the altitude of the triangle?

    (A) 6π

    (B) 8π

    (C) 10π

    (D) 12π

15. The vertex angle of an isosceles triangle is p degrees. How many degrees are there in one of the base angles?

    (A) $180 - p$

    (B) $90 - \dfrac{p}{2}$

    (C) $180 - 2p$

    (D) $180 - \dfrac{p}{2}$

16. In a circle with center O, the measure of arc $RS = 132$ degrees. How many degrees are there in angle RSO?

    (A) 66°

    (B) 48°

    (C) 24°

    (D) 22°

17. The ice compartment of a refrigerator is 8 inches long, 4 inches wide, and 5 inches high. How many ice cubes will it hold if each cube is 2 inches on an edge?

    (A) 8

    (B) 10

    (C) 12

    (D) 16

18. In the figure, PSQ is a straight line and $\overline{RS}$ is perpendicular to $\overline{ST}$. If the measure of angle $RSQ = 48°$, how many degrees are there in angle PST?

    (A) 48°

    (B) 90°

    (C) 132°

    (D) 138°

19. A cylindrical pail has a radius of 7 inches and a height of 9 inches. If there are 231 cubic inches to a gallon, approximately how many gallons will this pail hold?

(A) $\dfrac{12}{7}$

(B) 6

(C) 7.5

(D) 8.2

20. In triangle PQR, $\overline{QS}$ and $\overline{SR}$ are angle bisectors and the measure of angle $P = 80°$. How many degrees are there in angle QSR?

(A) 115°

(B) 120°

(C) 125°

(D) 130°

21. In the figure below, the circle has center O. If $b = 40$, what is the value of a?

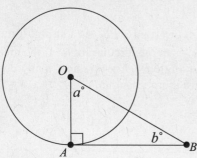

(A) 30

(B) 40

(C) 45

(D) 50

22. One end of a wire is attached to the top of a 70-foot-high pole, and the other end is attached to a stake in the ground. If the wire makes a 30° angle with the ground, how long is the wire?

(A) 70 feet

(B) $70\sqrt{3}$ feet

(C) 140 feet

(D) $140\sqrt{2}$ feet

23. What is the equation of the line containing the points (4,6) and (3,8)?

(A) $y = -2x + 14$

(B) $y = 2x + 14$

(C) $y = -2x + 2$

(D) $y = 2x - 2$

24. Which of the following represents the equation of a line with a slope of -7 and a y-intercept of 12?

(A) $y = 7x - 12$

(B) $y = -7x + 12$

(C) $y = 7x + 12$

(D) $y = 12x - 7$

25. Which of the following represents the equation of a line parallel to the line $y = 7x - 6$ and containing the point (1,7)?

(A) $y = 7x$

(B) $y = 7x - 7$

(C) $y = -7x + 7$

(D) $y = -7x$

ANSWER KEY AND EXPLANATIONS

1. B	6. D	11. B	16. C	21. D
2. C	7. C	12. B	17. D	22. C
3. B	8. C	13. D	18. D	23. A
4. C	9. B	14. D	19. B	24. B
5. C	10. D	15. B	20. D	25. A

1. **The correct answer is (B).** Represent the angles as $2x$, $3x$, and $7x$.
$$2x + 3x + 7x = 180°$$
$$12x = 180°$$
$$x = 15°$$
The angles are 30°, 45°, and 105°. The smallest angle is 30°.

2. **The correct answer is (C).**
$$V = \frac{1}{3}s^2h$$
$$V = \frac{1}{3}(25)^2(34.2)$$
$$V = 7125$$

3. **The correct answer is (B).** If the radii of the two circles have a ratio of 10:9, the areas have a ratio of 100:81. Therefore, the decrease is 19 out of 100, or 19%.

4. **The correct answer is (C).**
$$5^2 + 10^2 = x^2$$
$$25 + 100 = x^2$$
$$x^2 = 125$$
$$x = \sqrt{125} = \sqrt{25}\sqrt{5} = 5\sqrt{5}$$

5. **The correct answer is (C).** The volume of the sphere is calculated using the formula
$$V = \frac{4}{3}\pi r^3 : V = \frac{4}{3}\pi(1.5)^3 = 4.5\pi.$$
The volume of the cone is calculated using formula $V = \frac{1}{3}\pi r^2 h$:
$$V = \frac{1}{3}\pi(1.5)^2(10) = 7.5\pi.$$
Since $7.5\pi - 4.5\pi = 3\pi$, the volume of the cone is 3π bigger than the volume of the sphere.

6. **The correct answer is (D).** The consecutive angles of a parallelogram are supplementary, so $x + 4x = 180°$
$$5x = 180°$$
$$x = 36°$$
Angle P is 4(36), or 144°.

7. **The correct answer is (C).**

Since $\overline{QR} \cong \overline{RS}$, $\angle RQS \cong \angle RSQ$. There are 80° left in the triangle, so each of these angles is 40°. $\angle SQP$ is supplementary to $\angle SQR$, making it 140°. Since $\overline{QP} \cong \overline{QS}$, $\angle QPS \cong \angle QSP$. There are 40° left in the triangle, so each of these angles is 20°.

8. **The correct answer is (C).** The area of a sector of a circle is the product of the ratio $\dfrac{\text{measure of the arc}}{360°}$ and the area of the circle. Since the radius of a circle is 6 cm and the measure of the arc is 60°, the area of the sector is $\dfrac{60°}{360°} \bullet \pi(6)^2 = 6\pi$.

9. **The correct answer is (B).** Change 18 inches to 1.5 feet. Letting each side of the base be x, the volume is $1.5x^2$.

$$1.5x^2 = 6$$
$$15x^2 = 60$$
$$x^2 = 4$$
$$x = 2$$

10. **The correct answer is (D).** The surface area of a cube is made up of 6 equal squares. If each edge of the cube is x, then

$$6x^2 = 150$$
$$x^2 = 25$$
$$x = 5$$

$$\text{Volume} = (\text{edge})^3 = 5^3 = 125$$

11. **The correct answer is (B).**

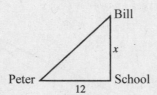

The direct distance from Peter's house to Bill's can be represented by means of the Pythagorean theorem as $\sqrt{144 + x^2}$.

Then:

$$\sqrt{144 + x^2} = (12 + x) - 6$$
$$\sqrt{144 + x^2} = x + 6$$

Square both sides.

$$144 + x^2 = x^2 + 12x + 36$$
$$144 = 12x + 36$$
$$108 = 12x$$
$$9 = x$$

12. **The correct answer is (B).**

The diagonal of the square will be a diameter of the circle.

$$\pi r^2 = 18\pi$$
$$r^2 = 18$$
$$r = \sqrt{18} = \sqrt{9}\,\sqrt{2} = 3\sqrt{2}$$

The diameter is $6\sqrt{2}$ and, since the triangles are 45°-45°-90°, a side of the square is 6.

13. **The correct answer is (D).** To find the area in square feet, change y yards to $3y$ feet. The area is then $(3y)(f)$, or $3yf$ square feet. If each square foot costs x cents, change this to dollars by dividing x by 100. Thus, each square foot costs $\dfrac{x}{100}$ dollars. The cost of $3yf$ square feet will then be $\dfrac{3xyf}{100}$. Since $\dfrac{3}{100} = 0.03$, the correct answer is choice (D).

14. **The correct answer is (D).** The area of the circle is $(6)^2\pi$, or 36π. In the triangle

$$\frac{1}{2}(6)(h) = 36\pi$$
$$3h = 36\pi$$
$$h = 12\pi$$

15. **The correct answer is (B).** There are $(180 - p)$ degrees left, which must be divided between 2 congruent angles. Each angle will contain $\dfrac{(180 - p)}{2}$, or $90 - \dfrac{p}{2}$ degrees.

16. The correct answer is (C).

By extending *SO* until it hits the circle at *P*, arc *PRS* is a semicircle. Therefore, the measure of arc *PR* = 48°, and the measure of the inscribed angle *RSO* = 24°.

17. The correct answer is (D).

The compartment will hold 2 layers, each of which contains 2 rows of 4 cubes each. This leaves a height of 1 inch on top empty. Therefore, the compartment can hold 16 cubes.

18. The correct answer is (D).

Since ∠*RST* is a right angle, 42° are left for ∠*QST*. Since ∠*PSQ* is a straight angle of 180°, ∠*PST* contains 138°.

19. The correct answer is (B). The volume of the pail is found using the formula $V = \pi r^2 h$. Since the answers are not in terms of π, it is best to use $\dfrac{22}{7}$ as a value for π because the 7 will divide out r^2:

$$V = \frac{22}{\cancel{7}} \cdot \overset{7}{\cancel{49}} \cdot 9$$

Rather than multiply this out, which will take unnecessary time, divide by 231 and cancel wherever possible.

$$\frac{\overset{2}{\cancel{22}} \cdot \cancel{7} \cdot \overset{3}{\cancel{9}}}{\underset{\underset{\cancel{3}}{33}}{\cancel{231}}} = 6$$

20. The correct answer is (D). If m∠ *P* = 80°, there are 100° left between ∠*PQR* and ∠*PRQ*. If they are both bisected, there will be 50° between ∠*SQR* and ∠*SRQ*, leaving 130° in triangle *SRQ* for ∠*QSR*.

21. The correct answer is (D). The line segment $\overline{AB}$ is tangent to the circle, and therefore is perpendicular to radius $\overline{OA}$.

This means that ∠*OAB* is a right angle. Therefore, one of the angles in the triangle measures 90°, and another angle measures 40°. Since the sum of the three angles in a triangle is 180°, the measure of the missing angle must be 50°.

22. The correct answer is (C). Begin by making a diagram of the situation described in the problem.

There are two ways to solve this problem. The first is to notice that the triangle is a 30°-60°-90° triangle, and in such a triangle, the length of the side opposite the 30° angle is half of the length of the hypotenuse. Thus, the length of the wire, which is represented by the hypotenuse in the triangle, would be 2 × 70 feet = 140 feet.

The problem can also be solved by using trigonometry. Let w stand for the length of the wire, then write sine $30° = \dfrac{70}{w}$. Since

sine $30° = \dfrac{1}{2}$, the equation is $\dfrac{70}{w} = \dfrac{1}{2}$. Cross-

multiply. $w = 140$ feet.

23. The correct answer is (A). The formula

for the slope of a line is $\dfrac{(y_2 - y_1)}{(x_2 - x_1)}$ where

(x_1, y_1) and (x_2, y_2) are any two points on the line. In this problem, the two points are (4,6) and

(3,8), so $m = \dfrac{(y_2 - y_1)}{(x_2 - x_1)} = \dfrac{8 - 6}{3 - 4} = \dfrac{2}{-1} = -2.$

Use either point and the slope to complete the equation.

$$y = mx + b$$
$$6 = (-2)(4) + b$$
$$6 = -8 + b$$
$$14 = b$$

So the equation of the line is $y = -2x + 14$.

24. The correct answer is (B). In the formula $y = mx + b$, m represents the slope of the line, and b represents the y-intercept. Thus, the equation $y = -7x + 12$ represents the equation of a line with a slope of -7 and y-intercept of 12.

25. The correct answer is (A). Since parallel lines have the same slope, the slope of the line to be determined is the same as the slope of $y = 7x - 6$, which is 7. Therefore, the equation of the unknown line can be written as $y = 7x + b$, where b represents the y-intercept. In order to find the value of b, substitute the point (1,7) into $y = 7x + b$.

$y = 7x + b$ 　　　　　Substitute (1,7).

$$7 = 7(1) + b$$
$$7 = 7 + b$$
$$b = 0$$

Therefore, the equation of the line is $y = 7x$.

Note that a faster way to solve this problem is the trial-and-error method. Of the four answer possibilities, choices (A) and (B) represent lines with slopes of 7, but only choice (A) contains the point (1,7).

SUMMING IT UP

- Lines and line segments are the basic building blocks for most geometry problems.

- If a geometry problem provides a figure, mine it for clues. If a geometry problem doesn't provide a figure, sketch one.

- If a geometry problem deals with a quadrilateral or circle, look to form triangles by drawing lines through the figure.

- Geometry diagrams on the SAT® are not always drawn to scale. If the diagram is not drawn to scale, you may want to redraw it.

Functions and Intermediate Algebra Review

chapter 12

OVERVIEW

- Functions
- Integer and rational exponents
- Solving complex equations
- Linear, quadratic, and exponential functions
- Summing it up

FUNCTIONS

Definitions and Notation

Let D and R be any two sets of numbers. A *function* is a rule that assigns to each element of D one and only one element of R. The set D is called the *domain* of the function, and the set R is called the *range*. A function can be specified by listing all of the elements in the first set next to the corresponding elements in the second set, or by giving a rule or a formula by which elements from the first set can be associated with elements from the second set.

As an example, let the set $D = \{1, 2, 3, 4\}$ and set $R = \{5, 6, 7, 8\}$. The diagram below indicates a particular function, f, by showing how each element of D is associated with an element of R.

This diagram shows that the domain value of 1 is associated with the range value of 5. Similarly, 2 is associated with 6, 3 is associated with 7, and 4 is associated with 8. The function f can also be described in words by saying that f is the function that assigns to each domain value x the range value $x + 4$.

Typically, the letter x is used to represent the elements of the domain and the letter y is used to represent the elements of the range. This enables us to write the equation $y = x + 4$ to express the rule of association for the function above.

Note that as soon as a domain value x is selected, a range value y is determined by this rule. For this reason, x is referred to as the *independent variable*, and y is called the *dependent variable*.

Often, the rule of association for a function is written in *function notation*. In this notation, the symbol $f(x)$, which is read "f of x," is used instead of y to represent the range value. Therefore, the rule for our function can be written $f(x) = x + 4$. If you were asked to determine which range value was associated with the domain value of, say, 3, you would compute $f(x) = f(3) = 3 + 4 = 7$. Note that, in this notation, the letter f is typically used to stand for "function," although any other letter could also be used. Therefore, this rule could also be written as $g(x) = x + 4$.

Using function notation, write the rule for a function that associates, to each number in the domain, a range value that is 7 less than 5 times the domain value.

$f(x) = 5x - 7$

Use the function from the problem above to determine the range value that is associated with a domain value of −12.

$f(-12) = 5(-12) - 7 = -60 - 7 = -67$

If $f(x) = 8x + 9$, determine the value of $f(5), f(q), f(p^2)$, and $f(r + 3)$.

$f(5) = 8(5) + 9 = 40 + 9 = 49$

In the same way, to determine the value of $f(q)$, simply substitute q for the value of x in the rule for $f(x)$. Therefore, $f(q) = 8q + 9$.

Similarly, $f(p^2) = 8(p^2) + 9 = 8p^2 + 9$.

Similarly, $f(r + 3) = 8(r + 3) + 9 = 8r + 24 + 9 = 8r + 33$.

Families of Functions

A *family* of functions is a group of functions with similar characteristics. The *parent function* is the most basic function in a family.

A linear function is a function whose graph is a straight line. $f(x) = x$ is the parent function for all linear functions. A quadratic function is a function whose graph is a parabola. The graph shown, $f(x) = x^2$, is the parent function for all quadratic functions.

Compare $f(x) = 2x^2$ to $f(x) = x^2$.

The graphs $f(x) = 2x^2$ and $f(x) = x^2$ both open up, have (0,0) as its vertex, and have the same axis of symmetry $x = 0$. The graph $f(x) = 2x^2$ is narrower than the graph of $f(x) = x^2$.

How does the graph $f(x) = x^2 + 2$ compare to the parent function $f(x) = x^2$?

The graph $f(x) = x^2 + 2$ is two units higher than $f(x) = x^2$. The function $f(x) = x^2$ has been shifted up 2 units. The shifting, or *translating*, of a function is called a *transformation*. To move a function up, add a value b to the function: $f(x) = x^2 + b$. To move a function down, subtract a value b from the function: $f(x) = x^2 - b$.

The function $f(x) = (x + 2)^2$ looks like the following:

Its graph has been shifted to the left 2 units. To shift a function to the left, add a value b to inside the function: $f(x) = (x + b)^2$. To shift a function to the right, subtract a value b to inside the function: $f(x) = (x - b)^2$.

The function $-f(x)$ is $f(x)$ flipped upside down, while $f(-x)$ is the mirror of $f(x)$:

Describe how the function $f(x) = -2x^2 + 3$ compares with the graph $f(x) = x^2$.

Both graphs have the same axis of symmetry but the graph $f(x) = -2x^2 + 3$ opens downward and is narrower than the graph of $f(x) = x^2$. The vertex of $f(x) = -2x^2 + 3$ is 3 units higher than the vertex of $f(x) = x^2$.

Perform Operations on Functions and Compositions

You can add, subtract, multiply, and divide any two functions.

Let $f(x) = 4x^2$ and $g(x) - x^2 + 9x + 6$.

$f(x) + g(x) = 4x^2 + (x^2 + 9x + 6) = 5x^2 + 9x + 6$

$f(x) - g(x) = 4x^2 - (x^2 + 9x + 6) = 3x^2 - 9x - 6$

$f(x) \cdot g(x) = 4x^2 (x^2 + 9x + 6) = 4x^4 + 36x^3 + 24x^2$

$$\frac{f(x)}{g(x)} = \frac{4x^2}{x^2 + 9x + 6}$$

The composition of functions involves applying two functions in succession. The composition of a function $g(x)$ with a function $f(x)$ is written as $g(f(x))$, read as "g of f of x".

Let $f(x) = 6x^3 + 2$ and $g(x) = 2x^2 - 8$.

Find $f(g(3))$ and $g(f(3))$.

To evaluate $f(g(3))$, first find $g(3)$.

$g(3) = 2(3)^2 - 8 = 10$

Then $f(g(3)) = f(10) = 6(10)^3 + 2 = 6002$.

To evaluate $g(f(3))$, first find $f(3)$.

$f(3) = 6(3)^3 + 2 = 164$

Then $g(f(164)) = g(164) = 2(164)^2 - 8 = 53,784$.

Generally, $f(g(x)) \neq g(f(x))$.

EXERCISES: FUNCTIONS

Directions: Work out each problem. Circle the letter of your choice.

1. What is the effect on the graph of the function $f(x) = 2x^2 + 5$ when it is changed to $f(x) = 2x^2 - 3$.

   (A) The graph gets narrower.

   (B) The graph opens down.

   (C) The graph gets wider.

   (D) The graph shifts down the y-axis.

2. Which function opens down?

   (A) $y = -7x^2 - 3$

   (B) $y = 0.5x^2 + 2$

   (C) $y = 10x^2 - 1$

   (D) $y = 7x^2 + 9$

3. If $h(x) = 3x^2 + 5$, and $j(x) = \dfrac{3}{(x-4)^2}$, what is the value of $h(5) - j(5)$?

   (A) 0

   (B) 77

   (C) 83

   (D) 87

4. The profit from selling x number of sweatshirts can be described by the function $p(x) = 22x - 230$. What is the profit if 200 sweatshirts are sold?

   (A) $4170

   (B) $4280

   (C) $4400

   (D) $4630

5. The number of blue blankets in stock can be modeled by the equation $f(x) = 2x^2 - 8x + 20$ and the number of red blankets in stock can be modeled by the equation $h(x) = 3x^2 + 4x + 30$. Which function models the total number of blankets in stock?

   (A) $-x^2 - 4x + 50$

   (B) $5x^2 - 12x + 50$

   (C) $5x^2 - 4x + 50$

   (D) $-x^2 + 4x + 20$

6. A company sells designer keychains. Its monthly revenue is modeled by $R(x) = 27x$ and its costs are modeled by $C(x) = 7x + 1200$, where x is the number of keychains sold. Find $R(x) - C(x)$.

   (A) $-34x + 1200$

   (B) $20x + 1200$

   (C) $20x - 1200$

   (D) $34x - 1200$

7. You have a $25 gift certificate to a clothing store. The store is having a 30%-off sale. You decide to purchase an outfit that costs $100 before the sale. What is the final cost of the outfit if the gift certificate is applied before the 30% discount?

   (A) $22.50

   (B) $30

   (C) $45

   (D) $52.50

8. You earn $17.50 per hour at your job. You are given a raise of 2% after 5 months. In addition, you receive $1 per hour for being a model employee. Find your new hourly wage if the $1 raise is applied before the 2% raise.

   (A) $18.13

   (B) $18.15

   (C) $18.85

   (D) $18.87

ANSWER KEY AND EXPLANATIONS

1. D	3. B	5. C	7. D
2. A	4. A	6. C	8. D

1. **The correct answer is (D).** The vertex of the graph changes from $(0, 5)$ to $(0, -3)$. The original graph is translated down.

2. **The correct answer is (A).** The graph opens down since the coefficient in front of the x^2 term is less than 0.

3. **The correct answer is (B).**

$$h(5) - j(5) = 3\left(5^2\right) + 5 - \frac{3}{\left(5-4\right)^2} =$$

$$3(25) + 5 - 3 = 77$$

4. **The correct answer is (A).**

$p(200) = 22(200) - 230 = 4170$. The profit is $4170.

5. **The correct answer is (C).**

$$f\left(x\right) + h\left(x\right) = 2x^2 - 8x + 20 + 3x^2 + 4x + 30$$
$$= 5x^2 - 4x + 50$$

6. **The correct answer is (C).**

$$R\left(x\right) - C\left(x\right) = 27x - \left(7x + 1200\right)$$
$$= 27x - 7x - 1200$$
$$= 20x - 1200$$

7. **The correct answer is (D).** Let x be the regular price. The function for the gift certificate is $f(x) = x - 25$. The function for the 30% discount is $g(x) = x - 0.30x - 0.7x$. The composition $g(f(x))$ represents the sale price when the $25 gift certificate is applied before the 30% discount.

$$g(f(x)) = g(x - 25)$$
$$= 0.7(x - 25)$$
$$= 0.7(100 - 25)$$
$$= 0.7(75)$$
$$= 52.50$$

So, you pay $52.50.

8. **The correct answer is (D).** Let x be your hourly wage. The function for the 2% raise is $f(x) = x + 0.2x = 1.02x$. The function for the $1 raise is $g(x) = x + 1$. The composition $f(g(x))$ represents the hourly wage when the $1 raise is applied before the 2% raise.

$$f(g(x)) = f(x + 1)$$
$$= 1.02(x + 1)$$
$$= 1.02(17.5 + 1)$$
$$= 1.02(18.50)$$
$$= 18.87$$

So your new hourly wage is $18.87.

INTEGER AND RATIONAL EXPONENTS

Chapter 10: Basic Algebra Review contains the definitions and the rules for positive integer exponents. The following section extends these definitions to integer and rational exponents.

Integer Exponents

Negative exponents are defined in the following way:

For any positive integer n, $x^{-n} = \dfrac{1}{x^n}$. Therefore, for example, $4^{-2} = \dfrac{1}{4^2} = \dfrac{1}{16}$.

Similarly, $\left(\dfrac{2}{3}\right)^{-4} = \left(\dfrac{3}{2}\right)^{4} = \dfrac{3^4}{2^4} = \dfrac{81}{16}$.

All of the properties of exponents discussed in Chapter 11 apply to expressions with negative exponents as well. Thus, the expression $x^{-7} \times x^4$ is equal to $x^{-3} = \dfrac{1}{x^3}$, and

$$\dfrac{y^{-5}}{y^{-11}} = y^{-5-(-11)} = y^{-5+11} = y^{6}.$$

Determine the value of the following expressions:

a. $8^{-2} \cdot 8^{4}$

b. $x^{5} \cdot x^{-5}$

c. $\dfrac{y^4}{y^{-9}}$

d. $\dfrac{x^{-2}y^9}{x^7 y^3}$

a. $8^{-2} \cdot 8^{4} = 8^{2} = 64$

b. $x^{5} \cdot x^{-5} = x^{0} = 1$

c. $\dfrac{y^4}{y^{-9}} = y^4 y^9 = y^{13}$

d. $\dfrac{x^{-2}y^9}{x^7 y^3} = \dfrac{y^{9-3}}{x^{7-(-2)}} = \dfrac{y^6}{x^9}$

If $f(x) = 5^{-x}$, what is the value of $f(-2)$?

If $f(x) = 5^{-x}$, what is the value of $f(2)$?

$f(-2) = 5^{-(-2)} = 5^2 = 25$

$f(2) = 5^{-2} = \dfrac{1}{5^2} = \dfrac{1}{25}$

Rational Exponents

The definition of exponents can also be extended to include rational numbers:

For a rational number, x to the power of $\frac{1}{n}$ is defined as the nth root of x. In other words, $x^{\frac{1}{n}}$ is equal to $\sqrt[n]{x}$.

Therefore, for example, $\sqrt{5}$ can be written as $5^{\frac{1}{2}}$.

Similarly, $8^{\frac{1}{3}}$ represents $\sqrt[3]{8}$ and is thus equal to 2.

Next, $x^{\frac{m}{n}}$ is defined to mean $\left(x^{\frac{1}{n}} \right)^m$, for $x > 0$, and $n > 0$. Therefore, when you are given a number

with a rational exponent, the numerator represents the power to which the number is to be raised, and

the denominator represents the root to be taken. The expression $16^{\frac{5}{4}}$ tells you to take the fourth root of

16 and then raise the result to the fifth power. This expression can be evaluated in the following way:

$$16^{\frac{5}{4}} = \left(\sqrt[4]{16} \right)^5 = (2)^5 = 32$$

In summary, all of the properties of exponents apply to expressions with rational exponents.

Determine the value of the following expressions:

a. $27^{\frac{1}{3}}$

b. $64^{-\frac{2}{3}}$

c. $2x^{\frac{5}{6}} \cdot 3x^{-\frac{1}{3}}$

a. $27^{\frac{1}{3}} = \sqrt[3]{27} = 3$

b. $64^{-\frac{2}{3}} = \left(\frac{1}{64} \right)^{\frac{2}{3}} = \left(\sqrt[3]{\frac{1}{64}} \right)^2 = \left(\frac{1}{4} \right)^2 = \frac{1}{16}$

c. $2 \cdot 3x^{\frac{5}{6}} x^{-\frac{1}{3}} = 6x^{\frac{5}{6} - \frac{1}{3}} = 6x^{\frac{1}{2}}$

Simplify the following expressions:

a. $\left(25a^6\right)^{\frac{1}{2}}$

b. $\dfrac{b^{\frac{1}{3}}}{b^{-\frac{2}{3}}}$

c. $\left(c^{-\frac{1}{8}}d^{\frac{3}{4}}\right)^{16}$

d. $\sqrt{4x^3} \bullet \sqrt{8x^5}$

a. $\left(25a^6\right)^{\frac{1}{2}} = 25^{\frac{1}{2}}\left(a^6\right)^{\frac{1}{2}} = \sqrt{25}a^3 = 5a^3$

b. $\dfrac{b^{\frac{1}{3}}}{b^{-\frac{2}{3}}} = b^{\frac{1}{3}}b^{\frac{2}{3}} = b^{\frac{1}{3}+\frac{2}{3}} = b^1 = b$

c. $\left(c^{-\frac{1}{8}}d^{\frac{3}{4}}\right)^{16} = \left(c^{-\frac{1}{8}}\right)^{16}\left(d^{\frac{3}{4}}\right)^{16} = c^{-2}d^{12} = \dfrac{d^{12}}{c^2}$

d. $\sqrt{4x^3}\Sigma\sqrt{8x^5} = 4^{\frac{1}{2}}x^{\frac{3}{2}}\Sigma 8^{\frac{1}{2}}x^{\frac{5}{2}}$

$\qquad\qquad = 4^{\frac{1}{2}}\Sigma 8^{\frac{1}{2}}x^{\frac{3}{2}}x^{\frac{5}{2}}$

$\qquad\qquad = 2(2\sqrt{2})x^{\frac{3}{2}+\frac{5}{2}}$

$\qquad\qquad = 4\sqrt{2}x^4$

EXERCISES: INTEGER AND RATIONAL EXPONENTS

Directions: Work out each problem. Circle the letter of your choice.

1. Simplify the expression: $\sqrt{8x} \cdot \sqrt{4x^3}$

   (A) $32x^{\frac{3}{2}}$

   (B) $16\sqrt{2x^4}$

   (C) $4x^4$

   (D) $4\sqrt{2}x^2$

2. Simplify the expression: $\sqrt{25x^4y^6} \cdot \sqrt{3x^3y^5}$

   (A) $3x^{\frac{7}{2}}y^{\frac{11}{2}}$

   (B) $5\sqrt{3}x^{\frac{7}{2}}y^{\frac{11}{2}}$

   (C) $15x^{12}y^{11}$

   (D) $75x^7y^{11}$

3. Which of the following is equal to $(xy^{-3})^2$?

   (A) $\dfrac{x}{y}$

   (B) $\dfrac{x}{y^6}$

   (C) $\dfrac{x^2}{y^6}$

   (D) $\dfrac{x^2}{y}$

4. Simplify the expression: $\dfrac{a^5b^{-2}c^{-3}}{a^{-2}b^4c^{-2}} =$

   (A) $\dfrac{a^7}{b^6c}$

   (B) $\dfrac{a^7c}{b^2}$

   (C) $\dfrac{a^3}{b^2c}$

   (D) $\dfrac{a^3c^5}{b^2}$

5. Simplify the expression: $(a^{-2}b^7c^{-3})^{-4} =$

   (A) $\dfrac{b^3}{a^6c}$

   (B) $\dfrac{b^3}{a^6c^7}$

   (C) $\dfrac{a^8c^{12}}{b^{28}}$

   (D) $\dfrac{b^{28}}{a^8c^{12}}$

6. Simplify the expression: $(49x^4y^8z^{-6})^{\frac{1}{2}}$

   (A) $49x^2y^4z^6$

   (B) $7x^3y^4z^3$

   (C) $\dfrac{y^4}{7x^2z^3}$

   (D) $\dfrac{7x^2y^4}{z^3}$

7. Simplify the expression: $\sqrt[4]{256x^2} \cdot \sqrt[4]{16x^4}$

   (A) $8x\sqrt{x}$

   (B) $16\sqrt[4]{x^6}$

   (C) $8x^4\sqrt{x^4}$

   (D) $32x^2\sqrt{x}$

8. Simplify the expression: $\sqrt[3]{-125x^6} \sum \sqrt[3]{64y^3}$

   (A) $-40x^6y^9$

   (B) $-20x^2y$

   (C) $-9x^6\sqrt{y}$

   (D) $20x^3y^3\sqrt{x}$

ANSWER KEY AND EXPLANATIONS

1. D	3. C	5. C	7. A
2. B	4. A	6. D	8. B

1. **The correct answer is (D).**

$$\sqrt{8x}\sum\sqrt{4x^3}=(8x)^{\frac{1}{2}}(4x^3)^{\frac{1}{2}}$$
$$=(2\sqrt{2}x^{\frac{1}{2}})(2x^{\frac{3}{2}})$$
$$=4\sqrt{2}x^2$$

2. **The correct answer is (B).**

$$(25x^4y^6)^{\frac{1}{2}}(3x^3y^5)^{\frac{1}{2}}=5x^2y^3\sum3^{\frac{1}{2}}x^{\frac{3}{2}}y^{\frac{5}{2}}$$
$$=5\sum3^{\frac{1}{2}}x^{2+\frac{3}{2}}y^{3+\frac{5}{2}}$$
$$=5\sqrt{3}x^{\frac{7}{2}}y^{\frac{11}{2}}$$

3. **The correct answer is (C).**

$$\left(xy^{-3}\right)^2=x^2y^{-6}=\frac{x^2}{y^6}$$

4. **The correct answer is (A).**

$$\frac{a^5b^{-2}c^{-3}}{a^{-2}b^4c^{-2}}=a^{5-(-2)}b^{-2-4}c^{-3-(-2)}=a^7b^{-6}c^{-1}=\frac{a^7}{b^6c}$$

5. **The correct answer is (C).**

$$\left(a^{-2}b^7c^{-3}\right)^{-4}=a^8b^{-28}c^{12}=\frac{a^8c^{12}}{b^{28}}$$

6. **The correct answer is (D).**

$$(49x^4y^8z^{-6})^{\frac{1}{2}}=49^{\frac{1}{2}}x^{\frac{4}{2}}y^{\frac{8}{2}}z^{\frac{-6}{2}}$$
$$=7x^2y^4z^{-3}$$
$$=\frac{7x^2y^4}{z^3}$$

7. **The correct answer is (A).**

$$\sqrt[4]{256x^2}\bullet\sqrt[4]{16x^4}=256^{\frac{1}{4}}x^{\frac{1}{2}}\bullet16^{\frac{1}{4}}x^1$$
$$=4x^{\frac{1}{2}}\bullet2x$$
$$=8x\sqrt{x}$$

8. **The correct answer is (B).**

$$\sqrt[3]{-125x^6}\sum\sqrt[3]{64y^3}=-5x^{\frac{6}{3}}(4y^{\frac{3}{3}})$$
$$=-20x^2y$$

SOLVING COMPLEX EQUATIONS

Chapter 10: Basic Algebra Review describes how to solve linear and quadratic equations. The following section discusses how to solve some of the more complex equations and inequalities that appear on the SAT®.

Equations Involving Rational Expressions

A *rational expression* is a fraction that contains variables in the numerator and/or the denominator. The quickest way to solve equations containing rational expressions is to determine the least common denominator (LCD) of all of the fractions in the equation and then to eliminate the fractions by multiplying each term in the equation by this LCD. The four steps in solving such an equation are:

1 Find the LCD of all of the rational expressions in the equation.

2 Multiply *every* term on both sides of the equation by this LCD.

3 Solve the resulting equation using the methods previously explained.

4 Check the solution to make certain that it actually solves the equation.

Note that step 4, checking the solution, is crucial because sometimes the process produces a solution that does not actually solve the equation. Such solutions are called *extraneous* solutions and need to be eliminated.

Solve for x: $\dfrac{7x}{5} + \dfrac{3}{8} = 10$

The LCD of the two fractions in the equation is 40, so every term must be multiplied by 40.

$$40\left(\frac{7x}{5}\right) + 40\left(\frac{3}{8}\right) = 40(10)$$ Perform the multiplications.

$$8(7x) + 5(3) = 400$$

$$56x + 15 = 400$$ Subtract 15 from both sides.

$$56x = 385$$ Divide both sides by 56.

$$x = \frac{385}{56} = \frac{55}{8} = 6\frac{7}{8}$$

Check that the answer is correct by substituting $\dfrac{55}{8}$ into the original equation.

Solve for x: $\dfrac{5}{x-4} - \dfrac{3}{x+4} = \dfrac{36}{x^2 - 16}$

Begin by finding the LCD of the three fractions. Note that since $x^2 - 16 = (x - 4)(x + 4)$, the LCD is $(x - 4)(x + 4)$. Each term must be multiplied by this.

$$(x-4)(x+4)\left(\frac{5}{x-4}\right) - (x-4)(x+4)\left(\frac{3}{x+4}\right) = \left(\frac{36}{x^2-16}\right)(x-4)(x+4)$$

$$(x+4)(5)-(x-4)(3)=36 \qquad \text{Distribute.}$$
$$5x+20-3x+12=36 \qquad \text{Combine like terms.}$$
$$2x+32=36 \qquad \text{Subtract 32 from both sides.}$$
$$2x=4 \qquad \text{Divide by 2.}$$
$$x=2$$

To check the solution, substitute 2 into the equation:

$$\frac{5}{x-4}-\frac{3}{x+4}=\frac{36}{x^2-16}$$
$$\frac{5}{2-4}-\frac{3}{2+4}=\frac{36}{2^2-16}$$
$$-\frac{5}{2}-\frac{3}{6}=-\frac{36}{12}$$
$$-3=-3$$

Therefore, the solution is $x = 2$.

Solve for x: $\dfrac{1}{5}-\dfrac{1}{6}=\dfrac{1}{x}$

The LCD is $30x$. Multiply all terms by the LCD.

$$(30x)\left(\frac{1}{5}\right)-(30x)\left(\frac{1}{6}\right)=\left(\frac{1}{x}\right)(30x)$$
$$6x-5x=30$$
$$x=30$$

If you check the value $x = 30$ in the original equation, you will find that it works.

Radical Equations

Equations that have variables in their radicands are called radical equations. For example, $\sqrt{x}=16$ is a radical equation. To solve this radical equation, square both sides:

$$\sqrt{x}=16$$
$$(\sqrt{x})^2=16^2$$
$$x=256$$

Check $x = 256$ in the original equation.

$$\sqrt{x}\overset{?}{=}16$$
$$\sqrt{256}\overset{?}{=}16$$
$$16=16$$

The solution works.

Extraneous solutions may occur when you raise both sides of a radical equation to an even power. For example, if you square both sides of the equation $x = 5$ you get $x^2 = 25$. This new equation has two solutions, -5 and 5, but only 5 is the solution to the original equation.

The steps to solve a radical equation are:

1 Isolate the radical on one side of the equation.

2 Raise both sides of the equation to the same power to eliminate the radical.

3 Solve the resulting equation.

4 Check the solution.

Solve each equation.

a. $\sqrt{2x+3} = 7$

b. $\sqrt[3]{4x-5} = 3$

c. $\sqrt[4]{2x+8} - 2 = 2$

d. $x + 2 = \sqrt{11x+12}$

a.

$$\sqrt{2x+3} = 7$$
$$(\sqrt{2x+3})^2 = 7^2$$
$$2x+3 = 49$$
$$2x = 46$$
$$x = 23 \quad \text{Check the solution.}$$

$$\sqrt{2x+3} = 7$$
$$\sqrt{2(23)+3} = 7\,?$$
$$\sqrt{49} = 7\,?$$
$$7 = 7 \qquad\qquad \text{The solution is 7.}$$

b.

$$\sqrt[3]{4x-5} = 3$$
$$(\sqrt[3]{4x-5})^3 = 3^3$$
$$4x-5 = 27$$
$$4x = 32$$
$$x = 8 \quad \text{Check the solution.}$$

$$\sqrt[3]{4x-5} = 3$$
$$\sqrt[3]{4(8)-5} = 3\,?$$
$$\sqrt[3]{27} = 3\,?$$
$$3 = 3 \qquad\qquad \text{The solution is 8.}$$

c.

$$\sqrt[4]{2x+8} - 2 = 2$$
$$\sqrt[4]{2x+8} = 4$$
$$(\sqrt[4]{2x+8})^4 = (4)^4$$
$$2x+8 = 256$$
$$2x = 248$$
$$x = 124 \quad \text{Check the solution.}$$

$$\sqrt[4]{2x+8} - 2 = 2$$
$$\sqrt[4]{2(124)+8} - 2 = 2\,?$$
$$\sqrt[4]{256} - 2 = 2\,?$$
$$4 - 2 = 2\,?$$
$$2 = 2 \qquad\qquad \text{The solution is 124.}$$

d.

$$x + 2 = \sqrt{11x + 12}$$

$$(x + 2)^2 = (\sqrt{11x + 12})^2$$

$$x^2 + 4x + 4 = 11x + 12$$

$$x^2 - 7x - 8 = 0$$

$$(x - 8)(x + 1) = 0$$

$$x = 8, \ x = -1$$

$$x + 2 = \sqrt{11x + 12}$$

$$8 + 2 = \sqrt{11(8) + 12} \ ?$$

$$10 = \sqrt{100} \ ?$$

Check the solution $x = 8$. $\quad 10 = 10$ $\qquad$ The solution is 8.

$$x + 2 = \sqrt{11x + 12}$$

$$-1 + 2 = \sqrt{11(-1) + 12} \ ?$$

$$1 = \sqrt{1} \ ?$$

Check the solution $x = -1$. $\quad 1 = 1$ $\qquad$ The solution is -1.

The solutions are $x = 8$ and $x = -1$.

EXERCISES: SOLVING COMPLEX EQUATIONS

Directions: Work out each problem. Circle the letter of your choice.

1. Solve for x: $\dfrac{2}{x-2} - \dfrac{5}{x+2} = \dfrac{2}{x^2-4}$

   (A) $x = -4$
   (B) $x = -2$
   (C) $x = 2$
   (D) $x = 4$

2. Solve for y: $\dfrac{4}{y-2} - \dfrac{3}{y+2} = \dfrac{12}{y^2-4}$

   (A) $y = -4$
   (B) $y = -2$
   (C) $y = 2$
   (D) There are no solutions.

3. Solve for a: $\dfrac{3}{a-7} + \dfrac{5}{a^2-13a+42} = \dfrac{7}{a-6}$

   (A) $a = -18$
   (B) $a = -9$
   (C) $a = 9$
   (D) $a = 18$

4. Solve for b: $\dfrac{b}{8} + \dfrac{b}{12} + \dfrac{b}{24} > 2$

   (A) $b > 4$
   (B) $b > 8$
   (C) $b > 12$
   (D) $b > 18$

5. Solve the equation: $\sqrt[3]{8x} = 4$
   (A) $x = 8$
   (B) $x = 6$
   (C) $x = 4$
   (D) $x = 2$

6. Solve the equation: $\sqrt[4]{3x-2} + 1 = 6$
   (A) $x = 1$
   (B) $x = 9$
   (C) $x = 17$
   (D) $x = 209$

7. Solve the equation: $-5\sqrt[3]{9x} + 10 = -5$
   (A) $x = 3$
   (B) $x = 1$
   (C) $x = -1$
   (D) $x = -3$

8. Solve the equation: $x = \sqrt{16x+225}$
   (A) $x = 45$
   (B) $x = 25$
   (C) $x = -9$
   (D) $x = -25$

9. Solve for t: $\dfrac{t}{4} + \dfrac{2t}{9} \geq \dfrac{3t-14}{6}$
   (A) $t \leq 84$
   (B) $t \leq 42$
   (C) $t \geq 42$
   (D) $t \geq 84$

10. Solve the equation: $\sqrt{16x-32} = \sqrt{2x+10}$
    (A) $x = \dfrac{11}{7}$
    (B) $x = \dfrac{7}{3}$
    (C) $x = 2$
    (D) $x = 3$

ANSWER KEY AND EXPLANATIONS

1. D	3. C	5. A	7. A	9. A
2. D	4. B	6. D	8. B	10. D

1. **The correct answer is (D).** The LCD of the fractions in the equation $\dfrac{2}{x-2} - \dfrac{5}{x+2} = \dfrac{2}{x^2-4}$ is $(x-2)(x+2)$. Multiply all terms by the LCD.

$$(x-2)(x+2)\frac{2}{x-2} - (x-2)(x+2)\frac{5}{x+2}$$
$$= \frac{2}{x^2-4}(x-2)(x+2)$$
$$2(x+2) - 5(x-2) = 2$$
$$2x+4-5x+10 = 2$$
$$3x = 12$$
$$x = 4$$

Remember that you should check the answer to make certain that it solves the equation.

2. **The correct answer is (D).** The LCD of the fractions in the equation $\dfrac{4}{y-2} - \dfrac{3}{y+2} = \dfrac{12}{y^2-4}$ is y^2-4.

$$(y-2)(y+2)\frac{4}{y-2} - (y-2)(y+2)\frac{3}{y+2}$$
$$= (y-2)(y+2)\frac{12}{y^2-4}$$
$$4(y+2) - 3(y-2) = 12$$
$$4y+8-3y+6 = 12$$
$$y+14 = 12$$
$$y = -2$$

Note that when you substitute $y=-2$ into the equation, two of the denominators become 0 and are, therefore, undefined. This means that $y=-2$ is an extraneous solution, and the equation actually has no solutions.

3. **The correct answer is (C).** Note that $a^2 - 13a + 42 = (a-7)(a-6)$, so the LCD of the fractions in the equation is $(a-7)(a-6)$. Now, multiply by the LCD.

$$(a-7)(a-6)\frac{3}{a-7} +$$
$$(a-7)(a-6)\frac{5}{(a-7)(a-6)} =$$
$$\frac{7}{a-6}(a-7)(a-6)$$
$$3a-18+5 = 7(a-7)$$
$$3a-13 = 7a-49$$
$$4a = 36$$
$$a = 9$$

This solution checks.

4. **The correct answer is (B).** In the inequality $\dfrac{b}{8} + \dfrac{b}{12} + \dfrac{b}{24} > 2$, multiply by the LCD of 24.

$$(24)\frac{b}{8} + (24)\frac{b}{12} + (24)\frac{b}{24} > 2(24)$$
$$3b+2b+b > 48$$
$$6b > 48$$
$$b > 8$$

5. The correct answer is (A).

$$\sqrt[3]{8x} = 4$$
$$(\sqrt[3]{8x})^3 = 4^3$$
$$8x = 64$$
$$x = 8$$

6. The correct answer is (D).

$$\sqrt[4]{3x - 2} + 1 = 6$$
$$\sqrt[4]{3x - 2} = 5$$
$$3x - 2 = 625$$
$$3x = 627$$
$$x = 209$$

7. The correct answer is (A).

$$-5\sqrt[3]{9x} + 10 = -5$$
$$5\sqrt[3]{9x} = -15$$
$$\sqrt[3]{9x} = 3$$
$$9x = 27$$
$$x = 3$$

8. The correct answer is (B).

$$x = \sqrt{16x + 225}$$
$$x^2 = 16x + 225$$
$$x^2 - 16x - 225 = 0$$
$$(x - 25)(x + 9) = 0$$
$$x = 25, -9$$

Note when you substitute $x = -9$ into the equation, you get $-9 = 9$. This means that -9 is an extraneous solution. The only solution is 25.

9. The correct answer is (A). To solve $\dfrac{t}{4} + \dfrac{2t}{9} \geq \dfrac{3t - 14}{6}$, multiply by the LCD of 36.

$$(36)\frac{t}{4} + (36)\frac{2t}{9} \geq (36)\frac{3t - 14}{6}$$
$$9t + 8t \geq 6(3t - 14)$$
$$17t \geq 18t - 84$$
$$-t \geq -84$$
$$t \leq 84$$

10. The correct answer is (D).

$$\sqrt{16x - 32} = \sqrt{2x + 10}$$
$$16x - 32 = 2x + 10$$
$$14x = 42$$
$$x = 3$$

LINEAR, QUADRATIC, AND EXPONENTIAL FUNCTIONS

A *linear function* is a function of the form $f(x) = mx + b$, where m and b are real numbers. A *quadratic function* is a function of the form $g(x) = ax^2 + bx + c$, where $a \neq 0$, and a, b, and c are real numbers. An *exponential function* is a function of the form $f(x) = ab^x$ where base b is a positive integer greater than one. These functions are important, because they can be used to model many real-world occurrences.

Applications of Linear Functions

In order to manufacture a new car model, a carmaker must initially spend \$750,000 to purchase the equipment needed to start the production process. After this, it costs \$7500 to manufacture each car. In this case, the *cost function* that associates the cost of manufacturing cars to the number of cars manufactured is $C(x) = 7500x + 750,000$, where x represents the number of cars manufactured, and $C(x)$ represents the cost of x cars. For example, the cost of making 7 cars is $C(7) = 7500(7) + 750,000 = 52,500 + 750,000 = \$802,500$.

The above cost function is a linear function with $b = 750,000$ and $m = 7500$. What is the domain of this function? Note that even though nothing has been specifically said about the domain, the only values that make sense as domain values are the non-negative integers, 0, 1, 2, 3, 4, 5,... In such a situation, assume that the domain only contains the values that make sense.

> Using the cost function for the carmaker discussed in the example above, how much would it cost to make 24 cars?

To solve this, you need to determine the value of $C(24)$.

$C(24) = 7500(24) + 750,000 = 180,000 + 750,000 = \$930,000$

> Using the same cost function, determine how many cars could be made for \$990,000.

In this problem, you are told that the value of $C(x)$ is \$990,000, and you need to find the value of x. To do this, solve the equation:

$990,000 = 75,000(x) + 750,000$ Subtract 750,000 from both sides.

$240,000 = 7500x$

Divide by 7500.

$32 = x$

Therefore, for \$990,000, 32 cars can be manufactured.

> In the town of Kenmore, a taxi ride costs \$2.50 plus an extra \$0.50 per mile. Write a function that represents the cost of taking a taxi ride, using x to represent the number of miles traveled.

$C(x) = \$2.50 + 0.50x$

If a ride costs \$0.50 a mile, then the cost for x miles will be \$0.50x. Add to this the initial fee of \$2.50 a ride.

> You purchased shorts for $8 per pair, plus a shirt for $6. Write a function that represents the cost of your purchases, where x represents the number of pairs of shorts you purchase. How much did you spend if you purchased 5 pairs of shorts?

$f(x) = 8x + 6$

Let $x = 5$, so $f(5) = 8(5) + 6 = 46$.

> A bus pass has a starting value of $60. Each ride costs $2.50. Write a function that represents the remaining balance on the bus pass, where x represents the number of rides taken. How much money is left on the pass after 12 rides?

$f(x) = 60 - 2.5x$

Let $x = 12$, so $f(12) = 60 - 2.5(12) = 30$.

There is $30 remaining on the pass after 12 rides.

The Graph of a Linear Function

Typically, when a function is graphed, the independent variable is graphed along the x-axis, and the dependent variable is graphed along the y-axis.

The taxi ride function from the previous problem is a linear function. In order to graph this function, you must first determine the domain. Note that the domain, once again, must consist of non-negative numbers. Next, determine a few values that satisfy the rule for the function. For example, when $x = 0$, $C(0) = \$2.50 + 0.50(0) = \$2.50$. A few additional simple computations will lead to the following table of values.

x	$C(x)$
0	$2.50
1	$3.00
2	$3.50
3	$4.00

If these points are plotted on a graph, you will see that they all lie on the same line. The entire graph of the taxi ride cost function is shown below.

In general, the graph of any linear function is either a straight line or (depending on the domain) a portion of a straight line. The value of m represents the slope of the line, and the value of b is the y-intercept.

Applications of Quadratic Functions

Quadratic functions can also be used to model certain real-world happenings. To understand these functions better, suppose a coffee manufacturer has a revenue function given by $R(x) = 40,000x - 2000x^2$, where x represents the amount of coffee produced in tons per week. Let's consider some of the values for this function.

If $x = 0$, $R(x) = 40,000(0) - 2000(0)^2 = 0$ represents the obvious fact that if no coffee is produced there is no revenue.

That $R(1) = 40,000 - 2000 = 38,000$ tells that the revenue from 1 ton of coffee is $38,000.

Similar computations show that $R(10) = \$200,000$ and $R(11) = \$198,000$.

Note that the revenue is smaller if 11 tons of coffee are produced than if 10 tons are produced. There are a number of possible reasons for this. Perhaps, for example, at the 11-ton level, more is produced than can be sold, and the coffee company must pay to store the overage.

The function $h(t) = -16t^2 + h_0$ models the height of an object dropped from an initial height h_0 (in feet) after t seconds.

> An object is dropped from the roof of a building that is 80 ft. tall. How long will it take the object to hit the ground? Round your answer to the nearest hundredth of a second.

$h(t) = -16t^2 + h_0$

Here $h_0 = 80$, so $h(t) = -16t^2 + 80$.

Substitute 0 in for $h(t)$ and solve the equation for t.

$$0 = -16t^2 + 80$$
$$16t^2 = 80$$
$$t^2 = 5$$
$$t \approx \pm 2.24$$

> Suppose you drop a ball from a window that is 36 ft. above the ground and it lands on a porch that is 4 ft. above the ground. How long does it take for the ball to land on the porch? Round your answer to the nearest hundredth of a second.

$h(t) = -16t^2 + h_0$

Here $h_0 = 36$, so $h(t) = -16t^2 + 36$.

Substitute 4 for $h(t)$, because the ball will hit the porch at 4 feet above 0, or ground level. Solve the equation for t.

$$4 = -16t^2 + 36$$
$$16t^2 = 32$$
$$t^2 = 2$$
$$t \approx \pm 1.41$$

It will take approximately 1.41 seconds for the object to land on the porch.

The Graph of a Quadratic Function

As you just saw, the graph of a linear function is always a straight line. To determine what the graph of a quadratic function looks like, consider the graph of the quadratic function $R(x) = 40{,}000x - 2000x^2$. Negative numbers must be excluded from the domain. A few computations lead to the table below.

x	R(x)
0	0
3	102,000
5	150,000
9	198,000
10	200,000
11	198,000
15	150,000
17	102,000
20	0

The graph of $R(x)$ is shown below.

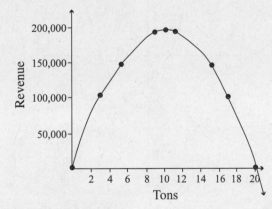

The graph shown above is called a *parabola*. This parabola is said to "open down." The highest point on the parabola, (10, 200,000), is called the *extreme point*.

Recall that the general form of a quadratic function is $g(x) = ax^2 + bx + c$. In general, the graph of any quadratic function will be a parabola. If $a > 0$, the parabola will "open up," and if $a < 0$, the parabola will "open down." If the parabola opens up, its extreme point is the minimum value of the function, and if the parabola opens down, its extreme point is the maximum value of the function.

The coordinates of the extreme point of a parabola are $\left[\dfrac{-b}{2a}, f\left(\dfrac{-b}{2a} \right) \right]$.

Sketch the graph of the function $f(x) = x^2 - x - 2$.

Since the function is quadratic, the graph will be a parabola. Note that the value of a, the number in front of the x^2-term is 1, so the parabola opens up. The x-coordinate of the minimum point is $x = \dfrac{-b}{2a} = \dfrac{-(-1)}{2(1)} = \dfrac{1}{2}$, and the y-coordinate of this point is

$$f\left(\frac{1}{2}\right) = \left(\frac{1}{2}\right)^2 - \frac{1}{2} - 2 = \frac{1}{4} - \frac{1}{2} - 2 = -2\frac{1}{4}.$$

In order to sketch a parabola, it is helpful to determine a few points on either side of the extreme point.

x	$f(x)$
-2	4
-1	0
0	-2
1	-2
2	0
3	4

The graph is shown below.

What is the relationship between the graph of the function $h(x) = ax^2 + bx$ and the graph of the function $j(x) = ax^2 + bx + 7$?

If (x,y) is a point on the graph of $h(x)$, then $(x, y + 7)$ will be a point on the graph of $j(x)$. Therefore, the two graphs have exactly the same size and shape. The graph of $j(x)$ can be obtained by taking the graph of $h(x)$ and "lifting" each point 7 units, that is, increasing the y-coordinate of each point by 7.

Applications of Exponential Functions

If a>0 and b>1, then the function $f(x) = ab^x$ is an *exponential growth function* and b is called the *growth factor*. If a>0 and 0<b<1, then the function $f(x) = ab^x$ is an *exponential decay function* and b is called the *decay factor*.

An exponential growth function can model the number of students in a high school. Suppose the number of students in 2011 is given by $f(x) = 1250(1.13)^x$, where x is the number of years since 2011. Let's consider some of the values for this function. If $x = 0$, then $f(x) = 1250(1.13)^0 = 1250$ represents the student population in 2011. If $x = 1$, then $f(x) = 1250(1.13)^1 = 1413$ represents the student population after 1 year. Similar computations show that $f(x) = 1596$ when $x = 2$ and $f(x) = 2303$ when $x = 5$.

An exponential decay function can model the value of an automobile. Suppose the value of the automobile is given by $f(x) = 35,000(0.85)^x$, where x is the number of years since the automobile was purchased. Let's consider some of the values for this function. If $x = 0$, then $f(x) = 35,000(0.85)^0 = 35,000$ represents the value of the automobile at the time of purchase. If $x = 2$, then $f(x) = 35,000(0.85)^2 = 25,287.50$ represents the value of the automobile after 2 years. Similar computations show that $f(x) = 15,529.69$ when $x = 5$ and $f(x) = 3057.40$ when $x = 15$.

The Graph of an Exponential Function

To determine what the graph of an exponential function looks like, consider the graph of the exponential function $f(x) = 5250(0.9)^x$, where $f(x)$ is the value of a jet ski in dollars after x years.

The initial value of the jet ski is $5250 and the percent of decrease per year is 10%. Some of the computations along with the graph of $f(x)$ is a curve that falls from left to right and gets less and less steep as x increases. The x-axis is a horizontal asymptote.

x	$f(x)$
0	5250
1	4725
5	3100.00
8	2260
12	1482.8
15	1080.0
25	339.21

Comparing Linear and Exponential Growth Functions

Suppose you can choose how you will get your allowance. First option is to get $5 a week every week. The second option is to get $0.50 for the first week, $1 for the second week, $2 for the third, and so on, by doubling the amount each week. Which option will pay you more?

Option 1: $y = 5x$, where x is the number of weeks you were paid your allowance and y is the total amount of money you have been paid so far.

Option 2: $y = (0.5)(2)^{x-1}$, where x is the number of weeks you were paid your allowance and y is the total amount of money you have been paid so far.

As you can see from the tables, option 1 pays more until the 8th week. After that Option 2 will always pay more since you are doubling a larger number.

Option 1: $y = 5x$

x (week)	1	2	3	4	5	6	7	8	9	10
y (total)	5	10	15	20	25	30	35	40	45	50

Option 2: $y = (0.5)(2)^{x-1}$

x (week)	1	2	3	4	5	6	7	8	9	10
y (total)	0.5	1	2	4	8	16	32	64	128	256

Option 1 is a linear function that is increasing at a constant rate and option 2 is an exponential function that is increasing rapidly as x gets bigger. You would chose option 2 to be paid the most.

EXERCISES: LINEAR, QUADRATIC, AND EXPONENTIAL FUNCTIONS

Directions: Work out each problem. Circle the letter of your choice.

1. A taxi company charges $2.25 for the first mile and $0.45 for each mile thereafter. If x stands for the number of miles a passenger travels, which of the following functions relates the length of the trip to its cost?

   (A) $f(x) = 2.25 + 0.45(x + 1)$

   (B) $f(x) = 2.25 + 0.45(1 - x)$

   (C) $f(x) = 2.25 + 0.45(x - 1)$

   (D) $f(x) = 2.25 + 0.45x$

2. The Amp Corporation manufactures home video systems. The cost function for the Amp45 system is $C(x) = 3x^2 - 2x + 7$, where x represents the number of systems manufactured, and the cost is in dollars. How much does it cost to manufacture 18 of these systems?

   (A) $943

   (B) $972

   (C) $974

   (D) $2903

3. Which of the following best describes the graph of the function $f(x) = 5x - 7$?

   (A) A horizontal line

   (B) A line that increases from left to right

   (C) A line that decreases from left to right

   (D) A parabola that opens up

4. Which of the following best describes the graph of the function $g(x) = -5x^2 + 7x - 23$?

   (A) A horizontal line

   (B) A line that increases from left to right

   (C) A line that decreases from left to right

   (D) A parabola that opens down

5. At the Four Seasons bowling alley, it costs $1.50 to rent shoes and $2.50 for each game played. Which of the following functions relates the number of games played, x, to the cost in dollars?

   (A) $f(x) = 4.00x$

   (B) $f(x) = 2.50 + 1.50x$

   (C) $f(x) = 1.50x - 2.50$

   (D) $f(x) = 2.50x + 1.50$

6. In order to raise money for a charity, Deb makes cakes to sell at a school bake sale. Her profit function is $P(x) = \$4.50x - \$15$. How many cakes must she sell in order to earn $66 for the charity?

   (A) 15

   (B) 16

   (C) 18

   (D) 20

7. For which domain values of the function $f(x) = x^2 + 3x - 10$ does $f(x) = 0$?

   (A) 2

   (B) −2

   (C) −5

   (D) 2 and −5

8. At which point does the graph of the function $g(x) = -12x + 6$ cross the y-axis?

   (A) $(0,6)$

   (B) $(6,0)$

   (C) $(0,2)$

   (D) $(0,\frac{1}{2})$

9. The functions $f(x) = 16x - 7$ and $g(x) = 16x + 5$ are graphed on the same coordinate axis. Which of the following best describes the appearance of the graph?

(A) Two intersecting lines, one with y-intercept of -7, the other with y-intercept of 5

(B) Two parallel lines, one with y-intercept of -7, and the other with y-intercept of 5

(C) Two parallel lines, one with y-intercept of 7, and the other with y-intercept of -5

(D) Two intersecting lines, one with y-intercept of 7, the other with y-intercept of -5

10. What is the x-coordinate of the extreme point of the function $f(x) = 7x^2 - 28x + 16$?

(A) $x = \dfrac{1}{2}$

(B) $x = -\dfrac{1}{2}$

(C) $x = 2$

(D) $x = -2$

11. You purchase a new bike for $850 and the value of the bike decreases by 20% per year. Approximately, when will the value of the bike will be less than $500?

(A) After 3 years

(B) After 2.5 years

(C) After 2 years

(D) After 1.5 years

12. What is the asymptote of the graph of $f(x) = (0.75)^x + 2$?

(A) $f(x) = -2$

(B) $f(x) = 0$

(C) $f(x) = 0.75$

(D) $f(x) = 2$

13. A ball is dropped from a height of 20 ft. above the ground. How long will it be before the ball hits the ground?

(A) About 2.0 seconds

(B) About 1.56 seconds

(C) About 1.12 seconds

(D) About 0.89 seconds

14. The value of a car can be modeled by the equation $f(x) = 38{,}000(0.89)^x$, when x is the number of years since the car was purchased and $f(x)$ is the value of the car. What is the approximate value of the car after 6 years?

(A) About $19,000

(B) About $22,000

(C) About $28,000

(D) About $30,000

ANSWER KEY AND EXPLANATIONS

1. C	4. D	7. D	10. C	13. B
2. A	5. D	8. A	11. B	14. A
3. B	6. C	9. B	12. D	

1. **The correct answer is (C).** The cost for the first mile on a trip of x miles is $2.25. After this, there are still $x - 1$ miles to go, and the cost for each of these miles is $0.45. Therefore, the total cost of the trip, in dollars, is $2.25 + 0.45(x - 1)$.

2. **The correct answer is (A).** You need to determine the value of $C(18)$.

   $$C(18) = 3(18)^2 - 2(18) + 7$$
   $$= 3(324) - 36 + 7$$
   $$= 972 - 36 + 7$$
   $$= 943$$

3. **The correct answer is (B).** The function $f(x) = 5x - 7$ is a linear function, which means that its graph is a straight line. The slope of the line is the coefficient of x, that is, 5. A line with a positive slope increases from left to right.

4. **The correct answer is (D).** The function $g(x) = -5x^2 + 7x - 23$ is a quadratic function, so its graph will be a parabola. Because the coefficient of the x^2-term is negative, the parabola opens down.

5. **The correct answer is (D).** The cost of x games, at $2.50 a game, is $2.50x$. Adding the $1.50 cost of shoe rental to this leads to the function $f(x) = 2.50x + 1.50$.

6. **The correct answer is (C).** You are asked to find the value of x for which $4.50x - 15 = 66$.

   $$4.50x - 15 = 66$$
   $$4.50x - 15 = 66 \quad \text{Add 15 to both sides.}$$
   $$4.50x = 81 \quad \text{Divide by 450.}$$
   $$x = 18$$

   Therefore, Deb must sell 18 cakes to make $66.

7. **The correct answer is (D).** In order to answer this question, you need to solve the quadratic equation $x^2 + 3x - 10 = 0$.

   $$x^2 + 3x - 10 = 0 \quad \text{Factor the left-hand side.}$$
   $$(x + 5)(x - 2) = 0 \quad \text{Set each factor equal to 0.}$$
   $$x + 5 = 0 \qquad x - 2 = 0$$
   $$x = -5 \qquad x = 2$$

   Thus, $f(x) = x^2 + 3x - 10 = 0$ at $x = -5$ and $x = 2$.

8. **The correct answer is (A).** For a linear function, the y-intercept is equal to the value of the constant. Therefore, $g(x) = -12x + 6$ crosses the y-axis at $(0,6)$.

9. **The correct answer is (B).** The two functions are both linear, so their graphs are straight lines. Note that the coefficient of the x-term in each case is 16. Since this coefficient represents the slope of the function, both functions are lines with slopes of 16. Lines with the same slopes are parallel. The constant term of a linear function is the y-intercept, so one line has a y-intercept of -7, and the other has a y-intercept of 5.

10. **The correct answer is (C).** The extreme point of a quadratic function is given by the formula $x = \dfrac{-b}{2a}$, where a is the coefficient of the x^2-term and b is the coefficient of the x-term. In this case, then, the extreme point is

$$x = \frac{-b}{2a} = \frac{-(-28)}{2(7)} = \frac{28}{14} = 2.$$

11. **The correct answer is (B).** The model giving the bike's value $f(x)$ in dollars after x years is: $f(x) = 850(0.8)^x$. Substitute 500 in for $f(x)$ and solve the equation. The value of the bike will be less than $500 after approximately 2.5 years.

12. **The correct answer is (D).** The graph of $f(x) = ab^{x-h} + k$ is the translation of the graph of $f(x) = ab^x$. So $f(x) = (0.75)^x + 2$ is translated up 2 units. The graph's asymptote is the line $f(x) = 2$.

13. **The correct answer is (C).** The model giving the height h of the ball (in feet) after t seconds is $h(t) = -16t^2 + 20$. Substitute 0 in for $h(t)$ and solve the equation. The ball will hit the ground about 1.12 seconds after it is dropped.

14. **The correct answer is (A).** Substitute 6 for x in the equation $f(x) = 38{,}000(0.89)^x$, and solve the equation. The car will be worth approximately $19,000 after 6 years.

SUMMING IT UP

- A function is a rule that assigns exactly one output to each input. In other words, each member of the domain corresponds to exactly one member of the range.

- The four steps in solving an equation involving rational expressions are:

    1 Find the LCD of all of the rational expressions in the equation.

    2 Multiply *every* term on both sides of the equation by this LCD.

    3 Solve the resulting equation using the methods previously explained.

    4 Check the solution to make certain that it actually solves the equation.

- The steps to solve a radical equation are:

    1 Isolate the radical on one side of the equation.

    2 Raise both sides of the equation to the same power to eliminate the radical.

    3 Solve the resulting equation.

    4 Check the solution.

Data Analysis, Statistics, and Probability Review

chapter 13

OVERVIEW

- Averages
- Weighted average
- Probability
- Data interpretation
- Statistics
- Summing it up

AVERAGES

Arithmetic Mean, Median, Mode, and Range

Typically, when asked to find the *average* of a group of n numbers, students add up all the numbers in the group and then divide by n. This type of average, which is more precisely called the *arithmetic mean,* is just one of a number of different types of averages, each of which is computed in a different way and conveys a different type of information. There are three additional ways to describe a set of data. Two of these are also types of averages, known as the median and the mode of the data. A third value, range, is used to describe data. These will also occasionally appear on the SAT®.

In order to avoid ambiguity, when an SAT® question involves the computation of the arithmetic mean, it will use the word *average* followed by the words *arithmetic mean* in parentheses. When an SAT® average question involves the median, the mode, or the range, the words *median*, *mode*, and *range* will be specifically used. The arithmetic mean is by far the most common type of average used on the SAT®.

The Arithmetic Mean

To find the average (arithmetic mean) of a group of n numbers, simply add the numbers and divide by n.

Find the average (arithmetic mean) of 32, 50, and 47.

$$
\begin{array}{r}
32 \\
50 \\
\underline{+47} \\
129
\end{array}
\qquad
3\overline{\smash{)}129}^{\,43}
$$

Another type of arithmetic mean problem gives you the arithmetic mean and asks for the missing term.

The average (arithmetic mean) of three numbers is 43. If two of the numbers are 32 and 50, find the third number.

Using the definition of arithmetic mean, write the equation:

$$\frac{32+50+x}{3} = 43$$
$$32+50+x = 129$$
$$82+x = 129$$
$$x = 47$$

Median and Mode

In order to find the *median* of a group of numbers, list the numbers in numerical order from smallest to largest. The median is the number in the middle. For example, the median of the numbers 3, 3, 5, 9, and 10 is 5. Note that, typically, the median and the arithmetic mean are not the same. In this problem, for example, the arithmetic mean is $30 \div 5 = 6$.

If there is an even number of numbers, the median is equal to the arithmetic mean of the two numbers in the middle. For example, to find the median of 3, 3, 5, 7, 9, and 10, note that the two middle numbers are 5 and 7. The median, then, is $\frac{5+7}{2} = 6$.

The *mode* of a group of numbers is simply the number that occurs most frequently. Therefore, the mode of the group of numbers 3, 3, 5, 7, 9, and 10 is 3. If all of the numbers in a group only appear once, then there is no mode.

What is the product of the arithmetic mean, the median, and the mode of the following group of eight numbers?

2, 7, 8, 9, 9, 9, 10, and 10

The sum of the eight numbers is 64, so the arithmetic mean is $64 \div 8 = 8$.

The median is the arithmetic mean of the two numbers in the middle. Since these numbers are both 9, the median is $\frac{9+9}{2} = 9$.

The mode is the number that occurs most often, which is also 9. The product of these three "averages" is $8 \times 9 \times 9 = 648$.

Range

The range, or the spread, of a data set is the difference between the greatest and least data values. To find the range of a set of data, first write the values in ascending order to make sure that you have found the least and greatest values. Here is an example:

Celia kept track of the average price of a gallon of gas over the last 10 years. Her data is shown in the table below. What is the range in the average price of gas?

Year	Average price/ gallon in U.S. dollars
2005	2.00
2006	2.08
2007	2.44
2008	3.40
2009	2.85
2010	2.90
2011	3.50
2012	4.20
2013	3.80
2014	3.25

Write the data in order from least to greatest:

2.00 2.08 2.44 2.85 2.90 3.25 3.40 3.50 3.80 4.20

Subtract the least value from the greatest value: $4.20 - 2.00 = 2.20$.

$2.20 is the range or spread of the data.

WEIGHTED AVERAGE

If asked to find the arithmetic mean of a group of numbers in which some of the numbers appear more than once, simplify the computation by using the *weighted average* formula. For example, suppose the question asks for the average (arithmetic mean) age of a group of 10 friends. If four of the friends are 17, and six of the friends are 19, determine the average in the usual way:

$$\text{Average age} = \frac{17+17+17+17+19+19+19+19+19+19}{10} = \frac{182}{10} = 18.2$$

However, the computation can be done more quickly by taking the *weights* of the ages into account. The age 17 is weighted four times, and the age 19 is weighted six times. The average can then be computed as follows:

$$\text{Average age} = \frac{4(17)+6(19)}{10} = \frac{182}{10} = 18.2$$

> Andrea has four grades of 90 and two grades of 80 during the spring semester of calculus. What is her average (arithmetic mean) in the course for this semester?

$$
\begin{array}{ll}
90 & \text{or} \qquad 90 \cdot 4 = 360 \\
90 & \\
90 & \\
90 & \qquad\qquad +80 \cdot 2 = \underline{160} \\
80 & \\
\underline{+80} & \\
6)\underline{520} & \qquad\qquad 6)\underline{520} \\
= 86\dfrac{2}{3} & \qquad\qquad = 86\dfrac{2}{3}
\end{array}
$$

Be sure not to average 90 and 80, since there are four grades of 90 and only two grades of 80.

Average Rate

The *average rate* for a trip is the total distance covered, divided by the total time spent. Recall that distance can be determined by multiplying the rate by the time, that is, $d = rt$.

> In driving from New York to Boston, Mr. Portney drove for 3 hours at 40 miles per hour and 1 hour at 48 miles per hour. What was his average rate for this portion of the trip?

$$\text{Average rate} = \frac{\text{Total distance}}{\text{Total time}}$$

$$\text{Average rate} = \frac{3(40)+1(48)}{3+1}$$

$$\text{Average rate} = \frac{168}{4} = 42 \text{ miles per hour}$$

Since more of the trip was driven at 40 mph than at 48 mph, the average should be closer to 40 than to 48, which it is. This will help you to check your answer, or to pick out the correct choice in a multiple-choice question.

EXERCISES: AVERAGES

Directions: Work out each problem. Circle the letter next to your choice.

1. Dan had an average (arithmetic mean) of 72 on his first four math tests. After taking the next test, his average (arithmetic mean) dropped to 70. Which of the following is his most recent test grade?

   (A) 60

   (B) 62

   (C) 66

   (D) 68

2. What is the average (arithmetic mean) of $\sqrt{0.64}$, 0.85, and $\frac{9}{10}$?

   (A) $\frac{21}{25}$

   (B) 2.55

   (C) 85%

   (D) $\frac{4}{5}$

3. The costs of five different airlines' tickets from Dallas to Boston are shown in table below.

Airline	Ticket Cost
A	$356
B	$298
C	$312
D	$304
E	$283

   A sixth airline also offers flights from Dallas to Boston. The median price of the tickets from the six airlines, including those shown in the table is $308. The range of the ticket prices is $77. What is the cost of the sixth airline's ticket?

   (A) $385

   (B) $360

   (C) $279

   (D) $231

4. A high school theater department is using sale information from previous years' sales for the annual musical to determine how many seats will be needed. The sale information is shown in the table below.

Year	Seats
2010	185
2011	203
2012	205
2013	197

   Which correctly shows the median and range of the data?

   (A) Median = 200; Range = 20

   (B) Median = 204; Range = 12

   (C) Median = 200; Range = 12

   (D) Median = 204; Range = 20

5. What is the average (arithmetic mean) of the first 15 positive integers?

   (A) 7

   (B) 7.5

   (C) 8

   (D) 8.5

6. A man travels a distance of 20 miles at 60 miles per hour and then returns over the same route at 40 miles per hour. What is his average rate for the round trip in miles per hour?

   (A) 50

   (B) 48

   (C) 47

   (D) 46

7. Max is selling his car. He looks at the selling prices of the same type of car at five local car dealerships to determine a fair price for his car. The selling prices are listed below.

$7505; $7630; $7995; $7029; $7135; $7995

What is the approximate average (arithmetic mean) selling price for the type of car Max is trying to sell?

(A) $7995
(B) $7548
(C) $7512
(D) $7505

8. Susan has an average (arithmetic mean) of 86 in three examinations. What grade must she receive on her next test to raise her average (arithmetic mean) to 88?

(A) 90
(B) 94
(C) 96
(D) 100

9. The heights of the 5 high jumpers on Redwood High's track team are 5'11", 6'3", 6', 6'6", and 6'2". The average (arithmetic mean) height of these players is

(A) 6'2".
(B) 6'3".
(C) 6'4".
(D) 6'5".

10. The age of the 14 most recent U.S. Presidents at inauguration are listed below in order of their presidencies. Which of the following correctly compares the average (arithmetic mean), median, and mode of their ages?

54　51　60　62　43　55　56　61　52　69　64　46　54　47

(A) mode < mean < median
(B) mode < median < mean
(C) median < mode < mean
(D) median < mean < mode

11. A basketball team has 5 top scoring players. The average (arithmetic mean) points per game scored by the 5 players during one season are shown in the list below.

15.5, 16.2, 18, 16.5, 17.4

There are 10 games during the season. What is the average points scored per player for the season for the 5 top scoring players?

(A) 16.72
(B) 18.72
(C) 134.8
(D) 167.2

12. Amaya drives on two types of roads for her trip. She averages 53 miles per hour on city roads and 59 miles per hour on the highway. Amaya drives her car on a trip that has twice as many highway miles as city road miles. She drives a total of 552 miles. What is her average gas mileage for the whole trip? Round your answer to the nearest whole.

(A) 55 miles per hour
(B) 56 miles per hour
(C) 57 miles per hour
(D) 58 miles per hour

ANSWER KEY AND EXPLANATIONS

1. B	4. A	7. B	10. B
2. C	5. C	8. B	11. D
3. B	6. B	9. A	12. C

1. **The correct answer is (B).**

$$\frac{4(72)+x}{5}=70$$
$$288+x=350$$
$$x=62$$

2. **The correct answer is (C).** In order to find the average (arithmetic mean) of these three numbers, they should all be expressed as decimals.

$$\sqrt{0.64}=0.8$$
$$0.85=0.85$$
$$\frac{9}{10}=0.9$$

$$\text{Average}=\frac{0.8+0.85+0.9}{3}=\frac{2.55}{3}=0.85$$

(arithmetic mean)

This is equal to 85%.

3. **The correct answer is (B).**

List the given ticket costs from least to greatest:

$283, $298, $304, $312, $356

Add $77 to the least cost to determine if the unknown cost is also the greatest cost:

283 + 77 = 360

Use the value to find the median of the tickets:

$283, $298, $304, $312, $356, $360

Find the average (mean) of $304 and $312, which is $308.

The unknown ticket cost is $360.

4. **The correct answer is (A).** List the given number of seats from least to greatest:

185, 197, 203, 205

The median is the middle value of the list. Since the list does not have a distinct middle value, add the two middle values 197 and 203, then divide by 2 to find the median.

197 + 203 = 400; 400/2 = 200

The median is 200.

To find the range, subtract the least from the greatest value:

205 − 185 = 20

The range is 20.

5. **The correct answer is (C).** Positive integers begin with 1.

$$\frac{1+2+3+4+5+6+7+8+9+10+11+12+13+14+15}{15}$$

Since these numbers are evenly spaced, the average (arithmetic mean) will be the middle number, 8.

6. **The correct answer is (B).**

$$\text{Average rate} = \frac{\text{Total distance}}{\text{Total time}}$$

Total distance = 20 + 20 = 40

Since $\text{time} = \dfrac{\text{distance}}{\text{rate}}$, time for first part of the trip is $\dfrac{20}{60}$, or $\dfrac{1}{3}$ hour, while time for the second part of the trip is $\dfrac{20}{40}$, or $\dfrac{1}{2}$ hour.

Total time $= \dfrac{1}{3} + \dfrac{1}{2}$, or $\dfrac{5}{6}$ hour

Average rate $= \dfrac{40}{\dfrac{5}{6}} = 40 \cdot \dfrac{6}{5} = 48$ mph

7. **The correct answer is (B).**

$$\frac{7505 + 7630 + 7995 + 7029 + 7135 + 7995}{6} = \frac{45,289}{6}$$
$$= 7548.167$$

The approximate average of the cars' selling prices is $7548.

8. **The correct answer is (B).**

$$\frac{3(86) + x}{4} = 88$$
$$258 + x = 352$$
$$x = 94$$

9. **The correct answer is (A).**

    5'11"
    6'3"
    6'0"
    6'6"
    6'2"

29'22" = 5)30'10"
              6'2"

10. **The correct answer is (B).** First put the ages of the presidents in order.

    43, 46, 47, 51, 52, 54, 54, 55, 56, 60, 61, 62, 64, 69

    The mode of their ages is 54, which is the only repeated age.

    The median of their ages is the middle number, which is the average of 54 and 55 or 54.5.

    The average or arithmetic mean is found by adding their ages and dividing by 14.

    $$\frac{43+46+47+51+52+54+54+55+56+60+61+62+64+69}{14} = \frac{774}{14} = 55.3$$

    Now order the three values: $54 < 54.5 < 55.3$, which means that mode < median < mean.

11. **The correct answer is (D).**

    To find the average points scored for the season by all 5 players, you can first find the total number of points each player scored during the season. Each player played 10 games, so to find their total number of points scored, multiply the average points per game by 10 games.

    $15.5 \times 10 = 155$

    $16.2 \times 10 = 162$

    $18 \times 10 = 180$

    $16.5 \times 10 = 165$

    $17.4 \times 10 = 174$

    Average points for the season:

    $$\frac{155+162+180+165+174}{5} = \frac{836}{5} = 167.2 \text{ points per season}$$

12. **The correct answer is (C).** Amaya drove for a time on city roads at 53 miles/hour and twice as much time on the highway at 59 miles/hour, so her average speed was:

    $$\frac{53x+59(2x)}{3x} = \frac{171x}{3x} = 57$$

    The average speed for the entire trip was 57 miles per hour.

PROBABILITY

In the study of probability, an *experiment* is a process that yields one of a certain number of possible outcomes. For example, tossing a coin is an experiment with two possible outcomes: heads or tails. Throwing a die is an experiment with six possible outcomes because there are six sides: 1, 2, 3, 4, 5, or 6.

Probability is a numerical way of measuring the likelihood that a specific outcome will happen. The probability of a specific outcome is always a number between 0 and 1. An outcome with a probability of 0 cannot possibly happen, and an event with probability of 1 will definitely happen. Therefore, the nearer the probability of an event is to 0, the less likely the event is to happen, and the nearer the probability of an event is to 1, the more likely the event is to happen.

If an experiment has n possible equally likely outcomes, the probability of each specific outcome is defined to be $\frac{1}{n}$. In the coin-tossing experiment, the probability of heads is $\frac{1}{2}$, since heads is one of the two equally likely outcomes. When a die is thrown, the probability of tossing an odd number is $\frac{3}{6}$ or $\frac{1}{2}$, since tossing an odd number is 3 of six equally likely outcomes.

Here is a helpful formula for computing simple probabilities:

The probability of an event occurring $= \dfrac{\text{The number of favorable outcomes}}{\text{The number of possible outcomes}}$

Independent Events

What is the probability of tossing two coins that both land heads up, if the first penny has already been tossed and landed heads up?

The result of the first toss does not affect the result of the second toss, so the conditional probability is equal to the probability of B (the second coin toss).

$P(B) = \dfrac{1}{2}$

What is the probability of tossing two coins and having them both land heads up?

Neither coin has been tossed, so the conditional probability of both coins landing heads up is determined using the probability of both events. In this case, the probability of event A and event B both happening is found by multiplying the probability of each event.

$P(A \text{ and } B) = \dfrac{1}{2} \times \dfrac{1}{2} = \dfrac{1}{4}$

The probability of tossing two coins and having them both land heads up is $\dfrac{1}{4} = 0.25$.

Dependent Events

If events A and B are dependent, then the probability of event B is affected by the result of event A.

> What is the probability of choosing a black 5 and then a red 5 from the same standard deck of cards?

There are two red 5s and two black 5s in a standard deck of 52 cards. Removing a black 5 from the deck will leave only 51 cards in the deck so the probability can be found by:

$$P(A \text{ and } B) = \frac{2}{52} \times \frac{2}{51} = \frac{1}{663}$$

Conditional Probability

The probability of an event occurring after another event has already occurred, is called *conditional probability*.

The notation for conditional probability is $P(B|A)$, which is read "the probability of B given A."

If both events A and B are *independent*, where the result of B is not affected by the result of A, then the conditional probability of B is equal to the probability of B only.

$$P(B|A) = P(B)$$

If both events A and B are *dependent*, where the result of B is affected by the result of A, then the conditional probability of B may be calculated using a few different methods. In probability situations involving dependent events, the way in which the question is asked will determine which of the following equations to use.

$$\frac{P(A \text{ and } B)}{P(A)} \quad \text{OR} \quad \frac{P(A \text{ and } B)}{P(B)} \quad \text{OR}$$

$$P(A \text{ and } B) = P(\mathbf{A}) \times P(B|A)$$

> Of 100 people who work out at a gym there are 45 people who take yoga classes, 60 people who take weight lifting classes, and 15 people who take both yoga and weight lifting. What is the probability that one of the people who works out at the gym is chosen at random who takes both yoga and weight lifting classes?

This question is asking you to find the probability that a person is taking a yoga class and weight-lifting class (A and B), given that the person is in a yoga class (A).

$$\frac{P(A \text{ and } B)}{P(A)} = \frac{0.15}{0.45} = \frac{1}{3}$$

The conditional probability that a person who takes yoga, is in a weight-lifting class is $\frac{1}{3}$.

Two-Way Tables and Probability

Data on the SAT® is often represented in two-way tables like the one in the example below. Be careful to read the correct row or column that represents the information in the problem. These tables are often used for two to three problems in a row.

Hattie is a member of the honor society. All members of the society are polled to determine how many hours they spend studying per week and whether they prefer math or science classes. The results are shown in the table below.

	Science	Math	Total
0–3 hours per week	4	2	6
4–6 hours per week	6	7	13
Total	10	9	19

What is the probability that an honor society member selected at random prefers math, given that the member studies 4–6 hours per week?

There are a total of 13 students who study 4–6 hours per week, and 7 of them prefer math. So the probability is $\frac{7}{13}$.

EXERCISES: PROBABILITY

Directions: Work out each problem. Circle the letter next to your choice.

1. A school cafeteria offers students three meal choices: salad, grilled chicken, and pot roast. There are 4 side choices: grilled vegetables, baked potato, rice, or soup. What is the probability that a student who randomly chooses a meal and a side chose the grilled vegetables after having chosen the grilled chicken?

   (A) $\frac{1}{3}$

   (B) $\frac{1}{4}$

   (C) $\frac{1}{7}$

   (D) $\frac{1}{12}$

2. A poll asked 100 visitors at a national park the distance they hiked during their visit. The table shows the data collected based on the visitors' ages and hiking distances.

	18–25 years old	26–35 years old	Total
0–2 miles	16	22	38
2–4 miles	20	17	37
4+ miles	11	14	25
Total	47	53	100

   What is the probability that a visitor hiked greater than 4 miles, given that the visitor was 18–25 years old?

   (A) $\frac{11}{14}$

   (B) $\frac{11}{25}$

   (C) $\frac{11}{36}$

   (D) $\frac{11}{47}$

3. A game uses letter tiles that are selected randomly out of a bag. The letters that are remaining in the bag after each player has taken 4 turns are shown below.

   S, U, G, R, A, O, E, T, V, E, A, H, S, E

   What is the probability of the player selecting two vowel tiles if the player selects two tiles from the letters that remain?

   (A) $\frac{3}{13}$

   (B) $\frac{1}{4}$

   (C) $\frac{6}{13}$

   (D) $\frac{1}{2}$

4. In a movie theater, there are 32 people who bought popcorn, 25 who bought a drink, and 12 people who bought popcorn and a drink. What is the probability that a randomly selected person who bought popcorn, also bought a drink?

(A) $\dfrac{3}{8}$

(B) $\dfrac{12}{25}$

(C) $\dfrac{25}{32}$

(D) $\dfrac{12}{13}$

5. The two-way frequency table below shows the results of a poll regarding video game play. The poll asked 150 randomly selected people the amount of time they spent playing video games each week and the type of game they most like to play. The table shows relative frequencies of each category.

	1–3 hours	3–5 hours	5+ hours	Total
Role-playing	12	15	16	43
Platform	24	19	18	61
Action	33	35	28	96
Total	69	69	62	200

What is the probability that a person plays 3–5 hours of games per week, given that they prefer platform games?

(A) $\dfrac{19}{35}$

(B) $\dfrac{19}{42}$

(C) $\dfrac{19}{61}$

(D) $\dfrac{19}{69}$

6. Which question below is the probability of two dependent events?

(A) Two coins are flipped. What is the probability of the second coin landing heads up, if the first coin landed tails up?

(B) Two number cubes are rolled. What is the probability of rolling two even numbers?

(C) A card is selected from a deck of 52 cards. What is the probability of selecting 3 hearts in a row, if each card is replaced after selected?

(D) A bag contains 5 red marbles and 6 blue marbles. What is the probability of selecting two marbles of different colors, without replacement of the marbles?

7. A summer camp held a fishing tournament. The participants selected the type of bait they would use. The data in the table shows the first type of fish caught by each participant and the bait they used.

	Perch	Bass	Trout	Catfish	Total
Live Bait	10	4	4	6	24
Artificial Bait	5	5	2	0	12
Total	15	9	6	6	36

What is the probability that a participant will catch a bass, given that artificial bait was used?

(A) $\frac{1}{4}$

(B) $\frac{5}{9}$

(C) $\frac{5}{12}$

(D) $\frac{5}{36}$

8. At a school dance, the DJ offers five kinds of music: Electronic, Rap, Pop, Swing, and Rock. If the kind of music played is selected at random, what is the probability that the next two songs the DJ will play will be an Electronic song and then a Pop song?

(A) $\frac{1}{25}$

(B) $\frac{1}{10}$

(C) $\frac{1}{5}$

(D) $\frac{2}{5}$

9. During a science experiment, two studies of chemical reactions are conducted. Each experiment required a hypothesis. Hypothesis A is correct $\frac{5}{7}$ of the times the experiment is conducted. Hypothesis B is correct $\frac{3}{4}$ of the time the experiment is conducted. If the two hypotheses do not affect the other, what is the probability that both hypotheses A and B are correct?

(A) $\frac{15}{28}$

(B) $\frac{5}{7}$

(C) $\frac{3}{4}$

(D) $\frac{8}{11}$

10. Gustav finds that during daily marching band practice he correctly completes all steps $\frac{7}{8}$ of the time. During daily symphonic band practice he correctly plays each piece of music $\frac{11}{12}$ of the time. The probability that completes all steps in marching band and plays each piece of music correctly in symphonic band during the same day is $\frac{3}{5}$. What is the probability that he correctly completes all steps during marching band given the he has attended symphonic band?

(A) $\frac{24}{35}$

(B) $\frac{36}{55}$

(C) $\frac{11}{20}$

(D) $\frac{21}{40}$

ANSWER KEY AND EXPLANATIONS

1. B	3. A	5. C	7. C	9. A
2. D	4. B	6. D	8. A	10. B

1. **The correct answer is (B).** The probability of choosing grilled vegetables is independent of choosing grilled chicken. There are 4 sides to choose from, and grilled vegetables is one of those four choices, or $\frac{1}{4}$.

2. **The correct answer is (D).** There are a total of 47 visitors who are 18–25 years old. In that age group, 11 of those visitors walked more than 4 miles, so the probability is $\frac{11}{47}$.

3. **The correct answer is (A).** Seven of the 14 tiles are vowels, so the probability of selecting one vowel is $\frac{7}{14}=\frac{1}{2}$. For the second tile, there are only 13 tiles to choose from and 6 vowel tiles remaining.
$$P(A \text{ and } B) = P(A) \times P(B)$$
$$= \frac{1}{2} \times \frac{6}{13}$$
$$= \frac{6}{26}$$
$$= \frac{3}{13}$$

4. **The correct answer is (B).** The probability that the student has popcorn, given the student has a drink can be found using the equation, $P(A \text{ and } B)$ is the probability of someone having both and $P(B)$ is the probability of someone having a drink.
$$\frac{P(A \text{ and } B)}{P(B)} = \frac{12}{25}$$

5. **The correct answer is (C).** There are 61 total people who play platform games. Of those 61 people, 19 of them play for 3–5 hours, so the probability is $\frac{19}{61}$.

6. **The correct answer is (D).** Situations that state there is no replacement, have an event that is dependent on the other. In this case, the second chosen marble is dependent on the marble that was chosen first because there will be one less marble in the bag and it must be a different color.

7. **The correct answer is (C).** There are 12 total fish caught using artificial bait. The number of bass caught out of those 12 is 5, so the probability is $\frac{5}{12}$.

8. **The correct answer is (A).** The probability of each type of song being played are independent of each other. The probability of an Electronic song being played is $\frac{1}{5}$ and the probability of a Pop song being played is $\frac{1}{5}$. The probability that an Electronic song and then a Pop song will be played is found by $\frac{1}{5} \times \frac{1}{5} = \frac{1}{25}$.

9. **The correct answer is (A).** The probability of each hypothesis is independent of the other. The probability of both events occurring can be found by
$$P(A \text{ and } B) = P(A) \times P(B) = \frac{5}{7} \times \frac{3}{4} = \frac{15}{28}$$

10. **The correct answer is (B).** The probability of correctly completing the marching steps correctly, given he has attended symphonic band can be found by
$$\frac{P(A \text{ and } B)}{P(B)} = \frac{\frac{3}{5}}{\frac{11}{12}} = \frac{3}{5} \times \frac{12}{11} = \frac{36}{55}.$$

DATA INTERPRETATION

Working with Data in Tables

Some SAT® questions ask you to solve mathematical problems based on data contained in tables. All such problems are based on problem-solving techniques that have already been reviewed. The trick when working with tables is to make certain that you select the correct data needed to solve the problem. Take your time reading each table so that you understand exactly what information the table contains. Carefully select data from the correct row and column. As you will see, things are even trickier when a problem involves more than one table.

In order to illustrate problem solving with tables, consider the two tables below. The three following questions are based on the data within these tables.

Paul, Mark, and Bob are computer salespeople. In addition to their regular salaries, they each receive a commission for each computer they sell. The number of computers that each salesperson sold during a particular week, as well as their commission amounts, is shown in the tables below.

NUMBER OF COMPUTERS SOLD

	Monday	Tuesday	Wednesday	Thursday	Friday
Paul	9	3	12	6	4
Mark	6	3	9	1	5
Bob	8	4	5	7	8

COMMISSION PER SALE

Paul	$15
Mark	$20
Bob	$25

> What is the total amount of the commissions that Bob earned over the entire week?

This problem only concerns Bob, so ignore the information for Mark and Paul. Over the course of the week, Bob sold $8 + 4 + 5 + 7 + 8 = 32$ computers. The second table tells us that Bob earns $25 per sale, so the total amount of his commission would be $25 \times 32 = 800.

> What is the total amount of commission money earned by Paul, Mark, and Bob on Thursday?

To solve this problem, focus only on what happened on Thursday. Ignore the data for the other four days. Be careful not to add the number of computers sold by the three people, since they each earn a different commission per sale.

- On Thursday, Paul sold 6 computers and earned a $15 commission for each computer sold, so Paul earned $15 \times 6 = 90.

- Mark sold 1 computer, so, based on his $20 commission, he earned $20.

- Bob sold 7 computers and earned a $25 commission per machine, so he made $25 \times 7 = 175.

- Overall, the amount of commission on Thursday is $90 + $20 + $175 = 285.

On what day did Paul and Mark earn the same amount in commission?

You can save yourself a lot of time if you look at the tables before you start to compute. Note that Mark's commission is larger than Paul's, and so the only way they could have earned the same amount is if Paul sold more computers than Mark. The only days that Paul sold more computers than Mark were Monday, Wednesday, and Thursday, so those are the only days that need to be considered.

- By observation, you can see that on Thursday Paul made much more in commission than Mark, so eliminate Thursday.

- On Monday, Paul earned $15 \times 9 = \$135$ and Mark earned $20 \times 6 = \$120$. This means that the answer must be Wednesday.

- To be certain, note that on Wednesday Paul earned $15 \times 12 = \$180$, and Mark earned $20 \times 9 = \$180$ also.

Correlation and Scatterplots

If two variables have a relationship such that when one variable changes, the other changes in a predictable way, the two variables are *correlated*. For example, there is a correlation between the number of hours an employee works each week and the amount of money the employee earns—the more hours the employee works, the more money the employee earns. Note that in this case, as the first variable increases, the second variable increases as well. These two variables are *positively correlated*.

Sometimes, when one variable increases, a second variable decreases. For example, the more that a store charges for a particular item, the fewer of that item will be sold. In this case, these two variables are *negatively correlated*.

Sometimes two variables are not correlated, that is, a change in one variable does not affect the other variable in any way. For example, the number of cans of soda that a person drinks each day is not correlated with the amount of money the person earns.

One way to determine whether two variables are correlated or not is to sketch a *scatterplot*. A scatterplot is a graph on which the *x*-axis represents the value of one variable and the *y*-axis represents the value of the other variable. Several values of one variable and the corresponding values of the other variable are measured and plotted on the graph:

- If the points appear to form a straight line, or are close to forming a straight line, then it is likely that the variables are correlated.

- If the line has a positive slope (rises up left to right), the variables are positively correlated.

- If the line has a negative slope (goes down left to right), the variables are negatively correlated.

- If the points on the scatterplot seem to be located more or less at random, then it is likely that the variables are not correlated.

Positive Correlation   Negative Correlation   No Correlation

It is rare that the points on a scatterplot will all lie exactly on the same line. However, if there is a strong correlation, it is likely that there will be a line that could be drawn on the scatterplot that comes close to all of the points. Statisticians call the line that comes the closest to all of the points on a scatterplot the "line of best fit." Without performing any computations, it is possible to visualize the location of the line of best fit, as the diagrams below show:

Which of the following slopes is the closest to the slope of the line of best fit for the scatterplot below?

(A) 3

(B) 1

(C) 0

(D) −1

Begin by sketching in the line of best fit in its approximate location.

This line has a negative slope, since it decreases from left to right. In addition, the slope appears to be about -1, because if you move one unit horizontally from a point on the line, you need to move one unit vertically downward to return to the line. **The correct answer is choice (D).**

Equation of Line of Best Fit

You may see questions that ask you to create a line of best fit and give the equation for this line. Again, there is some approximation involved in determining a line of best fit. Look at the scatterplot below. Imagine a line that would come closest to all the data points and includes an equal number of data points on either side of the line.

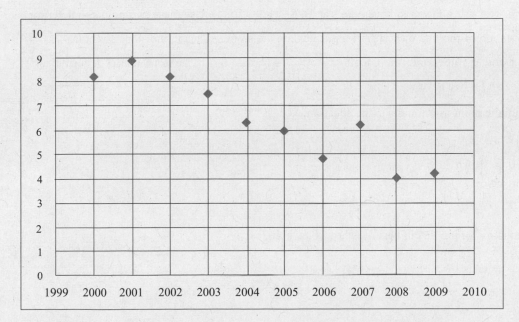

Notice the line of best fit below has 5 points above and 5 points below the line.

Note that the line of best fit does not have to cross any of the data points. It goes through the middle of the data and may not include any of the actual data points.

To determine the equation of the line of best fit, choose two points that lay on the line of best fit. You may have to approximate points if the line does not have points that are exactly on an intersection. The line appears to have points at (3, 8.2) and (10, 4). Use these two points to determine the equation of the line of best fit. First, calculate the slope, m, using the slope formula $\frac{y_1 - y_2}{x_1 - x_2}$. Plug x and y values into the equation: $\frac{8.2 - 4}{3 - 10} = \frac{4.2}{-7} = -0.6$. The slope-intercept formula $y = mx + b$. So far, we have $y = -0.6x + b$.

Plug in one point into x and y in the equation.

(10, 4):

$4 = -0.6(10) + b$

$4 = -6 + b$

$b = 10$

The equation of the line of best fit is: $y = -0.6x + 10$.

Making Predictions

Assume the same previous scatterplot has real-world data. The following scatterplot now shows the average number of books borrowed on a weekly basis for years 2000–2009 at a local library.

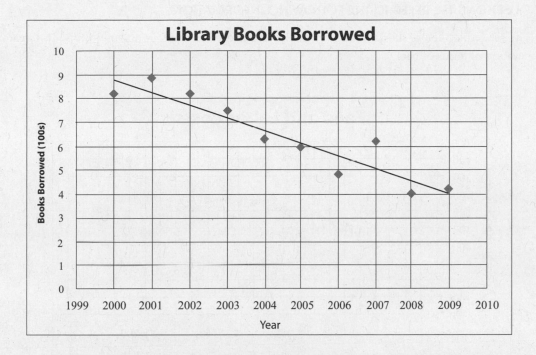

 If the trend continued, about how many books were borrowed in 2010?

To solve this problem, use the slope of the line to make predictions about data points that are not shown. According to the slope, the average number of books borrowed weekly goes down approximately $0.6 \times 100 = 60$ books every year. Multiply by 100 because, according to the title of the vertical axis, the numbers are in the 100s. The expected value for the number of books borrowed in 2009 was 400. The slope says we should expect that number to decrease by 60 every year, so you can predict that there were 340 books borrowed in 2010.

EXERCISES: DATA INTERPRETATION

> **Directions:** Work out each problem. Circle the letter of your choice.

QUESTIONS 1–3 REFER TO THE FOLLOWING INFORMATION.

The scatterplot below shows average monthly feed and labor costs in dollars to raise different numbers of heads of beef cattle.

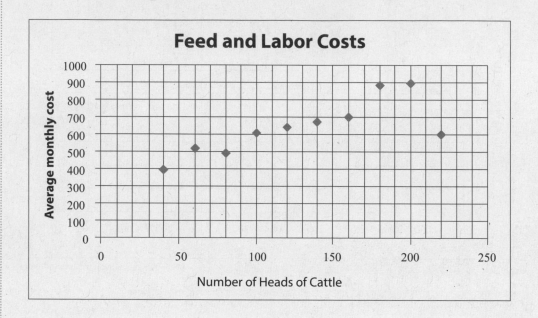

1. Which of the following is closest to the slope of a line of best fit for this data?

   (A) 200

   (B) $\dfrac{1}{2}$

   (C) $\dfrac{10}{9}$

   (D) 2

2. Based on the scatterplot, what is the equation of the line of best fit?

   (A) $y = 200x + 400$

   (B) $y = 2x + 320$

   (C) $y = 2x + 380$

   (D) $y = \dfrac{1}{2}x + 380$

3. If the trend continued, what would be the average monthly feed and labor costs to raise 500 heads of beef cattle?

   (A) $1,380.00

   (B) $1,000.00

   (C) $880.00

   (D) $600.00

QUESTIONS 4–6 REFER TO THE FOLLOWING INFORMATION.

Geographic Area	Attended college	Did not attend college	No response	TOTAL
northeast	72,404	68,350	29,542	170,296
northwest	88,960	125,487	48,960	263,407
southeast	115,488	96,541	65,880	277,909
southwest	79,880	65,874	13,840	159,594
TOTAL	356,732	356,252	158,222	871,206

A survey was conducted in different geographic areas of a large state, covering the entire state population, about whether people over the age of 30 attended college. The table above displays a summary of the survey results.

4. According to the table, for which group did the highest percentage of people report that they had attended college?

(A) northeast

(B) northwest

(C) southeast

(D) southwest

5. Of the people living in the northeast who reported that they did not attend college, 1,000 people were selected at random to do a follow-up survey where they were asked if they were interested in attending adult education classes. There were 665 people who said they were interested in attending adult education classes. Using the data from both the initial survey and the follow-up survey, which of the following is most likely to be an accurate statement?

(A) About 48,149 people living in the northeast who did not attend college would be interested in adult education classes.

(B) About 45,453 people living in the northeast who did not attend college would be interested in adult education classes.

(C) About 19,645 people living in the northeast who did not attend college would be interested in adult education classes.

(D) Most people in the state are not interested in taking adult education classes.

6. What is the relative frequency of the number of people who attended college statewide, according to the survey?

(A) 0.18

(B) 0.41

(C) 0.43

(D) 0.5

QUESTIONS 7–8 REFER TO THE FOLLOWING INFORMATION.

In this election, Haynes and Cogswell were the only ones who received votes.

	District A	District B	District C	District D
Cogswell	150	350	300	200
Haynes	100	200	450	150

7. What percent of the votes cast in District C did Haynes receive?

   (A) 40%

   (B) 45%

   (C) 60%

   (D) 65%

8. What is the ratio of the total number of votes received by Cogswell to the total number of votes received by Haynes?

   (A) 10:9

   (B) 5:4

   (C) 4:5

   (D) 9:10

9. The scatterplot below depicts the relationship between two variables, x and y. Which of the following best describes the line that best fits the data in the scatterplot?

   (A) The slope of the line of best fit is -3.

   (B) The slope of the line of best fit is -1.

   (C) The slope of the line of best fit is 1.

   (D) The slope of the line of best fit is 3.

10. Below is a scatterplot depicting the relationship between the variable a and the variable b. Which of the following best describes the relationship depicted in the graph?

   (A) There is a strong positive correlation between the two variables.

   (B) There is a strong negative correlation between the two variables.

   (C) The two variables are not correlated.

   (D) As the value of a increases, the value of b decreases.

ANSWER KEY AND EXPLANATIONS

1. D	3. A	5. B	7. C	9. E
2. C	4. D	6. B	8. B	10. C

1. **The correct answer is (D).** Use two points that would be on the line of best fit, which would look something like this:

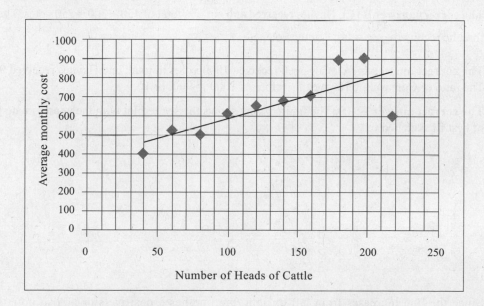

Choose 2 points on this line: (60, 500) and (160, 700) look like they lay on, or close to, the line.

Use these coordinates in the slope formula: $\dfrac{y_2 - y_1}{x_2 - x_1} = \dfrac{700 - 500}{160 - 60} = \dfrac{200}{100} = 2$.

2. **The correct answer is (C).** Using $m = 2$ as the slope (from Question 1), insert a set of xy coordinates into the point-slope formula $y = mx + $ b: $500 = (2)(60) + b$; $500 - 120 = b$; $b = 380$. This gives you the equation $y = 2x + 380$.

3. **The correct answer is (A).** Use the equation of the line of best fit to make predictions. Plug in 500 for the x value: $y = 2(500) + 380 = 1,000 + 380 = 1,380$.

4. **The correct answer is (D).** The percentage of people who attended college in the southwest region is $\dfrac{79,880}{159,594} \cong 0.5 = 50\%$. The percentages for the other areas are:

northeast: $\dfrac{72,404}{170,296} = 0.425 \cong 43\%$

northwest: $\dfrac{88,960}{263,407} = 0.337 \cong 34\%$

southeast: $\dfrac{115,488}{277,909} = 0.415 \cong 42\%$

5. **The correct answer is (B).** Extrapolating from the 2nd survey, we can predict that $\frac{665}{1,000} = 66.5\%$ of the total population of the northeast will likely be interested in taking adult education classes. Applying this to the total northeast population who reported that they did not attend college: $68,350 \times 0.665 = 45,453$ people in this population are likely to be interested in adult education classes.

6. **The correct answer is (B).** The relative frequency of college graduates in the survey is calculated by taking the total number of people who reported having attended college and dividing by the total number of people in the survey: $\frac{356,732}{871,206} = 0.409 \cong 0.41$.

7. **The correct answer is (C).** Haynes received 450 out of a total of $450 + 300 = 750$ votes. Therefore, he received $\frac{450}{750} = 60\%$ of the vote.

8. **The correct answer is (A).** Cogswell received 1000 votes in total, and Haynes received 900. The ratio of Cogswell to Haynes, therefore, is 1000 to 900, or 10:9.

9. **The correct answer is (D).** The figure below shows the scatterplot with the approximate line of best fit sketched in.

Since the line increases from left to right, the line has a positive slope. Also note that, if you move one unit horizontally away from a point on the line, you need to move approximately 3 units vertically to return to the line. Therefore, the slope of the line of best fit is approximately 3.

10. **The correct answer is (C).** The points on the scatterplot appear to be randomly arranged on the graph. This is an indication that the values of a and b are not correlated.

STATISTICS

Comparing Data Sets Using Shape, Center, and Spread

Statistics questions on the SAT® require using measures of central tendency, meaning the mean (average), median, and mode of a data set. You will need to be familiar with the shape, center, and spread of data. The shape of the data refers to the normal distribution curve, which we examine below. The center could be the average (arithmetic mean) or the median of the data values in the set. The spread is the range of the data, or the standard deviation of the data that describes the distance between values in a data set.

Data may be presented in tables, bar graphs, and other methods, so it is important to be familiar with different types of data presentation.

Standard Deviation—Normal Distribution

A standard deviation describes how far the data values in a set are from the mean, or how much they 'deviate' from the mean. The graphs below are both normal distribution curves. In the graph on the left, because much of the data clusters closely around the mean, there is a small standard deviation. In the graph on the right, because the data is more spread out, there is a large standard deviation. If these were sets of test scores for Class A and Class B on a math exam, most of the scores in Class A would be very close to the average score, but in Class B, the scores would be more varied.

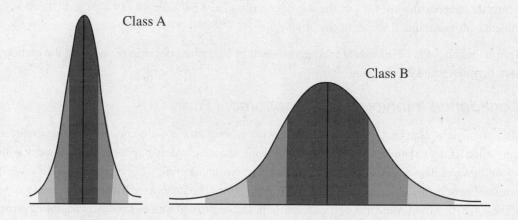

Class A

Class B

What You Really Need To Know About Standard Deviation

You won't have to calculate the standard deviation, but it is important to understand how to use it. If data has a normal distribution, the empirical rule states that:

- Approximately 68% of the data falls within 1 standard deviation of the mean.

- Approximately 95% of the data falls within 2 standard deviations of the mean.

- Approximately 99¾% of the data falls within 3 standard deviations of the mean.

Let's see how this works with a table of data. The table below lists the number of students enrolled in six different sections of algebra, A, B, C, D, E, and F, offered by a college. First calculate the mean.

	A	B	C	D	E	F
Number of Students	18	23	15	19	28	11

$$\text{mean} = \frac{18+23+15+19+28+11}{6} = \frac{114}{6} = 19$$

The mean is always in the middle. Here, it is 19, and each standard deviation is a distance of 5 from the mean of 19.

The standard deviation of this data set is given as 5. In this example, the standard deviation of 5 means that approximately 68% of the algebra sections have between 14 (19 − 5) and 24 (19 + 5) students, plus or minus 1 standard deviation.

Approximately 95% of the algebra sections lie within 2 standard deviations, meaning the sections have between 9 and 29 students.

Confidence Intervals and Measurement Errors

Measurement or sampling errors will usually occur when data cannot be collected about an entire population. If, for example, we are trying to determine the mean salary of people living in a city with 3.5 million people, we would probably use a smaller random sample of several hundred to several thousand people that was representative of the population. The difference between the mean salary of the actual population and that of the sample population is called a measurement or sampling error. The sampling error decreases as the sample size increases, because there is more data that should more accurately reflect the true population. Here's an example:

A packaging company is gathering data about how many oranges it can fit into a crate. It takes a sample of 36 crates out of a total shipment of 5,540 crates. The sample mean is 102 oranges with a sampling error of 6 oranges at a 95% confidence interval.

What does the confidence interval mean?

In this case, it means that based on the sample, you can be 95% confident that the true population mean for the entire shipment is between 102 − 6 and 102 + 6, or 96 and 108 oranges per crate.

A confidence interval tells you how close the sample mean is to the actual mean of the entire population.

Comparing Data Sets Using Mean and Standard Deviation

You may have two sets of data with similar means and ranges but different standard deviations. For the data set with the greater standard deviation, more of the data are farther from the mean.

Sample Question

A coach is deciding between 2 baseball players to recruit to his team. He is looking at player performance over the past 10 seasons. Both players have the same mean batting average of 0.270 and the same range of batting averages (0.080) over the past 10 seasons. However, Player A's batting averages have a higher standard deviation than Player B's batting averages. What does this indicate about each player?

(A) Player A is more likely to hit better than his mean batting average.

(B) Player B is more likely to hit better than his mean batting average.

(C) Player A's batting average is more erratic.

(D) Player B's batting average is more erratic.

A greater standard deviation in a data set means that the data values are more spread out, or erratic, meaning his performance varied more. Essentially, Player B's batting average is more dependable; he more frequently batted close to his batting average than did Player A. So, if the manager is looking for reliability, he may want to choose Player B for his team. **The correct answer is (C).**

Making Inferences Using Sample Data

Frequently a population is too large for every data value to be measured. Instead, a random sample of the population is used to make inferences about the true population.

Sample Question

An online retailer wants to determine the average dollar value of an order that it receives on a daily basis. Based on a random sample of 200 orders, the mean dollar value is $72.00 and the standard deviation is $5.00.

The normal distribution curve would look like this:

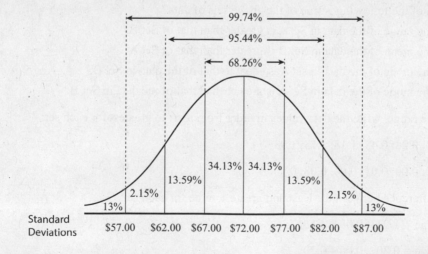

If the sample used is representative of the true population, what can be concluded about the true population of shoppers?

(A) The mean of the true population is $72.00.

(B) Most shoppers spend between $62.00 and $82.00.

(C) All shoppers spend between $57.00 and $87.00.

(D) The mode of the size of an order is $72.00.

Choice (B) is the best answer. Shoppers who spent between $62.00 and $82.00 fall within two standard deviations of the mean of the sample population. Approximately 95% of the shoppers fall within two standard deviations of the mean. Thus, it can be concluded that most shoppers spend between $62.00 and $82.00. Though the sample is representative, it does not entail that the mean of the true population is equal to the mean of the sample population, so choice (A) is incorrect. Approximately 99¾% of the population lies within 3 standard deviations of the mean, which, in this case, is between $57.00 and $87.00—but this is not all shoppers, so choice (C) is not fully supported. We don't know the mode of the data, so choice (D) is not correct. **The correct answer is (B).**

Comparing Data Sets Using Spread

The spread is simply the difference between the least and greatest value in a set.

Sample Question

Todd's meteorology class researched weekly precipitation in a tropical region during two 6-week periods. The data in Set A covers a period from January through mid-February, and the data in Set B is from July through mid-August. The results appear in the tables below.

Set A: Weeks 1–6 (January–February)					
0.43	1.73	1.93	0.28	0.08	1.18

Set B: Weeks 27–32 (July–August)					
0.20	0.01	0.00	0.08	0.04	0.00

Which of the following is true of the above sets of data?

(A) The range of the data in Set A is greater than that of Set B.

(B) The mean of the data in Set B is greater than that of Set A.

(C) The mode of the data in set A is equal to that of the data in Set B.

(D) The mode of the data in Set A is greater than that of the data in Set B.

To calculate range, write the data values in order from least to greatest for each set:

Set A: 0.08; 0.28; 0.43; 1.18; 1.73; 1.93

Set B: 0.00; 0.00; 0.01; 0.04; 0.08; 0.20

Find the difference between the least and greatest value for each set:

Set A: Range = 1.93 − 0.08 = 1.85

Set B: Range = 0.20 − 0.00 − 0.20

The range in Set A is greater. **The correct answer is (A).**

Comparing Data Sets Using Median and Mode

Using the same data sets about tropical precipitation, let's look at problems involving median and mode.

Sample Question

Set A: Weeks 3–8 (January–February)					
0.43	1.73	1.93	0.28	0.08	1.18

Set B: Weeks 29–34 (July–August)					
0.20	0.01	0.00	0.08	0.04	0.00

Which is true about the two sets of data above, Set A and Set B?

(A) The mode of Set A is greater than the mode of Set B.

(B) The mode of Set B is greater than the mode of Set A.

(C) The median of Set A is greater than the median of Set B.

(D) The median of Set B is greater than the median of Set A.

In this case, Set A does not have a mode, because there is no data value that appears more than once. So we cannot make any statements involving the mode of Set A.

Calculate the median of both sets of data. The median is the number in the middle of a data set when all the values are written in increasing order:

Set A: 0.08   0.28   0.43   1.18   1.73   1.93

Here the two middle numbers are 0.43 and 1.18, so we take their average:

Median of Set A: $\dfrac{0.43+1.18}{2}=\dfrac{1.61}{2}=0.805$

We perform the same set of calculations for set B:

Set B: 0.00   0.00   0.01   0.04   0.08   0.20

Median of Set B: $\dfrac{0.01+0.04}{2}=\dfrac{0.05}{2}=0.025$

From this we can see that the median of Set A is greater than the median of Set B. **The correct answer is (C).**

Evaluating Reports and Surveys

To evaluate a report about a set of data, it is important to consider the appropriateness of the data collection method.

Sample Question

A local politician wants to gauge how her constituents feel about the installation of a gas pipeline that will border her district. Which of the following would allow the politician to make a valid conclusion about the opinions of her constituents?

(A) Sending an electronic survey via e-mail

(B) Surveying people at several local movie theaters

(C) Surveying people at several local supermarkets

(D) Having people call in their opinion to a local radio show

Let's analyze each of these options. First is the e-mail survey in choice (A). This may seem like a good option, but does everyone in the district have an e-mail address? Will a representative group respond? Next, choice (B), is the option to survey people at local movie theaters. This may work, but it would exclude people who don't go to the movies on a regular basis. Choice (C) is probably best because everyone eats, and the probability is high that most, if not all, people in the politician's district go to the supermarket at some point. Finally, choice (D), is not correct, because few people will listen to any particular radio show, and even fewer will voluntarily call to voice their opinion. **The correct answer is (C).**

When considering whether the data in a report is representative of a population, it is important to consider the demographics of the population being studied. Their habits, behaviors, and perhaps incomes will influence their decisions and even their ability to be included in the report. The type of survey that will include the widest range of habits, behaviors, and incomes of the people being studied is likely the most representative.

EXERCISES: STATISTICS

Directions: Work out each problem. Circle the letter next to your choice.

1. The tables below show the number of employees in two different groups of an organization in different age ranges.

PRODUCTION	
Age Range	**Number of Employees**
20–24	4
25–29	8
30–34	25
35–39	19
40–44	17

DESIGN	
Age Range	**Number of Employees**
20–24	2
25–29	4
30–34	6
35–39	33
40–44	38

Which of the following conclusions can be made about the data above?

(A) The range of ages is greater in production than in design.

(B) The range of ages is greater in design than in production.

(C) The median age is greater in production than in design.

(D) The median age is greater in design than in production.

2. A nursery wants to know if a certain fertilizer is helping their rose bushes grow more roses per bush. The nursery uses the fertilizer on one plot, Plot A, of rose bushes but does not use fertilizer on another plot, Plot B. All the rose bushes in both plots were planted at the same time. The charts below show the number of flowers on each bush for the two plots.

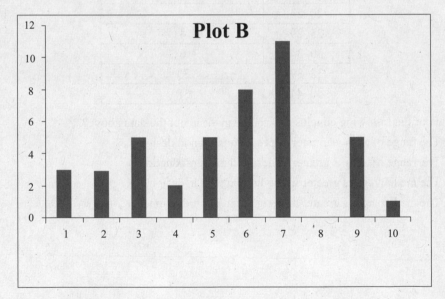

Which of the following conclusions could be logically drawn based on the data?

(A) The mean number of roses in Plot A is greater, so plot A likely benefitted from the fertilizer.

(B) The mean number of roses in Plot B is greater; so plot B likely benefitted from NOT having the fertilizer.

(C) The fertilizer had no effect on the rose bushes.

(D) There is not enough information to make any conclusion.

3. If two 90% confidence intervals are of different sizes, then the smaller interval provides a

   (A) more precise estimate of the population mean.

   (B) less precise estimate of the population mean.

   (C) larger standard deviation.

   (D) smaller standard deviation.

4. A property development company wants to see if a new movie complex would be a profitable venture in a suburban area. The location is 15 miles away from an existing movie complex in a region with approximately 650,000 residents with a mean age of 48. The company conducts a survey of 200 people coming out of a midnight movie on a Wednesday evening to see what they think of the idea.

   What can be said about this data collection method?

   (A) The population surveyed is likely a good representative population.

   (B) The survey probably didn't include movie theater employees.

   (C) The sample is likely skewed toward people younger than the mean.

   (D) The sample is likely skewed toward out-of-towners.

5. A coffee retailer kept track of number of customers during the same 6-hour period over the course of two days and recorded them in the table below.

	1 p.m.	2 p.m.	3 p.m.	4 p.m.	5 p.m.	6 p.m.
Sunday	24	22	28	35	38	35
Monday	11	18	18	22	44	30

   Which of the following is a valid conclusion to be drawn from the data in the tables?

   (A) The coffee shop is busier later in the day.

   (B) There are probably never more than 50 customers in the coffee shop.

   (C) The average number of customers is higher on the weekends than during the week.

   (D) The range of data on the two days is equal.

6. A farmer weighs eggs produced by his chickens. He samples 36 eggs from a population of over 2,000 eggs. The sample mean weight is 63.8 grams, with a sampling error of 9.2 grams at a 90% confidence interval. Which of the following is true, based on the sample?

   (A) You can be 90% confident that another sample will have a mean for the eggs between 54.6 and 73 grams.

   (B) You can be 90% confident that the true population mean for the eggs is between 54.6 and 73 grams.

   (C) You can be 90% confident that the standard deviation of each measurement is 9.2 grams.

   (D) You can be 90% confident that the true population mean is 63.8 grams.

7. Using the same data from question 6, if you calculate a 90% confidence interval for the mean given a sample size of 72 eggs, what is the effect?

   (A) It increases the sample mean.

   (B) It decreases the sample mean.

   (C) It decreases the margin of error.

   (D) It increases the margin of error.

8. The margin of error is +/– 20 points for a 95% confidence interval for a given set of data. The researcher in charge of the data wants to report a lower margin of error. Which of the following would give a true representation of the data and a lower margin of error?

   (A) Increase the confidence level to 98%.

   (B) Decrease the confidence level to 90%.

   (C) Increase the sample size.

   (D) Decrease the sample size.

9. A poll was taken by the local university to determine which candidate is most likely to win the upcoming congressional race. The poll was conducted by randomly talking to people walking downtown in the largest city of the congressional district. Which of the following best describes the poll?

   (A) The poll is a representative sample because it was done in the largest city in the district.

   (B) The poll is a representative sample because it was done randomly.

   (C) The poll is not a representative sample because it was done only in the largest city in the district.

   (D) The poll is not a representative sample because it was done randomly.

10. The double occupancy room rates at 40 five-star hotels in Los Angeles is normally distributed with a mean of $280 and a standard deviation of $48.25. Which is the range of values, in dollars, around the mean that includes 95% of the room rates?

    (A) $280.00–$328.25

    (B) $231.75–$280.00

    (C) $231.75–$328.25

    (D) $183.50–$376.50

ANSWER KEY AND EXPLANATIONS

1. D	3. D	5. A	7. C	9. C
2. A	4. C	6. B	8. B	10. D

1. **The correct answer is (D).** We don't have exact ages, which is why we can't conclude anything about the range of ages and can eliminate choices (A) and (B). However, if we wrote all the ages of the employees by age group, the median of the data for the design group is in the 35–39 age range. There are 73 employees in the production group, so the median age is the 37th data value when the ages are written in ascending order, which would be in the 30–34 age range. There are 83 employees in the design group. The median age is the 42nd data value, which falls in the 35–39 age range. Thus the median age for the design group is higher.

2. **The correct answer is (A).** First focus on the mean number of roses on the bushes in Plot A:

$$\frac{6+6+4+5+9+5+5+8+5+4}{10} = \frac{57}{10}$$
$$= 5.7$$

Then, look at those in Plot B:

$$\frac{3+3+5+2+5+8+11+0+5+1}{10} = \frac{43}{10}$$
$$= 4.3$$

On average the bushes in Plot A grew more roses so thus likely benefitted from the fertilizer.

3. **The correct answer is (D).** A 90% confidence interval means that those who conducted the survey have proved with 90% precision that the estimate for the mean is within a given range, so eliminate choices (A) and (B). If the range of a confidence interval is less, then the standard deviation is also less, so choice (D) is correct.

4. **The correct answer is (C).** People who are out after midnight are probably younger than the mean age, since they are not likely to be getting up early after a late night movie. It is probably not representative of the general population. There is no reason to believe the sample is skewed toward out-of-towners, choice (D), and 200 people is probably a good sample size, so choice (A) is incorrect. Whether the survey included movie theater employees, choice (B), is not relevant to the validity of the data.

5. **The correct answer is (A).** Given that on both days, the number of customers at 5 p.m. and 6 p.m. is more than twice the number of customers at 1 p.m. and 2 p.m. It is difficult to conclude that there are never more than 50 customers in the shop, as choice (B) says, because we don't have enough data. As for choice (C), while the mean for Sunday is higher than the mean for Monday, the sample size of 2 days is not enough to conclude about the weekends versus the weekdays in general. The range of the two data sets are not equal to each other, so choice (D) is incorrect.

6. **The correct answer is (B).** The confidence interval gives us the ability to estimate a range for the true mean of the population, not for a sample mean.

7. **The correct answer is (C).** The mean will likely be different, but there is no reason to believe it will only increase or only decrease. But, increasing sample size decreases the margin of error.

8. **The correct answer is (B).** The data has already been collected, so increasing the sample size is not possible without redoing the study, and it would not be an accurate representation of this data. Decreasing the confidence level would decrease the margin of error.

9. **The correct answer is (C).** A representative sample should allow for random selection within the entire population, not just random selection from one part of the population.

10. **The correct answer is (D).** Ninety-five percent of the population falls within 2 standard deviations of the mean, meaning within $48.25 × 2 = $96.50 of the mean price of $280.00 and 280.00 + 96.50 = 376.50 and 280.00 – 96.50 = 183.50.

SUMMING IT UP

- Not all problems that deal with averages will ask you to solve for the average of a set of quantities.

- The trick when working with tables is to make sure you select the correct data needed to solve the problem.

- Take your time reading each table.

- Observe trends with scatter plots, and use lines or curves to predict unknown values.

- Read data representations carefully when comparing data sets.

- Pay attention to sampling methods when you evaluate survey data.

PART VII

FIVE PRACTICE TESTS

Preface to the Practice Tests

chapter 14

OVERVIEW

- Simulate test-taking conditions
- Timing drills can help when you are short on time
- Summing it up

The practice tests in this book make up one of the most important parts of your SAT® preparation. Use them as benchmarks as you work through the other chapters in this book. Each test gives you a great opportunity to gauge your progress and focus your ongoing study. Together, the tests map the growth of your skills and demonstrate your SAT® readiness. And, when you take the practice exams under simulated test-taking conditions, they give you a wonderful opportunity to adjust to the test-taking environment. When you enter the testing room, you'll know what to expect—and you'll be ready to score high on the exam.

SIMULATE TEST-TAKING CONDITIONS

Above and beyond everything else, the five practice exams in this part of the book help you prepare for the experience of taking a timed, standardized test. Taking these tests will improve your familiarity with the SAT®, reduce your number of careless errors, and increase your overall level of confidence. To make sure that you get the most out of this practice, you should do everything in your power to simulate actual test-taking conditions. The following sections outline the best methods for simulating testing conditions when you work through the practice exams.

Find a Block of Time

Because the SAT® is administered in one long block of time, the best way to simulate test-taking conditions is to take an entire practice exam in one sitting. This means that you should set aside 3½–4 hours of consecutive time to take the practice tests.

If you find it difficult to find approximately 4 quiet hours at home, maybe take the test in the library. If you decide to take a test at home, take precautions. Turn off the ringer on all nearby phones, ask your parents to hold your calls, and convince siblings to stay out of your room. Easier said than done, right? Although infrequent interruptions won't completely invalidate your testing experience, you should try to avoid them.

Work at a Desk and Wear a Watch

Don't take a practice test while you are lounging on your bed. After all, the SAT® proctors won't let you take the test lying down! Clear off sufficient space on a desk or table to work comfortably. Wear a watch to properly administer the sections under timed conditions. Or use a timer. The time for each section is marked on the section, so check the beginning of each section and set your timer or your watch for that amount of time.

You are not allowed to explore other sections on the test while you are supposed to be working on a particular one. So when you take your practice tests, don't look ahead or back. Take the full time to complete each section.

Practice on a Weekend Morning

Since the SAT® is typically administered at 8:30 a.m. on Saturday (or Sunday for religious observers), why not take the exam at the exact same time on a weekend morning? You should be most energetic in the morning anyway. If you are not a morning person, now is a good time to become one since that's when you'll have to take the actual SAT®! When you take the practice test, allow yourself two breaks. Give yourself a 5-minute break after Section 2: Writing and Language Test to run to the bathroom, eat a snack, and resharpen your pencils. You can take another 5-minute break after Section 4: Math Test—Calculator.

Remember that your goal is to take these practice tests in as true an environment as possible so that you're prepared to take the real SAT®. You will be accustomed to sitting for a long period of time, but you will get two breaks. This knowledge will make you considerably less anxious on test day.

The following table puts all of the SAT® section times in a one-stop format, so you can refer to it often when planning your SAT® study time.

Section	Number of Questions	Time Allowed
Reading	52	65 minutes
Writing and Language	44	35 minutes
Math Test—No Calculator	20	25 minutes
Math Test—Calculator	38	55 minutes
Essay		50 minutes

SUMMING IT UP

If you are going to take a full practice examination, try to simulate test-taking conditions by doing the following:

- To take a full-length practice test, you'll need approximately 4 quiet hours.

- Work at a desk and wear a watch when you take the practice exams.

- If temptation may lead you to sneak a peak at the answers during the practice exam, cover them up before you start the test.

- Whenever possible, take the full practice tests on weekend mornings.

Practice Test 1

On test day, you will see these important reminders on the first page of your SAT® test booklet:

- You must use a No. 2 pencil when taking the test; you may not use a pen or mechanical pencil.

- You may not share any questions with anyone. This is considered a violation of College Board's "Test Security and Fairness" policies, and it could cause your scores to be canceled.

- You are not permitted to take the test booklet out of the testing room.

In addition to filling in your name and Test Center information on your answer sheet, you'll be asked to fill in two different codes that will be on your test booklet. Each test booklet has a unique code, and there will be a grid-in form to fill in with your "TEST ID" and "FORM CODE" letters and numbers.

The general directions for the test will look something like this:

- You may only work on one section at a time.

- If you complete a section before time is called, check your work on that section only. You are not permitted to work on any other section.

The directions for marking your answers will likely include the following recommendations:

- Mark your answer sheet properly—be sure to <u>completely</u> fill in the answer bubble.

- Be careful to mark only one answer for each question.

- Don't make any stray marks on the answer sheet.

- If you need to erase your answer, make sure you do so completely.

- Be sure to use the answer spaces that correspond to the question numbers.

You will be able to use your test booklet for scratch work, but you won't get credit for any work done in your test booklet. When time is called at the end of each section, you will not be permitted to transfer answers from your test booklet to your answer sheet.

Any information, ideas, or opinions presented in any of the passages you will see on the redesigned SAT® that have been taken from other sources or published material do not represent the opinions of the College Board.

Scoring on the SAT® is as follows:

- You will receive one point for each correct answer.

- You will not lose points for wrong answers, so you should attempt to answer every question even if you aren't completely sure of the correct answer.

Your testing supervisor will announce when to open the test booklet, so be sure to wait until you're told to do so. For the purposes of this practice test, be sure you have a timer to set for 65 minutes for the Section 1: Reading Test.

The answer sheets for each test section, including lined paper for the essay, appear on the next five pages. Following the Answer Key and Explanations for this Practice Test, you will find details on how to score your work.

ANSWER SHEET PRACTICE TEST 1

Section 1: Reading Test

1. Ⓐ Ⓑ Ⓒ Ⓓ   12. Ⓐ Ⓑ Ⓒ Ⓓ   23. Ⓐ Ⓑ Ⓒ Ⓓ   33. Ⓐ Ⓑ Ⓒ Ⓓ   43. Ⓐ Ⓑ Ⓒ Ⓓ

2. Ⓐ Ⓑ Ⓒ Ⓓ   13. Ⓐ Ⓑ Ⓒ Ⓓ   24. Ⓐ Ⓑ Ⓒ Ⓓ   34. Ⓐ Ⓑ Ⓒ Ⓓ   44. Ⓐ Ⓑ Ⓒ Ⓓ

3. Ⓐ Ⓑ Ⓒ Ⓓ   14. Ⓐ Ⓑ Ⓒ Ⓓ   25. Ⓐ Ⓑ Ⓒ Ⓓ   35. Ⓐ Ⓑ Ⓒ Ⓓ   45. Ⓐ Ⓑ Ⓒ Ⓓ

4. Ⓐ Ⓑ Ⓒ Ⓓ   15. Ⓐ Ⓑ Ⓒ Ⓓ   26. Ⓐ Ⓑ Ⓒ Ⓓ   36. Ⓐ Ⓑ Ⓒ Ⓓ   46. Ⓐ Ⓑ Ⓒ Ⓓ

5. Ⓐ Ⓑ Ⓒ Ⓓ   16. Ⓐ Ⓑ Ⓒ Ⓓ   27. Ⓐ Ⓑ Ⓒ Ⓓ   37. Ⓐ Ⓑ Ⓒ Ⓓ   47. Ⓐ Ⓑ Ⓒ Ⓓ

6. Ⓐ Ⓑ Ⓒ Ⓓ   17. Ⓐ Ⓑ Ⓒ Ⓓ   28. Ⓐ Ⓑ Ⓒ Ⓓ   38. Ⓐ Ⓑ Ⓒ Ⓓ   48. Ⓐ Ⓑ Ⓒ Ⓓ

7. Ⓐ Ⓑ Ⓒ Ⓓ   18. Ⓐ Ⓑ Ⓒ Ⓓ   29. Ⓐ Ⓑ Ⓒ Ⓓ   39. Ⓐ Ⓑ Ⓒ Ⓓ   49. Ⓐ Ⓑ Ⓒ Ⓓ

8. Ⓐ Ⓑ Ⓒ Ⓓ   19. Ⓐ Ⓑ Ⓒ Ⓓ   30. Ⓐ Ⓑ Ⓒ Ⓓ   40. Ⓐ Ⓑ Ⓒ Ⓓ   50. Ⓐ Ⓑ Ⓒ Ⓓ

9. Ⓐ Ⓑ Ⓒ Ⓓ   20. Ⓐ Ⓑ Ⓒ Ⓓ   31. Ⓐ Ⓑ Ⓒ Ⓓ   41. Ⓐ Ⓑ Ⓒ Ⓓ   51. Ⓐ Ⓑ Ⓒ Ⓓ

10. Ⓐ Ⓑ Ⓒ Ⓓ   21. Ⓐ Ⓑ Ⓒ Ⓓ   32. Ⓐ Ⓑ Ⓒ Ⓓ   42. Ⓐ Ⓑ Ⓒ Ⓓ   52. Ⓐ Ⓑ Ⓒ Ⓓ

11. Ⓐ Ⓑ Ⓒ Ⓓ   22. Ⓐ Ⓑ Ⓒ Ⓓ

Section 2: Writing and Language Test

1. Ⓐ Ⓑ Ⓒ Ⓓ   10. Ⓐ Ⓑ Ⓒ Ⓓ   19. Ⓐ Ⓑ Ⓒ Ⓓ   28. Ⓐ Ⓑ Ⓒ Ⓓ   37. Ⓐ Ⓑ Ⓒ Ⓓ

2. Ⓐ Ⓑ Ⓒ Ⓓ   11. Ⓐ Ⓑ Ⓒ Ⓓ   20. Ⓐ Ⓑ Ⓒ Ⓓ   29. Ⓐ Ⓑ Ⓒ Ⓓ   38. Ⓐ Ⓑ Ⓒ Ⓓ

3. Ⓐ Ⓑ Ⓒ Ⓓ   12. Ⓐ Ⓑ Ⓒ Ⓓ   21. Ⓐ Ⓑ Ⓒ Ⓓ   30. Ⓐ Ⓑ Ⓒ Ⓓ   39. Ⓐ Ⓑ Ⓒ Ⓓ

4. Ⓐ Ⓑ Ⓒ Ⓓ   13. Ⓐ Ⓑ Ⓒ Ⓓ   22. Ⓐ Ⓑ Ⓒ Ⓓ   31. Ⓐ Ⓑ Ⓒ Ⓓ   40. Ⓐ Ⓑ Ⓒ Ⓓ

5. Ⓐ Ⓑ Ⓒ Ⓓ   14. Ⓐ Ⓑ Ⓒ Ⓓ   23. Ⓐ Ⓑ Ⓒ Ⓓ   32. Ⓐ Ⓑ Ⓒ Ⓓ   41. Ⓐ Ⓑ Ⓒ Ⓓ

6. Ⓐ Ⓑ Ⓒ Ⓓ   15. Ⓐ Ⓑ Ⓒ Ⓓ   24. Ⓐ Ⓑ Ⓒ Ⓓ   33. Ⓐ Ⓑ Ⓒ Ⓓ   42. Ⓐ Ⓑ Ⓒ Ⓓ

7. Ⓐ Ⓑ Ⓒ Ⓓ   16. Ⓐ Ⓑ Ⓒ Ⓓ   25. Ⓐ Ⓑ Ⓒ Ⓓ   34. Ⓐ Ⓑ Ⓒ Ⓓ   43. Ⓐ Ⓑ Ⓒ Ⓓ

8. Ⓐ Ⓑ Ⓒ Ⓓ   17. Ⓐ Ⓑ Ⓒ Ⓓ   26. Ⓐ Ⓑ Ⓒ Ⓓ   35. Ⓐ Ⓑ Ⓒ Ⓓ   44. Ⓐ Ⓑ Ⓒ Ⓓ

9. Ⓐ Ⓑ Ⓒ Ⓓ   18. Ⓐ Ⓑ Ⓒ Ⓓ   27. Ⓐ Ⓑ Ⓒ Ⓓ   36. Ⓐ Ⓑ Ⓒ Ⓓ

Section 3: Math Test—No Calculator

1. Ⓐ Ⓑ Ⓒ Ⓓ   4. Ⓐ Ⓑ Ⓒ Ⓓ   7. Ⓐ Ⓑ Ⓒ Ⓓ   10. Ⓐ Ⓑ Ⓒ Ⓓ   13. Ⓐ Ⓑ Ⓒ Ⓓ
2. Ⓐ Ⓑ Ⓒ Ⓓ   5. Ⓐ Ⓑ Ⓒ Ⓓ   8. Ⓐ Ⓑ Ⓒ Ⓓ   11. Ⓐ Ⓑ Ⓒ Ⓓ   14. Ⓐ Ⓑ Ⓒ Ⓓ
3. Ⓐ Ⓑ Ⓒ Ⓓ   6. Ⓐ Ⓑ Ⓒ Ⓓ   9. Ⓐ Ⓑ Ⓒ Ⓓ   12. Ⓐ Ⓑ Ⓒ Ⓓ   15. Ⓐ Ⓑ Ⓒ Ⓓ

16.   17.   18.   19.   20.

(grid-in bubble grids for questions 16–20, each with digits 0–9)

Section 4: Math Test—Calculator

1. Ⓐ Ⓑ Ⓒ Ⓓ   7. Ⓐ Ⓑ Ⓒ Ⓓ   13. Ⓐ Ⓑ Ⓒ Ⓓ   19. Ⓐ Ⓑ Ⓒ Ⓓ   25. Ⓐ Ⓑ Ⓒ Ⓓ
2. Ⓐ Ⓑ Ⓒ Ⓓ   8. Ⓐ Ⓑ Ⓒ Ⓓ   14. Ⓐ Ⓑ Ⓒ Ⓓ   20. Ⓐ Ⓑ Ⓒ Ⓓ   26. Ⓐ Ⓑ Ⓒ Ⓓ
3. Ⓐ Ⓑ Ⓒ Ⓓ   9. Ⓐ Ⓑ Ⓒ Ⓓ   15. Ⓐ Ⓑ Ⓒ Ⓓ   21. Ⓐ Ⓑ Ⓒ Ⓓ   27. Ⓐ Ⓑ Ⓒ Ⓓ
4. Ⓐ Ⓑ Ⓒ Ⓓ   10. Ⓐ Ⓑ Ⓒ Ⓓ   16. Ⓐ Ⓑ Ⓒ Ⓓ   22. Ⓐ Ⓑ Ⓒ Ⓓ   28. Ⓐ Ⓑ Ⓒ Ⓓ
5. Ⓐ Ⓑ Ⓒ Ⓓ   11. Ⓐ Ⓑ Ⓒ Ⓓ   17. Ⓐ Ⓑ Ⓒ Ⓓ   23. Ⓐ Ⓑ Ⓒ Ⓓ   29. Ⓐ Ⓑ Ⓒ Ⓓ
6. Ⓐ Ⓑ Ⓒ Ⓓ   12. Ⓐ Ⓑ Ⓒ Ⓓ   18. Ⓐ Ⓑ Ⓒ Ⓓ   24. Ⓐ Ⓑ Ⓒ Ⓓ   30. Ⓐ Ⓑ Ⓒ Ⓓ

31.   32.   33.   34.   35.

(grid-in bubble grids for questions 31–35, each with digits 0–9)

answer sheet

36.

	/	/	
.	.	.	.
	0	0	0
1	1	1	1
2	2	2	2
3	3	3	3
4	4	4	4
5	5	5	5
6	6	6	6
7	7	7	7
8	8	8	8
9	9	9	9

37.

	/	/	
.	.	.	.
	0	0	0
1	1	1	1
2	2	2	2
3	3	3	3
4	4	4	4
5	5	5	5
6	6	6	6
7	7	7	7
8	8	8	8
9	9	9	9

38.

	/	/	
.	.	.	.
	0	0	0
1	1	1	1
2	2	2	2
3	3	3	3
4	4	4	4
5	5	5	5
6	6	6	6
7	7	7	7
8	8	8	8
9	9	9	9

Section 5: Essay

_____

_____

_____

_____

_____

_____

_____

_____

_____

_____

_____

_____

_____

_____

_____

_____

_____

_____

_____

answer sheet

SECTION 1: READING TEST

65 Minutes • 52 Questions

TURN TO SECTION 1 OF YOUR ANSWER SHEET TO ANSWER THE QUESTIONS IN THIS SECTION.

Directions: Each passage (or pair of passages) in this section is followed by a number of multiple-choice questions. After reading each passage, select the best answer to each question based on what is stated or implied in the passage or passages and in any supplementary material, such as a table, graph, chart, or photograph.

QUESTIONS 1–10 ARE BASED ON THE FOLLOWING PASSAGE.

The following passage has been taken from the "The Bride Comes to Yellow Sky," by Stephen Crane. It is a western short story that was first published in 1898. The protagonist is Jack Potter, who returns to the town of Yellow Sky with his bride.

The great Pullman was whirling onward with such dignity of motion that a glance from the window seemed simply
Line to prove that the plains of Texas were
5 pouring eastward. Vast flats of green grass, dull-hued spaces of mesquite and cactus, little groups of frame houses, woods of light and tender trees, all were sweeping into the east, sweeping over the
10 horizon, a precipice.

A newly married pair had boarded this coach at San Antonio. The man's face was reddened from many days in the wind and sun, and a direct result of his new black
15 clothes was that his brick-colored hands were constantly performing in a most conscious fashion. From time to time he looked down respectfully at his attire. He sat with a hand on each knee, like a man
20 waiting in a barber's shop. The glances he devoted to other passengers were furtive and shy.

The bride was not pretty, nor was she very young. She wore a dress of
25 blue cashmere, with small reservations of velvet here and there, and with steel buttons abounding. She continually twisted her head to regard her puff sleeves, very stiff, straight, and high.
30 They embarrassed her. It was quite apparent that she had cooked, and that she expected to cook, dutifully. The blushes caused by the careless scrutiny of some passengers as she had entered the car
35 were strange to see upon this plain, under-class countenance, which was drawn in placid, almost emotionless lines.

They were evidently very happy. "Ever been in a parlor-car before?" he asked,
40 smiling with delight.

"No," she answered; "I never was. It's fine, ain't it?"

"Great! And then after a while we'll go forward to the diner, and get a big
45 layout. Finest meal in the world. Charge a dollar."

"Oh, do they?" cried the bride. "Charge a dollar? Why, that's too much—for us—ain't it Jack?"

50 "Not this trip, anyhow," he answered bravely. "We're going to go the whole thing."

Later he explained to her about the trains. "You see, it's a thousand miles
55 from one end of Texas to the other; and this train runs right across it, and never stops but for four times." He had the pride of an owner. He pointed out to her the dazzling fittings of the coach,
60 and in truth her eyes opened wider as she contemplated the sea-green figured velvet, the shining brass, silver, and glass, the wood that gleamed as darkly brilliant as the surface of a pool of oil. At one end
65 a bronze figure sturdily held a support for a separated chamber, and at convenient places on the ceiling were frescoes in olive and silver.

To the minds of the pair, their
70 surroundings reflected the glory of their marriage that morning in San Antonio.

This was the environment of their new estate; and the man's face in particular
Line beamed with an elation that made him
75 appear ridiculous to the negro porter. This individual at times surveyed them from afar with an amused and superior grin. On other occasions he bullied them with skill in ways that did not make it exactly
80 plain to them that they were being bullied. He subtly used all the manners of the most unconquerable kind of snobbery. He oppressed them, but of this oppression they had small knowledge, and they
85 speedily forgot that infrequently a number of travelers covered them with stares of derisive enjoyment. Historically, there was supposed to be something infinitely humorous in their situation.

1 The passage might best be described as

(A) an analysis of a man's acceptance of his social status.

(B) an account of a couple's anticipation of married life.

(C) a description of train travel in nineteenth-century Texas.

(D) a criticism of class consciousness in the nineteenth century.

2 It can be inferred from the passage that Jack

(A) wants to impress his new bride.

(B) is likely a farmhand or rancher.

(C) is used to being treated as an inferior.

(D) wants to change his station in life.

3 Which choice provides the best evidence for the answer to the previous question?

(A) Lines 17–20 ("From time … barber's shop.")

(B) Lines 23–30 ("The bride … embarrassed her.")

(C) Lines 43–52 ("'Great! … whole thing.")

(D) Lines 69–75 ("To the … negro porter.")

4 As used in line 2, "dignity" most nearly means

(A) splendor.

(B) respectability.

(C) superiority.

(D) gracefulness.

5 Jack and his bride might best be described as

(A) firm and resolute in their decisions.

(B) nervous and fearful about their trip.

(C) awkward and self-conscious in the setting.

(D) amazed and bewildered by the landscape.

6 Which choice provides the best evidence for the answer to the previous question?

(A) Lines 5–10 ("Vast flats … precipice.")

(B) Lines 17–22 ("From time … furtive and shy.)

(C) Lines 41–46 ("'No,' she … a dollar'.")

(D) Lines 69–75 ("To the … negro porter")

7 In lines 32–37 ("The blushes … emotionless lines."), why does the narrator note that the bride's blushing seemed so out of place on her face?

(A) To emphasize the degree to which other passengers are staring

(B) To express the bride's extreme happiness with her marriage

(C) To communicate that the bride is lacking in self-confidence

(D) To underscore that the bride is strikingly unattractive

8 As used in line 73, "estate" most nearly means

(A) project.

(B) interests.

(C) property.

(D) standing.

9 In lines 75–87 ("This individual … derisive enjoyment."), the narrator maintains that the

(A) porter mocks the couple, making Jack and his bride believe they are being catered to.

(B) couple barely notices the contemptuous way they are treated by the porter.

(C) porter is openly hostile to the couple, making the trip painful for them.

(D) couple has become used to the rude behavior of the porter.

10 What is the main rhetorical effect of lines 14–18 ("and a … his attire")?

(A) To illustrate how nervous and awkward the groom is

(B) To show how much the groom is used to using his hands

(C) To convey how unaccustomed the groom is to wearing dress clothes

(D) To show how happy the groom is about being married

QUESTIONS 11–21 ARE BASED ON THE FOLLOWING PASSAGE.

The following passage has been taken from American Ornithology by Alexander Wilson, a Scottish-American naturalist. Dubbed "the Father of American Ornithology," Wilson is regarded as the greatest American ornithologist after Audubon. His nine-volume American Ornithology was published between 1808 and 1814.

About the twenty-fifth of April
the Hummingbird usually arrives in
Pennsylvania; and about the tenth of May
Line begins to build its nest. This is generally
5 fixed on the upper side of a horizontal
branch, not among the twigs, but on
the body of the branch itself. Yet I have
known instances where it was attached
by the side to an old moss-grown trunk;
10 and others where it was fastened on a
strong rank stalk, or weed, in the garden;
but these cases are rare. In the woods it
very often chooses a white oak sapling to
build on; and in the orchard, or garden,
15 selects a pear tree for that purpose. The
branch is seldom more than ten feet from
the ground. The nest is about an inch in
diameter, and as much in depth. A very
complete one is now lying before me,
20 and the materials of which it is composed
are as follows: —The outward coat is
formed of small pieces of bluish grey
lichen that vegetates on old trees and
fences, thickly glued on with the saliva of
25 the bird, giving firmness and consistency
to the whole, as well as keeping out
moisture. Within this are thick matted
layers of the fine wings of certain flying
seeds, closely laid together; and lastly, the
30 downy substance from the great mullein,
and from the stalks of the common fern,
lines the whole. The base of the nest is
continued round the stem of the branch,
to which it closely adheres; and, when
35 viewed from below, appears a mere
mossy knot or accidental protuberance.
The eggs are two, pure white, and of
equal thickness at both ends. … On a
person's approaching their nest, the little
40 proprietors dart around with a humming
sound, passing frequently within a few
inches of one's head; and should the
young be newly hatched, the female will
resume her place on the nest even while
45 you stand within a yard or two of the
spot. The precise period of incubation I
am unable to give; but the young are in
the habit, a short time before they leave
the nest, of thrusting their bills into the
50 mouths of their parents, and sucking
what they have brought them. I never
could perceive that they carried them any
animal food; tho, from circumstances that
will presently be mentioned, I think it
55 highly probable they do. As I have found
their nest with eggs so late as the twelfth
of July, I do not doubt but that they

GO TO THE NEXT PAGE

Line

frequently, and perhaps usually, raise two broods in the same season.

60   The hummingbird is extremely fond of tubular flowers, and I have often stopt, with pleasure, to observe his maneuvers among the blossoms of the trumpet flower. When arrived before a thicket of
65   these that are full blown, he poises, or suspends himself on wing, for the space of two or three seconds, so steadily, that his wings become invisible, or only like a mist; and you can plainly distinguish
70   the pupil of his eye looking round with great quickness and circumspection; the glossy golden green of his back, and the fire of his throat, dazzling in the sun, form altogether a most interesting
75   appearance. The position into which his body is usually thrown while in the act of thrusting his slender tubular tongue into the flower, to extract its sweets, is exhibited in the figure on the plate. When
80   he alights, which is frequently, he always prefers the small dead twigs of a tree, or bush, where he dresses and arranges his plumage with great dexterity. His only note is a single chirp, not louder than
85   that of a small cricket or grasshopper, generally uttered while passing from flower to flower, or when engaged in fight with his fellows; for when two males meet at the same bush, or flower, a battle
90   instantly takes place; and the combatants ascend in the air, chirping, darting and circling around each other, till the eye is no longer able to follow them. The conqueror, however, generally returns to
95   the place, to reap the fruits of his victory. I have seen him attack, and for a few moments tease the King-bird; and have also seen him, in his turn, assaulted by a humble-bee, which he soon put to flight.
100   He is one of those few birds that are universally beloved; and amidst the sweet dewy serenity of a summer's morning, his appearance among the arbours of honeysuckles, and beds of flowers, is
105   truly interesting.

---

11 The author is mostly concerned with

(A) describing the characteristics of the hummingbird.

(B) explaining how hummingbirds build their nests.

(C) discussing the reasons hummingbirds are interesting.

(D) interpreting the meaning of certain hummingbird behaviors.

---

12 Based on lines 1–4 ("About the twenty-fifth of April … to build its nest."), it can generally be assumed that hummingbirds

(A) take two weeks to build their nests.

(B) migrate elsewhere for the winter.

(C) cannot be found in places farther north.

(D) are mostly solitary animals.

---

13 As used in line 5, "fixed" most nearly means

(A) adjusted.

(B) intended.

(C) aligned.

(D) fastened.

---

14 In lines 18–36 ("A very complete one … accidental protuberance."), the author describes the hummingbird nest in layers most likely to establish that the hummingbird

(A) uses nearby plant debris in the nest.

(B) builds compact, complicated nests.

(C) builds the nest over a period of time.

(D) constructs a nest that is waterproof.

15 It can be inferred from the passage that hummingbirds

(A) stay in the nest for a short period of time.

(B) are fiercely protective of their eggs and young.

(C) have a sweet, though notably quiet, song.

(D) feed only on the sweet nectar of flowers.

16 Which choice provides the best evidence for the answer to the previous question?

(A) Lines 38–46 ("On a person's … the spot.")

(B) Lines 46–51 ("The precise … brought them.")

(C) Lines 51–55 ("I never … they do.")

(D) Lines 83–88 ("His only … with his fellows;")

17 As it is used in line 82, "dresses" most nearly means

(A) oils.

(B) clothes.

(C) shuffles.

(D) smooths.

18 In lines 68–69, the author notes that the hummingbird's "wings become invisible, or only like a mist" to

(A) show how transparent the wings are.

(B) emphasize how fast the wings are moving.

(C) point out that the sun reflects off the wings.

(D) reiterate that the hummingbird is beautiful.

19 In lines 93–95 ("The conqueror … fruits of his victory."), "fruits of his victory" refers to

(A) the dead twigs of a tree.

(B) a female hummingbird.

(C) the nectar of a flower.

(D) the other combatant.

20 Which choice provides the best evidence for the answer to the previous question?

(A) Lines 1–4 ("About the twenty-fifth … its nest.")

(B) Lines 75–79 ("The position … on the plate.")

(C) Lines 79–83 ("When he alights, … dexterity.")

(D) Lines 90–93 ("and the combatants … follow them.")

21 The author most likely references both the kingbird and the bee in lines 96–99 ("I have seen him … put to flight.") to

(A) highlight the many dangers that confront hummingbirds.

(B) describe how the hummingbird stays close to its nest.

(C) show that the hummingbird's size does not limit its ability to defend itself.

(D) emphasize that the hummingbird is an especially aggressive bird.

QUESTIONS 22–31 ARE BASED ON THE FOLLOWING PASSAGE AND SUPPLEMENTARY MATERIAL.

The passage is excerpted from information provided by the National Oceanic and Atmospheric Administration (NOAA) at http://www.noaa.gov.

Over half a mile taller … than Mt. Everest, Mauna Kea in Hawai'i is more than 6 miles tall, from its base on the

Line ocean floor to its summit two miles above
5 the surface of the Pacific Ocean. This island mountain is only one of many features found on the ocean floor. Besides

GO TO THE NEXT PAGE

being the base for islands, the ocean floor
Line also includes continental shelves and
10 slopes, canyons, oceanic ridges, trenches,
fracture zones, abyssal hills, abyssal
plains, volcanoes, and seamounts. Not
just rock and mud, these locations are the
sites of exotic ecosystems that have rarely
15 been seen or even explored.

Plate Tectonics and the Ocean Floor

The shape of the ocean floor, its
bathymetry, is largely a result of a process
called plate tectonics. The outer rocky
layer of the Earth includes about a dozen
20 large sections called tectonic plates that
are arranged like a spherical jigsaw
puzzle floating on top of the Earth's hot
flowing mantle. Convection currents in
the molten mantle layer cause the plates
25 to slowly move about the Earth a few
centimeters each year. Many ocean floor
features are a result of the interactions
that occur at the edges of these plates.

The shifting plates may collide
30 (converge), move away (diverge), or slide
past (transform) each other. As plates
converge, one plate may dive under the
other, causing earthquakes, forming
volcanoes, or creating deep ocean
35 trenches such as the Mariana Trench.
Where plates are pulled away (diverge)
from each other, molten magma flows
upward between the plates, forming
mid-ocean ridges, underwater volcanoes,
40 hydrothermal vents, and new ocean floor
crust. The Mid-Atlantic Ridge is an
example of this type of plate boundary ....

Marine Life and Exploration on the Ocean Floor

Over the last decade, more than 1500
new species have been discovered in the
45 ocean by marine biologists and other
ocean scientists. Many of these newly
discovered species live deep on the
ocean floor in unique habitats dependent
on processes resulting from plate
50 movement, underwater volcanoes, and
cold water seeps. The discovery of deep
ocean hydrothermal vent ecosystems in
1977 forced scientists to redefine living
systems on our planet. Considered one of
55 the most important scientific discoveries

of the last century, organisms in this deep,
dark ecosystem rely on chemicals and
a process called chemosynthesis as the
base of their food web and not on sunlight
60 and photosynthesis as in other previously
described ecosystems ....

Hydrothermal vents form along mid-
ocean ridges, in places where the sea
floor moves apart very slowly (6 to 18
65 cm per year) as magma wells up from
below. (This is the engine that drives
Earth's tectonic plates apart, moving
continents and causing volcanic eruptions
and earthquakes.) When cold ocean water
70 seeps through cracks in the sea floor
to hot spots below, hydrothermal vents
belch a mineral-rich broth of scalding
water. Sometimes, in very hot vents,
the emerging fluid turns black, creating
75 a "black smoker," because dissolved
sulfides of metals (iron, copper, and
several heavy metals) instantaneously
precipitate out of solution when they mix
with the cold surrounding seawater.
80 Unlike plants that rely on sunlight,
bacteria living in and around the dark
vents extract their energy from hydrogen
sulfide (HS) and other molecules that
billow out of the seafloor. Just like plants,
85 the bacteria use their energy to build
sugars out of carbon dioxide and water.
Sugars then provide fuel and raw material
for the rest of the microbes' activities.

Why is chemosynthesis important?

Chemosynthetic deep-sea bacteria
90 form the base of a varied food web that
includes shrimp, tubeworms, clams, fish,
crabs, and octopi. All of these animals
must be adapted to endure the extreme
environment of the vents—complete
95 darkness; water temperatures ranging
from 2°C (in ambient seawater) to about
400°C (at the vent openings); pressures
hundreds of times that at sea level; and
high concentrations of sulfides and other
100 noxious chemicals.

Why is photosynthesis important?

Aquatic and terrestrial plants form the
base of varied food webs that may include
small fish and crabs, larger fish, and
eventually, humans.

22 Which best describes the function of the opening sentence ("Over half a mile taller … the Pacific Ocean.")?

(A) It shows how unusual and extraordinary some ocean features are.

(B) It emphasizes that Mt. Everest is not the world's tallest mountain.

(C) It describes the geography of island mountains in the Pacific Ocean.

(D) It compares the geography of Mt. Everest to that of Mauna Kea.

23 The author uses the simile "like a spherical jigsaw puzzle" (lines 21–22) to illustrate that

(A) each plate plays a critical role.

(B) the earth is sphere-shaped.

(C) each plate is asymmetrical.

(D) the plates fit together.

24 The movement of the earth's tectonic plates is a function of

(A) earthquakes and volcanoes.

(B) the moving ocean currents.

(C) new ocean floor crust.

(D) the moving molten mantle layer.

25 Which inference can you correctly make about the discovery of deep ocean hydrothermal vent ecosystems in 1977?

(A) Before the discovery, scientists thought that all living systems relied on photosynthesis as the basis of their food web.

(B) Before the discovery, scientists believed that deep ocean hydrothermal vents were caused by colliding plates.

(C) After the discovery, scientists determined that some sea life can move easily between shallow waters and deep sea environments.

(D) After the discovery, scientists sought ways to mine the minerals that spew from the hydrothermal vents.

26 Which choice provides the best evidence for the answer to the previous question?

(A) Lines 43–46 ("Over the … ocean scientists.")

(B) Lines 54–61 ("Considered one … described ecosystems.")

(C) Lines 62–66 ("Hydrothermal vents … from below.")

(D) Lines 73–79 ("Sometimes, in … surrounding seawater.")

27 As it is used in line 84, "billow" most nearly means

(A) swell.

(B) blow.

(C) break.

(D) spout.

28 The author devotes the first half of the passage to an explanation of plate tectonics in order to

(A) describe the geography of the ocean floor.

(B) explain the conditions that create hydrothermal vents.

(C) compare hydrothermal vents to underwater volcanoes.

(D) argue that hydrothermal vents are a unique ecosystem.

29 Which choice provides the best evidence for the answer to the previous question?

(A) Lines 8–12 ("Besides being … and seamounts.")

(B) Lines 46–51 ("Many of … water seeps.")

(C) Lines 62–66 ("Hydrothermal vents … from below.")

(D) Lines 66–69 ("This is the engine … and earthquakes.")

30 As used in line 100, "noxious" most nearly means

(A) harmful.

(B) annoying.

(C) offensive.

(D) unusual.

31 Based on the diagram, what eventually happens to the dissolved sulfides of metals that belch out of the black smoker?

(A) They are carried by ocean currents.

(B) They are deposited on the sea bed.

(C) They rise to the surface of the sea.

(D) They drop back into the black smoker.

QUESTIONS 32–42 ARE BASED ON THE FOLLOWING PASSAGE AND SUPPLEMENTARY MATERIAL.

The passage is an excerpt from "How the Other Half Lives," by Jacob Riis. It was published in 1890 and documented the squalid living conditions in the tenements of New York City.

The old question, what to do with the boy, assumes a new and serious phase in the tenements. Under the best conditions
Line found there, it is not easily answered. In
5 nine cases out of ten he would make an excellent mechanic, if trained early to work at a trade, for he is neither dull nor slow, but the short-sighted despotism of the trades unions has practically closed
10 that avenue to him. Trade-schools, however excellent, cannot supply the opportunity thus denied him, and at the outset the boy stands condemned by his own to low and ill-paid drudgery, held
15 down by the hand that of all should labor to raise him.

Home, the greatest factor of all in the training of the young, means nothing to him but a pigeon-hole in a coop along
20 with so many other human animals. Its influence is scarcely of the elevating kind, if it have any. The very games at which he takes a hand in the street become polluting in its atmosphere.
25 With no steady hand to guide him, the boy takes naturally to idle ways. Caught in the street by the truant officer, or by the agents of the Children's Societies, peddling, perhaps, or begging, to help out
30 the family resources, he runs the risk of being sent to a reformatory, where contact with vicious boys older than himself soon develop the latent possibilities for evil that lie hidden in him. The city has
35 no Truant Home in which to keep him, and all efforts of the children's friends to enforce school attendance are paralyzed by this want. The risk of the reformatory is too great. What is done in the end is to
40 let him take chances—with the chances all against him. The result is the rough young savage, familiar from the street. Rough as he is, if any one doubt that this child of common clay have in him the

45 instinct of beauty, of love for the ideal of which his life has no embodiment, let him put the matter to the test. Let him take into a tenement block a handful of flowers from the fields and watch the brightened
50 faces, the sudden abandonment of play and fight that go ever hand in hand where there is no elbow-room, the wild entreaty for "posies," the eager love with which the little messengers of peace
55 are shielded, once possessed; then let him change his mind. I have seen an armful of daisies keep the peace of a block better than a policeman and his club, seen instincts awaken under their
60 gentle appeal, whose very existence the soil in which they grew made seem a mockery ….

Yet, as I knew, that dismal alley with its bare brick walls, between which
65 no sun ever rose or set, was the world of those children. It filled their young lives. Probably not one of them had ever been out of the sight of it. They were too dirty, too ragged, and too generally
70 disreputable, too well hidden in their slum besides, to come into line with the Fresh Air summer boarders.

With such human instincts and cravings, forever unsatisfied, turned into
75 a haunting curse; with appetite ground to keenest edge by a hunger that is never fed, the children of the poor grow up in joyless homes to lives of wearisome toil that claims them at an age when the
80 play of their happier fellows has but just begun. Has a yard of turf been laid and a vine been coaxed to grow within their reach, they are banished and barred out from it as from a heaven that is not for
85 such as they. I came upon a couple of youngsters in a Mulberry Street yard a while ago that were chalking on the fence their first lesson in "writin'."

And this is what they wrote: "Keeb of
90 te Grass." They had it by heart, for there was not, I verily believe, a green sod within a quarter of a mile. Home to them is an empty name.

GO TO THE NEXT PAGE

32 The passage is mainly concerned with establishing that

(A) there are very few job opportunities available for poor people.

(B) the condition of the tenements condemns children to lives of misery.

(C) more education is needed to help elevate the children of the poor.

(D) children who live in poverty naturally turn to crime to support themselves.

33 As it is used in line 24, "polluting" most nearly means

(A) dirty.

(B) dangerous.

(C) corrupting.

(D) rowdy.

34 In lines 13–14, "condemned by his own" means that the boy is

(A) denounced because of his character.

(B) criticized by his family members.

(C) held back by his own community.

(D) ridiculed by teachers in his school.

35 In line 19, the author uses the metaphor of the pigeon coop to establish that the tenement

(A) is as filthy as a cage for animals.

(B) provides little privacy for its tenants.

(C) is the only housing available for the boy.

(D) provides no positive training or education.

36 As it is used in line 26, "idle" most nearly means

(A) unproductive.

(B) vain.

(C) immature.

(D) inactive.

37 The author suggests in lines 34–41 that a truant home

(A) is no different from a reformatory.

(B) does not enforce school attendance.

(C) is full of vicious young boys.

(D) is necessary but unavailable.

38 The author suggests taking flowers to the tenement child to show that

(A) he has the capacity to appreciate exquisite things.

(B) he is always bored and will play with anything.

(C) there are few flowers growing in the tenements.

(D) the policemen patrolling the tenements are brutal.

39 Which choice provides the best evidence for the answer to the previous question?

(A) Lines 41–42 ("The result … the street.")

(B) Lines 44–47 ("Rough as … the test.")

(C) Lines 56–62 ("I have … a mockery.")

(D) Lines 63–66 ("Yet as … those children.")

40 The author's photos of tenement children best support which of the following ideas from his argument?

(A) Tenement children never get to enjoy childhood.

(B) Tenement children are always hungry and malnourished.

(C) Tenement children are subject to police brutality.

(D) Tenement children learn nothing at home.

41 The author provides the story of the "writin'" in the last paragraph to show that tenement children

(A) do not know how to spell.

(B) are in need of good schools.

(C) have no access to green spaces.

(D) are prone to vandalism.

42 Which choice provides the best evidence for the answer to the previous question?

(A) Lines 81–85 ("Has a … as they.")

B) Lines 85–88 ("I came … in writin'.")

C) Lines 89–90 ("And this … te Grass.")

D) Lines 92–93 ("Home to … empty name.")

QUESTIONS 43–52 ARE BASED ON THE FOLLOWING TWO PASSAGES.

Passage 1 is a letter written by Robert Schumann to Clara Wieck in 1838.

Passage 2 is a letter from Napoleon Bonaparte to his wife Josephine, written in 1796.

Passage 1—Robert Schumann to Clara Wieck (1838)

I have a hundred things to write to you, great and small, if only I could do it neatly, but my writing grows more and
Line more indistinct, a sign, I fear, of heart
5 weakness. There are terrible hours when your image forsakes me, when I wonder anxiously whether I have ordered my life as wisely as I might, whether I had any right to bind you to me, my angel,
10 or can really make you as happy as I should wish. These doubts all arise, I am inclined to think, from your father's attitude towards me. It is so easy to accept other people's estimate of oneself. Your
15 father's behaviour makes me ask myself if I am really so bad—of such humble standing—as to invite such treatment from anyone. Accustomed to easy victory over difficulties, to the smiles of fortune,
20 and to affection, I have been spoiled by having things made too easy for me, and now I have to face refusal, insult, and calumny. I have read of many such things in novels, but I thought too highly
25 of myself to imagine I could ever be the hero of a family tragedy of the Kotzebue sort myself. If I had ever done your father an injury, he might well hate me; but I cannot see why he should despise me and,
30 as you say, hate me without any reason. But my turn will come, and I will then

GO TO THE NEXT PAGE

show him how I love you and himself;
for I will tell you, as a secret, that I really
Line love and respect your father for his many
35 great and fine qualities, as no one but
yourself can do. I have a natural inborn
devotion and reverence for him, as for
all strong characters, and it makes his
antipathy for me doubly painful. Well, he
40 may some time declare peace, and say to
us, "Take each other, then."

You cannot think how your letter has
raised and strengthened me. ... You are
splendid, and I have much more reason
45 to be proud of you than of me. I have
made up my mind, though, to read all
your wishes in your face. Then you will
think, even though you don't say it, that
your Robert is a really good sort, that
50 he is entirely yours, and loves you more
than words can say. You shall indeed have
cause to think so in the happy future. I
still see you as you looked in your little
cap that last evening. I still hear you call
55 me *du*. Clara, I heard nothing of what you
said but that *du*. Don't you remember?

**Passage 2—Napoleon Bonaparte to
Josephine Bonaparte (1796)**

I have not spent a day without loving
you; I have not spent a night without
embracing you; I have not so much as
60 drunk a single cup of tea without cursing
the pride and ambition which force me to
remain separated from the moving spirit
of my life. In the midst of my duties,
whether I am at the head of my army
65 or inspecting the camps, my beloved
Josephine stands alone in my heart,
occupies my mind, fills my thoughts. If
I am moving away from you with the
speed of the Rhône torrent, it is only that
70 I may see you again more quickly. If I
rise to work in the middle of the night, it
is because this may hasten by a matter of
days the arrival of my sweet love. Yet in
your letter of the 23rd and 26th Ventôse,
75 you call me vous. Vous yourself! Ah!
wretch, how could you have written this
letter? How cold it is! And then there are
those four days between the 23rd and
the 26th; what were you doing that you
80 failed to write to your husband? ... Ah,

my love, that *vous*, those four days make
me long for my former indifference. Woe
to the person responsible! May he, as
punishment and penalty, experience what
85 my convictions and the evidence (which
is in your friend's favour) would make
me experience! Hell has no torments
great enough! *Vous! Vous!* Ah! How will
things stand in two weeks? ... My spirit
90 is heavy; my heart is fettered and I am
terrified by my fantasies. ... You love me
less; but you will get over the loss. One
day you will love me no longer; at least
tell me; then I shall know how I have
95 come to deserve this misfortune. ...

43 Both passages are primarily concerned
with the subject of

(A) jealousy.

(B) commitment.

(C) work.

(D) being apart.

44 As it is used in line 39, "antipathy" most
nearly means

(A) indifference.

(B) mistrust.

(C) rudeness.

(D) dislike.

45 We can infer from Passage 1 that Clara's
father's feelings about Robert have caused
Robert to

(A) dislike Clara's father.

(B) question his and Clara's future.

(C) doubt Clara's love for him.

(D) question Clara's character.

46 Which choice provides the best evidence for the answer to the previous question?

(A) Lines 5–13 ("There are … towards me.")

(B) Lines 14–18 ("Your father's … from anyone.")

(C) Lines 31–36 ("But my … can do.")

(D) Lines 47–51 ("Then you … can say.")

47 Napoleon's letter to Josephine suggests that he thinks she

(A) is tired of his long absence.

(B) has little to occupy her time.

(C) may be having an affair.

(D) regrets her marriage to him.

48 Which choice provides the best evidence for the answer to the previous question?

(A) Lines 59–63 ("I have … my life.")

(B) Lines 73–77 ("Yet in … this letter?")

(C) Lines 82–87 ("Woe to … me experience!")

(D) Lines 92–95 ("One day … this misfortune.")

49 As it is used in line 72, "hasten" most nearly means

(A) stretch out.

(B) speed up.

(C) force.

(D) cause.

50 We can infer that Clara's letter to Robert was different from Josephine's letter to Napoleon in that Clara's letter

(A) made Robert doubt himself.

(B) made Robert question her loyalty.

(C) left Robert feeling encouraged.

(D) left Robert feeling confused.

51 In each passage, the author recollects something their beloved said. But the effect of Josephine's words (lines 73–77) differ from the effect of Clara's words (lines 54–56) in that

(A) Josephine's words have hurt Napoleon.

(B) Clara's words have offended Robert.

(C) Josephine's words have calmed Napoleon.

(D) Clara's words have humbled Robert.

52 We can infer that both Robert and Napoleon

(A) are modest people.

(B) anger quickly.

(C) tend to be indecisive.

(D) suffer from self-doubt.

STOP

**If you finish before time is called, you may check your work on this section only.
Do not turn to any other section.**

No Test Material On This Page

SECTION 2: WRITING AND LANGUAGE TEST

35 Minutes • 44 Questions

Directions: Each passage below is accompanied by a number of multiple-choice questions. For some questions, you will need to consider how the passage might be revised to improve the expression of ideas. Other questions will ask you to consider how the passage might be edited to correct errors in sentence structure, usage, or punctuation. A passage may be accompanied by one or more graphics—such as a chart, table, or graph—that you will need to refer to in order to best answer the question(s).

Some questions will direct you to an underlined portion of a passage—it could be one word, a portion of a sentence, or the full sentence itself. Other questions will direct you to a particular paragraph or to certain sentences within a paragraph, or you'll be asked to think about the passage as a whole. Each question number refers to the corresponding number in the passage.

After reading each passage, select the answer to each question that most effectively improves the quality of writing in the passage or that makes the passage follow the conventions of Standard Written English. Many questions include a "NO CHANGE" option. Select that option if you think the best choice is to leave that specific portion of the passage as it is.

QUESTIONS 1–11 ARE BASED ON THE FOLLOWING PASSAGE.

Burma: has it truly changed?

A **1** rigid red-and-white sign erected on a rural road in Burma reads, "[The Military] AND THE PEOPLE IN ETERNAL UNITY. ANYONE ATTEMPTING TO DIVIDE THEM IS OUR ENEMY."

It's no wonder that Burma, also known as Myanmar, inspired two of the most well-known books about totalitarianism: **2** *Animal Farm* and *Nineteen Eighty-Four*? The books sprang from the mind of a man who, as a teenager, sought adventure with the British Imperial Police Force in the 1920s. Five years after Eric Arthur Blair began his tour of duty in the far-flung, **3** obscure Asian colony, he returned to his homeland, shed his uniform, changed his name to George Orwell, and started a new career as a novelist.

1

(A) NO CHANGE
(B) graphic
(C) rare
(D) stark

2

(A) NO CHANGE
(B) *Animal Farm* and *Nineteen Eighty-Four.*
(C) *Animal Farm* and *Nineteen Eighty-Four,*
(D) *Animal Farm* and *Nineteen Eighty-Four!*

3

(A) NO CHANGE
(B) darkened
(C) obvious
(D) uncertain

The contrasts Orwell saw still exist. This land of haunting beauty, with its history of human rights violations, **4** had also sparked filmmaker Ron Fricke's imagination. He and his crew traveled to 25 countries to shoot images for his non-verbal film "Samsara" (2013). Samsara means "the ever-turning wheel of life" in Sanskrit. The sequences shot in Bagan, Burma, are almost dreamlike in quality, especially because, as in the rest of the film, there is no dialogue or narration. **5** Only music accompanies scenes of hundreds of Buddhist temples as they seemingly float upon seas of green foliage. Watching these scenes, it is hard to believe that Burma has seen violent years of civil war, ethnic cleansing, and forced labor. But such problems, as well as those of economic stagnation and corruption, can usually be traced back to the military regime, which took power in 1962 through a coup. The military manages **6** the country's major industries and has also been accused of controlling Burma's substantial heroin exports.

The Irish rock band U2 dedicated their song "Walk On" to Burmese academic Aung San Suu Kyi, who was under house arrest from 1989 until 2010 because of her pro-democracy stance. **7** The members of U2 have a history of incorporating their political views into their music. Her National League for Democracy (NLD) won the 1990 elections

4

(A) NO CHANGE
(B) has also sparked
(C) also sparked
(D) will also spark

5

(A) NO CHANGE
(B) As they seemingly float above seas of green foliage, only music accompanies scenes of hundreds of Buddhist temples.
(C) Only music accompanies scenes, as they seemingly float above seas of green foliage, of hundreds of Buddhist temples.
(D) Only music accompanies scenes, of hundreds of Buddhist temples, as they seemingly float above a sea of green foliage.

6

(A) NO CHANGE
(B) the countries major industries
(C) the countrys major industries
(D) the countries' major industries

7 The writer is considering deleting the underlined sentence. Should the writer do this?

(A) Yes, because the sentence does not support the main idea of the paragraph.
(B) Yes, because the sentence should be moved to the beginning of the paragraph.
(C) No, because the sentence expands upon the main idea of the paragraph.
(D) No, because the sentence introduces an important detail about Burma.

with an overwhelming majority, but she was not allowed to serve. In 1991, she received the Nobel Peace Prize, **8** an honor given out to people and organizations by the Nobel Committee since 1901.

The lyrics of the song are about doing what's right, even if it requires personal sacrifice. **9** Not surprisingly, the album was banned and not allowed to be distributed in Burma. Anyone caught attempting to smuggle it into the country would have been imprisoned for three to twenty years for smuggling.

8 Which choice most effectively maintains support for claims or points in the text?

(A) NO CHANGE
(B) though she only heard about it on the radio while confined in her home.
(C) but she was not able to accept the award until almost two decades later in 2012.
(D) in recognition of her commitment to a nonviolent struggle for democracy in Burma.

9

(A) NO CHANGE
(B) Not surprisingly, the album was banned. Anyone caught attempting to smuggle it into the country would have been imprisoned for three to twenty years.
(C) Not surprisingly, the album was banned and not allowed to be distributed in Burma. Anyone caught attempting to smuggle it into the country would have been imprisoned for three to twenty years.
(D) Not surprisingly, the album was banned. Anyone caught attempting to smuggle it into the country would have been imprisoned for three to twenty years for smuggling.

GO TO THE NEXT PAGE

Military rule supposedly ended in 2011. Then-Secretary of State Hilary Clinton visited in 2011 and President Obama in 2012. The European Union has lifted sanctions against Burma and offered them financial aid. **10** There are signs that the country is emerging from **11** their isolation. However, it's too soon to be sure that the people of this land are finally free of the ever-watching gaze of Big Brother.

10 At this point, the writer is considering adding the following sentence:

> In 2010, things started to change in Burma with the end of house arrest for Aung San Suu Kyi.

Should the writer make this addition here?

(A) Yes, because it provides additional historical detail in the paragraph.

(B) Yes, because it aids the flow of ideas in the paragraph.

(C) No, because the sentence should be added at the beginning of the paragraph.

(D) No, because the sentence provides information that is irrelevant to the paragraph and doesn't support the main idea.

11

(A) NO CHANGE
(B) its isolation
(C) our isolation
(D) your isolation

QUESTIONS 12–22 ARE BASED ON THE FOLLOWING PASSAGE.

John Dewey and Education

John Dewey, an American educator and philosopher of education, was a prolific writer on the subject. He was particularly interested in the place of education in a democratic republic.

The place of public education within a democratic society has been widely discussed and debated through the years. Perhaps no one has written more widely on the subject in the United States than John Dewey, **12** <u>a philosopher and teacher,</u> whose theories on education have a large social component, that is, an emphasis on education **13** <u>as a social act, and the classroom or learning environment as a replica of society.</u>

Dewey defined various aspects or charactcristics of education. First, **14** <u>they were</u> a necessity of life inasmuch as living beings needed to maintain themselves through a process of renewal. Therefore, just as humans needed **15** <u>sleep; food; water; and shelter</u> for physiological renewal, they also needed education to renew their minds, assuring that their socialization kept pace with physiological growth.

12 Which choice provides the most relevant detail?

(A) NO CHANGE

(B) sometimes called "the father of public education,"

(C) the son of a grocer in Burlington, Vermont,

(D) a university professor who taught ethics and logic,

13

(A) NO CHANGE

(B) as a social act, and the classroom, or learning environment, as a replica of society

(C) as a social act and the classroom or learning environment as a replica of society

(D) as a social act and the classroom, or learning environment, as a replica of society

14

(A) NO CHANGE

(B) it was

(C) we were

(D) he was

15

(A) NO CHANGE

(B) sleep: food: water: and shelter

(C) sleep, food, water; and shelter

(D) sleep, food, water, and shelter

GO TO THE NEXT PAGE

16 Another aspect of education was its social component, which was to be accomplished by providing the young with an environment that would provide a nurturing atmosphere to encourage the growth of their as yet undeveloped social customs.

A third aspect of public education was the provision of direction to youngsters, who might otherwise **17** be left in uncontrolled situations without the steadying and organizing influences of school. Direction was not to be of an **18** autonomous nature, but rather indirect through the selection of the school situations in which the youngster participated.

19 On the other hand, Dewey saw public education as a catalyst for growth. Since the young came to school capable of growth, it was the role of education to provide opportunities for that growth to occur. The successful school environment is one in which a desire for continued growth is created—a desire that extends throughout one's life beyond the end of formal education.

…

16 The writer is considering revising the underlined portion of the sentence to read:

   A second aspect of education was its social component,

Should the writer make this revision here?

(A) Yes, because the change improves the organization.

(B) Yes, because the change clarifies the aspects of education.

(C) No, because the change eliminates information that supports the main idea of the paragraph.

(D) No, because the change makes the organization of this part of the passage unclear.

17

(A) NO CHANGE

(B) who might get wild and crazy if not for a teacher keeping them in check.

(C) who might change direction, much like the wind, with no one to guide them.

(D) who might be lost, forlorn without school to steer them toward moral clarity.

18

(A) NO CHANGE

(B) uncertain

(C) overt

(D) abstract

19

(A) NO CHANGE

(B) Finally,

(C) In retrospect,

(D) Therefore,

Neither did Dewey's model see education as a means by which the past was recapitulated. Instead **20** education was a continuous reconstructions of experiences, grounded very much in the present environment.

21 The nature of the larger society that supports the educational system, since Dewey's model places a heavy emphasis on the social component, is of paramount importance. The ideal larger society, according to Dewey, is one in which the interests of a group are all shared by all of its members and in which interactions with other groups are free and full. According to Dewey, education in such a society should provide members of the group a stake or interest in social relationships and the ability to **22** subjugate change without compromising the order and stability of the society.

20

(A) NO CHANGE
(B) educations were continuous reconstructions of experiences
(C) education was a continuous reconstruction of experience
(D) education was experiences being continuously reconstructed

21

(A) NO CHANGE
(B) The nature of the larger society that supports the educational system is of paramount important since Dewey's model places a heavy emphasis on the social component.
(C) Of paramount importance, since Dewey's model places a heavy emphasis on the social component, is the nature of the larger society that supports the educational system.
(D) Since Dewey's model places a heavy emphasis on the social component, the nature of the larger society that supports the educational system is of paramount importance.

22

(A) NO CHANGE
(B) negotiate
(C) complicate
(D) obfuscate

practice test

QUESTIONS 23–33 ARE BASED ON THE FOLLOWING PASSAGE.

The study of plant life is very different from the study of animal life because of unique plant characteristics. The following passage provides an overview of those characteristics, along with some plant classifications that are of interest to scientists.

23 Compared to animals, plants present unique problems in demographic studies. The idea of counting living individuals becomes difficult given perennials that reproduce vegetatively **24** by sending out runners or rhizomes, splitting at the stem base, or by producing arching canes that take root where they touch the ground. In these ways some individuals, given sufficient time, can extend out over a vast area.

Each plant life span has a basic associated life form. *Annual plants* live for 1 year or less. Their average life span is 1–8 months, depending on the species and on the environment where they are located (the same desert plant may complete **25** its life cycle in 8 months one year and in 1 month the next, depending on the amount of rain it receives). Annuals with extremely short life cycles are classified as *ephemeral* plants. An example of an ephemeral is *Boerrhavia repens* of the Sahara Desert, which can go from seed to seed in just 10 days. Annuals are herbaceous, which means that they lack a secondary meristem that produces lateral, woody tissue. They complete their life cycle after seed production for several reasons: nutrient depletion, hormone changes, or inability of non-woody

23 What choice provides the most logical introduction to the sentence?

(A) NO CHANGE

(B) There are five typical plant life spans, and each presents

(C) Plants are an important source of food, and they present

(D) Annual is one type of plant, and it presents

24

(A) NO CHANGE

(B) by sending out runners or rhizomes, a split at the stem base, or the production of arching canes that take root where they touch the ground.

(C) by sending out runners or rhizomes, splitting at the stem base, or in the production of arching canes that take root where they touch the ground.

(D) by sending out runners or rhizomes, splitting at the stem base, or producing arching canes that take root where they touch the ground.

25

(A) NO CHANGE

(B) it's

(C) its'

(D) it is

tissue to withstand unfavorable environmental conditions following the growing season. A few species can persist for more than a year in uncommonly favorable conditions.

Biennial plants are also herbaceous, but usually live for 2 years. **26** Their first year is spent in vegetative growth, which generally takes place more below ground than above. Reproduction occurs in the second year, and this is followed by the completion of the life cycle. Under poor growing conditions, or by experimental manipulation, the vegetative stage can be drawn out for more than 1 year.

Herbaceous perennials typically live for 20–30 years, although some species have been known to live for 400–800 years. These plants die back to the root system and root crown at the end of each growing season. The root system becomes woody, but the above-ground system is herbaceous. **27** They bloom and reproduce yearly after an initial vegetative state, making them popular landscaping plants. Sometimes they bloom only once at the conclusion of their life cycle. Because herbaceous perennials have no growth rings, it is difficult to age them. Methods that have been used to age them include counting leaf scars and **28** reducing the rate of spread in *tussock* (clumped) forms.

29 *Suffrutescent* shrubs (hemixyles) falls somewhere between herbaceous perennials and true shrubs. They develop perennial,

26 The writer is considering deleting the underlined sentence. Should the writer do this?

(A) Yes, because it doesn't support the main idea of the paragraph.

(B) Yes, because it is out of place in the paragraph.

(C) No, because it describes vegetative growth.

(D) No, because it describes what happens in the first year.

27 Which choice most effectively maintains the paragraph's focus on relevant information and ideas?

(A) NO CHANGE

(B) Their initial vegetative state lasts 2–8 years, which is an adaptation that is not seen in animals.

(C) Blooming and reproducing early, herbaceous perennials include such plants as hollyhocks, aster, and yarrow.

(D) They have a juvenile, vegetative stage for the first 2–8 years, then bloom and reproduce yearly.

28

(A) NO CHANGE
(B) hedging
(C) estimating
(D) valuing

29

(A) NO CHANGE
(B) *Suffrutescent* shrubs (hemixyles) fall
(C) *Suffrutescent* shrub (hemixyles) fall
(D) *Suffrutescent* shrubs (hemixyles) has fallen

GO TO THE
NEXT PAGE

woody tissue only near the base of their **30** stems. The rest of the shoot system is herbaceous and dies back each year. They are small and short-lived compared to true shrubs.

31 *Woody perennials (trees and shrubs) have the longest life spans.* Shrubs live on average 30–50 years. Broadleaf trees (angiosperm) average 200–300 years, and conifer (needles) trees average 500–1,000 years. Woody perennials spend approximately the first 10 percent of their life span in a juvenile, totally vegetative state before they enter a combined reproductive and vegetative state, achieving a peak of reproduction several years before the conclusion of their life cycle.

32 Irregardless of the life span, annual or perennial, one can identify about eight important age states in an individual plant or population. They are: (1) viable seed, (2) seedling, (3) juvenile, (4) immature, (5) mature, (6) initial reproductive, (7) maximum vigor (reproductive and vegetative), and (8) senescent. If a population shows all eight states, it is **33** stable and is most likely a part of a *climax* community. If it shows only the last four states, it may not maintain itself and may be part of a *seral* community.

30 Which choice most effectively combines the two sentences at the underlined portion?

(A) stems, the rest of the shoot system
(B) stems because the rest of the shoot system
(C) stems: the rest of the shoot system
(D) stems; the rest of the shoot system

31

(A) NO CHANGE
(B) *Woody perennials*—trees and shrubs—have the longest life spans.
(C) *Woody perennials,* trees and shrubs, have the longest life spans.
(D) *Woody perennials* "trees and shrubs" have the longest life spans.

32

(A) NO CHANGE
(B) Regardless
(C) Inregardless
(D) Regarding less

33 Which choice is most consistent with the style and tone of the passage?

(A) NO CHANGE
(B) diminishing
(C) ephemeral
(D) uniform

QUESTIONS 34–44 ARE BASED ON THE FOLLOWING PASSAGE.

Variations in wage

34 [1] Within certain fields, workers are especially likely to receive different salaries. [2] According to the Bureau of Labor Statistics (BLS), large differences in wages can be explained by a variety of factors. [3] Commercial pilots, for example, had a median annual wage **35** of $75,620: more than double the median for all occupations in May 2014. [4] But that median figure **36** diminishes the fact that the gap between the 90th percentile wage and the 10th percentile wage was more than $100,000. [5] In other words, just because someone chooses to be a commercial pilot does not necessarily mean he or she will earn as much as the top earners in the field.

Why wages vary

37 Everyone is unique. Each person comes to a position with her own set of skills, a capacity for adapting to the demands of the

34 For the sake of the cohesion of this paragraph, sentence 1 should be placed

(A) where it is now.
(B) after sentence 2.
(C) after sentence 3.
(D) after sentence 4.

35

(A) NO CHANGE
(B) of $75,620 more than double
(C) of $75,620; more than double
(D) of $75,620—more than double

36

(A) NO CHANGE
(B) contradicts
(C) conceals
(D) equivocates

37 The writer is considering revising the underlined sentence to read:

Everyone likes to have a job that suits his or her own needs.

Should the writer make this revision?

(A) Yes, because this strengthens the relationship between the first sentence and the second.
(B) Yes, because it is generally a true statement, and it adds detail to the paragraph.
(C) No, because it does not support the main idea of the paragraph as described in the next sentence.
(D) No, because it is just a restatement of the information provided in the next sentence.

practice test

job, and **38** their own personal strengths and weaknesses. In addition, job titles can be **39** deceiving. No two jobs are identical. In some fields, this allows for opportunity to advance dramatically in terms of rank and earnings. There are the fields in which these differences are very obvious, such as professional sports or the entertainment field.

In occupations with less variability among workers, wage differences are usually small. Fast food cooks, for example, earn similar wages. Workers in this occupation have fewer opportunities for advancement and **40** higher pay than other occupations. Nevertheless, there are a variety of factors that **41** effect how much you earn.

Credentials. In some jobs, having advanced education is necessary for advancement. In other careers, holding a professional license or training credentials will increase a worker's wage.

Experience. Experienced workers usually earn more than those newer to the field. Employers will pay more for a skilled employee, especially in fields in which they are in high demand.

Job tasks. **42** Jobs that are more complex or that demand more responsibility often pay more. Sometimes even within the same company, two workers with the same job title will be given different tasks and receive different wages as a result.

Location. In the U.S., a worker doing the same job as another in a different state may

38
(A) NO CHANGE
(B) our
(C) its
(D) her

39
(A) NO CHANGE
(B) tenuous
(C) impractical
(D) incidental

40
(A) NO CHANGE
(B) higher pay than workers with other opportunities
(C) higher pay than workers in other occupations
(D) higher pay than other workers with occupations

41
(A) NO CHANGE
(B) affect
(C) infect
(D) reflect

42 Which choice most effectively establishes the main topic of the paragraph?

(A) The duties tied to a specific job often dictate the pay.
(B) Wages among different companies can frequently vary.
(C) Workers with the same job title are often given different tasks.
(D) Variability in job titles often leads to differences in wages.

earn a very different salary. **43** <u>Some of the factors behind this variation: cost of living and the local demand for the skill.</u> For example, in New York City, the cost of living is high and workers will be paid more than their counterparts in Billings, Montana.

Performance. In highly competitive fields, such as sports, only a small percentage of athletes will experience great success. There

43

(A) NO CHANGE

(B) Cost of living and the local demand for the skill: some of the factors behind this variation.

(C) Some of the factors behind this variation, cost of living and the local demand for the skill.

(D) Some of the factors behind this variation include cost of living and the local demand for the skill.

TABLE 1. ARTS, ENTERTAINMENT, AND SPORTS OCCUPATIONS WITH MORE THAN $100,000 WAGE DIFFERENCE, MAY 2014					
Occupation	**Employment**	**Median wage**	**10th percentile wage**	**90th percentile wage[1]**	**Wage difference[2]**
Actors[3]	59,210	$41,230	$18,720	>$187,200	>$168,480
Athletes and sports competitors	11,520	43,350	20,190	>187,200	>167,010
Producers and directors	97,300	69,100	31,380	>187,200	>155,820
Broadcast news analysts	4,310	61,450	28,210	182,470	154,260
Art directors	33,140	85,610	45,060	168,040	122,980
Film and video editors	24,460	57,210	25,520	145,620	120,100
Musicians and singers[3]	38,900	50,250	18,680	137,510	118,830

Footnotes:

(1) BLS does not publish specific estimates for percentile wages above $187,200 per year. Where the percentile wage is greater than $187,200, the wage is shown with a greater-than sign (>).

(2) Wage differences with a greater-than sign (>) were calculated using $187,200, the highest percentile wage that BLS publishes.

(3) In occupations in which workers typically are paid by the hour and work less than the standard 2,080 hours per year, BLS reports only hourly wages. For comparison purposes in calculating wage differences, the hourly wage was multiplied by 2,080 to get an annual wage.

Source: Occupational Employment Statistics survey, Bureau of Labor Statistics

GO TO THE NEXT PAGE

will be many athletes who experience only little or moderate success, **44** <u>and consequently their median wage will rank below everyone except broadcast news analysts.</u>

Below are occupations in the field of arts, entertainment, and sports that had a wage difference of more than $100,000 in May 2014, higher than the $71,710 wage difference for all workers.

44 Which choice completes the sentence with accurate data based on the supplementary table?

(A) NO CHANGE.

(B) and consequently their median wage will rank below everyone except actors.

(C) and consequently their median wage will rank above only singers and musicians.

(D) and consequently their median wage will rank above only film and video editors.

STOP

If you finish before time is called, you may check your work on this section only. Do not turn to any other section.

SECTION 3: MATH TEST—NO CALCULATOR

20 Questions • 25 minutes

TURN TO SECTION 3 OF YOUR ANSWER SHEET TO ANSWER THE QUESTIONS IN THIS SECTION.

Directions: For Questions 1–15, solve each problem, select the best answer from the choices provided, and fill in the corresponding oval on your answer sheet. **For Questions 16–20,** solve the problem and enter your answer in the grid on the answer sheet. The directions **before Question 16** will provide information on how to enter your answers in the grid.

ADDITIONAL INFORMATION:

- The use of a calculator in this section **is not permitted.**

- All variables and expressions used represent real numbers unless otherwise indicated.

- Figures provided in this test are drawn to scale unless otherwise indicated.

- All figures lie in a plane unless otherwise indicated.

- Unless otherwise specified, the domain of a given function f is the set of all real numbers x for which $f(x)$ is a real number.

1 One angle of a triangle measures 82°. The other two angles have a ratio of 2:5. Find the number of degrees in the smallest angle of the triangle.

(A) 14
(B) 28
(C) 38
(D) 82

2 $$\left(\sqrt{18} - \sqrt{8}\right)^2 =$$

(A) 1
(B) $\sqrt{2}$
(C) 2
(D) 10

3 If $f(x) = x^2 + 2$ and $g(x) = x - 1$, which expression represents $f(g(a))$?

(A) $a^2 + 1$

(B) $a^2 - 2$

(C) $a^2 + 2a - 3$

(D) $a^2 - 2a + 3$

4 Which expression is equivalent to $(2x - y)(x - y) - xy$?

(A) $2x^2 + y^2$

(B) $2x^2 - xy + y^2$

(C) $2x^2 - 2xy + y^2$

(D) $2x^2 - 4xy + y^2$

5 Simplify:

$$\frac{x^2 - y^2}{x - y}$$

(A) $\dfrac{xy}{x + y}$

(B) $\dfrac{x + y}{xy}$

(C) $x + y$

(D) xy

6 Which of the following complex numbers is equivalent to $(3 - i)(8 + 4i)$?

(A) $20 - (-4i)$

(B) $20 + 4i$

(C) $24 - 4i$

(D) $28 + 4i$

7 Which of these expressions is equivalent to $(x + y)^2 - (x - y)^2$?

(A) 0

(B) $2y^2$

(C) $4xy$

(D) $4xy + 2y^2$

8 An economist studied the labor forces in several randomly selected states. He found the average minimum wage of these states was $7.50, with a 95% confidence interval of ±0.25. How should the economist interpret the data?

(A) States that have a minimum wage below $7.75 represent 95% of the states.

(B) States that have a minimum wage above $7.25 represent 95% of the states.

(C) There is a 95% probability that a randomly selected state will have a minimum wage between $7.25 and $7.75.

(D) There is a 95% probability that the actual average minimum wage of all states is between $7.25 and $7.75.

9

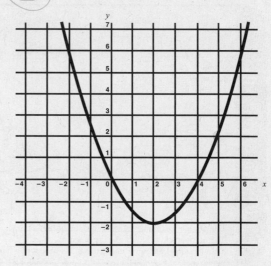

The curve shown on the *xy*-plane represents the function $f(x)$. Which of these equations represents the same function?

(A) $y = \dfrac{1}{2}x^2 - 2x$

(B) $y = x^2 - 4x$

(C) $y = x^2 + 4x$

(D) $y = \dfrac{1}{2}x^2 + 2x$

10 A 10% saline solution is to be mixed with a 40% saline solution to obtain 5 liters of a 20% saline solution. Which system of equations can be used to find the number of liters of the 10% solution, x, that will be needed to be combined with the number of liters of the 40% solution, y?

(A) $0.1x + 0.4y = 1$
$x + y = 5$

(B) $0.1x + 0.4y = 5$
$x + y = 5$

(C) $0.1x + 0.4y = 1$
$x + y = 1$

(D) $0.1x + 0.4y = 5$
$x + y = 1$

11 The function $f(t) = -4.9t^2 + 40t + 4$ is used to model the height of a ball, in meters, above the ground t seconds after being thrown. Which statement accurately describes the meaning of the number 40 in this function?

(A) The ball will achieve a maximum height of 40 meters.

(B) The ball will achieve its maximum height after 40 seconds.

(C) The ball was thrown upwards at a velocity of 40 meters per second.

(D) The ball was initially thrown from a height 40 meters above the ground.

12 $2x + 3y = 3$
$x = 2 - 9y$

If (x,y) is the solution of the system of equations above, what is the value of y?

(A) $-\dfrac{7}{15}$

(B) $\dfrac{1}{15}$

(C) $\dfrac{2}{9}$

(D) $\dfrac{3}{2}$

13 What is the equation of the line that is parallel to $y = 5x + 7$ and contains the point $(1, 3)$?

(A) $y = -5x + 8$
(B) $y = 5x - 2$
(C) $y = 5x + 3$
(D) $y = 5x + 2$

14 When Rafael parked his car in the city garage for 3 hours, the charge was $5. When he parked his car for 5 hours, the charge was $6.50. If the cost of parking a car in the city garage is a linear function of time in hours, which function represents the charge, y, to park for x hours?

(A) $y = \dfrac{5}{3}x$

(B) $y = 1.3x$

(C) $y = 3x + 5$

(D) $y = 0.75x + 2.75$

15 What is the solution of the equation $3(x - 9) = 4x + 3(1 - 2x)$?

(A) -4
(B) 6
(C) 12
(D) 30

GO TO THE
NEXT PAGE

practice test

Directions: For Questions 16–20, solve the problem and enter your answer in the grid, as described below, on the answer sheet.

1.   Although not required, it is suggested that you write your answer in the boxes at the top of the columns to help you fill in the circles accurately. You will receive credit only if the circles are filled in correctly.

2.   Mark no more than one circle in any column.

3.   No question has a negative answer.

4.   Some problems may have more than one correct answer. In such cases, grid only one answer.

5.   **Mixed numbers** such as $3\frac{1}{2}$ must be gridded as 3.5 or $\frac{7}{2}$.

     If $3\frac{1}{2}$ is entered into the grid as $\overline{3\ 1\ /\ 2}$, it will be interpreted as $\frac{31}{2}$, not $3\frac{1}{2}$.)

6.   **Decimal answers:** If you obtain a decimal answer with more digits than the grid can accommodate, it may be either rounded or truncated, but it must fill the entire grid.

16 How many degrees are in $\dfrac{4\pi}{5}$ radians?
(Do not grid in the degree symbol.)

17 What is the solution of the equation $\dfrac{3}{2}x + 7 = 4x$?

18 What is a solution of $x^2 + 4 = 9x - x^2$?

19 What is the x-intercept of the graph of $y - 3 = 5(x - 2)$?

20 Find a solution of $\sqrt{x+3} = x - 3$.

STOP

**If you finish before time is called, you may check your work on this section only.
Do not turn to any other section.**

practice test

SECTION 4: MATH TEST—CALCULATOR 🖩

38 Questions • 55 minutes

TURN TO SECTION 4 OF YOUR ANSWER SHEET TO ANSWER THE QUESTIONS IN THIS SECTION.

Directions: For **Questions 1–30,** solve each problem, select the best answer from the choices provided, and fill in the corresponding oval on your answer sheet. For **Questions 31–38,** solve the problem and enter your answer in the grid on the answer sheet. The directions **before question 31** will provide information on how to enter your answers in the grid.

ADDITIONAL INFORMATION:

- The use of a calculator is **permitted**.

- All variables and expressions used represent real numbers unless otherwise indicated.

- Figures provided in this test are drawn to scale unless otherwise indicated.

- All figures lie in a plane unless otherwise indicated.

- Unless otherwise specified, the domain of a given function f is the set of all real numbers x for which $f(x)$ is a real number.

Circle:
$C = 2\pi r$
$A = \pi r^2$

Rectangle:
$A = lw$

Triangle:
$A = \frac{1}{2}bh$

$a^2 + b^2 = c^2$

Rectangular Solid:
$V = lwh$

Cylinder:
$V = \pi r^2 h$

Sphere:
$V = \frac{4}{3}\pi r^3$

Cone:
$V = \frac{1}{3}\pi r^2 h$

Rectangular Based Pyramid:
$V = \frac{1}{3}lwh$

Reference Information

The number of degrees of arc in a circle is 360.
The number of radians in the arc of a circle is 2π.
The sum of the measures in degrees of the angles of a triangle is 180.

1 A salesperson earns twice as much in December as in each of the other months of a year. What part of this salesperson's entire year's earnings is earned in December?

(A) $\frac{1}{7}$

(B) $\frac{2}{13}$

(C) $\frac{1}{6}$

(D) $\frac{2}{11}$

2 Village A has a population of 6,800, which is decreasing at a rate of 120 per year. Village B has a population of 4,200, which is increasing at a rate of 80 per year. Which equation can be used to find the number of years, y, until the population of the two villages will be equal?

(A) $6800 - 120y = 4200 + 80y$
(B) $6800 + 120y = 4200 - 80y$
(C) $6800 - 120y = 4200 - 80y$
(D) $6800 + 120y = 4200 + 80y$

3

	Candidate A	Candidate B	Candidate C	Candidate D
Male	27	29	35	24
Female	24	49	45	17

The table above shows the results of a survey of a random sample of likely voters. What is the probability that a male voter who responded to the survey supports candidate C?

(A) $\frac{7}{50}$

(B) $\frac{7}{23}$

(C) $\frac{7}{16}$

(D) $\frac{7}{9}$

4 The formula for converting temperatures from degrees Fahrenheit to degrees Celsius is $C = \frac{5}{9}(F - 32)$.

Solve the formula for F.

(A) $F = \frac{5}{9}(C + 32)$

(B) $F = \frac{5}{9}(C - 32)$

(C) $F = \frac{9}{5}C - 32$

(D) $F = \frac{9}{5}C + 32$

5 A recent study showed that 15% of the salmon that pass through a turbine in hydroelectric dams are killed. If an initial population of 50,000 salmon must pass through n turbines, which function models the number of salmon that will survive?

(A) $A(n) = 50,000 - 0.15n$
(B) $A(n) = 50,000 - 0.85n$
(C) $A(n) = 50,000 \times 0.15^n$
(D) $A(n) = 50,000 \times 0.85^n$

6 The equation $f(x) = 1.5x + 15$ models the growth of a bamboo shoot, where x represents the number of days and $f(x)$ represents the height of the shoot in feet. Determine how many days it will take the bamboo shoot to reach a height of 19.5 feet.

(A) 1
(B) 2
(C) 3
(D) 4

7 What part of the total quantity is represented by a 24-degree sector of a circle graph?

(A) $6\frac{2}{3}\%$

(B) 12%

(C) $13\frac{1}{3}\%$

(D) 15%

8 A high school principal wanted to estimate the mean of the grade point averages of students in her school. She randomly selected a group of students and found the mean grade point average to be 2.8 on a four-point scale, with a 95% confidence interval of ±0.2. How should the principal interpret the data?

(A) Students with a grade point average below 3.0 make up 95% of the students in the school.

(B) Students with a grade point average above 2.6 make up 95% of the students in the school.

(C) There is a 95% probability that a randomly selected student will have a grade point average between 2.6 and 3.0.

(D) There is a 95% probability that the actual mean grade point average of all students in the school is between 2.6 and 3.0.

9

A pulley having a 9-inch diameter is belted to a pulley having a 6-inch diameter, as shown in the figure. If the large pulley runs at 120 rpm, how fast does the small pulley run, in revolutions per minute?

(A) 80

(B) 100

(C) 160

(D) 180

10

$$y = x^2 - 7x + 10$$
$$x - y = 4$$

If (x, y) is a solution of the system of equations above, what is the value of y^2?

(A) 2

(B) $\frac{9}{2}$

(C) $18 - 8\sqrt{2}$

(D) 14

11 The water level of a swimming pool, 75 feet by 42 feet, is to be raised 4 inches. How many gallons of water must be added to accomplish this? (7.48 gal. = 1 cubic ft.)

(A) 1,684

(B) 7,854

(C) 12,600

(D) 94,248

12 If $\frac{3}{7}$ of a bucket can be filled in 1 minute, how many minutes will it take to fill the rest of the bucket?

(A) $\frac{7}{3}$

(B) $\frac{4}{3}$

(C) $\frac{3}{4}$

(D) $\frac{4}{7}$

13 The distance from the center of a circle to a chord is 5. If the length of the chord is 24, what is the length of the radius of the circle?

(A) 5

(B) 10

(C) 13

(D) 26

14 A 40-pound bag of garden soil contains 0.8 cubic feet of soil. What is the weight, in pounds, of the garden soil needed to cover a 12-foot by 12-foot square garden to a depth of 3 inches?

(A) 1152

(B) 1800

(C) 4608

(D) 5760

15 The demand for a certain product can be defined by the function $y = 500 - 12x$, where y is the number of units of the product that can be sold at a price of x dollars. Which statement must be true?

(A) If the price of the product decreases by \$1, the number of units that can be sold decreases by 12.

(B) If the price of the product increases by \$12, the number of units that can be sold decreases by 1.

(C) The y-intercept of the graph of the function represents the units of the product that can be sold at a cost of \$1.

(D) The x-intercept of the graph of the function represents the price at which no units of the product will be sold.

16 $y = (x - 5)(x + 1)$

The equation above represents a parabola. Which of the following equivalent forms of the equation shows the coordinates of the vertex of the parabola as constants or coefficients?

(A) $y = x^2 - 4x - 5$

(B) $y = (x - 2)^2 - 9$

(C) $y = x(x - 4) - 5$

(D) $y + 5 = x^2 - 4x$

GO TO THE
NEXT PAGE

practice test

QUESTIONS 17–19 REFER TO THE FOLLOWING GRAPH.

This scatterplot shows the scores for 10 students on their most recent Algebra and Chemistry tests.

17. What is the arithmetic mean of the students' algebra test scores?

(A) 68
(B) 70
(C) 79
(D) 80

18 A line of best fit of the data is given by $y = 0.76x + 27.6$, where x is a student's algebra test score, and y is a student's chemistry test score. Which interpretation is valid?

(A) The average chemistry test score is 27.6 points higher than the average algebra test score.

(B) The average algebra test score is 0.76 times the average chemistry test score.

(C) Students with higher algebra test scores tended to have higher chemistry test scores.

(D) There is not enough information to determine a relationship between the students' chemistry test scores and their algebra test scores.

19 Using the line of best fit, $y = 0.76x + 27.6$, what is the predicted algebra test score of a student with a chemistry test score of 70, rounded to the nearest whole number?

(A) 50
(B) 56
(C) 77
(D) 81

20 The velocity of an object dropped from a tower is given by the function $v(t) = -9.8t$, where t is the number of seconds after the object was dropped and $v(t)$ is given in meters per second. If the object hits the ground and stops moving after 4 seconds, which inequality shows the possible values of $v(t)$?

(A) $-39.2 \le v(t) \le 0$
(B) $-2.45 \le v(t) \le 0$
(C) $0 \le v(t) \le 2.45$
(D) $0 \le v(t) \le 39.2$

21 To predict the results of an election for city council, a polling company surveyed 200 randomly selected likely voters within the city. Of those surveyed, 80 planned to vote for candidate A. The polling company reported a margin of error of 3.5%. What is a reasonable estimate of the percentage of likely voters who support candidate A?

(A) Between 36.5% and 43.5%
(B) Between 46.5% and 53.5%
(C) Between 56.5% and 63.5%
(D) Between 76.5% and 83.5%

22 Corporate Average Fuel Economy sets targets for fuel economy for cars and light trucks. The target for the year 2020 is 42 miles per gallon, and for 2025, it is 54.5 miles per gallon. Which function can be used to estimate progress toward the goal y years after 2020 until 2025?

(A) $g(y) = 54.5 - 2.5y$

(B) $g(y) = 42 - 2.5y$

(C) $g(y) = 54.5 + 2.5y$

(D) $g(y) = 42 + 2.5y$

23 A municipal light plant buys energy from windmill farms that have two sizes of windmills. Small windmills produce 1.45 megawatts of power, and large windmills produce 2.75 megawatts of power. Which inequality represents the number of small windmills, x, and large windmills, y, needed to supply the light plant with a total power supply of at least 200 megawatts?

(A) $2.75x + 1.45y \leq 200$

(B) $1.45x + 2.75y \geq 200$

(C) $2.75x + 1.45y \geq 200$

(D) $1.45x + 2.75y \leq 200$

24 If x_1 and x_2 are the solutions of $x^2 - 4x = 3$, what is $|x_2 - x_1|$?

(A) 0

(B) 2

(C) 4

(D) $2\sqrt{7}$

25 A group of 18 coins has a total value of $3.10. If the coins consist only of quarters and nickels, how many more quarters are there than nickels?

(A) 3

(B) 4

(C) 7

(D) 11

26 Which graph would be drawn to represent an economy that is growing at a fixed percentage rate?

(A)

(B)

(C)

(D)

27 The graph of the line $2x + 3y = 15$ is drawn on the coordinate plane. What is the equation of the perpendicular line with the same y-intercept?

(A) $y = \frac{2}{3}x + \frac{15}{2}$

(B) $y = -\frac{2}{3}x + \frac{15}{2}$

(C) $y = \frac{3}{2}x + 5$

(D) $y = -\frac{3}{2}x + 5$

GO TO THE
NEXT PAGE

28

$$x + 3y < 1$$
$$x + y > 1$$

Which of these points is in the solution set of the system of inequalities above?

(A) (4, 2)

(B) (−4, −2)

(C) (4, −2)

(D) (−4, −2)

? same ?!

29

A polynomial function $p(x)$ is shown on the xy-coordinate plane. If $q(x)$ is a quadratic function, which of these equations can represent $p(x)$?

(A) $p(x) = (x − 1)q(x)$

(B) $p(x) = (x + 2)q(x)$

(C) $p(x) = (x − 3)q(x)$

(D) $p(x) = (x + 4)q(x)$

30 The points (−3, 2) and (3, 2) are the endpoints of a diameter of a circle. Which equation represents the circle?

(A) $(x − 2)^2 + y^2 = 3$

(B) $(x − 2)^2 + y^2 = 6$

(C) $x^2 + (y − 2)^2 = 9$

(D) $x^2 + (y − 2)^2 = 16$

🖩

Directions: For **questions 31–38,** solve the problem and enter your answer in the grid, as described below, on the answer sheet.

1. Although not required, it is suggested that you write your answer in the boxes at the top of the columns to help you fill in the circles accurately. You will receive credit only if the circles are filled in correctly.

2. Mark no more than one circle in any column.

3. No question has a negative answer.

4. Some problems may have more than one correct answer. In such cases, grid only one answer.

5. **Mixed numbers** such as $3\frac{1}{2}$ must be gridded as 3.5 or $\frac{7}{2}$.

   If $3\frac{1}{2}$ is entered into the grid as $\overline{3\,|\,1\,/\,2}$, it will be interpreted as $\frac{31}{2}$, not $3\frac{1}{2}$.)

5. **Decimal answers:** If you obtain a decimal answer with more digits than the grid can accommodate, it may be either rounded or truncated, but it must fill the entire grid.

GO TO THE
NEXT PAGE

practice test

🖩

31 A local politician requested donations to pay for the cost of a radio ad. Twelve donors offered to split the cost equally, so they each paid $75. If the politician was able to find 20 donors to equally split the same cost, how much would each pay?

33 Jessica caught five fish with an average weight of 10 pounds. If three of the fish weigh 9, 9, and 10 pounds, respectively, what is the average (arithmetic mean) weight of the other two fish?

32

In the figure above, $\angle N = (9x - 40)°$, $\angle J = (4x + 30)°$, and $\angle JLR = (8x + 40)°$. What is the measure of $\angle J$? (Do not grid the degree symbol.)

34 In 2012, Algeria had a population of approximately 37.44 million. In 2013, the population had grown to 38.19 million. If the function $p(t) = a \cdot b^t$ is used to model the population in millions, $p(t)$, t years after 2012, what is the value of b? Round your answer to the nearest hundredth.

35 Juliette runs 20 miles a week. She would like to increase her running distance by 10% each week. How many miles should Juliette run after 2 times of increasing her distance by 10%?

37
$$3.6x + 2.4y = 12$$
$$x - y = 2$$

If (x,y) is a solution of the system of equations above, what is the value of y?

36 For which value of a will the equation $5(x + 7) - ax = ax + 35$ have infinitely many solutions?

38 The function $f(x) = x^2 - 4$ is translated 3 units to the right to create function $g(x)$. What is the value of $g(9)$?

STOP

If you finish before time is called, you may check your work on this section only.
Do not turn to any other section.

practice test

SECTION 5: ESSAY

50 Minutes • 1 Essay

Directions: The essay gives you an opportunity to show how effectively you can read and comprehend a passage and write an essay analyzing the passage. In your essay, you should demonstrate that you have read the passage carefully, present a clear and logical analysis, and use language precisely.

Your essay will need to be written on the lines provided in your answer booklet. You will have enough space if you write on every line and keep your handwriting to an average size. Try to print or write clearly so that your writing will be legible to the readers scoring your essay.

As you read the passage below, consider how Elizabeth Roberts-Pedersen uses the following:

- Evidence, such as facts, statistics, or examples, to support claims.
- Reasoning to develop ideas and to connect claims and evidence.
- Stylistic or persuasive elements, such as word choice or appeals to emotion, to add power to the ideas expressed.

Adapted from "From Shell Shock to PTSD: Proof of War's Traumatic History" by Elizabeth Roberts-Pedersen, originally published by The Conversation *on April 14, 2015. Elizabeth Roberts-Pedersen is a lecturer in history at the University of Western Sydney in Australia. (This passage was edited for length. To read the complete article, see http://theconversation.com.)*

1   2015 marks several important First World War anniversaries: the centenary of the first use of poison gas in January; the centenary of the Gallipoli landings and the Armenian genocide in April. It is also 100 years since *The Lancet* published Charles S. Myers' article, "A Contribution to the Study of Shell Shock."

The study of shell shock

2   Myers' article is generally regarded as the first use of the term "shell shock" in medical literature. It was used as a descriptor for "three cases of loss of memory, vision, smell and taste" in British soldiers admitted to a military hospital in France.

3   While Myers presented these cases as evidence of the spectacular concussive effects of artillery on the Western Front, British medical opinion soon came to regard these symptoms as psychological in origin. The men presenting to medical officers with tics, tremors, and palpitations, as well as more serious symptoms of "functional" blindness, paralysis, and loss of speech, were not concussed—but nor were they necessarily cowards or malingerers.

4   Instead, these were men simply worn down by the unprecedented stresses of trench warfare—in particular, the effort required to push out of one's mind the prospect of joining the ranks of the maimed or the corpses lying in no man's land ....

5   For contemporaries and later for historians, shell shock came to encapsulate all the horror of this new form of industrialized warfare. As historian Jay Winter suggests, it moved "from a diagnosis into a metaphor." …

Developing a diagnosis

6   It is tempting to view shell shock as the unambiguous turning point in psychiatry's history, popularizing the idea that unconscious processes might produce symptoms that operate separately from moral qualities such as endurance and courage. However, scholarship over the last 15 years suggests that this position was far from widely accepted.

7   … The notion that many patients had some "predisposing" weakness—independent of their combat experiences—persisted throughout the interwar period and into the Second World War.

8   It wasn't until the Vietnam War that this formulation was reversed, which in turn bridged the gap between combatant syndromes and the civilian sphere.

9   This development is only comprehensible as part of a broader political context. The notion that the Vietnam War exacted a form of psychic damage on American soldiers was championed by the anti-war activists of Vietnam Veterans Against the War (VVAW) and psychiatrists Chaim Shatan and Robert Jay Lifton. "Post-Vietnam syndrome," Shatan wrote, was caused by the "unconsummated grief" of a brutal and brutalizing war.

10   The VVAW's advocacy was instrumental in securing official recognition for this condition. It was included in 1980 in the third edition of the *Diagnostic and Statistical Manual of Mental Disorders* (*DSM-III)* as "post-traumatic stress disorder."

11   PTSD's inclusion in *DSM-III* legitimated the suffering of Vietnam veterans and held out the possibility of subsidized medical care and compensation. But the *DSM-III* definition of PTSD was significant in two additional ways.

12   First, it identified the disorder as a condition that could afflict soldiers and civilians alike—not a diagnosis exclusive to combat, like shell shock.

13   Second, it focused attention on the continuing effects of a traumatic experience, rather than on the personality and constitution of the patient.

14   The ramifications of these changes have been immense. PTSD and a broader field of "traumatology" are now entrenched in psychiatric and popular discourse. In Australia, we now assume that warfare is objectively traumatizing, and that governments ought to provide medical and financial support for affected service personnel, even if a recent Four Corners program confirmed that this is not always the case.

How is PTSD viewed today?

15   Though PTSD has its origins in opposition to the Vietnam War, the politics of the condition are now largely ambivalent, with its significance shifting according to circumstance.

16   This point is well illustrated by the film *American Sniper*, which demonstrates the possibility of two contrary positions. After his return to civilian life, SEAL sniper Chris Kyle (Bradley Cooper) is shown to be suffering from some characteristic after-effects of combat. …

…

GO TO THE
NEXT PAGE

17 The real Chris Kyle was shot dead by Eddie Ray Routh [another veteran] in 2013. At trial, the accused's lawyers pursued a defense of insanity, compounded by the inadequate care provided by veterans' mental health services. Routh was found guilty of Kyle's murder in March of 2015.

18 In the 100 years since Myers' article on shell shock, the psychological consequences of war remain as relevant as ever.

Write an essay in which you explain how the writer builds an argument to persuade her audience that she is offering proof of war's traumatic history. In your essay, analyze how Elizabeth Roberts-Pedersen uses one or more of the features listed above (or features of your own choice) to strengthen the logic and persuasiveness of her argument. Be sure that your analysis focuses on the most relevant aspects of the passage.

Your essay should not explain whether you agree with the writer's claims, but rather explain how she builds an argument to persuade her audience.

STOP

If you finish before time is called, you may check your work on this section only.
Do not turn to any other section.

ANSWER KEY AND EXPLANATIONS

Section 1: Reading Test

1. B	12. B	23. D	34. C	45. B
2. A	13. D	24. D	35. D	46. A
3. C	14. B	25. A	36. A	47. C
4. D	15. B	26. B	37. D	48. C
5. C	16. A	27. A	38. A	49. B
6. B	17. D	28. B	39. B	50. C
7. A	18. B	29. C	40. A	51. A
8. D	19. C	30. B	41. C	52. D
9. B	20. B	31. B	42. A	
10. C	21. C	32. B	43. B	
11. A	22. A	33. C	44. D	

READING TEST RAW SCORE
(Number of correct answers) ☐

1. **The correct answer is (B).** The narrator's description of Jack and his bride, of their wonder at their surroundings and happiness at their marriage, makes choice (B) the correct answer. Choice (A) is incorrect because though Jack seems awkward in his surroundings, he does not seem aware of his lower social standing compared to other passengers. Though the passage provides a great deal of insight about the people who traveled on trains and the luxury in which they traveled, choice (C) is incorrect because the primary focus is on the newly married couple and their interactions. While Jack and his bride do seem self-conscious on the train, and while other passengers seem to regard them with derision, the passage does not delve deeply into issue of class and class consciousness, so choice (D) is also incorrect.

2. **The correct answer is (A).** The couple's trip on the opulent train, as well as specific luxuries that Jack points out to his bride, makes choice (A) the correct answer.

Choice (B) is misleading, as Jack's face is "reddened from many days in the wind and sun," suggesting that he works outside but not necessarily as a farmhand or rancher. Choice (C) is incorrect because, while the couple seem to shrug off the stares of other passengers, readers get the distinct impression that they are not used to being around people of a higher social standing. Choice (D) is not correct because Jack does not suggest through deeds or words that he wants more than he has.

3. **The correct answer is (C).** Jack's enthusiastic tone in responding to his bride's delight ("Great!") and his "brave" assurance that they are "going to go the whole thing" when she questions if they can afford the dining car make choice (C) the correct answer. While choice (A) suggests that Jack is aware of his formal clothes and may want to make a good impression, it is not clear that he wants to impress his bride with his appearance. Therefore, choice (A) is incorrect. Because it involves the bride and the other

passengers' perceptions of her, choice (B) is also incorrect. Though (D) suggests that the couple views their marriage favorably, there is no indication in these lines that Jack wants to impress his bride.

4. **The correct answer is (D).** In the first sentence, the phrase "whirling onward with such dignity of motion that a glance from the window seemed simply to prove that the plains of Texas were pouring eastward" suggests that the train was moving very smoothly, so choice (D) is the correct answer as "gracefulness" suggests a lack of turbulence. Choices (A) and (C) are incorrect because, while they may suggest that the ride is better than expected, they do not describe the smooth movement that the sentence emphasizes. Choice (B) is a synonym of "dignity," but it does not suit the context of the sentence.

5. **The correct answer is (C).** The expressions of both Jack and his bride, as well as the intimation that they are not wholly comfortable in their attire, make choice (C) correct. The pair seems happy about their marriage, but there is no suggestion that they are resolute about their decision to marry or about any other decision, so choice (A) is incorrect. Choice (B) is a distortion because, while they seem slightly nervous, there is no evidence to suggest that they are nervous about the trip itself. Choice (D) is incorrect because, although they are amazed at the train's interior, they do not seem to notice the landscape.

6. **The correct answer is (B).** The couple's awkwardness and self-consciousness is best supported by Jack's nervous and shy countenance, choice (B). The description of the landscape is a distraction and does not support the inference that the couple feels self-conscious, so choice (A) is incorrect. Choice (C) is off-base because it suggests the bride is concerned about the cost, rather than how the couple might appear to others. Choice (D) is incorrect because the narrator's likening the state of their marriage to their surroundings does not suggest that they were either comfortable or uncomfortable in their surroundings.

7. **The correct answer is (A).** The narrator notes the other passengers' "careless scrutiny" and emphasizes that the bride's countenance is "emotionless." The inference is that the other passengers were staring to such a degree that the bride's usually "placid" face flushed red with embarrassment, making choice (A) correct. While the narrator notes in the following sentence that the pair are "very happy," there is no evidence to suggest that she is blushing from happiness, so choice (B) is not correct. While the "careless scrutiny" likely led to self-consciousness, there is no evidence to support the idea that the bride is generally lacking in self-confidence. Therefore, choice (C) is incorrect. Choice (D) is misleading, because the narrator only notes that the bride is plain, not unattractive.

8. **The correct answer is (D).** In the preceding sentence the narrator notes that "their surroundings reflected the glory of their marriage that morning in San Antonio." The glory of their new estate, then, refers to their new standing as a married couple, so choice (D) is correct. While "estate" can refer to social standing, in this case the couple's newly married status helps to give context to the word, so choice (A) is incorrect. Choice (B) is off-base, as "interests" do not fit the context. While "estate" does refer to property, the context of the sentence does not support this definition of the word. Therefore, choice (C) is incorrect.

9. **The correct answer is (B).** The narrator notes that the couple "had small knowledge" of the porter's bullying, so choice (B) is correct. There is no indication they are being openly mocked, nor that the couple feels catered to, so choice (A) is incorrect. The narrator describes the couple's enjoyment and does not suggest that anyone was openly hostile to them, thus choice (C) is not correct. The couple "had small knowledge" of the porter's bullying, so choice (D) cannot be correct because they could not have become used to behavior they had small knowledge of.

10. **The correct answer is (C).** Because the author describes the new black suit as the cause when he says the groom's "brick-

colored hands were constantly performing in a most conscious fashion," choice (C) is the correct answer. Although the groom is nervous in general, here the focus is on how his clothes have led to certain hand gestures, so choice (A) is incorrect. Choice (B) is off-base because although the author brings up the weathered condition of the groom's hands, he uses it as a contrast to the new clothes; the reader can assume that the groom's hands are clean. (D) is incorrect because the groom's happiness is not described in this part of the story, and when he expresses happiness, it is with a natural openness. For example, he smiles with delight or beams with elation.

11. **The correct answer is (A).** The passage covers nest building, feeding, and other behaviors, so choice (A) is correct. Choice (B) is incorrect, because the passage does not deal exclusively or mostly with nest building. Choice (C) is also incorrect because while the author notes that the hummingbird is interesting, it is not an argument the author makes throughout the passage. Choice (D) is also incorrect because the author does not, for example, explain why the hummingbird builds nests where it does, but rather describes its behavior.

12. **The correct answer is (B).** By noting that the birds arrive "about the twenty-fifth of April," the author is implying that hummingbirds are elsewhere before that. There is a certain presumption that the reader understands that many birds migrate for the winter, thus choice (B) is the correct answer. The time span the author gives is between the time the birds arrive and the time they begin building their nest, so choice (A) is incorrect. There is no indication that some birds do not migrate farther north of Pennsylvania, so choice (C) is not a correct assumption. By referring to "the Hummingbird," the author is not referring to a singular one, but rather to those species that migrate to Pennsylvania. Therefore, choice (D) is also incorrect.

13. **The correct answer is (D).** The author is describing how the nest is stuck to the branch and provides a context clue in the form of a synonym ("attached") in line 8, so choice

(D) is correct. Because neither choice (A) nor choice (B) make sense in the context of the sentence, they are incorrect. While choice (C) makes sense in the context, it does not make sense when the synonym ("attached") in line 8 is taken into account, and so it is incorrect.

14. **The correct answer is (B).** The author notes the materials in each layer and uses phrases like "firmness and consistency" and "closely laid together," making choice (B) the correct answer. While the author does cite a number of different plants that go into the nest, the way in which the hummingbird layers the materials and fuses them to the nest is the focus, so choice (A) is incorrect. Though it might be assumed that such an intricate nest takes time to build, the author does not note time as a factor, so choice (C) is not correct. While the author notes that the bird's saliva helps keep out moisture, there is no mention of this characteristic as the author describes the other layers, so choice (D) is also incorrect.

15. **The correct answer is (B).** The author notes the female's reaction when a person comes near, which makes choice (B) correct. There is no mention of how long hummingbird chicks stay in the nest, so choice (A) is incorrect. Though the author mentions that hummingbird chirps are "not louder than that of a small cricket or grasshopper," it is also noted that a hummingbird's "only note is a single chirp," making choice (C) incorrect. The author notes that the females most likely carry "animal food" to their young, so choice (D) is also incorrect.

16. **The correct answer is (A).** The author notes the female hummingbird's reaction when a person comes near, inferring her fierce protection of her eggs and nest. So, choice (A) is the correct answer. Choice (B) refers to the duration that chicks are in the nest, and thus does not support the inference. Choice (C) refers to what hummingbirds eat, and it also does not support the inference. Choice (D) is incorrect because it includes details about a hummingbird's voice and does not support the idea that the female guards her young.

17. The correct answer is (D). Choice (D) is correct because the bird is putting its feathers in order, as supported by the word "arrange." Choice (A) is incorrect because no oil or supporting words are mentioned in the passage. Choice (B) is misleading because in this instance, the author doesn't compare the bird's plumage to clothes. Choice (C) would be a possibility except that the author describes the dexterity of the bird and uses the word "arrange," which implies precision. Shuffle is a word commonly associated with clumsiness.

18. The correct answer is (B). The author notes that the hummingbird "poises, or suspends himself on wing, for the space of two or three seconds." To accomplish this, the hummingbird would have to move its wings at a high speed, making choice (B) the correct answer. While the description of the wings as "only like a mist" may sound as if they are transparent, there is no other evidence to support this inference. Therefore, choice (A) is incorrect. The sun reflecting off the wings would not make them "become invisible," so choice (C) is also incorrect. While the author praises the hummingbird, the description of the wings does not emphasize beauty, thus choice (D) is not correct.

19. The correct answer is (C). In lines 88–90, the author notes that, "for when two males meet at the same bush, or flower, a battle instantly takes place." When the author says the victor "returns to the same place," the reference must be the bush or flower, a conclusion reinforced by line 78 in which the author describes how the hummingbird "extracts its sweets" from the flower. Thus, choice (C) is correct. Though the author notes in line 81 that the hummingbird tends to alight on the "dead twigs of a tree," there is no indication that this is the place the bird returns to after battle, so choice (A) is incorrect. Similarly, although the two combatants are male, the author has not indicated that the males are battling over females. Rather, the battle seems to be over access to food, so choice (B) is also incorrect. Choice (D) is off-base, as the author only mentions the conqueror returning "to the same place."

20. The correct answer is (B). The author's description of the hummingbird extracting nectar from a flower serves to introduce the idea that hummingbirds feed on flower nectar (Lines 75–79), thus supporting the notion that the two males are fighting over a food source (the flower). So choice (B) is correct. While the author begins the passage with a description of the nesting habits of females, nesting and mating are not discussed in the second paragraph, so choice (A) is incorrect. The reference to dead twigs is not to any specific territory, making choice (C) incorrect. The reference to another male hummingbird provides no support for the idea that "fruits of his victory" refers to the nectar of flowers, so choice (D) is incorrect.

21. The correct answer is (C). The name "kingbird" infers that the bird is large, while the bee is small. The author notes that the hummingbird "teases" the kingbird and chases off the bee, showing that, despite its small size, the hummingbird defends itself against both large and small assailants. Choice (C) is the correct answer. The author pointedly notes how the hummingbird is successful in both instances, making choice (A) incorrect. Choice (B) is also incorrect, as the author describes the female hummingbird as staying on its nest and these lines refer to the male. While choice (D) may seem plausible given how the hummingbird "teases" the kingbird, the interaction with the bee is slightly different in that the bee harasses the hummingbird.

22. The correct answer is (A). By invoking Mt. Everest, the world's tallest mountain, the author is intent on showing that there are equally extraordinary and exotic geographical features on the ocean floor, making choice (A) the correct answer. While the author does emphasize that Mauna Kea is actually taller, that isn't the point of the opening sentence. Instead, the author continues describing the many geographical features found on the ocean floor. Therefore, choice (B) is incorrect. The author does not describe the geography of Mauna Kea or any other island mountain, so choice (C) is incorrect. Because there is no other mention of Mt. Everest in the passage, choice (D) is also incorrect.

23. **The correct answer is (D).** In lines 26–28, the author points out that the way the edges of the plates fit together determines the geography of the ocean floor. Thus, choice (D) is correct. As the author does not note individual plates and the role each plays, choice (A) is incorrect. Comparing the earth to a jigsaw puzzle does not underscore the spherical shape of the earth, so choice (B) is incorrect. Because the author does not describe the shape of each plate, choice (C) is also incorrect.

24. **The correct answer is (D).** The author describes the tectonic plates as "floating on top of the Earth's hot flowing mantle" and notes that "convection currents in the molten mantle layer cause the plates to slowly move," so choice (D) is correct. Earthquakes and volcanoes are a result of the movement of the plates, so choice (A) is incorrect. The author mentions "convection currents," not ocean currents, causing the plates to move, thus choice (B) is also incorrect. The upward flow of magma in diverging plates causes new ocean floor crust, so choice (D) is not correct.

25. **The correct answer is (A).** In lines 53–61, the author notes that the discovery forced scientists to "redefine living systems on our planet" and then goes on to note "other previously described ecosystems" that rely on sunlight and photosynthesis as the basis of their food web. Therefore, choice (A) is the correct answer. It can be inferred that deep ocean hydrothermal vents were discovered at the same time that the ecosystems that thrive in and around them, thus choice (B) is incorrect. In lines 89–104, the author describes the food web found in this ecosystem and notes that these animals must be adapted to survive in the extreme environment. There is no indication that the animals move between environments, so choice (C) is incorrect. While there are many metals that spew from the vents, the depth and extreme conditions imply that mining would be difficult, so choice (D) is also incorrect.

26. **The correct answer is (B).** In lines 53–61, the author notes that the discovery forced scientists to "redefine living systems on

our planet" and then goes on to note "other previously described ecosystems" that rely on sunlight and photosynthesis as the basis of their food web. This makes choice (B) the correct answer. Lines 43–46 do not provide evidence because the author has not yet tied the new species to the existence of an ecosystem that relies on chemosynthesis, so choice (A) is incorrect. The way hydrothermal vents are formed does not support the inference about ecosystems that are based on photosynthesis, so choice (C) is incorrect. Similarly, the kinds of metals that spew from the vents support bacteria that form the base of the chemosynthetic food web, but the existence of these metals does not support the inference that before 1977 scientists believed that all ecosystems were based on photosynthesis. Thus, choice (D) is also incorrect.

27. **The correct answer is (A).** In lines 83–84, the author describes "molecules that billow out of the seafloor." Because of the context, we know that the molecules are somehow emerging from the seafloor, but there is no indication that it is forceful, so choice (A) seems the most reasonable answer. Answer choices (B), (C), and (D) indicate a degree of force or type of movement that is not indicated in the context of the sentence.

28. **The correct answer is (B).** At the beginning of the second paragraph, the author notes, "The shape of the ocean floor, its bathymetry, is largely a result of a process called plate tectonics." The author goes on to describe how the movement of plates causes hydrothermal vents, so choice (B) is the correct answer. While the author does describe the geography of the ocean floor, this description is general and doesn't tie into the discussion of hydrothermal vents, so choice (A) is incorrect. The suggestion that hydrothermal vents are created by the same forces that create volcanoes is tangential, thus choice (C) is also incorrect. While the author describes the ecosystems around hydrothermal vents as different from those that rely on photosynthesis, the discussion of plate tectonics does not support the inference that they are unusual. Therefore, choice (D) is not correct.

29. The correct answer is (C). The passage describes the features of hydrothermal vents, so the discussion of plate tectonics serves to explain how hydrothermal vents are formed. In lines 62–66, the author explains how the movement of the plates causes the formation of hydrothermal vents, so choice (C) is correct. In lines 8–12, the author introduces the geography of the ocean floor but has not yet mentioned hydrothermal vents, so choice (A) is incorrect. In lines 46–51, the author notes that many species have been discovered in this unique environment, but there is no general discussion of the formation of hydrothermal vents. Thus, choice (B) is not correct. Lines 66–69 note that the main causes of hydrothermal vents are also responsible for volcanoes and earthquakes, but the information is parenthetical and not as extensive as in the previous lines, so choice (D) is also incorrect.

30. The correct answer is (B). The description of an "extreme environment," including darkness and extreme temperatures that would kill most other forms of life, signals that choice (B) is the answer. Neither choice (A) nor choice (C) supports the idea of the extremely inhospitable environment that the author is describing in the paragraph. Likewise, choice (D) is incorrect because while the environment described is unusual, the focus is more on the idea that it is inhospitable, i.e., harmful to most forms of life that we know.

31. The correct answer is (B). Based on the arrows, we know that the metals go up through the vent. But once they separate from the solution, the only indication we have of what happens to them is the label of "metalliferous sediment" on the sea bed. We can infer that "metalliferous sediment" is sediment made up of metals, so choice (B) is correct. There are no arrows to indicate that the metals are moved by ocean currents, nor arrows to show that they rise to the surface, so choices (A) and (C) are incorrect. The arrows in the black smoker only go up, making choice (D) incorrect.

32. The correct answer is (B). The passage begins with a sentence that focuses on boys who live in the tenements. Further, the passage ends with the idea that "Home to them is an empty name," referring again to the tenements, so choice (B) is correct. Though much of the first paragraph is a discussion of the few job opportunities, the focus is still on the lack of opportunities *in the tenements*, so choice (A) is not correct. The author does allude to education in the last paragraph, but it is not the focus of the passage, thus choice (C) is also incorrect. The second paragraph deals with delinquency, but it is within the context of the tenements. Therefore, choice (D) is incorrect.

33. The correct answer is (C). Both the preceding and following sentences discuss the idea that the tenements are not "elevating" and contribute to "idle" ways, so the context makes choice (C) the correct answer. While polluting can mean "dirty," the author here is concerned more with the child's character development, so choice (A) is incorrect. There is no evidence to suggest that the games are dangerous, thus choice (B) is also incorrect. Similarly, the context does not suggest that the author is referring to the games as having a noisy character, so choice (D) is not correct.

34. The correct answer is (C). The context of the tenements and the rest of the sentence ("held down by the hand that of all should labor to raise him") help make clear that the author is referring to the child's surroundings, the people who make up his community. Thus, choice (C) is the correct answer. Because the author's reference to "the boy" is a reference to all boys in the tenement, choice (A) cannot be correct. Choice (B) is incorrect because the author's discussion is more about the corrosive effects of the entire community, not of the smaller family unit. There is no indication that the children go to school, so choice (D) is also incorrect.

35. The correct answer is (D). Again, the author's focus is on the tenements as spirit crushing, as supported by the following sentence, "Its influence is scarcely of the elevating kind, if it have any." Thus, choice (D) is the correct answer. While the author speaks of "so many other human animals," creating an image of packed cages, there is no suggestion that the tenements are filthy, only that they don't provide an environment that helps grow a boy's character, so choice (A) is incorrect. Likewise, choices (B) and (C) are incorrect because they do not take into account the preceding sentence about home being "the greatest factor of all in the training of the young," as well as the context of the tenements as soul-crushing.

36. **The correct answer is (A).** The author demonstrates the meaning of "idle" in the sentence that follows the word, in which the author describes the boy doing things that will not help him and may lead him into trouble. Thus, choice (A) is the correct answer. The context of the sentence, the implication that "idle" ways will lead to trouble does not support choice (B), "vain," as an answer. Similarly, there is no indication that the boy acts younger than he is, so choice (C) is incorrect. While "idle" can mean inactive, the sentence that follows indicates that the author is not referring to inactivity, so choice (D) is also incorrect.

37. **The correct answer is (D).** The author notes that "The city has no Truant Home" and that efforts to get the child to go to school "are paralyzed by this want," or this need for a truant home, so choice (D) is the correct answer. The author notes in the lines that precede lines 34–41 that a reformatory is full of "vicious boys," but the author sees a "want" or need for a truant home, so choices (A) and (C) are incorrect. The suggestion that the city needs a truant home because the boy won't go to school suggests the opposite of choice (B).

38. **The correct answer is (A).** The author notes in lines 43–47: "Rough as he is, if any one doubt that this child of common clay have in him the instinct of beauty, of love for the ideal of which his life has no embodiment, let him put the matter to the test." Thus, choice (A) is the correct answer. Because the context suggests the author is speaking of the child's "instinct for beauty," choice (B) is incorrect. While there is a suggestion that no flowers grow in the tenements, choice (C) is incorrect because the author's focus here is on the child and his (or her) potential, as evidenced by the sentence cited above. Similarly, the reference to the police and

their tactics suggests brutality in dealing with the children. The focus, again, is on the child's potential, so choice (D) is incorrect.

39. **The correct answer is (B).** The lines, "if anyone doubt that this child of common clay have in him the instinct of beauty, of love for the ideal of which his life has no embodiment," support the idea that the tenement child has a capacity to appreciate beauty, so choice (B) is the correct answer. Neither choice (A) nor choice (D) suggests the child has the capacity to appreciate beauty, given his (or her) surroundings. While choice (C) suggests the calming effect of flowers and juxtaposes this with the image of a policeman's brutal tactics, it does not suggest the capacity to appreciate the "ideal."

40. **The correct answer is (A).** In lines 78–81, the author notes that tenement children lead lives of "wearisome toil" as opposed to "their happier fellows" whose play "has but just begun." The author is maintaining that tenement children aren't allowed to play and just be children, so choice (A) is the correct answer. While the author notes in a preceding sentence that they have a "hunger that is never fed," the author is referring more to a spiritual hunger, so choice (B) is incorrect. The author says that the children are more likely to be moved by flowers than by a policeman with a club, but there is no discussion of police brutality. The fact that the children can sleep on the street suggests that the police look the other way. Therefore, choice (C) is also incorrect. Choice (D) is incorrect because, although the author says "Home is an empty name," there is no direct correlation between that idea and the photos. The boy in the factory might have a viable home, nevertheless, he is working at too young an age.

41. **The correct answer is (C).** In lines 83–85, the author notes that tenement children "banished and barred" from "a yard of turf" as from "a heaven that is not for such as they," and notes later that there was not "a green sod within a quarter of a mile." Thus, choice (C) is the correct answer. While the author notes that this is "their first lesson in 'writin'," the point is more about what they wrote, so choice (A) is not correct.

Similarly, choice (B) is incorrect, as the author does not mention lack of schooling in this paragraph. There is no support for choice (D), as the focus in this paragraph is on children's play.

42. **The correct answer is (A).** In lines 81–85, the author notes that tenement children are "banished and barred" from "a yard of turf" as from "a heaven that is not for such as they," supporting the idea that there are no available green spaces for them, so choice (A) is the correct answer. Choice (B) does not support the idea that there are no available green spaces, as it merely recounts seeing children write on a fence. While choice (C) notes that the children tried to write "keep off the grass," it does not provide a wider context for why they wrote it. Choice (D) is incorrect because it provides no direct evidence to support the idea that there are no available green spaces.

43. **The correct answer is (B).** In line 50, Robert expresses his devotion to Clara by saying that he is "entirely yours," and likewise, Napoleon begins his letter by noting that "I have not spent a day without loving you; I have not spent a night without embracing you." Both letters express a devotion and commitment to the relationship, so choice (B) is the correct answer. While Napoleon's letter betrays his jealousy, Robert's letter contains no note of jealousy, so choice (A) is incorrect. Napoleon's letter notes his "pride and ambition" that force him away from Josephine, a reference to his work, but Robert's letter mentions no such reference, so choice (C) is incorrect. Likewise, choice (D) is incorrect, as Robert's letter does not lament that the two are apart.

44. **The correct answer is (D).** The author notes in lines 28–30, "but I cannot see why he should despise me and, as you say, hate me without any reason." Thus, choice (D) is correct. The synonyms "despise" and "hate" suggest that choice (A) is incorrect, as indifference implies little feeling. Similarly, choices (B) and (C) are incorrect, as "hate" and "despise" suggest dislike, not mistrust or rudeness.

45. **The correct answer is (B).** In lines 6–9, the author notes, "I wonder anxiously whether … I had any right to bind you to me, my angel" and then goes on to write in lines 11–13, "These doubts all arise, I am inclined to think, from your father's attitude towards me." Thus, choice (B) is correct. Choice (A) is incorrect, as Robert notes in lines 33–34, "I really love and respect your father." There is no indication that he doubts Clara's love for him. In fact, lines 42–43 suggest otherwise: "You cannot think how your letter has raised and strengthened me." Therefore, choice (C) is incorrect. In lines 43–45, Robert writes, "You are splendid, and I have much more reason to be proud of you than of me," so choice (D) is also incorrect.

46. **The correct answer is (A).** In lines 7–9, the author notes, "I wonder anxiously whether … I had any right to bind you to me, my angel" and then goes on to write in lines 11–13, "These doubts all arise, I am inclined to think, from your father's attitude towards me." Thus, choice (A) is correct. Choice (B) is incorrect, as Robert doubts himself in these lines, not his relationship with Clara. In Lines 31–39, Robert expresses his admiration for Clara's father, sentiments that do not support the inference, so choice (C) is incorrect. Likewise, (D) suggests a new commitment by Robert to their relationship, so choice (D) is also incorrect.

47. **The correct answer is (C).** Napoleon writes in lines 82–87: "Woe to the person responsible! May he, as punishment and penalty, experience what my convictions and the evidence (which is in your friend's favour) would make me experience!" thus suggesting that choice (C) is the correct answer. While Napoleon himself does not like being away from Josephine (lines 59–63), there is no indication that she has grown tired of his absence, so choice (A) is incorrect. Choice (B) is also incorrect, as Napoleon questions whether she is too busy to write to her husband (lines 77–80). There is nothing to suggest that Napoleon thinks Josephine questions her marriage, so choice (D) is also incorrect.

48. **The correct answer is (C).** Napoleon writes in lines 82–87: "Woe to the person responsible! May he, as punishment and penalty, experience what my convictions

and the evidence (which is in your friend's favour) would make me experience!" This makes choice (C) the correct answer. While Napoleon himself does not like being away from Josephine (lines 59–63), this sentiment does not support the inference that he thinks she's having an affair, so choice (A) is incorrect. Choice (B) is also incorrect, as Napoleon condemns the coldness of her letter but does not question her fidelity in these lines. While Napoleon questions Josephine's commitment in the last lines of the passage, the lines do not reflect his mistrust, so choice (D) is also incorrect.

49. **The correct answer is (B).** The context—Napoleon's desire to see Josephine—and the phrase "by a matter of days" suggest that choice (B) is the correct answer. Choice (A) is incorrect, as stretching out the time would delay his ability to see Josephine. "Force" does not make sense when added to the phrase "by a matter of days," so choice (C) is incorrect. Likewise, choice (D) is incorrect because "cause" does not suggest the idea that Napoleon wants to make the days go by more quickly.

50. **The correct answer is (C).** In lines 42–43, Robert writes to Clara: "You cannot think how your letter has raised and strengthened me. …" whereas Napoleon writes to Josephine in lines 75–77: "Ah! wretch, how could you have written this letter? How cold it is!" Thus, choice (C) is the correct answer. While Robert does indeed express doubts, those doubts seem to stem from the attitude of Clara's father, not Clara's letter, so choice (A) is incorrect. Robert does not question Clara's loyalty, though Napoleon does question Josephine's, thus choice (B)

is also incorrect. Clara's letter to Robert only seems to have strengthened his love for her, rather than made him feel confused, so choice (D) is not correct.

51. **The correct answer is (A).** Napoleon is incensed and crushed that Josephine used *vous* (a formal way of addressing someone) in her letter, whereas Robert is delighted by the memory of Clara calling him *du*. Therefore, choice (A) is the correct answer, and choice (B) is incorrect. Likewise, choice (C) is incorrect because rather than calming Napoleon, the use of *vous* has made him angry. Choice (D) is incorrect, as there is no evidence that Robert feels humbled by her words.

52. **The correct answer is (D).** In lines 13–14, Robert notes, "It is so easy to accept other people's estimate of oneself." Similarly, Napoleon writes in lines 91–95, "You love me less; but you will get over the loss. One day you will love me no longer; at least tell me; then I shall know how I have come to deserve this misfortune …." Choice (D) then is the correct answer. Neither Robert nor Napoleon show any evidence of being modest, thus choice (A) is incorrect. There is no evidence to support the idea that Robert angers quickly, whereas Napoleon seems quick to anger. Thus, choice (B) is not correct. While Robert seems indecisive, Napoleon does not. In fact, he seems to make up his mind about Josephine quickly, so choice (C) is also incorrect.

Section 2: Writing and Language Test

1. D	11. B	21. D	31. A	41. B
2. B	12. B	22. B	32. B	42. A
3. A	13. C	23. B	33. A	43. D
4. C	14. B	24. D	34. B	44. B
5. A	15. D	25. A	35. D	
6. A	16. A	26. D	36. C	
7. A	17. A	27. D	37. C	
8. D	18. C	28. C	38. D	
9. B	19. B	29. B	39. A	
10. C	20. C	30. D	40. C	

WRITING AND LANGUAGE TEST RAW SCORE
(Number of correct answers)

1. **The correct answer is (D).** Choice (D) is correct because it conveys the clear and attention-grabbing nature of the boldly colored red-and-white sign. Choice (A) is incorrect because the context does not suggest that the sign is unbending or stiff. Choice (B) is incorrect because it suggests that the sign is potentially disturbing. Choice (C) is incorrect because it suggests that the sign is one-of-a-kind or unique.

2. **The correct answer is (B).** Choice (B) is correct because the sentence is declarative and therefore requires a period. Choice (A) is incorrect because the sentence is not a question. Choice (C) is incorrect because it creates a run-on. Choice (D) is incorrect because the sentence is not an exclamation.

3. **The correct answer is (A).** Choice (A) is correct because "obscure" supports the characterization of the colony as "far-flung" and out-of-the-way. Choice (B) is incorrect because there is no indication that the colony is not well-lit. Choice (C) is incorrect because the colony is the opposite of obvious. Choice (D) is incorrect because

the word implies vagueness, which isn't intended here.

4. **The correct answer is (C).** Choice (C) is correct because the sentence requires the simple past tense. Choice (A) is incorrect because this is past perfect tense. Choice (B) is incorrect because it is in the present perfect tense. Choice (D) is incorrect because it is in the future tense.

5. **The correct answer is (A).** Choice (A) is correct because the phrase "as they seemingly float above seas of green foliage" modifies, and thus must follow, "Buddhist temples." Choices (B) and (C) are incorrect because they make it unclear what the modifying clause refers to. Choice (C) is incorrect because the use of commas is wrong.

6. **The correct answer is (A).** Choice (A) is the correct because "country's" is a singular possessive noun referring to Burma. Choice (B) is incorrect because it is plural, not possessive. Choice (C) is incorrect because it requires an apostrophe before the *s*. Choice (D) is incorrect because it is plural possessive.

7. **The correct answer is (A).** The sentence should be deleted because it is irrelevant to the passage. Choice (B) is incorrect because it does not belong in the passage at all. Choice (C) is incorrect because it does not expand upon the main idea but introduces an unrelated detail. Choice (D) is incorrect, because it is a detail about the rock band, not the country.

8. **The correct answer is (D).** Choice (D) is correct because it supports the paragraph's focus on Aung San Suu Kyi's pro-democracy struggle and her Nobel Peace Prize and adds important information about why she was awarded the prize. Choices (A), (B), and (C) are incorrect because while the information they provide is interesting, it is not as relevant to the main focus of the paragraph.

9. **The correct answer is (B).** Only choice (B) eliminates redundancies while still communicating that the album was banned and that smugglers were punished. Choice (A) is incorrect because "not allowed to be distributed in Burma" and "for smuggling" are redundant. Choice (C) is incorrect because "not allowed to be distributed in Burma" is redundant. Choice (D) is incorrect because "for smuggling" is redundant.

10. **The correct answer is (C).** The sentence should be added at the beginning of the paragraph because the paragraph is organized chronologically, and this sentence talks about an event that happened before the other events mentioned in the paragraph. Choice (A) is incorrect because although it provides historical detail, the sentence is misplaced in the paragraph. Choice (B) is incorrect because the sentence disrupts rather than helps the flow of ideas since it is out of place chronologically. Choice (D) is incorrect because the information in the sentence is relevant to the paragraph.

11. **The correct answer is (B).** Choice (B) is correct because the pronoun "its" refers to "the country," which is a singular noun. Choices (A), (C), and (D) are wrong because they do not correctly refer to the antecedent, "the country."

12. **The correct answer is (B).** Noting that Dewey is known as "the father of public education" sets up the rest of the passage and provides information that supports the main idea of the passage. Although accurate, choices (A), (C), and (D) do not support the main idea of the paragraph and introduce ideas that are not developed in the passage.

13. **The correct answer is (C).** Choice (C) is correct because this part of an extended prepositional phrase introduced by the phrase "emphasis on." Because of this, no commas are necessary as they would separate the preposition from its other subjects ("the classroom" or "learning environment"). Choice (A) is incorrect because the comma causes confusion about the subject of the preposition "on." Choice (B) is incorrect for the same reason and also because "or learning environment" is a restrictive phrase and does not require commas. Choice (D) is incorrect because "or learning environment" is a restrictive phrase and does not require commas.

14. **The correct answer is (B).** Choice (B) is correct because the antecedent is "education," which means the pronoun should be "it." Choice (A) is incorrect because it implies that the antecedent is "aspects or characteristics." Choice (C) is incorrect because the passage is not written in the first person and there is no antecedent it could logically refer to. Choice (D) is incorrect because it implies that the antecedent is Dewey, which is incorrect.

15. **The correct answer is (D).** Choice (D) is correct because semicolons are only necessary when the list items themselves contain commas. Since they don't, this series only requires commas. Choices (A) and (C) are incorrect because they misuse semicolons. Choice (B) is incorrect because it misuses colons.

16. **The correct answer is (A).** Changing "another" to "a second" improves the organization because it includes an ordinal number as the previous and following paragraphs do. Choice (B) is incorrect because it does not clarify the aspects of education. Choice (C) is incorrect because the change does not eliminate supporting information. Choice (D) is incorrect because the change does not negatively affect the organization.

answers PRACTICE TEST 1

17. **The correct answer is (A).** Choice (A) is correct because it matches and maintains the formal and objective tone of the passage. Choice (B) is incorrect because the tone and diction are informal. Choice (C) is incorrect because, while the diction is formal, the tone is overly dramatic. Choice (D) is incorrect because the tone is subjective.

18. **The correct answer is (C).** Choice (C) is correct because the context clue "but rather" suggests a word that is the opposite of "indirect," and "overt" comes closest to this meaning. Choices (A), (B), and (D) are incorrect because they do not make sense in the context of the sentence.

19. **The correct answer is (B).** Choice (B) is correct because it effectively sets up the fourth and final item in a list of examples. Choice (A) is incorrect because it implies a contrast which is unsupported by the context. Choice (C) is incorrect because it suggests the author is looking back, which is unsupported by the context. Choice (D) is incorrect because it suggests a conclusion, which the paragraph is not.

20. **The correct answer is (C).** Choice (C) is correct because the noun "education" must agree in number with "reconstruction." Choices (A), (B), and (D) are incorrect because "education" must be singular in order to be in agreement with "reconstruction."

21. **The correct answer is (D).** In choice (D), the subordinate clause that begins with "since" should precede the second part of the sentence that it qualifies. Choice (A) is incorrect because the subordinate clause is illogical in the middle of the sentence. Choice (B) is incorrect because the subordinate clause helps set up the rest of the sentence and belongs at the beginning. Choice (C) is incorrect because the arrangement of the clauses is awkward and difficult to follow.

22. **The correct answer is (B).** Choice (B) supports the implication that members of the group could find a way to enact and undergo change without causing social instability. Choice (A) is incorrect because it suggests that change is a negative thing that must be overcome. Choices (C) and (D) are incorrect because they both imply meanings that are not supported by the context of the sentence.

23. **The correct answer is (B).** The introduction in choice (B) best leads into the rest of the sentence and the passage that follows. Choice (A) is incorrect because animals are not referenced at all in the passage. Choice (C) is incorrect because it is not relevant to the idea presented. Choice (D) is incorrect because it is too specific to one aspect of the passage.

24. **The correct answer is (D).** Choice (D) accurately employs parallel structure. Choice (A) is incorrect because the word "by" before "producing arching canes" is unnecessary and prevents the clause from being parallel. Choice (B) is incorrect because each part of the clause is constructed in a different way ("by sending," "a split," "the production"). Choice (C) is incorrect because the last part of the clause ("in the production . . .") is not constructed like the rest of the clause.

25. **The correct answer is (A).** Choice (A) is correct because "its" is a possessive determiner that refers to "desert plant." Choice (B) is incorrect because it is a contraction of "it is." Choice (C) is incorrect because it is not a word. Choice (D) is incorrect because it does not make sense in the sentence.

26. **The correct answer is (D).** The sentence should not be deleted because it maintains the organizational pattern and flow of ideas. Choice (A) is incorrect because this information does support the main idea of the paragraph. Choice (B) is incorrect because the current placement of the sentence is correct in the organization of the paragraph. Choice (C) is incorrect because the primary purpose of the sentence is not to describe vegetative growth.

27. **The correct answer is (D).** Choice (D) is correct because the focus of the passage is on the scientific characteristics of plants, and only this choice remains focused on these characteristics without adding extraneous information or comparisons. Choice (A) is incorrect because the author has not discussed plants in terms of their landscaping advantages. Choice (B) is incorrect because the distinction between plants and animals is erroneous and irrelevant. Choice (C) is incorrect because the author has refrained from naming specific kinds of plants in each category.

28. **The correct answer is (C).** Choice (C) is correct because the context of the sentence suggests a word that refers to an attempt to determine a number. Choices (A) and (B) are incorrect because "reducing" and "hedging" suggest actions that are not supported by the context of the sentence. Choice (D) is incorrect because it suggests a valuation of quality and worth rather than an attempt at counting.

29. **The correct answer is (B).** Choice (B) is correct because the subject "*suffrutescent* shrubs (hemixyles)" is plural and must be followed by the plural verb, "fall." Choice (A) is incorrect because the subject is plural and the verb is singular. Choice (C) is incorrect because the subject is singular and the verb is plural. Choice (D) is incorrect because the subject is plural and the verb is singular and not in the present tense.

30. **The correct answer is (D).** Choice (D) is correct because both sentences are closely related, independent clauses. Choice (A) is incorrect because a comma is not sufficient to join two independent clauses. Choice (B) is incorrect because there is no cause/effect relationship present, which the word "because" implies. Choice (C) is incorrect because a colon is only used to separate independent clauses when the second clause explains or amplifies the first, which is not the case here.

31. **The correct answer is (A).** The parentheses in choice (A) correctly indicate that the phrase "trees and shrubs" is supplemental information and not necessary for understanding the rest of the sentence. Choice (B) is incorrect because dashes are used to call attention to the text that they surround, which is not intended here. Choice (C) is incorrect because it makes it unclear whether woody perennials are trees and shrubs, or if the author is talking about them in addition to trees and shrubs. Choice (D) is not correct because quotation marks are not used to set off extraneous information, but rather to highlight specific words or to cast doubt on a word or phrase.

32. **The correct answer is (B).** Choice (B) is correct because "regardless" is the correct form of this conventional expression.

Choices (A), (C), and (D) are incorrect variations of this phrase.

33. **The correct answer is (A).** Choice (A) is correct because the context suggests that if the eight age states exist, the population is healthy, viable, and not going anywhere. Choice (B) is incorrect because it suggests the population is shrinking, which is not implied by the context. Choice (C) is incorrect because it suggests impermanence, which is not implied by the text. Choice (D) is incorrect because it suggests that the population is homogenous, which is not implied by the context.

34. **The correct answer is (B).** Choice (B) is correct because sentence 2 makes a broad statement about differences in wages and makes the most sense as an introductory statement. Choice (A) is incorrect because sentence 1 is not the best introductory statement. Choices (C) and (D) are incorrect because sentences 3 and 4 expand on an idea presented in sentence 2."

35. **The correct answer is (D).** Choice (D) is correct because the dash helps draw attention to the supplemental information that follows it. Choice (A) is incorrect because a colon is not used to introduce a dependent clause that expands on an independent clause. Choice (B) is incorrect because there should be punctuation to separate the number from the rest of the sentence. Choice (C) is incorrect because a semicolon is used to join two independent clauses.

36. **The correct answer is (C).** Choice (C) is correct because the context implies that the author wants to suggest that the median figure hides the fact that the gap was more than $100,000. Choice (A) is incorrect because it does not make sense in the sentence—the median figure doesn't reduce the fact. Choice (B) is incorrect because the author is not presenting a disagreement. Choice (D) is incorrect because the context does not suggest vagueness and it is grammatically incorrect."

37. **The correct answer is (C).** The existing sentence sets up the next sentence, supporting the main idea of the paragraph, so, as choice (C) correctly states, the author does not need to revise it. Choice (A) is incorrect

because there is no clear relationship between the information in the revised sentence and the information in the next sentence. Choice (B) is incorrect because although it might seem to add detail to the paragraph, it does not support the main idea. Choice (D) is incorrect because the information in the revised sentence is very different from the information in the next sentence; they do not say the same thing.

38. **The correct answer is (D).** Choice (D) is correct because the antecedent in this sentence is "each person," and the pronoun "she" was used previously to refer to the antecedent. Choices (A), (B), and (C) are incorrect because they do not align with "her" in number and gender.

39. **The correct answer is (A).** Choice (A) is correct because the author's point is that "no two jobs are identical" and that because of this, job titles can be misleading. Choice (B) is incorrect as it suggests a weak or unconvincing connection, which doesn't make sense in the context of the sentence. Choice (C) is incorrect because the sentence is not talking about the practicality of job titles. Choice (D) is incorrect because the sentence is not suggesting job titles are unplanned or unimportant.

40. **The correct answer is (C).** Choice (C) is correct because the comparison is between workers in different occupations. Choice (A) is incorrect because it suggests a comparison between workers and occupations. Choice (B) is incorrect because the sentence is talking about occupations, not opportunities. Choice (D) is incorrect because the phrase "workers with occupations" doesn't make sense.

41. **The correct answer is (B).** Choice (B) is correct because the author is listing the factors that influence, lead to, or affect, how much a person earns. Choice (A) is incorrect because the verb "effect" is used to suggest someone has succeeded in making something happen, which is not intended here. Choices (C) and (D) are incorrect because they do not make sense in the context of the sentence.

42. **The correct answer is (A).** Choice (A) is correct because the focus of the paragraph is on "job tasks" and how different responsibilities can lead to different wages. Choice (B) is incorrect because the author does not make this point. Choice (C) is incorrect because it does not link this fact to different wages. Choice (D) is incorrect because the author is not suggesting that job titles lead to different pay, but that job tasks do.

43. **The correct answer is (D).** Choice (D) corrects the fact that this sentence lacks a verb and is incomplete by adding "include." Choices (A), (B), and (C) are incorrect because they are not complete sentences.

44. **The correct answer is (B).** Choice (B) is correct because the only job with a lower median wage than athletes is actor. Choice (A) is incorrect because broadcast news analysts do not have a lower median wage than actors. Choices (C) and (D) are incorrect because only actors have a median wage lower than athletes' median wage.

Section 3: Math Test—No Calculator

1. B	**5.** C	**9.** A	**13.** B	**17.** 14/5 or 2.8
2. C	**6.** D	**10.** A	**14.** D	**18.** 4 or 1/2
3. D	**7.** C	**11.** C	**15.** B	**19.** 1.4 or 7/5
4. D	**8.** D	**12.** B	**16.** 144	**20.** 6

MATH TEST—NO CALCULATOR RAW SCORE
(Number of correct answers)

1. **The correct answer is (B).** Let the other two angles be $2x$ and $5x$. Thus,

$$2x + 5x + 82 = 180$$
$$7x = 98$$
$$x = 14$$
$$2x = 28$$
$$5x = 70$$

The smallest angle $= 28°$.

2. **The correct answer is (C).**

$$\left(\sqrt{18} - \sqrt{8}\right)^2 = \left(3\sqrt{2} - 2\sqrt{2}\right)^2 = \left(\sqrt{2}\right)^2 = 2$$

3. **The correct answer is (D).**

$$g(a) = a - 1$$
$$f(a-1) = (a-1)^2 + 2 = a^2 - 2a + 1 + 2$$
$$f(g(a)) = a^2 - 2a + 3$$

4. **The correct answer is (D).**

$$(2x - y)(x - y) - xy = 2x^2 - 2xy - xy + y^2 - xy$$
$$= 2x^2 - 4xy + y^2$$

5. **The correct answer is (C).** The numerator is the difference between perfect squares; $x^2 - y^2$ is equal to the product of $(x+y)$ and $(x-y)$.

Therefore, $\dfrac{x^2 + y^2}{x - y} = \dfrac{(x+y)(x-y)}{x-y} = x + y$

6. **The correct answer is (D).**

$$(3 - i)(8 + 4i) = 24 + 12i - 8i - 4i^2$$
$$= 24 + 4i - (-4)$$
$$= 28 + 4i$$

7. **The correct answer is (C).**

$$(x+y)^2 - (x-y)^2 = x^2 + 2xy + y^2 - (x^2 - 2xy + y^2)$$
$$= x^2 + 2xy + y^2 - x^2 + 2xy - y^2$$
$$= 4xy$$

8. **The correct answer is (D).** The confidence interval indicates the interval that the estimated population parameter is likely to fall within. A 95% confidence interval of ± 0.25 means that it can be said, with 95% confidence, that the average minimum wage of all states will fall $0.25 above the average of the randomly selected states and $0.25 below the average of the randomly selected states. The economist found the average of the randomly selected states to be $7.50, so $7.50 + $0.25 = $7.75, and $7.50 − $0.25 = $7.25. Therefore, the average minimum wage of all states will be found within the range of $7.25 and $7.75, with 95% confidence.

9. **The correct answer is (A).** Since we know the roots of the quadratic function are 0 and 4, the equation must take the form $y = ax(x - 4)$. We can use the vertex, $(2, -2)$, to find the value of a:

$$-2 = a(2)(2 - 4) = -4a \rightarrow a = \frac{1}{2}$$

Substituting this value into the equation, we get:

$$y = \frac{1}{2}x(x - 4)$$
$$= \frac{1}{2}x^2 - 2x$$

10. **The correct answer is (A).** The amount of the solutions x and y combined must equal 5 liters, so $x + y = 5$. The amount of salt in the two solutions, $0.1x$ and $0.4y$, must combine to equal the amount of salt in the total: $(0.2)(5) = 1$

11. **The correct answer is (C).** In the standard equation for ballistic motion, $y = \frac{1}{2}at^2 + bt + c$, the coefficient of the first-degree term is determined by the initial velocity. So the ball was thrown upwards at a velocity of 40 meters per second.

12. **The correct answer is (B).** Substitute the expression equivalent to x from the second equation into the first equation and solve:

$$2(2 - 9y) + 3y = 3$$
$$4 - 18y + 3y = 3$$
$$4 - 15y = 3$$
$$-15y = -1$$
$$y = \frac{1}{15}$$

13. **The correct answer is (B).** The slope of the line $y = 5x + 7$ is 5, and a line parallel to this line would have the same slope. Therefore, the desired line is of the form $y = 5x + b$. Substitute $(1, 3)$ into this equation to compute the value of b:

$$3 = 5 \times 1 + b$$
$$-2 = b$$

Thus, the equation of the line is $y = 5x - 2$.

14. **The correct answer is (D).** Find the equation of a line that passes through the points $(3, 5)$ and $(5, 6.5)$, by finding the slope, then substituting one of the ordered pairs in the slope–intercept form of an equation to find b.

$$m = \frac{6.5 - 5}{5 - 3} = 0.75$$
$$5 = 0.75(3) + b \rightarrow b = 5 - 0.75(3) = 2.75$$
$$y = 0.75x + 2.75$$

15. **The correct answer is (B).**
$$3(x - 9) = 4x + 3(1 - 2x)$$
$$3x - 27 = 4x + 3 - 6x$$
$$3x - 27 = -2x + 3$$
$$5x = 30$$
$$x = 6$$

16. **The correct answer is 144.**
$$\frac{4\pi}{5} \times \frac{180}{\pi} = \frac{720}{5} = 144$$

17. **The correct answer is 14/5 or 2.8**
$$\frac{3}{2}x + 7 = 4x$$
$$7 = 4x - \frac{3}{2}x$$
$$7 = \frac{5}{2}x$$
$$\frac{14}{5} = x$$

18. **The correct answer is 4 or 1/2.** (Either is acceptable.)
$$x^2 + 4 = 9x - x^2$$
$$2x^2 - 9x + 4 = 0$$
$$(2x - 1)(x - 4) = 0$$
$$x = \frac{1}{2} \text{ or } x = 4$$

19. **The correct answer is 1.4 or 7/5.**

To find the x-intercept, set y equal to 0 and solve for x:
$$0 - 3 = 5(x - 2)$$
$$-3 = 5x - 10$$
$$7 = 5x$$
$$\frac{7}{5} = x$$

20. **The correct answer is 6.**
$$\sqrt{x + 3} = x - 3$$
$$\left(\sqrt{x + 3}\right)^2 = (x - 3)^2$$
$$x + 3 = x^2 - 6x + 9$$
$$0 = x^2 - 7x + 6$$
$$0 = (x - 6)(x - 1)$$
$$x = 6 \text{ or } x = 1$$

Because $\sqrt{1 + 3} = 2 \neq 1 - 3 = -2$, only $x = 6$ is an actual solution.

Section 4: Math Test—Calculator

1. B	**9.** D	**17.** A	**25.** B	**33.** 11
2. A	**10.** A	**18.** C	**26.** A	**34.** 1.02
3. B	**11.** B	**19.** B	**27.** C	**35.** 24.2
4. D	**12.** B	**20.** A	**28.** C	**36.** 5/2 or 2.5
5. D	**13.** C	**21.** A	**29.** A	**37.** 0.8
6. C	**14.** B	**22.** D	**30.** C	**38.** 32
7. A	**15.** D	**23.** B	**31.** 45	
8. D	**16.** B	**24.** D	**32.** 70	

MATH TEST—CALCULATOR RAW SCORE
(Number of correct answers)

1. **The correct answer is (B).** Let x = amount earned each month. Since the salesperson earned twice as much in December as in every other month, $2x$ = amount earned in December. Then, the entire earnings are

   $11x + 2x = 13x$. $\dfrac{2x}{13x} = \dfrac{2}{13}$.

2. **The correct answer is (A).** Because the population of village A is decreasing by 120 per year, the population in year y will be $6800 - 120y$. Because the population of village B is increasing by 80 per year, the population in year y will be $4200 + 80y$. Set the two expressions equal to find when the populations will be the same:

   $6800 - 120y = 4200 + 80y$.

3. **The correct answer is (B).** There are a total of $27 + 29 + 35 + 24 = 115$ males who responded to the survey. Of the 115 males, 35 supported candidate C:

   $\dfrac{35}{115} = \dfrac{7}{23}$

4. **The correct answer is (D).**

   $$C = \frac{5}{9}\left(F - 32\right)$$

   $$\frac{9}{5}C = F - 32$$

   $$\frac{9}{5}C + 32 = F$$

   $$F = \frac{9}{5}C + 32$$

5. **The correct answer is (D).** Because this is a recursive percent decrease, an exponential model is appropriate. A model for exponential decay is $f(t) = a(1 - r)^t$, where a is the initial amount, and r is the decay rate. The initial amount is 50,000 and the decay rate is 0.15, so the appropriate model in this case is $A(n) = 50,000(1 - 0.15)^n = 50,000 \times 0.85^n$.

6. **The correct answer is (C).** Substitute 19.5 for $f(x)$ and solve the resulting equation for x:

   $$19.5 = 1.5x + 15$$

   $$4.5 = 1.5x$$

   $$3 = x$$

7. **The correct answer is (A).** There are 360 degrees in a circle. A 24-degree sector is

    $\dfrac{24}{360} = 0.067$, or about $6\dfrac{2}{3}\%$ of a circle.

8. **The correct answer is (D).** The confidence interval indicates the interval into which the estimated population parameter is likely to fall.

9. **The correct answer is (D).** This is an inverse proportion; that is:

    $\dfrac{9}{6} = \dfrac{x}{120}$

    $6x = 1080$

    $x = 180$

10. **The correct answer is (A).** Since $x - y = 4$, $y = x - 4$. Set the equations equal to each other. Then combine like terms and use the quadratic formula to solve for x. To solve for y, substitute the value for x into one of the given equations. The answer will be y^2:

    $x - 4 = x^2 - 7x + 10$

    $0 = x^2 - 8x + 14$

    $x = \dfrac{-(-8) \pm \sqrt{(-8)^2 - 4(1)(14)}}{2(1)} = 4 \pm \sqrt{2}$

    $y = x - 4 = (4 \pm \sqrt{2}) - 4 = \pm\sqrt{2}$

    $y^2 = 2$

11. **The correct answer is (B).** Four inches is $\dfrac{1}{3}$ ft. The volume of the added level is

    $75 \times 42 \times \dfrac{1}{3} = 1050$ cubic ft.

    There are 7.48 gallons in 1 cubic ft., so 1050 cubic ft. × 7.48 gal./cubic ft. = 7,854 gallons.

12. **The correct answer is (B).** Let x = number of minutes to fill

    $\dfrac{4}{7}$ of bucket. Then, $\dfrac{\frac{3}{7}}{1} = \dfrac{\frac{4}{7}}{x}$,

    $3x = 4$

    or $\dfrac{3}{1} = \dfrac{4}{x}$ $x = \dfrac{4}{3}$

13. **The correct answer is (C).**

    A radius drawn perpendicular to a chord bisects the chord. Construct the radius as shown above.

    $5^2 + 12^2 = r^2$

    $25 + 144 = r^2$

    $169 = r^2$

    $13 = r$

14. **The correct answer is (B).** Three inches equal 0.25 feet. To cover the garden, we'll need 12 feet × 12 feet × 0.25 feet = 36 cubic feet of garden soil.

    $\dfrac{x \text{ pounds}}{36 \text{ cubic feet}} = \dfrac{40 \text{ pounds}}{0.8 \text{ cubic feet}}$

    $x = \dfrac{(40)(36)}{0.8}$

    $x = 1800$

15. **The correct answer is (D).** The x-intercept occurs at the point where $y - 0$, or where no products will be sold.

answers PRACTICE TEST 1

16. **The correct answer is (B).** To find the equation that shows the vertex of the parabola, change from factored form to standard form, and then complete the square:

$$y = (x - 5)(x + 1)$$
$$y = x^2 - 4x - 5$$
$$y = x^2 - 4x + 4 - 5 - 4$$
$$y = (x - 2)^2 - 9$$

17. **The correct answer is (A).** The arithmetic mean of the algebra test scores is $50 + 50 + 60 + 60 + 70 + 70 + 70 + 80 + 80 + 90 = 680 \div 10 = 68$.

18. **The correct answer is (C).** The slope of the line of best fit is positive, indicating that the y-variable tends to increase as the x-variable increases.

19. **The correct answer is (B).** Set $y = 70$ and solve for x:

$$70 = 0.76x + 27.6$$
$$42.4 = 0.76x$$
$$x = \frac{42.4}{0.76} \approx 56$$

20. **The correct answer is (A).** At $t = 0$, the object is moving at $-9.8(0) = 0$ meters per second. At $t = 4$ seconds, the object is moving at a $-9.8(4) = -39.2$ meters per second. The velocity must be equal to or between these two extremes.

21. **The correct answer is (A).**

$$\frac{80}{200} = 40\%$$
$$40\% - 3.5\% = 36.5\%$$
$$40\% + 3.5\% = 43.5\%$$

22. **The correct answer is (D).** Since we are interpolating, we can use a linear model as the basis for the estimate. The rate of change is

$$\frac{54.5 - 42}{2025 - 2020} = 2.5 .$$ In 2020, the target is 42, and the target increases by 2.5 each year.

23. **The correct answer is (B).** Multiply 1.45 by x and 2.75 by y. The total power supply must be at least 200, so the inequality is $1.45x + 2.75y \geq 200$.

24. **The correct answer is (D).** First, find the solutions:

$$x^2 - 4x = 3$$
$$x^2 - 4x + 4 = 7$$
$$(x - 2)^2 = 7$$
$$x - 2 = \pm\sqrt{7}$$
$$x = 2 \pm \sqrt{7}$$

Then, find the absolute value of the difference of the solutions:

$$\left|\left(2 + \sqrt{7}\right) - \left(2 - \sqrt{7}\right)\right| = 2\sqrt{7}$$

25. **The correct answer is (B).** Let n be the number of nickels and q be the number of quarters. Then, solve the resulting system of equations:

$$0.05n + 0.25q = 3.10$$
$$n + q = 18 \rightarrow q = 18 - n$$
$$0.05n + 0.25(18 - n) = 3.10$$
$$0.05n + 4.5 - 0.25n = 3.10$$
$$-0.2n = -1.4$$
$$n = 7$$

Since there are 7 nickels, there must be 11 quarters: $11 - 7 = 4$.

26. **The correct answer is (A).** Because the rate of growth is a fixed percentage, an exponential graph is appropriate.

27. **The correct answer is (C).** Put the equation into slope–intercept form to find the slope and intercept:

$$2x + 3y = 15$$
$$3y = -2x + 15$$
$$y = -\frac{2}{3}x + 5$$

The perpendicular line will have the opposite reciprocal as its slope and the same y-intercept:

$$y = \frac{3}{2}x + 5$$

28. **The correct answer is (C).** Rewrite the inequalities as

$$y < \frac{1}{3}x + \frac{1}{3}$$

and $y > -x + 1$. Then, sketch the inequalities to observe that only $(4, -2)$, choice (C), is in the overlapping region.

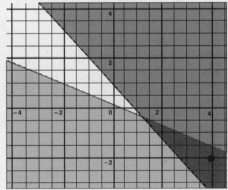

29. **The correct answer is (A).** Since 1 is a 0 of the graph, $(x - 1)$ is a factor of the polynomial.

30. **The correct answer is (C).** Since $(-3, 2)$ and $(3, 2)$ are the endpoints of a diameter of a circle, the center of the circle is at $(0, 2)$ and the radius of the circle is 3. The general form of the equation of a circle with center

(a,b) and radius r is $(x - a)^2 + (y - b)^2 = r^2$. Substituting the values for a, b, and r, we obtain $x^2 + (y - 2)^2 = 9$.

31. **The correct answer is 45.**

$$\frac{x}{12} = 75$$
$$x = 900$$
$$\frac{900}{20} = 45$$

32. **The correct answer is 70.**

An exterior angle of a triangle is equal to the sum of the two remote interior angles.

$$8x + 40 = (9x - 40) + (4x + 30)$$
$$8x + 40 = 13x - 10$$
$$5x = 50$$
$$x = 10$$
$$\angle J = (4x + 30)° = (40 + 30)° = 70°$$

33. **The correct answer is 11.**

$$\frac{9 + 9 + 10 + x + y}{5} = 10$$
$$28 + x + y = 50$$
$$x + y = 22$$

The average of x and y is

$$\frac{x + y}{2} = \frac{22}{2} = 11$$

34. **The correct answer is 1.02.** Because this is an exponential growth model, divide the population in 2013 by the population in 2012 to find the value of b: (38.19 million) ÷ (37.44 million) ≈ 1.02.

answers PRACTICE TEST 1

35. The correct answer is 24.2.

$20 \times 1.1 = 22$

$22 \times 1.1 = 24.2$

36. The correct answer is 5/2 or 2.5.

$$5(x+7) - ax = ax + 35$$

$$5x + 35 - ax = ax + 35$$

$$5x - 2ax = 0$$

$$x(5 - 2a) = 0$$

This equation has solutions when $x = 0$ or for any value of x when

$$a = \frac{5}{2}$$

37. The correct answer is 0.8.

$$3.6x + 2.4y = 12$$

$$x - y = 2$$

Multiply the second equation by 3.6 and subtract it from the first equation. Then, solve for y:

$$3.6x + 2.4y = 12$$

$$\underline{3.6x - 3.6y = 7.2}$$

$$6y = 4.8$$

$$y = 0.8$$

38. The correct answer is 32. Since $g(x)$ is a translation of $f(x)$ 3 units to the right,

$$g(x) = f(x-3): g(9) = f(9-3) = f(6) = 6^2 - 4 = 32.$$

Section 5: Essay

Analysis of Passage

The following is an analysis of the passage by Elizabeth Roberts-Pedersen, noting how the writer used evidence, reasoning, and stylistic or persuasive elements to support her claims, connect the claims and evidence, and add power to the ideas she expressed. Check to see if you evaluated the passage in a similar way.

Adapted from "From Shell Shock to PTSD: Proof of War's Traumatic History" by Elizabeth Roberts-Pedersen, originally published by The Conversation on April 14, 2015. Elizabeth Roberts-Pedersen is a lecturer in history at the University of Western Sydney in Australia. (This passage was edited for length. To read the complete article, see http://theconversation.com.)

1 2015 marks several important First World War anniversaries: the centenary of the first use of poison gas in January; the centenary of the Gallipoli landings and the Armenian genocide in April. It is also 100 years since *The Lancet* published Charles S. Myers' article, "A Contribution to the Study of Shell Shock."

1 *The writer provides a historical context to support her central idea: people have long known that war is psychologically traumatic.*

The study of shell shock

2 Myers' article is generally regarded as the first use of the term "shell shock" in medical literature. It was used as a descriptor for "three cases of loss of memory, vision, smell and taste" in British soldiers admitted to a military hospital in France.

2 *The writer lays the groundwork for her argument by providing facts about and describing the symptoms of this trauma, which was initially called "shell shock."*

3 While Myers presented these cases as evidence of the spectacular concussive effects of artillery on the Western Front, British medical opinion soon came to regard these symptoms as psychological in origin.

3 *The writer supports her argument with facts that show that "shell shock," which was at first used to describe symptoms caused by "concussive effects of artillery," came to be seen as "psychological in origin."*

4   The men presenting to medical officers with tics, tremors, and palpitations, as well as more serious symptoms of "functional" blindness, paralysis, and loss of speech, were not concussed—but nor were they necessarily cowards or malingerers.

5   Instead, these were men simply worn down by the unprecedented stresses of trench warfare—in particular, the effort required to push out of one's mind the prospect of joining the ranks of the maimed or the corpses lying in no man's land ….

6   For contemporaries and later for historians, shell shock came to encapsulate all the horror of this new form of industrialized warfare. As historian Jay Winter suggests, it moved "from a diagnosis into a metaphor."

…

Developing a diagnosis

7   It is tempting to view shell shock as the unambiguous turning point in psychiatry's history, popularizing the idea that unconscious processes might produce symptoms that operate separately from moral qualities such as endurance and courage. However, scholarship over the last 15 years suggests that this position was far from widely accepted.

8   … The notion that many patients had some "predisposing" weakness—independent of their combat experiences—persisted throughout the interwar period and into the Second World War.

---

4   *The writer strengthens her argument with facts that demonstrate those suffering from shell shock were suffering genuine psychological trauma, and were not, as often believed, cowards or people trying to avoid combat. The author's examples of "functional" problems shows that even without physical damage, people can become deaf, mute, or paralyzed because of psychological damage.*

5   *The writer offers evidence that shows the psychological effects of combat.*

6   *The writer quotes a historian who views shell shock not only as devastating in itself, but as absolute confirmation of the horrors of war.*

7   *The writer makes the point that even though shell shock was being generally accepted as a legitimate condition, there was still resistance to the idea.*

8   *Continuing to trace resistance to the validity of shell shock, the writer cites one opposing argument. She also provides additional historical perspective, saying that resistance continued even into WWII.*

9   It wasn't until the Vietnam War that this formulation was reversed, which in turn bridged the gap between combatant syndromes and the civilian sphere.

9   *The writer completes this part of her argument, providing a specific time frame (the Vietnam War) for when shell shock was fully legitimized as a combat-related condition. She also identifies this period as a time when the concept of trauma-caused damage began to be extended to civilian experiences outside of military participation.*

10 This development is only comprehensible as part of a broader political context. The notion that the Vietnam War exacted a form of psychic damage on American soldiers was championed by the anti-war activists of Vietnam Veterans Against the War (VVAW) and psychiatrists Chaim Shatan and Robert Jay Lifton.

10 *The writer provides historical, political, and social contexts for this acceptance.*

11 "Post-Vietnam syndrome," Shatan wrote, was caused by the "unconsummated grief" of a brutal and brutalizing war.

11 *The writer uses the evocative words brutal and brutalizing to communicate the particular horrors of the Vietnam War.*

12 The VVAW's advocacy was instrumental in securing official recognition for this condition. It was included in 1980 in the third edition of the *Diagnostic and Statistical Manual of Mental Disorders* (*DSM-III*) as "post-traumatic stress disorder."

12 *The writer provides facts and dates to show when "shell shock" was officially recognized as a legitimate condition and when it was renamed post-traumatic stress disorder (PTSD).*

13 PTSD's inclusion in *DSM-III* legitimated the suffering of Vietnam veterans and held out the possibility of subsidized medical care and compensation. But the *DSM-III* definition of PTSD was significant in two additional ways.

    First, it identified the disorder as a condition that could afflict soldiers and civilians alike—not a diagnosis exclusive to combat, like shell shock.

    Second, it focused attention on the continuing effects of a traumatic experience, rather than on the personality and constitution of the patient.

13 *The writer explains why official recognition of PTSD was so important. She details how the shift in emphasis from the patient to the experience removed the stigma from those suffering from PTSD.*

14 The ramifications of these changes have been immense. PTSD and a broader field of "traumatology" are now entrenched in psychiatric and popular discourse. In Australia, we now assume that warfare is objectively traumatizing, and that

14 *The writer cites benefits that sufferers of PTSD can now receive as a consequence of the improved attitude toward PTSD.*

answers PRACTICE TEST 1

governments ought to provide medical and financial support for affected service personnel, even if a recent Four Corners program confirmed that this is not always the case.

How is PTSD viewed today?

15 Though PTSD has its origins in opposition to the Vietnam War, the politics of the condition are now largely ambivalent, with its significance shifting according to circumstance.

This point is well illustrated by the film *American Sniper*, which demonstrates the possibility of two contrary positions. After his return to civilian life, SEAL sniper Chris Kyle (Bradley Cooper) is shown to be suffering from some characteristic after-effects of combat ....

…

The real Chris Kyle was shot dead by Eddie Ray Routh [another veteran], in 2013. At trial, the accused's lawyers pursued a defense of insanity, compounded by the inadequate care provided by veterans' mental health services. Routh was found guilty of Kyle's murder in March of 2015.

16 In the 100 years since Myers' article on shell shock, the psychological consequences of war remain as relevant as ever.

15 *The writer addresses the perception of PTSD today, citing two recent examples of former soldiers linked to PTSD.*

16 *The writer concludes her argument by juxtaposing these modern instances of PTSD with the article that introduced the term "shell shock," and restating her central idea: The psychological consequences of war are as relevant and deserving of attention today as they were 100 years ago. By referring to the 100 years since Myers' article on shell shock, the writer reinforces her central idea that she is offering "proof of war's traumatic history."*

Sample Essays

The following are examples of a high-scoring and low-scoring essay, based on the passage by Elizabeth Roberts-Pedersen.

High-Scoring Essay

Elizabeth Roberts-Pedersen claims that the psychological consequences of war have always been with us; it just took time for us to realize it. To convince us, she uses evidence and reasoning that carefully develop and reinforce her premise. With a few persuasive elements, her article brings us to the same conclusion: war has severe consequences that don't disappear when peace is declared.

Roberts-Pedersen begins the discussion of PTSD by citing an article published 100 years ago that contained the first mention of a condition known at the time as shell shock. Soldiers suffering from shell shock were described as having physical symptoms, such as blindness and paralysis. At first attributed to the effects of artillery, the medical community soon accepted the cause as the stress and exhaustion of combat rather than physical injury. Unfortunately, the men were considered to be weak individuals by popular medical opinion of the time.

In the section titled "Developing a diagnosis," Roberts-Pedersen uses reason to explain how popular opinion toward this condition changed and uses evidence to prove that the change occurred. She credits the Vietnam War and the public's response to the war for the change. Anti-war activists and psychiatrists promoted a description of Vietnam veterans' condition as grief caused by a "brutal and brutalizing war." The phrasing shows us that the soldiers with this condition are victims of the war, just as soldiers who are physically wounded in combat are. The image of veterans with shell shock morphed from "weak individuals" to "noble heroes who suffer from brutal acts of war." The evidence she cites for this claim is the addition of post-traumatic stress disorder (PTSD) to the official medical manual, *Diagnostic and Statistical Manual of Mental Disorders* (*DSM-III*). She explains the consequences by showing the cause (including the condition in the manual) with its effects (people with PTSD are now treated well by the military).

In the final section, Roberts-Pedersen reminds us of the *American Sniper* movie. Both the hero and the villain in the movie have combat experience. Regardless of the men's conditions, the audience easily distinguishes the hero from the villain. Understanding of the medical condition first described 100 years ago is needed to understand the movie. This final piece of evidence persuades us that PTSD is a condition that continues to affect lives today, and we need to see it with clear eyes.

Low-Scoring Essay

Elizabeth Roberts-Pedersen is a writer familiar with shell shock, which is called PTSD today. She first discovered shell shock 100 years ago and wrote about it in a medical book. Shell shock was a head injury that happens when men close to the bomb are shocked when the bomb explodes. The light is bright enough to blind them and the sound can make them deaf and dumb or paralyze them. They studied this in three British soldiers who were in a French hospital.

Doctors studied this a long time and changed the name to PTSD. They changed the name because the same thing can happen when people who aren't in the military get shocked by something bad. Now, it's a stress disorder that doctors can treat with medicine. Civilians can get it now after a bad thing happens like a riot or a bombing but they don't get as stressed about it anymore. Now they can cure it or at least treat it.

The writer uses a movie I saw called American Sniper. The sniper does some stuff during the war and gets PTSD. A bad guy who was also in a military unit killed the sniper. He tries to tell people that he had PTSD and that's why he killed the sniper.

The writer says that the story in the movie, which is true, is proof that PTSD still happens today. You hear about it in the news pretty often. That makes it important for people to know about, which is why she wrote about it and why we should know about it.

COMPUTING YOUR SCORES

To get a sense of your progress in preparing for the SAT®, follow these instructions and the following conversion tables. Keep in mind that these formulas have been simplified to give you a "quick and dirty" sense of where you are scoring—it's not a perfectly precise score.

To Determine Your Practice Test Scores

1 After you go through each of the test sections (Reading, Writing and Language, Math—No Calculator, and Math—Calculator) and determine which answers you got right, be sure to enter the number of correct answers in the box below the answer key for each of the sections.

2 Your total score on the SAT® practice test is the sum of your Evidence-Based Reading and Writing Section score and your Math Section score. To get your total score, convert the raw score—the number of questions you got right in a particular section—into the "scaled score" for that section, and then you'll calculate the total score. It sounds a little confusing, but we'll take you through the steps.

To Calculate Your Evidence-Based Reading and Writing Section Score

Your Evidence-Based Reading and Writing Section score is on a scale of 200–800. First determine your Reading Test score, and then determine your score on the Writing and Language Test.

1 Count the number of correct answers you got on the **Section 1: Reading Test.** Remember that there is no penalty for wrong answers. **The number of correct answers is your raw score.**

2 Go to Raw Score Conversion Table 1: Section and Test Scores on page 571. Look in the "Raw Score" column for your raw score, and match it to the number in the "Reading Test Score" column.

4 Do the same with **Section 2: Writing and Language Test** to determine that score.

4 Add your Reading Test score to your Writing and Language Test score.

5 Multiply that number by 10. This is your Evidence-Based Reading and Writing Section score.

To Calculate Your Math Section Score

YOUR MATH SECTION SCORE IS ALSO ON A SCALE OF 200–800.

1 Count the number of correct answers you got on the **Section 3: Math Test—No Calculator** and the **Section 4: Math Test—No Calculator** practice tests. Again, there is no penalty for wrong answers. **The number of correct answers is your raw score.**

2 Add the number of correct answers on the Section 3: Math Test—No Calculator and the Section 4: Math Test—No Calculator practice tests.

3 Use the **Raw Score Conversion Table 1: Section and Test Scores** on page 571 and convert your raw score into your Math Section score.

answers PRACTICE TEST 1

To Obtain Your Total Score

Add your score on the Evidence-Based Reading and Writing Section to the Math Section score. This is your total score on this SAT® Practice Test, on a scale of 400–1600.

Subscores Provide Additional Information

Subscores offer you greater details about your strengths in certain areas within literacy and math. The subscores are reported on a scale of 1–15 and include Heart of Algebra, Problem Solving and Data Analysis, Passport to Advanced Math, Expression of Ideas, Standard English Conventions, Words in Context, and Command of Evidence.

Heart of Algebra

The **Heart of Algebra subscore** is based on questions from the Math Test—No Calculator and Math Test—Calculator (Sections 3 and 4) that focus on linear equations and inequalities.

- Add up your total correct answers from these sections:
- Math Test—No Calculator: Questions 8, 10, 12–15, 17, 19
- Math Test—Calculator: Questions 2, 6, 15, 20, 22, 23, 25, 27, 28, 36, 37
- Your Raw Score = the total number of correct answers from all of these questions.
- Use the **Raw Score Conversion Table 2: Subscores** on page 572 to determine your **Heart of Algebra** subscore.

Problem Solving and Data Analysis

The **Problem Solving and Data Analysis subscore** is based on questions from the Math Test that focus on quantitative reasoning, the interpretation and synthesis of data, and solving problems in rich and varied contexts.

- Add up your total correct answers from these sections:
- Math Test—No Calculator: No Questions
- Math Test—Calculator: Questions 1, 3, 5, 7–9, 11, 12, 14, 17–19, 21, 26, 33, 35
- Your Raw Score = the total number of correct answers from all of these questions.
- Use the **Raw Score Conversion Table 2: Subscores** on page 572 to determine your **Problem Solving and Data Analysis** subscore.

Passport to Advanced Math

The **Passport to Advanced Math subscore** is based on questions from the Math Test that focus on topics central to your ability to progress to more advanced math, such as understanding the structure of expressions, reasoning with more complex equations, and interpreting and building functions.

- Add up your total correct answers from these sections:
- Math Test—No Calculator: Questions 2–5, 7, 9, 11, 18, 20
- Math Test—Calculator: Questions 4, 10, 16, 24, 29, 34, 38
- Your Raw Score = the total number of correct answers from all of these questions.
- Use the **Raw Score Conversion Table 2: Subscores** on page 572 to determine your **Passport to Advanced Math** subscore.

Expression of Ideas

The **Expression of Ideas subscore** is based on questions from the Writing and Language Test that focus on topic development, organization, and rhetorically effective use of language.

- Add up your total correct answers from Section 2: Writing and Language Test:
- Questions 1, 3, 7–10, 16–18, 19, 22, 23, 26–28, 30, 33, 34, 36, 37, 37, 42, 44
- Your Raw Score = the total number of correct answers from all of these questions.
- Use the **Raw Score Conversion Table 2: Subscores** on page 572 to determine your Expression of Ideas subscore.

Standard English Conventions

The **Standard English Conventions subscore** is based on questions from the Writing and Language Test that focus on sentence structure, usage, and punctuation.

- Add up your total correct answers from Section 2: Writing and Language Test:
- Questions 2, 4–6, 11, 13–15, 20, 21, 24, 25, 29, 31, 32, 35, 38, 40, 41, 43
- Your Raw Score = the total number of correct answers from all of these questions.
- Use the **Raw Score Conversion Table 2: Subscores** on page 572 to determine your **Standard English Conventions** subscore.

Words in Context

The **Words in Context subscore** is based on questions from the Reading Test and the Writing and Language Test that address word/phrase meaning in context and rhetorical word choice.

- Add up your total correct answers from Sections 1 and 2:
- Reading Test: Questions 4, 8, 13, 17, 27, 30, 33, 36, 44, 49
- Writing and Language Test: Questions 1, 3, 18, 22, 28, 33, 36, 39
- Your Raw Score = the total number of correct answers from all of these questions.
- Use the **Raw Score Conversion Table 2: Subscores** on page 572 to determine your **Words in Context** subscore.

Command of Evidence

The **Command of Evidence subscore** is based on questions from the Reading Test and the Writing and Language Test that ask you to interpret and use evidence found in a wide range of passages and informational graphics, such as graphs, tables, and charts.

- Add up your total correct answers from Sections 1 and 2:
- Reading Test: Questions 3, 6, 16, 20, 26, 29, 39, 42, 46, 48
- Writing and Language Test: Questions 7, 10, 12, 16, 23, 26, 37, 42
- Your Raw Score = the total number of correct answers from all of these questions.
- Use the **Raw Score Conversion Table 2: Subscores** on page 572 to determine your **Command of Evidence** subscore.

Cross-Test Scores

The new SAT®also reports two cross-test scores: Analysis in History/Social Studies and Analysis in Science. These scores are based on questions in the Reading Test, Writing and Language Test, and both Math Tests that ask you to think analytically about texts and questions in these subject areas. Cross-test scores are reported on a scale of 10–40.

Analysis in History/Social Studies

- Add up your total correct answers from these sections:
- Reading Test: Questions 32–52
- Writing and Language Test: Questions 1, 3, 7–10
- Math Test—No Calculator: Question 8
- Math Test—Calculator: Questions 2, 3, 21, 22, 26, 31, 34
- Your Raw Score = the total number of correct answers from all of these questions.
- Use the **Raw Score Conversion Table 3: Cross-Test Scores** on page 573 to determine your **Analysis in History/Social Studies** cross-test score.

Analysis in Science

- Add up your total correct answers from these sections:
- Reading Test: Questions 11–31
- Writing and Language Test: Questions 23, 26–28, 30, 33
- Math Test—No Calculator: Questions 10, 11
- Math Test—Calculator: Questions 4–6, 9, 20, 23
- Your Raw Score = the total number of correct answers from all of these questions.
- Use the **Raw Score Conversion Table 3: Cross-Test Scores** on page 573 to determine your **Analysis in Science** cross-test score.

Raw Score Conversion Table 1: Section and Test Scores

Raw Score	Math Section Score	Reading Test Score	Writing and Language Test Score	Raw Score	Math Section Score	Reading Test Score	Writing and Language Test Score	Raw Score	Math Section Score	Reading Test Score	Writing and Language Test Score
0	200	10	10	20	450	22	23	40	610	33	36
1	200	10	10	21	460	23	23	41	620	33	37
2	210	10	10	22	470	23	24	42	630	34	38
3	230	11	10	23	480	24	25	43	640	35	39
4	240	12	11	24	480	24	25	44	650	35	40
5	260	13	12	25	490	25	26	45	660	36	
6	280	14	13	26	500	25	26	46	670	37	
7	290	15	13	27	510	26	27	47	670	37	
8	310	15	14	28	520	26	28	48	680	38	
9	320	16	15	29	520	27	28	49	690	38	
10	330	17	16	30	530	28	29	50	700	39	
11	340	17	16	31	540	28	30	51	710	40	
12	360	18	17	32	550	29	30	52	730	40	
13	370	19	18	33	560	29	31	53	740		
14	380	19	19	34	560	30	32	54	750		
15	390	20	19	35	570	30	32	55	760		
16	410	20	20	36	580	31	33	56	780		
17	420	21	21	37	590	31	34	57	790		
18	430	21	21	38	600	32	34	58	800		
19	440	22	22	39	600	32	35				

Conversion Equation 1 Section and Test Scores

Raw Score Conversion Table 2: Subscores

Raw Score (# of correct answers)	Expression of Ideas	Standard English Conventions	Heart of Algebra	Problem Solving Data Analysis	Passport to Advanced Math	Words in Context	Command of Evidence
0	1	1	1	1	1	1	1
1	1	1	1	1	3	1	1
2	1	1	2	2	5	2	2
3	2	2	3	3	6	3	3
4	3	2	4	4	7	4	4
5	4	3	5	5	8	5	5
6	5	4	6	6	9	6	6
7	6	5	6	7	10	6	7
8	6	6	7	8	11	7	8
9	7	6	8	8	11	8	8
10	7	7	8	9	12	8	9
11	8	7	9	10	12	9	10
12	8	8	9	10	13	9	10
13	9	8	9	11	13	10	11
14	9	9	10	12	14	11	12
15	10	10	10	13	14	12	13
16	10	10	11	14	15	13	14
17	11	11	12	15		14	15
18	11	12	13			15	15
19	12	13	15				
20	12	15					
21	13						
22	14						
23	14						
24	15						

Conversion Equation 2 Subscores

HEART OF ALGEBRA RAW SCORE (0–19)	EXPRESSION OF IDEAS RAW SCORE (0–24)	COMMAND OF EVIDENCE RAW SCORE (0–18)	PROBLEM SOLVING AND DATA ANALYSIS RAW SCORE (0–17)
CONVERT	CONVERT	CONVERT	CONVERT
HEART OF ALGEBRA SUBSCORE (1–15)	EXPRESSION OF IDEAS SUBSCORE (1–15)	COMMAND OF EVIDENCE SUBSCORE (1–15)	PROBLEM SOLVING AND DATA ANALYSIS SUBSCORE (1–15)

STANDARD ENGLISH CONVENTIONS RAW SCORE (0–20)	WORDS IN CONTEXT RAW SCORE (0–18)	PASSPORT TO ADVANCED MATH RAW SCORE (0–16)
CONVERT	CONVERT	CONVERT
STANDARD ENGLISH CONVENTIONS SUBSCORE (1–15)	WORDS IN CONTEXT SUBSCORE (1–15)	PASSPORT TO ADVANCED MATH SUBSCORE (1–15)

Raw Score Conversion Table 3: Cross-Test Scores

Raw Score (# of correct answers)	Analysis in History/Social Studies Cross-Test Score	Analysis in Science Cross-Test Score	Raw Score (# of correct answers)	Analysis in History/Social Studies Cross-Test Score	Analysis in Science Cross-Test Score
0	10	10	18	28	26
1	10	11	19	29	27
2	11	12	20	30	27
3	12	13	21	30	28
4	14	14	22	31	29
5	15	15	23	32	30
6	16	16	24	32	30
7	17	17	25	33	31
8	18	18	26	34	32
9	20	19	27	35	33
10	21	20	28	35	33
11	22	20	29	36	34
12	23	21	30	37	35
13	24	22	31	38	36
14	25	23	32	38	37
15	26	24	33	39	38
16	27	24	34	40	39
17	28	25	35	40	40

answers PRACTICE TEST 1

Conversion Equation 3: Cross-Test Scores

TEST	ANALYSIS IN HISTORY/SOCIAL STUDIES		ANALYSIS IN SCIENCE	
	QUESTIONS	RAW SCORE	QUESTIONS	RAW SCORE
Reading Test	32–52		11–31	
Writing and Language Test	1, 3, 7–10		23, 26–28, 30, 33	
Math Test—No Calculator	8		10, 11	
Math Test—Calculator	2. 3. 21, 22, 26, 31, 34		4–6, 9, 20, 23	
TOTAL				

ANALYSIS IN HISTORY/
SOCIAL STUDIES
RAW SCORE (0–35)

CONVERT

ANALYSIS IN HISTORY/
SOCIAL STUDIES
CROSS-TEST SCORE (10–40)

ANALYSIS IN SCIENCE
RAW SCORE (0–35)

CONVERT

ANALYSIS IN SCIENCE
CROSS-TEST SCORE (1–15)

Practice Test 2

On test day, you will see these important reminders on the first page of your SAT® test booklet:

- You must use a No. 2 pencil when taking the test; you may not use a pen or mechanical pencil.
- You may not share any questions with anyone. This is considered a violation of College Board's "Test Security and Fairness" policies, and it could cause your scores to be canceled.
- You are not permitted to take the test booklet out of the testing room.

In addition to filling in your name and Test Center information on your answer sheet, you'll be asked to fill in two different codes that will be on your test booklet. Each test booklet has a unique code, and there will be a grid-in form to fill in with your "TEST ID" and "FORM CODE" letters and numbers.

The general directions for the test will look something like this:

- You may only work on one section at a time.
- If you complete a section before time is called, check your work on that section only. You are not permitted to work on any other section.

The directions for marking your answers will likely include the following recommendations:

- Mark your answer sheet properly—be sure to <u>completely</u> fill in the answer bubble.
- Be careful to mark only one answer for each question.
- Don't make any stray marks on the answer sheet.
- If you need to erase your answer, make sure you do so completely.
- Be sure to use the answer spaces that correspond to the question numbers.

You will be able to use your test booklet for scratch work, but you won't get credit for any work done in your test booklet. When time is called at the end of each section, you will not be permitted to transfer answers from your test booklet to your answer sheet.

Any information, ideas, or opinions presented in any of the passages you will see on the redesigned SAT® that have been taken from other sources or published material do not represent the opinions of the College Board.

Scoring on the SAT® is as follows:

- You will receive one point for each correct answer.
- You will not lose points for wrong answers, so you should attempt to answer every question even if you aren't completely sure of the correct answer.

Your testing supervisor will announce when to open the test booklet, so be sure to wait until you're told to do so. For the purposes of this practice test, be sure you have a timer to set for 65 minutes for the Section 1: Reading Test.

The answer sheets for each test section, including lined paper for the essay, appear on the next five pages. Following the Answer Key and Explanations for this Practice Test, you will find details on how to score your work.

practice test 2

ANSWER SHEET PRACTICE TEST 2

Section 1: Reading Test

1. Ⓐ Ⓑ Ⓒ Ⓓ   12. Ⓐ Ⓑ Ⓒ Ⓓ   23. Ⓐ Ⓑ Ⓒ Ⓓ   33. Ⓐ Ⓑ Ⓒ Ⓓ   43. Ⓐ Ⓑ Ⓒ Ⓓ

2. Ⓐ Ⓑ Ⓒ Ⓓ   13. Ⓐ Ⓑ Ⓒ Ⓓ   24. Ⓐ Ⓑ Ⓒ Ⓓ   34. Ⓐ Ⓑ Ⓒ Ⓓ   44. Ⓐ Ⓑ Ⓒ Ⓓ

3. Ⓐ Ⓑ Ⓒ Ⓓ   14. Ⓐ Ⓑ Ⓒ Ⓓ   25. Ⓐ Ⓑ Ⓒ Ⓓ   35. Ⓐ Ⓑ Ⓒ Ⓓ   45. Ⓐ Ⓑ Ⓒ Ⓓ

4. Ⓐ Ⓑ Ⓒ Ⓓ   15. Ⓐ Ⓑ Ⓒ Ⓓ   26. Ⓐ Ⓑ Ⓒ Ⓓ   36. Ⓐ Ⓑ Ⓒ Ⓓ   46. Ⓐ Ⓑ Ⓒ Ⓓ

5. Ⓐ Ⓑ Ⓒ Ⓓ   16. Ⓐ Ⓑ Ⓒ Ⓓ   27. Ⓐ Ⓑ Ⓒ Ⓓ   37. Ⓐ Ⓑ Ⓒ Ⓓ   47. Ⓐ Ⓑ Ⓒ Ⓓ

6. Ⓐ Ⓑ Ⓒ Ⓓ   17. Ⓐ Ⓑ Ⓒ Ⓓ   28. Ⓐ Ⓑ Ⓒ Ⓓ   38. Ⓐ Ⓑ Ⓒ Ⓓ   48. Ⓐ Ⓑ Ⓒ Ⓓ

7. Ⓐ Ⓑ Ⓒ Ⓓ   18. Ⓐ Ⓑ Ⓒ Ⓓ   29. Ⓐ Ⓑ Ⓒ Ⓓ   39. Ⓐ Ⓑ Ⓒ Ⓓ   49. Ⓐ Ⓑ Ⓒ Ⓓ

8. Ⓐ Ⓑ Ⓒ Ⓓ   19. Ⓐ Ⓑ Ⓒ Ⓓ   30. Ⓐ Ⓑ Ⓒ Ⓓ   40. Ⓐ Ⓑ Ⓒ Ⓓ   50. Ⓐ Ⓑ Ⓒ Ⓓ

9. Ⓐ Ⓑ Ⓒ Ⓓ   20. Ⓐ Ⓑ Ⓒ Ⓓ   31. Ⓐ Ⓑ Ⓒ Ⓓ   41. Ⓐ Ⓑ Ⓒ Ⓓ   51. Ⓐ Ⓑ Ⓒ Ⓓ

10. Ⓐ Ⓑ Ⓒ Ⓓ   21. Ⓐ Ⓑ Ⓒ Ⓓ   32. Ⓐ Ⓑ Ⓒ Ⓓ   42. Ⓐ Ⓑ Ⓒ Ⓓ   52. Ⓐ Ⓑ Ⓒ Ⓓ

11. Ⓐ Ⓑ Ⓒ Ⓓ   22. Ⓐ Ⓑ Ⓒ Ⓓ

Section 2: Writing and Language Test

1. Ⓐ Ⓑ Ⓒ Ⓓ   10. Ⓐ Ⓑ Ⓒ Ⓓ   19. Ⓐ Ⓑ Ⓒ Ⓓ   28. Ⓐ Ⓑ Ⓒ Ⓓ   37. Ⓐ Ⓑ Ⓒ Ⓓ

2. Ⓐ Ⓑ Ⓒ Ⓓ   11. Ⓐ Ⓑ Ⓒ Ⓓ   20. Ⓐ Ⓑ Ⓒ Ⓓ   29. Ⓐ Ⓑ Ⓒ Ⓓ   38. Ⓐ Ⓑ Ⓒ Ⓓ

3. Ⓐ Ⓑ Ⓒ Ⓓ   12. Ⓐ Ⓑ Ⓒ Ⓓ   21. Ⓐ Ⓑ Ⓒ Ⓓ   30. Ⓐ Ⓑ Ⓒ Ⓓ   39. Ⓐ Ⓑ Ⓒ Ⓓ

4. Ⓐ Ⓑ Ⓒ Ⓓ   13. Ⓐ Ⓑ Ⓒ Ⓓ   22. Ⓐ Ⓑ Ⓒ Ⓓ   31. Ⓐ Ⓑ Ⓒ Ⓓ   40. Ⓐ Ⓑ Ⓒ Ⓓ

5. Ⓐ Ⓑ Ⓒ Ⓓ   14. Ⓐ Ⓑ Ⓒ Ⓓ   23. Ⓐ Ⓑ Ⓒ Ⓓ   32. Ⓐ Ⓑ Ⓒ Ⓓ   41. Ⓐ Ⓑ Ⓒ Ⓓ

6. Ⓐ Ⓑ Ⓒ Ⓓ   15. Ⓐ Ⓑ Ⓒ Ⓓ   24. Ⓐ Ⓑ Ⓒ Ⓓ   33. Ⓐ Ⓑ Ⓒ Ⓓ   42. Ⓐ Ⓑ Ⓒ Ⓓ

7. Ⓐ Ⓑ Ⓒ Ⓓ   16. Ⓐ Ⓑ Ⓒ Ⓓ   25. Ⓐ Ⓑ Ⓒ Ⓓ   34. Ⓐ Ⓑ Ⓒ Ⓓ   43. Ⓐ Ⓑ Ⓒ Ⓓ

8. Ⓐ Ⓑ Ⓒ Ⓓ   17. Ⓐ Ⓑ Ⓒ Ⓓ   26. Ⓐ Ⓑ Ⓒ Ⓓ   35. Ⓐ Ⓑ Ⓒ Ⓓ   44. Ⓐ Ⓑ Ⓒ Ⓓ

9. Ⓐ Ⓑ Ⓒ Ⓓ   18. Ⓐ Ⓑ Ⓒ Ⓓ   27. Ⓐ Ⓑ Ⓒ Ⓓ   36. Ⓐ Ⓑ Ⓒ Ⓓ

Section 3: Math Test—No Calculator

1. Ⓐ Ⓑ Ⓒ Ⓓ   4. Ⓐ Ⓑ Ⓒ Ⓓ   7. Ⓐ Ⓑ Ⓒ Ⓓ   10. Ⓐ Ⓑ Ⓒ Ⓓ   13. Ⓐ Ⓑ Ⓒ Ⓓ

2. Ⓐ Ⓑ Ⓒ Ⓓ   5. Ⓐ Ⓑ Ⓒ Ⓓ   8. Ⓐ Ⓑ Ⓒ Ⓓ   11. Ⓐ Ⓑ Ⓒ Ⓓ   14. Ⓐ Ⓑ Ⓒ Ⓓ

3. Ⓐ Ⓑ Ⓒ Ⓓ   6. Ⓐ Ⓑ Ⓒ Ⓓ   9. Ⓐ Ⓑ Ⓒ Ⓓ   12. Ⓐ Ⓑ Ⓒ Ⓓ   15. Ⓐ Ⓑ Ⓒ Ⓓ

16.   17.   18.   19.   20.

[Grid-in bubble answer boxes for questions 16–20, each with columns of digits 0–9]

Section 4: Math Test—Calculator

1. Ⓐ Ⓑ Ⓒ Ⓓ   7. Ⓐ Ⓑ Ⓒ Ⓓ   13. Ⓐ Ⓑ Ⓒ Ⓓ   19. Ⓐ Ⓑ Ⓒ Ⓓ   25. Ⓐ Ⓑ Ⓒ Ⓓ

2. Ⓐ Ⓑ Ⓒ Ⓓ   8. Ⓐ Ⓑ Ⓒ Ⓓ   14. Ⓐ Ⓑ Ⓒ Ⓓ   20. Ⓐ Ⓑ Ⓒ Ⓓ   26. Ⓐ Ⓑ Ⓒ Ⓓ

3. Ⓐ Ⓑ Ⓒ Ⓓ   9. Ⓐ Ⓑ Ⓒ Ⓓ   15. Ⓐ Ⓑ Ⓒ Ⓓ   21. Ⓐ Ⓑ Ⓒ Ⓓ   27. Ⓐ Ⓑ Ⓒ Ⓓ

4. Ⓐ Ⓑ Ⓒ Ⓓ   10. Ⓐ Ⓑ Ⓒ Ⓓ   16. Ⓐ Ⓑ Ⓒ Ⓓ   22. Ⓐ Ⓑ Ⓒ Ⓓ   28. Ⓐ Ⓑ Ⓒ Ⓓ

5. Ⓐ Ⓑ Ⓒ Ⓓ   11. Ⓐ Ⓑ Ⓒ Ⓓ   17. Ⓐ Ⓑ Ⓒ Ⓓ   23. Ⓐ Ⓑ Ⓒ Ⓓ   29. Ⓐ Ⓑ Ⓒ Ⓓ

6. Ⓐ Ⓑ Ⓒ Ⓓ   12. Ⓐ Ⓑ Ⓒ Ⓓ   18. Ⓐ Ⓑ Ⓒ Ⓓ   24. Ⓐ Ⓑ Ⓒ Ⓓ   30. Ⓐ Ⓑ Ⓒ Ⓓ

31.   32.   33.   34.   35.

[Grid-in bubble answer boxes for questions 31–35, each with columns of digits 0–9]

answer sheet

36.

	/	/	
⊙	⊙	⊙	⊙
	0	0	0
1	1	1	1
2	2	2	2
3	3	3	3
4	4	4	4
5	5	5	5
6	6	6	6
7	7	7	7
8	8	8	8
9	9	9	9

37.

	/	/	
⊙	⊙	⊙	⊙
	0	0	0
1	1	1	1
2	2	2	2
3	3	3	3
4	4	4	4
5	5	5	5
6	6	6	6
7	7	7	7
8	8	8	8
9	9	9	9

38.

	/	/	
⊙	⊙	⊙	⊙
	0	0	0
1	1	1	1
2	2	2	2
3	3	3	3
4	4	4	4
5	5	5	5
6	6	6	6
7	7	7	7
8	8	8	8
9	9	9	9

Section 5: Essay

_____

_____

_____

_____

_____

_____

_____

_____

_____

_____

_____

_____

_____

_____

_____

_____

_____

_____

_____

_____

_____

answers PRACTICE TEST 2

SECTION 1: READING TEST

65 Minutes • 52 Questions

TURN TO SECTION 1 OF YOUR ANSWER SHEET TO ANSWER THE QUESTIONS IN THIS SECTION.

Directions: Each passage or pair of passages below is followed by a number of questions. After reading each passage or pair of passages, choose the best answer to each question based on what is stated or implied in the passage or passages and in any accompanying graphics (such as a table, chart, or graph).

QUESTIONS 1–11 ARE BASED ON THE FOLLOWING PASSAGE AND SUPPLEMENTARY CHART.

"A Menace to U.S. Public Health" was authored by Rob Wilkins, a member of the National Federation of Professional Trainers (NFPT). The NFPT certifies personal fitness trainers to understand the fundamental exercise science principles in order to provide safe and effective fitness programs to individuals or small groups. The following article is taken from the NFPT's website, http://www.nfpt.com.

"In the United States, even the Grim Reaper is flabby." – Dr. Frank W. Booth, University of Missouri-Columbia

Line
Being fat and physically inactive now
5 has a name—Sedentary Death Syndrome or "SeDS." Approximately 2.5 million Americans will die prematurely in the next ten years due to SeDS, a number greater than all alcohol, guns, motor
10 vehicles, illicit drug use, and sexual behavior related deaths combined.

Research has identified SeDS as the second largest threat to public health (heart disease remains the number one
15 cause of death for Americans) and is expected to add as much as $3 trillion to healthcare costs over ten years, more than twice the tax cut recently passed by the U.S. Senate. Frank W. Booth, a professor
20 at the University of Missouri-Columbia, stated that he invented the term SeDS to emphasis his point that, in the United States, even the Grim Reaper is flabby.

Professor Booth's goal is to make the
25 public and the federal government pay more attention and spend more money on getting the average American to become more physically active. "We knew that there were approximately 250,000 people
30 in the United States each year dying of inactivity-related diseases, but the phrase inactivity-related disease lacks pizzazz," Booth said. Without a catchy name, the condition wasn't getting enough attention,
35 he said. "One day while I was out jogging, it hit me: Why not call it SeDS?"

Approximately two-thirds of American adults are currently overweight or obese according to the Center for Science in the
40 Public Interest (CSPI). Due to the fact that more than one-fourth of Americans are not physically active in their leisure time, obesity has doubled, and Type 2 diabetes (also known as adult-onset
45 diabetes) has increased tenfold. Type 2 diabetes is a devastating disease that may lead to complications such as blindness, kidney failure, heart disease, circulatory problems that can result in amputation,
50 and premature death.

Between 1982–1994, one third of all new cases of Type 2 diabetes were among people ages 10–19. The then-Surgeon General of the United States recently
55 observed that, "We are raising the most overweight youngsters in American history." In 2011–2012, 8.4% of 2- to 5-year-olds had obesity compared with 17.7% of 6- to 11-year-olds, and 20.5% of
60 12- to 19-year-olds.

Studies indicate that currently about 17% of the nation's children are obese. This is not surprising, considering that the average American child spends 900
65 hours per year in school but 1,200 hours

GO TO THE NEXT PAGE

watching television, according to the TV-Turnoff Network.

The problem is made worse by the fact that fewer than 3 in 10 high school
70 students get at least 60 minutes of physical activity every day. Less than half (48%) of all adults meet the 2008 Physical Activity Guidelines.

"Our bodies were designed to be
75 physically active," said Scott Gordon of East Carolina University. The trouble is that hard work, from farming to simply doing household chores without appliances, is no longer part of ordinary
80 life for most people, he said. Gordon called for activity to be put back in. "In adults, this may mean planning exercise into your daily routine," he said. "However, it may be as simple as
85 taking the stairs instead of the elevator a couple of times a day." Booth and his supporters said a special effort must be made to reach children, so they won't turn fat and weak like their parents and,
90 also like their parents, get sick and die early. "Perhaps the greatest tragedy is that ailments previously associated with the

middle-aged and older population will now affect our children and will serve
95 to drastically decrease their quality of life," said researcher Ron Gomes of the University of Delaware.

All Americans may incur a severe decline in their health due to consistent
100 physical inactivity. Thirty-five known conditions are exacerbated by physical inactivity; they include arthritis pain, arrhythmias, breast cancer, colon cancer, congestive heart failure, depression,
105 gallstone disease, heart attack, hypertension, obesity, osteoporosis, peripheral vascular disease, respiratory problems, Type 2 diabetes, sleep apnea, and stroke.
110 Providing enjoyable experiences is a potent strategy for increasing activity levels in youth, their attitude about the value of exercise, and ultimately long-term health outcome. Introducing
115 and making exercise fun for young children may help them develop commitment and a positive attitude toward physical activity as they go through adolescence and adulthood.

Number in Thousands of New Cases of Diagnosed Diabetes Among Adults Aged 18–79 Years, U.S. 1980–2011

1 The idea the author presents in lines 16–23 that the cost of SeDS is twice that of a recent tax cut is analogous to an automaker that

(A) investigates a faulty brake system in one of its models and issues a recall.

(B) apologizes to its customers for a faulty brake system in one of its models and assures them that next year's model has already been redesigned.

(C) compensates all the customers whose brakes have failed by offering them a free paint job for their car.

(D) gives classes to teach its customers how to install a fix for a faulty brake system in one of its models.

2 The structure of the article is designed to

(A) present opinions backed up by factual detail.

(B) frighten readers who are ignoring their weight issues.

(C) offer testimonials from those who are most affected.

(D) focus on statistical data and how it is being interpreted.

3 What effect on meaning and tone does the mention of the Grim Reaper add to the article?

(A) It encourages weight loss by alluding to the Grim Reaper's gaunt form.

(B) It links preventable health issues with a symbol of mortality.

(C) It uses a symbolic figure to make a humorous point.

(D) It relies on valid scientific conclusions from past studies.

4 Based on the passage, which choice best describes the relationship between the design of our bodies and the fact that obesity has doubled?

(A) Humans are naturally prone to obesity.

(B) Weight gain is passed from parents to children.

(C) People eat more in order to perform modern activities.

(D) Hard work is no longer part of most people's lives.

5 As used in line 5, "sedentary" most nearly means

(A) inactive.

(B) robust.

(C) sudden.

(D) obese.

6 In lines 12–15 ("Research has … for Americans."), what is the most likely reason the author compares SeDS with heart disease?

(A) To compare the symptoms of obesity with those of heart disease

(B) To make readers think of the many warnings against heart disease

(C) To demonstrate how heart disease often leads to issues with obesity

(D) To emphasize that poor health is not the issue, but a fatal outcome is

7 Which choice provides the best evidence for the answer to the previous question?

(A) Lines 6–11 ("Approximately … combined")

(B) Lines 35–36 ("One day … SeDS")

(C) Lines 53–57 ("The then-Surgeon … history")

(D) Lines 115–119 ("Introducing … adulthood")

GO TO THE NEXT PAGE

8 It can reasonably be inferred from the passage and the chart that steady increases in new cases of Type 2 diabetes began around

(A) 1980.

(B) 1988.

(C) 1998.

(D) 2009.

9 As used in line 32 , "pizzazz" most nearly means

(A) research.

(B) oomph.

(C) seriousness.

(D) action.

10 The passage most strongly suggests which of the following?

(A) A catchy name will motivate people to lose weight.

(B) Moving the body is essential to health.

(C) Type 2 diabetes is another form of obesity.

(D) Children can have good habits despite poor role models.

11 Which choice provides the best evidence for the answer to the previous question?

(A) Lines 24–28 ("Professor … active")

(B) Lines 40–45 ("Due to … tenfold")

(C) Lines 45–50 ("Type 2 … death")

(D) Lines 91–97 ("Perhaps … Delaware")

QUESTIONS 12–22 ARE BASED ON THE FOLLOWING PASSAGE.

This passage is excerpted from Helen Hunt Jackson's A Century of Dishonor, *published in 1881. In 1879, Jackson became a Native American rights activist after witnessing a speech by Ponca chief Standing Bear.*

There are within the limits of the United States between two hundred and fifty and three hundred thousand

Line Indians, exclusive of those in Alaska. The
5 names of the different tribes and bands
as entered in the statistical table, so the
Indian Office Reports, number nearly
three hundred.

There is not among these three
10 hundred bands of Indians one which has
not suffered cruelly at the hands either of
the Government or of white settlers. The
poorer, the more insignificant, the more
helpless the band, the more certain the
15 cruelty and outrage to which they have
been subjected. This is especially true
of the bands on the Pacific slope. These
Indians found themselves all of a sudden
surrounded by and caught up in the great
20 influx of gold-seeking settlers, as helpless
creatures on a shore are caught up in a
tidal wave. There was not time for the
Government to make treaties; not even
time for communities to make laws. The
25 tale of the wrongs, the oppressions, the
murders of the Pacific-slope Indians in
the last thirty years would be a volume by
itself, and is too monstrous to be believed.

It makes little difference, however,
30 where one opens the record of the history
of the Indians; every page and every year
has its dark stain. The story of one tribe is
the story of all, varied only by differences
of time and place; but neither time nor
35 place makes any difference in the main
facts. Colorado is as greedy and unjust in
1880 as was Georgia in 1830, and Ohio in
1795; and the United States Government
breaks promises now as deftly as then,
40 and with an added ingenuity from long
practice.

One of its strongest supports in so
doing is the wide-spread sentiment
among the people of dislike to the Indian,
45 of impatience with his presence as a
"barrier to civilization" and distrust of
it as a possible danger. The old tales
of the frontier life, with its horrors of
Indian warfare, have gradually, by two
50 or three generations' telling, produced
in the average mind something like an
hereditary instinct of questioning and
unreasoning aversion which it is almost
impossible to dislodge or soften.

55 President after president has appointed commission after commission to inquire into and report upon Indian affairs, and to make suggestions as to the best methods of managing them. The reports are filled
60 with eloquent statements of wrongs done to the Indians, of perfidies on the part of the Government; they counsel, as earnestly as words can, a trial of the simple and unperplexing expedients of
65 telling truth, keeping promises, making fair bargains, dealing justly in all ways and all things. These reports are bound up with the Government's Annual Reports, and that is the end of them.

70   The history of the Government connections with the Indians is a shameful record of broken treaties and unfulfilled promises. The history of the border white man's connection with the
75 Indians is a sickening record of murder, outrage, robbery, and wrongs committed by the former, as the rule, and occasional savage outbreaks and unspeakably barbarous deeds of retaliation by the
80 latter, as the exception.

      Taught by the Government that they had rights entitled to respect, when those rights have been assailed by the rapacity of the white man, the arm which should
85 have been raised to protect them has ever been ready to sustain the aggressor.

      The testimony of some of the highest military officers of the United States is on record to the effect that, in our Indian
90 wars, almost without exception, the first aggressions have been made by the white man …. Every crime committed by a white man against an Indian is concealed and palliated. Every offense committed
95 by an Indian against a white man is borne on the wings of the post or the telegraph to the remotest corner of the land, clothed with all the horrors which the reality or imagination can throw around it. Against
100 such influences as these are the people of the United States need to be warned.

12 The author's description of government inquiries into the handling of Native American affairs in lines 55–69 suggests that the author

(A) believes the government recognizes the need to be fairer in its dealings with the Native Americans.

(B) is doubtful that the government is inquiring into Native American affairs with the intention of making substantive changes.

(C) supposes that presidents have been more critical of the government's dealings with the Native Americans than the commissions.

(D) acknowledges that the government understands the problem but is not equipped to determine a viable solution.

13 The author refers to different states and different times (lines 29–41) as a way of

(A) citing specific abuses that were spread over a century.

(B) pointing out which states had the worst records of abuse.

(C) showing that these abuses no longer occur in America.

(D) defining where abuses in the Pacific slope area occurred.

14 Which choice provides the best evidence for the answer to the previous question?

(A) Lines 9–12 ("There is not … white settlers.")

(B) Lines 24–28 ("The tale … believed")

(C) Lines 29–32 ("It … stain")

(D) Lines 70–73 ("The history … promises")

GO TO THE NEXT PAGE

15 What explanation does the author give for the abuse of Native Americans as described in lines 22–28?

(A) The author blames old tales of Native Americans attacks on the frontier.

(B) The author cites a record of broken treaties and abuse of the laws.

(C) The author says that the settlers surrounded Native Americans.

(D) The author describes the Pacific-slope area as lawless and chaotic.

16 In what year did serious abuses of Native. Americans occur in Georgia?

(A) 1795

(B) 1830

(C) 1855

(D) 1880

17 The author chose a text structure designed to

(A) follow the historical chronology of how settlers in the United States dealt with Native Americans over time.

(B) dispel some of the common misconceptions of the dealings between the United States and Native Americans.

(C) categorize causes and effects in explaining the US government's treatment of Native Americans.

(D) present opposing viewpoints as to why the United States has had conflicts with Native Americans.

18 As used in line 94, "palliated" most nearly means

(A) intensified.

(B) confused.

(C) eased.

(D) excused.

19 Which of the following summaries of the last paragraph is the most accurate?

(A) The generals of the U.S. Army suggest that they had to be aggressive to keep Native Americans from defeating them and that sometimes there were crimes committed against Native Americans. Both sides spread their interpretation of events across the nation.

(B) In court hearings, soldiers discussed how the white man often took the fight to Native Americans in order to move them off the land and that there were occasions when this resulted in savage behavior by both parties.

(C) Proof that the white man was the aggressor in almost every conflict comes from the U.S. Army itself and the offenses of white men are disguised while the few offenses of Native Americans are widely exaggerated.

(D) The history of the conflicts between Native Americans and white men is one of gross injustice and extreme crimes against the tribes most of the time, while horrible crimes against white people are generally few and far between.

20 The central theme of the passage is that

(A) Native Americans have been victimized by the U.S. government.

(B) what happened to one tribe happened to all the tribes eventually.

(C) the U.S. government has done little to help Native Americans.

(D) Native Americans and white settlers had conflicts with each other in the past.

21 Which choice provides the best evidence for the answer to the previous question?

(A) Lines 12–16 ("The poorer … subjected")

(B) Lines 29–32 ("It makes … stain")

(C) Lines 32–36 ("The story … facts")

(D) Lines 73–80 ("The history … exception")

22 As used in line 79, "barbarous" most nearly means with

(A) silent determination.

(B) steadfast revenge.

(C) calculated antagonism.

(D) wild brutality.

QUESTIONS 23–32 ARE BASED ON THE FOLLOWING PASSAGE AND SUPPLEMENTARY MATERIAL.

Robert E. Lee and his family lived on a plantation estate in Arlington, Virginia, up until 1861. When Civil War broke out, he and his family departed for safer quarters. Lee became the commander of the Rebel field forces in 1862. His former home is now a National Park site. The full-length text of the following passage, provided by the National Park Service, can be found at http://www.nps.gov/arho/learn/historyculture/slavery.htm.

Slavery at Arlington

From its earliest days, Arlington House was home not only to the Custis and Lee families who occupied the mansion, but
Line to dozens of slaves who lived and labored
5 on the estate.

For nearly sixty years, Arlington functioned as a complex society made up of owners and slaves, whites and blacks. To some observers, on the surface,
10 Arlington appeared as a harmonious community in which owner and slave often lived and worked side by side. Yet an invisible gulf separated the two, as slaves were the legal property of their
15 owners. The enslaved possessed no rights, could not enter into legally binding contracts, and could be permanently separated from their families at a moment's notice.
20 In 1802, the first slaves to inhabit Arlington arrived with their owner, George Washington Parke Custis. The grandson of Martha Washington and adopted grandson of George Washington,
25 Custis had grown up at Mount Vernon, as had many of his slaves. Upon Martha Washington's death, Custis inherited her slaves and purchased others who belonged to his mother. In all, Custis
30 owned nearly 200 slaves and as many as 63 lived and worked at Arlington. The others worked on his other two plantations near Richmond, Virginia.

Once at Arlington, the slaves
35 constructed log cabins for their homes and began work on the main house. Using the red clay soil from the property and shells from the Potomac river, they made the bricks and stucco for the walls
40 and exterior of the house. The slaves also harvested timber from the Arlington forest, which was used for the interior flooring and supports. The slaves were responsible for keeping up the house and
45 laboring on the plantation, working to harvest corn and wheat, which was sold at market in Washington.

Custis saw his daughter marry Lt. Robert E. Lee at Arlington in 1831.
50 Robert and Mary Anna came to call Arlington home and Custis was a prominent figure in the lives of the seven Lee children. In his later years, Custis did not stray far from Arlington. He made his
55 will in 1855, and he increasingly relied on his son-in-law, Col. Lee, to handle his tangled business affairs. Until his death, Custis retained his old bedchamber in the north wing of the mansion, where he died
60 after a short illness on October 10, 1857.

Some slaves had very close relationships with the family members, though these relationships were governed by the racial hierarchy that existed
65 between slaves and slaveholders. Mr. Custis relied heavily on his carriage driver, Daniel Dotson, and Mrs. Lee had a personal relationship with the head housekeeper, Selina Gray. As Mary's

70 arthritis increasingly restricted her activities through the years, she depended on Selina for assistance. As evidence of their close bond, Mrs. Lee entrusted Selina with the keys to the plantation at 75 the time of the Lees' evacuation in May 1861.

There is evidence that some slaves at Arlington had opportunities not widely afforded to slaves elsewhere. Mrs. Custis, 80 a devout Episcopalian, tutored slaves in basic reading and writing so that they could read the Bible. Mrs. Lee and her daughters continued this practice even though Virginia law had prohibited the 85 education of slaves by the 1840s. Mrs. Custis also persuaded her husband to free several women and children.

Some of these emancipated slaves settled on the Arlington estate, including 90 Maria Carter Syphax who lived with her husband on a seventeen-acre plot given to her by the Custises at the time of her emancipation around 1826.

While such allowances may have 95 improved the quality of life for the Arlington slaves, most black men and women on the estate remained legally in bondage until the Civil War. In his will, Custis stipulated that all the Arlington 100 slaves should be freed upon his death if the estate was found to be in good financial standing or within five years otherwise. When Custis died in 1857, Robert E. Lee—the executor of the 105 estate—determined that the slave labor was necessary to improve Arlington's financial status. The Arlington slaves found Lee to be a more stringent taskmaster than his predecessor. Eleven 110 slaves were "hired out" while others were sent to the other estates. In accordance with Custis's instructions, Lee officially freed the slaves on December 29, 1862.

WEST ELEVATION

NORTH ELEVATION

FIRST FLOOR PLAN

The room at the east end on the lower level housed the summer kitchen, with cooks' quarters above. The center room at the lower level was a washroom, with the washerwoman's quarters above. The rooms at the west end housed various domestic slaves, including the coachmen, gardener, and housekeeper.

23 What is the most likely purpose of the passage?

(A) To inform people about the evils of slavery

(B) To persuade people that slavery was not so terrible

(C) To describe the history of Arlington House

(D) To illustrate how slaves lived before the Civil War

24 Why did Mrs. Custis teach her slaves to read?

(A) So they could teach other slaves and become self-sufficient

(B) So they could read their contracts with their owners

(C) So they could teach her children to read

(D) So they could read the Bible

25 What did George Washington Parke Custis inherit from his grandmother Martha Washington?

(A) Land and slaves

(B) Slaves

(C) A house with land and slaves

(D) Three plantations

26 How was the life of Selina Gray different from that of other slaves?

(A) She didn't have to work as hard.

(B) She was trusted by Mrs. Lee.

(C) She took care of the Lee children.

(D) She ran the whole plantation.

27 Which of the following statements is true based on the graphic and the passage.

(A) The slaves lived in one enormous house built just for slaves.

(B) The slaves' quarters were adequate for the needs of the slaves.

(C) The slaves lived in very tight quarters.

(D) The slave quarters were located next to the main house of the plantation.

28 How was Robert E. Lee related to George Washington?

(A) Lee married the daughter of Washington's grandson.

(B) Lee married George Washington's granddaughter.

(C) Lee's son married Martha Washington's granddaughter.

(D) Lee's father was Martha Washington's nephew.

29 What evidence in the passage suggests that Lee was more of a practical man than an idealist?

(A) Lines 53–57 ("Custis did not … business affairs")

(B) Lines 79–85 ("Mrs. Custis … by the 1840's")

(C) Lines 103–107 ("When Custis … financial status")

(D) Lines 112–113 ("Lee officially … December 29, 1862")

GO TO THE NEXT PAGE

30 Which of the following best illustrates that slaves were considered property in the era described in the passage?

(A) Lines 6–9 ("Arlington functioned … and blacks")

(B) Lines 27–29 ("Custis inherited … his mother")

(C) Lines 82–85 ("Mrs. Lee … the 1840s")

(D) Lines 85–87 ("Mrs. Custis … and children")

31 How does the author use the phrase "invisible gulf" (line 13)?

(A) As a figure of speech—related to differences in stature

(B) As a martime definition—related to a hidden body of water

(C) As a geographical reference—related to a ravine or abyss

(D) As an architectural description—related to building placement

32 In the context of the passage, what is the best definition of the word "afforded" (line 79)?

(A) Spared or given up without risk

(B) Had sufficient money to pay for

(C) Provided or supplied

(D) Purchased in exchange for

QUESTIONS 33–42 ARE BASED ON THE FOLLOWING PASSAGES.

Passage 1 is excerpted from the U.S. Environmental Protection Agency website. Passage 2 is excerpted from the article "Science Has Spoken: Global Warming Is a Myth" by Oregon Institute of Science and Medicine chemists, Arthur B. Robinson and Zachary W. Robinson. This article was published in the Wall Street Journal *in 1997.*

Passage 1

Climate change is happening

Our Earth is warming. Earth's average temperature has risen by 1.4°F over the past century and is projected to rise another 2 to 11.5°F over the next hundred years. Small changes in the average temperature of the planet can translate to large and potentially dangerous shifts in climate and weather.

The evidence is clear. Rising global temperatures have been accompanied by changes in weather and climate. Many places have seen changes in rainfall, resulting in more floods, droughts, or intense rain, as well as more frequent and severe heat waves. The planet's oceans and glaciers have also experienced some big changes—oceans are warming and becoming more acidic, ice caps are melting, and sea levels are rising. As these and other changes become more pronounced in the coming decades, they will likely present challenges to our society and our environment.

Humans are largely responsible for recent climate change. Over the past century, human activities have released large amounts of carbon dioxide and other greenhouse gases into the atmosphere. The majority of greenhouse gases come from burning fossil fuels to produce energy, although deforestation, industrial processes, and some agricultural practices also emit gases into the atmosphere.

Greenhouse gases act like a blanket around Earth, trapping energy in the atmosphere and causing it to warm. This phenomenon is called the greenhouse effect and is natural and necessary to support life on Earth. However, the buildup of greenhouse gases can change Earth's climate and result in dangerous effects to human health and welfare and to ecosystems.

Our lives are connected to the climate. Human societies have adapted to the relatively stable climate we have enjoyed since the last ice age, which ended several thousand years ago. A warming climate will bring changes that can affect our water supplies, agriculture, power and transportation systems, the natural environment, and even our own health and safety.

Some changes to the climate are
55 **unavoidable.** Carbon dioxide can stay in
the atmosphere for nearly a century, so
Earth will continue to warm in the coming
decades. The warmer it gets, the greater
the risk for more severe changes to the
60 climate and Earth's system. Although it's
difficult to predict the exact impacts of
climate change, what's clear is that the
climate we are accustomed to is no longer
a reliable guide for what to expect in the
65 future.

**We can reduce the risks we will face
from climate change.** By making choices
that reduce greenhouse gas pollution
and preparing for the changes that are
70 already underway, we can reduce risks
from climate change. Our decisions today
will shape the world our children and
grandchildren will live in.

Passage 2

[The global warming] hypothesis
75 predicts that global temperatures will
rise significantly, indeed catastrophically,
if atmospheric carbon dioxide rises.
Most of the increase in atmospheric
carbon dioxide has occurred during
80 the past 50 years, and the increase has
continued during the past 20 years. Yet
there has been no significant increase
in atmospheric temperature during
those 50 years, and during the 20 years
85 with the highest carbon dioxide levels,
temperatures have decreased.

In science, the ultimate test is the
process of experiment. If a hypothesis
fails the experimental test, it must be
90 discarded. Therefore, the scientific
method requires that the global warming
hypothesis be rejected.

Why, then, is there continuing
scientific interest in "global warming"?
95 There is a field of inquiry in which
scientists are using computers to try
to predict the weather—even global
weather over very long periods. But
global weather is so complicated that
100 current data and computer methods are
insufficient to make such predictions.
Although it is reasonable to hope that
these methods will eventually become

useful, for now computer climate models
105 are very unreliable.

So we needn't worry about human use
of hydrocarbons warming the Earth. We
also needn't worry about environmental
calamities, even if the current, natural
110 warming trend continues: After all the
Earth has been much warmer during the
past 3,000 years without ill effects.

But we should worry about the effects
of the hydrocarbon rationing being
115 proposed at Kyoto. Hydrocarbon use has
major environmental benefits. A great
deal of research has shown that increases
in atmospheric carbon dioxide accelerate
the growth rates of plants and also permit
120 plants to grow in drier regions. Animal
life, which depends upon plants, also
increases.

---

33 Upon which concepts do both passages
fully agree?

(A) That global warming has been proven
by evidence

(B) That an increase in overall
temperature is manageable

(C) That levels of atmospheric carbon
dioxide have increased

(D) That usual weather patterns have
been affected

---

34 Which choice provides the best evidence
for the answer to the previous question?

(A) Lines 5–8 ("Small changes … and
weather.")

(B) Lines 39–43 ("However, the … to
ecosystems.")

(C) Lines 78–81 ("Most of the … 20
years.")

(D) Lines 113–115 ("But we should … at
Kyoto.")

GO TO THE
NEXT PAGE

35 Which point of view characterizes both passages?

(A) One of scientists taking neutral positions

(B) One of fanatics defending a cause

(C) One of humans concerned for global well-being

(D) One of debaters directly addressing readers as "you"

36 In making their arguments, the authors of both passages fail to

(A) provide sources of proof for their claims.

(B) account for recent advances in the field.

(C) acknowledge dissenting opinions.

(D) provide definitions for their terminology.

37 The word choice of the first passage (potentially dangerous, severe, challenges, dangerous effects) and the second passage (no significant, rejected, insufficient, unreliable) differ in that

(A) the first is employing colorful language to describe, and the second is relying on simpler language to define.

(B) Passage 1 uses scientific terms and Passage 2 uses layperson's terms.

(C) the first passage attempts to reassure readers, and the second passage tries to motivate them.

(D) Passage 1 is sounding a warning, and Passage 2 is negating any cause for alarm.

38 As used in line 21, "pronounced" most nearly means

(A) articulated.

(B) announced.

(C) inconspicuous.

(D) noticeable.

39 In both passages, the authors present information by

(A) listing a sequence of events that begins in the past and continues into the future.

(B) discussing the causes of a situation and the resulting effects or lack of effects.

(C) comparing two different approaches to a problem and determining which will be most effective.

(D) defining the problems the world faces and then offering solutions to them.

40 The essential difference between the arguments the two sets of authors present is whether or not

(A) atmospheric hydrogen should be controlled.

(B) climate and weather can be modified by humans.

(C) atmospheric hydrogen poses a threat to human life.

(D) the production of hydrocarbons is a natural result of human activity.

41 Which choice provides the best evidence for the answer to the previous question?

(A) Lines 29–30 ("The majority … into the atmosphere.")

(B) Lines 55–58 ("Carbon dioxide … coming decades")

(C) Lines 74–77 ("The global … dioxide rises")

(D) Lines 116–120 ("A great … drier regions")

42 As used in line 7, "translate" most nearly means

(A) comprehend.

(B) expand.

(C) transform.

(D) explain.

QUESTIONS 43–52 ARE BASED ON THE FOLLOWING PASSAGE.

The following is an excerpt from a short story, "Miss Tempy's Watchers," by Sarah Orne Jewett, a novelist and short-story writer who lived from 1849–1909. In the story, two women watch over their deceased friend on the evening before her funeral and share their memories of her.

The time of year was April; the place was a small farming town in New Hampshire, remote from any railroad.

Line One by one the lights had been blown out
5 in the scattered houses near Miss Tempy Dent's, but as her neighbors took a last look out of doors, their eyes turned with instinctive curiosity toward the old house where a lamp burned steadily. They gave
10 a little sigh. "Poor Miss Tempy!" said more than one bereft acquaintance; for the good woman lay dead in her north chamber, and the lamp was a watcher's light. The funeral was set for the next day
15 at one o'clock.

The watchers were two of her oldest friends. Mrs. Crowe and Sarah Ann Binson. They were sitting in the kitchen because it seemed less awesome than
20 the unused best room, and they beguiled the long hours by steady conversation. One would think that neither topics nor opinions would hold out, at that rate, all through the long spring night, but there
25 was a certain degree of excitement just then, and the two women had risen to an unusual level of expressiveness and confidence. Each had already told the other more than one fact that she had
30 determined to keep secret; they were again and again tempted into statements that either would have found impossible by daylight. Mrs. Crowe was knitting a blue yarn stocking for her husband; the
35 foot was already so long that it seemed as if she must have forgotten to narrow it at the proper time. Mrs. Crowe knew exactly what she was about, however; she was of a much cooler disposition than Sister
40 Binson, who made futile attempts at some sewing, only to drop her work into her lap whenever the talk was most engaging.

Their faces were interesting—of the dry, shrewd, quick-witted New England
45 type, and thin hair twisted neatly back out of the way. Mrs. Crowe could look vague and benignant, and Miss Binson was, to quote her neighbors, a little too sharp-set, but the world knew that she
50 had need to be, with the load she must carry supporting an inefficient widowed sister and six unpromising and unwilling nieces and nephews. The eldest boy was at last placed with a good man to learn
55 the mason's trade. Sarah Ann Binson, for all her sharp, anxious aspect never defended herself, when her sister whined and fretted.

She was told every week of her life
60 that the poor children would never have had to lift a finger if their father had lived, and yet she had kept her steadfast way with the little farm, and patiently taught the young people many useful things for
65 which, as everybody said, they would live to thank her. However pleasureless her life appeared to outward view, it was brimful of pleasure to herself.

Mrs. Crowe, on the contrary, was
70 well-to-do, her husband being a rich farmer and an easy-going man. She was a stingy woman, but for all of that she looked kindly; and when she gave away anything, or lifted a finger to help
75 anybody, it was thought a great piece of beneficence, and a compliment, indeed, which the recipient accepted with twice as much gratitude as double the gift that came from a poorer and more generous
80 acquaintance. Everybody liked to be on good terms with Mrs. Crowe. Socially, she stood much higher than Sarah Ann Binson.

GO TO THE
NEXT PAGE

43 The two women are in Miss Tempy Dent's house because they are

(A) waiting to tell other friends and family that she has died.

(B) staying with the body so it isn't alone until it is buried.

(C) conducting a funeral service following Miss Tempy's requests.

(D) visiting Miss Tempy Dent, but she has died.

44 The theme of this excerpt can best be described as

(A) old friends often grow closer when they lose a friend.

(B) the bonds of friendship remain strong even in death.

(C) trying to stay awake all night isn't hard for dear friends.

(D) the living carry on the traditions of the dead.

45 In lines 33–42, the author uses the activities of knitting and sewing to show that

(A) the two women are so lost in conversation that they neglect their work.

(B) there are a lot of things that need to be done by morning.

(C) the women are so upset by the death that they find it hard to work.

(D) the two elderly women are getting absent-minded and weak.

46 Even though these two women are very different, the author shows that they are getting closer by

(A) having them sit in the kitchen instead of the best room.

(B) having Mrs. Crowe give Sarah Ann something nice.

(C) explaining that Sarah Ann was actually very happy.

(D) explaining they were telling each other secrets.

47 Which choice provides the best evidence for the answer to the previous question?

(A) Lines 22–28 ("One would … and confidence.")

(B) Lines 46–53 ("Mrs. Crowe … nieces and nephews.")

(C) Lines 59–66 ("She was … thank her.")

(D) Lines 69–71 ("Mrs. Crowe … easy-going man.")

48 Which choice provides the best summary of what happened between Mrs. Crowe and Sarah Ann Binson in Miss Tempy's kitchen?

(A) Both women found it hard to fill up the long hours.

(B) Both women had become excited by the intimacy they shared.

(C) Mrs. Crowe did not reveal as much as Sarah Ann Binson.

(D) Sarah Ann Binson revealed her love of pleasure and freedom.

49 Although they were both friends to Miss Tempy Dent, the relationship between Mrs. Crowe and Sarah Ann Binson could be described as not

(A) all that close, but enjoying the same pleasures.

(B) the same age, but close enough to understand.

(C) united in purpose, but learning to work together.

(D) from the same social status, but intimate.

50 Which choice provides the best evidence for the answer to the previous question?

(A) Lines 1–3 ("The time of … any railroad.")

(B) Lines 28–33 ("Each had … by daylight.")

(C) Lines 37–42 ("Mrs. Crowe … most engaging.")

(D) Lines 81–83 ("Socially … Sarah Ann Binson.")

51 As used in line 49, "sharp-set" most nearly means

(A) hungry.

(B) restless.

(C) willy-nilly.

(D) close-fisted.

52 As used in line 76, "beneficence" most nearly means

(A) furniture.

(B) succor.

(C) magnanimity.

(D) scrupulousness.

STOP

**If you finish before time is called, you may check your work on this section only.
Do not turn to any other section.**

No Test Material On This Page

SECTION 2: WRITING AND LANGUAGE TEST

35 MINUTES • 44 QUESTIONS

TURN TO SECTION 2 OF YOUR ANSWER SHEET TO ANSWER THE QUESTIONS IN THIS SECTION.

Directions: Each passage below is accompanied by a number of multiple-choice questions. For some questions, you will need to consider how the passage might be revised to improve the expression of ideas. Other questions will ask you to consider how the passage might be edited to correct errors in sentence structure, usage, or punctuation. A passage may be accompanied by one or more graphics—such as a chart, table, or graph—that you will need to refer to in order to best answer the question(s).

Some questions will direct you to an underlined portion of a passage—it could be one word, a portion of a sentence, or the full sentence itself. Other questions will direct you to a particular paragraph or to certain sentences within a paragraph, or you'll be asked to think about the passage as a whole. Each question number refers to the corresponding number in the passage.

After reading each passage, select the answer to each question that most effectively improves the quality of writing in the passage or that makes the passage follow the conventions of Standard Written English. Many questions include a "NO CHANGE" option. Select that option if you think the best choice is to leave that specific portion of the passage as it is.

QUESTIONS 1–11 ARE BASED ON THE FOLLOWING PASSAGE.

Code Talking

In September of 1992, a group of American heroes who had gone unrecognized for many years was honored by the United States Pentagon. Consisted of thirty-five Navajo code talkers.

During World War II, the United States Marines needed to develop a code, for communicating top-secret information.

1

(A) NO CHANGE
(B) Having consisted of
(C) A group which were made of
(D) It consisted of

2

(A) NO CHANGE
(B) code for communicating
(C) code, for communicating,
(D) code for communicating,

GO TO THE
NEXT PAGE

3 It being the case that they would then have access to information about United States Marines tactics and troop movements, it was crucial that enemy forces not be able to decipher the code.

The military recruited a small group of Navajos to create a code based on their language. **4** The Navajo language was chosen because many of the top military officials at the time were Navajo. First, it was extremely difficult to learn and virtually unknown outside the Navajo community in the American Southwest. **5** However, the Navajo language does not have a written form; it uses no alphabet. Its complexity and **6** obscurity made it the perfect basis for a code.

The first group of Navajo recruits attended boot camp in 1942. Afterward, they set to work developing a vast dictionary of code words for military terms based on the Navajo language. Each code talker had to memorize the dictionary before being sent to a Marine unit. Once they were stationed with a unit, the code talkers used telephones and radios to transmit encoded orders and information.

3

(A) NO CHANGE
(B) It was crucial to the United States, that enemy forces not be able to decipher the code, having access to information about Marines tactics and troop movements.
(C) It was crucial that enemy forces be unable to decipher the code because, if they did, they would have access to information about the Marines' tactics and troop movements.
(D) Crucially, the enemy forces were unable to decipher the code, which would have access to the Marines' tactics and troop movements.

4 Which choice most effectively sets up the information that follows?

(A) NO CHANGE
(B) The Navajo language was chosen because the Navajo people were famous for their military history.
(C) The Navajo people had often been called on to help the American government in the past.
(D) The Navajo language made an excellent code for several essential reasons.

5

(A) NO CHANGE
(B) Furthermore
(C) Likewise
(D) As a result

6

(A) NO CHANGE
(B) uncertainty
(C) intricacy
(D) clarity

While the Navajo language was complicated, the code was even more complex. A code talker receiving a message heard a stream of Navajo words. **7** <u>The receiver had to translate the words into English. Then the receiver had to use the first letter of each English equivalent to spell out a word.</u> Adding to the difficulty of breaking the code was the fact that most letters could be indicated by the code talkers with more than one Navajo word.

Though able to crack the codes of other military branches, enemy forces never managed to **8** perceive what the Marines' Navajo code talkers said. The code talkers were renowned for the **9** speed, and accuracy, with which they **10** worked.

7 Which choice most effectively joins the two sentences?

(A) The receiver had to translate the words into English, and then the receiver had to use the first letter of each English equivalent to spell out a word.

(B) The receiver had to translate the words into English and then use the first letter of each English equivalent to spell out a word.

(C) The receiver had to translate the words into English even though the receiver had to then use the first letter of each English equivalent to spell out a word.

(D) The receiver had to translate the words into English because the receiver had to use the first letter of each English equivalent to spell out a word.

8

(A) NO CHANGE
(B) fathom
(C) elucidate
(D) decipher

9

(A) NO CHANGE
(B) speed, and accuracy
(C) speed and accuracy
(D) speed and accuracy,

10

(A) NO CHANGE
(B) will work.
(C) are working.
(D) have been working.

practice test

GO TO THE NEXT PAGE

11 Because the Navajo language <u>was common only in the American Southwest,</u> the work of the code talkers remained unacknowledged until quite recently. Half a century later, in 1992, thirty-five former code talkers and their families attended the dedication of the Navajo Code Talker Exhibit at the United States Pentagon, and officially took their place in military history.

11 Which choice provides information that best supports the claim made by the sentence?

(A) NO CHANGE

(B) had to be translated into English words and letters

(C) took a long time to decode by people who didn't speak English

(D) remained part of a classified code for many years

QUESTIONS 12–22 ARE BASED ON THE FOLLOWING PASSAGE.

Who was Dian **12** <u>Fossey.</u> Dian Fossey was a researcher, a visionary, and a pioneer in the field of animal conservation. More specifically, Fossey dedicated her life to preserving Africa's endangered mountain gorilla.

Fossey **13** <u>was born in San Francisco and made her first trip to Africa in 1963.</u> At the time, she was 31 years old. In the course of her trip, she met Dr. Louis Leakey, a **14** <u>prominent</u> archaeologist and anthropologist.

12

(A) NO CHANGE

(B) Dian Fossey?

(C) Dian Fossey,

(D) Dian Fossey!

13 The writer is considering deleting the underlined portion of the sentence. Should the writer make this deletion?

(A) Yes, because this information should be provided earlier in the passage.

(B) Yes, because this information doesn't support the main idea of the paragraph.

(C) No, because this information supports the main idea of the paragraph.

(D) No, because this information is important to the organization of the passage.

14

(A) NO CHANGE

(B) imminent

(C) infamous

(D) egregious

Dr. Leakey believed in the importance of research on large apes and encouraged Fossey to undertake such a study. **15** After accepting the research challenge from Dr. Leakey, mountain gorillas became a research topic.

Fossey began her work in the African country of Zaire, but was forced to leave because of political unrest. She moved to another African country, Rwanda, where she established a research camp in a national park. **16** They're, she spent thousands of hours observing the behavior of gorillas. Her steadfast patience won the trust of the animals, and they began to **17** except her presence among them. As a result, she was able to observe behaviors that had never been seen by humans before.

Spending so much time observing the gorillas, Fossey naturally distinguished among them and had particular favorites. One of these favorites was a young male gorilla named Digit. Digit was later killed by a poacher, an illegal hunter of protected animals. **18** Fossey was really, really sad. She began a public campaign to raise awareness about the problem of gorilla poaching, a practice that threatened their continued existence. **19** The rhinoceros, too, has faced grave danger from poaching. Fossey's campaign earned worldwide attention and support, and she continued to live and work in Africa for many years thereafter.

15

(A) NO CHANGE
(B) After accepting the research challenge from Dr. Leakey, Fossey chose mountain gorillas as the topic of her research.
(C) Mountain gorillas, after accepting the research challenge from Dr. Leakey, became the topic of Fossey's research.
(D) Fossey chose mountain gorillas after accepting the research challenge from Dr. Leakey, as her research topic.

16

(A) NO CHANGE
(B) Their
(C) There
(D) Where

17

(A) NO CHANGE
(B) undertake
(C) assume
(D) accept

18

(A) NO CHANGE
(B) Fossey was crushed.
(C) Fossey was super-duper sad.
(D) Fossey was stunned and saddened.

19 Which sentence most effectively fits with the main idea of the paragraph?

(A) NO CHANGE
(B) Organizations like the African Wildlife Foundation help to prevent poaching, too.
(C) Mountain gorillas, after all, have a life expectancy of 35 years in the wild.
(D) In 1989, it was predicted that there were only 620 mountain gorillas left.

GO TO THE NEXT PAGE

20 In 1980, Fossey took a teaching position at Cornell University and wrote a book, *Gorillas in the Mist*, that brought further attention to the **21** deteriorating numbers of mountain gorillas. Afterward, Fossey returned to Rwanda, and spent the rest of her life working to protect the mountain gorilla. Even after her mysterious death, Fossey's work continued make an impact.

Today, **22** the population of mountain gorillas in Rwanda is rising thanks to the legacy of Dian Fossey.

20 At this point, the writer is considering adding the following sentence:

> She had always been interested in teaching and decided to seek employment at the university level.

Should the writer make this addition here?

(A) Yes, because this information provides information necessary to understand the paragraph.

(B) Yes, because this information makes a good transition from the previous paragraph.

(C) No, because this information is not necessary and doesn't support the main idea of the paragraph.

(D) No, because this information should be placed at the end of the passage.

21

(A) NO CHANGE

(B) declining

(C) demeaning

(D) degrading

22

(A) NO CHANGE

(B) the population of mountain gorillas in Rwanda are rising.

(C) the population of mountain gorillas in Rwanda were rising.

(D) the population of mountain gorillas in Rwanda rises.

QUESTIONS 23–33 ARE BASED ON THE FOLLOWING PASSAGE.

Tamarin Families

Deep in the rainforests of Brazil, tiny creatures known as "kings of the jungle" inhabit the trees. These creatures, similar in size to squirrels, have bright, reddish-orange coats and hairless faces; their fur **23** obscures their faces like the mane of a lion. Accordingly, these highly endangered monkeys are called golden lion tamarins.

Tamarins live in small family units of up to nine individuals. **24** Offspring are generally born in pairs, and all members of the group will pitch in to help care for them. Tamarins that participate in caring for their newborn siblings tend to become **25** better parents.

23

(A) NO CHANGE
(B) encircles
(C) covers
(D) marks

24 The writer is considering deleting the underlined sentence. Should the writer do this?

(A) No, because it provides information necessary to understand the next sentence.
(B) No, because it explains why family units are relatively small.
(C) Yes, because it should be placed earlier in the paragraph.
(D) Yes, because this information interrupts the flow of the paragraph.

25

(A) NO CHANGE
(B) better parents than tamarins that do not.
(C) better parents than other tamarins.
(D) better parents than older tamarins.

GO TO THE
NEXT PAGE

practice test

[1] Tamarins are diurnal, meaning **26** they are active during the daytime. [2] At night, they seek shelter in tree hollows. [3] They are omnivorous, eating fruits, insects, and occasionally small lizards and snakes, which are **27** one in the same to them. [4] Tamarins spend their time in trees, using their fingers to grip the branches. **28** [5] However, they dislike direct sunlight, and so are well-suited to the dense foliage of the forest.

Golden lion tamarins inhabit a distinct ecological **29** niche, they are found only in the eastern rainforests of Brazil. As farmers clear the rainforest to grow cash crops, the habitat of the tamarins has decreased drastically; as a result, the survival of the species is in extreme danger. Ecologists estimate that there are only one thousand tamarins remaining in the wild.

26

(A) NO CHANGE
(B) it is
(C) he is
(D) it will be

27

(A) NO CHANGE
(B) one with the same
(C) one and the same
(D) one the same

28 To make this paragraph the most logical, sentence 5 should be placed

(A) where it is now.
(B) before sentence 1.
(C) before sentence 2.
(D) before sentence 4.

29 Which choice most effectively combines the two sentences at the underlined portion?

(A) NO CHANGE
(B) niche they,
(C) niche they
(D) niche; they

30 In the 1970s, a conservation campaign was initiated to save the tamarins. The movement began as a collaboration between the National Zoological Park in Washington, the Smithsonian Institute, and the Rio de Janeiro Primate Center. **31** It has grown to address the problem from several angles, including managing and restoring the disappearing habitat of the tamarins, breeding tamarins in captivity and in the wild, and reintroducing tamarins into their natural environment. As part of this effort, a number of zoos around the world have participated in helping to breed tamarins in captivity. **32**

30 Which choice most effectively establishes the main topic of paragraph 5?

(A) A collaborative effort to save the tamarins was established in 1970 and over time has developed a multi-faceted approach to solving the problem of tamarin endangerment.

(B) The effort to save the tamarins includes managing and restoring the disappearing habitat of the tamarins, breeding tamarins in captivity and in the wild, and reintroducing tamarins into their natural environment.

(C) The collaborative effort to save tamarins includes the National Zoological Park in Washington, the Smithsonian Institute, and the Rio de Janeiro Primate Center.

(D) The continued effort of zoos to breed the tamarin in captivity has saved the tamarin from extinction.

31

(A) NO CHANGE
(B) The campaign
(C) The problem
(D) They

32 Which choice adds accurate data to the paragraph based on the graph (next page)?

(A) Unfortunately, the participation rate among zoos has fallen dramatically while the tamarin population has climbed.

(B) While the population of tamarins in captivity has fluctuated since 2000, the number of participating zoos has remained relatively steady.

(C) Although the population of tamarins has fallen since 2000, the participation rate of zoos has risen substantially in recent years.

(D) Sadly, both the number of participating zoos and the population of tamarins has fallen significantly since 2000.

GO TO THE NEXT PAGE

So far, efforts to return these animals back into their natural habitat have been **33** <u>fruitful</u>, making the golden lion tamarin one of very few species to be successfully reintroduced into the wild.

33

(A) NO CHANGE
(B) problematic
(C) lucrative
(D) delayed

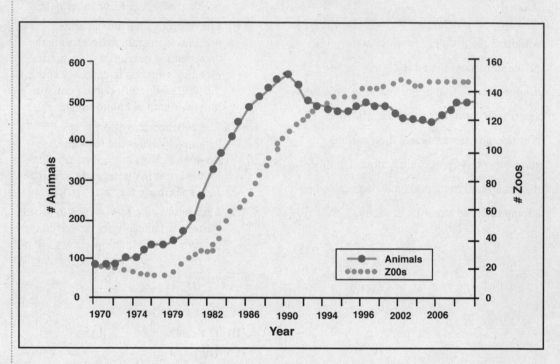

Used with permission. Ballou, J. D., J. Mickelberg, D. Field, and N. Lindsey. 2009. Population Management Recommendations for the International Ex-situ Population of Golden Lion Tamarins (*Leontopithecus rosalia*). National Zoological Park, Washington, D.C.

QUESTIONS 34–44 ARE BASED ON THE FOLLOWING PASSAGE.

Classical architecture, the origins of which can be traced to ancient Rome, is characterized by a strict and **34** terminable adherence to the principles of coherence, exactness, and detail.

35 The basis of the classical style was the manner in which a building's space was divided so as to create a coherent whole. An example of a plan for the division of a building's space was **36** the tripartite plan. This plan would divide the space in a particular building into three equal parts. Such a plan would be followed no matter what the purpose of the building—churches, homes, or public government buildings could all be designed with such a plan. Even gardens, designed in the classical style, might have a three-part plan.

34

(A) NO CHANGE
(B) inclement
(C) rigorous
(D) contentious

35 At this point, the writer is considering adding the following sentence:

> Over time, the classical tripartite plan spilled over from architecture to other arts—music, poetry, and dance—and it is not uncommon to have a three-part hierarchy within those artistic areas as well.

Should the writer make this addition here?

(A) Yes, because it adds interesting detail to the paragraph.
(B) Yes, because it provides an accurate introduction to the paragraph.
(C) No, because this information should be added at the end of the paragraph.
(D) No, because this information does not support the main idea of the paragraph.

36 Which choice most effectively combines the sentences at the underlined portion?

(A) the tripartite plan, and this plan would
(B) the tripartite plan would
(C) the tripartite plan, it would
(D) the tripartite plan, which would

Once the framework of a building designed in the classical style was established, architectural elements were added. While **37** columns are fairly typical architectural element, there are five types in particular that are the most **38** common: the *Doric, Ionic, Corinthian, Tuscan,* and *Composite.* Each column was distinctive and of a certain specified proportion, base to top. Just as the building follows a tripartite plan, so the columns themselves have a three-part organization. Above the column is a horizontal piece, called the *entablature*; then comes the column itself, which is tall and cylindrical; and finally comes the platform, or *crepidoma,* upon which the column rests.

Each of these elements also maintains a three-part organization. The *entablature* is divided into three parts— **39** cornice, the frieze, and the architrave. The column includes the capital, the shaft, and the base. **40** .

37
(A) NO CHANGE
(B) columns are fairly typical architectural elements
(C) column is a fairly typical architectural elements
(D) columns is fairly typical architectural elements

38
(A) NO CHANGE
(B) common: the Doric and Ionic, Corinthian, and Tuscan, and Composite.
(C) common: the Doric; Ionic; Corinthian; Tuscan; and Composite.
(D) common: the Doric and Ionic; Corinthian, Tuscan, and Composite.

39
(A) NO CHANGE
(B) cornice, frieze, and the architrave.
(C) the cornice, the frieze, and the architrave.
(D) the cornice, the frieze, and architrave.

40 Which of the following choices supports the topic of the paragraph with relevant information?

(A) The *crepidoma* was a single solid mass of steps that supported the rest of the column.
(B) The *crepidoma* sometimes included a sloping ramp, particularly in large temples.
(C) The *crepidoma* maintains the three-part division with its three steps.
(D) The *crepidoma,* though, was not often used in Doric columns.

Classical architecture is filled with conventions that while not obvious to most viewers, become apparent upon closer analysis. For example, **41** classical buildings must stand free; it cannot touch the sides of other buildings because, in the view of the classicist, each building is a world within a world of **42** his own. Consequently, organizing groups of buildings became problematic for rule-following, classical architects because of **43** differentiated violations of spatial conventions. The classical mode required adherence to formal rules that were sometimes impossible to impose on groups of buildings. **44**

41

(A) NO CHANGE
(B) a classical building must stand free; we cannot touch
(C) classical buildings must stand free; you cannot touch
(D) classical buildings must stand free; they cannot touch

42

(A) NO CHANGE
(B) their
(C) its
(D) the buildings

43

(A) NO CHANGE
(B) perceived
(C) comprehended
(D) extricated

44 Which choice most effectively establishes the main topic of the final paragraph?

(A) The rules of classical architecture, which become apparent on close examination, often organize a building and its features into tripartite groups of three.
(B) Classical architects often had trouble following the rules and building groups of buildings.
(C) A classical building must stand free and be a world unto itself, which is why no classical buildings connect to each other.
(D) The numerous and strict conventions of classical architecture, such as the idea that a building must stand on its own, were not always easy for classical builders to abide by.

STOP

**If you finish before time is called, you may check your work on this section only.
Do not turn to any other section.**

SECTION 3: MATH TEST—NO CALCULATOR

20 Questions • 25 minutes

TURN TO SECTION 3 OF YOUR ANSWER SHEET TO ANSWER THE QUESTIONS IN THIS SECTION.

Directions: For Questions 1–15, solve each problem, select the best answer from the choices provided, and fill in the corresponding oval on your answer sheet. **For Questions 16–20,** solve the problem and enter your answer in the grid on the answer sheet. The directions **before Question 16** will provide information on how to enter your answers in the grid.

ADDITIONAL INFORMATION:

- The use of a calculator in this section **is not permitted.**

- All variables and expressions used represent real numbers unless otherwise indicated.

- Figures provided in this test are drawn to scale unless otherwise indicated.

- All figures lie in a plane unless otherwise indicated.

- Unless otherwise specified, the domain of a given function f is the set of all real numbers x for which $f(x)$ is a real number.

The number of degrees of arc in a circle is 360.
The number of radians in the arc of a circle is 2π.
The sum of the measures in degrees of the angles of a triangle is 180.

1 Simplify the expression

$$(4x^2 - 5x + 8) - (3x^2 - 5 - 2x).$$

- **(A)** $x^2 - 3x + 13$
- **(B)** $x^2 - 3x + 3$
- **(C)** $x^2 - 7x + 13$
- **(D)** $x^2 - 7x + 3$

2 Which expression is equivalent to

$$x^{\frac{2}{3}} \cdot x^{\frac{-4}{3}} ?$$

- **(A)** $-\sqrt[3]{x^8}$
- **(B)** $-\sqrt[3]{x^2}$
- **(C)** $\sqrt[3]{x^2}$
- **(D)** $\dfrac{1}{\sqrt[3]{x^2}}$

3 Which expression is equivalent to

$$\frac{3}{4}(3x - 4y) + \frac{2}{3}(-3y + 5x)\ ?$$

(A) $\dfrac{67x}{12} - 5y$

(B) $\dfrac{x}{4} + \dfrac{y}{3}$

(C) $\dfrac{19x}{12} - 5$

(D) $\dfrac{17x}{4} + \dfrac{19y}{3}$

4 $8x - 9 = x^2 - y$

Which of the following equations is equivalent to the equation above and in a form that includes the vertex of the parabola as coefficients?

(A) $y = (x + 1)(x - 9)$

(B) $y = (x - 4)^2 - 7$

(C) $y = x^2 - 8x + 9$

(D) $x = \sqrt{y + 7} + 4$

5 If $a + 4b = 16$, what is the value of

$3(a + 4b)$?

(A) 48

(B) 24

(C) 16

(D) $5\dfrac{1}{3}$

6 $S = 2\pi r^2 + 2\pi rh$

The formula above gives the suface area S of a cylinder with a radius r and height h. Which of the following gives h in terms of S and r?

(A) $h = \dfrac{S}{2\pi r} - r$

(B) $h = \dfrac{S}{2\pi r} + r$

(C) $h = \dfrac{2\pi r^2 - S}{2\pi r}$

(D) $h = \dfrac{S + 2\pi r^2}{2\pi r}$

7 A group of economists performed a study on the decreasing population in a small town for a time period of 10 years. They determined that as a result of factors such as loss of jobs and a poor economy, the population of the town decreased by about 3.5% each year. Write an equation for the population of thc town, P, in terms of its initial population, P_0, and n, the number of years of the study.

(A) $P = P_0(0.965)^n$

(B) $P = P_0(0.965)n$

(C) $P = P_0(1.035)^n$

(D) $P = P_0(1.035)n$

8 If f is a linear function and if $f(4) = 2$ and $f(6) = 10$, which of the following could be the function f?

(A) $f(x) = x - 2$

(B) $f(x) = 2x - 2$

(C) $f(x) = 2x - 6$

(D) $f(x) = 4x - 14$

GO TO THE NEXT PAGE

9

Figure not drawn to scale.

In the figure above, lines p and q are parallel. If $y = x + 1$ represents the equation of line p, what is the y-intercept of line q?

(A) 2

(B) 3

(C) 4

(D) 5

10 A certain brand of yogurt is sold in either large or small cups. If 3 small cups and 2 large cups hold 30 ounces of yogurt, and 4 small cups and 1 large cup hold 25 ounces of yogurt, how much yogurt, in ounces, does a large cup of yogurt hold?

(A) 2 ounces

(B) 4 ounces

(C) 7 ounces

(D) 9 ounces

11

Figure not drawn to scale.

In the figure above, DE is parallel to BC and $AD = 3$. What is the length of segment AB?

(A) 2

(B) 3

(C) 4

(D) 6

12 A student opened a savings account that earns r% annual interest compounded monthly. The equation that shows the total amount of money in the account at any time is $A = P\left(1 + \dfrac{r}{1200}\right)^{12t}$.

What does t represent in the equation?

(A) The initial investment in the savings account

(B) The rate of interest

(C) The number of years the money has been in the account

(D) The total amount of money in the account

13 If $(x + 2)^2 - (x - 3)^2 = 0$, which of the following are possible values of x?

(A) $\frac{1}{2}$ only

(B) -2 and 3

(C) -3 and 2

(D) -2 and $\frac{1}{2}$

15 A line in the xy-plane with the slope $-\frac{4}{5}$ passes through the point $(3, 4)$. Which of the following points lies on the line?

(A) $(-5, 12)$
(B) $(-2, 0)$
(C) $(7, -1)$
(D) $(13, -4)$

14

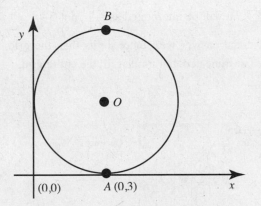

If AB is a diameter of the circle with center O, and AB is parallel to the y-axis, which equation represents the circle?

(A) $(x - 3)^2 + (y - 3)^2 = 3$
(B) $(x - 3)^2 + y^2 = 3$
(C) $(x - 3)^2 + (y - 3)^2 = 9$
(D) $(x - 3)^2 + y^2 = 9$

practice test

GO TO THE
NEXT PAGE

Directions: For Questions 16–20, solve the problem and enter your answer in the grid, as described below, on the answer sheet.

1. Although not required, it is suggested that you write your answer in the boxes at the top of the columns to help you fill in the circles accurately. You will receive credit only if the circles are filled in correctly.

2. Mark no more than one circle in any column.

3. No question has a negative answer.

4. Some problems may have more than one correct answer. In such cases, grid only one answer.

5. **Mixed numbers** such as $3\frac{1}{2}$ must be gridded as 3.5 or $\frac{7}{2}$.

    If $3\frac{1}{2}$ is entered into the grid as $\overline{3\,1\,/\,2}$, it will be interpreted as $\frac{31}{2}$, not $3\frac{1}{2}$.

6. **Decimal answers:** If you obtain a decimal answer with more digits than the grid can accommodate, it may be either rounded or truncated, but it must fill the entire grid.

16 Miguel is making a new garden. He is buying a new wheelbarrow and bags of peat moss. Each bag weighs 32 pounds and the wheelbarrow weighs 65 pounds. If his truck can carry a maximum of 1500 pounds in the bed, what is the greatest number of whole bags of peat moss he can carry in the bed of his truck, along with the wheelbarrow?

17

A sign is made by cutting four identical right triangles out of a square, as shown above. What is the perimeter of the sign, in inches?

18 What is the value for b that will make the equation below true?

$$\frac{5x+2}{x-4} = 5 + \frac{b}{x-4}$$

19 $y = 3x - 4$

$y = 2x - 5$

According to the system of equations above, what is the value of xy?

20 $6x - 5y = 9$

$ax + by = -27$

What value of b will make the system of equations above have infinitely many solutions?

STOP

**If you finish before time is called, you may check your work on this section only.
Do not turn to any other section.**

practice test

SECTION 4: MATH TEST—CALCULATOR 🖩

38 Questions • 55 minutes

TURN TO SECTION 4 OF YOUR ANSWER SHEET TO ANSWER THE QUESTIONS IN THIS SECTION.

Directions: For Questions 1–30, solve each problem, select the best answer from the choices provided, and fill in the corresponding oval on your answer sheet. **For Questions 31–38,** solve the problem and enter your answer in the grid on the answer sheet. The directions **before Question 31** will provide information on how to enter your answers in the grid.

ADDITIONAL INFORMATION:

- The use of a calculator **is permitted.**

- All variables and expressions used represent real numbers unless otherwise indicated.

- Figures provided in this test are drawn to scale unless otherwise indicated.

- All figures lie in a plane unless otherwise indicated.

- Unless otherwise specified, the domain of a given function f is the set of all real numbers x for which $f(x)$ is a real number.

Reference Information

Circle:
$C = 2\pi r$
$A = \pi r^2$

Rectangle:
$A = lw$

Triangle:
$A = \frac{1}{2}bh$
$a^2 + b^2 = c^2$

Rectangular Solid:
$V = lwh$

Cylinder:
$V = \pi r^2 h$

Sphere:
$V = \frac{4}{3}\pi r^3$

Cone:
$V = \frac{1}{3}\pi r^2 h$

Rectangular Based Pyramid:
$V = \frac{1}{3}lwh$

The number of degrees of arc in a circle is 360.
The number of radians in the arc of a circle is 2π.
The sum of the measures in degrees of the angles of a triangle is 180.

---

1 A large bottle of soda holds 3 times as much as a small bottle of soda, which holds 12 fluid ounces. How many large bottles are completely filled by 120 fluid ounces of soda?

(A) 2

(B) 3

(C) 4

(D) 5

2 If $4(x + 10) - 3(x + 10) = 0$, what is the value of x?

(A) −40

(B) −10

(C) 2

(D) 20

3 In the 1908 London Olympics, the 400-meter race was introduced. Wyndham Halswelle of Great Britain won with a time of 50.0 seconds. In 1996, Michael Johnson of the United States ran the 400-meter race with a time of 43.18 seconds, which is the current record. If they had been racing together, approximately how many meters would Halswelle still have had to run after Johnson finished the race?

(A) 10
(B) 25
(C) 55
(D) 100

4 If $18 - 6x$ is 4 less than -8, what is the value of $-3x$?

(A) -15
(B) -5
(C) 5
(D) 15

5 1000 milligrams = 1 gram

1000 grams = 1 kilogram

Ibuprofen is an over-the-counter drug used to treat arthritis and relieve pain, fever, and swelling. The dose contained in a standard tablet is 200 mg. If ibuprofen is sold in cartons of 24 bottles with 250 standard tablets per bottle, how much pain medication is in the carton in all?

(A) 0.12 kilograms
(B) 1.2 kilograms
(C) 12 kilograms
(D) 120 kilograms

6 A local newspaper reported a poll of 100 adults that found 80% of respondents were in favor of building a new school. The poll was taken by asking random parents picking up their students after school. Which of the following statements about the sampling method for this poll is NOT true?

(A) The sampling method was not representative of the town as a whole because some students take the bus home.

(B) The sampling method was not representative of the town as a whole because not everyone has children who go to school.

(C) The sampling method was not representative of the town as a whole because the population of the town is much greater than 100.

(D) The sampling method was not representative of the town as a whole because people who do not have students in school are less likely to support a new school.

QUESTIONS 7 AND 8 REFER TO THE FOLLOWING INFORMATION.

The graph below shows the population of a small town, from the years 2007 through 2015.

7   Assuming that the population growth trend continues, what is the best prediction for the town's population in 2016?

(A) 850

(B) 900

(C) 950

(D) 1,025

8   Which of the following best describes the relationship between the population of the small town and the number of years?

(A) The relation is an example of linear growth, because a line can be drawn between any two points on the grid that exactly shows the relation.

(B) The relation is an example of linear growth, because all of the points lie on a single line.

(C) The relation is an example of exponential growth, because the slope of the line between any two points is increasing as the x-values increase.

(D) The relation is an example of exponential decay, because the vertical space between the points gets greater as the number of days increases.

9   The median salary at a large biotech company is $45,000. The mean income is $60,000. Which of the following statements best explains the difference between the mean and the median?

(A) There are a few people at the biotech company with very low salaries.

(B) There are a few people at the biotech company with very high salaries.

(C) Most of the salaries at the biotech company are between $45,000 and $60,000.

(D) All of the salaries at the biotech company are within a small range.

10   Mount Asgard in Auyuittuq (pronounced: *ow-you-eet-took*) National Park, Baffin Island, Nunavut, was used in the opening scene for the James Bond movie *The Spy Who Loved Me*. A stuntman skis off the edge of the mountain, free-falls for several seconds, and then opens a parachute. The height, h, in meters, of the stuntman above the ground t seconds after he opens the parachute is represented by the equation $h(t) = -10.5t + 980$. What does the 980 in the equation represent?

(A) The speed of the stuntman

(B) The height of the mountain

(C) The height of the stuntman when he opens the parachute

(D) The total length of time the stuntman is in the air

11   According to Einstein's theory of relativity, no object can travel faster than the speed of light, which is approximately 180,000 miles per second. Which inequality represents this information?

(A) $x \leq 180,000$

(B) $x \geq 180,000$

(C) $x = 180,000$

(D) $x > 180,000$

12

What is the value of z in right triangle ABC?

(A) 15

(B) 18

(C) 30

(D) 36

🖩

13 In 1992, the first AA lithium battery was released. Suppose a pack of 4 AA lithium batteries costs x dollars. At this rate, how much do 100 batteries cost?

(A) $5x$

(B) $10x$

(C) $25x$

(D) $100x$

14 What is the value of y if

$$\frac{7}{4}+\frac{6}{y}=1?$$

(A) -24

(B) -8

(C) -4

(D) 6

15 A food truck sells sandwiches for $5.95 each and drinks in cans or bottles. Which of the following statements is true about the equation that represents the food truck revenue, $5.95x + 1.75y = z$?

(A) x is the number of customers served

(B) z is the number of customers served

(C) y is the number of beverages sold

(D) y is the number of sandwiches sold

16
$$2x + y \geq a$$
$$x + 2y \geq b$$

In the xy-plane, if $(-1, -1)$ is a solution to the system of inequalities above, which of the following relationships must be true about a and b?

(A) $a > b > 0$

(B) $a < b < 0$

(C) $b < a < 0$

(D) $a < 0$ and $b < 0$

17 Alex is baking cupcakes and cookies. The cupcake pan holds 15 cupcakes and the cookie pan holds 18 cookies. Alex wants to make at least twice as many cookies as cupcakes, but no more than 165 total cookies and cupcakes. Which of the following system of inequalities fits the situation?

(A) $18x + 15y \leq 165$
$\quad\quad x \leq 2y$

(B) $18x + 15y \leq 165$
$\quad\quad x \geq 2y$

(C) $18x + 15y < 165$
$\quad\quad x < 2y$

(D) $18x + 15y < 165$
$\quad\quad x > 2y$

18 Which of the following equals x, if

$$3\sqrt{x} + 8 = 20?$$

(A) 4

(B) 8

(C) 12

(D) 16

19 According to historians, Archimedes proved that a crown made for his king was not pure gold. Suppose the crown had a density of 800 grams and a volume of 50 grams. The density of gold is about 19 grams per cc, and the density of silver is about 10.5 grams per cc. The system below models this relationship (G = volume of gold, S = volume of silver).

$$G + S = 50$$
$$19G + 10.5S = 800$$

If the crown contained both silver and gold, about what percent of the crown is silver?

(A) 19 percent

(B) 36 percent

(C) 62 percent

(D) 81 percent

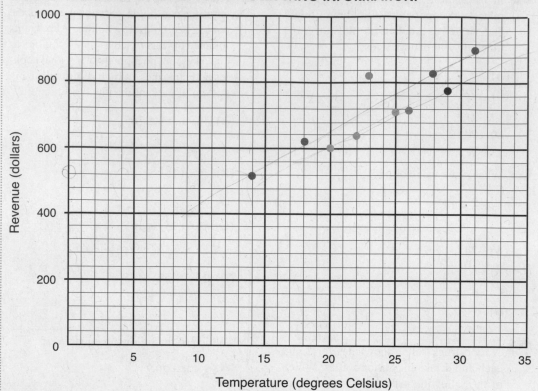

QUESTIONS 20 AND 21 REFER TO THE FOLLOWING INFORMATION.

The graph above displays the total revenue R in dollars for an ice cream shop when the temperature is T degrees Celsius.

20 Which of the following best describes the association between R and T?

(A) Strong positive correlation

(B) Strong negative correlation

(C) Weak positive correlation

(D) Weak negative correlation

21 Which of the following is the best fit equation for the data in the graph?

(A) $y = 500 + 1.2x$

(B) $y = 1.33x$

(C) $y = 20x + 250$

(D) $y = 725$

22 Simplify $(5 - 3i)(4 + 2i)$.

(A) $20 - 2i$

(B) $20 - 6i$

(C) $26 - 2i$

(D) $26 - 6i$

23 If $(x - 1)$ and $(x + 5)$ are factors of $f(x)$, which of the following graphs shows a possible graph of the function f?

(A)

(B)

(C)

(D)

24 The graph of a parabola has x-intercepts at 4 and -2 and a y-intercept at 8. Which of the following could be the equation of the graph?

(A) $y = -(x - 1)^2 + 9$

(B) $y = x^2 - 2x + 8$

(C) $y = (x - 1)^2 - 9$

(D) $y = x^2 + 2x - 8$

25 A population of bacteria in a sample increases in number by 30% every hour. Which best describes the relation between the time h in hours and the number of bacteria B in the sample?

(A) The relation between B and h is linear, because the population increases by the same percent each hour.

(B) The relation between B and h is linear, because the population increases by the same amount each hour.

(C) The relation between B and h is exponential, because the population increases by the same percent each hour.

(D) The relation between B and h is exponential, because the population increases by the same amount each hour.

GO TO THE NEXT PAGE

▦

26 If k is a negative constant less than -1, which of the following could be the graph of $y = kx^2 + bx + c$?

(A)

(C)

(B)

(D)

An educational researcher chose 200 randomly selected college students and asked them how they would best categorize their political inclinations. The results are shown in the table below.

	Liberal	Moderate	Conservative
Seniors	6	18	34
Juniors	20	42	30
Sophomores	8	6	4
Freshmen	22	8	2

27 What is the probability that a junior of this group is a conservative?

(A) $\dfrac{17}{29}$

(B) $\dfrac{9}{15}$

(C) $\dfrac{2}{9}$

(D) $\dfrac{15}{46}$

28 If there were a total of 4,000 students at the college, about how many of those students would categorize themselves as moderates?

(A) About 74

(B) About 1,120

(C) About 1,400

(D) About 1,480

29 A recent poll found that 11% of the respondents approve of the job that the U.S. Congress is doing. The margin of error for the poll was ± 3% with 95% confidence interval. Which of the following statements is a conclusion that can accurately be drawn from this poll?

(A) The true percentage of people who disapprove of the job that the U.S. Congress is doing is between 86% and 92%.

(B) The true percentage of people who approve of the job that the U.S. Congress is doing is between 8% and 14%.

(C) The pollsters are 95% confident that the true percentage of people who approve of the job that the U.S. Congress is doing is between 86% and 92%.

(D) The pollsters are 95% confident that the true percentage of people who approve of the job that the U.S. Congress is doing is between 8% and 14%.

30 Line m intersects the x-axis at $(3, 0)$ and the y-axis at $(0, -2)$. Line n passes through the origin and is perpendicular to line m. Which of the following is an equation of line n?

(A) $y = \dfrac{3}{2}x$

(B) $y = \dfrac{2}{3}x$

(C) $y = -\dfrac{3}{2}x$

(D) $y = -\dfrac{2}{3}x$

Directions: For Questions 31–38, solve the problem and enter your answer in the grid, as described below, on the answer sheet.

1. Although not required, it is suggested that you write your answer in the boxes at the top of the columns to help you fill in the circles accurately. You will receive credit only if the circles are filled in correctly.

2. Mark no more than one circle in any column.

3. No question has a negative answer.

4. Some problems may have more than one correct answer. In such cases, grid only one answer.

5. **Mixed numbers** such as $3\frac{1}{2}$ must be gridded as 3.5 or $\frac{7}{2}$.

    If $3\frac{1}{2}$ is entered into the grid as $\overline{3\,|\,1\,|/\,|2}$, it will be interpreted as $\frac{31}{2}$, not $3\frac{1}{2}$.

5. **Decimal answers:** If you obtain a decimal answer with more digits than the grid can accommodate, it may be either rounded or truncated, but it must fill the entire grid.

31 A baboon troop has 60 members, 35% of which are male. What is the ratio of males to females in the baboon troop? (Grid your answer as a fraction.)

32 During a recent baseball season, 2 hitters on a team had a total of 66 home runs. Batter B had 14 fewer home runs than batter A. How many home runs did batter A hit?

33 A community radio station operates 24 hours per day, every day of the week. Each radio show lasts 90 minutes. What is the total number of shows that the radio station will broadcast Monday through Friday?

34 $3(5 - 2x) = -4(cx + 4)$

What value for c in the equation above will make the equation have no solutions?

35 If a cube with a surface area of 600 square centimeters holds 1 liter, how many liters are held in a cube with a surface area of 5400 square centimeters?

36
$$f(x) = 3x^2 - 4x + 8$$
$$g(x) = 2x - 5$$

Use the functions above to find the value of $g(f(-2))$.

37 $y = 2x - 3$

$y = -3(x-1)^2 + 4$

According to the system of equations above, what is one value of x?

38 The total rainfall in Plainville increased by 25% from 2012 to 2013. The rainfall decreased by 30% from 2013 to 2014. Then, it increased again by 40% from 2014 to 2015. What was the percent of increase in rainfall from 2012 to 2015? Write your answer as a percent, but do not write in the percent symbol.

STOP

If you finish before time is called, you may check your work on this section only.
Do not turn to any other section.

SECTION 5: ESSAY

50 Minutes • 1 Essay

Directions: The essay gives you an opportunity to show how effectively you can read and comprehend a passage and write an essay analyzing the passage. In your essay, you should demonstrate that you have read the passage carefully, present a clear and logical analysis, and use language precisely.

Your essay will need to be written on the lines provided in your answer booklet. You will have enough space if you write on every line and keep your handwriting to an average size. Try to print or write clearly so that your writing will be legible to the readers scoring your essay.

As you read the passage below, consider how Jessica Smartt Gullion uses the following:

- Evidence, such as facts, statistics, or examples, to support claims.

- Reasoning to develop ideas and to connect claims and evidence.

- Stylistic or persuasive elements, such as word choice or appeals to emotion, to add power to the ideas expressed.

Will guns on campus lead to grade inflation?

Adapted from "Will Guns on Campus Lead to Grade Inflation?" by Jessica Smartt Gullion, originally published in The Conversation on April 27, 2015. Jessica Smartt Gullion is an assistant professor of sociology at Texas Woman's University. (This passage was edited for length. For the complete article, see http://theconversation.com.)

1   Texas college professors may soon face a dilemma between upholding professional ethics and protecting their lives.

2   The Texas legislature appears poised to approve a bill that would allow college students to carry firearms to class. Called "campus carry," public universities in Texas will not be allowed to ban guns on their campuses, once the law is passed, although private schools could enact their own prohibitions.

3   Its backers argue that students have the right to protect themselves on campuses with handguns. The lobbying extends to sponsoring crash courses such as the NRA University, a two-hour seminar course for college students.

4   With this proposed law, a question coming up for many academics is whether they would be forced to give As to undeserving students, just so they can avoid being shot.

5   This is not as farfetched as it sounds. In my five years as a college professor, I have had experience with a number of emotionally distressed students who resort to intimidation when they receive a lesser grade than what they feel they deserve.

GO TO THE NEXT PAGE

Threats on campus

6   Here is an example of one such threatening experience: One evening in a graduate course, after I handed back students' papers, a young woman stood up and pointed at me. "This is unacceptable!" she screamed as her body shook in rage.

7   She moved toward the front of the class waving her paper in my face and screamed again, "unacceptable!" After a heated exchange, she left the room and stood outside the door sobbing.

8   All this was over receiving a B on a completely low-stakes assignment.

9   What followed was even more startling. The following week, the student brought along a muscle-bound man to class. He watched me through the doorway window for the entire three hours of the class, with his arms folded across his chest.

10   And if this wasn't enough, the young woman's classmates avoided me on campus because, they said, they were afraid of getting caught in the crossfire should she decide to shoot me.

11   After that, every time she turned in a paper I cringed and prayed that it was good so that I wouldn't have to give her anything less than an A.

12   Learning from this experience, now I give papers back only at the end of the class or just "forget" to bring them with me.

13   I was lucky that the student didn't have a gun in my classroom. Other professors have not been so lucky.

14   Last year, a student at Purdue shot his instructor in front of a classroom of students. In another incident in 2009, a student at Northern Virginia Community College tried to shoot his math professor on campus. And, in 2000, a graduate student at the University of Arkansas shot his English professor.

15   In each of these states, carrying handguns on campus was illegal at the time of the shooting, although a bill was introduced in Arkansas earlier this year to allow students to carry guns.

Grade inflation

16   Despite these and other shootings, a new trend has emerged across the U.S. that supports guns on college campuses.

17   Eight states allow firearms onto college campuses, and 11 states are now considering similar legislation.

18   We know that some students will carry guns whether it is legal or not. One study found that close to 5 percent of undergraduates had a gun on campus and that almost two percent had been threatened with a firearm while at school.

…

19   Who would want to give a student a low grade and then get shot for it?

20 Many majors are highly competitive and require certain GPAs for admission. Students on scholarships and other forms of financial aid must maintain high grades to keep their funding. It's no surprise that some students might resort to any means necessary to keep up their GPAs.

21 An international student once cried in my office and begged me to change his F to an A, as without it, his country would no longer pay for him to be in the U.S. I didn't. He harassed me by posting threatening messages on Facebook.

22 So, the question is, will we soon see a new sort of grade inflation, with students earning a 4.0 GPA with their firepower rather than brain power? And if so, what sort of future citizenry will we be building on our campuses?

Write an essay in which you explain how the writer builds an argument to persuade her audience that she is offering proof of war's traumatic history. In your essay, analyze how Jessica Smartt Gullion uses one or more of the features listed previously (or features of your own choice) to strengthen the logic and persuasiveness of her argument. Be sure that your analysis focuses on the most relevant aspects of the passage.

Your essay should not explain whether you agree with the writer's claims, but rather explain how she builds an argument to persuade her audience.

STOP

**If you finish before time is called, you may check your work on this section only.
Do not turn to any other section.**

No Test Material On This Page

ANSWER KEY AND EXPLANATIONS

Section 1: Reading Test

1. C	12. B	23. C	34. B	45. A
2. A	13. A	24. D	35. C	46. D
3. B	14. D	25. B	36. A	47. A
4. D	15. D	26. B	37. D	48. B
5. A	16. B	27. C	38. D	49. D
6. D	17. B	28. A	39. B	50. B
7. A	18. D	29. C	40. C	51. A
8. C	19. C	30. B	41. C	52. C
9. B	20. A	31. A	42. C	
10. B	21. D	32. C	43. B	
11. B	22. D	33. C	44. A	

READING TEST RAW SCORE
(Number of correct answers) [   ]

1. **The correct answer is (C).** An automaker providing a free paint job to customers with cars that have failing breaks offers generous but irrelevant compensation for an error that could have life or death consequences. Similarly, a tax cut is a pleasant bonus, but in the author's opinion, if the seriousness of SeDS were addressed instead, the savings for the U.S. treasury would be enormous, and the benefits to U.S. citizens would be incalculable. Choice (A) is incorrect because the automaker is taking appropriate steps to remedy its error, as well as allocating its funds responsibly, which is the opposite of what the author sees happening in the U.S. Choices (B) and (D) are incorrect because they show acknowledgement of the problem but offer nonsensical solutions.

2. **The correct answer is (A).** The article presents the opinions of Frank Booth first, accompanied by factual details. These are followed by quotes from Scott Gordon and Ron Gomes, along with other facts and charts

illustrating statistics about diabetes. Choice (B) is incorrect because the information is not presented in a sensational manner; it is concerned with facts and opinions from experts. Those affected are not quoted, so choice (C) is also incorrect. Choice (D) focuses only on statistics, and the article does not discuss how the statistics are interpreted, so it is incorrect as well.

3. **The correct answer is (B).** The Grim Reaper is a traditional image of the inevitability of death, and the article suggests that diseases caused by obesity hasten death. Choice (A) is incorrect because in this article, the Grim Reaper is referred to as "flabby." Choice (C) is partially correct because the idea of a flabby Grim Reaper is ironic; however, the article is about a larger attempt to educate the public about the causes of a health crisis. Choice (D) is also incorrect, confusing statistical details with the fantastical image of death as embodied by the Grim Reaper.

4. **The correct answer is (D).** The article says that the human body has evolved over time to do hard work like farming and household chores, but machines now do much of that work, which leads to obesity. Choice (A) focuses on obesity without recognizing the causes. Choice (B) confuses the fact that children do inherit different body types, but inactivity is not an inherited trait. Choice (C) is in direct contradiction to the point made in the article, which is that people are now more sedentary than in previous generations.

5. **The correct answer is (A).** Frank Booth wanted to emphasize that a lack of exercise or activity leads to obesity and even death, so he chose "sedentary" as a synonym for "inactive" to add pizzazz to a condition that needs greater attention. Choice (B) is actually the opposite meaning, referring to health and energy. Choice (C) echoes another health issue: Sudden Death Syndrome, which refers to children who die mysteriously as infants. The process the article discusses is not sudden or restricted to children. Choice (D) describes the result of inactivity, but does not define it.

6. **The correct answer is (D).** The author links a well-known killer—heart disease—to a health concern that is usually considered less critical: obesity. Choice (A) focuses on similar symptoms but is incorrect; the author is comparing the outcomes, not the symptoms. Choice (B) doesn't take into account one half of the comparison, so it is incorrect. Choice (C) is incorrect because the connection is reversed. Obesity leads to heart disease.

7. **The correct answer is (A).** Choice (A) emphasizes that SeDs is a bigger killer than the sum of several causes that readers know well. Choice (B) is incorrect because it refers to Booth having a revelation about the name of the disease. Choice (C) is a statement from the then-Surgeon General about the disease, but it does not relate the answer to the previous question. Choice (D) is incorrect because it talks about one way to prevent obesity in children.

8. **The correct answer is (C).** In 1998, new cases of Type 2 diabetes began to increase and grow continuously every year, until the number peaked in 2009. Choice (A) is the start of the chart, and although it shows an increasing trend overall, there are many decreases as well. Choice (D) is the highest number of new cases reported, but it is not the beginning of continuing increases because the number of cases falls off the following year.

9. **The correct answer is (B).** Booth wanted to come up with a catchy name, something that would get people's attention. Choice (A) makes sense within the context of the sentence, but it doesn't convey the idea of a catchy name. Choice (C) suggests that "inactivity-related disease" is too frivolous, with the author saying it's not going to catch the public's attention. Choice (D) ties the idea of "inactivity-related" to a lack of "action," but it doesn't match other ideas in the sentence.

10. **The correct answer is (B).** The author offers activity or exercise as a solution to the rise in obesity. Although this connection is not explained in detail, it forms the basis of the article. Choice (A) is incorrect because the author sees a catchy name as simply a way to make people aware of the problem. Choice (C) is incorrect because although the article connects the rise in Type 2 diabetes with obesity, it is only one health issue the article discusses. Choice (D) is also incorrect because of the narrowness of its focus. The article brings up the importance of children developing better habits than their parents, but is not the overarching theme of the passage.

11. **The correct answer is (B).** Choice (B) establishes a clear link between the number of Americans who are not physically active and the doubling of the obesity rate. Choice (A) mentions the fact that one person wants more money to be allocated to helping Americans be more active, but doesn't link obesity to fitness. Choice (C) describes the complications of Type 2 diabetes but doesn't refer to obesity. Choice (D) explains the connection between children and ailments associated with obesity but doesn't indicate how essential it is for all human beings to be physically active.

12. **The correct answer is choice (B).** Although the government professes that wrongs done to the Native Americans should be corrected, the author's use of the phrase "simple and unperplexing expedients" suggests that the author believes the government's intentions are not sincere. For this reason, choice (A) is incorrect. Choice (C) is also incorrect, as the author does not make a distinction between the presidents and the commissions in their approach to Native American affairs. Choice (D) is incorrect because the author does not suggest that the government is unable to determine a viable solution, only that the government seems uninterested or unwilling to do so.

13. **The correct answer is (A).** The author is making two points. First, she is citing specific places and times where some of the worst abuses occurred, and second, is describing "countless" abuses over the course of a century. Choice (B) is incorrect because, although specific states are mentioned, that is not the overall thrust of the passage. Choice (C) implies that because the dates cited are not recent, the problems have stopped, yet the second half of the sentence explains that the government "breaks promises now as deftly as then."

14. **The correct answer is (D).** Lines 32–33 make the point that "every page and every year has its dark stain." This phrase supports the author's assertion that abuse was widespread throughout the century. Choice (A) makes the point that there were many tribes that were abused, but it does not reference the time period in which these abuses took place. Choice (B) stresses the abuse specific to the Pacific-slope Indians but not the scope of the overall abuse. Choice (D) describes the whole scope of the abuse but only with regard to broken treaties and unfulfilled promises.

15. **The correct answer is (D).** The correct answer is Choice (D) because in lines 22–24 (There … laws), the author talks about an area that was settled so quickly that there wasn't a chance to create laws. Settlers could do whatever they wanted to the tribes, unregulated by any treaty. Choice (A) explains general prejudices but not the specific abuse of Native Americans. Choice (B) is incorrect because there were no treaties or laws to break. Choice (C) is partially correct because it describes Native Americans as being outnumbered, but it doesn't explain the fundamental dangers of the time and place.

16. **The correct answer is (B).** The article specifically refers to abuse in Georgia in 1830. Choice (A) is associated with Ohio; choice (C) is associated with the Pacific-slope and the Gold Rush of 1849; and choice (D) is associated with Colorado.

17. **The correct answer is (B).** Choice (B) best describes the purpose of the majority of the paragraphs of the passage. The author notes what others have thought or said about the shared history of these groups and makes the point that the United States has consistently mistreated Native Americans. Choice (A) is incorrect because the author is interested in building an argument rather than establishing a chronological account. Choice (C) is incorrect because, while the author touches on some causes and effects, they are secondary to the argument. Choice (D) is inaccurate because the author is presenting only one viewpoint, not opposing viewpoints.

18. **The correct answer is (D).** The author repeatedly refers to concealing or explaining away the offenses of white settlers against Native Americans. Choice (A) has the opposite meaning of "palliated." Although concealment sometimes takes the form of confusion, based on the context, choice (B) is incorrect because the sentences that follow the sentence contrast how offenses against white settlers are spread with the way offenses against Native Americans are spread. "Palliated" can be used to refer to easing medical symptoms, but that meaning is not applicable here, so choice (C) is incorrect.

19. **The correct answer is (C).** Choice (C) is the best summary because it accurately states that the army admits they were the aggressor. The few times Native Americans did something horrible, the events were played up as worse than they were, while the army's crimes were played down. Choice (A) gets some of the facts wrong and makes assumptions that aren't in the original

paragraph. Choice (B) does the same and interprets "testimony" as literally referring to a courtroom. Choice (D) is too simplistic and leaves out much of the pertinent information of the paragraph.

20. **The correct answer is A.** Choice (A) stresses the inequality in the way Native Americans were treated and any part they had in the conflict between the settlers taking their land and their attacking settlers. Choice (B) is only one idea that is part of the larger, more comprehensive theme. Choice (C) may be true, but it is not really covered by the passage. Choice (D) is incorrect because the passage clearly states that it is a continuing problem, not one that existed only in the past.

21. **The correct answer is (D)** Choice (D) makes a sweeping statement of the situation and points out how one-sided the conflict between Native Americans and white settlers has been. Choice (A) focuses on the fact that weaker tribes suffered more than others, not that all tribes were victims. Choice (B) focuses more on a timeline of abuse rather than who is to blame. Choice (C) points out that all tribes were mistreated in a like manner but doesn't place the blame on white settlers.

22. **The correct answer is (D).** Choice (D) suggests the wildness of cruelty that white settlers perceived in the retaliation by Native Americans, which further spread fear and hatred of the tribes and helped to publicize the need to remove them. Choice (A) misinterprets "unspeakable," which refers to something so outrageous it shouldn't be said out loud, instead of the nature of the acts themselves. Choice (B) references the idea of retaliation but does not characterize the acts correctly. Choice (C) refers to some of the anger and aggression Native Americans felt in striking back but suggests careful planning and strategy, an interpretation that is not supported by the passage.

23. **The correct answer is (C).** The main theme in the passage describes the people who lived at Arlington House—slaves and owners—and includes information about how the house was constructed and by whom as well as the history of the plantation's owner-

ship. There is no language that suggests the author wished to persuade readers, choice (B). Although the author makes it clear how disadvantaged slaves were, the passage does not focus on the evils of slavery, choice (A). Although the passage includes some information about the lives of slaves, choice (D), its overall focus is the history of the plantation.

24. **The correct answer is (D).** The text explains that Mrs. Custis taught the slaves to read the Bible (lines 79–82) because she was a very religious woman. There is no indication that she wanted them to be able to teach the skills to anyone else, choices (A) and (C), or read any other material, choice (B).

25. **The correct answer is (B).** The text states that Custis inherited slaves. It does not say how he acquired the land for his plantations, so we cannot assume that it was granted to him by Martha Washington, choice (A). The passage describes how Custis went about building the house, so it's safe to say that he did not inherit a house with land and slaves, choice (C). The text states that Custis had three plantations in all, but it does not say how he acquired them, choice (D).

26. **The correct answer is (B).** The text tells us that Selina was given the keys to the plantation, which implies great trust in the days of slavery. As head housekeeper, she may also have cared for the Lee children, choice (C), but that information is not in the passage. Being head of housekeeping is not the same as running the whole plantation, choice (D); while housekeeping of a large mansion is hard work, the text doesn't compare it to the fieldwork of other slaves, choice (A).

27. **The correct answer is (C).** From the blueprint and the caption, it is clear that there were a lot of slaves housed in a small space, even if an exact number is not supplied. It is one house, but it's hardly large, especially given the number of people living there, choice (A), and so it was not adequate, choice (B). It is not possible to tell from the drawing where the main house is located in relation to these slave quarters, choice (D).

28. **The correct answer is (A).** Robert E. Lee was related to George Washington through marriage. Paragraph 5 explains the rela-

tionship: Custis's daughter, Mary Anna, married Robert E. Lee, and Lee came to Arlington to live with the Custis family. Custis was the adopted grandson of Martha and George Washington, which made his daughter—Mary Anna—Washington's great granddaughter.

29. **The correct answer is (C).** The first sentence in the last paragraph states that the slaves would only be freed if the estate were in good financial standing. The slaves were not freed immediately because Lee determined that their labor was still needed to get his father-in-law's financial affairs in order. The fact that Custis relied on Lee, choice (A), shows that Custis believed Lee was a good financial manager, but it doesn't show that it is true. Lee freed the slaves, choice (D), because it was part of Custis's wishes. The reader does not learn whether or not Lee agreed with those wishes. While this is true that Mrs. Custis taught slaves how to read, choice (B), the passage does not report how Lee felt about this act.

30. **The correct answer is (B).** Custis could inherit slaves because they were legally equivalent to any other property—a good that could be bought and sold. Choice (B) illustrates this point. Simply being able to free a slave (D) doesn't illustrate the concept of property ownership; it illustrates the concept of physical freedom. Choice (A) is a general description of the complexity of the relationships on the plantation, but doesn't show how slaves were property to be bought and sold.

31. **The correct answer is (A).** The "invisible gulf" the author mentions is one of separation between slaves and owners in terms of privilege and human rights. While "gulf" can describe a body of water, as in choice (B); a chasm, as in choice (C); or a physical gap, as in choice (D), here the author's use is metaphorical.

32. **The correct answer is (C).** In this context, "afford" does not refer to money as in choice (B), but to things provided to others. Since slaves were property, and treated as such, few owners thought about teaching them to read or write. There is no risk implied in this use of the word, choice (A), or any suggestion

of the tutoring being given in exchange for something else as in choice (D).

33. **The correct answer is (C).** Both passages agree that the amount of carbon dioxide in our atmosphere has increased. However, choice (A) is disputed by the second passage, and choice (B) is disputed by the first passage. Choice (D) is refuted by the second passage as being too complicated to prove or predict.

34. **The correct answer is (B).** Only choice (B) contains the admission by the author of the second passage that atmospheric carbon dioxide is increasing, which the first passage also states. Choice (A) discusses some of the effects of carbon dioxide levels but does not confirm their increase. Choice (B) discusses the changes to the atmosphere without specifically mentioning increased hydrogen levels. Choice (D) directly counters any attempts to limit carbon dioxide but doesn't support the fact there are increases.

35. **The correct answer is (C).** Both passages address the reader as "we" or "our," indicating a shared interest among humans. Each passage is trying to persuade the reader to one viewpoint, thus making choice (A) incorrect. Choice (B) is too strong a description since both passages try to convince with logic rather than pure emotionalism. Choice (D) is incorrect because there are no second-person or "you" statements in the passages.

36. **The correct answer is (A).** Neither passage provides sources for the information, observations, and conclusions that they are advancing. Choice (B) ignores some of the computer simulation that is discussed. Choice (C) is incorrect because at least one of the passages mentions dissenting opinions. Choice (D) is only partially correct, as some terms are defined at least through context.

37. **The correct answer is (D).** The purpose of the first passage is to convince readers that global warming is a danger, while the second passage is attempting to refute any cause for concern. Choice (A) misses the point that both passages use persuasive terms. Neither is limited to description or definition. Choice (B) is not applicable because both passages use a variety of terms. Choice (C) reverses the purpose of the two passages.

38. The correct answer is (D). The sentence refers to symptoms of climate change becoming more recognizable. "Pronounced" can refer to the way something is said; however, that meaning doesn't fit the context, choice (A). Choice (C) has the opposite meaning from the meaning of "pronounced" as used in the passage. "Pronounced" can refer to a declaration or announcement, choice (B), but that meaning also does not fit the context.

39. The correct answer is (B). Although the authors of these passages disagree, they are focused on the causes and effects of certain problems, choice (B), not solutions, choice (D). Choice (A) suggests a timeline of events. Although both authors reference past and future events, information is not presented sequentially. Choice (C) is something the reader might unconsciously do, but the authors don't take this approach.

40. The correct answer is (C). The first passage focuses only on the negative effects of atmospheric hydrogen, and the second passage states that atmospheric carbon dioxide does not have a negative effect. Choice (A) is about human control, which is only a minor element of each argument. Choice (B) focuses on the weather and climate argument, which is also a lesser issue. Choice (D) references hydrocarbon production, which is only one part of the larger argument.

41. The correct answer is (C). The author of the second passage is quoting those he or she disagrees with, such as the author of the first passage. Choice (A) only highlights the sources of greenhouse gases and does not encapsulate the major differences between these arguments. Choice (B) focuses on the long-term effects of carbon dioxide but doesn't summarize the two competing arguments. Choice (D) focuses only on beneficial effects of increased atmospheric carbon dioxide.

42. The correct answer is (C). Choice (C) correctly fits with the idea of changes becoming shifts and suggests that the effects of climate change may be unpredictable. Language translation, choice (A), is the process of converting words and meaning from one language into another; however, that is not

the way in which "translate" is used here. The effects the authors mention could include expansion, but that is too narrow a definition for the context, which makes choice (B) incorrect. Choice (D) refers to helping someone understand something, which does not fit the context of the sentence.

43. The correct answer is (B). The two women are fulfilling a tradition common to many cultures, in which the living stay with the body of a friend or family member so it doesn't have to be alone. The tradition partly grew out of the possibility that the deceased might revive, as sometimes happened in the days before doctors were readily available. Choice (A) is incorrect; it is clear that word has already spread that Miss Tempy died. Choice (C) has no supporting evidence in the story. Choice (D) is a presumption that is also unsupported by details in the story.

44. The correct answer is (A). While performing a duty to a friend, two of her oldest, dearest friends draw closer to each other. Choice (B) is incorrect because the focus of the story is the relationship between the two remaining friends. Choice (C) may be true but is incidental. Choice (D) may also be true but is not central to the story.

45. The correct answer is (A). Mrs. Crowe forgets to pay attention to her knitting because she's so enjoying her talk with Sarah Ann Binson. Sarah Ann Binson, on the other hand, abandons her sewing completely when she's preoccupied. Choice (B) is a presumption unsupported by the details of the story. Choice (C) is contradicted by the way the women are portrayed in the story. Although both women are elderly, the author portrays them as energetic and intelligent, albeit somewhat eccentric.

46. The correct answer is (D). Choice (D) shows that under this special circumstance, the women are bonding. Choice (A) is a minor detail that doesn't reflect their friendship. Choice (B) does not happen in the story, although it is mentioned as a trait of Mrs. Crowe's. Choice (C) is part of the author's description of Sarah Ann, but it doesn't indicate closeness to Mrs. Crowe.

47. The correct answer is (A). Choice (A) best shows that, despite her burdens, Sarah

Ann Binson could be excited, expressive, and confident. Choice (B) merely describes Sarah Ann's situation and doesn't provide insight into other aspects of her life. Choice (C) spells out what she had done for her relatives, but it doesn't tell us much about her joy. Choice (D) provides details about Mrs. Crowe but not about Sarah Ann Binson.

48. **The correct answer is (B).** During the long night together talking, both women reveal secrets and say things they would never have said under normal circumstances. Choice (A) is a supposition the author makes, presuming they wouldn't have enough to talk about all night long, but that doesn't prove to be the case. Choice (C) reflects the characterization of Mrs. Crowe as "knowing exactly what she was about" and "a cooler disposition," yet she is so involved in her conversation that she doesn't notice she is knitting a sock that is too long. Choice (D) reflects the author's comment that her life is filled with pleasure, but she also says that, to outward appearances, Sarah Ann Binson was burdened by caring for her family.

49. **The correct answer is (D).** Choice (D) is correct because despite Mrs. Crowe's higher social standing, the women easily fill a long night with intimate talk. Choice (A) may be true, but the reader couldn't know this. Choice (B) assumes they are the same age, but this detail isn't mentioned. Choice (C) is contradicted by the fact that they work well together.

50. **The correct answer is (B).** The sharing of secrets is evidence that the two women are becoming good friends despite their different positions in life. Choice (A) only discusses sharing memories, which even distant acquaintances might do. Choice (C) describes their dispositions but doesn't give much insight into their friendships. Choice (D) only describes Mrs. Crowe and doesn't explain their friendship.

51. **The correct answer is (A).** Sarah Ann would have to be eager and hungry to carry the load of her family as discussed in the rest of the sentence. Although Sarah Ann may be restless, the focus of the sentence is on how much responsibility she shoulders for her relatives, which makes choice (B) incorrect. Choice (C) is not a term usually applied to a person. Choice (D) applies more closely to Mrs. Crowe as she is described later in the passage.

52. **The correct answer is (C).** Giving something away is being generous or magnanimous. Choice (A) is a confusion with a piece of furniture. Choice (B) is a confusion with lifting a finger or helping someone. Choice (D) is a confusion with thoroughness being an act of kindness.

Section 2: Writing and Language Test

1. D	**11.** D	**21.** B	**31.** B	**41.** D
2. B	**12.** B	**22.** A	**32.** B	**42.** C
3. C	**13.** B	**23.** B	**33.** A	**43.** B
4. D	**14.** A	**24.** A	**34.** C	**44.** D
5. B	**15.** B	**25.** B	**35.** C	
6. A	**16.** C	**26.** A	**36.** D	
7. B	**17.** D	**27.** C	**37.** B	
8. D	**18.** D	**28.** C	**38.** A	
9. C	**19.** D	**29.** D	**39.** C	
10. A	**20.** C	**30.** C	**40.** C	

WRITING AND LANGUAGE TEST RAW SCORE
(Number of correct answers)

1. **The correct answer is (D).** This sentence is a fragment requiring a subject, which the pronoun "it" provides. Choices (B) and (C) do not work because the specific subject doesn't have a verb—"having" and "were" are part of the descriptive phrase, not the direct action of the subject.

2. **The correct answer is (B).** The phrase "for communicating" is set off by a comma in the passage, but because the description "for communicating" modifies "code" by defining the purpose of that code, "for communicating" is a restrictive phrase and should not be separated from the word or phrase it modifies. This makes choices (A) and (C) incorrect because the comma after "code" separates the restrictive phrase and the word it modifies. Choice (D) is incorrect because the comma after "communicating" is incorrect.

3. **The correct answer is (C).** Choice (C) is the only choice that makes clear who has the access and the only choice that states the intended purpose concisely. Choice (A) is

incorrect because the construction "it being the case that they would" is wordy. Choice (D) places "enemy forces" near the beginning of the sentence, but it creates confusion in the second clause that implies that the code, not the enemy forces, would have access to the tactics and troop movements. Choice (B) is incorrect because "having access" is ambiguous.

4. **The correct answer is (D).** This sentence accurately introduces the next sentence and supports the main idea of the paragraph. Choices (A), (C), and (D) are incorrect because they do not support the main idea of the passage. They might or might not be true, but they introduce ideas that are not developed in the passage.

5. **The correct answer is (B).** This sentence provides an additional reason why the Navajo language made an excellent code, which makes "furthermore" the best choice. Choice (A) is incorrect because "However" indicates a contrast, which is not implied by the context. Choice (C) is incorrect because

"Likewise" would make sense only if the sentence were making a comparison. Choice (D) is incorrect because "As a result" suggests that the sentence is drawing a conclusion, but this is not supported by the context.

6. **The correct answer is (A).** Choice (A) maintains the paragraph's implication that the Navajo language is largely unknown or obscure, a quality that would make the language ideal for the Marines' purpose. Choice (B) is incorrect because it implies that the language is nonsensical and incomprehensible, which is not the point. Choice (C) is incorrect because "intricacy" is synonymous with "complexity," making it redundant. Choice (D) is incorrect because "clarity" is not a desirable quality for a code that is intended to be unbreakable.

7. **The correct answer is (B).** Choice (B) correctly joins two independent clauses with a comma and a coordinating conjunction. Choice (A) does not effectively combine the two sentences because it repeats the subject, forming an awkward sentence. Choices (C) and (D) are incorrect because they imply that the second clause is dependent on the first clause, which changes the meaning of the sentence.

8. **The correct answer is (D).** Choice (D) accurately suggests that the enemy forces attempted, but did not succeed, in interpreting (or deciphering) the code. Choices (A) and (B) are incorrect because they do not fit the intended meaning of the sentence and therefore do not make sense in the context. Choice (C) is incorrect because "elucidate" the enemy forces were trying to decipher the code, not explain it.

9. **The correct answer is (C).** No commas are needed to separate "speed and accuracy" from the rest of the sentence, as this adverbial phrase does not need to be set off from the verb (the work of the code talkers). For this reason, choices (A) and (D) are incorrect. Choice (B) is incorrect because "speed and accuracy" contains a conjunction and does not require a comma.

10. **The correct answer is (A).** Choice (A) maintains the simple past tense, which is established earlier in the sentence. Choices

(B), (C), and (D) are incorrect because they contain inappropriate shifts in verb tense.

11. **The correct answer is (D).** This sentence best explains the rest of the sentence; it gives the most logical reason for the time span between World War II and the recognition of the code talkers. Choices (A), (B), and (C) are incorrect because, although they are mostly true, they do not explain the long time span between WWII and the recognition of the code talkers. They offer irrelevant details that do not support the main idea of the passage.

12. **The correct answer is (B).** "Who is Dian Fossey" is a question and thus requires a question mark. Choices (A), (C), and (D) are incorrect because they do not include a question mark.

13. **The correct answer is (B).** Knowing where Fossey was born is irrelevant to the rest of the passage; it doesn't support the main idea of the paragraph or the passage, which is Fossey's work with gorillas. Choice (A) is incorrect because this information does not need to be included anywhere in the passage. Choice (C) is incorrect because the information does not support the main idea of the paragraph. Choice (D) is incorrect because the organization of the passage is built on dates, not places.

14. **The correct answer is (A).** Choice (A) correctly portrays Dr. Louis Leakey as a well-known and well-respected scholar in the field. Choice (B) is incorrect because "imminent" refers to something that is about to happen and therefore does not make sense. Choices (C) and (D) both imply that Dr. Leakey is bad or disreputable, which is not supported by the context.

15. **The correct answer is (B).** Choice (B) corrects the dangling modifier by making it clear that Fossey decided to focus her research on mountain gorillas. Choice (A) is incorrect because it contains a dangling modifier. Choice (C) and (D) are incorrect because they contain misplaced modifiers.

16. **The correct answer is (C).** The sentence is attempting to show where Fossey observed gorillas, so "There" is the correct word to start the sentence. Choice (A) is incorrect

because it is a contraction. Choice (B) is incorrect because it is a possessive determiner and does not fit in this context. Choice (D) is incorrect because it makes the sentence a fragment.

17. **The correct answer is (D).** Choice (D) is correct because the sentence is talking about how the animals welcomed Fossey. Choice (A) is incorrect because it confuses "except," which refers to something that is apart from other things, with the word "accept." Choices (B) and (C) are incorrect because they are used incorrectly in this context.

18. **The correct answer is (D).** Only choice (D) maintains the tone and style of the rest of the passage. Choices (A), (B), and (C) are incorrect because they are much more informal than the rest of the passage.

19. **The correct answer is (D).** Choice (D) provides relevant information concerning the endangerment of the mountain gorilla, which is the subject of the paragraph. Choice (A) is incorrect because the information about rhinoceroses is unrelated to the topic of the paragraph and passage. Choice (B) is incorrect because the paragraph is about the endangerment of the mountain gorilla, not the protection efforts. Choice (C) is incorrect because while the information is about mountain gorillas, it is unrelated to the topic of the paragraph.

20. **The correct answer is (C).** The writer should not add the sentence because, while the information might or might not be true, the writer doesn't expand on it, and it doesn't support the main idea of the paragraph—that Fossey continued to work to save gorillas for the rest of her life. Choice (A) is incorrect because the information does not support the main idea of the paragraph. Choice (B) is incorrect because the information is not necessary to the transition between paragraphs. Choice (D) is incorrect because the information is not necessary anywhere in the passage.

21. **The correct answer is (B).** Choice (B) is correct because "declining" accurately communicates that the number of gorillas as falling. Choice (A) is incorrect because it suggests a diminishment of quality, not number. Choices (C) and (D) both imply

humiliation, which is not supported by the context.

22. **The correct answer is (A).** Choice (A) is the correct answer because the singular verb "is rising" agrees with the singular noun "population." Choice (B) is incorrect because the verb "are" is plural. Choice (C) is incorrect because the verb "were" is plural and past tense. Choice (D) is incorrect because the verb "rise" is in the present tense rather than in the present progressive tense.

23. **The correct answer is (B).** Choice (B) is correct because "encircles" maintains the comparison the author makes between a tamarin's fur and a lion's mane. Choices (A) and (C) are incorrect because the first part of the sentence describes their "hairless faces," so the notion of fur obscuring or covering the face is inappropriate. Choice (D) is incorrect because it is vague and ambiguous.

24. **The correct answer is (A).** The writer should not delete the underlined sentence. This information supports the main idea of the paragraph, and the sentence appears in the correct place in the logical organization of the paragraph. Choice (B) is incorrect because this sentence does not explain the previous sentence; rather, it adds a detail that is further explained in the next sentence. Choice (C) is incorrect because moving the sentence would interrupt the organizational flow of the paragraph. Choice (D) is incorrect because this information does not interrupt the flow of ideas in the paragraph.

25. **The correct answer is (B).** Choice (B) clarifies the comparison between tamarins that assist in the care of newborns with those that do not. Choice (A) is incorrect because the failure to note what is being compared leads to confusion. Choices (C) and (D) are incorrect because the comparisons are vague or incorrect.

26. **The correct answer is (A).** The pronoun "they" correctly refers to the plural antecedent "tamarins" and the verb "are" is in the present tense like the rest of the paragraph. Choices (B) and (D) are incorrect because the pronoun "it" is singular. Choice (C) is incorrect because "tamarins" are gender-neutral.

27. **The correct answer is (C).** Choice (C) corrects the conventional expression to "one and the same." Choices (A), (B), and (D) are incorrect because they do not reflect the proper use of this conventional expression.

28. **The correct answer is (C).** Sentence 5 provides more information about tamarins' diurnal activities, and thus should naturally follow sentence 1. The word "however" also implies that the sentence provides information that somehow contrasts with the previous sentence, and the idea that tamarins dislike sunlight contrasts with the notion that they are active during the day. Choices (A), (B), and (D) are incorrect because sentence 5 does not make sense in those positions.

29. **The correct answer is (D).** The semicolon in choice (D) correctly connects two independent clauses. Choice (A) is incorrect because a comma may not be used to separate independent clauses without the use of a coordinating conjunction. Choices (B) is incorrect because it doesn't fix the commas splice, it just moves it. Choice (C) is incorrect because the sentence requires punctuation to fix the grammatical error.

30. **The correct answer is (C).** The graph shows that the number of tamarins in zoos between 1970 and 1978 ranged from fewer than 100 in 1970 to about 150 in 1978. Choice (A) is incorrect because it includes incorrect information from the chart. There were about 140 zoos participating in 2006, not in the 1970s. Choice (B) is incorrect because the graph shows fewer than 100 zoos participating in the 1970s. Choice (D) is incorrect because the graph shows that the number of tamarins in zoos between 1970 and 1978 ranged from fewer than 100 in 1970 to about 150 in 1978.

31. **The correct answer is (B).** Choice (B) clarifies the ambiguous pronoun "it" by inserting the reference to "the campaign." Choice (C) is incorrect because "it" does not refer to "the problem." Choice (D) is incorrect because it simply replaces one pronoun with another, which does nothing to clarify what the pronoun refers to.

32. **The correct answer is (B).** Choice (B) accurately states that tamarin populations have fluctuated in recent years while the number of zoos participating in the program

have not. Choice (A) is incorrect because the graph does not show any decline in the participation of zoos. Choice (C) is incorrect because the participation rate of zoos has not risen substantially in recent years. Choice (D) is incorrect because neither the number of participating zoos nor the population of tamarins has fallen significantly since 2000.

33. **The correct answer is (A).** Choice (A) accurately suggests the efforts have been successful. Choice (B) is incorrect because the sentence suggests success rather than a problem. Choice (C) is incorrect because the sentence does not mention making money. Choice (D) is incorrect because it suggests their plan is off schedule, but this is not supported by the sentence.

34. **The correct answer is (C).** Choice (C) supports the idea of "strict" adherence to principles. Choice (A) is incorrect because it suggests the adherence is temporary, which is not supported by the context. Choices (B) and (D) are incorrect because they do not make sense in the context of the sentence.

35. **The correct answer is (C).** This information supports the main idea of the paragraph and provides a logical conclusion to the paragraph, so it should be placed at the end. Choice (A) is incorrect because, although the information might be interesting, it is out of place and disrupts the flow of ideas in the paragraph. Choice (B) is incorrect because it is a conclusion, not an introduction. Choice (D) is incorrect because, although the information supports the main idea of the paragraph, it is out of place.

36. **The correct answer is (D).** Only choice (D) uses a transition word and a comma to combine the sentences in way that is grammatically correct and concise. Choice (A) is incorrect because "and" suggests additional but equal information, but the second clause modifies the first and is not equal. Choice (B) is incorrect because it is syntactically incorrect. Choice (C) is incorrect because it separates two independent clauses with a comma.

37. **The correct answer is (B).** In choice (B), the plural noun "columns" is in agreement with the second plural noun "elements," and the statement contains the plural verb

"are." Choice (A) is incorrect because the plural noun "columns" is not in agreement with the singular noun "element." Choice (C) is incorrect because the singular noun "column" is not in agreement with the plural noun "elements." Choice (D) is incorrect because the noun "columns" is plural and the verb "is" is singular.

38. **The correct answer is (A).** The items in the list need only be separated by commas. Choice (B) is incorrect because the conjunction "and" is incorrectly used in several places. Choices (C) and (D) are incorrect because they incorrectly and unnecessarily use a semicolon.

39. **The correct answer is (C).** Only choice (C) maintains parallel structure by including "the" before each of item in the series. Choices (A), (B), and (D) are incorrect because they use "the" inconsistently and thus fail to maintain parallel structure.

40. **The correct answer is (C).** Choice (C) correctly continues and supports the paragraph's purpose of providing examples of how each element is divided into three parts. The paragraph currently discusses how the entablature and column are divided into three parts, and choice (C) continues that purpose by describing the three parts of the crepidoma, the third element. Choices (A), (B), and (D) are incorrect because they do not support the purpose or topic of the paragraph.

41. **The correct answer is (D).** The antecedent "classical buildings" is plural, which means the pronoun must also be plural. Choices (A), (B), and (C) are incorrect because they contain antecedents and pronouns that are not in agreement.

42. **The correct answer is (C).** "Its" is a possessive determiner that refers to the singular noun "building." Choices (A) and (B) are incorrect because the antecedent is "building," so the pronoun should be gender neutral and singular. Choice (D) is incorrect because "buildings" should be singular possessive.

43. **The correct answer is (B).** "Perceived" means recognized, which fits with the meaning of the sentence. Choice (A) is incorrect because it describes the violations as being different, which is not what the author intends. Choices (C) and (D) are incorrect because neither makes sense in the context of the sentence.

44. **The correct answer is (D).** Choice (D) follows the paragraph's focus on the difficulty of following the strict conventions of classical architecture. Choice (A) is incorrect because it focuses on information from a previous paragraph. Choice (B) is incorrect because it is a vague generalization. Choice (C) is incorrect because it makes a hyperbolic generalization that is not supported by the paragraph.

Section 3: Math Test—No Calculator

1. A	**5.** A	**9.** A	**13.** A	**17.** 48
2. D	**6.** A	**10.** D	**14.** C	**18.** 22
3. A	**7.** A	**11.** D	**15.** D	**19.** 7
4. B	**8.** D	**12.** C	**16.** 44	**20.** 15

MATH TEST—NO CALCULATOR TEST RAW SCORE ☐
(Number of correct answers)

1. **The correct answer is (A).** Subtract like terms when simplifying the expression: $4x^2 - 3x^2 = x^2$, $-5x - (-2x) = -3x$, and $8 - (-5) = 13$. Put together, we get the expression: $x^2 - 3x + 13$.

2. **The correct answer is (D).** To simplify the expression, first add the exponents, and then use the rule that a negative exponent is equal to the reciprocal of the positive exponent of the same number. Finally, rewrite the rational exponent in radical form:

$$x^{\frac{2}{3}} \bullet x^{-\frac{4}{3}} = x^{-\frac{2}{3}}$$
$$= \frac{1}{x^{\frac{2}{3}}}$$
$$= \frac{1}{\sqrt[3]{x^2}}$$

3. **The correct answer is (A).** Multiply, combine like terms, and simplify:

$$\frac{3}{4}(3x - 4y) + \frac{2}{3}(-3y + 5x) = \frac{9x}{4} - 3y - 2y + \frac{10x}{3}$$
$$= \frac{9x}{4} + \frac{10x}{3} - 5y$$
$$= \frac{27x}{12} + \frac{40x}{12} - 5y$$
$$= \frac{67x}{12} - 5y$$

4. **The correct answer is (B).** Solve the equation for y, then complete the square to write it in vertex form.

$$y = x^2 - 8x - 9$$
$$(x^2 - 8x + 16) - 9 - 16$$
$$(x - 4)^2 - 25$$

In vertex form, the constants are the coordinates of the vertex for the parabola. Choices (A) and (C) show equations equivalent to the given equation, but in intercept form and standard form instead of vertex form. Choice (D) includes the coordinates of the vertex, but it is not equivalent to the given equation; it only represents half of the parabola.

5. **The correct answer is (A).** If a + 4b = 16, then three times that quantity equals 3 × (16), or 48.

6. **The correct answer is (A).** Divide both sides by $2\pi r$ to simplify. Then set the equation equal to h:

$$S = \frac{2\pi r^2 + 2\pi rh}{2\pi r}$$
$$\frac{S}{2\pi r} = r + h$$
$$\frac{S}{2\pi r} - r = h$$

7. **The correct answer is (A).** The population will be reduced by 3.5% each year, so each year the population is multiplied by $(1 - 0.035)$, or (0.965). The only answer choice that shows repeated multiplication of (0.965), through the use of the exponent n, is choice (A): $P = P_0(0.965)^n$.

8. **The correct answer is (D).** Substitute the values 4 and 6 for x and check which equation has the correct function values for both, or calculate the slope between the points and substitute one point to find the y-intercept:

$$\frac{10-2}{6-4} = 4$$
$$y = 4x + b$$
$$2 = 4(4) + b$$
$$-14 = b$$
$$y = 4x - 14$$

9. **The correct answer is (A).** The standard Slope-Intercept form of the equation of a line is $y = mx + b$, where m is the slope of the line and b is the y-intercept. Therefore, the slope of line p equals 1. Since lines p and q are parallel, their slopes are equal. Therefore, the slope of line q equals 1. Let line q be represented by the standard equation of a line, $y = mx + b$. Since the slope of line q equals 1, substitute $m = 1$ in the equation: $y = x + b$.

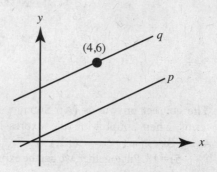

Figure not drawn to scale.

From the above figure, we know that point $(4, 6)$ lies on line q. Therefore, $x = 4$ and $y = 6$ must satisfy the equation of the line. Substitute these values in the above equation and solve for b, which is the y-intercept:

$$6 = 4 + b$$
$$2 = b$$

Therefore, the y-intercept of line q equals 2.

10. **The correct answer is (D).** Write equations based on the information given; let s = a small cup and L = a large cup. Multiply the first equation by 4 and the second one by 3, so that s gets eliminated during the subtraction. Then solve for L:

$$4(3s + 2L = 30)$$
$$-3(4s + L = 25)$$
$$\overline{5L = 45}$$
$$L = 9$$

11. **The correct answer is (D).** If the angles of a triangle are equal to the corresponding angles of another triangle, the two triangles are similar. Also remember that when two triangles are similar, their corresponding sides are proportional.

Figure not drawn to scale.

Since DE is parallel to BC, then $\angle ABC = \angle ADE$ and $\angle ACB = \angle AED$. Also, the angle at point A is common to both triangles. Thus, all three angles of triangle ABC are congruent with the corresponding angles of triangle ADE.

Therefore, triangle ABC and triangle ADE are similar and their corresponding sides are proportional.

Now set up a proportion of their corresponding sides and solve for the length of segment AB:

$$\frac{AB}{AD} = \frac{BC}{DE}$$

$$\frac{AB}{3} = \frac{4}{2}$$

$$\frac{AB}{3} = 2$$

$$AB = 6$$

Therefore, the length of segment $AB = 6$.

12. **The correct answer is (C).** The compound interest formula is

$$A = P\left(1 + \frac{r}{n}\right)^{nt},$$

where A is the total amount of money in the account including interest, P is the initial investment in the account, r is the rate of interest, n is the number of times the interest is compounded, and t is the number of years the amount is in the account. In the problem, the exponent is $12t$. Since the account has interest that is compounded monthly, the number of times in one year that it compounds is 12, so $n = 12$. This means that t equals the number of years the money has been in the account.

13. **The correct answer is (A).** You can work backward with the answer choices to determine the value of x. None of the values works except

$$x = \frac{1}{2} : (x+2)^2 + (x-3)^2 = \left(\frac{5}{2}\right)^2 + \left(-\frac{5}{2}\right)^2$$

$$= \frac{25}{4} - \frac{25}{4}$$

$$= 0$$

answers PRACTICE TEST 2

14. The correct answer is (C).

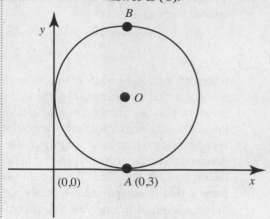

The center of the circle is at the point (3, 3), and because the circle is tangent to the *x*- and *y*-axes, the horizontal and vertical distance between the center and the axes must be equal. The standard form for the equation of a circle is $(x-h)^2 + (y-k)^2 = r^2$, where (h, k) is the center and r is the radius. So an equation for the circle is $(x-3)^2 + (y-3)^2 = 9$.

15. The correct answer is (D). Check each answer choice to see if the slope between the point $(3, 4)$ and the given coordinates is $-\dfrac{4}{5}$.

Only choice (D) gives us this answer:

$$\frac{y-4}{x-3} = -\frac{4}{5}$$

$$\frac{-4-4}{13-3} =$$

$$\frac{-8}{10} = -\frac{4}{5}$$

16. The correct answer is 44. Let x be the number of 32-pound bags that Miguel can safely carry. Because his truck can safely carry only a maximum of 1500 pounds, the weight of the bags plus the weight of the wheelbarrow has to be equal to or less than that, which gives us the inequality $32x + 65 \le 1500$. Solve for x to get the number of bags:

$$32x + 65 \le 1500$$

$$32x \le 1435$$

$$x \le 44.84375$$

Because Miguel can't take partial bags, he can safely take 44 bags.

17. The correct answer is 48.

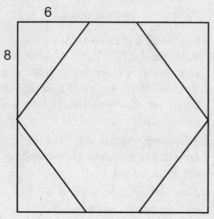

We know that each side of the square has length 16 since two triangle sides of length 8 form one side of the square. From this, we know that the shortest sides of the hexagonal sign must equal 4: the square side − 2 triangle edges = 16 − 2(6) = 4. Now all we have to do is find the hypotenuse of one triangle and multiply it by 4.

Use the Pythagorean Theorem: $a^2 + b^2 = c^2$, where c is the length of the hypotenuse. In this case: $8^2 + 6^2 = c^2$,

$64 + 36 = c^2$, $100 = c^2$, and $10 = c$.

So the perimeter of the sign is

$10(4) + 4(2) = 40 + 8 = 48$ inches.

18. The correct answer is 22. To solve for b, first multiply both sides by $x - 4$ to get $5x + 2 = 5x - 20 + b$. Then, subtract $5x - 20$ from both sides to get $22 = b$.

$$\frac{5x + 2}{x - 4} = \frac{5x - 20 + 22}{x - 4}$$
$$= \frac{5x - 20}{x - 4} + \frac{22}{x - 4}$$
$$= 5 + \frac{22}{x - 4}$$
$$b = 22$$

19. The correct answer is 7.
$$3x - 4 = 2x - 5$$
$$x = -1$$
$$y = 3(-1) - 4 = -7$$
$$xy = (-1)(-7) = 7$$

20. The correct answer is 15.
$$-3(6x - 5y) = -3(9)$$
$$-18x + 15y = -27$$

Multiplying the first equation by -3 will yield an equivalent equation, so if the second equation actually had the coefficients of -18 and 15 for a and b, there would be infinitely many solutions. So, $b = 15$ is the answer.

Section 4: Math Test—Calculator

1. B	**9.** B	**17.** B	**25.** C	**33.** 80
2. B	**10.** C	**18.** D	**26.** D	**34.** 1.5
3. C	**11.** A	**19.** B	**27.** D	**35.** 27
4. A	**12.** A	**20.** A	**28.** D	**36.** 51
5. B	**13.** C	**21.** C	**29.** D	**37.** 2
6. C	**14.** A	**22.** C	**30.** C	**38.** 22.5
7. D	**15.** C	**23.** B	**31.** 7/13	
8. C	**16.** D	**24.** A	**32.** 40	

MATH TEST—CALCULATOR RAW SCORE
(Number of correct answers)

1. **The correct answer is (B).** We know that a small bottle holds 12 ounces of soda, and so a large bottle holds three times that amount, or 36 ounces. The key to solving this problem lies in the phrasing, "how many large bottles are *completely* filled." With 120 ounces of soda, we know that three bottles can be filled completely (108 ounces), leaving 12 ounces. But since this remaining amount isn't enough to fill an additional large bottle completely, the correct answer is choice (B).

2. **The correct answer is (B).** Simplify the algebraic expression:

$$4(x+10) - 3(x+10) = 0$$
$$4x + 40 - 3x - 30 = 0$$
$$x + 10 = 0$$
$$x = -10$$

3. **The correct answer is (C).** Johnson ran the 400-meter race in 43.18 seconds. In that time, Halswelle ran at a rate of 8 meters per second (400 meters/50 seconds = 8 meters/second). So he would have run 43.18 seconds × 8 meters/second = 345.44 meters. So Halswelle would have had about 55 more meters to run before reaching the end of the 400-meter race.

4. **The correct answer is (A).** The description can be written as $18 - 6x = -8 - 4$, which is equivalent to $18 - 6x = -12$. Subtracting 18 from both sides gives $-6x = -30$. Since $-3x$ is half of $-6x$, dividing both sides by 2 gives $-3x = -15$.

5. **The correct answer is (B).** The total amount of pain medication is 24(250)(200) = 1,200,000 milligrams. The answers are all in kilograms, so convert the measure in milligrams to kilograms one step at a time: 1,200,000 milligrams = 1200 grams, and 1200 grams = 1.2 kilograms.

6. **The correct answer is (C).** A sample is not equivalent to the population, and just because a sample is smaller than the population does not mean that it is not representative.

7. **The correct answer is (D).** The slope of the curve is increasing as the number of years increases, and between the years of 2014 and 2015, the population increased by approximately 175 people, so the best prediction for the population in 2016 is 1,025.

8. **The correct answer is (C).** The slope is increasing as the number of years increases, which models exponential growth.

9. **The correct answer is (B).** If the mean is significantly greater than the median, there must be some values that are much greater than the rest in order to increase the mean.

10. **The correct answer is (C).** In the equation $h(t) = -0.5t + 980$, 980 represents the height above the ground of the stuntman when he opens the parachute.

11. **The correct answer is (A).** The speed of the object must be less than or equal to ($\leq$) 180,000.

12. **The correct answer is (A).** We know that the internal angles of a triangle always add up to 180; the fact that the triangle may or may not be drawn to scale is irrelevant. In this case, we have:
$$90 + 5z + z = 180$$
$$90 + 6z = 180$$
$$6z = 90$$
$$z = 15$$

13. **The correct answer is (C).** This is a good question to plug in numbers. Let's use a number instead of x. We can make x equal anything as long as it makes sense, so let's try $x = 10$. If it costs 10 dollars for a pack of 4 batteries, then how much would it cost to buy 100 batteries? Using proportions, we find:
$$\frac{\$10}{4} = \frac{y}{100}$$
$$y = \frac{\$10(100)}{4}$$
$$y = \$250$$

Substituting 10 for x in each of the answer choices will show that the correct answer is choice (C), since it is the only expression that equals $250.

14. **The correct answer is (B).** You could solve this problem by working backwards. Start with answer choice (C). If $y = -4$, then
$$\frac{7}{4} + \frac{6}{-4} = \frac{1}{4},$$
which does not equal 1. Eliminate this choice. Try answer choice (B): If $y = -8$, then
$$\frac{7}{4} + \frac{6}{-8} = \frac{14}{8} - \frac{6}{8} = \frac{8}{8} = 1.$$
This is correct, so there is no need to check the other answer choices.

15. **The correct answer is (C).** If $5.95 is the cost per sandwich, then $5.95x$ is the revenue from sandwiches, and y must be the number of beverages sold, since the number of beverages sold is an unknown value, and z must be the total revenue.

16. **The correct answer is (D).** Both coefficients must be negative to make the system of inequalities true, but neither must be greater than the other.

17. The correct answer is (B). The number of cookies and cupcakes that Alex bakes are $18x$ and $15y$ respectively. The number of cookies and cupcakes are x and y respectively. Since the number of pans of cookies is "at least" twice as many, the "greater than or equal to" symbol should be used. Also "no more than 165" means to use the "less than or equal to" symbol.

18. The correct answer is (D). Isolate $\sqrt{x}$ on one side of the equation and then square both sides to solve.

$$3\sqrt{x} + 8 = 20$$
$$3\sqrt{x} = 12$$
$$\sqrt{x} = 4$$
$$x = 16$$

19. The correct answer is (B). First, solve the system of equations for S:

$$G + \quad\; S = 50$$
$$\underline{19G + 10.5S = 800}$$
$$19G + \quad 19S = 950$$
$$\underline{19G + 10.5S = 800}$$
$$8.5S = 150$$
$$S = 17.65$$
$$S \approx 18$$

Then divide the total volume of the crown by 50:

$$\frac{18}{50} = 0.36$$
$$= 36\%$$

20. The correct answer is (A). The trend of the graph is positive, and most of the data points are close to a line, so the association is a strong positive correlation.

21. The correct answer is (C). The trend of the graph is positive and most of the data points are close to a line, and the line for $y = 20x + 250$ goes through the center of the data. The other graphs don't go through the center or don't follow the trend of data.

22. The correct answer is (C). Use FOIL to multiply:

$$(5 - 3i)(4 + 2i) = 20 + 10i - 12i - 6i^2$$
$$= 20 - 2i - 6(-1)$$
$$= 26 - 2i$$

23. The correct answer is (B). Because the function f has $(x - 1)$ and $(x + 5)$ as factors, the function should have zeros when $x - 1 = 0$ and $x + 5 = 0$. The only graph that shows a curve that has x-intercepts at 1 and -5 is choice (B).

24. The correct answer is (A). Only the graphs of (A) and (B) have y-intercepts at 8. Only the graphs of (A) and (C) have x-intercepts at 4 and -2.

25. The correct answer is (C). The relation between the number of bacteria and the time in hours should be an equation like $B = A(1.3)^h$, where A is the initial population of bacteria, h is the number of hours, 0.3 is the rate of growth, and B is the sample population after h hours.

26. The correct answer is (D). If $k < -1$, then the graph must open downward and be relatively steep.

27. The correct answer is (D). There were 92 juniors, and, of those, 30 students categorized themselves politically as conservative:

$$\frac{30}{92} = \frac{15}{46}$$

28. **The correct answer is (D).** Of the 200 students surveyed, there were 74 students total who categorized themselves as moderates.

$$\frac{74}{200} \times 4000 = 1480$$

29. **The corect answer is (D).** The 95% confidence that the margin of error is ± 3% is important, and choices (A) and (B) ignore the confidence interval. Choice (C) is not correct because there are likely people who don't know or have no opinion of the job that the U.S. Congress is doing. Only choice (D) accurately uses the confidence interval and the data given in the problem.

30. **The correct answer is (C).** First, find the slope of line m using the points on the line:

$$\frac{-2-0}{0-3} = \frac{2}{3}$$

A line that is perpendicular to line m will have a slope that is the negative reciprocal of that slope, so the slope of line n is $-\frac{3}{2}$, which means that choice (C) is correct.

31. **The correct answer is 7/13.** First, determine how many male baboons there are in the troop; 35% of 60 equals 21. So, there are 21 males and 39 females. Since the fraction $\frac{21}{39}$ won't fit into the grid, you must reduce. Divide both the numerator and the denominator by 3 to get $\frac{7}{13}$.

32. **The correct answer is 40.** Write and solve an equation that represents the home runs hit by batters A and B and solve for the desired number.

n = number of home runs by batter A

$n - 14$ = number of home runs by batter B

$$n + n - 14 = 66$$
$$2n - 14 = 66$$
$$2n = 80$$
$$n = 40$$

33. **The correct answer is 80.** First, calculate how many hours there are in five days:

5(24 hrs.) = 120 hrs.

Then, convert the length of each show to hours:

$$90 \text{ min.} \left(\frac{1 \text{ hr.}}{60 \text{ min.}}\right) = \frac{3}{2} \text{ hrs.}$$

Finally, divide the number of hours by the length of each show:

$$\frac{120 \text{ hrs.}}{\frac{3}{2} \text{ hrs.}} = 80$$

34. **The correct answer is 1.5.** First simplify the equation, and then determine which value of c will make the equation have no solutions, which is when the coefficient for $x = 0$.

$$3(5 - 2x) = -4(cx + 4) \qquad 4c - 6 = 0$$
$$15 - 6x = -4cx - 16 \qquad 4c = 6$$
$$4cx - 6x = -31 \qquad\qquad c = 1.5$$

35. The correct answer is 27. A cube has 6 equally sized faces, which means that each face has an area of 100 square centimeters, since the total surface area is 600 square centimeters. One edge of the cube must equal 10 centimeters, the square root of 100 square centimeters. The volume of the cube is $l \times w \times h = 10 \text{ cm} \times 10 \text{ cm} \times 10 \text{ cm} = 1000$ cubic centimeters. So 1000 cubic centimeters hold 1 liter.

The larger cube has a combined surface area of 5400 centimeters; one face will have a surface area of 900 square centimeters. One edge of the cube must equal 30 centimeters $(30 \times 30 = 900)$. So the volume of the cube is $30 \text{ cm} \times 30 \text{ cm} \times 30\text{cm} = 27,000$ cubic centimeters. If 1000 cubic centimeters hold 1 liter, then 27,000 cubic centimeters hold 27 liters.

36. The correct answer is 51.

$$f(-2) = 3(-2)^2 - 4(-2) + 8 = 28$$
$$g(28) = 2(28) - 5 = 51$$
$$g(f(-2)) = 51$$

37. The correct answer is 2. First, combine the equations by substituting $2x - 3$ for y in the second equation. Then solve for x:

$$2x - 3 = -3(x - 1)^2 + 4$$
$$2x - 3 = -3x^2 + 6x - 3 + 4$$
$$0 = -3x^2 + 4x + 4$$
$$0 = (3x + 2)(-x + 2)$$
$$x = -\frac{2}{3}, 2$$

Negative answers cannot be gridded, so the only correct answer is 2.

38. The correct answer is 22.5. To find the percent of change, multiply $1.25(1-0.3)$ (1.4) to show the three years of change as (1.225). This is equivalent to a 22.5% increase. The problem asks to write the answer as a percent without a percent symbol, so the answer is 22.5.

Section 5: Essay

Analysis of Passage

The following is an analysis of the passage by Jessica Smartt Gullion, noting how the writer used evidence, reasoning, and stylistic or persuasive elements to support her claims, connect the claims and evidence, and add power to the ideas she expressed. Check to see if you evaluated the passage in a similar way.

Will guns on campus lead to grade inflation?

By Jessica Smartt Gullion, Assistant Professor of Sociology at Texas Woman's University

(Passage was edited for length. For the complete article, see The Conversation, April 27, 2015 at http://theconversation.com)

1   Texas college professors may soon face a dilemma between upholding professional ethics and protecting their lives.

2   The Texas legislature appears poised to approve a bill that would allow college students to carry firearms to class. Called "campus carry," public universities in Texas will not be allowed to ban guns on their campuses, once the law is passed, although private schools could enact their own prohibitions.

3   Its backers argue that students have the right to protect themselves on campuses with handguns. The lobbying extends to sponsoring crash courses such as the NRA University, a two-hour seminar course for college students.

4   With this proposed law, a question coming up for many academics is whether they would be forced to give As to undeserving students, just so they can avoid being shot.

5   This is not as farfetched as it sounds. In my five years as a college professor, I have had experience with a number of emotionally distressed students who resort to intimidation when they receive a lesser grade than what they feel they deserve.

1   *The writer starts her argument by articulating her central concern: Texas college professors may soon be forced to put fear for their safety above professional ethics.*

2   *The writer states her reason for this concern: a pending Texas law that permits college students to carry guns on campuses.*

3   *The writer establishes her credibility and fairness by stating the reason why some legislators support this bill.*

4   *The writer returns to her central concern, expressing it in more detail: some instructors might give undeserved high grades to avoid being shot.*

5   *The writer provides facts about herself: she has been a college professor for five years and has had experience with students who intimidate instructors. By citing her background, the writer establishes her credentials as someone qualified to write about this topic and make this argument.*

www.petersons.com

Threats on campus

6　Here is an example of one such threatening experience: One evening in a graduate course, after I handed back students' papers, a young woman stood up and pointed at me. "This is unacceptable!" she screamed as her body shook in rage.

7　She moved toward the front of the class waving her paper in my face and screamed again, "unacceptable!" After a heated exchange, she left the room and stood outside the door sobbing.

8　All this was over receiving a B on a completely low-stakes assignment.

9　What followed was even more startling. The following week, the student brought along a muscle-bound man to class. He watched me through the doorway window for the entire three hours of the class, with his arms folded across his chest.

10　And if this wasn't enough, the young woman's classmates avoided me on campus because, they said, they were afraid of getting caught in the crossfire should she decide to shoot me.

11　After that, every time she turned in a paper I cringed and prayed that it was good so that I wouldn't have to give her anything less than an A.

6　*The writer provides a specific example drawn from her own experience. This makes her argument more personal and further strengthens her credibility—she truly knows what she is talking about. In addition, the writer makes this story extremely vivid using powerful words (screamed; shook in rage).*

7　*The writer continues to use evocative words (waving her paper in my face; heated exchange; sobbing).*

8　*The writer underscores the volatility of this student by using the phrase all this and pointing out that she received a respectable grade (a B) on an assignment that wasn't particularly important. The writer is implying that this woman's response to the grade was not rational, and she might have been angrier (and potentially more dangerous) if this were a major assignment.*

9　*The writer adds more details to the story, again carefully choosing words to paint a vivid picture (a muscle-bound man; the entire three hours; arms folded across his chest). Here, the writer evokes sympathy for herself and, by extension, all college teachers who have experienced (or who might experience) something similar.*

10　*The writer points out that the consequence of this experience went beyond her and one student, extending to her interactions with her other students.*

11　*The writer concludes the story by relating the effects this experience had on her, driving home the point that she is speaking from personal experience and eliciting more sympathy from the reader. She chooses her words carefully (cringed; prayed) for maximum impact.*

12 Learning from this experience, now I give papers back only at the end of the class or just "forget" to bring them with me.

12 *The writer makes the reader aware that this experience has had a lasting effect on her.*

13 I was lucky that the student didn't have a gun in my classroom. Other professors have not been so lucky.

13 *The writer returns to her central point: students having guns on campuses.*

14 Last year, a student at Purdue shot his instructor in front of a classroom of students. In another incident in 2009, a student at Northern Virginia Community College tried to shoot his math professor on campus. And, in 2000, a graduate student at the University of Arkansas shot his English professor.

14 *The writer cites three other incidents in which college students shot or tried to shoot instructors on a college campus.*

15 In each of these states, carrying handguns on campus was illegal at the time of the shooting, although a bill was introduced in Arkansas earlier this year to allow students to carry guns.

15 *The writer points out that in these incidents carrying handguns on campus was illegal. Thus she implies that things could get much worse on campuses where carrying handguns is allowed.*

Grade Inflation

16 Despite these and other shootings, a new trend has emerged across the U.S. that supports guns on college campuses.

16 *The writer points that even with the issue of students shooting instructors, there is support for guns on college campuses.*

17 Eight states allow firearms onto college campuses and 11 states are now considering similar legislation.

17 *The writer uses statistics to support this claim.*

18 We know that some students will carry guns whether it is legal or not. One study found that close to five percent of undergraduates had a gun on campus and that almost two percent had been threatened with a firearm while at school.

18 *The writer underscores her point that guns on campus are a big problem and cites a study to support this claim.*

...

19 Who would want to give a student a low grade and then get shot for it?

19 *The writer asks a rhetorical question to support her argument that guns on campus could motivate instructors to give undeserved high grades.*

20   Many majors are highly competitive and require certain GPAs for admission. Students on scholarships and other forms of financial aid must maintain high grades to keep their funding. It's no surprise that some students might resort to any means necessary to keep up their GPAs.

20   *The writer provides reasons why some students are desperate to maintain good grades, bolstering her claim that students can become violent if they receive disappointing grades.*

21   An international student once cried in my office and begged me to change his F to an A, as without it, his country would no longer pay for him to be in the U.S. I didn't. He harassed me by posting threatening messages on Facebook.

21   *Citing another example from her past, the writer describes what a student who was dependent on good grades did to her. She is again showing that her concern is well-founded and arousing the reader's sympathy by relating a personal experience.*

22   So, the question is, will we soon see a new sort of grade inflation, with students earning a 4.0 GPA with their firepower rather than brain power? And if so, what sort of future citizenry will we be building on our campuses?

22   *The writer concludes her argument with two rhetorical questions. She also chooses words that create strong images ("students earning a 4.0 GPA with their firepower rather than brain power" and "what sort of future citizenry will we be building on our campuses").*

Sample Essays

The following are examples of a high-scoring and low-scoring essay, based on the passage by Jessica Smartt Gullion.

High-Scoring Essay

The right to bear arms is highly contested in the United States. Rather than entering the national fray, Jessica Smartt Gullion focuses on only the right of college students to carry guns on campus. To persuade readers that college students should not be allowed to carry guns, she uses examples from her experience as a college professor to demonstrate the connection between grades and violence directed at the professors who assign those grades. Examples of violent incidents at other universities show that her experience is not unique. She brings the examples to life with words that evoke emotion, revealing the stress and fear that classroom violence creates. Gullion concludes by posing rhetorical questions that ask readers to consider the effect of guns in the college classroom.

Gullion presents the issue in a single clear sentence. At first, the claim seems extreme—professors might be killed for giving students poor grades for poor performance. She provides some background information, explaining the "campus carry" bill that would permit students at public universities in Texas to carry guns on campus. To balance the article's viewpoint, the writer briefly explains the opposing view that students should be armed to protect themselves. The article then circles back, bringing the information together by reminding readers that her concern is that professors who give poor grades for poor performance put themselves in danger.

To ward off readers' first impression that her concern is unrealistic, she admits that it may seem farfetched. However, she states that students have tried to intimidate her into giving better grades a number of times in the five years that she has been a college professor. In the next section, she uses emotional words that bring a threatening situation to life.

By simply placing the words "threats" and "campus" together, the "Threats on campus" heading brings an immediate sense of danger to a location where readers expect to feel safe. Gullion recounts a story of a violent event in her classroom. Emotional words such as "screamed" and "body shook with rage" help readers feel the shock and fear the exchange generated. The writer points out that the student's reaction was caused by getting a decent grade on an unimportant assignment. Without actually saying it, Gullion has made readers wonder what could have happened if the grade had been lower, if the assignment were more important, or if the student had been armed. The confrontation in the classroom didn't end there. The tale of the muscle-bound man watching her silently for three hours increased the "creepiness" rating of the incident and demonstrated some long-term effects. Even without a "campus carry" law, other students worried about the possibility of a shooting. Gullion describes how she cringed when the student turned in assignments after that.

Reinforcing the danger by supporting her personal experience with facts, Gullion identifies three separate incidents in which students shot their teachers. She makes the possibility of being shot for giving bad grades to students seem like it is not farfetched at all.

Sometimes, Gullion reasons, more is at stake for a student than grades. Poor grades can cause a student to be rejected for admission to a particular field of study, lose a scholarship, or lose the opportunity to study in the United States. Any of these results could change a student's life forever.

The rhetorical questions in the conclusion ask readers what they think about "campus carry" laws after the information she presented. Using the words "firepower" and "brain power" lays out the two options side by side. Firepower is the physical, violent option. Brain power is the smart, nonviolent option. She clearly wants readers to choose brain power by voting against any law that would allow students to carry guns on campus. If readers don't choose brain power, Gullion fears for the result.

Low-Scoring Essay

The Texas legislature thinks it would be safer if people carried guns everywhere they go, including college classes. Jessica Smartt Gullion disagrees. She has been a college professor for five years. In five years, she has been threatened by students a number of times. She's afraid that if students can carry guns, she might be shot.

Jessica Gullion thinks students might shoot her if she gives them bad grades. She tells stories about two times that she was threatened. One of the students brought a stalker to class with her just to threaten the teacher after getting a bad grade. The stalker might have shot the teacher if guns were allowed. Later, she talks about another stalker who threatened her on Facebook before he was forced to leave the country because his grades were bad.

The writer gives some statistics that show that five percent of college students already carry guns on college campuses. Making it legal, would mean that even more students would carry guns. Although the writer worries about being shot by a student on purpose, she could also worry about being shot accidentally if students try to shoot each other in the classroom.

At the end of the article, the writer asks if teachers will give better grades to students who are armed. She thinks students who get good grades by threatening teachers will make worse citizens than students who are smart and study to get good grades.

COMPUTING YOUR SCORES

To get a sense of your progress in preparing for the SAT®, follow these instructions and the following conversion tables.

To Determine Your Practice Test Scores

1 After you go through each of the test sections (Reading, Writing and Language, Math—No Calculator, and Math—Calculator) and determine which answers you got right, be sure to enter the number of correct answers in the box below the answer key for each of the sections.

2 Your total score on the SAT® practice test is the sum of your Evidence-Based Reading and Writing Section score and your Math Section score. To get your total score, convert the raw score—the number of questions you got right in a particular section—into the "scaled score" for that section, and then you'll calculate the total score. It sounds a little confusing, but we'll take you through the steps.

To Calculate Your Evidence-Based Reading and Writing Section Score

Your Evidence-Based Reading and Writing Section score is on a scale of 200–800. First determine your Reading Test score, and then determine your score on the Writing and Language Test.

1 Count the number of correct answers you got on the **Section 1: Reading Test.** Remember that there is no penalty for wrong answers. **The number of correct answers is your raw score.**

2 Go to Raw Score Conversion Table 1: Section and Test Scores on page 663. Look in the "Raw Score" column for your raw score, and match it to the number in the "Reading Test Score" column.

3 Do the same with **Section 2: Writing and Language Test** to determine that score.

4 Add your Reading Test score to your Writing and Language Test score.

5 Multiply that number by 10. This is your Evidence-Based Reading and Writing Section score.

To Calculate Your Math Section Score

YOUR MATH SECTION SCORE IS ALSO ON A SCALE OF 200–800.

1 Count the number of correct answers you got on the Section 3: Math Test—No Calculator and the Section 4: Math Test—No Calculator practice tests. Again, there is no penalty for wrong answers. **The number of correct answers is your raw score.**

2 Add the number of correct answers on the Section 3: Math Test—No Calculator and the Section 4: Math Test—No Calculator practice tests.

3 Use the **Raw Score Conversion Table 1: Section and Test Scores** on page 663 and convert your raw score into your Math Section score.

To Obtain Your Total Score

Add your score on the Evidence-Based Reading and Writing Section to the Math Section score. This is your total score on this SAT® Practice Test, on a scale of 400–1600.

Subscores Provide Additional Information

Subscores offer you greater details about your strengths in certain areas within literacy and math. The subscores are reported on a scale of 1–15 and include Heart of Algebra, Problem Solving and Data Analysis, Passport to Advanced Math, Expression of Ideas, Standard English Conventions, Words in Context, and Command of Evidence.

Heart of Algebra

The **Heart of Algebra subscore** is based on questions from the Math Test—No Calculator and Math Test—Calculator (Sections 3 and 4) that focus on linear equations and inequalities.

- Add up your total correct answers from these sections:
- Math Test—No Calculator: Questions 3, 8, 9, 10, 15, 16, 19, 20
- Math Test—Calculator: Questions 2, 4, 10, 11, 15–17, 19, 30, 32, 34
- Your Raw Score = the total number of correct answers from all of these questions.
- Use the **Raw Score Conversion Table 2: Subscores** on page 664 to determine your **Heart of Algebra** subscore.

Problem Solving and Data Analysis

The **Problem Solving and Data Analysis subscore** is based on questions from the Math Test that focus on quantitative reasoning, the interpretation and synthesis of data, and solving problems in rich and varied contexts.

- Add up your total correct answers from these sections:
- Math Test—No Calculator: None
- Math Test—Calculator: Questions 1, 5, 6–9, 13, 20, 21, 25, 27–29, 31, 33, 35, 38
- Your Raw Score = the total number of correct answers from all of these questions.
- Use the **Raw Score Conversion Table 2: Subscores** on page 664 to determine your **Problem Solving and Data Analysis** subscore.

Passport to Advanced Math

The **Passport to Advanced Math subscore** is based on questions from the Math Test that focus on topics central to your ability to progress to more advanced math, such as understanding the structure of expressions, reasoning with more complex equations, and interpreting and building functions.

- Add up your total correct answers from these sections:
- Math Test—No Calculator: Questions 1, 2, 4–7, 12, 13, 18
- Math Test—Calculator: Questions 14, 18, 23, 24, 26, 36, 37
- Your Raw Score = the total number of correct answers from all of these questions.
- Use the **Raw Score Conversion Table 2: Subscores** on page 664 to determine your **Passport to Advanced Math** subscore.

Expression of Ideas

The **Expression of Ideas subscore** is based on questions from the Writing and Language Test that focus on topic development, organization, and rhetorically effective use of language.

- Add up your total correct answers from Section 2: Writing and Language Test
- Questions 3–6, 8, 11, 13, 14, 18–21, 23, 24, 28, 30, 32–36, 39, 43, 44
- Your Raw Score = the total number of correct answers from all of these questions.
- Use the **Raw Score Conversion Table 2: Subscores** on page 664 to determine your **Expression of Ideas** subscore.

Standard English Conventions

The **Standard English Conventions subscore** is based on questions from the Writing and Language Test that focus on sentence structure, usage, and punctuation.

- Add up your total correct answers from Section 2: Writing and Language Test:
- Questions 1, 2, 7, 9, 10, 12, 15–17, 22, 25–27, 29, 31, 37, 38, 40–42
- Your Raw Score = the total number of correct answers from all of these questions.
- Use the **Raw Score Conversion Table 2: Subscores** on page 664 to determine your **Standard English Conventions** subscore.

Words in Context

The **Words in Context subscore** is based on questions from the Reading Test and the Writing and Language Test that address word/phrase meaning in context and rhetorical word choice.

- Add up your total correct answers from Sections 1 and 2:
- Reading Test: Questions 5, 9, 18, 22, 31, 32, 38, 42, 51, 52
- Writing and Language Test: Questions 6, 8, 14, 21, 23, 33, 34, 43
- Your Raw Score = the total number of correct answers from all of these questions.
- Use the **Raw Score Conversion Table 2: Subscores** on page 664 to determine your **Words in Context** subscore.

Command of Evidence

The **Command of Evidence subscore** is based on questions from the Reading Test and the Writing and Language Test that ask you to interpret and use evidence found in a wide range of passages and informational graphics, such as graphs, tables, and charts.

- Add up your total correct answers from Sections 1 and 2:
- Reading Test: Questions 7, 11, 14, 21, 29, 30, 34, 41, 47, 50
- Writing and Language Test: Questions 4, 11, 13, 20, 24, 30, 35, 44
- Your Raw Score = the total number of correct answers from all of these questions.
- Use the **Raw Score Conversion Table 2: Subscores** on page 664 to determine your **Command of Evidence** subscore.

answers PRACTICE TEST 2

Cross-Test Scores

The new SAT® also reports two cross-test scores: Analysis in History/Social Studies and Analysis in Science. These scores are based on questions in the Reading Test, Writing and Language Test, and both Math Tests that ask you to think analytically about texts and questions in these subject areas. Cross-test scores are reported on a scale of 10–40.

Analysis in History/Social Studies

- Add up your total correct answers from these sections:
- Reading Test: Questions 12–32
- Writing and Language Test: Questions 3–6, 8, 11
- Math Test—No Calculator: Question 7
- Math Test—Calculator: Questions 3, 6–8, 27–29
- Your Raw Score = the total number of correct answers from all of these questions.
- Use the **Raw Score Conversion Table 3: Cross-Test Scores** on page 665 to determine your **Analysis in History/Social Studies** cross-test score.

Analysis in Science

- Add up your total correct answers from these sections:
- Reading Test: Questions 1–11, 33–42
- Writing and Language Test: Questions 23, 24, 28, 30, 32, 33
- Math Test—No Calculator: None
- Math Test—Calculator: Questions 5, 9–11, 13, 19, 25, 31
- Your Raw Score = the total number of correct answers from all of these questions.
- Use the **Raw Score Conversion Table 3: Cross-Test Scores** on page 665 to determine your **Analysis in Science** cross-test score.

Raw Score Conversion Table 1: Section and Test Scores

Raw Score	Math Section Score	Reading Test Score	Writing and Language Test Score	Raw Score	Math Section Score	Reading Test Score	Writing and Language Test Score	Raw Score	Math Section Score	Reading Test Score	Writing and Language Test Score
0	200	10	10	20	450	22	23	40	610	33	36
1	200	10	10	21	460	23	23	41	620	33	37
2	210	10	10	22	470	23	24	42	630	34	38
3	230	11	10	23	480	24	25	43	640	35	39
4	240	12	11	24	480	24	25	44	650	35	40
5	260	13	12	25	490	25	26	45	660	36	
6	280	14	13	26	500	25	26	46	670	37	
7	290	15	13	27	510	26	27	47	670	37	
8	310	15	14	28	520	26	28	48	680	38	
9	320	16	15	29	520	27	28	49	690	38	
10	330	17	16	30	530	28	29	50	700	39	
11	340	17	16	31	540	28	30	51	710	40	
12	360	18	17	32	550	29	30	52	730	40	
13	370	19	18	33	560	29	31	53	740		
14	380	19	19	34	560	30	32	54	750		
15	390	20	19	35	570	30	32	55	760		
16	410	20	20	36	580	31	33	56	780		
17	420	21	21	37	590	31	34	57	790		
18	430	21	21	38	600	32	34	58	800		
19	440	22	22	39	600	32	35				

Conversion Equation 1 Section and Test Scores

Raw Score Conversion Table 2: Subscores

Raw Score (# of correct answers)	Expression of Ideas	Standard English Conventions	Heart of Algebra	Problem Solving Data Analysis	Passport to Advanced Math	Words in Context	Command of Evidence
0	1	1	1	1	1	1	1
1	1	1	1	1	3	1	1
2	1	1	2	2	5	2	2
3	2	2	3	3	6	3	3
4	3	2	4	4	7	4	4
5	4	3	5	5	8	5	5
6	5	4	6	6	9	6	6
7	6	5	6	7	10	6	7
8	6	6	7	8	11	7	8
9	7	6	8	8	11	8	8
10	7	7	8	9	12	8	9
11	8	7	9	10	12	9	10
12	8	8	9	10	13	9	10
13	9	8	9	11	13	10	11
14	9	9	10	12	14	11	12
15	10	10	10	13	14	12	13
16	10	10	11	14	15	13	14
17	11	11	12	15		14	15
18	11	12	13			15	15
19	12	13	15				
20	12	15					
21	13						
22	14						
23	14						
24	15						

Conversion Equation 2 Subscores

HEART OF ALGEBRA RAW SCORE (0–19)	EXPRESSION OF IDEAS RAW SCORE (0–24)	COMMAND OF EVIDENCE RAW SCORE (0–18)	PROBLEM SOLVING AND DATA ANALYSIS RAW SCORE (0–17)
CONVERT	CONVERT	CONVERT	CONVERT
HEART OF ALGEBRA SUBSCORE (1–15)	EXPRESSION OF IDEAS SUBSCORE (1–15)	COMMAND OF EVIDENCE SUBSCORE (1–15)	PROBLEM SOLVING AND DATA ANALYSIS SUBSCORE (1–15)

STANDARD ENGLISH CONVENTIONS RAW SCORE (0–20)	WORDS IN CONTEXT RAW SCORE (0–18)	PASSPORT TO ADVANCED MATH RAW SCORE (0–16)
CONVERT	CONVERT	CONVERT
STANDARD ENGLISH CONVENTIONS SUBSCORE (1–15)	WORDS IN CONTEXT SUBSCORE (1–15)	PASSPORT TO ADVANCED MATH SUBSCORE (1–15)

Raw Score Conversion Table 3: Cross-Test Scores

Raw Score (# of correct answers)	Analysis in History/Social Studies Cross-Test Score	Analysis in Science Cross-Test Score	Raw Score (# of correct answers)	Analysis in History/Social Studies Cross-Test Score	Analysis in Science Cross-Test Score
0	10	10	18	28	26
1	10	11	19	29	27
2	11	12	20	30	27
3	12	13	21	30	28
4	14	14	22	31	29
5	15	15	23	32	30
6	16	16	24	32	30
7	17	17	25	33	31
8	18	18	26	34	32
9	20	19	27	35	33
10	21	20	28	35	33
11	22	20	29	36	34
12	23	21	30	37	35
13	24	22	31	38	36
14	25	23	32	38	37
15	26	24	33	39	38
16	27	24	34	40	39
17	28	25	35	40	40

answers PRACTICE TEST 2

Conversion Equation 3: Cross-Test Scores

TEST	ANALYSIS IN HISTORY/SOCIAL STUDIES		ANALYSIS IN SCIENCE	
	QUESTIONS	RAW SCORE	QUESTIONS	RAW SCORE
Reading Test	12–32		1–11, 33–42	
Writing and Language Test	3–6, 8, 11		23, 24, 28, 30, 32, 33	
Math Test—No Calculator	7		None	
Math Test—Calculator	3, 6–8, 27–29		5, 9–11, 13, 19, 25, 31	
TOTAL				

ANALYSIS IN HISTORY/
SOCIAL STUDIES
RAW SCORE (0–35)

CONVERT

ANALYSIS IN HISTORY/
SOCIAL STUDIES
CROSS-TEST SCORE (10–40)

ANALYSIS IN SCIENCE
RAW SCORE (0–35)

CONVERT

ANALYSIS IN SCIENCE
CROSS-TEST SCORE (1–15)

Practice Test 3

On test day, you will see these important reminders on the first page of your SAT® test booklet:

- You must use a No. 2 pencil when taking the test; you may not use a pen or mechanical pencil.
- You may not share any questions with anyone. This is considered a violation of College Board's "Test Security and Fairness" policies, and it could cause your scores to be canceled.
- You are not permitted to take the test booklet out of the testing room.

In addition to filling in your name and Test Center information on your answer sheet, you'll be asked to fill in two different codes that will be on your test booklet. Each test booklet has a unique code, and there will be a grid-in form to fill in with your "TEST ID" and "FORM CODE" letters and numbers.

The general directions for the test will look something like this:

- You may only work on one section at a time.
- If you complete a section before time is called, check your work on that section only. You are not permitted to work on any other section.

The directions for marking your answers will likely include the following recommendations:

- Mark your answer sheet properly—be sure to completely fill in the answer bubble.
- Be careful to mark only one answer for each question.
- Don't make any stray marks on the answer sheet.
- If you need to erase your answer, make sure you do so completely.
- Be sure to use the answer spaces that correspond to the question numbers.

You will be able to use your test booklet for scratch work, but you won't get credit for any work done in your test booklet. When time is called at the end of each section, you will not be permitted to transfer answers from your test booklet to your answer sheet.

Any information, ideas, or opinions presented in any of the passages you will see on the redesigned SAT® that have been taken from other sources or published material do not represent the opinions of the College Board.

Scoring on the SAT® is as follows:

- You will receive one point for each correct answer.
- You will not lose points for wrong answers, so you should attempt to answer every question even if you aren't completely sure of the correct answer.

Your testing supervisor will announce when to open the test booklet, so be sure to wait until you're told to do so. For the purposes of this practice test, be sure you have a timer to set for 65 minutes for the Section 1: Reading Test.

The answer sheets for each test section, including lined paper for the essay, appear on the next five pages. Following the Answer Key and Explanations for this Practice Test, you will find details on how to score your work.

practice test 3

ANSWER SHEET PRACTICE TEST 3

Section 1: Reading Test

1. Ⓐ Ⓑ Ⓒ Ⓓ   12. Ⓐ Ⓑ Ⓒ Ⓓ   23. Ⓐ Ⓑ Ⓒ Ⓓ   33. Ⓐ Ⓑ Ⓒ Ⓓ   43. Ⓐ Ⓑ Ⓒ Ⓓ
2. Ⓐ Ⓑ Ⓒ Ⓓ   13. Ⓐ Ⓑ Ⓒ Ⓓ   24. Ⓐ Ⓑ Ⓒ Ⓓ   34. Ⓐ Ⓑ Ⓒ Ⓓ   44. Ⓐ Ⓑ Ⓒ Ⓓ
3. Ⓐ Ⓑ Ⓒ Ⓓ   14. Ⓐ Ⓑ Ⓒ Ⓓ   25. Ⓐ Ⓑ Ⓒ Ⓓ   35. Ⓐ Ⓑ Ⓒ Ⓓ   45. Ⓐ Ⓑ Ⓒ Ⓓ
4. Ⓐ Ⓑ Ⓒ Ⓓ   15. Ⓐ Ⓑ Ⓒ Ⓓ   26. Ⓐ Ⓑ Ⓒ Ⓓ   36. Ⓐ Ⓑ Ⓒ Ⓓ   46. Ⓐ Ⓑ Ⓒ Ⓓ
5. Ⓐ Ⓑ Ⓒ Ⓓ   16. Ⓐ Ⓑ Ⓒ Ⓓ   27. Ⓐ Ⓑ Ⓒ Ⓓ   37. Ⓐ Ⓑ Ⓒ Ⓓ   47. Ⓐ Ⓑ Ⓒ Ⓓ
6. Ⓐ Ⓑ Ⓒ Ⓓ   17. Ⓐ Ⓑ Ⓒ Ⓓ   28. Ⓐ Ⓑ Ⓒ Ⓓ   38. Ⓐ Ⓑ Ⓒ Ⓓ   48. Ⓐ Ⓑ Ⓒ Ⓓ
7. Ⓐ Ⓑ Ⓒ Ⓓ   18. Ⓐ Ⓑ Ⓒ Ⓓ   29. Ⓐ Ⓑ Ⓒ Ⓓ   39. Ⓐ Ⓑ Ⓒ Ⓓ   49. Ⓐ Ⓑ Ⓒ Ⓓ
8. Ⓐ Ⓑ Ⓒ Ⓓ   19. Ⓐ Ⓑ Ⓒ Ⓓ   30. Ⓐ Ⓑ Ⓒ Ⓓ   40. Ⓐ Ⓑ Ⓒ Ⓓ   50. Ⓐ Ⓑ Ⓒ Ⓓ
9. Ⓐ Ⓑ Ⓒ Ⓓ   20. Ⓐ Ⓑ Ⓒ Ⓓ   31. Ⓐ Ⓑ Ⓒ Ⓓ   41. Ⓐ Ⓑ Ⓒ Ⓓ   51. Ⓐ Ⓑ Ⓒ Ⓓ
10. Ⓐ Ⓑ Ⓒ Ⓓ   21. Ⓐ Ⓑ Ⓒ Ⓓ   32. Ⓐ Ⓑ Ⓒ Ⓓ   42. Ⓐ Ⓑ Ⓒ Ⓓ   52. Ⓐ Ⓑ Ⓒ Ⓓ
11. Ⓐ Ⓑ Ⓒ Ⓓ   22. Ⓐ Ⓑ Ⓒ Ⓓ

Section 2: Writing and Language Test

1. Ⓐ Ⓑ Ⓒ Ⓓ   10. Ⓐ Ⓑ Ⓒ Ⓓ   19. Ⓐ Ⓑ Ⓒ Ⓓ   28. Ⓐ Ⓑ Ⓒ Ⓓ   37. Ⓐ Ⓑ Ⓒ Ⓓ
2. Ⓐ Ⓑ Ⓒ Ⓓ   11. Ⓐ Ⓑ Ⓒ Ⓓ   20. Ⓐ Ⓑ Ⓒ Ⓓ   29. Ⓐ Ⓑ Ⓒ Ⓓ   38. Ⓐ Ⓑ Ⓒ Ⓓ
3. Ⓐ Ⓑ Ⓒ Ⓓ   12. Ⓐ Ⓑ Ⓒ Ⓓ   21. Ⓐ Ⓑ Ⓒ Ⓓ   30. Ⓐ Ⓑ Ⓒ Ⓓ   39. Ⓐ Ⓑ Ⓒ Ⓓ
4. Ⓐ Ⓑ Ⓒ Ⓓ   13. Ⓐ Ⓑ Ⓒ Ⓓ   22. Ⓐ Ⓑ Ⓒ Ⓓ   31. Ⓐ Ⓑ Ⓒ Ⓓ   40. Ⓐ Ⓑ Ⓒ Ⓓ
5. Ⓐ Ⓑ Ⓒ Ⓓ   14. Ⓐ Ⓑ Ⓒ Ⓓ   23. Ⓐ Ⓑ Ⓒ Ⓓ   32. Ⓐ Ⓑ Ⓒ Ⓓ   41. Ⓐ Ⓑ Ⓒ Ⓓ
6. Ⓐ Ⓑ Ⓒ Ⓓ   15. Ⓐ Ⓑ Ⓒ Ⓓ   24. Ⓐ Ⓑ Ⓒ Ⓓ   33. Ⓐ Ⓑ Ⓒ Ⓓ   42. Ⓐ Ⓑ Ⓒ Ⓓ
7. Ⓐ Ⓑ Ⓒ Ⓓ   16. Ⓐ Ⓑ Ⓒ Ⓓ   25. Ⓐ Ⓑ Ⓒ Ⓓ   34. Ⓐ Ⓑ Ⓒ Ⓓ   43. Ⓐ Ⓑ Ⓒ Ⓓ
8. Ⓐ Ⓑ Ⓒ Ⓓ   17. Ⓐ Ⓑ Ⓒ Ⓓ   26. Ⓐ Ⓑ Ⓒ Ⓓ   35. Ⓐ Ⓑ Ⓒ Ⓓ   44. Ⓐ Ⓑ Ⓒ Ⓓ
9. Ⓐ Ⓑ Ⓒ Ⓓ   18. Ⓐ Ⓑ Ⓒ Ⓓ   27. Ⓐ Ⓑ Ⓒ Ⓓ   36. Ⓐ Ⓑ Ⓒ Ⓓ

Section 3: Math Test—No Calculator

1. Ⓐ Ⓑ Ⓒ Ⓓ   4. Ⓐ Ⓑ Ⓒ Ⓓ   7. Ⓐ Ⓑ Ⓒ Ⓓ   10. Ⓐ Ⓑ Ⓒ Ⓓ   13. Ⓐ Ⓑ Ⓒ Ⓓ

2. Ⓐ Ⓡ Ⓒ Ⓓ   5. Ⓐ Ⓑ Ⓒ Ⓓ   8. Ⓐ Ⓑ Ⓒ Ⓓ   11. Ⓐ Ⓑ Ⓒ Ⓓ   14. Ⓐ Ⓑ Ⓒ Ⓤ

3. Ⓐ Ⓑ Ⓒ Ⓓ   6. Ⓐ Ⓑ Ⓒ Ⓓ   9. Ⓐ Ⓑ Ⓒ Ⓓ   12. Ⓐ Ⓑ Ⓒ Ⓓ   15. Ⓐ Ⓑ Ⓒ Ⓓ

16. 17. 18. 19. 20.

Section 4: Math Test—Calculator

1. Ⓐ Ⓑ Ⓒ Ⓓ   7. Ⓐ Ⓑ Ⓒ Ⓓ   13. Ⓐ Ⓑ Ⓒ Ⓓ   19. Ⓐ Ⓑ Ⓒ Ⓓ   25. Ⓐ Ⓑ Ⓒ Ⓓ

2. Ⓐ Ⓑ Ⓒ Ⓓ   8. Ⓐ Ⓑ Ⓒ Ⓓ   14. Ⓐ Ⓑ Ⓒ Ⓓ   20. Ⓐ Ⓑ Ⓒ Ⓓ   26. Ⓐ Ⓑ Ⓒ Ⓓ

3. Ⓐ Ⓑ Ⓒ Ⓓ   9. Ⓐ Ⓑ Ⓒ Ⓓ   15. Ⓐ Ⓑ Ⓒ Ⓓ   21. Ⓐ Ⓑ Ⓒ Ⓓ   27. Ⓐ Ⓑ Ⓒ Ⓓ

4. Ⓐ Ⓑ Ⓒ Ⓓ   10. Ⓐ Ⓑ Ⓒ Ⓓ   16. Ⓐ Ⓑ Ⓒ Ⓓ   22. Ⓐ Ⓑ Ⓒ Ⓓ   28. Ⓐ Ⓑ Ⓒ Ⓓ

5. Ⓐ Ⓑ Ⓒ Ⓓ   11. Ⓐ Ⓑ Ⓒ Ⓓ   17. Ⓐ Ⓑ Ⓒ Ⓓ   23. Ⓐ Ⓑ Ⓒ Ⓓ   29. Ⓐ Ⓑ Ⓒ Ⓓ

6. Ⓐ Ⓑ Ⓒ Ⓓ   12. Ⓐ Ⓑ Ⓒ Ⓓ   18. Ⓐ Ⓑ Ⓒ Ⓓ   24. Ⓐ Ⓑ Ⓒ Ⓓ   30. Ⓐ Ⓑ Ⓒ Ⓓ

31. 32. 33. 34. 35.

answer sheet

36.

	/	/	
.	.	.	.
	0	0	0
1	1	1	1
2	2	2	2
3	3	3	3
4	4	4	4
5	5	5	5
6	6	6	6
7	7	7	7
8	8	8	8
9	9	9	9

37.

	/	/	
.	.	.	.
	0	0	0
1	1	1	1
2	2	2	2
3	3	3	3
4	4	4	4
5	5	5	5
6	6	6	6
7	7	7	7
8	8	8	8
9	9	9	9

38.

	/	/	
.	.	.	.
	0	0	0
1	1	1	1
2	2	2	2
3	3	3	3
4	4	4	4
5	5	5	5
6	6	6	6
7	7	7	7
8	8	8	8
9	9	9	9

Section 5: Essay

_____

_____

_____

_____

_____

_____

_____

_____

_____

_____

_____

_____

_____

_____

_____

_____

_____

_____

_____

_____

_____

answer sheet

_____

_____

_____

_____

_____

_____

_____

_____

_____

_____

_____

_____

_____

_____

_____

_____

_____

_____

_____

_____

_____

_____

_____

_____

_____

_____

SECTION 1: READING TEST

65 Minutes • 52 Questions

TURN TO SECTION 1 OF YOUR ANSWER SHEET TO ANSWER THE QUESTIONS IN THIS SECTION.

Directions: Each passage (or pair of passages) below is followed by a number of multiple-choice questions. After reading each passage, select the best answer to each question based on what is stated or implied in the passage or passages and in any supplementary material, such as a table, graph, chart, or photograph.

QUESTIONS 1–11 ARE BASED ON THE FOLLOWING PASSAGE.

The U.S. Geological Survey (USGS) is a government agency whose goal is to provide reliable scientific information about the Earth, including minimizing loss from natural disasters. This excerpt is from the organization's website. For the full passage, please visit http://earthquake.usgs.gov/learn.

Earthquakes, Megaquakes, and the Movies

Throughout the history of Hollywood, disaster films have been sure-fire winners for moviemakers .... With amazing special
Line effects, it's easy to get caught up in the
5   fantasy disaster epic. What makes a great science fantasy film often bears no relation to real facts or the hazards people truly face.

The U.S. Geological Survey is the lead federal agency responsible for
10   researching, monitoring and forecasting geologic hazards such as earthquakes, volcanoes and landslides .... Let's start with some **science-based information** on earthquakes.

15   **Earthquakes are naturally occurring events outside the powers of humans to create or stop.** An earthquake is caused by a sudden slip on a fault, much like what happens when you snap your
20   fingers. Before the snap, you push your fingers together and sideways. Because you are pushing them together, friction keeps them from slipping. When you apply enough stress to overcome this
25   friction, your fingers move suddenly, releasing energy. The same "stick-slip" process goes on in the earth. Stresses in the Earth's outer layer push the sides of the fault together. The friction across

30   the surface of the fault holds the rocks together so they do not slip immediately when pushed sideways. Eventually enough stress builds up and the rocks slip suddenly, releasing energy in waves
35   that travel through the rock to cause the shaking that we feel during an earthquake.

Earthquakes typically originate several to tens of miles below the surface of the Earth. It takes decades
40   to centuries to build up enough stress to make a large earthquake, and the fault may be tens to hundreds of miles long. People cannot prevent earthquakes from happening or stop
45   them once they've started—giant nuclear explosions at shallow depths, like those in some movies, won't actually stop an earthquake.

It's well known that California, the
50   Pacific Northwest, and Alaska all have frequent earthquakes, some of which are quite damaging. Some areas of the country are more at risk than others, but, in fact, **42 of the 50 states could**
55   **experience damaging ground shaking** from an earthquake in 50 years (which is the typical lifetime of a building), and 16 states have a relatively high likelihood of experiencing damaging ground shaking.
60   **The two most important variables affecting earthquake damage are the intensity of ground shaking and the quality of the engineering of structures in the region.** The level of shaking
65   is controlled by the proximity of the earthquake source to the affected region and the types of rocks that seismic waves pass through en route (particularly those at or near the ground surface). Generally,

GO TO THE NEXT PAGE

70 the bigger and closer the earthquake, the stronger the shaking. But there have been large earthquakes with very little damage because they caused little shaking or because the buildings were

75 built to withstand that shaking. In other cases, moderate earthquakes have caused significant damage because the shaking was locally amplified, or because the structures were poorly engineered.

80   The idea of a "Mega-Quake"—an earthquake of magnitude 10 or larger—is very unlikely. Earthquake magnitude is based in part on the length of faults— the longer the fault, the larger the

85 earthquake. **The simple truth is that there are no known faults capable of generating a magnitude 10 or larger "mega-quake." ...**

Then there's this business of

90 **California falling off into the ocean. NOT TRUE!** The ocean is not a great hole into which California can fall, but is itself land at a somewhat lower elevation with water above it.

95 It's impossible that California will be swept out to sea. Instead, southwestern California is moving slowly (2 inches per year) towards Alaska. 15 million years (and many earthquakes) from now,

100 Los Angeles and San Francisco will be next-door neighbors.

   Another popular cinematic and literary device is a fault that opens during an earthquake to swallow up an inconvenient

105 character. But the ground moves parallel to a fault during an earthquake, not away from it. If the fault could open, there would be no friction. Without friction, there would be no earthquake. Shallow

110 crevasses can form during earthquake-induced landslides, lateral spreads, or other types of ground failures. **Faults, however, do not gape open during an earthquake.**

115   So when you see the next big disaster film, rest assured that movies are just entertainment. Enjoy them! And then go learn about the real-world science behind disasters, and if you live in an area where

120 hazards exist, take the suggested steps to protect you and your family.

1 Which of the following best describes the author's purpose in writing this article?

(A) To counter the myths about earthquakes driven by fictional films

(B) To explain to people the causes and effects of earthquakes

(C) To show how Hollywood distorts science

(D) To give people advice about what to do if an earthquake strikes

2 What is the main cause of an earthquake?

(A) A fault in the Earth's crust

(B) Friction caused by stresses built up in rocks

(C) Stresses in the Earth's outer layer

(D) Energy waves through the rocks in the Earth's crust

3 Who is the target audience of the article?

(A) The general public

(B) Scientists

(C) Filmmakers

(D) Science teachers

4 How does the article counter the claim that in the future, part of California may fall off into the ocean?

(A) It states that it would be a disaster.

(B) It states that sea level rise will prevent it.

(C) It explains the similarity between California and Alaska.

(D) It explains how the ocean is just land covered by water.

5 Which choice provides the best evidence for the answer to the previous question?

(A) Lines 91–94 ("The ocean … above it.")

(B) Lines 95–96 ("It's impossible … out to sea.")

(C) Lines 96–98 ("Instead, southwestern … towards Alaska.")

(D) Lines 98–101 ("15 million years … neighbors.")

6 As used in line 24, "stress" most nearly means

(A) anxiety.

(B) weight.

(C) pressure.

(D) emphasis.

7 Based only on information in the article, what is the most likely reason that Haiti experienced such extensive damage in the earthquake of 2010?

(A) The earthquake source was very near the affected region and the buildings were poorly constructed.

(B) Haiti has had earthquakes many times before, and they were all destructive.

(C) The people are poor and were unprepared for the earthquake of 2010.

(D) The faults were deep and numerous across the country.

8 Which choice provides the best evidence for the answer to the previous question?

(A) Lines 17–29 ("An earthquake is … the fault together.")

(B) Lines 37–43 ("Earthquakes typically … miles long.")

(C) Lines 60–64 ("The two most important … in the region.")

(D) Lines 105–108 ("But the ground … be no friction")

9 In line 78, "amplified" most nearly means

(A) lifted.

(B) supplemented.

(C) intensified.

(D) augured.

10 How does the use of the phrase "inconvenient character"(lines 104–105) affect the tone of the passage?

(A) It reveals a negative attitude about unscientific data.

(B) It illustrates a mocking tone toward how the storylines are written.

(C) It reveals a scholarly attitude about science.

(D) It communicates a warning about inaccurate scientific information.

11 How does the author refute the idea that an earthquake could cause the earth to open up and swallow people and things?

(A) By pointing out that the idea of the Earth opening up is portrayed in movies

(B) By noting that there are no known faults capable of producing a "mega quake"

(C) By explaining that the ground moves parallel to a fault during an earthquake

(D) By suggesting that subsequent landslides can cause crevasses to open up

GO TO THE NEXT PAGE

QUESTIONS 12–22 ARE BASED ON THE FOLLOWING TWO PASSAGES.

After the Constitution was drafted, it had to be ratified by at least nine of the thirteen states. The following two passages illustrate the debate over ratification. Passage 1 is from a speech made on June 5, 1788 by Patrick Henry, the governor of Virginia, at the state's convention, called specifically to ratify the Constitution. Passage 2 is from an essay written by James Madison, which first appeared in a New York newspaper on June 6, 1788, and later became part of what is now known as the Federalist Papers.

Passage 1

If you make the citizens of this
country agree to become the subjects
of one great consolidated empire of
Line America, your government will not have
5 sufficient energy to keep them together.
Such a government is incompatible
with the genius of republicanism. There
will be no checks, no real balances, in
this government. What can avail your
10 specious, imaginary balances, your rope-
dancing, chain-rattling ridiculous ideal
checks and contrivances? But, sir, "we are
not feared by foreigners; we do not make
nations tremble." Would this constitute
15 happiness or secure liberty? I trust, sir,
our political hemisphere will ever direct
their operations to the security of those
objects.

This Constitution is said to have
20 beautiful features; but when I come to
examine these features, sir, they appear
to me horribly frightful. Among other
deformities, it has an awful squinting;
it squints toward monarchy, and does
25 not this raise indignation in the breast
of every true American? Your president
may easily become king. Your Senate
is so imperfectly constructed that your
dearest rights may be sacrificed to what
30 may be a small minority; and a very
small minority may continue for ever
unchangeably this government, altho
horridly defective. Where are your checks
in this government? Your strongholds will
35 be in the hands of your enemies. It is on a

supposition that your American governors
shall be honest that all the good qualities
of this government are founded; but its
defective and imperfect construction puts
40 it in their power to perpetrate the worst
of mischiefs should they be bad men;
and, sir, would not all the world, blame
our distracted folly in resting our rights
upon the contingency of our rulers being
45 good or bad? Show me that age and
country where the rights and liberties of
the people were placed on the sole chance
of their rulers being good men without
a consequent loss of liberty! I say that
50 the loss of that dearest privilege has ever
followed, with absolute certainty, every
such mad attempt.

Passage 2

In order to lay a due foundation for
that separate and distinct exercise of the
55 different powers of government, which to
a certain extent is admitted on all hands
to be essential to the preservation of
liberty; it is evident that each department
should have a will of its own; and
60 consequently should be so constituted that
the members of each should have as little
agency as possible in the appointment
of the members of the others .... It is
equally evident that the members of each
65 department should be as little dependent
as possible on those of the others for the
emoluments annexed to their offices.
Were the executive magistrate, or the
judges, not independent of the legislature
70 in this particular, their independence in
every other would be merely nominal.
But the great security against a gradual
concentration of the several powers in
the same department, consists in giving
75 to those who administer each department
the necessary constitutional means and
personal motives to resist encroachments
of the others. The provision for defense
must in this, as in all other cases, be made
80 commensurate to the danger of attack.
Ambition must be made to counteract
ambition. The interest of the man must be
connected with the constitutional rights
of the place. It may be a reflection on

85 human nature, that such devices should
be necessary to control the abuses of
government. But what is government
itself, but the greatest of all reflections
on human nature? If men were angels, no
90 government would be necessary. If angels
were to govern men, neither external nor
internal controls on government would be
necessary. In framing a government which
is to be administered by men over men,
95 the great difficulty lies in this: you must
first enable the government to control the
governed; and in the next place oblige
it to control itself. A dependence on the
people is, no doubt, the primary control
100 on the government; but experience has
taught mankind the necessity of auxiliary
precautions.

12 Which of the following best represents the
differences in point of view of the authors
of the two passages?

(A) Henry was concerned about the
balance of power and Madison was
concerned about concentration of
wealth.

(B) Henry worried about too much power
in the hands of the government
and Madison worried about too
much power in any one branch of
government.

(C) Henry was focused on states' rights
and Madison was focused on adding
the Bill of Rights to the Constitution.

(D) Henry was afraid of a return to
monarchy and Madison was afraid of
government corruption.

13 Which represents the best summary of
Patrick Henry's objection to the drafted
Constitution?

(A) Its structure is unstable and will lead
to loss of liberty.

(B) It leaves too much power in the
hands of the people.

(C) It does not centralize power enough.

(D) It makes government dependent on
people who are flawed.

GO TO THE NEXT PAGE

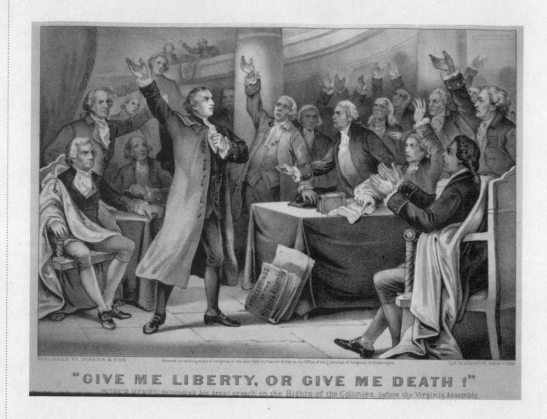

"GIVE ME LIBERTY, OR GIVE ME DEATH !"
PATRICK HENRY delivering his great speech on the Rights of the Colonies, before the Virginia Assembly,

14 Examine the illustration that shows Patrick Henry delivering his most famous speech; the one in which he declared, "Give me liberty or give me death!" Choose the option that best explains how the artist's portrayal applies to Henry's speech about the Constitution.

(A) The artist shows Henry as an important man with a message, surrounded by many people who react strongly his speech. Henry delivers his speech to the state Assembly as an important figure—governor of Virginia.

(B) The artist shows Henry as a calm, persuasive speaker, using logic and reasoning to persuade his listeners. Henry uses order and reasoning in his speech about the Constitution. He asks his listeners logical questions to persuade them that he is right.

(C) The artist shows Henry standing on his feet making dramatic gestures and speaking with passion. In the speech about the Constitution, Henry uses dramatic phrases and figures of speech to try to persuade his listeners.

(D) The artist shows Henry as an extremist so carried away by his own emotions that people think he's a madman. This view contrasts sharply with Henry's speech, in which he slowly builds his argument, appealing to the listener's sense of patriotism.

15 What was Madison's strongest counter-argument to those who were concerned about a strong central government?

(A) Men are inherently flawed.

(B) No one is perfect.

(C) Government would ultimately be controlled by the people.

(D) So long as the powers are separated, power will not be concentrated.

16 Which choice provides the best evidence for the answer to the previous question?

(A) Lines 72–78 ("But the great … of the others.")

(B) Lines 81–82 ("Ambition must … counteract ambition.")

(C) Lines 89–90 ("If men were … would be necessary.")

(D) Lines 98–102 ("A dependence on … auxiliary precautions.")

17 What do these two statements show about how their authors viewed human nature?

Henry, lines 45–49: "Show me that age and country where the rights and liberties of the people were placed on the sole chance of their rulers being good men without a consequent loss of liberty!"

Madison, lines 90–93: "If angels were to govern men, neither external nor internal controls on government would be necessary."

(A) Henry believed humans are naturally dishonest and self-interested and Madison believed that humans are basically honest and good, but not perfect.

(B) Henry believed past rulers were generally good men who lost their way; Madison believed humans tend to be dishonest.

(C) Henry didn't trust ordinary men to be rulers and Madison believed all people could be trusted to rule.

(D) Henry believed that government is unnecessary for a free people; Madison believed that government needs to be regulated.

18 Who is Patrick Henry quoting in lines 12–14 But, sir, "we are not feared by foreigners; we do not make nations tremble"?

(A) An omniscient narrator

(B) The framers of the Constitution

(C) The general public

(D) The people of Virginia

19 What kind of government does Henry think is best?

(A) Monarchy

(B) Republic

(C) Autocracy

(D) Plutocracy

practice test

20 Which choice provides the best evidence for the answer to the previous question?

(A) Lines 3–4 ("one great … of America.")

(B) Line 7 ("the genius … republicanism.")

(C) Line 24 ("it squints … monarchy")

(D) Lines 26–27 ("Your president … become king.")

21 As it is used in line 58, "department" most nearly means

(A) an executive in the government.

(B) an office in the government.

(C) a level of government.

(D) a branch of government.

22 As used in line 80, "commensurate" most nearly means

(A) proportional.

(B) provisional.

(C) dependent.

(D) relevant.

QUESTIONS 23–32 ARE BASED ON THE FOLLOWING PASSAGE AND SUPPLEMENTARY MATERIAL.

This article is excerpted from the National Oceanic and Atmospheric Administration Fisheries website (NOAA). The public agency provides science news and scientific findings related to the Earth and the Earth's atmosphere. This article describes the finding of a tiny, rare shark. For the full passage, please visit www. nmfs.noaa.gov/stories.

NOAA and Tulane researchers identify second possible specimen ever found.

A very small and rare species of shark is swimming its way through scientific literature. But don't worry, the chances of
Line this inches-long vertebrate biting through
5 your swimsuit is extremely slim, because if you ever spotted one, you'd be the third person to ever do so.

This species common name is the "pocket shark," though those in the
10 field of classifying animals refer to it by its scientific name *Mollisquama* sp., according to a new study published in the international journal of taxonomy *Zootaxa*. While it is small enough to,
15 yes, fit in your pocket, it's dubbed "pocket" because of the distinctive orifice above the pectoral fin—one of many physiological features scientists hope to better understand.

20 "The pocket shark we found was only 5 and a half inches long, and was a recently born male," said Mark Grace of NOAA Fisheries' Pascagoula, Miss., Laboratory, lead author of the new
25 study, who noted the shark displayed an unhealed umbilical scar. "Discovering him has us thinking about where mom and dad may be, and how they got to the Gulf. The only other known specimen
30 was found very far away, off Peru, 36 years ago."

Interestingly, the specimen Grace discovered wasn't found it the ocean, per se, but rather in the holdings of NOAA's
35 lab in Pascagoula. It was collected in the deep sea about 190 miles offshore Louisiana during a 2010 mission by the NOAA Ship *Pisces* to study sperm whale feeding. Grace, who was part of that
40 mission after the rare shark was collected, and upon uncovering the sample at the lab years later, recruited Tulane University researchers Michael Doosey and Henry Bart, and NOAA Ocean Service genetics
45 expert Gavin Naylor, to give the specimen an up-close examination.

A tissue sample was collected, and by tapping into the robust specimen collection of Tulane University's
50 Biodiversity Research Institute, scientists were able to place the specimen into the genus *Mollisquama*. Further genetic analysis from Naylor indicates that pocket sharks are closely related to the
55 kitefin and cookie cutter species, fellow members of the shark family *Dalatiidae*. Like other *Dalatiidae* shark species it is possible that pocket sharks when hungry may remove an oval plug of flesh from

60 their prey (various marine mammals, large fishes, and squid).

The specimen is part of the Royal D. Suttkus Fish Collection at Tulane University's Biodiversity Research

65 Institute in Belle Chasse, La., and it is hoped that further study of the specimen will lead to many new discoveries. Already, the specimen—when compared to the 1979 specimen taxonomic

70 description—is found to have a series of glands along the abdomen not previously noted. Partners at the Smithsonian National Museum of Natural History in Washington, D.C., and American Natural

75 History Museum in New York City have also contributed to the study of this shark.

"This record of such an unusual and extremely rare fish is exciting, but it's also an important reminder that we still

80 have much to learn about the species that inhabit our oceans," Grace added.

23 What does the article illustrate about how scientific information is gathered?

(A) Sometimes information can be lost for years but may be useful when found and shared.

(B) Scientists conduct many different kinds of tests on animals to get information about them.

(C) All scientific research is recorded in journals.

(D) Scientists in different locations often share their findings.

24 Why were scientists surprised at finding the shark?

(A) Scientists didn't know about it before.

(B) It was discovered by accident in a lab.

(C) It was thought to be extinct.

(D) Scientists thought it lived in colder waters.

25 Why was the finding reported in a journal of taxonomy?

(A) Because scientists wanted to test the DNA of this shark

(B) Because the scientific community was excited about a new species

(C) Because the journal specializes in marine animals

(D) Because scientists wanted to report such a rare species and how they classified it

26 Which choice provides the best evidence for the answer to the previous question?

(A) Lines 25–26 ("the shark … umbilical scar.")

(B) Lines 50–56 ("scientists were … Dalatiidae.")

(C) Lines 66–67 ("the specimen … new discoveries.")

(D) Lines 68–72 ("Already, the … previously noted.")

27 What information did scientists need to determine the species of the shark?

(A) The length of the shark

(B) The "pocket" feature that made it unique

(C) Tissue samples to provide genetic information

(D) Its position in the food chain

GO TO THE NEXT PAGE

Credit: Dr. Mark Grace, *Zootaxa 3948 (3): 587–600*

28 Based on the diagram above, where is the shark's pocket located?

(A) Above the pectoral fin
(B) Between the eye and the pectoral fin
(C) Above the eye on both sides of the shark
(D) In the spiracle

29 Why were scientists excited about the find?

(A) They expect to learn more about the habitat of the pocket shark.
(B) They will be able to learn more about what they eat.
(C) They can figure out how they are related to other sharks.
(D) They expect to be able to discover many new things about sharks.

30 Which choice provides the best evidence for the answer to the previous question?

(A) Lines 32–35 ("Interestingly … in Pascagoula")
(B) Lines 65–67 ("it is hoped that … new discoveries")
(C) Lines 52–55 ("Further genetic … cutter species")
(D) Lines 72–76 ("Partners at the … of this shark")

31 Based on its use in line 48, "robust" most nearly means

(A) typical.
(B) healthy.
(C) varied.
(D) distinguished.

32 As it is used in line 59, "plug" most nearly means

(A) lump.
(B) a protrusion.
(C) obstruction.
(D) scar.

QUESTIONS 33–42 ARE BASED ON THE FOLLOWING PASSAGE.

The following passage is excerpted from Mark Twain's essay, "Fenimore Cooper's Literary Offenses" (1895). James Fenimore Cooper (1789–1851) was a popular writer whose works were published in the first half of the 19th century.

[James Fenimore] Cooper's art has some defects. In one place in *Deerslayer*, and in the restricted space of two-thirds

Line of a page, Cooper has scored 114 offences
5 against literary art out of a possible 115.

…In his little box of stage properties he kept six or eight cunning devices. A favorite one was to make a moccasined person tread in the tracks of the
10 moccasined enemy, and thus hide his own trail. Cooper wore out barrels and barrels of moccasins in working that trick. Another stage-property that he pulled out of his box pretty frequently was his
15 broken twig. Every time a Cooper person is in peril, and absolute silence is worth four dollars a minute, he is sure to step on a dry twig. There may be a hundred handier things to step on, but … Cooper
20 requires him to turn out and find a dry twig; and if he can't do it, go and borrow one. In fact, the Leather Stocking Series ought to have been called the Broken Twig Series.
25 If Cooper had any real knowledge of Nature's ways of doing things, he had a most delicate art in concealing the fact. For instance: one of his acute Indian experts, Chingachgook (pronounced Chicago, I
30 think), has lost the trail of a person he is tracking through the forest. Neither you nor I could ever have guessed out the way to find it. It was very different with Chicago. He turned a running stream out of
35 its course, and there, in the slush in its old bed, were that person's moccasin-tracks. The current did not wash them away, as it would have done in all other like cases— no, even the eternal laws of Nature have
40 to vacate when Cooper wants to put up a delicate job of woodcraft on the reader.

…In the *Deerslayer* tale, Cooper has a stream which is fifty feet wide where it flows out of a lake; it narrows to twenty
45 as it meanders along for no given reason; and yet when a stream acts like that it ought to be required to explain itself. Cooper narrowed it to less than twenty to accommodate some Indians. He bends a
50 "sapling" to the form of an arch over this narrow passage, and conceals six Indians in its foliage. They are "laying" for a settler's scow or ark, which is coming up the stream on its way to the lake. Its rate of progress
55 cannot be more than a mile an hour.

The ark is one hundred and forty feet long; the dwelling is ninety feet long. The idea of the Indians is to drop softly and secretly from the arched sapling as the ark
60 creeps along under it. It will take the ark a minute and a half to pass under. It will take the ninety-foot dwelling a minute to pass under. Now, then, what did the six Indians do? It would take you thirty years
65 to guess. Their chief warily watched the canal-boat as it squeezed along under him, and when he had got his calculations fined down to exactly the right shade, as he judged, he let go and dropped. And
70 missed the house! He missed the house and landed in the stern of the scow. It was not much of a fall, yet it knocked him silly. He lay there unconscious. If the house had been ninety-seven feet long he
75 would have made the trip. The fault was Cooper's, not his. There still remained in the roost five Indians.

The boat has passed under and is now out of their reach. Let me explain what
80 the five did—you would not be able to reason it out for yourself. No. 1 jumped for the boat, but fell in the water astern of it. Then No. 2 jumped for the boat, but fell in the water still farther astern of it.
85 Then No. 3 jumped for the boat and fell a good way astern of it. Then No. 4 jumped for the boat and fell in the water away astern. Then even No. 5 made a jump for the boat—for he was a Cooper Indian ….
90 I may be mistaken, but it does seem to me that *Deerslayer* is not a work of art in any sense; it does seem to me that it is destitute of every detail that goes to the making of a work of art; in truth, it seems
95 to me that *Deerslayer* is just simply a literary delirium tremens.

GO TO THE NEXT PAGE

33 What is the most likely reason that Twain wrote this essay?

(A) To point out flaws in Cooper's works

(B) To make fun of a writer he didn't like

(C) To criticize Cooper's treatment of Native Americans

(D) To show the importance of literary criticism

34 Which of the following words best describe the tone of Twain's critique?

(A) Arrogant

(B) Scholarly

(C) Cheery

(D) Humorous

35 Which choice provides the best evidence for the answer to the previous question?

(A) Lines 4–5 ("Cooper has … possible 115.")

(B) Lines 11–12 ("Cooper wore … that trick")

(C) Line 89 ("for he … Cooper Indian")

(D) Lines 92–94 ("it does seem … work of art")

36 As used in line 6, "stage properties" most nearly means

(A) literary tricks.

(B) dramatic license.

(C) stage rules.

(D) scripts for a drama.

37 Why did Twain include a pronunciation guide to the Native American Indian name Chingachgook (line 29)?

(A) To make it easier for people to read his essay

(B) To mock Cooper's plot

(C) To show respect for the Native American tribe

(D) To illustrate that Cooper's work was about actual Native American peoples

38 Overall, what is the basic criticism Twain had of Cooper's work?

(A) His books are too long and complicated.

(B) His work has no artistic or literary value.

(C) His plots are unrealistic and not believable.

(D) His stories are boring.

39 Which choice provides the best evidence for the answer to the previous question?

(A) Lines 4–5 ("Cooper has … possible 115.")

(B) Lines 48–49 ("Cooper narrowed … some Indians.")

(C) Lines 79–81 ("Let me … for yourself.")

(D) Lines 88–89 ("Then even … Cooper Indian.")

40 According to Twain's criticism in the passage, how did Cooper characterize Native Americans?

(A) They were athletic and smart.

(B) They were simple-minded and inept.

(C) They were awkward and sneaky.

(D) They were sneaky and agile.

41 In line 50, Twain most likely puts "sapling" in quotation marks to emphasize that

(A) the word is not generally used anymore.

(B) Cooper uses the word excessively in his works.

(C) the description of the tree does not sound like a sapling.

(D) sapling is a Latin word used to describe certain kinds of trees.

42 As used in line 93, "destitute" most nearly means

(A) impoverished.

(B) full.

(C) void.

(D) capable.

QUESTIONS 43–52 ARE BASED ON THE FOLLOWING PASSAGE.

Pulitzer prize-winning writer Willa Cather worked as a reporter and also wrote several novels and short stories. This excerpt is from one of her more popular short stories, written in 1905.

Paul's Case: A Study in Temperament

It was Paul's afternoon to appear before the faculty of the Pittsburgh High School to account for his various
Line misdemeanors. He had been suspended
5 a week ago, and his father had called at the Principal's office and confessed his perplexity about his son. Paul entered the faculty room suave and smiling. His clothes were a trifle outgrown, and the tan
10 velvet on the collar of his open overcoat was frayed and worn; but for all that there was something of the dandy in him, and he wore an opal pin in his neatly knotted black four-in-hand, and a red carnation in
15 his buttonhole. This latter adornment the faculty somehow felt was not properly significant of the contrite spirit befitting a boy under the ban of suspension.

Paul was tall for his age and very
20 thin, with high, cramped shoulders and a narrow chest. His eyes were remarkable for a certain hysterical brilliancy, and he

continually used them in a conscious, theatrical sort of way, peculiarly offensive
25 in a boy. The pupils were abnormally large, as though he was addicted to belladonna, but there was a glassy glitter about them which that drug does not produce.
30 When questioned by the Principal as to why he was there Paul stated, politely enough, that he wanted to come back to school. This was a lie, but Paul was quite accustomed to lying; found it,
35 indeed, indispensable for overcoming friction. His teachers were asked to state their respective charges against him, which they did with such a rancor and aggrievedness as evinced that this was not
40 a usual case. Disorder and impertinence were among the offenses named, yet each of his instructors felt that it was scarcely possible to put into words the cause of the trouble, which lay in a sort of
45 hysterically defiant manner of the boy's; in the contempt which they all knew he felt for them, and which he seemingly made not the least effort to conceal. Once, when he had been making a synopsis
50 of a paragraph at the blackboard, his English teacher had stepped to his side and attempted to guide his hand. Paul had started back with a shudder and thrust his hands violently behind him.
55 The astonished woman could scarcely have been more hurt and embarrassed had he struck at her. The insult was so involuntary and definitely personal as to be unforgettable. In one way and another
60 he had made all of his teachers, men and women alike, conscious of the same feeling of physical aversion. In one class he habitually sat with his hand shading his eyes; in another he always looked out the
65 window during the recitation; in another he made a running commentary on the lecture, with humorous intention.

His teachers felt this afternoon that his whole attitude was symbolized by
70 his shrug and his flippantly red carnation flower, and they fell upon him without mercy, his English teacher leading the pack. He stood through it smiling, his pale lips parted over his white teeth. (His

GO TO THE NEXT PAGE

75 lips were constantly twitching, and he
    had a habit of raising his eyebrows that
    was contemptuous and irritating to the
    last degree.) Older boys than Paul had
    broken down and shed tears under that
80 baptism of fire, but his set smile did not
    once desert him, and his only sign of
    discomfort was the nervous trembling of
    the fingers that toyed with the buttons of
    his overcoat, and an occasional jerking of
85 the other hand that held his hat. Paul was
    always smiling, always glancing about
    him, seeming to feel that people might
    be watching him and trying to detect
    something. This conscious expression,
90 since it was as far as possible from boyish
    mirthfulness, was usually attributed to
    insolence or "smartness."

43 Based on the passage, what is the best way
     to describe the story?

(A) It's a character study.

(B) It's an account of a real-life character.

(C) It's a psychological story with a
    complicated plot.

(D) It's a story that emphasizes the
    setting.

44 What was the reason that Paul was asked
     to go to the principal's office?

(A) To explain to the teachers why he
    wanted to return to school

(B) To explain to the faculty why he had
    been misbehaving

(C) To explain to the principal why he
    was late for class

(D) To explain to his parents why he had
    been suspended

45 Why did Paul wear a red carnation?

(A) To show respect for the faculty

(B) To show remorse

(C) To make himself appear wealthy

(D) To defy the faculty

46 We can infer from the passage that the feel-
     ings of Paul's teachers toward him may be
     described as mostly

(A) frustration and anger.

(B) sadness and confusion.

(C) scorn and disdain.

(D) hope and tenderness.

47 Which choice provides the best evidence
     for the answer to the previous question?

(A) Lines 4–7 ("He had been … about his
    son.")

(B) Lines 15–18 ("This latter … ban of
    suspension.")

(C) Lines 36–40 ("His teachers … not a
    usual case.")

(D) Lines 59–62 ("In one way …
    physical aversion.")

48 From whose perspective or viewpoint is
     the story told?

(A) Paul

(B) The narrator

(C) A psychologist

(D) The school principal

49 How does Cather show a connection be-
     tween Paul's feelings and his actions?

(A) She describes how subtle signals
    reflect Paul's mood or disposition.

(B) She describes his reactions compared
    to how others would react in similar
    circumstances.

(C) She gives details about his physical
    appearance and that of the teachers.

(D) She provides details about his
    behavior and the way it is interpreted
    by others.

50 Which choice provides the best evidence for the answer to the previous question?

(A) Lines 78–85 ("He stood … white teeth.")

(B) Lines 74–78 ("His lips were … last degree.")

(C) Lines 78–85 ("Older boys … his hat.")

(D) Lines 89–92 ("This conscious … or 'smartness.'")

51 Based on the passage, which meaning of the word "temperament" best fits the story?

(A) Complexion

(B) Adjustment

(C) Mood

(D) Personality

52 As in line 12, "dandy" most nearly means someone who

(A) is first-rate in his class.

(B) dresses with elegance and care.

(C) is carefree.

(D) is brilliant.

STOP

**If you finish before time is called, you may check your work on this section only.
Do not turn to any other section.**

practice test

No Test Material On This Page

SECTION 2: WRITING AND LANGUAGE TEST

35 Minutes • 44 Questions

TURN TO SECTION 2 OF YOUR ANSWER SHEET TO ANSWER THE QUESTIONS IN THIS SECTION.

Directions: Each passage below is accompanied by a number of multiple-choice questions. For some questions, you will need to consider how the passage might be revised to improve the expression of ideas. Other questions will ask you to consider how the passage might be edited to correct errors in sentence structure, usage, or punctuation. A passage may be accompanied by one or more graphics—such as a chart, table, or graph—that you will need to refer to in order to best answer the question(s).

Some questions will direct you to an underlined portion of a passage—it could be one word, a portion of a sentence, or the full sentence itself. Other questions will direct you to a particular paragraph or to certain sentences within a paragraph, or you'll be asked to think about the passage as a whole. Each question number refers to the corresponding number in the passage.

After reading each passage, select the answer to each question that most effectively improves the quality of writing in the passage or that makes the passage follow the conventions of Standard Written English. Many questions include a "NO CHANGE" option. Select that option if you think the best choice is to leave that specific portion of the passage as it is.

QUESTIONS 1–11 ARE BASED ON THE FOLLOWING PASSAGE.

Elizabeth Blackwell, the Doctor

On January 23, 1849, in the town of Geneva, New York, Elizabeth Blackwell stepped onto the altar of the Presbyterian church and received her medical degree from the president of Geneva Medical College. **1** In doing so, she took her place in history. Blackwell had **2** denounced the expectations of most of her teachers and classmates to become the country's first female doctor.

As a young woman, Blackwell had worked as a school teacher, but she found herself unsatisfied. Once she realized that her dream was to be a doctor, she faced tremendous obstacles. There had never before been a

1 The writer is considering deleting the underlined sentence. Should the writer do this?

(A) Yes, because the historical importance of this event is irrelevant.

(B) Yes, because Blackwell has already been introduced.

(C) No, because it establishes the importance of Blackwell's accomplishment.

(D) No, because it tells us what Blackwell did to become famous.

2

(A) NO CHANGE
(B) defied
(C) incited
(D) encountered

GO TO THE
NEXT PAGE

female physician in America. At the time, educating a boy was considered **3** far more important than a girl. Blackwell's education did not prepare her for the challenges of medical school, and she had to work hard just to catch up. **4** To make up for the gaps in her education, the household of a physician became her home for the next several years. There, she had access to educational resources and received some medical training.

5 As she prepared to apply to medical school, Blackwell sought advice from physicians in New York and Philadelphia. She found that they **6** doubted she would be admitted to medical school; at least one advisor went so far as to suggest that she might disguise herself as a man in order to gain admittance. **7** Their advisors were not far from wrong in their prediction. Blackwell applied to well over a dozen medical colleges, but she received admission to only one— Geneva Medical College.

3
(A) NO CHANGE
(B) far more important than it was to a girl.
(C) far more important than educating a girl.
(D) far more important than opportunities for girls.

4
(A) NO CHANGE
(B) A physician's household, to make up for the gaps in her education, became her home for the next several years.
(C) Her home for the next several years, to make up for the gaps in her education, became a physician's household.
(D) To make up for the gaps in her education, she arranged to live in the household of a physician for the next several years.

5 Which choice provides the most logical introduction to the sentence?
(A) NO CHANGE
(B) After finishing medical school,
(C) While attending university,
(D) Before she applied to be a psychologist,

6
(A) NO CHANGE
(B) debated
(C) insisted
(D) supposed

7
(A) NO CHANGE
(B) Her
(C) His
(D) Your

Gaining admission to the college **8** <u>has become</u> the first in a long line of obstacles for Blackwell. She discovered that her fellow **9** <u>students all of whom were men had</u> elected as a joke to admit her to the medical program and were astonished when she actually showed up at the college to enroll for classes. The students were embarrassed by her presence in lectures on topics—such as human anatomy—that they considered unsuitable for mixed company.

Steadily, and with perseverance, Blackwell gained acceptance among the students and faculty. After she completed her degree, she continued **10** <u>to face prejudice, biases against her because she was a woman, and outright barriers to her career.</u> She was unable to establish the private practice she had hoped for. Nevertheless, Blackwell was successful, **11** <u>but when she went to study at a hospital in Paris, she was assigned the same duties as young girls with no education at all.</u>

8

(A) NO CHANGE
(B) becomes
(C) became
(D) will become

9

(A) NO CHANGE
(B) students all, of whom, were men had
(C) students all of whom, were men had
(D) students, all of whom were men, had

10

(A) NO CHANGE
(B) to face prejudice and outright barriers to her career
(C) to face barriers, many of which included prejudice and bias against her
(D) to face barriers that obstructed her career and included bias because she was a woman

11 Which choice most effectively maintains support for claims or points in the text?

(A) NO CHANGE
(B) but she is remembered for having been the first woman in America to receive a medical degree
(C) and she had a distinguished career as a promoter of preventative medicine and as a champion of medical opportunities for women
(D) but she lived an interesting life and had many opportunities to travel widely and meet new people

GO TO THE NEXT PAGE

QUESTIONS 12–22 ARE BASED ON THE FOLLOWING PASSAGE.

Rachel Carson, Protector of the Environment

Today we can hardly imagine a world without newspapers and magazines that express concern about the environment. **12** Carson, a former marine biologist for the Fish and Game Service, **13** <u>ruffled the feathers of a ton of people</u> who had a vested interest in maintaining the status quo where the environment was concerned. Her credibility as a scientist and her personal courage enabled Carson to withstand the criticism heaped on her during her lifetime.

12 At this point, the writer is considering adding the following sentence:

But in 1962, when Rachel Carson's *Silent Spring* was published, this was not the case.

Should the writer do this?

(A) Yes, because it provides the reader with an exact date.

(B) Yes, because it establishes historical attitudes about the environment.

(C) No, because it inserts irrelevant information about an unimportant book.

(D) No, because it divides the paragraph's focus between the book and Carson.

13

(A) NO CHANGE
(B) aggravated a lot of folks
(C) inflamed the outsized egos of those
(D) disturbed many

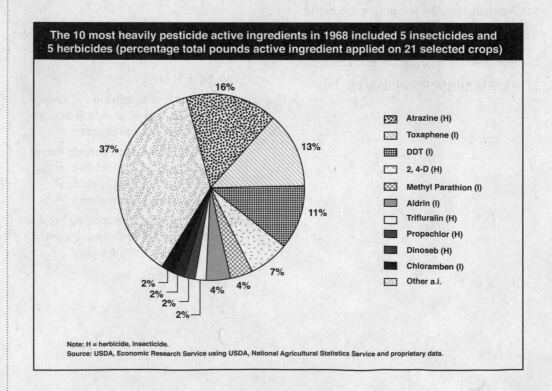

The 10 most heavily pesticide active ingredients in 1968 included 5 insecticides and 5 herbicides (percentage total pounds active ingredient applied on 21 selected crops)

Atrazine (H)
Toxaphene (I)
DDT (I)
2, 4-D (H)
Methyl Parathion (I)
Aldrin (I)
Trifluralin (H)
Propachlor (H)
Dinoseb (H)
Chloramben (I)
Other a.i.

Note: H = herbicide, insecticide.
Source: USDA, Economic Research Service using USDA, National Agricultural Statistics Service and proprietary data.

And what exactly was it that Rachel Carson did that was so **14** disturbing. She pointed out the dangers of **15** pesticides—DDT in particular—to the environment. DDT was designed to contain insect pests in gardens and on farmland after World War II. Most people considered it a "wonder chemical," **16** and by 1968, they used DDT to cover approximately 11% of all farmland.

Rachel Carson believed, however, that the pesticides were **17** dehydrating the soil and the rivers, and adhering to tree leaves and branches that were the home for birds and beneficial insects. She contended that the levels of chemical pesticides in plants, animals, and humans had already reached alarming levels. In her view, **18** they were so potent that they were able to penetrate systems and remain

14

(A) NO CHANGE
(B) disturbing?
(C) disturbing!
(D) disturbing:

15

(A) NO CHANGE
(B) pesticides—DDT in particular to
(C) pesticides DDT in particular,
(D) pesticides (DDT) in particular to

16 Which choice completes the sentence with accurate data based on the chart?

(A) NO CHANGE
(B) and in fact, by 1968, DDT accounted for 11% of all pesticides used.
(C) as it was believed to contain approximately 11% of all garden pests.
(D) though only about 11% of all farmers and gardeners actually used it.

17

(A) NO CHANGE
(B) appropriating
(C) transcending
(D) permeating

18

(A) NO CHANGE
(B) it was
(C) the pesticides were
(D) everything was

practice test

there for years, **19** giving way to possible improvements in general health and well-being.

The furor caused by Carson's writing was mostly felt by the chemical companies that produced pesticides. Not willing to **20** contradict the potential hazards of their products, they resisted by seeking to discredit Carson. And despite her credentials, Carson was discredited for a period of time. However, in 1970, with the establishment of the Environmental Protection Agency, the nation became more concerned with issues that Carson had raised.

Since 2001, DDT has been banned for agricultural use worldwide except in small quantities and only as part of a plan to transition to safer alternatives. The only places in which DDT is still allowed are those countries in which it is being used to combat malaria. **21** Since malaria kills more than 800,000 people every year, most of them children in Sub-Saharan Africa, Carson has been blamed for "millions of deaths," despite the studies that show that the pesticide can contribute to cancers, male infertility, miscarriages, developmental delay in children, and damage to the liver and nervous system.

Were it not for those like Rachel Carson, **22** DDT would probably still be seen as "wonder chemicals," and the only way to combat malaria. Though still controversial, she was a scientist of vision and determination who changed the course of history and brought environmental issues to the world's attention.

19 Which choice best completes the sentence and remains consistent with Carson's argument about pesticides?

(A) NO CHANGE
(B) providing a definitive link between cancer and pesticides.
(C) leading to an alarming decrease in local bird populations.
(D) potentially leading to a breakdown in tissue and immune systems.

20

(A) NO CHANGE
(B) acknowledge
(C) propagate
(D) solicit

21

(A) NO CHANGE
(B) Although malaria kills 800,000 people every year, most of them children in Sub-Saharan Africa, Carson
(C) Malaria kills 800,000 people every year, most of them children in Sub-Saharan Africa. Carson
(D) Malaria kills 800,000 people every year, most of them children in Sub-Saharan Africa; however, Carson

22

(A) NO CHANGE
(B) pesticides with DDT would probably still be seen as a "wonder chemical,"
(C) DDT would probably still be seen as a "wonder chemical,"
(D) DDT would probably still be seen as chemicals that are wondrous.

QUESTIONS 23–33 ARE BASED ON THE FOLLOWING PASSAGE.

A Mayan Worldview

The ancient Mayans inhabited the area that now consists of **23** Mexico; Guatemala, Belize, Honduras; and El Salvador. Their rich civilization flourished from the third through the ninth centuries. **24** Among the many notable achievements of this society were the Mayan understanding of astronomy, which was manifest not only in Mayan science but in every aspect of the culture.

Ancient Mayans kept meticulous records of the movements of **25** the Sun, Moon, the planets' movement, and the stars that were visible to the naked eye. Based on the solar year, they created a calendar which they used to keep track of time. So **26** astute were the Mayans' observations that they could predict such events as solar and lunar eclipses, and **27** the movement of the planets.

23

(A) NO CHANGE
(B) Mexico, Guatemala, Belize, Honduras, and El Salvador.
(C) Mexico, Guatemala, Belize, Honduras; El Salvador.
(D) Mexico; Guatemala; Belize; Honduras; El Salvador.

24

(A) NO CHANGE
(B) Among the many notable achievements of this society are the Mayan understanding of astronomy,
(C) Among the many notable achievements of this society is the Mayan understanding of astronomy,
(D) Among the many notable achievements of this society was the Mayan understanding of astronomy,

25

(A) NO CHANGE
(B) the Sun, Moon, planets, and the movement of the stars
(C) the Sun, the Moon, the planets, and the stars
(D) the Sun and Moon, the movement of the planets, and the stars

26

(A) NO CHANGE
(B) inept
(C) distinguished
(D) profound

27 Which choice gives a supporting example that is most similar to the example already in the sentence?

(A) NO CHANGE
(B) the migration of birds.
(C) the direction of the winds.
(D) the flow of the tides.

GO TO THE NEXT PAGE

practice test

For the ancient Mayans, astronomy was not just a science; it was a combination of science, religion, and philosophy that found **28** it's way into many aspects of their lives, including architecture. Mayan ceremonial buildings, for example, were exactly aligned with compass points, so that at the fall and spring equinoxes, light would flood the interior of the building. These buildings were designed and built as acts of worship to the **29** Mayan gods. Science, architecture, and religion, then, were all intricately and beautifully blended.

Government, too, was **30** correspondingly linked with astronomy. The beginning and ending of the reigns of Mayan leaders appear to have been timed to coincide with astronomical events. Ancient Mayan artwork, carvings and murals show royalty wearing **31** symbols: relating to the sun, moon, and sky. The Mayans believed that the Sun and Moon were guided across the sky by benevolent gods, and that these gods needed human help to thwart the evil gods who wanted to stop them. Human intervention took the form of different rituals, including sacrifice. It was considered an honor to die for this cause, and those who were sacrificed were believed to have gained eternal life.

The planet Venus, which can often be seen by the unaided eye, played a large role in Mayan life. The Mayans used the appearance of Venus in the sky as a means of timing when they attacked enemies. The night sky, among its other duties, could then serve as a **32** harvest calendar.

28

(A) NO CHANGE
(B) its'
(C) its
(D) its's

29 Which choice most effectively combines the two sentences at the underlined portion?

(A) Mayan gods: science
(B) Mayan gods; science
(C) Mayan gods, science
(D) Mayan gods, but

30

(A) NO CHANGE
(B) ostensibly
(C) comparatively
(D) inextricably

31

(A) NO CHANGE
(B) symbols, relating to the sun, moon, and sky.
(C) symbols relating to the sun, moon, and sky.
(D) symbols; relating to the sun, moon, and sky.

32 Which choice provides information that best supports the focus of this paragraph?

(A) NO CHANGE
(B) reminder of the season
(C) reference point for direction
(D) call to war

33 In short, the ancient Mayans, in looking to the night sky for guidance, discovered a natural order around which they were able to base a rich and textured civilization.

33

(A) NO CHANGE
(B) However,
(C) Moreover,
(D) Incidentally,

QUESTIONS 34–44 ARE BASED ON THE FOLLOWING PASSAGE.

The Real World

Our college employment counseling center recommended that students have mock interviews before setting out into the world for the real thing. **34** For reasons that I still don't understand, I believed that this applied to other people but not to me. Midway **35** thorough my senior year of college, I sent out resumes to several law firms in the area. I didn't consult with anybody about how to begin seeking a job. My plan was to work at a law firm for a couple of years before attending law school. I received a couple of responses and was thrilled to set up **36** our first interview, at a prestigious law firm that had offices all over the world. **37** It was exactly the type of environment in which I envisioned myself.

34 Which choice provides the most logical introduction to the sentence?

(A) NO CHANGE
(B) Because I already had a job,
(C) Now that I was ready,
(D) Based on what they suggested,

35

(A) NO CHANGE
(B) threw
(C) though
(D) through

36

(A) NO CHANGE
(B) his
(C) my
(D) their

37 Which choice most effectively maintains the paragraph's focus on relevant information and ideas?

(A) NO CHANGE
(B) I had heard from my aunt that my cousin once applied for a job there.
(C) I had worked for other big companies, including a fast-food restaurant in high school.
(D) Growing up, my next-door neighbor was a successful lawyer for a big law firm.

GO TO THE NEXT PAGE

The position for which I was interviewing was a clerical job that, the interviewer made clear from the outset, would require long hours, late nights and a great deal of filing and photocopying. I confidently announced to the interviewer that I didn't mind long hours and thankless assignments. **38** And then happily informed him that I wanted to work my way up and someday be his boss. I figured the surprised look on his face was because he wasn't used to seeing young men as ambitious and **39** enigmatic as I was. I would have kept going, had he not suggested moving on to another topic.

[1] I'm sorry to say that here I left nothing to the imagination. [2] I believed that my interviewer would value my stark honesty when I told him that my greatest **40** weakness's included not getting along with other people very well and a tendency to make more enemies than friends. **41** [3] In the next phase of the interview, I was asked to list my strengths and weaknesses. [4] The interviewer raised his eyebrows but said nothing, and I was certain that he knew he'd found his candidate. [5] After all, **42** I could've cared less about getting along with other people and I figured I wouldn't need to get along with people to photocopy and file, so I'd hit upon the perfect answer to a tricky question.

38

(A) NO CHANGE
(B) After happily informing him that I wanted to work my way up and someday be his boss.
(C) Which is why I happily informed him that I wanted to work my way up and someday be his boss.
(D) Then I happily informed him that I wanted to work my way up and someday be his boss.

39

(A) NO CHANGE
(B) articulate
(C) conspicuous
(D) incoherent

40

(A) NO CHANGE
(B) weaknesses'
(C) weaknesses
(D) weakness'

41 For the sake of cohesion, sentence 3 of this paragraph should be placed

(A) where it is now.
(B) before sentence 1.
(C) before sentence 2.
(D) before sentence 5.

42

(A) NO CHANGE
(B) I could have cared less
(C) I could of cared less
(D) I couldn't have cared less

43 I did not get offered that job, nor the next several for which I interviewed at other firms. Eventually I paid a **44** deferred trip to the college job counseling office and got a few pointers on my technique. I am happy to say that while I never did end up going to law school, I have become a high school guidance counselor who specializes in helping students find internships in community businesses.

43 Which choice most effectively establishes the main topic of the paragraph?

(A) After being turned down for several jobs, the narrator eventually sought help for his interviewing technique and now helps students find internships.

(B) Because the narrator was turned down for several jobs, he decided against becoming a lawyer and instead became a high school guidance counselor.

(C) Because the narrator told the interviewer that he didn't care about getting along with others, he was not offered the job.

(D) The narrator eventually became a high school guidance counselor who specializes in helping his students find internships.

44

(A) NO CHANGE
(B) belated
(C) hastened
(D) disparaged

STOP

If you finish before time is called, you may check your work on this section only. Do not turn to any other section.

No Test Material On This Page

SECTION 3: MATH TEST—NO CALCULATOR

20 Questions • 25 minutes

TURN TO SECTION 3 OF YOUR ANSWER SHEET TO ANSWER THE QUESTIONS IN THIS SECTION.

Directions: For Questions 1–15, solve each problem, select the best answer from the choices provided, and fill in the corresponding oval on your answer sheet. **For Questions 16–20,** solve the problem and enter your answer in the grid on the answer sheet. The directions **before Question 16** will provide information on how to enter your answers in the grid.

ADDITIONAL INFORMATION:

- The use of a calculator in this section **is not permitted.**
- All variables and expressions used represent real numbers unless otherwise indicated.
- Figures provided in this test are drawn to scale unless otherwise indicated.
- All figures lie in a plane unless otherwise indicated.
- Unless otherwise specified, the domain of a given function *f* is the set of all real numbers *x* for which *f(x)* is a real number.

The number of degrees of arc in a circle is 360.
The number of radians in the arc of a circle is 2π.
The sum of the measures in degrees of the angles of a triangle is 180.

1 Jared is beginning to track the number of steps he walks each day. Yesterday he walked 950 steps. He set a goal of increasing his steps per day by 125, with an eventual goal of walking at least 3,000 steps per day. Which of the following functions can be used to determine the number of steps Jared plans to take *d* days from yesterday?

(A) $f(d) = 3000 - (950 + 125d)$

(B) $f(d) = 3000 - 125d$

(C) $f(d) = 950 + 125d$

(D) $f(d) = 950 - 125d$

2 If $f(1) = 3$, $f(3) = -1$, $g(3) = 1$, and $g(-1) = 3$, what is the value of $f(g(3))$?

(A) -3

(B) -1

(C) 1

(D) 3

3 The amount of radioactive iodine 131 that remains in an object after d days is found using the formula

$$y = a(0.5)^{\frac{d}{8.02}}.$$

What does a represent in the formula?

(A) The number of days for the object to lose half of its radioactive iodine 131

(B) The initial amount of radioactive iodine 131

(C) The amount of radioactive iodine 131 after d days

(D) The amount of radioactive iodine 131 lost each day

4 An architect is designing the roof of a house. The peak of the roof is 8 ft. above the house. If the outside of the roof is separated into two parts, how long is each part from the peak of the roof to its edge?

(A) 15 ft.

(B) 17 ft.

(C) 23 ft.

(D) 31 ft.

5 $y = 2(x - 5)^2 - 2$

Which equation is equivalent to the equation above and shows the x-intercepts as constants?

(A) $y = 2x^2 - 20x + 48$

(B) $y = 2(x^2 - 10x + 24)$

(C) $y = 2(x - 4)(x - 6)$

(D) $y = (2x - 8)(x - 6)$

6 Which of the following graphs represents the equation $3x + y = 4$?

(A)

(B)

(C)

(D)

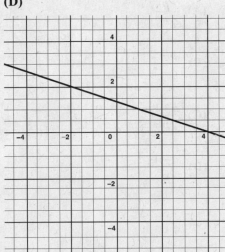

7 Which of the following is an equation for the line through the point (2, 3) with a slope of –1?

(A) $2x + 3y = -1$

(B) $3x + 3y = 15$

(C) $3x + 2y = 10$

(D) $x + y = -5$

8 Which of the following expressions is equivalent to

$$\frac{3}{4}(x-4)(3+5x)?$$

(A) $\dfrac{3x^2}{4} - 15x - 9$

(B) $\dfrac{9x^2}{4} - \dfrac{7x}{4} - 15$

(C) $\dfrac{15x^2}{4} - \dfrac{51x}{4} - 9$

(D) $\dfrac{15x^2}{4} - \dfrac{69x}{4} - 9$

9

Which of the following is equal to $x^{\frac{3}{4}}$?

(A) $4x^3$

(B) $3x^4$

(C) $\sqrt[4]{x^3}$

(D) $\sqrt[3]{x^4}$

10 Which of the following is the equation for the graph of a parabola that has a vertex at (3, –5) and a y-intercept at 13?

(A) $y - 28 = (x - 3)(x + 5)$

(B) $y = 2(x - 3)^2 - 5$

(C) $y = (x - 3)^2 - 13$

(D) $y = x^2 - 6x + 13$

GO TO THE NEXT PAGE

practice test

11 The admission cost for a play is $12 for adults and $7 for children. Which system of equations can be used to determine the number of adults and number of children that attended if 117 people attended the play and the total amount collected for admission was $1,079?

(A) $12x + 7y = 117$
$x + y = 1079$

(B) $12x + y = 117$
$x + 7y = 1079$

(C) $12x + 7y = 1079$
$x + y = 117$

(D) $x + 7y = 117$
$12x + y = 1079$

12 Which of the following is equivalent to $\dfrac{4 - i}{3 + i}$

that can be found by multiplying by the complex conjugate of the denominator?

(A) $\dfrac{1}{3}$

(B) $\dfrac{17}{11 + 7i}$

(C) $\dfrac{11 - 7i}{10}$

(D) $\dfrac{13 + i}{8}$

13 What is the solution to the equation $-6(t + 1) = 2(1 - 3t) - 8$?

(A) −8
(B) −6
(C) No solution
(D) Infinitely many solutions

14 A small city in Spain grows at an average rate of 1.7% a year. The population of the city in 1980 was 2,845. The equation that models the city's population in 1990 is $P = 2845e^{(0.017)(10)}$. What does 10 represent in the equation?

(A) The city's population in 1980
(B) The number of years
(C) The city's average grown rate
(D) The factor of increase of the city's population each year

15 If p and q are positive and $\dfrac{2p + 2n}{qn} = 2$,

which of the following is equivalent to n?

(A) $\dfrac{p}{q - 1}$

(B) $\dfrac{p - 1}{q - 1}$

(C) $\dfrac{q + 1}{p}$

(D) $\dfrac{q - 1}{p}$

Directions: For Questions 16-20, solve the problem and enter your answer in the grid, as described below, on the answer sheet.

1. Although not required, it is suggested that you write your answer in the boxes at the top of the columns to help you fill in the circles accurately. You will receive credit only if the circles are filled in correctly.

2. Mark no more than one circle in any column.

3. No question has a negative answer.

4. Some problems may have more than one correct answer. In such cases, grid only one answer.

5. **Mixed numbers** such as $3\frac{1}{2}$ must be gridded as 3.5 or $\frac{7}{2}$.

   If $3\frac{1}{2}$ is entered into the grid as $\boxed{3\,1\,/\,2}$, it will be interpreted as $\frac{31}{2}$, not $3\frac{1}{2}$.)

6. **Decimal answers:** If you obtain a decimal answer with more digits than the grid can accommodate, it may be either rounded or truncated, but it must fill the entire grid.

GO TO THE
NEXT PAGE

16 If $\sqrt{x+1} - 2 = 3$, what is the value of x?

19
$$y = 3x + 7$$
$$4x - ty = 5$$

According to the system of equations above, what is the value of b that makes the system of equations have no solutions?

17 If $f(x) = 3x - 2$, for what value of x does $f(x)$ equal 1?

20 A spherical scoop of ice cream is placed on top of a hollow ice cream cone. The scoop and cone have the same radius. The ice cream melts completely and it fills the cone to the top. How many times greater is the height of the cone than the radius of the cone?

18
$$\frac{3x^2 - 4x - 18}{x + 3} = 3x - c + \frac{21}{x + 3}$$

What is the value for c that will make the equation above true?

STOP

If you finish before time is called, you may check your work on this section only.
Do not turn to any other section.

SECTION 4: MATH TEST—CALCULATOR 🖩

38 Questions • 55 minutes

TURN TO SECTION 4 OF YOUR ANSWER SHEET TO ANSWER THE QUESTIONS IN THIS SECTION.

Directions: **For Questions 1–30,** solve each problem, select the best answer from the choices provided, and fill in the corresponding oval on your answer sheet. **For Questions 31–38,** solve the problem and enter your answer in the grid on the answer sheet. The directions **before Question 31** will provide information on how to enter your answers in the grid.

ADDITIONAL INFORMATION:

- The use of a calculator is **permitted.**

- All variables and expressions used represent real numbers unless otherwise indicated.

- Figures provided in this test are drawn to scale unless otherwise indicated.

- All figures lie in a plane unless otherwise indicated.

- Unless otherwise specified, the domain of a given function f is the set of all real numbers x for which f(x) is a real number.

Reference Information

Circle:
$C = 2\pi r$
$A = \pi r^2$

Rectangle:
$A = lw$

Triangle:
$A = \dfrac{1}{2}bh$
$a^2 + b^2 = c^2$

Rectangular Solid:
$V = lwh$

Cylinder:
$V = \pi r^2 h$

Sphere:
$V = \dfrac{4}{3}\pi r^3$

Cone:
$V = \dfrac{1}{3}\pi r^2 h$

Rectangular Based Pyramid:
$V = \dfrac{1}{3}lwh$

The number of degrees of arc in a circle is 360.
The number of radians in the arc of a circle is 2π.
The sum of the measures in degrees of the angles of a triangle is 180.

1 A certain insect is estimated to travel 1,680 feet per year. At this rate, about how many months would it take for the insect to travel 560 feet?

(A) 0.75
(B) 3
(C) 4
(D) 5.5

2 A librarian is tracking the circulation of books at the library. In one day of checking books, 18 were renewed, 46 were returned on time, and 11 were returned late. At this rate, about how many books will be renewed if the library loans 25,000 books each year?

(A) 4,000
(B) 6,000
(C) 9,000
(D) 15,000

🔲

3

	Smalltown	Littletown	Total
Male	175	210	385
Female	195	205	400
Total	370	415	785

Smalltown and Littletown are two towns in Tinytown County. The table above shows the distribution of population of males and females of the towns. If a person from the county is selected at random, what is the probability that the person will be either a male from Littletown or a female from Smalltown?

(A) $\dfrac{39}{74}$

(B) $\dfrac{42}{83}$

(C) $\dfrac{56}{157}$

(D) $\dfrac{81}{157}$

4 A pink dogwood tree has an average growth rate of 0.36 inches per week. Based on the average growth rate, if a pink dogwood tree was newly planted, what would its height, in inches, be in 10 years?

(A) 43.2 inches

(B) 187.2 inches

(C) 218 inches

(D) 360 inches

5 Glen earns $10.25 per hour and pays $12.50 per day to commute to and from work on the bus. He wants to make sure that he works long enough to earn at least three times as much as he spends commuting. Which of the following inequalities best represents this situation?

(A) $10.25h \geq 3(12.50)$

(B) $3(10.25) \geq 12.50h$

(C) $3(10.25h) \geq 12.50$

(D) $h \geq 3(12.50)(10.25)$

6 Nadia spent 7 more hours on math homework last month than Peter. If they spent total of 35 hours doing math homework last month, how many hours did Peter spend on math homework?

(A) 7

(B) 14

(C) 21

(D) 28

7 If c is 22 percent of e and d is 68 percent of e, what is $d - c$ in terms of e?

(A) $90e$

(B) $46e$

(C) $0.9e$

(D) $0.46e$

8

$$2x - 9y < 12$$
$$-3x + 4y > 5$$

Which of the following is a solution to the system of inequalities shown above?

(A) $(-4, -4)$

(B) $(-4, 4)$

(C) $(4, -4)$

(D) $(4, 4)$

9 If n = 7, what is $2m(16 - 6n)$ in terms of *m*?

(A) $-52m$

(B) $-15m$

(C) $-14m$

(D) $32m$

10 Tessa wants to raise a total of $250 for her favorite charity. She has already raised $145. Tessa asks for $15 contributions from each person she contacts. Which equation best represents this situation?

(A) $15x = 250$

(B) $145(15x) = 250$

(C) $145 + 15x = 250$

(D) $145 - 15x = 250$

QUESTIONS 11 AND 12 REFER TO THE FOLLOWING INFORMATION.

A class raised money selling t-shirts, and then began selling hats. The graph represents the total amount of money in the class account as the number of hats sold increases.

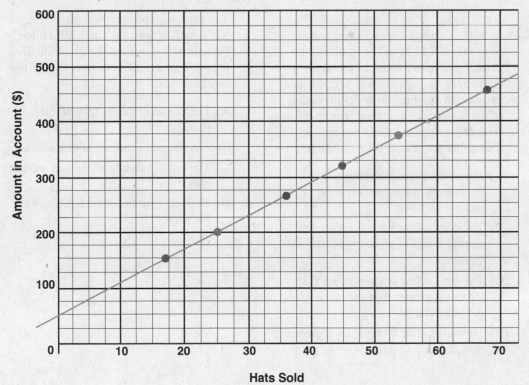

11 According to the graph, which of the following best approximates the number of hats that must be sold for the class to have raised a total of $400

(A) 54

(B) 58

(C) 64

(D) 68

12 What does the slope of the line signify?

(A) The amount of money already raised

(B) The amount of money raised by selling each hat

(C) The number of hats that are sold

(D) The number of hats that must be sold to meet the fundraising goal

GO TO THE
NEXT PAGE

🔢

13 A survey was conducted to determine whether the voters in a city of 38,000 would support funding a new park. A sample of 18 voters randomly selected from the voting list revealed that 11 voters favored funding the park, 4 voters did not want to fund the park, and 3 voters had no preference. Which of the following makes it least likely that a reliable conclusion can be drawn from the data?

(A) The size of the sample population

(B) The size of the city's population

(C) The number of people with no preference

(D) How the sample population was selected

14 In 2010, a census showed a city had a population of 22,500. The results of the census also showed that the mean income of the population was $72,350, and the median income was $65,580. Which of the following could describe the difference between the mean income and the median income of the population?

(A) Most of the income values are between the mean and median income values.

(B) There are a few income values that are much less than the other income values.

(C) There are a few income values that are much greater than the other income values.

(D) The range in income values is greater than the income value.

15 A group of h neighbors has 1,230 CDs they are selling at a yard sale. If each neighbor sells on average x CDs per day for j days of the yard sale, which of the following represents the total number of CDs that will be left when the yard sale is over?

(A) $1230 - jhx$

(B) $1230 - hx - j$

(C) $1230 - \dfrac{jx}{h}$

(D) $1230 + \dfrac{jx}{h}$

16 $y = -16x^2 + 50x + 2$

The equation above represents the height y of a ball, in feet, x seconds after it has been thrown upwards. Which of the following best describes the meaning of the coefficient 50?

(A) The height of the ball when it is thrown

(B) The height of the ball after x seconds

(C) The initial velocity of the ball when it is thrown

(D) The acceleration of the ball's upward velocity

QUESTIONS 17 AND 18 REFER TO THE FOLLOWING INFORMATION.

Quinn is moving across the state and needs to rent a moving truck that will fit her belongings. The table below shows the mileage rate and daily rental cost for trucks from three different companies.

	Mileage rate, b, in cents per mile	Rental rate, a, in dollars per day
Company J	15	19
Company K	10	30
Company L	12	25

The total cost, y, for renting the truck for one day and driving x miles is found by using the formula $y = a + 0.01bx$.

17 For which numbers of miles x is the cost of renting from Company J less than renting from Company K?

(A) $x < 44$
(B) $x < 55$
(C) $x < 220$
(D) $x < 980$

18 If the relationship between the total cost, y, of renting the truck from Company L and driving it x miles for one day is graphed in the xy-plane, what does the slope of the line represent?

(A) The daily rental cost for the truck
(B) The cost to drive the truck each mile
(C) The total cost for the miles driven
(D) The total cost for renting and driving the truck

QUESTIONS 19 AND 20 REFER TO THE FOLLOWING INFORMATION.

A sample of the population in two neighborhood towns, Town A and Town B, was surveyed in order to determine the most popular types of house styles. The results of the survey are shown in the table.

TYPES OF HOUSES

House Style	Ranch	Colonial	Cape Cod	Victorian
Town A	75	25	53	20
Town B	62	65	43	32

19 According to the table above, what is the probability that a randomly selected house in Town B is a colonial house?

(A) $\dfrac{65}{202}$

(B) $\dfrac{17}{18}$

(C) $\dfrac{31}{45}$

(D) $\dfrac{25}{62}$

20 What is the probability that a house randomly selected from Town A is a Victorian house?

(A) $\dfrac{5}{13}$

(B) $\dfrac{20}{43}$

(C) $\dfrac{4}{75}$

(D) $\dfrac{32}{375}$

GO TO THE NEXT PAGE

21 Which of the following are the solutions to the equation $y - 5 = 3x^2 - 5x - 7$?

(A) $2, -\dfrac{1}{3}$

(B) $3, -1\dfrac{1}{3}$

(C) $\dfrac{5 \pm \sqrt{109}}{6}$

(D) $\dfrac{5}{6}$

22

Figure not drawn to scale.

In the figure above, if $QP = 11.5$, $TQ = 15$, and $QR = 46$, what is the value of SQ?

(A) 65

(B) 60

(C) 49.5

(D) 42.5

23

$$1 = \dfrac{3}{x-4} + \dfrac{4}{x-3}$$

Which of the following are the values of x in the equation above?

(A) $7 \pm 2\sqrt{3}$

(B) $7 \pm \sqrt{62}$

(C) $7 \pm \sqrt{86}$

(D) $1, 13$

24 A certain type of weather radar, known as a Base Reflectivity Radar, has a circumference of 572π miles. The central angle of a sector of the circle that the radar makes is $\dfrac{3\pi}{4}$.

What is the area, in square miles, of the sector of the circle?

(A) 858π square miles

(B) $\dfrac{429\pi}{4}$ square miles

(C) $\dfrac{61{,}347\pi}{2}$ square miles

(D) $81{,}796\pi$ square miles

25 If c is a negative constant less than 1 and b is a positive constant greater than 1, which of the following could be the graph of $y = a(x + b)(x + c)$?

(A)

(B)

(C)

(D)

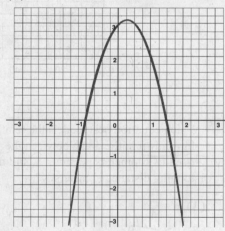

26 $2x - 5y < 6$

$x + ay < -3$

Which of the following must be true if the system of inequalities has solutions only in quadrants II and III?

(A) $a < 0$

(B) $a = 0$

(C) $0 \le a \le 2.5$

(D) $a > 2.5$

QUESTIONS 27 AND 28 REFER TO THE FOLLOWING INFORMATION.

The graph below shows the results of a study to see how far a vehicle travels before coming to a complete stop at different speeds.

27 Which equation best models the relationship shown in the graph between the
speed in kilometers per hour, x, and the
stopping distance in meters, y?

(A) $y = \frac{1}{4}x$

(B) $y = x - 10$

(C) $y = 4.82(1.03)^x$

(D) $y = 4.82x^{1.03}$

28 Which of the following best describes
the relationship represented in the graph?

(A) The relationship between the initial
speed and the stopping distance is
linear, because the points are close to
a line.

(B) The relationship between the initial
speed and the stopping distance is
linear, because the points are all on a
line.

(C) The relationship between the initial
speed and the stopping distance is
modeled by exponential growth,
because the slope of the line
connecting any two points increases
as the initial speed increases.

(D) The relationship between the initial
speed and the stopping distance
is modeled by exponential decay,
because the slope of the line
connecting any two points increases
as the initial speed increases.

29 A recent national poll of adults in the United States found that 64% favor stricter emissions on power plants. The margin of error for the poll was ± 4% with 95% confidence. Which of the following statements is a conclusion that can accurately be drawn from this poll?

(A) The true percentage of people who oppose stricter emissions of power plants is definitely between 32% and 40%.

(B) The true percentage of people who support stricter emissions of power plants is definitely between 60% and 68%.

(C) The pollsters are 95% confident that the true percentage of people who oppose stricter emissions of power plants is between 32% and 40%.

(D) The pollsters are 95% confident that the true percentage of people who support stricter emissions of power plants is between 60% and 68%.

30 The equation for the graph of a circle in the xy-plane is $x^2 + y^2 - 10x + 4y = -20$. What are the coordinates of the center of the circle?

(A) $(5, -2)$

(B) $(-5, 2)$

(C) $(10, -4)$

(D) $(-10, 4)$

GO TO THE
NEXT PAGE

Directions: For Questions 31–38, solve the problem and enter your answer in the grid, as described below, on the answer sheet.

1. Although not required, it is suggested that you write your answer in the boxes at the top of the columns to help you fill in the circles accurately. You will receive credit only if the circles are filled in correctly.

2. Mark no more than one circle in any column.

3. No question has a negative answer.

4. Some problems may have more than one correct answer. In such cases, grid only one answer.

5. **Mixed numbers** such as $3\frac{1}{2}$ must be gridded as 3.5 or $\frac{7}{2}$.

    If $3\frac{1}{2}$ is entered into the grid as $\boxed{3\,|\,1\,|\,/\,|\,2}$, it will be interpreted as $\frac{31}{2}$, not $3\frac{1}{2}$.)

6. **Decimal answers:** If you obtain a decimal answer with more digits than the grid can accommodate, it may be either rounded or truncated, but it must fill the entire grid.

31. A bowling alley charges $4.50 per hour to use a lane. They also charge $2.50 to rent a pair of bowling shoes. Miguel and his friend rent a pair of bowling shoes each. The total cost before taxes is $16.25. How many hours did they bowl?

32. If $4s - 3 < 2$ and s is an integer, what is the greatest possible value of $4s + 5$?

33. If $2a - b = 7$ and $2a + 2b = 16$, what is the value of $3a + 7b$?

34. The current population of a certain type of organism is about 100 million. The population is currently increasing at an annual rate that will make the population double in 18 years. If this pattern continues, what will the population of this country be, in millions of organisms, 54 years from now?

35. Sally sold pieces of her pottery for x dollars each at an art show. Paul sold pieces of his pottery for y dollars each at the same show. Paul sold four pieces of pottery for a total of $85 and Sally sold five pieces for a total of $40 more than Paul. How much more, in dollars, did Sally charge for each piece of her pottery than Paul charged for his? (Ignore the dollar sign when gridding in your answer.)

36 Carl knitted 4 more scarves this year than last year. If he knitted 16% more scarves this year than last year, how many did he knit this year?

38 The average weekly median household income in a country from 2010 through 2014 was $1,007. What is the least average weekly median household income for 2015 that would keep an average of at least $1,000? Grid in your answer without the dollar sign.

37

$$y = 2x + 5$$

$$y = -2(x+1)^2 + 3$$

If (x, y) is a solution to the system of equations above, what is one possible value of y?

STOP

If you finish before time is called, you may check your work on this section only.
Do not turn to any other section.

SECTION 5: ESSAY

50 Minutes • 1 Essay

Directions: The essay gives you an opportunity to show how effectively you can read and comprehend a passage and write an essay analyzing the passage. In your essay, you should demonstrate that you have read the passage carefully, present a clear and logical analysis, and use language precisely.

Your essay will need to be written on the lines provided in your answer booklet. You will have enough space if you write on every line and keep your handwriting to an average size. Try to print or write clearly so that your writing will be legible to the readers scoring your essay.

As you read the passage below, consider how Catherine Anderson uses the following:

- Evidence, such as facts, statistics, or examples, to support claims.

- Reasoning to develop ideas and to connect claims and evidence.

- Stylistic or persuasive elements, such as word choice or emotional, intellectual, and ethical appeals to emotion, to add power to the ideas expressed.

Adapted from "Michael Graves sought to create joy through superior design" by Catherine Anderson, originally published in The Conversation on March 25, 2015. Catherine Anderson is an Assistant Professor of Interior Architecture and Design at George Washington University. (This passage was edited for length. For the complete article, see http:// theconversation.com)

1   Visit the website of designer Michael Graves, and you'll be greeted with the words "Humanistic Design = Transformative Results." The mantra can double as Graves' philosophy. For Graves—who passed away at 80 earlier this month—paid no heed to architectural trends, social movements or the words of his critics. Instead, it was the everyday human being—the individual—who inspired and informed his work.

2   During a career that spanned over 50 years, Graves held firm to the belief that design could effect tremendous change in people's day-to-day lives. From small-scale kitchen products to immense buildings, a thread runs throughout his products: accessible, aesthetic forms that possess a sense of warmth and appeal.

3   Early in his career, Graves was identified as one of the New York Five, a group of influential architects who whole-heartedly embraced Modernism, the architectural movement that subscribed to the use of simple, clean lines, forms devoid of embellishments and modern materials such as steel and glass.

4   However, Graves is best described as a Post-Modernist. He eschewed the austerity of Modernism and its belief that "less is more," instead embracing history and references to the past. He rejected the notion that decoration, or ornament, was a "crime" (as Austrian architect Adolf Loos wrote in 1908); rather, he viewed it as a way for his architecture to convey meaning.

5   As the noted architectural historian Spiro Kostof explains in his book A History of Architecture: Settings and Rituals, "Post Modernists turn to historical memory … to ornament, as a way of enriching the language of architecture."

6   … Along these lines, Graves loathed the idea of intellectualizing his structures. Instead, he sought to make them accessible, understandable, and poignant to all passersby. …

7   In addition to designing buildings, Graves embarked upon a long and highly successful partnership with the Italian kitchenware company Alessi. … Graves' most famous Alessi design is his iconic teakettle … which had a cheerful red whistling bird and sky-blue handle. On sale since 1985, the best-selling product is still in production today.

8   In 1999, Minneapolis-based discount retail giant Target approached Graves with an offer to design a line of kitchen products, ranging from toasters to spatulas.

9   While some might have shied away from having their work associated with a mega-corporation like Target, Graves wholly embraced the project. …

10 In all, Graves' collaboration with Target would last 13 years; during this time, the designer would become a household name, with millions of units of his products appearing in American homes.

11 Many of Graves' designs for Target—his spatula, can opener, and ice cream scoop—had chunky, sky-blue handles. Other appliances that were white … were sprinkled with touches of color. … Black and beige had no place in Graves' palette.

12 The option to select a better-looking product with a slightly higher price versus the same article but with a less expensive, nondescript appearance is now the norm for most consumers: good design (and function) are part and parcel of the customer experience (nowhere is this more evident than in Apple's rise to dizzying heights as arguably one of the world's most valuable brands).

13 It's an idea that's democratic in nature, and thinking about design through this lens led Graves to create thoughtful, appealing, and affordable products for the masses. …

14 As Graves' popularity rose, his critics leveled blistering commentaries about what they deemed a precipitous fall from grace—from a "trend beyond compare" to a "stale trend," as architecture critic Herbert Muschamp noted in a 1999 New York Times article. The notion that he had commodified design—and had somehow "cheapened" it—drew the disdain of those who once lauded his works.

15 Yet Graves remained true to his beliefs even into the last phase of his life. In 2003, after an illness left him paralyzed below the waist, he realized that the design of hospitals and equipment … could be redesigned and made more functional, comfortable, and visually appealing. He then went on to improve ubiquitous devices such as wheelchairs and walking canes. …

16 Consumers may not have ever known his architecture or what the critics thought of his work (or even realized they were buying one of his products). Graves didn't seem to mind. His goal was to provide well-designed items for everyday use rather than impress his detractors.

17 As he told NPR in 2002, "It's the kind of thing where you pick something up or use it with a little bit of joy … it puts a smile on your face."

Write an essay in which you explain how Catherine Anderson builds an argument to persuade her audience that Michael Graves' central concern was creating designs that helped "the everyday human being." In your essay, analyze how the writer uses one or more of the features listed previously (or features of your own choice) to strengthen the logic and persuasiveness of her argument. Be sure that your analysis focuses on the most relevant aspects of the passage.

Your essay should not explain whether you agree with the writer's claims, but, rather, explain how she builds an argument to persuade her audience.

STOP

If you finish before time is called, you may check your work on this section only. Do not turn to any other section.

practice test

No Test Material On This Page

ANSWER KEY AND EXPLANATIONS

Section 1: Reading Test

1. A	12. B	23. D	34. D	45. D
2. B	13. D	24. B	35. B	46. A
3. A	14. C	25. D	36. A	47. C
4. D	15. D	26. B	37. B	48. B
5. A	16. A	27. C	38. C	49. A
6. C	17. A	28. A	39. B	50. C
7. A	18. B	29. D	40. C	51. D
8. C	19. B	30. B	41. C	52. B
9. C	20. B	31. C	42. C	
10. B	21. D	32. A	43. A	
11. C	22. A	33. B	44. B	

READING TEST RAW SCORE ☐
(Number of correct answers)

1. **The correct answer is (A).** The overall main points of the article are all meant to dispel the myths surrounding earthquakes: how and why they occur. The article provides supporting details about the science of earthquakes, which also counter the Hollywood myths. Thus, choice (A) is the correct answer. While the author does explain the causes and effects of earthquakes, it is to dispel the myths created by Hollywood, thus choice (B) is incorrect. Choice (C) is incorrect, as the passage applies to earthquakes only and not to science in general. Choice (D) is incorrect as this topic is not covered in the passage.

2. **The correct answer is (B).** The text proves that "eventually enough stress builds up and the rocks slip suddenly, releasing energy in waves that travel through the rock to cause the shaking that we feel during an earthquake" (lines 32–36). Although all of the factors listed in choices (A), (C), and (D) are contributing causes, the main cause of

earthquakes is friction, as stated in choice (B). Therefore, choices (A), (C), and (D) are incorrect.

3. **The correct answer is (A).** The article is intended to separate fact from fiction for those who might be misinformed. Although there are a lot of scientific facts in the passage, the tone is casual and almost scolding in its refutation of the myths surrounding earthquakes. Choice (C) is incorrect because filmmakers would not be particularly interested. Choices (B) and (D) are incorrect as both science teachers and scientists would already know these facts.

4. **The correct answer is (D).** The article counters the myths by pointing out in lines 91–94 that the ocean isn't a hole into which a land mass can fall, as the ocean is itself just land at a lower elevation. Thus, choice (D) is the correct answer. Choice (A) is incorrect because it accepts the myth as fact rather than countering it. Choice (B) is incorrect because while the author talks

about the land mass under the ocean as being at a lower sea level than California, it is only in explaining the geography of the region. Choice (C) is incorrect because the author does not explain that California and Alaska are similar but rather that southern California is moving slowly toward Alaska.

5. **The correct answer is (A).** The author notes in lines 91–96 that California cannot break off, as it is part of the land that makes up the ocean floor, only at a higher elevation. Thus, choice (A) is the correct answer. Choice (B) is incorrect, as it is not an explanation as much as a refutation. Choices (C) and (D) are incorrect, as they merely point out another feature of the geology of California; they do not clarify why California will not be swept out into the ocean.

6. **The correct answer is (C).** In the context of this passage, "stress" is pressure that builds up in rocks. Only in human interactions does "stress" describe the pressure that builds up in people, causing worry and/or anxiety. Stress does not imply the idea of weight in the context of this passage, making choice (C) incorrect. It also does not mean "emphasis," so choice (D) is incorrect.

7. **The correct answer is (A).** The passage makes it clear that the closer a region is to the earthquake source, the more that region will be affected. The most likely reason for devastation in Haiti (or any place) is that these variables were in place: lack of buildings that could withstand the shaking from an earthquake and an earthquake that was probably very strong. The combination can be deadly. Choices (B) and (C) may be partially true, but neither choice completely accounts for why Haiti experienced such extensive damage. Therefore, choices (B) and (C) are both incorrect. Choice (D) is incorrect because the passage does not support this statement.

8. **The correct answer is (C).** Lines 64–69 clearly explain that the effects of an earthquake are dependent on the proximity of the earthquake source to the affected region as well as the structure of the buildings that are shaken by the earthquake. Choice (B) is incorrect because these lines discuss the creation of an earthquake, but do not mention the affected region of an earthquake. Similarly, choices (A) and (D) both contain lines that regard the attributes and causes of an earthquake, but fail to address why a region is affected. Therefore, choices (A) and (D) are incorrect.

9. **The correct answer is (C).** The context, that moderate earthquakes have caused significant damage because the shaking was locally amplified, suggests that amplified means made stronger, so choice (C) is the correct answer. Choice (A) is incorrect, as shaking would not be lifted. Choice (B) is incorrect, as "supplemented" or "added to" does not make sense in the context of an earthquake. Choice (C) is incorrect because whether or not an earthquake was predicted would have no bearing on the shaking that is felt locally.

10. **The correct answer is (B).** The phrase reveals that disaster movies are made more dramatic for effect at the expense of scientific accuracy. Using the word "inconvenient" mocks the story; it implies that the earthquake is used as an easy way to write a character out of the story. Choices (A), (C), and (D) are incorrect because the use of the referenced phrase does not directly relate to scientific information within the passages, as stated in these choices.

11. **The correct answer is (C).** The passage explains that friction is required for an earthquake (lines 108–109), making the idea of a gaping fault impossible, as a fault line could only open up without friction. Choice (A) is incorrect because although the concept is portrayed in movies, which use the image, that fact does not refute the myth. Choices (B) and (D) are both incorrect because they are true statements that do not refute the premise.

12. **The correct answer is (B).** Patrick Henry lashes out against concentrated power (Passage 1, lines 1–5). Madison, on the other hand, explains that power is essential, but separating the power of the government into different departments (branches) will act as a check on that power, ensuring that it cannot get out of control (Passage 2, sentence 1). Choices (A), (C), and (D) are incorrect because the statements made in them do not reflect the content of the passages.

13. **The correct answer is (D).** Henry addresses the issue of concentrating power and says that it rests "on a supposition that your American governors shall be honest" (lines 35–37), which, in his view, is a dangerous and unnecessarily risky assumption to make. Choice (A) is incorrect because it is never implied in the passage that the structure of the Constitution is unstable. Choices (B) and (C) are both incorrect because neither correlate with the views of Henry and would therefore not be an objection of his.

14. **The correct answer is (C).** The artist portrays Henry as a passionate speaker. This mirrors the dramatic phases Henry uses in his speech, such as calling the features of the Constitution "horribly frightful" and the government "horridly defective." Choice (A) is incorrect because the reader has no way of knowing how people react to Henry's speech. The artist does not portray Henry as calm; instead Henry appears impassioned, making choice (B) incorrect. The artist shows Henry as impassioned, but not necessarily an extremist. Some spectators look excited; some look angry or sullen, but there is no indication Henry is perceived as a madman. Henry does appeal to the listener's patriotism, but his argument is not built slowly. The structure is logical, but the pacing is quick and the tone urgent. Therefore, choice (D) is also incorrect.

15. **The correct answer is (D).** Madison argues that a government whose powers are separated by design will act as controls, each branch on the other, and avoid concentration of power. Choices (A) and (B) are incorrect because they both relate an idea that would be detrimental to use in order to address concerns about a strong central government. Choice (C) is incorrect because it is not a point made by Madison anywhere in Passage 2.

16. **The correct answer is (A).** Lines 73–80 describe how Madison believes the government should be divided into branches that would check and balance each other. This would serve to counteract the idea that the government is too centralized because the branches would allow for the power to be divided and would make it so that one branch

would not have too much power. Choice (C) would be detrimental to use as a counterargument, and is therefore incorrect. Choices (B) and (D) are both incorrect because they do not pertain to the counterargument.

17. **The correct answer is (A).** Henry's statement shows a skepticism about human nature and the ability of humans to resist corruption. He says that never in human history has there been a benevolent government that automatically grants its people rights; governments only grant the people rights and liberties if their power is threatened. This statement shows Henry's belief that human beings are inherently dishonest and self-concerned. Madison, on the other hand, believes that although humans are not perfect beings, with the proper controls, it is possible for humans to govern themselves without resorting to tyranny. Choices (B), (C), and (D) are all incorrect because they contain information that is not substantiated in the passage.

18. **The correct answer is (B).** Henry is addressing the Virginia Convention and attempting to persuade them to vote against ratification (introduction). In this part of his speech, Henry is responding to the idea of checks and balances in the government, calling them "imaginary." He refers rhetorically to what the opposition (i.e., the framers) are saying about how such a government would work with balanced branches and a centralized government. Henry also discusses the "ridiculous ideal checks and contrivances" and how the opposition's idea of checks and balances would not work. Choice (A) is incorrect because Henry is giving a speech and would therefore not be referring to a narrator. Choices (C) and (D) are incorrect because, in the speech, Henry is addressing the opposition and not all of the general public or the people of Virginia are in the opposition.

19. **The correct answer is (B).** In line 7 ("the genius of republicanism"), Henry praises a republican form of government (i.e., one that has elected representatives and is not run by a monarchy) Henry indicates that such a centralized government, as outlined in the Constitution, cannot work with the goals of

forming a republican government. Choices (A), (C), and (D) are incorrect because Henry is adamant about his opposition towards anything similar to a monarchial government, autocracy and plutocracy included.

20. **The correct answer is (B).** Line 7 ("the genius of republicanism") clearly states that Henry believes that the ideal form of government is republicanism where all the people are represented. Choices (C) and (D) are similar because they both have to do with the United States becoming a monarchy. Therefore, these choices are both incorrect. Choice (A) is incorrect because it does not have to do with Henry's preference in forms of government.

21. **The correct answer is (D).** Madison's reference to "department" refers to the branches of the government that are outlined in the Constitution (executive, legislative, judicial), which is apparent from the context. Choice (A), (B), and (C) are incorrect because they do not make sense in the context of the paragraph.

22. **The correct answer is (A).** In the context of the sentence, Madison is referring to how the checks on one department (or branch) would be in turn proportional to the checks on another department. One department would hold another in check to maintain a balance of power so that power would not get concentrated in one branch. Choices (B), (C), and (D) do not make sense in the context and are therefore incorrect.

23. **The correct answer is (D).** The article mentions multiple scientists and institutions who all worked on identifying the shark and sharing their information so that it could be correctly catalogued and understood. The overall conclusion about methodology, therefore, shows that science can be a collaborative endeavor. Choice (A) is incorrect because it is not relevant to the passage. Choice (B) is incorrect because it contains information that is not fully supported by the passage. Choice (C) is also incorrect, as it is not suggested in the passage.

24. **The correct answer is (B).** Lines 32–35 show that the scientists discovered the shark by accident when it was found in a controlled lab. Choice (A) is incorrect

because while it is true, it does not explain why the scientists were surprised. Choices (C) and (D) are incorrect because neither is suggested in the passage.

25. **The correct answer is (D).** Scientific journals report news relevant to the field of the journal's specialty. Taxonomy is a specific field that studies the classification of animals and plants, which is shown by the interest in determining the genus and species of the pocket shark. Choices (A) and (B) are incorrect because, although they could be true, they do not explain why the finding was reported in the journal of taxonomy. Choice (C) is incorrect because the question notes that the finding was reported in a journal of taxonomy, not a journal that specializes in marine animals.

26. **The correct answer is (B).** Choice (B) describes how scientists were able to classify the specimen and genetically analyze the specimen. This explains why the finding was published in the journal of taxonomy, which is the classification of species. Choice (A) and choice (C) do not relate to the reasons for why the finding was published in the journal of taxonomy and are therefore incorrect. Although choice (D) relates to taxonomy, it does not explain where the finding was published. Therefore, choice (D) is also incorrect.

27. **The correct answer is (C).** Paragraph 5 explains that tissue samples were analyzed to get genetic information that could be compared to other specimens. Using this data, scientists could then determine how to classify the pocket shark. Choices (A), (B), and (D) could all help to determine the species of the shark, but they do not provide the exact information that scientists need to determine the species of the shark.

28. **The correct answer is (A).** In Part A of the diagram, there is a lighter spot above the fin, though it is not labeled there. But on part C, the pocket gland is labeled and is shown in the same place and on the light spot in part A. Based on this, it can be inferred that this is the place where the pocket is located. Choices (B), (C), and (D) are incorrect because neither the image nor the text provides

evidence to suggest that the pockets are located in any of these locations.

29. **The correct answer is (D).** Lines 66–67 explain that scientists "hoped that further study of the specimen will lead to many new discoveries." The specifics aren't discussed because scientists cannot anticipate what they will discover, but it can be assumed that it will be related to sharks. Choices (A), (B), and (C) are incorrect because they all relate directly to the pocket shark; scientists hope to discover new information about sharks in general.

30. **The correct answer is (B).** Lines 65–67 explain how the discovery of the pocket shark could lead to further discoveries in the future, a prospect that would excite scientists. Choice (A), (C), and (D) are all incorrect because they involve information about the pocket shark that, although probably exciting to some, is very specific and does not provide a broad explanation of why the find may be exciting in general, as choice (B) does.

31. **The correct answer is (C).** "Robust" in this context describes a collection that has variety. A specimen is a sample used for testing, so it makes sense for the lab to have a large, substantial collection of marine animal samples for testing. Choices (A), (B), and (D) are incorrect because it cannot be inferred, based on the passage, that the "robust specimen collection" is how these choices describe it.

32. **The correct answer is (A).** The author refers to pocket sharks, which, when hungry, take an "oval plug of flesh" from prey, so "plug" is this context means lump or piece. Choice (B) is incorrect because there is no indication that the flesh that the shark bites off actually protrudes from the prey's body. Choice (C) is incorrect because "obstruction of flesh" does not make sense. Choice (D) is also incorrect because it, too, makes no sense in the context of the sentence.

33. **The correct answer is (B).** In spite of the humor, Twain makes it clear that he does not approve of either the story, which he finds unrealistic and boring, or the style, which he finds repetitive. While he does point out the flaws in the work, he does so by using

sarcasm and satire, to show why it cannot be considered any kind of literary art, making choice (A) incorrect. Choice (C) is incorrect because only a portion of the passage deals with the Native Americans. Although Twain does criticize Cooper based on his work, he never shows the importance of literary criticism in the passage. For this reason, choice (D) is also incorrect.

34. **The correct answer is (D).** For the entirety of the passage, Twain mocks Cooper's story, but he does so in a humorous way. For example, in the second to the last paragraph (lines 79–81), he describes the action of the novel, saying: "Let me explain what the five did—you would not be able to reason it out for yourself." This is sarcasm making mockery of the action of the characters in the book. It is light-hearted and expresses incredulity, thus setting a humorous tone. Choice (A) is incorrect because arrogance implies an exaggerated sense of self-importance that is not expressed in the passage. The voice of the passage is somewhat informal and, as a result, not scholarly. This makes choice (B) incorrect. The tone of the passage is humorous; however, it is not cheery and does not suggest optimism, making choice (C) incorrect.

35. **The correct answer is (B).** Lines 11–12 illustrate the hyperbole that Twain uses to humorously describe how Cooper took liberty with his description of the techniques Native Americans used to track footprints to find and/or attack enemy tribes. In this line, Twain's description of wearing out the moccasins in the process of following a trail pokes fun at the erroneous nature of Cooper's characterization. Choices (A), (C), and (D) are all critiques, but they do not express humor.

36. **The correct answer is (A).** Twain refers to Cooper's use of various literary devices as "stage properties," as a way to mock Cooper. The "barrels and barrels of moccasins" is a satire on the moccasins referred to by Cooper's character who is tracking a Native American through footprints made by the moccasins. The "stage properties" Twain refers to do not have anything to do with drama or theater, making choices (B), (C), and (D) incorrect.

37. **The correct answer is (B).** The pronunciation guide is another way of mocking Cooper's book. Here, Twain describes the plot and throws in, as an aside, the pronunciation key to indicate how far Cooper veers from reality, so much so that the Native Americans he describes might as well be called Chicago. Choices (A) and (C) are incorrect because Twain is writing satirically and does not actually intend for the reader to pronounce the Native American's name correctly. As the work is satire, Twain only intends to criticize Cooper, and illustrating that Cooper's work was about actual Native Americans would achieve this goal. Therefore, choice (D) is incorrect.

38. **The correct answer is (C).** The biggest and most frequent criticism Twain makes in the passage is to show how unrealistic the plot and characters are. For example, in describing the ark (paragraph 5), he explains how the timing is off for the entire scene, making its occurrence totally unreasonable. And here he jokes and ridicules the outcome: "He missed the house and landed in the stern of the scow. It was not much of a fall, yet it knocked him silly." (Lines 70–73) showing how absurd the story line is. Choices (A), (B), and (D) are not substantiated by the passage and are therefore incorrect.

39. **The correct answer is (B).** Lines 48–49 refer to Cooper's changes in the width and flow of a river, which Twain deems unrealistic and therefore defective. Twain makes the case that Cooper's description of the natural world is mistaken and at odds with reality and therefore defective. Choice (A) is merely a hyperbolic description of Twain's list of defects, and choice (C) illustrates Twain's style of satire. Therefore, both choices (A) and (C) are incorrect. Choice (D) does not show how the jump was unrealistic or how in itself it mischaracterizes the way something would happen, making choice (D) incorrect.

40. **The correct answer is (C).** Twain criticizes Cooper's characterization of the Native Americans as dim-witted, inept, and deceitful. The Native Americans bumble through every attempt they make to attack the settlers (for example, they can't jump onto a very slow-moving boat, because they

miscalculate the timing). Choices (A), (B), and (D) describe the Native Americans as more intelligent and competent than Cooper is credited with describing them.

41. **The correct answer is (C).** Twain notes that Cooper "conceals six Indians in its (the sapling's) foliage" (lines 51–52). A sapling is a young, immature tree, so it is illogical to assume that six people could be hidden in the foliage of a sapling. Thus, choice (C) is the correct answer. Choice (A) is incorrect, as it is untrue. Choice (B) is incorrect, as the audience would not necessarily know that this is why he put it in quotation marks. Choice (D) is incorrect, as it is untrue.

42. **The correct answer is (C).** In the context of the sentence, "destitute" means that the work is void of the variables that make a story artful. Although the word can mean impoverished, that meaning does not fit this context, making choice (A) incorrect. Choices (B) and (D) are both incorrect because they do not make sense in this context.

43. **The correct answer is (A).** The overall descriptions are of the character Paul. The passage describes how he looks, his actions and reactions, and his emotions. Through the use of a narrator telling the story, it also describes how others react to him, giving the reader an outside perspective of the character. Thus, choice (A) is the correct answer. Choice (B) is incorrect because the passage description notes that it is from a short story and therefore fiction. Choice (C) is incorrect because there is no plot in the passage. Choice (D) is incorrect because it is the character of Paul—not any one setting—that is emphasized.

44. **The correct answer is (B).** The author notes in lines 1–4 that it "was Paul's afternoon to appear before the faculty of the Pittsburgh High School to account for his various misdemeanors." Thus, choice (B) is the correct answer. Choice (A) is incorrect because while the author notes that Paul does tell the principal that he wants to return to school, this was not the reason why he was asked to appear before the faculty. Choice (C) is incorrect because tardiness is not mentioned as one of Paul's infractions. Choice (D) is incorrect because while he father calls the

principal after Paul's suspension confessing that he is perplexed by his son's behavior, there is no mention that Paul's parents are in the principal's office at this time.

45. **The correct answer is (D).** The carnation is obvious on his coat lapel, and it is a contrast to the way he is dressed in shabby clothes, as if he didn't care. And yet the carnation adds a note of frivolity and mockery to the seriousness of the event. It is a way of subtly communicating that he will do as he pleases, in defiance of the wishes of the faculty, thus choice (D) is the correct answer. Choice (A) is incorrect, as Paul does not wish to show respect to the faculty. Choice (B) is incorrect because Paul does not intend to show remorse. In fact, he intends to show defiance. Choice (C) is incorrect because if Paul wanted to appear wealthy, he would not wear shabby clothes.

46. **The correct answer is (A).** The author notes in lines 38–40 that his teachers stated their charges against him with "such a rancor and aggrievedness as evinced that this was not a usual case." Thus, choice (A) is the correct answer. Choice (B) is incorrect because while the teachers may not understand Paul's behavior, they are too offended by it to be sad or confused. Choice (C) is incorrect because "scorn and disdain" imply that the teachers have made a value judgment, determining that Paul is despicable and unworthy. Instead, their actions suggest anger. Choice (D) is incorrect because nothing in the text suggests such feelings.

47. **The correct answer is (C).** In lines 38–40, the author notes that Paul's teachers stated their charges with "rancor and aggrievedness," words that suggest anger and frustration. Thus, choice (C) is the correct answer. Choice (A) is incorrect because these lines refer to Paul's father's feelings. Choice (B) is incorrect because while it suggests that the teachers did not feel that Paul was contrite, it does not support the idea that they were angry and frustrated. Choice (D) is incorrect because these lines explain how the teachers interpreted Paul's feelings toward them.

48. **The correct answer is (B).** An unnamed narrator describes Paul, using great detail to show how others perceived him. The narrator allows for an objective look at an adolescent by observing his actions, reactions, and appearance. Choice (B) is the correct answer. Choices (A) and (D) are incorrect because both Paul and the principal are referred to in the third person. Choice (C) is incorrect because a psychologist is not noted in the introduction or the text.

49. **The correct answer is (A).** Paul's appearance is described in great detail and his outer appearance is often betrayed by behavior that gives away his true feelings. For example, he smiles but his fingers tremble and play with the buttons on his coat (lines 80–84). Choices (B), (C), and (D) are incorrect because they do not describe Paul's actions and feelings; rather, they describe contrasts with others and their appearance and reactions.

50. **The correct answer is (C).** Cather notes in her description of Paul playing with the buttons on his coat that it was the only outward sign of his discomfort, thus in lines 82–85, she connects his outer actions to his inner feelings, allowing the reader inside Paul's emotional state. Choice (C) then is the correct answer. Choices (A) and (B) are incorrect, as the lines do not interpret the meaning of Paul's facial expression. Choice (D) is incorrect, as the interpretation noted here is made by others and not necessarily reflective of Paul's feelings.

51. **The correct answer is (D).** The word as used in the title suggests that the story is focused on the personality makeup of the protagonist. Thus, choice (D) is the correct answer. Choice (A) is incorrect because the narrator does not describe Paul's complexion. Choice (B) is incorrect, as the word does not make sense in the context. Choice (C) is incorrect, because the story is a description of a boy's behavior over a period of time, and mood suggests one particular moment or feeling.

52. **The correct answer is (B).** A dandy is a person who is meticulous in the way he dresses and takes extreme care in his appearance. The paragraph in which the word is used is in the context of Paul's clothing, and "dandy" suits the characterization of Paul, so choice (B) is the correct answer. Choices (A), (C), and (D) are incorrect because the context is a description of Paul's dress.

Section 2: Writing and Language Test

1. C	11. C	21. A	31. C	40. C
2. B	12. A	22. C	32. D	41. B
3. C	13. D	23. B	33. A	42. D
4. D	14. B	24. D	34. B	43. A
5. A	15. A	25. C	35. D	44. B
6. A	16. B	26. A	36. C	
7. B	17. D	27. A	37. A	
8. C	18. C	28. C	38. D	
9. D	19. A	29. B	39. B	
10. B	20. B	30. D		

WRITING AND LANGUAGE TEST RAW SCORE
(Number of correct answers)

1. **The correct answer is (C).** This introductory paragraph establishes that in 1849, Elizabeth Blackwell became the first female doctor in the United States, defying expectations. The only choice that reflects this point is choice (C). Choice (A) is incorrect because it misses the point about Blackwell becoming the first female doctor in the country. Choice (B) is incorrect because it doesn't explain what her degree was in, nor why she took her place in history. Choice (D) is also incorrect because it reflects points made in the second paragraph, not the first.

2. **The correct answer is (B).** The context of the paragraph makes clear that the expectations of those around her were that she would fail in becoming a doctor, and that Blackwell had ignored or disregarded those expectations. Thus, choice (B) is the correct answer. Choice (A) is incorrect because her achievement was not a condemnation or criticism of the expectation that she would fail; it simply flouted it. Choice (C) is incorrect because "incite" means to encourage or inspire, and the context does not support the idea that she inspired the expectation that she would fail. Choice (D) is incorrect because the context makes clear that in earning her degree, Blackwell did not meet the expectations of her peers. Rather, she disregarded them.

3. **The correct answer is (C).** The comparison here is between educating a boy and educating a girl, thus choice (C) is the correct answer. Choice (A) is incorrect because it illogically compares educating a boy to a girl, rather than to educating a girl. Choice (B) is incorrect because it is illogically compares educating a boy to a girl's preference for education. Choice (D) is incorrect because it illogically compares educating a boy to opportunities for girls.

4. **The correct answer is (D).** The phrase, "To make up for the gaps in her education," modifies "she" or Blackwell and should directly precede a reference to Blackwell to avoid confusion. Therefore, choice (D) is the correct answer. Choice (A) is incorrect because the phrase appears to modify household. Choices (B) and (C) are incorrect

because the phrase appears awkwardly in the middle of the sentence and it is unclear what it modifies.

5. **The correct answer is (A).** Though this paragraph alludes to the discrimination and attitudes that Blackwell faced, the point of the paragraph is that she had a hard time getting into medical school because she was a woman and that she gained admission to only one school. Thus, choice (A) is correct because it is the only answer choice that makes both these points. Choice (B) is incorrect because it misses the point of the paragraph and incorrectly suggests that physicians would help her gain admission rather than advise her. Choice (C) is incorrect because it misses the point of the paragraph and incorrectly suggests that Blackwell considered disguising herself as a man. Choice (D) is not correct because while it illustrates the attitudes of the times, it fails to note that she did gain admission to one school after applying to over a dozen.

6. **The correct answer is (A).** You can tell from context that the underlined word should be something that means "didn't believe," so choice (A), "doubted," is the correct answer. Choice (B), "debated" is incorrect because it implies that some physicians thought she might be admitted to medical school—a notion that is not supported by the text. Choices (C) and (D) are incorrect because both imply that physicians thought she would get in, and that is not the case.

7. **The correct answer is (B).** The antecedent of the pronoun is Blackwell, so the pronoun should be "her," making choice (B) the correct answer. Choices (A), (C), and (D) do not agree with the antecedent "Blackwell."

8. **The correct answer is (C).** The sentence should be written in the simple past tense: *became* agrees with the verb tense used in the sentences that follow, thus choice (C) is the correct answer. Choice (A) is incorrect because it is in the present perfect tense while the sentence that follows is in the simple past tense. Choice (B) is incorrect because it is in the present tense, and all of the events take place in the distance past. Choice (D) is incorrect because it is in the future tense.

9. **The correct answer is (D).** The phrase, "all of whom were men" is nonrestrictive, which means it must be set off by commas. Only choice (D) has the commas in the appropriate place to set off the entire phrase, so choice (D) is the correct answer. Choice (A) is incorrect, as there are no commas to set off the nonrestrictive phrase. Choices (B) and (C) are incorrect because the commas are in the wrong place.

10. **The correct answer is (B).** Only choice (B) avoids wordiness and redundancy, thus it is the correct answer. Choice (A) is incorrect because "biases" is the same as prejudice, making the phrasing redundant. Choice (C) is incorrect, because while barriers could include prejudice, including "bias" in the wording is redundant. Choice (D) is incorrect because "obstructed her career" is implicit in the word "barriers," making the wording redundant.

11. **The correct answer is (C).** Only choice (C) supports the idea that although she faced barriers, she was successful by distinguishing herself as a promoter of preventative medicine and medical opportunities for women. Choice (A) is incorrect because it does not support the idea that she was successful and it does not refer to her career after she graduated from medical school. Choice (B) is incorrect because it does not describe anything that Blackwell went on to do after she got her degree. Choice (D) is incorrect because it does not describe anything that Blackwell did in her career.

12. **The correct answer is (A).** Only choice (A) includes the idea that few people in 1962 expressed concern about the environment, that Carson was brave for speaking out, and that she was heavily criticized for doing so. Choice (B) is not correct, as it does not include the idea that Carson spoke out during a time when no one else did. Choice (C) is incorrect because it does not mention Carson and the criticism she endured. Choice (D) is incorrect because it does not mention that she spoke out during a time when no one else did.

13. **The correct answer is (D).** The style of the passage is formal and objective, and only choice (D) corresponds with this style. Thus, choice (D) is the correct answer. Choices (A)

and (B) are incorrect because they employ an informal style. Choice (C) is incorrect because it is not objective in referring to "outsized egos."

14. **The correct answer is (B).** The sentence is a question and so requires a question mark at the end. Choice (B), then, is the correct answer. Choices (A), (C), and (D) are incorrect because the sentence is interrogative and requires a question mark.

15. **The correct answer is (A).** In this sentence, the phrase "DDT in particular" represents a sharp break in thought and so should be set off by dashes. The sentence as it is written is correct, so choice (A) is the correct answer. Choice (B) is incorrect because a dash must be used at the beginning and end of the phrase to set it off from the rest of the sentence. Choice (C) is incorrect because while commas could be used to separate the phrase, they must be used before and after the phrase to be correct. While parenthesis could be used to set off the phrase, in choice (D), they are only used to set off part of it, making it incorrect.

16. **The correct answer is (B).** The information above the pie chart indicates that the chart refers to the most heavily used pesticides by percentage in 1968. Only choice (B) accurately notes this by referencing that DDT accounted for 11% of all pesticides used in that year. Thus, choice (B) is the correct answer. Choice (A) is incorrect because the chart does not show the amount of farmland that was sprayed with DDT. Choice (C) is incorrect because the chart does not indicate the percentage of pests contained by DDT. Choice (D) is incorrect because the chart does not show the percentage of farmers and gardeners that used DDT.

17. **The correct answer is (D).** The context of the paragraph as well as the point later in the paragraph that pesticides "they were able to penetrate systems and remain there for years" indicate that the pesticides were seeping into, or permeating, the soil and rivers. Therefore, choice (D) is the correct answer. Choice (A) is incorrect because there is no support for the idea that the pesticides sapped the water from soil and rivers. Choice (B) is incorrect because the pesticides could not seize the soil and rivers. Choice (C) is

not correct because "transcend" does not make sense in the context.

18. **The correct answer is (C).** In the original text, it is unclear what the pronoun "they" refers to. For clarity, the sentence must restate the antecedent, thus choice (C) is the correct answer. Choice (A) is incorrect because it is unclear whether "they were" refers to the pesticides; the levels; or the plants, animals, and humans. Choice (B) is incorrect because "it" does not agree with any antecedent in the preceding sentence. Choice (D) is incorrect because the sentence goes on to reference "they," making "everything" illogical in the context.

19. **The correct answer is (A).** The paragraph establishes that companies producing pesticides deflected blame and criticism by turning the argument around and questioning Carson's credentials. Only choice (A) includes all of these points. Choice (B) is incorrect because the paragraph does not tie the establishment of the EPA to Carson. Choice (C) is incorrect because it fails to cite what the companies did to Carson. Choice (D) is incorrect because the paragraph does not suggest that chemical companies were discredited upon the establishment of the EPA.

20. **The correct answer is (B).** The context of the paragraph suggests that the chemical companies were not willing to accept or admit the potential hazards of their product, thus, choice (B) is the correct answer. Choice (A) is incorrect because here, "contradict" suggests that they agreed with Carson, an idea not supported by the context. Choice (C) is incorrect because while it is likely true that chemical companies were not willing to "propagate" or communicate the potential hazards of their product, the fact that they discredited Carson suggests that they were even stronger in their reaction to her claims. Choice (D) is incorrect because "solicit" or try to obtain doesn't make sense in the context.

21. **The correct answer is (A).** The first part of the sentence is a subordinating clause, and the subordinating conjunction "since" helps establish the clause's connection to the rest of the sentence. It explains why Carson is blamed for the deaths. Therefore, choice (A) is the correct answer. Choice (B) is not correct because the subordinating conjunction

"although" implies that despite the fact that malaria kills thousands, Carson is blamed for the deaths—an illogical connection. Choice (C) is incorrect because creating two sentences fails to establish the essential link between the two, that because malaria kills so many, Carson is blamed for their deaths. Choice (D) is also incorrect because "however" suggests that there is a contradiction in the two clauses rather than a cause/effect relationship.

22. **The correct answer is (C).** The noun DDT must agree in number with "wonder chemical," thus choice (C) is the correct answer. Choice (A) is incorrect because DDT does not agree in number with "wonder chemicals." Likewise, choice (B) is incorrect because "pesticides" does not agree in number with "wonder chemical." Choice (D) is also incorrect because DDT does not agree in number with "chemicals."

23. **The correct answer is (B).** Because this is a simple list of countries, the items in the series should be set off by commas, choice (B). Choices (A) and (C) are incorrect because the items are set off by both commas and semicolons. Choice (D) is incorrect because semicolons are not necessary here.

24. **The correct answer is (D).** The subject and verb in a sentence must agree in number. In this case, only choice (D) reflects agreement of the subject and verb as well as appropriate verb tense. Thus, choice (D) is the correct answer. Choice (A) is incorrect because the subject of the sentence, "the Mayan understanding of astronomy," is singular and requires a singular verb, and "were" is plural. Choice (B) is incorrect because "are" is plural and is in the present tense rather than the past tense. Choice (C) is incorrect because while the verb "is" agrees with the subject, it is in the present tense, while the passage is written in the past tense.

25. **The correct answer is (C).** All of the items in the list should be in the same form, or parallel. Only choice (C) reflects a parallel structure, so choice (C) is the correct answer. Choice (A) is incorrect because "the planet's movement" is redundant, as "movement of" preceded the list, and it lacks parallel structure. Likewise, choice (B) is incorrect because it contains a similar awkward struc-

ture with the inclusion of "the movement of" before "the stars." Choice (D) is also incorrect because it contains the same structure, with "the movement of" before "the planets."

26. **The correct answer is (A).** The context of the sentence suggests that the Mayans' observations were accurate, as they could predict eclipses and the movement of the planets. Only "acute" reflects this level of accuracy, so choice (A) is correct. Choice (B) is incorrect, as "inept" suggests the Mayans weren't skilled at making observations. Choice (C) is incorrect, as "distinguished" suggests success but does not invoke the idea of accuracy that the rest of the sentence points to. Choice (D) is incorrect because "profound" suggest intensity, which doesn't make sense in the context.

27. **The correct answer is (A).** The main point of the paragraph is the way in which the Mayans blended science (or astronomy), religion, and architecture in their ceremonial buildings. Only choice (A) includes only these important points. Choice (B) is incorrect because it omits the idea that they blended the three disciplines. Choice (C) is incorrect because it is based on information in the preceding paragraph. Choice (D) is incorrect because it does not mention that the Mayans blended astronomy, architecture, and religion in certain buildings.

28. **The correct answer is (C).** "Its" is a possessive determiner and does not require an apostrophe, thus choice (C) is the correct answer. Choice (A) is incorrect because "it's" is a contraction of "it is." Choices (B) and (D) are incorrect because they are not words.

29. **The correct answer is (B).** A semicolon is used to join two related sentences that can stand on their own. Thus, choice (B) is the correct answer. Choice (A) is incorrect because a colon is not used to join two independent clauses. Choice (C) is incorrect because a comma may only be used to join two independent clauses if it is followed by a conjunction. Choice (D) is incorrect because while it is followed by a conjunction, "but" indicates that the second clause is somehow at odds with the first.

30. **The correct answer is (D).** The paragraph suggests that the link between government

and astronomy was so complete that the two were inseparable, so choice (D) is the correct answer. The word "inextricably" means in a manner that is impossible to separate. Choice (A) is incorrect because "correspondingly" suggests that the link between the government and astronomy was somehow related to the link that connected science, religion, and architecture. Choice (B) is incorrect because it suggests that the two appeared to be linked but perhaps were not. Choice (C) is incorrect because the word suggests that the link was not so strong.

31. **The correct answer is (C).** No punctuation is required after "symbols" because the phrase that follows it is restrictive, or necessary for identifying which symbols. Only choice (C) contains no punctuation after "symbols," so it is the correct answer. Choice (A) is incorrect because while a list follows "symbols," it is separated by the word "relating," and so a colon is not correct. Choice (B) is incorrect because the comma sets the restrictive phrase off from "symbols." Choice (D) is incorrect because a semicolon is used only to separate two independent clauses, and "relating to the sun, moon, and sky" is not an independent clause.

32. **The correct answer is (D).** The paragraph is concerned with how the Mayans also used the night sky to time warfare. Their signal was the appearance of Venus. Choice (D) is the correct answer, as it is the only choice that makes these two important points. Choice (A) is incorrect because the author does not suggest that Venus's appearance caused them to go to war, only that they waited for the appearance of Venus before engaging in warfare. Choice (B) is incorrect because it does not accurately note how the Mayans used Venus to time wars. Choice (C) is incorrect because it combines information from the preceding paragraph with information from this paragraph in a way that is misleading.

33. **The correct answer is (A).** The last paragraph is a short summary of the rest of the passage, as the phrase "in short," suggests. Thus, choice (A) is the correct answer. Choice (B) is incorrect because "however" indicates a contrast with information that

preceded it. Choice (C) is incorrect because "moreover" suggests that the paragraph will include new information, which it does not. Choice (D) is also incorrect because "incidentally" suggests that a digression or side topic will follow.

34. **The correct answer is (B).** The point of this opening paragraph is to establish that the narrator did not seek advice about how to get a job and instead tried to find a job on his own without interview experience. Only choice (B) makes these important points. Choice (A) is incorrect because it omits the idea that the narrator did not learn how to apply for jobs before he sent out resumes. Choice (C) is incorrect because it incorrectly suggests the narrator believed he was destined to work at a prestigious law firm and that this belief led him to ignore advice about seeking interview experience. Choice (D) is incorrect because it omits the central point that the narrator ignored the advice to get interview experience and instead sought jobs on his own.

35. **The correct answer is (D).** The narrator has intended to use the preposition "through" here, and only choice (D) reflects the correct spelling. Thus, choice (D) is the correct answer. Choice (A) is incorrect because "thorough" is an adjective that means complete or exhaustive. Choice (B) is also incorrect because "threw" is the past tense of "throw." Choice (C) is not correct because "though" functions as either an adverb meaning however or a conjunction meaning while.

36. **The correct answer is (C).** Because it is clear that the narrator is seeking a job, the correct possessive noun must be "my," as the passage is written in the first person and the narrator is referring to himself and no one else. Thus, choice (C) is the correct answer. Choice (A) is incorrect because "our" is plural in number and refers to the narrator and others, an incorrect reference. Choice (B) is not correct because there is no antecedent for "his" and the interview clearly belongs to the narrator. Choice (D) is also incorrect because there is no antecedent for "their."

37. **The correct answer is (A).** The paragraph's focus is the narrator's attempt to seek a job in a law firm. Only choice (A) maintains

this focus by noting the kind of environment the narrator hoped to work in. Choices (B), (C), and (D) are incorrect, as they do not add information that is relevant to the narrator's attempts to secure a job in a law firm.

38. **The correct answer is (D).** A complete sentence contains both a subject and a predicate. The sentence as it stands is a fragment, as it does not contain a subject. Only choice (D) contains both a subject ("I") and a predicate ("informed"). Choice (A) is incorrect because, as previously noted, it does not contain a subject. Choice (B) is incorrect, as it is a dependent clause, containing neither a subject nor a predicate. Choice (C) is incorrect because it, too, is a dependent clause.

39. **The correct answer is (B).** The context of the paragraph suggests that the narrator thinks that he is ambitious and well-spoken, as he has articulated his goals to the interviewer. Only choice (B) fits with the context. Choice (A) is incorrect because "enigmatic" means mysterious, and there is nothing mysterious about the narrator. Further, the narrator wouldn't assume that the interviewer thought he was mysterious. Choice (C) is incorrect because "conspicuous" means noticeable. While this could potentially work, it is not usually considered an admirable trait in a job interview. In this case, "articulate" is a better fit. Choice (D) is incorrect because "incoherent" means unable to be understood, and the narrator clearly thinks he has made a good impression on the interviewer.

40. **The correct answer is (C).** The context requires the plural form of "weakness," which is "weaknesses." Thus, choice (C) is the correct answer. Choice (A) is incorrect because it is a possessive form of "weakness." Choice (B) is incorrect because it is the possessive form of the plural "weaknesses," rather than just the plural. Choice (D) is not correct because it neither accurately reflects the plural of "weakness," nor the possessive of the word.

41. **The correct answer is (B).** Sentence 3 introduces the topic of the paragraph, which is the narrator's listing of his strengths and weaknesses. Because the sentence clearly introduces the main point of the paragraph, it belongs at the beginning of the paragraph. Choice (B), then, is the correct answer.

Choices (A) and (D) are incorrect because it makes no sense to place the sentence after the sentences that tell the narrator's response to the interviewer's question. Choice (C) is incorrect because sentence 1 only makes sense if it is placed after sentence 3, as sentence 3 helps explain it.

42. **The correct answer is (D).** The conventional phrase, "I couldn't have cared less," expresses apathy, as the speaker cannot care any less. Only choice (D) reflects the correct usage. Choice (A) is incorrect because the narrator is suggesting that he actually *could* have cared less than he already does—the degree of care can be reduced. Choices (B) and (C) are incorrect for the same reason, though choice (C) also incorrectly uses "of" instead of "have."

43. **The correct answer is (A).** The narrator's point in this final paragraph is that he was turned down for the job he sought and realized he needed tips on what to say during an interview. He ends by revealing that he now helps high school students find internships in his capacity as a guidance counselor. Only choice (A) includes all of these points. Choices (B), (C), and (D) are incorrect because they all omit the idea that the narrator eventually sought guidance for his job hunt after being turned down for several jobs. Choices (B) and (C) also omit the idea that the narrator now works as a guidance counselor helping students find internships.

44. **The correct answer is (B).** The word "eventually," along with the narrator's admission in the first paragraph that he did not go to the college job counseling office when first advised to, suggests that the correct term here is "belated," or overdue. Thus, choice (B) is the correct answer. Choice (A) is incorrect because "deferred" implies that he put off the trip with the intention of going at a later time, and there is no indication that the narrator did this. Choice (C) is incorrect because "hastened" suggests that the narrator made a speedy trip. Choice (D) is also incorrect, as "disparaged" means belittled or criticized, an adjective that doesn't make sense in the context of describing his trip to the college job counseling office.

Section 3: Math Test—No Calculator

1. C	**5.** C	**9.** C	**13.** D	**17.** 1
2. D	**6.** B	**10.** B	**14.** B	**18.** 13
3. B	**7.** B	**11.** C	**15.** A	**19.** 4/3
4. B	**8.** C	**12.** C	**16.** 24	**20.** 4

MATH TEST—NO CALCULATOR TEST RAW SCORE
(Number of correct answers)

1. **The correct answer is (C).** The question asks for Jared's goal in steps per day after d days. He increases his goal by 125 steps each day, so after 1 day it will go up 125(1), after 2 days it will go up by 125(2), and after d days it will go up by 125d from his original amount of 950.

2. **The correct answer is (D).** Use the correct order of evaluating functions. First evaluate $g(3) = 1$, then substitute in $f(g(3))$ as $f(1)$ to find that $f(g(3)) = 3$.

3. **The correct answer is (B).** The formula for exponential decay is $y = a(1-r)^n$, where r is the rate of change, n is the number of times the rate is applied, a is the initial amount, and y is the amount remaining.

4. **The correct answer is (B).** First, find half the length of the horizontal distance, which is 15 ft. Then, use the Pythagorean Theorem to find the length of each of the slanted sides.

$$a^2 + b^2 = c^2$$
$$8^2 + 15^2 = c^2$$
$$64 + 225 = c^2$$
$$289 = c^2$$
$$17 = c$$

5. **The correct answer is (C).** Since $y = 2(x - 4)(x - 6)$ is equivalent to the equation, and it is given in the form $y = a(x - b)(x - c)$, it shows the x-intercepts (4 and 6) as constants.

6. **The correct answer is (B).** Find the x- and y-intercepts of the given equation.

$$3x + y = 4$$
$$3(0) + y = 4$$
$$y = 4$$
$$3x + 0 = 4$$
$$x = \frac{4}{3}$$

Check the intercepts on the graph of each line to see if they match the intercepts of the equation in the problem. Only choice (B) has intercepts at $(0, 4)$ and $\left(\frac{4}{3}, 0\right)$.

7. **The correct answer is (B).** Use the point slope form of a linear equation to write the slope-intercept form of the equation:

$$y - y_1 = m(x - x_1)$$
$$y - 3 = -1(x - 2)$$
$$y - 3 = -x + 2$$
$$y = -x + 5$$

Then find the equation that is equivalent to the slope-intercept form:

$$3x + 3y = 15$$
$$3y = -3x + 15$$
$$y = -x + 15$$

8. **The correct answer is (C).** Use FOIL to solve:

$$\frac{3}{4}(x-4)(3+5x) = \frac{3}{4}\left(3x + 5x^2 - 12 - 20x\right)$$
$$= \frac{3}{4}\left(5x^2 - 17x - 12\right)$$
$$= \frac{15x^2}{4} - \frac{51x}{4} - 9$$

9. **The correct answer is (C).** To solve this problem, you need to remember the rule of fractional exponents, which states that if x is a nonzero rational number and m and n are positive integers, then $x^{\frac{m}{n}}$ equals the nth root of x^m:

$$x^{\frac{m}{n}} = \sqrt[n]{x^m}$$
$$x^{\frac{3}{4}} = \sqrt[4]{x^3}$$

10. **The correct answer is (B).** The equation for a parabola with a vertex at (h, k) is $y = a(x - h)^2 - k$, and if the y-intercept is 13, then $(0, 13)$ is a point on the parabola and $13 = a(0 - h)^2 - k$. Since $13 = 2(0 - 3)^2 - 5$, choice (B) is correct.

11. **The correct answer is (C).** The amount per each type of admission is $12 and $17, so the total admission of $1079 based upon number of adults and children is $12x + 7y$. The total number of people, 117, is represented by $x + y$.

12. **The correct answer is (C).**

$$\frac{4-i}{3+i} \times \frac{3-i}{3-i} = \frac{11-7i}{10}$$

13. **The correct answer is (D).** Solve the equation:

$$-6(t+1) = 2(1-3t) - 8$$
$$-6t - 6 = 2 - 6t - 8$$
$$-6 = -6$$

The equation has infinitely many solutions.

14. **The correct answer is (B).** The formula for population growth is $P = P_o e^{rt}$, where P represents the total population, P_o represents the initial population, e represents the constant value, r represent the rate of growth, and t represents the time. The "10" in the problem represents the time, in years, between the two years of interest—the initial year 1980 and the city's population in 1990. There are 10 years between 1980 and 1990.

15. **The correct answer is (A).** It's probably easiest to answer this question by plugging in numbers. We want to select easy numbers to represent the variables p and q. It is always a good idea stay away from numbers like 0 and 1, which have special properties; for this question, we also want to avoid the number 2, since it already appears in the equation. So, let's say that $p = 4$ and $q = 3$. If we plug these numbers into the original equation, we get:

$$\frac{2(4) + 2n}{3n} = 2$$
$$8 + 2n = 6n$$
$$8 = 4n$$
$$2 = n$$

When we plug the numbers 4 and 3 in for the variables p and q in each of the answer choices, we see that the expression in choice (A) works out to be 2, and that none of the other choices work.

$$\frac{p}{q-1} = \frac{4}{3-1} = 2$$

16. The correct answer is 24. To solve this problem, first isolate $\sqrt{x+1}$ on one side of the equation. Then, square both sides:

$$\sqrt{x+1} - 2 = 3$$
$$\sqrt{x+1} = 5$$
$$x+1 = 25$$
$$x = 24$$

17. The correct answer is 1. To solve this problem, substitute the value of $f(x) = 1$ in the given equation and solve for x:

$$f(x) = 3x - 2$$
$$1 = 3x - 2$$
$$3 = 3x$$
$$1 = x$$

18. The correct answer is 13. To find the value of c, divide the numerator by the denominator using either long division or synthetic division. Remember that the remainder can be written as a fraction, with the remainder as the numerator and the divisor as the denominator.

$$\frac{3x^2 - 4x - 18}{x+3} = x+3\overline{)3x^2 - 4x - 18}^{\;3x - 13R21}$$

Here, the remainder is 21, so the fraction is equal to $3x - 13 + \dfrac{21}{x+3}$. Set this equal to the expression in the equation to find that $c = 13$.

$$\frac{3x^2 - 4x - 18}{x+3} = 3x - 13 + \frac{21}{x+3}$$
$$c = 13$$

19. The correct answer is $\dfrac{4}{3}$. The equations need to have the same slope but different y-intercepts. The first equation is already written in slope-intercept form. First, re-write the second equation so that it is in slope-intercept form, then find the value for t that make the slope 3. This should make the y-intercept different than 7.

$$4x - ty = 5$$
$$-ty = -4x + 5 \qquad \text{So, } \frac{-4}{-t} = 3$$
$$y = \frac{-4x + 5}{-t} \qquad\qquad -4 = 3t$$
$$y = \frac{-4x}{-t} + \frac{5}{-t} \qquad\quad t = \frac{4}{3}$$

To check that the y-intercept is not 7:

$$\frac{5}{-t} = \frac{5}{-\frac{4}{3}}$$
$$= 5\left(-\frac{3}{4}\right)$$
$$= -\frac{15}{4}$$

20. The correct answer is 4. Use the formula for the volume of a sphere and of a cone and set the formulas equal to each other since their volumes are equal. Then solve for the value of $\dfrac{h}{r}$.

$$V_{cone} = V_{scoop}$$
$$\frac{1}{3}\pi r^2 h = \frac{4}{3}\pi r^3$$
$$h = \frac{\cancel{3}\left(\frac{4}{\cancel{3}}\cancel{\pi}r^{\cancel{3}^2}\right)}{\cancel{\pi}\cancel{r}}$$
$$h = 4r$$
$$\frac{h}{r} = 4$$

Section 4: Math Test—Calculator

1. C	**9.** A	**17.** C	**25.** B	**33.** 36
2. B	**10.** C	**18.** B	**26.** C	**34.** 800
3. D	**11.** B	**19.** A	**27.** C	**35.** 3.75
4. B	**12.** B	**20.** C	**28.** C	**36.** 29
5. A	**13.** A	**21.** A	**29.** D	**37.** 1 or 3
6. B	**14.** C	**22.** B	**30.** A	**38.** 965
7. D	**15.** A	**23.** A	**31.** 2.5	
8. B	**16.** C	**24.** C	**32.** 9	

MATH TEST—CALCULATOR RAW SCORE ☐
(Number of correct answers)

1. **The correct answer is (C).** We must first determine how many feet the insect travels in an average month. Then we can determine how many months it will take for the insect to travel 560 feet. To determine the number of feet the insect travels per month, we divide the yearly total by 12:

$$\frac{1680}{12} = 140$$

The insect travels 140 feet each month. To determine how many months it would take the insect to travel 560 feet, we divide the total number of feet (560) by the amount of feet that the insect travels in a month (140):

$$\frac{560}{140} = 4$$

Traveling at a rate of 140 feet per month, it would take the insect 4 months to travel 560 feet.

2. **The correct answer is (B).** The question asks for the number of books that will be renewed if the library loans 25,000 books. Use a proportion to solve.

$$\frac{18}{75} = \frac{x}{25,000}$$
$$75x = 18(25,000)$$
$$x = \frac{18(25,000)}{75}$$
$$x = 6000$$

3. **The correct answer is (D).** The number of males in Littletown is 210, and the number of females in Smalltown is 195. The probability of choosing a male who lives in Littletown is $\frac{210}{785}$ and the probability of choosing a woman who lives in Smalltown is $\frac{195}{785}$.

The probability of choosing one or the other is the sum of the individual probabilities:

$$\frac{210}{785} + \frac{195}{785} = \frac{405}{785} = \frac{81}{157}$$

4. **The correct answer is (B).** There are 52 weeks in a year, so multiplying 0.36 inches by 52 weeks is 18.72 inches. If the tree grows 18.72 inches in a year, then it will grow $18.72 \times 10 = 187.2$ inches in ten years.

5. **The correct answer is (A).** The total amount that Glen earns in one day is $10.25h$ where h is the number of hours Glen works and $3(12.50)$ is three times what he spends commuting. If he wants to earn at least three times what he spends commuting, then choice (A) is the only answer that represents the situation.

6. **The correct answer is (B).** If Peter spent x hours, then Nadia spent $x + 7$ hours on math homework, and together they spent $x + (x + 7) = 35$ hours. Solve for x:

$$x + (x + 7) = 35$$
$$2x + 7 = 35$$
$$2x = 28$$
$$x = 14$$

7. **The correct answer is (D).** Since c is 22 percent of e, c equals $(e \times 0.22)$, or $= 0.22e$. Likewise, because d is 68 percent of e, d equals $(e \times 0.68)$, or $= 0.68e$. To find the value of $d - c$, in terms of e, we can set up an equation:

$$d - c = \left(0.68e - 0.22e\right)$$
$$d - c = \left(0.46e\right)$$

8. **The correct answer is (B).** Graph the inequalities and look for where they overlap, or substitute each point into both inequalities to determine which point satisfies both inequalities.

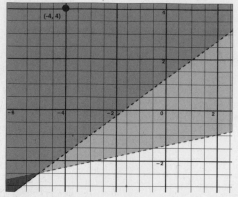

Only choice (B) is correct:

$$2x - 9y < 12 \qquad\qquad -3x + 4y > 5$$
$$2(-4) - 9(4) < 12 \qquad -3(-4) + 4(4) > 5$$
$$-8 - 36 < 12 \qquad\qquad 12 + 16 > 5$$

9. **The correct answer is (A).** The question is just asking us to substitute the value that we are given for n and then to simplify the expression. We're asked to provide an answer in terms of m, or in other words, an answer that contains the variable m. Let's see what we get when we substitute 7 for n:

$$2m(16 - 6n) = 2m\left[16 - 6(7)\right]$$
$$= 2m(16 - 42)$$
$$= 2m(-26)$$
$$= -52m$$

10. **The correct answer is (C).** The total amount that she has raised is $145. If she gets $15 from each additional donor, then the total contributions will be equal to $145 + 15x$, where x is the number of contributions she gets from this point forward.

11. **The correct answer is (B).** Read the graph and look for where the line has a vertical coordinate of $400. The closest approximation is 58 hats.

12. **The correct answer is (B).** The x-axis of the graph shows the number of hats sold, and the y-axis shows the amount of money raised. Consequently, the slope of the line shows the amount of money received per hat.

13. **The correct answer is (A).** A sample size of 18 people is not large enough to make a conclusion for a city of 38,000. The sample population was randomly selected, the size of the city population alone doesn't affect the reliability, and the number of people with no preference does not affect the reliability.

14. **The correct answer is (C).** When the mean and median of a set of data are not the same, outliers tend to affect the mean more than the median. If some income values are much greater than the others, the mean will be greater than the median.

15. **The correct answer is (A).** The amount of CDs sold would be equal to the number of days in the sale (j) times the number of neighbors (h) times the average number of CDs sold (x), or jhx. To determine the number of CDs that will be *left* after the total number of CDs, (jhx), are sold, we subtract jhx from 1230. This value can be expressed as $1230 - jhx$.

16. **The correct answer is (C).** The formula that is useful for this problem is the formula for projectile motion: $y = 0.5at^2 + vt + h$, where a is the acceleration, v is the upward velocity, h is the initial height, t is the time in seconds, and y is the height after t seconds. Here, the coefficient, v, equals 50, so the correct answer must be choice (C).

17. **The correct answer is (C).** First, write inequalities that represent the price for each company. Then let the price from Company J be less than the price for Company K and solve the inequality.

Company J $= 0.15x + 19$

Company K $= 0.10x + 30$

$$0.15x + 19 < 0.1x + 30$$
$$0.05x < 11$$
$$x < 220$$

18. **The correct answer is (B).** The daily rental cost for the truck is the y-intercept. The slope of the graph of this relationship is the per mile cost. The total cost for the miles driven in the truck is $0.12x$. The total cost for driving the truck the entire distance is $0.12x + 25$.

19. **The correct answer is (A).** To find the probability that a randomly chosen house in Town B is a colonial house, first find the total number of houses that are in Town B: $62 + 65 + 43 + 32 = 202$. Then write and simplify a ratio of colonial houses in Town B to the total number of houses in Town B in the survey: $\dfrac{65}{202}$

20. **The correct answer is (C).** The total number of houses in the survey is 375. The number of Victorian houses in Town A is 20. The probability that a randomly selected house is chosen from Town A and is a Victorian house is $\dfrac{20}{375} = \dfrac{4}{75}$.

answers PRACTICE TEST 3

21. The correct answer is (A). To solve the quadratic equation, first add 5 to both sides of the equation: $y = 3x^2 - 5x - 2$. Then, use the quadratic formula with $a = 3$, $b = -5$, $c = -2$ and simplify the expression.

$$x = \frac{-(-5) \pm \sqrt{(-5)^2 - 4(3)(-2)}}{2(3)}$$

$$= \frac{5 \pm \sqrt{49}}{6}$$

$$= 2, \ -\frac{1}{3}$$

22. The correct answer is (B). The key to solving this geometry problem is to recognize that the figure contains two similar triangles. We know that the triangles are similar because their corresponding angles are equal ($x = x$, $y = y$, and the two right angles are equal). Since the triangles have equal corresponding angles, we know that the sides are in proportion to one another.

We want to determine the ratio between the corresponding sides in the larger triangle, SQR, and the smaller triangle, TQP. We can do this by comparing the two corresponding sides for which we have measures. We're given the length of QP in the smaller triangle as 11.5. We're also given the length of its corresponding leg from the larger triangle, QR, as 46. How many times bigger is QR than QP? If we divide 46 by 11.5, we see that QR is 4 times as large as QP.

The question asks us to determine the length of SQ, which is a side of the larger triangle, SQR. We know that the measure of its corresponding side in the smaller triangle, TQP, is TQ, which measures 15. We also know that all corresponding sides in the larger triangle, SQR, are 4 times as long as the ones in the smaller triangle, TQP, so SQ measures 4 times as much as TQ, or $4 \times 15 = 60$.

23. The correct answer is (A). First, rewrite the equation as a quadratic one:

$$1 = \frac{3}{x-4} + \frac{4}{x-3}$$

$$(x-3)(x-4) = (x-3)(x-4)\left[\frac{3}{x-4} + \frac{4}{x-3}\right]$$

$$x^2 - 7x + 12 = 3x - 9 + 4x - 16$$

$$x^2 - 14x + 37 = 0$$

Now use the quadratic formula with $a = 1$, $b = 14$, and $c = 37$ to simplify:

$$x = \frac{14 \pm \sqrt{(-14)^2 - 4(37)}}{2}$$

$$x = \frac{14 \pm \sqrt{196 - 148}}{2}$$

$$x = 7 \pm 2\sqrt{3}$$

24. The correct answer is (C). Use the circumference of the circle to find the radius.

$$C = 2\pi r$$

$$572\pi = 2\pi r$$

$$286 = r$$

Then use the measure of the central angle and the radius to find the area of the sector:

$$A = \frac{\frac{3\pi}{4}}{2\pi}\pi(r)^2$$

$$A = \frac{3}{8}\pi(286)^2$$

$$A = \frac{61,347\pi}{2}$$

25. The correct answer is (B). If $b < -1$ and $c > 1$, then the x-intercepts of the graph must greater than 1 and less than -1.

26. The correct answer is (C). If a is any value less than 0, then the border of $x + ay < -3$ will intersect the y-axis and there will be solutions in quadrant I. Eliminate choice (A). If a is greater than 2.5 then there will be solutions in quadrant IV. Eliminate choice (D). If $0 \le a \le 2.5$, then there are only solutions in quadrants II and III. Since a can take on values other than 0, choice (B) is incorrect.

27. **The correct answer is (C).** The slope increases between the points, so it is not a linear relationship. Eliminate choices (A) and (B). An exponential relationship uses the x-variable for the exponent. Eliminate choice (D). Checking approximate points (32, 13), (80, 54) and (96, 75) using choice (C):

$$y = 4.82(1.03)^x \rightarrow 4.82(1.03)^{32} \rightarrow y \approx 12.4$$

$$y = 4.82(1.03)^x \rightarrow 4.82(1.03)^{80} \rightarrow y \approx 51.3$$

$$y = 4.82(1.03)^x \rightarrow 4.82(1.03)^{96} \rightarrow y \approx 82.3$$

The equation approximately models the data, so choice (C) is correct.

28. **The correct answer is (C).** The relationship between the initial speed and the stopping distance is modeled by exponential growth, because the slope of the line connecting any two points increases as the initial speed increases. While the points are close to a line, an exponential growth curve better approximates the relationship.

29. **The correct answer is (D).** The 95% confidence that the margin of error is +/− 34 is important, and choices (A) and (B) ignore the confidence interval. Choice (C) is not correct because there are likely people who don't know or have no opinion on whether there should be stricter emissions standards for power plants. Only choice (D) accurately uses the confidence interval and the data given in the problem.

30. **The correct answer is (A).** Use completing the square to find the coordinates of the center of the circle. Separate the equation x- and y-terms:

$$x^2 + y^2 - 10x + 4y = -20$$
$$x^2 - 10x + y^2 + 4y = -20$$
$$(x^2 - 10x + 25) + (y^2 + 4y + 4) = -20 + 25 + 4$$
$$(x - 5)^2 + (y + 2)^2 = 9$$

The center is (5, −2), because the standard form of the circle is $(x - h)^2 + (y - k)^2 = r^2$.

31. **The correct answer is 2.5.** Write an equation to represent the situation, and then solve:

$$16.25 = 2.5(2) + 4.5x$$
$$11.25 = 4.5x$$
$$2.5 = x$$

32. **The correct answer is 9.** Solve for the expression requested in the inequality, then interpret the answer in the context of the question asked:

$$4s - 3 < 2$$
$$4s < 5$$
$$s < \frac{5}{4}$$

Since s is an integer, s must be 1, and so $4s + 5 = 4(1) - 5 = 9$. The greatest integer value that is less than 10 is 9.

33. **The correct answer is 36.** Use the method of combination to determine the values of a and b. Start by subtracting the first equation from the second equation:

$$2a + 2b = 16$$
$$-(2a - b) = -(7)$$
$$\overline{3b = 9}$$
$$b = 3$$

Insert $b = 3$ into the first equation:

$$2a - (3) = 7$$
$$2a = 10$$
$$a = 5$$

Now you are ready to plug both values into the expression in question:

$$3a + 7b = 3(5) + 7(3)$$
$$= 15 + 21$$
$$= 36$$

34. The correct answer is 800. The formula for population growth is given in terms of n, the number of years. In order to solve this problem, plug the value of n, in this case 54, into the formula and calculate the value of the expression $100(2)^{\frac{n}{18}}$:

Population in millions after n years $= 100(2)^{\frac{n}{18}}$

$$= 100(2)^{\frac{54}{18}}$$
$$= 100(2)^3$$
$$= 800$$

35. The correct answer is 3.75. Read the question carefully; it asks for the difference in the prices of one object, not the difference between the amounts of money they made, or any other quantity.

Since Paul sold four pieces of pottery for $85, he made $y = \frac{85}{4} = \$21.25$ per piece. Sally made $40 more than Paul did for all of her pieces, so she made $85 + $40 = $125 in total. Since she sold five pieces, she made $x = \frac{125}{5} = \$25.00$ per piece. Per piece, Sally made $x - y = \$25 - \$21.25 = \$3.75$ more than Paul did. The correct answer is 3.75.

36. The correct answer is 29. First, find the original amount using a percent proportion. Then add 4 to find the new total.

$$\frac{16}{100} = \frac{4}{x}$$
$$16x = 400$$
$$x = \frac{400}{16}$$
$$x = 25$$
$$25 + 4 = 29$$

37. The correct answer is 1 or 3. First, combine the equations by substituting $2x + 5$ for y in the second equation. Then solve for x. Next, substitute the x-values back in and solve for y:

$$2x + 5 = -2(x+1)^2 + 3$$
$$2x + 5 = -2x^2 - 4x - 2 + 3$$
$$0 = -2x^2 - 6x - 4$$
$$0 = -2(x+2)(x+1)$$
$$x = -1, -2$$
$$y = 2(-1) + 5 = 3$$
or
$$y = 2(-2) + 5 = 1$$

38. The correct answer is 965. If the average of the 2010–2014 weekly median income is $1,007, and the average after 2015 is at least $1,000, then an equation can be written to solve for the least amount that the weekly median income amount can be for 2015:

$$\frac{1,007 \cdot 5 + x}{6} = 1,000$$
$$5,035 + x = 6,000$$
$$x = 965$$

Therefore, the least average weekly median household income for 2015 that will keep the average of at least $1,000 is $965.

Section 5: Essay

Analysis of Passage

The following is an analysis of the passage by Catherine Anderson, noting how the writer used evidence, reasoning, and stylistic or persuasive elements to support her claims, connect the claims and evidence, and add power to the ideas she expressed. Check to see if you evaluated the passage in a similar way.

Adapted from "Michael Graves sought to create joy through superior design" by Catherine Anderson, Assistant Professor of Interior Architecture and Design at George Washington University. From The Conversation, March 25, 2015 [http://theconversation.com]

1 Visit the website of designer Michael Graves, and you'll be greeted with the words "Humanistic Design = Transformative Results."

2 The mantra can double as Graves' philosophy.

3 For Graves—who passed away at 80 earlier this month—paid no heed to architectural trends, social movements or the words of his critics. Instead, it was the everyday human being—the individual—who inspired and informed his work.

4 During a career that spanned over 50 years, Graves held firm to the belief that design could effect tremendous change in people's day-to-day lives. From small-scale kitchen products to immense buildings, a thread runs throughout his products: accessible, aesthetic forms that possess a sense of warmth and appeal.

5 Early in his career, Graves was identified as one of the New York Five, a group of influential architects who whole-heartedly embraced Modernism, the architectural movement that subscribed to the use of simple, clean lines, forms devoid of embellishments and modern materials such as steel and glass.

6 However, Graves is best described as a Post-Modernist.

1 *Anderson lays the groundwork for the validity of her argument by referring the reader to an authoritative source on this subject—the website of Michael Graves.*

2 *The writer uses evocative words and phrases such as mantra, double as, philosophy, paid no heed, and trends.*

3 *The writer clearly states her central argument.*

4 *Anderson continues using evocative phrases: held firm, effect tremendous change, immense buildings, a thread runs throughout, a sense of warmth and appeal.*

5 *She provides historical context by discussing Graves' early career and establishing his status as a Modernist architect. She also defines Modernism for the reader.*

6 *The writer expands her historical context by claiming that Graves was really a Post-Modernist. She then explains exactly what this means.* www.petersons.com

7   He eschewed the austerity of Modernism and its belief that "less is more," instead embracing history and references to the past.

8   He rejected the notion that decoration, or ornament, was a "crime" (as Austrian architect Adolf Loos wrote in 1908); rather, he viewed it as a way for his architecture to convey meaning.

9   As the noted architectural historian Spiro Kostof explains in his book *A History of Architecture: Settings and Rituals*, "Post Modernists turn to historical memory … to ornament, as a way of enriching the language of architecture."

10 …Along these lines, Graves

11 loathed the idea of intellectualizing his structures. Instead, he sought to make them accessible, understandable and poignant to all passersby. …

12 In addition to designing buildings, Graves embarked upon a long and highly successful partnership with the Italian kitchenware company Alessi …

13 Graves' most famous Alessi design is his iconic teakettle … which had a cheerful red whistling bird and sky-blue handle. On sale since 1985, the best-selling product is still in production today.

14 In 1999, Minneapolis-based discount retail giant Target approached Graves with an offer to design a line of kitchen products, ranging from toasters to spatulas.

15 While some might have shied away from having their work associated with a mega-corporation like Target, Graves wholly embraced the project. …

7   *The writer uses evocative phrases to paint pictures for the reader: eschewed the austerity, embracing history, rejected the notion.*

8   *Anderson enlivens her writing with a vivid word (crime) used by an authority and cites her source.*

9   *Anderson quotes an authoritative source to support her claim that Graves was a Post-Modernist.*

10 *The writer builds on this quotation to advance her argument that Graves was a Post-Modernist.*

11 *The writer uses evocative phrases to make her argument vivid: "loathed the idea," intellectualizing his structures," "poignant to all passersby."*

12 *Anderson points out that Graves did more than design buildings, mentioning his partnership with the Italian kitchenware company Alessi.*

13 *She also mentions one of Graves' famous creations for Alessi and points out that it sold extremely well.*

14 *Continuing her discussion of Graves' non-architectural creations, the writer refers to his work designing kitchen products for Target.*

15 *The writer anticipates a possible negative reaction to this work, pointing out that Graves "embraced" it.*

16 In all, Graves' collaboration with Target would last 13 years; during this time, the designer would become a household name, with millions of units of his products appearing in American homes.

17 Many of Graves' designs for Target—his spatula, can opener and ice cream scoop— had chunky, sky-blue handles. Other appliances that were white … were sprinkled with touches of color. … Black and beige had no place in Graves' palette.

18 The option to select a better-looking product with a slightly higher price versus the same article but with a less expensive, nondescript appearance is now the norm for most consumers: good design (and function) are part and parcel of the customer experience

19 (nowhere is this more evident than in Apple's rise to dizzying heights as arguably one of the world's most valuable brands).

20 It's an idea that's democratic in nature, and thinking about design through this lens led Graves to create thoughtful, appealing and affordable products for the masses. …

21 As Graves' popularity rose, his critics leveled

22 blistering commentaries about what they deemed a precipitous fall from grace— from a "trend beyond compare" to a "stale trend," as

23 architecture critic Herbert Muschamp noted in a 1999 New York Times article. The notion that he had commodified design—and had somehow "cheapened" it—drew the disdain of those who once lauded his works.

16 *Anderson legitimizes Graves' work with Target, saying his creations sold millions of units and that he became "a household name."*

17 *She gives the reader a strong sense of Graves' practical, everyday Target creations, naming specific products and describing what they looked like.*

18 *Anderson cites the significance of Graves' work with Target, pointing out that better design in everyday products has become the norm.*

19 *She supports this claim by citing Apple as an example of a company that routinely offers customers good design in its products.*

20 *The writer reasserts the importance of Graves' place in the movement to create "affordable products for the masses."*

21 *The writer provides historical context to trace the negative reaction to Graves' work with Target.*

22 *She brings this reaction to life using evocative phrases: blistering commentaries, precipitous fall from grace, commodified design, drew the disdain of those who once lauded his works.*

23 *The writer cites a source to support her claim that there was a negative reaction to Graves' Target products.*

24   Yet Graves remained true to his beliefs even into the last phase of his life. In 2003, after an illness left him paralyzed below the waist, he realized that the design of hospitals and equipment … could be redesigned and made more functional, comfortable and visually appealing. He then went on to improve ubiquitous devices such as wheelchairs and walking canes. …

24   *Anderson provides additional historical context for Graves' later designs for common things and gives specific examples.*

25   Consumers may not have ever known his architecture or what the critics thought of his work (or even realized they were buying one of his products). Graves didn't seem to mind. His goal was to provide well-designed items for everyday use rather than impress his detractors.

25   *The writer provides psychological insight into Graves' personality and reasserts his primary goal: "to provide well-designed items for everyday use."*

26   As he told NPR in 2002, "It's the kind of thing where you pick something up or use it with a little bit of joy …it puts a smile on your face."

26   *The writer concludes her argument with a quotation from Graves that supports her claim that his primary concern was quality design for the everyday human being.*

Sample Essays

The following are examples of a high-scoring and low-scoring essay, based on the passage by Catherine Anderson.

High-Scoring Essay

Catherine Anderson is clearly a fan of Michael Graves's architecture and product design. Anderson identifies the everyday human being as Graves's inspiration. She gives a history of Graves' work, explaining how his focus on people inspired him. Anderson's word choices and descriptions bring Graves's products to life. Anderson's words are as warm and appealing as the products she describes. Supporting her descriptions with a history of Graves's designs and biographical details convinces readers to admire the products he designed and, perhaps, to buy one that fits in their own kitchens.

Anderson tells readers that Graves's career started as an architect in New York 50 years ago. She provides historical context by identifying Graves as one of an elite group of Modernist architects who designed simple, plain buildings constructed of the modern materials steel and glass. Because her description of Modernist architecture sounds cold and empty, Anderson hastens to say that Graves was actually a Post-Modernist architect whose creations were less plain and more inviting. He used embellishments in his architectural designs to convey meaning, which sounds more warm and comforting than the Modernist architectural style she described with the words *plain*, *steel and glass*, and *austerity*.

To support her statements, Anderson cites a well-known architectural expert who describes Post Modernists architecture as enriched by ornamentation. She then uses appealing words to attract readers to Graves's work—*accessible*, *understandable*, and *poignant*.

Graves didn't design architecture only. He also designed common items, such as teakettles and spatulas, for common people. His most famous design is a quirky teakettle that has a sky-blue handle and a bright red bird that whistles when the water is hot enough to make tea. Just the image Anderson created of the whistling bird on the teakettle makes Graves's work sound fun and appealing. The kitchen products Graves designed are sold by Target, a store where the people who inspired Graves could afford to shop. They must be buying his products because millions of them have been purchased at Target and are still selling today.

While Graves's popularity rose among Target shoppers, it dropped among architecture critics. Anderson informs readers of the critics' changing attitudes by quoting their comments such as "stale trend" and "cheapened." Graves, however, heroically "remained true to his beliefs" by continuing to design attractive products that could be bought by average people.

In 2003 an illness made Graves a paraplegic. Instead of becoming bitter, like many people would have in the same situation, Graves looked around at the poorly designed medical products and decided that he could make improvements. Even a hospital environment benefited from his design abilities. He created products, such as wheelchairs and canes, that Anderson said were "more functional, comfortable and visually attractive."

Anderson closed the article by quoting Graves's comment that he hoped his products would make people smile. Anderson showed that throughout his life, Graves's main concern was creating designs for the average person. Just as he had hoped, his products have inspired, and continue to inspire, joy in the people who inspired him—especially when making tea.

Low-Scoring Essay

Catherine Anderson started the article by focusing on Michael Graves's mantra of "Humanistic Design = Transformative Results." This means that focusing on people can make things better.

Michael Graves focused on people to design buildings and things they could use like teakettles and wheelchairs. Because Michael Graves likes people, he designed things that they would like, things that would make them happy.

Catherine Anderson says his products are warm and appealing. She describes a teakettle that's fun to use because it whistles. The buildings he designed have historical meaning because he added a lot of decorations. He said it's not a crime to build decorated buildings.

Michael Graves worked with Alessi to design attractive kitchen products that people liked a lot, like the whistling teakettle. He used warm colors like red to make it more appealing. Catherine Anderson describes his kitchen products as "chunky" and colorful. This makes them sound like things everyone would want to have. Because millions were sold at Target, he probably made a lot of money on them. That's a good reason to ignore the critics who didn't like his designs. The critics said his kitchen products were "stale," which is a clever food-related way to say they were old and boring. Regardless of the critics, his stuff is popular.

Michael Graves was pretty old when he got sick and couldn't walk. Because he couldn't walk, he designed wheelchairs and canes that he and other people could use. Catherine Anderson says they're "functional, comfortable and visually appealing." If Target sold them, they would probably be as popular as his teakettle.

Michael Graves died in 2015 when he was 80 years old. His buildings and products followed his mantra of "Humanistic Design = Transformative Results." He made things better by focusing on people. He improved a lot of things that he designed and made a lot of people happy. Catherine Anderson proved that the things he made were attractive and made people happy.

COMPUTING YOUR SCORES

To get a sense of your progress in preparing for the SAT®, follow these instructions and the following conversion tables.

To Determine Your Practice Test Scores

❶ After you go through each of the test sections (Reading, Writing and Language, Math—No Calculator, and Math—Calculator) and determine which answers you got right, be sure to enter the number of correct answers in the box below the answer key for each of the sections.

❷ Your total score on the SAT® practice test is the sum of your Evidence-Based Reading and Writing Section score and your Math Section score. To get your total score, convert the raw score   the number of questions you got right in a particular section—into the "scaled score" for that section, and then you'll calculate the total score. It sounds a little confusing, but we'll take you through the steps.

To Calculate Your Evidence-Based Reading and Writing Section Score

Your Evidence-Based Reading and Writing Section score is on a scale of 200–800. First determine your Reading Test score, and then determine your score on the Writing and Language Test.

❶ Count the number of correct answers you got on the **Section 1: Reading Test.** Remember that there is no penalty for wrong answers. **The number of correct answers is your raw score.**

❷ Go to Raw Score Conversion Table 1: Section and Test Scores on page 755. Look in the "Raw Score" column for your raw score, and match it to the number in the "Reading Test Score" column.

❸ Do the same with **Section 2: Writing and Language Test** to determine that score.

❹ Add your Reading Test score to your Writing and Language Test score.

❺ Multiply that number by 10. This is your Evidence-Based Reading and Writing Section score.

To Calculate Your Math Section Score

YOUR MATH SECTION SCORE IS ALSO ON A SCALE OF 200–800.

❶ Count the number of correct answers you got on the Section 3: Math Test—No Calculator and the Section 4: Math Test—No Calculator practice tests. Again, there is no penalty for wrong answers. **The number of correct answers is your raw score.**

❷ Add the number of correct answers on the Section 3: Math Test—No Calculator and the Section 4: Math Test—No Calculator practice tests.

❸ Use the **Raw Score Conversion Table 1: Section and Test Scores** on page 755 and convert your raw score into your Math Section score.

To Obtain Your Total Score

Add your score on the Evidence-Based Reading and Writing Section to the Math Section score. This is your total score on this SAT® Practice Test, on a scale of 400–1600.

Subscores Provide Additional Information

Subscores offer you greater details about your strengths in certain areas within literacy and math. The subscores are reported on a scale of 1–15 and include Heart of Algebra, Problem Solving and Data Analysis, Passport to Advanced Math, Expression of Ideas, Standard English Conventions, Words in Context, and Command of Evidence.

Heart of Algebra

The **Heart of Algebra subscore** is based on questions from the Math Test—No Calculator and Math Test—Calculator (Sections 3 and 4) that focus on linear equations and inequalities.

- Add up your total correct answers from these sections:
- Math Test—No Calculator: Questions 1, 6, 7, 11, 13, 14, 17, 19
- Math Test—Calculator: Questions 5, 6, 8, 10, 15, 17, 18, 26, 31, 32, 33
- Your Raw Score = the total number of correct answers from all of these questions.
- Use the **Raw Score Conversion Table 2: Subscores** on page 756 to determine your **Heart of Algebra** subscore.

Problem Solving and Data Analysis

The **Problem Solving and Data Analysis subscore** is based on questions from the Math Test that focus on quantitative reasoning, the interpretation and synthesis of data, and solving problems in rich and varied contexts.

- Add up your total correct answers from these sections:
- Math Test—No Calculator: None
- Math Test—Calculator: Questions 1–4, 7, 11–14, 19, 20, 27–29, 35, 36, 38
- Your Raw Score = the total number of correct answers from all of these questions.
- Use the **Raw Score Conversion Table 2: Subscores** on page 756 to determine your **Problem Solving and Data Analysis** subscore.

Passport to Advanced Math

The **Passport to Advanced Math subscore** is based on questions from the Math Test that focus on topics central to your ability to progress to more advanced math, such as understanding the structure of expressions, reasoning with more complex equations, and interpreting and building functions.

- Add up your total correct answers from these sections:
- our total correct answers from these sections:
- Math Test—No Calculator: Questions 2, 3, 5, 8–10, 15, 16, 18
- Math Test—Calculator: Questions 9, 16, 21, 23, 25, 34, 37
- Your Raw Score = the total number of correct answers from all of these questions.
- Use the **Raw Score Conversion Table 2: Subscores** on page 756 to determine your **Passport to Advanced Math** subscore.

Expression of Ideas

The **Expression of Ideas subscore** is based on questions from the Writing and Language Test that focus on topic development, organization, and rhetorically effective use of language.

- Add up your total correct answers from Section 2: Writing and Language Test
- Questions 1, 2, 5, 6, 10–13, 16, 17, 19, 20, 26, 27, 29, 30, 32–34, 37, 39, 41, 43, 44
- Your Raw Score = the total number of correct answers from all of these questions.
- Use the **Raw Score Conversion Table 2: Subscores** on page 756 to determine your **Expression of Ideas** subscore.

Standard English Conventions

The **Standard English Conventions subscore** is based on questions from the Writing and Language Test that focus on sentence structure, usage, and punctuation.

- Add up your total correct answers from Section 2: Writing and Language Test:
- Questions 3, 4, 7–9, 14, 15, 18, 28, 31, 35, 36, 38, 40, 42
- Your Raw Score = the total number of correct answers from all of these questions.
- Use the **Raw Score Conversion Table 2: Subscores** on page 756 to determine your **Standard English Conventions** subscore.

Words in Context

The **Words in Context subscore** is based on questions from the Reading Test and the Writing and Language Test that address word/phrase meaning in context and rhetorical word choice.

- Add up your total correct answers from Sections 1 and 2:
- Reading Test: Questions 6, 9, 21, 22, 31, 36, 42, 51, 52
- Writing and Language Test: Questions 2, 6, 17, 20, 26, 30, 39, 44
- Your Raw Score = the total number of correct answers from all of these questions.
- Use the **Raw Score Conversion Table 2: Subscores** on page 756 to determine your **Words in Context** subscore.

Command of Evidence

The **Command of Evidence subscore** is based on questions from the Reading Test and the Writing and Language Test that ask you to interpret and use evidence found in a wide range of passages and informational graphics, such as graphs, tables, and charts.

- Add up your total correct answers from Sections 1 and 2:
- Reading Test: Questions 5, 8, 16, 20, 26, 30, 35, 39, 47, 50
- Writing and Language Test: Questions 1, 5, 12, 19, 27, 32, 34, 43
- Your Raw Score = the total number of correct answers from all of these questions.
- Use the **Raw Score Conversion Table 2: Subscores** on page 756 to determine your **Command of Evidence** subscore.

Cross-Test Scores

The new SAT®also reports two cross-test scores: Analysis in History/Social Studies and Analysis in Science. These scores are based on questions in the Reading Test, Writing and Language Test, and both Math Tests that ask you to think analytically about texts and questions in these subject areas. Cross-test scores are reported on a scale of 10–40.

Analysis in History/Social Studies

- Add up your total correct answers from these sections:
- Reading Test: Questions 12–22, 33–42
- Writing and Language Test: Questions 26, 27, 29, 30, 32, 33
- Math Test—No Calculator: Question 14
- Math Test—Calculator: Questions 3, 13, 14, 19, 20, 29, 38
- Your Raw Score = the total number of correct answers from all of these questions.
- Use the **Raw Score Conversion Table 3: Cross-Test Scores** on page 757 to determine your **Analysis in History/Social Studies** cross-test score.

Analysis in Science

- Add up your total correct answers from these sections:
- Reading Test: Questions 1–11, 23–32
- Writing and Language Test: Questions 12, 13, 16, 17, 19, 20
- Math Test—No Calculator: Question 3
- Math Test—Calculator: Questions 1, 4, 16, 24, 27, 28, 34
- Your Raw Score = the total number of correct answers from all of these questions.
- Use the **Raw Score Conversion Table 3: Cross-Test Scores** on page 757 to determine your **Analysis in Science** cross-test score.

Raw Score Conversion Table 1: Section and Test Scores

Raw Score	Math Section Score	Reading Test Score	Writing and Language Test Score	Raw Score	Math Section Score	Reading Test Score	Writing and Language Test Score	Raw Score	Math Section Score	Reading Test Score	Writing and Language Test Score
0	200	10	10	20	450	22	23	40	610	33	36
1	200	10	10	21	460	23	23	41	620	33	37
2	210	10	10	22	470	23	24	42	630	34	38
3	230	11	10	23	480	24	25	43	640	35	39
4	240	12	11	24	480	24	25	44	650	35	40
5	260	13	12	25	490	25	26	45	660	36	
6	280	14	13	26	500	25	26	46	670	37	
7	290	15	13	27	510	26	27	47	670	37	
8	310	15	14	28	520	26	28	48	680	38	
9	320	16	15	29	520	27	28	49	690	38	
10	330	17	16	30	530	28	29	50	700	39	
11	340	17	16	31	540	28	30	51	710	40	
12	360	18	17	32	550	29	30	52	730	40	
13	370	19	18	33	560	29	31	53	740		
14	380	19	19	34	560	30	32	54	750		
15	390	20	19	35	570	30	32	55	760		
16	410	20	20	36	580	31	33	56	780		
17	420	21	21	37	590	31	34	57	790		
18	430	21	21	38	600	32	34	58	800		
19	440	22	22	39	600	32	35				

Conversion Equation 1 Section and Test Scores

Raw Score Conversion Table 2: Subscores

Raw Score (# of correct answers)	Expression of Ideas	Standard English Conventions	Heart of Algebra	Problem Solving Data Analysis	Passport to Advanced Math	Words in Context	Command of Evidence
0	1	1	1	1	1	1	1
1	1	1	1	1	3	1	1
2	1	1	2	2	5	2	2
3	2	2	3	3	6	3	3
4	3	2	4	4	7	4	4
5	4	3	5	5	8	5	5
6	5	4	6	6	9	6	6
7	6	5	6	7	10	6	7
8	6	6	7	8	11	7	8
9	7	6	8	8	11	8	8
10	7	7	8	9	12	8	9
11	8	7	9	10	12	9	10
12	8	8	9	10	13	9	10
13	9	8	9	11	13	10	11
14	9	9	10	12	14	11	12
15	10	10	10	13	14	12	13
16	10	10	11	14	15	13	14
17	11	11	12	15		14	15
18	11	12	13			15	15
19	12	13	15				
20	12	15					
21	13						
22	14						
23	14						
24	15						

Conversion Equation 2 Subscores

HEART OF ALGEBRA RAW SCORE (0–19)	EXPRESSION OF IDEAS RAW SCORE (0–24)	COMMAND OF EVIDENCE RAW SCORE (0–18)	PROBLEM SOLVING AND DATA ANALYSIS RAW SCORE (0–17)
CONVERT	CONVERT	CONVERT	CONVERT
HEART OF ALGEBRA SUBSCORE (1–15)	EXPRESSION OF IDEAS SUBSCORE (1–15)	COMMAND OF EVIDENCE SUBSCORE (1–15)	PROBLEM SOLVING AND DATA ANALYSIS SUBSCORE (1–15)

STANDARD ENGLISH CONVENTIONS RAW SCORE (0–20)	WORDS IN CONTEXT RAW SCORE (0–18)	PASSPORT TO ADVANCED MATH RAW SCORE (0–16)
CONVERT	CONVERT	CONVERT
STANDARD ENGLISH CONVENTIONS SUBSCORE (1–15)	WORDS IN CONTEXT SUBSCORE (1–15)	PASSPORT TO ADVANCED MATH SUBSCORE (1–15)

Raw Score Conversion Table 3: Cross-Test Scores

Raw Score (# of correct answers)	Analysis in History/Social Studies Cross-Test Score	Analysis in Science Cross-Test Score	Raw Score (# of correct answers)	Analysis in History/Social Studies Cross-Test Score	Analysis in Science Cross-Test Score
0	10	10	18	28	26
1	10	11	19	29	27
2	11	12	20	30	27
3	12	13	21	30	28
4	14	14	22	31	29
5	15	15	23	32	30
6	16	16	24	32	30
7	17	17	25	33	31
8	18	18	26	34	32
9	20	19	27	35	33
10	21	20	28	35	33
11	22	20	29	36	34
12	23	21	30	37	35
13	24	22	31	38	36
14	25	23	32	38	37
15	26	24	33	39	38
16	27	24	34	40	39
17	28	25	35	40	40

answers PRACTICE TEST 3

Conversion Equation 3: Cross-Test Scores

TEST	ANALYSIS IN HISTORY/SOCIAL STUDIES		ANALYSIS IN SCIENCE	
	QUESTIONS	RAW SCORE	QUESTIONSs	RAW SCORE
Reading Test	12–22, 33–42		1–11, 23–32	
Writing and Language Test	26, 27, 29, 30, 32, 33		12, 13, 16, 17, 19, 20	
Math Test—No Calculator	14		3	
Math Test—Calculator	3, 13, 14, 19, 20, 29, 38		1, 4, 16, 24, 27, 28, 34	
TOTAL				

ANALYSIS IN HISTORY/
SOCIAL STUDIES
RAW SCORE (0–35)

CONVERT

ANALYSIS IN HISTORY/
SOCIAL STUDIES
CROSS-TEST SCORE (10–40)

ANALYSIS IN SCIENCE
RAW SCORE (0–35)

CONVERT

ANALYSIS IN SCIENCE
CROSS-TEST SCORE (1–15)

Practice Test 4

On test day, you will see these important reminders on the first page of your SAT® test booklet:

- You must use a No. 2 pencil when taking the test; you may not use a pen or mechanical pencil.

- You may not share any questions with anyone. This is considered a violation of College Board's "Test Security and Fairness" policies, and it could cause your scores to be canceled.

- You are not permitted to take the test booklet out of the testing room.

In addition to filling in your name and Test Center information on your answer sheet, you'll be asked to fill in two different codes that will be on your test booklet. Each test booklet has a unique code, and there will be a grid-in form to fill in with your "TEST ID" and "FORM CODE" letters and numbers.

The general directions for the test will look something like this:

- You may only work on one section at a time.

- If you complete a section before time is called, check your work on that section only. You are not permitted to work on any other section.

The directions for marking your answers will likely include the following recommendations:

- Mark your answer sheet properly—be sure to <u>completely</u> fill in the answer bubble.

- Be careful to mark only one answer for each question.

- Don't make any stray marks on the answer sheet.

- If you need to erase your answer, make sure you do so completely.

- Be sure to use the answer spaces that correspond to the question numbers.

You will be able to use your test booklet for scratch work, but you won't get credit for any work done in your test booklet. When time is called at the end of each section, you will not be permitted to transfer answers from your test booklet to your answer sheet.

Any information, ideas, or opinions presented in any of the passages you will see on the redesigned SAT® that have been taken from other sources or published material do not represent the opinions of the College Board.

Scoring on the SAT® is as follows:

- You will receive one point for each correct answer.

- You will not lose points for wrong answers, so you should attempt to answer every question even if you aren't completely sure of the correct answer.

Your testing supervisor will announce when to open the test booklet, so be sure to wait until you're told to do so. For the purposes of this practice test, be sure you have a timer to set for 65 minutes for the Section 1: Reading Test.

The answer sheets for each test section, including lined paper for the essay, appear on the next five pages. Following the Answer Key and Explanations for this Practice Test, you will find details on how to score your work.

ANSWER SHEET PRACTICE TEST 4

Section 1: Reading Test

1. Ⓐ Ⓑ Ⓒ Ⓓ   12. Ⓐ Ⓑ Ⓒ Ⓓ   23. Ⓐ Ⓑ Ⓒ Ⓓ   33. Ⓐ Ⓑ Ⓒ Ⓓ   43. Ⓐ Ⓑ Ⓒ Ⓓ

2. Ⓐ Ⓑ Ⓒ Ⓓ   13. Ⓐ Ⓑ Ⓒ Ⓓ   24. Ⓐ Ⓑ Ⓒ Ⓓ   34. Ⓐ Ⓑ Ⓒ Ⓓ   44. Ⓐ Ⓑ Ⓒ Ⓓ

3. Ⓐ Ⓑ Ⓒ Ⓓ   14. Ⓐ Ⓑ Ⓒ Ⓓ   25. Ⓐ Ⓑ Ⓒ Ⓓ   35. Ⓐ Ⓑ Ⓒ Ⓓ   45. Ⓐ Ⓑ Ⓒ Ⓓ

4. Ⓐ Ⓑ Ⓒ Ⓓ   15. Ⓐ Ⓑ Ⓒ Ⓓ   26. Ⓐ Ⓑ Ⓒ Ⓓ   36. Ⓐ Ⓑ Ⓒ Ⓓ   46. Ⓐ Ⓑ Ⓒ Ⓓ

5. Ⓐ Ⓑ Ⓒ Ⓓ   16. Ⓐ Ⓑ Ⓒ Ⓓ   27. Ⓐ Ⓑ Ⓒ Ⓓ   37. Ⓐ Ⓑ Ⓒ Ⓓ   47. Ⓐ Ⓑ Ⓒ Ⓓ

6. Ⓐ Ⓑ Ⓒ Ⓓ   17. Ⓐ Ⓑ Ⓒ Ⓓ   28. Ⓐ Ⓑ Ⓒ Ⓓ   38. Ⓐ Ⓑ Ⓒ Ⓓ   48. Ⓐ Ⓑ Ⓒ Ⓓ

7. Ⓐ Ⓑ Ⓒ Ⓓ   18. Ⓐ Ⓑ Ⓒ Ⓓ   29. Ⓐ Ⓑ Ⓒ Ⓓ   39. Ⓐ Ⓑ Ⓒ Ⓓ   49. Ⓐ Ⓑ Ⓒ Ⓓ

8. Ⓐ Ⓑ Ⓒ Ⓓ   19. Ⓐ Ⓑ Ⓒ Ⓓ   30. Ⓐ Ⓑ Ⓒ Ⓓ   40. Ⓐ Ⓑ Ⓒ Ⓓ   50. Ⓐ Ⓑ Ⓒ Ⓓ

9. Ⓐ Ⓑ Ⓒ Ⓓ   20. Ⓐ Ⓑ Ⓒ Ⓓ   31. Ⓐ Ⓑ Ⓒ Ⓓ   41. Ⓐ Ⓑ Ⓒ Ⓓ   51. Ⓐ Ⓑ Ⓒ Ⓓ

10. Ⓐ Ⓑ Ⓒ Ⓓ   21. Ⓐ Ⓑ Ⓒ Ⓓ   32. Ⓐ Ⓑ Ⓒ Ⓓ   42. Ⓐ Ⓑ Ⓒ Ⓓ   52. Ⓐ Ⓑ Ⓒ Ⓓ

11. Ⓐ Ⓑ Ⓒ Ⓓ   22. Ⓐ Ⓑ Ⓒ Ⓓ

Section 2: Writing and Language Test

1. Ⓐ Ⓑ Ⓒ Ⓓ   10. Ⓐ Ⓑ Ⓒ Ⓓ   19. Ⓐ Ⓑ Ⓒ Ⓓ   28. Ⓐ Ⓑ Ⓒ Ⓓ   37. Ⓐ Ⓑ Ⓒ Ⓓ

2. Ⓐ Ⓑ Ⓒ Ⓓ   11. Ⓐ Ⓑ Ⓒ Ⓓ   20. Ⓐ Ⓑ Ⓒ Ⓓ   29. Ⓐ Ⓑ Ⓒ Ⓓ   38. Ⓐ Ⓑ Ⓒ Ⓓ

3. Ⓐ Ⓑ Ⓒ Ⓓ   12. Ⓐ Ⓑ Ⓒ Ⓓ   21. Ⓐ Ⓑ Ⓒ Ⓓ   30. Ⓐ Ⓑ Ⓒ Ⓓ   39. Ⓐ Ⓑ Ⓒ Ⓓ

4. Ⓐ Ⓑ Ⓒ Ⓓ   13. Ⓐ Ⓑ Ⓒ Ⓓ   22. Ⓐ Ⓑ Ⓒ Ⓓ   31. Ⓐ Ⓑ Ⓒ Ⓓ   40. Ⓐ Ⓑ Ⓒ Ⓓ

5. Ⓐ Ⓑ Ⓒ Ⓓ   14. Ⓐ Ⓑ Ⓒ Ⓓ   23. Ⓐ Ⓑ Ⓒ Ⓓ   32. Ⓐ Ⓑ Ⓒ Ⓓ   41. Ⓐ Ⓑ Ⓒ Ⓓ

6. Ⓐ Ⓑ Ⓒ Ⓓ   15. Ⓐ Ⓑ Ⓒ Ⓓ   24. Ⓐ Ⓑ Ⓒ Ⓓ   33. Ⓐ Ⓑ Ⓒ Ⓓ   42. Ⓐ Ⓑ Ⓒ Ⓓ

7. Ⓐ Ⓑ Ⓒ Ⓓ   16. Ⓐ Ⓑ Ⓒ Ⓓ   25. Ⓐ Ⓑ Ⓒ Ⓓ   34. Ⓐ Ⓑ Ⓒ Ⓓ   43. Ⓐ Ⓑ Ⓒ Ⓓ

8. Ⓐ Ⓑ Ⓒ Ⓓ   17. Ⓐ Ⓑ Ⓒ Ⓓ   26. Ⓐ Ⓑ Ⓒ Ⓓ   35. Ⓐ Ⓑ Ⓒ Ⓓ   44. Ⓐ Ⓑ Ⓒ Ⓓ

9. Ⓐ Ⓑ Ⓒ Ⓓ   18. Ⓐ Ⓑ Ⓒ Ⓓ   27. Ⓐ Ⓑ Ⓒ Ⓓ   36. Ⓐ Ⓑ Ⓒ Ⓓ

Section 3: Math Test—No Calculator

1. Ⓐ Ⓑ Ⓒ Ⓓ 4. Ⓐ Ⓑ Ⓒ Ⓓ 7. Ⓐ Ⓑ Ⓒ Ⓓ 10. Ⓐ Ⓑ Ⓒ Ⓓ 13. Ⓐ Ⓑ Ⓒ Ⓓ
2. Ⓐ Ⓑ Ⓒ Ⓓ 5. Ⓐ Ⓑ Ⓒ Ⓓ 8. Ⓐ Ⓑ Ⓒ Ⓓ 11. Ⓐ Ⓑ Ⓒ Ⓓ 14. Ⓐ Ⓑ Ⓒ Ⓓ
3. Ⓐ Ⓑ Ⓒ Ⓓ 6. Ⓐ Ⓑ Ⓒ Ⓓ 9. Ⓐ Ⓑ Ⓒ Ⓓ 12. Ⓐ Ⓑ Ⓒ Ⓓ 15. Ⓐ Ⓑ Ⓒ Ⓓ

16. _(grid-in)_ 17. _(grid-in)_ 18. _(grid-in)_ 19. _(grid-in)_ 20. _(grid-in)_

Section 4: Math Test—Calculator

1. Ⓐ Ⓑ Ⓒ Ⓓ 7. Ⓐ Ⓑ Ⓒ Ⓓ 13. Ⓐ Ⓑ Ⓒ Ⓓ 19. Ⓐ Ⓑ Ⓒ Ⓓ 25. Ⓐ Ⓑ Ⓒ Ⓓ
2. Ⓐ Ⓑ Ⓒ Ⓓ 8. Ⓐ Ⓑ Ⓒ Ⓓ 14. Ⓐ Ⓑ Ⓒ Ⓓ 20. Ⓐ Ⓑ Ⓒ Ⓓ 26. Ⓐ Ⓑ Ⓒ Ⓓ
3. Ⓐ Ⓑ Ⓒ Ⓓ 9. Ⓐ Ⓑ Ⓒ Ⓓ 15. Ⓐ Ⓑ Ⓒ Ⓓ 21. Ⓐ Ⓑ Ⓒ Ⓓ 27. Ⓐ Ⓑ Ⓒ Ⓓ
4. Ⓐ Ⓑ Ⓒ Ⓓ 10. Ⓐ Ⓑ Ⓒ Ⓓ 16. Ⓐ Ⓑ Ⓒ Ⓓ 22. Ⓐ Ⓑ Ⓒ Ⓓ 28. Ⓐ Ⓑ Ⓒ Ⓓ
5. Ⓐ Ⓑ Ⓒ Ⓓ 11. Ⓐ Ⓑ Ⓒ Ⓓ 17. Ⓐ Ⓑ Ⓒ Ⓓ 23. Ⓐ Ⓑ Ⓒ Ⓓ 29. Ⓐ Ⓑ Ⓒ Ⓓ
6. Ⓐ Ⓑ Ⓒ Ⓓ 12. Ⓐ Ⓑ Ⓒ Ⓓ 18. Ⓐ Ⓑ Ⓒ Ⓓ 24. Ⓐ Ⓑ Ⓒ Ⓓ 30. Ⓐ Ⓑ Ⓒ Ⓓ

31. _(grid-in)_ 32. _(grid-in)_ 33. _(grid-in)_ 34. _(grid-in)_ 35. _(grid-in)_

answer sheet

36.

	/	/	
.	.	.	.
	0	0	0
1	1	1	1
2	2	2	2
3	3	3	3
4	4	4	4
5	5	5	5
6	6	6	6
7	7	7	7
8	8	8	8
9	9	9	9

37.

	/	/	
.	.	.	.
	0	0	0
1	1	1	1
2	2	2	2
3	3	3	3
4	4	4	4
5	5	5	5
6	6	6	6
7	7	7	7
8	8	8	8
9	9	9	9

38.

	/	/	
.	.	.	.
	0	0	0
1	1	1	1
2	2	2	2
3	3	3	3
4	4	4	4
5	5	5	5
6	6	6	6
7	7	7	7
8	8	8	8
9	9	9	9

Section 5: Essay

_____

_____

_____

_____

_____

_____

_____

_____

_____

_____

_____

_____

_____

_____

_____

_____

_____

_____

_____

_____

answer sheet

SECTION 1: READING TEST

65 Minutes • 52 Questions

TURN TO SECTION 1 OF YOUR ANSWER SHEET TO ANSWER THE QUESTIONS IN THIS SECTION.

Directions: Each passage (or pair of passages) below is followed by a number of multiple-choice questions. After reading each passage, select the best answer to each question based on what is stated or implied in the passage or passages and in any supplementary material, such as a table, graph, chart, or photograph.

QUESTIONS 1–10 ARE BASED ON THE FOLLOWING PASSAGE AND SUPPLEMENTARY MATERIAL.

From his humble beginnings, Herbert Hoover made his fortune in the mining industry. He earned his reputation as a humanitarian and skilled administrator during and after World War I and later served as Secretary of Commerce under both Presidents Harding and Coolidge. In 1928, he was nominated for president by the Republican Party. The following is an excerpt from a speech he gave at the end of his campaign against the Democratic nominee, New York Governor Alfred E. Smith.

During one hundred and fifty years
we have builded up a form of self
government and a social system which is
Line peculiarly our own. It differs essentially
5 from all others in the world. It is the
American system. … It is founded upon
the conception that only through ordered
liberty, freedom and equal opportunity
to the individual will his initiative and
10 enterprise spur on the march of progress.
And in our insistence upon equality of
opportunity has our system advanced
beyond all the world.

During [World War I] we necessarily
15 turned to the government to solve
every difficult economic problem. The
government having absorbed every
energy of our people for war, there was
no other solution. For the preservation of
20 the state the Federal Government became
a centralized despotism which undertook
unprecedented responsibilities, assumed
autocratic powers, and took over the
business of citizens. To a large degree, we

25 regimented our whole people temporally
into a socialistic state. However justified
in war time, if continued in peace-time
it would destroy not only our American
system but with it our progress and
30 freedom as well.

When the war closed, the most
vital of issues both in our own country
and around the world was whether
government should continue their
35 wartime ownership and operation of
many [instruments] of production and
distribution. We were challenged with
a … choice between the American system
of rugged individualism and a European
40 philosophy of diametrically opposed
doctrines, doctrines of paternalism and
state socialism. The acceptance of these
ideas would have meant the destruction of
self-government through centralization …
45 [and] the undermining of the individual
initiative and enterprise through which
our people have grown to unparalleled
greatness. …

I would like to state to you the effect
50 that … [an interference] of government
in business would have upon our system
of self-government and our economic
system. That effect would reach to the
daily life of every man and woman. It
55 would impair the very basis of liberty and
freedom. …

Let us first see the effect on self-
government. When the Federal
Government undertakes to go into
60 commercial business it must at once set
up the organization and administration
of that business, and it immediately finds
itself in a labyrinth. … Commercial

GO TO THE NEXT PAGE

business requires a concentration of responsibility. Our government to succeed in business would need to become in effect a despotism. There at once begins the destruction of self-government ….

Liberalism is a force truly of the spirit, a force proceeding from the deep realization that economic freedom cannot be sacrificed if political freedom is to be preserved. [An expansion of the government's role in the business world] would cramp and cripple the mental and spiritual energies of our people. It would extinguish equality and opportunity. It would dry up the spirit of liberty and progress. … For a hundred and fifty years liberalism has found its true spirit in the American system, not in the European systems.

I do not wish to be misunderstood. … I am defining general policy. … I have already stated that where the government is engaged in public works for purposes of flood control, of navigation, of irrigation, of scientific research or national defense … it will at times necessarily produce power or commodities as a by-product.

Nor do I wish to be misinterpreted as believing that the United States is a free-for-all and devil-take-the-hindmost. The very essence of equality of opportunity and of American individualism is that there shall be no domination by any group or [monopoly] in this republic. … It is no system of *laissez faire*. …

I have witnessed not only at home but abroad the many failures of government in business. I have seen its tyrannies, its injustices, its destructions of self-government, its undermining of the very instincts which carry our people forward to progress. I have witnessed the lack of advance, the lowered standards of living, the depressed spirits of people working under such a system. …

And what has been the result of the American system? Our country has become the land of opportunity to those born without inheritance, not merely because of the wealth of its resources and industry but because of this freedom of initiative and enterprise. Russia has natural resources equal to ours. … But she has not had the blessings of one hundred and fifty years of our form of government and our social system.

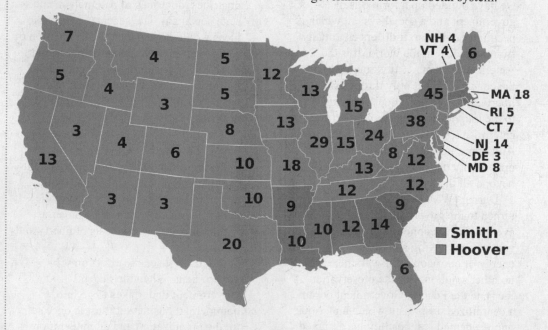

This map shows the electoral votes for each state in the presidential election of 1928, which Herbert Hoover won in a landslide.

1 Based on the excerpt, which statement is true of Hoover's ideas about government?

(A) Socialism is justified during wartime, but not at other times.

(B) Government cannot solve economic problems.

(C) A strong government stifles individual liberty.

(D) A democratic government is always superior to other governments.

2 Why did Hoover believe it was necessary to strengthen the federal government during wartime?

(A) The United States was fighting despotism and therefore had to become despotic.

(B) Only a socialistic government can function during wartime.

(C) Most resources went toward the war effort, draining them for other uses in the economy.

(D) Businesses acting by themselves could interfere with the war effort.

3 How does Hoover's speech change in lines 83–110 ("I do not wish … under such a system.")?

(A) He changes his attitude.

(B) He shows he wants to be understood.

(C) He shows that his ideas are moderate.

(D) He clarifies his position by providing details about his philosophy.

4 What is the most likely reason that Hoover includes lines 83–110 in his speech?

(A) He wanted to appeal to more voters.

(B) He wanted to preempt criticism.

(C) He wanted to soften his position.

(D) He wanted to provide context for his views.

5 How did Hoover view European governments?

(A) Tyrannical/despotic

(B) Democratic/republican

(C) Socialistic/paternalistic

(D) Autocratic/monarchical

6 Based on the map, what is a landslide?

(A) A popular vote

(B) A close contest

(C) A hard-won election

(D) A decisive victory

7 Which of the following lines in the text explain how the U.S. changed course during WWI?

(A) Lines 1–4 ("During one hundred … our own.")

(B) Lines 14–16 ("During [World War I] … economic problem.")

(C) Lines 53–54 ("That effect … and woman.")

(D) Lines 89–91 ("it will at times … a by-product.")

8 How does Hoover indicate that he believes the American form of government is superior to others?

(A) Lines 6–10 ("It is founded … of progress.")

(B) Lines 69–73 ("Liberalism is … be preserved.")

(C) Lines 99–100 ("It is no … laissez faire.")

(D) Lines 117–118 ("Our country … of opportunity")

9 As used in line 63, "labyrinth" most nearly means

(A) maze.

(B) cave.

(C) bind.

(D) landmine.

GO TO THE NEXT PAGE

10 As used in line 25, "regimented" most nearly means

(A) organized.

(B) militarized.

(C) bullied.

(D) established.

QUESTIONS 11–21 ARE BASED ON THE FOLLOWING TWO PASSAGES AND SUPPLEMENTARY MATERIAL.

Passage 1 is an excerpt from a letter written by Harriet Beecher Stowe, the abolitionist and author of the best-selling novel Uncle Tom's Cabin (1852). The book describes the horrors of slavery and is said to have helped promote the abolitionists' cause. The recipient of the letter, Mrs. Follen, a fellow abolitionist, was also a poet, editor, and novelist. Passage 2 is an excerpt from the memoir of Frederick Douglass, an active abolitionist who had escaped from slavery in 1838. After gaining his freedom, Douglass published Narrative of the Life of Frederick Douglass, An American Slave, Written by Himself (1845). The passage describes how he planned his escape.

Passage 1

Harriet Beecher Stowe, from a letter to Mrs. Follen (1853)

I had two little curly-headed twin daughters to begin with, and my stock in this line was gradually increased, till I
Line have been the mother of seven children,
5 the most beautiful and the most loved of whom lies buried near my Cincinnati residence. It was at his dying bed and at his grave that I learned what a poor slave mother may feel when her child is torn
10 away from her. In those depths of sorrow which seemed to me immeasurable, it was my only prayer to God that such anguish might not be suffered in vain. There were circumstances about his death of
15 such peculiar bitterness, of what seemed almost cruel suffering, that I felt that I could never be consoled for it unless this crushing of my own heart might enable

me to work out some great good to
20 others …

I allude to this here because I have often felt that much that is in that book ("Uncle Tom") had its root in the awful scenes and bitter sorrows of that summer.
25 It has left now, I trust, no trace on my mind except a deep compassion for the sorrowful, especially for mothers who are separated from their children ….

I am now writing a work which will
30 contain, perhaps, an equal amount of matter with *Uncle Tom's Cabin*. It will contain all the facts and documents upon which that story was founded, and an immense body of facts, reports of trial,
35 legal documents, and testimony of people now living South, which will more than confirm every statement in *Uncle Tom's Cabin*. I must confess that till I began the examination of facts in order to write this
40 book, much as I thought I knew before, I had not begun to measure the depth of the abyss. The law records of courts and judicial proceedings are so incredible as to fill me with amazement whenever
45 I think of them. It seems to me that the book cannot but be felt, and, coming upon the sensibility awaked by the other, do something. I suffer exquisitely in writing these things. It may be truly said that I
50 suffer with my heart's blood. Many times in writing *Uncle Tom's Cabin* I thought my heart would fail utterly, but I prayed earnestly that God would help me till I got through, and still I am pressed beyond
55 measure and above strength ….

Passage 2—Recollection of Frederick Douglass

… It is impossible for me to describe my feelings as the time of my contemplated start grew near. I had a number of warm-hearted friends in
60 Baltimore,—friends that I loved almost as I did my life,—and the thought of being separated from them forever was painful beyond expression. It is my opinion that thousands would escape from slavery,
65 who now remain, but for the strong cords of affection that bind them to their

friends. The thought of leaving my friends was decidedly the most painful thought with which I had to contend. The love of
70 them was my tender point, and shook my decision more than all things else. Besides the pain of separation, the dread and apprehension of a failure exceeded what I had experienced at my first attempt. The
75 appalling defeat I then sustained returned to torment me. I felt assured that, if I failed in this attempt, my case would be a hopeless one—it would seal my fate as a slave forever. I could not hope to get
80 off with anything less than the severest

punishment, and being placed beyond the means of escape. It required no very vivid imagination to depict the most frightful scenes through which I would have to
85 pass, in case I failed. The wretchedness of slavery, and the blessedness of freedom, were perpetually before me. It was life and death with me. But I remained firm and according to my resolution, on the
90 third day of September, 1838, I left my chains, and succeeded in reaching New York without the slightest interruption of any kind.

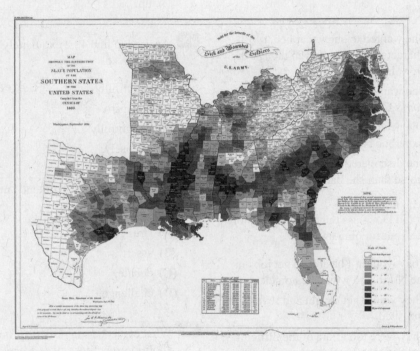

This map shows population and density of slaves in 1860.
(Credit: Historical Map & Chart Collection, Office of Coast Survey, NOAA)

11 What was the common thread of the experiences that stimulated the writing of Stowe and Douglass?

(A) Loss of close friends

(B) Death in the family

(C) Witness to cruelty of slavery

(D) Permanent loss of loved ones

12 Why would Stowe be sympathetic to Douglass' experience?

(A) She was appalled at the idea of slavery.

(B) She had lost a young child.

(C) She knew freed slaves who told her their stories.

(D) She had family members who had been enslaved.

13 What is the most likely reason that Stowe wrote *Uncle Tom's Cabin*?

(A) She wanted to earn her own money.

(B) She wanted to document her own experience with slavery.

(C) She wanted to show others why slavery should be abolished.

(D) She wanted to express her concerns about freed slaves in the North.

14 Why did Stowe want to write another book after the success of *Uncle Tom's Cabin*?

(A) She wanted to show that her characters were real even though the work is a novel.

(B) She wanted to confirm that *Uncle Tom's Cabin* was based on the truth.

(C) She needed to prove her point to sell more books.

(D) She discovered that slavery was worse than she had thought.

15 What did Douglass think prevented more slaves from running away?

(A) They wouldn't be able to get jobs in the North and would be homeless.

(B) They would get caught and severely punished.

(C) They were too afraid of the difficult and dangerous journey.

(D) They were afraid that they would never see their loved ones again.

16 Why might Douglass have given his narrative its title?

(A) He was almost illiterate and liked the way it sounded.

(B) He wanted people to know that he actually was the author.

(C) He wanted to make sure no one else could take his identity.

(D) He wanted to promote the abolitionist cause.

17 What do the passages suggest about the abolition movement in the mid-nineteenth century?

(A) It was made up of people who opposed slavery based on reading about it.

(B) There were many people writing to expose the evils of slavery in an effort to abolish it.

(C) People in the North were angry that slavery was legal.

(D) The conflict over slavery was heating up.

18 As used in line 48, "exquisitely" most nearly means

(A) beautifully.

(B) exhaustively.

(C) delightfully.

(D) intensely.

19 As used in line 69, "contend" most nearly means

(A) struggle.

(B) assert.

(C) debate.

(D) challenge.

20 What evidence suggests that Stowe's abolitionist activism was a way to memorialize her lost child?

(A) Lines 7–9 ("It was at … mother may feel")

(B) Lines 16–20 ("that I felt … good to others")

(C) Lines 22–24 ("that book … that summer")

(D) Lines 49–50 ("It may be … heart's blood")

21 Why does Stowe believe she needs to do research for her next book?

(A) Lines 25–27 ("It has left … the sorrowful")

(B) Lines 40–42 ("much as I … the abyss.")

(C) Lines 42–43 ("The law records … so incredible")

(D) Lines 50–52 ("Many times … fail utterly")

QUESTIONS 22–31 ARE BASED ON THE FOLLOWING PASSAGE AND SUPPLEMENTARY MATERIAL.

The following passage is a news item published on May 4, 2015, from the Jet Propulsion Laboratory at the California Institute of Technology. The lab is part of NASA and is dedicated to the robotic exploration of space.

Traffic Around Mars Gets Busy

NASA has beefed up a process of traffic monitoring, communication, and maneuver planning to ensure that Mars
Line orbiters do not approach each other too
5 closely.

Last year's addition of two new spacecraft orbiting Mars brought the census of active Mars orbiters to five, the most ever. NASA's Mars Atmosphere and
10 Volatile Evolution (MAVEN) and India's Mars Orbiter Mission joined the 2003 Mars Express from ESA (the European Space Agency) and two from NASA: the 2001 Mars Odyssey and the 2006
15 Mars Reconnaissance Orbiter (MRO). The newly enhanced collision-avoidance process also tracks the approximate location of NASA's Mars Global Surveyor, a 1997 orbiter that is no longer
20 working.

It's not just the total number that matters, but also the types of orbits missions use for achieving their science goals. MAVEN, which reached Mars
25 on Sept. 21, 2014, studies the upper atmosphere. It flies an elongated orbit, sometimes farther from Mars than NASA's other orbiters and sometimes closer to Mars, so it crosses altitudes
30

occupied by those orbiters. For safety, NASA also monitors positions of ESA's and India's orbiters, which both fly elongated orbits.
    …
35 Traffic management at Mars is much less complex than in Earth orbit, where more than 1,000 active orbiters plus additional pieces of inactive hardware add to hazards. As Mars exploration
40 intensifies, though, and will continue to do so with future missions, precautions are increasing. The new process was established to manage this growth as new members are added to the Mars orbital
45 community in years to come.

All five active Mars orbiters use the communication and tracking services of NASA's Deep Space Network, which is managed at JPL [Jet Propulsion
50 Laboratory]. This brings trajectory information together, and engineers can run computer projections of future trajectories out to a few weeks ahead for comparisons.
55 "It's a monitoring function to anticipate when traffic will get heavy," said Joseph Guinn, manager of JPL's Mission Design and Navigation Section. "When two spacecraft are predicted to
60 come too close to one another, we give people a heads-up in advance so the project teams can start coordinating about whether any maneuvers are needed."

The amount of uncertainty in the
65 predicted location of a Mars orbiter a few days ahead is more than a mile (more than two kilometers). Calculating projections for weeks ahead multiplies the uncertainty to dozens of miles, or
70 kilometers. In most cases when a collision cannot be ruled out from projections two weeks ahead, improved precision in the forecasting as the date gets closer will rule out a collision with no need for
75 avoidance action. Mission teams for the relevant orbiters are notified in advance when projections indicate a collision is possible, even if the possibility will likely disappear in subsequent projections.
80 This situation occurred on New Year's weekend, 2015.

GO TO THE NEXT PAGE

On Jan. 3, automated monitoring determined that two weeks later, MAVEN and MRO could come within about two
85 miles (three kilometers) of each other, with large uncertainties remaining in the exact passing distance. Although that was a Saturday, automatic messages went out to the teams operating the orbiters.

90   "In this case, before the timeline got short enough to need to plan an avoidance maneuver, the uncertainties shrank, and that ruled out the chance of the two spacecraft coming too near each other,"
95 Guinn said. This is expected to be the usual pattern, with the advance warning kicking off higher-level monitoring and initial discussions about options.

    If preparations for an avoidance
100 maneuver were called for, spacecraft commands would be written, tested, and approved for readiness, but such commands would not be sent to a

spacecraft unless projections a day or two
105 ahead showed probability of a hazardous conjunction. The amount of uncertainty about each spacecraft's exact location varies, so the proximity considered unsafe also varies. For some situations, a day-
110 ahead projection of two craft coming within about 100 yards (100 meters) of each other could trigger a maneuver.

    The new formal collision-avoidance process for Mars is part of NASA's
115 Multi-Mission Automated Deep-Space Conjunction Assessment Process. A side benefit of it is that information about when two orbiters will be near each other—though safely apart—could be
120 used for planning coordinated science observations. The pair could look at some part of Mars or its atmosphere from essentially the same point of view simultaneously with complementary
125 instruments.

This graphic depicts the relative shapes and distances from Mars for five active orbiter missions plus the planet's two natural satellites. It illustrates the potential for intersections of the spacecraft orbits.

22 Which of the following is the best summary of passage?

(A) Gathering information from space requires careful and complex monitoring of spacecraft satellites.

(B) The multiple satellites orbiting around Mars could collide even though they are not traveling in the same orbits.

(C) Planning for space satellites around other planets takes skilled teamwork.

(D) Monitoring traffic around the Earth is more complex than monitoring the traffic around Mars.

23 Which countries are involved in monitoring of the Mars satellites?

(A) The United States, Russia, and India

(B) Europe and the United States

(C) India, Europe, and the United States

(D) The United States, China, and Russia

24 According to information in the passage, what happened on New Year's weekend 2015?

(A) Data indicated that there could be a collision.

(B) Data gave scientists new information about the orbit of the satellites.

(C) The collision alert turned out to be a false alarm.

(D) Two satellites almost collided.

25 Based on information given in the passage, which of the following career fields would the workers at the Jet Propulsion Lab most likely be qualified for?

(A) Disaster preparedness planner

(B) Meteorologist

(C) Airplane pilot

(D) Road construction worker

26 Which are the natural satellites of Mars?

(A) MRO and Phobos

(B) Phobos an MAVEN

(C) Deimos and Odyssey

(D) Phobos and Deimos

27 Based on the graphic, which satellite is least likely to have collision problem?

(A) Phobos, because it has a more elongated orbit

(B) MOM, because its orbit extends farthest from Mars

(C) Deimos, because it only intersects with one other satellite

(D) MAVEN, because its path is controlled by NASA engineers

28 Which lines in the passage explain why scientists must constantly monitor the satellites' orbits?

(A) Lines 24–26 ("MAVEN, which … upper atmosphere")

(B) Lines 26–29 ("It flies … to Mars")

(C) Lines 35–36 ("Traffic management … Earth orbit")

(D) Lines 46–48 ("All five … Space Network")

29 What evidence in the passage supports the idea that the distances between satellites are related to the degree of danger they pose?

(A) Lines 75–78 ("Mission teams … is possible")

(B) Lines 83–85 ("MAVEN and … each other")

(C) Lines 106–109 ("The amount … also varies")

(D) Lines 113–116 ("The new formal … Assessment Process.")

practice test

30 As used in line 106, "conjunction" most nearly means

(A) connection between the satellites.

(B) divergence between orbits.

(C) linking of Mars and a satellite.

(D) alignment of two satellites.

31 As used in line 52, "projections" most nearly means

(A) use of trajectory information.

(B) reference to future trajectories.

(C) comparisons to other trajectories.

(D) engineers can make comparisons.

QUESTIONS 32–42 ARE BASED ON THE FOLLOWING PASSAGE.

Potatoes were first cultivated in Peru by the Incas between 8000 and 5000 BCE. Today, potatoes make up the fourth largest food crop in the world. In a ground-breaking agreement between the International Potato Center (known by its Spanish acronym CIP), the nonprofit organization ANDES, and the Association of the Potato Park communities, scientists are helping Peruvian farmers test and monitor many varieties of potatoes. One of their goals is to ensure continued diversity in potatoes—an action that could prevent disasters such as the Irish Potato Famine.

As world leaders gather in Lima to negotiate a new global climate deal at the UN Climate conference, this innovative,

Line inclusive work shows the importance
5 of new kinds of partnerships between scientists and farmers for adaptation to climate change.

In the Peruvian highlands near Cusco, climate change has already impacted
10 farmers in a fundamental way. Rising temperatures are correlated with increased pests and diseases, making it difficult to grow potatoes, their staple food.

The effects of these temperature
15 changes are very pronounced in the Potato Park, a valley outside of Cusco, where just 30 years ago, cultivation of native potato was routinely done at 3,800 meters.

Now, native potato cultivation starts
20 at around 4,000 meters. In just 30 years, challenges associated with a warming climate have pushed potato cultivation up by 200 meters. The speed of this change in planting zones due to a warming climate is
25 unprecedented as it is pushing the farmers to the top of the mountain, beyond which there is no more soil or land.

In addition to moving to higher elevation for potato cultivation,
30 Quechua farmers in the Potato Park are also responding to this challenge by stewarding over 1,440 cultivars of native potato. These include their own varieties plus cultivars that different entities have
35 provided to the Park, 410 of which have come from CIP.

The five communities that make up the Potato Park are also working with CIP scientists in the characterization of
40 potato diversity, monitoring changes in potato varieties used over time and testing of varieties in different parts of the landscape, a combined territory of over 9,000 hectares.
45 Planting a diversity of potatoes provides a vital safeguard against crop failure–if disaster strikes, the farmers will always have food. This strategy to reduce risk comes from their ancestors.
50 The agreement with CIP has brought back varieties which had been collected from the communities in the 1960s but had since been lost. The resulting landscape-based gene bank is actively
55 managed by the five Potato Park communities.

It provides a critical source of climate-resilient crops for adaptation, both locally and globally. Although gene banks
60 conserve many food crops, they cannot safeguard them all, and their collections are no longer evolving in response to climatic changes or accessible to farmers.

Alejandro Argumedo, Director of
65 Programs of the Peruvian NGO ANDES explained: "The landmark agreement between CIP and the Potato Park for repatriation and monitoring of native potatoes represents a fundamental shift
70 in approach. Rather than only collecting

crops from farmers, scientists have also given farmers crops from their gene bank in return. The disease-free seeds and scientific knowledge gained have
75 boosted food security, and the new varieties have enhanced income, enabling the communities to develop novel food products."

Head of the CIP Genetic Resources-
80 Genebank David Ellis said: "Through the agreement, first signed in 2004, CIP is increasing its understanding of how climate change is affecting potato diversity and agro-ecosystems, and
85 through collaborative and mutually beneficial research with the farmers, it has continued to enhance knowledge, adaptation to climate change and capacity development for sustaining potato
90 production and traditional knowledge.

In Asia and Africa, hardy local landraces and livestock breeds are also proving a vital resource in the struggle to cope with more extreme weather such as
95 droughts.

Krystyna Swiderska, Principal Researcher at IIED [International Institute for Environment and Development] said: "From China to Kenya, farmers have
100 improved both resilience and productivity by crossing resilient landraces with high-yielding modern varieties."

32 What is the relationship between plant diversity and climate change?

(A) Plant diversity can provide some protection from crop failure due to climate change.

(B) Increasing plant diversity with ancient varieties of potatoes may be more resilient to the higher temperatures associated with climate change.

(C) Some varieties of potatoes are more adaptable to climate change than others.

(D) The potato gene bank tries to ensure plant diversity by saving seeds of all varieties from extinction.

33 How are potato farmers trying to combat climate change?

(A) They will be attending the UN summit on climate change.

(B) They are forming new partnerships with scientists.

(C) They are planting more diverse seeds and plants.

(D) They are experimenting with a different kind of staple food.

34 What kind of climate is best suited for potatoes?

(A) Tropical

(B) Cool

(C) Warm

(D) Cold

35 How does plant diversity help reduce crop failure?

(A) If one variety of plant fails, there are likely to be others that succeed.

(B) Different communities of farmers can share their seeds to make sure at least some seeds germinate.

(C) Some plants act as guards against others because they are more resistant to insects.

(D) Different kinds of plants enable scientists to experiment with plants and save them in gene banks.

GO TO THE NEXT PAGE

36 Which of the following is the best summary of the passage?

(A) New farming techniques are helping Peruvian farmers adapt to a changing climate.

(B) Peruvian farmers are part of an international group trying to fight the effects of climate change.

(C) Ancestral growing techniques combined with new scientific methods are proving to be useful in combating the effects of climate change on Peruvian farmers.

(D) Extreme weather conditions are proving difficult challenges for farmers all over the world.

37 What are the implications of climate change on world hunger?

(A) It won't be affected.

(B) It may enable the development of new crops to feed the world.

(C) With the right scientific intervention, it could alleviate hunger.

(D) It may get worse.

38 Why would the Peruvian farmers want other nations to advocate for the UN summit to take steps to mandate that countries act to alleviate climate change?

(A) Peru is a small country and doesn't have much power.

(B) Climate change is directly affecting their livelihoods and their ability to feed their population.

(C) Peru won't be attending the conference.

(D) Because of its high altitude, climate change has a larger impact on Peruvian farmers.

39 What evidence in the passage illustrates the effects of climate change in Peru?

(A) Lines 10–13 ("Rising temperatures … staple food")

(B) Lines 45–47 ("Planting a … crop failure").

(C) Lines 59–63 ("Although gene … climatic changes")

(D) Lines 85–86 ("CIP is … the farmers")

40 What evidence does the text provide to show that potatoes were eaten by people thousands of years ago?

(A) Lines 33–35 ("These include … the Park")

(B) Lines 38–41 ("Potato Park … over time")

(C) Lines 48–49 ("This strategy …their ancestors")

(D) Lines 50–53 ("The agreement … been lost")

41 As used in line 32, "stewarding" most nearly means

(A) managing.

(B) controlling.

(C) regulating.

(D) developing.

42 As used in line 15, "pronounced" most nearly means

(A) articulated.

(B) official.

(C) well-known.

(D) noticeable.

QUESTIONS 43–52 ARE BASED ON THE FOLLOWING PASSAGE.

In his leisure time, Thomas Bulfinch (1796–1867) enjoyed writing condensed summaries of classical literature. Written for the general reader, "to popularize mythology and extend the enjoyment of elegant literature," his three volumes of classics were published under the title Bullfinch's Mythology. This passage is an excerpt from chapter XXVII, The Trojan War.

Minerva was the goddess of wisdom, but on one occasion she did a very foolish thing; she entered into competition with
Line Juno and Venus for the prize of beauty. It
5 happened thus: At the nuptials of Peleus and Thetis all the gods were invited with the exception of Eris, or Discord. Enraged at her exclusion, the goddess threw a golden apple among the guests,
10 with the inscription, "For the fairest." Thereupon Juno, Venus, and Minerva each claimed the apple. Jupiter, not willing to decide in so delicate a matter, sent the goddesses to Mount Ida, where
15 the beautiful shepherd Paris was tending his flocks, and to him was committed the decision. The goddesses accordingly appeared before him. Juno promised him power and riches, Minerva glory and
20 renown in war, and Venus the fairest of women for his wife, each attempting to bias his decision in her own favor. Paris decided in favour of Venus and gave her the golden apple, thus making the
25 two other goddesses his enemies. Under the protection of Venus, Paris sailed to Greece, and was hospitably received by Menelaus, king of Sparta. Now Helen, the wife of Menelaus, was the very woman
30 whom Venus had destined for Paris, the fairest of her sex. She had been sought as a bride by numerous suitors, and before her decision was made known, they all, at the suggestion of Ulysses, one of their
35 number, took an oath that they would defend her from all injury and avenge her cause if necessary. She chose Menelaus, and was living with him happily when Paris became their guest. Paris, aided by
40 Venus, persuaded her to elope with him, and carried her to Troy, whence arose the famous Trojan war, the theme of the greatest poems of antiquity, those of Homer and Virgil.
45 Menelaus called upon his brother chieftains of Greece to fulfill their pledge, and join him in his efforts to recover his wife. They generally came forward, but Ulysses, who had married Penelope, and
50 was very happy in his wife and child, had no disposition to embark in such a troublesome affair. He therefore hung back and Palamedes was sent to urge him. When Palamedes arrived at Ithaca,
55 Ulysses pretended to be mad. He yoked an ass and an ox together to the plough and began to sow salt. Palamedes, to try him, placed the infant Telemachus before the plough, whereupon the father turned
60 the plough aside, showing plainly that he was no madman, and after that could no longer refuse to fulfill his promise. Being now himself gained for the undertaking, he lent his aid to bring in other reluctant
65 chiefs, especially Achilles. This hero was the son of that Thetis at whose marriage the apple of Discord had been thrown among the goddesses. Thetis was herself one of the immortals, a sea-nymph, and
70 knowing that her son was fated to perish before Troy if he went on the expedition, she endeavoured to prevent his going. She sent him away to the court of King Lycomedes, and induced him to conceal
75 himself in the disguise of a maiden among the daughters of the king. Ulysses, hearing he was there, went disguised as a merchant to the palace and offered for sale female ornaments, among which
80 he had placed some arms. While the king's daughters were engrossed with the other contents of the merchant's pack, Achilles handled the weapons and thereby betrayed himself to the keen eye of
85 Ulysses, who found no great difficulty in persuading him to disregard his mother's prudent counsels and join his countrymen in the war.

practice test

43 Which of the following is a theme used in this myth?

(A) Humans use deception to achieve goals.

(B) The gods have special powers of to control events.

(C) The bonds of marriage tie people's loyalties to one another.

(D) War is a dangerous undertaking that threaten human life.

44 Which of the following could characterize Ulysses' decision not to participate in the war?

(A) Rational

(B) Wise

(C) Hypocritical

(D) Practical

45 Why was the golden apple referred to as the "Apple of Discord"?

(A) It was sought after by Eris.

(B) It started a war.

(C) It was rotten.

(D) It was claimed by several goddesses.

46 Why did Thetis try to prevent Achilles from going to Troy?

(A) She thought his presence might start a war.

(B) She didn't want him to marry Helen.

(C) She wanted him to ask King Lycomedes for his help.

(D) She didn't want her son to be killed in battle.

47 Based on the myth, what started the Trojan War?

(A) A fight over an apple

(B) A fight for the hand of Helen

(C) A test of Ulysses' loyalty

(D) The marriage of Peleus and Thetis

48 What is the relationship between Telemachus and Ulysses?

(A) Telemachus was Ulysses' son.

(B) Telemachus was a god and Ulysses human.

(C) Telemachus was a prince and Ulysses was king of Sparta.

(D) Telemachus was an old man and Ulysses was his son.

49 Which of the following lines from the text explain why the Spartans go to war with the Trojans?

(A) Lines 33–37 ("they all … if necessary.")

(B) Lines 54–55 ("When Palamedes … be mad.")

(C) Lines 73–76 ("She sent … the king.").

(D) Lines 83–88 ("Achilles handled … the war.")

50 Which of the following lines from the text illustrate powers ascribed to the gods and goddesses in the myth?

(A) Lines 8–9 ("the goddess … the guests")

(B) Lines 25–27 ("Under the … to Greece")

(C) Lines 68–69 ("Thetis was … the immortals")

(D) Lines 77–78 ("[Ulysses] went disguised as … the palace")

51 As used in line 87, "prudent counsels" most nearly mean

(A) cautious plans.

(B) wise advise.

(C) legal documents.

(D) sensible recommendations.

52 As used in line 5, "nuptials" most nearly means

(A) wedding ceremony.

(B) beauty contest.

(C) spring ritual.

(D) religious rite.

STOP

**If you finish before time is called, you may check your work on this section only.
Do not turn to any other section.**

practice test

No Test Material On This Page

SECTION 2: WRITING AND LANGUAGE TEST

35 Minutes • 44 Questions

TURN TO SECTION 2 OF YOUR ANSWER SHEET TO ANSWER THE QUESTIONS IN THIS SECTION.

Directions: Each passage below is accompanied by a number of multiple-choice questions. For some questions, you will need to consider how the passage might be revised to improve the expression of ideas. Other questions will ask you to consider how the passage might be edited to correct errors in sentence structure, usage, or punctuation. A passage may be accompanied by one or more graphics—such as a chart, table, or graph—that you will need to refer to in order to best answer the question(s).

Some questions will direct you to an underlined portion of a passage—it could be one word, a portion of a sentence, or the full sentence itself. Other questions will direct you to a particular paragraph or to certain sentences within a paragraph, or you'll be asked to think about the passage as a whole. Each question number refers to the corresponding number in the passage.

After reading each passage, select the answer to each question that most effectively improves the quality of writing in the passage or that makes the passage follow the conventions of Standard Written English. Many questions include a "NO CHANGE" option. Select that option if you think the best choice is to leave that specific portion of the passage as it is.

QUESTIONS 1-11 ARE BASED ON THE FOLLOWING PASSAGE AND SUPPLEMENTARY MATERIAL.

The Fight for African American Progress

The struggle of African Americans to make economic and political progress within the socioeconomic structure of the United States has been long and filled with setbacks. The following passages document some of the events in that long struggle and seek to explain why it has been so difficult.

The Economic Picture

Slavery—which lasted until 1865—and inadequate education guaranteed that African Americans remained socioeconomically disadvantaged until well into the twentieth century. **1** Segregated schools were rarely on par with schools for whites; consequently, African Americans often found they could not compete with whites for jobs.

1 Which choice provides the most relevant detail?

(A) NO CHANGE
(B) Public schools afforded African Americans the opportunity to gain basic skills
(C) Segregated schools remained an obstacle for equality
(D) Public schools remained segregated until the Civil Rights Act in 1964

GO TO THE NEXT PAGE

Increased opportunities for African Americans followed in the wake of **2** the civil rights movement, African Americans were finally able to gain higher levels of education and achieve better positions in a variety of professions. In the 1980s, large numbers of African Americans moved into the upper middle class.

Median Net Worth of Households, 2005 and 2009
in 2009 dollars

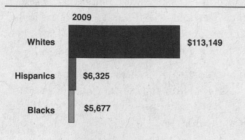

2009

Whites	$113,149
Hispanics	$6,325
Blacks	$5,677

2005

Whites	$134,992
Hispanics	$18,359
Blacks	$12,124

Source: Pew Research Center tabulation of Survey of Income and Program Particpation data
PEW RESEARCH CENTER

3 However, by the 1990s, there was a noticeable gap between low-income African Americans and those who were able to improve their socioeconomic status. By 2010, the economic status of many African American households had declined, **4** with the median net worth in 2009 less than half of what it had been in 2005. Today, many low-income African Americans do not have a

2

(A) NO CHANGE
(B) the civil rights movement and African Americans
(C) the civil rights movement African Americans
(D) the civil rights movement. African Americans

3

(A) NO CHANGE
(B) Moreover,
(C) To begin with,
(D) Incidentally,

4 Which choice most effectively reflects information in the chart?

(A) NO CHANGE
(B) though the median net worth in 2009 was several times more than what it had been in 2005.
(C) whereas the median net worth of white households grew by 50% from 2005 to 2009.
(D) while the median net worth of white and Hispanic households grew modestly.

place in the class structure because of poverty and underlying racial prejudice, particularly in urban areas. **5** Too often, urban neighborhoods become a place of high crime, poor schools, and substandard housing.

The Political Picture

6 Only, with the enforcement of the Reconstruction Act of 1867 and the ratification of the Fifteenth Amendment did African Americans first win seats in Congress. On February 25, 1870, Hiram Revels of Mississippi became the first African American Senator. Later that same year, Joseph Rainey of South Carolina became the first African American member of the House of Representatives.

African Americans throughout the South became politically active soon after the close of the Civil War. A generation of African American leaders emerged, almost all of whom supported the Republican Party because **7** they had **8** discerned their rights.

During the 1890s and early 1900s, however, no African American won election to

5

(A) NO CHANGE
(B) Too often, urban neighborhoods become places of high crime, poor schools, and substandard housing.
(C) Too often, urban neighborhoods become a high-crime place with poor schools and substandard housing.
(D) Too often, an urban neighborhood becomes places of high crime, poor schools, and substandard housing.

6

(A) NO CHANGE
(B) Only with the enforcement of the Reconstruction Act of 1867, and the ratification of the Fifteenth Amendment,
(C) Only with the enforcement of the Reconstruction Act of 1867 and the ratification of the Fifteenth Amendment
(D) Only with the enforcement of the Reconstruction Act of 1867, and the ratification of the Fifteenth Amendment

7

(A) NO CHANGE
(B) he
(C) we
(D) it

8

(A) NO CHANGE
(B) evinced
(C) championed
(D) disputed

practice test

GO TO THE NEXT PAGE

Congress, in part because of **9** restricted state election codes in some southern states. During World War I and in the following decade, African Americans who migrated to northern cities created the foundations for political organization in urban centers. Over the next three decades, African Americans won congressional seats in New York City, Detroit, and Philadelphia. In the wake of the civil rights movement, African Americans regained seats in the South. **10** Since the 1930s, nearly all African American representatives have been Democrats.

These members of Congress have traditionally served as advocates for all African Americans, not just their constituencies. During Reconstruction and the late nineteenth century, they worked to protect the voting rights of African Americans. They also called for expanded educational opportunities and land grants for freed slaves. In the mid-twentieth century, they focused on urban communities and urged federal programs for improved housing and job training. **11** The Congressional Black Caucus demonstrated a special concern for the protection of civil rights, the guarantee of equal opportunity in education, employment, and housing, and a broad array of foreign and domestic policy issues.

9

(A) NO CHANGE
(B) conflicting
(C) irrelevant
(D) expansive

10 The writer is considering deleting the underlined sentence. Should the writer do this?

(A) No, because it provides relevant details about the main topic of the paragraph.
(B) No, because it provides context for the following paragraph.
(C) Yes, because it introduces a detail that is not directly related to the topic of the paragraph.
(D) Yes, because it creates a transition to the next paragraph.

11

(A) NO CHANGE
(B) The Congressional Black Caucus demonstrated a special concern for the protection of civil rights; the guarantee of equal opportunity in education, employment, and housing; and a broad array of foreign and domestic policy issues.
(C) The Congressional Black Caucus demonstrated a special concern for the protection of civil rights—the guarantee of equal opportunity in education, employment, and housing—and a broad array of foreign and domestic policy issues.
(D) The Congressional Black Caucus demonstrated a special concern for the protection of civil rights, the guarantee of equal opportunity in education; employment; and housing, and a broad array of foreign and domestic policy issues.

QUESTIONS 12–22 ARE BASED ON THE FOLLOWING PASSAGE.

Morocco has many rich musical traditions stemming from **12** their unique geographical conditions and a long history of intermingled cultures. For the past century, Morocco has attracted musicians and other artists from the west who wanted to learn from the country's creative and hospitable people. For instance, Jimi Hendrix's style of guitar playing was influenced by his travels to Marrakesh and Essaouira, where he discovered the rhythmic music of the Ganawa tribe. The Rolling Stones were fascinated with Morocco's music and made several trips there to hear it. During one of the Stones' stays, Brian Jones recorded an album of village folk music. **13** The Rolling Stones have also been influenced by such legendary African American musicians as Muddy Waters, Chuck Berry, and James Brown.

Morocco is located on the northeastern corner of Africa, only a few miles from the southern tip of Spain across the Strait of Gibraltar. Mountain ranges from the "backbone" of the country, running from the northeast to the southwest. Fertile plains stretch from the northern side of these mountains to the Mediterranean Sea and Atlantic Ocean. **14** This area covered with farmland and several large cities and towns is the most prosperous part of the country. Although the mountains themselves are quite rugged and rocky, there is plenty of water to support fruit orchards and

12

(A) NO CHANGE
(B) our
(C) its
(D) your

13 Which choice most effectively maintains the paragraph's focus on relevant information and ideas?

(A) NO CHANGE
(B) Jazz musicians such as Pharaoh Sanders and Ornette Coleman have also made pilgrimages, in search of Morocco's earthy, trance-inducing rhythms, and complex melodies.
(C) The band once made a trip to Morocco in the late 1960s while waiting for the verdict on drug charges made against them in Great Britain.
(D) Today, raj, a type of music from Algeria, is popular among young Moroccans for the way it mixes western rock with Jamaican reggae and Moroccan pop.

14

(A) NO CHANGE
(B) This area covered with farmland and several large cities and towns, is the most prosperous part of the country.
(C) This area, covered with farmland and several large cities and towns, is the most prosperous part of the country.
(D) This area, covered with farmland and several large cities and towns is the most prosperous part of the country.

GO TO THE NEXT PAGE

isolated villages of goatherds. The southern side of the mountains is more arid, with rocky plateaus and several fertile river valleys descending gradually into the Sahara Desert. The river valleys are dotted with towns and villages that get smaller as the rivers dry up along the desert's edge. Several nomadic tribes travel among the villages and desert oases.

15 Throughout the ages, the Berbers have been the largest ethnic group in Morocco. **16** There ancestors lived all along the North African coast until frequent invasions brought foreign rulers to many of the countries, including Morocco. However, invading Greeks, Romans, Vandals, and Turks found it all but impossible to control the Berbers who lived in the rugged and isolated mountain ranges. Despite ruling the country, foreigners could not conquer the stubborn Berber spirit. The Romans gave them their name, which eventually evolved into the term *barbarian*, although this is a **17** misnomer for such gracious and hospitable people.

Beginning in the seventh century, Arab legions invaded Morocco on several occasions. These invasions began to affect the region not only politically, but religiously as well. Eventually the Berbers and most of the other **18** notorious tribes became Islamic and adopted some elements of Arabic culture, including classical Arabic music. The strongest Arabic musical influence is found in their lyrics, which often praise Allah or refer to the Qur'an.

15 Which choice most effectively establishes the main topic of the paragraph?

(A) Foreign invaders found it impossible to conquer the Berbers.

(B) The Berbers have long been the largest ethnic group in Morocco.

(C) Ancestors of the Berbers lived in rugged, isolated mountain ranges.

(D) Berbers are hospitable people, despite the origins of their name.

16

(A) NO CHANGE

(B) They're

(C) Theyre

(D) Their

17

(A) NO CHANGE

(B) euphemism

(C) locution

(D) reflection

18

(A) NO CHANGE

(B) autonomous

(C) indigenous

(D) illustrious

Despite these additional influences, the Berbers were still able to maintain most of their own beliefs and traditions. Traditional Berber music was performed solo or in larger ensembles, sometimes accompanied by dancers. Musicians could be found performing in the medina marketplaces in the older parts of towns. The musicians often got a performance started with improvisational banter, referring to one another and to people in the gathering crowd. Then they began to warm up their instruments as they continued jesting: **19** drum skins that had been heated over lanterns were thumped, someone played a few chords on a flute or a lute, some castanets clacked, or a few dance steps were stomped out. This buildup set the dramatic tone for the frenzied music about to be played; it also encouraged the audience to toss out a few more coins.

Tribes of Saharan nomads, such as the Ganawa and the Tuareg, brought the music and musical traditions of West Africa to Morocco. **20** It traveled with the gold and salt caravans through Timbuktu and up to Marrakesh just across the Atlas Mountains. The most notable instruments were large, metal, double-castanets clapped between the fingers to make a galloping rhythm. Hand clapping, fast drumming, and harmonized chanting were also common elements of these southern Moroccan tribes.

19

(A) NO CHANGE
(B) drummers thumped drum skins that had been heated over lanterns, someone played a few chords on a flute or a lute, some castanets clacked, or a few dance steps were stomped out.
(C) drum skins that had been heated over lanterns were thumped, a few chords on a flute or a lute were played, some castanets were clacked, or dancers stomped out few dance steps.
(D) drum skins that had been heated over lanterns were thumped, a few chords on a flute or a lute were played, some castanets were clacked, or a few dance steps were stomped out.

20

(A) NO CHANGE
(B) They
(C) This music
(D) Everything

GO TO THE NEXT PAGE

Morocco's musical traditions were additionally influenced by the country's northern neighbor, Spain. Arabs had lived in southern Spain for several centuries before they were driven out during the Spanish Inquisition. Arab musicians from the Spanish region of Andalusia brought a sophisticated and intricate style of music back to North Africa. Much of this Andalusian music was played on the oud, an Arabian lute with a pear-shaped body, three rounded sound holes, a short, fretless neck, and five pairs of strings. **21** Some researchers believe that Andalusian music found its way into the poetry of the troubadours. Andalusian music, with its distinctly western classic sound, had in fact influenced the troubadours who played in the medieval courts of Europe. A good deal of southern European folk music, such as Flamenco, was influenced by Andalusian music.

Today many Moroccan musicians adeptly blend these various musical styles, perhaps playing an Andalusian melody over a Ganawa rhythm while chanting in praise of Allah. Their lively mixes are as naturally eclectic as the rest of Moroccan culture. A few musicians, such as Nouamane Lahlou, have taken practically the reverse path of Jimi Hendrix and Ornette Coleman, blending their Moroccan musical traditions with modern styles. **22** Yet the result is similar. They have created popular songs that have a more international appeal.

21 Which choice gives a second supporting example that is most similar to the example that precedes it in the paragraph?

(A) NO CHANGE

(B) The rebec, a predecessor of the violin, was also an instrument in Andalusian musical traditions.

(C) Today, there are two basic types of ouds: Arabic and Turkish.

(D) Folk traditions of Andalusia were embedded in the music of the region.

22 Which choice most effectively combines the two sentences at the underlined portion?

(A) similar; they

(B) similar—they

(C) similar: they

(D) similar, they

QUESTIONS 23–33 ARE BASED ON THE FOLLOWING PASSAGE.

Heralded as "The Queen of Carbon," Mildred Dresselhaus is a pioneer for women in science, especially physics and electrical engineering. **23** Born into a poor household in the Bronx, New York, Dresselhaus had **24** <u>a stroke in luck</u> when her brother won a scholarship to attend a music school in New York City. Dresselhaus soon joined him, and through music she became **25** <u>cognizant</u> of the fact that there were schools within the city that could offer her a better education. She secured a place at Hunter College High School—a school open only to girls.

After high school, she attended Hunter College with the goal of becoming a teacher. **26** <u>This was a common career path for women in this era.</u> Fortunately, during her

23 At this point, the writer is considering adding the following sentence:

With all the honors Dresselhaus has received, she has never forgotten those who helped her, and she continues to help others pursue the field she loves.

Should the writer make this addition here?

(A) Yes, because it provides a detail to reinforce the passage's main idea.

(B) Yes, because it serves as an introduction to her childhood.

(C) No, because it detracts from the main idea.

(D) No, because it should be included later in the passage.

24

(A) NO CHANGE
(B) stroke and luck
(C) stroke of luck
(D) stroke of lucky

25

(A) NO CHANGE
(B) apprehensive
(C) dismayed
(D) astute

26 Which choice best supports the statement made in the previous sentence?

(A) NO CHANGE

(B) Hunter College was established in 1870 and is located in New York City.

(C) Dresselhaus later received her master's degree from Radcliffe College.

(D) By this point, she was not as interested in music.

second year at Hunter, **27** Dresselhaus met the celebrated Rosalyn Yalow—a woman who would eventually gain recognition for winning the Nobel Prize in Medicine. With **28** Yalows encouragement, Dresselhaus began to explore science and became passionate about physics. After seeing a notice on a bulletin board, Dresselhaus applied for a Fulbright Scholarship in physics, despite having already been accepted into a graduate program for math. To her delight, she won a scholarship.

[1] The Fulbright Scholarship sent her to the Cavendish Laboratory in Cambridge, England. [2] In 1958, Dresselhaus received her Ph.D. in physics from the University of Chicago. **29** [3] There, only she had often been the woman in her classes. [4] Dresselhaus continued her research on the microwave properties of superconductors at Cornell University— after winning a two-year NSF post-doctoral fellowship. **30** [5] After Dresselhaus returned to the United States, her mentor Yalow persuaded her to continue her research.

After her two years at Cornell, Dresselhaus accepted a position at MIT. She first worked as a researcher for Lincoln Laboratories and later as a visiting professor of electrical engineering and computer science. While at MIT, Dresselhaus shifted her research from semiconductors to the structure of semimetals, especially graphite.

27

(A) NO CHANGE
(B) Dresselhaus met Rosalyn Yalow—a woman who would eventually win the Nobel Prize in Medicine.
(C) Dresselhaus met Rosalyn Yalow—a woman who would, a little later in her career, win one of the most prestigious awards in her field—the Nobel Prize in Medicine.
(D) Dresselhaus met Rosalyn Yalow—a woman who would eventually, but later, win the Nobel Prize in Medicine.

28

(A) NO CHANGE
(B) Yalows'
(C) Yalow
(D) Yalow's

29

(A) NO CHANGE
(B) There, she had often been the only woman in her classes.
(C) There, she had often only been the woman in her classes.
(D) Only there, she had often been the woman in her classes.

30 For the sake of cohesion, sentence 5 of this paragraph should be placed

(A) where it is now.
(B) before sentence 1.
(C) before sentence 2.
(D) before sentence 3.

In 1968, she became a full professor, teaching condensed matter physics to engineering students, while continuing her research. Shortly thereafter, Dresselhaus began to achieve recognition for her work, recognition that has continued up to the present. She is celebrated as an **31** eminent scientist. In 2014, when President Obama awarded her the Medal of Freedom, he said, "Her influence is all around us, in the cars we drive, the energy we generate, the electronic devices that power our lives."

Although Dresselhaus is pleased to be recognized for her work in physics, perhaps her greatest enjoyment comes from her mentoring of numerous PhD **32** students—about 20 percent of them women. Despite her age, Dresselhaus's **33** complacency with physics has not diminished. She says, "I am excited by my present research and am not yet anxious to stop working."

31
(A) NO CHANGE
(B) immanent
(C) imminent
(D) emigrant

32
(A) NO CHANGE
(B) students: about 20 percent of them women.
(C) students; about 20 percent of them women.
(D) students—about 20 percent of them: women.

33
(A) NO CHANGE
(B) preoccupation
(C) compulsion
(D) fascination

QUESTIONS 34–44 ARE BASED ON THE FOLLOWING PASSAGE.

Sense of Smell

Smell is considered to be the most delicate of our five senses. It has many practical functions—allowing us, for example, to determine whether food has gone bad or to detect smoke when something is burning. **34** Scent is integral to warning us of danger; our noses are powerful tools for recognizing familiar people and places or recalling old memories: smells can remind us of our aunt's cooking or our second-grade classroom, just as an infant identifies the individual scents of its mother and father. Smell also factors into romance, which is why the perfume industry labors to extract and mix pleasure-provoking aromas. **35** The nose will even play a complementary role in tasting: if you plug your nose while eating, you will find that your food seems to lose some of its taste. It is certainly true that we can perceive much more subtle olfactory variations than visual or auditory ones.

Despite all of these known applications, our knowledge of just *how* the nose knows **36** is less than the knowledge of our other senses. First of all, it's often difficult to describe how something smells. It's relatively easy to identify a D major chord or paint a verbal picture of something that is silvery-blue, but the fragrance of a rose is more **37** concordant. The scent of one rose might be "flowery and sweet, with a touch of citrus,"

34 Which choice most effectively sets up the examples given at the end of the sentence?

(A) NO CHANGE
(B) Dogs have a stronger sense of smell;
(C) It also offers emotional functions;
(D) Other senses are more acute than smell;

35

(A) NO CHANGE
(B) The nose even plays a complementary role in tasting:
(C) The nose even played a complementary role in tasting:
(D) The nose has played a complementary role in tasting:

36

(A) NO CHANGE
(B) is less than our other senses.
(C) is less than that of how our other senses operate.
(D) is less than how our other senses operate.

37

(A) NO CHANGE
(B) distinct
(C) ineffable
(D) elusive

while that of another might be more "like honey and freshly-cut grass." **38** Therefore, scents have been classified by scientists into 10 groups, each of which is characterized by its volatile compounds.

Sights and sounds are measured in terms of their wavelengths, **39** allowing us to perceive shades of color and decibels of sounds, which can be assessed with scientific instruments. Scent molecules are not as easy to quantify. **40** We know that molecules up to a certain mass have scents, but there are conflicting theories as to what determines their smell and how the nose records and transmits this information to the brain. Until recently, most experts believed us able to recognize a certain smell based on a molecule's shape. Such a theory asserts that when a scent molecule of a certain shape enters the nose and touches a receptor, like a key, it unlocks and triggers a particular smell, which is then sent to the brain. Likewise, a variety of different scent molecules can open a combination of locks, sending a mixture of scent signals to the brain ("smells like this spaghetti sauce has basil and garlic in it"). This "lock-and-key" theory does hold true for the shape and smell of many molecules. For instance, most molecules that contain an amine group will have a fishy smell. There are, however, many instances of similarly shaped molecules with different smells, and vice versa. For example, two differently

38 Which choice most effectively maintains support for claims or points in the text?

(A) NO CHANGE
(B) Even those employed in the perfume and food industries often have trouble agreeing on how to describe and categorize particular scents.
(C) Yet many studies of scents attempt to classify new and interesting fragrance mediums.
(D) Even wine aromas have been assigned to twelve different categories, each represented by a section of a wine aroma wheel.

39 The writer is considering deleting the underlined part of the sentence. Should the writer do this?

(A) No, because it provides scientific details about the measurement of two of the senses.
(B) No, because it provides comparative data about perception.
(C) Yes, because it should be placed later in the passage.
(D) Yes, because it adds irrelevant details.

40

(A) NO CHANGE
(B) We know that molecules up to a certain mass have scents because there are
(C) Since we know that molecules up to a certain mass have scents, there are
(D) We know that molecules up to a certain mass have scents, and there are

GO TO THE NEXT PAGE

shaped compounds will still **41** stink like rotten eggs if they both contain sulfur.

Luca Turin, a biophysicist and perfume enthusiast, questioned these discrepancies and resolved to form a new theory of his own. Turin has performed many experiments that **42** thwart the lock-and-key theory. He believes that out of literally millions of different smells, there are too many cases in which the shape does *not* determine the smell. He once demonstrated this assertion by comparing a hydrocarbon called camphane (the main component of camphor, sometimes used in cold medicines) with decaborane. Decaborane resembles camphane structurally, except that it has boron atoms where camphane has carbon atoms. According to the lock-and-key theory, both compounds should smell like camphor. However, the decaborane instead smells like rotten eggs (which is surprising, as it contains no sulfur). This example proves that molecular shape is not always the determining factor of smell.

41

(A) NO CHANGE
(B) smell like rotten eggs
(C) emit a disgusting odor like rotten eggs
(D) have a nasty smell like rotten eggs

42

(A) NO CHANGE
(B) sanction
(C) instigate
(D) refute

Then what exactly *is* the determining **43** factor—Turin theorizes that the *vibration* of a molecule's atoms provides its signature smell. **44** The number of atoms and electrons connected within a molecule determine that molecule's particular vibration. The result of these minute shakes and quivers can be recorded as a particular frequency. The receptors in the nose, therefore, actually record the vibration of the molecules and transmit that information to the brain as a scent. This theory puts smell in the same category as sight and sound. Colors can be measured along a spectrum of light according to their wavelengths; tones can be measured along a spectrum of octaves according to their wavelengths. Turin claims that the same types of measurements can be taken with smells. Although the frequencies of scents are much more complicated to measure, measuring them is exactly what Turin has set out to do.

43

(A) NO CHANGE
(B) factor?
(C) factor.
(D) factor!

44

(A) NO CHANGE
(B) The number of atoms and electrons within a molecule determines
(C) The number of atoms and electrons within a molecule have determined
(D) The number of atoms and electrons within a molecule will have determined

STOP

If you finish before time is called, you may check your work on this section only. Do not turn to any other section.

practice test

No Test Material On This Page

SECTION 3: MATH TEST—NO CALCULATOR

20 Questions • 25 minutes

TURN TO SECTION 3 OF YOUR ANSWER SHEET TO ANSWER THE QUESTIONS IN THIS SECTION.

Directions: For **Questions 1–15,** solve each problem, select the best answer from the choices provided, and fill in the corresponding oval on your answer sheet. For **Questions 16–20,** solve the problem and enter your answer in the grid on the answer sheet. The directions **before Question 16** will provide information on how to enter your answers in the grid.

ADDITIONAL INFORMATION:

- The use of a calculator in this section **is not permitted.**

- All variables and expressions used represent real numbers unless otherwise indicated.

- Figures provided in this test are drawn to scale unless otherwise indicated.

- All figures lie in a plane unless otherwise indicated.

- Unless otherwise specified, the domain of a given function f is the set of all real numbers x for which $f(x)$ is a real number.

The number of degrees of arc in a circle is 360.
The number of radians in the arc of a circle is 2π.
The sum of the measures in degrees of the angles of a triangle is 180.

1 If $x + x + x + 7 = x + x + 9$, what is the value of x?

(A) 1
(B) 2
(C) 3
(D) 5

2 Which shows the simplified form of $(3x^2 - 7x + 5) - (-6x^2 + 5x - 4)$?

(A) $-3x^2 - 2x + 1$
(B) $-3x^2 - 12x + 9$
(C) $9x^2 - 2x + 1$
(D) $9x^2 - 12x + 9$

3

$$y \leq 3x - 4$$
$$5x + 4y \geq 6$$

Which point is a solution to the system of inequalities?

(A) (0, 0)

(B) (−1, 5)

(C) (2, −3)

(D) (3, 4)

4 Angie took $3x$ hours to make it on time for her brother's birthday party in another state, and she drove the route at an average of z miles per hour. If b is the number of hours Angie spent at rest stops, when she was NOT traveling, which of the following represents the total distance Angie traveled to get to her brother's party?

(A) $z(b - 3x)$

(B) $b - 3x$

(C) $z(3x - b)$

(D) $3xz - b$

5 If $3s - r = 9$ and $6s = 36$, what is the value of r?

(A) 3

(B) 6

(C) 9

(D) 12

6 Gary deposits $50 into an existing savings account. Each month he plans to increase the amount he deposits by $7. Using $y = 50 + 7(x − 1)$ to represent this situation, what is the meaning of y in the equation?

(A) The total amount that Gary has in the account after x months

(B) The number of months that Gary has been making deposits

(C) The amount that Gary deposits into his account in month x

(D) The increase in the monthly amount of Gary's deposits

7 If $f(x) = cx - \dfrac{d}{x}$, which of the following represents $f\left(\dfrac{1}{c}\right)$?

(A) $1 - cd$

(B) $1 + cd$

(C) $c^2 - \dfrac{d}{c}$

(D) $\dfrac{d}{c} - c^2$

8 The graph of a function has a y-intercept at 3 and an x-intercept at 1.5. Which of the following could be the equation for that function?

(A) $y = -\dfrac{3}{x - 3} + 2$

(B) $y = \dfrac{1}{x - 3} + 2$

(C) $y = \dfrac{3}{x - 3} + 2$

(D) $y = \dfrac{3}{x - 1} + 2$

9 The x-intercepts of the function $g(x)$ are −2, 3, and 5. Which of the following is a factor of $g(x)$?

(A) $x + 2$

(B) $x + 3$

(C) $x - 15$

(D) $x - 30$

10 The ratio of marbles in each package of marbles is 2 red: 3 green: 4 blue. How many green and blue marbles does Ina have if she bought 108 marbles?

(A) 12

(B) 36

(C) 48

(D) 84

11 What is the value of a, if

$$x^{\frac{1}{5}} \bullet x^{\frac{4}{5}} = x^{-a} ?$$

(A) -5

(B) -1

(C) 1

(D) 5

12 In the figure above, lines p and q are parallel. If point (x, y) lies on line q, which of the following represents the relationship between x and y?

(A) $x + y = 0$

(B) $x - y = 0$

(C) $x + y = 1$

(D) $x - y = -1$

13

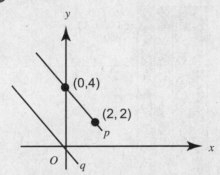

In a right triangle DEF, $\sin F = \dfrac{2}{3}$ and $m\angle E = 90°$. Which of the following statements is true?

(A) $\cos F = \dfrac{1}{3}$

(B) $\tan F = 2$

(C) $\cos D = \dfrac{2}{3}$

(D) $\sin D = \dfrac{1}{3}$

14 A circle is drawn on an xy-plane. The diameter of the circle has endpoints at $(-9, 7)$ and $(15, -3)$. Which of the following is an equation for the graph of the circle?

(A) $(x - 3)^2 + (y - 2)^2 = 169$

(B) $(x - 3)^2 + (y - 2)^2 = 676$

(C) $(x - 6)^2 + (y - 4)^2 = 169$

(D) $(x - 6)^2 + (y - 4)^2 = 676$

15

$$\frac{3x^2 - 5x + 9}{x - 3}$$

Which expression is equivalent to the expression above?

(A) $3x + 4 + \dfrac{21}{x - 3}$

(B) $3x - 5 - \dfrac{6}{x - 3}$

(C) $3x + 9 + \dfrac{36}{x - 3}$

(D) $3x - 14 + \dfrac{51}{x - 3}$

GO TO THE
NEXT PAGE

Directions: For Questions 16-20, solve the problem and enter your answer in the grid, as described below, on the answer sheet.

1. Although not required, it is suggested that you write your answer in the boxes at the top of the columns to help you fill in the circles accurately. You will receive credit only if the circles are filled in correctly.

2. Mark no more than one circle in any column.

3. No question has a negative answer.

4. Some problems may have more than one correct answer. In such cases, grid only one answer.

5. **Mixed numbers** such as $3\frac{1}{2}$ must be gridded as 3.5 or $\frac{7}{2}$.

   If $3\frac{1}{2}$ is entered into the grid as $\overline{3\,|\,1\,/\,2}$, it will be interpreted as $\frac{31}{2}$, not $3\frac{1}{2}$.)

6. **Decimal answers:** If you obtain a decimal answer with more digits than the grid can accommodate, it may be either rounded or truncated, but it must fill the entire grid.

16 A ball is tossed into the air from 6 meters off of the ground, with a velocity of 13 meters per second. The equation that represents the height of the ball (h, in meters) at time (t, in seconds) is $h = 6 + 13t - 5t^2$. How many seconds will it take for the ball to hit the ground?

19 What is the value of x, if

$$\sqrt{x+10} - \sqrt{2x-5} = 0\ ?$$

17 If $b = 6$ is a solution to the equation $6b + m = 270$, where m is a constant, what is the value of m?

20
$$fx + gy = -16$$
$$3x - 8y = 32$$

In the system of equations above, f and g are constants. If the system has infinitely many solutions, what is the value of $-\dfrac{g}{f}$?

18

In the figure above, $ACED$ is a rectangle and B is the midpoint of $\overline{AD}$. What is the value of $\overline{AD}$?

STOP

**If you finish before time is called, you may check your work on this section only.
Do not turn to any other section.**

No Test Material On This Page

SECTION 4: MATH TEST—CALCULATOR ▦

38 Questions • 55 minutes

TURN TO SECTION 4 OF YOUR ANSWER SHEET TO ANSWER THE QUESTIONS IN THIS SECTION.

Directions: For **Questions 1–30,** solve each problem, choose the best answer from the choices provided, and fill in the corresponding circle on your answer sheet. For **Questions 31–38,** solve the problem and enter your answer in the grid on the answer sheet. Please refer to the directions **before Question 31** on how to enter your answers in the grid.

ADDITIONAL INFORMATION:

- The use of a calculator is permitted.
- All variables and expressions used represent real numbers unless otherwise indicated.
- Figures provided in this test are drawn to scale unless otherwise indicated.
- All figures lie in a plane unless otherwise indicated.
- Unless otherwise specified, the domain of a given function f is the set of all real numbers x for which f(x) is a real number.

The number of degrees of arc in a circle is 360.
The number of radians in the arc of a circle is 2π.
The sum of the measures in degrees of the angles of a triangle is 180.

---

1 A 6-pound bag of flour is poured into 24 containers, with the same amount in each container. How many ounces of flour is in each container?

(A) 2   (C) 6
(B) 4   (D) 8

2 A major city performed a recent study to see the effect that snowfall totals have on the number of drivers on the road. The results of the study are represented in the scatterplot, where the x-axis represents the amount of snowfall and the y-axis represents the number of drivers. Which statement best describes the results of the study?

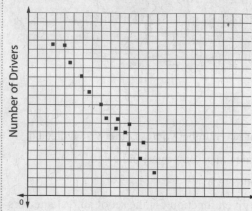

Amount Of Snowfall

(A) There is no correlation between the amount of snowfall and the number of drivers on the road.

(B) There is a positive correlation between the amount of snowfall and the number of drivers on the road.

(C) There is a negative correlation between the amount of snowfall and the number of drivers on the road.

(D) The scatterplot does not display enough data to interpret a correlation between the amount of snowfall and the number of drivers on the road.

3 How many quarters must Lilly charge for a box of cookies in order to make $18 after selling 3 boxes of cookies of equal value?

(A) 6
(B) 10
(C) 14
(D) 24

4 Martina earns $480 per week plus 15% commission on all of her sales. Which shows the amount she earns each week as a function of her total sales, x?

(A) $f(x) = 480(0.15x)$
(B) $f(x) = 480 + 0.15x$
(C) $f(x) = 480(15x)$
(D) $f(x) = 480 + 15x$

5 The city of Smallville had an increase of 8% in its tax revenues from last year to this year. For next year, the mayor projects the city's tax revenues to increase by 10% from this year. What will be the total percent increase from last year to next year's projection?

(A) 18%
(B) 18.8%
(C) 19%
(D) 19.8%

6 A random sample of people in a county were asked whether or not they drive more when gas prices decrease. Of the 682 people who responded, 471 of them said they do not drive more when gas prices decrease. If there are about 898,000 people living in the county, about how many people would be expected to not drive more when gas prices decrease?

(A) 280,000
(B) 320,000
(C) 580,000
(D) 620,000

7 A scale model drawing of the Moon shows its diameter as 6 inches. The scale of the drawing is 1 inch = 360 miles. What is the approximate diameter of the actual Moon?

(A) 2,160 miles
(B) 2,260 miles
(C) 3,060 miles
(D) 3,360 miles

8   There are 380 seats in a movie theater. The theater must collect at least $600 in admission per movie screening in order to make a profit. The prices for admission are $6.50 for children and $8.25 for adults. Which system of inequalities best describes this situation?

(A) $x+y \geq 380$
$6.5x+8.25y \leq 600$

(B) $x+y < 380$
$6.5x+8.25y > 600$

(C) $x+y \leq 380$
$6.5x+8.25y \leq 600$

(D) $x+y \leq 380$
$6.5x+8.25y \geq 600$

9   A couch is on sale for 15% off the retail price r. A 6% sales tax is added to the sale price. Which expression represents the total cost of the couch, including the sales tax?

(A) $0.85r + 1.06$
(B) $0.85r + 1.06r$
(C) $0.85r \times 1.06$
(D) $0.85r \times 1.06r$

10   A hiking club bought energy bars for $2.25 each and reusable water bottles for $12.50 each and spent a total of $447.50. Which equation can be used to determine the number of energy bars x and water bottles y that the club bought?

(A) $2.25x + 12.5y = 447.5$
(B) $12.5x + 2.25y = 447.5$
(C) $14.75(x + y) = 447.5$
(D) $\dfrac{x}{2.25}+\dfrac{y}{12.5}= 447.5$

11   If $b \neq 1$ and…hich of the following expressions is equivalent to $\dfrac{a-3}{3b-3}$?

(A) $-b$
(B) $-\dfrac{1}{b}$
(C) $-a$
(D) $\dfrac{1}{a}$

12   Which of the following is equivalent to $3\sqrt[4]{x^3}$?

(A) $3x^{\frac{4}{3}}$
(B) $3x^{\frac{3}{4}}$
(C) $3\left(x^3\right)^4$
(D) $3\left(x^4\right)^{\frac{1}{3}}$

13   Aaron earns $9 working part-time at the pool and $11 working part-time at the bakery. He needs to make at least $215 each week, but he cannot work more than a total of 25 hours each week. Which system of inequalities represents this situation?

(A) $9x+11y \geq 215$
$x+y \leq 25$

(B) $9x+11y < 215$
$x+y < 25$

(C) $9x+11y < 215$
$x+y > 25$

(D) $9x+11y > 215$
$x+y \leq 25$

GO TO THE NEXT PAGE

14 A book company sells science textbooks and science laboratory activity books. If the maximum weight for one shipment of books is 50 pounds, which inequality can be used to determine the number of each book that can be shipped when the textbooks weigh 2.5 pounds each and the laboratory books weigh 1.25 pounds each?

(A) $2.5x + 1.25y > 50$

(B) $2.5x + 1.25y < 50$

(C) $2.5x + 1.25y \geq 50$

(D) $2.5x + 1.25y \leq 50$

15 What is the y-intercept of the line whose equation is $3x + 4y = 16$?

A) $\left(\dfrac{3}{4}, 0\right)$

(B) $(4, 0)$

(C) $\left(0, \dfrac{3}{4}\right)$

(D) $(0, 4)$

QUESTIONS 16 AND 17 REFER TO THE FOLLOWING INFORMATION.

The graph below shows the amount of radioactive material in y grams that remains after x days in a container. Each point shows a measured amount that remains, and the best fit relation between those points is drawn to connect those points.

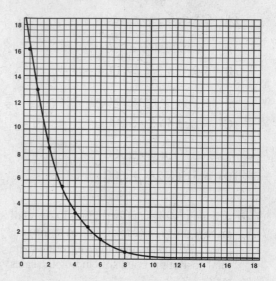

16 Which of the statements describes the relation between the amount of radioactive material and the number of days that have passed?

(A) Linear increasing

(B) Linear decreasing

(C) Exponential growth

(D) Exponential decay

17 About how much radioactive material remained after 9 days?

(A) 0.25 gram

(B) 0.5 gram

(C) 0.75 gram

(D) 1 gram

18

Figure not drawn to scale.

In the rectangle *FGHI* above, what is the value of ∠*b*?

(A) 17°

(B) 20°

(C) 33°

(D) 45°

19 The population of a country has been growing at an annual rate of about 2.5%. The population in the year 2014 was estimated at 339,800. Which of the following equations shows the projected population of the country *x* years after 2010?

(A) $y = 339,800(1.025)^x$

(B) $y = 339,800(1.025)^{x-4}$

(C) $y = 339,800(2.5)^x$

(D) $y = 339,800(2.5)^{x-4}$

20 A city newspaper randomly surveyed 250 subscribers about their support for the mayor. Of the respondents, 27% said they supported the mayor, and the results had a margin of error of 3%. The newspaper ran a headline that less than 30% of city residents support the mayor. Which of the following statements best explains why the results do not support the conclusion stated in the headline?

(A) The sample size is too small.

(B) The percent of supporters could be exactly 30.

(C) The margin of error is too large to make any conclusions.

(D) The sample is likely biased and not representative of the city.

21 If $a > 0$ and $\left(3^{-a}\right)^{\frac{2}{3}} = \left(9^{\frac{1}{a}}\right)^{-6}$ what is the value of *a*?

(A) $3\sqrt{3}$

(B) $3\sqrt{2}$

(C) $2\sqrt{3}$

(D) $2\sqrt{2}$

QUESTIONS 22 AND 23 REFER TO THE FOLLOWING INFORMATION.

The tables below give the number of days of rain per month for one year in Town A and Town B.

Town A		Town B	
Days of Rain	Frequency	Days of Rain	Frequency
5	1	1	1
6	3	3	3
7	2	5	2
8	1	9	1
9	2	12	2
10	1	15	1
11	2	19	2

22 Which of the following is true about the data shown in the table?

(A) The median number of days of rain is greater in Town A.

(B) The median number of days of rain is greater in Town B.

(C) The median number of days of rain is the same in both towns.

(D) There is not enough information to compare the mean, median, or mode.

23 Which of the following is true about the standard deviation of the data shown in the tables?

(A) The standard deviation of days of rain per month in Town A is greater.

(B) The standard deviation of days of rain per month in Town B is greater.

(C) The standard deviation of days of rain per month is the same in both towns.

(D) There isn't enough information to calculate the standard deviations.

24 The graph of a linear function has intercepts at $(a, 0)$ and $(0, a)$. Which of the following is true about the slope of the graph of the function?

(A) It is positive.

(B) It is negative.

(C) It is zero.

(D) It is undefined.

25 What is the value of x in the diagram below?

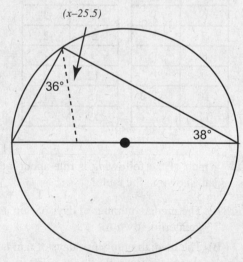

not drawn to scale

(A) 16

(B) 41.5

(C) 54

(D) 79.5

QUESTIONS 26 AND 27 REFER TO THE FOLLOWING INFORMATION.

A poll surveyed 300 randomly selected voters for an upcoming city election. Of the respondents, 31% said that they will vote for Candidate A. The margin of error for the results was ± 4% with 95% confidence.

26 Which of the following statements is best supported by the data?

(A) The sample size is too small to make an inference about the election.

(B) The margin of error is too large to make an inference about the election.

(C) The sample is likely biased, so an inference about the election cannot be made.

(D) The sample is likely unbiased and large enough to make an inference about the election.

27 Which of the following statements can be best drawn from this data?

(A) The actual percentage of voters who will vote for Candidate A is 27%.

(B) The actual percentage of voters who will vote for Candidate A is 35%.

(C) The actual percentage of voters who will vote for Candidate A is most likely between 27% and 35%.

(D) The actual percentage of voters who will vote for Candidate A is most likely between 91% and 99%.

28 The diameter of Pluto's largest moon Charon is about 750 miles. The diameter of Pluto is about 2 times greater than the diameter of Charon. Which of the following best describes the volume of Pluto?

(A) The volume of Pluto is about two times as great as the volume of Charon.

(B) The volume of Pluto is about four times as great as the volume of Charon.

(C) The volume of Pluto is about six times as great as the volume of Charon.

(D) The volume of Pluto is about eight times as great as the volume of Charon.

29 $y = -2$

$y = ax^2 - b$

Which of the following values for a and b will make the system of equations have one solution?

(A) $a = 3, b = -3$

(B) $a = -2, b = -2$

(C) $a = -2, b = 2$

(D) $a = 3, b = 3$

30 $h(x) = -(x - 8)(x + 2)$

Which of the following is an equivalent form of the function h above in which the maximum value of h appears as a constant or coefficient?

(A) $h(x) = -x^2 + 16$

(B) $h(x) = -x^2 + 6x + 16$

(C) $h(x) = -(x + 3)^2 - 7$

(D) $h(x) = -(x - 3)^2 + 25$

GO TO THE NEXT PAGE

Directions: For Questions 31-38, solve the problem and enter your answer in the grid, as described below, on the answer sheet.

1. Although not required, it is suggested that you write your answer in the boxes at the top of the columns to help you fill in the circles accurately. You will receive credit only if the circles are filled in correctly.

2. Mark no more than one circle in any column.

3. No question has a negative answer.

4. Some problems may have more than one correct answer. In such cases, grid only one answer.

5. **Mixed numbers** such as $3\frac{1}{2}$ must be gridded as 3.5 or $\frac{7}{2}$.

   If $3\frac{1}{2}$ is entered into the grid as $\boxed{3\,|\,1\,/\,2}$, it will be interpreted as $\frac{31}{2}$, not $3\frac{1}{2}$.

6. **Decimal answers:** If you obtain a decimal answer with more digits than the grid can accommodate, it may be either rounded or truncated, but it must fill the entire grid.

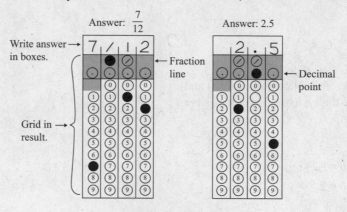

Answer: $\frac{7}{12}$ Answer: 2.5

Write answer in boxes. →   ← Fraction line   ← Decimal point

Grid in result.

Answer: 201
Either position is correct.

Acceptable ways to grid $\frac{2}{3}$ are:

31 Sorin rents a car for $49, plus mileage, for the weekend. The car rental company charges a fee for every mile over 100 miles driven. The equation $y = 49 + 0.24(x - 100)$ shows the total cost to rent the car and drive x miles. What is the fee, in cents per mile, for more than 100 miles?

32 Amber has $25 to spend. She wants to buy a book for $12 and pens that cost $2.75 each. What is the greatest number of pens she can buy?

33 A team scored 74 points in a basketball game, not including foul shots. They scored on a total of 33 field goals, including 2-point shots and 3-point shots. How many 2-point shots did the team score in the game?

QUESTIONS 34 AND 35 REFER TO THE FOLLOWING INFORMATION:

The data provided in the table shows the results of a 2010 census showing the estimated population of four countries, in millions of people, divided into males and females in each country.

	Canada	China	Mexico	United States	Total
Males	16.9	696.3	55.9	153.1	922.2
Females	17.1	645.0	57.5	157.2	876.8
Total	34	1,341.3	113.4	310.3	1,799.0

34 If a person is chosen at random, what is the probability that the person is a female from China? Express your answer as a decimal rounded to the nearest hundredth?

35 If a person is chosen at random, what is the probability that the person is NOT male? Express your answer as a decimal rounded to the nearest hundredth.

36
$$g(x) = \frac{1}{(x-6)^2 + 2(x-6) + 1}$$

For what value of x is the function g above undefined?

QUESTIONS 37 AND 38 REFER TO THE FOLLOWING INFORMATION.

The value of a famous painting last sold for $300,000 ten years ago. Similar paintings have increased by about 14% annually in that time. The current owner of the painting is using the equation $V = 300(r)^t$ to model the value, V, in thousands of dollars t years after it was last sold.

37 What value should the current owner use for r?

38 What is the estimated value, to the nearest whole thousands of dollars, of the painting today? (Disregard the dollar sign when gridding your answer.)

STOP

If you finish before time is called, you may check your work on this section only.
Do not turn to any other section.

SECTION 5: ESSAY

50 Minutes • 1 Essay

Directions: The essay gives you an opportunity to show how effectively you can read and comprehend a passage and write an essay analyzing the passage. In your essay, you should demonstrate that you have read the passage carefully, present a clear and logical analysis, and use language precisely.

Your essay will need to be written on the lines provided in your answer booklet. You will have enough space if you write on every line and keep your handwriting to an average size. Try to print or write clearly so that your writing will be legible to the readers scoring your essay.

As you read the passage below, consider how the writer, Marc de Rosnay, uses the following:

- Evidence, such as facts, statistics, or examples, to support claims.

- Reasoning to develop ideas and to connect claims and evidence.

- Stylistic or persuasive elements, such as word choice or appeals to emotion, to add power to the ideas expressed.

Adapted from "Milestones: what is the 'right' age for kids to travel alone, surf the web, learn about war?" by Marc de Rosnay, originally published by The Conversation *on January 4, 2015. Marc de Rosnay is a Professor and Head of Early Start at the School of Education at University of Wollongong, Australia. (This passage was edited for length. To read the complete article, see http://theconversation.com/.)*

1   Being a parent presents some problems. Irrespective of what you want, your children are going to take actions or be exposed to things that you may not relish. There is the ever-present possibility that they will experience things that you want to actively protect them from. The web provides some salient examples, like pornography. I really don't want my eight-year-old seeing pornography.

2   However, when my eight-year-old asks me an important Dungeons & Dragons question like, "Dad, can a paladin do magic and wear armour?" or he wants to know how solar panels operate, I always encourage him to look on the web. I've taught him to search on Google, to follow his curiosity, and I sometimes do it with him.

3   Ultimately, I want him to be able to seek answers to the questions that are interesting to him independently. He is guaranteed to run into something dodgy on the web, and my wife and I can take ordinary precautions.

4   To our way of thinking, however, more extreme precautions—prohibiting unsupervised internet use and high-level parental control—start to present their own risks.

5   One might ask, at what age should I allow my child to use the web unsupervised?

6   From the perspective of developmental and educational psychology, this is a slightly odd question. Let me explain. Most parents are familiar with the idea that certain developmental

GO TO THE
NEXT PAGE

achievements happen at specific ages. Thus, infants become more wary of strangers at about nine months of age (stranger wariness), and they start to point communicatively by about 12 months of age (declarative pointing). These kinds of developments in the child's capacity are to be expected in all children given a typical environment; we call them developmental milestones.

…

7   I spoke recently to a friend who wanted her ten-year-old daughter to be able to get to school, in the city, on public transport from the inner-west by herself. This particular young girl is very intelligent and responsible, I'm sure that she could have gotten herself to school at seven years of age. But there is no way her parents would have felt comfortable about that.

8   Why? For her parents to give her the independence to travel to school alone, they need to be satisfied not just that she can present her ticket, change trains, and get on the right bus, they need to be confident that she understands the importance of staying on the path, like Little Red Riding Hood.

9   This understanding is largely derived from countless conversations in which the parents have been able to convey important information about the world and the risks it presents to their daughter.

10   We know that children seek information from the people they trust, and from people who have a good record at providing useful information; actually, these two things are not unconnected. Between early childhood and mid-adolescence children have to understand all sort of things for which they need information from people they trust.

11   The information we convey to our children, and the manner in which we do it, helps prepare them for life. For most things, like knowledge about their bodies and sexuality, there is no particular moment at which children are ready for specific knowledge or experience, and much of this we can't control anyway.

12   But what we can do is answer their questions honestly in a manner that is appropriate for their age and conveys our values. The risks of overprotection are simple: children will grow up anyway but they won't have access to good information from people that they trust.

So what age is a good age?

13   It is very difficult to put an age on when a child should or shouldn't be able to grasp a new domain of independence. Your decisions will depend on specific circumstances … Managing risk is critical.

14   The web provides a salient example. By year five or six, today's children should have some freedom to search for the information they need independently. They can do this in a family space rather than in their bedroom. Talk to them honestly about the unsavoury content on the web; this will give them a framework for managing troubling or embarrassing content with you.

15   Independent action is also very important for children. Think back to your own childhood, there is a good chance that some of your fondest memories don't involve adults. Sometimes,

children can walk to the shops before they are 12 years old, and around this time, they should be able to stay in the house for a little while as well.

…

16 Independence is linked to responsibility and much can be done to build responsibility in children before they undertake fully independent actions. But when you give your children independence you provide them with evidence that you trust them, and that trust fortifies responsibility in a way that supervised activity cannot.

Write an essay in which you explain how Marc de Rosnay builds an argument to persuade his audience that being overly protective of children can be as risky as not protecting them enough. In your essay, analyze how the writer uses one or more of the features previously listed (or features of your own choice) to strengthen the logic and persuasiveness of his argument. Be sure that your analysis focuses on the most relevant aspects of the passage.

Your essay should not explain whether you agree with the writer's claims, but rather explain how this writer builds an argument to persuade his audience.

STOP

If you finish before time is called, you may check your work on this section only.
Do not turn to any other section.

No Test Material On This Page

ANSWER KEY AND EXPLANATIONS

Section 1: Reading Test

1. A	**12.** B	**23.** C	**34.** B	**45.** B
2. C	**13.** C	**24.** A	**35.** A	**46.** D
3. D	**14.** B	**25.** A	**36.** C	**47.** B
4. B	**15.** D	**26.** D	**37.** D	**48.** A
5. C	**16.** B	**27.** C	**38.** B	**49.** A
6. D	**17.** B	**28.** B	**39.** A	**50.** B
7. B	**18.** D	**29.** C	**40.** C	**51.** B
8. D	**19.** A	**30.** D	**41.** A	**52.** A
9. A	**20.** D	**31.** B	**42.** D	
10. A	**21.** B	**32.** A	**43.** A	
11. D	**22.** B	**33.** C	**44.** C	

READING TEST RAW SCORE
(Number of correct answers)

1. **The correct answer is (A).** Hoover held that economic success is only possible if people have economic freedom (lines 8–10) but he justifies the stronger centralized government, which he characterizes as socialist, bordering on despotic, as necessary during wartime (lines 14–15).

2. **The correct answer is (C).** Hoover thought that the best way to have a strong economy was to allow individual freedom, but that during wars, it was necessary to allocate resources to the war effort. Only the federal government is able to control resources so that they could be put to best use depending on need for the war.

3. **The correct answer is (D).** In these two paragraphs, Hoover explains that his general statements are not to be interpreted as extreme positions, and in doing so, he provides some details to clarify his position. His attitude remains the same. He does want to be understood, but that does not indicate a change in the overall speech.

4. **The correct answer is (B).** These lines show that Hoover not only was addressing his immediate audience, he was communicating his ideas to the country as a whole. He was arguing for a democratic form of government that was free from government interference, which he believed was the best kind of government. However, he acknowledges possible criticisms and addresses them head on by explaining that is not taking extreme positions and that his statements are generalities.

5. **The correct answer is (C).** Hoover describes the philosophy of European governments as being made of "diametrically opposed" doctrines—paternalism and socialism—that would undermine self-government and individual initiative and enterprise.

6. **The correct answer is (D).** The map shows the electoral votes being wildly in Hoover's favor, with him winning all but a handful of states, mostly in the South. A landslide is

something won by a wide margin and thus a decisive victory.

7. **The correct answer is (B).** Hoover describes his strong beliefs about government and economic liberty but tempers it by showing that the country needs to be flexible so that when necessary, the government can change sufficiently to control resources in order to respond to a crisis, as in wartime.

8. **The correct answer is (D).** Hoover's argument is that progress can only be achieved when people are free to pursue their own economic interests without interference. However, none of the other statements indicate a superiority to other forms of governance. In this statement he says that the result of American government policies has enabled the country to surpass other nations.

9. **The correct answer is (A).** A labyrinth is a maze or a puzzle, which in the context of the sentence shows that Hoover is referring to the problems that will ensue if government gets into business. The result, he says, will be a tangled mess of bureaucracy rather than a smooth operation.

10. **The correct answer is (A).** In the context of this sentence, the word regiment refers to the organization of people or government. Although the context is military, the regimen here refers to the civilian population.

11. **The correct answer is (D).** Both passages describe some kind of loss that is associated with slavery. Stowe recalls how she was deeply affected by the loss of her young child, and she relates this experience to that of slaves who are often separated from their families. Douglass describes the anxiety around losing one's loved ones when escaping from slavery, a permanent loss since once escaped, there would be no way to return to visit or to keep in contact.

12. **The correct answer is (B).** Stowe describes the loss of her young child and relates it to how slaves must feel when they lose their children in the slave market. Stowe's loss was traumatic, and she recognizes the depth of the loss regardless of circumstance. Because Douglass escaped and would never again see his loved ones, Stowe would be sympathetic to his feelings of loss.

13. **The correct answer is (C).** As an abolitionist, Stowe worked with others in the movement to try to get the practice outlawed. One of the methods she used to accomplish this goal was to write about slavery in an effort to persuade people to oppose it. *Uncle Tom's Cabin,* although a work of fiction, told stories about slavery that made people more aware of its horrors.

14. **The correct answer is (B).** In lines 29–38, Stowe suggests that people were prone to doubt the factual basis for *Uncle Tom's Cabin.* She describes the lengths she goes to in order to research the facts about the slave experience and how she was even more horrified than she expected. So she says that in her next book, she will document the facts as they were used in the novel to prove the validity of the book.

15. **The correct answer is (D).** Douglass laments about the loss of loved ones when he thinks about his plan to escape. It states that he believes this deep loss is a major reason that more slaves don't attempt to flee. All of the other reasons in choices (A), (B), and (C) are also true, but choice (D) is the main reason Douglass cites.

16. **The correct answer is (B).** The addition of "An American Slave, Written by Himself" reinforces the idea that it was unusual for a slave to write anything, no less a complete book. We can infer from the inclusion of this information in the title that Douglass wanted to make sure no one thought someone else had written the work.

17. **The correct answer is (B).** The passages are but two examples of how abolitionists were drawing attention to the plight of the slaves. Stowe discusses how she planned to write more, and the introductory material describes *Uncle Tom's Cabin* as a best-seller, indicating that it was widely read. The fact that Douglass' book was published shows that people were interested in his story. The popularity of these works suggests that there were also many others who were doing similar work to advance the cause.

18. **The correct answer is (D).** The only meaning of the word that makes sense in the sentence is choice (D). Here Stowe is talking about the intense pain she felt when

discovering that the slave experience was even worse than she had thought. Although *exquisite* can mean beautiful or delightful, in this context its meaning is intensely.

19. The correct answer is (A). In this part of the narrative, Douglass describes his feelings about leaving his friends when he escapes. These feelings are part of his struggle to make the final decision to attempt the escape, so in this context, he is contending with his feelings of pain about the decision.

20. The correct answer is (B). In this part of the passage, Stowe expresses her deep sorrow and says that what would make her feel better would be knowing that she could use her loss for some greater purpose. Her belief in the evil of slavery and acting on that belief through the abolitionist movement was one way she used to come to terms with her child's death.

21. The correct answer is (B). The fact that Stow felt she had to document what she wrote in the book indicates that some people questioned the validity of the premise of *Uncle Tom's Cabin*. Her research lead her to discover, not that the book got it wrong, but that the treatment of slaves was even worse than she had imagined when writing *Uncle Tom's Cabin*. Choice (B) suggests that whatever ideas Stowe recorded in the book were incomplete, and she needed more work to further the truth.

22. The correct answer is (B). The main idea of the passage is how NASA and its partners monitor the satellites orbiting around Mars to make sure they don't collide. A summary must include the main idea along with some other information that provides an overview of the entire text. Choice (B) includes both the main idea and the detail that explains the reason the satellites need monitoring. The passage doesn't discuss gathering information, choice (A), and choice (D) is a detail.

23. The correct answer is (C). The passage details the various spacecraft currently in orbit around Mars and their sponsoring countries. Four belong to the United States, one to India, and one to the European Union.

24. The correct answer is (A). The passage describes a close call in which a collision

alert was sounded, triggering the plans put in place for such an event. The alarms are set so that the orbits can be closely monitored and steps taken to prevent a collision should they be needed. Over that weekend, the alarms went off, but no action was needed because it was determined that the satellites were not that close to each other after all, a fact the scientists could not predict earlier. It was not a false alarm since it was a possibility at the time that the alarm went off, choice (C). It turned out that it was not a very close call after all, choice (D).

25. The correct answer is (A). The passage describes the procedures that the scientists at the lab put in place in case of emergency. In this case, the emergency isn't one of human life at risk, but the lives of the satellites, the data they are sending to Earth, and the time and money spent on the project could be at risk if there were to be a collision. These are the same kinds of steps taken for people who make plans in case of disasters such as floods, hurricanes, or major fires.

26. The correct answer is (D). The two natural satellites or moons can be determined by eliminating the satellites that are named in the passage and using the graphic to identify all of the satellites in orbit.

27. The correct answer is (C). In the graphic, you can see that Deimos, one of the natural satellites, orbits Mars at the greatest distance. It intersects with only one other satellite's orbit, making it least likely to have a collision.

28. The correct answer is (B). An elongated orbit means that the distance from the orbit to Mars changes as the satellite makes its way around the planet. Because it is constantly changing, it can't be predicted accurately.

29. The correct answer is (C). A satellite could collide if its path in orbit crosses the path in orbit of another satellite at the same time. Choice (C) explains this relationship. None of the other choices describe this relationship.

30. The correct answer is (D). Conjunction here is used to describe the meeting of the celestial bodies, that is, when the satellites are aligned. It does not refer to a collision;

rather, the conjunction is the alignment. If the conjunction is hazardous, it means the satellites may be colliding. If *conjunction* included in its meaning the idea of collision, the word *hazardous* would be not necessary.

31. **The correct answer is (B).** The word *future* explains when the data will be used, from which it can be inferred that projection is something forecast for later or at a future time. In this case the data consists of forecasts about the paths of the satellites in the future as they travel in their orbits.

32. **The correct answer is (A).** Because climate change is already affecting the potato crops in Peru, especially those at high altitudes, diversity of crops can help determine which varieties are better suited for the higher altitudes and warmer temperatures. Some ancient varieties could be resilient to warmer temperatures, but the statement does not explain how diversity of crops can be resilient to the effects of climate change—choice (B). Choice (C) is true of higher temperatures, but it does not explain how crop diversity is related to climate change. Choice (D) does not explain how the gene bank and preserving seeds from extinction is related to climate change.

33. **The correct answer is (C).** Diversity of crops can help alleviate disease and enhance adaptation to different environments, and the farmers are using more diverse plants and seedlings. This tactic will help fight crop failure and also help the crops to adapt to changing conditions as the farmers experiment with breeds of plants and seeds. The partnerships with scientists are helpful, but they are not necessarily all related to climate change. The passage does not suggest that the farmers are trying out a different kind of staple food, choice (D).

34. **The correct answer is (B).** The passage describes how the farmers had to move their crops to higher altitudes for them to survive because the temperature was too high where they had been planted. This suggests that the potatoes need cooler temperatures since the air temperature would be cooler at higher altitudes.

35. **The correct answer is (A).** Diversity is important to ensure that there is always at least one crop that succeeds and can feed people. Sharing information and seeds is important, but that doesn't in itself reduce crop failure, choice (B), nor do gene banks guarantee that a particular variety of plant will succeed where others have failed, choices (C) and (D).

36. **The correct answer is (C).** Choice (C) is best because it includes the main idea of the passage—Peruvian farmers are working to combat the effects of climate change—and the idea that the strategies include both the old and the new. Choice (A) includes only one facet of this concept, and choices (B) and (D) are details that are not needed in a summary.

37. **The correct answer is (D).** The passage describes the effects of farming the potato, a staple crop for thousands of people, and how climate change is reducing output of the crop. Although farmers and scientists are working together in Peru and other places, it will be challenging to stay ahead of the changes already occurring. These changes, as described in the passage, for example, having to move crops to higher altitudes, may have limited use; as the article states, the land at higher altitudes is scarce and rockier. The passage also states that efforts to maintain a gene bank to increase crop diversity are limited, and sometimes the crops don't respond well and/or not all farmers have access to the gene banks. These factors suggest that the problem could grow worse.

38. **The correct answer is (B).** Because they are deeply affected by the changes in climate, Peruvian farmers have a big stake in what is decided at the UN summit. If enough nations agree to pursue policies that will help alleviate the effects, the farmers will be helped. The problem is worldwide, as the passage suggests, so the wishes of the farmers is not dependent on the size of the country or who attends the conference. The last paragraph indicates that there are deep problems faced by countries around the world and it is not confined to issues of high altitudes.

39. **The correct answer is (A).** The text states clearly the relationship between rising temperatures—one aspect of climate change—and the increase in farming problems like

pest control and disease. Crop diversity, choice (B) is one response to climate change, as are gene banks and seed sharing, choice (C) and sharing information and research, choice (D).

40. The correct answer is (C). The word "ancestors" suggests something that or someone who existed hundreds of generations ago, so the sentence in choice (C) indicates that the potato is a food that was grown for food perhaps thousands of years ago. Choices (A) and (D) refer to past practices, but neither took place that long ago.

41. The correct answer is (A). This sentence refers to how the farmers care for their native plants; they are managing them as they try to find breeds that are hardier at higher altitudes and withstand some of the effects of higher temperatures. None of the other words convey this exact meaning—the farmers can't control the seedlings, choice (B); nor can they regulate them, choice (C). The farmers are not developing the crops, choice (D); scientists are working on that aspect.

42. The correct answer is (D). In some contexts, the word *pronounced* can mean to articulate, choice (A), but here it is used to refer to how noticeable the temperature changes are, choice (D). None of the other choices provide a meaning that makes sense in the sentence.

43. The correct answer is (A). The myth includes two examples of deception to achieve goals: one when Thetis sends Achilles to the court of King Lycomedes disguised as a young girl and the other when Ulysses disguises himself as a merchant to gain access to the royal palace. Both acts show people trying to deceive others to get what they want. The gods aren't shown to control events so much as cleverly intervene in human endeavors, so choice (B) is wrong. Marriage loyalties are shown as bonds that can be broken (Helen willingly went off with Paris though she was married to Menelaus), making choice (C) incorrect. There are several references to the dangers of war, choice (D), but the men are encouraged to join the war efforts.

44. The correct answer is (C). Ulysses had urged others to swear to defend Helen, but when he was called upon to do the same, he opted out because he didn't want to upset his happy life. This decision was hypocritical, choice (C). Although he may have viewed his decision as rational, practical, or wise—choices (A), (B), and (D)—those answers are not correct. Ulysses eventually changed his mind and joined forces with the others in their attempt to capture Helen.

45. The correct answer is (B). The apple began the dispute among the goddesses, each trying to prove that that she was "the fairest of all." This set off a chain of events in which Helen was taken from her home by Paris, who wanted her for his wife. An earlier pact among the Spartans had stipulated that they would defend Helen at all costs. The war was an effort to recapture Helen from Paris and bring her back to her husband Menelaus, the King of Sparta.

46. The correct answer is (D). Lines 70–71 states that Thetis was afraid that Achilles might perish if he went to war. The battle was already beginning, so choice (A) is incorrect. Her objections were based on her fear for his safety, not any ideas about his future marriage plans, making choice (B) incorrect. Her plan for Achilles to go to King Lycomedes was not to ask for help, choice (D), but rather so he could avoid being drafted to fight by concealing his true identity.

47. The correct answer is (B). Paris wanted the much-prized Helen for his wife. Although she was married to Menelaus, he persuaded her to go with him and leave the palace, setting in motion a pact agreed to by the men of Sparta to protect the beautiful Helen. The men set out to bring Helen back to her rightful husband.

48. The correct answer is (A). Lines 58–59 reveal that Telemachus is Ulysses' son when the young child is put in danger, and Ulysses had to drop his guise as a madman to save him. Both Telemachus and Ulysses were humans, but neither was royalty, making choices (B) and (C) incorrect.

49. The correct answer is (A). It describes the pledge made by the Spartans to find Helen and bring her back to Sparta. It was that oath to defend Helen that started the war.

Ulysses' pretense at anger was meant to deflect Palamedes's requests that Ulysses join forces with Achilles—choice (B). It was an action that contributed to the start of the war. Thetis's disguise was designed to save him from fighting—choice (C)—it was not a cause of the war. Choice (D) describes how Ulysses persuaded Achilles to join the cause; the war had already been declared.

50. **The correct answer is (B).** One of the roles of the gods and goddesses was to protect the humans from their own human foibles a well as from dangers from one another. Lines 25–27 show shows that the gods were offering to protect Paris on his journey. None of the other choices illustrate text that shows the powers of the gods. Choice (A) shows Eris in action, but it does not illustrate her powers. Choice (C) defines Thetis as one of the gods, and choice (D) describes the actions of a human.

51. **The correct answer is (B).** The context of the sentence indicates that *prudent counsels* is associated with something told to Achilles by his mother. His mother had advised Achilles to adopt the disguise to avoid participating in the war. A mother's counsel is generally thought of as wise, though in this case Ulysses may be questioning that description since he wants Achilles to ignore her advice.

52. **The correct answer is (A).** *Nuptials* refers to wedding ceremonies. This can be inferred from the context, which makes it clear that it is an invitation-only event related to Peleus and Thetis. There is nothing that suggests a religious context, choice (D), nor a ritual, choice (C). The beauty contest, choice (B), was not part of the nuptials; the contest occurred when Eris was angry at being excluded.

Section 2: Writing and Language Test

1. A	**11.** B	**21.** B	**31.** A	**41.** B
2. D	**12.** C	**22.** C	**32.** A	**42.** D
3. A	**13.** B	**23.** D	**33.** D	**43.** B
4. A	**14.** C	**24.** C	**34.** C	**44.** B
5. B	**15.** B	**25.** A	**35.** B	
6. C	**16.** D	**26.** A	**36.** C	
7. D	**17.** A	**27.** B	**37.** D	
8. C	**18.** C	**28.** D	**38.** B	
9. A	**19.** D	**29.** B	**39.** D	
10. C	**20.** C	**30.** C	**40.** A	

WRITING AND LANGUAGE TEST RAW SCORE ☐
(Number of correct answers)

1. **The correct answer is (A).** Choice (A) explains why the segregated school system was a major factor in keeping African Americans disadvantaged. Choice (B) is not an accurate statement. Choice (C) does not explain why the segregated schools kept African Americans from competing on equal grounds. Choice (D) is irrelevant as it relates to a period after the timeframe in the paragraph.

2. **The correct answer is (D).** This sentence contains two independent clauses that are neither separated by appropriate punctuation nor connected with a coordinating conjunction, making it a run-on sentence. Only choice (D) provides the appropriate punctuation in the form of a period, and thus it is correct. Choice (A) is incorrect, as a comma alone is inadequate to separate two independent clauses. Choice (B) is incorrect, as a coordinating conjunction like "and" must be preceded by a comma. Choice (C) is incorrect because it includes no punctuation at all.

3. **The correct answer is (A).** The third paragraph contains information that contrasts with information presented in the second paragraph. The introductory word "however" is the best choice to connect these two contrasting ideas. Thus, choice (A) is the correct answer. Choice (B) is incorrect because "moreover" is used to introduce additional information to support the preceding idea. Choice (C) is incorrect because "to begin with" does not generally connect two ideas. Choice (D) is also incorrect because "incidentally" is used to add information that is unconnected to the preceding idea.

4. **The correct answer is (A).** The chart shows the median net worth of households dropped from 2005 to 2009, with Black households showing a drop from $12,124 to $5,677. Thus, choice (A) is the correct answer, as the median net worth of Black households did drop to less than half of what it had been in 2005. Choice (B) is incorrect, as the median net worth *dropped*, not *rose*. Choices (C) and (D) are not correct because the median

net worth of *all* households fell in the same time period.

5. **The correct answer is (B).** In this sentence "urban neighborhoods" must agree in number with "places," so choice (B) is the correct answer as both are plural. Choices (A) and (C) are incorrect because "place" is singular. Choice (D) is also incorrect because while "places" is plural, "neighborhood" is singular.

6. **The correct answer is (C).** The first part of this sentence requires no punctuation, so choice (C) is correct. Choice (A) is incorrect because "only" should not be set off by a comma. Choice (B) is incorrect because "and the ratification of the Fifteenth Amendment" should not be separated by a comma from the preposition "with" as it is part of the prepositional phrase. Choice (D) is incorrect, as the entire phrase is an adverbial phrase that modifies "did win" and should not be separated by a comma.

7. **The correct answer is (D).** The pronoun antecedent is "Republican Party," so the pronoun that refers to it should be singular and gender neutral. Thus, choice (D) is correct. Choice (A) is incorrect because "they" does not agree with the antecedent in number. Choice (B) is incorrect, as "he" is an incorrect shift in pronoun person. Choice (C) is also incorrect, as "we" is an incorrect shift in both person and number.

8. **The correct answer is (C).** The context in this paragraph suggests that African Americans supported the Republican Party because the party somehow aided them in gaining rights. The best choice, then, is *championed,* choice (C), as it implies that the Republican Party fought for the rights of African Americans. Choice (A) is incorrect because *discern* means "to perceive," which doesn't suggest a good enough reason for African Americans to support the party. Choice (B) is incorrect, as *evinced* means "reveal" and that, too, is not a strong enough reason for African Americans to support the party. Choice (D) is incorrect because African Americans would not support the Republican Party if the party disputed or argued against their rights.

9. **The correct answer is (A).** The context suggests that the state election codes were

somehow limiting for African American candidates, as they were not elected because of the codes. Thus, choice (A) is the correct answer. Choice (B) is incorrect, as "conflicting" does not necessarily suggest that the codes were designed to prevent African American candidates from winning. Choice (C) is incorrect, because if the codes were "irrelevant," they could not be a contributing factor to African American losses. Choice (D) is incorrect, as "expansive" suggests that the codes allowed a greater number of people to compete in the elections.

10. **The correct answer is (C).** The writer should delete the sentence because it introduces a detail that is not directly related to the topic of the paragraph—the political party of the congressional representatives is not discussed in the passage. Choice (A) is incorrect because its details are irrelevant. Choice (B) is incorrect because the political party of African Americans is not necessary context for the following paragraph. Choice (D) is incorrect because the sentence does not provide a transition for the paragraph that follows.

11. **The correct answer is (B).** A semicolon is used to link lists of items in which commas are used. Thus, choice (B) is the correct answer, as the semicolons help to avoid confusion by linking lists of items that already contain commas. Choice (A) is incorrect, as there is no way to discern the lists. Choice (C) is incorrect, as dashes are used to indicate a break in thought, not to separate items in a list. Choice (D) is incorrect because the semicolons should be used to separate the lists, not items within each list.

12. **The correct answer is (C).** The antecedent in this sentence is Morocco, so the pronoun "its" must be used for agreement. Thus, choice (C) is the correct answer. Choice (A) is incorrect because "they" does not correctly refer to Morocco but rather to Moroccans, a noun that is not used in this sentence. Choices (B) and (D) are incorrect, as there are no logical antecedents to which "our" and "your" might refer.

13. **The correct answer is (B).** The paragraph is about the influence that Moroccan music has had on non-Moroccan musicians, and only choice (B) maintains this focus by

pointing out how some jazz musicians were influenced by Moroccan music. Choices (A) and (C) are incorrect because the sentences take the focus off Moroccan music and on the people who influenced the Rolling Stones. Choice (D) is incorrect because it talks about how other types of music have influenced Moroccan music.

14. **The correct answer is (C).** The clause "covered with farmland and several large cities and towns" is a nonrestrictive phrase, which means that it is not necessary for understanding the sentence; thus it should be set off with commas, choice (C). Choice (A) is incorrect, as commas are necessary to indicate that the information contained within them is additional and nonessential. Choices (B) and (D) are incorrect because other commas are necessary in the sentences.

15. **The correct answer is (B).** The point of this paragraph is to note who the Berbers are, and only choice (B) explains that they are the largest ethnic group in Morocco. Choice (A) is incorrect because, although the author mentions foreign invaders, the main topic is to explain who the Berbers are. Choice (C) is incorrect because the author's focus is on who the Berbers are, not where their ancestors lived. Choice (D) is incorrect because this is a minor point in the paragraph.

16. **The correct answer is (D).** Here, the possessive determiner "their," choice (D), is correct, as the word describes ancestors belonging to the Berbers. Choice (A) is incorrect because "there" is an adverb telling where. Choice (B) is incorrect because "they're" is a contraction of "they are." Similarly, choice (C) is incorrect because "theyre" is the contraction of "they are" spelled incorrectly.

17. **The correct answer is (A).** The context suggests that the word *barbarian* does not fit the Berber people, and *misnomer* means "inaccurate name." Thus, choice (A) is the correct answer. Choice (B) is incorrect, as *euphemism* means "a milder word for one considered too harsh," which is not what the context suggests. Choice (C) is incorrect, as *locution* refers to the way a word is pronounced. Choice (D) is incorrect because the context, that the Berbers are gracious and hospitable people, is not a reflection

of the term *barbarian*, which suggests the opposite of gracious and hospitable.

18. **The correct answer is (C).** The author explains that the Berbers and most of the other tribes became Islamic. The context, then, suggests that the other tribes were like the Berbers, which means they were indigenous, or native to the area. Choice (C) is the correct answer. Choice (A) is incorrect because "notorious" means famous, usually for something bad, and there is no indication that this was so. Choice (B) is incorrect because "autonomous" means independent, and the idea of autonomy, for the Berbers or any tribe, is not noted anywhere else. Choice (D) is incorrect because "illustrious" means distinguished and this, too, is not supported by the context.

19. **The correct answer is (D).** This sentence requires parallel structure, which means that each clause uses the same pattern of words to show that they all have the same level of importance. In this case, each clause should be in the passive voice, as the author wants to call attention to each action. Choice (D) is the only choice that employs all passive voice, so it is correct. Choice (A) is incorrect because two of the clauses (flute and castanets) are in the active voice, while the rest is in the passive voice. Choice (B) is incorrect because all clauses except the last are in the active voice. Choice (C) is incorrect because all clauses but the last are in the active voice.

20. **The correct answer is (C).** It is unclear what the pronoun here refers to. For clarity, the sentence must restate the antecedent, thus choice (C) is correct. Choice (A) is incorrect because it is unclear whether "it" refers to the music, the traditions, or Morocco. Choice (B) is incorrect because "they" presumably refers to the tribes, which doesn't make sense in the context. Choice (D) is incorrect because the rest of the paragraph focuses on the music and musical traditions, not everything that the caravans carried.

21. **The correct answer is (B).** This answer provides another example of the instruments used in Andalusian music. Choice (A) is not an example; it describes another aspect of Andalusian traditions. Choice (C) gives a detail about the example given rather than

a second example. Choice (D) provides further information about Andalusian culture and is not a further example of the types of instruments used.

22. **The correct answer is (C).** The second sentence is an explanation of the first, and thus a colon, choice (C), should be used to separate the independent clauses. Choice (A) is incorrect because although a semicolon is used to separate two independent clauses, in this case a colon is more appropriate as the second clause actually expands on the first. Choice (B) is incorrect, as dashes are used to set off material for emphasis and not to separate two independent clauses. Choice (D) is also incorrect, as a comma alone is never used to separate two independent clauses. It must instead be combined with a conjunction.

23. **The correct answer is (D).** The sentence would work better later in the passage, after Dresselhaus's honors have been described and before her mentoring is discussed. Choice (A) is incorrect because the sentence is not a detail that supports the main idea. Choice (B) is incorrect because the sentence is about her work later in life, not her childhood. Choice (C) is incorrect because the sentence does not detract from the main idea.

24. **The correct answer is (C).** The conventional expression used here is "stroke of luck," which means a fortunate occurrence. Only choice (C) is an accurate representation of this expression. Choices (A), (B), and (D) are incorrect because they are inaccurate expressions.

25. **The correct answer is (A).** The context suggests that Dresselhaus became aware that there were better schools in the area, as she later got into a school for girls. Choice (A) means the same as *aware*, thus it is correct. Choice (B) is incorrect, as *apprehensive* means "worried," and there is no indication that Dresselhaus was worried. Choice (C) is incorrect, as *dismayed* means "alarmed," and there is no sense that she was alarmed. Choice (D) is incorrect, as *astute* doesn't fit the context.

26. **The correct answer is (A).** The statement in the passage provides more information about why Dresselhaus's original goal was to become a teacher, so choice (A) is cor-

rect. Choice (B) is incorrect because it offers more information about Hunter College, rather than Dresselhaus's goals. Choice (C) is incorrect because it would better fit in later in the passage. Choice (D) is incorrect because it does not relate to why Dresselhaus wanted to be a teacher.

27. **The correct answer is (B).** Only choice (B) avoids wordiness and redundancy, making it the correct answer. Choice (A) is incorrect because "celebrated" and "gain recognition" make the sentence unnecessarily wordy. Choice (C) is incorrect because it is also wordy: "a little later in her career" could easily be substituted for "eventually," and "one of the most prestigious awards in her field" is unnecessary. Choice (D) is incorrect because "but later" is redundant.

28. **The correct answer is (D).** In this sentence, "Yalow" is possessive, and thus must be followed by *'s*. Only choice (D) reflects the correct spelling of this possessive noun. Choice (A) is incorrect because there is no apostrophe before the *s*. Choice (B) incorrectly places the apostrophe after the *s* instead of before it. Choice (C) is incorrect because it contains no apostrophe or *s*.

29. **The correct answer is (B).** The context of the paragraph makes clear that often, there were no other women in the classes Dresselhau attended. The modifier "only" must appear directly before the word it modifies, in this case "woman." Thus, choice (B) is the correct answer. Choice (A) is incorrect because placing the modifier before "she" makes the sentence unclear. Choice (C) is incorrect because "only" modifies the verb "had been," again making the sentence unclear. Choice (D) is incorrect because "only" modifies "there," suggesting that "there" was the only place she had been a woman.

30. **The correct answer is (C).** The first sentence of the paragraph notes that Dresselhaus studied in Cambridge, England. And the second sentence notes that she received her Ph.D. from the University of Chicago. Since sentence 5 is about Dresselhaus returning to the United States to continue her research, it most logically fits between sentences 1 and 2. Thus, choice (C) is the correct answer. Choices (A), (B), and (D)

are incorrect because they do not reflect a logical sequence of events.

31. **The correct answer is (A).** The author's intention is to point out that Dresselhaus is a distinguished scientist, and only choice (A) reflects the correct spelling of the word *eminent*. Choices (B) and (C) are incorrect, as *immanent* means "inherent or within," and *imminent* means "impending or close at hand." Choice (D) is incorrect, as an emigrant is someone who leaves his or her own country to settle in another.

32. **The correct answer is (A).** In this sentence, the phrase "about 20 percent of them women" represents a sharp break in thought, and it should be set off by a dash. The sentence as it is written is correct, so choice (A) is the correct answer. Choice (B) is incorrect because a colon is used before a list or explanation, and the phrase "about 20 percent of them women" is neither a list nor an explanation. Instead, it is additional information. A dash is more appropriate in this case. Choice (C) is incorrect because a semicolon is used to separate items in a series or two independent clauses. Choice (D) is incorrect because it employs a dash correctly but includes a colon before "women," an addition that is unnecessary and incorrect.

33. **The correct answer is (D).** The context makes clear that Dresselhaus enjoys her work and is interested in it. Only *fascination* conveys this idea, thus choice (D) is the correct answer. Choice (A) is incorrect, as *complacency* means "self-satisfied," but the word is usually used in the context of being stuck in a position and unwilling to move forward. Choice (B) is incorrect, as *preoccupation* refers to a fixation or obsession, rather than an interest in how things work. Choice (C) is incorrect because it, too, suggests an obsession or a pressure that is not apparent in the context.

34. **The correct answer is (C).** Choice (C) correctly introduces the emotional concepts discussed at the end of the sentence. Choice (A) is incorrect because it is related to the previous examples, not the ones at the end of the sentence. Choice (B) is incorrect because the focus is on humans rather than

dogs. Choice (D) is incorrect because it focuses on other senses rather than on smell.

35. **The correct answer is (B).** The paragraph is written in the present tense, as is the conditional clause that follows the colon. Thus, this clause must be written in the present tense, making choice (B) the correct answer. Choice (A) is incorrect, as the clause makes an inappropriate shift to the future tense. Choice (C) is incorrect because the clause makes an inappropriate shift to the past tense. Choice (D) is incorrect because the clause makes an inappropriate shift to the present perfect tense.

36. **The correct answer is (C).** The comparison here is between our knowledge of how the nose works and our knowledge of how other senses work, thus choice (C) is the correct answer. Choice (A) is incorrect because it illogically compares our knowledge of how the nose works to our general knowledge about the other senses. Choice (B) is incorrect because it illogically compares our knowledge of how the nose works to our other senses, without specifying any particular thing about the other senses. Choice (D) is incorrect because it illogically compares our knowledge of how the nose works to how our other senses work, without mentioning the word *knowledge*.

37. **The correct answer is (D).** The context of the paragraph suggests that the fragrance of a rose is difficult to pin down, as the author contrasts it with identifying a D major chord or describing something that is silvery-blue. The word *elusive* best captures this sense, as it means "difficult to capture or pin down." Thus, choice (D) is the correct answer. Choice (A) is incorrect because *concordant* means "consistent," which is not what the author is trying to convey. Choice (B) is incorrect because *distinct* means "recognizably different or distinguishable," and the author's point is that a rose's scent, while recognizable, is difficult to describe. Choice (C) is also incorrect, as *ineffable* does mean "difficult to express" but difficult because of the greatness of the subject.

38. **The correct answer is (B).** The paragraph makes the point that our knowledge of how the nose differentiates odors and our ability

to categorize those odors is limited. Only choice (B) supports this point by noting that people who make scent their job have a hard time agreeing on how to classify or categorize scents. Choice (A) is incorrect because the fact that scientists have classified scents into 10 groups directly contradicts the point the author is making in the paragraph that our ability to categorize scents is limited. Choice (C) is incorrect because while it doesn't contradict the author's main point, it also doesn't support it. Choice (D) is incorrect because it also contradicts the author's main point that scents are hard to categorize, as wine aromas have been assigned to twelve different categories.

39. **The correct answer is (D).** The writer should delete the underlined part of the sentence because it adds irrelevant details that are not related to the rest of the passage. Choices (A) and (B) are incorrect because they suggest adding irrelevant or erroneous information. Choice (C) is incorrect because it is irrelevant and shouldn't be included at all.

40. **The correct answer is (A).** The context of the paragraph makes clear two points: We know that molecules up to a certain mass have scents and that there are conflicting theories as to what determines their smell and how the nose records and transmits this information to the brain. The second independent clause contrasts with the first, as it presents uncertainty while the first points out what we know. Thus, the coordinating conjunction "but" is the best way to join these two clauses. Choice (A) is the correct answer. Choices (B) and (C) are incorrect as they set up a causal relationship that is inaccurate. Choice (D) is incorrect as it doesn't accurately establish the contrast information presented in the two clauses.

41. **The correct answer is (B).** The style of the passage is formal and objective, and only choice (B) corresponds with this style. Choices (A), (B), and (C) are incorrect because they employ an informal and subjective style, using words like "stink," "disgusting," and "nasty."

42. **The correct answer is (D).** Turin's questioning of the lock-and-key theory along with the results of his experiments suggest that he has disproved the theory, which makes choice (D) the correct answer. Choice (A) is incorrect, as *thwart* means "to hinder or stop." Choice (B) is incorrect, as *sanction* means "to support," and Turin's experiments did not support the theory. Choice (C) is incorrect, as *instigate* means "to bring about or induce," which doesn't make sense in the context.

43. **The correct answer is (B).** The sentence is clearly interrogative and thus requires a question mark at the end. Choice (B), then, is the correct answer. Choice (A) is incorrect, as a dash is not used as end-of-sentence punctuation. Choice (C) is incorrect, as a period is used for a declarative sentence, and this sentence is interrogative. Choice (D) is incorrect because an exclamation point is used for an exclamatory statement, and this one is not.

44. **The correct answer is (B).** The subject of the sentence is "number," which is singular, so the verb should agree in number. Only "determines" agrees in number with the subject, so choice (B) is the correct answer. Choice (A) is incorrect, as "determine" is a plural verb. Choices (C) and (D) are incorrect because both contain plural verbs as well as shifts in tense.

Section 3: Math Test—No Calculator

1. B	**5.** C	**9.** A	**13.** C	**17.** 234
2. D	**6.** C	**10.** D	**14.** A	**18.** 16
3. D	**7.** A	**11.** B	**15.** A	**19.** 15
4. C	**8.** A	**12.** A	**16.** 3	**20.** 8/3 or 2.66 or 2.67

MATH TEST—NO CALCULATOR TEST RAW SCORE
(Number of correct answers)

1. **The correct answer is (B).** One way to solve this problem is to add the xs and the numbers. When you do this, you'll get $3x + 7 = 2x + 9$. Then put all the xs on one side of the equation and all the numbers on the other to get $x = 2$.

   Another way to solve this problem is to work backwards. Plug in the numbers in the answer choices for x and see if the sides are equal. If you use answer choice (C), 3, you'll get

   $3 + 3 + 3 + 7 = 3 + 3 + 9$, or $16 = 15$.

   This is not true, so choice (C) is not correct. Try choice (B), 2, and you'll get

   $2 + 2 + 2 + 7 = 2 + 2 + 9$, or $13 = 13$,

   which is true. That means choice (B) is the correct answer.

2. **The correct answer is (D).** Subtract the two polynomials by combining like terms:

   $(3x^2 - 7x + 5) - (-6x^2 + 5x - 4) = (3x^2 - (-6x^2))$
   $+ (-7x - 5x) + (5 - (-4)) = 9x^2 - 12x + 9$

3. **The correct answer is (D).** To determine which point is correct, substitute each value into each inequality:

   $$0 \le 3(0) - 4$$
   (A) $5(0) + 4(0) \ge 6$ Wrong

   $$5 \le 3(-1) - 4$$
   (B) $5(-1) + 4(5) \ge 6$ Wrong

   $$-3 \le 3(2) - 4$$
   (C) $5(2) + 4(-3) \ge 6$ Wrong

   $$4 \le 3(3) - 4$$
   (D) $5(3) + 4(4) \ge 6$ Correct

4. **The correct answer is (C).** Pick values for the numbers. Suppose $x = 1$. That means Angie took 3×1, or 3, hours to get to the party. If it took her 3 hours to get to the party, she could have stopped for 1 hour ($b = 1$) and driven 30 miles per hour ($z = 30$). If she took 3 hours to get to the party and she stopped for 1 hour, then she was only driving for 2 hours. That means that she must have driven 30×2, or 60, miles total. Now try the answer choices. Plug in $x = 1$, $b = 1$, and $z = 30$. The answer choice that is correct will also total 60. Choice (C) results in:

$$30(3 \times 1 - 1) = 30(3 - 1) = 30(2) = 60$$

It is the correct answer.

You can also solve this problem by thinking it through. You are looking for a distance, and distance = rate × time. The rate is z miles per hour. The time is the amount of time it took Angie to arrive at the party ($3x$) minus any time she stopped during the trip (b). So the time is $3x - b$. If you multiply the rate by the time to find the distance, you get $z(3x - b)$, which is choice (C).

5. **The correct answer is (C).** First, solve for s: $6s = 36$; $s = 6$. Now plug in 6 for s to solve for r: $3s - r = 9$; $3(6) - r = 9$; $18 - r = 9$; $-r = -9$; $r = 9$.

Another way you could solve this is to work backwards. After finding the value of s to be 6, plug in each answer choice as a value for r. For example, if you started with choice (A): $3(6) - 3 = 18 - 3 = 15$, which is not 9, so eliminate choice (A). You could try out each answer choice until you reached choice (C) and found that: $3(6) - 9 = 18 - 9 = 9$, so (C) is correct.

6. **The correct answer is (C).** The value of y is dependent on the number of x months of increasing deposits, so y represents the amount that Gary deposits into his account in month x, making choice (C) the correct answer. Choice (A) incorrectly assumes that the equation is totaling the amounts added each month, when it is only calculating the amount deposited each month based on the previous month. Choice (B) is incorrect because the formula is calculating a total amount; the variable x represents the number of months. Choice (D) is incorrect because calculating the increase would involve a comparison of the previous month(s).

7. **The correct answer is (A).** In order to find the value of $f\left(\dfrac{1}{c}\right)$ plug $x = \dfrac{1}{c}$ into the given function and simplify:

$$f\frac{1}{c} = c\left(\frac{1}{c}\right) - \frac{d}{\frac{1}{c}} = 1 - cd$$

8. **The correct answer is (A).** Substitute $(0, 3)$ and $(1.5, 0)$ into each equation to determine which will have those intercepts. Use your understanding of intercepts to find the equation of the function.

$$y = -\frac{3}{x-3} + 2 \qquad y = -\frac{3}{x-3} + 2$$

$$3 = -\frac{3}{0-3} + 2 \qquad 0 = -\frac{3}{1.5-3} + 2$$

$$3 = 1 + 2 \qquad \text{and} \qquad 0 = -2 + 2$$

9. **The correct answer is (A).** The factors of a function can be found from its x-intercepts through a process like below:

$$x = -2, x = 3, x = 5$$

$$x + 2 = 0, x - 3 = 0, x - 5 = 0$$

$$g(x) = f(x)(x + 2)(x - 3)(x - 5)$$

10. **The correct answer is (D).** The total per package is 9 marbles, and 108 marbles is $9 \times 12 = 108$. So the number of each color needs to be multiplied by 12; $3 \times 12 = 36$, $4 \times 12 - 48$, $36 + 48 = 84$.

11. **The correct answer is (B).** When multiplying exponential terms with the same base, exponents are added:

$$x^{\frac{1}{5}} \bullet x^{\frac{4}{5}} = x^{-a}$$

$$x^{\frac{1}{5} + \frac{4}{5}} = x^{-u}$$

$$x^{\frac{5}{5}} = x^{-a}$$

$$x^1 = x^{-a}$$

$$-a = 1$$

$$a = -1$$

12. **The correct answer is (A).** When two lines are parallel, their slopes are equal. Since you know that line p passes through points $(0, 4)$ and $(2, 2)$, you can use this information to find the slope of p:

$$\text{Slope of } p = \frac{y_2 - y_1}{x_2 - x_1}$$

$$= \frac{2 - 4}{2 - 0}$$

$$= \frac{-2}{2}$$

$$= -1$$

Since lines p and q are parallel, their slopes must be equal. This means that the slope of q is also equal to -1.

Since you know that line q passes through points $(0, 0)$ and (x, y) and the slope is -1, you can write an equation representing the relationship between x and y:

$$\text{Slope of } q = \frac{y_2 - y_1}{x_2 - x_1}$$

$$= \frac{y - 0}{x - 0}$$

$$= \frac{y}{x}$$

$$\frac{y}{x} = -1$$

$$y = -x$$

$$x + y = 0$$

Therefore, the relationship between x and y can be represented by the equation $x + y = 0$.

13. **The correct answer is (C).** In any right triangle the sine of one acute angle is equal to the cosine of the other acute angle.

$$\sin F = \frac{\text{opposite}}{\text{hypotenuse}}$$

$$= \frac{f}{e} = \frac{2}{3}$$

$$\cos D = \frac{\text{adjacent}}{\text{hypotenuse}}$$

$$= \frac{f}{e} = \frac{2}{3}$$

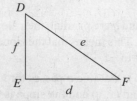

14. **The correct answer is (A).** First, find the center of the circle by finding the midpoint of its diameter. The distance between the x-values is $15 - (-9) = 24$ units. Half that distance is:

$$\left(\frac{-9+15}{2}, \frac{7+(-3)}{2} \right) \rightarrow \left(\frac{6}{2}, \frac{4}{2} \right) \rightarrow (3, 2)$$

Next, find the radius of the circle by finding half the length of the diameter:

$$\frac{\sqrt{(-9-15)^2 + (7-(-3))^2}}{2} = 13$$

Then, plug the center and the radius into the standard form for the equation of a circle and simplify:

$$(x-h)^2 + (y-k)^2 = r^2$$
$$(x-3)^2 + (y-2)^2 = 13^2$$
$$(x-3)^2 + (y-2)^2 = 169$$

15. **The correct answer is (A).** Divide the two expressions using either long division or synthetic division:

$$\begin{array}{r} 3x+4 \\ x-3{\overline{\smash{\big)}\,3x^2 - 5x + 9}} \\ \underline{-(3x^2 - 9x)} \\ 0x^2 + 4x + 9 \\ \underline{-(4x - 12)} \\ 0x^2 + 0x + 21 \end{array}$$

Alternatively, you can use the remainder theorem to solve. Substitute 3 for x in the numerator, and the value should be the remainder:

$$3(3)^2 - 5(3) + 9 = 27 - 15 + 9 = 21$$

16. **The correct answer is 3.** To find a solution, first set the equation equal to 0, since the height of the ball when it hits the ground is 0. Then, solve the equation for t using factoring.

$$0 = 6 + 13t - 5t^2$$
$$0 = 5t^2 - 13t - 6$$
$$0 = (5t + 2)(t - 3)$$
$$5t + 2 = 0; \quad t = 3$$

$$t = -\frac{2}{5}; \qquad t = 3$$

Since the time cannot be negative, the solution is $t = 3$. The ball will hit the ground in 3 seconds.

17. **The correct answer is 234.** Since m is a constant, that means that m must always have the same value. So use $b = 6$ to solve for m.

$$6b + m = 270$$
$$6(6) + m = 270$$
$$36 + m = 270$$

After subtracting 36 from both sides of the equation, you will get $m = 234$.

18. **The correct answer is 16.** You know that opposite sides of a rectangle are equal, so since $\overline{ED} = 6$, $\overline{CA}$ must also equal 6. You know from the diagram that $\overline{CB} = 10$. Since $\triangle ABC$ is a right triangle, you can use the Pythagorean Theorem or what you know about 3-4-5 triangles to find the length of $\overline{AB}$.

Using the Pythagorean Theorem:
$a^2 + b^2 = c^2$; $6^2 + b^2 = 10^2$; $36 + b^2 = 100$; $b^2 = 64$; $b = 8$.

So now you know that $\overline{AB} = 8$. You know that B is the midpoint of $\overline{AD}$ and that the midpoint divides a segment in half. That means that $\overline{AB} = \overline{BD}$. Since $\overline{AB} = 8$, $\overline{BD}$ also equals 8. That means that the length of $\overline{AD} = 8 + 8 = 16$.

19. **The correct answer is 15.** Transfer the radical expressions on the opposite sides of the equation and then square both sides:

$$\sqrt{x+10} - \sqrt{2x-5} = 0$$
$$\sqrt{x+10} = \sqrt{2x-5}$$
$$\left(\sqrt{x+10}\right)^2 = \left(\sqrt{2x-5}\right)^2$$
$$x + 10 = 2x - 5$$
$$10 + 5 = 2x - x$$
$$x = 15$$

20. **The correct answer is 8/3.** For a system of linear equations to have infinitely many solutions, the equations must be equivalent. To make the first equation equivalent to the second equation, we must multiply by –2:

$$-2(fx + gy = -16) = -2fx - 2gy = 32$$
$$-2fx - 2gy = 32$$
$$3x - 8y = 32$$
$$-2f = 3 \rightarrow f = -\frac{2}{3}$$
$$2g = 8 \rightarrow g = 4$$

Then write and simplify the ratio that is asked for in the problem:

$$f = -\frac{3}{2}, g = 4$$
$$-\frac{g}{f} = -\frac{4}{-\frac{3}{2}} = \frac{4}{\frac{3}{2}} = \frac{8}{3}$$

The correct answer is $\frac{8}{3}$, which you would grid as 8/3.

Section 4: Math Test—Calculator

1. B	**9.** C	**17.** B	**25.** D	**33.** 25
2. C	**10.** A	**18.** C	**26.** D	**34.** .36
3. D	**11.** B	**19.** B	**27.** C	**35.** .49
4. B	**12.** B	**20.** D	**28.** D	**36.** 5
5. B	**13.** A	**21.** B	**29.** C	**37.** 1.14
6. D	**14.** D	**22.** A	**30.** D	**38.** 1112
7. A	**15.** D	**23.** B	**31.** 24	
8. D	**16.** D	**24.** B	**32.** 4	

MATH TEST—CALCULATOR RAW SCORE
(Number of correct answers)

1. **The correct answer is (B).** Using 1 pound = 16 ounces, multiply 6 by 16 to find that there are 96 ounces of flour in the bag. Then, divide the overall number of ounces by the number of containers, $96 \div 24 = 4$. Each container has 4 ounces of flour, which is choice (B).

2. **The correct answer is (C).** A negative correlation is a relationship between two variables such that when one variable increases, the other variable decreases. The points on the scatterplot show that as the amount of snowfall increases, the number of drivers on the road decreases. Therefore, the scatterplot shows a negative correlation.

3. **The correct answer is (D).** $\$18 \div 3 = \$6$ for each box of cookies. $\$6 \div \$0.25 = 24$ quarters. Another way to solve this would be to figure out that she must sell each box for $6, and then to multiply each number of quarters in the answer choices by $0.25 to see which equals $6.

4. **The correct answer is (B).** The amount of $480 is constant, and the amount she makes in commission depends on her total sales. The term that represents her commission should include the variable, and since she makes 15% of her total sales x, the term $0.15x$ represents the amount of commission. Adding both of these amounts together results in $f(x) = 480 + 0.15x$.

5. **The correct answer is (B).** Choose an initial amount for the tax revenue for the town of $100,000. An increase of 8% would be an increase of $8,000 to $108,000. An additional 10% increase the next year would be another $10,800, for total revenue of $118,800. This is 18.8% more than the original $100,000.

6. **The correct answer is (D).** 471 of the 682 respondents is about $\frac{471}{682} \approx 0.69 = 69\%$. To estimate the number of people in the county who will not drive more if gas prices drop, multiply the entire population by the percent in the random sample.

   $898,000(0.69) = 619,620$

   The answer that comes closest to this calculation is choice (D).

7. **The correct answer is (A).** The model drawing of the Moon's diameter is 6 inches. To find the diameter of the actual Moon, use the scale: $6 \times 360 = 2160$. Therefore, the approximate diameter of the actual Moon is 2,160 miles.

8. **The correct answer is (D).** There are 380 seats in the theater, so the total number of tickets that can be sold is at most 380. They will sell x student tickets and y adult tickets for a maximum of 380 tickets, or $x + y \leq 380$.

   The income from tickets will be $6.50 per child, or $6.5x$, and $8.25 per adult, or $8.25y$. The total amount they collect, $6.5x + 8.25y$, has to be at least $600, or $6.5x + 8.25y \geq 600$. Only choice (D) shows both of these inequalities.

9. **The correct answer is (C).** The discount is 15%, or $1 - 0.15 = 0.85$ of the retail price, which is $0.85r$. The 6 % sales tax is added to this discounted cost, which is the same as multiplying by 1.06. The expression combining those two is $0.85r \times 1.06$.

10. **The correct answer is (A).** The cost of buying energy bars can be represented by $2.25x$. The cost of buying the water bottles can be represented by $12.5y$. The total cost is represented by $2.25x + 12.5y = 447.5$.

11. **The correct answer is (B).** You know that b cannot equal 1. Pick values for a and b. For example, suppose $b = 6$. That would mean that $a = 0.5$, because $ab = 3$. Plug in these values for the expression given:

$$\frac{a-3}{3b-3} = \frac{0.5-3}{3(6)-3}$$
$$= \frac{-2.5}{15}$$
$$= -\frac{5}{2} \times \frac{1}{15}$$
$$= -\frac{1}{6}$$

Since $b = 6$, $-\frac{1}{6} = -\frac{1}{b}$, which matches choice (B).

12. **The correct answer is (B).** Simplify the expression:

$$3\sqrt[4]{x^3} = 3\left(x^3\right)^{\frac{1}{4}} = 3x^{\frac{3}{4}}$$

13. **The correct answer is (A).** The amount earned per hour is $9x$ for the pool and $11x$ for the bakery, and needs to be at least $215, so $9x + 11y \geq 215$ represents this. The total number of hours needs to be at most 25, so at so $x + y \leq 25$ represents this. Only choice (A) shows both of these inequalities.

14. **The correct answer is (D).** The weight has to be less than or equal to 50 pounds, and the weight of each type of book is represented by $2.5x$ and $1.25y$, so the inequality that represents this situation is $2.5x + 1.25y \leq 50$.

answers PRACTICE TEST 4

15. **The correct answer is (D).** The Slope-Intercept form of the equation of a line is $y = mx + b$, where m is the slope of the line and b is the y-intercept. The coordinates of the y-intercept are $(0, b)$.

In order to solve this problem, transform the given equation into the slope-intercept form:

$$3x + 4y = 16$$
$$4y = -3x + 16$$
$$y = -\frac{3}{4}x + 4$$

Comparing the above equation with the slope-intercept equation, $y = mx + b$, you can see that $b = 4$.

Therefore, the coordinates of the y-intercept are $(0, 4)$.

16. **The correct answer is (D).** The graph shows that the slope decreases between subsequent pairs of points, so the relationship is exponential. The y-values decrease as the x-values increase, indicating exponential decay.

17. **The correct answer is (B).** Use the curve on the graph and draw a line up from 9 along the x-axis to the curve. Then connect that intersection horizontally to the y-axis. Note the scale along the y-axis to see that 0.5 is closest to the value at $x = 9$ on the curve.

18. **The correct answer is (C).** You know that the angles labeled $3a$, $4a$, and $47°$ all lie on the same line. You know that a straight line measures $180°$, so you can find the value of a by adding:

$$3a + 4a + 47° = 180°$$
$$7a + 47° = 180°$$
$$7a = 133°$$
$$a = 19°$$

If $a = 19°$, then $3a = 3(19°) = 57°$. Angle I and the angles labeled b and $3a$ form a triangle. The sum of the angles of a triangle is $180°$. Since $FGHI$ is a rectangle, you know that angle $I = 90°$. So:

$$180° = 57° + 90° + b$$
$$180° = 147 + b$$
$$33° = b$$

19. **The correct answer is (B).** Note that in the question it asks for the projected population x years after 2010, but gives the population in 2014. The equation must take into account this difference.

The formula for exponential growth is $y = a(1 + r)^n$, where a is the initial amount, r is the rate at which the amount is increasing, and n is the number of times that the amount increases at that rate. In this question $a = 339,800$, $r = 0.025$, and $n = x - 4$. Plugging these values into the formula, we get $y = 339,800(1 + 0.025)^{x-4}$, which is choice (B).

20. **The correct answer is (D).** The sample is likely biased since they only asked subscribers of their newspaper. Also, subscribers of the newspaper may not live in the city.

21. **The correct answer is (B).** To solve this problem, first convert 9 into an exponential term with base 3, so that both sides have the same base. Then equate powers on both sides. Also remember that when raising an exponential term with another power, exponents are multiplied, thus $(x^m)^n = x^{m \times n}$

$$\left(3^{-a}\right)^{\frac{2}{3}} = \left(9^{\frac{1}{a}}\right)^{-6}$$

$$\left(3^{-a}\right)^{\frac{2}{3}} = \left[\left(3^2\right)^{\frac{1}{a}}\right]^{-6}$$

$$3^{\frac{-2a}{3}} = 3^{\frac{-12}{a}}$$

$$-2a^2 = -36$$

$$a^2 = 18$$

$$a = \sqrt{18}$$

$$a = \sqrt{9 \times 2}$$

$$a = \sqrt{9} \times \sqrt{2}$$

$$a = 3\sqrt{2}$$

22. **The correct answer is (A).** The median for Town A is 7.5 and for Town B is 7, so the median is greater for Town A. This is the only statement among the answer choices that is true.

23. **The correct answer is (B).** The numbers of days of rain have a much greater variation in Town B than in Town A. Since standard deviation is a measure of variation, choice (B) is correct.

24. **The correct answer is (B).** Consider an example that would make the statement in the question true. If the intercepts of a function are at $(a, 0)$ and $(0, a)$, then they could be at $(3, 0)$ and $(0, 3)$. The slope of the line through those points is:

$$\frac{3-0}{0-3} = \frac{3}{-3} = -1 \quad \text{OR} \quad \frac{a-0}{0-a} = \frac{a}{-a} = -1$$

The same is true when a is negative:

$$\frac{-a-0}{0-(-a)} = \frac{-a}{a} = -1$$

25. **The correct answer is (D).** An inscribed triangle that passes through the center forms a right triangle. So the missing angle measure is $90 - 36 = 54$. Using the given expression $x - 25.5 = 54$, $x = 79.5$.

26. **The correct answer is (D).** There is nothing to indicate that the sample is biased or too small, or that the margin of error is too large, so choice (D) is best supported by the data.

27. **The correct answer is (C).** The 95% confidence that the margin of error is ±4% means that there is a high probability that the actual percent of the voters that will vote for Candidate A is most likely 31%, ±4%, or between 27% and 35%.

28. The correct answer is (D). We can calculate and compare their actual volumes or the ratio of their volumes.

$$V_{Charon} = \frac{4}{3}\pi r^3$$

$$= \frac{4}{3}\pi\left(\frac{750}{2}\right)^3$$

$$\approx 220,781,250$$

$$V_{Pluto} = \frac{4}{3}\pi r^3$$

$$= \frac{4}{3}\pi(750)^3$$

$$\approx 1,766,250,000$$

$$\frac{1,766,250,000}{220,781,250} = 8$$

OR

$$\frac{V_{Pluto}}{V_{Charon}} = \frac{\frac{4}{3}\pi(2r)^3}{\frac{4}{3}\pi r^3}$$

$$= \frac{8r^3}{r^3}$$

$$= 8$$

The volume comparison of any two spheres where the diameter of one sphere is twice the diameter of the other sphere is always 8 to 1.

29. The correct answer is (C). For the system to have exactly one real solution, the graph of the system will be a line and a parabola that is tangent to the line. For the parabola to be tangent to the line, it must have its vertex along that line. Since the graph of $y = ax^2$ has its vertex along the line $y = 0$, then $y = ax^2 - 2$ has its vertex along the line $y = -2$.

30. The correct answer is (D). Remember that the vertex form of a quadratic equation is $h(x) = a(x - h)^2 + k$, where k is the minimum or maximum value of the function. Since in this question h is the equation for a parabola that opens down, it will have a maximum at k when written in vertex form. Choices (C) and (D) are both in vertex form, but only choice (D) is equivalent to the original function. Check by writing both in standard form:

$$-(x - 8)(x + 2) = -(x - 3)^2 + 25$$

$$-(x^2 - 6x - 16) = -(x^2 - 6x + 9) + 25$$

$$-x^2 + 6x + 16 = -x^2 + 6x + 16$$

31. The correct answer is 24. To use the formula to find the answer, find the total cost for driving one additional mile, or 101 miles.

$$y = 49 + 0.24(x - 100)$$

$$y = 49 + 0.24(101 - 100)$$

$$y = 49 + 0.24$$

$$y = 49.24$$

32. The correct answer is 4. Write and solve an inequality to find the number of pens she can buy, and then interpret the answer, including the remainder.

$$2.75x + 12 \le 25$$

$$2.75x \le 13$$

$$x \le 4.\overline{72}$$

Since she can't buy fractions of a pen, the greatest number of pens that Amber can buy is 4.

33. The correct answer is 25. Write and solve a system of equations. Let x = the number of 2-point shots made and y = the number of 3-point shots made.

$$x + y = 33$$
$$2x + 3y = 74$$

Multiply the first equation by 2:

$$2(x + y) = 2 \times 33$$
$$2x + 2y = 66$$

Now subtract the second equation from this new one:

$$2x + 2y = 66$$
$$\underline{-(2x + 3y) = 74}$$
$$-y = -8$$
$$y = 8$$

Substitute $y = 8$ into the initial equation:

$$x + y = 33$$
$$x + 8 = 33$$
$$x = 25$$

34. The correct answer is .36. The number of females in China is 645 million. The total number of people represented in the table is 1,799 million. The probability that a random person chosen in this census is a female in China is:

$$\frac{645}{1799} = 0.358 = 0.36$$

35. The correct answer is .49. The probability that a person chosen is not a male is the same as the probability that a random person chosen is female. The total number of females in the census is 876.8 million, and the total number of people represented in the table is 1,799 million. Therefore, the probability that a random person chosen is not male is:

$$\frac{876.8}{1799} = 0.487 = 0.49$$

36. The correct answer is 5. A function like g is undefined when the denominator is equal to 0, so set the denominator equal to 0 and solve for x:

$$(x - 6)^2 + 2(x - 6) + 1 = 0$$
$$x^2 - 12x + 36 + 2x - 12 + 1 = 0$$
$$x^2 - 10x + 25 = 0$$
$$(x - 5)^2 = 0$$
$$x - 5 = 0$$
$$x = 5$$

37. The correct answer is 1.14. Substitute 1.14 for r because there is an increase of 14%, so r should be $1 + 0.14$, or 1.14, in order to match the standard form for exponential growth.

38. The correct answer is 1112. Substitute 1.14 for r to represent a 14% increase and 10 for t to represent 10 years after it was last sold:

$$V = 300(1.14)^{10}$$
$$= 1112.166$$

This is rounded to 1112, which is 1112 thousands of dollars.

Section 5: Essay

Analysis of Passage

The following is an analysis of the passage by Marc de Rosnay, noting how the writer used evidence, reasoning, and stylistic or persuasive elements to support his claims, connect the claims and evidence, and add power to the ideas he expressed. Check to see if you evaluated the passage in a similar way.

Adapted from "Milestones: what is the 'right' age for kids to travel alone, surf the web, learn about war?" by Marc de Rosnay, originally published by The Conversation on January 4, 2015. Marc de Rosnay is a Professor and Head of Early Start at the School of Education at University of Wollongong, Australia. (This passage was edited for length. To read the complete article, see http://theconversation.com/.)

1   Being a parent presents some problems. Irrespective of what you want, your children are going to take actions or be exposed to things that you may not relish. There is the ever-present possibility that they will experience things that you want to actively protect them from.

1   *The writer begins his argument by pointing out that there are problems inherent in raising a child, naming the issue that is central to his essay: children are going to do things or be exposed to things a parent will not like.*

2   The web provides some salient examples, like pornography. I really don't want my eight-year-old seeing pornography.

2   *The writer then cites a specific example: the web.*

3   However, when my eight-year-old asks me an important Dungeons & Dragons question like, "Dad, can a paladin do magic and wear armour?" or he wants to know how solar panels operate, I always encourage him to look on the web.

3   *The writer establishes his legitimacy to write about this topic by mentioning that he is the parent of an eight-year-old boy.*

4   I've taught him to search on Google, to follow his curiosity, and I sometimes do it with him.

4   *Using his relationship with his son as an example, the writer describes a situation in which a parent gives a child free access to the web.*

5   Ultimately, I want him to be able to seek answers to the questions that are interesting to him independently.

5   *The writer states why he believes he is right to give his child free access to the web.*

6   He is guaranteed to run into something dodgy on the web, and my wife and I can take ordinary precautions.

7   To our way of thinking, however, more extreme precautions—prohibiting unsupervised internet use and high-level parental control—start to present their own risks.

8   One might ask, at what age should I allow my child to use the web unsupervised?

9   From the perspective of developmental and educational psychology, this is a slightly odd question. Let me explain. Most parents are familiar with the idea that certain developmental achievements happen at specific ages. Thus, infants become more wary of strangers at about nine months of age (stranger wariness), and they start to point communicatively by about 12 months of age (declarative pointing). These kinds of developments in the child's capacity are to be expected in all children given a typical environment; we call them developmental milestones.

. . .

10 I spoke recently to a friend who wanted her ten-year-old daughter to be able to get to school, in the city, on public transport from the inner-west by herself. This particular young girl is very intelligent and responsible, I'm sure that she could have gotten herself to school at seven years of age. But there is no way her parents would have felt comfortable about that.

11 Why? For her parents to give her the independence to travel to school alone, they need to be satisfied not just that she can present her ticket, change trains, and get on the right bus, they need to be confident that she understands the importance of staying on the path, like Little Red Riding Hood.

6   *De Rosnay returns to the issue of children being exposed to things a parent will not like, admitting that his son "is guaranteed" to encounter something objectionable on the web. He then raises the possibility of taking precautions against this situation. However, these precautions are "ordinary," or reasonable.*

7   *The writer states his central argument: extreme precautions can present their own risks.*

8   *Proceeding with his argument, the writer asks a rhetorical question.*

9   *The writer answers his question by explaining that some developmental achievements (developmental milestones) occur at specific ages.*

10 *Again referring to his personal experience, the writer cites a specific example of a parent wrestling with the question of how much freedom to give her child.*

11 *The writer explores the problems this question raises, citing some of the specific issues a parent must address.*

This understanding is largely derived from countless conversations in which the parents have been able to convey important information about the world and the risks it presents to their daughter.

12 We know that children seek information from the people they trust, and from people who have a good record at providing useful information; actually, these two things are not unconnected. Between early childhood and mid-adolescence children have to understand all sort of things for which they need information from people they trust.

13 The information we convey to our children, and the manner in which we do it, helps prepare them for life.

14 For most things, like knowledge about their bodies and sexuality, there is no particular moment at which children are ready for specific knowledge or experience, and much of this we can't control anyway.

15 But what we can do is answer their questions honestly in a manner that is appropriate for their age and conveys our values.

16 The risks of overprotection are simple: children will grow up anyway but they won't have access to good information from people that they trust.

So what age is a good age?

17 It is very difficult to put an age on when a child should or shouldn't be able to grasp a new domain of independence. Your decisions will depend on specific circumstances… Managing risk is critical.

12 *The writer changes perspective from the personal to the objective to discuss how children seek and acquire information.*

13 *The writer lays the foundation for his argument by talking about the importance of parents allowing children to acquire information: it helps prepare them for life.*

14 *De Rosnay strengthens his argument by pointing out that often there is no ideal moment to communicate "specific knowledge or experience." He also points out that parents have little or no control over when their children acquire specific knowledge or experience.*

15 *The writer supports his central argument by stating what parents do have control over: answering children's questions honestly and appropriately.*

16 *The writer strengthens his central argument by citing the risks of overprotection: children will not gain good information from people they trust.*

17 *De Rosnay returns to the essay's central question (the ideal age to let a child acquire new independence), stressing the crucial role played by the different factors in each situation.*

18 The web provides a salient example.

19 By year five or six, today's children should have some freedom to search for the information they need independently.

20 They can do this in a family space rather than in their bedroom. Talk to them honestly about the unsavoury content on the web; this will give them a framework for managing troubling or embarrassing content with you.

Independent action is also very important for children. Think back to your own childhood, there is a good chance that some of your fondest memories don't involve adults. Sometimes, children can walk to the shops before they are 12 years old, and around this time, they should be able to stay in the house for a little while as well.

. . .

21 Independence is linked to responsibility and much can be done to build responsibility in children before they undertake fully independent actions. But when you give your children independence you provide them with evidence that you trust them, and that trust fortifies responsibility in a way that supervised activity cannot.

18 *The writer returns to his first specific example: the web.*

19 *The writer suggests an age at which a child should have "some freedom" to use the web independently.*

20 *The writer suggests some precautions parents can take as they give children this freedom.*

21 *The writer concludes his argument by summing up his reasoning: giving children independence shows that you trust them, which in turn teaches children to be responsible; denying children independence by overprotecting them does not give them the same trust-fosters-responsibility experience.*

Sample Essays

The following are examples of a high-scoring and low-scoring essay, based on the passage by Marc de Rosnay.

High-Scoring Essay

The central argument in this article is that parents have to give their children a certain amount of freedom to help them grow up to be responsible, independent adults. Marc de Rosnay says that children will be exposed to things that parents won't like, but a good parent gives a child freedom and support. If a parent teaches the child how to handle things that are unpleasant or dangerous, the child learns to be independent and stay safe. Overprotecting children can pose risks because these children may not learn to protect themselves. To convince us of his viewpoint, de Rosnay uses knowledge about childhood development, examples from his experience as a parent, and logic.

As they grow up, children will be exposed to things that parents won't like, such as Internet pornography. De Rosnay establishes his qualification to write about this topic by revealing that he has an eight-year-old son and he's encouraged him to search for information on the Internet. This gives us an example of a danger—pornography on the Internet—and de Rosnay's response—allowing his son to use the Internet. He explains that he taught his son to use Google and he sometimes uses the Internet with him.

De Rosnay uses logic to explain this decision. (1) He wants his son to be able to use the Internet without his help. (2) He takes precautions (which he calls "ordinary") to protect his son from objectionable material. (3) Forms of overprotection, like forbidding his son to use the Internet without supervision or setting up a high level of parental control, can also cause problems.

The author poses a rhetorical question to ask how old a child should be to use the Internet without supervision. This question is really about how a parent determines when a child is old enough to do anything, and de Rosnay uses logic to answer it. He uses the term "developmental milestone" to discuss the age at which most children acquire a skill, such as declarative pointing at the age of 12 months. More complex skills aren't acquired at a particular age because the skill is more complicated and factors like the environment and the child's maturity are different.

De Rosnay provides an example of a complex skill. His friend wanted her ten-year-old daughter to be able to use public transportation to go to school. However, the girl would have to change trains and take a bus to get from home to school. More importantly, she had to understand the dangers she could face and how to avoid them, which meant her parents had to prepare her.

Using this example, the author connects to how parents can prepare their children for life— where children will face all kinds of new experiences, including some that are dangerous. He argues that the best a parent can do is answer questions in a way that is honest and appropriate for the child's age, and conveys good values. Children taught this way will trust their parents and go to their parents for information and help when they need it. He contrasts this with overprotected children who have not learned that they can get good information from their parents, and so won't turn to their parents for help.

The author acknowledges that it is difficult to say how much independence a child should have at a specific age. He cites differences in parents, children, and the amount of risk in a situation (like a bad neighborhood). He does say that children should have some independence on the Internet by the age of five or six, but also suggests that parents take the precaution of making access available in a family space (as opposed to the child's bedroom). He also gives milestones for other independent activities like staying home alone.

To wrap up his argument, de Rosnay uses logic to link responsibility, independence, and trust. He believes that trusting children makes them more responsible. Responsibility leads to giving a child more independence. Giving more independence shows more trust. The cycle starts with trusting the child. As the cycle continues, the child eventually grows up and becomes an independent, responsible adult. De Rosnay's examples and logic create a solid argument for giving a child as much independence as the child can handle while providing a framework to help the child mature.

Low-Scoring Essay

In his article called "Milestones: what is the 'right' age for kids to travel alone, surf the web, learn about war?" Marc de Rosnay looks at what ages kids should be allowed to do certain things like surfing the Internet, walking to school, and watching the news.

Marc de Rosnay is the head of a school in Australia, which is why he knows about child development. In his own life, Marc determined that his eight-year-old son was old enough to use the Internet alone. He thinks his son would probably use the Internet alone anyway, so trying to keep him from using it would cause problems.

Marc de Rosnay asks when children should be allowed to do other things like riding a bike. He says that Dutch people start riding bikes at 2 because riding bikes is really popular there. They learn how to ride by watching other people do it and then imitating them.

Marc de Rosnay gives ages when children should be able to do certain things. They should go to the store alone at 10-14 years, surf the Internet at 5-6 years old, stay home alone at 11 years old, visit a war memorial at 6-8 years old, and watch the news or read the newspaper at 7-9 years old.

In conclusion, Marc de Rosnay says it's hard to know when children can do some things alone. Parents just have to trust their children.

COMPUTING YOUR SCORES

To get a sense of your progress in preparing for the SAT®, follow these instructions and the following conversion tables.

To Determine Your Practice Test Scores

1. After you go through each of the test sections (Reading, Writing and Language, Math—No Calculator, and Math—Calculator) and determine which answers you got right, be sure to enter the number of correct answers in the box below the answer key for each of the sections.

2. Your total score on the SAT® practice test is the sum of your Evidence-Based Reading and Writing Section score and your Math Section score. To get your total score, convert the raw score—the number of questions you got right in a particular section—into the "scaled score" for that section, and then you'll calculate the total score. It sounds a little confusing, but we'll take you through the steps.

To Calculate Your Evidence-Based Reading and Writing Section Score

Your Evidence-Based Reading and Writing Section score is on a scale of 200–800. First determine your Reading Test score, and then determine your score on the Writing and Language Test.

1. Count the number of correct answers you got on the **Section 1: Reading Test.** Remember that there is no penalty for wrong answers. **The number of correct answers is your raw score.**

2. Go to Raw Score Conversion Table 1: Section and Test Scores on page 850. Look in the "Raw Score" column for your raw score, and match it to the number in the "Reading Test Score" column.

3. Do the same with **Section 2: Writing and Language Test** to determine that score.

4. Add your Reading Test score to your Writing and Language Test score.

5. Multiply that number by 10. This is your Evidence-Based Reading and Writing Section score.

To Calculate Your Math Section Score

YOUR MATH SECTION SCORE IS ALSO ON A SCALE OF 200–800.

1. Count the number of correct answers you got on the Section 3: Math Test—No Calculator and the Section 4: Math Test—No Calculator practice tests. Again, there is no penalty for wrong answers. **The number of correct answers is your raw score.**

2. Add the number of correct answers on the Section 3: Math Test—No Calculator and the Section 4: Math Test—No Calculator practice tests.

3. Use the **Raw Score Conversion Table 1: Section and Test Scores** on page 850 and convert your raw score into your Math Section score.

To Obtain Your Total Score

Add your score on the Evidence-Based Reading and Writing Section to the Math Section score. This is your total score on this SAT® Practice Test, on a scale of 400–1600.

Subscores Provide Additional Information

Subscores offer you greater details about your strengths in certain areas within literacy and math. The subscores are reported on a scale of 1–15 and include Heart of Algebra, Problem Solving and Data Analysis, Passport to Advanced Math, Expression of Ideas, Standard English Conventions, Words in Context, and Command of Evidence.

Heart of Algebra

The **Heart of Algebra subscore** is based on questions from the Math Test—No Calculator and Math Test—Calculator (Sections 3 and 4) that focus on linear equations and inequalities.

- Add up your total correct answers from these sections:
- Math Test—No Calculator: Questions 1, 3–6, 12, 17, 20
- Math Test—Calculator: Questions 4, 8–10, 13–15, 24, 31–33
- Your Raw Score = the total number of correct answers from all of these questions.
- Use the **Raw Score Conversion Table 2: Subscores** on page 851 to determine your **Heart of Algebra** subscore.

Problem Solving and Data Analysis

The **Problem Solving and Data Analysis subscore** is based on questions from the Math Test that focus on quantitative reasoning, the interpretation and synthesis of data, and solving problems in rich and varied contexts.

- Add up your total correct answers from these sections:
- Math Test—No Calculator: Question 10
- Math Test—Calculator: Questions 1–3, 5–7, 16, 17, 19, 20, 22, 23, 26, 27, 34, 35, 38
- Your Raw Score = the total number of correct answers from all of these questions.
- Use the **Raw Score Conversion Table 2: Subscores** on page 851 to determine your **Problem Solving and Data Analysis** subscore.

Passport to Advanced Math

The **Passport to Advanced Math subscore** is based on questions from the Math Test that focus on topics central to your ability to progress to more advanced math, such as understanding the structure of expressions, reasoning with more complex equations, and interpreting and building functions.

- Add up your total correct answers from these sections:
- our total correct answers from these sections:
- Math Test—No Calculator: Questions 2, 7–9, 11, 15, 16, 19
- Math Test—Calculator: Questions 11, 12, 19, 21, 29, 30, 36, 37
- Your Raw Score = the total number of correct answers from all of these questions.
- Use the **Raw Score Conversion Table 2: Subscores** on page 851 to determine your **Passport to Advanced Math** subscore.

Expression of Ideas

The **Expression of Ideas subscore** is based on questions from the Writing and Language Test that focus on topic development, organization, and rhetorically effective use of language.

- Add up your total correct answers from Section 2: Writing and Language Test
- Questions 1, 3, 4, 8–10, 13, 15, 17, 18, 21–23, 25–27, 30, 33, 34, 37–39, 41, 42
- Your Raw Score = the total number of correct answers from all of these questions.
- Use the **Raw Score Conversion Table 2: Subscores** on page 851 to determine your **Expression of Ideas** subscore.

Standard English Conventions

The **Standard English Conventions subscore** is based on questions from the Writing and Language Test that focus on sentence structure, usage, and punctuation.

- Add up your total correct answers from Section 2: Writing and Language Test:
- Questions 2, 5–7, 11, 12, 14, 16, 19, 20, 24, 28, 29, 31, 32, 35, 36, 40, 43, 44
- Your Raw Score = the total number of correct answers from all of these questions.
- Use the **Raw Score Conversion Table 2: Subscores** on page 851 to determine your **Standard English Conventions** subscore.

Words in Context

The **Words in Context subscore** is based on questions from the Reading Test and the Writing and Language Test that address word/phrase meaning in context and rhetorical word choice.

- Add up your total correct answers from Sections 1 and 2:
- Reading Test: Questions 10, 11, 19, 20, 31, 32, 41, 42, 51, 52
- Writing and Language Test: Questions 8, 9, 17, 18, 25, 33, 37, 42
- Your Raw Score = the total number of correct answers from all of these questions.
- Use the **Raw Score Conversion Table 2: Subscores** on page 851 to determine your **Words in Context** subscore.

Command of Evidence

The **Command of Evidence subscore** is based on questions from the Reading Test and the Writing and Language Test that ask you to interpret and use evidence found in a wide range of passages and informational graphics, such as graphs, tables, and charts.

- Add up your total correct answers from Sections 1 and 2:
- Reading Test: Questions 8, 9, 21, 22, 29, 30, 39, 40, 49, 50
- Writing and Language Test: Questions 1, 10, 15, 21, 23, 26, 34, 39
- Your Raw Score = the total number of correct answers from all of these questions.
- Use the **Raw Score Conversion Table 2: Subscores** on page 851 to determine your **Command of Evidence** subscore.

Cross-Test Scores

The new SAT®also reports two cross-test scores: Analysis in History/Social Studies and Analysis in Science. These scores are based on questions in the Reading Test, Writing and Language Test, and both Math Tests that ask you to think analytically about texts and questions in these subject areas. Cross-test scores are reported on a scale of 10–40.

Analysis in History/Social Studies

- Add up your total correct answers from these sections:
- Reading Test: Questions 1–21
- Writing and Language Test: Questions 13, 15, 17, 18, 21, 22
- Math Test—No Calculator: None
- Math Test—Calculator: Questions 5, 6, 19, 20, 26, 27, 34, 35
- Your Raw Score = the total number of correct answers from all of these questions.
- Use the **Raw Score Conversion Table 3: Cross-Test Scores** on page 852 to determine your **Analysis in History/Social Studies** cross-test score.

Analysis in Science

- Add up your total correct answers from these sections:
- Reading Test: Questions 22–42
- Writing and Language Test: Questions 34, 37–39, 41, 42
- Math Test—No Calculator: Question 16
- Math Test—Calculator: Questions 2, 7, 16, 17, 22, 23, 28
- Your Raw Score = the total number of correct answers from all of these questions.
- Use the **Raw Score Conversion Table 3: Cross-Test Scores** on page 852 to determine your **Analysis in Science** cross-test score.

Raw Score Conversion Table 1: Section and Test Scores

Raw Score	Math Section Score	Reading Test Score	Writing and Language Test Score	Raw Score	Math Section Score	Reading Test Score	Writing and Language Test Score	Raw Score	Math Section Score	Reading Test Score	Writing and Language Test Score
0	200	10	10	20	450	22	23	40	610	33	36
1	200	10	10	21	460	23	23	41	620	33	37
2	210	10	10	22	470	23	24	42	630	34	38
3	230	11	10	23	480	24	25	43	640	35	39
4	240	12	11	24	480	24	25	44	650	35	40
5	260	13	12	25	490	25	26	45	660	36	
6	280	14	13	26	500	25	26	46	670	37	
7	290	15	13	27	510	26	27	47	670	37	
8	310	15	14	28	520	26	28	48	680	38	
9	320	16	15	29	520	27	28	49	690	38	
10	330	17	16	30	530	28	29	50	700	39	
11	340	17	16	31	540	28	30	51	710	40	
12	360	18	17	32	550	29	30	52	730	40	
13	370	19	18	33	560	29	31	53	740		
14	380	19	19	34	560	30	32	54	750		
15	390	20	19	35	570	30	32	55	760		
16	410	20	20	36	580	31	33	56	780		
17	420	21	21	37	590	31	34	57	790		
18	430	21	21	38	600	32	34	58	800		
19	440	22	22	39	600	32	35				

Conversion Equation 1 Section and Test Scores

Raw Score Conversion Table 2: Subscores

Raw Score (# of correct answers)	Expression of Ideas	Standard English Conventions	Heart of Algebra	Problem Solving Data Analysis	Passport to Advanced Math	Words in Context	Command of Evidence
0	1	1	1	1	1	1	1
1	1	1	1	1	3	1	1
2	1	1	2	2	5	2	2
3	2	2	3	3	6	3	3
4	3	2	4	4	7	4	4
5	4	3	5	5	8	5	5
6	5	4	6	6	9	6	6
7	6	5	6	7	10	6	7
8	6	6	7	8	11	7	8
9	7	6	8	8	11	8	8
10	7	7	8	9	12	8	9
11	8	7	9	10	12	9	10
12	8	8	9	10	13	9	10
13	9	8	9	11	13	10	11
14	9	9	10	12	14	11	12
15	10	10	10	13	14	12	13
16	10	10	11	14	15	13	14
17	11	11	12	15		14	15
18	11	12	13			15	15
19	12	13	15				
20	12	15					
21	13						
22	14						
23	14						
24	15						

answers PRACTICE TEST 4

Conversion Equation 2 Subscores

HEART OF ALGEBRA RAW SCORE (0–19)	EXPRESSION OF IDEAS RAW SCORE (0–24)	COMMAND OF EVIDENCE RAW SCORE (0–18)	PROBLEM SOLVING AND DATA ANALYSIS RAW SCORE (0–17)
CONVERT	CONVERT	CONVERT	CONVERT
HEART OF ALGEBRA SUBSCORE (1–15)	EXPRESSION OF IDEAS SUBSCORE (1–15)	COMMAND OF EVIDENCE SUBSCORE (1–15)	PROBLEM SOLVING AND DATA ANALYSIS SUBSCORE (1–15)

STANDARD ENGLISH CONVENTIONS RAW SCORE (0–20)	WORDS IN CONTEXT RAW SCORE (0–18)	PASSPORT TO ADVANCED MATH RAW SCORE (0–16)
CONVERT	CONVERT	CONVERT
STANDARD ENGLISH CONVENTIONS SUBSCORE (1–15)	WORDS IN CONTEXT SUBSCORE (1–15)	PASSPORT TO ADVANCED MATH SUBSCORE (1–15)

Raw Score Conversion Table 3: Cross-Test Scores

Raw Score (# of correct answers)	Analysis in History/Social Studies Cross-Test Score	Analysis in Science Cross-Test Score	Raw Score (# of correct answers)	Analysis in History/Social Studies Cross-Test Score	Analysis in Science Cross-Test Score
0	10	10	18	28	26
1	10	11	19	29	27
2	11	12	20	30	27
3	12	13	21	30	28
4	14	14	22	31	29
5	15	15	23	32	30
6	16	16	24	32	30
7	17	17	25	33	31
8	18	18	26	34	32
9	20	19	27	35	33
10	21	20	28	35	33
11	22	20	29	36	34
12	23	21	30	37	35
13	24	22	31	38	36
14	25	23	32	38	37
15	26	24	33	39	38
16	27	24	34	40	39
17	28	25	35	40	40

Conversion Equation 3: Cross-Test Scores

TEST	ANALYSIS IN HISTORY/SOCIAL STUDIES		ANALYSIS IN SCIENCE	
	QUESTIONS	RAW SCORE	QUESTIONS	RAW SCORE
Reading Test	1–21		22–42	
Writing and Language Test	13, 15, 17, 18, 21, 22		34, 37–39, 41, 42	
Math Test—No Calculator	None		16	
Math Test—Calculator	5, 6, 19, 20, 26, 27, 34, 35		2, 7, 16, 17, 22, 23, 28	
TOTAL				

ANALYSIS IN HISTORY/
SOCIAL STUDIES
RAW SCORE (0–35)

CONVERT

ANALYSIS IN HISTORY/
SOCIAL STUDIES
CROSS-TEST SCORE (10–40)

ANALYSIS IN SCIENCE
RAW SCORE (0–35)

CONVERT

ANALYSIS IN SCIENCE
CROSS-TEST SCORE (1–15)

Practice Test 5

On test day, you will see these important reminders on the first page of your SAT® test booklet.

- You must use a No. 2 pencil when taking the test; you may not use a pen or mechanical pencil.
- You may not share any questions with anyone. This is considered a violation of College Board's "Test Security and Fairness" policies, and it could cause your scores to be canceled.
- You are not permitted to take the test booklet out of the testing room.

In addition to filling in your name and Test Center information on your answer sheet, you'll be asked to fill in two different codes that will be on your test booklet. Each test booklet has a unique code, and there will be a grid-in form to fill in with your "TEST ID" and "FORM CODE" letters and numbers.

The general directions for the test will look something like this:

- You may only work on one section at a time.
- If you complete a section before time is called, check your work on that section only. You are not permitted to work on any other section.

The directions for marking your answers will likely include the following recommendations:

- Mark your answer sheet properly—be sure to <u>completely</u> fill in the answer bubble.
- Be careful to mark only one answer for each question.
- Don't make any stray marks on the answer sheet.
- If you need to erase your answer, make sure you do so completely.
- Be sure to use the answer spaces that correspond to the question numbers.

You will be able to use your test booklet for scratch work, but you won't get credit for any work done in your test booklet. When time is called at the end of each section, you will not be permitted to transfer answers from your test booklet to your answer sheet.

Any information, ideas, or opinions presented in any of the passages you will see on the redesigned SAT® that have been taken from other sources or published material do not represent the opinions of the College Board.

Scoring on the SAT® is as follows:

- You will receive one point for each correct answer.
- You will not lose points for wrong answers, so you should attempt to answer every question even if you aren't completely sure of the correct answer.

Your testing supervisor will announce when to open the test booklet, so be sure to wait until you're told to do so. For the purposes of this practice test, be sure you have a timer to set for 65 minutes for the Section 1: Reading Test.

The answer sheets for each test section, including lined paper for the essay, appear on the next five pages. Following the Answer Key and Explanations for this Practice Test, you will find details on how to score your work.

ANSWER SHEET PRACTICE TEST 5

Section 1: Reading Test

1. Ⓐ Ⓑ Ⓒ Ⓓ   12. Ⓐ Ⓑ Ⓒ Ⓓ   23. Ⓐ Ⓑ Ⓒ Ⓓ   33. Ⓐ Ⓑ Ⓒ Ⓓ   43. Ⓐ Ⓑ Ⓒ Ⓓ
2. Ⓐ Ⓑ Ⓒ Ⓓ   13. Ⓐ Ⓑ Ⓒ Ⓓ   24. Ⓐ Ⓑ Ⓒ Ⓓ   34. Ⓐ Ⓑ Ⓒ Ⓓ   44. Ⓐ Ⓑ Ⓒ Ⓓ
3. Ⓐ Ⓑ Ⓒ Ⓓ   14. Ⓐ Ⓑ Ⓒ Ⓓ   25. Ⓐ Ⓑ Ⓒ Ⓓ   35. Ⓐ Ⓑ Ⓒ Ⓓ   45. Ⓐ Ⓑ Ⓒ Ⓓ
4. Ⓐ Ⓑ Ⓒ Ⓓ   15. Ⓐ Ⓑ Ⓒ Ⓓ   26. Ⓐ Ⓑ Ⓒ Ⓓ   36. Ⓐ Ⓑ Ⓒ Ⓓ   46. Ⓐ Ⓑ Ⓒ Ⓓ
5. Ⓐ Ⓑ Ⓒ Ⓓ   16. Ⓐ Ⓑ Ⓒ Ⓓ   27. Ⓐ Ⓑ Ⓒ Ⓓ   37. Ⓐ Ⓑ Ⓒ Ⓓ   47. Ⓐ Ⓑ Ⓒ Ⓓ
6. Ⓐ Ⓑ Ⓒ Ⓓ   17. Ⓐ Ⓑ Ⓒ Ⓓ   28. Ⓐ Ⓑ Ⓒ Ⓓ   38. Ⓐ Ⓑ Ⓒ Ⓓ   48. Ⓐ Ⓑ Ⓒ Ⓓ
7. Ⓐ Ⓑ Ⓒ Ⓓ   18. Ⓐ Ⓑ Ⓒ Ⓓ   29. Ⓐ Ⓑ Ⓒ Ⓓ   39. Ⓐ Ⓑ Ⓒ Ⓓ   49. Ⓐ Ⓑ Ⓒ Ⓓ
8. Ⓐ Ⓑ Ⓒ Ⓓ   19. Ⓐ Ⓑ Ⓒ Ⓓ   30. Ⓐ Ⓑ Ⓒ Ⓓ   40. Ⓐ Ⓑ Ⓒ Ⓓ   50. Ⓐ Ⓑ Ⓒ Ⓓ
9. Ⓐ Ⓑ Ⓒ Ⓓ   20. Ⓐ Ⓑ Ⓒ Ⓓ   31. Ⓐ Ⓑ Ⓒ Ⓓ   41. Ⓐ Ⓑ Ⓒ Ⓓ   51. Ⓐ Ⓑ Ⓒ Ⓓ
10. Ⓐ Ⓑ Ⓒ Ⓓ   21. Ⓐ Ⓑ Ⓒ Ⓓ   32. Ⓐ Ⓑ Ⓒ Ⓓ   42. Ⓐ Ⓑ Ⓒ Ⓓ   52. Ⓐ Ⓑ Ⓒ Ⓓ
11. Ⓐ Ⓑ Ⓒ Ⓓ   22. Ⓐ Ⓑ Ⓒ Ⓓ

Section 2: Writing and Language Test

1. Ⓐ Ⓑ Ⓒ Ⓓ   10. Ⓐ Ⓑ Ⓒ Ⓓ   19. Ⓐ Ⓑ Ⓒ Ⓓ   28. Ⓐ Ⓑ Ⓒ Ⓓ   37. Ⓐ Ⓑ Ⓒ Ⓓ
2. Ⓐ Ⓑ Ⓒ Ⓓ   11. Ⓐ Ⓑ Ⓒ Ⓓ   20. Ⓐ Ⓑ Ⓒ Ⓓ   29. Ⓐ Ⓑ Ⓒ Ⓓ   38. Ⓐ Ⓑ Ⓒ Ⓓ
3. Ⓐ Ⓑ Ⓒ Ⓓ   12. Ⓐ Ⓑ Ⓒ Ⓓ   21. Ⓐ Ⓑ Ⓒ Ⓓ   30. Ⓐ Ⓑ Ⓒ Ⓓ   39. Ⓐ Ⓑ Ⓒ Ⓓ
4. Ⓐ Ⓑ Ⓒ Ⓓ   13. Ⓐ Ⓑ Ⓒ Ⓓ   22. Ⓐ Ⓑ Ⓒ Ⓓ   31. Ⓐ Ⓑ Ⓒ Ⓓ   40. Ⓐ Ⓑ Ⓒ Ⓓ
5. Ⓐ Ⓑ Ⓒ Ⓓ   14. Ⓐ Ⓑ Ⓒ Ⓓ   23. Ⓐ Ⓑ Ⓒ Ⓓ   32. Ⓐ Ⓑ Ⓒ Ⓓ   41. Ⓐ Ⓑ Ⓒ Ⓓ
6. Ⓐ Ⓑ Ⓒ Ⓓ   15. Ⓐ Ⓑ Ⓒ Ⓓ   24. Ⓐ Ⓑ Ⓒ Ⓓ   33. Ⓐ Ⓑ Ⓒ Ⓓ   42. Ⓐ Ⓑ Ⓒ Ⓓ
7. Ⓐ Ⓑ Ⓒ Ⓓ   16. Ⓐ Ⓑ Ⓒ Ⓓ   25. Ⓐ Ⓑ Ⓒ Ⓓ   34. Ⓐ Ⓑ Ⓒ Ⓓ   43. Ⓐ Ⓑ Ⓒ Ⓓ
8. Ⓐ Ⓑ Ⓒ Ⓓ   17. Ⓐ Ⓑ Ⓒ Ⓓ   26. Ⓐ Ⓑ Ⓒ Ⓓ   35. Ⓐ Ⓑ Ⓒ Ⓓ   44. Ⓐ Ⓑ Ⓒ Ⓓ
9. Ⓐ Ⓑ Ⓒ Ⓓ   18. Ⓐ Ⓑ Ⓒ Ⓓ   27. Ⓐ Ⓑ Ⓒ Ⓓ   36. Ⓐ Ⓑ Ⓒ Ⓓ

Section 3: Math Test—No Calculator

1. Ⓐ Ⓑ Ⓒ Ⓓ   4. Ⓐ Ⓑ Ⓒ Ⓓ   7. Ⓐ Ⓑ Ⓒ Ⓓ   10. Ⓐ Ⓑ Ⓒ Ⓓ   13. Ⓐ Ⓑ Ⓒ Ⓓ
2. Ⓐ Ⓑ Ⓒ Ⓓ   5. Ⓐ Ⓑ Ⓒ Ⓓ   8. Ⓐ Ⓑ Ⓒ Ⓓ   11. Ⓐ Ⓑ Ⓒ Ⓓ   14. Ⓐ Ⓑ Ⓒ Ⓓ
3. Ⓐ Ⓑ Ⓒ Ⓓ   6. Ⓐ Ⓑ Ⓒ Ⓓ   9. Ⓐ Ⓑ Ⓒ Ⓓ   12. Ⓐ Ⓑ Ⓒ Ⓓ   15. Ⓐ Ⓑ Ⓒ Ⓓ

16. **17.** **18.** **19.** **20.**

Section 4: Math Test—Calculator

1. Ⓐ Ⓑ Ⓒ Ⓓ   7. Ⓐ Ⓑ Ⓒ Ⓓ   13. Ⓐ Ⓑ Ⓒ Ⓓ   19. Ⓐ Ⓑ Ⓒ Ⓓ   25. Ⓐ Ⓑ Ⓒ Ⓓ

2. Ⓐ Ⓑ Ⓒ Ⓓ   8. Ⓐ Ⓑ Ⓒ Ⓓ   14. Ⓐ Ⓑ Ⓒ Ⓓ   20. Ⓐ Ⓑ Ⓒ Ⓓ   26. Ⓐ Ⓑ Ⓒ Ⓓ

3. Ⓐ Ⓑ Ⓒ Ⓓ   9. Ⓐ Ⓑ Ⓒ Ⓓ   15. Ⓐ Ⓑ Ⓒ Ⓓ   21. Ⓐ Ⓑ Ⓒ Ⓓ   27. Ⓐ Ⓑ Ⓒ Ⓓ

4. Ⓐ Ⓑ Ⓒ Ⓓ   10. Ⓐ Ⓑ Ⓒ Ⓓ   16. Ⓐ Ⓑ Ⓒ Ⓓ   22. Ⓐ Ⓑ Ⓒ Ⓓ   28. Ⓐ Ⓑ Ⓒ Ⓓ

5. Ⓐ Ⓑ Ⓒ Ⓓ   11. Ⓐ Ⓑ Ⓒ Ⓓ   17. Ⓐ Ⓑ Ⓒ Ⓓ   23. Ⓐ Ⓑ Ⓒ Ⓓ   29. Ⓐ Ⓑ Ⓒ Ⓓ

6. Ⓐ Ⓑ Ⓒ Ⓓ   12. Ⓐ Ⓑ Ⓒ Ⓓ   18. Ⓐ Ⓑ Ⓒ Ⓓ   24. Ⓐ Ⓑ Ⓒ Ⓓ   30. Ⓐ Ⓑ Ⓒ Ⓓ

31. **32.** **33.** **34.** **35.**

answer sheet

36.

	/	/	
.	.	.	.
	0	0	0
1	1	1	1
2	2	2	2
3	3	3	3
4	4	4	4
5	5	5	5
6	6	6	6
7	7	7	7
8	8	8	8
9	9	9	9

37.

	/	/	
.	.	.	.
	0	0	0
1	1	1	1
2	2	2	2
3	3	3	3
4	4	4	4
5	5	5	5
6	6	6	6
7	7	7	7
8	8	8	8
9	9	9	9

38.

	/	/	
.	.	.	.
	0	0	0
1	1	1	1
2	2	2	2
3	3	3	3
4	4	4	4
5	5	5	5
6	6	6	6
7	7	7	7
8	8	8	8
9	9	9	9

Section 5: Essay

_____

_____

_____

_____

_____

_____

_____

_____

_____

_____

_____

_____

_____

_____

_____

_____

_____

_____

_____

answer sheet

SECTION 1: READING TEST

65 Minutes • 52 Questions

TURN TO SECTION 1 OF YOUR ANSWER SHEET TO ANSWER THE QUESTIONS IN THIS SECTION.

> **Directions:** Each passage (or pair of passages) below is followed by a number of multiple-choice questions. After reading each passage, select the best answer to each question based on what is stated or implied in the passage or passages and in any supplementary material, such as a table, graph, chart, or photograph.

QUESTIONS 1–11 ARE BASED ON THE FOLLOWING PASSAGE.

Snail-Sniffing Dogs in the Galapagos

The Galapagos Islands, which belong to Ecuador, are located approximately 906 km (563 mi.) west of the mainland. Because of their isolation, these volcanic islands are home to a variety of unique species, such as gigantic land tortoises and marine iguanas. As more people have visited and settled on the islands, however, it has become increasingly difficult to protect the native plants and animals.

The following text has been adapted from "Eco-system Restoration: Invasive Snail Detection Dogs," which was originally published by Galapagos Conservancy (www.galapagos.org). Galapagos Conservancy is a conservation group that collaborates with scientists worldwide to ensure protection of the Galapagos Islands. (For the complete article, see http://galapagos.org/conservation.)

In Galapagos, native species are threatened by introduced, invasive species such as goats, rats, pigs, and cats,

Line among many others. While much has
5 been accomplished in the management of existing invasive species, the islands are constantly at risk of new unwanted species arriving each day. The Giant African Land Snail (GALS)—the largest
10 species of snail found on land, growing to nearly 8 inches in length—is one such new invasive that has taken up residence in Galapagos. Known to consume at least 500 different types of plants, scientists
15 consider the GALS to be one of the most destructive snail species in the world. It

now poses a serious threat to the native snails and plants of Galapagos.

Invasive Giant African Land Snails
20 were first detected on Santa Cruz Island in 2010, and currently less than 20 hectares (50 acres) are infested—but the snails are expanding their range every wet season. Experience has shown that once
25 an invasive species becomes established, it is almost impossible to remove. At this point in time, it is still possible to eradicate the GALS from Galapagos if additional management techniques are
30 integrated into current activities.

Previously, staff from the Galapagos Agency for the Regulation and Control of Biosecurity and Quarantine (ABG) had to search for and collect GALS
35 on rainy nights using headlamps—an extremely challenging and unsustainable solution to the permanent eradication of the snails. Dogs, on the other hand, have an incredible sense of smell and can be
40 trained to detect scents imperceptible to the human nose, making them ideal for the detection of the GALS. Detection dogs have been used for finding contraband drugs and shark fins in
45 Galapagos, but not for other purposes. This project entails utilizing two scent detection dogs to detect GALS in order to help clear currently affected areas and search for previously undetected
50 populations in the islands.

During the first phase of the project, which took place in the fall of 2014, two detection dogs were trained by Dogs for Conservation (DFC) in the United States
55 to specifically detect GALS. Darwin, a

GO TO THE NEXT PAGE

golden Labrador retriever, was rescued after he was unable to successfully complete a service dog training program,
Line and Neville, a black Labrador retriever,
60 was saved from a shelter. Darwin and Neville were selected for this project based on their detection abilities and temperament for working with multiple handlers, in preparation for work with
65 new handlers in Galapagos. In December of 2014, the dogs were brought to Galapagos where six ABG staff were trained as handlers for this and future detection projects. Many had never
70 worked with dogs before and had to learn the basics of canine behavior, learning theory, scent theory, training methods, and handling skills. New kennels were built by ABG personnel with materials
75 funded through this project in order to house the dogs.

   Both dogs required a period of acclimation to Galapagos and to their new roles. The dogs could only be trained on
80 dead snails in the U.S. due to biosecurity risks for this highly invasive species, so additional training was needed upon their arrival in Galapagos to transition them to live snails and snail eggs. Darwin and
85 Neville have now been fully trained to detect the invasive snails, and the dogs will be regularly assisting with GALS eradication and monitoring on Santa Cruz.
90   DFC continues to provide guidance and support to the GALS K9 team, with whom they are in weekly communication. Future updates to the project will be posted … as they occur. This project
95 is also serving as a pilot to establish a permanent canine detection program in the Galapagos. Expertly trained dogs and experienced handlers will be a highly cost-effective detection tool for ongoing
100 biosecurity programs aimed at eliminating targeted invasive species that threaten the unique and fragile ecosystems of Galapagos.

1 What is the purpose of this article?

(A) To bring tourists to the Galapagos

(B) To raise money for the organization

(C) To inform the public about the problems of invasive species

(D) To persuade people that it is important to keep species of animals and plants from becoming extinct

2 Which statement best represents the main idea of the passage?

(A) Dogs can help reduce invasive species in the Galapagos.

(B) Dogs can be trained to hunt for snails.

(C) Galapagos ecosystems include unique species.

(D) Organizations are working together to rid the Galapagos of invasive species.

3 Why do the Galapagos have a unique ecosystem?

(A) Islands can only support certain kinds of species.

(B) There were no mammals there until humans brought them.

(C) Only certain types of animals and plants can live there because of the climate.

(D) It was isolated for a long time, so humans did not interfere with the native species.

4 Which best describes the threat of GALS to the Galapagos islands?

(A) Their growth patterns

(B) Their eating habits

(C) Their ability to hide from detection

(D) Their ability to survive in hot climates

5 How have people increased the fragility of the ecosystems in Galapagos?

(A) They brought trained dogs to the islands.

(B) They added to the wealth and attractiveness of the islands.

(C) They introduced nonnative species to the islands.

(D) They made others aware of the native species on the islands.

6 What evidence does the passage provide to explain the difficulty of maintaining the ecosystems in the Galapagos?

(A) Lines 13–16 ("Known to … the world")

(B) Lines 24–26 ("Experience has … to remove")

(C) Lines 31–38 ("Previously, staff … the snails")

(D) Lines 79–81 ("The dogs … biosecurity risks")

7 What information from the text answers the question of how dogs contribute to biosecurity in the Galapagos?

(A) Lines 38–41 ("Dogs, on … human nose")

(B) Lines 52–55 ("Two detection … detect GALS")

(C) Lines 79–81 ("The dogs … invasive species")

(D) Lines 97–101 ("Expertly trained … invasive species")

8 Why did the scientists decide to try using dogs to find the GALS?

(A) They are friendly animals that are easy to train.

(B) They can also be trained to find illicit drugs.

(C) They can smell things that humans can't.

(D) They didn't require special training for the handlers.

9 As used in lines 80–100, "biosecurity" most nearly means

(A) safe handling of animals.

(B) safety from dangerous animals and plants.

(C) protection to keep wildlife from extinction.

(D) protection of an ecosystem from invasive species.

10 As used in line 78, "acclimation" is best defined as

(A) adjusting to changes in the environment.

(B) conforming to one's surroundings.

(C) adaptation of a species.

(D) modification of behavior.

11 Why are dogs considered an invasive species to the Galapagos?

(A) The dogs' sense of smell helps them find native species and use them for food.

(B) The dogs there required time to get acclimated to the environment.

(C) The dogs did not inhabit the Galapagos until brought there by humans.

(D) The dogs once thrived on the Galapagos, but they had depleted their limited food sources.

QUESTIONS 12–22 ARE BASED ON THE FOLLOWING PASSAGE.

The following is an excerpt from a speech given by President Jimmy Carter, spoken and broadcast from the White House library two weeks after he took office. Prior to Carter's election, the country had faced a severe oil shortage and rising prices for oil and related products.

Report to the American People (February 2, 1977)

The extremely cold weather this winter has dangerously depleted our supplies of natural gas and fuel oil and forced
Line hundreds of thousands of workers off the
5 job. I congratulate the Congress for its quick action on the Emergency Natural Gas Act, which was passed today and signed just a few minutes ago. But the real problem—our failure to plan for the
10 future or to take energy conservation seriously—started long before this winter, and it will take much longer to solve.

I realize that many of you have not believed that we really have an energy
15 problem. But this winter has made all of us realize that we have to act.

Our program will emphasize conservation. The amount of energy being wasted which could be saved is
20 greater than the total energy that we are importing from foreign countries. We will also stress development of our rich coal reserves in an environmentally sound way; we will emphasize research on
25 solar energy and other renewable energy sources; and we will maintain strict safeguards on necessary atomic energy production.

The responsibility for setting energy
30 policy is now split among more than 50 different agencies, departments, and bureaus in the Federal Government. Later this month, I will ask the Congress for its help in combining many of these agencies
35 in a new energy department to bring order out of chaos. Congressional leaders have already been working on this for quite a while.

We must face the fact that the energy
40 shortage is permanent. There is no way we can solve it quickly. But if we all

cooperate and make modest sacrifices, if we learn to live thriftily and remember the importance of helping our neighbors,
45 then we can find ways to adjust and to make our society more efficient and our own lives more enjoyable and productive. Utility companies must promote conservation and not consumption. Oil
50 and natural gas companies must be honest with all of us about their reserves and profits. We will find out the difference between real shortages and artificial ones. We will ask private companies to
55 sacrifice, just as private citizens must do.

All of us must learn to waste less energy. Simply by keeping our thermostats, for instance, at 65 degrees in the daytime and 55 degrees at night we
60 could save half the current shortage of natural gas.

There is no way that I, or anyone else in the Government, can solve our energy problems if you are not willing to help.
65 I know that we can meet this energy challenge if the burden is borne fairly among all our people—and if we realize that in order to solve our energy problems we need not sacrifice the quality of our
70 lives.

The Congress has made great progress toward responsible strip-mining legislation, so that we can produce more energy without unnecessary destruction
75 of our beautiful lands. My administration will support these efforts this year. We will also ask Congress for its help with legislation which will reduce the risk of future oil tanker spills and help deal with
80 those that do occur.

I would like to tell you now about one of the things that I have already learned in my brief time in office. I have learned that there are many things that a President
85 cannot do. There is no energy policy that we can develop that would do more good than voluntary conservation. There is no economic policy that will do as much as shared faith in hard work, efficiency, and
90 in the future of our system

12 What is the most likely reason that Carter gave this speech?

(A) He wanted to reassure people that as president he was going to make the United States energy independent.

(B) As a new president, he wanted to start a dialogue with the people.

(C) He wanted to explain the severity of the energy crisis and what needed to be done to address it.

(D) He wanted people to understand the limitations of the president.

13 What is the theme of the speech?

(A) The United States has a long-term energy problem.

(B) There are many ways to conserve energy.

(C) People need to use less energy in their homes.

(D) The government cannot solve environmental problems.

14 Which of the following actions does Carter propose that the government take to help solve the problem?

(A) Lowering the thermostats

(B) Forming a new energy department

(C) Developing coal reserves

(D) Protecting the environment from oil spills

15 Which of the following best represents the belief system illustrated in Carter's speech?

(A) The idea that the United States should be energy independent

(B) The concept of shared sacrifice

(C) The idea that the environment needs to be protected by volunteers

(D) The concept of equal powers among the three branches of government

16 What does Carter think should be the foundation for conserving energy?

(A) The renewed use of strip mining to produce more energy

(B) The reduction of indoor temperatures to conserve fuel

(C) The use of solar and other renewable energy sources

(D) A voluntary policy in which people share in creating efficiency

17 How does Carter try to convince the public that everyone needs to participate to solve the problem?

(A) He describes how utility companies are also promoting conservation, not consumption.

(B) He explains that people waste a lot of energy.

(C) He tells the public to lower the thermostats in their homes, which can save natural gas.

(D) He explains that sacrifices must be made by everyone alike.

18 Which of the following best explains the tone of the speech?

(A) Carter speaks bluntly about the problem, but also tries to be persuasive and optimistic in order to encourage everyone to work together.

(B) Carter is speaking on national television and wants his audience to keep listening to him, so his tone is light and informal, even though the topic is a serious one.

(C) Carter is deeply concerned over the energy problem so the tone of the speech is stern and authoritative because he wants people to follow his requests.

(D) Carter wants to be taken seriously, so he avoids persuasive language; instead, he speaks with informative, matter-of-fact neutrality.

GO TO THE NEXT PAGE

19 What language in the speech indicates that Carter has great respect for the land and the concept of conservation?

(A) Lines 21–28 ("We will … energy production")

(B) Lines 39–40 ("We must … is permanent")

(C) Lines 73–75 ("we can … beautiful lands")

(D) Lines 68–70 ("in order … our lives")

20 Which of the following might be used by some people as evidence to claim that Carter was anti-business?

(A) Lines 17–18 ("Our program … emphasize conservation")

(B) Lines 26–28 ("we will … energy production")

(C) Lines 39–30 ("We must … is permanent")

(D) Lines 49–52 ("Oil and … and profits")

21 As used in line 2, "depleted" most nearly means

(A) consumed.

(B) replaced.

(C) weakened.

(D) wasted.

22 Explain how the word "reserves" is used in line 21 and line 53.

(A) In the first use, "reserves" refers to something protected in order to prevent easy access to it; in the second use, it refers to something that is difficult to obtain.

(B) In the first use, "reserves" refers to something discarded; in the second use; it refers to something set aside in case of emergencies.

(C) In the first use, "reserves" refers to something saved in case of future needs; in the second use, it refers to being set aside in order to raise prices.

(D) In the first use, "reserves" refers to something not used because there is an excess; in the second use, it refers to something that belongs to someone else.

QUESTIONS 23–32 ARE BASED ON THE FOLLOWING PASSAGE.

Rudyard Kipling (1865–1936) was one of the most popular English writers of his era, authoring stories, novels, and poems, many of which take place in colonial India, where he was born and lived as a young child and returned to as a young adult. "The Arrest of Lieutenant Golightly," one of his earliest stories, was first published in an English language newspaper in India where Kipling worked as a journalist. The following is an excerpt from that story.

If there was one thing on which Golightly prided himself more than another, it was looking like "an Officer
Line and a gentleman." He said it was for
5 the honor of the Service that he attired himself so elaborately; but those who knew him best said that it was just personal vanity. There was no harm about Golightly. … He recognized a horse
10 when he saw one, … he played a very fair game at billiards, and was a sound man at the whist-table. Everyone liked him; and nobody ever dreamed of seeing him handcuffed on a station platform as a
15 deserter. But this sad thing happened.

He was going down from Dalhousie, at the end of his leave—riding down. He

had cut his leave as fine as he dared, and
wanted to come down in a hurry.

20   It was fairly warm at Dalhousie [a
town in India in the hills, used as a
summer retreat for British personnel]
and knowing what to expect below, he
descended in a new khaki suit—tight

25 fitting—of a delicate olive-green; a
peacock-blue tie, white collar, and a
snowy white solah [a plant made into
fabric used in hat-making] helmet. He
prided himself on looking neat even when

30 he was riding post. He did look neat, and
he was so deeply concerned about his
appearance before he started that he quite
forgot to take anything but some small
change with him. He left all his notes at

35 the hotel. His servants had gone down the
road before him, to be ready in waiting at
Pathankote with a change of gear.

        Twenty-two miles out of Dalhousie it
began to rain—not a mere hill-shower,

40 but a good, tepid monsoonish downpour.
Golightly bustled on, wishing that he
had brought an umbrella. The dust on
the roads turned into mud, and the pony
mired a good deal. So did Golightly's

45 khaki gaiters. But he kept on steadily and
tried to think how pleasant the coolth was.

        His next pony was rather a brute at
starting, and Golightly's hands being
slippery with the rain, contrived to get rid

50 of Golightly at a corner. He chased the
animal, caught it, and went ahead briskly.
The spill had not improved his clothes or
his temper, and he had lost one spur. He
kept the other one employed. By the time

55 that stage was ended, the pony had had as
much exercise as he wanted, and, in spite
of the rain, Golightly was sweating freely.
At the end of another miserable half-hour,
Golightly found the world disappear

60 before his eyes in clammy pulp. The rain
had turned the pith of his huge and snowy
solah-topee into an evil-smelling dough,
and it had closed on his head like a half-
opened mushroom. Also the green lining

65 was beginning to run.

        Golightly did not say anything worth
recording here. He tore off and squeezed
up as much of the brim as was in his eyes
and ploughed on. The back of the helmet

70 was flapping on his neck and the sides
stuck to his ears, but the leather band and
green lining kept things roughly together,
so that the hat did not actually melt away
where it flapped.

75   Presently, the pulp and the green stuff
made a sort of slimy mildew which ran
over Golightly in several directions—
down his back and bosom for choice.
The khaki color ran too … and sections

80 of Golightly were brown, and patches
were violet, and contours were ochre, and
streaks were ruddy red, and blotches were
nearly white, according to the nature and
peculiarities of the dye. When he took out

85 his handkerchief to wipe his face and the
green of the hat-lining and the purple stuff
that had soaked through on to his neck
from the tie became thoroughly mixed,
the effect was amazing.

90   He went to the Station-Master to
negotiate for a first-class ticket to Khasa,
where he was stationed. The booking-
clerk said something to the Station-
Master, the Station-Master said something

95 to the Telegraph Clerk, and the three
looked at him with curiosity. They asked
him to wait for half-an-hour, while they
telegraphed to Umritsar for authority.
So he waited, and four constables came

100 and grouped themselves picturesquely
round him. Just as he was preparing to
ask them to go away, the Station-Master
said that he would give the Sahib [term
of respect; like calling someone "sir" in

105 English] a ticket to Umritsar, if the Sahib
would kindly come inside the booking-
office. Golightly stepped inside, and the
next thing he knew was that a constable
was attached to each of his legs and arms,

110 while the Station-Master was trying to
cram a mailbag over his head.

---

23 Which of the following best describes
the tone of the story?

(A) Disgust

(B) Mocking

(C) Ironic

(D) Proud

24 Even though the author says "this sad thing happened," which detail from the passage shows that Kipling considers Golightly to be responsible for what happened to him?

(A) He did look neat, and he was so deeply concerned about his appearance before he started that he quite forgot to take anything but some small change with him.

(B) He prided himself on looking neat even when he was riding post.

(C) Golightly bustled on, wishing that he had brought an umbrella.

(D) His next pony was rather a brute at starting, and Golightly's hands being slippery with the rain, contrived to get rid of Golightly at a corner.

25 Which of the following best explains the identity and actions of the main character, Golightly?

(A) He's a proper military man leaving his post.

(B) He's a British soldier trying to escape capture by the Indian government.

(C) He's an outlaw trying to escape capture.

(D) He's a British businessman on a trip overseas.

26 How does Kipling make fun of his character Golightly?

(A) His explanation of Golightly's vanity is satiric.

(B) His description of Golightly's experience shows how he has trouble coping with the severe rainstorms in India.

(C) He gives a detailed description of how silly Golightly looks.

(D) He shows that Golightly had difficulty riding the horse.

27 Why did Kipling provide such detail about Golightly's looks?

(A) To make fun of his vanity and usual appearance

(B) To show how intense the climate is in India

(C) To help the reader understand the setting

(D) To describe the problems of the British military in India

28 How is lines 66–67 distinguished from the rest of the text in the passage?

(A) Kipling describes the character's verbal response to the situation.

(B) The narrator interjects his own viewpoint.

(C) It adds internal dialogue to the story.

(D) The narrator describes Golightly's thoughts rather than his appearance.

29 Which description of Golightly shows that Kipling was making fun of the character?

(A) Lines 50–51 ("He chased … ahead briskly")

(B) Lines 69–74 ("The back … it flapped")

(C) Lines 79–84 ("The khaki … the dye")

(D) Lines 84–89 ("When he … was amazing")

30 Which of the following lines from the text show that Golightly is relatively wealthy?

(A) Lines 4–6 ("He said … so elaborately")

(B) Lines 35–36 ("His servants … before him")

(C) Lines 47–48 ("His next … at starting")

(D) Lines 105–107 ("if the … the booking office")

31 What is the meaning of the sentence: "He had cut his leave as fine as he dared." (lines 17–19)

(A) He dared to take leave without telling the authorities.

(B) He arranged to take as much time as he could without getting in trouble.

(C) He was daring in leaving the military post because it was dangerous.

(D) He wanted to leave, but was afraid he'd get caught.

32 Which of the following surrounding words best help you figure out the meaning of the word "mired" (line 44)?

(A) "the pony"

(B) "roads turned into mud"

(C) "wishing that he had brought an umbrella"

(D) "So did Golightly's khaki gaiters"

QUESTIONS 33–42 ARE BASED ON THE FOLLOWING TWO PASSAGES AND SUPPLEMENTARY MATERIAL.

Passage 1 is an excerpt from a speech modeled on the Declaration of Independence, written and read by Elizabeth Cady Stanton at the Woman's Rights Convention, held in Seneca Falls, New York, July 19, 1848. About 300 people attended the event and about a third (68 women and 32 men) signed the declaration.

Passage 2 is excerpted from The Narrative of Sojourner Truth, the memoir of a slave in pre-Civil War New York. Born into slavery as Isabella, after being freed in 1827, she took the name Sojourner Truth to express her strong faith. Because Truth was illiterate, she dictated her story to the writer Olive Gilbert, whom she had met in Massachusetts. The book was published in 1850 and was widely distributed by Abolitionists to help further their cause.

Passage 1

Declaration of Sentiments

The history of mankind is a history of repeated injuries and usurpations on the part of man toward woman, having

Line in direct object the establishment of an
5 absolute tyranny over her. To prove this, let facts be submitted to a candid world.

He has never permitted her to exercise her inalienable right to the elective franchise.

10 He has compelled her to submit to laws, in the formation of which she had no voice.

He has withheld from her rights which are given to the most ignorant
15 and degraded men—both natives and foreigners.

Having deprived her of this first right of a citizen, the elective franchise, thereby leaving her without representation in the
20 halls of legislation, he has oppressed her on all sides.

He has made her, if married, in the eye of the law, civilly dead.

He has taken from her all right in
25 property, even to the wages she earns.

He has made her, morally, an irresponsible being, as she can commit many crimes with impunity, provided they be done in the presence of her
30 husband. In the covenant of marriage, she is compelled to promise obedience to her husband, he becoming, to all intents and purposes, her master—the law giving him power to deprive her of her liberty, and to
35 administer chastisement.

He has so framed the laws of divorce, as to what shall be the proper causes, and in the case of separation, to whom the guardianship of the children shall
40 be given, as to be wholly regardless of the happiness of women—the law, in all cases, going upon a false supposition of the supremacy of man, and giving all power into his hands.

45 After depriving her of all rights as a married woman, if single, and the owner of property, he has taxed her to support a government which recognizes her only when her property can be made profitable
50 to it ….

He has endeavored, in every way that he could, to destroy her confidence in her own powers, to lessen her self-respect, and to make her willing to lead a
55 dependent and abject life. …

GO TO THE NEXT PAGE

(Credit: Women's Political Union,
1911. Library of Congress)

Passage 2

From: The Narrative of Sojourner Truth

After emancipation had been decreed
by the State, some years before the time
fixed for its consummation, Isabella's
master told her if she would do well,
60 and be faithful, he would give her "free
papers," one year before she was legally
free by statute. In the year 1826, she had
a badly diseased hand, which greatly
diminished her usefulness; but on the
65 arrival of July 4, 1827, the time specified
for her receiving her "free papers," she
claimed the fulfillment of her master's
promise; but he refused granting it, on
account (as he alleged) of the loss he had
70 sustained by her hand. She plead that
she had worked all the time, and done
many things she was not wholly able
to do, although she knew she had been
less useful than formerly; but her master
75 remained inflexible. Her very faithfulness
probably operated against her now, and he
found it less easy than he thought to give
up the profits of his faithful Bell, who had
so long done him efficient service.

80   But Isabella inwardly determined that
she would remain quietly with him only
until she had spun his wool—about one
hundred pounds—and then she would
leave him, taking the rest of the time to
85 herself. "Ah!" she says, with emphasis
that cannot be written, "the slaveholders
are TERRIBLE for promising to give you
this or that, or such and such a privilege,
if you will do thus and so; and when the
90 time of fulfillment comes, and one claims
the promise, they, forsooth, recollect
nothing of the kind; and you are, like as
not, taunted with being a LIAR; or, at
best, the slave is accused of not having
95 performed *his* part or condition of the
contract." "Oh!" said she, "I have felt as
if I could not live through the *operation
sometimes*. Just think of us! *so* eager for
our pleasures, and just foolish enough
100 to keep feeding and feeding ourselves
up with the idea that we should get what
had been thus fairly promised; and when
we think it is almost in our hands, find
ourselves flatly denied! Just think! how
105 *could* we bear it?"

33 What was Stanton's purpose in writing
and speaking the Declaration of Sentiments?

(A) She wanted to show that women
could write important documents.

(B) She wanted to shock the audience in
upstate New York.

(C) She wanted to show why women
needed rights.

(D) She wanted to gain support for equal
protection of minorities.

34 What is the effect of repeating the phrase "He has"?

(A) It shows how strongly she feels about how women were treated.

(B) It emphasizes the transgressions of men against women.

(C) It makes the speech dull because it repeats the same words.

(D) It makes the speech more like the Declaration of Independence.

35 Which lines in the text are best illustrated by the graphic?

(A) Lines 13–16: ("He has withheld … and foreigners")

(B) Lines 22–23: ("He has made … civilly dead.")

(C) Lines 42–44: (" … going upon a … into his hands.").

(D) Lines 47–50: (" … he has taxed … profitable to it").

36 How does Stanton support her argument that women have been forced into obedience?

(A) She explains that women can't work outside the home.

(B) She expresses anger at the idea that women are not allowed to vote.

(C) She expresses dismay at how children can be taken from mothers in cases of divorce or separation.

(D) She explains how marriage legally compels women to obey their husbands.

37 What does Stanton mean by "elective franchise" as used in line 18?

(A) The sport of elections

(B) The business of elections

(C) The team needed for elections

(D) The right to vote

38 What do the two passages suggest about what women and slaves had in common?

(A) Neither women nor slaves could get paid for their work.

(B) Both women and slaves had to take care of the children in a family.

(C) Women had to obey their husbands; slaves had to obey their masters.

(D) Men made and broke promises to both women and slaves.

39 Which of the following statements is true about the two passages?

(A) They both display a tone of anger at their lack of freedom.

(B) Stanton's tone is angry and Truth's tone is sad.

(C) Truth's tone is bitter; Stanton's tone is outrage.

(D) They both show a tone of frustration.

40 Which of the following lines from the text indicate why Truth says her master did not want to let her be free as he had promised?

(A) Lines 75–76 ("Her very faithfulness … her now.")

(B) Lines 76–78 ("he found it … faithful Bell")

(C) Lines 86–89 ("the slaveholders … thus and so")

(D) Lines 93–96 ("at best … of the contract.")

41 What set Isabella's master apart from other slaveholders?

(A) He didn't mistreat her.

(B) He allowed her to learn to read and write.

(C) He finally did set her free before he had to.

(D) He made promises he didn't keep.

42 In lines 75–76, Truth says that her "faith-fulness probably operated against her." What does she mean by this phrase?

(A) Her faith in God would help her through the difficulties operating against her.

(B) Her loyalty made her more important and valuable to her master.

(C) She needed to be faithful to her God so that her master would not break his promises.

(D) She needed to be faithful in the face of her master's inflexibility.

QUESTIONS 43–52 ARE BASED ON THE FOLLOWING PASSAGE AND SUPPLEMENTARY MATERIAL.

The following passage has been adapted from "New Dinosaur's Keen Nose Made it a Formidable Predator, Penn Study Finds" by Katherine Unger Baillie, originally published by the University of Pennsylvania, May 11, 2015. (This passage was edited for length. For the complete article, see http://upenn.edu/pennnews.)

New Dinosaur's Keen Nose Made It a Formidable Predator

A researcher from the University of Pennsylvania has identified a species of dinosaur closely related to *Velociraptor*,
Line the group of creatures made infamous
5 by the movie *Jurassic Park*. The newly named species likely possessed a keen sense of smell that would have made it a formidable predator.

Steven Jasinski, a doctoral student
10 in the School of Arts & Science's Department of Earth and Environmental Science at Penn, and acting curator of paleontology and geology at the State Museum of Pennsylvania, discovered
15 the new species while investigating a specimen originally assigned to a previously known species. His analysis suggests the fossil—part of the dinosaur's skull—actually represents a brand new
20 species, which Jasinski has named *Saurornitholestes sullivani*. The creature's genus name Saurornitholestes, which means "lizard bird thief," gives a sense of

what the prehistoric predator would have
25 looked like. These animals were lightly built with long legs and jaws lined with teeth, and they are believed to be very distant relatives of today's birds.

...

30 The specimen, roughly 75 million years old, was discovered by paleontologist Robert Sullivan in the Bisti/De-Na-Zin Wilderness Area of New Mexico in 1999. When first
35 described, scientists believed it was a member of *Saurornitholestes langstoni*, a species of theropod dinosaurs in the Dromaeosauridae family that had been found in present-day Alberta, Canada.
40 But when Jasinski … began a comparative analysis of the specimen to other *S. langstoni* specimens, he found subtle differences. Notably, he observed that the surface of the skull corresponding
45 with the brain's olfactory bulb was unusually large. This finding implies a powerful sense of smell.

"This feature means that *Saurornitholestes sullivani* had a
50 relatively better sense of smell than other dromaeosaurid dinosaurs, including *Velociraptor, Dromaeosaurus*, and *Bambiraptor*," Jasinski said. "This keen olfaction may have made *S. sullivani*
55 an intimidating predator as well."

S. sullivani comes from the end of the time of dinosaurs, or the Late Cretaceous, and represents the only named dromaeosaur from this period in North
60 America south of Montana.

At the time *S. sullivani* lived, North America was split into two continents separated by an inland sea. This dinosaur lived on the western shores
65 in an area called Laramidia. Numerous dromaeosaurs, which are commonly called raptors, are known from more northern areas in Laramidia, including Alberta, Canada, and Montana. However,
70 *S. sullivani* represents the only named dromaeosaur from the Late Cretaceous of southern Laramidia.

S. sullivani shared its world with numerous other dinosaurs. …Though a
75 distinct species, *S. sullivani* appears to be

closely related to *S. langstoni*. Finding the two as distinct species further shows that differences existed between dinosaurs between the northern and southern parts
80 of North America.

At less than 3 feet at its hip and roughly 6 feet in length, *S. sullivani* was not a large dinosaur. However, previous findings of related species suggest the
85 animal would have been agile and fast, perhaps hunting in packs and using its acute sense of smell to track down prey.

"Although it was not large, this was not a dinosaur you would want to mess
90 with," Jasinski said.

A pair of S. sullivani attack a young hadrosaur. (Illustration by Mary P. Williams)

43 Which of the following is the best statement of the main idea of the article?

(A) The *S. sullivani* was a predator aided by its keen sense of smell.

(B) The new species resembled today's birds.

(C) Scientific discoveries make important contributions to our knowledge of prehistoric animals.

(D) Recent fossil evidence identified a new species of dinosaur.

44 What conclusion can you draw from the way the *S. sullivani* species was discovered?

(A) Students can sometimes make amazing discoveries.

(B) Scientific investigations can yield surprising results.

(C) Students do important work with academics in their field of studies

(D) Some discoveries are attributable to chance.

45 Why would a strong sense of smell help a predator?

(A) It would help a predator find food.

(B) It could help a predator sense danger.

(C) It would make up for poor eyesight.

(D) It could help a predator find a mate.

46 What does the name of the new species tell us about this dinosaur?

(A) Dinosaurs are named after real people.

(B) The name tells us where the dinosaur fossils were found.

(C) Dinosaurs are given names based on where they lived.

(D) The name suggests what it might have looked like.

47 How did scientists recognize that the fossil they found was a new species?

(A) The fossil was larger than others that they had found previously.

(B) By comparing it to other fossils, they noticed differences in the skull.

(C) By looking at its closest relatives, they realized this was a different species.

(D) The fossil had different markings than other species.

48 How is the information in the passage supported by the graphic?

(A) It shows that *S. sullivani* lived about 75 million years ago.

(B) It shows that *S. sullivani* stood less than 3 feet at its hip and about 6 feet in length.

(C) It shows that *S. sullivani* had a very keen sense of smell, which helped it hunt other dinosaurs.

(D) It shows that *S. sullivani* had legs and feet that resemble those of birds, and in fact may be distantly related to birds.

49 Which lines from the text best describe part of the scientific process?

(A) Lines 34–36 ("When first … *Saurornitholestes langstoni*")

(B) Lines 40–42 ("But when … *S. langstoni* specimens")

(C) Lines 76–80 ("Finding the … North America")

(D) Lines 81–83 ("At less … large dinosaur")

50 Which lines from the text best show what made Jasinski's work newsworthy?

(A) Lines 1–5 ("A researcher … movie *Jurassic Park*.")

(B) Lines 17–20 ("analysis suggests … new species.")

(C) Lines 30–34 ("The specimen … New Mexico.")

(D) Lines 61–63 ("At the time … an inland sea.")

51 As used in line 8, "formidable" most nearly means

(A) dreadful.

(B) inspiring.

(C) impressive.

(D) solid.

52 What words in lines 43–47 provide a clue to the meaning of the word "olfactory"?

(A) Bulb

(B) Sense of smell

(C) Surface of the skull

(D) Unusually large

STOP

If you finish before time is called, you may check your work on this section only.
Do not turn to any other section.

SECTION 2: WRITING AND LANGUAGE TEST

35 Minutes • 44 Questions

TURN TO SECTION 2 OF YOUR ANSWER SHEET TO ANSWER THE QUESTIONS IN THIS SECTION.

Directions: Each passage below is accompanied by a number of multiple-choice questions. For some questions, you will need to consider how the passage might be revised to improve the expression of ideas. Other questions will ask you to consider how the passage might be edited to correct errors in sentence structure, usage, or punctuation. A passage may be accompanied by one or more graphics—such as a chart, table, or graph—that you will need to refer to in order to best answer the question(s).

Some questions will direct you to an underlined portion of a passage—it could be one word, a portion of a sentence, or the full sentence itself. Other questions will direct you to a particular paragraph or to certain sentences within a paragraph, or you'll be asked to think about the passage as a whole. Each question number refers to the corresponding number in the passage.

After reading each passage, select the answer to each question that most effectively improves the quality of writing in the passage or that makes the passage follow the conventions of Standard Written English. Many questions include a "NO CHANGE" option. Select that option if you think the best choice is to leave that specific portion of the passage as it is.

QUESTIONS 1–11 ARE BASED ON THE FOLLOWING PASSAGE.

The Glass Ceiling

"The Glass Ceiling" is a metaphor that refers to the imperceptible and subversive forms of discrimination women in the workforce encounter when pursuing upper-level management positions. A popular phrase in the 1980s, it has become less widely used over the ensuing years. **1** Other phrases from past decades are still in frequent use. However, as recent data makes clear, "The Glass Ceiling" remains a solid barrier to women working in **2** America!

1 The writer is considering deleting the underlined sentence. Should the writer do this?

(A) No, because it provides a detail that supports the main topic of the paragraph.

(B) No, because it acts as a transition to the next paragraph.

(C) Yes, because it repeats information that has been provided.

(D) Yes, because it is a detail that is irrelevant to the main topic of the paragraph.

2

(A) NO CHANGE
(B) America.
(C) America?
(D) America...

According to data from the U.S. Bureau of Labor Statistics and the Pew Research Center, women make up 57.2% of the nation's workforce **3** but hold 5 percent only of CEO positions in Fortune 500 companies. Women also account for only 17% of board membership at Fortune 500 companies. While these percentages note a minimal increase in female leadership over the **4** passed thirty years, barriers still seem to exist.

5 In 1995, a bipartisan Federal Glass Ceiling Commission was formed; to determine the root of gender discrimination within corporate America. The committee, headed by Secretary of Labor Robert Reich, noted that "At the highest levels of corporations the promise of reward for preparation and pursuit of excellence is not equally available to members of all groups." Two barriers that contributed most to "The Glass Ceiling" **6** effect were "supply barriers" and "internal business barriers."

3

(A) NO CHANGE
(B) but hold only 5 percent of CEO positions in Fortune 500 companies
(C) but hold 5 percent of only CEO positions in Fortune 500 companies
(D) but hold 5 percent of CEO positions only in Fortune 500 companies

4

(A) NO CHANGE
(B) passing
(C) passive
(D) past

5

(A) NO CHANGE
(B) In 1995, a bipartisan Federal Glass Ceiling Commission, was formed to determine the root of gender discrimination within corporate America
(C) In 1995, a bipartisan Federal Glass Ceiling Commission was formed to determine the root of gender discrimination within corporate America
(D) In 1995 a bipartisan Federal Glass Ceiling Commission was formed to determine the root of gender discrimination; within corporate America.

6

(A) NO CHANGE
(B) affect
(C) effective
(D) affection

"Supply barriers" represent the lack of leadership, education, and experience women are given access to during high school and college. Corporations have viewed this lack of access as an educational reform issue, not a business issue, and **7** <u>they do not think it's their responsibility to fix it</u>. However, corporations are equipped with both financial and educational resources to overcome this "supply barrier." If corporations are serious about ending discrimination in the workplace, they need to invest in educational programs that train women to be future leaders. This includes creating more mentoring programs and school-to-work initiatives and providing more educational scholarships. **8**

9 <u>The difference between what corporate executives say they want to do. In regard to discrimination</u>, and efforts being made (or not made) to end discriminatory practices is another issue. Talking the talk and not walking the walk is what the "internal business barrier" is all about. The reason for this discrepancy is that many white males working in the highly competitive corporate America believe they are "losing the corporate game, losing control, and losing opportunity." In essence, white men in corporate leadership feel threatened by including women in their ranks.

7 Which choice provides information that best supports the claim made by this sentence?

(A) NO CHANGE
(B) they are working to provide more education.
(C) they have not worked to eliminate these supply barriers.
(D) they have noticed other barriers as well.

8 Which statement from this paragraph best supports the answer to the previous question?

(A) "Supply barriers" represent the lack of leadership, education, and experience women are given access to during high school and college.
(B) Traditionally, corporations have viewed this lack of access as an educational reform issue, not a business issue.
(C) However, corporations are equipped with both financial and educational resources to overcome this "supply barrier."
(D) This includes creating more mentoring programs and school-to-work initiatives, and providing more educational scholarships.

9

(A) NO CHANGE
(B) The difference between what corporate executives say they want to do; in regard to discrimination, and
(C) The difference between what corporate executives say they want to do and in regard to discrimination
(D) The difference between what corporate executives say they want to do in regard to discrimination and

GO TO THE NEXT PAGE

10 Ending discrimination against women in the workforce is an involved, complicated process. While many efforts have been made to prevent overt discriminatory practices, 65% of women still see gender bias as a barrier they have to overcome. 11 Until women can be as equals accepted in the corporate sphere, "The Glass Ceiling" will remain firmly intact.

10

(A) NO CHANGE
(B) Ending discrimination against women in the workforce is a process.
(C) Ending discrimination against women in the workforce is a complicated process.
(D) Ending discrimination and bias against women in the workforce is a complicated process.

11

(A) NO CHANGE
(B) Until women can be accepted as equals in the corporate sphere, "The Glass Ceiling" will remain firmly intact.
(C) Until women can be accepted as equally in the corporate sphere, "The Glass Ceiling" will remain firmly intact.
(D) Until women can be accepted in the corporate sphere as equally, "The Glass Ceiling" will remain firmly intact.

QUESTIONS 12–22 ARE BASED ON THE FOLLOWING PASSAGE AND SUPPLEMENTARY CHART.

The Library of Congress

The Library of Congress is the world's largest and most open library. **12** <u>With collections numbering</u> more than 158 million items on 838 miles of shelving, it includes materials in 470 languages; the basic manuscript collections of 23 Presidents of the United States; maps and atlases that have aided explorers and navigators in charting both the world and outer space; and the earliest motion pictures and examples of recorded sound, as well as the latest databases and software packages. **13** <u>The Library's services extend, not only to members and committees of Congress, but also to the executive, and judicial branches of government, to libraries throughout the nation and the world, and to scholars,</u> researchers, artists, and scientists who use its resources.

14 <u>This was not always the case.</u> When President John Adams signed the bill that provided for the removal of the seat of government to the new capital city of Washington in 1800, he created a reference library for Congress only. The bill provided, among other items, $5,000 "for the purchase of such books as may be necessary for the use of Congress—and for putting up a suitable apartment for containing them therein … ."

12 Which choice provides the most logical introduction to the sentence?

(A) NO CHANGE

(B) It is difficult to maintain such a vast collection—

(C) Among the collections of

(D) Already collections number

13

(A) NO CHANGE

(B) The Library's services extend not only to members and committees of Congress, but also to the executive and judicial branches of government; to libraries throughout the nation and the world; and to scholars, researchers, artists, and scientists

(C) The Library's services extend not only to members and committees of Congress, but also to the executive and judicial branches, of government, to libraries throughout the nation, and the world and to scholars, researchers, artists, and scientists

(D) The Library's services, extend not only to members and committees of Congress, but also to the executive and judicial branches of government to libraries, throughout the nation and the world, and to scholars, researchers, artists, and scientists

14

(A) NO CHANGE

(B) A little history is in order here.

(C) Nevertheless, John Adams signed a bill to create the library.

(D) We're lucky we have this institution.

GO TO THE NEXT PAGE

After this small congressional library was destroyed by fire along with the Capitol building in 1814, former President Thomas Jefferson offered therein "… as a **15** substitute his personal library, accumulated over a span of fifty years." It was considered to be one of the finest in the United States. Congress accepted Jefferson's offer. Thus the foundation was laid for a great national library.

By the close of the Civil War, the collections of the Library of Congress had grown to 82,000 volumes and were still principally used by members of Congress and committees. In 1864, President Lincoln appointed as Librarian of Congress a man who was to transform the Library: Ainsworth Rand Spofford, who opened the Library to the public and greatly expanded **16** it's collections. Spofford successfully advocated a change in the copyright law so that the **17** Library would receive two, free copies of every book, map, chart, dramatic, or musical composition, engraving, cut, print, or photograph submitted for copyright. Predictably, Spofford soon filled all the Capitol's library rooms, attics, and hallways. In 1873, he then won another lobbying effort, for a new building to permanently house the nation's growing collection and reading rooms to serve scholars and the reading public. The result was the Thomas Jefferson Building, completed in 1897. Since then, two more buildings have been constructed to house the Library's **18** ever-expanding collection.

15
(A) NO CHANGE
(B) replacement
(C) stand-in
(D) copy

16
(A) NO CHANGE
(B) it collections
(C) its collections
(D) its' collections

17
(A) NO CHANGE
(B) Library would receive two free copies of every book, map, chart, dramatic or musical composition engraving, cut, print, or photograph, submitted for copyright.
(C) Library would receive two, free copies of every book, map, chart, dramatic or musical composition; engraving, cut, print, or photograph submitted for copyright
(D) Library would receive two free copies of every book, map, chart, dramatic or musical composition, engraving, cut, print, or photograph submitted for copyright.

18
(A) NO CHANGE
(B) ever-existing
(C) ever-expending
(D) ever-expounding

The first librarian in the new building was a newspaperman with no previous library experience, John Russell Young. He quickly realized that the Library had to get control of the collections that had been overflowing the rooms in the Capitol. Young set up organizational units and devised programs that changed the Library. **19** Instead of being essentially an acquisitions operation, it became an efficient processing factory that organized the materials and made them useful.

20 Formerly head of the Boston Public Library, Herbert Putnam succeeded Young. Putnam served as Librarian of Congress for 40 years. While Librarian, Spofford had collected the materials, Young had organized them, and Putnam set out to ensure that they would be used. **21** They took the Library of Congress directly into the national library scene and made its holdings known and available to the smallest community library in the most distant part of the country.

In about 1912, both Librarian Putnam and members of Congress became concerned about the distance that was widening between the Library and its employer, the Congress. Various states had begun to set up "legislative reference bureaus," which brought together skilled teams of librarians, economists, and political scientists whose purpose was to respond quickly to questions that arose in the

19 Which choice most effectively sets up the information that follows?

(A) NO CHANGE
(B) In spite of being essentially an acquisitions operation,
(C) Once it was essentially an acquisitions operation,
(D) In addition to it being essentially an acquisitions operation,

20 Which choice represents the best transition between paragraphs?

(A) NO CHANGE
(B) Young was succeeded. Herbert Putnam had formerly been head of the Boston Public Library.
(C) Young was succeeded by someone else—Herbert Putnam, former head of the Boston Public Library.
(D) Young was succeeded after only two years by Herbert Putnam, formerly the head of the Boston Public Library.

21

(A) NO CHANGE
(B) Them
(C) He
(D) We

practice test

legislative process. Congress wanted the same kind of service for itself, so Putnam designed such a unit for the Library of Congress. Called the Legislative Reference Service, it went into operation in 1914 to prepare indexes, digests, and compilations of law that the Congress might need, but it quickly became a specialized reference unit for information transfer and research. This service was the forerunner of the Library's current Congressional Research Service. **22**

22 Which choice best describes a conclusion that can be drawn from the chart?

(A) There are more public university than private university libraries that are similar in scope and scale to the Library of Congress.

(B) University Libraries of the same scope and scale as the Library of Congress are more common than one would expect.

(C) When it comes to university libraries of the same scope and scale as the Library of Congress, the private sector is doing more to create them than the public sector.

(D) As the years go on, university libraries of the same scope and scale as the Library of Congress are rapidly increasing.

NUMBER OF LIBRARIES IN VOLUME CATEGORY

INSTITUTIONAL CHARACTERISTIC	Less than 5,000	5,000–9,999	10,000–19,999	20,000–29,999	30,000–49,999	50,000–99,999	100,000–249,999	250,000–499,999	500,000–999,999	1,000,000 or more
All higher education institutions	320	158	241	450	450	691	747	275	153	160
CONTROL										
Public	43	57	77	145	297	362	231	146	106	109
Private	277	101	136	96	153	329	516	129	47	51
LEVEL										
Total 4-year and above	115	48	90	89	155	361	673	273	151	160
Doctor's	12	6	8	5	14	35	131	83	93	151
Master's	35	19	24	22	39	177	378	151	51	9
Bachelor's	68	23	58	61	102	148	164	39	7	0
Less than 4-year	205	110	123	152	295	330	74	2	2	0
SIZE (FTE ENROLLMENT)										
Less than 1,500	309	138	186	193	257	352	363	36	4	1
1,500 to 4,999	9	20	26	47	185	249	297	135	36	7
5,000 or more	2	0	1	1	8	90	87	104	113	152
CARNEGIE CLASSIFICATION (1994)										
Research I and II	0	0	0	0	0	0	1	1	10	113
Doctoral I and II	1	0	0	0	0	0	10	20	44	35
Master's I and II	1	0	3	4	3	47	211	164	76	9
Baccalaureate I and II	1	5	5	6	26	178	292	66	17	3
Associate of Arts	150	75	85	150	317	328	74	2	1	0
Specialized	50	33	67	60	82	116	126	21	3	0
Not classified	117	45	53	21	2	22	33	1	2	0

Source: U.S. Department of Education, National Center for Education Statistics, 1996 Integrated Postsecondary Education Data System, "Academic Libraries Survey" (IPEDS-L: 1996).

QUESTIONS 23–33 ARE BASED ON THE FOLLOWING PASSAGE.

Lavinia & Emily

The Homestead was quiet and still, a preternatural quiet Lavinia Dickinson had become all too accustomed to. Looking around her sister **23** Emily's now forever empty bedroom that contained nothing, Lavinia recalled some verses penned by Emily many years ago:

> *The bustle in a house*
> *The morning after death*
> *Is solemnest of industries*
> *Enacted upon earth, —*
>
> *The sweeping up the heart,*
> *And putting love away*
> *We shall not want to use again*
> *Until eternity.*

24 Some people wondered at Emily's seeming preoccupation with death. But Lavinia found it natural for her **25** sisters inquisitive mind to be drawn to exploring this final journey in the cycle of life, especially since Emily had seen so many loved ones pass into eternal slumber. Emily had always had a curious mind, and a voracious appetite for learning. She also greatly enjoyed being in nature. Faith was something she refused to accept blindly, without thought, much to the chagrin of the Calvinist community around her. For Emily, faith was more than rote belief.

23

(A) NO CHANGE
(B) Emily's now forever empty bedroom, Lavinia recalled some verses
(C) Emily's bedroom, Lavinia recalled some verses
(D) Emily's now forever empty bedroom, Lavinia recalled some verses and poetry

24 Which choice is a sentence that is not relevant to the main topic of the paragraph?

(A) Some people wondered at Emily's seeming preoccupation with death.
(B) Emily had always had a curious mind and a voracious appetite for learning.
(C) She also greatly enjoyed being in nature.
(D) For Emily, faith was more than rote belief.

25

(A) NO CHANGE
(B) sister's.
(C) sisters'
(D) sister

GO TO THE
NEXT PAGE

Faith is a fine invention
For gentlemen who see;
But microscopes are prudent
In an emergency!

26 Emily had felt very fully her isolation as one "standing alone in rebellion" of faith. Reading **27** <u>through</u> her letters and the poems Emily had hidden away, Lavinia realized just how isolated her beloved sister had felt. Perhaps that was why the self-professed "belle of Amherst" had withdrawn so much from the public sphere.

Emily felt, quite keenly, the limitations of womanhood. Lavinia still remembered the indignation Emily had expressed during the Whig Convention of 1852 when women were not allowed to be delegates. "Why can't *I* be a Delegate? ...don't I know all about Daniel Webster, and the Tariff and the Law?" **28**

Yes, it seemed to Lavinia that her sister had most decidedly felt the trappings of being a woman. And, as much as **29** <u>they</u> tried to

26 Which choice best expresses the main idea of the paragraph?

(A) One reason for Emily's sense of isolation was her resistance to common ideas of her time.

(B) One reason for Emily's sense of isolation was her refusal to take part in social events.

(C) One reason for Emily's sense of isolation was her need to be alone to write poetry.

(D) One reason for Emily's sense of isolation was her house's remote location.

27

(A) NO CHANGE
(B) tough
(C) though
(D) thought

28 At this point, the writer is considering adding the following sentence:

But Lavinia also knew that her sister was not cut out for politics and all the socializing and public display it would entail.

Should the writer make this addition here?

(A) Yes, because it adds more information about Emily's personality.

(B) Yes, because it explains the contrast between Emily's words and actions.

(C) No, because it detracts from the point about women's issues.

(D) No, because it is not relevant to Emily's life.

29

(A) NO CHANGE
(B) we
(C) she
(C) her

eschew them **30** by not becoming a wife or mother, she still felt trapped by society's strict bonds.

ESCAPE.

I never hear the word "escape"
Without a quicker blood,
A sudden expectation,
A flying attitude.

I never hear of prisons broad
By soldiers battered down,
But I tug childish at my bars, —
Only to fail again!

Emily never understood the power of the gift she had been **31** given?

THE DUEL.

I took my power in my hand.
And went against the world;
'T was not so much as David had,
But I was twice as bold.

I aimed my pebble, but myself
Was all the one that fell.
Was it Goliath was too large,
Or only I too small?

Sitting in the stillness of Emily's room, surrounded by her internal monologue expressed through thousands of poems, **32** it was decided by Lavinia that it was time the world knew the full treasure her sister was. **33** And that world would never know what hit it.

30 Which choice best fits with the style and tone of the passage?

(A) NO CHANGE
(B) by never being a wife or mother
(C) by postponing choosing to be a wife or mother
(D) by refusing the role of wife or mother

31

(A) NO CHANGE
(B) given!
(C) given.
(D) given;

32

(A) NO CHANGE
(B) Lavinia decided
(C) it had been decided by Lavinia
(D) it was being decided by Lavinia

33 Which choice is most consistent with the style and tone of the passage?

(A) NO CHANGE
(B) That world was about to receive a gift it would long cherish.
(C) That world would line up to thank Lavinia for years to come.
(D) That world didn't know it yet, but it would soon have a new superstar.

QUESTIONS 34–44 ARE BASED ON THE FOLLOWING PASSAGE.

What Is Sleep?

Scientists have known for some years that sleep is important to human health. In fact, cases of long-term sleep deprivation have even led to death. **34** Yet, scientists are still studying this unique state in which humans spend a third of their lives.

35 [1] It isn't only current scientists who are intrigued with sleep. [2] Throughout history, people have attempted to understand this remarkable experience. [3] Many centuries ago, for example, sleep was regarded as a type of anemia of the brain. [4] Alcmaeon, a Greek scientist, believed that blood retreated into the blood vessels, and the partially starved brain went to sleep. [5] Plato supported the idea that the soul left the body during sleep, wandered through the world, and woke up the body when it returned. [6] During the twentieth century, great strides were made in the study of sleep.

Recently, more scientific explanations of sleep have been proposed. Looking at them, we see a variety of ideas about the nature of sleep. **36** Research may be able to help people who have sleep disorders. According to one theory, the brain is put to sleep by a chemical agent that accumulates in the body when it is awake. Another theory is that weary branches of certain nerve cells break connections with neighboring cells. The flow of impulses required for staying awake is then

34

(A) NO CHANGE
(B) Scientists are yet studying
(C) Scientists are studying yet
(D) Yet, scientists study still

35 Which sentence in this paragraph should be moved to the fourth paragraph to create a more logical sequence?

(A) Sentence 1
(B) Sentence 2
(C) Sentence 4
(D) Sentence 6

36 Which choice most effectively sets up the information that follows?

(A) NO CHANGE
(B) Some of the newer ideas may yield important data about the science of sleep.
(C) Although science has not yet solved the mysteries of sleep, breakthroughs are imminent.
(D) However, some of the old ideas may prove to be correct.

disrupted. These more recent theories have to be subjected to laboratory research.

Why do we sleep? Why do we dream? Modern sleep research is said to have begun in the 1920s with the **37** discovery of a machine that could measure brain waves, the electroencephalograph (EEG). The study of sleep was further enhanced in the 1950s, **38** and Eugene Aserinsky, a graduate student at the University of Chicago, and Nathaniel Kleitman, his professor, observed periods of rapid eye movements (REMs) in sleeping subjects. When awakened during these REM periods, subjects almost always remembered dreaming. **39** Nevertheless when awakened during non-REM phases of sleep, the subjects rarely could recall their dreams. Aserinsky and Kleitman used EEGs and other machines in an attempt to learn more about REMs and sleep patterns.

40 Guided by REMs, it became possible for investigators to "spot" dreaming from outside and then **41** awakening the sleeper to collect dream stories. They could also **42** altar the dreamers' experiences with noises, drugs, or other stimuli before or during sleep. Thankfully, it appears the body takes care of itself by temporarily paralyzing muscles during REM sleep, preventing the dreamer from "acting out" dream activities.

37
(A) NO CHANGE
(B) invention
(C) idea
(D) suggestion

38
(A) NO CHANGE
(B) when
(C) or
(D) so

39
(A) NO CHANGE
(B) Even so,
(C) As predicted,
(D) On the other hand,

40 Which choice sets up the most logical introduction to the sentence?
(A) NO CHANGE
(B) Guided by EEGs,
(C) No longer hampered by REMs,
(D) Nevertheless, with REMs,

41
(A) NO CHANGE
(B) quickly awakening
(C) awakened
(D) awaken

42
(A) NO CHANGE
(B) alter
(C) alternate
(D) alternative

GO TO THE NEXT PAGE

Since the mid-1950s researchers has been drawn into sleep laboratories. Initial studies attempted to answer questions about why people sleep and what happens in the brain and the body during sleep. There, bedrooms adjoin other rooms that contain EEGs and other equipment. The EEG amplifies signals from sensors on the face, head, and other parts of the body, which together yield tracings of respiration, pulse, muscle tension, and changes of electrical potential in the brain that are sometimes called brain waves. These recordings supply clues to the changes of the sleeping person's activities. These sleep studies have changed long-held beliefs that sleep was an inactive, or passive, state only used for rest and recuperation. As scientists have learned more about the purpose of sleep and dreams during REM sleep. They are now turning to the study of sleep disorders to learn more about problems during sleep.

(A) NO CHANGE
(B) were been drawn
(C) have been drawn
(D) was drawn

(A) NO CHANGE.
(B) sleep—they
(C) sleep; they
(D) sleep, they

STOP

**If you finish before time is called, you may check your work on this section only.
Do not turn to any other section.**

SECTION 3: MATH TEST—NO CALCULATOR

20 Questions • 25 minutes

TURN TO SECTION 3 OF YOUR ANSWER SHEET TO ANSWER THE QUESTIONS IN THIS SECTION.

Directions: For Questions 1–15, solve each problem, select the best answer from the choices provided, and fill in the corresponding oval on your answer sheet. **For Questions 16–20,** solve the problem and enter your answer in the grid on the answer sheet. The directions **before Question 16** will provide information on how to enter your answers in the grid.

ADDITIONAL INFORMATION:

- The use of a calculator in this section **is not permitted.**

- All variables and expressions used represent real numbers unless otherwise indicated.

- Figures provided in this test are drawn to scale unless otherwise indicated.

- All figures lie in a plane unless otherwise indicated.

- Unless otherwise specified, the domain of a given function f is the set of all real numbers x for which $f(x)$ is a real number.

The number of degrees of arc in a circle is 360.
The number of radians in the arc of a circle is 2π.
The sum of the measures in degrees of the angles of a triangle is 180.

1

If $\dfrac{x+2}{5} = m$ and $m = -3$, what is the value of x?

(A) −17
(B) −15
(C) −5
(D) −1

2

If $d = m - \dfrac{50}{m}$, and m is a positive number, then as m increases in value, d

(A) increases in value.
(B) decreases in value.
(C) increases, then decreases.
(D) decreases, then increases.

GO TO THE NEXT PAGE

3 Pieces of wire are soldered together so as to form the edges of a cube whose volume is 64 cubic inches. The number of inches of wire used is

(A) 24.

(B) 48.

(C) 64.

(D) 96.

4 Myra baked 6 sheets of cookies with r cookies on each sheet. Neil baked 7 sheets of cookies with p cookies on each sheet. Which of the following represents the total number t of cookies baked by Myra and Neil?

(A) $t = 13pr$

(B) $t = 42pr$

(C) $t = 6r + 7p$

(D) $t = 7r + 6p$

5 If $2y = \dfrac{1}{3}$, then $\dfrac{1}{4y} =$

(A) $\dfrac{3}{2}$

(B) $\dfrac{3}{4}$

(C) $\dfrac{1}{5}$

(D) $\dfrac{4}{3}$

6
$$y = \frac{(x-3)^3}{4}$$

Which expression is equivalent to x?

(A) $\sqrt{4y} + 3$

(B) $\sqrt{4y + 3}$

(C) $\sqrt[3]{4y} + 3$

(D) $\sqrt[3]{4y + 3}$

7 Hannah recently purchased a plant that grows 4.5 centimeters each week. The height of Hannah's plant can be found using the equation $h = 4.5w + 6$, where h is the height of the plant in centimeters, and w is the number of weeks. What is the meaning of the 6 in the equation?

(A) Hannah's plant will be 6 centimeters tall after 4.5 weeks.

(B) Hannah's plant grows 6 centimeters each week.

(C) Hannah's plant will grow for 6 weeks.

(D) Hannah's plant was initially 6 centimeters tall.

8 $(x)^6 + (2x^2)^3 + (3x^3)^2 =$

(A) $5x^5 + x^6$

(B) $17x^5 + x^6$

(C) $6x^6$

(D) $18x^6$

QUESTION 9 REFERS TO THE FOLLOWING GRAPH.

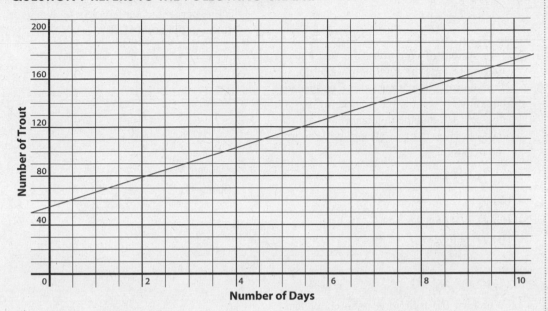

9 Stephen was studying the population of a certain trout pond. When he started his study, there were 55 trout in the pond. He observed the pond each day for 10 days and observed that there were 12 new trout each day. The graph above represents the relationship between the number of trout in the pond and the number of days. Which of the following is an equation for the graph?

(A) $y = 12x + 55$

(B) $y = 10x + 12$

(C) $y = 55x + 12$

(D) $y = 12x + 10$

10 Which of the following is equal to $\left(-\dfrac{27}{8}\right)^{\frac{1}{3}}$?

(A) $-\dfrac{3}{2}$

(B) $-\dfrac{2}{3}$

(C) $\dfrac{2}{3}$

(D) $\dfrac{3}{2}$

11 The area of a square is $49x^2$. What is the length of a diagonal of the square?

(A) $7x$

(B) $7x\sqrt{2}$

(C) $14x$

(D) $\dfrac{7x}{\sqrt{2}}$

12 The distance, s, in feet that an object falls in t seconds when dropped from a height is obtained by use of the formula $s = 16t^2$. When graphed, what is the meaning of the slope between any two points in the graph?

(A) The height in feet from where the object falls

(B) The speed in feet per second of the object as it falls

(C) The time in seconds it takes for the object to fall to the ground

(D) The acceleration in feet per second squared of the object as it falls

GO TO THE
NEXT PAGE

13 $D + B = 24$

$4D + 2B = 84$

In a system of equations, the first equation represents the total number of dogs, D, and birds, B, in a pet store. The second equation represents the number of legs a dog has, $4D$, and the number of legs a bird has, $2B$. How many dogs and birds are in the pet store?

(A) $D = 6; B = 18$

(B) $D = 18; B = 6$

(C) $D = 24; B = 84$

(D) $D = 60; B = 24$

14 $f(x) = x^2 - 4x - 21$

Which of the following is an equivalent equation that shows the zeros of the function as coefficients or constants?

(A) $f(x) = (x - (-7))(x - 3)$

(B) $f(x) = (x - 7)(x - (-3))$

(C) $f(x) = (x - 2)^2 - 21$

(D) $f(x) = (x - 2)^2 - 25$

15 Which equation represents the equation of a line perpendicular to $y = 3x - 2$ that goes through the point $(1, 3)$?

(A) $y = -3x + 6$

(B) $y = -\dfrac{1}{3}x + \dfrac{10}{3}$

(C) $y = -\dfrac{1}{3}x + \dfrac{9}{3}$

(D) $y = 3x$

Directions: For Questions 16-20, solve the problem and enter your answer in the grid, as described below, on the answer sheet.

1. Although not required, it is suggested that you write your answer in the boxes at the top of the columns to help you fill in the circles accurately. You will receive credit only if the circles are filled in correctly.

2. Mark no more than one circle in any column.

3. No question has a negative answer.

4. Some problems may have more than one correct answer. In such cases, grid only one answer.

5. **Mixed numbers** such as $3\frac{1}{2}$ must be gridded as 3.5 or $\frac{7}{2}$.

    If $3\frac{1}{2}$ is entered into the grid as $\overline{3\ |\ 1\ /\ 2}$, it will be interpreted as $\frac{31}{2}$, not $3\frac{1}{2}$.)

6. **Decimal answers:** If you obtain a decimal answer with more digits than the grid can accommodate, it may be either rounded or truncated, but it must fill the entire grid.

GO TO THE
NEXT PAGE

practice test

16

70°

120°

$x°$

In the figure above, $x =$

19

$$\sqrt{4 - x^2} = \sqrt{3x}$$

What is one solution to the equation?

17 The factors of the function f are $(x + 3)^2$ and $(3x - 2)$. What is a zero of the function?

20

$$2x + 3y = 7$$
$$ax - 12y = b$$

According to the system of equations above, what is the value of ab that will make the system of equations have an infinite number of solutions?

18 $5(4 - 8x) = d(5 - 6x) - 4x$

What value of d will make the equation have no solutions?

STOP

**If you finish before time is called, you may check your work on this section only.
Do not turn to any other section.**

SECTION 4: MATH TEST—CALCULATOR 🖩

38 Questions • 55 minutes

TURN TO SECTION 4 OF YOUR ANSWER SHEET TO ANSWER THE QUESTIONS IN THIS SECTION.

Directions: For Questions 1–30, solve each problem, select the best answer from the choices provided, and fill in the corresponding oval on your answer sheet. **For Questions 31–38,** solve the problem and enter your answer in the grid on the answer sheet. The directions **before Question 31** will provide information on how to enter your answers in the grid.

ADDITIONAL INFORMATION:

- The use of a calculator **is permitted.**

- All variables and expressions used represent real numbers unless otherwise indicated.

- Figures provided in this test are drawn to scale unless otherwise indicated.

- All figures lie in a plane unless otherwise indicated.

- Unless otherwise specified, the domain of a given function f is the set of all real numbers x for which $f(x)$ is a real number.

Reference Information

Circle:
$C = 2\pi r$
$A = \pi r^2$

Rectangle:
$A = lw$

Triangle:
$A = \frac{1}{2} bh$

$a^2 + b^2 = c^2$

Rectangular Solid:
$V = lwh$

Cylinder:
$V = \pi r^2 h$

Sphere:
$V = \frac{4}{3} \pi r^3$

Cone:
$V = \frac{1}{3} \pi r^2 h$

Rectangular Based Pyramid:
$V = \frac{1}{3} lwh$

The number of degrees of arc in a circle is 360.
The number of radians in the arc of a circle is 2π.
The sum of the measures in degrees of the angles of a triangle is 180.

---

1 If $9x + 5 = 23$, what is the numerical value of $18x + 5$?

(A) 46

(B) 41

(C) 36

(D) 32

2 A pickup truck has maximum load capacity of 1,500 pounds. Bruce is going to load small radiators, each weighing 150 pounds, and large radiators, each weighing 250 pounds, into the truck. There are 15 radiators to choose from. Which system of linear inequalities represents this situation?

(A) $x + y < 15$
    $150x + 250y < 1500$

(B) $x + y \geq 15$
    $150x + 250y \geq 1500$

(C) $x + y > 15$
    $150x + 250y > 1500$

(D) $x + y \leq 15$
    $150x + 250y \leq 1500$

3 If 15 cans of food are needed for 7 adults for two days, how many cans are needed to feed 4 adults for seven days?

(A) 15
(B) 20
(C) 25
(D) 30

4 Fiona earns $28 per hour working for herself. She saves 25% of her income to pay taxes. Which function can be used to determine the non-taxed amount Fiona earns for working x hours,?

(A) $f(x) = 28(0.25x)$
(B) $f(x) = 28 + 0.25x$
(C) $f(x) = 28(0.75x)$
(D) $f(x) = 28 + 0.75x$

QUESTIONS 5 AND 6 REFER TO THE FOLLOWING INFORMATION.

TOTAL ANNUAL SALES

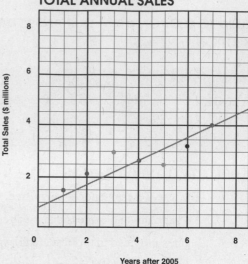

The graph above represents the sales for a company after 2005.

5 Which phrase best describes the correlation between the years after 2005 and the total sales?

(A) Weak negative
(B) Strong negative
(C) Weak positive
(D) Strong positive

6 Which equation best models the data shown in the graph?

(A) $y = 0.4x + 1$
(B) $y = x + 0.5$
(C) $y = 1.5^x$
(D) $y = 0.5^x$

7 If a box of notepaper costs $4.20 after a 40% discount, what was its original price?

(A) $2.52
(B) $5.88
(C) $7.00
(D) $10.50

8 The average attendance to basketball games at a local university over the last 10 years can be modeled by the equation $y = 329x + 6489$, where y represents the average attendance at basketball games x years after 2004. Which of the following describes the meaning of 329 in the equation?

(A) The average attendance at basketball games in 2004

(B) The total attendance at basketball games in 2004

(C) The annual increase in average attendance to basketball games.

(D) The total increase in average attendance to basketball games for the last 10 years.

9 A local theater company sells t-shirts and tote bags at all of their performances. They charge $20 for each t-shirt and $12.50 for each tote bag. Which expression can be used to determine the total amount the company earns from selling x t-shirts and y tote bags?

(A) $12.5(x + y)$

(B) $20(x + y)$

(C) $20x + 12.5y$

(D) $12.5x + 20y$

10 A local library had 25,825 books at the beginning of 2010. Since then, it has added 375 books each year. The library can fit a maximum of 35,000 books. If x represents the number of years after the start of 2010, which inequality shows the number of years that the library can continue adding books at this pace without adding space?

(A) $35,000 - 375 \leq x$

(B) $35,000 \leq 375x$

(C) $35,000 \geq 375x - 25,825$

(D) $35,000 \geq 375x + 25,825$

11 Which of the following is equivalent to $(6 - 5i)(3 + 2i)$?

(A) $8 - 3i$

(B) $18 - 10i$

(C) $28 - 3i$

(D) 28

12 A study was performed to determine if a new medication, Z, helps people who suffer from a certain affliction. A group of 500 randomly selected people who have the affliction were included in the study. Of the group, 200 people were given Z, 200 people were given an old medication, Y, and another 100 people received no treatment. The data showed that people who received Z had significantly decreased effects of the affliction, more than people who received no treatment or who were given medicine Y. Based on the design and results of the study, which of the following is an appropriate conclusion?

(A) Z is likely to lessen the effects of the affliction in people who suffer from the affliction.

(B) Z is likely to lessen the effects of the affliction better than any other medication.

(C) Z is likely to lessen the effects of the affliction for anyone who takes the medication.

(D) Z is likely to lessen the effects of the affliction for those who received no treatment.

13 A group of 27 people visit a city. The people rent either a bicycle or rollerblades. People pay $7 to rent a bicycle for the day or $5 to rent rollerblades for an hour. If the total cost for rentals is $171, how many people rent bicycles?

(A) 9

(B) 12

(C) 15

(D) 18

GO TO THE NEXT PAGE

14 Scientists are creating a new pesticide spray that will help control the mosquito population. When the pesticide spray is complete and on the market, consumers will be able to buy it in a container that can be set on a circular-rotating mechanism in the middle of a yard. The spray will shoot out and cover a distance of 60 feet. If 60 feet represents the radius of the circle created by the rotating mechanism, what is the area of the sector of the circle created by a 60-degree angle at its center?

(A) 360π

(B) 600π

(C) 840π

(D) 1000π

15
$$y = 2x - 5$$
$$y = (x - 2)^2 - 9$$

Which choice shows the solutions to the system of equations?

(A) $(-1, 0), (5, 0)$

(B) $(0, -5), (3, -8)$

(C) $(0, -5), (6, 7)$

(D) $(5, 0), (6, 7)$

QUESTIONS 16 AND 17 REFER TO THE FOLLOWING INFORMATION.

The graph provided shows the population of California, in millions, from the years 1860 to 1980. Each point represents the population at a particular year. The best fit relation between the points is drawn to connect them.

16 Which phrase describes the relationship between the population and the number of years?

(A) Linear increasing

(B) Linear decreasing

(C) Exponential growth

(D) Exponential decay

17 Based on the graph, which of the following would be the best prediction of the population of California in 1990?

(A) 20 million

(B) 23 million

(C) 25 million

(D) 30 million

18 A rectangular sign is cut down by 10% of its height and 30% of its width. What percent of the original area remains?

(A) 37%

(B) 57%

(C) 63%

(D) 70%

19 A recent report states that if you were to eat each meal in a different restaurant in New York City, it would take you more than 19 years to cover all of New York City's eating places, assuming that you eat three meals a day. On the basis of this information, the number of restaurants in New York City

(A) exceeds 20,500.

(B) is closer to 20,000 than 21,000.

(C) exceeds 21,000.

(D) exceeds 21,000 but does not exceed 21,500.

20 If a cubic inch of gold weighs 0.70 pounds, how much does a cubic foot of gold weigh?

(A) 700 pounds

(B) 1,210 pounds

(C) 1,296 pounds

(D) 1,728 pounds

21

$$\frac{3x-1}{2x+3} - \frac{2x+3}{3x-1}$$

Which of the following is equivalent to the expression above?

(A) $\dfrac{5x^2 - 18x - 8}{6x^2 + 7x - 3}$

(B) $\dfrac{x-4}{6x^2 + 7x - 3}$

(C) $\dfrac{5x^2 + 10}{6x^2 + 7x - 3}$

(D) $\dfrac{5x^2 - 12x - 8}{6x^2 + 7x - 3}$

22

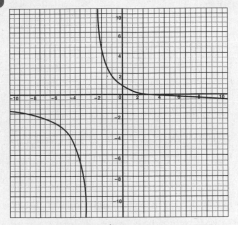

Which of the following is an equation for the graph?

(A) $y = \dfrac{6}{x+3} - 1$

(B) $y = \dfrac{6}{x-3} - 1$

(C) $y = \dfrac{1}{x+3} - 1$

(D) $y = \dfrac{1}{x-3} - 1$

23

$$f(x) = \frac{3}{x-1}$$

$$g(x) = (x-4)^2$$

What is the value of $g(f(4))$?

(A) –3

(B) 0

(C) 1

(D) 9

24 The number of people living in a certain city has been growing at a constant rate of about 3.8% each year since 1980. The population in 2000 was 38,500. If y is the population of the city x years after 1980, which equation best represents this situation?

(A) $y = 18,260(1.038)^x$

(B) $y = 38,500(1.38)^x$

(C) $y = 38,500(1.038)^x$

(D) $y = 81,172(1.38)^x$

GO TO THE NEXT PAGE

25 If $f(x) = x^2 - 2x - 8$, for which value(s) of x does $f(x) = 0$?

(A) $x = -4, 2$

(B) $x = 2, 4$

(C) $x = -4, -2$

(D) $x = -2, 4$

QUESTIONS 26 AND 27 REFER TO THE FOLLOWING INFORMATION.

A recent poll surveyed a random selection of 850 likely voters in a state election. Of the sample, 31% say that they favor candidate A, and 18% say that they favor candidate B. The margin of error reported for this was ± 3.4% with 95% confidence.

26 Which of the following statements can accurately be drawn from this data?

(A) The margin of error is too large to make any conclusions.

(B) The sample of likely voters don't represent all voters.

(C) The sample size is too small to represent the voters across the entire state.

(D) The sample was randomly selected and is large enough to make conclusions.

27 Which of the following statements can accurately be drawn from this data?

(A) The true percentage of likely voters who will vote for candidate A is 31%.

(B) The true percentage of likely voters who will vote for candidate A is most likely between 27.6% and 34.4%.

(C) The true percentage of likely voters who will vote for candidate B is 18%.

(D) The true percentage of likely voters who will vote for someone other than candidate A or candidate B is most likely between 45.6% and 52.4%.

28 In a certain course, a student takes eight tests, all of which count equally. When figuring out the final grade, the instructor drops the best and the worst grades and averages the other six. The student calculates that his average for all eight tests is 84%. After dropping the best and the worst grades, the student averages 86%. What was the average of the best and the worst grades?

(A) 68

(B) 73

(C) 78

(D) 88

29 $x^2 + y^2 - 8x + 12y = 144$

What is the length of the radius of the circle with the equation above?

(A) 6

(B) 12

(C) 14

(D) 24

30

$$2(2x + 3) = n\left(x + \frac{6}{8}\right) - 4x$$

Which value of n gives the equation above an infinite number of solutions?

(A) 2

(B) 4

(C) 6

(D) 8

Directions: For Questions 31–38, solve the problem and enter your answer in the grid, as described below, on the answer sheet.

1. Although not required, it is suggested that you write your answer in the boxes at the top of the columns to help you fill in the circles accurately. You will receive credit only if the circles are filled in correctly.

2. Mark no more than one circle in any column.

3. No question has a negative answer.

4. Some problems may have more than one correct answer. In such cases, grid only one answer.

5. **Mixed numbers** such as $3\frac{1}{2}$ must be gridded as 3.5 or $\frac{7}{2}$.

   If $3\frac{1}{2}$ is entered into the grid as $\overline{3\,|\,1\,/\,2}$, it will be interpreted as $\frac{31}{2}$, not $3\frac{1}{2}$.)

6. **Decimal answers:** If you obtain a decimal answer with more digits than the grid can accommodate, it may be either rounded or truncated, but it must fill the entire grid.

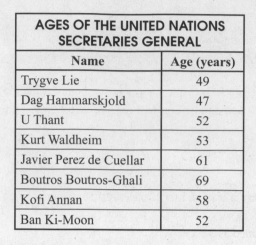

AGES OF THE UNITED NATIONS SECRETARIES GENERAL	
Name	Age (years)
Trygve Lie	49
Dag Hammarskjold	47
U Thant	52
Kurt Waldheim	53
Javier Perez de Cuellar	61
Boutros Boutros-Ghali	69
Kofi Annan	58
Ban Ki-Moon	52

32 If $\frac{x}{12} + \frac{x}{18} = 1$, what is the value of x?

31 The table above lists the ages of the first eight United Nations Secretaries General at the beginning of each term in office. What is the mean age? (Round your answer to the nearest tenth.)

33 An African elephant can lift a total of approximately 660 pounds with its trunk. A small bundle of twigs weighs 12 pounds. If an African elephant lifts a small log that weighs 50 pounds, what is the greatest number of small twig bundles that it could theoretically lift in addition to the log?

QUESTIONS 34 AND 35 REFER TO THE FOLLOWING INFORMATION.

Population of United States by Gender and Age in 2010 (in millions)

	0–24 years	25–49 years	50–74 years	75–100 years	Total
Males	53.6	52.2	38.6	7.3	151.7
Females	51.2	52.6	41.8	11.2	156.8
Total	104.8	104.8	80.4	18.5	308.5

34 What percent of males were 49 years or younger in 2010? Round your answer to the nearest tenth.

35 What is the probability that a randomly selected female is between the ages of 25 and 74? Write your answer as a decimal to the nearest hundredth.

36. $5x + 4y = 11$
$6x - 8y = 10$

In the system of equations above, what is the value of y?

37. A car travels from town A to town B, a distance of 360 miles, in 9 hours. How many hours would the same trip have taken had the car traveled 5 mph faster?

38. $$\frac{2}{x+2} + \frac{3}{x-5} = \frac{4x+7}{x^2-3x-10}$$

What is the solution to the equation shown above?

STOP

**If you finish before time is called, you may check your work on this section only.
Do not turn to any other section.**

practice test

SECTION 5: ESSAY

50 Minutes • 1 Essay

Directions: The essay gives you an opportunity to show how effectively you can read and comprehend a passage and write an essay analyzing the passage. In your essay, you should demonstrate that you have read the passage carefully, present a clear and logical analysis, and use language precisely.

Your essay will need to be written on the lines provided in your answer booklet. You will have enough space if you write on every line and keep your handwriting to an average size. Try to print or write clearly so that your writing will be legible to the readers scoring your essay.

As you read the passage below, consider how the writers, Alex Jensen and Susan M. McHale, use the following:

- Evidence, such as facts, statistics, or examples, to support claims.

- Reasoning to develop ideas and to connect claims and evidence.

- Stylistic or persuasive elements, such as word choice or appeals to emotion, to add power to the ideas expressed.

Adapted from "What makes siblings from the same family so different? Parents" by Alex Jensen and Susan M. McHale, originally published by The Conversation, July 6, 2015. Alex Jensen is an Assistant Professor of Human Development at Brigham Young University. Susan M. McHale is a Professor of Human Development and Family Studies at Pennsylvania State University.

What makes siblings from the same family so different? Parents

1   A colleague related the following story: while running errands with her 11- and 7-year-old daughters, a back seat battle began to rage. My colleague's attempts to defuse the situation only led to a shouting match about who was to blame for the skirmish. Finally the 11-year-old proclaimed to her sister, "You started it the day you were born and took away Mom's love!"

2   This pair of sisters fight frequently, and from their mother's perspective, part of the reason is that the two have little in common. As it turns out, their situation is not unique.

3   Despite the fact that siblings are, on average, 50% genetically similar, are often raised in the same home by the same parents, attend the same schools and have many other shared experiences, siblings are often only as similar to each other as they are to children who are growing up across town or even across the country.

4   So, what is it that makes two siblings from the same family so different?

What makes the difference?

5   As researchers of sibling and family relationships, we knew that at least one answer to this question comes from theory and data showing that, at least in some families, siblings try to be different from one another and seek to establish a unique identity and position in their family.

6   From a child's perspective, if an older brother excels at school, it may be easier to attract her parents' attention and praise by becoming a star athlete than by competing with her brother to get the best grades. In this way, even small differences between siblings can become substantial differences over time.

7   But parents may also play a role. For instance, when parents notice differences between their children, children may pick up on parents' perceptions and beliefs about those differences. This, in turn, can increase sibling differences.

8   We wanted to test these ideas to see what makes siblings different. So, we used data from first- and second-born teenage siblings from 388 two-parent families to examine sibling differences in school performance.

9   We asked mothers and fathers to report on whether they thought the two siblings differed in their academic abilities, and if so, which sibling was more capable. We also collected school grades from both siblings' report cards.

Preference for the firstborn

10 Our analyses showed some interesting results: parents tended to believe that the older sibling was better in school. This was even when older siblings did not actually receive better grades, on average.

11 This may be a product of parents having greater expectations for firstborns or that, at any given time, the older sibling is undertaking more advanced school work.

12 There was, however, an exception to this pattern: in families with older brothers and younger sisters, parents rated the younger sibling as being more capable. In fact, in those families, younger sisters received better grades than their older brothers.

13 Our findings also showed that it was not sibling differences in school grades that predicted parents' ratings of their children's abilities. Rather, parents' beliefs about differences in their children's abilities predicted later sibling differences in school grades.

14 In other words, when parents believed one child was more capable than the other, that child's school grades improved more over time than their sibling's.

Sustaining beliefs

15 Although we expected that children's school grades and parents' beliefs about their children's relative abilities would be mutually influential, it turned out that parents' beliefs did not change much over their children's teenage years.

16 Instead, sibling differences in school grades did change and were predicted by parents' beliefs. In this way, parents' beliefs about differences between their children may encourage the development of actual sibling difference.

17 The above comment by an 11-year-old highlights that children are sensitive to their place and value in the family—relative to those of their siblings. Parents may strive to show their love for their children, but they also should be aware that small differences in how they treat their children can have large effects—including on their children's development and adjustment and also on the sibling relationship.

GO TO THE
NEXT PAGE

18 Indeed, some research suggests that sibling conflict arises when children try to be different from their siblings.

19 My colleague may be correct that her daughters fight frequently because they have nothing in common. But their conflicts may also be motivated by her daughter's perception that their differences started on the day her sister was born "and took away Mom's love."

Write an essay in which you explain how the writers build an argument to persuade their audience that parents are the reason why siblings from the same family behave differently. In your essay, analyze how Alex Jensen and Susan M. McHale use one or more of the features previously listed or features of your own choice) to strengthen the logic and persuasiveness of their argument. Be sure that your analysis focuses on the most relevant aspects of the passage.

Your essay should not explain whether you agree with the writers' claims, but rather explain how they build an argument to persuade their audience.

STOP

**If you finish before time is called, you may check your work on this section only.
Do not turn to any other section.**

ANSWER KEY AND EXPLANATIONS

Section 1: Reading Test

1. C	12. C	23. B	34. B	45. A
2. A	13. A	24. A	35. A	46. D
3. D	14. C	25. A	36. D	47. B
4. B	15. B	26. C	37. D	48. D
5. C	16. D	27. A	38. C	49. B
6. B	17. B	28. B	39. D	50. C
7. D	18. A	29. D	40. D	51. C
8. C	19. C	30. B	41. C	52. B
9. D	20. D	31. B	42. B	
10. A	21. A	32. B	43. D	
11. C	22. C	33. C	44. C	

READING TEST RAW SCORE [   ]
(Number of correct answers)

1. **The correct answer is (C).** The overall idea of the article emphasizes the problem of GALS, an invasive species that threatens the ecosystems of the islands. The article is informational and does not attempt to persuade readers, choice (D), or encourage them to visit, choice (A), or raise money, choice (B).

2. **The correct answer is (A).** The main discussion of the article is about how scientists are trying to contain and eliminate GALS by using trained dogs to detect them. Choice (C) is a true statement, but it is not the main idea of the article. Choice (D) is also true, but the article does not focus on how organizations are collaborating; rather its emphasis is on training dogs to help solve the specific problem of one invasive species.

3. **The correct answer is (D).** The article mentions the location of the islands, which are quite a distance from any mainland. This fact of geography likely kept people from settling there for a long time. This meant that the natural ecosystems were in balance.

4. **The correct answer is (B).** The article explains that the GALS is very destructive because it eats so many different types of plants and animals. Once this snail enters a population, it takes over by reproducing quickly and eating all the other species that keep the ecosystems in balance. While their ability to hide, choice (C), makes them difficult to find, the threat comes from their eating habits.

5. **The correct answer is (C).** The article explains that people first introduced animals that were nonnative to the islands. The fact that GALS and likely other species as well have taken over can be ascribed to the people who arrive with plants and animals—sometimes intentionally and sometimes unintentionally. These nonnative species have a tendency to take over and wipe out the native species, upsetting the ecosystem. The trained dogs were brought in to help relieve the problem, choice (A). By visiting the islands both for research and tourism, people have learned much about the native

species and shared this information with people off the islands. This has not made the islands more fragile.

6. **The correct answer is (B).** Choice (B) shows how getting rid of invasive species is a problem and invasive species often upset the balance in an ecosystem. Finding GALS is difficult, but that's not why the ecosystem is hard to maintain. Choice (A) is true, but it is not why maintaining the ecosystem is difficult.

7. **The correct answer is (D).** Dogs can track and find GALS effectively, and the cost to train and maintain them is reasonable relative to the service they provide, so choice (D) is the correct answer. The other choices provide additional information about the dogs and their training, but they don't answer the question of how dogs contribute to biosecurity.

8. **The correct answer is (C).** Dogs have a very highly developed sense of smell and can be trained to follow a scent that humans cannot detect. Dogs were not chosen based on their ease of interaction with people or for their ability to find drugs. The specific dogs described in the article were able to be trained for the specific task. Choice (D) is not true because the handlers did require special training.

9. **The correct answer is (D).** "Biosecurity" is a combined form of the prefix *bio-* (meaning life) and *security*. As used in the passage, the word refers to security from harmful biological species. The word is not related to handling of plants or animals, choices (A) and (B). The article does not mention extinction, choice (C); the word is not used in this context. Here, "biosecurity" is protection of the ecosystems.

10. **The correct answer is (A).** "Acclimation," as used in the context provided, describes how the dogs had to adjust to the Galapagos, which was not their native environment. "Conforming," choice (B), suggests blending in rather than adjusting. "Adaptation," choice (C), is a process that takes many years, not a few days or weeks. Training is a type of behavior modification, choice (D), but it is unrelated to acclimation.

11. **The correct answer is (C).** Dogs are not native to the Galapagos, which are islands far from any mainland, inhabited mostly by species unique to the islands, such as giant tortoises and iguanas. Dogs were brought to the islands by people to help them find the invasive species that are upsetting the balance found on the islands. The dogs' sense of smell makes them good hunters for the invasive species on the islands, but that does not explain why they are invasive, so choice (A) is incorrect. The text explains that the dogs had to be acclimated both to the islands and their trainers, but their adjustment was so that they could be trained properly for their role as hunters. This acclimation does not explain why they would be considered invasive, so choice (B) is incorrect. Choice (D) is incorrect because the text does not say that dogs ever thrived on the islands or were predators of any native species; it only stated that the dogs brought by the project helped in finding a particular invasive species so that it could be eradicated.

12. **The correct answer is (C).** Carter explains in the beginning of the speech how important it was for people to grasp the severity of the energy problem. He then goes on to explain how he plans to address the problem. Although energy independence was cited as a goal, it was not a reason for his speech. He could start a dialogue with the public at any time, choice (B), so this speech was not a casual, friendly dialogue. Carter does mention at the end of his speech how he understands the limitations of the office, but that idea is not the reason for addressing the public.

13. **The correct answer is (A).** The overriding idea that Carter emphasizes is that the energy problem is not new; it is complex; it will take a long time to fix it; and many people, the public included, will have to work together to change it. There are many ways to conserve energy, choice (B), but this is not the specific focus of the passage. Carter's urging people to use less energy in their homes, choice (C), is a detail. Carter never claims that government cannot solve environmental problems, choice (D).

14. **The correct answer is (C).** Carter proposes that people lower their thermostats, but that is not a government action. He also proposes consolidating different agencies to form a new cabinet-level department, but that is not an action that would solve the energy problem. Protection from oil spills would help mitigate pollution and stop the waste of energy, but it is not mentioned as a way to solve the problem. Developing coal reserves is an example of how the United States could decrease its dependence on foreign sources of energy.

15. **The correct answer is (B).** Throughout his speech, Carter references the public and its role in addressing the problem. He emphasizes that the problem affects everyone and everyone needs to participate to help solve it. He says that the sacrifices needed to be made by the public should be "borne fairly among all our people" (lines 66–67). Choice (A) is true, but it is not a belief system. Choice (D) is referenced when he explains the limitations of presidential power, but that is not a belief system; it is a part of the Constitution.

16. **The correct answer is (D).** Carter explains how he believes that if everyone cooperates and contributes to conservation, the problem will get solved more easily and quickly. Although he mentions all of the other choices as actions that can be taken, his main thrust is to appeal to people acting together as a nation to be more energy efficient.

17. **The correct answer is (B).** By explaining various sources of waste, Carter shows people that it won't be all that difficult to conserve energy; simple, small changes can make a difference if enough people participate. The other choices are all ideas that he mentions, but they are not statements that support his argument that people can make a difference by conserving the energy they now waste.

18. **The correct answer is (A).** Because Carter is addressing the public, he makes suggestions that people can easily do and tries to encourage conservation. He speaks directly and plainly to the people in an effort to get them on board. The fact that he is on television, choice (B), was irrelevant. The speech is not authoritarian, choice (C)—it is the opposite: an effort to enlist the citizenry in solving a national problem. Because he recognized the depth of the problem and needs to persuade the citizenry about participating, his tone is not merely informational, so choice (D) is incorrect.

19. **The correct answer is (C).** Carter's reference to the land of America as "beautiful" indicates how he respects the land and wants to make sure it is not destroyed. The other choices are examples of ways to fix the problem, and they show Carter's resolve in accomplishing the task, but they do not specifically show the respect of and awe at the beauty of the land.

20. **The correct answer is (D).** Choice (D) suggests that Carter doesn't trust oil and gas companies because he is questioning their honesty. Some might interpret that as anti-business, whether or not he meant it that way. None of the other choices specifically and directly references companies and/or business.

21. **The correct answer is (A).** In the context of this sentence, *depleted* means "consumed or used up." Carter is speaking about the overall supplies, not individual waste. The supplies were used during the cold winter months. The energy sources were not weakened, choice (C), or wasted, choice (D). They might be replaced by renewables, but he is not discussing those sources in this part of the speech, so choice (B) is incorrect.

22. **The correct answer is (C).** In both of these sentences, the word *reserves* refers to something that is saved for future use. In the first use ("We will also stress development of our rich coal reserves in an environmentally sound way…"), the reserves are lands that contain coal that has not yet been mined; they are reserved for future use. In the second use ("Oil and natural gas companies must be honest with all of us about their reserves and profits."), the reserves are oil and gas supplies that are set aside in order to raise prices.

23. **The correct answer is (B).** The attention to detail is designed to show how ridiculous Golightly looked. Contrasted with his vanity, the picture Kipling paints is mocking. The adjectives, for example, "clammy pulp" (line 60) and "evil-smelling dough" (line 62) go beyond a simple description of someone caught in the rain. There is no

irony shown nor disgust, so choices (A) and (C) are incorrect. The descriptions show the character to be helpless in the face of a normal event—a rainstorm.

24. **The correct answer is (A).** In the passage, Kipling states that Golightly's focus on his appearance led to him not taking enough money with him. This results in him negotiating with the Station-Master for a first-class ticket and subsequent arrest. His pride, lack of an umbrella, and fall from his horse may have been contributing factors to his arrest, but none is the best answer: It was not pride alone that led to the arrest; even with an umbrella, Golightly would still have had no money for a ticket; and Golightly was not responsible for the fall, as it was an accident.

25. **The correct answer is (A).** Golightly is described as an officer. We are told he was taking a leave of his post, which would indicate a military post. There is no indication that he was an elected official or that he worked in a company.

26. **The correct answer is (C).** Kipling piles on the missteps Golightly makes, each one adding to the other, making Golightly look silly and inept. For a person whose title is "officer," Golightly does not show professionalism or skill at handling a relatively minor problem. The rainstorm, choice (B), is a backdrop for the setting in which he falters and is not in itself a way to make fun of the character. There is no satire shown, so choice (A) is incorrect. Golightly's trouble with the horse, choice (D), went beyond "difficulty."

27. **The correct answer is (A).** It is the detail of the descriptions that give the story its mocking tone and attitude. Kipling sets up the character by describing his intense vanity, which contrasts with the way he looks when caught in the rainstorm. The details are not relevant to any of the other choices.

28. **The correct answer is (B).** Throughout the excerpt, Kipling uses an omniscient narrator to tell the story. But in this line, the narrator editorializes and injects his own opinion. Instead of describing the character's response, the narrator judges it and then continues to describe Golightly's behavior. The narrator does not report the character's verbal response or add dialogue.

29. **The correct answer is (D).** Choice (D) shows a tongue-in-cheek response by the narrator and is mocking in its tone: "When he took out his handkerchief to wipe his face and the green of the hat-lining and the purple stuff that had soaked through on to his neck from the tie became thoroughly mixed, the effect was amazing." The other choices are all descriptions of the environment and Golightly's responses to events as they unfold.

30. **The correct answer is (B).** Among the details that illustrate that Golightly was a man of privilege is that he had servants who were meeting him so he could change his clothes. Golightly's attire was a result of his vanity, not his wealth (choice A). The title Sahib indicates respect, not wealth, so choice (D) is incorrect.

31. **The correct answer is (B).** This sentence from the passage is an idiomatic way of saying that Golightly was pushing the envelope to the greatest extent possible without ruffling feathers in the line of command. His capture by the authorities was a result of misidentification because he was so unrecognizable from being out in the rainstorm and falling off the horse. He was doing what was expected, so there was nothing to get caught doing, choice (D), except that he looked suspicious to others in his disheveled state. Choice (A) is contrary to the meaning of the text; he had told his superiors. The sentence is about how much leave he could take, not about leaving without permission.

32. **The correct answer is (B).** The word *mired* means to become covered with dirt or muck. In the sentence, the word *mud* is a clue that the word is not just related to the road condition, but to the effect of the conditions. Although the sentence describes the pony, choice (A), *pony* does not help establish the meaning of mired.

33. **The correct answer is (C).** The content of the speech shows Stanton's concern about how women were treated unfairly, with few rights. Although some people at the time may have been shocked by her speech, her purpose was not shock value, choice (B), but to inform and persuade. Although she was sympathetic to the plight of minorities/African Americans, this speech was focused on women's issues, so choice (D) is incorrect.

34. **The correct answer is (B).** Stanton repeats the phrase "He has" to list each of the transgressions of men against women's rights. The repetition emphasizes and magnifies these transgressions and makes the point that they can't be ignored. Stanton did feel strongly, choice (A), but the use of repetition does not indicate strength of feeling, it shows strength of her argument. Although Stanton did use the Declaration of Independence as a model, choice (D), the repetition is not part of that model.

35. **The correct answer is (A).** The graphic is a cover from an old newspaper that was published by a women's group. The drawing shows a policeman holding back the women from voting while he points to the ballot box for the inmates, who are shown by their stereotypical striped prison clothes. The message is clear: criminals can vote but woman can't, which is the sentiment reflected in choice (A): "He has withheld from her rights which are given to the most ignorant and degraded men—both natives and foreigners."

36. **The correct answer is (D).** In lines 30–35, Stanton shows how women have been enslaved by the legal system and by men, who are considered superior. Some women did have jobs outside the home, as is implied by lines 24–25, choice (A), but Stanton explains that they were not allowed to keep their wages. Women were not allowed to vote, and Stanton includes this in her list of grievances, but voting rights is not directly related to obedience. Choice (C) is implied by lines 38–41, but this issue is not directly related to obedience.

37. **The correct answer is (D).** "Franchise" is another word for the right to vote. By pairing the word with *elective,* the focus is on the right to vote in elections. Stanton emphasizes how women are deprived of this basic right. A more modern meaning of franchise is in sports, indicating a team that is a member of a larger group or league. At the time of the speech, there were no such sports leagues, and the word was commonly used to refer to the right to vote.

38. **The correct answer is (C).** The commonality is in the necessity for obedience. For women, obedience to their husbands was the rule of law; for slaves, it was a given that they had to obey their masters. In some cases, women did get paid for their work, choice (A), and women, whether or not they were slaves, were generally in charge of children, whether their own or others', choice (B). While some men may break promises, only the Sojourner text discusses how her master continually broke his promises to her.

39. **The correct answer is (D).** Stanton's list of grievances shows her frustration and resulting anger at the system that has denied women basic rights. Truth's narrative is second-hand, but it expresses her feelings of frustration at being promised her freedom only to have it denied. Truth doesn't show anger, choice (A); sadness, choice (B); or bitterness, choice (C); she shows resolve and determination to get her freedom.

40. **The correct answer is (D).** In the lines *"… at best, the slave is accused of not having performed his part or condition of the contract."* Truth explains that the master's ploy is always to say that there is some piece of work that has not been completed, which he claims voids their contract. Choice (A) describes what Truth thinks has become an obstacle for her leaving—not a reason given by her master. Choice (C) shows Truth exclaiming that slaveholders in general don't keep their promises, but it does not show why her master denied her freedom as he had promised. Although financial concerns may have played a role in why her master didn't want to let her go, this was not what Truth was told was the reason, so choice (B) is incorrect.

41. **The correct answer is (C).** Lines 60–62 tells us that he was willing to give her freedom before he had to and the introduction tells us that she was granted her freedom in 1827, before it was legally mandated. Forcing her to work longer than he had originally said was a form of mistreatment. He did not allow her to learn to read and write, which was why her narrative is told through someone else's voice, choice (B). Although he did make promises that he didn't keep, choice (D), Truth suggests that all slaveholders used this tactic to get more work out of their slaves.

42. **The correct answer is (B).** Although Truth had great religious faith, the faithfulness referred to here is not about religion, choices (A) and (C); it is about loyalty. Truth reminisces here about her service to her master. He had asked that she be a faithful servant (line xx), which she was, but then she recognizes that, ironically, this is exactly why she has become so valuable to her master.

43. **The correct answer is (D).** The overall main idea encompasses the discovery and its meaning (a new species). Choices (A) and (B) are details that support the main idea. Choice (C) is a general statement that could be a conclusion, but it is not the main idea.

44. **The correct answer is (C).** The article describes how the discovery was made by a student and other researchers. The discovery was important because it identified a new species and will help scientists and researchers continue to add to our body of knowledge about prehistoric mammals. The discovery wasn't totally by chance because Jasinski was conducting related research, choice (D). Choices (A) and (B) are general statements that could have general application, but they are not conclusions based on facts in the article.

45. **The correct answer is (A).** A predator kills and eats other animals. To find its prey, a strong sense of smell could be a useful in the hunt. Such a trait would probably not help detect danger. The text does not discuss eyesight or finding a mate.

46. **The correct answer is (D).** The genus name *Saurornitholestes* means "lizard bird thief," which indicates its appearance. None of the Latin names indicate either where the fossils were found, choice (B), or where the dinosaurs lived, choice (C). The discovered species was named after a human, as are others on occasion, but the name does not reveal anything about the dinosaur.

47. **The correct answer is (B).** The story explains the process of Jasinski's discovery, and he noticed that the species he was examining differed from the description of what was expected. In the comparison, he realized that the fossil he had was actually a different species. He didn't recognize this because of either the size of the fossil, choice (A), or its markings, choice (D). Scientists did not know what its closest relatives were because they had not yet realized that it was a different species, so choice (C) is incorrect.

48. **The correct answer is (D).** Looking at the drawing, the traits shown on the *S. sullivani* are as described in the text. The drawing is made to reflect what scientists think this dinosaur looked like based on the fossil evidence and research. Choices (A) and (C) are facts in the text that are unrelated to the drawing. Choice (B) describes its size, but the drawing displays only relative size.

49. **The correct answer is (B).** Part of the scientific process is to test theories by comparing evidence. Jasinski was comparing the fossils, which led to his discovery. The other choices indicate some of the data scientists had, but they do not illustrate the scientific process.

50. **The correct answer is (B).** The information in the article was in the news because Jasinski's discovery identified a new species of dinosaur, adding to our scientific knowledge of evolution and paleontology. Choice (D) is incorrect because the discovery itself was not related to determining where the species lived—that was determined after identifying the species. The mention of the film *Jurassic Park* helps readers envision the new species, but the relationship of the discovery to the film is not the news, so choice (A) is incorrect. Choice (C) is incorrect because the naming of the species is a detail that, in itself, is not newsworthy.

51. **The correct answer is (C).** "Formidable" means impressive. It can mean impressive in the sense of its size or power, and in this context the predator—the newly discovered species—was one that would have been threatening to other species. A predator might have been dreaded, but not dreadful, so choice (A) is incorrect.

52. **The correct answer is (B).** The two sentences together connect the meaning by indicating that the olfactory bulb is related to the sense of smell. The organs that are used for smell are contained in that part of the skull, which was unusually large, but the clue is in the next sentence that defines "olfactory."

Section 2: Writing and Language Test

1. D	11. B	21. C	31. C	41. D
2. B	12. A	22. A	32. B	42. B
3. B	13. B	23. B	33. B	43. C
4. D	14. A	24. C	34. A	44. D
5. C	15. B	25. B	35. D	
6. A	16. C	26. A	36. B	
7. C	17. D	27. A	37. B	
8. C	18. A	28. C	38. B	
9. D	19. A	29. C	39. D	
10. C	20. D	30. D	40. A	

WRITING AND LANGUAGE TEST RAW SCORE
(Number of correct answers)

1. **The correct answer is (D).** The underlined sentence should be deleted because other phrases from the 1980s are not related to the Glass Ceiling. Choices (A) and (B) are incorrect because the sentence should not be kept. It does not support the main topic nor does it act as a transition. Choice (C) is incorrect because it is not information that has already been shared.

2. **The correct answer is (B).** The proper end punctuation for this sentence is a period. Any other punctuation will be grammatically incorrect or inappropriately change the tone or intent of the sentence. Thus, choice (B) is the correct answer. Choice (A) is incorrect because ending the sentence with an exclamation point injects emotion that is missing from the rest of the passage. It is like shouting at the reader. Choice (C) is incorrect because this sentence is not a question. Choice (D) is incorrect because ending the sentence with ellipses suggests the thought isn't finished, which is not the case.

3. **The correct answer is (B).** As written, the text has a syntax error. The intention of the writer is to say that the number of women in CEO positions in Fortune 500 companies is just 5% of the total. To convey this, the modifier *only* has to be placed correctly in the sentence—before 5%. Choice (B) does this, so that's the correct answer. Choices (A) and (C) are incorrect because they say women hold 5% of CEO positions (but may or may not hold that percentage of any other positions), and they take the emphasis off the low figure of 5% and place it on CEO positions; this is not what the writer means to say. Choice (D) is incorrect because it says women hold 5% of CEO positions in Fortune 500 companies (but may or may not hold that percentage in other kinds of companies), and it takes the emphasis off the low figure of 5% and places it on Fortune 500 companies; this is not what the writer means to say.

4. The correct answer is (D). This sentence requires a word that means "having existed or taken place in a period before the present," which is what *past* means. Therefore, choice (D) is the correct answer. Choice (A) is incorrect because *passed* is the past tense of *pass*. (*Past* and *passed* are commonly confused words.) Choice (B) is incorrect because *passing* doesn't have the right meaning for this sentence. While it refers to time going by, it changes the sense of the sentence by referring to passing years rather than events that have taken place. Choice (C) is incorrect because the word *passive* doesn't make sense in this sentence.

5. The correct answer is (C). The only internal punctuation this sentence requires is a comma after the introductory phrase "In 1995," making choice (C) the correct answer. Choice (A) is incorrect because it includes a semicolon after *formed*, which makes the rest of the sentence a fragment. Choice (B) is incorrect because while it removes the incorrect semicolon, it introduces a new error by including a second comma after *Commission*. Choice (D) is not correct because, while it removes the incorrect semicolon, it introduces a new error by placing a semicolon after *discrimination,* which creates a sentence fragment.

6. The correct answer is (A). This sentence requires a word that means "result," or "something caused by something else," which is the meaning of *effect*—a noun that means "the result of something." Therefore, choice (A) is the correct answer. Choice (B) is incorrect because *affect* is the wrong word for this sentence. It is a verb that means "to bring about a result." (*Effect* and *affect* are commonly confused words. One way to know the difference between them is to remember that after you *affect* something, there is an *effect*.) Choice (C) is incorrect because the word *effective* doesn't make sense in this sentence. Choice (D) is incorrect because the word *affection* doesn't make sense in this sentence.

7. The correct answer is (C). Choice (C)—"they have not worked to eliminate these supply barriers."—supports the claim that corporations do not think the supply barriers are a business issue. Choice (A) is incorrect because it repeats the claim rather than supporting it. Choice (B) is incorrect because it is contrary to the claim. Choice (D) is incorrect because it offers an additional claim, and it does not support the one in the sentence.

8. The correct answer is (C). The writer's main argument regarding supply barriers is "Corporations could overcome this barrier to women's advancement if they wanted to." Choice (C) gives specific reasons why the writer believes this. Therefore, choice (C) is the correct answer. Choice (A) explains what supply barriers are; it does not support the writer's claim. Choice (B) gives a reason why corporations have not acted to address this issue; it does not support the writer's claim. Choice (D) might seem like a correct answer, but it simply provides additional information after the writer has supported the argument with the statement in choice (C). Therefore, choice (C) is a better answer than choice (D).

9. The correct answer is (D). The original punctuation creates a sentence fragment. Combining the text eliminates the fragment, so choice (D) is the correct answer. Choice (A) is incorrect because the period after *do* creates a sentence fragment. Choice (B) is incorrect because while it eliminates the incorrect period, it introduces a new error by replacing the period with a semicolon to separate the two dependent clauses. Choice (C) is not correct because, although it removes the incorrect period, it introduces a new error by including the conjunction *and*. With this addition, the sentence no longer makes sense.

10. The correct answer is (C). As written, this sentence contains a redundancy—*involved* and *complicated* mean the same thing, so only one of these words is necessary. Choice (C) eliminates this redundancy, so it is correct. Choice (A) is incorrect because *involved* and *complicated* mean the same thing, making the phrasing redundant. Choice (B) is incorrect because, while it eliminates the redundancy, it changes the meaning of the sentence. The intent of the sentence is not to say that ending discrimination against women in the work force is a process—its intent is to say that this is a *complicated* process. Choice (D) is incorrect because although it eliminates the original redundancy, it adds a new one: *discrimination* and *bias* mean the same thing.

11. **The correct answer is (B).** The writer is saying that women must be accepted "as equals" in the corporate sphere. Only choice (B) places this modifier after *accepted*, the correct position in the sentence. Therefore, choice (B) is the correct answer. Choice (A) is incorrect because the modifying phrase "as equals" is not placed in the right part of the sentence, creating a syntax error. Choice (C) is incorrect because while it repositions the modifying phrase, it introduces a new error by using the adverb form of *equal*. Choice (D) is incorrect because, while it repositions the modifying phrase (which could be correct in this part of the sentence), it, too, uses the adverb form of *equal*.

12. **The correct answer is (A).** The sentenced as is introduces details that describe the entire collection. Choice (B) adds information not supported by the passage. Choice (C) implies the examples are not inclusive. Choice (D) is incorrect because "Already" has no meaning in the context of the sentence.

13. **The correct answer is (B).** Semicolons are needed when items in a series already contain commas. Choice (B) correctly shows the proper separation of items in a series with semicolons and commas. Choice (A) incorrectly places commas after *extend* and *executive*. Choice (C) incorrectly places a comma after *branches* and incorrectly eliminates the comma after *world*. Choice (D) incorrectly places a comma after *services* and incorrectly eliminates the comma after *government*.

14. **The correct answer is (A).** The author is introducing a new topic (going from an overview of the modern Library of Congress to its beginnings), and pointing out the Library did not start out as big as it is today. The sentence in the original text is the best transition phrase for cohesion, so choice (A) is the correct answer. Choice (B) might sound correct, but it changes the tone of the passage from formal to informal, so it is not the best answer. Choice (C) is incorrect because it changes the sense and meaning of the text and creates a sentence that does not support the main idea of the

paragraph. Choice (D) might appear to be correct, but like choice (B), it changes the tone of the passage from formal to informal, so it is not the best answer.

15. **The correct answer is (B).** After the original Library of Congress was destroyed, the nation needed a new, similar institution. In other words, the library had to be replaced. Therefore, choice (B) is the correct answer. Choice (A) is incorrect because while it suggests a new library, it also suggests the continued presence of the original library, which was not the case. Choice (B) is the better answer because it is a more precise word in this context. Choice (C) also indicates a new library, but like choice (A), it suggests the continued presence of the original library. Choice (D) is not correct because the new library was a replacement as opposed to a copy of the old library.

16. **The correct answer is (C).** "Its" is a possessive determiner and does not require an apostrophe. Thus, choice (C) is the correct answer. Choice (A) is incorrect because *it's* is a contraction of "it is." Choice (B) is incorrect because it makes no sense. Choice (D) is incorrect because *its'* is not a word.

17. **The correct answer is (D).** This text requires seven commas, and only choice (D) has all the necessary commas in the right places. Choice (A) incorrectly places commas after *two* and *dramatic*. Choice (B) incorrectly leaves out a comma after *composition* and incorrectly places a comma after *photograph*. Choice (C) incorrectly places a comma after *two* and a semicolon after *composition*.

18. **The correct answer is (A).** The library's collection keeps growing—it is ever-expanding. Thus, choice (A) is the correct answer. Choice (B) is incorrect because it changes the meaning of the sentence to say that the library's collection always exists. This is not what the author means. Choice (C) is incorrect because it changes the meaning of the sentence to say that the library's collection is always paying out, which makes no sense. Choice (D) is incorrect because it changes the meaning of the sentence to say that the library's collection is always explaining, which makes no sense.

answers PRACTICE TEST 5

19. **The correct answer is (A).** Choice (A) best expresses the idea that Young instigated the change. Choice (B) is incorrect because it implies that there was opposition to the change. Choice (C) implies that it had to be an acquisitions library first before making the change. Choice (D) is incorrect because the introductory phrase implies that there was an addition to the operation rather than a replacement of one system for another.

20. **The correct answer is (D).** In this paragraph the author is shifting from John Russell Young to Herbert Putnam. Choice D adds the phrase "after only two years," a detail with additional information that gives the reader a fuller sense of this story and creates a smoother transition. Therefore, choice (D) is the correct answer. Choices (A), (B), and (C) make the shift from Russell to Putnam, but none of them have the additional information or make as smooth a transition as choice (D), so none of them is the best answer.

21. **The correct answer is (C).** This paragraph is mainly about Herbert Putnam, and Putnam (in the previous sentence) is the antecedent of the pronoun that starts this sentence. Putnam is one person, so the singular pronoun *he* is required. Therefore, choice (C) is the correct answer. Choice (A) is incorrect because if *they* is used, the meaning of the sentence changes—it means Spofford, Young, and Putnam "took the Library of Congress directly into the national library scene." Choice (B) is incorrect because *them* is the objective case, and this sentence requires a pronoun in the subjective case. Choice (D) is incorrect because the antecedent of the pronoun that starts this sentence is Putnam, so a singular pronoun is required.

22. **The correct answer is (A).** The last column of the chart shows information for the largest libraries (the category for the Library of Congress). According to the chart, there are 109 of these in the private sector, as opposed to 51 in the private sector. So there are more public than private libraries similar in scope and scale to the Library of Congress, making choice (A) correct. Choices (B), (C), and (D) are incorrect because the chart does not support these conclusions.

23. **The correct answer is (B).** As written, this sentence contains a redundancy—empty and contained nothing mean the same thing. Only choice (B) eliminates this redundancy. Choice (A) is incorrect because empty and contained nothing mean the same thing, making the phrasing redundant. Choice (C) is not the best answer because while it eliminates the redundancy, it changes the sense and intent of the sentence, taking away the weight and urgency of the bedroom being "forever empty." Choice (D) is incorrect because although it eliminates the original redundancy, it adds a new one: verses and poetry are the same thing.

24. **The correct answer is (C).** The paragraph is mainly about Emily's independence and keen intellect. Choice (C) tells readers that she also liked being in nature, which is a facet of her personality unrelated to her intellectual pursuits. This isn't relevant to the main topic of the paragraph, so choice (C) is the correct answer. Choice (A) is relevant because it introduces Lavinia's musings on Emily's "inquisitive mind." Choice (B) is relevant because it refers to Emily's "curious mind" and "voracious appetite for learning." Choice (D) is relevant because it refers to Emily's intellectual independence.

25. **The correct answer is (B).** Emily is the sister in question, so this sentence calls for a singular possessive pronoun. Choice (B) is the possessive pronoun for *sister*, so it is the correct answer. Choice (A) is incorrect because it is the plural of *sister*, not the possessive pronoun for the word. Choice (C) is incorrect because it is a plural possessive pronoun (for *sisters*), not a singular possessive pronoun (for *sister*). Choice (D) is incorrect because it is not a possessive pronoun.

26. **The correct answer is (A).** The paragraph is mainly about Emily's isolation and the reason for it. In Emily's own words, she was "one 'standing alone in rebellion' of faith" as she resisted ideas common to her time. Only choice (A) refers to this, which makes it the correct answer. Choice (B) might seem like a good answer, but Emily's refusal to take part in social events stemmed from her sense of isolation rather than acting as the cause of it. The passage

does not say she became isolated after refusing to participate in social events; it implies her refusal to be social was a decision she made because she felt so isolated. Choices (C) and (D) are incorrect because they are not supported by the passage. The author does not say either of these reasons caused Emily's sense of isolation.

27. **The correct answer is (A).** Choice (A) is the only choice that supplies the correct word "through" for this sentence. Choices (B), (C), and (D) are all incorrect because none of these words makes sense in the sentence.

28. **The correct answer is (C).** The writer should not add the sentence because it detracts from the point about women's issues. The added sentence focuses on the idea of Emily being involved in politics, which is not the point Lavinia is making. Choices (A) and (B) are incorrect because the information is not directly related to the point being made by Lavinia. Choice (D) is incorrect because although the statement is about Emily's life, it is misplaced in the midst of Lavinia's thoughts about how Emily viewed the limitations society imposed on women.

29. **The correct answer is (C).** Because it is clear that it was Emily who avoided "the trappings of being a woman," the required word is the singular subjective pronoun *she*. Thus, choice (C) is the correct answer. Choice (A) is incorrect because *they* is plural. If *they* is used, the sentence appears to be saying that both Emily and Lavinia "tried to eschew" the trappings of being a woman, which is not supported by the passage; in addition, the rest of the sentence will make no sense because *her* is used toward the end of the sentence. Choice (B) is incorrect because there is no antecedent for *we*. Choice (D) is incorrect because the sentence calls for a subjective pronoun; *her* is a possessive or an objective pronoun.

30. **The correct answer is (D).** The passage is written in a formal style and has a literary tone. Instead of saying Emily did not accept the role of women, the author writes she "eschewed" "the trappings of being a woman." Only choice (D) matches this style and tone, so it is the correct answer. Choices (A), (B), and (C) are incorrect because while each

conveys this same thought, the uninspired word choice in each answer does not match the style or tone of the passage. Choice (C) is also unnecessarily wordy.

31. **The correct answer is (C).** The proper end punctuation for this sentence is a period. Most other punctuation will be grammatically incorrect or inappropriately change the tone or intent of the sentence. Thus, choice (C) is the correct answer. Choice (A) is incorrect because this sentence is not a question. Choice (B) is incorrect because ending the sentence with an exclamation point injects emotion that is missing from the rest of the passage and is inappropriate here. Choice (D) is not correct because it is incorrect to end a sentence with a semicolon.

32. **The correct answer is (B).** The paragraph is written in the active voice, which should be maintained throughout. Only choice (B) is written in the active voice, so choice (B) is the correct answer. Choices (A), (C), and (D) are incorrect because they are all written in the passive voice.

33. **The correct answer is (B).** The passage is written in a formal style and has a literary tone ("her internal monologue expressed through thousands of poems;" "it was time the world knew the full treasure her sister was"). Only choice (B) matches this style and tone, so it is the correct answer. Choices (A), (C), and (D) are incorrect because they change the tone to one that is informal and conversational, and they use modern phrases and expressions.

34. **The correct answer is (A).** The point of this opening paragraph is to establish the fact that even though scientists have long known that sleep is important to human health, they continue to study sleep. The "even though" part of this idea is conveyed by the word *yet*, which must be placed in the right part of the sentence if the sentence is to make sense. Only choice (A) does this, making it the correct answer. Choices (B) and (C) are incorrect because they change the meaning of the sentence by eliminating the "even though" element that the writer wants to convey, and they demonstrate clumsy syntax. Choice (D) is incorrect because while it

places *yet* correctly in the sentence, the rest of this answer demonstrates clumsy syntax.

35. **The correct answer is (D).** This paragraph is mainly concerned with past theories about sleep. The fourth paragraph addresses sleep study in the twentieth century. Sentence 6, choice (D), refers to advances in the study of sleep that were made during the twentieth century, so the passage would have a more logical sequence if this sentence were moved to the fourth paragraph. Thus, choice (D) is the correct answer. Choices (A) and (B) are incorrect because the first two sentences serve as transitions to the topic of past theories about sleep and should remain in this paragraph. Choice (C), sentence 4, is incorrect because it describes one of these past theories about sleep. Therefore, it, too, should remain in this paragraph.

36. **The correct answer is (B).** The sentence in choice (B) leads to the introduction of the theories that follow. Choice (A) is incorrect because it is irrelevant to this part of the passage. Choices (C) and (D) are incorrect because the text does not imply either statement.

37. **The correct answer is (B).** This sentence tells the reader that modern sleep research began with a machine. Machines are created, or invented, and only choice (B) conveys this idea. Choices (A), (C), and (D) are incorrect because each conveys a different idea. A machine isn't discovered, choice (A), though a new use for a machine may be discovered. The passage makes it clear that sleep study went beyond the idea, choice (C), or suggestion, choice (D), of a machine; the machine was created (invented) and used.

38. **The correct answer is (B).** The second part of the sentence is a subordinate clause, and a subordinating conjunction is necessary to establish the clause's connection to the beginning of the sentence: The study of sleep was enhanced *as a result of* Aserinsky and Kleitman's work. Choice (B) is the only answer with a subordinating conjunction. Therefore, choice (B) is the correct answer. Choices (A), (C), and (D) are not correct because they are all coordinating conjunctions that, if used, change the meaning of the sentence. Choice (A) makes the

enhancement of sleep study and Aserinsky and Kleitman's work separate and equal things rather than one being the result of the other. Choice (C) creates a sentence that does not make sense. Choice (D) changes the cause and effect: it means that Aserinsky and Kleitman did their work *because* the study of sleep was enhanced.

39. **The correct answer is (D).** The link between the ideas in this sentence and the previous sentence is contradiction. Subjects awakened during REM sleep almost always remembered dreaming; *but* subjects awakened during non-REM sleep could rarely recall dreams. To convey this idea, a contradictory transition word or phrase is required. Only choice (D) provides the right phrase. Choices (A) and (B) are incorrect because while these phrases can indicate contradiction, in this case each creates a sentence that does not make sense. Choice (C) is incorrect because the passage does not say any predictions were made about what would happen during this study.

40. **The correct answer is (A).** The underlined phrase leads directly to the idea presented in the second part of the sentence. Choice (B) is incorrect because this part of the passage is not about EEGs. Choice (C) is incorrect because it contains an erroneous implication. Choice (D) is incorrect because the adverb used implies that there is contradictory text preceding it, which there is not.

41. **The correct answer is (D).** As written, this sentence lacks parallel construction. Choice (D) makes the verbs *spot*, *awaken*, and *collect* parallel in tense and form, so it is the correct answer. Choices (A), (B), and (C) are incorrect because they don't correct the lack of parallel construction, and they are incorrect verb-tense or verb-form changes.

42. **The correct answer is (B).** The intent of this sentence is to talk about changing dreamers' experiences. Only choice (B) is the correct word to communicate this (*alter* means "to change"), so choice (B) is the correct answer. Choice (A) is incorrect because the definition of *altar* is "a usually raised structure or place on which sacrifices are offered or incense is burned in worship." (*Alter* and *altar* are frequently confused words.) Choice (C) is

incorrect because it creates a sentence that means scientists could switch dreamers' various experiences for one another. Choice (D) is incorrect because it creates a sentence that does not make sense. (*Alternate* and *alternative* are frequently confused words.)

43. **The correct answer is (C).** The subject and verb in a sentence must agree in number. The subject of this sentence (*researchers*) is plural, so a plural verb in the right tense is required. Only choice (C) reflects agreement between the subject and verb, as well as appropriate verb tense. Choice (A) is incorrect because the subject of the sentence (*researchers*) is plural, and *has been drawn* is singular. Choice (B) is plural but there is no such verb as *were been drawn*. Choice (D) is incorrect because *was drawn* is singular.

44. **The correct answer is (D).** The original punctuation creates a sentence fragment. Combining the text in a grammatically correct way eliminates the fragment, and only choice (D) does this. Choice (A) is incorrect because the period after *sleep* creates the sentence fragment. Choice (B) is incorrect because while it eliminates the incorrect period after *sleep*, replacing the period with a dash creates a sentence that does not make sense. Choice (C) is not correct because although it removes the incorrect period, it introduces a different error by replacing it with a semicolon. Semicolons are used with complete thoughts. The first part of this sentence is not a complete thought, so choice (C) does not correct the original fragment.

Section 3: Math Test—No Calculator

1. A	**5.** A	**9.** A	**13.** B	**17.** 2/3, or .666, or .667
2. A	**6.** C	**10.** B	**14.** B	**18.** 6
3. B	**7.** D	**11.** B	**15.** B	**19.** 1
4. C	**8.** D	**12.** B	**16.** 50	**20.** 224

MATH TEST—NO CALCULATOR TEST RAW SCORE
(Number of correct answers)

1. **The correct answer is (A).** Substitute the value for m and solve for x:

$$\frac{x+2}{5} = m$$
$$\frac{x+2}{5} = -3$$
$$x + 2 = -15$$
$$x = -17$$

2. **The correct answer is (A).** If h is any positive quantity, then letting $d_h = (m+h) - \frac{50}{m+h}$, we can see that d_h is greater than d, since h is greater than zero, and $\frac{50}{m}$ is greater than $\frac{50}{m+h}$. Therefore, d increases as m does.

3. **The correct answer is (B).** The volume of a cube is $V = s^3$. A side of this cube is $\sqrt[3]{64}$ in. Since there are 12 edges to a cube, the amount of wire needed is 12×4 in., or 48 inches.

4. **The correct answer is (C).** The total number of cookies is equal to the sum of the cookies that Myra baked plus the cookies Neil baked. Myra baked 6 sheets of r cookies, or $6r$ cookies, and Neil baked 7 sheets of p cookies, or $7p$ cookies. The total number of cookies must be $6r + 7p$.

5. **The correct answer is (A).**

$$2y = \frac{1}{3}$$
$$6y = 1$$
$$y = \frac{1}{6}$$
$$\frac{1}{4y} = \frac{1}{4\left(\frac{1}{6}\right)} = \frac{1}{\frac{2}{3}} = \frac{3}{2}$$

6. **The correct answer is (C).**

$$y = \frac{(x-3)^3}{4}$$
$$4y = (x-3)^3$$
$$\sqrt[3]{4y} = x - 3$$
$$\sqrt[3]{4y} + 3 = x$$

7. **The correct answer is (D).** The plant grows 4.5 centimeters a week, and that is represented by the $4.5w$ in the equation. Since the 6 is a constant in the equation, this represents the initial height of the plant. Therefore, the plant must have been 6 centimeters tall when Hannah bought it.

8. **The correct answer is (D).**
$$x^6 + (2x^2)^3 + (3x^3)^2 = x^6 + 8x^6 + 9x^6 = 18x^6$$

9. **The correct answer is (A).** The graph shows that the y-intercept is approximately at the point $(0, 55)$. The equation that shows a y-intercept of 55 is in choice (A). To further verify, substitute points in for the number of days to find the corresponding number of trout. For example, substitute 10 in for x: $y = 12(10) + 55 = 120 + 55 = 175$. The point $(10,175)$ is on the graph.

10. **The correct answer is (B).**
$$\left(-\frac{27}{8}\right)^{-\frac{1}{3}} = \left(-\frac{8}{27}\right)^{\frac{1}{3}} = -\frac{2}{3}x$$

11. **The correct answer is (B).** If the area is $49x^2$, the side of the square is $7x$. Therefore, the diagonal of the square must be the hypotenuse of a right isosceles triangle of leg $7x$. Hence the diagonal $= 7x\sqrt{2}$.

12. **The correct answer is (B).** The slope of the graph of a function is its vertical variable divided by its horizontal variable. In this case, the slope is feet divided by seconds, so the answer must be choice (B).

13. **The correct answer is (B).** Solve the system of equations by solving for one of the variables in the first equation, and then substituting that expression into the second equation:
$$D = 24 - B$$
$$4(24 - B) + 2B = 84$$
$$96 - 4B + 2B = 84$$
$$96 - 2B = 84$$
$$-2B = -12$$
$$B = 6$$

Then, substitute $B = 6$ into the other equation, and solve for D:
$$D + 6 = 24$$
$$D = 18$$

Therefore, the number of dogs in the pet store is 18, and the number of birds in the pet store is 6.

14. **The correct answer is (B).** Both choices (B) and (D) are equivalent to the original function. This can be shown by multiplying the binomial factors and simplifying the product. The form of the equation in choice (D) gives coordinates of the vertex as its coefficients, and choice (B) is in intercept form, where 7 and –3 are the x-intercepts of the function.

15. **The correct answer is (B).** The slope of a line perpendicular to another line will be the negative reciprocal of the slope of the first line. So the slope of the new line must be $-\frac{1}{3}$. The only equations with that slope are choices (B) and (C). Check which equation is correct by substituting the given point. Using choice (B), you will see that it is correct:
$$y = -\frac{1}{3}x + \frac{10}{3}$$
$$3 = -\frac{1}{3}(1) + \frac{10}{3}$$
$$3 = \frac{9}{3}$$

16. The correct answer is 50.

$$120 = 70 + x$$
$$x = 50$$

17. The correct answer is 2/3 or .666 or .667.
If $(x + 3)^2$ is a factor of the function, then $(x + 3)^2 = 0$, $x + 3 = 0$, and $x = -3$, but that cannot be gridded. If $(3x - 2)$ is a factor of the function, then $3x - 2 = 0$, $3x = 2$, and $x = \dfrac{2}{3}$ or .666 or .667.

18. The correct answer is 6. The equation will have no solutions when the coefficient for x is the same on both sides of the equation, but the constant terms are different. So simplify the equations so that the variable terms are the same, and see if the constant are different:

$$5(4 - 8x) = d(5 - 6x) - 4x$$
$$20 - 40x = 5d - 6dx - 4x$$
$$-40x + 20 = (-6dx - 4x) + 5d$$

For $(-6dx - 4x)$ to equal $-40x$, $-6dx$ must be equal to $-36x$, so d must be equal to 6. This leads to $-40x + 20 = -40x + 30$.

19. The correct answer is 1.

$$\sqrt{4 - x^2} = \sqrt{3x}$$
$$4 - x^2 = 3x$$
$$0 = x^2 + 3x - 4$$
$$0 = (x + 4)(x - 1)$$
$$x = -4, x = 1$$

Only 1 works because although

$$\sqrt{4 - (-4)^2} = \sqrt{3(-4)}$$
$$\sqrt{-12} = \sqrt{-12}$$, negative numbers cannot be gridded.

20. The correct answer is 224. The system will have an infinite number of solutions when the two equations are equivalent, so multiply each term in the first equation by -4 to find the values for a and b, then find their product:

$$-4(2x + 3y) = -4(7)$$
$$-8x - 12y = -28$$

For the two equations to be equivalent, a must be -8 and b must be -28.

$$-8x - 12y = -28$$
$$ax - 12y = b$$
$$a = -8$$
$$b = -28$$
$$ab = -8(-28) = 224$$

Section 4: Math Test—Calculator

1. B	**9.** C	**17.** D	**25.** D	**33.** 50
2. D	**10.** D	**18.** C	**26.** D	**34.** 69.7
3. D	**11.** C	**19.** A	**27.** B	**35.** .60
4. C	**12.** A	**20.** B	**28.** C	**36.** 1/4 or .25
5. D	**13.** D	**21.** A	**29.** C	
6. A	**14.** B	**22.** A	**30.** D	**37.** 8
7. C	**15.** C	**23.** D	**31.** 55.1	**38.** 11
8. C	**16.** C	**24.** A	**32.** 7.2 or 36/5	

MATH TEST—CALCULATOR RAW SCORE [   ]
(Number of correct answers)

1. **The correct answer is (B).** If $9x + 5 = 23$, $9x = 18$, and $x = 2$. Thus, $18x + 5 = 36 + 5 = 41$.

2. **The correct answer is (D).** There can be at most 15 radiators, so $x + y \leq 15$. Each small radiator weighs 150 pounds, represented by $150x$. Each large radiator weighs 250 pounds, represented by $250y$. The maximum load can be equal to but not exceed 1,500 pounds: $150x + 250y \leq 1500$.

3. **The correct answer is (D).** Each adult needs 15 cans/7 adults $= \dfrac{15}{7}$ cans in two days, or $\left(\dfrac{1}{2}\right)\left(\dfrac{15}{7}\right) = \dfrac{15}{14}$ cans per adult per day. Multiply this by the number of adults and by the number of days: $\dfrac{15}{14}$ (4 adults)(7 days) = 30 cans of food .

4. **The correct answer is (C).** Fiona's non-taxed amount is 75% of what she earns each hour, or $0.75x$. This can be multiplied by the hourly rate, which in this case is $28, leading to the expression $28(0.75x)$.

5. **The correct answer is (D).** The data is increasing and stays relatively close to a line of best fit that would pass through the center of the points. This means that the company has strong positive sales numbers.

6. **The correct answer is (A).** Using a line that passes through (2, 1.9) and (6, 3.5), the slope is

$$\frac{3.5 - 1.9}{6 - 2} = \frac{1.6}{4} = 0.4$$

The line passes through (0, 1), making the equation $y = 0.4x + 1$.

7. **The correct answer is (C).** Let $x =$ original price. Then: $0.60x = \$4.20$

or $6x = \$42.00$

$x = \$7.00$

8. **The correct answer is (C).** The number 329 represents the slope of the graph of the equation, which is the rate of increase in attendance.

9. **The correct answer is (C).** Consider what each term represents:

   $20x$ means $20 earned for each t-shirt.

   $12.5x$ means $12.50 earned for each t-shirt.

   The correct answer equals the sum of $20x$ and $12.5y$. Only answer choice (C) includes the correct terms and expression.

10. **The correct answer is (D).** The number of books that the library adds is $375x$, or 375 times the number of years. The total number of books must be the sum of $375x$ and 25,825 (the number they already have), not to exceed 35,000.

11. **The correct answer is (C).**
$$(6 - 5i)(3 + 2i) = 6(3) + 6(2i) + (-5i)(3) + (-5i)(2i)$$
$$= 18 + 12i - 15i - 10i^2$$
$$= 18 - 3i - 10(-1)$$
$$= (18 + 10) - 3i$$
$$= 28 - 3i$$

12. **The correct answer is (A).** Choice (C) is incorrect because we cannot say with certainty that a medication will help all people who need it. Choice (D) doesn't make sense; the medication cannot help people who don't take it. Choice (B) is incorrect because we only compared Z against one other medication, Y. The inference can be applied only to the given medications and populations.

13. **The correct answer is (D).** Write equations to represent the situation. Let x be the number of bicycles rented and y be the number of pairs of rollerblades rented. Then solve the system using elimination:

   $$x + y = 27$$
   $$7x + 5y = 171$$

   Multiply $x + y = 27$ by -5 to solve by elimination:

   $$-5x - 5y = -135$$
   $$7x + 5y = 171$$
   $$2x = 36$$
   $$x = 18$$

14. **The correct answer is (B).**

   $$A = \frac{x}{360}\pi r^2$$
   $$= \frac{60}{360}\pi(60)^2$$
   $$= \frac{1}{6}(3600)\pi$$
   $$= 600\pi$$

15. **The correct answer is (C).** Solve the system by substitution:

   $$y = 2x - 5$$
   $$y = (x - 2)^2 - 9$$
   $$2x - 5 = (x - 2)^2 - 9$$
   $$2x - 5 = x^2 - 4x + 4 - 9$$
   $$0 = x^2 - 6x$$
   $$0 = x(x - 6)$$
   $$0 = x, 6 = x$$

   Then substitute x-values into both equations to check for the y-values:

   $$-5 = 2(0) - 5$$
   $$-5 = (0 - 2)^2 - 9$$
   $$-5 = -5$$
   $$2(6) - 5 = (6 - 2)^2 - 9$$
   $$7 = 7$$

16. The correct answer is (C). The graph shows points connected by a curve with an increasing positive slope that approximates an exponential graph, so this is exponential growth.

17. The correct answer **is (D).** The graph shows an exponential growth curve, and the population of California in 1980 is approximately 24 million. Therefore, choices (A) and (B) can be eliminated, because based on the exponential growth, the population in 1990 would be more than the population in 1980. And because it is exponential growth, 30 million would be the best prediction.

18. The correct answer is (C). Let the original sign be 10 by 10.

```
        10
  ┌──────────────┐     7
10│ Area = 100   │  9┌────────┐
  │              │   │Area=63 │
  └──────────────┘   └────────┘
```

Then, the new sign is 9 by 7.

$$\frac{63}{100} = 63\%$$

19. The correct answer is (A). Three meals a day times 365 days per year means there are $3 \times 365 = 1095$ meals in one year. Over 19 years, there are $1095 \times 19 = 20,805$ meals. Therefore, the number of restaurants in New York City exceeds 20,500.

20. The correct answer is (B). One cubic foot equals 12^3, or 1,728 cubic inches. One cubic foot of gold weighs $1728 \times 0.70 = 1210$ pounds.

21. The correct answer is (A). Subtract by writing using a common denominator, and then simplify:

$$\frac{3x-1}{2x+3} - \frac{2x+3}{3x-1} = \frac{(3x-1)(3x-1)}{(2x+3)(3x-1)} - \frac{(2x+3)(2x+3)}{(3x-1)(2x+3)}$$
$$= \frac{(3x-1)^2 - (2x+3)^2}{(2x+3)(3x-1)}$$
$$= \frac{5x^2 - 18x - 8}{6x^2 + 7x - 3}$$

22. The correct answer is (A). The graph is a hyperbola which is of the general form $y = \frac{a}{x-b} + c$. There are asymptotes at $x = -3$ and $y = -1$, $b = -3$ and $c = -1$. To determine whether choice (A) or (C) is the correct equation, locate points on the graph and check against both equations. (0, 1) is a point on the graph.

$$y = \frac{6}{x+3} - 1 \qquad y = \frac{1}{x+3} - 1$$
$$1 = \frac{6}{0+3} - 1 \qquad 1 = \frac{1}{0+3} - 1$$
$$1 = 2 - 1 \qquad 1 \neq -\frac{2}{3}$$

Only answer choice (A) works.

23. The correct answer is (D).
$$g(f(x)) = g(f(4))$$
$$= g\left(\frac{3}{4-1}\right)$$
$$= g(1)$$
$$= (1-4)^2$$
$$= 9$$

24. The correct answer is (A). To write an exponential equation for this situation, you need to find the population in 1980:

$$38,500 = P(1+0.038)^{20}$$

$$\frac{38,500}{(1.038)^{20}} = P$$

$$18,260 \approx P$$

So, the correct answer is choice (A).

25. The correct answer is (D). In order to determine when $f(x) = 0$, solve the equation $x^2 - 2x - 8 = 0$.

$x^2 - 2x - 8 = 0$ Factor the left-hand side.

$(x-4)(x+2) = 0$ Set each factor equal to 0.

$x - 4 = 0,\ x + 2 = 0$ Solve each equation.

$$x = 4, -2$$

26. The correct answer is (D). The sample size leads to the margin of error that is given with the data. As long as the margin of error is considered when making conclusions, those conclusions are reasonable.

27. The correct answer is (B). The 95% confidence that the margin of error is ± 3.4% is important, and choices (A) and (C) ignore the confidence interval. Choice (D) is not correct, because this interval is centered around 49%, instead of 51%, which is the number of people who support a different candidate or no candidate at this time. Only choice (B) accurately uses the confidence interval and the data given in the problem.

28. The correct answer is (C). If the average for the eight tests is 84%, then the sum of the eight tests must be 8 times 84, or 672. For the six tests, the sum must be 6 times 86, or 516. The two dropped tests must have accounted for 156 points. 156 divided by 2 is 78.

29. The correct answer is (C). Complete the square to write the equation in standard form for a circle:

$$x^2 + y^2 - 8x + 12y = 144$$

$$x^2 - 8x + y^2 + 12y = 144$$

$$\left(x^2 - 8x + 16\right) + \left(y^2 + 12y + 36\right) = 144 + 16 + 36$$

$$\left(x-4\right)^2 + \left(y+6\right)^2 = 196$$

Since 196 is 14^2, the radius is 14.

30. The correct answer is (D). An equation with an infinite number of solutions simplifies to $x = x$.

Simplifying the given equation leads to:

$$2(2x+3) = n\left(x + \frac{6}{8}\right) - 4x$$

$$4x + 6 = nx + n\frac{6}{8} - 4x$$

So $nx - 4x$ must equal $4x$, which is satisfied by $n = 8$.

And $n\frac{6}{8}$ must equal 6, which is also satisfied by $n = 8$.

31. The correct answer is 55.1. Add the eight numbers and divide by 8. Then round to the nearest tenth.

$$\frac{49 + 47 + 52 + 53 + 61 + 69 + 58 + 52}{8} = 55.125$$

The average age is 55.1.

32. The correct answer is 7.2 or 36/5. Begin by multiplying all terms of the equation by the LCD of 36:

$$36\left(\frac{x}{12}\right) + 36\left(\frac{x}{18}\right) = 1(36)$$

$$3x + 2x = 36$$

$$5x = 36$$

$$x = \frac{36}{5} = 7\frac{1}{5} = 7\frac{2}{10} = 7.2$$

33. **The correct answer is 50.** Write and solve an inequality that represents the situation. Then interpret the solution:

$$50 + 12x \le 660$$
$$12x \le 610$$
$$25x \le 380$$
$$x \le 50.8$$

Since the elephant cannot lift part of a bundle, the greatest number of bundles it can lift is 50.

34. **The correct answer is 69.7.** The males who are 49 years old or younger are in the 0–24 range and the 25–49 range. First, find this sum: $53.6 + 52.2 = 105.8$.

Then, divide it by the total number of males, which is 151.7 million:

$$\frac{105.8}{151.7} = 0.697$$
$$= 69.7\%$$

35. **The correct answer is .60.** The probability is the number of females who are in the age range of 25 to 74 (52.6 + 41.8 = 94.4) divided by the total number of females, which is 156.8 million:

$$\frac{94.4}{156.8} = 0.602$$
$$\approx 0.60$$

36. **The correct answer is 1/4 or .25.** Solve using elimination so that the x-terms are eliminated:

$$-6(5x + 4y) = -6(11)$$
$$5(6x - 8y) = 5(10)$$

$$-30x - 24y = -66$$
$$+\ 30x - 40y = 50$$
$$\overline{-64y = -16}$$
$$y = \frac{16}{64}$$
$$= \frac{1}{4}$$

37. **The correct answer is 8.** Distance = rate × time:

$$360 = r(9)$$
$$40 = r$$

If r were $40 + 5 = 45$

$$d = rt$$
$$360 = 45t$$
$$t = 8$$

38. **The correct answer is 11.** Solve using a common denominator, and check your answer:

$$\frac{2}{x+2} + \frac{3}{x-5} = \frac{4x+7}{x^2 - 3x - 10}$$
$$\frac{2(x-5)}{(x+2)(x-5)} + \frac{3(x+2)}{(x-5)(x+2)} = \frac{4x+7}{x^2 - 3x - 10}$$
$$\frac{2x - 10 + 3x + 6}{x^2 - 3x - 10} = \frac{4x+7}{x^2 - 3x - 10}$$
$$5x - 4 = 4x + 7$$
$$x = 11$$

$$\frac{2}{11+2} + \frac{3}{11-5} = \frac{4(11)+7}{(11)^2 - 3(11) - 10}$$
$$\frac{2}{13} + \frac{3}{6} = \frac{51}{78}$$
$$\frac{2(6)}{13(6)} + \frac{3(13)}{6(13)} = \frac{51}{78}$$
$$\frac{51}{78} = \frac{51}{78}$$

answers PRACTICE TEST 5

Section 5: Essay

Analysis of Passage

The following is an analysis of the passage by Alex Jensen and Susan M. McHale, noting how the writers used evidence, reasoning, and stylistic or persuasive elements to support their claims, connect the claims and evidence, and add power to the ideas the writers expressed. Check to see if you evaluated the passage in a similar way.

Adapted from "What makes siblings from the same family so different? Parents" by Alex Jensen and Susan M. McHale, originally published by The Conversation, July 6, 2015. Alex Jensen is an Assistant Professor of Human Development at Brigham Young University. Susan M. McHale is a Professor of Human Development and Family Studies at Pennsylvania State University.

What makes siblings from the same family so different? Parents

1   A colleague related the following story: while running errands with her 11- and 7-year-old daughters, a back seat battle began to rage. My colleague's attempts to defuse the situation only led to a shouting match about who was to blame for the skirmish. Finally the 11-year-old proclaimed to her sister, "You started it the day you were born and took away Mom's love!"

2   This pair of sisters fight frequently, and from their mother's perspective, part of the reason is that the two have little in common. As it turns out, their situation is not unique.

3   Despite the fact that siblings are, on average, 50% genetically similar, are often raised in the same home by the same parents, attend the same schools and have many other shared experiences,

4   siblings are often only as similar to each other as they are to children who are growing up across town or even across the country.

1   *The writers begin the essay with an anecdote drawn from personal experience. This story (which includes the evocative statement "You... took away Mom's love!") immediately makes the essay more personal and prepares the reader to engage with the writers' argument.*

2   *The writers broaden their point of view from the personal to the objective, and give the reader more perspective on the topic.*

3   *The writers use statistics and factual information to provide context for and lay the foundation of their argument.*

4   *Jensen and McHale clearly state a key premise of their argument — siblings are rarely similar. Having said this, they now have to support the rest of their argument: parents are the reason for these differences.*

5 So, what is it that makes two siblings from the same family so different?

What makes the difference?

6 As researchers of sibling and family relationships, we knew that at least one answer to this question comes from

7 theory and data showing that, at least in some families, siblings try to be different from one another and seek to establish a unique identity and position in their family.

8 From a child's perspective, if an older brother excels at school, it may be easier to attract her parents' attention and praise by becoming a star athlete than by competing with her brother to get the best grades. In this way, even small differences between siblings can become substantial differences over time.

9 But parents may also play a role. For instance, when parents notice differences between their children, children may pick up on parents' perceptions and beliefs about those differences. This, in turn, can increase sibling differences.

10 We wanted to test these ideas to see what makes siblings different. So, we used data from first- and second-born teenage siblings from 388 two-parent families to examine sibling differences in school performance.

11 We asked mothers and fathers to report on whether they thought the two siblings differed in their academic abilities, and if so, which sibling was more capable. We also collected school grades from both siblings' report cards.

5 *The writers pose a rhetorical question to introduce support for their argument.*

6 *The writers provide their backgrounds, which show why they're qualified to be making this argument: they are researchers of sibling and family relationships.*

7 *The writers refer to theory and data that support their argument: "some siblings try to be different from one another, and seek to establish a unique identity and position in their family."*

8 *The writers go into more detail about this information, presenting a concrete example that is easily understood by the reader.*

9 *The writers now discuss the role of parents in sibling differences, paving the way to support the central point in their argument: parents are a major force in sibling differences.*

10 *The writers explain how they tested the validity of their argument.*

11 *The writers provide more detailed information about the study they conducted to test the validity of their argument.*

Preference for the firstborn

12 Our analyses showed some interesting results: parents tended to believe that the older sibling was better in school. This was even when older siblings did not actually receive better grades, on average.

12 *The writers provide results of their study that revealed parents' perceptions of and ideas about older siblings. Specifically, parents tended to believe that the older sibling was better in school (whether this was true or not).*

13 This may be a product of parents having greater expectations for firstborns or that, at any given time, the older sibling is undertaking more advanced school work.

13 *The writers go into more detail about parents' perceptions of and ideas about older siblings.*

14 There was, however, an exception to this pattern: in families with older brothers and younger sisters, parents rated the younger sibling as being more capable. In fact, in those families, younger sisters received better grades than their older brothers.

14 *The writers go into further detail about results of their study. This detail shows a difference in how parents regarded their children, apparently favoring girls over boys in the area of academic capability.*

15 Our findings also showed that it was not sibling differences in school grades that predicted parents' ratings of their children's abilities. Rather, parents' beliefs about differences in their children's abilities predicted later sibling differences in school grades.

15 *The writers provide additional details form their study, showing parental beliefs and attitudes toward their children's abilities greatly affected sibling differences regarding academic performance.*

16 In other words, when parents believed one child was more capable than the other, that child's school grades improved more over time than their sibling's.

16 *Jensen and McHale explain these details and show how they support their argument: When parents believed one child was more academically capable than the other, that child's school grades improved more over time than their sibling's.*

Sustaining beliefs

17 Although we expected that children's school grades and parents' beliefs about their children's relative abilities would be mutually influential, it turned out that parents' beliefs did not change much over their children's teenage years.

17 *The writers provide information showing that once parents form perceptions and beliefs about their children's academic abilities, these attitudes and ideas do not greatly change.*

18 Instead, sibling differences in school grades did change and were predicted by parents' beliefs. In this way, parents' beliefs about differences between their children may encourage the development of actual sibling difference.

19 The above comment by an 11-year-old highlights that children are sensitive to their place and value in the family—relative to those of their siblings. Parents may strive to show their love for their children, but they also should be aware that small differences in how they treat their children can have large effects—including on their children's development and adjustment, and also on the sibling relationship.

20 Indeed, some research suggests that sibling conflict arises when children try to be different from their siblings.

21 My colleague may be correct that her daughters fight frequently because they have nothing in common.

22 But their conflicts may also be motivated by her daughter's perception that their differences started on the day her sister was born "and took away Mom's love."

18 Jensen and McHale use the information revealed by their study to prove their argument: While parents' beliefs about their children's academic abilities did not change, sibling differences in school grades did. Thus, "parents' beliefs about differences between their children may encourage the development of actual sibling difference."

19 The writers strengthen their argument by returning to their introductory anecdote and summing up what their study revealed: "Children are sensitive to their place and value in the family," and differences in how parents treat their children can have "large effects" on them.

20 The writers conclude the essay by referring to research that supports the mother's statement in the introductory anecdote: sibling conflict can be created "when children try to be different from their siblings."

21 While this may seem like the writers are giving up on their argument, acknowledging their colleague might be right about the cause of her daughters' conflicts demonstrates the writers' honesty and objectivity.

22 Jensen and McHale then end the essay by offering additional insight about their colleague's daughters. Here, they provide an alternative explanation for the girls' differences, restating their argument and repeating the 11-year-old girl's evocative remark: the conflict between these two siblings may also be motivated by the girl's belief that the birth of her younger sister changed their mother's behavior toward the older girl because the younger sister "took away Mom's love.

Sample Essays

The following are examples of a high-scoring and low-scoring essay, based on the passage by Alex Jenson and Susan M. McHale.

High-Scoring Essay

No two siblings are alike. Alex Jenson and Susan M. McHale are two university professors who investigated the reasons for the differences between siblings. They concluded that parents cause the differences. To explain their conclusion, they use professional authority, personal experience, statistics, results of a study they conducted, and references to other research.

Professional authority is established immediately—both authors are identified as university professors in the area of human development. In the second section, they reinforce their authority by stating that they are researchers of sibling and family relationships. This demonstrates their knowledge specifically in the area of siblings. Readers can trust their conclusions.

The article begins with a personal story of two young siblings who constantly fight. During a particular fight, the 11-year-old girl accuses her 7-year-old sister of starting the fight when she was born and "took away mom's love." This harsh accusation hooks readers into wondering about the real cause of sibling differences.

A quick look at statistics provided by the authors reveals many reasons for siblings to be similar rather that different. Siblings are 50% genetically similar and share the same parents, schools, and other experiences. Again, this makes the reader wonder about the cause of sibling differences.

The answer comes from theory and data, reinforcing their role as authorities in the subject. One cause, the authors state, is that siblings try to be different from each other to be unique in the family. They support this with an example of how one sibling can choose to excel at athletic pursuits because an older sibling already excels in academics. Over time, one small choice made to be different, such as joining a soccer team, causes other, bigger differences. One sibling becomes an athlete while the other becomes a scholar.

Finally, the authors address the role of parents in sibling differences. They theorize that parents notice small differences between children and children react to their parents' perceptions by becoming even more different. To confirm their theory, the authors conducted a study of the first and second siblings in 388 two-parent homes. Readers can easily see the study as a reasonable approach to determining the cause of the differences. The authors asked parents about their perceptions of their children's academic abilities and compared the perceptions to the children's report cards. In effect, they compared parents' perceptions to actual performance.

The authors present the analysis of the study results. Parents seem to expect the oldest sibling to perform better than the younger child, even though it wasn't always true. They describe an exception: If the older sibling is male and the younger sibling is female, the parents expect the girl to perform better academically, and the girl does get better grades than her brother.

The authors present their findings. Overall, the authors determined that parents' perception caused siblings' academic performance. If the parents believed that Suzy would perform better that Sally, Suzy's grades would improve until they were better than Sally's. Over time, parents' perceptions caused behaviors to change; behaviors did not cause parents' perceptions to change.

Parents have a large role in shaping their children and the relationship between their children. The authors briefly cite other research that points to differences between siblings as the cause of conflict between siblings.

At the end of the article, the authors return to the personal story told at the beginning of the article. The authors' colleague says that the conflict between her daughters is caused by the differences between the daughters. After reading the authors' findings though, readers can conclude that the differences are caused by the parents. Hence, the conflict between the siblings is actually caused by the parents. The authors have successfully presented their theory and their results to convince readers that parents should be more aware of the effect they have on their children.

Low-Scoring Essay

Alex Jenson and Susan M. McHale are two professors who researched the cause of sibling rivalry. They start the article with a story about two sisters having a fight in the backseat of a car. One of the girls accuses the other of stealing Mom's love. It refers to the age-old argument that "Mom loves you best."

The researchers look at some of the reasons that siblings fight even though they share so many of the same things, including genes, parents, schools, and probably clothes. They conclude that siblings try to be different on purpose so they can have a unique place in the family. The differences might start as things their parents notice like, "You're better at math than Mike," or "You run faster than Jake." Eventually, the small differences that parents notice become big things. Jake becomes an accountant because he's better at math. Mike becomes a gym teacher and coaches at the local high school because he's a better athlete.

The authors talk about a study they did about sibling rivalry. The differences between the siblings are caused by the way that parents expect the children to act. Children act the way they do to get attention.

The authors tell us that parents should be careful about the characteristics they encourage in their children and the perceptions they talk about. The "Mom loves you best" argument can shape children's lives. Parents should be careful to say good things about their children and interact evenly with both children. Then, no one will win the "Mom loves you best" argument and siblings will fight less.

COMPUTING YOUR SCORES

To get a sense of your progress in preparing for the SAT®, follow these instructions and the following conversion tables.

To Determine Your Practice Test Scores

1 After you go through each of the test sections (Reading, Writing and Language, Math—No Calculator, and Math—Calculator) and determine which answers you got right, be sure to enter the number of correct answers in the box below the answer key for each of the sections.

2 Your total score on the SAT® practice test is the sum of your Evidence-Based Reading and Writing Section score and your Math Section score. To get your total score, convert the raw score—the number of questions you got right in a particular section—into the "scaled score" for that section, and then you'll calculate the total score. It sounds a little confusing, but we'll take you through the steps.

To Calculate Your Evidence-Based Reading and Writing Section Score

Your Evidence-Based Reading and Writing Section score is on a scale of 200–800. First determine your Reading Test score, and then determine your score on the Writing and Language Test.

1 Count the number of correct answers you got on the **Section 1: Reading Test.** Remember that there is no penalty for wrong answers. **The number of correct answers is your raw score.**

2 Go to Raw Score Conversion Table 1: Section and Test Scores on page 938. Look in the "Raw Score" column for your raw score, and match it to the number in the "Reading Test Score" column.

3 Do the same with **Section 2: Writing and Language Test** to determine that score.

4 Add your Reading Test score to your Writing and Language Test score.

5 Multiply that number by 10. This is your Evidence-Based Reading and Writing Section score.

To Calculate Your Math Section Score

YOUR MATH SECTION SCORE IS ALSO ON A SCALE OF 200–800.

1 Count the number of correct answers you got on the Section 3: Math Test—No Calculator and the Section 4: Math Test—No Calculator practice tests. Again, there is no penalty for wrong answers. **The number of correct answers is your raw score.**

2 Add the number of correct answers on the Section 3: Math Test—No Calculator and the Section 4: Math Test—No Calculator practice tests.

3 Use the **Raw Score Conversion Table 1: Section and Test Scores** on page 938 and convert your raw score into your Math Section score.

To Obtain Your Total Score

Add your score on the Evidence-Based Reading and Writing Section to the Math Section score. This is your total score on this SAT® Practice Test, on a scale of 400–1600.

Subscores Provide Additional Information

Subscores offer you greater details about your strengths in certain areas within literacy and math. The subscores are reported on a scale of 1–15 and include Heart of Algebra, Problem Solving and Data Analysis, Passport to Advanced Math, Expression of Ideas, Standard English Conventions, Words in Context, and Command of Evidence.

Heart of Algebra

The **Heart of Algebra subscore** is based on questions from the Math Test—Calculator and Math Test—No Calculator (Sections 3 and 4) that focus on linear equations and inequalities.

- Add up your total correct answers from these sections:
- Math Test—No Calculator: Questions 1, 4, 7, 9, 13, 15, 18, 20
- Math Test—Calculator: Questions 1, 2, 4, 8–10, 13, 30, 32, 33, 36
- Your Raw Score = the total number of correct answers from all of these questions.
- Use the **Raw Score Conversion Table 2: Subscores** on page 939 to determine your **Heart of Algebra** subscore.

Problem Solving and Data Analysis

The **Problem Solving and Data Analysis subscore** is based on questions from the Math Test that focus on quantitative reasoning, the interpretation and synthesis of data, and solving problems in rich and varied contexts.

- Add up your total correct answers from these sections:
- Math Test—No Calculator: None
- Math Test—Calculator: Questions 3, 5–7, 12, 16–20, 26–28, 31, 34, 35, 37
- Your Raw Score = the total number of correct answers from all of these questions.
- Use the **Raw Score Conversion Table 2: Subscores** on page 939 to determine your **Problem Solving and Data Analysis** subscore.

Passport to Advanced Math

The **Passport to Advanced Math subscore** is based on questions from the Math Test that focus on topics central to your ability to progress to more advanced math, such as understanding the structure of expressions, reasoning with more complex equations, and interpreting and building functions.

- Add up your total correct answers from these sections:
- our total correct answers from these sections:
- Math Test—No Calculator: Questions 2, 5, 6, 8, 10, 12, 14, 17, 19
- Math Test—Calculator: Questions 15, 21–25, 38
- Your Raw Score = the total number of correct answers from all of these questions.
- Use the **Raw Score Conversion Table 2: Subscores** on page 939 to determine your **Passport to Advanced Math** subscore.

Expression of Ideas

The **Expression of Ideas subscore** is based on questions from the Writing and Language Test that focus on topic development, organization, and rhetorically effective use of language.

- Add up your total correct answers from Section 2: Writing and Language Test
- Questions 1, 3, 4, 7, 8, 10, 12, 14, 15, 19, 20, 22–24, 26, 28, 30, 33–37, 39, 40
- Your Raw Score = the total number of correct answers from all of these questions.
- Use the **Raw Score Conversion Table 2: Subscores** on page 939 to determine your **Expression of Ideas** subscore.

Standard English Conventions

The **Standard English Conventions subscore** is based on questions from the Writing and Language Test that focus on sentence structure, usage, and punctuation.

- Add up your total correct answers from Section 2: Writing and Language Test:
- Questions 2, 5, 6, 9, 11, 13, 16–18, 21, 25, 27, 29, 31, 32, 38, 41–44
- Your Raw Score = the total number of correct answers from all of these questions.
- Use the **Raw Score Conversion Table 2: Subscores** on page 939 to determine your **Standard English Conventions** subscore.

Words in Context

The **Words in Context subscore** is based on questions from the Reading Test and the Writing and Language Test that address word/phrase meaning in context and rhetorical word choice.

- Add up your total correct answers from Sections 1 and 2:
- Reading Test: Questions 9, 10, 20, 21, 31, 32, 37, 42, 51, 52
- Writing and Language Test: Questions 4, 6, 15, 18, 23, 27, 37, 42
- Your Raw Score = the total number of correct answers from all of these questions.
- Use the **Raw Score Conversion Table 2: Subscores** on page 939 to determine your **Words in Context** subscore.

Command of Evidence

The **Command of Evidence subscore** is based on questions from the Reading Test and the Writing and Language Test that ask you to interpret and use evidence found in a wide range of passages and informational graphics, such as graphs, tables, and charts.

- Add up your total correct answers from Sections 1 and 2:
- Reading Test: Questions 6, 7, 18, 19, 29, 30, 35, 40, 49, 50
- Writing and Language Test: Questions 1, 7, 12, 19, 26, 28, 36, 40
- Your Raw Score = the total number of correct answers from all of these questions.
- Use the **Raw Score Conversion Table 2: Subscores** on page 939 to determine your **Command of Evidence** subscore.

Cross-Test Scores

The new SAT® also reports two cross-test scores: Analysis in History/Social Studies and Analysis in Science. These scores are based on questions in the Reading Test, Writing and Language Test, and both Math Tests that ask you to think analytically about texts and questions in these subject areas. Cross-test scores are reported on a scale of 10–40.

Analysis in History/Social Studies

- Add up your total correct answers from these sections:
- Reading Test: Questions 12–22, 33–42
- Writing and Language Test: Questions 12, 14, 15, 19, 20, 22
- Math Test—No Calculator: None
- Math Test—Calculator: Questions 16, 17, 24, 26, 27, 31, 34, 35
- Your Raw Score = the total number of correct answers from all of these questions.
- Use the **Raw Score Conversion Table 3: Cross-Test Scores** on page 940 to determine your **Analysis in History/Social Studies** cross-test score.

Analysis in Science

- Add up your total correct answers from these sections:
- Reading Test: Questions 1–11, 43–52
- Writing and Language Test: Questions 34–37, 39, 40
- Math Test—No Calculator: Question 7, 9, 12, 13
- Math Test—Calculator: Questions 12, 14, 20, 33
- Your Raw Score = the total number of correct answers from all of these questions.
- Use the **Raw Score Conversion Table 3: Cross-Test Scores** on page 940 to determine your **Analysis in Science** cross-test score.

Raw Score Conversion Table 1: Section and Test Scores

Raw Score	Math Section Score	Reading Test Score	Writing and Language Test Score	Raw Score	Math Section Score	Reading Test Score	Writing and Language Test Score	Raw Score	Math Section Score	Reading Test Score	Writing and Language Test Score
0	200	10	10	20	450	22	23	40	610	33	36
1	200	10	10	21	460	23	23	41	620	33	37
2	210	10	10	22	470	23	24	42	630	34	38
3	230	11	10	23	480	24	25	43	640	35	39
4	240	12	11	24	480	24	25	44	650	35	40
5	260	13	12	25	490	25	26	45	660	36	
6	280	14	13	26	500	25	26	46	670	37	
7	290	15	13	27	510	26	27	47	670	37	
8	310	15	14	28	520	26	28	48	680	38	
9	320	16	15	29	520	27	28	49	690	38	
10	330	17	16	30	530	28	29	50	700	39	
11	340	17	16	31	540	28	30	51	710	40	
12	360	18	17	32	550	29	30	52	730	40	
13	370	19	18	33	560	29	31	53	740		
14	380	19	19	34	560	30	32	54	750		
15	390	20	19	35	570	30	32	55	760		
16	410	20	20	36	580	31	33	56	780		
17	420	21	21	37	590	31	34	57	790		
18	430	21	21	38	600	32	34	58	800		
19	440	22	22	39	600	32	35				

Conversion Equation 1 Section and Test Scores

Raw Score Conversion Table 2: Subscores

Raw Score (# of correct answers)	Expression of Ideas	Standard English Conventions	Heart of Algebra	Problem Solving Data Analysis	Passport to Advanced Math	Words in Context	Command of Evidence
0	1	1	1	1	1	1	1
1	1	1	1	1	3	1	1
2	1	1	2	2	5	2	2
3	2	2	3	3	6	3	3
4	3	2	4	4	7	4	4
5	4	3	5	5	8	5	5
6	5	4	6	6	9	6	6
7	6	5	6	7	10	6	7
8	6	6	7	8	11	7	8
9	7	6	8	8	11	8	8
10	7	7	8	9	12	8	9
11	8	7	9	10	12	9	10
12	8	8	9	10	13	9	10
13	9	8	9	11	13	10	11
14	9	9	10	12	14	11	12
15	10	10	10	13	14	12	13
16	10	10	11	14	15	13	14
17	11	11	12	15		14	15
18	11	12	13			15	15
19	12	13	15				
20	12	15					
21	13						
22	14						
23	14						
24	15						

Conversion Equation 2 Subscores

HEART OF ALGEBRA
RAW SCORE (0–19)

CONVERT

HEART OF ALGEBRA
SUBSCORE (1–15)

EXPRESSION OF IDEAS
RAW SCORE (0–24)

CONVERT

EXPRESSION OF IDEAS
SUBSCORE (1–15)

COMMAND OF EVIDENCE
RAW SCORE (0–18)

CONVERT

COMMAND OF EVIDENCE
SUBSCORE (1–15)

PROBLEM SOLVING AND DATA
ANALYSIS RAW SCORE (0–17)

CONVERT

PROBLEM SOLVING AND DATA
ANALYSIS SUBSCORE (1–15)

STANDARD ENGLISH CONVENTIONS
RAW SCORE (0–20)

CONVERT

STANDARD ENGLISH CONVENTIONS
SUBSCORE (1–15)

WORDS IN CONTEXT
RAW SCORE (0–18)

CONVERT

WORDS IN CONTEXT
SUBSCORE (1–15)

PASSPORT TO ADVANCED
MATH RAW SCORE (0–16)

CONVERT

PASSPORT TO ADVANCED
MATH SUBSCORE (1–15)

Raw Score Conversion Table 3: Cross-Test Scores

Raw Score (# of correct answers)	Analysis in History/Social Studies Cross-Test Score	Analysis in Science Cross-Test Score	Raw Score (# of correct answers)	Analysis in History/Social Studies Cross-Test Score	Analysis in Science Cross-Test Score
0	10	10	18	28	26
1	10	11	19	29	27
2	11	12	20	30	27
3	12	13	21	30	28
4	14	14	22	31	29
5	15	15	23	32	30
6	16	16	24	32	30
7	17	17	25	33	31
8	18	18	26	34	32
9	20	19	27	35	33
10	21	20	28	35	33
11	22	20	29	36	34
12	23	21	30	37	35
13	24	22	31	38	36
14	25	23	32	38	37
15	26	24	33	39	38
16	27	24	34	40	39
17	28	25	35	40	40

Conversion Equation 3: Cross-Test Scores

TEST	ANALYSIS IN HISTORY/SOCIAL STUDIES		ANALYSIS IN SCIENCE	
	QUESTIONS	RAW SCORE	QUESTIONS	RAW SCORE
Reading Test	12–22, 33–42		1–11, 43–52	
Writing and Language Test	12, 14, 15, 19, 20, 22		34–37, 39, 40	
Math Test—No Calculator	None		7, 9, 12, 13	
Math Test—Calculator	16, 17, 24, 26, 27, 31, 34, 35		12, 14, 20, 33	
TOTAL				

ANALYSIS IN HISTORY/
SOCIAL STUDIES
RAW SCORE (0–35)

CONVERT

ANALYSIS IN HISTORY/
SOCIAL STUDIES
CROSS-TEST SCORE (10–40)

ANALYSIS IN SCIENCE
RAW SCORE (0–35)

CONVERT

ANALYSIS IN SCIENCE
CROSS-TEST SCORE (1–15)

answers PRACTICE TEST 5

PART VIII

APPENDIX

Parents' Guide to College Admission Testing

Parents' Guide to College Admission Testing

GETTING INVOLVED

The first step in creating a plan to help your teen prepare for college-admissions tests is to define your role. As a parent, you already play a variety of roles in raising your children, wearing different hats at different times. You may find yourself acting as mentor, chauffeur, cook, coach, mediator, or even prison warden. All of these roles require different time commitments and often even require you to acquire new skills.

When it comes to helping your teen tackle the SAT® or ACT®, you might feel confused about which role to take. Many parents find becoming involved with their teen's education a bit challenging. Teenagers can have a hard time accepting their parents as teachers. Sometimes, when parents try to teach their teen, their efforts lead to the three "Fs": *failure, friction,* and *frustration*. When these experiences arise, parents may conclude that they have no role to play in their child's education.

Of course, nothing could be further from the truth. In fact, there are many roles parents should choose to play in helping their teens prepare for college-admissions tests.

ROLES FOR PARENTS

You can play a variety of roles in helping your teen prepare for college-admissions tests. In guiding your teen, you may choose to be one, or any combination, of the following:

- Buyer
- Advocate
- Supporter
- Helper
- Organizer
- Manager
- Tutor

The Buyer

"Here's a check to buy the SAT® books you want."

This parent feels that it is the teenager's job to prepare for college-admissions tests, and the parent's job is to offer financial support. The teenager is the main decision maker and is responsible for obtaining the necessary materials and services. This parental role is supportive and not too time-consuming, although it may present problems for parents who are on a tight budget.

NOTE

Educators and legislators recognize the importance of having parents involved in their children's education. Research shows that parents can successfully teach their teens, when they have been taught how to do it.

The Advocate

"How does your school help juniors prepare for the SAT® or ACT®?"

This parent believes that it is the school's job to prepare students for the test. The parent starts the ball rolling and requests information from school personnel about what services are available. The teenager may or may not be involved in this information-gathering process. Most parents feel comfortable in this role, as it requires little time and is accepted by both school personnel and teachers.

The Supporter

"I know it's a tough test. I see you're working hard and spending a lot of time studying for it."

This parent believes that the teenager has the major responsibility in preparing for the test. The teenager is the decision maker, and the parent offers suggestions and support. The parent is understanding, empathetic, and non-critical. This can be a comfortable parental role since it is non-threatening to the teenager, is positive, and requires a minimal amount of time.

The Helper

"I picked up this SAT® practice book and made a list of some tutoring courses for you."

This parent believes that it is the parent's job to help the teenager with his plans, but that it is up to the teenager to make the final decisions. This parent only helps when asked and follows the teen's timetable when possible. This is a comfortable role since it is supportive, non-threatening, and not time-consuming. However, this role might pose problems for working parents who do not have flexible schedules.

The Organizer

"I've signed you up to take a test-prep course."

This parent feels that the teenager should not be responsible for the arrangements involved in test preparation. The parent assumes a major role in establishing a timetable, finding out about resources, arranging for services, and purchasing materials. The teenager's responsibility is to follow the parent's game plan. In short, the parent provides the framework so that the teenager can spend her time preparing effectively. This role is time-consuming and parent-directed.

The Manager

"After you study your vocabulary words for 30 minutes, you can use the car."

This parent believes that good intentions are not enough to make her child perform well on the SAT®. She believes in the rule "work first, then play." Firm guidelines and consequences are established to keep the ball rolling. The degree to which the teenager is involved in planning and implementing this approach depends on a number of factors, such as the teenager's maturity and motivation.

Your comfort with this role is related to the extent to which you believe in the "work first, then play" philosophy. If you already ascribe to this rule in raising your children, extending it to SAT® or ACT® test preparation will be an easy task. Patience and willingness to check on study behavior are also important factors to consider when thinking about the role of manager.

The Tutor

"I'll explain the algebra problem to you."

Parents who take on the role of tutor believe that they can work effectively with their teenager on academic subjects. These parents offer direct instruction in one or more of the SAT® or ACT® areas, such as vocabulary, reading comprehension, geometry, or science.

WHICH ROLE IS FOR YOU?

Defining your role requires two steps:

- Collecting information about yourself
- Using this information systematically, as you decide which role you want to take on and when

To collect information about yourself, take the following "Parent Survey."

PARENT SURVEY

Directions: Read each question and circle the answer that best describes you. You may find that you mark some questions low, others medium, and still others high.

	LOW	MEDIUM	HIGH
1. How much money is available for test preparation, tutoring books, etc.?	Up to $25 for books	$25–$150 for books and tutoring	More than $150 for courses, books, etc.
2. Do you question school personnel?	Never. I feel uncomfortable.	Sometimes, if it is important.	Usually. It's my right.
3. Do you make supportive statements about academic achievements?	Not usually. I don't want to spoil my child.	Sometimes, if grades are good.	Frequently, especially about trying hard.
4. What resources are available in your school or community?	I don't have the faintest idea!	I thought I saw an advertisement for an SAT® course,	I know a tutor and saw an SAT® book in the store.
5. How involved do you feel?	I don't know if I should be involved.	I'll do what I can if I'm asked.	This is important! I'll help whenever I can.
6. How much time are you willing to devote to SAT® preparation?	1–3 hours total	1–2 hours per week	3 or more hours per week
7. How efficient is your decision making?	It's either too slow or too hasty.	Sometimes good, but it's a tiresome process.	Usually good. I consider options and select one.
8. Who should be the primary decision maker?	Not me. It's not my job!	I'll make decisions sometimes.	Me. I have more experience.
9. How organized are you?	I lose papers, forget dates, and am often late.	I write schedules but forget to follow them.	A place for everything and everything in its place!
10. How comfortable are you with your teenager?	It's tough being around my child.	Some days are good, others aren't.	Minor problems, but we get along.

TIP

Remember, no single role is superior to the other. Find roles that are best suited to you and your teenager's needs.

	LOW	MEDIUM	HIGH
11. How firm or consistent are your limits?	No one listens to me. I nag and yell.	My children know the rules, but I forget to enforce them.	My children follow the rules.
12. Do you have reading and math skills?	Minimal skills; low confidence.	Some skills; average confidence.	Strong skills; high confidence.
13. How effective are you as your teenager's teacher?	We always end up fighting.	Sometimes it works, sometimes it doesn't.	It's not easy, but we work together.

Choosing Your Role by Interpreting Your Survey Responses

While there are no hard and fast rules to use in choosing a role, your answers to the survey questions will help you select your role in a systematic way. Using your survey responses, you can use the following guidelines to identify which roles to try first. Remember that any combination of roles is good. To help clarify:

- **The roles of buyer, advocate, and supporter** are appropriate if a majority of your answers fall in the low or medium columns. These roles demand the least amount of direct parent-as-teacher involvement, yet they are an important part of test preparation. Most parents can assume these roles.

- **The roles of helper, organizer, and manager** require that the majority of your answers fall in the medium or high columns. These roles involve more constant and direct interaction with your teen. Some parents can assume these roles.

- **The role of tutor** is the most demanding role and requires that at least eleven out of thirteen responses fall in the medium or high columns. There are few parents who can comfortably and successfully assume this role.

Depending on your time and resources, you may, for example, want to begin in the advocate and supporter roles, followed by that of a buyer. If necessary, you could find someone else to act as a manager and tutor. Or, alternatively, you might find yourself best suited to being an organizer, manager, helper, and supporter right away.

BECOMING ACTIVE

Parents entrust their most valuable assets—their children—to the schools. As an investor in your child's education, you have the same concerns as any other person investing in the future. Unfortunately, sometimes parents are made to feel that the school is the "expert." In some schools, parents are viewed as meddlers if they ask for, or insist upon, information about their children's progress. As a parent, you can, and should, be involved in your teen's education, even at the secondary level. Don't be afraid to pursue information on your teen's behalf—you need to be informed, ask questions, offer suggestions, and reject suggestions if they aren't the right solutions to the problems!

HOW TO APPROACH YOUR TEENAGER

For the first time, your teen may be striving for independence and questioning himself or herself and the future. These changes may make your role as a parent additionally tough, and you may find it hard to help your teen prepare for college-admissions tests. The key to reaching your teen is to focus on where he or she is academically and personally.

GETTING INFORMATION FROM DIFFERENT SOURCES

To design your SAT® or ACT® preparation plan, you'll need to get up-to-date information about your teenager from several sources, including yourself, your teenager, and the school. Your child's guidance counselor is a primary source of information, since he or she can provide information from classroom teachers and across various subject areas.

You and Your Teen

The first source of information is you. Parents must neither overestimate nor underestimate the importance of their own information about their teenager. You can be most effective if you know which questions to ask and whom to ask. You need to know about your teenager's concerns, goals, attitudes, academics, work habits, general behavior, and special strengths and weaknesses.

To initiate this step, ask your teen to meet with you for an hour to discuss college plans and how he or she feels about preparing for the SAT® or ACT®. You can begin by asking your teen for his or her opinions on matters concerning his or her education and future goals. In this first conversation, you can ask about colleges he or she is considering. Because many colleges suggest that its applicants' test scores fall within a certain range, information about the college's requirements is important. The required scores may affect the amount of time and the kind of commitment required for SAT® or ACT® preparation.

You may also want to ask your teen to evaluate his or her study skills and the kind of study skills needed to prepare for the SAT® or ACT®. Some teenagers work effectively in groups. Others are uncomfortable or distracted when studying in a group. Students' work habits and interactions with other people also influence their attitudes toward college-admissions tests and toward their scores. Your teenager's reaction to tests in general is an important factor to take into consideration.

Don't feel rejected if your teen says, "I don't want to meet. I know what to do." Don't push it; just try again later. The timing may be right on the second go-around.

The School

Another important source of information is the school. Guidance counselors, teachers, and others; such as coaches or band directors, can tell you about your teenager's attitudes and interactions with peers and adults outside the home. These attitudes may influence your teen's college selection and in turn lead you to the most appropriate type of preparation for the college-admissions tests.

Your teen's guidance counselor can review previous standardized test scores with you and discuss differences in performance between tests and grades. Reviewing standardized test scores and grades can help you establish realistic guidelines for SAT® or ACT® preparation.

Teachers and counselors can also describe specific weaknesses that might block an otherwise solid test performance. In addition, they can offer information about your child's work habits, such as whether homework is submitted on time or how well-organized his or her papers are.

Additional Options

Independent school counselors, or educational consultants, are another alternative to consider. These types of counselors are not affiliated with a school and work as private consultants. If you lack confidence in your teen's counselor or feel that the counselor is too busy to provide the extensive work necessary for appropriate college planning, you may want to work with an educational consultant.

A private consultant may work with students from all over the United States and foreign countries. This broader perspective can provide more diverse options for your child. Many independent counselors also have firsthand experience as college-admissions officers and therefore are aware of the kind of information that should be collected and ways of presenting such information to colleges.

WHAT TO ASK

The following is a list of questions you'll want to ask yourself, your teen, and school personnel or educational consultants.

Goals

- What career choices is your teen considering?
- Are there specific colleges your teen wants to attend?
- What range of SAT® or ACT® scores do those colleges require? (Or are SAT® or ACT® scores optional?)

Attitudes

- How confident is your teen about his or her ability to succeed?
- What attitude does your teen have toward school and school personnel?
- Are your teen's friends a good influence in terms of future plans?
- How helpful is the family in terms of school success?
- What is your teen's attitude toward college-admissions tests?

Academics

- How has your teen done on other standardized tests?
- Do standardized test scores accurately reflect your teen's skills or abilities?
- Do your teen's grades accurately reflect his or her skills or abilities?
- What are your teen's areas of strength?
- What are your teen's areas of weakness?

Work Habits

- How effective are your teen's organizational and study skills?
- Does your teen the student do better with certain study procedures (e.g., in a group or listening to recorded lectures)?
- How effective are your teen's test-taking skills?
- Are there obstacles that might interfere with effective test preparation (e.g., a job or extracurricular activities)?
- Are there barriers to effective test-taking; (e.g., struggles with long reading passages or not liking multiple-choice tests)?

Behavior

- To what degree does your teen need or accept help?
- To what degree is your teen a good decision maker?
- How good is your teen at self-managing or being a self-starter?
- To what degree does your teen test limits or rules?
- How well does your teen cope with stress or adversity?
- How well does your teen relate to school personnel and teachers?
- How well does your teen relate to peers and classmates?
- How well does your teen relate to family members?
- With whom will your teen talk about problems (e.g., a sibling or a neighbor)?

Special Issues

- Does your teen have special talents or abilities?
- Does your teen have special challenges or obstacles?
- Have special challenges or obstacles been addressed previously?
- In what way will any of these issues affect preparation for the college-admissions tests?

SAT® and/or ACT®

- How do students in your school perform on the SAT® or ACT®?
- How did your teen perform on other college-admissions tests?
- How do your teen's test scores compare with others in the class?
- How do your teen's test scores compare with others nationally?

- How have other students prepared for the SAT® or ACT®?
- What services do school personnel provide for SAT® or ACT® preparation?
- What remedial services do school personnel provide?
- What remedial or preparatory services are available in the community (e.g., tutors or courses)?

By asking these questions, you can really focus on your teenager. By answering these questions now, you'll reveal information gaps, identify consistencies or inconsistencies in opinions or behaviors, highlight strengths and weaknesses, and begin your systematic plan for helping your teen.

HOW TO USE THE INFORMATION

To get the most out of the information you have collected, pay particular attention to the following issues:

- **Consistency of answers provided by each of the sources**—for example, whether the counselor's answers conflict with your teenager's answers
- **Trends that emerge**—such as better work this year or more anxiety than last year
- **Gaps in information**—such as no previous standardized test scores available
- **Strengths and weaknesses**—such as being well organized or having poor reading comprehension

YOUR TEEN'S STRENGTHS

All teenagers have strengths. However, some teenagers' strengths are more obvious than others. Your job as a parent includes:

- Identifying, highlighting, maintaining, and increasing existing strengths
- Providing opportunities for new strengths to develop

Strengths may be grouped into several broad categories—knowledge, work habits, attitude, behavior, and special. To help clarify:

- **Strengths in the knowledge area** include mastering basic skills, achieving good grades, and having a potential for learning.
- **Strengths in the area of work habits** include applying skills and knowledge in an organized and effective way and achieving desired goals.
- **Strengths in the area of attitude** include having clear goals, optimism, motivation, and self-confidence.
- **Strengths in the behavior category** refer to the teenager's ability to cope, follow rules, and get along with peers and adults.
- **Special strengths** may include talents in areas such as music, art, writing, or science.

Too frequently, both parents and teachers forget to accent the positive. They zero in on the weaknesses rather than on the strengths. To avoid this common mistake, review the information you have collected and list your teen's strengths and special talents in the following chart. We'll come back to filling in the problem areas later.

SOURCE		KNOWLEDGE	WORK HABITS	ATTITUDE	BEHAVIOR	SPECIAL
Parent	Strength					
	Problem					
Teenager	Strength					
	Problem					
School	Strength					
	Problem					

Remember to discuss these strengths with your teenager, especially if he or she does not recognize his or her own strengths or talents. Building your teen's confidence is important and will pay off enormously.

IDENTIFYING SPECIFIC PROBLEM AREAS

Several kinds of problems may become obvious as you collect information about your teenager. These problem areas may be grouped into the same five categories we used to identify strengths.

Knowledge Problems

Students with knowledge problems may make statements such as: "I'm not even sure about getting all the ratio and proportion problems right," or "I hate reading," or "I never do those vocabulary parts—I skip most of them."

Knowledge problems include:

- Lack of mastery of basic skills, such as arithmetic.
- Lack of understanding of rules and concepts in more advanced areas, such as geometry.
- Lack of experience, which leaves gaps in some areas covered on the SAT® or ACT®.
- Difficulties in one or more of the following: remembering previously learned material, analyzing material, or putting information together (e.g., as in a report).

Your teenager may have a knowledge problem in only one area, which may or may not have an effect on any other area. For example, Marcus, a 10th-grader, had a reading problem, and testing showed that he read two years below his present grade level. His computation skills were good, and he did well in algebra. However, word problems were his downfall. In this case, a knowledge problem in one area had an effect on another area.

Work-Habits Problems

Statements such as "I can't find my notes," "I think I left my books at school," or "I'll study later, after my favorite TV show" signal work-habits problems.

Work-habits problems include:

- Poor study habits
- Test anxiety

- Ineffective test-taking skills
- Lack of organization
- Difficulty estimating how long a task will take

Teenagers with work-habit problems lack the skills necessary to study effectively or to apply the knowledge they have during a testing situation. These teenagers may work too slowly and be unable to complete portions of the test, or they may work too quickly and inadvertently skip questions and make careless errors.

Attitude Problems

Students with attitude problems may make statements such as: "It doesn't matter how much I study, I'll never be able to do it," or "I don't care—the SAT® doesn't matter anyway."

Attitude problems involve:

- Unrealistic self-image and academic goals
- Over- or under-estimation of the importance of the SAT® or ACT®

On the one hand, teenagers may be overly optimistic in thinking that they are smart, do not need to prepare for the SAT® or ACT®, and can get into any college on the basis of grades alone. On the other hand, teenagers may have an overly negative view of their ability and therefore avoid school, worry about grades, panic on tests, and can be difficult or quarrelsome.

Attitude problems can influence the degree to which teenagers are willing to spend time and energy preparing for the SAT® or ACT®.

Behavior Problems

Teenagers with behavior problems are likely to make statements such as: "I don't have to study just because you say so," or "I know I should study, but I just can't make myself do it," or "I keep getting headaches when I think about the SAT®."

Behavior problems include:

- Poor self-control
- Lack of responsible behavior
- Inability to get along with peers, adults, or family
- Inability or unwillingness to follow rules and maintain commitments in school and in the community
- Drug and/or alcohol abuse

Teenagers with behavior problems usually use ineffective ways of coping with stress, are overly dependent or rebellious, are unable to control anger, and are unwilling to face or discuss problems with adults.

Special Problems

Teenagers with special problems may make statements such as: "I've always had trouble with spelling and reading," or "I know I have physical problems, but I want to try to go to college," or "I can do those questions; I just need more time."

Special problems include:

- Specific learning disabilities
- Severe physical, sensory, or emotional limitations
- Language barriers
- Disadvantaged backgrounds that may result in a lack of culturally enriching experiences

Special problems may prevent or affect your teen's ability to take the test. If your teenager is eligible, he or she may be able to take the SAT® with certain accommodations, such as extended time. Be sure to review the options and eligibility requirements and submit an accommodations request well in advance, as it can take several weeks to be approved.

To begin designing an SAT® or ACT® plan, you need to review your teenager's problems. List these problems on the same chart where you have already listed the teenager's strengths. When discussing these problems with your teenager, remember to talk about his or her strengths as well.

HOW TO USE THE INFORMATION ABOUT YOUR TEEN

After collecting information about your teenager, you should summarize the information by reviewing the chart you completed. Remember that strengths, along with weaknesses, may exist in each area. Keep the following in mind as you evaluate and summarize the information you have gathered:

- The number of sources that agree or disagree
- The number of objective measures that agree or disagree, such as tests, grades, or reports
- The number of times you are aware of the strength or problem—for example, your teenager always seems to be studying or is always complaining

WORKING WITH YOUR TEEN'S GUIDANCE COUNSELOR

Relative to college-admissions tests, the counselor's role is to help students understand the nature of these tests, the benefits of study and coaching, what test to take and when, and whether to retake a test in order to achieve a higher score.

The counselor can help you and your teen summarize information about how prepared your teen is for the SAT® or ACT® and can discuss strengths and weaknesses in light of current and past test results and grades. Making an appointment with your teen's guidance counselor now will enable you to make reasonable decisions about a course of action.

DEVELOPING EFFECTIVE WORK HABITS

In addition to assessing knowledge of English, math, and other content areas, the SAT® and ACT® test how well your teen takes standardized tests. Part of becoming a successful test-taker involves developing effective work habits. Developing these habits now will save your teen lots of frustration, time, and energy and will inevitably improve his or her test scores.

MANAGING TIME

Consider the following example. John is a fairly good student and earns Bs and Cs in his high school courses. He is concerned about the SAT® and wants to do well. During a practice SAT® test, he plods through each section and spends extra time on some of the more difficult questions. He doesn't finish parts of the test. His practice SAT® scores are unnecessarily low because he didn't have time to answer all of the questions he could have easily handled. John's test behavior indicates that he needs help in work habits, especially in learning to manage his time and pace himself during the test.

When people work in factories or offices, they are usually told how much time should be spent on different tasks. This process ensures productivity, allowing workers to know what is expected of them and helping them pace themselves so that they get the most done in the least amount of time. Similarly, your teen will also benefit from learning how to manage the time he has to take the SAT® or ACT®. Before taking the tests, he or she should know the following:

- How many questions are on each section of the test
- How much time is provided for each section
- Approximately how much time can be given to each question if he or she is to complete the test and if all of the questions are of equal difficulty
- The kinds of questions that he or she can't do and should skip until completing those questions he or she can definitely answer correctly

With test-taking, managing time means that your teen can predict what he or she has to do, how long it should take, how to pace himself or herself to get the job done, and how to leave time to check his or her work. Although most testing centers have clocks, your teen should wear a watch during the test (and practice tests) to keep track of time and check his or her pacing.

GETTING ORGANIZED AND STICKING TO TASKS

Now consider the case of another test-taker, Emma. The following takes place in her parents' kitchen after dinner:

7:05 p.m.	"Mom, did you see my SAT® practice book?"
7:10 p.m.	"Mom, I found some paper. Where are some pencils?"
7:15 p.m.	"Oh, I'd better text Liam to see if I have a ride tomorrow!"
7.20 p.m.	"What time is it?"
7:22 p.m.	"I need to get on the computer."
7:25 p.m.	"That's enough math! I think I'll do some vocabulary."
7:40 p.m.	"I hate vocabulary! I'll go back to math."

Emma displays several work-habits problems. One problem is that she hasn't recognized what she can't do during study time—for example, disrupting herself by sending a text message. Another problem is that Emma jumps from task to task, breaking her own concentration.

Good work habits entail being organized. Teenagers need to learn how to organize materials, list what has to be done, and specify how much time might be needed to complete each job. Study styles may differ, but teenagers must find the most effective ways to use their time and follow their own plans.

Students like Emma benefit from guidelines to follow during study time, such as:

- Spend at least 20–30 minutes on each activity, maintaining concentration, and building up skills.
- Stick to some basic study rules, including not avoiding work because it is too difficult or boring.
- Invoke the rule: "Work first and then play." For example, text, go online, or make phone calls only after work is completed.

Sticking to a task is an essential work habit. Unless she changes her habits, Emma will not reach the critical test-related goal: accurately completing the greatest number of problems she can within specific time limits. Emma is also operating under some misconceptions. She really believes that she is working hard and that her fatigue is a result of studying. She may also begin to think that she is not so bright as her friends because they are getting better results on practice tests. All of these potential problems can be resolved by changing her work habits.

IF IT WORKS, DON'T CHANGE IT

Another 10th-grader, Caleb, likes his comforts. He loads up on soda and chips before he settles down to work. The radio is an essential part of his lifestyle. When his mother and sisters pass by his room, they see him sprawled on his bed with a small light turned on and papers and books all over the floor. Sometimes he's sound asleep. Because he seems so casual, everybody stops by and talks to him.

Some parents might assume that the manner in which Caleb goes about studying is totally ineffective. It doesn't appear that any teenager could concentrate and maintain attention curled up in bed with music blaring, people walking in and out, poor lighting, and a nap now and then. Most parents would be right. Caleb's parents had been concerned and were annoyed by his work habits. However, Caleb earns high grades in school, and on the first SAT® he took, he scored more than 600 on the reading and writing sections. He has also shown his parents how his speed is increasing on certain practice SAT® exercises. In this case, the parents have specific information and assurance that their son's work habits work for him, despite appearing inefficient.

Your objective here is to check the effectiveness of your teenager's work habits. Consider what effect these habits have on classroom or college-admissions test performance. Remember to have your teen take a practice test under actual SAT® or ACT® conditions to see how his or her work habits hold up.

TAMING THE PROCRASTINATOR

Procrastination is a common problem for teens. Leslie is an 11th-grader having a conversation with her father, Mr. Rand.

Mr. Rand: "Did you start to study for the SAT®?"

Leslie: "No, it's in two months."

Mr. Rand: "Shouldn't you start now?"

Leslie: "I wish you would stop nagging me. I can take care of myself."

Here's another scenario, between Mrs. Sanchez and her 11th-grader, Ricky:

Mrs. Sanchez: "I haven't seen that SAT® book around. Are you studying in school?"

Ricky: "I started looking at it, but it's so long I'll never get through it."

Putting off work occurs when people feel overwhelmed, don't know where to begin, feel pressured to get other things done, or are distracted by other things they would rather do. Parents who recognize this work-habit problem in their teenagers may have similar habits themselves.

Procrastination becomes a particular problem because:

- Time is limited; when time is limited, people feel pressure.
- There can be a penalty for delay—for example, you might miss the SAT® or ACT® because your check was mailed late.
- Avoiding work increases the load, rather than decreases it.

By taking into account the time available before the SAT® or ACT® and the preparation that has to be done, you can help your teenager create a sensible plan that divides one seemingly overwhelming task into smaller and more manageable ones. Predicting what has to be done, and doing those tasks one by one, gives teenagers control over feelings of being swamped and unable to cope.

A WORK-HABITS CHECKLIST

To help your teenager develop effective work habits, ask him or her questions regarding time management, materials, atmosphere, and space. You may want to use the following checklist.

Time Management

❏ Are there signals to others that this is a study time (e.g., a "Do Not Disturb" sign)?

❏ Are there rules set up for the study time (e.g., no phone calls or no visitors)?

❏ Is a time schedule agreed upon and posted?

❏ Are study breaks scheduled?

Materials

❏ Is a clock or kitchen timer available?

❏ Are supplies handy (e.g., pencils, eraser, computer)?

❏ Does the seating encourage attention and alert behavior (e.g., a chair and a desk rather than a bed)?

Atmosphere

❏ Is the lighting adequate?

❏ Is the noise level low?

❏ Is the area visually nondistracting?

❏ Is the area well-ventilated and does it have a moderate temperature?

Space

❑ Is there a special place designated (e.g., desk, room, or area) for studying?

❑ Is this space away from the main traffic of the home?

❑ Is the space large enough to allow for writing?

❑ Is there space available for storing or filing materials?

HOW TO HELP YOUR TEEN WITH WORK HABITS

Teenagers have difficulty finding time to do homework or household chores, but they usually seem to have a lot of time to text or talk on the phone, go online, or hang out with friends. Managing time comes down to establishing priorities. Here are some guidelines that you can use to help your teenager use his or her time more effectively:

- Set a realistic study schedule that doesn't interfere too much with normal activities.

- Divide the task into small and manageable parts—for example, instead of trying to memorize 2,000 vocabulary words in two weeks, have your teen learn and use five new words a day, three times a week.

- Use what has just been learned whenever possible—for example, talk about, joke about, and use new vocabulary words.

- Find times that are best for concentration and, if possible, have your teen avoid studying at times when he or she is tired, hungry, or irritable.

- Plan a variety of study breaks, such as music or jogging, to revive concentration.

Using Study Groups

You may also want to encourage your teenager to get a group of friends together to practice taking the SAT® or ACT®, review test items, compare answers, and/or discuss the ways they used to solve the problems. Such a group can range in size from two to six students.

Consider this example: Ms. Franklin realized that her daughter, Barbara, liked to be with other teenagers and studied best in a group. If she waited for Barbara to begin studying independently, Ms. Franklin was afraid that Barbara would put off studying until it was too late.

Ms. Franklin asked her daughter if she would like to organize a study group. Ms. Franklin also volunteered to provide the house and find a tutor. Barbara's responsibilities were to call her friends and tell them which materials to buy, how much each session would cost, and where and when the group would meet. By doing this, Ms. Franklin provided a real service to a group of motivated students who needed some direction.

So, if you want to help set up a study group, you can:

- Make the initial arrangements

- Provide the space for meetings

- Set up a "study atmosphere" in your home

- Help other parents to set up such groups

More Tips on Organization

When reading about Ms. Franklin, you might think that she is very organized and efficient. Nope! In fact, she is usually disorganized and is a procrastinator herself. She rarely plans ahead, and there is a lot of confusion in her home when deadlines must be met.

Ms. Franklin's behavior shows that it really is possible for an otherwise hassled parent to become more organized and efficient for a short time just for the SAT® or ACT®. During this brief window, you can help your teen by doing the following:

- Save papers and announcements with dates and requirements for the SAT® or ACT®.

- Make copies of all correspondence, applications, checks, and bills and find one place to store or file these papers.

- Write the SAT® and/or ACT® date and your teenager's study-session schedule on your own calendar.

- Write notes to yourself so that you don't forget to do what you said you'd do, such as making phone calls or picking up materials.

WHY CREATE A PLAN?

It takes more than good intentions to do well on a college-admissions test. It takes time, organization, and hard work. A test-prep plan provides the means for converting good intentions into meaningful test preparation. An effective plan specifies:

- Goals
- Responsibilities of parent and teenager
- Available resources
- Schedules
- Budgets
- Instruction
- Possible problems or concerns

By clearly establishing who is responsible for what, a test-prep plan removes many sources of conflict between parent and teenager and allows each person to channel all of his or her efforts toward the goal of improving test scores.

CREATING TEST-PREP PLANS

Let's look at some step-by-step ways of creating test-prep plans and what to expect as you create a plan for your teen.

Make Time to Plan

Family life is hectic. Finding time to sit down and talk together is frequently a problem. Like a well-managed business, families with educational concerns and goals also need to have planning meetings. They need to find the time and place that will allow for discussion and working together.

Setting up a time to talk about a plan with your teen will work best if you approach him or her when he or she is most apt to be receptive. How you proceed is as important as what you do. A first step in developing a plan is to set goals.

List Goals

Goals help identify in a concrete way what you want to happen, such as your teen raising his or her verbal score by 40 to 60 points. Sometimes teenagers choose goals that are too general, such as doing geometry problems more accurately or completing the reading section more rapidly. Goals should be specific to the SAT® or ACT® even when they include study skills. For example, just having a goal of studying for 30 minutes a night does not guarantee improvement. The following list contains some sample goals.

For accuracy:	Increase the number of correct math and vocabulary test answers.
For speed:	Decrease the time needed to read comprehension exercises while maintaining an understanding of what is read.
For speed and accuracy:	Decrease the time needed to read comprehension exercises and increase understanding of what is read.
For quantity:	Increase the number of problems tried or completed.
For frequency:	Study vocabulary words and do essay writing practice exercises for about 30 minutes at least three times per week.
For duration:	Increase study sessions to 1 hour, adding additional practice math problems.

After outlining the goals, the next step in planning is to prepare a schedule.

TIP

Some teenagers need to review a specific skill or subject; others have problems that require intensive instruction and practice. Since each teenager is unique, each test-prep plan must be individually tailored to fit specific needs.

Remember to take
action in a way that
is sensitive to your
teen's needs and
schedules.

Make a Schedule

A test-preparation schedule should include a timetable and weekly or daily activity lists. First make
the timetable. You can use a regular calendar that covers the time between the current date and the
date of the SAT® or ACT®. To make your timetable, write down all activities related to preparing
for the test and the test date on the calendar.

You should also keep weekly and/or daily lists to identify specific tasks, such as the type or number
of practice exercises to be completed. Such scheduling spells out the tasks ahead of time, reduces
unnecessary worrying, and allows for more realistic planning. Often, teenagers become overwhelmed
by the thought of all that has to be done and end up doing nothing. Writing a list and assigning times
to each task tends to make these jobs more doable and more realistic.

Talk About Costs

Although you want to do everything possible for your teen's college-admissions test preparation,
cost is an important consideration. Most families' budgets are already strained without adding the
expenses of materials, tutors, or commercial courses—especially since test preparation comes at a
time when parents are trying to save money for college tuition.

Regardless of who pays the bill—the parent, the teenager, or both—budgets should be discussed.
The estimated costs of various alternatives should also be outlined. Any budget limits and expected
responsibilities should be proposed. By discussing these issues up front, you clarify problems and
provide a realistic basis for decision making.

Find Out About Resources

Your community may have a variety of resources to help teenagers prepare for college-admissions tests. However, it may take a little detective work to find them. For example, many religious groups and local organizations, such as your department of recreation, senior center, or the town library, sponsor young-adult activities. These groups usually know skilled people within the community who would be willing to help teenagers study for the SAT® or ACT®. In addition, parent or community groups may also be willing to sponsor special activities if they are aware of teenagers' needs.

Match Materials to Your Teen's Goals

You and your teen should now select which books, equipment, and/or specialized materials will be used. You should match these materials to your teenager's goals. Consider drawing on information from teachers or counselors, previous standardized tests, and test-prep books that analyze the SAT® or ACT®. Material can be purchased, borrowed, or shared by several teenagers.

Locate a Tutor

In finding a tutor, you should consider someone who has experience with the college-admissions tests. You may actually hire more than one tutor, since instruction may be provided by volunteers, peers, schoolteachers, or professional tutors. Discuss various tutoring options with your teen.

Find a Place to Practice and Study

Regardless of your plan's specifics, your teen needs a suitable place in which to study. Teenagers who register for courses or who receive tutoring have to practice test-taking at home too. It is important to select a quiet study place at home or at school for SAT® or ACT® homework assignments or for sessions with the tutor. It is also smart to turn off phones, the TV, and computers to reduce interruptions and distractions while your teen is preparing for the test. Some students do well working in a library or another area set aside for quiet study.

Do a Subtle Sell Job

Doing a subtle sell job means helping your teenager realize that the long-term benefits of test preparation outweigh the short-term costs of studying. As you prepare to make a test-prep plan with your teen, you may want to use the following chart to guide your thinking about the plan's importance.

		COSTS (TIME, MONEY, ENERGY)	BENEFITS (SUPPORT, CHALLENGE, ACHIEVEMENT)
PARENTS	**SHORT-TERM**	"It takes me 20 minutes to drive to the tutor." "I've already spent $20 on books." "I'm tired of thinking and talking about the SAT®." "I got a lot of resistance when I suggested an SAT® course."	"I know I helped." "Her scores went up." "I feel good." "He knows we care."
	LONG-TERM	"I ought to have spent more time." "It's costing twice as much now." "I should have been firmer about SAT® studying." "I wish I had been more aware."	"He did the best he could." "She got into three colleges." "Now I can relax." "She knows we all worked to help her."
TEENAGERS	**SHORT-TERM**	"I'd rather be sleeping." "The SAT® fee is so high!" "I'm tired of studying." "I don't feel like caring." "Suppose I don't do well?" "No one else is studying."	"Studying takes time, but it's OK." "I stopped worrying when I started studying." "I'm learning how to take tests." "My math is actually improving." "I'm learning new words." "This is a first step toward being a lawyer."
	LONG-TERM	"I didn't get into the college I wanted. I hope I can transfer later." "I could have done better." "I should have listened to my parents." "I wish I had tried harder."	"My scores were high, and I won a scholarship." "I did the best I could." "I had a good choice of colleges." "My parents helped a lot."

WRITE YOUR PLAN

As you create your plan and revise it, you and your teen should list specific responsibilities, as well as the expected and actual costs. Use the following outline to help you keep notes.

Describe the planning time:

Identify goals:

Set schedules and agendas:

List possible materials, instructors, and/or locations:

Identify resources:

Assign responsibilities and roles:

Specify costs and budgets:

Review and Revise Your Plan

After writing an initial plan, you should review it to make sure it's realistic. Remember that you can and should revise your plan as you go along. The following questions will help you and your teenager determine whether your plan is relevant, realistic, and useful.

Planning Time

❑ Has a specific time been selected?

❑ Has a quiet, comfortable place been chosen?

❑ Has all the necessary information been collected?

❑ Have costs and benefits been discussed?

❑ Have roles for both the parent and teenager been discussed?

Goals

❑ Have the teen's strengths been discussed?

❑ Have problems been identified and prioritized according to time and/or financial constraints?

❑ Have goals been discussed and written?

❑ Are the goals realistic?

❑ Are the goals listed in the order of their importance?

❑ Has a range of outcomes been considered (such as increasing scores by 25 to 50 points on a particular section)?

Schedule

❑ Has a timetable that specifies all time commitments been designed?

❑ Does the schedule seem realistic in terms of goals and limitations?

❑ Have tutoring sessions been scheduled?

❑ Have study or practice sessions been scheduled?

❑ Have time limits been specified for those sessions?

Materials

❑ What materials are needed?

❑ How are materials matched with goals or problems?

❑ How will materials be used?

❑ Who is responsible for acquiring the materials?

Coaches and Instructors

❑ Who will provide the coaching or instruction?

❑ Does this person have the necessary skills?

❑ Are other teachers or tutors necessary?

Location

❑ Where will instruction occur?

❑ Has transportation been arranged?

❑ When studying at home, where will it be done?

❑ Will these places be available when needed?

Budget

❑ Have financial costs and resources been discussed?

❑ Have financial responsibilities been specified?

❑ If costs are a problem, have alternatives been considered and discussed?

❑ Are adjustments or alternatives necessary?

Resources

❑ Have the necessary or desired resources been identified?

❑ Who is responsible for selecting and contacting these resources?

❑ How will decisions be made about the usefulness of these resources?

ANTICIPATE POSSIBLE HURDLES

Some common problems that arise during the test-prep process include:

- The teenager doesn't work well with the tutor.

- The instructor gets sick.

- The study group falls apart.

- One of the parents loses a job, so money is no longer available for a commercial course.

More subtle problems can occur when:

- Teenagers set unrealistic goals and then feel tired, frustrated, and angry.

- Parents become worried that their teenager isn't making enough progress.

- Parents feel angry and disappointed when things don't work out exactly as planned.

When managing a plan, you must assume that problems will arise and that plans have to be changed to deal with these problems. Helping your teenager shift gears and learn how to make adjustments is vital preparation for the real world and a valuable skill for him or her to learn now.

WAYS TO TRACK PROGRESS

Here are some ways you can check on your teen's performance progress:

- Keep records for each study session.

- Keep track of the number of problems completed correctly.

- Keep track of how much time it takes to complete the work.

- Review the records to see if changes to the plan need to be made.

- Make sure your teen is focused on the specific SAT® or ACT® sections or questions that need special attention.

Teenagers can check on their progress in several ways. These methods include calendars, checklists, charts, and graphs. The best method is the one that your teen will regularly use.

Timing Your Comments

You should comment on performance when the progress has occurred, not a week or two later. Teenagers usually do not want anyone to know that they are studying for the tests, so it's best to comment when no one else is around. You should also be especially sensitive to how your teenager will receive any comments about his or her work. Teenagers often view these helpful hints as criticism, even when they are offered in a positive way. You may find it easier to use notes or humor as a way of making a point that can be accepted by your teen. For example, Anne's father wrote her the following note:

> *Dear Anne:*
>
> *I see that you're keeping track of the number of problems you complete for the SAT. Looks as if you're doing at least 2–3 more problems each time—HOORAY!*

FIXING PROBLEMS

TIP

Research suggests that tracking progress can positively influence a student's performance. Remember the days when you hung your children's drawings on the refrigerator? Recognition still goes a long way. Post progress charts where they can be seen and acknowledged.

When teenagers are not progressing as anticipated, parents frequently jump to conclusions and think that the teenager has done something wrong. It may appear that the teenager is lazy. In fact, he or she may just be feeling overwhelmed, confused, and exhausted. When you become aware of problems, you may need to take a second look at the situation, looking for specific performance obstacles.

Rather than blaming your teenager, or labeling his or her behavior as right or wrong, you might consider behavior in terms of its being efficient or inefficient. To help you pinpoint what's going on, you may want to ask your teenager two questions:

- How is your study schedule working?
- Are you learning what you thought you would?

Your teen can give you the information to zero in on the specific problem. Some common problems teenagers face stem from unrealistic goals, unsuitable materials, and inefficient organization.

Applying Solutions

Usually there is more than one solution for every identified problem. Here are some common SAT® and ACT® test-prep problems and a variety of possible solutions.

Problem: The teen seems to give up because it appears to him or her that the material is too complicated.

Solution: Remind the teen that habits are like muscles. The first time someone goes for a run, it may seem very difficult, but it gets easier each time the person does it. Incorporating regular studying time for the SAT® into the day will become easier the more the teen does it. If necessary, have the teen start small so she or he will be energized by successes.

NOTE

Keep in mind that the idea is to study more effectively, not necessarily longer.

Problem:	Progress is slower than anticipated and there isn't enough time left to reach the original goal.
Solutions:	Lower the expectations about the scores.
	Rearrange the study schedule.
	Provide more intensive instruction.
	Schedule the test at a later date.
	Shoot for a later college-admissions date.
Problem:	The teenager is studying, but he or she does not remember anything the next day.
Solutions:	Change from group to individual tutoring.
	Change from reading the information to listening to some of the information.
	Practice aloud before doing the test exercises.
	Study in a different place.
	Check that the teaching materials match the required skills. Also try to determine how the teen learns best and use the information to leverage those strengths. For example, some students remember better if they write things down by hand rather than if they type them. Other students benefit from talking out loud as they work through the steps of a difficult concept.
Problem:	The teenager is studying, but he or she seems to lose things and waste time.
Solution:	Give him or her information and techniques that will help him or her to become better organized.
Problem:	The teenager seems frantic and appears to be spending too much time studying.
Solution:	Provide some written material that will help him or her rank what has to be done in order of importance.

Review the goals, costs, and benefits, but keep in mind that the test is part of a larger picture.

Using Checklists to Manage Problems

It is important that teenagers try to manage their own problems. However, sometimes they lack the information they need to effectively deal with these problems. Provide the following questionnaire and encourage the teen to apply the solutions to manage the obstacles to his or her success.

Do You:	**Then Try To:**
❑ Have papers and books that you haven't looked at for months?	❑ Schedule periodic clean-ups. Throw out the things you don't use.
❑ Waste time and break up your concentration looking for things you have misplaced?	❑ Find the necessary papers and materials before starting to study.
❑ Lose test registration papers, exercise sheets, or materials?	❑ Arrange your materials in a systematic manner, such as by using folders.
❑ Have a study area that is a mess?	❑ Make a labeled file or box for different kinds of materials.
❑ Let things pile up because you don't know where to put them?	❑ Store your materials and supplies in an easy-to-spot place.

Do You:	**Then Try To:**
❑ Let assignments pile up because you can't decide what to do first?	❑ Write down all your assignments—by the week or by the day—putting those that should be done first at the top of the list.
❑ Forget regular school assignments that you can't study for as you had planned?	❑ Ask teachers for all future test or project dates and write them down on your calendar.
❑ Have a hard time sticking to your study schedule?	❑ See how long you can study and regularly increase this time in 5- to 10-minute intervals.
❑ Forget to do errands, like picking up materials or making phone calls?	❑ Write yourself notes and put them on your backpack or wallet. This looks funny, but it works.
❑ Find that your attention wanders when you begin to study?	❑ Ask yourself, "At what time do I study best?" Change your study time if necessary.

Do You:	**Then Try To:**
❑ Try to cram everything in?	❑ Be selective. Do only those tasks that are the most important.
❑ Feel anxious if you don't have every minute planned?	❑ Make sure that you allow time to relax and exercise.
❑ Feel uncomfortable if you need to change your schedule?	❑ Tell yourself, "Relax and be flexible. I have a schedule and I'll do the best I can."
❑ Feel overburdened by the responsibilities of test preparation?	❑ Get a study buddy you can call when you get discouraged.
❑ Want to study but don't, because someone asks you to do something else?	❑ Practice saying, "No. I'd really like to, but I'm studying."
❑ Find the work difficult?	❑ Give yourself a pep talk and say, "This is hard, but it can be done."

MOTIVATING YOUR TEENAGER

Once you get the plan going, the next step is to keep it going. Studying for the test usually isn't fun. It is hard work and teenagers need encouragement to keep going.

Sometimes teenagers are motivated because they immediately taste success. For example, Rico studied for a chemistry test and received an A. It is highly likely that he will study for the next test because he saw that his work paid off.

Checking on progress on the SAT® or the ACT® practice tests is important. Doing so gives your teenager the opportunity to realize that his or her work does pay off and progress is being made.

Sometimes parents need to boost motivation when they see signs of fatigue or signals that their teenager is being turned off to studying. If you are trying to find ways to encourage your teenager, consider the following:

- Make positive statements, such as "I know you're working hard."

- Provide extra treats, such as a special dinner or extra use of the car.

- Leave a small, humorous gift in their room, such as a giant pencil or a silly figurine.

- Organize some special event, such as going to the movies, a concert, or out to eat with another family whose teenager is also taking the test.

- Do some chore for your teenager so that your teen has more time to study.

Setting Up Rewards

Like everyone else, not all teenagers are motivated the same way. This is why it's helpful to know as much as possible about your teen's personality. Some teens feel very comfortable with a lot of structure and being held accountable by a tutor, parent, or teacher. Others are fine with a lot of structure as long as the purpose behind it makes sense to them. Highly independent teens may perceive it as "being told what to do," however. Challenge teens for whom choice is essential to come up with their own plan for test preparation. These teens can be very good at "thinking outside the box" and may be more motivated by proving they can succeed doing things their way than by any other reward.

Sometimes, you need to put into practice methodical and consistent ways to make sure that plans are followed. In other words, you may need to make sure that certain events occur after, and only after, a task is completed. The following examples show how you can build in rewards for work accomplished.

- Ron tends to be forgetful. For a month, he had not done the vocabulary exercises he agreed to do. He and his parents worked out a plan so that if a certain number of exercises were completed on Tuesday and Thursday nights, he could have the car on Fridays.

- Diana, on the other hand, did not want the car—she loved talking on the phone. Her family devised a plan that required her to work on her writing exercises for 30 minutes, three nights a week, before she could talk on the phone.

- You can also set up a tracking system using counters such as paper clips, to record short blocks of study time—a half hour, for example. Each counter can represent something the student can use as he or she wishes. For example, each paper clip might represent a dollar or a half hour that can be spent with friends or playing sports.

TIP

Regardless of the system of rewards, remember to be positive, low-key, and avoid negative or punishing situations. The goal is to encourage and support effective studying, not to control your teenager. By establishing realistic goals and rewards, you help your teenager do his or her best and show him or her that you really care.

Research also shows that linking habits—also called anchoring or stacking habits—makes a person more likely to accomplish them. Have the student choose an activity he or she performs every day, then link a desired new habit to an existing one. For example, if Rose takes 5 minutes every night before she brushes her teeth to be sure that she's written out her study plan for the next day and gathered all the materials she will need, she's more likely to do so. The new habit, writing the study plan, is linked to an established habit, brushing her teeth.

This final list of questions is provided to help you check on your teen's progress and iron out problems. When plans are well-managed, trouble spots are easily identified and changes can usually be made without anyone feeling that he or she has failed, especially the teenager.

Managing Your Plan: A Checklist

☐ Is progress being checked using charts, checklists, graphs, or other means?

☐ Do charts or graphs show any problems?

☐ What adjustments are necessary?

☐ Have alternative solutions been considered?

☐ Are any additional resources or checklists necessary?

☐ Has progress been made toward the goals?

Originally published in a slightly different form in *Parent's Guide to the SAT® & ACT®* (Lawrenceville, NJ: Peterson's, 2005), 27–133. Reprinted by permission of the authors.

notes